INTERNATIONAL DIRECTORY
OF PSYCHOLOGISTS

EXCLUSIVE OF THE U.S.A.

PUBLICATION 520

NATIONAL ACADEMY OF SCIENCES - NATIONAL RESEARCH COUNCIL

WASHINGTON, D.C.

INTERNATIONAL DIRECTORY
OF PSYCHOLOGISTS

EXCLUSIVE OF THE U.S.A.

PREPARED FOR THE NATIONAL ACADEMY OF SCIENCES
NATIONAL RESEARCH COUNCIL

BY

THE COMMITTEE ON AN
INTERNATIONAL DIRECTORY OF PSYCHOLOGISTS
DIVISION OF ANTHROPOLOGY AND PSYCHOLOGY, N.A.S.-N.R.C.

Chairman: E. G. Boring

EUGENE H. JACOBSON, *editor*
H. C. J. DUIJKER, *European Co-editor*

1958

ROYAL VAN GORCUM & COMP. LTD. - G. A. HAK & DR. H. J. PRAKKE
ASSEN - THE NETHERLANDS

U.S. *Library of Congress catalog card number: 57-60048*

Printed in the Netherlands by Royal VanGorcum Ltd., Assen

THE COMMITTEE ON AN INTERNATIONAL DIRECTORY OF PSYCHOLOGISTS,

DIVISION OF ANTHROPOLOGY AND PSYCHOLOGY, NATIONAL ACADEMY OF SCIENCES-NATIONAL RESEARCH COUNCIL:

E. G. BORING, Harvard University, Cambridge, Mass.

LEE J. CRONBACH, University of Illinois, Urbana, Ill.

FRANK A. GELDARD, University of Virginia, Charlottesville, Virg.

JANE HILDRETH, American Psychological Association, Washington D.C.

OTTO KLINEBERG, Columbia University, New York, N.Y.

H. S. LANGFELD, Princeton University, Princeton, N. J.

R. B. MACLEOD, Cornell University, Ithaca, N.Y.

E. B. NEWMAN, Harvard University, Cambridge, Mass.

While this Directory was being prepared, the death occurred of Professor H. S. Langfeld. The other members of the Committee and the Editors cherish his memory as an outstanding scholar and as an indefatigable pioneer of international co-operation among psychologists. They regret deeply that Professor Langfeld has not lived to see the completion of this work, to which he has contributed so greatly.

socy., society
SP, Sveriges Psykologforbund
spec., special, specialist
SPS, Suomen Psykologinen Seura
SPT, Society for Projective Techniques
sq., square
sr., senior
SSP, Swiss Society of Psychology (Société Suisse de Psychologie et de Psychologie Appliquée; Schweizerische Gesellschaft für Psychologie und Ihre Anwendungen
St., Street, Saint
sta., station
stat., statistics, statistical, statistician
str., strasse, straat
stud., student
superv., supervisor, supervision
supt., superintendent
Swed., Sweden, Swedish
Switz., Switzerland
Tas., Tasmania
TB, tuberculosis
tchng., teaching
tchr., teacher
tech., technical, technician, technology
tel, telephone
Terr., Terrace
ther., therapy, therapeutic, therapist

transport., transportation
trng., training
trtmt., treatment
tstng., testing
TV, television
Twp., Township
UK, United Kingdom
univ., university, universidad, université
USSR, Union of Socialist Soviet Republics
utiliz., utilization
Vets., Veterans
vis.,visiting
vocat., vocational
W., West
W.A., Western Australia
WAPOR, World Association for Public Opinion Research
welf., welfare
WFMH, World Federation for Mental Nealth
wrkr, worker
YPA, Yugoslav Psychological Association (Udruzenje Psihologa FNRJ; Psychological Association of the Federal People's Republic of Yugoslavia)
Yugo., Yugoslavia
Yuk., Yukon
zool., zoology, zoological

Man., Manitoba
Mar, March
math., mathematics
MB, BS, BCH, Bachelor of Medicine, Bachelor of Surgery
MD, Doctor of Medicine
mech., mechanical, mechanics
med., medical, medicine
memor., memorial
ment., mental
metrop., metropolitan
mfg., manufacturing
mgr., manager
milit., military
mkt., market
MPs, Master of Psychology
MPsSc, Master of Psychological Science
msmt., measurement
munic., municipal
N., North.
N.B., New Brunswick
natl., national
nerv., nervous
Neth., The Netherlands (Holland)
ner., neurology, neurological
Newf., Newfoundland
NIPP, Netherland Institute of Practising Psychologists (Nederlands Instituut voor Praktizeerende Psychologen)
N.Ire., Northern Ireland
No., Northern
Nor., Norway, Norwegian
Nov, November
NP, Norsk Psykologforening
nrsng., nursing
N.S., Nova Scotia
N.S.W., New South Wales
N.T., Northern Territory
N.Z., New Zealand
observ., observer
occupat., occupation, occupational
Oct, October
off., office, officer
OGP, Osterreichische Gesellschaft für Psychologie
Ont., Ontario
oper., operation
optom., optometry
organiza., organization
pathol., pathology
pediat., pediatrics
P.E.I., Prince Edward Island
penit., penitentiary
pers., personnel
PH.B, Bachelor of Philosophy
PH.D, Doctor of Philosophy
philos., philosphy
PH.L, Licence in Philosophy
PH.M, Master of Philosophy
phys., physician
physiol., physiology
pkwy., Parkway
Pl., Place, Plaza

plng., planning
P.O., Post Office
polit., political
PPC, Pakistan Philosophical Congress
P.Q., Province of Quebec
prac., practice
pres., president
preven., preventive
prin., principal
priv., private
prob., probation
prof., professor
profes., professional
prog., program
proj., project
psych., psychology, psychological
psychiat., psychiatry, psychiatric
psychoanal., psychoanalysis, psychoanalytic
psychomet., psychometric, psychometrician
psychother., psychotherapy
psych't., psychologist
PTP, Polskie Towarzystwo Psychologiczne
pub., public
Que., Quebec
Rd., Road
recreatl., recreational
reform., reformatory
reg., regional
rehab., rehabilitation
relat., relation
relig., religious, religion
remed., remedial
rep., representative
res., research
resid., resident
ret., retired
Rev., Reverend
RMPA, Royal Medico Psychological Association
S., South
S.A., South Africa
sanitar, sanitarium
SAPA, South African Psychological Association
Sask., Saskatchewan
SBP, Société Belge de Psychologie
sch., school
sci., science, scientific, scientist
Scot., Scotland
SCP, Society of Clinical Psychology (Japan)
sect., section
secy., secretary
sel., selection
semin., seminary
SEP, Sociedad Española de Psicología
Sept, September
serv., service
SFP, Société Française de Psychologie
SIP, Sociedad Interamericano de Psicología (Interamerican Society of Psychology)
SNPPD, Syndicat National des Psychologues Practiciens Diplômés
So., Southern
soc., social
sociol, sociology, sociological

consult., consultant, consulting
coop., cooperative
coord., coordinator, coordination
corp., corporation
correctl., correctional
correctn., correction
counc., council
couns., counselor, counseling
CPA, Canadian Psychological Association
crim., criminal
criminol., criminology
CSc, Candidate of Science
ct., court
Czech., Czechoslovakia
Dec., December
def., defense
defic., deficiency
deleg., delegate
Den., Denmark
dept., department
devel., development, developmental
DGP,, Deutsche Gesellschaft für Psychologie
diag., diagnostic
Dipl., Diploma, Diplôme
dir., director, directorate
discip., disciplinary
dispens., dispensary
dist., district
div., division
DLit, Doctor of Literature
DLitt, Doctor of Letters
domes., domestic
dorm., dormitory
DP, Dansk Psykologforening
DPM, Diploma in Psychological Medicine
dpto., departamento (office, apartment)
Dr., Drive, Doctor, Docteur, Dottore
Drs., Doctorandus
D.SC, Doctor of Science
dynam., dynamics
E., East
econ., economics
ed., editor, editorial
ED.B, Bachelor of Education
ED.D, Doctor of Education
ED.M, Master of Education
educ., education, educational
EEG, electroencephalography
elec., electric, electronic
elem., elementary
emer., emeritus, emergency
empl., employment
Eng., England
engr., engineering, engineer
equip., equipment
eval., evaluation
exam., examiner, examining, examination
excep., exceptional
exec., executive
exper., experimental
ext., extension
fac., faculty, facultad
fam., family

Feb, February
fed., federal, federation
found., foundation
Fr., France, French
gd., ground
genl., general
Ger., Germany, German
govt., government
grad., graduate
grp., group
grtr., greater
guid., guidance
hlth., health
hosp., hopital
HPS, Hellenic Psychological Society
hq., headquarters
hrng., hearing
hse., house
hyg., hygiene
ICWP, International Council of Women Psychologists
indep., independent
indiv., individual
indus., industrial
info., information
ins., insurance
inst., institute, institution, instituto, institut
instr., instructor, instruction
int., international
interv., interviewer
inves., investigation, investigator
IPA, Indian Psychological Association
Ire., Ireland
IRRA, Industrial Relations Research Association
ISCA, Indian Science Congress Association
IsPA, Israel Psychological Association
It., Italy, Italian
IUSP, International Union of Scientific Psychology
JAEP, Japanese Association of Educational Psychology
Jan, January
Jap., Japanese
JPA, Japanese Psychological Association
jr., junior
JSAP, Japan Society of Applied Psychology
juv., juvenile
KPA, Korean Psychological Association
lab., laboratory, laboratoire
Lab., Labrador
lect., lecturer
lib., library, librarian
Lib. Doc., Libero Docente, Libera Docenza
lic., licensed
Lic., Licence, Licenciado, Licenciatura
LL.D., Doctor of Law
LPs, Licence in Psychology
lrng., learning
Lt., Lieutenant
MA, Master of Arts
Mag., Magister
Maj., Major

ABBREVIATIONS

Abbreviations are used wherever possible to achieve maximum brevity. In general, they have been used for geographic names, academic degrees, psychological society names, and words commonly used in describing the positions and places of employment held by psychologists.

For purposes of clarity and comprehension, no abbreviations have been used in the section of each entry describing the psychologist's activities and interests.

abn., abnormal
Acad., Academy
ACOF, Association des Conseillers d'Orientation de France
acous., acoustical
A.C.T., Australian Capital Territory
activ., activity, activities
adj., adjunct
admin., administrator, administration, administrative
adol., adolescence
adv., advertising
advanc., advancement, advanced
advis., advisor
AE.SC, Academy of Educational Sciences (USSR)
affil., affiliate
agric., agricultural
AIOP, Association Internationale d'Orientation Professionnelle
AIPA, Association Internationale de Psychologie Appliquée
Alta., Alberta
Amer., American
anal., analyst, analysis, analytic
anat., anatomy
anthrop., anthropology, anthropological
APA, American Psychological Association
APPD, Association Professionnelle des Psychotechniciens Diplômés
appl., applied
Apr, April
APSLF, Association de Psychologie Scientifique de Langue Française
apt., apartment
aptit., aptitude
assn., association
assoc., associate
asst., assistant
Aug, August
Austl., Australia, Australian
Ave., Avenue, Avenida
aviat., aviation
BA, Bachelor of Arts
BAAP, Brazilian Association of Applied Psychologists (Associação Brasileira de Psicotécnica)
B.C., British Colombia
BCom, Bachelor of Commerce
bd., board
BDP, Berufsverband Deutscher Psychologen

BE, Bachelor of Engineering
beh., behavior
Bel., Belgium, Belgian
biol., biological, biology
bldg., building
Blvd., Boulevard
BLP, Berufsverband Osterreichischer Psychologen
BPA, Brazilian Psychological Association (Associação Brasileira de Psicologos)
BPs, Bachelor of Psychology
B.PS, British Psychological Society
BPS-A, British Psychological Society, Australian Branch
BPS-NZ, British Psychological Society, New Zealand Branch
br., branch
Br., British
BRF, British Rorschach Forum
Bros., Brothers
B.SC, Bachelor of Science
B.RH, Bachelor of Theology
bur., bureau
bus., business
Can., Canada, Canadian
Cand., Candidate
Cath., Catholic
CBSc, Candidate of Biological Sciences
cen., center, central
cert., certificate, certification
CESc, Candidate of Educational Sciences
child., children
chmn., chairman
ChPA, Chinese Psychological Association
CJSc, Candidate of Juridical Sciences
classif., classification
clin., clinical, clinic, clinician
Cmd., Command
CMSc, Candidate of Medical Sciences
CNSc, Candidate of Natural Sciences
Co., Company
Col., Colonel
coll., college
comm., committee, commission
commr., commissioner
commun., community
communic., communication
comp., comparative
conf., conference
cong., congress
conserv., conservation

Ecuador:	Dr. Edmundo Carbo, Quito.
Guatemala:	Dr. Richard N. Adams, East Lansing, Michigan, U.S.A.
Honduras:	Dr. Victor Donaire Funes, Tegucigalpa.
Mexico:	Professor Guillermo Davila, Mexico City; Professora Zara Margarita Zendejas, Mexico City; Dr. Werner Wolff, Annandale on Hudson, New York, U.S.A.
Panama:	Mr. Andres O. Ponce A., Panama City.
Paraguay:	Miss Mary C. Albert, Asuncion.
Peru:	Dr. Walter Blumenfeld, Lima; Dr. Enrique Solari, President, Sociedad de Psicologia, Lima.
Uruguay:	Mr. Nicholas Altuchow, Monteviedeo.
Venezuela:	Dr. John Boulger, Caracas; Dr. F. Oliver Brachfeld, Caracas; Dr. Edwin R. Henry, New York City, U.S.A.

MIDDLE EAST

Dr. Bradford B. Hudson, Houston, Texas, U.S.A. and Professor E. Terry Prothro, Beirut, Lebanon, were of major assistance in assembling names of psychologists in Egypt, Iraq, Lebanon and Syria.

Egypt:	Dr. Chafik A. Chamass, UNESCO, Cairo; Professor Abdul Aziz El-Koussy, Cairo; Dr. A. Z. Selah, Cairo.
Iran:	Dr. Iraj Ayman, Tehran.
Iraq:	Professor Ibrahim A. Muhyi, Baghdad.
Israel:	Membership lists of the Israel Psychological Society were made available through Dr. Erwin Arnstein, IPS President in Jerusalem. Professor Albert Rabin, East Lansing, Michigan, U.S.A. was helpful in establishing contact with the Israel Society.
Syria:	Dr. George F. Miller, Aleppo.
Turkey:	Dr. Walter, R. Miles, Istanbul; Professor Orhan Tuna, Istanbul; Dr. John Volkmann, Massachusetts, U.S.A.

Notwithstanding the fact that many efforts were made to ensure both completeness and correctness, the editors are well aware that this Directory has many shortcomings. They hope that those of their colleagues who discover mistakes both of omission and of commission will not be discouraged from giving their indispensable assistance whenever an attempt will be made to publish a second edition of this Directory. For an enterprise like this can succeed only by a common effort from psychologists all over the world.

Poland:	Professor Stefan Blachowski, Poznan; Polskie Towarzystwo Psychologiczne.
Rumania:	Professor M. Ralea, Bucharest.
Spain:	Professor J. Germain, Madrid; Professor M. Yela, Madrid. Spanish Psychological Society.
Sweden:	Kjell Härnqvist, Stockholm; David Magnusson, Stockholm; Swedish Psychological Association. The editors express their gratitude to Mr. Magnusson for checking the Swedish entries.
Switzerland:	Professor Bärbel Inhelder, Geneva; Swiss Psychological Association.
Union of Soviet Socialist Republics:	Professor A. N. Leontiev, Moscow; Academy of Educational Sciences of the U.S.S.R., U.S.S.R. Psychological Association. Very special thanks are due to Professor Leontiev. He arranged to have the questionnaire translated into Russian, distributed and collected, and had the completed questionnaires translated into English.
United Kingdom:	Dr. Arthur Summerfield, London; British Psychological Society. Dr. Summerfield's assistance has been particularly valuable. He has both distributed and assembled the questionnaires in the United Kingdom.
Yugoslavia:	Dr. Borislav Petz, Belgrade; Psychological Association of the Federal People's Republic of Yugoslavia.

LATIN AMERICA

The primary sources of names for Latin America were the Inter-American Society of Psychology; the Pan American Union; Dr. Margaret Hall Powers, Chicago, U.S.A.; a report of the first Argentine Psychological Congress and UNESCO. Special thanks are also due to individuals who were helpful in locating psychologists in various countries as follows:

Argentina:	Dr. Mauricio Knobel, Buenos Aires; Dr. Carlos A. Pourteau Agote, Buenos Aires; Dr. H. J. A. Rimoldi, Chicago, Illinois, U.S.A.
Brazil:	Dr. Dante Moriera Leite, Lawrence, Kansas, U.S.A.; Miss Odette Lourencau, Secretary, Sociedade de Psicologia de Sao Paulo; Dr. Joel Martins, President, Associacao Brasileira de Psicologos, Sao Paulo; Dr. Emilio Mira y Lopez, Secretary, Brazilian Association of Applied Psychologists, Rio de Janeiro; and Mrs .Ruth Nobre Scheefer, Brazilian Association of Applied Psychologists, Rio de Janeiro.
British West Indies:	Dr. H. D. Huggins, Jamaica.
Chile:	Professor Carlos Nassar, Santiago.
Colombia:	Professor Rafael Nunez, Bogota; Mr. Ernesto Camacho Leyva, Bogota.
Cuba:	Dr. Guillermo Francovich, UNESCO, Havana.
Dominican Republic:	Dr. Andres Avelino, Cuidad Trujillo.

names with the presidents of the Provincial Psychological Associations: Dr. E. P. Friesen, British Columbia; Dr. Jean Garneau, Quebec; Dr. C. A. McMurray, Saskatchewan; Dr. R. H. Nicholson, Ontario; and Dr. F. H. Page, Maritime Psychological Association.

EUROPE

Acknowledgements are due to the various national Psychological Societies and a large number of individual psychologists, without whose co-operation and advice it would not have been possible to reach so many psychologists in nearly all European countries. In particular, the editors want to express their gratitude to the following persons and organizations:

Austria:	Professor H. Rohracher, Vienna; Berufsverband Oesterreichischer Psychologen; Dr. Otto Pawlik, Vienna.
Belgium:	Professor J. Nuttin, Louvain; Belgian Association of Psychology.
Czechoslovakia:	Dr. Vaclav Prihoda, Prague.
Denmark:	Poul W. Perch, Copenhagen; Danish Psychological Association. Special thanks are due to Mr. Perch for checking the Danish entries.
Finland:	Christel Svedlin, Helsinki; Finnish Psychological Society. The editors gratefully acknowledge the trouble taken by Miss Svedlin in checking the Finnish entries.
France:	Professor P. Fraisse, Paris; Dr. J. Bonnaire, Paris; Société Française de Psychologie. Association Professionnelle des Psychotechniciens Diplomés. Professor Fraisse and the French Psychological Society have contributed materially to an adequate representation of France, both by screening the address lists and by checking the completed entries.
Germany:	Professor A. Wellek, Mainz; Deutsche Gesellschaft für Psychologie; Berufsverband Deutscher Psychologen. Professor Wellek had made a great and valuable effort in assembling and making available to the editors not only the names of the members of both German societies, but also of those qualified psychologists who were not members of either of them.
Greece:	Professor G. Sakellariou, Athens; Hellenic Psychological Association.
Hungary:	Professor Lajos Kardos, Budapest. Hungarian Psychological Society.
Iceland:	Dr. B. Johanesson; Icelandic Psychological Association.
Ireland:	Dr. Nico Steemens, S.M.A., Wilton, Cork.
Italy:	Professor A. Gemelli, Milan; Professor C. L. Musatti, Milan; Professor A. Marzi, Florence; Societa Italiana di Psicologia.
Norway:	Arvid As, Oslo; P. A. Holter, Oslo; Jarle Rotevatn, Oslo; Norwegian Psychological Association. The editors want to express their thanks to the officers of the Norwegian Psychological Association for checking the completed entries.

	Schuelke, USIA, Madras; Dr. J. D. N. Versluys, UNESCO, Calcutta.
Indonesia:	Professor H. J. Heeren, Djakarta.
Japan:	We are particularly grateful to Professor Sadaji Takagi, Tokyo Joshi Daigaku, President, and Professor Matsusaburo Yokoyama, Keio University, Executive Director of the Japanese Psychological Association, who collected Directory questionnaires in Japan, and supervised preliminary editing and screening of the translated questionnaires in Japan before sending them to the editorial offices. Questionnaires were collected from members of the J.P.A. and the Japanese Society of Applied Psychology, the Society of Clinical Psychology, the Japanese Association of Educational Psychology, the Japanese Society of Animal Psychology, Japanese Association of Correctional Psychology.
	Special help was provided to the Directory Project by Professor Koje Sato, Kyoto University, who visited the Directory offices in Ann Arbor frequently during the project. Professor Hiroshi Kaneko, Hiroshima University, and Mr. Jyuji Misumi, in residence at Ann Arbor, were also of assistance.
Malaya:	Mr. K. Spelling, UNESCO, Kuala Lumpur.
Pakistan:	Professor Ghulam Jilani, Dacca; Colonel Rafi Z. Khan, Karachi; Dr. Randolph C. Sailer, Lahore; and Professor M. M. Sharif, Lahore.
Philippines:	Dr. Alfredo Lagmay, Manila.
South Korea:	Professor Koje Sato, Kyoto, Japan; Professor Soon Duk Koh, Seoul; Professor Suk-Jay Kim, Seoul.
Taiwan-Formosa:	Professor Chien-hou Hwang, Tapei; Professor Hsiang-Yu Su, Taipei; Professor Koje Sato, Kyoto, Japan; Dr. J. D. N. Versluys, Unesco, Calcutta, India.
Thailand:	Dr. Frederick L. Ayer, Bangkok; Dr. L. M. Hanks, Jr., North Bennington, Vermont, U.S.A.

AUSTRALIA AND NEW ZEALAND

Australia:	The Australian Branch of the British Psychological Society, through its President, Professor O. A. Oeser, Melbourne, and its Secretary, Dr. R. A. Champion, Sydney, made the membership lists of the Branch available to us.
New Zealand:	The New Zealand Branch of the British Psychological Society, through its President, Dr. T. H. Scott, Christchurch, made the membership lists of the Branch available to us.

CANADA

The Canadian Psychological Association through its Officers, Professor D. O. Hebb, McGill University, Montreal, Professor Noël Mailloux, University of Montreal, and Dr. Dalbir Bindra, McGill University, provided membership lists for the CPA. Through the CPA we were directed to correspond for additional

National Academy of Sciences-National Research Council Committee for the Directory included Drs. Lee Cronbach, Frank Geldard, Robert B. MacLeod and Edwin B. Newman whose extensive knowledge of professional psychology and psychologists was made available to the project throughout its course.

As Executive Secretary of the Division of Anthropology and Psychology of the National Academy of Sciences-National Research Council, Dr. Glen Finch has devoted much time and energy to guiding the project, from its original efforts to obtain funds through the publishing phase.

During 1955 and 1956, Dr. Finch was working with Dr. Harry Harlow as Chairman of the Division of Anthropology and Psychology. In 1957, Dr. Clyde Kluckhohn succeeded Dr. Harlow as Chairman of the Division.

In the various countries, the Directory project was assisted by many people. Among them are:

AFRICA

For initial contacts in Africa, Mrs. M. E. M. Chilver, former Secretary, Colonial Social Science Research Council, London, England; Dr. G. Latouche, Brazza-ville, French Equatorial Africa; Dr. Th. Monod, Dakar, French West Africa, and Professor Josef Nuttin, University of Louvain, Belgium, were generous in their help.

In the various countries, the following individuals assisted us in locating psychologists:

Belgian Congo: Dr. Paul Verhaegen, Elizabethville.
Camerouns: Dr. P. Stoerckel, Duala.
Ethiopia: Mr. Mekuria Worku, Addis Ababa.

French West Africa: Mr. R. Durand, Dakar.
Ghana: Dr. G. Jahoda, Glasgow, Scotland.
Nigeria: Mr. P. Morton-Williams, Ibadan; Dr. T. A. Lambo, Aro Abeokuta.

Union of South Africa: The officers of the South African Psychological Association: Dr. S. Biesheuvel, Johannesburg; Professor A. J. LaGrange, Stellenbosch, and Dr. H. Reuning, Johannesburg, provided membership lists for the Association.

ASIA

Ceylon: Professor T. L. Green, Colombo.
Mainland China: Professor Koje Sato, Kyoto, Japan.
India: In India we were most fortunate to have the co-operation of the Indian Government and a number of officers of psy-chological societies, UNESCO and the universities. Among the many who helped us assemble names are:
Under-Secretary Shri T. S. Bhatia, New Delhi; Professor L. J. Bhatt, Baroda; Professor G. D. Boaz, Madras; Pro-fessor Sudhir K. Bose, Bangalore; Dr. Kamla Chowdrhy, Ahmedebad; Dr. D. Ganguli, Calcutta; Dr. D. A. Mehta, New Delhi; Dr. Raj Narain, Lucknow; Mr. Herbert Theodore

clearly were not in the field of professional psychology or whose entries were received too late for publishing deadlines.

Questionnaire mailing was begun in 1955, reached its peak in 1956, and continued until the first months of 1957. Questionnaires returned after the summer of 1957 have not been included. Approximately 13,000 questionnaires were sent out and approximately 7,000 were returned completed.

The Editors realize that, although we made a conscientious effort to establish contact with psychologists in the various countries, we have not been uniformly successful in representing psychologists in all communities.

Format of Entries

More material was obtained from the questionnaires than is included in this Directory. For the purpose of publication, the following items were selected:

1. The name and title of the respondent. In all cases titles were simplified, and an attempt was made to achieve uniformity in presenting academic degrees.
2. Preferred mailing address. This is the address to which the respondent prefers to have his mail sent.
3. Date of birth.
4. Place of birth.
5. Highest earned academic degree.
6. University granting degree and year in which degree was granted.
7. Membership in professional societies.
8. Editorial responsibilities.
9. Current occupation.
10. Primary fields of interest in psychology.
11. Sex.

In many cases, it was impossible to represent the respondent's education, academic achievements, professional society memberships or professional interests and occupations fully. Because of space limitations, we did not include any information about publications, but publications were used to confirm data about professional interests.

Acknowledgements

The initial planning of the Directory benefited from the advice of Dr. Melville Herskovits, Editor of the International Directory of Anthropologists for the National Research Council; Dr. George Kish, Chairman of the Committee of the International Geographical Union that published the World Directory of Geographers; Dr. Jane Hildreth, former Editor of the Directory of the American Psychological Association; Dr. H. S. Langfeld, former Secretary-General of the International Union of Scientific Psychology; Dr. Otto Klineberg, former Director of the Applied Social Sciences Division of Unesco, now Secretary-General of the International Union of Scientific Psychology; Dr. Theo R. Crevenna of the Pan American Union; Dr. Donald McGranahan of the United Nations; Dr. Werner Wolff, Secretary-General of the Inter-American Society of Psychology, and Dr. Samy Friedman, Editor, International Social Science Bulletin, Division of International Development of Social Sciences, Unesco.

In addition to Drs. Boring, Langfeld, Klineberg and Hildreth the sponsoring

EDITOR'S INTRODUCTION AND ACKNOWLEDGEMENTS

How the Directory Project was Organized

The major planning for the Directory has been the task of the Committee on an International Directory of Psychologists of the National Academy of Sciences-National Research Council, led by Professors Edwin G. Boring and Herbert S. Langfeld. The responsibility for finding subventions has been assumed by Dr. Glen Finch of the Council's Division of Anthropology and Psychology.

The availability of substantial National Science Foundation and U.S. Air Force support left the Editors free to devote their energies to finding psychologists. To accomplish this we established two editorial offices. At the Psychological Laboratory at the University of Amsterdam, Netherlands, Professor H. C. J. Duijker, Director of the Laboratory, set up procedures for collecting questionnaires from his colleagues in Europe. In the Institute for Social Research of the University of Michigan, at Ann Arbor, Michigan, Dr. Eugene Jacobson maintained central records, collected questionnaires from countries outside of Europe, and prepared entries.

The Ann Arbor office was under the direction of editorial assistants Mrs. Elman Service and Mrs. Doris Slesinger who organized and supervised the day to day work of mailing out questionnaires, receiving them and drafting entries.

When the entries were written, they were sent to Professor Duijker for final checking and publishing.

Who are the Psychologists Listed in the Directory?

Because the American Psychological Association publishes a readily available Directory of Psychologists in the United States, it was decided that the International Directory should not duplicate that effort but, rather, should represent psychologists in all countries outside of the United States.

In countries where psychological societies exist, the membership lists of those societies have been the primary source of names for the Directory. In countries where there are no active societies, contacts have been made through a variety of professional sources, including international professional groups, universities, UNESCO representatives, research institutes, local agencies, and individual psychologists.

When names were assembled in our editorial offices, a questionnaire was sent to every person who might ultimately be listed in the Directory. The last section of the questionnaire provided space for the respondent to list additional names and addresses of psychologists known to him who might not otherwise come to the attention of the editors.

It was the intention of the advisory committee and the Editors to produce a directory that would include a large percentage of the professional psychologists, rather than one limited to a smaller group of better known persons in each of the countries. Because psychology is developing at different rates in different countries, it was not considered desirable or possible to set common standards for inclusion. Directory entries were prepared for all persons who returned questionnaires with the exception of a relatively small group who a member, with the addition of Otto Klineberg and Robert B. MacLeod, with Boring retained as chairman. In the fall Lee J. Cronbach and Frank A. Geldard were added to the Committee.

A prime mover in this undertaking has been Dr. Glen Finch, the Executive Secretary of the Division of Anthropology and Psychology of the National Research Council. He kept the project active until there were editors to take over, and he has persistently sought and found the necessary subventions. Some of the needed money could come from the National Research Council's fund that was derived from royalties on certain psychological tests and books that the Council had published. More support was promised by the Air Force, since the data on foreign research psychologists was information that the Air Force needed. Later assistance came from the National Science Foundation.

The new committee's first move was to find an Editor who could take over the project as administrative officer. It considered ten persons and in the spring of 1955 chose Eugene H. Jacobson, who, with Finch's support, relieved the sponsoring committee of activity other than oversight and approval.

It soon became evident to Jacobson and the Committee that a European Co-Editor was needed. After careful consideration, later in 1955, the Committee persuaded Dr. H. C. J. Duijker of Amsterdam to undertake this responsibility.

Since then the project has moved ahead under the cooperative enthusiasms of Jacobson, Duijker and Finch, with a speed and success that have both surprised and delighted the Committee. The further account of how the world psychologists were selected, how the data were secured, how the new directory, much larger than had been anticipated, was ultimately financed and manufactured, the Chairman leaves to the Editor, under whose superintendence the project was completed.

EDWIN G. BORING, CHAIRMAN

Committee on an International Directory of Psychologist[S]
Exclusive of the United States
U.S. National Research Council-National
Academy of Sciences.

AN INTRODUCTORY STATEMENT
for the International Directory of Psychologists by the
Chairman of the N.R.C. Committee

Science is advantaged by communication, and the broader the spread of communication the better for civilization and progress. When many nations are working in the same field, it is important to keep scientific communication and personal acquaintance as international as possible. In psychology a great service to international understanding and acquaintance was rendered in 1932 by Carl Murchison's publication of the *Psychological Register*, a volume that listed the vitae and bibliographies of 1156 psychologists in 38 countries including the United States. As this volume became more and more superanuated, the demand for an up-dated edition increased, especially after the Second World War, when the number of American psychologists was increasing exponentially and the Americans were failing to make contact with their new European and other foreign colleagues, and they with each other.

In 1932, when the *Psychological Register* was published, the membership of the American Psychological Association was 1510. In 1940 it was 2739. In 1950 it had grown to 7273. In 1957 it is 15,545. This phenomenal growth had the effect of making the Americans so concerned with their own complicated affairs that most of them were becoming unaware of the activities of psychologists on the other five continents. A small group of Americans sought, however, to keep contact abroad, especially with the Europeans, and to strengthen the weak bonds, but at first they had but little success.

Meanwhile printing costs had gone up. It had become impossible to reproduce a volume like the *Register* with complete bibliographies, or to plan an international directory that would include the Americans, who in 1957 are 13 times as numerous as Murchison's entire 1156 world psychologists in 1932. Some of us, then, in association with Dr. Herbert S. Langfeld, chairman of the U.S. National Research Council's Committee on International Relations in Psychology, proposed seeking a subvention for a directory without the bibliographies and excluding the overwhelmingly numerous psychologists of the United States. Such a project seemed to lie within the realm of practicality. The American Psychological Association considered sponsoring the project but decided that its role is chiefly national and that it ought not to get so deeply involved in international psychology. Then Langfeld's committee put the matter in 1953 to the National Research Council, which appointed, under his Committee, a subcommittee to examine the desirability and feasibility of the project: H. S. Langfeld (ex-officio), Jane D. Hildreth, Edwin B. Newman, and Edwin G. Boring (Chairman).

This committee polled 245 Fellows of the American Psychological Association and 64 members of the Society of Experimental Psychologists. The response was almost entirely favorable although not highly enthusiastic. The indications were that many Americans would buy the directory if it were published. The clinical psychologists were as favorable as the experimentalists; the older persons were somewhat more favorable than the younger. On these grounds the National Research Council in the spring of 1954 decided to go ahead. It made the subcommittee into an independent committee, with Langfeld still

CONTENTS

ALGERIA

BACKES-THOMAS, Mrs. Madeleine. 12 Rue
Hydra, Algiers. b. 26 Jan 1913 Boufarik.
Diplôme '37 Univ. of Geneva, Switz.
PSYCHOANALYST, priv. prac. Member: Swiss
Psychoanal. Socy, Int. Psychoanal. Socy.
Psychotherapy, research, testing, clinical
analysis; psychoanalysis, projective tech-
niques.   F
DELMAS, Mr. Centre Orientation Profession-
nelle, Bône. b. 16 Apr 1917 Les Lèves,
Gironde, Fr. Conseiller, Univ. of Paris, Fr.
DIRECTOR, Centre d'Orientation Profession-
nelle. Member: ACOF. Consulting, guidance,
applied and industrial psychology, teaching
characterology, social psychology.   M
MALMEJAC, Prof. Jean. Fac. of Med.Univ.
of Algiers, Algeria. b. 5 June 1903 Arras,
Fr. Prof, Univ. of Algiers, Algeria. PROF. of
PHYSIOL, Univ. of Algiers; DIRECTOR, Inst.
for Psychotech, Univ. of Algiers. Member:
SFP, APSLF. Research, teaching, testing;
aviation psychology, psychophysiology.   M
MAZZIOTTA, André. 32 Rue Joseph Bosco,
Constantine. b. 10 Nov 1921 Constantine.

Diplôme d'état '54 Univ. of Paris, Fr.
VOCAT. GUID. COUNS, Centre d'Orientation
Professionnelle, Musée Mercier Condiat,
Constantine. Guidance, testing, clinical
analysis, applied, educational and in-
dustrial psychology.   M
RONCEVICH, Mr. Henri. 56 Rue Alaize,
Sidi-Mabrouk, Constantine. b. 3 Sept 1921
Constantine. Diplôme d'état, Constantine,
Algeria. VOCAT. GUID. COUNS, Centre
d'Orientation Professionnelle, Constantine.
Member: ACOF. Consulting, clinical
practice, guidance, applied, educational and
industrial psychology, testing, clinical
analysis.   M
SALASCA, Georges. Centre d'Orientation
Professionnelle, Musée Mercier, Constantin
b. 30 June 1920 Letourneux. Diplôme
d'état '50 Univ. of Paris, France. DIRECTOR,
Centre Pub. d'Orientation Professionnelle.
Research, administration, consulting,
clinical practice, guidance; social psychology, learning, guidance of secondary
school students.   M

ARGENTINA

ANSELMO, Prof. Dr. Victorio. Casilla 74,
Suc. 1 B, Buenos Aires. b. 5 July 1921
Buenos Aires. MD, Univ. of Buenos Aires,
Argentina. DIRECTOR, Mental Hyg. Clinic,
Hosp. de Merlo, Buenos Aires; CHIEF, Med.
Serv, Casa Tow, Whiteaway, Laidlaw and
Co. Member: Argentine Med. Assn.
Clinical practice, testing and clinical
analysis, teaching, research; psychotherapy,
mental tests, personality of the criminal. M
ARIAS, Prof. Arturo Horacio. Ave. Santa Fe
3242, piso 8, dpto. D, Buenos Aires. b.
4 Apr 1921 Buenos Aires. Prof. Inst.
Superior de Pedagogía, Argentina. DIREC-
TOR, Educ. and Vocat. Guid. Cen, Inst.
,,F. F. Bernasconi," Ministry of Educ,
Pedro Echagüe 2750, Buenos Aires; PROF.
of APPL. PSYCH. Escuela Superior Técnica,
Ministry of Soc. Assistence and Pub. Hlth.
Member: Argentine Psych. Socy. Applied
psychology, consulting, vocational and
educational guidance, teaching; characterology, psychology of learning, aptitude
measurement.   M
ASTI VERA, Prof. Armando Antonio. Campos
Salles 2190, Sucursal 29, Buenos Aires.
b. 25 June 1914 Buenos Aires. Prof. '46
Univ. of Buenos Aires, Argentina. PROF-
ESSOR, Fac. of Philos.and Letters,Viamonte
430, Buenos Aires. Teaching, research,
professional writing; parapsychology,
oriental psychology, psychology of religion,

methodology and epistemology of psychology.   M
AYBAR, Dr. Benjamín. Calle San Martín
51, San Miguel de Tucumán. b. 14 Apr 1896
San Miguel de Tucumán. PhD '19 Univ.
Gregoriana, Rome, Italy. PROF. EMER. of
EXPER. PSYCH, Natl. Univ. of Tucumán.
Research, applied, educational and industrial psychology, teaching; vocational
guidance, moral conduct and the origin of
conflict, theory of telepathy, paramnesia,
and suggestion.   M
BADANO, Prof. Hector Ceferino. General Paz
756, San Isidro. b. 26 Aug. 1913, Ex. de la
Cruz. Prof. Inst. of Psych, Argentina.
PRINCIPAL, Primary School No. 1, Rivadavia
349, San Isidro; PROFESSOR, Inst. of Psych.
Teaching, applied and educational psycho-
logy, consulting, guidance; ergologia,
vocational guidance.   M
BELBEY, Dr. José. Ave. Callao 232, Buenos
Aires. b. 1 Jan 1894, Parana. MD '20
Univ. of Buenos Aires, Argentina. DIRECTOR
Priv. Psychiat. Clin, Ave. San Martín 2880,
Buenos Aires; PROF. TITULAR of LEGAL MED,
Natl. Univ. of La Plata, and Univ. of
Buenos Aires. Member: SIP, Argentine
Psych. Socy, Socy. of Neur, Psychiat. and
Neurosurgery. Psychotherapy, consulting,
clinical practice, guidance; social per-
ception   M
BERNARD, Dr. Ernestina Mercedes. Santa

Ana 2140, Córdoba. b. 28 Nov. 1928 Córdoba. Lic. '49 Natl. Univ. of Córdoba, Argentina. PSYCHOLOGIST, Serv. of Child Psychopathol, Hosp. de Niños, Corrientes 643, Córdoba; PROFESSOR, Escuela Normal Alejandro Carbo, Córdoba. Testing, clinical analysis, psychological re-education of retarded children; projective techniques, intelligence tests, methods of teaching. F

BERNSTEIN, Prof. Jaime. Cabildo 1695, piso 8, dpto. 25, Buenos Aires. b. 25 Aug 1917 Buenos Aires. Prof. of Pedagogy '42 Univ. of Buenos Aires, Argentina. PROF. of EDUC. PSYCH. and DIRECTOR, Psych. Inst, Univ. of the Litoral, Entre Ríos 758, Rosario. Member: Argentine Cen. for Pedagogical Studies. Teaching, research, educational psychology; child psychology and guidance. M

BERRUEZO, Dr. Juan José. General Urquiza 358, Buenos Aires. b. 29 Oct 1919 La Plata. MD '46 Univ. of Buenos Aires, Argentina. DIRECTOR, Serv. of Psychosomatic Med, Natl. Inst. of Allergy Illnesses, Cangallo 1435, Buenos Aires. Member: Argentine Socy. of Psychosomatic Med, Argentine Socy. of Med. Anthropology. Psychotherapy, teaching, professional writing; psychosomatic medicine, existential a-nalysis. M

BIANCHI, Prof. Ariel Edgardo. 24 de Noviembre 405, Buenos Aires. b. 12 Apr 1926 Rosario. Prof. '47 Univ. of Buenos Aires, Argentina. PROF. of PSYCH, Colegio Militar de la Nación, El Palomar. Teaching, testing, clinical analysis, research; projective techniques, attitude measurement, military psychology. M

BIEDMA, Dr. Carlos José. Escuela Argentina Modelo, Rio Bamba 1059, Buenos Aires. b. 11 Mar 1915 Buenos Aires. PH.D, Univ. of Buenos Aires, Argentina. DIRECTOR, Escuela Argentina Modelo. Testing, educational psychology, teaching; projective and creative tests, personality tests. M

BLOTTA, Prof. María Alba. San Luis 401, Rosario. b. 31 May 1926 Rosario. Prof. Natl. Univ. of the Litoral, Argentina. PROFESSOR, Escuela Normal de Profesoras No. 1, Corrientes 1197, Rosario; CHIEF, Vocat. Guid. Dept, Inst. of Psych, Natl. Univ. of the Litoral. Teaching, educational psychology, student; projective techniques, educational and vocational guidance. F

BONO, Prof. Humberto Miguel. Viel 664, piso 1, dpto. D, Buenos Aires. b. 7 Oct 1913 Buenos Aires. Prof. '38 Univ. of Buenos Aires, Argentina. PSYCHOLOGIST, Asesoría Etnica Militar, Ing. Huergo 251, Buenos Aires; PROF. of EDUC. PSYCH, Inst. del Profesorado en Lenguas Vivas "Juan R. Fernández," Buenos Aires. Testing,

clinical analysis, teaching; ethnic psychology, projective techniques, intelligence tests. M

BONOLI CIPOLLETTI, Dr. Hector. San Martin 58, Moron, Buenos Aires. b. 9 Mar 1912 Mendoza. Diplôme '49 Univ. of Buenos Aires, Argentina. PSYCHIATRIST, Inst. of Surgery of Haedo, Buenos Aires; PROFESSOR, School of Psychiat. Soc. Work, Ministry of Pub. Hlth. Clinical practice, teaching, research; projective techniques, child development, psychotherapy. M

BOTTO, Dr. Jorge Armando. Colegio Militar de la Nacion, El Palomar. b. 4 Nov 1919 Buenos Aires. MD '44 Univ. of Buenos Aires, Argentina. CHIEF, Hlth. Serv, Colegio Militar; PSYCHIATRIST, Policlínico Bancario. Member: Argentine Med. Assn. Psychotherapy, testing, clinical practice, guidance; aptitude measurement, projective and achievement tests, psychosomatic medicine. M

BRAGE, Dr. Diego. Carlos Pellegrini 1336, Buenos Aires. b. 12 June 1920 Entre Ríos. Docente Libre de Neurología, Univ. of Buenos Aires, Argentina. DOCENT of NEUR, Fac. of Med, Univ. of Buenos Aires; NEUROLOGIST, Natl. Neuropsychiat. Hosp. for Women, Buenos Aires. Member: SIP, Socy. of Neur, Psychiat. and Neurosurgery. Teaching, clinical practice, student; projective techniques, attitude measurement, group processes. M

BRENER DE SCHEINER, Prof. Julia. Pasteur 556, piso 3, Buenos Aires. b. 7 Sept 1924 Buenos Aires. Prof. '49 Univ. of Buenos Aires, Argentina. ASSISTANT, Dept. of Stud. Hlth, Ministry of Educ, Saavedra 15, Buenos Aires; PROF. of PSYCH. and EDUC, Escuela Normal de San Martín. Teaching, consulting, guidance, testing; infant psychology, educational guidance. F

BRUGGER, Prof. Dr. Heriberto Juan Bernardo. Inst. of Psychotechnics and Vocat. Guid, José Evaristo Uriburu 619, piso 5, dpto. B, Buenos Aires. b. 14 Aug. 1896, Austria. PH.D '28 Univ. of Innsbruck, Austria. DIR. and PROF, Inst. of Psychotechnics and Vocat. Guid. Member: Buenos Aires Psych. Assn, Argentine Assn. for the Advanc. of Sci. Research, teaching, testing, applied psychology; psychostructural relationships of intelligence, will, sensory perception and personality. M

CÁCERES, Miss María Etelvina. Alsina 532, Bolívar. b. 19 Sept 1899 Bolívar. Maestra normal, Normal Sch. of La Plata, Argentina PROF. of GENL. and EDUC. PSYCH, Inst. Adscripto Jesús Sacramentado, Ave. San Martín 583, Bolívar. Teaching, educational psychology, testing; attitude measurement, social psychology. F

CALDERADO, Prof. José Domingo. Melian

2237, Buenos Aires. b. 23 Feb 1894 Buenos Aires. PROF. of PSYCHOPEDAGOGY and PSYCH, Fac. of Humanities, Natl. Univ. of La Plata. Teaching, educational psychology, professional writing. M

CAMBIAGGIO, Prof. Miss Delmirà F. General Hornos 1110, 3 A, Buenos Aires. b. 11 June 1906 Buenos Aires. Prof, Radecki Psych School. Member: Latin American Coordinating Comm. of Psych. Industrial psychology, consulting, guidance; social psychology, educational problems. F

CANAVESIO, Dr. Orlando. Rivadavia 4144, Buenos Aires. b. 13 Jan 1916 Rafaela. MD, Univ. of Córdoba, Argentina. CHIEF of ENCEPHALOGRAPHIC SERV, Inst. of Neuroses, Fac. of Med, Paraguay and Uriburu, Buenos Aires. Member: Argentine Socy. of Psychosomatic Med, Argentine Socy. of Psychiat, Neur. and Neurosurgery, Argentine Socy. of Psych. and Psychoanal. Clinical practice, psychotherapy, research; electroencephalography. M

CASASOLA, Prof. Dr. Luis Antonio. San Lorenzo 2600, Santa Fe. b. 20 Dec 1915 Rosario. PH.D, Natl. Univ. of Córdoba, Argentina. PROF. of PSYCH. and PHILOS, Military Lyceum "Gral. Belgrano," Santa Fe. Member: SIP. Teaching, educational psychology, research; group process, sociology. M

CASTILLO SALAS, Prof. Dr. Cesar Rafael. Ave. Belgrano 1386, 3-A, Buenos Aires. b. 15 May 1904 Graneros. MD '27 Univ. of Buenos Aires, Argentina. DIRECTOR, Centro Antinervioso, Montevideo 855, Buenos Aires. Member: Socy. of Legal Med. and Toxicology, Argentine Socy. of Neur, Psychiat. and Neurosurgery, Argentine Assn. of Existential Logotherapy, Assn. of Med. Psychother. (Vienna). Psychotherapy, guidance, teaching; forensic psychiatry, criminology, social perception, existential analysis. M

CHUIT, Roberto Alejandro. Pasaje Soria 82, Córdoba. b. 11 Apr 1925 Pergamino. Lic, Natl. Univ. of Córdoba, Argentina. PROF. of PHILOS, Liceo Militar "General Paz," Km. 5½ Camino a Jesús María, Córdoba. Member: Asociación Iberoamericana para la Eficiencia y Satisfacción el el Trabajo (Madrid). Teaching, testing, consulting, guidance, industrial psychology; tests, vocational guidance, psychophysical methods of increasing production. M

CICCHITTI, Dr. Amadeo José. Chile 1350, Mendoza. b. 19 Dec 1914 Mendoza. MD '39 Univ. of Buenos Aires, Argentina. DIRECTOR, Dirección de Readaptación, San Martín 2165, Mendoza; DIRECTOR, Priv. Inst. of Appl. Psych; CHIEF, Serv. of Neuropsychiat. Inst. Member: Argentine Psych. Socy, Argentine Assn. of Psych'ts. Clinical

practice, guidance, psychotherapy; psychiatry, educational psychology. M

CORTADA, Prof. Nuria E. G. Salguero 1361, Buenos Aires. b. 5 Nov 1921 Mendoza. Prof. '45 Natl. Univ. of Cuyo, Argentina; MA '47 Ohio State Univ, USA. DIR. of SEMINARIES, Univ. of Buenos Aires, Viamonte 434, Buenos Aires. Member: SIP, AIPA. Teaching, research, testing; projective techniques, psychometrics, group psychotherapy for children. F

D'ALFONSO, Dr. Pedro Giordano. Medrano 391, Buenos Aires. b. 28 Aug 1907 Milan, Italy. PH.D, Univ. of Buenos Aires, Argentina. PROF. of CHILD PSYCH, Fac. of Philos. and Letters, Viamonte 420, Buenos Aires; DIRECTOR, Inst. Caracterológico. Member: Sociedad de Logoterapia. Consulting and vocational guidance, industrial psychology, teaching; characterology. M

DALMA, Prof. Dr. Giovanni Juan. Marcos Paz 419, dpto. D, Tucumán. b. 18 June 1895 Fiume, Italy. MD '20 Univ. of Padua, Italy. PROF. of PSYCHIAT, Fac. of Med, Natl. Univ. of Tucumán, Ayacucho 482, Tucumán. Member: SIP. Teaching, research, applied psychology, psychotherapy; dynamic psychology, history of psychology, social psychology. M

DAVID, Dr. Pedro R. Buenos Aires 263, San Miguel de Tucumán. b. 21 July 1929 Villa Alberdi. Dr. en Derecho, Univ. of Tucumán Argentina. CRIMINOLOGIST, Carcel Penitenciaria de Salta. Member: Latin Amer. Assn. of Sociol, Socy. of Criminol. and Legal Med. of Tucumán, Psych. Socy. of Salta. Applied psychology, professional writing, research; criminology, juvenile delinquency, psychology of the delinquent. M

DICK, Dr. José Guillermo Osman. Juncal 3626, Buenos Aires. b. 25 June 1194 La Rioja. MD '45 Univ. of La Plata, Argentina. DIRECTOR, Priv. Inst. "Argentino," Juncal 3626; PSYCHIAT. CONSULT, Hosp. Sirio Libanés, Buenos Aires. Member: SIP, Argentine Socy. of Psychosomatic Med, Argentine Eugenics Socy. Psychotherapy, testing, clinical analysis, consulting; psychosomatic medicine. M

ESCARDO, Prof. Florencio. Teodoro Garcia 1890, Buenos Aires. b.13 Aug 1904 Mendoza. MD '42 Univ. of Buenos Aires, Argentina. DIRECTOR, Neuropsychiat. Serv, Hospital de Niños, Gallo 1330, Buenos Aires. Member: SIP, Argentine Socy. of Criminol. Teaching, consulting, guidance, research; pediatrics, psychosomatic medicine, intrafamilial integration of the child, pathology of the family. M

FARRÉ, Dr. Luis. Las Piedras 530, piso 4, dpto. N, San Miguel de Tucumán. b. 12 Jan 1902 Montblanch, Spain. PH.D. PROFESSOR, Inst of Philos, San Martín 891, Tucumán.

Member: Argentine Psych. Socy. Professional writing, teaching, research; psychology of esthetics and art.   M
FEBBRARO, Prof. Dr. Enrique Ernesto. Casilla 67, Suc. 1, Buenos Aires. b. 7 July 1914 Buenos Aires. Egresado, Univ. of Buenos Aires, Argentina. PROF. of PSYCH, Inst. Educational Rivadavia, Belgrano 2736, Buenos Aires. Member: Argentine Socy. of Psychosomatic Med, Italian Socy. of Psychosomatic Studies. Teaching, psychotherapy; psychology of art, use of art in psychotherapy.   M
FERNÁNDEZ GUIZZETTI, Prof. Germán M. A. Natl. Univ. of the Litoral, Entre Rios 1443, Rosario. b. 9 Nov. 1930 Rosario. Prof. '54 Natl. Univ. of the Litoral, Argentina. CHAIRMAN, Dept. of Social Anthrop; PROF. ADSCRIPTO, Chair of Linguistics, Fac. of Philos, Letters and Sci. of Educ, Natl. Univ. of the Litoral, Entre Rios 1443. Member: Argentine Socy. of Americanists. Research, professional writing, teaching, ethnolinguistics, American Indian cultures and languages.   M
FIGUERAS, Dr. Aniceto. Montevideo 1958, piso 3, dpto. A, Buenos Aires. b. 17 Sept 1916 Buenos Aires. Docente libre '53 Univ. of Buenos Aires, Argentina. DOCENTE LIBRE of CLIN. PSYCHIAT, Fac. of Med, Paraguay 2155, Buenos Aires. Member: Psychoanal. Assn. of Argentina. Research, psychotherapy, teaching; projective techniques.
FIGUEROA ROMAN, Prof. Miguel. Balcarce 748, Tucumán. b. 22 Nov 1901 Tucumán. MD '44 Univ. of Córdoba, Argentina. DIRECTOR, Inst. of Sociography and Planning, Natl. Univ. of Tucumán. Research, teaching; social psychology, parapsychology.   M
FINGERMANN Prof. Gregorio. Montevideo 471, Buenos Aires. b. 1 May 1890 Villaguay. Prof. Diplômé, Univ. of Buenos Aires, Argentina. DIRECTOR, Inst. of Vocat. Guid, Ave. Corrientes 1723, Buenos Aires. Member: SIP, AIPA, Natl. Inst. of Indus. Psych. (London). Teaching, research, testing, vocational guidance; intelligence tests, psychotechnics, measurement of occupational aptitudes.   M
FUCHS, Prof. Sara. Alberti 151, Buenos Aires. b. 29 Nov 1924 Buenos Aires. Prof, Fac. of Philos. and Letters, Univ. of Buenos Aires, Argentina. DIRECTOR, Escuela de Libre Expresión, Amenabar 1045, Buenos Aires. Research, professional writing, teaching; psychotherapy.   F
GARCÍA DE ONRUBIA, Prof. Dr. Luis Felipe. Roca 136, Adrogué, Buenos Aires. b. 1 Aug 1914 Buenos Aires. PH.D '47 Univ. of Buenos Aires, Argentina. HEAD, Inst. of Psych, Univ. of Buenos Aires, Viamonte 430. Member: SIP. Teaching, testing,

administration; personality, child psychology, psychoanalysis.   M
GARMA, Dr. Angel. Ave. Libertador G. San Martín 2392, Buenos Aires. b. 24 June 1904 Bilbao, Spain. MD '24 Univ. of Madrid, Spain. PSYCHIATRIST, priv. prac. Member: Argentine Psychoanal. Assn, Socy. of Neur. and Psychiat, Int. Psychoanal. Assn. Psychotherapy, research, teaching; psychosomatic medicine, psychoanalysis of dreams.   M
GERMANO, Prof. Santiago Jesús. Marcos Avellaneda 1120, Tucumán. b. 3 June 1928 Tucumán. Prof, Univ. of Tucumán, Argentina. ASST. PROF. of VOCAT. GUID, Natl. Univ. of Tucumán, Ayacucho 482, Tucumán; CHIEF of PSYCH. SECT, Neurosurgery Dept, Padilla Hosp, Tucumán. Member: SIP. Teaching, testing, industrial psychology; projective techniques, achievement tests, job analysis.   M
GONZÁLEZ, Prof. Hilario. 25 de Mayo 1649, Córdoba. b. 28 Feb 1920 Resistencia. Lic. '46 Univ. of Córdoba, Argentina. PROFESSOR, Colegio de Lassale, Argüello. Teaching, research; educational psychology.   M
GONZÁLEZ RÍOS, Prof. Francisco. Obligado 1720, dpto. A, Buenos Aires. b. 10 Oct 1913 Buenos Aires. Prof. '41 Inst. Nacional de Profesorado Secundario, Argentina. PROF. of PHILOS. and PSYCH, Inst. Nacional de Profesorado, Secundario, José Hernández 2247, Buenos Aires; HEAD, Dept. of Psychotechnics and Psych, Natl. Military School, El Palomar. Teaching, research, testing; projective techniques, social perception, group process, psychological theory.   M
GRAND RUIZ, Prof. Dr. Beatriz Hilda. Hipólito Yrigoyen 2757, dpto. D, Buenos Aires. b. 28 Feb. 1930 Buenos Aires. PH.D '54 Univ. of Buenos Aires, Argentina. PROFESSOR, Inst. of Philos, Reconquista 694, Buenos Aires. Member: Argentine Psych. Socy. Research, teaching, applied psychology; graphology, juvenile delinquency, social perception, group process.   F
GRINBERG, Dr. Leon. Paraguay 2669, Buenos Aires. b. 23 Feb. 1921 Buenos Aires. MD '46 Univ. of Buenos Aires, Argentina. PSYCHOANALYST, priv. prac; EDITOR, *Revista de Psicoanálisis*. Member: Argentine Psychoanal. Assn, Int. Psychoanal. Assn, Group Psychotherapy Assn. Psychotherapy, applied psychology, teaching, research; psychoanalysis and group psychotherapy.   M
GUERRERO, Prof. Dr. Luis Juan. Cuba 2281, Buenos Aires. b. 8 Feb 1899 Baradero. PH.D '25 Univ. of Zurich, Switz. PROF. of PSYCH, Univ. of the Litoral, Rosario; PROF. of ESTHETICS, Univ. of Buenos Aires.

Teaching, research, professional writing; psychology of art, imagination, social behavior. M

GUIJO DE VAZQUEZ LORENZO, Miss Ana. Viamonte 920 2-B, Buenos Aires. b. 21 Jan 1915 Buenos Aires. Prof. '48 Univ. of Buenos Aires, Argentina. DIRECTOR of PROJECTIVE TECHNIQUES SEMINARS, Fac. of Philos. and Letters, Viamonte 440, Buenos Aires; PSYCHODIAGNOSTICIAN, Natl. Hosp. of Neuropsychiat, Buenos Aires. Teaching projective techniques, testing, clinical practice, student; projective techniques. F

HORAS, Prof. Plácido Alberto. Mitre 1073, San Luis. b. 11 Dec 1916 Mendoza. Prof. '42 Univ. of Buenos Aires, Argentina. PROF. of CHILD PSYCH, Fac. of Sci. of Educ, Natl. Univ. of Cuyo, Pedernera y Chacabuco, San Luis; DIRECTOR, Inst. of Pedagogic Res, Univ. of Cuyo; CHIEF, Psychopedagogic Div, Dirección de Menores, San Luis; EDITOR, *Anales del Instituto de Investigaciones Pedagógicas.* Member: SIP. Teaching, applied and educational psychology, testing, research; child and adolescent psychology, differential psychology, learning theory, projective techniques, intelligence tests. M

IMBRIANO, Prof. Dr. Aldo Enrique. José Cubas 3131, piso 1, A, Buenos Aires. b. 24 Aug. 1919 Buenos Aires. Prof. '54 Univ. of Buenos Aires, Argentina. HEAD, Dept. of Electroencephalography, Hosp. Militar Central, Ave. L. M. Campos 800, Buenos Aires; EDITOR, Psych. Sec. of *Semana Médica.* Member: Argentine Psych. Socy, Amer. Psych. Socy. (Mexico). Research, applied psychology, teaching; achievement tests, electroencephalography, psychotherapeutic effects of drugs. M

IMPERATRICE, Prof. Nélida N. Buenos Aires 1743, Rosario. b. 8 Nov. 1919 Serodino. Prof. '41 Escuela Normal de Profesoras de Rosario, Argentina. A. de DOCENCIA, Inst. of Psych, Natl. Univ. of the Litoral, Rosario. Member: SIP. Teaching, testing, research; psycho-social interaction, intelligence tests, projective techniques. F

KNOBEL, Dr. Mauricio. Larrea 608, piso 2, Buenos Aires. b. 19 Mar 1922 Buenos Aires. MD '50 Univ. of Buenos Aires, Argentina. PSYCHIATRIST, Inst. of Psychosomatic Studies, Inst. of Phonoaudiology, San Eduardo 578, Buenos Aires; PRIV. DOCENT in ANATOMY, Fac. of Med, Univ. of Buenos Aires. Member: SIP, APA, Argentine Socy. of Med. Psych. Psychotherapy, consulting, clinical practice, teaching; psycho-organic interaction, social perception, child psychotherapy. M

KOCH, Dr. Hans Albert. Rua Freire 2450, dpto. G, Buenos Aires. b. 23 Sept 1897 Berlin, Germany. Dr. phil. habil. '36 Univ. of Würzburg, Germany. NATL. SUB-DIR,

Dirección Nacional de Investigaciones Científicas y Técnicas, Paseo Colón 255, piso 9, Buenos Aires. Member: DGP. Research on manpower utilization, teaching administration; inheritance of psychic characteristics, military psychology. M

KRAPF, Prof. Dr. E. Eduardo. 16 Parc Château Banquet, Geneva, Switzerland. b. 4 July 1901 Nürnberg, Germany. MD '23 Univ. of Leipzig, Ger; Privat Dozent '33 Univ. of Cologne, Ger; MD '36 Univ. of Buenos Aires, Argentina; Assoc. Prof. '48 Univ. of Buenos Aires, Argentina. CHIEF, Ment. Hlth. Sect, World Hlth. Organiz, Palais des Nations, Geneva; ED. BD, *Acta Psychotherapeutica, International Journal of Social Psychiatry, Excerpta Medica* (Psychiat. Sect.), *Revista de Psquiatria y Psicología Médica.* Member: BPS, APSLF, SIP, Int. Psychoanal. Assn, Swiss Psychoanal. Socy, Buenos Aires Psych. Socy. Administration, research, professional writing, consulting and teaching in the field of mental health; psychopathology, social psychology, group process. M

LAGUINGE, Prof. Carlos. Peredo 125, Córdoba. b. 19 Nov 1915 Argentina. Lic. '47 Univ. of Córdoba, Argentina. PROFESSOR Univ. of Córdoba; PSYCHOLOGIST, Military School of Paratroops, Córdoba. Teaching, military psychology, testing; vocational guidance, professional selection. M

LAMBRUSCHINI, Prof. Dr. Carlos A. H. Santa Fe 2121, Rosario. b. 21 Oct 1905 Parana. MD '32 Univ. of the Litoral, Argentina. PROF. EMER, Natl. Univ. of the Litoral; MED. CONSULT. in CHILD PSYCHIAT. Consulting, clinical practice, psychotherapy testing, clinical analysis; projective techniques, psychodynamics of abnormal behavior. M

LAMBRUSCHINI, Prof. Erminda Lucrecia Benítez de. Santa Fe 2121, Rosario. b. 23 Nov 1900 Rosario. Prof. '22 Escuela Normal de Rosario, Argentina. PROF. of PSYCH, Colegio Nacional "D. F. Sarmiento," 9 de Julio 80, Rosario. Member: Psych. Socy. of Rosario. Teaching, research, tests, vocational tests, psychoanalysis of dreams of adolescents. F

LAURITI, Prof. Carmen. San Juan 2071, Buenos Aires. b. 13 Aug 1923 Buenos Aires. Prof. '48 Inst. of Psych, Buenos Aires, Argentina. Member: Latin Amer. Psych. Comm. General, individual and social psychology and psychopathology; applied psychology, testing, guidance, consulting, research, readaptation of abnormal children. F

LUCHINA, Dr. Isaac León. Pumacahua 292 2-P, dpto. D, Buenos Aires. b. 24 June 1921 Buenos Aires. Diploma '46 Fac. of Med. Sci, Univ. of Buenos Aires, Argentina.

ASST. CHIEF, Pabellon Inchauspe de Cardiologia, Hosp. Ramos Mejia, Buenos Aires; CHIEF, Psychosomatic Dept, Hosp. Ramos Mejia. Member: Argentine Socy. of Med. Psych. and Psychoanal. Psychotherapy, research, clinical analysis; psychobiology, psychosomatic medicine, psychoanalysis. M

LUSTIG, Dr. Elfriede Susana. Malabia 2847, Buenos Aires. b. 20 May 1930 Vienna, Austria. MD, Univ. of Buenos Aires, Argentina. INTERNE, Children's Hosp. of Buenos Aires, Bustamonte, Buenos Aires. Member: Argentine Psychoanal. Assn, Buenos Aires Med. Psych. Socy. Psychotherapy, clinical practice, psychoanalytic trainee; psychoanalytic treatment, group analysis, neuropsychiatric pediatrics. F

MAHIEU, Prof. Jaime María de. Tapiales 1270, Vicente López, Buenos Aires. b. 31 Oct 1915 Paris, France. Lic. ès lettres, Univ. d'Aix-Marseille, France. DIRECTOR, Psycho-sociological Dept, Inst. Lanús, Ave. Roque Sáenz Peña 636, Buenos Aires; EDITOR, *Investigaciones de Mercado*. Member: Argentine Acad. of Sociol. Market research, public opinion studies, editorial and professional writing; anthropological psychology, biopsychology, public opinion research. M

MANSILLA, Prof. José Raúl. Muñecas 1203, San Miguel de Tucumán. b. 30 May 1920 Santiago. Prof, Univ. of Tucumán, Argentina. PROF. SECUNDARIO, Gymnasium, Natl. Univ. of Tucumán, 25 de Mayo 621; ADJUNCT PROF. of CHILD PSYCH, Natl. Univ. of Tucumán. Teaching, testing, clinical analysis, consulting, vocational guidance; projective techniques, Rorschach psychodiagnosis, psychology of adolescence. M

MÉNDEZ MOSQUERA, Dr. Jorge L. Serrano 2226, Buenos Aires. b. 15 Oct 1923 Buenos Aires. MD '53 Univ. of Buenos Aires, Argentina. CHIEF, Clin. Serv, Natl. Hosp. of Neuropsychiatry, Vieytes 307, Buenos Aires. Member: Argentine Assn. of Psych, Psychoanal, and Psychosomatic Med. Psychotherapy, clinical practice, student; group psychotherapy, use of drugs in psychoanalysis. M

MONDRÍA, Prof. Dr. Julio Andrés. Donato, Alvarez 480, Buenos Aires. b. 2 Jan 1903 Buenos Aires. MD, Univ. of Buenos Aires, Argentina. TECH. ADVISOR, Ministry of Social Assistance and Public Health, Bernardo de Irigoyen 248, Buenos Aires; PROF. of BIOL. SCI, Colegio Nacional Mariano Moreno, Buenos Aires; GUIDANCE COUNS, Colegio Militar de la Nación. Member: Argentine Psych. Socy. Teaching, testing, guidance; applied psychology. M

MONTDOR DE COHEN, Prof. Ana Matilde. Añasco 84, Buenos Aires. b. 2 Mar 1917

Buenos Aires. Travailleur d' higiene mental '43 Fac. of Med, Univ. of Buenos Aires, Argentina. TECHNICAL COUNSELOR, Dirección de Psicología y Orientacion Profesional, Ministry of Educ, 53-1006, La Plata. Psychotherapy, consulting, clinical practice, applied psychology; psychophoniatrics, child psychotherapy. F

MORALES, Prof. Dr. Eugenio Miguel. Gallardo 752, Suc. 8, Buenos Aires. b. 12 Feb 1911 Buenos Aires. MD '35 Univ. of Córdoba, Argentina. PROF. of PSYCH, Escuela Normal Nacional; PEDIATRICIAN, Social Service, Ministerio de Hacienda, San Martín 877, Buenos Aires. Member: SIP. Teaching, applied psychology, consulting, clinical practice; educational tests, psychodiagnosis. M

MURAT, Dr. Franco. Calle Ferroviarios Argentinos 625, Mendoza. b. 21 Apr 1923 Milan, Italy. Dr. '50 Univ. of Urbino, Italy. PSYCHOLOGIST, Patronato de Menores, Calle E. Civit 235, Mendoza; TCHR. of PSYCH, Natl. Univ. of Cuyo, Mendoza. Testing, clinical analysis, consulting, teaching; projective techniques, statistics in psychology and education. M

NÖLLMANN, Dr. Jorge Enrique. Pereyra Lucena 2580, Buenos Aires. b. 17 Oct 1909 Buenos Aires. MD '50 Natl. Univ. of Buenos Aires, Argentina. PSYCHOANALYST; EDITOR, *Revista* of Argentine Psychoanal. Assn. Member: Argentine Psychoanal. Assn, Argentine Socy. of Neur. and Psychiat, Argentine Psych. Socy. Psychotherapy, consulting, clinical practice, research; psychopathology. M

OÑATIVIA, Prof. Oscar Venancio. Santiago del Estero 1138, Salta. b. 19 May 1919 Salta. Prof. '45 Univ. of Buenos Aires, Argentina. DIRECTOR, Inst. of Psych. and Sci. of Educ, Ave. Sarmiento 201, piso 2, Salta. Member: SIP, Socy. of Criminol. and Legal Med. Research, consulting, teaching; projective techniques, emotional conflicts, maladjustment. M

PITA, Prof. Enrique Bernardo. Colegio del Salvador, Callao 542, Buenos Aires. b. 20 Aug 1900 Paraná. PH.D, Pontifical Univ. of Buenos Aires, Argentina. PROF. and DEAN, Fac. of Philos, Colegio Máximo San José, Bartolomé Mitre, San Miguel; DEAN, Superior Inst. of Philos, Colegio del Salvador. Teaching, research; cognition. M

POURTEAU AGOTE, Prof. Carlos Alberto. Pedernera 510, dpto. C, Buenos Aires. b. 23 Feb 1924 Buenos Aires. Prof. '52 Univ. of Buenos Aires, Argentina. INDUS. PSYCH. COORDINATOR, Esso S. A. Petrolera Argentina, Ave. Roque Sáenz Peña 567, Ofic. 550, Buenos Aires. Applied and industrial psychology, personnel research, teaching; selection and evaluation of personnel, industrial instruction. M

PRÓ, Prof. Diego Francisco. Amadeo Jacques 19, San Miguel de Tucumán. b. 4 June 1915 Resistencia. Prof. '39 Univ. of Paraná, Argentina. PROF. of EDUC. and PHILOS, Univ. of Tucumán, Muñecas 850, Tucumán; DIRECTOR, Inst. of Philos, San Martín 981, Tucumán. Research, testing, teaching; social psychology, projective tests. M

PROSDOCIMI, Dr. Virginia. Ituzaingo 1060, Buenos Aires. b. 17 Feb. 1922 Vittorio V, Italy. PH.D '48 Natl. Univ. of Milan, Italy. RES. ASST. and LECT, Fac. of Philos. and Letters, Univ. of Buenos Aires, Viamonte 430. Member: SIP, Argentine Psych. Socy. Testing, teaching, student; standardization of mental tests, mental testing of children with cerebral injuries, projective techniques F

PUCHETA MORCILLO, Prof. Raúl. Caseros 852, Córdoba. b. 14 June 1904 Córdoba. Prof. Adj. '47 Univ. of Córdoba, Argentina; MD '27 Univ. of Córdoba, Argentina. NEUROPSYCHIATRIST, priv. prac. Member: Argentine Socy. of Psychiat, Neur. and Neurosurgery. Psychotherapy, teaching, consulting, clinical practice; psychogenesis and psychotherapy of neuroses, mental hygiene. M

QUILLES, Prof. Dr. Ismael. Fac. of Philos. and Theology, San Miguel. b. 4 July 1906 Pedralba, Spain. PH.D '29 Univ. of Barcelona, Spain. PROF. and DEAN, Fac. of Philos. El Salvador, Callao 542, Buenos Aires. Teaching, research; psychology of personality, social psychology, metaphysics and psychology. M

RADAELLI, Prof. Mrs. Amalia Lucas de. Calle Carlos Pellegrini 485, piso 7, F, Buenos Aires. b. 16 Jan 1915 Buenos Aires. Professor, Fac. of Philos. and Letters, Univ. of Buenos Aires, Argentina. PROF. of PSYCH, Escuela Superior de Comercio, Univ. of Buenos Aires; PSYCHOLOGIST, Child Psych. and Psychiat. Cen, Hosp. Nacional de Clínicas, Univ. of Buenos Aires. Psychotherapy, guidance,teaching; educational psychology, projective techniques. F

RADECKA, Dr. Halina. Calle Piedras 813, Buenos Aires. b. 5 July 1897 Warsaw, Poland. MD, Univ. of Warsaw, Poland. PROFESSOR, Inst. of Psych, Presidente Luis Sáenz Peña 471, Buenos Aires. Teaching, research, applied and educational psychology; social and general psychology and its application to education and to work. F

RASCOVSKY, Dr. Arnaldo. Suipacha 1368, Buenos Aires. b. 1 Jan 1907 Córdoba. MD '28 Univ. of Buenos Aires, Argentina. PRES. and CHMN. of SCI. ACTIVITIES, Argentine Socy. of Med. Psych, Psychoanal, and Psychosomatic Med, Santa Fé 1171, Buenos Aires; PSYCHOTHERAPIST, priv.

prac. Member: Int. Psychoanal. Assn, Argentine Psychoanal. Assn, Argentine Socy. for Group Psych. and Psychother. Psychotherapy, research, teaching; psychoanalysis, prenatal psychological conditioning, psychosomatic research. M

RAVAGNAN, Prof. Luis María. Calle Margarita Weild 217, Lanús, Buenos Aires. b. 30 Aug 1902 Buenos Aires. PROFESSOR, Fac. of Philos and Letters, Univ. of Buenos Aires, Viamonte 430. Research, teaching; psychic functions, psychophysical unity, phenomenology. M

RAVASCHINO DE VÁZQUEZ, Prof. Ofelia Thelma. José María Moreno 25, Lanús, Buenos Aires. b. 25 Aug 1924 Buenos Aires. Prof. '51 Inst. Nacional del Profesorado Secundario, Argentina. DIRECTOR, Psych. Dept, Gath y Chaves, Ltd, Florida y Cangallo, Buenos Aires; PROF. of GENL. and CHILD PSYCH, Inst. Nacional del Profesorado Secundario, and Escuela Normal de Maestras No. 1, Buenos Aires. Personnel recruitment, assignment and promotion, testing, teaching; aptitude measurement, intelligence tests, job placement. F

RENDO, Rogelio. Argentine Lab. of Psych. "Prof. Dr. W. Radecki," Aconquija 3464, Buenos Aires. b. 5 Nov 1925 Buenos Aires. CHIEF, Argentine Lab. of Psych. "Prof. Dr. W. Radecki." Member: Latin Amer. Coordinating Comm. of Psych. (Montevideo). Research, psychotherapy, construction of psychology laboratory equipment; general psychology, readaptation, psycho-organic functionalism. M

RIMOLDI, Dr. Horacio J. A. 5640 Kimbark Ave, Chicago 37, Illinois, USA. b. 11 Apr 1913 Buenos Aires, Argentina. PH.D '49 Univ. of Chicago, USA; MD '39 Univ. of Buenos Aires, Argentina. ASSOC. PROF, Loyola Univ, 820 N. Michigan Ave, Chicago, Illinois, USA. Member: APA, AAAS, SIP, AIPA, Argentine Assn. for the Advanc. of Sci, Psychometric Socy. Research, teaching, administration; problem solving, factorial techniques, scaling procedures, experimental design. M

RODRIGUE, Dr. Emilio. Ayacucho 1534, Buenos Aires. b. 9 Jan 1923 Buenos Aires. MD '47 Univ. of Buenos Aires, Argentina. PSYCHIATRIST, priv. prac. Member: Argentine Psychoanal Assn, Argentine Assn. of Psych. and Group Psychother, British Psychoanal Socy. Psychotherapy, applied psychology, teaching seminars in psychoanalysis and group psychotherapy; symbolism in tranference situation, psychoanalytic approach to psychoses and group phenomena. M

RODRÍGUEZ, Miss Elsa Carmen Josefina. Campillo 2639, Buenos Aires. b. 17 Sept 1907 Buenos Aires. Prof. '46 Inst. of

Psych, Buenos Aires, Argentina. PRO-
FESSOR, Inst. of Psych, Luis Sáenz Peña
471, Buenos Aires. Teaching, educational
psychology, student; general, individual
and social psychology. F
RODRÍGUEZ ZELADA, Dr. Carlos. Ave.
Avellaneda 199, Tucumán. b. 15 July 1918
Tucumán. MD '47 Univ. of Córdoba,
Argentina. PROFESSOR, Psychotechnic
Inst, Univ. of Tucumán, 9 de Julio 629,
Tucumán; NEUROLOGIST, Neuropsychiat.
Clin, Children's Hosp. and Santillán
Women's Hosp, Tucumán. Member: Socy.
of Neur. and Psychopathology of Tucumán.
Socy. of Criminol. and Penal Sciences.
Teaching experimental psychology, clinical
practice; maturation and learning tests,
encephalography, psycho-physiology. M
ROMERO VILLANUEVA, Miss Olimpia.
Conde 1462, Buenos Aires. b. 1 Nov 1916
Buenos Aires. Phonoaudiologist '50,
Argentina. ASST. DIR, Sch. of Social Work;
PSYCHIAT. SOCIAL WORKER, Centro de
Rehabilitacion de Paralíticos Cerebrales,
Hosp. Rawson. Applied psychology,
testing, clinical analysis, consulting, guidance
teaching; group process, psychology of the
disabled, industrial psychology. F
SALERA, Dr. Adolfo Mateo. Willard State
Hosp, Willard, New York, USA. b. 6 Dec
1907 Ataliva, Argentina. MD '43 Natl.
Univ. of the Litoral, Argentina. DIRECTOR,
Sanatorio Vieytes, Vieytes 374, Rosario;
RESID. in MED, Willard State Hosp.
Psychiatry. M
SALERA, Dr. María del Carmen Foz de.
Willard State Hosp, Willard, New York,
USA. b. 4 Apr 1918 Rosario, Argentina.
MD, Natl. Univ. of the Litoral, Argentina.
CO-DIRECTOR, Sanatorio Vieytes, Vieytes
374, Rosario. Testing, clinical practice,
psychotherapy, research, teaching; psycho-
pathology, Rorschach test, psychology of
adolescence. F
SARRULLE, Prof. Oscar Emilio. Muñecas
223, San Miguel de Tucumán. b. 9 Apr 1917
San Pedro. Lic, Natl. Univ. of Córdoba,
Argentina. PROF. of PSYCH, Escuela Normal
de Tucumán, Muñecas 119, San Miguel de
Tucumán. Teaching, educational psy-
chology; psychology of adolescence. M
SAURI, Prof. Dr. Jorge Joaquin. Córdoba 435,
Buenos Aires. b. 6 Aug 1923 Buenos Aires.
MD '49 Univ. of Buenos Aires, Argentina.
PROFESSOR, Inst. of Psych. of El Salvador,
Callao 542, Buenos Aires; PSYCHIATRIST.
Member: Argentine Socy. of Rorschach
Psychodiagnosis. Psychotherapy, con-
sulting, clinical practice, teaching; pro-
jective techniques, depth psychology,
existential analysis. M
SCHEINSON, Prof. María Ethel. Tucumán
881, piso 5, Buenos Aires. b. 6 Feb. 1925

Buenos Aires. Psychologist '48 Inst. of
Psych, Univ. of Buenos Aires, Argentina.
PSYCHOLOGIST, Inst. of Phonoaudiology,
Ministry of Pub. Hlth, Dr. Pedro Aranguren
578, Buenos Aires. Testing, student,
teaching; projective techniques, testing,
phonoaudiology. F
TAVELLA, Nicolás M. Córdoba 2086, Buenos
Aires. b. 9 Feb 1918 Gálvez. MED. '41
Escuela Normal, Argentina. TECH. COORDI-
NATOR, Dept. of Educ. Psych. and Student
Assistance, Ministry of Educ, 1006 Calle 53,
La Plata; DIRECTOR, Psych. Sect, Neuro-
psychiat. Clin. and Rehab. Cen. for Spastic
Children, Hosp. Rawson, Buenos Aires;
PSYCHOLOGIST, Rehab. Serv, Hosp. Fiorito,
Buenos Aires. Technical coordination of
educational psychology, vocational
guidance, and social assistance for students,
testing, applied psychology, research;
psychological testing, psychometric tech-
niques, learning theory. M
UCHA, Dr. Selva E. Defensa 1165, dpto. 11,
Buenos Aires. b. 10 Apr 1925 Santa Fe.
PH.D, Univ. of the Litoral, Argentina. DIR.
of RES. and PSYCHOSTAT, Inst. of Psycho-
technics and Vocat. Guid, Laprida 1860,
Buenos Aires. Member: AIPA. Research,
testing, applied psychology; intelligence
tests, attitude measurement, projective
techniques. F
UCHA MARTÍNEZ, Prof. Sirio Albor. 4 de
Enero 2115, Santa Fe. b. 17 Dec 1923
Santa Fe. Prof., Inst. Profesorado de
Paraná, Argentina. DIRECTOR, Inst. of
Psychotechnics and Vocat. Guid, San
Martín 1805, piso 2, Santa Fe. Member:
Asociación Iberoamericana para la Efi-
ciencia y Satisfacción en el Trabajo (Spain).
Vocational selection and guidance, testing,
applied psychology; attitude measurement,
achievement tests. M
VALLEJOS MEANA, Prof. Dr. Nestor H.
Ave. Santa Fé 1111, Buenos Aires. b. 29
May 1907 Buenos Aires. MD, Univ. of
Buenos Aires, Argentina. DIRECTOR and
PROF. of PSYCH. RES, Socy. for Protection of
Children, Paraguay 2567, Buenos Aires;
DIRECTOR, Priv. Inst. of Psych, Educ. and
Assistance (P.E.Y.A.I.). Member: Argentine
Socy. of Med. Psych, Socy. of Social Med,
Assn. of Argentine Psych'ts. Teaching, re-
search, educational psychology, testing,
guidance; personality and attitude measure-
ment, group guidance, learning theory. M
VICTORIA, Prof. Marcos. Arenales 1441,
Buenos Aires. b. 8 Mar 1901 Tucumán.
MD, Univ. of Buenos Aires, Argentina.
PROF. of PSYCH, Univ. of Buenos Aires,
Viamonte 430, Buenos Aires; DIRECTOR,
Inst. of Psych, Univ. of Buenos Aires;
CHIEF of NEUROPSYCHIAT, Ministry of the
Navy. Member: Société Médico-Psycho-

logique (Paris), Neurological Socy. (Paris). Teaching, research, psychotherapy; psychophysiology, psychology of values, phenomenology. M

VILLAVERDE, Prof. Aníbal. Vallejos 3858, Buenos Aires. b. 21 July 1918 Buenos Aires. PH.D '44 Univ. of Buenos Aires, Argentina. PROF. of PSYCHOPEDAGOGY, Inst. Nacional de Profesorado Secundario, José Hernández 2247, Buenos Aires. Member: Argentine Cen. of Pedagogical Studies, Socy. of Psych. of San Pablo.

Teaching, educational psychology, guidance; research on the teaching profession, application of psychoanalysis to education. M

VILLAVERDE, Dr. Juan. Vallejos 3858, Buenos Aires. b. 17 Oct 1911 Buenos Aires. Prof. '37 Univ. of Buenos Aires, Argentina. INDUS. PSYCH'T, Industrias Fiat, Sarmiento 767, piso 4, Buenos Aires. Industrial psychology, research, teaching; social and psychological problems of work, human relations. M

AUSTRALIA

ALLEY, Selby George. Dept. of Tech. Educ, Tech. Coll, Tighes Hill, N.S.W. b. 24 June 1902 Nowra. BA '35 Univ. of Sydney, Austl. CHIEF GUID. OFF, Dept. of Tech. Educ, Tech.Coll. Member: BPS-A. Psychotherapy, guidance, testing, teaching; counseling and psychotherapy with young adults. M

ANDERSON, Dr. Mrs. Betty Martha. 57 New South Head Rd, Vaucluse, N.S.W. b. 8 June 1926 Wellington, New Zealand. PH.D '51 Univ. of London, Eng. LECT. in APPL. PSYCH, New South Wales Univ. of Tech, Kensington; HONORARY PLAY THER, Child Guid. Clin; CHILD PSYCH'T, priv. prac. Member: BPS, British Rorschach Forum. Teaching, consulting, guidance, clinical practice, psychotherapy; social and personality maladjustment in child development, play therapy, parent counseling. F

ANDERSON, Donald S. Stud. Couns. Off, Univ. of Melbourne, Victoria. b. 10 Nov 1926 Melbourne. MA '56 Univ. of Melbourne, Austl. ASST. STUD. COUNS, Univ. of Melbourne. Member: BPS-A. Counseling, research, teaching; group process, social forces, determinants of academic success. M

BADDELEY, Ronald Charles. Flat 5, 202 Clovelly Rd, Randwick, N.S.W. b. 7 Aug 1922 Perth. BA '49 Univ. of Western Australia. OFF. in CHARGE, N.S.W. Br, Commonwealth Acoustic Labs, Circular Quay, Sydney. Testing, consulting, administration, teaching lip-reading; social perception, attitude measurement, projective techniques. M

BAKER, Bruce Peter. 8 Kavanagh St, Canning Bridge, W.A. b. 27 Aug 1914 Mundaring. BA '45 Univ. of Western Australia. SUPT. of GUID. and SPEC. EDUC, EDUC. Dept. of W.A., Barrack St, Perth, W.A. Member: BPS-A. Administration, educational psychology; educational guidance, social perception. M

BAKER, Maurice Arthur William. 80 Comer St, Como, W.A. b. 6 July 1922 London, Eng. BA' 52 Univ.of Western Australia. Member: BPS-A. Projective techniques, achievement

tests. M

BARKER, Ray McCredie. 9 Barwell Rd, Medina, W.A. b. 26 Aug 1920 Sydney. MA '54 Univ. of Leeds, Eng. TRNG. OFF, Australasian Petroleum Refinery Ltd, Box 131, Fremantle, W.A. Member: BPS. Teaching, administration, industrial psychology; attitude measurement, selection, achievement testing, assessment form construction. M

BARRATT, Mrs. Constance Shirley. 26 Handel St, Armidale, N.S.W. b. 9 Apr 1922 Sydney. BA '44 Univ. of Sydney, Austl. DEMONSTRATOR, Univ. of New England, Armidale. Teaching, supervision of laboratory classes, research; history and systems, experimental psychology, learning and perception, aptitudes. F

BARRATT, Paul Eric Hunter. Dept. of Psych, Univ. of New England, Armidale, N.S.W. b. 23 Dec 1917 Kalgoorlie. MA '52 Univ. of Sydney, Austl. SR. LECT, Univ. of New England. Member: BPS-A. Teaching, research, professional writing; application of electroencephalography to psychological problems, cognition, learning theory. M

BARRETT, Kelvin Lindsay. Child Guid. Clin, Pub. Sch, Parramatta Rd, Camperdown, N.S.W. b. 5 May 1919 Adelaide. B.ED '48 Univ. of Melbourne, Austl. PSYCHOLOGIST, Dept. of Pub. Hlth, 52 Bridge St, Sydney. Member: BPS-A. Diagnostic testing, psychotherapy, guidance; psychodynamic theory, projective techniques. M

BARRETT-LENNARD, Godfrey Trevor. The Counseling Cen, Univ. of Chicago, 5737 Drexel Ave, Chicago 37, Illinois, USA. b. 6 Apr 1926 Northam. BA '50 Univ. of Western Australia. PSYCHOMETRIST and INTERN, The Couns. Cen, Univ. of Chicago. Member: BPS-A. Research, testing, psychotherapeutic counseling; speech therapy, study of satisfaction in work. M

BASSETT, Dr. George William. Teachers' Coll, Mossman St, Armidale, N.S.W. b. 26 Mar 1910 Orange. PH.D '40 Univ. of London, Eng. PRINCIPAL, Teachers' Coll; HEAD,

Dept. of Educ, Univ. of New England, Armidale. Member: BPS-A. Administration, educational psychology, teaching; learning theory, group process. M

BEAN, Alan Graham Stewart. 24 Goldsmith Rd, Claremont, W.A. b. 15 Sept 1926 Bruce-Rock. BA '53 Univ. of Melbourne, Austl. STAFF MGR, Commonwealth Oil Refineries Ltd, 189 St. Georges Terrace, Perth, W.A. Member: BPS-A. Aust. Inst. of Pers. Management. Industrial and personnel psychology, counseling, administration; group behavior and social roles, vocational guidance, communication in industry and its effect on personnel. M

BENJAMIN, Eric. Guid. and Spec. Educ. Br, Educ. Dept, 35 Subiaco Rd, Perth, W.A. b. 12 Feb. 1915 Wuppertal, Germany. BA '56 Univ. of Western Australia. GUID. OFF, Guid. Br. and Spec. Educ, Educ. Dept; EDITOR, *Our Children.* Member: BPS-A. Educational and vocational counseling, social case work, testing, editorial; social learning of mentally deficient children. M

BENNETT, Dr. Ivy V. P. 32 Bellevue Terrace, Perth, W.A. b. Wagin. PH.D '51 Univ. of London, Eng. PSYCHOANALYST, priv. prac. Member: BPS-A, British Psychoanal. Socy, Austl. Socy. of Psychoanal, British Assn. of Child Psychotherapists. Child and adult psychoanalysis, professional writing, research; delinquency and neurosis in children. F

BENNING, Herbert Francis. Box 481, GPO, Sydney. b. 5 May 1907 Gunnedah. MA '30 Univ. of Sydney, Austl. SECRETARY, Austl. Gas Light Co, Pitt St, Sydney. Member: BPS-A, Austl. Inst. of Indus. Psych, Austl. Psych. Assn, Austl. Inst. of Pers. Management. Industrial psychology, teaching, administration; application of psychology to personnel administration. M

BENTLEY, William John. 34 Dress Circle Rd, Avalon Beach, N.S.W. b. 30 Apr 1912 Sydney. B.EC '50 Univ. of Sydney, Austl. GUID. OFF, New South Wales Univ. of Tech, Dept. of Tech. Educ, 45 Broadway, Sydney. Member: BPS-A. Educational guidance and counseling, testing; use of projective techniques in child guidance, remedial reading, educational psychology. M

BLANK, Leon. 410 Toorak Rd, Toorak S.E. 2, Victoria. b. 11 Mar 1928 Perth. BA '51 Univ. of Western Australia. SR. TUTOR, Dept. of Psych, Univ. of Melbourne, Carlton N. 3, Melbourne. Member: BPS-A, Austl. Rorschach Socy. Research, teaching, student; psychodiagnostics, social perception, group process. M

BLOMGREN, Anthony James. 14 Tulloch Ave, Concord West, Sydney, N.S.W. b. 22 Nov 1915 Sydney. BA '38 Univ. of Sydney Austl. VOCAT. GUID. OFF, Parramatta Br,

Dept. of Labour, Indus. and Soc. Welf, 53 Martin Pl, Sydney. Member: BPS-A. Vocational and educational guidance, administration; performance tests. M

BODLEY, Miss Edith A. 56A Telegraph Rd, Pymble, Sydney. b. 20 Apr 1931 Sydney. BA '50 Univ. of Sydney, Aust. TRNG. OFF, Commonwealth Off. of Educ, Wembley Chambers, 104 Hunter St, Sydney. Member: BPS-A. Administration of training programs for Asian students in Australia; personnel psychology. F

BONNETTE, Miss Mareta. 2 Queen Victoria St, Drummoyne, Sydney. b. 16 Jan 1901 Sydney. B.SC '21 Univ. of Sydney, Austl. DIST. SCH. COUNS, Dept. of Educ, Bridge St, Sydney. Member: BPS-A. Testing, educational and clinical guidance; achievement and intelligence tests, learning theory, problem behavior. F

BOSTOCK, Prof. John. Univ. of Queensland, George St, Brisbane, Queensland. b. 20 Jan 1892 Glasgow, Scot. MB, BS, Univ. of London, Eng. RES. PROF. of MED. PSYCH, Univ. of Queensland. Member: BPS-A. Research; social psychology, history of psychiatry, evolution of personality traits in childhood. M

BOWNES, Arthur Frederick. 473 Stirling Highway, Cottesloe, W.A. b. 16 May 1925 Gourock, Scot. BA '51 Univ. of Western Australia. PSYCHOLOGIST, Ment. Hlth. Serv, Claremont, W.A. Member: BPS-A, W.A. Clin. Psych. Socy. Testing, psychotherapy, student; projective techniques, group process in therapy, juvenile and adult delinquency. M

BRAMICH, Roger Garfield. 44 Goldsmith Rd, Claremont, W.A. b. 1 June 1918 Burnie. BA '48 Univ. of Western Australia. PSYCHOLOGIST, Dept. of the Navy, Cliff St, Fremantle, W.A. Member: BPS-A. Naval selection and personnel work, guidance, research. M

BRERETON, Miss Beatrice Le Gay. 38 Eastern Rd, Turramurra. b. 10 Aug 1914 Sydney. MA '45 Univ. of Sydney, Austl. EDUC. RES. OFF, Spastic Centre, Mosman, N.S.W. Member: BPS-A. Research, testing, teaching psychology and speech therapy; intelligence and achievement tests for physically handicapped children, study of perceptive processes. F

BROWN, William Joseph. Res. and Guid. Br, Block A, Tech. Coll. Bldgs, George St, Brisbane, Queensland. b. 25 June 1916 Rockhampton. B.ED .51 Univ. of Queensland, Austl. SR. GUID. OFF, Dept. of Pub. Instr, Res. Guid. Br. Member: BPS-A. Guidance, testing, educational psychology; aptitude testing, vocational selection. M

BUBNA-LITIC, Mrs. Barbara Constance. 37 Beatrice Rd, Dalkeith, W.A. b. 11 Apr 1929

Perth. BA '49 Univ. of Western Australia. GUID. OFF, Guid. and Spec. Educ. Br, Educ. Dept, Subiaco and Coll. Rds, Subiaco. Member: BPS-A. Educational and vocational guidance and counseling in high school, testing; developmental vocational guidance, job selection. F

BUCKLE, Dr. Donald Fergus. World Health Organiza, Reg. Off. for Europe, Palais des Nations, Geneva, Switzerland. b. 7 May 1911 Melbourne. MB, BS '33 Melbourne Univ, Austl; Dr Psych Med '37 Univ. of London, Eng. REGIONAL OFFICER for MENT. HLTH, World Hlth. Organiza. Member: BPS-A, SPT, RMPA, Australasian Assn. of Psychiatrists. Research, administration; psychoanalysis, projective techniques, small group process. M

BUCKLOW, Mrs. Maxine. Staff Dept, Commonwealth Bank of Austl, Pitt St, Sydney. b. 27 Nov 1921 Sydney. BA '43 Univ. of Sydney, Austl. STAFF PSYCH'T, Commonwealth Bank of Austl. Member: BPS-A. Personnel selection and training, research, testing, student; research on clerical aptitude tests, staff turnover, supervisor training. F

BURNHEIM, Ronald Bede. Child Guid. Cen, Dept. of Pub. Hlth, Brisbane St, Sydney. b. 14 May 1921 Sydney. BA '51 Univ. of Sydney, Austl. PSYCHOLOGIST, Child Guid. Cen; PSYCHOLOGIST, Honorary Med. Panel, Royal Blind Socy, Sydney. Member: BPS-A. Diagnostic testing, child psychotherapy and guidance; projective techniques, clinical testing, psychoanalysis with children. M

BURTON, Rongomai George. Teachers' Coll, Geelong, Victoria. b. 9Feb 1909 Wanganui, New Zealand. BA '48 Univ. of Melbourne, Austl. LECTURER, Educ. Dept, Melbourne. Member: Victorian Inst. for Educ. Res. Teaching, administration, educational psychology; learning theory, adchievement tests, attitude measurements. M

BUTLER, William Peter. 29 Kent Grove, Caulfield, Victoria. b. 30 Dec 1930 Melbourne. BA '52 Univ. of Melbourne, Austl. RES. OFF, Dept. of Labour and Natl. Serv, 125 Swanston St, Melbourne. Personnel psychology, research, professional writing; motivation in work, selection tests. M

CAINE, Jack Alfred James. Dept. of Labour and Natl. Serv, 125 Swanston St, Melbourne Victoria. b. 3 Nov 1916 Gatton. BA '41 Univ. of Queensland, Austl. OFF. in CHARGE, Occupat. Res. Sect, Dept. of Labour and Natl. Serv. Member: BPS-A. Vocational guidance and classification, administration, research; occupational research, aptitude testing, learning theory. M

CAINE, Mrs. Mollie Beris. Dept. of Labour and Natl. Serv, 125 Swanston St, Mel-

bourne. b. 15 May 1927 Brisbane. BA '48 Univ. of Queensland, Austl. VOCAT. GUID. OFF, Dept. of Labour and Natl. Serv. Member: BPS. Test construction, research in vocational guidance techniques, consulting; human relations in industry, characteristics of older workers. F

CAMPBELL, Lt. Col. Edward Francis. "Launceston," 589 Nepean Highway, Carrum, Victoria. b. 7 Jan 1908 Kalgoorlie. BA '35 Univ. of Western Australia. DIRECTOR, Austl. Army Psych. Corps, Dept. of the Army, St. Kilda Rd, Melbourne, Victoria; HONORARY PSYCH'T, Royal Melbourne Hosp; LECTURER, Univ. of Melbourne. Member: BPS-A, APA, Austl. Rorschach Socy. Administration, personnel psychology, testing, consulting; military personnel selection, group process, attitude measurement. M

CAMPBELL, Dr. William John. Dept. of Educ, Univ. of Sydney, Broadway, Sydney, N.S.W. b. 5 Jan 1922 Winton, N.Z. PH.D '51 Univ. of London, Eng. SR. LECT. in EDUC, Univ. of Sydney. Member: BPS. Teaching, research, testing; educational guidance, group process in the classroom, ethnocentrism in industry. M

CARDNO, Prof. James Alexander. Univ. of Tasmania,, Box 647-C, GPO, Hobart. b. 5 Jan 1915 Longside, Aberdeenshire, Scot. MA '46 Univ. of Cambridge, Eng. ASSOC. PROF. and HEAD, Dept. of Psych, Univ. of Tasmania. Member: BPS-A. Teaching, research, administration; history of British psychology, time perception, psychological interpretation of literature. M

CATHCART, Keith Mountford. 23 Dower St, Burwood E 13, Victoria. b. 16 Aug 1905 Melbourne. M.ED '39 Univ. of Melbourne, Austl. INSPECTOR, Mental Deficiency Trng, Ment. Hygiene Authority, 300 Queen St, Melbourne. Member: BPS-A, Austl. Rorschach Socy. Supervision and guidance of centers for mentally retarded children, testing, teaching; mental deficiency, achievement tests, projective techniques. M

CATTERALL, Kelvyn Henry Edward. 197 Royal St, Mt. Yokine, W.A. b. 6 Jan 1924 Wollongong. GUID. OFF, Guid. Br, Educ. Dept. of W.A, 35 College St, Subigco, W.A.; PSYCHOLOGIST, Austl. Army. Member: BPS-A. Educational and vocational guidance, testing, clinical analysis; children's interests as related to maladjustment, aptitude tests. M

CHAMBERS, Ronald Kerwin. Melbourne Grammar Sch, Domain Rd, South Yarra, Melbourne, Victoria. b. 17 Dec 1921 Austl. B.EC '47 Univ. of Sydney, Austl. GUID. MASTER, Melbourne Grammar Sch; PSYCHOLOGIST, Royal Austl. Air Force Member: BPS-A. Counseling, testing, vocational and educational guidance, teaching, consulting; personnel selection, educational psychology.   M

CHAMPION, Richard Annells. Dept. of Psych, Univ. of Sydney, Sydney, N.S.W. b. 6 Jan 1925 Largs Bay. MA '54 State Univ. of Iowa, USA. SR. LECT, Univ. of Sydney. Member: BPS-A. Teaching, research, administration; learning theory, measurement and methodology in experimental psychology, motivation.   M

CHAMPNESS, Dr. John Howard. Mt. Moriac Estate, Mt. Moriac, Via. Geelong, Victoria. b. 9 June 1921 Kaniva. PH.D '53 Univ. of London, Eng. EDUC, CONSULT, Geelong Grammar Sch, Corio, Victoria; LECT. in INDUS. MANAGEMENT, Gordon Inst. of Tech, Geelong. Member: BPS-A, APA. Educational and industrial psychology, administration of test program, clinical diagnosis, counseling; learning theory and personality dynamics in mentally handicapped, achievement tests, special aptitude assessment.   M

CHANDLER, Alfred Thomas. A'Beckett's Rd, Upper Beaconsfield, Victoria. b. 29 Sept 1921 Melbourne. BA '48 Univ. of Melbourne, Austl. PERS. CONSULT, W.D. Scott and Co. Pty. Ltd, Management Consultants, 401 Collins St, Melbourne; LECT. in APPL. PSYCH, Occupat. Ther. Sch. of Victoria. Member: BPS-A, Assn. of Profes. Psych'ts. Industrial psychology, personnel selection and training, testing, consulting; learning theory applied to industrial training, group process and attitude formation in industry.   M

CHARLESWORTH, Miss Mary Evelyn Joyce. Vocat. Guid. Bur, Dept. of Labour and Indus, 100 Macquarie St, Parramatta, N.S.W. b. 21 Aug 1913 Sydney. BA '44 Univ. of Sydney, Austl. GUID. OFF, Vocat. Guid. Bur. Vocational guidance, professional writing, testing; motivation, integration, social perception.   F

CLARK, Alfred William. 66 Balcombe Rd, Mentone, Melbourne. b. 31 Aug 1925 Melbourne. BA '56 Univ. of Melbourne, Austl. GUID. OFF, Educ. Dept. of Victoria. Member: BPS-A. Educational psychology, consulting and guidance service for primary schools, psychotherapy; social psychology of the classroom.   M

CLARK, Prof. John Faithfull. 48 Kallaroo Rd, Lane Cove, N.S.W. b. 20 Apr 1911 Sydney. PH.D '50 Univ. of London, Eng. PROF. and HEAD, Sch. of Appl. Psych. New South Wales Univ. of Tech, Anzac Parade, Kensington, N.S.W. Member: BPS-A. Teaching and research in industrial psychology, administration, consulting; interests and attitudes, personality of technologists and executives, group process. M

CLARKE, Dr. Bryan Robert. 45 Hex St,

Tottenham W. 12, Melbourne. b. 30 Mar 1922 Murchison. PH.D '53 Univ. of Manchester, Eng. LECTURER, Trng. Cen. for teachers of the Deaf, 17 Marshall Ave, Kew E 4, Melbourne. Member: BPS-A. Teaching, testing, research; audiology, selection procedures.   M

CLUNIES-ROSS, Mrs. Jane. c/o Austl. and New Zealand Bank, Pitt and Hunter Streets, Sydney. b. 13 July 1891 Sydney. BA '12 Univ. of Sydney, Austl. LECT. in PSYCH, Nursery Sch. Trng. Coll, Sydney Day Nursery and Nursery Schools Assn. Inc, 39 Park St, Sydney; TUTORIAL LECT. in PSYCH, Dept. of Tutorial Classes, Univ. of Sydney. Member: BPS-A, Australasian Assn. of Psych. and Philos. Teaching, educational psychology, counseling; preschool child education, adult education in psychology.   F

COCHRANE, Rupert Gordon. 49 Ernest St, Woody Pt, Queensland. b. 11 Feb 1909 Armidale. BA '50 Univ. of Queensland, Austl. LECT. in EDUC, Univ. of Queensland, St. Lucia, Queensland; ASST, ED, *The Slow Learning Child.* Member: BPS-A. Testing, guidance, educational psychology, teaching; intelligence, achievement and diagnostic testing, remedial teaching.   M

COLEMAN, Francis G. Sydney Teachers' Coll, Univ. Grounds, Newtown, Sydney. b. 24 Feb. 1909 Sydney. BA '50 Univ. of Sydney, Austl. LECTURER, Sydney Teachers' Coll. Member: BPS-A. Teaching, research, educational psychology, student counseling; learning theory and motivation, mental hygiene, philosophical foundations of psychology.   M

COOK, Dr. Philip Halford. Dept. of Labour and Natl. Serv, 125 Swanston St, Melbourne C 1. b. 10 Oct 1912 Benalla. PH.D '41 Univ. of Kansas, USA. ASST. SECY, Dept. of Labour and Natl. Serv; CONSULT. PSYCH'T, Psychiat. Clin, Prince Henry's Hosp, Melbourne; ASSOC. ED, *Australian Journal of Psychology.* Member: BPS-A, SPT, Austl. Rorschach Socy. Administration, industrial psychology, consulting; communication and group process in industry, projective techniques, vocational problems in national employment service.   M

COOPER, Miss Daphne Daisy. 60 Trevallyn Rd, Launceston, Tas. b. 30 Apr 1919 Sydney. MA '55 Univ. of Tasmania, Austl. SR. PSYCH'T, Educ. Dept, Macquarie St, Hobart, Tas. Member: BPS-A. Student and parent guidance, testing, applied psychology; juvenile delinquency, child development, projective techniques.   F

COUCH, Dr. Victor James. 41 Cammeray Rd, Cammeray, N.S.W. b. 27 July 1912 Hawthorn. PH.D '55 Univ. of London, Eng. LECT. in CHARGE, Tech. Teacher Trng.

Annexe, Sydney Teachers' Coll, Dept. of Educ, Bridge St, Sydney. Member: BPS-A, N.S.W. Inst. of Educ. Res. Administration, teaching, educational psychology; social perception, attitude measurement, projective techniques. M

COX, Francis Nicol. Dept. of Psych, Univ. of Melbourne, Carlton, Victoria. b. 7 July 1924 Perth. MS '53 Yale Univ, USA. LECTURER, Univ. of Melbourne; HONORARY PSYCH'T, Royal Melbourne Hosp, Parkville, Victoria. Member: BPS-A, APA. Teaching, research, testing; learning theory, child development, abnormal psychology. M

CRAGO, Ian Hamilton. Box 3, Ballina, N.S.W. b. 2 Aug 1915 Yass. BA '46 Univ. of Sydney, Austl. INSPECTOR of SCHOOLS, Dept. of Educ, Box 33, GPO, Sydney. Member: BPS-A. Administration, teaching, educational psychology; educational guidance, special education, remedial teaching techniques. M

CRAIG, James Douglas. 20 Merton St, Ivanhoe N. 21, Victoria. b. 6 May 1922 Yarram. BA '50 Univ. of Melbourne, Austl. VOCAT. GUID. OFF, Dept. of Labour and Natl. Serv, 37 Swanston St, Melbourne, Victoria. Member: BPS-A. Vocational guidance, testing, applied psychology; aptitude testing, attitude measurement, social perception. M

CRANE, Allan Robert. Teachers' Coll, Armidale, N.S.W. b. 10 Feb 1914 Picton. MA '40 Univ. of Sydney, Austl. SR. LECT. in EDUC, Teachers' Coll, Armidale; LECT. in CHILD DEVEL, Univ. of New England, Armidale. Member: BPS-A. Teaching, testing, educational guidance, research; group process, personality development, reading difficulties of children. M

CULLEN, James Sylvester. 20 Hardinge St, Beaumaris. b. 29 Mar 1923 Melbourne. BA '48 Univ. of Melbourne, Austl. VOCAT. GUID. OFF, Dept. of Labour and Natl. Serv, 37 Swanston St, Melbourne. Member: BPS-A, Austl. Rorschach Socy, Austl. Assn. of Profes. Psychologists. Vocational guidance, applied psychology, testing; social perception, test interpretation. M

CUNNINGHAM, Dr. Kenneth Stewart. "Kentucky", Park Rd, Mt. Waverley, Victoria. b. 3 Feb 1890 Ballorat. PH.D '27 Teachers Coll, Columbia Univ, USA. EDUC. ADVIS, UNESCO Tech. Assistance Mission, Djakarta, Indonesia. Member: BPS-A. Retired, educational research; experimental education, achievement and intelligence tests. M

CURRIE, Keith. "Stirling," 21 Lissadell St, Floreat Park, W.A. b. 11 July 1915 Fremantle. B.ED '53 Univ. of Western Australia. SUPERV. of PRAC. TCHNG, Teachers' Coll, Claremont, W.A.; LECT. in

EDUC, Univ. of Western Australia, Perth. Member: BPS-A, W.A. Inst. of Educ. Res. Teaching education, student counseling and guidance, administration, testing; personality development, group dynamics, attitude measurement, learning theory, projective techniques. M

DASH, Robert Allan. 24 Cobham Ave, Ermington, N.S.W. b. 14 Sept 1911 Sydney. BA '47 Univ. of Sydney, Austl. VOCAT. ADVIS, Dept. of Educ, Bridge St, Sydney, N.S.W. Member: BPS-A. Administration, vocational guidance, educational psychology; aptitude and ability tests, educational and vocational guidance. M

DAVIES, Evan Edwin. 334 Livingstone Rd, Marrickville, N.S.W. b. 1 Apr 1923 Sydney. MA '54 Univ. of Sydney, Austl. LECTURER, N.S.W. Univ. of Tech, P.O. Box 1, Kensington, N.S.W.; CONSULTANT, Royal Austl. Air Force; HONORARY PSYCH'T, Royal Prince Alfred Hosp, Sydney. Member: BPS-A. Teaching, industrial psychology, consulting, research; personality theory, industrial psychology. M

DAWSON, Miss Hazel Copeland. Box 900 GPO, Sydney, N.S.W. b. 29 Sept 1915 Sydney. MA '39 Univ. of Sydney, Austl. Member: BPS-A. Retired; child guidance, consulting, psychotherapy, testing. F

DAY, Dr. Ross Henry. Dept. of Psych, Univ. of Sydney, Sydney, N.S.W. b. 20 Mar 1927 Albany. PH.D '54 Univ. of Bristol, Eng. LECTURER, Univ. of Sydney. Member: BPS-A. Teaching, research, consulting; human skill, physiology of visual perception. M

DERWENT, Sydney Conrad. 22 Adderstone Ave, N. Sydney, N.S.W. b. 8 May 1915 Sydney. BA '42 Univ. of Sydney, Austl. INSPECTOR of PERS. and TRNG, N.S.W. State Pub. Serv. Bd, 19 O'Connell St, Sydney; LECTURER, N.S.W. Univ. of Tech. Member: BPS-A. Administration and development of personnel policy and practice, research, teaching; achievement and selection tests, training principles and practices, attitude measurement. M

DINGLE, John Tor. Youth Welf. Sect, Dept. of Labour and Indus, 4 Albert St, Sydney, N.S.W. b. 18 Mar 1906 Sydney. BA '28 Univ. of Sydney, Austl. ASST. DIR. of YOUTH WELF, Dept. of Labour and Indus. Member: BPS-A. Administration, testing, vocational guidance, selection; vocational counseling, aptitude tests. M

DOUGHTON, Horace Edwin. 47 Alfred Rd, Dee Why, Sydney, N.S.W. b. 6 Sept 1910 Sydney. BA '38 Univ. of Sydney, Austl. CHIEF GUID. OFF, Div. of Res. Guid. and Adjustment, N.S.W. Dept. of Educ, Bridge St, Sydney; LECTURER, Univ. of Sydney and New South Wales, Univ. of Tech,

Sydney. Member: BPS-A, Austl. Socy. of Philos. and Psych. Administration of educational and vocational guidance services, testing; educational guidance, intelligence and achievement testing, projective techniques. M

DOUGLAS, Mrs. Alma B. Woodland Ave, Lugarmo, N.S.W. b. 27 Dec 1924 Ballarat. BA '48 Univ. of Melbourne, Austl. PSYCHOLOGIST, Child Guid. Clin, Brisbane St, Sydney. Member: BPS-A. Testing, clinical analysis, psychotherapy; methods of personality assessment, social factors in school adjustment. F

DRUMMOND, Miss Grace Adelaide. Psych. Dept, Univ. of Western Australia, Crawley, W.A. b. 6 Oct 1911 Perth. MA '47 Univ. of London, Eng. LECTURER, Univ. of W.A. Member: BPS-A. Teaching, educational psychology, testing. F

DUNN, Sydney Stephen. Austl. Counc. for Educ. Res, 147 Collins St, Melbourne. b. 9 July 1916 Balaklava. BA '46 Univ. of Adelaide, Austl. OFF. in CHARGE, Test Div, Austl. Counc. for Educ. Res. Educational and psychological test construction, research, administration. M

EDDY, Miss Margaret Mary. 16 Lillian St, Cottesloe, W.A. b. 5 Sept 1934 Perth. BA '53 Univ. of Western Australia. VOCAT. GUID. OFF, Dept. of Labour and Natl. Serv, 86 King St, Perth. Member: BPS. Testing, guidance, research; vocational guidance and counseling, aptitude tests. F

EDWARDS, Miss Anastasia Beatrice. 156 Grosvenor Rd, N. Perth, W.A. b. 29 Feb 1908 Perth. VOCAT. GUID. OFF, Commonwealth Govt. of Austl, Dept. of Labour and Natl. Serv, 86 King St, Perth. Member: BPS, Australasian Socy. of Psych. and Philos. Vocational guidance; aptitude tests, attitude measurement. F

EDWARDS, Mrs. Eileen Mary. 75 Stevenson St, Kew E 4, Melbourne. b. 18 Jan 1910 Surrey, Eng. MA '35 Univ. Coll, London, Eng. LECTURER, Kindergarten Trng. Coll, Nodden Grave, Kew E 4, Victoria. Member: BPS-A, Rorschach Socy. Teaching, clinical analysis, consulting; child development, diagnostic testing of young handicapped children. F

EDWARDS, Rev. Neil Russell. Commonwealth Off. of Educ, Grace Bldg, York St, Sydney. b. 2 Aug 1918 Moonee Ponds. BA '42 Univ. of Sydney, Austl. SR. EDUC. OFF, Commonwealth Oft. of Educ. Member: BPS-A. Research and supervision of research in education and educational psychology; achievement and ability tests, attitude measurement. M

EGLINGTON, Geoffrey Clarence. 11 Walker St, Five Dock, N.S.W. b. 10 June 1917 Murwillumbah. BA '40 Univ. of Sydney,

Austl. SR. GUID. OFF, Vocat. Guid. Bur, Youth Welf. Sect, N.S.W. Dept. of Labour and Indus, 266 A Pacific Highway, Crows Nest; COMMANDING OFF, N.S.W. Unit of Austl. Army Psych. Corp. Member: BPS-A. Vocational guidance, testing, administration, military psychology; aptitude and intelligence testing, occupational research. M

ELLIOTT, Gordon Charles. 35 Elizabeth St, Ashfield, N.S.W. b. 14 Apr 1914 Sydney. BA '34 Univ. of Sydney, Austl. LECT. in PSYCH, Teachers' Coll, Union St, Newcastle, N.S.W. Member: BPS-A. Teaching, educational psychology, psychotherapy; counseling, achievement tests, educational guidance. M

ELSNER, Mrs. Rhonda Lois. Flat 6, 3 Burtway, Perth, W.A. b. 17 Sept 1929 Perth. BA '50 Univ. of Western Australia. GUID. OFF, Educ. Dept, Barrack St, Perth. Testing, educational and clinical guidance of physically handicapped children, parent counseling; achievement tests, educational placement. F

EMERY, Dr. Frederick Edmund. Flat 4, 163 Flemington Rd, Melbourne N 1, Victoria. b. 27 Aug 1925 Narrogin. PH.D '53 Univ. of Melbourne, Austl. SR. LECT, Univ. of Melbourne, Carlton N 3, Melbourne Member: BPS-A. Teaching, research, applied psychology; role behavior, group process, mass communication. M

EVANS, Robert Cecil. 4 Merton St, Ivanhoe, Victoria. b. 2 Apr 1931 Perth. BA '54 Univ. Of Western Australia. INDUS. PSYCH'T, Dept. of Labour and Natl. Serv, 129 Swanston St, Melbourne; ED. STAFF, *Personnel Practice Bulletin.* Member: B.PS. Industrial psychology, research, testing; test construction and validation, personnel practice in industry, labor turnover problems. M

FARRANT, Roland Harvard. 19 Sluman St, West Ryde, N.S.W. b. 5 Aug 1921 Perth. BA '48 Univ. of Melbourne, Austl. SR. PSYCH'T, Commonwealth Acoustic Labs, Customs Hse, Circular Quay, Sydney, N.S.W. Member: BPS-A. Research in psychology and audiology, staff training, consulting; psychology and audiology tests and procedures for the deaf, child and parent guidance. M

FLACH, Mrs. Auguste. 46 Basin Rd, Launceston, Tas. b. 20 Mar 1891 Vienna, Austria. Diploma '26 Univ. of Vienna, Austria. CONSULT. PSYCH'T. and PROBAT. OFF, Children's Court, Hobart, Tas. Member: BPS-A, Socy. for Exper.Psych. (Berlin), Socy. for Appl. Psych. and Psychother. Research, testing, consulting; psychology of thinking, movement, and expression. F

FLECKER, Robert. 49 Evandale St, Floreat

Park, w.a. b. 3 June 1924 Perth. b.sc '51 Univ. of Western Australia. sr. lect, Psych. and Couns. Serv, Tech. Educ. Div, Educ. Dept, Mounts Bay Rd, Perth, w.a.; off. in charge, Citizen Milit. Force Army Psych. Unit. Member: bps-a, w.a. Clin. Socy. Teaching personnel and applied psychology, student and employee selection, guidance, counseling; group processes and communication, personality theory and non-directive theory, perception and needs. M

FLEMING, Henry John. 263 Elizabeth St, Sydney, n.s.w. b. 4 May 1919 Geelong. ba '51 Univ. of Melbourne, Austl. clin. psych't, priv. prac; honorary psych't, Sydney Hosp, Parramatta Dist. Hosp, Fam. Welf. Bur. Member: bps-a. Clinical practice, consulting, clinical testing and analysis, research, teaching; infant intelligence testing, development of new projective techniques. M

FRAGAR, Lester Reginald. Sydney Teachers' Coll, Univ. Grounds, Sydney, n.s.w. b. 14 Dec 1921 Sydney. ba '51 Univ. of Sydney, Austl. lect. in educ, Sydney Teachers' Coll. Educational psychology, teaching, administration; learning theory, group dynamics, social movements. M

FROST, Barry Philip. 171 Davey St, Hobart, Tas. b. 20 Sept 1926 Sydney. ba '51 Univ. of Sydney, Austl. guid. off, Psychologists Off, Educ. Dept, 307 Macquarie St, Hobart. Member: bps-a. Guidance, educational psychology, testing; projective techniques, group therapy, classroom dynamics. M

FROST, Mrs. Ruth. 171 Davey St, Hobart, Tas. b. 30 Oct 1924 Bunbury. ba '45 Univ. of Western Australia. sr. psych't, Psychologist's Off, Educ, Dept. of Tas, 307 Macquarie St, Hobart. Member: bps-a. Educational psychology and guidance, testing; mental retardation, classroom dynamics, social perception. F

GAULT, Miss Una. Dept. of Psych, Univ. of Sydney, n.s.w. b. 23 Dec 1925 Young. ba '47 Univ. of Sydney, Austl. clin. psych't, Psychiat. Div, Repatriation Commission, Grace Bldg, York St, Sydney. Member: bps-a. Testing, teaching, consulting; diagnostic testing procedures and personality evaluation. F

GIBB, Prof. Cecil Austin. Dept. of Psych, Canberra Univ. Coll, Canberra. b. 18 Aug 1913 Sydney. ph.d '49 Univ. of Illinois, usa. professor, Canberra Univ. Coll. Member: bps-a, apa. Teaching, research, administration; group process, leadership, human relations training. M

GOLDING, Neville William. 660 Kiewa St, Albury, n.s.w. b. 2 Nov 1914 Sydney. ba '45 Univ. of Sydney, Austl. dist. sch.

couns, Dept. of Educ, Bridge St, Sydney, n.s.w. Testing, guidance, clinical treatment of maladjusted pupils, educational psychology; intelligence and achievement testing, remedial reading. M

GORMAN, Dr. John. Mental Hygiene Authority, 300 Queen St, Melbourne, Victoria. b. 30 Aug 1905 Melbourne. mb, bs: Diploma Psych. Med. '53 Univ. of Melbourne, Austl. psychiatrist and supt, Ment. Hyg. Authority. Member: bps-a, Australasian Assn. of Psychiatrists. Consulting, psychotherapy, administration; neuro-anatomical and neuro-physiological basis of behavior, learning theory, psychological deviants. M

GRAHAM, Dr. Francis Walter. Melbourne Clin. for Psychoanal, 111 Collins St, Melbourne, Victoria. b. 28 Apr 1914 Ocean Island, Cen. Pacific. mb, bs '40 Univ. of Sydney, Austl; Diploma Psych. Med. '44 Univ. of Melbourne, Austl. director, Melbourne Clin. for Psychoanal; honorary asst. psychiatrist, Royal Melbourne Hosp, Parkville, Victoria. Member: bps-a, Australasian Assn. of Psychiatrists, Br. Psychoanal. Socy, Austl. Psychoanal. Socy, Austl. Rorschach Socy. Psychotherapy, consulting, teaching; clinical psychiatry, group psychotherapy, psychological effects of physical disability. M

GRAVES, Donald Edward. Dept. of Labour and Natl. Serv, 129 Swanston St, Melbourne, Victoria. b. 3 Apr 1918 Crayford, Kent, Eng. ba '40 Univ. of New Zealand. exec. off, Plng. and Res. Div, Dept. of Labour and Natl. Serv. Member: bps-a, Austl. Assn. of Profes. Psych'ts, Natl. Inst. of Indus. Psych. (London). Administration of section on manpower planning for national emergency, research, industrial and personnel psychology; occupational research, vocational guidance and selection, industrial application of psychological techniques. M

GRAY, George Andrew. 2 Georgann St, Turramurra, n.s.w. b. 19 June 1916 Goulburn. ba '48 Univ. of Sydney, Austl. prin. educ. off, n.s.w. Dept. of Techn. Educ, Broadway, n.s.w; lecturer, n.s.w. Univ. of Tech, Sydney. Member: bps-a. Administration of educational research and services, student counseling, teaching; vocational and educational counseling. M

GRAY, Kenneth Clive. 90 Hannah St, Beecroft, n.s.w. b. 11 Mar 1925 Sydney. ba '45 Univ. of Sydney, Austl. clin. psych't, Child Guid Clin, Parramatta Rd, Camperdown, Sydney; honorary Psych't, Royal Blind Socy. panel for pre-school blind children. Member: bps-a. Testing, clinical diagnosis, child psychotherapy, consulting; child guidance, projective techniques, theories of personality dynamics. M

GREEN, Mrs. Verona Edith. 24 Stanley St, Nedlands, w.a. b. 24 Oct 1932 Adelaide. BA '53 Univ. of Western Australia. PSYCH'T. and GUID. OFF, Educ. Dept. of Victoria, Treasury Place, Victoria. Educational guidance, testing; achievement tests, social perception, learning theory. F

GREIG, Alexander Ronald. 27 Bolton St, Spotswood W. 14, Victoria. b. 21 Nov 1911 Melbourne. BA '50 Univ. of Melbourne, Austl. SR. GUID. OFF, Psych. and Guid. Br, Educ. Dept, c/o State School 1406, Yarra Park, E. Melbourne, Victoria; LECT. in EDUC. PSYCH, Tech. Teachers' Coll, Victoria. Member: BPS-A. Educational and vocational guidance, counseling, teaching; group processes in education, psychotherapy, teacher training. M

GRIFFITHS, Major David McCracken. 11 Psych. Unit, N. Cmd. Pers. Depot, Enoggera, Brisbane. b. 22 Apr 1913 Brisbane. BA '38 Univ. of Queensland, Austl. DEPUTY ASST. DIR. of PSYCH, Austl. Reg. Army, 11 Psych Unit; ASSOCIATE, John P. Young and Assoc, Management Consultants. Member: BPS-A. Testing, personnel psychology, administration, consulting; intelligence and aptitude tests, projective techniques. M

GRIFFITHS, Francis Denis. Dept. of Labour and Natl. Serv, 37 Swanston St, Melbourne. b. 31 Oct 1930 Brisbane. BA '56 Univ. of Melbourne, Austl. VOCAT. GUID. OFF, Dept. of Labour and Natl. Serv. Member: BPS. Vocational guidance, testing, interviewing; rehabilitation of physically handicapped, social perception. M

GROH, Leslie Stephen. 58 Patterson St, Middle Park, Melbourne S.C. 6. b. 28 Oct 1928 Budapest, Hungary. BA '54 Univ. of Melbourne, Aust. PSYCHOLOGIST, Travancore Clin, Flemington St, Melbourne. Member: BPS-A. Intelligence and projective testing, play therapy, parent and educational guidance; developmental psychology, projective techniques. M

GWILLIAM, Malcolm Ross. 6 Ramsay Rd, Pennant Hills, N.S.W. b. 8 Nov 1919 Bathurst. BA '52 Univ. of Sydney, Austl. GUID. OFF, N.S.W. Educ. Dept, Univ. Br, Univ. Grounds, Sydney, N.S.W. Member: BPS-A. Educational and vocational guidance, consulting, administration; perception, cognition, learning theory. M

HALL, John Alexander. 11 Lower Heidelberg Rd, Ivanhoe, Victoria. b. 23 May 1911 Melbourne. BA '49 Univ. of Melbourne, Austl. PRIN. PSYCH'T. and GUID. OFF, Victoria Dept. of Educ, Treasury Bldgs, Melbourne. Member: BPS-A. Educational psychology, testing, administration; social factors affecting learning. M

HAMILTON, Miss Nancie. Child Guid. Clin, Childrens' Hosp, Herston Rd, Brisbane, Queensland. b. 18 Sept 1899 Toowoomba. BA '20 Univ. of Melbourne, Austl. PSYCHOLOGIST, Child Guid. Clin. Member: BPS-A. Intelligence and achievement testing, guidance, remedial teaching, play therapy; projective techniques, learning theory, social perception. F

HAMMER, Alfred Gordon. Dept. of Psych, Univ. of Sydney, Sydney. b. 10 Aug 1914 Sydney. MA '49 Univ. of Sydney, Austl. SR. LECT, Univ. of Sydney. Member: BPS-A, Australasian Assn. of Psych. and Philos. Teaching, research, psychotherapy; theory of psychotherapy, personality and psychopathology. M

HANNA, Ian. 66 Armstrong St, Middle Park S.C. 6, Melbourne, Victoria. b. 24 Feb 1923 Melbourne. BA '51 Univ. of Melbourne, Austl. DIR. of CLASSES, Counc. of Adult Educ, 114 Flinders St, Melbourne. Member: BPS-A. Administration, educational psychology, teaching; social participation. M

HARLAND, Ronald William. 12 Rowan St, Merewether 2N, N.S.W. b. 22 July 1912 Newcastle. BA '34 Univ. of Sydney, Austl. DIST. GUID. OFF, Dept. of Educ, 88 Scott St, Newcastle; AREA SUPERV, Adult Migrant Educ. Administration of clinical guidance service, testing; educational and vocational guidance, intelligence and achievement testing. M

HART, Wilfred Edmund. Dept. of Educ, Box 33 GPO, Sydney, N.S.W. b. 12 Oct 1912 Sydney. MA '39 Univ. of Sydney, Austl. DIST. INSPECTOR of SCHOOLS, Dept. of Educ, N.S.W; VICE PRIN, Teachers' Coll, Dept. of Educ, N.S.W. Member: BPS-A. Administration, teaching, research; personnel management, learning, measurement. M

HARVEY, Leslie Vincent. Commonwealth Empl. Serv, Box 1435 J, GPO, Adelaide, s.A. b. 2 Aug 1921 Swan Hill. BA '50 Univ. of Melbourne, Austl. OFF. in CHARGE, Profes. Serv. Off, Dept. of Labour and Natl. Serv, 99 Currie St, Adelaide. Member: BPS-A. Administration of employment service, vocational guidance, testing, consulting; aptitude and intelligence testing, group work, counseling, psychodiagnostic testing. M

HENDERSON, Dr. Norman Keith. Univ. of Queensland, St. Lucia, Brisbane, Queensland. b. 22 June 1914 Colac. PH.D '49 Univ. of London, Eng. SR. LECT. in EDUC, Univ. of Queensland. Member: BPS-A. Teaching, research administration; learning theory, psychometrics, social-emotional development. M

HERBERT, Miss Margaret Vera. 47 Adamson St, Wooloowin N. 3, Queensland. b. 6 July 1926 Brisbane. MA '56 Teachers Coll,

Columbia Univ, USA. GUID. OFF, Res. and Guid. Br, George St, Brisbane. Member: BPS-A. Guidance, educational psychology, testing; counseling, aptitude and interest tests, job studies. F

HINSHAW, Alfred Laurence. 22 Beardow St, Lismore, N.S.W. b. 25 Jan 1920 West Wallsend. BA '46 Univ. of Sydney, Austl. DIST. GUID. OFF, N.S.W. Educ. Dept., Bridge St, Sydney. Member: BPS-A. Educational psychology, testing, guidance and consulting; achievement and intelligence tests, educational and vocational guidance. M

HOHNE, Dr. Hans Hugo. Eltham South, Victoria. b. 24 Apr 1906 Chemnitz, Germany. PH.D '38 Univ. of Prague, Czechoslovakia. CHIEF CLIN. PSYCH'T, Melbourne Inst. for Psychoanal, 111 Collins St, Melbourne C. 1, Victoria. Member: BPS-A, Austl. Rorschach Socy. Research, testing, consulting; clinical diagnosis by projective and other tests, psychoanalysis, prediction of academic success. M

HOLT, Norman Francis. Diamond St, Eltham, Victoria. b. 4 May 1923 Melbourne. BA '50 Univ. of Melbourne, Austl. SR. INDUS. PSYCH'T, Dept. of Labour and Natl. Serv, 129 Swanston St, Melbourne; EDITOR *Personnel Practice Bulletin.* Member: BPS-A. Administration, research direction, and editorial work in industrial psychology; problems of personnel practice. M

HORN, Miss Margaret Heather. Box 2883 GPO, Sydney. b. 19 Sept 1929 Deniliquin. BA '49 Univ. of Sydney, Austl. VOCAT. GUID. OFF, Youth Welf. Sect, 4 Albert St, Sydney. Testing, guidance, interviewing; vocational psychology, child adoption, juvenile delinquency and the family. F

HORNER, Vincent. Graylands Teachers' Coll, Mimosa Ave, Graylands, Perth, W.A. b. 17 Oct 1923 Guildford. BA '52 Univ. of Western Australia. LECT. in PSYCH. and EDUC, Graylands Teachers' Coll. Teaching, educational psychology, testing; group processes, remedial techniques, learning. M

HOWARTH, Edgar. Dept. of Psych, Univ. of Melbourne, Carlton N. 3, Victoria. b. 5 May 1925 Blackburn, Eng. MS '53 Univ. of Manchester, Eng. LECTURER, Univ. of Melbourne. Member: BPS-A. Teaching, research; learning theory, visual perception neurophysiology. M

HOWE, Maurice Arthur. 164 Pittwater Rd, Manly, N.S.W. b. 5 Nov 1927 Cottesloe. BA '48 Univ. of Western Australia. OFF. in CHARGE, Profes. Serv. Off, Dept. of Labour and Natl. Serv, 77 York St, Sydney. Member: BPS-A. Administration of vocational guidance section, personnel psychology; aptitude and intelligence testing, counseling. M

HOWIE, Prof. Duncan. 11 Garibaldi St,

Armidale, N.S.W. b. 18 Apr 1904 Mearns, Scot. PH.D '35 Univ. of London, Eng. HEAD, Dept. of Psych, Univ. of New England, Armidale. Member: BPS-A. Teaching, research; factor analysis, personality theory and assessment. M

JAMES, Miss Ione May Vickery. Div. of Res, Guid. and Adjustment, N.S.W. Dept. of Educ, Bridge St, Sydney. b. 27 Aug 1914 Sydney. BA '35 Univ. of Sydney, Austl. SR. GUID. OFF, N.S.W. Dept. of Educ. Member: BPS-A. Organization of training for school counsellors, guidance, teaching; achievement and ability testing, educational guidance, school counseling. F

JENKINS, Norman Richard. 18 Anzac Pde, Newcastle. b. 21 June 1921 Sydney. BA, Univ. of Sydney, Austl. SR. GUID. OFF, Newcastle Educ. Guid. Clin, Dept. of Educ, Bridge St, Sydney; HONORARY PSYCH'T, Royal Newcastle Hosp; VIS. PSYCH'T, Newcastle and Stockton Ment. Hosps; LECT. in PSYCH, Newcastle Univ. Coll. Member: BPS-A. Educational guidance, diagnosis, therapy, testing, teaching; mental deficiency, brain injury and psychosis in children, special education for handicapped children. M

JONES, Paul. 21 Michael St, Beaumaris, Victoria. b. 17 Sept 1923 Dunedin, New Zealand. BA '50 Univ. of Melbourne, Austl. VOCAT. GUID. OFF, Commonwealth Dept. of Labour and Natl. Serv, 37 Swanston St, Melbourne. Member: BPS-A. Vocational guidance, clinical testing, counseling; interviewing and counseling techniques, nature of intelligence, interpretation of intelligence tests. M

JONES, Miss Rita Merlwyn. 63 Hobbs Ave, Nedlands, W.A. b. 25 May 1903 Waroona. BA '44 Univ. of Western Australia. GUID. OFF, Guid. and Spec. Educ. Br, W.A. Educ. Dept, 35 Subiaco Rd, Subiaco. Member: BPS-A. Testing and treatment of retarded children, research in educational psychology, remedial education, guidance and consulting; achievement testing. F

JORGENSEN, Dr. Christopher. 12 Kilby Rd, Kew, Victoria. b. 14 Aug 1903 Kerang. PH.D '33 Columbia Univ, USA. PSYCHOLOGIST, Repatriation Dept, Hanna St, South Melbourne, Victoria; HONORARY VOCAT. and EDUC. GUID. OFF, Returned Servicemen's League, Victoria. Member: BPS-A, Austl. Rorschach Socy. Clinical practice, testing, guidance; measurement of abilities, personality theory, adjustment. M

KAGI, Robert John. 99 Pangbourne St, Wembley Park, W.A. b. 18 May 1916 Perth. B.SC '49 Univ. of Western Australia. LECT. in EDUC, Teachers' Coll, Goldsworthy Rd, Claremont, Perth, W.A. Member: BPS-A, W.A. Clin. Psych. Socy. Teaching, guidance, administration, research, testing; educational psychology, group dynamics. M

KAWENOKA, Mrs. Maria. Psychologists Off, Educ. Dept, 307 Macquarie St, Hobart, Tas. b. 21 Jan 1914 Luck, Poland. MA '36 Univ. of Warsaw, Poland. PSYCHOLOGIST, Educ. Dept, Hobart. Member: BPS-A, Austl. Rorschach Socy. Educational psychology, testing, guidance; projective techniques, learning theory applied to school situation, child and adolescent psychotherapy. F

KEATS, Dr. John Augustus. Austl. Counc. for Educ. Res, 145 Collins St, Melbourne, Victoria. b. 24 Oct 1921 Port Pirie. PH.D '55 Princeton Univ, USA. STATISTICIAN, Austl. Counc. for Educ. Res. Member: BPS-A, Psychomet. Socy. Research in education and psychometrics; test theory and scaling, development of abilities, classroom roles. M

KEMP, Miss Elizabeth Armour. 91 Broadway, Punchbowl, N.S.W. b. 7 Feb 1913 Invercargill, New Zealand. BA '43 Univ. of Sydney, Austl. SR. GUID. OFF. and EDUC. CONSULT, Dept. of Educ, Bridge and Lottus Sts, Sydney, N.S.W. Member: BPS-A. Student counseling and guidance, educational psychology, clinical analysis, administration; learning theory, social development, development of attitudes. F

KEMP, Dr. Leslie Charles Dunstan. 106 Jeffrey St, Armidale, N.S.W. b. 12 Mar 1915 Sydney. PH.D '54 Univ. of London, Eng. VICE PRIN, Teachers' Coll, Mossman St, Armidale; LECTURER, Univ. of New England, Armidale. Member: BPS-A. Teaching, administration, educational research; personality, group behavior, achievement tests. M

KENNA, Charles Porter. Dept. of Appl. Psych, New South Wales Univ. of Tech, Harris St, Ultimo, Sydney. b. 28 July 1922 Sydney. BA '47 Univ. of Sydney, Austl. LECTURER, N.S.W. Univ. of Tech; HONORARY PSYCH'T, Austl. Inst. of Indus. Psych, 12 O'Connel St, Sydney. Member: BPS-A. Teaching, industrial psychology, consulting; achievement tests, industrial selection and counseling. M

KNAUERHASE, Oscar Carl. 29 Narinna Ave, Cumberland Park, S.A. b. 27 Apr 1911 Booleroo Centre. MA '43 Univ. of Adelaide, Austl. SR. MASTER, Adelaide Tech. High Sch, S.A. Sch. of Mines and Industries, North Terrace, Adelaide. Member: BPS-A. Teaching, research, educational psychology; psychology of personality and individual differences, achievement tests, attitude measurement. M

KNÖPFELMACHER, Dr. Frank. Dept. of Psych, Univ. of Melbourne, Victoria. b. 3 Feb 1923 Vienna, Austria. PH.D '53 Univ. of London, Eng. LECTURER, Univ. of

Melbourne. Member: BPS-A, Socy. for the Study of Animal Beh. (London). Teaching, research, administration; learning theory, methodology, experimental neurosis. M

LAFITTE, Dr. Paul. Dept. of Psych, Univ. of Melbourne, Carlton N. 3, Victoria. b. 21 Sept 1915 London, Eng. Litt D '56 Univ. of Melbourne, Austl. SR. LECT, Univ. of Melbourne. Member: BPS-A. Teaching, research, administration; theory and method of psychology, social behavior in industry, structure of projective techniques. M

LANGLEY, Philip Dacres. Dept. of Psych, Univ. of Melbourne, Grattan St, Carlton N. 3, Victoria. b. 11 Nov 1907 Sydney. B.ED '48 Univ. of Melbourne, Austl. SR. LECT, Univ. of Melbourne. Member: BPS-A. Teaching, administration, educational psychology; methodology. M

LASSCOCK, Edward David. 591 Brighton Rd, Seacliff, S.A. b. 8 Oct 1921 Adelaide. BA '50 Univ. of Melbourne, Austl. SR. GUID. OFF, Educ. Dept. of South Austl, Flinders St, Adelaide. Member: BPS-A. Educational psychology, counseling of school children, administration; relation of academic success to social status position and to participation in school activities. M

LAWRANCE, Miss Patricia. Commonwealth Employment Serv, Box 1435 J, GPO, Adelaide, S.A. b. 25 Feb 1923 Corrigin. BA '49 Univ. of Western Australia. VOCAT. GUID. OFF, Commonwealth Employment Serv, 99 Currie St, Adelaide. Member: BPS-A. Individual and group testing, interviewing, guidance. F

LEA, Ronald Charles Geoffrey. Psych. and Guid. Br, Educ. Dept. of Victoria, State Sch. 1406, Print Rd, E. Melbourne. b. 27 Aug 1914 Melbourne. B.ED '50 Univ. of Melbourne, Austl. SR. GUID. OFF, Educ. Dept. of Victoria, Treasury Bldgs, Melbourne. Member: BPS-A, Austl. Assn. of Profes. Psych'ts. Administration of primary school guidance services, educational psychology, testing; social psychology in the classroom, study of handedness and speech problems, post-hospitalization adjustment of schizophrenics. M

LEABEATER, Bruce. 56 Daunt Ave, Matraville, N.S.W. b. 5 Apr 1925 Sydney. BA '50 Univ. of Sydney, Austl. CLIN. PSYCH'T, Psychiat. Clin, Div. of Ment. Hyg, Dept. of Pub. H.lth, Broughton Hall, Wharf Rd, Leichhardt, Sydney; HONORARY PSYCH'T, Royal Blind Socy. and St. Andrews Marriage Guid. Cen. Member: BPS-A. Diagnostic testing, consulting, counseling, psychotherapy; projective techniques, organic pathologies, group therapy. M

LEAPER, Miss Patricia M. Commonwealth Trading Bank of Austl, Collins St, Melbourne C. 1. b. 22 Jan 1929 Melbourne.

MA '53 Univ. of Melbourne, Austl. ACTING
LECT, Sch. of Psych, Univ. of Melbourne,
Carlton N. 3, Melbourne. Member: BPS-A.
Teaching, clinical consulting, testing; social
psychological development of children,
theory of projective testing. F

LEWIS, Arthur Neil. 1 Acacia Ave, Klemzig,
S.A. b. 10 Apr 1923 Melbourne. BA '51
Univ. of Sydney, Austl. OFF. in CHARGE,
Commonwealth Acoustic Lab, Topham St,
Adelaide, S.A. Member: BPS. Clinical
audiology with children, testing, guidance,
administration; psychology of the deaf. M

LINDSAY, John S. B. Ballarat Mental Hosp,
Ballarat, Victoria. b. 5 June 1920 Christchurch, New Zealand. MD '53 Univ. of
New Zealand. PSYCHIATRIST, Ballarat
Ment. Hosp. Member: BPS-A, RMPA,
Australasian Assn. of Psychiatrists. Psycho
therapy, administration, research "therapeutic communities," group process, group
psychotherapy. M

LINK, Dr. Harold Selby. 335 St. Kilda St,
Melbourne S. 5. b. 11 Jan 1899 Melbourne.
MB, BS '22 Univ. of Melbourne, Austl.
PSYCHOTHERAPIST, priv. prac, 61 Collins
St, Melbourne. Member: BPS-A, Victorian
Rorschach Socy. Psychotherapy; analytic
psychology. M

LIVESEY, Peter James. 61 Tuart St, Tuart
Hill, W.A. b. 17 Oct 1919 Perth. MA '52
Univ. of Western Australia. OFF. in
CHARGE, Profes. Serv. Off, Commonwealth
Empl. Serv, 99 Wellington St, Perth.
Member: BPS-A. Vocational guidance,
placement of the physically handicapped,
research, teaching; aptitude measurement,
vocational counseling, learning theory. M

LOFTUS, Aaron Patrick Taparo. Parkside
Ment. Hosp, Adelaide, S.A. b. 19 Nov 1927
Melbourne. BA '50 Univ. of Melbourne,
Austl. PSYCHOLOGIST, Parkside Ment.
Hosp. Member: BPS-A. Testing, consulting,
research; projective techniques, group
dynamics, role perception. M

LOVELL, Allen Bruce. 79 Kensington Rd,
Norwood, Adelaide, S.A. b. 12 Feb 1929
Pernong. BA '52 Univ. of Melbourne, Austl.
SR. VOCAT. GUID. OFF, Dept. of Labour and
Natl. Serv, 99 Currie St, Adelaide. Member:
BPS-A. Consulting, testing, personnel psy-
chology, marriage counseling; projective
techniques, selection. M

LUMSDEN, James. Univ. of Western
Australia, Nedlands. b. 26 Jan 1920
Buckhaven, Scot. BA '51 Univ. of Sydney,
Austl. LECTURER, Univ. of W.A. Member:
BPS-A. Teaching, research, educational
psychology; measurement theory, edu-
cational measurement, development of
abilities. M

LUND, Dr. Ernest. Sydney Teachers' Coll,
Univ. Grounds, Newtown, N.S.W. b. 19 June

1908 Keighley, Eng. PH.D '41 Univ. of
Manchester, Eng. LECT. in EDUC, Sydney
Teachers' Coll. Member: BPS-A. Teaching,
guidance, research; educational psychology,
education of handicapped children, clinical
psychology. M

LYLE, Jack Greville. 7 Stephens St, North
Balwyn, Victoria. b. 25 Oct 1919 Sydney.
MA '53 Univ. of Melbourne, Austl. SR.
PSYCH'T, Ment. Hlth. Res. Inst, Dept. of
Ment. Hyg, Royal Park Ment. Hosp,
Melbourne. Member: BPS-A, Rorschach
Socy. Testing, clinical analysis, research,
counseling; projective techniques, child
psychotherapy, theories of psycho-
pathology. M

MacDOUGALL, Roderick Malcolm. 99 Ardross
St, Applecross, W.A. b. 31 July 1926 Perth.
BA '51 Univ. of Western Australia. GUID.
OFF, Educ. Dept, St. George's Tce, Perth,
W.A. Member: BPS-A. Teaching, vocational
counseling; group process, personnel psy-
chology, achievement tests. M

MacLEOD, Douglas. Warrandyte Rd,
Warrandyte S, Victoria. b. 4 Apr 1927
Melbourne. BA '49 Univ. of Melbourne,
Austl. TECH. SECY, Austl. Paper Manu-
facturers Ltd, Aikman St, S. Melbourne,
Victoria; CLIN. PSYCH'T, priv. prac.
Member: BPS-A. Industrial psychology,
administration, research, educational and
vocational guidance, testing, clinical analysis; sensation and perception experimentation, social adaptation of the physically handicapped, selection and placement
methods. M

MARSHALL, Dr. Alexander James. Dept. of
Psych, Univ. of Western Australia,
Nedlands, W.A. b. 18 Jan 1910 Pingelly.
PH.D '39 Univ. of London, Eng. READER
in PSYCH, Univ. of W.A. Member: BPS-A.
Teaching, research, administration; pattern
perception, night vision. M

MARTIN, Dr. Ian Holland. Cato Wing,
Epworth Hosp, Erin St, Richmond,
Victoria. b. 1 June 1919 Adelaide. MD '52
Univ. of Adelaide, Austl. PSYCHIATRIST,
priv. prac; CLIN. ASST, Royal Melbourne
Hosp, Grattan St, Parkville; VIS. MED. OFF,
Repatriation Dept. Hosp, "Rockingham,"
Barkers Rd, Kew, Melbourne, Victoria.
Member: BPS-A, Australasian Assn. of
Psychiatrists, Austl. Rorschach Socy.
Consulting, clinical practice, teaching,
psychotherapy; group interaction, psycho-
somatic clinical research. M

MARTIN, Miss Leonie Joyce. Div. of Ment.
Hyg, Pub. Hlth. Dept, 20 Murray St,
Hobart, Tas. b. 25 Sept 1917 Sydney.
BA, Univ. of Sydney, Aust. SR. PSYCH'T,
Div. of Ment. Hyg. Member: BPS-A.
Guidance, testing, clinical analysis, ad-
ministration, teaching; mental deficiency,

handicapped children, intelligence and personality measurement.   F

MARTIN, Reginald Thomas. Dept. of Appl. Psych, New South Wales Univ. of Tech, Sydney. b. 16 Oct 1916 Sydney. BA '50 Univ. of Sydney, Austl. LECTURER, New South Wales Univ. of Tech. Member: BPS-A, Australasian Assn. of Psych. and Philos. Teaching, psychotherapy, consulting; psychoanalytic theory, social psychology, ethics and psychology.   M

MAYFIELD, Captain Harry. Married Quarters, Hse. 8, Kapooka via Wagga, Wagga Wagga, N.S.W. b. 13 Sept 1926 Sydney. BA '53 Univ. of Sydney, Austl. OFF. COMMANDING, Psych. Detachment, Dept. of the Army, Kapooka. Member: BPS-A. Personnel psychology, testing, psychotherapy, guidance, administration; projective techniques, psychosomatics, interest patterns, psychological stress and leaderless group situations.   M

McCALL, James Arthur.   24 Neville Rd, Dalkeith, W.A. b. 13 Nov 1903 Kalgoorlie. BA '26 Univ. of Western Australia. DIRECTOR, Child Welf. Dept. of W.A., 508 Hay St, Perth. Member: BPS-A. Administration, consulting, guidance, testing; mental deficiency, delinquency, vocational guidance.   M

McCUBBING, Miss Pauline Judith. 8 Mann St, Cottesloe, W.A.   b. 3 Feb 1930 Perth. BA '50 Univ. of Western Australia. GUID. OFF, Educ. Dept. of W.A. Treasury Bldgs, Perth. Member: BPS-A. Consulting, parent guidance, psychotherapy, testing; projective techniques, intelligence and attainment testing.   F

McCULLOCH, Raymond William. Psychologist's Off, Tasmanian Educ. Dept, 307 Macquarie St, Hobart, Tas. b. 7 Dec. 1915 Sydney. B.ED '39 Univ. of Melbourne, Austl. CHIEF PSYCH'T and SUPT. of SPEC. CLASSES, Tasmanian Educ. Dept. Member: BPS-A, Austl. Rorschach Socy. Administration of educational guidance services, research and testing, special education; personality development, projective techniques, statistical theory.   M

McELWAIN, Prof. Donald William. Univ. of Queensland, St. Lucia, Brisbane, Queensland.   b. 8 May 1915 Wanganui, New Zealand. PH.D '37 Univ. of London, Eng. PROF. of PSYCH, Univ. of Queensland; EDITOR, *Australian Journal of Psychology*. Member: BPS-A, Biometrics Socy. Teaching, administration, editorial; measurement theory, perception, vocational selection. M

McLEAN, Miss Judith. Remedial Educ. Cen, Univ. of Queensland, Brisbane. b. 22 Aug 1935 Armidale. BA '55 Univ. of New England, Austl. GRAD. ASST, Remedial Educ. Cen, Univ. of Queensland; RESID.

TUTOR, Womens' Coll, Univ. of Queensland.   Testing, educational psychology, psychotherapy.   F

McLEOD, John Raymond.   71 Nell St, Greensborough, Victoria.   b. 28 Oct 1913 Hamilton. BA '37 Univ. of Melbourne, Austl. SR. GUID. OFF, Secondary Schools, Dept. of Educ, Treasury Place, Melbourne, Victoria. Member: BPS.   Group and individual testing, educational and vocational guidance; social perception, group process, learning theory.   M

McRAE, Prof. Christopher Ralph. Univ. of Sydney, Sydney. b. 25 Feb 1901 Glenpatrick. PH.D '25 Univ. of London, Eng. DEPUTY VICE CHANCELLOR, Univ. of Sydney; VICE PRES, Austl. Counc. for Educ. Res. Member: BPS-A. Administration, research, teaching; growth and development, achievement tests, learning theory.   M

MEADOWS, Dr. Arthur Wilkes. Dept. of Psych, Univ. of Adelaide, S.A. b. 11 June 1911 Wigan, Eng. PH.D '51 Univ. Coll. of London, Eng. HEAD, Dept. of Psych, Univ. of Adelaide; HONORARY PSYCH'T, Dept. of Psych, Royal Adelaide Hosp; ASSOC. ED, *Australian Journal of Psychology*. Member: BPS, Australasian Assn. of Psych. and Philos, Austl. Rorschach Socy. Administration, teaching, research, consulting; psychometrics, psychoanalysis, social psychology.   M

MEDDLETON, Dr. Ivor Graham. Univ. of Queensland, St. Lucia, Brisbane, Queensland. b. 13 Dec 1910 Maryborough. PH.D '54 Univ. of London, Eng. LECT. in EDUC, Univ. of Queensland. Member: BPS-A. Research, teaching, educational psychology; psychometrics, psychotherapy and diagnosis.   M

MICHAELIS, Mrs. Ann Margaret.   14 Sirius Ave, Mosman, N.S.W.   b. 12 Nov 1925 Amersham, Eng. B.SC '49 Univ. Coll. of London, Eng. PSYCHOLOGIST, Child Guid. Clin, Royal Alexandra Hosp. for Children, Pyrmont Bridge Rd, Camperdown, N.S.W.; CONSULT. PSYCH'T, priv. prac. Member: BPS-A.   Testing and clinical analysis of children, play therapy, interviewing parents consulting, educational psychology; projective techniques, intelligence tests, Rogerian theory.   F

MIDDLETON, Miss Margaret R. 2 Haileybury St, Hampton S. 7, Victoria. b. 10 Apr 1928 Melbourne. MA '51 Univ. of Melbourne, Austl. SR. RES. FELLOW, Univ. of Western Australia, Nedlands. Member: BPS-A. Research, teaching, student; concept formation in children, teaching methods, social determinants of consciousness.   F

MILLER, Emer. Prof. Dr. E. Morris. Univ. of Tasmania, Hobart. b. 14 Aug 1881 Pietermaritzburg, Natal, Union of South Africa.

LittD '18 Univ. of Melbourne, Austl. EMER. PROF. of PSYCH. and PHILOS, Univ. of Tasmania. Member: BPS, Austl. Assn. of Psych. and Philos. Retired; mental deficiency. M

MILLER, Miss Gwendoline Dorothy. 11 Glenroy Rd, Hawthorn E. 2, Victoria. b. 5 Feb 1927 Melbourne. MA '51 Univ. of Melbourne, Austl. PSYCHOLOGIST, Travancore Clin, Flemington St, Flemington W. 1, Victoria. Member: BPS-A. Testing, clinical analysis, guidance, research; group process, neurological abnormality and behavior, projective techniques. F

MILLER, Dr. Kenneth Maxwell. Univ. of Tasmania, Box 647 C, Hobart, Tas. b. 31 Mar 1923 Geelong. PH.D '54 Univ. Coll, London, Eng. LECT. in PSYCH, Univ. of Tas. Member: BPS-A, APA. Teaching, administration, research; attitude measurement, social perception, motivation. M

MILNE, Gordon Gerrard. Dept. of Labour and Natl. Serv, 71 Adelaide St, Brisbane, Queensland. b. 2 July 1914 Melbourne. BA '49 Univ. of Melbourne, Austl. VOCAT. GUID. OFF, Dept. of Labour and Natl. Serv; MARRIAGE COUNS, Queensland Marriage Guid Counc; LECT. in PERS. ADMIN, Dept. of Pub. Instr, Brisbane. Member: BPS-A, Austl. Rorschach Socy. Personnel psychology, testing, consulting, guidance, teaching; vocational and marriage counseling, projective and cognitive tests. M

MOORE, Mrs. Deirdre Janet. 20 John Pde, Merewether, Newcastle, N.S.W. b. 23 Oct 1921 Toronto. BA '42 Univ. of Sydney, Austl. VOCAT. GUID. OFF, Youth Welf. Sect, Dept. of Labour and Indus, 1 Bolton St, Newcastle. Member: BPS-A, Austl. Rorschach Socy. Research, teaching, interviewing and counseling, guidance, testing; diagnostic psychological testing. F

MOORE, James Francis Henry. Tasmanian Educ. Dept, 307 Macquarie St, Hobart. b. 7 Aug 1926 Melbourne. BA '49 Univ. of Melbourne, Austl. GUID. OFF, Tas. Educ. Dept. Member: BPS-A. Personal, educational and vocational guidance, psychotherapy, testing; projective techniques, group life, social perception. M

MOREY, Dr. Elwyn Aisne. Psych. Dept, Univ. of Western Australia, Nedlands, W.A. b. 17 Sept 1914 Stawell. PH.D '47 Univ. of California, USA. SR. LECT, Univ. of W.A. Member: APA, BPS, Int. Counc. for Except. Children, Amer. Assn. for Ment. Defic, Int. Assn. for Child Psychiat. Teaching, research, consulting; personality development in handicapped children, parent-child relationships, projective techniques. F

MORTIMER-TANNER, Richard Sutherland. Dept. of Psych, Univ. of Queensland, St. Lucia, Brisbane, Queensland. b. 26 Nov 1918 Ross. BA, Univ. of Queensland, Austl. LECTURER, Univ. of Queensland. Teaching, research; chronic alcoholism. M

MORTON, William Lonsdale. 10 Nottingham St, Prahran S. 1, Victoria. b. 2 July 1928 Melbourne. B.COM '48 Univ. of Melbourne, Austl. METHODS OFF, Shell Co. of Austl. Ltd, Williams St, Melbourne. Member: BPS-A, Austl. Rorschach Socy. Research on procedures and methods in clerical work; industrial psychology, selection procedures. M

MURPHY, Dr. Leo John. 36 Hawthorn Grove, Hawthorn, Victoria. b. 19 Aug 1912 Victoria. PH.D '52 Univ. of Manchester, Eng. PRINCIPAL, Trng. Cen. for Teachers of the Deaf, Educ. Dept, Treasury Pl, Melbourne C. 2. Member: BPS-A, Rorschach Socy. Administration, lecturing, psychotherapy, consulting; projective techniques, learning theory, social perception, group process. M

MURPHY, Patrick Alan. "Windbreak," 354 Nelson Rd, Rialannah, Hobart, Tas. b. 3 June 1925 Liverpool, Eng. BA '52 Univ. of Tasmania, Aust. PSYCH'T-in-CHARGE, Commonwealth Acoustic Lab, Stowell Ave, Battery Point, Hobart. Member: BPS-A. Testing and therapy in audiometry, consulting, administration; juvenile delinquency, aphasia, behavior and personality disorders resulting from deafness. M

NEAL, Walter Douglas. 98 Banksia Terr, S. Perth, W.A. b. 22 Feb. 1920 Bristol, Eng. B.ED '52 Univ. of Western Australia. SUPT. of RES. and CURRICULUM, Educ. Dept. of W.A, Barrack St, Perth; LECT. in STATISTICS, DEVEL. PSYCH, and EDUC, Univ. of Western Austl, Perth. Member: BPS-A. Educational research, administration, teaching; learning theory applied to maturation and group dynamics, achievement tests. M

NEWALL, Kenneth Comben. 11 Monash St, Box Hill E. 11, Victoria. b. 19 Mar 1929 Box Hill. BA '56 Univ. of Melbourne, Austl. RES. OFF, Dept. of Labour and Natl. Serv, 129 Swanston St, Melbourne, Victoria. Industrial and personnel psychology, research, testing; selection testing, employee attitude measurement, personnel practices. M

NEWLING, Paul Arthur. Newcastle Teachers' Coll, Union St, Newcastle, N.S.W. b. 4 Mar 1914 Sydney. MA '41 Univ. of Sydney, Austl. LECT. in EDUC, Newcastle Teachers' Coll; LECT. in SOC. PSYCH, N.S.W. Univ. of Tech. Teaching, educational and industrial psychology, consulting; achievement tests, teacher aptitude. M

OESER, Dr. Mary Drury. 5 William St, North Brighton, Melbourne. b. 1 May 1900 Ballarat. PH.D '30 Univ. of Cambridge, Eng. RES. FELLOW, Dept. of Psych, Univ. of

Melbourne. Member: BPS-A. Consulting, guidance, educational research; child guidance, social perception, family and educational adjustment problems.   F

OESER, Prof. Oscar A. Univ. of Melbourne, Carlton, Victoria. b. 21 Feb 1904 Pretoria, Union of South Africa. PH.D '31 Univ. of Cambridge, Eng. PROF. of PSYCH, Univ. of Melbourne; CONSULT. ED, *Australian Journal of Psychology*, *Psychological Review*, *Journal of Social Psychology*. Member: BPS-A, APA. Teaching, research, administration, industrial psychology, consulting; social perception, attitude measurement, social psychology in education.   M

OLLEY, Alan Keith. 15 Miller Ave, Bexley North, N.S.W. b. 21 May 1915 Sydney. BA '48 Univ. of Sydney, Austl. LECT. in APPL. PSYCH, New South Wales Univ. of Tech, Kensington. Member: BPS-A. Teaching, research in industrial psychology; group processes, human relations in industry, social perception.   M

OLPHERT, Warwick Bruce. Sch. of Educ, Univ. of Melbourne, Carlton N. 3, Victoria. b. 22 Dec 1924 Pukekohe, New Zealand. MA '50 Univ. of New Zealand. LECTURER, Univ. of Melbourne. Member: BPS-A, Austl. Rorschach Socy. Teaching, student, research; group dynamics, psychoanalytic theory, projective techniques, perception. M

O'NEIL, Prof. William Matthew. Dept. of Psych, Univ. of Sydney, Sydney. b. 15 June 1912 Sydney. MA '35 Univ. of Sydney, Austl. HEAD and PROF, Dept. of Psych, Univ. of Sydney; REVIEW ED, *Australian Journal of Psychology*. Member: BPS-A, Australasian Assn. of Psych. and Philos. Teaching, administration, research; psychological methods and theory, perception of space, measurement in psychology.   M

ORD, Capt. Ian Geoffry. 11 Psych. Unit, N. Cmd. Pers. Depot, Enoggera, Queensland. b. 14 Jan 1927 Kingaroy. BA '51 Univ. of Queensland, Austl. PSYCHOLOGIST, 11 Psych. Unit, Dept. of Army, AHQ, Melbourne. Member: BPS-A. Personnel psychology, testing, administration; attitude measurement, personnel selection, educational attainment and diagnostic testing.   M

OUTRIDGE, Miss Margaret. 16 Melton Rd, Toombul, Brisbane, Queensland. b. 30 Dec 1918 Eidsvold. BA '48 Univ. of Queensland, Austl. GUID. OFF, Res. and Guid. Br, Educ. Dept, Block A, Tech. Coll. Bldgs, George St, Brisbane. Clinical guidance of school children, testing, psychotherapy; stammering, the slow learning child, intelligence testing.   F

OWNER, Donald. Dept. of Educ, Port Moresby, Territory of Papua. b. 18 July 1913 Cootamundra. BA, Univ. of Sydney,

Austl. CHIEF, Non-Native Div, Dept. of Educ, Port Moresby, Papua. Member: BPS-A. Administration, inspection of schools, research, teaching; educational achievement tests, mental tests, research in educational methods, case work with non-normal children.   M

OXLADE, Miss Margery Nellie. 25 High St, Manly, Sydney, N.S.W. b. 10 June 1912 Sydney. BA '33 Univ. of Sydney, Austl. ASST. VOCAT. GUID. OFF, Dept. of Labour and Natl. Serv, York St, Sydney. Member: BPS-A. Personnel selection, vocational guidance, testing; aptitude testing, selection tests for industry, projective techniques.   F

PARKER, Henry Thomas. 41 Proctor's Rd, Hobart, Tas. b. 27 Apr 1890 Sydney. MA '20 Univ. of Tasmania, Aust. RETIRED. Member: BPS-A. Testing, teaching, research; achievement tests, educational guidance, educational planning.   M

PARKER, Leo Ronald. 35 Dresden St, Heidelberg N. 23, Victoria. b. 12 July 1916 Perth. B.SC '36 Univ. of Western Australia. CHIEF PSYCH'T, Dept. of the Navy, St. Kilda Rd, Melbourne. Member: BPS-A. Adminsitration, personnel psychology; selection techniques.   M

PAUL, Bruce Irvine. 59 Arthur St, W. Hobart, Tas. b. 9 Mar 1924 Molong. BA '49 Univ. of Sydney, Austl. VOCAT. GUID. OFF, Dept. of Labour and Natl. Serv, 81 Murray St, Hobart. Member: BPS-A. Personnel selection, guidance, testing; aptitude tests, non-directive counseling.   M

PEMBER, Mrs. Margary Lilian. Princess Margaret Hosp. for Children, Thomas St, Perth, W.A. b. 1 Jan 1922 Katanning. BA '46 Univ. of Western Australia. PSYCHOLOGIST, Princess Margaret Hosp. for Children; HONORARY PSYCH'T, Royal Perth Hosp. Member: BPS-A, W.A. Clin. Psych. Socy. Clinical testing and diagnosis, parent counseling, play therapy; projective techniques, emotional and social factors in medical syndromes, diagnosis and therapy of family relationships.   F

PENNY, Ronald. Div. of Soc. Sciences, Rockefeller Foundation, 49 W. 49 St, New York City, USA. b. 19 Mar 1924 Melbourne. BA '51 Univ. of Melbourne, Austl. RES. FELLOW, Austl. Natl. Univ, Canberra. Member: BPS-A. Research in communication processes, teaching, student; interpersonal and mass communication, group dynamics, use of projective techniques in primitive cultures, learning theory.   M

PENTONY, Patrick. Canberra Univ. Coll, Childers St, Canberra. b. 4 Oct 1915 Fremantle. MA '41 Univ. of Western Australia. SR. LECT, The Council, Canberra Univ. Coll. Member: BPS-A. Teaching, research, administration; social and clinical psychology, counseling. M

PETER, Robert Graham. 4 Grovedale Rd, Floreat Park, W.A. b. 13 June 1917 Geraldton. BA '40 Univ. of Western Australia. SR. LECT. and HEAD, Psych. Dept, Teachers' Coll, Claremont, W.A.; PERS. PSYCH'T, Royal Austl. Air Force. Member: BPS-A. Teaching, testing, consulting; prediction of teaching success, remedial education. M

PHILP, Hugh W. S. Dept. of Educ, Univ. of Sydney, N.S.W. b. 1 Jan 1919 Gourock, Scot. MA '51 Univ. of Sydney, Austl. SR. LECT, Univ. of Sydney. Member: BPS-A. Amer. Stat. Assn. Research, teaching; measurement theory and research design, attitude measurement, prejudice. M

PICK, Dr. Thomas. Psychologist's Off, Educ. Dept, 307 Macquarie St, Hobart, Tas. b. 15 Apr 1925 Szeged, Hungary. PH.D '47 Univ. of Budapest, Hungary. GUID. OFF, Psychologist's Off, Educ. Dept. Member: BPS-A. Testing, guidance, educational psychology; projective techniques, personality and child training, child guidance. M

PIDDINGTON, Lyndon Spencer. Psych. Branch, Educ. Dept, Govt. of South Austl. b. 30 May 1903 Sydney. B.SC '42 Univ. of London, Eng. SR. PSYCH''T, S.A. Educ. Dept. Member: BPS-A. Administration, educational psychology, testing, guidance; marriage guidance counseling. M

PITTY, William Warren. Div. of Ment. Hyg, Dept. of Pub. Hlth, 20 Murray St, Hobart, Tas. b. 28 Aug 1925 Echuca. BA '52 Univ. of Sydney, Austl. PSYCHOLOGIST, Div. of Ment. Hyg. Member: BPS-A. Testing, clinical analysis, consulting, research; description and measurement of personality, play therapy, hypnosis. M

POIDEVIN, Brian Leo. Indus. Serv. Div, Dept. of Labour and Natl. Serv, Century Bldg, Swanston St, Melbourne, Victoria. b. 6 Feb 1930 Brisbane. BA '52 Univ. of Queensland, Austl. INDUS. PSYCH''T, Indus. Serv. Div, Dept. of Labour and Natl. Serv. Member: BPS-A. Research in industrial psychology, consulting, professional writing; group processes, morale measurement, organization of work. M

POLLACK, Dr. Robert Harvey. Dept. of Psych, Univ. of Sydney, N.S.W. b. 26 June 1927 New York City, U.SA PH.D '53 Clark Univ, USA. LECTURER, Univ. of Sydney. Member: BPS-A, APA. Teaching, research; developmental psychology, perception, language behavior. M

PRINCE, Miss Edna Muriel. 61 Shirley Rd, Roseville, N.S.W. b. 22 Nov 1913 Sydney. BA '48 Univ. of Sydney, Austl. VOCAT. GUID. OFF, Dept. of Labour, Indus. and Soc. Welf, 266A Pacific Highway, Crow's Nest,

Sydney. Member: BPS-A. Vocational guidance, testing, personnel psychology; psychometrics, aptitude testing, interest analysis. F

PROCTOR, Arthur Craig. Toowoomba Ment. Hosp, Willowburn, Toowoomba, Queensland. b. 10 Feb 1922 Brisbane. BA '50 Univ. of Queensland, Austl. PSYCHOLOGIST, Dept. of Ment. Hyg. of the Dept. of Hlth. and Home Affairs, William St, Brisbane, Queensland. Member: BPS-A, Austl. Natl. Assn. for Ment. Hlth. Testing, consulting, psychotherapy; projective techniques, causes and prevention of delinquency, social patterns. M

RADCLIFFE, John Alfred. Dept. of Psych, Univ. of Sydney, N.S.W. b. 10 Jan 1919 Newcastle. BA '49 Univ. of Sydney, Austl. LECTURER, Univ. of Sydney. Member: BPS-A. Teaching, research, consulting; factor analysis, psychometric theory, dimensions of personality and ability. M

RADFORD, Dr. William Cropley. Australian Counc. for Educ. Res, 147 Collins St, Melbourne. b. 20 May 1913 Victoria. PH.D '54 Univ. of London, Eng. DIR. and ED, Austl. Counc. for Educ. Res. Member: BPS-A. Directing educational research and service, editorial, administration; child vocabulary, achievement tests, social psychology of the classroom. M

RENWICK, Ian Douglas. Newcastle Teachers' Coll, Union St, Cook's Hill, N.S.W. b. 29 Dec 1903 Edinburgh, Scot. M.ED '43 Univ. of Melbourne, Austl. SR. LECT, N.S.W. Dept. of Educ, Bridge St, Sydney, N.S.W. Member: BPS-A. Teaching, administration; educational psychology, vocational guidance and selection, dynamic psychology. M

RICHARDSON, James. Remedial Educ. Cen, Univ. of Queensland, George St, Brisbane, Queensland. b. 6 Oct 1915 Sheffield, Eng. MA '49 Univ. of Birmingham, Eng. DIRECTOR, Remed. Educ. Cen; EDITOR, *The Slow Learning Child.* Member: BPS-A. Clinical analysis, research, teaching, editorial; educational retardation, aptitude, achievement and diagnostic testing. M

ROBERTSON, Malcolm David. 126 Richmond St, Gordon Park, Brisbane N. 11, Queensland. b. 17 June 1912 Hobart. BA '42 Univ. of Tasmania, Austl. OFF. in CHARGE, Profes. Serv. Off, Dept. of Labour and Natl. Serv, 71 Adelaide St, Brisbane. Member: BPS-A, Austl. Inst. of Pers. Management. Administration of employment and vocational guidance office, teaching, personnel management consulting, marriage guidance counseling; labor-management relations, morale studies, interviewing techniques. M

ROHRLACH, Gordon Clarence. 103 Macleay St, Wagga Wagga, N.S.W. b. 20 Dec 1918 Lockhart. BA '48 Univ. of Sydney, Austl.

DIST. GUID. OFF, N.S.W. Dept. of Educ, Bridge St, Sydney. Member: BPS-A. Educational psychology, testing, guidance; psychometrics, individual and group testing, educational and vocational guidance. M

ROSE, Dennis Edward. Youth Welf. Sect, Dept. of Labour, Indus. and Soc. Welf, 4 Albert St, Sydney. b. 27 Dec 1911 Westcliff, Eng. MA '41 Univ. of Sydney, Austl. DIR. of YOUTH WELF, Dept. of Labour, Indus. and Soc. Welf, 53 Martin Pl, Sydney. Member: BPS-A. Administration of vocational guidance service for adolescents and adults; intelligence and aptitude testing, juvenile delinquency. M

ROSENBERG, Leslie Harry. 26 Clay St, Moorabbin S. 20, Victoria. b. 22 July 1930 Melbourne. BA '54 Univ. of Melbourne, Austl. PSYCHOLOGIST, Repatriation Dept, 121 Hanna St, S. Melbourne, Victoria. Member: BPS-A. Vocational guidance, testing, diagnosis, research; fundamentals of theory construction, personality theory, social perception. M

ROTHWELL, John Wilson. 8 Bilton St, Claremont, Tas. b. 1 Oct 1913 Hobart. BA '51 Univ. of Melbourne, Austl. VOCAT. GUID. OFF. in CHARGE, Profes. Serv. Off, Dept. of Labour and Natl. Serv, 81 Murray St, Hobart, Tas; LECTURER, Univ. of Tasmania. Member: BPS-A. Administration of vocational guidance and employment office, testing, research, teaching; personnel selection, techniques of interest measurement. M

ROUCH, Frank Lawrence. 169 Mont Albert Rd, Canterbury, Melbourne, Victoria. b. 4 Jan 1923 Melbourne. MA '54 Univ. of Melbourne, Austl. DIST. GUID. OFF, Educ. Dept,Treasury Bldgs,Spring St, Melbourne. Educational psychology, testing, consulting and guidance; adjustment to learning process, school counseling, therapy. M

ROUTH, Mrs. Margaret Ray. c/o R.M. Routh, Vocat. Guid. Sect, Commonwealth Empl. Serv, 71 Adelaide St, Brisbane, Queensland. b. 20 Dec 1925 Melbourne. BA '50 Univ. of Melbourne, Austl. CLIN. PSYCH'T, priv. prac. Member: BPS-A. Clinical practice, testing and analysis, consulting; projective techniques, diagnosis, interviewing. F

ROUTH, Russell Miller. Vocat. Guid. Sect, Commonwealth Empl. Serv, 71 Adelaide St, Brisbane, Queensland. b. 6 Mar 1921 Norwich, Eng. BA '50 Univ. of Melbourne, Austl. VOCAT. GUID. OFF, Dept. of Labour and Natl. Serv, Commonwealth Empl. Serv; LECT. in ADMIN, State Commercial High Sch. and Coll. Member: BPS-A. Vocational guidance, personnel psychology, teaching; aptitude tests. M

ROWLEY, Noel Reginald. Dept. of Educ,

Box 132, Wollongong, N.S.W. b. 20 Aug 1914 Mudgee. BA '38 Univ. of Sydney, Austl. DIST. GUID. OFF, Educ. Dept, Bridge St, Sydney, N.S.W. Educational psychology, testing, guidance and counseling; learning theory, student counseling, projective techniques. M

SANDERS, Prof. Colsell S. Fac. of Educ, Univ. of Western Australia, Nedlands, W.A. b. 1 May 1904 Adelaide. PH.D '38 Univ. of London, Eng. DEAN and PROF, Fac. of Educ, Univ. of W.A.; CO-EDITOR, Educand. Member: BPS-A. Teaching, research, administration. M

SARFATY, Peter. Commonwealth Acoustic Lab, 473 Wellington St, Perth, W.A. b. 12 Aug 1923 Sydney. BA '49 Univ. of Sydney, Austl. OFF. in CHARGE, Commonwealth Acoustic Lab. Member: BPS-A. Testing in audiology, administration, consulting; audiological assessment of children and exservicemen. M

SCARLETT, Grahame Yorke Dalley. Univ. of Sydney, Camperdown, N.S.W. b. 8 July1910 Sydney. BA '52 Univ. of Sydney, Austl. STUD. ADVIS, Univ. of Sydney. Member: BPS-A. Personal, vocational, and academic counseling, educational psychology, administration; failure in college adjustment. M

SCHNIERER, Dr. Irma. 44A Williams Rd, Prahran S. 1, Melbourne, Victoria. b. 19 Nov 1892 Vienna, Austria. PH.D '14 Univ. of Vienna, Austria. LECT. in PSYCH, Royal Melbourne Tech. Coll, 124 Latrobe St. and Coll. of Nrsng, 431 St. Hilda Rd. Member: BPS-A. Teaching, educational psychology, professional writing, consulting, testing; intelligence, projective tests, group process. F

SCHONELL, Dr. Florence Eleanor. Ivy St, Indooroopilly. b. 31 Oct 1902 Durban, Union of South Africa. PH.D '51 Univ. of Birmingham, Eng. LECTURER, Univ. of Queensland, St. Lucia S.W. 6, Queensland; HONORARY PSYCH'T, Queensland Spastic Children's League, New Farm, Brisbane, Queensland. Member: BPS-A. Testing, professional writing, teaching; spastic children, mental testing of children, language difficulties. F

SCHONELL, Prof. Fred Joyce. Dept. of Educ, Univ. of Queensland, St. Lucia S.W. 6, Queensland. b. 3 Aug 1900 Perth. D.Lit. '42 Univ. of London, Eng. HEAD and PROF, Dept. of Educ. and DIRECTOR, Remedial Educ. Cen, Univ. of Queensland; ED. CONSULT, Oliver and Boyd, The Slow Learning Child. Member: BPS-A, Amer. Assn. for Ment. Defic, Amer. Educ. Res. Assn. Teaching, research, testing; handicapped children, learning difficulties, diagnostic tests for scholastic backwardness. M

SCOTT, Dr. Wilma Alice. 32 Rushall St, Fairfield N. 10, Melbourne, Victoria. b. 8 June 1927 Melbourne. PH.D '54 Univ. of London, Eng. SR. TUTOR, Univ. of Melbourne, Carlton, Victoria. Member: BPS-A. Teaching, administration, testing; parent-child relations, cognitive development, socialization processes.   F

SEAGRIM, Gavin Nott. Canberra Univ. Coll, Childers St, Canberra. b. 18 June 1915 Dieppe, France. BA '52 Univ. Coll, London, Eng. LECT. and STUD. ADVIS, Canberra Univ. Coll. Member: BPS-A. Teaching, research, administration; visual perception, cognitive development, higher mental functions in animals.   M

SHADWELL, Mrs. Rae Mavis. Youth Welf. Sect, Dept. of Labour and Indus, 4 Albert St, Circular Quay, Sydney. b. 26 Nov 1926 Brisbane. BA '49 Univ. of Queensland, Austl. GUID. OFF, Dept. of Labour and Indus. Vocational guidance, personnel psychology, testing; speech development in deaf children, auditory training of the deaf.   F

SHAW, Mrs. J. Noel. 93 Princess St, Kew, Victoria. b. 17 Dec 1916 Kew. BA, Univ. of Western Australia. RES. OFF, Psych. Dept, Univ. of Melbourne, Carlton, Victoria; ASST. to HONORARY PSYCH'T, Royal Melbourne Hosp. Member: BPS-A. Research, testing.   F

SHEARS, Dr. Lawrence William. 17 Sturdee Rd, Black Rock, Melbourne, Victoria. b. 1 July 1921 Melbourne. PH.D '52 Univ. of London, Eng. SURVEY and PLANNING OFF, Educ. Dept, Treasury Buildings, Treasury Pl, Melbourne, Victoria; EDITOR, *Journal of Education*. Member: BPS-A. Administration of teacher training program, research, editorial; group process, adolescent development, peer group adjustment, learning techniques.   M

SIMPSON, Frank Noel. Repatriation Comm, King and York Sts, Sydney, N.S.W. b. 25 Dec 1920 Kurri Kurri. BA '47 Univ. of Sydney, Austl. PSYCHOLOGIST, Repatriation Comm. Member: BPS-A. Clinical testing of psychiatric cases, administration, counseling, guidance; aptitude and achievement test construction, projective techniques, learning theory.   M

SKY, Arthur William. Pub. Serv. Bd, Canberra. b. 22 June 1917 Sydney. BA '49 Univ. of Sydney, Austl. OFF. in CHARGE, Recruitment and Examinations, Pub. Serv. Bd, Broughton St, Barton. Member: BPS-A. Administration, personnel psychology, research; selection tests, staff rating, interview techniques.   M

SMITH, Ross Lamont. 57 Viewway, Nedlands, W.A. b. 11 May 1922 East Fremantle. BA '50 Univ. of Western Australia. CLIN.

PSYCH'T, Child. Guid. Clin, 590 Newcastle St, Perth, W.A. Member: BPS-A, W.A. Clin. Psych. Socy. Psychotherapy and psycho-diagnostic testing of children and parents, teaching, student; projective techniques, hypnosis research, parent education.   M

STAFFORD, Dr. Basil Frederick Roberts. Queensland State Govt, 274 George St, Brisbane, Queensland. b. 13 May 1900 Victoria. MB, BS '24 Univ. of Melbourne, Austl. DIR. of MENT. HYG. and DIR. of PSYCHIAT, Queensland State Govt. Member: BPS-A, British Med. Assn, Australasian Assn. of Psychiatrists. Administration, clinical psychiatry and psychology, forensic psychiatry, teaching.   M

STAINES, Dr. James Wilfred. Newcastle Teachers' Coll, Union St, Cooks Hill, N.S.W. b. 28 Apr 1912 Glen Innes. PH.D '54 Univ. of London, Eng. VICE PRIN, Teachers' Coll, Dept. of Educ, Bridge St, Sydney, N.S.W.; LECT. in PSYCH. and EDUC, Newcastle Univ. Coll. Member: BPS-A. Teaching, administration, research, self perception, psychotherapy.   M

ST. ELLEN, Joseph James. 749 Malvern Rd, Toorak S.E. 2, Victoria. b. 3 Nov 1912 Melbourne. BA '49 Univ. of Melbourne, Austl. LECT. in PSYCH. and EDUC, Burwood Teachers' Coll, Burwood Rd, Burwood, Victoria; ED. COMM, *Victorian Journal of Education*. Member: BPS-A. Educational psychology, teaching, editorial; social psychology, child development, learning theory.   M

STONEMAN, Dr. Ethel Turner. 71 Collins St, Melbourne. b. 10 Aug 1890 Perth. PH.D '33 Univ. of Edinburgh, Scot. CONSULT. PSYCH'T, priv. prac. Member: BPS-A, ICWP Psychotherapy, consulting, clinical practice, applied psychology, testing; resolution of stress and strain, character development. F

STURMER, Caryll Hugh Leigh von. 27 Delmar Pde, Dee Why, Sydney, N.S.W. b. 11 Jan 1921 Auckland, New Zealand. MA '47 Auckland Univ. Coll, N.Z. SR. RES. OFF, Dept. of Educ, Bridge St, Sydney. Member: BPS-A. Research on visual aids as educational media, administration, consulting; learning theory, atypical children, children's reading.   M

SUMMERS, Mrs. Betty. 62 David St, Turner, Canberra City. b. 20 Mar 1922 Stanthorpe. BA '51 Univ. of Queensland, Austl. CHILD PSYCH'T, priv. prac; HONORARY CONSULT. CHILD GUID. OFF, Canberra Community Hosp. Member: BPS-A. Child guidance, consulting, clinical practice, testing, psychotherapy; behavior problems in subnormal children, psychotherapeutic interviewing, social attitudes of the pre-school child   F

SUTCLIFFE, John Philip. Dept. of Psych, Univ. of Sydney, Sydney, N.S.W. b. 24 May

1926 Sydney. MA '54 Univ. of Sydney, Austl. LECTURER, Univ. of Sydney. Member: BPS-A. Teaching, research, professional writing; hypnosis, social psychology, experimental design and analysis. M

SWAN, Douglas Arthur. Railway Parade, Holbrook, N.S.W. b. 7 Feb 1927 West Maitland. BA '54 Univ. of Sydney, Austl. DEPUTY HEAD MASTER, Intermediate High Sch, Holbrook. Administration, guidance, educational psychology, teaching; level of aspiration, social learning, factor anlysis. M

TAFT, Dr. Ronald. Dept. of Psych, Univ. of Western Australia, Nedlands, W.A. b. 3 June 1920 Melbourne. PH.D '50 Univ. of California, USA. SR. LECT, Univ. of W.A. Member: BPS-A, APA. Teaching, research, social and industrial psychology; social attitudes, social assimilation, personality traits. M

THIELE, Dr. Harold William. Dept. of Psych, Univ. of Queensland, St. Lucia, Brisbane, Queensland. b. 19 Mar 1923 Mt. Morgan. PH.D '53 Univ. of London, Eng. LECTURER, Univ. of Queensland. Member: BPS-A. Teaching, research, industrial psychology; psychology of the physically handicapped, perception theory, problem of occupational adjustment. M

THOMAS, Malcolm Ernest. 378 Kingsway, Caringbah, N.S.W. b. 7 Aug 1913 Boggabri. MA '39 Univ. of Sydney, Austl. PRIN.RES. and GUID. OFF, Dept. of Educ, Sydney, N.S.W. Member: BPS-A. Guidance for handicapped and gifted children, educational psychology, research; counseling, guidance techniques, achievement tests, group dynamics. M

THOMSON, Richard James. 9 Ross St, Mitcham, Victoria. b. 10 Oct 1922 Sydney. BA '47 Univ. of Sydney, Austl. ASST. INSPECTOR, Div. of Pers. and Establishments, Dept. of Civil Aviation, 499 Little Collins St, Melbourne. Member: BPS-A. Research, administration of licensing examinations, personnel psychology; experimental and statistical methods, achievement and aptitude tests for staff selection. M

TINDALL, Kevin William Lewis. 3 Shackel Ave, Gladesville, N.S.W. b. 13 Mar 1924 Bathurst. BA '50 Univ. of Sydney, Austl. LECT. in PSYCH, Dept. of Educ, Sydney Teachers' Coll, Sydney, N.S.W. Member: BPS-A. Teaching, administration, research; psychology of learning, memory, attention. M

TOMPKINS, Robert Mervyn. 94 Gugeri St, Claremont, W.A. b. 25 Nov 1918 Narrogin. B.SC '44 Univ. of Western Australia. SR. GUID. OFF, Guid. And Spec. Educ. Br, Educ. Dept, 35 Subiaco Rd, Subiaco, W.A.

Member: BPS-A. Administration of field guidance officers, educational psychology, guidance; educational and vocational guidance, social perception. M

TRAYLEN, Neil Garratt. 24 Doonan Rd, Claremont. b. 24 Mar 1910 Guildford. MA '47 Univ. of Western Australia. PRINCIPAL, Graylands Teachers' Coll, Educ. Dept. of W.A, Barrack St, Perth; LECT. in EDUC, Univ. of W.A. Member: BPS-A, W.A. Clin. Psych. Socy. Administration, teaching education, educational psychology, study methods, assessment of teachers and student teachers. M

TROY, Adrian A. 29 Adams St, Harbord, N.S.W. b. 22 Feb 1916 Mittagong. BA '40 Univ. of Sydney, Austl. CLIN. PSYCH'T, priv. prac. Consulting, clinical practice, psychotherapy; child and youth behavior disorders, personality maladjustment. M

TROY, Capt. Mark Sybert. 12 Psych. Unit, 5th Head Barracks, Sydney. b. 23 Mar 1929 Manly. BA '56 Univ. of Sydney, Austl. PSYCH. OFF, Dept. of Army. Personnel selection, testing, consulting; aptitude and achievement tests, social perception, projective techniques. M

UNDERWOOD, Miss Elizabeth Jill. 2 Wattle Ave, Dalkeith, Perth, W.A. b. 17 June 1936 Perth. BA '55 Univ. of Western Australia. PSYCHOLOGIST, Child Guid. Clin, 590 Newcastle St, Perth. Testing, clinical analysis, play therapy, student; projective techniques, child psychotherapy, remedial teaching. F

UNDERWOOD, Keith Leslie. Tech. Coll, Gladstone Ave, Wollongong, N.S.W. b. 2 Aug 1925 Sydney. BA '46 Univ. of Sydney, Austl. GUID. OFF, Dir. of Tech. Educ, Mary Ann St, Broadway, Sydney. Member: BPS-A. Educational guidance and counseling, testing, administration; validation of aptitude tests, predictive value of attainment tests, factors in college success. M

VAN SOMMERS, Peter. 12 Seville St, Camberwell, Victoria. b. 30 June 1930 Melbourne. BA '55 Univ. of Melbourne, Austl. GUID. OFF, Educ. Dept. of Victoria, Treasury Bldgs, Melbourne C. 2. Member: BPS-A. Educational guidance. M

VERCO, David J. A. 7 Powell St, Killara, N.S.W. b. 22 Dec 1913 Sydney. MA '37 Univ. of Sydney, Austl. ASST. to DIR. GENL. of EDUC, Dept. of Educ, Bridge St, Sydney, N.S.W. Member: BPS-A. Administration, supervision of psychological services, educational psychology, teaching psychology to adult education classes; test construction and validation, counseling techniques, achievement testing and prognosis of academic achievement. M

VOLK, Henry. 25 Trevascus St, Caulfield S.E. 8, Victoria. b. 16 May 1904 Melbourne.

B.ED '53 Univ. of Melbourne, Austl. HEAD-MASTER, Albert Park Trng. Sch, Victorian Educ. Dept, Treasury Place, Melbourne. Member: BPS-A, Austl. Assn. of Profes. Psych'ts. Administration, supervision of educational and social adjustment of pupils, testing; educational and vocational guidance, achievement tests, social perception. M

WALKER, John Donald. Flat 4, 15 Trafalgar St, Stanmore, N.S.W. b. 28 Feb 1912 Sydney. BA '50 Univ. of Sydney, Austl. DIST. SCH. COUNS, Dept. of Educ, Hunter and Loftus Sts, Sydney, N.S.W; PERS. CONSULTANT, Royal Austl. Air Force. Member: BPS-A. Vocational counseling, testing, educational psychology, psychotherapy; student counseling, intelligence, vocational and achievement tests, general guidance. M

WALKER, Prof. Kenneth Frederick. Dept. of Psych, Univ. of Western Australia, Nedlands, W.A. b. 18 Nov 1918 Sydney. PH.D '53 Harvard Univ, USA. PROFESSOR, Univ. of W.A; CONSULTANT, Austl. Dept. of Labour. Member: BPS-A. Teaching, research, administration; ecological factors in behavior, attitudes and social perception in industry, gerontology. M

WALTERS, Sydney Herbert. 4 Hotham Court, Mont Albert, Melbourne, Victoria. b. 5 June 1899 Merthyr, Wales. BA '33 Univ. of Melbourne, Aust. SR. LECT. and HEAD, Dept. of Psych. and Educ, Toorak Teachers' Coll, Melbourne. Member: BPS-A. Teaching; learning theory, social perception, group process. M

WANT, Richard Langloh. 16 Weybridge St, Surrey Hills E. 10, Victoria. b. 9 Oct 1904 Glen Innes. MA '36 Univ. of Sydney, Austl. CHIEF PSYCH'T, Royal Austl. Air Force, Victoria Barracks, Melbourne. Member: BPS-A. Administration, applied psychology, research; psychometric testing, dream theory in relation to perception. M

WARD, Alfred Percy. 50 Esplanade, Brighton Beach S. 5, Victoria. b. 27 Mar 1912 Footscray. BA '50 Univ. of Melbourne, Austl. LECT. in EDUC. PSYCH, Victorian Educ. Dept, Spring St, Melbourne. Member: BPS-A. Teaching, administration of training of teachers of handicapped children; group process, problems of adolescence, achievement tests. M

WARE, Frank Raymond. 9 Grovedale Rd, Floreat Park, W.A. b. 1 Nov 1919 Subiaco. B.ED '54 Univ. of Western Australia. OFF. in CHARGE, Psych. and Couns. Serv, Tech. Educ. Div, Educ. Dept. of W.A. Barrack St, Perth. Member: BPS-A. Administration, educational and vocational guidance, industrial selection, teaching applied psychology. M

WATERHOUSE, Dr. Ian Kellie. Dept. of Psych, Univ. of Melbourne, Carlton N. 3, Victoria. b. 30 May 1921 Sydney. PH.D '53 Yale Univ, USA. SR. LECT, Univ. of Melbourne; HONORARY PSYCH'T, Royal Melbourne Hosp; ASST. ED, *Australian Journal of Psychology*. Member: BPS-A. Teaching, administration, research, editorial; learning theory and personality development, projective techniques, child development. M

WATKINS, Glynn Mayne. Teachers' Coll, Graylands, W.A. b. 22 Nov 1925 Collie. BA '48 Univ. of Western Australia. LECTURER, Educ. Dept. of W.A, Barrack St, Perth. Teaching, testing, research; achievement tests, learning theory, remedial teaching techniques. M

WATSON, William Crawford. Burwood Teachers' Coll, Burwood E. 13, Victoria. b. 26 Mar 1913 Warragul. B.ED '55 Univ. of Melbourne, Austl. LECT. in EDUC. and PSYCH, Burwood Teachers' Coll. Teaching, educational psychology, research; perception and learning, mental health of children and youth, child development. M

WATTS, Miss Nora Alice. 47 Hobbs Ave, Nedlands, W.A. b. 18 Apr 1919 Western Austl. BA '40 Univ. of Western Australia. PSYCHOLOGIST, Child Welf. Dept, Hay St, Perth, W.A. Member: BPS-A, W.A. Clin. Psych. Socy. Consulting, clinical practice, guidance, testing, clinical analysis, psychotherapy; delinquency, deprived children. F

WAUCHOPE, Miss Mavis Lorelie. 18 Park Rd, Kensington Park, Adelaide, S.A. b. 4 May 1898 Adelaide. MA '37 Univ. of Adelaide, Austl. SR. LECT, Adelaide Teachers' Coll; LECT. in EDUC. PSYCH, Univ. of Adelaide. Member: BPS-A, ICWP. Teaching, educational psychology, administration; learning theory, group process and group dynamics, attitude measurement. F

WEBSTER, Alfred Harold. Dept. of Educ, Bridge St, Sydney, N.S.W. b. 13 Nov 1913 Sydney. BA '46 Univ. of Sydney, Austl. CHIEF RES. OFF, Dept. of Educ. Member: BPS-A. Educational and administrative research, editorial; curriculum theory and construction, teaching methods, achievement and aptitude tests. M

WEEDEN, William John. Box 3879 GPO, Sydney, N.S.W. b. 10 Aug 1905 Tumut. MA '31 Univ. of Sydney, Austl. DIRECTOR, Commonwealth Off. of Educ, York St, Sydney. Member: BPS-A. Administration, educational research, guidance; learning theory. M

WERTHEIM, Mrs. Eleanor Sabina. 1 Deepdene Rd, Balwyn, Melbourne, Victoria. b. 11 Dec 1921 Warsaw, Poland. BA '52 Univ. of Melbourne, Austl. PSYCHOLOGIST, Psychiat. Clin, Royal Children's Hosp, Pelham St, Carlton, Melbourne. Member:

BPS-A, Austl. Rorschach Socy. Testing, clinical analysis, psychotherapy, teaching; mental testing, projective techniques, psychotherapy with children and parents. F

WHEELER, Dr. Daryl Kenneth. 18 Hovea Crescent, City Beach, W,A, b. 23 Mar 1911 Leonora. PH.D '48 Univ. Coll, London, Eng. SR. LECT. in EDUC, Univ. of Western Australia, Nedlands. Member: BPS-A. Teaching, research; experimental education, educational psychology. M

WHITE, Jeffrey Reginald Ernest. 6 Rheola St, W. Perth, W.A. b. 12 May 1924 Williams. BA '51 Univ. of Western Australia. PSYCHOLOGIST, Repatriation Genl. Hosp, Repatriation Comm, Monash Ave, Hollywood, Perth; HONORARY CONSULT. PSYCH'T, Royal Perth Hosp; SR. MARRIAGE GUID. COUNS, Marriage Guid. Counc. Member: BPS-A, W.A. Clin. Psych. Socy. Clinical testing, psychotherapy, consulting; narcoanalysis associated with hypnotherapy, projective techniques, art therapy. M

WHITE, Miss Ruth Doreen. 16 King George St, Victoria Park, W.A. b. 8 Dec 1902 Burbanks. BA '41 Univ. of Western Australia. GUID. OFF, W.A. Educ. Dept, Barrack St, Perth. Member: BPS-A, W.A. Clin. Psych. Socy. Parent and child guidance, testing, clinical analysis, play therapy, counseling. F

WHITEHOUSE, Miss Jean Marian Frances. Youth Welf. Sect, Dept. of Labour and Indus, 1A Bolton St, Newcastle, N.S.W. b. 26 Sept 1912 Brisbane. BA '34 Univ. of Queensland, Austl. GUID. OFF, Youth Welf. Sect. Member: BPS-A. Vocational guidance, personnel psychology, testing. F

WHITEMAN, Leonard Arthur. 4 Gillies St, Wollstonecraft, Sydney, N.S.W. b. 7 Aug 1913 Cowra. MA '50 Univ. of Sydney, Austl. CHIEF GUID. OFF, Univ. Br. Off, Dept. of Educ, Univ. Grounds, Sydney, N.S.W. Member: BPS-A. Administration of commonwealth scholarships, selection of teacher trainees, supervision of adult education, counseling; learning theory, vocational guidance, group testing. M

WHITFORD, Alfred Eugene. 302 North Terrace, Adelaide, S.A. b. 22 Oct 1911 Moonta. BA '48 Univ. of Sydney, Austl. CONSULT. PSYCH'T, priv. prac; LECTURER, adult educ. classes, S.A. Workers' Educ. Assn. Member: BPS-A. Educational and vocational guidance, personnel selection, clinical testing, teaching; intelligence and achievement testing, student selection for secondary education, vocational prediction. M

WHYTE, Peter Montgomery. 342 Albert St, E. Melbourne, Victoria. b. 6 Aug 1920 Melbourne. BA '48 Univ. of Melbourne, Austl. CONSULT. PSYCH'T, priv. prac;

HONORARY PSYCH'T, Alfred Hosp; CLIN. ASST, Royal Melbourne Hosp. Member: BPS-A, Austl. Rorschach Socy. Testing, applied and educational psychology, psychotherapy, vocational guidance; projective, sociometric and psychotherapeutic techniques, group process in schools. M

WILEY, Bryan John. 38 Swan Rd, Attadale, W.A. b. 10 July 1920 Perth. BA '48 Univ. of Western Australia. VOCAT. GUID. OFF, Commonwealth Dept. of Labour and Natl. Serv, Wellington St, Perth, W.A. Member: BPS-A. Vocational guidance, personnel selection, administration; achievement tests. M

WILLIAMS, Clive. Psychologist's Off, Educ. Dept. of Tas, 307 Macquarie St, Hobart, Tas. b. 9 Nov 1931 Brisbane. B.ED '56 Univ. of Queensland, Austl. GUID. OFF, Psychologist's Off, Educ. Dept. of Tas. Member: BPS. Educational, personal, and vocational guidance, testing; attitude measurement in industrial relations. M

WILLIAMS, Dr. Haydn Stanley. 35 Tareena St, Hollywood, W.A. b. 14 June 1917 Perth. PH.D '48 Univ. of London, Eng. ASST. SUPT. of TECHN. EDUC, Educ. Dept. of W.A, Barrack St, Perth. Member: BPS-A, Austl. Inst. of Pers. Management. Administration, applied psychology, teaching; aptitude tests, guidance and selection techniques, human relations in industry. M

WILLIAMS, Dr. John Francis. 12 Collins St, Melbourne, Victoria. b. 8 Oct 1899 Victoria. MD '26 Univ. of Melbourne, Austl. HONORARY CONSULT. PSYCHIATRIST, Royal Children's Hosp, Melbourne; HONORARY PSYCHIATRIST, Alfred Hosp, Prahran, Victoria. Member: BPS-A. Consulting, clinical practice, teaching, editorial. M

WILLIAMS, Captain John Ormond. 23 Bakewell Rd, Evandale, S.A. b. 15 Feb 1918 Melbourne. BA '51 Univ. of Melbourne Austl. DEPUTY DIR. of PSYCH, HQ Cen. Cmd, Austl. Army, Keswick Barracks, Keswick, S.A; HONORARY CONSULT. CLIN. PSYCH'T, Repatriation Dept. Member: BPS-A. Administration of psychological services, testing; aptitude and personality testing for military personnel selection and placement, group processes. M

WINFIELD, John Walton. 20 Nicholson Rd, Subiaco, W.A. b. 2 Feb 1931 Fremantle. BA '55 Univ. of Western Australia. VOCAT. GUID. OFF, Commonwealth Dept. of Labour and Natl. Serv, 86 King St, Perth, W.A. Member: BPS-A. Vocational guidance, counseling, and selection, testing, personnel psychology. M

WINSHIP, John Coates. 64 Villa St, Annerley, Queensland. b. 19 June 1913 Whitley Bay, Northumberland, Eng. MA '48 Univ. of Queensland, Austl. PSYCHOLOGIST, Repatriation Dept, Queensland Br, Elizabeth St, Brisbane. Member: BPS-A. Testing, clinical analysis, psychotherapy; diagnostic psychological examination, group psychotherapy, army psychology. M

WINTER, Dr. Karl Berthold. 219 North Terrace, Adelaide, S.A. b. 30 Mar 1898 Vietz, Germany. MD '24 Univ. of Berlin, Germany. PSYCHIATRIST, priv. prac; HONORARY PSYCHIATRIST, Psychiat. Clin, Royal Adelaide Hosp. Member: BPS-A, Australasian Assn. of Psychiatrists. Clinical practice, psychotherapy, teaching; psychotherapy of neuroses. M

WOOD, William. Res. and Guid. Br, Block A, Tech. Coll. Bldgs, George St, Brisbane, Queensland. b. 4 Oct 1910 Paisley, Scot. MA '37 Univ. of Queensland, Austl. PRIN. RES. and GUID. OFF, Commonwealth Scholarship Scheme, Dept. of Pub. Instr, Queen St, Brisbane, Queensland. Member: BPS-A. Administration, student counseling, research, adult education; educational and vocational guidance, construction of aptitude tests, achievement testing. M

WOODHOUSE, Mrs. Hilda Mary. 28 McIntosh St, Gordon, Sydney, N.S.W. b. 12 May 1898 Newcastle. B.SC '19 Univ. of Sydney, Austl. SCH. DIST. COUNS, Res. Div, Dept. of Educ, Bridge and Loftus Sts, Sydney. Member:

BPS-A. Lecturing to parents, educational and vocational guidance, intelligence and achievement testing; parent education. F

WORTHINGTON, Robert Norman. Starling St, Warner's Bay, Lake Macquarie, N.S.W. b. 18 Mar 1914 Sydney. MA '43 Univ. of Sydney, Austl. SECONDARY SCH. TCHR. and STUD. ADVIS, N.S.W. Dept. of Educ, Bridge St, Sydney. Member: BPS-A. Teaching, career guidance, testing; psychology of personality, vocational and educational guidance, aptitude tests. M

WYATT, Dr. Walter. Child. Guid. Clin, 590 Newcastle St, Perth, W.A. b. 10 Apr 1900 Edinburgh, Scot. MB, CH.B '24 Univ. of Edinburgh, Scot; Dr. Psych. Med. '27 Univ. of London, Eng. MED. SUPT, Child Guid. Clin, Med. Dept. of Western Australia, Murray St, Perth; HONORARY PSYCHIATRIST, Princess Margaret Hosp. for Child, Perth. Member: BPS-A. Child guidance, psychotherapy, administration. M

WYETH, Dr. Ezra Robert Harding. Sch. of Educ, Univ. of Melbourne, Carlton N. 3, Victoria. b. 13 Mar 1910 Toowoomba. ED.D '48 Univ. of California, USA. SR. LECT, Univ. of Melbourne. Member: BPS-A. Research, teaching, administration; prediction of academic success, utilization of talent, mass media. M

AUSTRIA

BAAR, Dr. phil. Edultrud. Blindengasse 38/30, Vienna 8. b. 9 Dec 1910 Vienna. PH.D '38 Univ. of Vienna, Austria. CHILD PSYCH'T, Municipality of Vienna, Sonder-Kindergarten "Schweizer Spende," Auer Welsbach Park, Vienna 14. Member: ICWP, Austrian Appl. Psych. Socy. Testing, educational psychology, research; testing of handicapped children, pre-school education of exceptional children, tests for deaf children, reading readiness. F

BARDODEJ, Dr. phil. Wilhelm. St. Petergasse 9, Vienna 17. b. 29 May 1914 Vienna. PH.D '39 Univ. of Vienna, Austria. INDEP. RES. and CO-WRKR, Inst. für Arbeitskunde und Berufseignungsforschung, Rochusgasse 2, Vienna. Member: BOP. Industrial psychology, research, guidance; job analysis psychology of personality. M

BAUER-DEBOIS, Dr. Karl. Scharitzerstr. 24/A, Linz-Donau. b. 29 Mar 1924 Vienna. Dr. '49 Univ. of Graz, Austria. EDUC. CONSULT, Jugendamt des Magistrates der Stadt Linz, Tummelplatz 19, Linz-Donau. Member: BOP. Child guidance; projective techniques, social perception, group process. M

BERKA, Dr. phil. Dipl. Psych. Marta de. Cottegeg. 62, Vienna 19. b. 26 Apr 1923

Vienna. PH.D '46 Univ. of Vienna, Austria. EDUC. PSYCH'T, priv. prac. Member: BOP. Consulting and guidance, testing, student; mental tests, projective techniques, cultural anthropology. F

BINDER, Dr. Richard. Kärtnerstr. 9/II, Graz. b. 28 Oct 1926 Stainz. Dr. '52 Univ. of Graz, Austria. PSYCHOLOGIST, Berufsvorschule "Jugend und Werk," Graz. Member: BOP. Teaching, testing, psychotherapy; testing and guidance for the mentally ill. M

BRANDSTÄTTER, Dipl. Psych. Hermann. Pernzell 38, Obergrünburg a.d. Steyr. b. 4 Jan 1930 Grünburg. Dipl. Psych. '54 Univ. of Munich, Ger. CO-WORKER, Psych. Inst. Munich-Schwabing, Römerstr. 28, Munich, Ger. Member: BDP. Applied psychology, research, testing; graphology, attitude measurement, psychology of human development. M

BREZINKA, Dozent Dr. phil. Wolfgang. Hallein-Au 146, Land Salzburg. b. 9 June 1928 Berlin, Ger. PH.D '51 Univ. of Innsbruck, Austria. DOZENT, Educ. Inst. of the Univ, Innrain 54, Innsbruck. Member: BOP. Clinical practice, applied and educational psychology, research, teaching; psychology of adolescence, socialisation of the child, habits and formation of character. M

BROSCH, Dr. phil. August. Wurzbachgasse 2/2/4, Vienna 15. b. 7 Aug 1921 Vienna. PH.D '51 Univ. of Vienna, Austria. TEACHER, Stadtschulrat für Wien, Türkenstr. 3, Vienna; TEACHER, Volkshochschule. Educational psychology, testing, research; group process, learning theory, achievement tests. M

CARUSO, Dr. Igor Alexander. Wiener Arbeitskreis für Tiefenpsych, 45 Lainzerstr, Vienna 13. b. 4 Feb 1914 Tiraspol, Russia. Docteur '37 Univ. of Louvain, Bel. DIR. and EDITOR, Wiener Arbeitskreis für Tiefenpsych; CO-ED, *Jahrbuch für Psychologie und Psychotherapie*, Würzburg; *Zeitschrift für Psycho-somatische Medizin*, Göttingen; *Acta Psychotherapeutica, Psychosomatica, Orthopaedagogica*, Basel. Member: BOP, Austrian Assn. for Ment. Hyg, Austrian Socy. for Psych. Consulting, clinical practice, guidance, research, teaching; anthropological fundamentals of psychoanalysis, epistemological significance of symbols, personality. M

DAIM, Dr. Wilfried. Heiligenstädterstr. 29/5, Vienna 19. b. 21 July 1923 Vienna. Dr. '48 Univ. of Vienna, Austria. PSYCHO-THERAPIST, priv. prac. Member: BOP. Research, psychotherapy, professional writing, graphology, theory of depth psychology and theological problems, pathological tendencies in social and political life, phenomenology. M

EHER, Dr. phil. Alfred. Inst. Geo-Graphik, Nonnbergstiege 2, Salzburg. b. 29 Apr 1914 Fratting, Czech. PH.D '41 Univ. of Prague, Czech. PSYCHOLOGIST, Inst. Geo-Graphik. Member: BOP. Applied and industrial psychology, color psychology; job analysis, color in graphic presentation. M

EPPEL, Dr. phil. Hedda. Am Modenapark 6, Vienna 3. b. 18 Dec 1919 Vienna. PH.D '49 Univ. of Vienna, Austria. PSYCHO-THERAPIST, priv. prac. Member: BOP. Psychotherapy, guidance, testing, applied and educational psychology; child psychoanalysis. F

EPPEL, Dr. phil. Heinz. Am Modenapark 6/8, Vienna 3. b. 24 Nov 1921 Vienna. PH.D '49 Univ. of Vienna, Austria. CHILD PSYCH'T. and DIR, Beratungsstelle und Privathort, Sebastianpl. 7/3, Vienna. Member: BOP. Child psychotherapy, educational and applied psychology, consulting, guidance; group development, counseling. M

ESTL, Dr. phil. Marianne. Zollergasse 16/14, Vienna 8. b. 23 Nov 1917 Vienna. PH.D '52 Univ. of Vienna, Austria. EDUC. COUNS, Jugendamt der Gemeinde Wien, Schottenring 22, Vienna. Member: BOP. Educational psychology, administration, testing, psycho-,

therapy; achievement tests, social perception, attitude measurement. F

FASCHING, Dr. phil. Hans. Janzgasse 8, Graz. b. 12 Dec 1915 Graz. PH.D '53 Univ. of Graz, Austria. TEACHER, Landesschulrat, Grabenstr, Graz. Member: BOP. Teaching, research, adult education; history of psychology, psychology of language, personality, mental hygiene. M

FASOLD, Dr. phil. Elfriede L. Pichelwangergasse 41, Vienna 21. b. 24 Apr 1901 Mhr. Ostrau, Czech. PH.D '38 Univ. of Vienna, Austria. CHIEF, Child Guid. Serv. and Observation Cen, Pub. Welf. Off, Schottenring 22, Vienna. Member: BOP. Guidance, testing, clinical analysis, counseling; intelligence measurement, projective techniques, conditioning, group process, institutional care. F

FELLNER, Dr. phil. Fritz. Ing. Etzel Str. 39, Innsbruck. b. 23 Feb 1911. Dr. '53 Univ. of Innsbruck, Austria. TCHR. and APPL. PSYCH'T, Sonderschule Innsbruck, Gilmstr. 4, Innsbruck; SECRETARY, Franklin Inst, Univ. of Innsbruck. Member: BOP. Teaching, educational psychology, testing; teaching and testing retarded children, psychology of human development. M

FISCHHOF, Dr. phil. Georg. Kölblgass 22/12, Vienna III. b. 23 May 1922 Vienna. PH.D '52 Univ. of Vienna, Austria. EDITOR, Forum-Verlag, Niederhofstr. 37, Vienna. Member: BOP. Editorial, professional writing, consulting, testing; psychology of sex, political psychology. M

FOPPA, Dr. phil. Klaus. Psych. Inst, Dommerschulstr. 13, Würzburg, Ger. b. 15 Aug 1930 Linz/Donau. PH.D '54 Univ. of Vienna, Austria. ASSISTANT, Psych. Inst; EDITOR, *Psychologie und Praxis*. Member: BOP. Research, applied psychology, editorial; learning theory, color vision, projective techniques. M

FOURMY, Dr. phil. Dipl. Psych. Nora. Einwanggasse 11, Vienna 14. b. 5 Aug 1923 Vienna. Dr. phil. '46 Univ. of Vienna, Austria. Member: BOP. Vocational guidance, intelligence tests, industrial research. F

GEBHART, Dr. Grete. Alserstr. 43/I/8 d, Vienna 8. b. 4 Dec 1909 Vienna. Dr. '43 Univ. of Vienna, Austria. SR. ASST. and LECT, Univ. of Vienna, Lammgasse 8/4, Vienna 8; DIRECTOR, Priv. Kindergarten. Member: BOP. Teaching, educational psychology, testing; evaluation of children's books, testing children. F

GRAF, Dr. Rudolf. Kurzbauergasse 2/20, Vienna II. b. 30 Aug 1921 Kitzbühel. Dr. '50 Univ. of Vienna, Austria. CLERK, Fiscal Off, Finanzlandesdirektion, Vordere Zollamtstr. 7, Vienna III; PSYCH. CONSULT, priv. prac. Member: BOP. Educational and applied psychology, testing, consulting; education of the mentally deficient and criminals. M

GRÜNEWALD, Dipl. Psych. Dr. phil. Eduard. Museumstr. 27, Innsbruck. b. 2 Apr 1924 Innsbruck. PH.D '46 Univ. of Innsbruck, Austria. DIRECTOR, Inst. für Psychodiagnostik und Angewandte Psych. Member: BOP, Int. Gesellschaft, Christlicher Tiefenpsychologen (Paris). Psychotherapy, industrial and educational psychology, testing; projective techniques, depth psychology. M

GUTTMANN, Dr. Maria. Josefsgasse 1, Vienna VIII. b. 7 Feb 1931 Vienna. Dr. '56 Univ. of Vienna, Austria. TEACHER, Stadtschulrat, Hütteldorferstr. 7, Vienna; PSYCHOLOGIST, Child Guid. Clin. Member: BOP. Guidance, clinical analysis, psychotherapy; scientific experimental psychology. F

HABADA, Dr. phil. Erich. Mozartstr. 13, Attnang-Puchheim. b. 19 June 1922 Linz. PH.D '53 Univ. of Vienna, Austria. SCH. TCHR, Land Oberösterreich-Hauptschule, Hauptstr. 31, Frankenmarkt. Member: BOP. Teaching, psychotherapy, testing; the use of leisure time by adolescent boys.M

HAUKE, Dr. phil. Johanna. Verlängerte Bachgasse 1088, Mödling. b. 1 Sept 1906 Baden. PH.D '51 Univ. of Vienna, Austria. PSYCHOLOGIST, Heilpädagogische Beobachtungsstation des Landes Niederösterreich, Wienerstr. 18, Mödling. Member: BOP. Testing. F

HENTSCHEL, Dr. phil. Herbert. Scherenbrandtnerhof Str. 8, Salzburg. b. 7 Aug 1915 Znaim, Czech. PH.D '40 Univ. of Prague, Czech. PSYCHOLOGIST, Forschungsinst. für Arbeitspsych. und Personalwesen (FORFA), Garkueche 3, Braunschweig, Ger. Member: BOP, BDP. Applied and industrial psychology, research; motivation research, typology, aviation psychology. M

HERZ, Dr. Franz. Kierlingerstr. 25c, Klosterneuburg, Vienna. b. 9 June 1909 Krems. Dr, Univ. of Vienna, Austria. HEAD, Schulpsych. Beratungsstelle, Tulln Sch. Dist, Tulln. Member: Austrian Socy. of Profes. Psych'ts. Applied and educational psychology, testing, guidance; psychology of art. M

HIFT, Dr. phil. Mrs. Erika. Köstlergasse 6, Vienna VI. b. 3 Feb 1929 Vienna. PH.D '52 Univ. of Vienna, Austria. CHILD PSYCH'T, Child. Ward, Univ. Clin. for Neur. and Psychiat, Lazarettgasse 14, Vienna IX; LECT. in CHILD PSYCH, Pädagogical Inst. of Vienna. Member: BOP. Consulting, child psychotherapy, testing; diagnosis of psychosis in children, abnormal development of young children. F

HOCHLEITNER, Dr. Adolf. Moosstr. 148,

Salzburg. b. 12 Feb 1915 Golling/Salzburg. Dr. '38 Univ. of Innsbruck, Austria. TEACHER, Gymnasium, Universitätsplatz 1, Salzburg; TEMPORARY LECT, Volkshochschule. Member: BOP. Teaching, educational psychology, research; social perception.M

HÖFER, Dr. Angela. Schwarzhorngasse 10/16, Vienna V. b. 16 Mar 1923 Vienna. PH.D '52 Univ. of Vienna, Austria. Educational and industrial psychology. F

HOFER, Dr. phil. Ernst. Bluetengasse 5/10, Vienna 3. b. 2 Dec 1924 Vienna. PH.D '51 Univ. of Vienna, Austria. APTITUDE PSYCH'T, Vocat. Guid. and Psych. Serv, Employment Off, Esteplatz 2, Vienna 3. Member: BOP. Testing, vocational guidance, industrial psychology; empirical and experimental research on social behavior and attitudes, construction and validation of tests. M

HOLZINGER, Dr. phil. Fritz. Klosterwiesg 77, Graz. b. 3 Dec 1911 Taufkirchen. PH.D '34, MD '48 Univ. of Vienna, Austria. DIRECTOR, Educ. Psych. Serv, Landesschulrat, Grabenstr. 56, Graz. Teaching, educational psychology, testing, research; achievement tests, learning theory. M

HOLZWARTH, Dipl. Psych. Dr. phil. Hermann. Mariahilferstr. 158/2/2, Vienna XV. b. 21 Sept 1922 Vienna. PH.D '48 Univ. of Vienna, Austria. INSTRUCTOR, Grammar Sch, Herthergasse 28, Vienna XII. Member: BOP, Austrian Assn. for Ment. Hyg. Educational psychology, guidance, teaching, research; learning theory, achievement tests. M

HÖNEL, Dr. phil. Herbert. Kosselgasse 50, Vienna XIX. b. 31 May 1916 Geisenheim/ Rhein, Ger. PH.D '50 Univ. of Vienna, Austria. GRAPHOLOGIST, priv. prac; EDITOR, *Zeitschrift für Menschenkunde.* Member: BOP, Austrian Socy. for Psych. Graphology, editorial; characterology. M

HUNGER-KAINDLSTORFER, Dr. phil. Maria. Maroltingergasse 102A, Vienna XVI. b. 9 Apr 1912 Vienna. PH.D '54 Univ. of Vienna, Austria. SCH. PSYCH'T, Zinckg 12-14, Vienna; PSYCHOLOGIST, priv. prac. Member: BOP, Indiv. Psych. Socy. Applied and educational psychology, consulting, research, psychotherapy; neurosis, cerebral disturbances. F

KAMPAS, Dr. phil. Herwig. Gabelsbergerstr. 36, Salzburg. b. 11 June 1921 Strengberg. PH.D '43 Univ. of Vienna, Austria. PSYCHOTHERAPIST and CONSULT. PSYCH'T, Dr. Robert Pavelka, Schwarzstr. 30, Salzburg. Member: BOP, Austrian Socy. for Psych. Psychotherapy, consulting, clinical analysis, guidance; psychosomatic research, personality, social perception, attitude measurement. M

KARAS, Dr. phil. Edwin. Karl Böttingerstr,

Salzburg. b. 1 May 1923 Krummnussbaum. PH.D '50 Univ. of Salzburg, Austria. EDUC. PSYCH'T, Landesschulrat für Salzburg, Mozartplatz 10, Salzburg. Member: BOP. Guidance, testing, teaching, educational psychology.   M

KETTNER, Dipl. Psych. Kurt. Mortaraplatz 2, Vienna 20. b. 30 Aug 1918 Djakovo, Yugo. Dipl. Psych. '45 Univ. of Vienna, Austria. MKT. and OPINION RES, priv. prac. Member: BOP, Austrian Socy. for Psych. Market and opinion research.   M

KIENESBERGER, Dr. phil. Alfred. Haydn-platz 5, Innsbruck. b. 20 May 1923 Wels. PH.D '52 Univ. of Innsbruck, Austria. APPL. PSYCH'T. and LABOR COUNS, Employment Off, Innsbruck. Member: BOP. Applied and industrial psychology, testing, administration; social psychology, mass psychology, group dynamics, projective techniques.   M

KLEBELSBERG, Dr. phil. Dieter von. Schillerstr. 13, Innsbruck. b. 14 Dec 1928 Innsbruck. PH.D '52 Univ. of Innsbruck, Austria. ASSISTANT, Inst. für Pyscho-diagnostik und Angewandte Psych, Museumstr. 27, Innsbruck. Testing, applied psychology, clinical practice; Gestalt theory, projective techniques, psychology of accidents.   M

KOHLER, Prof. Dr. phil. Ivo. Inst. for Exper. Psych, Schöpfstr. 41, Innsbruck. b. 27 July 1915 Schruns. PH.D '41 Univ. of Innsbruck, Austria. PROF. and HEAD, Psych. Dept, Inst. for Exper. Psych. Member: BOP, DGP. Teaching, research; sensation and perception, learning theory, rehabilitation.   M

KOS, Dr. phil. Marta. Nussdorferstr. 40, Vienna 9. b. 9 Sept 1919 Slany, Czech. PH.D '49 Univ. of Prague, Czech. CLIN. PSYCH'T, Children's Dept, Univ. Neur. and Psychiat. Clin, Lazarettg. 14, Vienna 9; APPL. PSYCH'T, Sch. City Serv, Vienna. Member: BOP. Child psychotherapy, clinical practice, research, testing; projective techniques.   F

KRAMMEL, Dr. phil. Franz. Währingerstr. 99, Vienna 18. b. 28 Feb 1920 Vienna. PH.D '55 Univ. of Vienna, Austria. VOCAT. COUNS, Employment Off, Hohenstaufen-gasse 2, Vienna 1. Member: BOP. Testing, test construction, industrial psychology; objective measurement research, factor analysis, social psychology in industry and army.   M

KRENEK, Dr. phil. Hans. Baumgartner-höhe 1, Wien XIV. b. 11 Mar 1903 Vienna. PH.D '38 Univ. of Vienna, Austria. DIRECTOR, Jugendfürsorge und Erziehungs-anstalten der Stadt Wien, Schottenring 22, Vienna I; PSYCHOLOGIST, priv. prac. Member: BOP. Psychotherapy, education-al psychology, teaching; medical psychology.   M

KUHN, Dr. Dietmar. Postgasse 4, Vienna I. b. 16 Feb 1928 Rankweil. Dr. '55 Univ. Of Vienna, Austria. GENL. SECY, Cath. Family Assn. of Austria, Singerstr. 8, Vienna I. Administration, guidance; social perception, attitude measurement. M

KURZ-BEITEL, Dr. phil. Leopoldine. Dionysius Andrassystr. 7, Vienna XIX/117. b. 18 Sept 1902 Gemeinlebarn. PH.D '39 Univ. of Vienna, Austria. HEAD, Vocat. Guid. and Psych. Serv, Employment Off, Weibburggasse 30, Vienna. Member: BOP. Administration, professional guidance, applied psychology; child psychology, psychology of adolescence.   F

LANG, Dr. phil. Ludwig. Schönbrunnerstr. 2, Vienna IV. b. 20 Apr 1902 Vienna. PH.D '28 Univ. of Vienna, Austria. MINISTERIAL-RAT, Ministry of Educ, Minoritenplatz 5, Vienna I. Member: BOP. Educational psychology, administration, research; psychology of human development, depth psychology, learning, social psychology. M

LECHNER, Dr. phil. Karl. Mommsengasse 6/VI/40, Vienna IV. b. 29 Oct 1917 Vienna. PH.D '49 Univ. of Vienna, Austria. PSY-CHOLOGIST, Employment Off, Hohen-staufengasse 3, Vienna I. Member: BOP. Administration, applied and industrial psychology, consulting; projective techniques, achievement tests, attitude measurement, analysis of tests.   M

LEHMANN, Dr. Paula. Keisslergasse 18a/IV/ 2/9, Vienna 14. b. 29 June 1926 Bad Vöslau. Dr. '49 Univ. of Vienna, Austria. PSYCHOLOGIST, Employment Off, Esteplatz 2, Vienna 3. Member: BOP. Testing, applied psychology, consulting; methods of aptitude testing, child and juvenile psychology.   F

LEHNER, Dr. Erich. Lustenauerstr. 29, Linz. b. 8 Nov 1916 Pilsen, Czech. Dr. '48 Univ. of Innsbruck, Austria. CLIN. PSYCH'T, Accident Hosp, Linz; VOCAT. COUNS, Employment Off, Blumauerplatz 1, Linz. Member: BOP. Administration, testing, clinical practice; industrial psychology, testing, clinical psychology, rehabilitation.   M

LESOVSKY, Dr. med. Dr. phil. Wilhelm Heinrich. Washington Sanitarium and Hosp. Oaklea, 7600 Carroll St, Takoma Park 12, Maryland, USA. b. 2 July 1901 Kranichsfeld/Maribor, Yugo. MD '44 Univ. of Graz, Austria. ASSISTANT, Washington Sanitarium and Hosp. Oaklea. Consulting, psychotherapy, testing, clinical analysis; child development, projective painting, religious behavior, psychosomatic diseases.   M

LESSING, Dr. phil. Friedrike. Ottakringerstr. 33/7, Vienna 16. b. 11 Nov 1926 Vienna.

PH.D. '49 Univ. of Vienna, Austria. EDUC. and CHILD GUID. COUNS, Children's Bur, City of Vienna, Schottenring 22, Vienna. Member: BOP. Guidance, testing, clinical analysis, educational psychology; interviewing, intelligence tests, projective techniques, conditioning.　　　　　　　　F

LINDNER, Dr. phil. Traugott Emanuel. Viktorgasse 9, Vienna 4. b. 18 Mar 1923 Brno, Czech. PH.D '51 Univ. of Vienna, Austria. ASST. to the DIR, Soc. Sci. Res. Lab, Univ. of Vienna, Vienna 1; INDUS. PSYCH'T, priv. prac. Member: BOP. Applied and industrial psychology, teaching, research; group process, leadership training, industrial consultation.　　　　　　　M

LINK, Dr. Hertha. Czerningasse 7/13, Vienna II. b. 6 Sept 1927 Vienna. Dr. '53 Univ. of Vienna, Austria. INDUS. PSYCH'T, Radiowerk Horny AG, Rennweg, Vienna; SECRETARY, Schiff and Stern, Untere Donaustr. 41, Vienna II. Member: BOP. Applied and industrial psychology, testing, research; social perception, group process, achievement tests, projective techniques. F

LÖDL, Dr. phil. Rudolf. Robert Blumgasse 1/26, Vienna XX. b. 16 Apr 1921 Liscovec, Czech. PH.D '50 Univ. of Vienna, Austria. BUNDESBAHNRAT, Generaldirektion der Osterreichischen Bundesbahnen, Elisabethstr. 9, Vienna I. Member: BOP. Personnel psychology, testing, administration; intelligence measurement, test construction and evaluation.　　　　　　　　M

LOIDOLT, Dr. Hans. Hydngasse 10, Graz. b. 18 Feb 1918 Graz. Dr. '56 Univ. of Graz, Austria. RES. ASST., Steirische Wasserkraft und Elektrizitäts AG, Opernring 7, Graz. Applied and industrial psychology, research, administration; research on human relations by critical incident techniques, employee rating, public relations.　　M

MANN, Dr. phil. Werner Emanuel. Baumeistergasse 1/19/3, Vienna XVI. b. 19 July 1921 Vienna. PH.D, Univ. of Vienna, Austria. TEST amd CLIN. PSYCH'T, Employment Off, Weihburggasse 30, Vienna I; LECT. in VOCAT. PSYCH, Univ. of Vienna; LECT. in SOC. PSYCH, Adult Educ. Inst. Member: BOP. Testing, teaching; guidance; application of tests, group dynamics, juvenile psychology.　　　　　　　M

MANSFELD, Dr. phil. Friedrich. Schaumburgergasse 11, Vienna IV. b. 31 Dec 1895 Vienna. PH.D, Univ. of Vienna, Austria. PROFESSOR, Bundes Blinden Erziehungs Inst, Vienna; EDITOR, *Blindenpsychologie*. Teaching; psychology of the blind.　　M

MARTE, Dr. phil. Hubert. Auf der Matte 19, Bregenz. b. 9 Mar 1915 Batschuns. PH.D, Univ. of Innsbruck, Austria. SPEC. PSYCH'T, Employment Off, Bahnhofstr. 43, Bregenz. Member: BOP, Austrian Socy. for Psych.

Applied psychology, testing, psychotherapy; psychology of impulses, instincts.　　　　　　　　　　　M

MARTERBAUER, Dr. Gerda. Jahnstr. 17, Tulln. b. 21 Jan 1927 Vienna. Dr. '55 Univ. of Vienna, Austria. TEACHER, Domes. Sci. Sch, Vienna 19. Member: BOP. Teaching, testing, research; developmental psychology, vocational guidance, learning theory.　　　　　　　　　　　F

MICKO, Dr. phil. Hans Christoph. Burggasse 100, Vienna VII. b. 5 June 1931 Berlin, Ger. PH.D '56 Univ. of Vienna, Austria. CONSULT PSYCH'T, Beratungsstelle für Berufsschüler, Mollardgasse, Vienna. Member: BOP. Testing, consulting, research; attitude, opinion, prejudice, religion, social psychology, intelligence, problem solving.　　　　　　　M

MITTENECKER, Dr. phil. Erich. Liebiggasse 5, Vienna I. b. 26 June 1922 Wiener Neustadt. PH.D '48 Univ. of Vienna, Austria. DOZENT, Psych. Inst, Univ. of Vienna. Member: BOP, DGP. Teaching, research, applied psychology, personality theory, experimental design, test construction.　　　　　　　　　　M

MÖRBE, Dr. phil. Editha. Zollerstr. 4, Innsbruck. b. 4 June 1923 Inzersdorf. PH.D '51 Univ. of Innsbruck, Austria. TEST PSYCH'T, Austrian Administration of Labor, Haydnplatz 5, Innsbruck. Member: BOP, Gesellschaft für Psychoter. und Angewandte Psych. Personnel psychology, testing, psychotherapy; projective techniques, industrial aptitude testing, counseling of alcoholics.　　　　　　　　F

MÜLLER, Dr. phil. Helmut. Adolf Bekk Str. 8, Salzburg. b. 23 Sept 1926 Salzburg. PH.D '49 Univ. of Innsbruck, Austria. SCH. PSYCH'T. and TCHR, Bundesrealgymnasium Salzburg, Franz Josephs Kai 41, Salzburg. Member: BOP. Teaching, educational psychology, testing; projective techniques, color phenomena, psychology of esthetics.　　　　　　　　M

MÜLLER-HARTBURG, Dr. phil. Helmut. Grundlsee/Bad Aussee, Styria. b. 27 Aug 1921 Vienna. PH.D '49 Leop. Franzens Univ. of Innsbruck, Austria. INDUS. CONSULT, priv. prac. Applied and industrial psychology, personnel work; group process, group dynamics, learning and teaching theory, didactics, testing.　　　　　M

NAVRATIL, Dr. med. Dr. Phil. Leo. Heilanstalt Gugging, Vienna 26. b. 3 July 1921 Türnitz. MD '46, PH.D '50 Univ. of Vienna, Austria. HEAD PHYSICIAN, Landes-Heil und Pflegeanstalt Gugging. Member: BOP. Psychotherapy, psychiatry, research; personality and constitution, psychodynamics of alcoholism, projective techniques.　　　　　　　　M

NEJEDLIK, Dr. phil. Rudolf. Fürstengasse 1/3, Vienna IX. b. 15 July 1922 Feldsberg, Czech. PH.D '51 Univ. of Vienna, Austria. PSYCHOLOGIST, Arbeitsamt für Jugendliche, Esteplatz 2, Vienna III. Member: BOP. Testing, personnel psychology, consulting; intelligence and achievement tests, projective methods. M

NEKULA, Dr. phil. Maria. Theergasse 3/9/10, Vienna 12. b. 27 May 1914 Vienna. PH.D '38 Univ. of Vienna, Austria. EDUC. COUNS, Pub. Welf. Off, Div. for Child. and Youth, Schottenring 22, Vienna I. Member: BOP. Guidance, testing, educational counseling; intelligence testing, projective techniques, learning theory, conditioning. F

NEUBAUER, Prof. Dr. phil. Vinzenz. Schubertstr. 18, Innsbruck. b. 3 Oct 1899 Vienna. PH.D '28 Univ. of Graz, Austria. HEAD, Profes. Guid. Serv. in Tyrol, Employment Off, Haydnplatz, Innsbruck; ASST. PROF, Univ. of Innsbruck. Member: BOP, DGP. Personnel psychology, teaching, psychotherapy, guidance; social psychology, projective techniques. M

OLSZEWSKI, Dr. Anton. Hadikgasse 100/9, Vienna 14. b. 3 Nov 1926 Vienna. Dr. '49 Univ. of Vienna, Austria. PSYCHOLOGIST, Arbeiterkammer Vienna, Ebendorferstr. 7, Vienna I. Member: BOP. Guidance, psychotherapy, applied psychology; diagnostic test methods, psychotherapy, clinical psychology, selection methods. M

OLSZEWSKI, Dr. Elfriede. Hadikagasse 100/9, Vienna 14. b. 20 Aug 1928 Vienna. Dr. '51 Univ. of Vienna, Austria. PSYCHOLOGIST, Employment Off, Esteplatz 2, Vienna 3. Member: BOP. Testing, applied and industrial psychology, guidance; projective techniques, performance tests, psychotherapy, clinical psychology, selection methods, diagnosis. F

PARTMANN, Dr. phil. Leo. Sautergasse 1/20, Vienna 17. b. 11 Sept 1930 Vienna. PH.D '53 Univ. of Vienna, Austria. TEACHER, Realgymnasium, Schopenhauerstr, Vienna. Member: BOP. Teaching. M

PAWLIK, Dr. phil. Otto. Schweglerstr. 47, Vienna 15. b. 26 May 1924 Vienna. PH.D '49 Univ. of Vienna, Austria. EDUC. COUNS, Pub. Welf. Off, Div. for Child. and Youth, Schottenring 22, Vienna 1. Member: BOP. Guidance, testing, educational counseling; intelligence tests, projective techniques, learning theory, conditioning. M

PETRI, Dr. phil. Gottfried. Gabriachgasse 21, Graz. b. 14 July 1924 Vienna. PH.D '49 Univ. of Graz, Austria. PSYCHOLOGIST, Employment Off, Permayerstr. 10, Eisenstadt. Member: BOP. Research, testing, consulting; theory of personality, projective techniques. M

PETRI-WOLDE, Dr. phil. Herma. Schörgel-

gasse 17/11, Graz. b. 12 Feb 1924 Klagenfurt. PH.D '49 Univ. of Graz, Austria. SCI. WRKR, Austrian Broadcasting Co, Radio Graz, Zusertalgasse 14a, Graz. Member: BOP. Educational psychology, consulting, guidance; child guidance, depth psychology, projective techniques. F

PETZ, Dr. Gertrud T. D. Zwerggasse 14, Graz. b. 11 July 1924 Graz. Dr. '49 Karl Franzens Univ. of Graz, Austria. PSYCHOLOGIST, Univ. Hosp, Riesstr. 1, Graz; PSYCHOLOGIST, priv. prac. Member: BOP. Testing, psychotherapy, research; projective tests, psychotherapeutic treatment of epilepsy. F

PIPEREK, Dr. phil. Maximilian. Hauptstr. 88, Vienna III. b. 30 Dec 1906 Vienna. PH.D '38 Univ. of Vienna, Austria. HEAD, Österreichische Berufsberatung, Bundesministerium für Soziale Verwaltung, Stubenring 1, Vienna I. Member: BOP, AIPA, Austrian Socy. of Profes. Psych'ts. Administration, industrial psychology, research, testing, consulting. M

PONISCH, Dr. phil. Gerhard. Merangasse 53, Graz. b. 11 Nov 1923 Maribor, Yugo. PH.D '50 Univ. of Graz, Austria. PSYCH'T, Employment Off, Bürgergasse 2, Graz. Member: BOP. Testing, vocational and child guidance; applied and industrial psychology; achievement tests, social psychology, projective techniques. M

PRESOL Y, Dr. phil. Elfriede. Schreberstr. 8, Linz. b. 4 Mar 1926 Traisen. PH.D '53 Univ. of Vienna, Austria. SECRETARY, Arbeitsunfallkrankenhaus Linz, Blumauerplatz 1, Linz; EDUC. COUNS, Child Guid. Cen, Linz. Member: BOP, Austrian Socy. for Psych. Educational and child guidance. F

REICH, Dipl. Psych. Elisabeth. Viktor Danklstr. 12, Innsbruck. b. 13 July 1918 Vienna. Dipl. Psych. '43 Univ. of Marburg/ L, Ger. PSYCHOLOGIST, priv. prac. Member: BOP, BDP, Austrian Socy. for Psych. Applied, educational and industrial psychology, testing, psychotherapy; developmental, child and adolescent psychology, children's drawings and play, family relations. F

REICH, Dr. phil. Ernst-Lothar. Viktor-Danklstr. 12, Innsbruck. b. 20 Nov 1914 Stolp/Pommern, Ger. PH.D '48 Univ. of Innsbruck, Austria. PSYCHOLOGIST, priv. prac. Member: BDP, Austrian Socy. for Psych. Applied and industrial psychology, psychotherapy, testing; color psychology, public and human relations. M

REPP, Dr. Günther. Salzburger Reichsstr. V 1096 Linz. b. 28 Jan 1926 Brunn, Czech. PH.D '50 Karl Franzens Univ. of Graz, Austria. LIBRARIAN, U.S.I.S. Linz, Amerikahaus, Landstr. 68 Linz. Member: BOP.

Library, editorial, psychotherapy; personnel psychology. M

RICHART, Dr. phil. Margarete. Salesianergasse 17/7, Vienna 3. b. 19 Aug 1930 Vienna. PH.D '54 Univ. of Vienna, Austria. Member: BOP. Educational psychology; intelligence, learning theory, child psychology, color perception. F

ROHRACHER, Dr. phil. Harald J. Wallriesstr. 125, Vienna 18. b. 24 Jan 1925 Spittal/ Drau. PH.D '49 Univ. of Vienna, Austria. CHIEF COMMISSIONER, Federal Railroads, Generaldirektion der Österreichischen Bundesbahnen, Elisabethstr. 9, Vienna 1. Member: BOP. Testing, personnel selection, administration; measurement of attitudes, projective techniques. M

ROHRACHER, Prof. Dr. phil. Hubert. Liebiggasse 5, Vienna I. b. 24 Apr 1903 Linz. PH.D '25 Univ. of Munich, Ger. PROF. and DIR, Dept. of Psych, Univ. of Vienna, Dr. Karl Lueger Ring, Vienna; EDITOR, *Wiener Archiv für Psychologie, Psychiatrie und Neurologie; Wiener Zeitschrift für Philosophie, Psychologie, Pädagogie; Zeitschrift für Experimentelle und Angewandte Psychologie.* Member: BOP, DGP. Teaching, research, editorial; memory and learning, physiological and neuro-psychology, evaluation of tests, accidents. M

ROTH, Dr. Franz Joseph. Karlsplatz 1/11, Vienna 1. b. 7 Feb 1924 Leobersdorf. Dr. '52 Univ. of Vienna, Austria. MUSICAL PROG. PLANNER, Austrian Broadcasting Co, Radio Vienna, Argentinierstr. 30a, Vienna IV. Administration, research; music in medicine and industry, eastern and medieval psychology, music psychology. M

SAGL, Dr. phil. Theodor. Wattmanngasse 12/10, Vienna 13. b. 18 Oct 1925 Vienna. PH.D '49 Univ. of Vienna, Austria. PSYCHOLOGIST, Jugendgerichtshof, Rüdengasse 7-9, Vienna 3; EDUC. and VOCAT. GUID. COUNS, priv. prac. Member: BOP. Testing, educational psychology, student; developmental psychology, psychology of adolescent and adult criminals, personality, methods of resocialization. M

SCHADEN, Dr. phil. Alfred. Hollandstr. 13, Vienna 2. b. 24 Mar 1927 Vienna. PH.D '54 Univ. of Vienna, Austria. CHILD PSYCH'T, Univ. Children's Hosp, Heilpädagogisch Abteilung, Lazarettgasse 14, Vienna 9; PSYCHOTHER, Vienna Child Guid. Clin, Heilingenstädterstr. 74, Vienna 19. Member: BOP. Testing, psychotherapy, guidance; achievement tests, projective techniques, child psychotherapy. M

SCHADEN, Dr. phil. Margarete. Hollandstr. 13, Vienna 2. b. 16 June 1924 Vienna. PH.D '49 Univ. of Vienna, Austria. CHILD PSYCH'T, Inst. für Erziehungshilfe, Heiligenstädterstr. 82/14, Vienna 19. Member: BOP.

Psychotherapy, guidance, testing; child therapy, projective techniques, group process. F

SCHALLEBÖCK, Dr. phil. Rudolf. Kaiserfeldgasse 6, Leoben. b. 6 Aug 1916 Vienna. PH.D '40 Univ. of Vienna, Austria. PSYCHOLOGIST, Employment and Vocat. Guid. Off, Leoben. Member: BOP. Testing, applied and industrial psychology, psychotherapy; characterology, graphology, depth psychology, psychology and religion. M

SCHENK-DANZIGER, Dr. Charlotte. Dornbacherstr. 29, Vienna XVII. b. 22 Dec 1905 Vienna. PH.D '30 Univ. of Vienna, Austria. DIRECTOR, Psych. Serv, Vienna Sch. Bd, Zinckgasse 12. Member: BOP, ICWP, Arbeitsgemeinschaft für Heilpädagogik. Testing, consulting, research; developmental testing, reading disability, left-handedness, school readiness, after effects of hospitalization. F

SCHERNHUBER, Dr. phil. Franz. Stelzhammerstr. 21, Wels. b. 7 Jan 1927 Wels. PH.D '52 Univ. of Innsbruck, Austria. EDUC. COUNS, Inst. für Erziehungshilfe, Tummelplatz 19, Linz. Member: BOP. Consulting, educational psychology, testing; group work, projective techniques, nondirective methods in guidance. M

SCHINDLER, Dr. phil. Sepp. Gerlgassel, Vienna 3. b. 14 Dec 1922 Vienna. PH.D '49 Univ. of Vienna, Austria. PSYCHOLOGIST, Inst. für Erziehungshilfe, Heiligenstädterstr. 82, Vienna 19; PSYCH'T. and EDUCATOR, Bundesanstalt für Erziehungsbedürftige, Kaiserebersdorferstr. 297, Vienna 11. Member: BOP. Educational psychology, consulting, testing, research; affective disturbances, selection of educators. M

SCHISCHITZA, Dr. phil. Anna. Strozzig 30, Vienna 8. b. 9 Aug 1930 Tschestereg, Yugo. PH.D, Univ. of Vienna, Austria. CHILD PSYCH'T, Dept. of Child Psychiat. and Neur, Univ. Clin, Lazarettg. 14, Vienna 9. Member: BOP, Socy. of Indiv. Psych'ts. Psychotherapy, clinical diagnosis, research; individual and group therapy. F

SCHMIDT, Dr. Friedrich. Schönbrunnerstr. 21/10, Vienna 5. b. 27 Mar 1922 Vienna. Dr. '49 Univ. of Vienna, Austria. MEMBER, Vienna Symphony Orchestra, Lothringerstr. 20, Vienna 3. Member: BOP. Consulting research; psychology of thought and intelligence, psychology of music. M

SCHÖCHL, Dr. Günther. Mayerhofweg 17, Salzburg. b. 15 June 1923 Vienna. Dr. '51 Univ. of Vienna, Austria. INDUS. PSYCH'T, Osterreichische Saurer Werke AG, Haidequerstr. 3, Vienna XI. Member: BOP. Industrial psychology; public opinion research, human relations, group psychology, depth psychology. M

SCHOTTKOWSKY, Mjr. Dr. phil. Friedrich.

Fasangartensiedlung 12, Vienna 12. b. 3 Dec 1913 Trieste. PH.D, Leopold Franzens Univ. of Innsbruck, Austria. DIRECTOR, Austrian Milit. Psych. Serv, Fasangartenkaserne, Vienna 12. Member: BOP, Austrian Socy. for Psych. Applied psychology; military psychology. M

SCHREIBER, Dr. Waltraut. Währingergurtel 35, Vienna 18. b. 20 Mar 1927 Vienna. Dr. psych. '52 Univ. of Vienna, Austria. TEACHER, Sonderschulen, Kulturministerium für Hessen, Luisenstr. 10, Wiesbaden, Ger. Member: BDP. Teaching, testing, guidance; learning theory, social perception, group process. F

SCHWARZENAUER, Dr. phil. Wilhelm. Inst. für Demoskopie, Allensbach/Bodensee, Ger. b. 21 July 1931 Salzburg, Austria. PH.D '56 Karl Franzens Univ, Graz, Austria. STUDENT, Inst. für Demoskopie. Member: BOP. Public opinion research; interests and drives, introspective method, projective techniques. M

SEYFRIED, Prof. Helmut. Weiler 46, Vorarlberg. b. 30 July 1923 Weiler. Gymnasiallehrer '49 Univ. of Innsbruck, Austria. PROF. and EDUC. and VOCAT, GUID. COUNS, Landesschulrat für Vorarlberg, Montfortstr. 12/1, Bregenz, Vorarlberg. Member: Gesellschaft für Psych. und Psychother, Int. Rorschach Socy. Guidance, applied and educational psychology, testing; projective techniques, color tests, group development and decadence, music and color. M

SIMON, Dr. phil. Maria Dorothea. Tuchlauben 17, Vienna 1. b. 6 Aug 1918 Vienna. PH.D '51 Univ. of Vienna, Austria. PSYCHO-THERAPIST, priv. prac. Member: BOP, APA, Austrian Psychoanal. Assn, Int. Psychoanal. Assn. Child psychotherapy, clinical analysis, consulting; child development, personality tests, therapy. F

SMEKAL-HUBER, Dr. phil. Dipl. Psych. Erika. Judenplatz 6, Vienna 1. b. 18 Nov 1899 Vienna. PH.D '45 Univ. of Vienna, Austria. PSYCH. CONSULT, priv. prac. Member: BOP, Austrian Socy. for Psych, Austrian Assn. for Ment. Hyg. Psychotherapy, applied psychology, testing, research; professional counseling, juvenile court consultant, welfare, psychoanalysis. F

SPINDLER, Dr. phil. Paul. Ernst Ludwiggasse 10/3/16, Vienna 10. b. 29 June 1922 Vienna. PH.D '53 Univ. of Vienna, Austria. ANTHROPOLOGIST, Anthrop. Inst, Univ. of Vienna, van Swietengasse 1, Vienna 9; PSYCHOLOGIST, Kinderabteilung Pav. XVII, Versorgungsheimplatz, Vienna 12. Member: BOP. Testing and clinical analysis, research, neurophysiology and ethology; human genetics, comparative psychology. M

SPRENGER, Dr. phil. Heinz. Schubertsstr. 15, Linz. b. 25 Mar 1926 Innsbruck. PH.D,

Univ. of Innsbruck, Austria. PSYCHOLOGIST Employment Off, Wiener Reichsstr. 7, Linz. Member: BOP. Consulting, personnel psychology, testing, teaching; projective techniques, achievement tests, social perception, group process. M

STOGER, Dr. phil. Herbert Josef. Schloss Bogenhofen, St. Peter am Hart. b. 18 Sept 1925 Bruck a. d. Mur. PH. D.'50 Univ. of Graz, Austria. PROFESSOR, Seminar Bogenhofen. Member: BOP. Teaching, consulting, educational psychology; child guidance, social perception, group process, orthopedagogy. M

STRAUHAL, Dr. phil. Mrs. Maria Anastasia. Alserstr. 57, Vienna VIII. b. 11 Aug 1905 Vienna. PH.D '41 Univ. of Berlin, Ger. APPL. and EDUC. PSYCH'T, priv. prac. Member: BOP. Applied and educational psychology; marriage problems, professional counseling. F

STRIGL, Dr. phil. Klaus. Harrachstr. 17, Linz. b. 13 June 1928 Linz. PH.D '50 Univ. of Vienna, Austria. PSYCHOLOGIST, Employment Off, Wiener Reichsstr. 7, Linz. Member: BOP. Testing, consulting, applied psychology; projective techniques, achievement tests, group process. M

STROHAL, Prof. Dr. Richard. Conradstr. 6, Innsbruck. b. 22 Aug 1888 Mähr. Schönberg, Czech. PH.D '13 Univ. of Innsbruck, Austria. PROFESSOR, Univ. of Innsbruck. Member: DGP. Research, teaching; psychology and philosophy, science and mathematics, educational psychology. M

THUMB, Dozent Dr. phil. Norbert. Rochusgasse 2/24, Vienna 3. b. 7 Nov 1903 Vienna. PH.D, Univ. of Vienna, Austria. CONSULTANT, Inst. für Arbeitskunde; TEACHER, Tech. Hochschule; TEACHER, Hochschule für Welthandel. Member: BOP, DGP. Teaching, industrial psychology, industrial consulting; human relations, group dynamics, vocational guidance, professional training, industrial selection. M

THURNER, Dr. phil. Franz. Psych. Inst, Univ. of Innsbruck, Schöpfstr. 41, Innsbruck. b. 10 Sept 1928 Innsbruck. PH.D '52 Univ. of Innsbruck, Austria. UNIV. ASST, Inst. for Exper. Psych, Univ. of Innsbruck. Member: BOP, Gesellschaft für Psychother. und Angewandte Psych. Research, teaching, psychotherapy, testing; projective techniques, influence of emotions on retention, recall and perception. M

TOMAN, Prof. Walter. Brandeis Univ, Waltham, Massachusetts, USA. b. 15 Mar 1920 Vienna. Dr. phil. habil. '51 Univ. of Vienna, Austria. ASST. PROF, Brandeis Univ; DOZENT, Univ. of Vienna. Member: BOP, Int. Psychoanal. Assn. Teaching, research, psychotherapy; theory of personality development. M

TREML, Dr. phil. Franz. Kobergerweg 14, Salzburg. b. 28 Dec 1918 Ahorn. PH.D '48 Univ. of Vienna, Austria. PSYCHOLOGIST, Employment Off, Ignaz Harrerstr. 4, Salzburg. Member: BOP. Testing, consulting, research, industrial psychology, teaching; projective techniques, aptitude tests, vocational guidance. M

TRÖBINGER, Dr. phil. Johann. Franckstr. 40a, Linz. b. 22 Feb 1921 Waldburg. PH.D '49 Univ. of Graz, Austria. INDUS. PSYCH'T, Osterreichische Stickstoffwerke AG, Linz. St. Peter 224, Linz. Member: BOP. Industrial psychology, testing, consulting and guidance; attitude measurement, projective techniques, group process, job analysis. M

TÜRSCHERL, Dr. phil. Wilhelm. Volksfeststr. 13a, Linz. b. 12 Apr 1915 Unterdambach. PH.D '39 Univ. of Vienna, Austria. MAGISTRATSRAT, Erziehungsberatungsstelle des Städtischen Jugendamtes, Tummelplatz 19, Linz. Member: BOP. Consulting, testing, applied psychology; depth psychology, intelligence and projective testing. M

WEGELER, Dr. phil. Adalbert P. Otto Bauergasse 5/12, Vienna 6. b. 2 Nov 1922 Feldkirch. PH.D '55 Univ. of Vienna, Austria. PSYCHOLOGIST, Inst. for Child Guid, Heiligenstädterstr. 82, Vienna 19; EDITOR, *Sitzungsberichte des Wiener Arbeitskreises für Tiefenpsychologie.* Testing, clinical analysis, psychotherapy, teaching; projective techniques, depth psychology, research on biological behavior patterns. M

WEGELER-TUTSCHEWA, Dr. phil. Anna. Otto Bauergasse 5/12, Vienna 6. b. 17 Aug 1916 Plovdiv, Bulgaria. PH.D '49 Univ. of Vienna, Austria. Member: BOP, Österreichische Gesellschaft für Angewandte Psych. Retired; applied child psychology, graphology, sociological research. F

WEGLEHNER, Dr. phil. Ignaz. Mühlkreisbahnstr. 3, Linz. b. 31 Dec 1911 Kefermarkt. PH.D '49 Univ. of Vienna, Austria. HEAD, Dept. of Vocat. Guid, Employment Off, Wiener Reichstr. 7, Linz. Member: BOP. Consulting, administration, industrial psychology; achievement tests, social psychology. M

WEINAND, Dr. Hartmann. Neudeggergasse 19, Vienna 8. b. 9 Dec 1921 Mautern. Dr. '51 Univ. of Vienna, Austria. PRIN. SCH. TCHR, Knaben Hauptschule, Neubaugasse 42, Vienna 7. Teaching; child and adolescent psychology, educational psychology. M

WEINHANDL, Prof. Dr. phil. Ferdinand. Morellenfeldgasse 5, Graz. b. 31 Jan 1896 Judenburg. PH.D '19 Univ. of Graz, Austria. PROF. and DIR, Inst. of Psych. and Inst. of Pedagogy, Universitätsplatz 2, Graz. Member: BOP. Research, teaching, applied and educational psychology; personality, psychology of feeling and emotions, Gestalt psychology. M

WILFERT, Dr. phil. Otto. Taborstr. 87/20, Vienna 2. b. 4 Mar 1924 Hainburg/D. PH.D '49 Univ. of Vienna, Austria. EDUC. DIR, Bundesanstalt für Erziehungsbedürftige in Kaiser-Ebersdorf, Vienna 11. Member: BOP, Int. Union for Child Welf. Educational psychology, administration, teaching; group dynamics, social work. M

WILLNAUER, Franz. Geblergasse 61/31, Vienna 17. b. 11 Nov 1933 Enns. PH.D '57 Univ. of Vienna, Austria. STUDENT, Psych. Inst, Liebiggasse 5, Vienna 1. Research, applied psychology, testing; psychology of music and art, accident psychology. M

WUNSCH, Dr. phil. Wolfgang. Baumgasse 3/17, Vienna 3. b. 27 May 1926 Neufeld, Burgenland. SCH. PSYCH'T, Stadtschulrat, Zinckgasse 12-14, Vienna. Member: BOP. Testing, psychotherapy, teaching; psychotherapy of criminals and old people, experiments on brain physiology, adult education. M

BELGIAN CONGO

LAROCHE, Mr. Jean-Louis René Gabriel. B.P. 2370 Elisabethville. b. 29 Oct 1923 Charleroi, Bel. Licence '52 Univ. of Louvain Bel. RES. WRKR, Cen. for Psych, Union Minière du Haut-Katanga, Elisabethville. Research, testing, clinical analysis, teaching; aptitude measurement, acculturation problems, phenomenology of conjugal love. M

LEBLANC, Miss Maria Anne. Cen. for Psych, Union Minière du Haut-Katanga, Elisabethville. b. 2 Mar 1926 Couillet, Bel. Licence '49 Univ. of Louvain, Bel. RES. WRKR, Cen. for Psych, UMHK. Member: SBP.

Research, testing, student; personality and attitudes, cultural psychology, social perception, child training. F

VAN SPEYBROEK, Constant Victor Albert. I.G.M.O.I., Otraco D.G., Léopoldville. b. 12 Feb 1917 London, Eng. Conseiller '46 Univ. of Ghent, Bel. PSYCHOTECHNICIAN, Otraco, Inspection Générale M.O.I., Leopoldville. Applied, and industrial psychology, testing, professional selection; achievement tests, job evaluation. M

VERHAEGEN, Dr. Paul K. M. Union Minière du Haut-Katanga, Elisabethville. b. 6 Feb 1926 Antwerp, Bel. MD '49 Cath. Univ. of

Louvain, Bel. DIRECTOR, Cen. for Psych. and Educ, UMHK; PSYCHIATRIST, priv. prac. Research, applied and educational psychology, administration; intelligence scales, learning potential of adults without school training in youth. M

BELGIUM

ADRIAENSSENS, Maurits J. B. Bisschopslaan 30, Beerse. b. 22 July 1930 Beerse. Lic. '52 Univ. of Ghent, Bel. ASSISTANT, Laboratoire de Psych. Appliquée, Univ. of Ghent, Coupure 86, Ghent. Member: AIPA. Applied psychology, research, teaching; group tests. M

BEIRLAEN, Jean-Pierre Rolland. 528 rue Vanderkindere, Brussels. b. 29 Nov 1924 Brussels. Psychotech. '51 Sch. of Ergology, Brussels, Bel. HEAD, Psychotech. Cen, Touring Secours, rue de la Loi 44, Brussels. Member: AIPA. Applied psychology, testing, professional writing; psychology of the motorist, road safety improvement. M

BEIRNAERT, Rev. Roger H. F. Bisschoppelijke Normal Sch, Kasteelstraat 8, Sint Niklaas. b. 21 Nov 1925 Antwerp. Lic. '55 Univ. of Louvain, Bel. TEACHER, Bisschoppelijke Normal Sch; TEACHER, Catholic Univ. for Women, Antwerp. Teaching, educational psychology; readiness for school, learning theory, mental health in the school. M

BEMELMANS, F. D. A. 54 rue de Hervé Grivegnée, Liège. b. 13 Sept. 1916 Liège. Doctor '46 Univ. of Liège, Bel. DIRECTOR, Centre Libre d'Orientation, 29 rue St. Gilles, Liège. Member: SBP, AIPA. Applied and educational psychology, consulting, guidance; projective techniques, aptitude and interest measurement. M

BEUN, Mrs. Lutgarde (Sister Gérarda). Inst. N.D. aux Epines, rue sud du Marais 131, Eeklo. b. 7 Feb 1886 Etterbeek, Brussels. Doctor '32 Univ. of Ghent, Bel. PROF. of PSYCH. and VOCAT. GUID, Inst. N.D. aux Epines; EDUC. COUNS, Medico-Pedagogic Inst. of Louvain. Member: AIPA. Teaching, educational psychology, guidance; research on moral judgment. F

BLOCH, Dr. Claude F. 58 Rue St. Bernard, Brussels. b. 10 Jan 1922 St. Gilles. MD '53 Univ. of Brussels, Bel. ASSISTANT, Inst. of Psychiat, Hosp. Univ. Brugmann, 4 Pl. A. van Gehuchten, Brussels; CLIN PSYCH'T, priv. prac. Member: Int. Rorschach Socy. Psychotherapy, testing, clinical analysis, clinical psychiatry; projective techniques.M

BOURDON, Dr. Jean Charles. 18 Rue Dodonée, Uccle, Brussels. b. 21 Oct 1924 Wavre. MD '49 Univ. of Brussels, Bel. ASSOC. PHYS, Inst. of Psychiat, Hosp. Brugmann, 4 Pl. Van Gehuchten, Brussels; PSYCHIATRIST, priv. prac. Member: SBP, APSLF. Psychotherapy, consulting, clinical practice, testing; projective techniques. M

BUYSE, Prof. Raymond L. Gh. Ibis, Rue St. Georges, Tournai. b. 8 Sept 1889 Tournai. Doctor '20 Univ. of Brussels, Bel. PROFESSOR, Fac. of Philos and Letters, Univ. of Louvain; DIRECTOR, Lab. of Exper. Pedagogy, Inst. du Spoelbergh, Rue Kaeken 3, Louvain; PRESIDENT, Cen. Natl. de Recherches Psychotechniques Scolaire, Brussels. Member: SBP, IUSP, AIPA. Research, educational psychology, testing; achievement and aptitude tests, experimental education, vocational guidance. M

CARDU, Dr. Bruno. 49 Ave. de Juillet, Brussels. b. 25 Feb. 1925 Olbia, Italy. Doctor '53 Univ. of Louvain, Bel. TEACHING ASST, Univ. of Louvain. Research, teaching; sensory processes, learning. M

CHRISTIAENS, Dr. Xavier A. J. Boulevard de la Croix Rouge 7, Tongres. b. 17 Mar 1928 Tongres. Lic. '54 Cath. Univ. of Louvain, Bel. PSYCH. COUNS, Centre d'Orientation Scolaire et Professionnelle, Boulevard Leopold 38, Tongres; PROFESSOR, Ecoles Sociales de Louvain. Guidance, teaching; projective techniques, juvenile crime, validity and reliability of tests. M

CLOOTS, Josef. Mosselweg 19 B, Genk. b. 12 Dec 1920 Elsene. Lic. '44 Univ. of Louvain, Bel. PSYCHOLOGIST, Centre Psycho-Medico-Sociale, 23 rue Winterslag, Genk. Applied psychology, testing, psychotherapy, guidance; projective techniques, achievement tests, attitude measurement.M

COETSIER, Leo. Dorp 1, Astene. b. 26 July 1908. Doctor '39 Univ. of Ghent, Bel. PROF. and DIR, Applied Psych. Lab, Univ. of Ghent. Member: SBP, AIPA, APSLF. Teaching, research, applied psychology; intelligence and aptitude tests, projective techniques. M

COLLETTE, Albert F. L. 18 Rue A. Magis, Liège. b. 2 Sept 1915 Liège. Lic. '51 Univ of Liège, Bel. ASSISTANT, l'Institut de Sciences Pédagogiques, Univ. of Liège, Boulevard Piercot 46, Liège; PROFESSOR, Normal School, Liège. Testing, teaching, psychotherapy; projective techniques, educational psychology, adolescent psychology. M

COLLINET, Dr. Marcel François Augustin. Rue Samuel Donnay, 112, Flemalle-Grande. b. 9 Oct 1901 Seraing-Sur-Meuse. Doctor, Univ. of Liège, Bel. ADV. DIR,

Centre Provincial d'O.S. et. P, Rue Grégoire Chapuis, 36, Seraing-Sur-Meuse; EDITOR, *Cahiers de Pédagogie et d'O.P.* Member: Assn. Int. de Psychotechnique, Assn. Natl. d'Orientation Professionnelle. Testing, applied psychology, editorial; achievement tests, projective techniques, aptitude tests. M

COULON-ALLEGRE, Mrs. Elvire. 46 Dreve Pittoresque, Uccle, Brussels. b. 16 Apr 1919 Marseille, France. Lic. '56 Univ. of Brussels, Bel. PSYCHOLOGIST, Centre Médico-psychologique, 207 Chaussée de Louvain, Brussels. Consulting, psychotherapy, testing; projective techniques, affective relations between parents and children, child psychology, analytical psychotherapy. F

DE BIE, Prof. Emiliaan. St. Clarastr, 171, Brugge. b. 24 July 1923 Heist-op-de-Berg. Lic. '53 Univ. of Louvain, Bel. PROFESSOR, Séminaire de Philosophie, P.P. Capucins; PSYCHOLOGIST, Marienhove. Teaching, consulting, educational psychology; projective techniques, counseling, learning theory. M

DE CLERCK, Dr. Julia J. M. M. Institut Médico Pédagogique, Rixensart. b. 6 Apr 1915 Antwerp. Doctor, Univ. of Louvain, Bel. DIRECTOR, Institut Médico Pédagogique. Member: SBP. Clinical analysis, applied psychology, teaching; personality problems of children. F

DE COSTER, Prof. Sylvain. 101 Ave. Vanderaye, Uccle, Brussels. b. 24 Aug 1907 Schaerbeek. Doctor '38 Univ. of Brussels, Bel. DIR. of PUB. INSTR, City of Brussels, 162 Boulevard Maurice Lemonnier, Brussels; PROFESSOR, Univ. of Brussels, Ave. Franklin Roosevelt. Member: SBP, APSLF. Teaching, administration; social psychology, applied and educational psychology, general psychology. M

DE COSTER, Dr. William. Papegaaistraat 52, Ghent. b. 1 Dec 1920 Gent. Doctor '52 Univ. of Ghent, Bel. DIRECTOR, Psych. Lab, Univ. of Ghent, Universiteitstraat 14, Ghent. Research, applied psychology, testing, teaching; social and cultural influence on personality and intelligence. M

DE CRAECKER, Prof. Raymond. 336 Ave. de Limburg-Stirum, Wemmel. b. 18 June 1910 St. Josse-Ten-Noode. Doctor '49 Univ. of Brussels, Bel. PROFESSOR, l'Ecole Normale Secundaire de Tirlemont, 1 Slicksteenvest, Tirlemont; PROFESSOR, l'Ecole d'Ergologie, Institut des Hautes Etudes de Belgique. Member: SBP. Teaching, applied psychology; gifted children, psychology of authority, adolescence. M

DEHAESELEER, Miss Simone. Rue Delft 24, Borgerhout, Antwerp. b. 16 Apr 1929 Borgerhout. Lic. '52 Univ. of Louvain, Bel.

ADV. DIR, Dienst voor Studie en Beroepsoriëntering, Statiestr. 28, Sint-Truiden. Guidance, testing, applied psychology; projective techniques, intelligence and character tests, child psychology. F

DELLAERT, Dr. René. 221 Italielei, Antwerp. b. 14 Feb 1906 Deynze. MD '31 Univ. of Louvain, Bel. DIRECTOR, Child and Adult Guid. Clin; PSYCH'T, priv. prac. Member: SBP. Applied psychology, consulting, psychotherapy; personality traits. M

DELYS, Prof. Louis. Ave. de Sept-Bonniers, 296, Forest-Brussels. b. 4 Nov 1905 Gages. Doctor '41 Univ. of Brussels, Bel. DIRECTOR Centre d'Etudes et de Recherches Psychotechniques des Forces Armées Belges, rue Léonard de Vinci, 11, Brussels; PROFESSOR, Univ. of Brussels. Member: SBP, APSLF. Research, teaching, administration, military psychology; achievement tests, group process, attitude measurement. M

DE MONTPELLIER, Prof. Gerard. 2 Place Cardinal Mercier, Louvain. b. 1 July 1906 Denée. Doctor '29 Univ. of Louvain, Bel. PROF. and DIR, Psych. Lab, Univ. of Louvain. Teaching, research. M

DERIVIERE, Dr. Raoul. 86 Rue du Merlo, Brussels. b. 15 Sept 1906 Neufvilles. Doctor '28 Univ. of Louvain, Bel. ADV. DIR, Centre Psycho-Médico Social, Avenue 11 Novembre, Etterbeek; PROFESSOR, Ecole d'Assitants Sociaux. Member: SBP, APSLF, Association Nationale d'Orientation Professionnelle. Applied psychology, teaching, guidance; vocational choice, projective techniques, scholastic achievement. M

DE SCHOUWER, Joseph Maurice. Teere Neuve 198, Brussels. b. 20 July 1918 Malines. Lic. '46, Univ. of Louvain, Bel. PREFET, Ecole Normale, St. Thomas. Administration, teaching; psychology of adolescents, intelligence and character tests. M

D'ESPALLIER, Prof. Dr. Victor. Koninklyke Laan 55 Berchem-Antwerpen. b. 22 Aug 1904. Doctor '29 Univ. of Louvain, Bel. PROFESSOR, Institut de Psychologie et de Pédagogie, Univ. of Louvain; EDITOR, *Katholieke Encyclopaedie voor Opvoeding en Onderwijs, Tijdschrift voor Opvoedkunde.* Member: B.SP. Teaching, educational psychology; psychology of the only child, educational psychology of primary teaching. M

DE WAEPENAERE, Mrs. Maria. Institut Notre Dame aux Epines, rue Sud du Marais 131, Eeklo. b. 14 Apr 1908 Merelbeke. Lic. '38 Univ. of Louvain, Bel. PROFESSOR, Institut Notre Dame aux Epines. Teaching educational psychology, testing. F

DIERKENS, Dr. Jean C. 34 Rue Jacques Jordaens, Brussels. b. 16 May 1926 Ghent.

MD '51 Univ. of Brussels, Bel. ASSISTANT, Institute of Psychiat, Hôpital Universitaire Brugmann, Place van Gehuchten, Brussels. Member: SBP, APSLF. Psychotherapy, clinical practice, testing, teaching; tests of organic deterioration, projective techniques. M

DOUTREPONT, Georges C. A. J. 50 Rue Fusch, Liège. b. 3 Feb 1926 Brussels. Lic. '52 Univ. of Liège, Bel. ASSISTANT, Univ. of Liège, 36 Blvd. Piercot, Liège. Member: APSLF, Association Internationale de Psychotechnique. Applied psychology, consulting, psychotherapy; projective techniques, individual psychotherapy, social psychology. M

DRABS, Prof. José. 134 Avenue Franklin Roosevelt, Brussels. b. 2 Aug 1896 Brussels. Doctor '36 Univ. of Brussels, Bel. PROFESSOR, l'Ecole Normale Secondaire, Brussels; DIRECTOR, l'Ecole d'Ergologie, Institut des Hautes Etudes de Belgique; CHARGE de COURS, Univ. of Brussels; EDITOR, *Ergologie*. Member: SBP, Belgian Socy. of Ergology, Association International de Psychotechnique. Teaching, research, educational psychology; aptitude measurement, motor phenomena, time perception. M

FAUVILLE, Prof. Arthur. 55 Ave. Van den Bempt, Héverlé, Louvain. b. 25 Feb 1894 Brussels. Doctor '21 Univ. of Louvain, Bel. PROF. and DIR, Inst. of Psych, Univ. of Louvain. Member: SBP, SFP. Teaching, research; experimental psychology. M

FLAMENT, Dr. Jacques. 65 Rue Ten Bosch, Ixelles-Brussels. b. 20 Nov 1921 Haine-Saint-Paul. MD '45 Univ. of Brussels, Bel. FIRST ASST, Inst. of Psychiat, Brugmann Univ. Hosp, 4 Place Van Gehuchten, Brussels; PROFESSOR, Nursing Sch, Univ. Hosp. Member: SBP, APSLF. Clinical practice, psychotherapy, testing, teaching; projective techniques, psychotherapy. M

FRANCK, Brother Emile Alphonse J. G. Institut Psychiatrique St. Camille, Bierbeek, Louvain. b. 3 Mar 1902 Antwerp. Lic, Univ. of Louvain. PSYCHOMETRIST, Institut Psychiatrique St. Camille. Testing, guidance, educational psychology; projective techniques, intelligence and achievement tests, vocational guidance. M

FRANSEN, Prof. Jan Frans. 20 Blvd. du Parc, Ghent. b. 11 Sept 1886 Ryckevorsel. MD '10 Univ. of Louvain, Bel. RETIRED PROF, Univ. of Ghent. Member: SBP. Teaching, educational psychology, retired; learning theory, gestalt psychology. M

GHEKIERE, Mrs. Josine. 194, Noordstr, Roeselare, W-Vlaanderen. b. 21 Jan 1930 Roeselare. Lic. '54 Univ. of Louvain, Bel. CONSULTANT, Bureau de Consultations pour Enfants, 21 B, Ave. du Fer Caheval, Bruges.

Guidance, psychotherapy, testing; play therapy, projective techniques, psychoanalysis, child psychology. F

GIBLET, Mrs. Christiane. 24 Rue Henri Maubel, Forest, Brussels. b. 10 July 1926 Forest, Brussels. Lic. '50 Univ. of Louvain, Bel. CLIN. PSYCH'T, Ligue Nationale Belge d'Hygiene Mentale, Rue Joseph Stallaert, 1, Ixelles, Brussels. Clinical practice, child guidance, testing, psychotherapy; projective techniques, achievement tests, group process. F

GIJS, Robert A. S. C.S.B.O. Thonissenlaan 6, Hasselt. b. 19 June 1931 Antwerp. Lic. '56 Univ. of Louvain, Bel. ADV. DIR, C.S.B.O. Limburg. Consulting, research, educational psychology; attitude measurement, projective techniques, social psychology. M

GIJSEN, Miss Elza. 54, O.L. Vrouwstr. Louvain. b. 26 Mar 1920 Louvain. Lic. '45 Univ. of Louvain, Bel. PSYCHOLOGIST, Medisch-Psychologische Kinderkliniek, 1, de Merodelei, Berchem-Antwerpen; ASSISTANT, Univ. of Louvain, Louvain. Testing, teaching, psychotherapy; achievement tests, projective techniques, child psychotherapy, child development. F

GODFRIND, Miss Jacqueline Paule. 147 Ave. Plasky, Brussels. b. 3 Aug 1933 Brussels. Lic. '56 Univ. of Brussels, Bel. PSYCHOLOGIST, Serv. de Pédiatrie, Hôpital St. Pierre, Rue Haute, Brussels. Testing, psychotherapy, clinical practice; psychotherapy, projective techniques, dyslexie. F

GOOSENS, Gerard. 16 Rue de Vriere, Brussels b. 18 July 1915 Laeken. Doctor '46 Univ. of Brussels, Bel. EDUC. COUNS. and DIR, Centre d'Orientation Scolaire et Professionelle, 54 Boulevard G. Van Haelen, Forest (Bt); EDITOR, *Revue Belge de Psychologie et de Pédagogie*. Member: SBP. Educational psychology, guidance, editorial; intelligence and achievement tests, academic adjustment, academic and vocational guidance. M

HAROUX, Prof. Hector Henry. 148 Chaussée de Haacht, Kampenhout. b. 10 Mar 118 Tournai. Doctor '47 Univ. of Louvain, Bel. PROFESSOR, Univ. of Louvain. Member: SBP, APSLF. Teaching, research, educational psychology; leadership. M

HUSQUINET, Albert Fernand. 122 Rue de Fragnée, Liège. b. 17 Oct 1923 Seraing. Lic. '44 Univ. of Liège, Bel. ASSISTANT, Univ. of Liège, Pl. du 20 Août, Liège. Research, consulting, testing, psychotherapy; socialization, projective techniques, child psychotherapy. M

JONCKHEERE, Prof. Tobie. 58 Blvd. Léopold II, Brussels. b. 3 Jan 1878 Brussels. Cert. '04 Iena, Germany. HON. PROF, Univ. of Brussels, Ave. Franklin Roosevelt 50,

Brussels. Member: SBP. Retired, educational psychology; intelligence and achievement tests. M

KLUPPELS, Rafael, G. J. Olmstraat 35, Waregem. b. 6 Aug 1923 Malines. Lic. '54 Univ. of Louvain, Bel. PROFESSOR, Ecole de Service Social, Rue de la Poste 111, Brussels. Consulting, testing, teaching; projective techniques, human relations, non-directive counseling. M

KNOPS, Prof. Leopold Nicolas Hupert. Psychologisch Institut, 96 Tiense St, Louvain. b. 2 Oct 1914 Maastricht, Netherlands. Doctor '46 Univ. of Louvain, Bel. PROFESSOR, Univ. of Louvain, 4 Kraekenstraat, Louvain. Member: SBP, APSLF. Teaching, research; visual perception, aptitude, achievement and personality tests, psychological measurement. M

KRIEKEMANS, Albert Jan Josef. Kwekerijstraat 28, Antwerp. b. 3 Jan 1906 Antwerp. Doctor '28 Univ. of Louvain, Bel. PROFESSOR, Univ. of Louvain. Educational psychology, teaching, research; child psychology. M

LEBLANC, André. 96 Av. de la Gare, Neufchateau. b. 10 Mar 1920 Neufchateau. Lic. '45 Univ. of Louvain, Bel. DIRECTOR, Office Libre d'O.S.P., 24 Rue d'Arlon, Neufchateau; PROFESSOR, Ecole Supérieure de Pédagogie du Luxembourg. Member: SBP. Consulting, teaching, testing; achievement tests, learning theory, aptitude measurement. M

LEBLANC, Mrs. Marguerite (Joris). 20 Blvd. Tirou, Charleroi. b. 8 June 1927 Couillet. Lic. '51 Univ. of Louvain, Bel. Teaching; child psychology. F

LEGRAND, Jacques G. J. A. G. 17 Rue de Waltzing, Arlon. b. 24 Sept 1929 Bléharies. Lic, Univ. of Louvain, Bel. DIRECTOR, Service Psycho-Médico-Social Libre du Luxembourg-Sud, 41 Rue des Deportes, Arlon. Guidance, testing, applied psychology; scholastic achievement, aptitude measurement, adaptation to the school environment. M

LEROY, Dr. Roger Octave. Rue A. Rodenbach 19, Bruges. b. 24 Nov 1923 Wervicq. Lic. '46 Univ. of Louvain, Bel. VOCAT. GUID. COUNS, Service d'Orientation Professionnelle et Scolaire, Rue Neuve 7, Bruges; PROFESSOR, Normaal School. Member: Association Internationale de Psychotechnique. Guidance, testing, teaching; intelligence tests, group process. M

LITWINSKI, Léon. 305 Ave. de Tervueren, Brussels. b. 11 Apr 1887 Warsaw, Poland. Doctor '09 Univ. of Liège, Bel. Member: SBP, BPS, APA, APSLF. Retired, professional writing; personality, psychoanalysis, gerontology. M

MACOURS, Dr. Felix. Rue Jonckeu 18,

Liège. b. 20 Jan 1907 Bressoux. Doctor '34 Univ. of Liège, Bel. PROFESSOR, Ecole Normale Professionnelle de l'Etat, Rue Basse Marcelle 6, Namur. Teaching, educational psychology, editing; intelligence tests, education of retarded children. M

MATTHYSSEN, Mme. Paula. Institut Notre Dame aux Epines, 131 Rue Sud du Marais, Eeklo. b. 24 June 1927. Lic. '55 Univ. of Louvain, Bel. PROFESSOR, Institut Notre Dame aux Epines. Teaching, educational psychology, testing. F

MERTENS de WILMARS, Prof. Dr. Charles. Balkermolen, Nederockerzeel. b. 20 Nov 1921 Louvain. MD '48 Univ. of Louvain, Bel. PROFESSOR, Univ. of Louvain; DIRECTOR, Centre de Recherches et d'Information de l'Institut de Psychologie Appliquée de l'Université de Louvain. Member: SBP, AIPA, APSLF. Teaching, research, consulting; psychological factors in social integration. M

MICHOTTE van den BERCK, Prof. Baron Albert Edward. 185 Chaussée de Tirlemont, Louvain. b. 13 Oct 1881 Brussels. Maître Agrégé de Philosophy '05, Univ. of Louvain. PROF. EMER, Univ. of Louvain; DIRECTOR, Laboratoire de Psychologie Experimentale, l'Institut Supérieur de Philosophie, 2 Place Cardinal Mercier, Louvain; EDITOR, *Etudes de Psychologie, Studia Psychologica.* Member: SBP, APSLF, Int. Union of Sci. Psych. Research, retired; perception. M

NUTTIN, Prof. Joseph R. 108 Tiense Straat, Louvain. b. 7 Nov 1909 Zwevegem, Bel. Doctor '41 Univ. of Louvain, Bel. PROFESSOR, Institute of Psychology, Univ. of Louvain, Place Cardinal Mercier 2, Louvain; CO-DIR, *Studia Psychologica, Universitaire Bibliotheek voor Psychologie.* Member: SBP, APSLF, BPS. Research, teaching; motivational and cognitive processes, learning theory, personality theory. M

OMBREDANE, Prof. Dr. André. 115 Ave. Ad. Buyl, Brussels. b. 19 Nov 1898 Parthenay, France. Doctor '47 Univ. of Paris, France. PROFESSOR, Univ. of Brussels, 50 Ave. Franklin Roosevelt, Brussels. Member: SBP, Int. Rorschach Socy. Teaching, research, editorial; aphasia, projective techniques, intellect capacity of African negroes, analysis of work. M

OSTERRIETH, Prof. Dr. Paul A. 39 Ave. Defré, Uccle, Brussels. b. 19 Sept 1916 The Hague, Netherlands. PH.D '44 Univ. of Geneva, Switz. PROFESSOR, Univ. of Brussels; CO-DIR, Centre Médico-Psychologique, 407 Chaussée de Louvain, Brussels; CHARGE du COURS, Univ. of Liège. Member: SBP, APSLF, AIPA, Int. Rorschach Socy. Teaching, educational psychology, research; child development, projective techniques. M

PASQUASY, René. 83 Rue Wazon, Liège. b. 31 July 1911 Xhoris. Doctor '47 Univ. of Liège, Bel. CHARGE du COURS, Institut Supérieur de Sciences Pédagogiques, Univ. of Liège, Bel. Piercot, Liège; EDITOR, *Bulletin d'Orientation Scolaire et Professionnelle.* Member: SBP, AIPA, APSLF. Teaching, research, guidance; graphology, occupational choise, aptitude and interest tests.   M

PAULUS, Prof. Jean-Joseph. 24 Rue Courtois, Liège. b. 16 Nov 1908 Liège. Doctor '38 Univ. of Liège, Bel. PROFESSOR, Univ. of Liège, Place du 20 Août, Liège. Member: SBP, BPS, APSLF. Teaching, research, consulting; psychological theory, personality, emotion.   M

PIERSON, Mrs. Colette (Robaye). 81 Ave. des Ortolans a Boitsfort, Brussels. b. 27 May 1929 Brussels. Lic. '56 Univ. of Brussels, Bel. STUDENT, Univ. of Brussels, 50 Ave. Franklin Roosevelt, Brussels. Student, psychotherapy, educational psychology; selection and training of saleswomen, psychotherapy and projective techniques. F

PIRET, Prof. Roger Octave Jules. Rue César Franck 47, Liège. b. 16 June 1912 Verviers. Doctor '45 Univ. of Liège, Bel. PROFESSOR, Univ. of Liège; CO-DIR, *Zeitschrift für Verkehrssicherheit*; *Bulletin de l'Association Internationale de Psychologie Appliquée.* Member: SBP, APSLF, AIPA. Teaching, industrial psychology, research; traffic accidents, work accidents, testing.   M

RAHIER, Mrs. Anne-Marie. 17 Rue des Aduatiques, Brussels. b. 19 Mar 1930 Brussels. Lic, Univ. of Brussels, Bel. ASSISTANT, Univ. of Brussels. Teaching, testing, psychotherapy; child psychology, projective techniques, drawings, games. F

ROBAYE, Francine. 115 Ave. A. Buyl, Brussels. b. 24 June 1925 Brussels. Lic. '53 Univ. of Brussels, Bel. RES. DIR, Fonds Nat. Belge de la Recherche Scientifique, Psych. Lab, Univ. of Brussels. Member: SBP. Research, psychotherapy, testing; projective techniques, psychoanalysis, research methods.   F

SEGERS, Jean-Emile. Rue Stevens Delannoy 66, Brussels. b. 20 July 1897 Diest. Doctor '32 Univ. of Brussels, Bel. PROFESSOR, Ecole Normale moyenne de l'Etat, 4 Rue Karel Bogaert, Brussels II; DIRECTOR Centre Médicopsycho-pédagogique, Saint Gilles-lez-Brussels. Member: SBP. Teaching educational psychology, testing; child psychology, educational psychology, achievement tests.   M

SMET, S.J, Walter Florent Francis. 4 Ursulinenstraat, Brussels. b. 25 Mar 1915 Hornchurch, England. Doctor '49 Univ. of Louvain, Bel. DIRECTOR, Sch. Psych. Serv, Verenigde Colleges van de Societeit van Jezus in België, 8 Haachtse Steenweg, Brussels; LECTURER, Katholieke Sociale School, Handels-Hogeschool St. Ignatius, Antwerp. Member: SBP, APA. Consulting, clinical analysis, teaching; educational psychology, pastoral psychology, achievement tests, projective techniques.   M

SPOO, Marc. Lendeledestraat 840 A, Kortrijk. b. 14 Oct 1925 Bruges. Lic. '55 Univ. of Louvain, Bel. ADV. DIR, C.S.B.O, Vlamingstraat 29, Kortrijk. Consulting, guidance, applied psychology, teaching, testing; attitude measurement, group process, sociometry.   M

SPOO-PETERS, Mrs. Rachel. Lendeledestraat 840 A, Kortrijk. b. 21 Feb 1929 Tildonk. Lic. '53 Univ. of Louvain, Bel. ADV. DIR, C.S.B.O, Bruggestraat 40, Tielt. Consulting, guidance, teaching, testing, applied psychology; social psychology, sociometry, group process, industrial psychology.   F

STIENLET, Felix L. N. Ave des Célestins 54, Heverlee. b. 25 Jan 1921 Louvain. Lic. '48 Univ. of Louvain, Bel. INDUS. PSYCH, Union Minière du Haut-Katanga, Rue Montagne du Parc 6, Brussels. Member: SBP, APSLF. Industrial psychology, guidance, teaching; human relations in industry, leadership, achievement tests. M

STINISSEN, Dr. Juul L. E. Heideberg, 181, Kessel-Lo. b. 2 June 1921 Antwerp. Doctor '53 Univ. of Louvain, Bel. INSTRUCTOR, Inst. of Psych. and Educ. Univ. of Louvain, Tiensestr. 96, Louvain. Member: SBP, APSLF, AIPA. Teaching, research, guidance; test construction, projective techniques, educational guidance. M

SWAELENS, Julia. 20 Market Place, Vorselaar. b. 15 Feb 1921 Dworp. Lic. '50 Univ. of Louvain, Bel. PROFESSOR, Normal School for Teaching of Infants. Teaching, research; teaching methods, pedagogic tests.   F

TANGHE, Dr. Marcel (Brother Gonzales). Bethanielei, 1 Sint-Job-in-'t-Goor, Antwerp. b. 10 Aug 1911 Woumen. Doctor '41 Univ. of Louvain, Bel. DIRECTOR, Christus-Koning Institut. Administration, clinical analysis, teaching; mentally deficient children, diagnostic and achievement tests.   M

THIENPONT, André Remi. 67 Hollenaarstraat, Oostakker bij Gent. b. 14 May 1914 Kalken. Lic. '48 Univ. of Ghent, Bel. ADV. DIR, Service Libre d'Orientation Scolaire et Professionnelle, 43 Holstraat, Ghent; PROFESSOR, Ecole Sociale; ED. COMM, *Tijdschrift voor Studie en Beroepsorientering.* Member: SBP, AIPA. Guidance, teaching, applied psychology; intelligence and memory tests, social perception.

THINES, Dr. Georges-Louis. Lab. of Zoophysiology, Univ. of Louvain, 71 Rue de Namur, Louvain. b. 10 Feb 1923 Liège. Doctor '55 Univ. of Louvain, Bel. DIR. of RESEARCH, Lab. of Zoophysiology. Member: SBP, APSLF, Royal Socy. of Zoology. Research, teaching; sense physiology and tropisms, animal ethology, visual perception. M

TORDEUR, Willem-Gustave. 1 Slicksteenvest, Tirlemont, Brabant. b. 3 Dec 1903 Schaerbeek. Doctor, Univ. of Brussels, Bel. DIRECTOR, Ecole Normale Provinciale. Member: SBP. Teaching, research, testing, guidance; vocational guidance techniques, projective techniques, differential psychology. M

VAN BOVEN, Roger-Charles. 23 Rue Georges Rency, Woluwe-St-Lambert, Brussels. b. 7 Oct 1933 Uccle, Brussels. Lic. '56 Univ. of Brussels, Bel. ASSISTANT, Centre Médico-Psychologique du Dr. Geeraerts, Chaussée de Louvain 407, Brussels. Psychotherapy, clinical practice, research; psycho-analytical theories, projective techniques. M

VAN BRABANT, Rev. Père Prof. Albert (Père Hubert M.O.F.M.) Collège Saint Antoine, Luikstraat 44, Lokeren. b. 8 Dec 1916 Hasselt. Lic. '48 Univ. of Louvain, Bel. PROFESSOR. Teaching, testing; intelligence tests, vocational guidance. M

VAN DE PUTTE, Dr. Jeanne (Sister Bernarda). Inst. Heilig Graf, Patersstraat, Turnhout. b. 2 Sept 1909 Antwerp. Doctor '49 Univ. of Louvain, Bel. HEAD MISTRESS and TCHR, Inst. Heilig Graf. Teaching, educational psychology, administration; adolescent psychology. F

VANDERGOTEN, Miss Elise Yvonne. 66, chaussée de Rodelbeel, Woluwe-St-Lambert. b. July 1926 Ixelles. Lic. '54 Univ. of Brussels, Bel. TEACHER, Ecole Normale Charles Buls, 110, Blvd. Maurice Lemonnier Brussels; ASSISTANT, l'Ecole des Sci. de l'Educ, de l'Univ. de Brussels. Teaching, educational psychology; developmental psychology, social psychology, projective techniques, psychotherapy. F

VAN HOVE, Dr. Werner. Prinses Jos. Charlottelaan, 123, Sint-Niklaas W, Bel. b. 23 Nov 1919 Sint-Niklaas W. Doctor '44 Univ. of Louvain, Bel. CHIEF COUNS, Acad. and Vocat. Guid. Center, Ankerstraat 61, Sint-Niklaas W; CHIEF ED, *Tijdschrift Voor Studie-en-Beroepsoriëntering*; CO-DIR, *Opvoeding, Onderwijs, Gezondheidszorg.* Member: SBP, AIPA. Applied psychology, teaching, editorial; learning processes, intelligence and achievement tests. M

VAN NYPELSEER, Dr. Jean-Louis. 80 Ave. de la Toison d'Or. b. 13 July 1921 Brussels. MD '46 Univ. of Brussels, Bel. ASSISTANT,

Univ. of Brussels, 50, Ave. Franklin Roosevelt, Brussels. Member: APSLF, Société Internationale Rorschach. Psychotherapy, testing, teaching; projective techniques, emotional processes, psychoanalysis. M

VAN PETEGHEM, Raymond. Scheldervde, Ghent. b. 12 Apr 1915 Munte. Doctor '54 Univ. of Ghent. ASSISTANT, Psych. Lab, Univ. of Ghent; HEAD PSYCH, Charbonnage de Houthalen, Limbourg. Member: SBP, AIPA. Applied psychology, testing, guidance; academic selection and guidance. M

VAN RIEBEKE, Kamiel Cyriel. Medisch-Pedagogisch Institut Sint-Josef, Heirweg-Noord, 217 Zwijnaarde. b. 17 May 1909 Zandwoorde bij Oostende. Lic. '37 Univ. of Louvain, Bel. DIRECTOR, Medisch-Pedagogisch Institut. Administration, teaching, guidance; intelligence and achievement tests, abnormal psychology. M

VERBIST, Prof. Dr. J. J. Richard. Rue Carnot 47, Antwerp. b. 26 July 1911 Antwerp. PROF. and DIR, Appl. Psych. Lab, Institut Supérieur des Sciences Pédagogiques, Univ. of Ghent, Rue de l'Université 14, Ghent. Teaching, research, educational psychology, testing; psychology of the thought, intelligence tests. M

VERHEYEN, Prof. J. Emile. Univ. of Ghent, Ghent. b. 15 May 1889 Kessel. Lic. '30 Univ. of Ghent, Bel. PROFESSOR, Univ. of Ghent. Research, teaching, writing; educational psychology. M

VERMOERE, Wilfried. Bruggesteenweg 367, Rosselare. b. 13 Oct 1920 Deerlijk. Lic. '48 Univ. of Louvain, Bel. ADV. DIR, Acad. and Vocat. Guid. Serv, H. Horriestr. 33, Roeselare; TEACHER, Social Work School. Member: AIPA. Guidance, testing, teaching; projective techniques, tests of cognitive functions. M

WENS, Dr. Maria. Avenue Rooigem 421, Ghent. b. 31 Dec 1919 Antwerp. Doctor '45 Univ. of Ghent, Bel. CHIEF CONSULTANT, Psychiat. Clin, Univ. of Ghent, 65 Rue Prof. Guislain, Ghent. Member: SBP, APSLF. Group psychotherapy, clinical practice, testing; intelligence tests, projective tests, child psychotherapy. F

WILLEMS, Emiel Frans. Weerstandlaan 8, Hasselt. b. 18 Nov 1923 Vorselaar. Lic. '48 Univ. of Louvain, Bel. SECRETARY, Provinciale Centrale voor Beroepsoriëntering v.z.w, Tramstraat 6, Hasselt. Member: SBP, AIPA. Guidance, testing, applied psychology; projective techniques, attitude measurement, group processes. M

WINDEY, Rev. Raphael Amand Gustave. Kasteelstraat 8, Sint-Niklaas. b. 27 Jan 1920 Moerzeke. Lic. '45 Univ. of Louvain, Bel. PROFESSOR, Cath. Normaal Sch, Sint-Niklaas. Teaching, educational psychology, editorial; psychology of religion, religious education. M

WITVROUW, Dr. Marcel. 3 Av. des Frênes, Neuville-en-Condroz. b. 2 Oct 1917. Doctor '49 Univ. of Liège, Bel. INDUS. PSYCH'T, S.A. Cockerill-Ougrée, Seraing; TEACHER, Social Service Schools. Applied psychology, teaching, testing; projective techniques, group process and group techniques. M

BOLIVIA

BLANCO CATACORA, Prof. Federico. Inst. Normal Superior, Núcleo Escolar de Miraflores, La Paz. b. 18 July 1926 Oruro. Professor '49 Inst. Normal Superior, Bolivia. PROF. of PHILOS, Inst. Normal Superior. Teaching, professional writing, testing; learning theory, Rorschach test. M

DURÁN P., Prof. Manuel. Casilla 204, Sucre. b. 14 Sept 1904 Sucre. Dr. en Derecho '25 Univ. of Chuquisaca, Bolivia. DEAN Fac. of Law, Calle Junín 501, Sucre; EDITOR, *Revista de Estudios Jurídicos, Políticos y Sociales*, Teaching, editorial, student; social psychology, group psychology, penal law. M

GOBILLARD RIBERA, Prof. Eduardo. Casilla 1932, La Paz. b. 28 Feb 1918 Uyuni. Diplome '53 Inst. of Applied Psych, Cuba. PROF. and COUNSELOR, Academia Nacional de Carabinero, La Paz. Consulting, clinical practice, guidance, psychotherapy, applied psychology; theory of the unconscious, psychology of women, relation between sex and personality. M

LÓPEZ-REY, Prof. Manuel. 541 E. 20th St, New York City, USA. b. 30 Sept 1902 Madrid, Spain. LL.D. '28 Univ. of Madrid, Spain. CHIEF, Section of Social Defence, United Nations Secretariat, New York City; EDITOR, *International Review of Criminal Policy*. Member: Int. Assn. of Penal Law, Int. Socy of Criminol. United Nations policy director on prevention of crime and treatment of offenders, editorial and professional writing, research; criminal psychology, social problems of industrialization and urbanization. M

OSORIO E., Dr. L. Fernando. Casilla 951, La Paz. b. 2 May 1914 Cochabamba. MD '47 Univ. of San Andrés, Bolivia. PSYCHOTHERAPIST, Servicio Cooperativo Interamericano de Salud Publica (SCISP), Plaza 14 de Septiembre, La Paz; DIRECTOR, Ment. Rehab. Inst. "Ernst," Red Cross of La Paz; PSYCHIATRIST, priv. prac. Psychotherapy, guidance, clinical practice, applied psychology, mental hygiene and sex edcuation; sexual psychology, emotional disturbances of children. M

BRAZIL

ABREU PAIVA, Dr. Jorge. Rua Paula Freitas 19, apt. 1203, Rio de Janeiro. b. 31 July 1916 Rio de Janeiro. MD '39 Faculdade Fluminense, Brazil. PSYCHOANALYST, priv. prac; PSYCHIATRIST, Pestalozzi Socy; PHYSICIAN, Indus. Hyg. Dept, Ministry of Labor, Industry and Commerce Member: BAAP, Brazilian Assn. of Indus. Med. Psychotherapy, clinica practice,. guidance, teaching; psychoanalysis, child neuropsychiatry, constitutional typology.M

ALMEIDA MAGALHÃES, Miss María Lourdes. Rua São Clemente 514, apt. 301, Botafogo, Rio de Janeiro. b. 24 Sept 1931 Rio de Janeiro. BA '56 Natl. Fac. of Philos, Brazil. COUNSELOR, Inst. de Seleção e Orientação Profissional (ISOP), Rua da Candelária 6, andar 3, Rio de Janeiro. Guidance, industrial psychology, testing; social perception, group process, psychotherapy. F

ALVES, Dulce Godoy. Dept. of Public Admin, Rua Florêncio de Abreu 848, São Paulo. b. 15 Dec 1918 Santos. Bacharel '42 Escola de Sociologia e Política, Brazil. CHIEF, Test Planning Sect, Personnel Selection Div, Dept. of Public Admin. Member: São Paulo Psych. Socy. Preparation of tests for selection of public employees, personnel psychology, administration, research; aptitude, intelligence and achievement tests. F

ALVIN, Mrs. Mariana. Fundação Getúlio Vargas, Rua da Candelária 6, andar 2, Rio de Janeiro. b. 8 Apr 1909 Rio de Janeiro. BA '41 Sch. of Social Work, Brazil. PSYCHOLOGIST, Inst. de Seleção e Orientação Profissional (ISOP), Fundação Getúlio Vargas. Member: BAAP. Consulting, guidance, testing, teaching; social work techniques, social perception, attitude measurement, projective and expressive techniques. F

AMARAL VIEIRA, Prof. José Antonio. Rua Costa Aguiar 635, São Paulo. b. 23 Nov. 1920 São Paulo. Lic. '45 Univ. of São Paulo, Brazil. PROF. of EDUC, PSYCHOTECHNICIAN, Sel. Serv, Estrada de Ferro Sorocabana, Alameda Cleveland 20, Caixa Postal 66 B, São Paulo. Member: São

Paulo Psych. Socy. Personnel selection, teaching, administration; psychology of learning, intelligence and aptitude tests, projective techniques. M

ANGELINI, Prof. Dr. Arrigo Leonardo. Rua D. Antonia de Queiroz 469, Apt. 302, São Paulo. b. 28 Sept 1924 Santo Andre. Livre Docente '54 Univ. of São Paulo, Brazil. PROF. of EDUC. PSYCH, Univ. of São Paulo, Rua Maria Antonia 294, São Paulo; EDITOR, Publications of Fac. of Philos, Sci. and Letters, Univ. of São Paulo. Member: APA, SIP, BPA, BAAP. Teaching and research in educational psychology; psychology of learning, motivation, personality measurement. M

ANTIPOFF, Daniel. Rua do Ouro 1527, Belo Horizonte. b. 31 Mar 1919 St. Petersburg, Russia. Bacharel, Fac. of Philos, Belo Horizonte, Brazil. CHIEF, Profes. Sel. and Guid. Serv, Reg. Dept. of Minas Gerais, Serviço Nacional de Apridizagem Comercial (SENAC), Belo Horizonte; ASST. PSYCH'T, Serviço Estadual do Transito, Belo Horizonte. Member: BAAP. Testing, clinical analysis, consulting, guidance, industrial psychology; projective techniques, aptitude measurement, employee placement. M

ANTUNHA, Prof. Heladio Cesar Gonçalves. Rua Voluntários da Pátria 3040, São Paulo. b. 28 Aug 1925 Santos. Lic. '48 Univ. of São Paulo, Brazil. DIRECTOR, Serv. of Educ. Measurement and Res, Rua Major Diogo 200, São Paulo; HEADMASTER, Colégio Estadual e Escola Normal. Research, teaching, administration; intelligence, personality, aptitude and a-chievement tests. M

ARAZÍ COHÉN, Jaime César. Rua Senador Furtado 113 c/XIV, apt. 101, Rio de Janeiro. b. 16 Oct 1907 Belo Horizonte. MD '46 Univ. of the Fed. Dist, Brazil. PSYCHOLOGIST, Inst. de Seleção e Orientação Profissional (ISOP), Rua¡da Candelária 6, andar 3, Rio de Janeiro. Member: BAAP. Teaching, testing, clinical analysis, personnel selection; study of personality, psychotherapy, genetic psychology, psychological typology. M

ARRUDA, Prof. Dr. Elso. Ave. Atlântica 720, apt. 302, Rio de Janeiro. b. 15 May 1916 Carangola. MD, Private Docent, Fac. of Med, Univs. of Brazil and Bahia. DIRECTOR, Inst. of Psychiat, Rua Ramiro Magalhães, Rio de Janeiro; CHIEF, Biopsych. Serv. of Fed. District Prison; EDITOR, *Arquivos do Inst. de Psiquiatria*, Bahia. Member: BAAP, Brazilian Assn. of Neur. and Psychiat, Int. Socy. of Criminol. Teaching, research, administration; projective techniques, personality tests, psychopathologic art and expressions, research on mental

diseases, criminal psychology. M

AVILEZ, Prof. Tito. Rua Bartolomeu Portela 10, apt. 201, Botafogo, Rio de Janeiro. b. 10 Dec 1921 Rio de Janeiro. PH.B '53 Univ. of the Fed. Dist, Brazil. PROF. of PORTUGUESE and PHILOS, Colégio Militar do Rio de Janeiro, Rua São Francisco Xavier 267, Rio de Janeiro. Member: BAAP. Teaching, research, testing; projective techniques, attitude measurement, achievement tests. M

AZEVEDO, Prof. Marcionilla Loureiro Costa de. Rua Djalma Ulrich 271, apt. 504, Rio de Janeiro. b. 30 Dec 1904 São Fidélis. PSYCHOTECHNICIAN, Inst. de Seleção e Orientação Profissional (ISOP), Rua da Candelária 6, andar 3, Rio de Janeiro. Member: BAAP. Applied psychology, teaching, testing; projective techniques, intelligence and personality tests. F

AZZI, Prof. Dr. Enzo. Inst. of Psych, Catholic Univ. of São Paulo, Rua Monte Alegre 984, São Paulo. b. 10 Dec 1921 Bozzolo, Italy. MD '47 Univ. of Parma, Italy. DIRECTOR, Inst. of Psych, Catholic Univ; EDITOR, *Revista de Psicologia Normal e Patologica*. Member: BAAP, São Paulo Psych. Socy, Italian Psych. Socy, Italian Psychiat. Socy. Psychotherapy, research, teaching; psychophysiology, perceptive processes, psychotherapeutic processes. M

BARIONI, Dr. Walther. Serviço Nacional de Aprendizagem Comercial (SENAC), Rua 24 de Maio 208, andar 2, São Paulo. b. 3 Nov 1900 São Paulo. Dr. en Droit '37 Univ. Fluminense, Brazil. DIRECTOR, Vocat. Guid. and Sel. Serv, Reg. Dept. of São Paulo, (SENAC). Member: BAAP, São Paulo Psych. Socy. Applied psychology, administration; techniques of learning, intelligence tests, aptitude measurement. M

BARRA, Prof. Elza. Instituto Aché, Ave. Lacerda Franco 527, Cambucí, São Paulo. b. 22 July 1915 São Paulo. Professor '31 Colégio de São Paulo, Brazil. PSYCHOLOGIST, Inst. Aché, and State Penitentiary, Carandirú, São Paulo. Member: Int. Rorschach Socy, São Paulo Psych. Socy, Paulista Assn. of Ment. Hyg. and Child Psychiat, São Paulo Rorschach Socy. Individual and group psychotherapy, testing, teaching; projective techniques, achievement tests, child and adolescent psychotherapy and guidance. F

BARROS SANTOS, Prof. Oswaldo. Serviço Nacional de Aprendizagem Industrial (SENAI), Rua Monsenhor Andrade 298, São Paulo. b. 8 Oct 1918 São Paulo. Lic. '50 Univ. of São Paulo, Brazil. DIR. of GUID. SERV, SENAI; PROF. of PSYCHOTECHNICS, Soc. Serv. Inst, São Paulo. Member: BPA, BAAP, São Paulo Psych. Socy. Consulting, guidance, testing, industrial psychology; tests and measurements employed in educational and vocational guidance, counseling. M

BENFATTI, Prof. Eros. Rua Gravatai 41, apt. 2, São Paulo. b. 4 Mar 1912 Mocóca. ASST. in RES, Serv. of Educ. Measurement and Res, Major Diogo 200, São Paulo; DIRECTOR, Primary School. Member: São Paulo Psych. Socy. Achievement testing, administration, psycho-pedagogical research, student; learning theory, achievement and personality tests. F

BENKÖ, Prof. Antonius. Colégio Anchieta, Nova Friburgo. b. 7 July 1920 Paks, Hungary. Dr. '56 Catholic Univ, Louvain, Belgium. PROF. of PSYCH, Fac. of Philos, Nossà Senhora Medianeira, Rua General Osório 181, Nova Friburgo. Teaching, research, applied, educational psychology; projective techniques, psychological theory, relation between scientific psychology and philosophy, perception. M

BOISSON CARDOSO, Prof. Ofélia. Praça Eugênio Jardim 48, andar 8, Rio de Janeiro. b. 17 Apr 1905 São Paulo. EDUC. CONSULT. and PSYCHOTECH, Inst. of Soc. Serv. of Rio de Janeiro, Ave. Presidente Roosevelt 115, andar 2, Rio de Janeiro. Member: BAAP, League of Mental Hygiene, Pestalozzi Socy. of Brazil. Educational guidance and consulting, research, teaching; speech defects, emotional and character disturbances in infants and adolescents. F

BRITO, Rubens de. Inst. dos Industriários, Ave. Alte. Barroso 78, Caixa Postal 1291, Rio de Janeiro. b. 3 Sept 1918 Rio de Janeiro. Psychotechnician '49 Fundação Getúlio Vargas, Brazil. ASSISTANT, Div. of Vocat. Guid, Inst. dos Industriários. Member: BAAP. Applied, industrial psychology, testing, teaching; personality tests, intelligence tests. M

BRUNO, Livre-Docente Dr. Antonio Miguel Leão. Rua Rodrigo Cláudio 404, São Paulo. b. 21 July 1903 São Paulo. MD '28 Univ. of São Paulo, Brazil. DOCENTE-LIVRE and ASST. to the CHAIR of LEGAL MED, Fac. of Med, Univ. of São Paulo, Rua Teodoro Sampaio 115, São Paulo. Member: São Paulo Psych. Socy, São Paulo Rorschach Socy. Teaching, research, forensic psychiatry; projective techniques, tests of character, attitude tests. M

CABRAL, Dr. Annita de Castilho. Rua Iquitos 212, São Paulo. b. 11 July 1910 Novo Horizonte. PH.D '45 Univ. of São Paulo, Brazil. PROF. and CHMN, Dept. of Psych, Fac. of Philos, Sci, and Letters, Univ. of São Paulo, Rua Maria Antonia 294, São Paulo; EDITOR, *Boletim de Psicologia*, Univ. of São Paulo. Member: BPA, APA, AAAS, São Paulo Psych. Socy. Teaching, research, administration; social

psychology, national character, child play and drawings. F

CAMERINHA, NASCIMENTO, Prof. Dr. José. Ave. São João, 1.009. apt. 43, São Paulo. b. 4 Dec 1918 São Paulo. EDUC. TECH, Educ. Guid. Sect, Serv. for Adult Educ, Secretary of Educ, Praça Da Se 108, andar 2, São Paulo; TCHR. of PSYCH, Teachers Coll, São Paulo; EDITOR, *Exedra, Revista de Educação* of the Dept. of Educ. of São Paulo. Member: São Paulo Psych. Socy. Teaching, research, applied and educational psychology; learning theory, group process, adult education, social perception. M

CAMPOS, Prof. Dr. Nilton. Ave. Copacabana 445, apt. 1001, Rio de Janeiro. b. 23 Aug 1898 Rio de Janeiro. MD '24 Univ. of Brazil; PH.D, Natl. Fac. of Philos, Univ. of Brazil. DIRECTOR, Inst. of Psych. and PROF. of PSYCH, Univ. of Brazil, Ave. Nilo Paçanha 155, Rio de Janeiro; EDITOR, *Boletim do Instituto de Psicologia, Monografias.* Member: SFP, APA, IUSP, Phenomenological Socy. Teaching, research, professional writing; psychological theory and methodology of research, neuropsychology, personality. M

CAMPOS PIRES, Prof. Nelson de. Rua Visconde de Ouro Preto 165, apt. 701, São Paulo. b. 7 Sept 1921 Botucatu. Lic. '46 Univ. of São Paulo, Brazil. HEAD, Psychotech. Lab, Serviço Nacional de Aprendizagem Industrial (SENAI), Monsenhor Andrade 298, São Paulo; ASSISTANT, Inst. of Exper. Psych, Catholic Univ, São Paulo. Member: BAAP, AIPA, São Paulo Psych. Socy. Consulting and guidance, testing, research; projective techniques, experimental psychology, aptitude tests. M

CARVALHAES, Prof. João. Companhia Municipal de Transportes Colectivos (CMTC), Luis Antonio 1367, São Paulo. b. 15 Aug 1917 Sta. Rita. PSYCHOTECHNICIAN, CMTC. Member: BAAP, São Paulo Psych. Socy. Industrial psychology, research, teaching; psychotechnics, psychology of selling. M

CARVALHO RIBEIRO, Mrs. Catarina de. Fundação Getúlio Vargas, Rua da Candelária 6, Rio de Janeiro. b. 16 July 1912 Rio de Janeiro. Certificate '50 Inst. of Social Work, Brazil. PSYCHOLOGIST, Fundação Getúlio Vargas. Member: BAAP. Testing, clinical analysis, consulting, guidance; projective techniques, learning theory, social perception, group process, play theory. F

CASTRO, Prof. Dr. Mrs. Amelia Domingues de. Caixa Postal 8105, São Paulo. b. 27 Dec 1920 Rio de Janeiro. PH.D '50 Univ. of São Paulo, Brazil. ASST. PROF, Univ. of São Paulo, Rua Maria Antonia 294, São

Paulo; ED. BD, *Revista de Pedagogia.*
Member: São Paulo Psych. Socy. Teaching
pedagogical methods, research, professional
writing, editorial; learning process, de-
velopmental psychology of child and
adolescent, achievement tests. F
CERQUEIRA, Dr. Luis. Inst. Ulisses Pernam-
bucano, Estrada Velha da Tijuca 954, Rio
de Janeiro. b. 31 Jan 1911 União dos
Palmares-Alagôas. Livre docente '45
Univ. of Bahia, Brazil. DIRECTOR, Inst.
Ulisses Pernambucano; PHYSICIAN, Clin.
for Child Guidance, Inst. of Psychiat,
Univ. of Brazil, Rio de Janeiro. Member:
BAAP, Brazilian Socy. of Psychother, São
Paulo Psych. Socy, São Paulo Rorschach
Socy. Guidance, psychotherapy, teaching;
psychoanalysis, projective techniques,
social psychology. M
CULLINAN, Dr. Dora de Barros. Rua
Engenheiro Alfredo Duarte 132, Rio de
Janeiro. b. 6 Nov 1910 Rio de Janeiro.
PH.D '40 Univ. of São Paulo, Brazil.
COUNSELOR, Inst. de Seleção e Orientação
Profissional (ISOP), Fundação Getúlio
Vargas, Rua Candelária 6, Rio de Janeiro.
Member: BAAP. Research, guidance,
teaching; study of personality, psychology
of adolescence. F
CUNHA, Prof. Mário Wagner Vieira da. Inst.
of Administration, Univ. of São Paulo,
Rua dr. Vila Nova 268, São Paulo. b. 3 Jan
1912 São Paulo. MA '43 Univ. of Chicago,
USA. DIRECTOR, Inst. of Admin, Univ. of
São Paulo; PROF. of PUBLIC and INDUS.
ADMIN, Fac. of Admin. and Econ. Sci,
Univ. of São Paulo; EDITOR, *Revista de
Administraçao.* Member: São Paulo Psych.
Socy. Administration of research, industrial
psychology; human relations in industry. M
**D'ALMEIDA BESSA, Prof. Mathilde Brasi-
liense.** Rua Antonio Carlos 302, São Paulo.
b. 6 July 1900 Piracicaga. Lic. '37 Univ.
of São Paulo, Brazil. TEACHER of EDUC.
PSYCH, Lar-Escola São Francisco, Rua
Franca Pinto 783, São Paulo. Member:
São Paulo Psych. Socy. Educational
guidance, teaching, research; learning. F
DIAS, José Augusto. Rua Cônego Eugênio
Leite 889, São Paulo. b. 15 Nov 1929 Santa
Cruz do Rio Pardo. Lic. '53 Univ. of São
Paulo, Brazil. PERSONNEL SEL. TECH, Dept.
Estadual de Administração, Rua Florencio
de Abreu 848, São Paulo: PRINCIPAL,
Ginásio Estadual "Sylas Gedeão Coutinho."
Member: São Paulo Psych. Socy. Testing,
administration, teaching; psychotechnics,
aptitude tests, statistics. M
DI LASCIO SANIOTO, Mrs. Cecília Maria D.
Rua Viscondessa do Livramento 246,
Recife. b. 22 Nov 1913 São Paulo. Bacharel
'42 Escola de Sociologia e Política, Brazil.
PSYCHOLOGIST, League of Ment. Hyg, Rua

Cônego Barata s/n, Casa Amarela, Recife.
Member: São Paulo Psych. Socy. Consulting, guidance, applied psychology,
psychotherapy; study of the family, social
attitudes, deviant opinions. F
DORIA SODRE, Prof. Celia. Catholic Univ,
Rua Marquês de Paranaguá 111, São Paulo.
b. 7 Oct 1916 Jaboticabal. PH.D '53
Catholic Univ. of São Paulo, Brazil. PROF.
of PSYCH. and DIR. of PSYCH. CLINIC,
Catholic Univ. "Sedes Sapientiae."
Member: BPA, São Paulo Psych. Socy.
Teaching, consulting, clinical practice,
testing, clinical analysis; structure of
personality, drives and emotions, behavior
disorders. F
EDELWEISS, Prof. Malomar Lund. Caixa
Postal 659, Pelotas. b. 11 Jan 1917 Santa
Cruz do Sul. LL.D. '52 "Athaeneum
Angelicum," Rome, Italy. DIR. and PROF,
Inst. of Psych, Rua Félix da Cunha 412,
Pelotas; PROFESSOR, Catholic Fac. of
Philos. of Pelotas; DIRECTOR, Brazilian
Circle for Depth Psych. Administration,
guidance, clinical practice, teaching; pro-
jective techniques, symbols in depth psy-
chology, neurosis. M
EDWIGES DE C., Dr. Florence. Dept. of
Psych. 407 Arps Hall, Ohio State Univ,
Columbus 10, Ohio, USA. b. 12 Aug 1912
Bahia, Brazil. PH.D '56 Ohio State Univ.
USA. ASST. PROF, Inst. Normal da Bahia,
Barbalho, Salvador, Brazil; INDUS.
PSYCH'T. INTERNE, Sears, Roebuck and Co,
Chicago, Illinois, USA. Member: APA.
Educational and industrial psychology,
research, teaching; test construction,
morale surveys, academic motivation. F
ESPÍNOLA, Prof. Ivone. Rua Cândido
Espinheira 18, apt. 41, São Paulo. b. 14
Apr 1924 Atibaia. BA '45 Univ. of São
Paulo, Brazil. PERSONNEL ADMIN, Dept. of
Public Administration, Rua Florencio de
Abreu 848, andar 5, São Paulo; EDITOR,
Boletim de Psicologia. Member: São Paulo
Psych. Socy. Personnel psychology, ad-
ministration, research; achievement, person-
ality, attitude and intelligence tests. F
FÉO, Prof. Joselina de. Rua Peixoto Gomide
1665, São Paulo. b. 26 Aug 1931 São Paulo.
Lic. '54 Univ. of São Paulo, Brazil. PROF.
PARTICULIER, Ment. Hyg. Serv. for Children
Rua Epitacio Pessoa, São Paulo. Member:
São Paulo Psych. Socy. Teaching, testing,
student; projective techniques, achievement
tests, psychotherapy. F
FERNANDES, Dr. Augusto José. Rua Tupi
651, São Paulo. b. 8 May 1912 São Paulo.
MD '39 Univ. of São Paulo, Brazil.
DIRECTOR, Maternity and Children's Div,
Legião Brasileira de Assitencia, Rua
Guaianases 1385, São Paulo; PSYCHIATRIST,
Pediatric Clinic. Member: São Paulo

Psych. Socy. Administration of medical and social work, testing, clinical practice; projective techniques, social perception, group process. M

FRALETTI, Dr. Paulo. Manicômio Judiciário do Estado de São Paulo, Rua Aroujo 165, andar 9, São Paulo. b. 4 Jan 1921 Pereiras. MD '47 Paulista Med. School, Brazil. PSYCHIATRIST, Manicômio Judiciário do Estado de São Paulo; ASSISTANT, Chair of Psychiat, Fac. of Med. of Sorocaba, São Paulo; DIRECTOR, *Boletim de Higiene Mental.* Member: São Paulo Socy. of Legal Med. and Criminol, Paulista League of Ment. Hyg, São Paulo Psych. Socy, Sociedade Médica Brasileira de Psicoterapia. Psychotherapy, clinical and forensic psychiatry, teaching, editorial; origin of neuroses, biotypology, morphology of the delinquent, art of the insane. M

FRANÇA, Prof. Lêda. Rua Fradique Coutinho 526, São Paulo. b. 7 Jan 1925 Franca. Prof. '48 Univ. of São Paulo, Brazil. EDUC. GUID. COUNSULT, Industrial School "Carlos de Campos," Rua Monsenhor Andrade 798, São Paulo. Member: BAAP. Applied, educational psychology, testing, teaching; achievement tests, professional and educational guidance. F

FREITAS, Jr., Dr. José Otavio de. Rua Dom Bosco 779-793, Recife. b. 11 June 1920 Recife. MD '43 Univ. of Recife, Brazil. PSYCHIATRIST, Inst. de Aposentadorias e Pensões Comerciarios, Avc. Guarapes, Recife; EDITOR, *Jornal de Medicina de Pernambuco, Neurobiologia.* Member: Société Médico-Psychologique (Paris), Brazilian Socy. of Psychotherapy. Consulting, clinical practice, teaching, applied psychology; psychodiagnostic techniques of personality, psychosomatics, psychopathology. M

GARCEZ, Miss Maria Dulce Nogueira. Rua Fagundes 122, São Paulo. b. 16 Dec 1915 Guaratinguetá. ED.D '53 Univ. of São Paulo, Brazil. ASST. PROF, Fac. of Philos, Sci. and Letters, Univ. of São Paulo, Rua Maria Antonia 258, São Paulo. Member: São Paulo Psych. Socy. Teaching, research; history of psychology, perception, intelligence. F

GINSBERG-MEYER, Dr. Mrs. Aniela. Rua Livreiro Sáraiva 48, São Paulo. b. 2 Oct 1902 Warsaw, Poland. PH.D '30 Univ. of Warsaw, Poland. DIRECTOR, Cen. for Psych. Guid, Catholic Univ. of São Paulo, Monte Alegre 984, São Paulo; CHIEF, Cen. of Profes. Guid, Inst. de Orgenização Racional do Trabalho (IDORT), Praça D. Gaspar 30, São Paulo. Member: BAAP, AIPA, São Paulo Psych. Socy. Educational and professional guidance, research; projective techniques, new methods of testing,

social psychology, national and social group differences, race prejudice, study of professional thieves. F

GRÜNSPUN, Dr. Haim. Rua Pamplona 822, São Paulo. b. 16 Aug 1927 Hotin, Rumania. MD '52 Univ. of São Paulo, Brazil. PSYCHIATRIST, Hosp. I.A.P.C, Ave. Brigadeiro Luiz Antonio 2651, São Paulo; LECT. in CHILD PSYCHIAT, Catholic Univ. of São Paulo. Member: Paulista Med. Assn, São Paulo Psych. Socy, Paulista Assn. of Ment. Hyg. and Child Psychiat. Clinical practice, psychotherapy, teaching; group psychotherapy, psychoses, behavior disorders. M

GUIMARÃES ALVES, Prof. Pórcia. Rua Visconde Guarapuava 3375, apt. 4, Curitiba b. 9 Nov 1917 Curitiba. BA '40 Univ. of Paraná, Brazil. FIRST ASST, Chair of Psych, Univ. of Paraná, Praça Santos Andrade, Curitiba; PRINCIPAL, Experimental Primary School. Teaching, educational psychology, guidance; learning theory, projective techniques, achievement tests. F

HADDAD, Mrs. Suad. Ave. Conceição 1464, São Paulo. b. 19 Mar 1933 Mirasol. CLIN. PSYCH'T, Casa de Saude Santana (Psychiat. Hosp.), Rua Valerio Giuli 12, São Paulo; TEACHER, secondary school. Member: São Paulo Psych. Socy. Teaching, clinical practice, psychotherapy, student; individual and group psychotherapy, projective techniques. F

JOSETTI, Dr. Newton Ferreira. Rua Manoel Niobey 61, apt. 301, Rio de Janeiro. b. 2 May 1916 Rio de Janeiro. MD '55 Univ. of Brazil. PSYCHOTHERAPIST, priv. prac, Rua Santa Luzia 732, Rio de Janeiro; ADMIN. and MED. ASST. to PERS. MGR, Ministry of Agriculture. Member: AIPA, BAAP. Psychotherapy, testing, clinical analysis, research on psychophysiology and psychopathology, medical and psychological techniques of treatment of neurosis. M

KATZENSTEIN, Dr. Betti. Psych. Guid. Clinic, Rua Avanhandava 801, apt. 1, São Paulo. b. 27 Aug 1906 Hamburg, Germany. PH.D '31 Univ. of Hamburg, Germany. DIRECTOR, Psych. Guid. Clinic. Member: ICWP, BAAP, AIPA, São Paulo Psych. Socy, Socy. for Mental Health and Child Psychiat. of São Paulo. Consulting, guidance, research, applied psychology; case studies, organization of psychological services for institutions of social welfare, study of children's drawings and other projective methods. F

KEGEL, Dr. Ilse Gertrud. Trav. Prof. Coelho Gomes 4, Niterói. b. 16 Jan 1928 Berlin, Germany. PH.D '53 Univ. of Hamburg, Germany. PSYCHOPEDAGOGICAL TECH, Cen. for Juvenile Guid, Ave. Rui Barbosa 716, Rio de Janeiro. Guidance, testing, research; projective techniques, achievement tests. F

KRYNSKI, Dr. Stanislau. Rua Pamplona 822, São Paulo. b. 8 Mar 1920 Warsaw, Poland. MD '43 Univ. of São Paulo, Brazil. PSYCHIATRIST and CHIEF of CHILD PAVILION, Hosp. de Juqueri, Franco da Rocha, São Paulo; PSYCHIATRIST, priv. prac; CHIEF, Ment. Hyg. and Child Psychiat. Sect, Fac. of Med, Univ. of São Paulo. Member: BPA, Paulista Med. Assn, Brazilian League of Ment. Hyg, Paulista Assn. of Ment. Hyg. and Child Psychiat, Int. Rorschach Socy, São Paulo Rorschach Socy. Clinical practice, child psychiatry, teaching, research; psychopathology of mental deficiency, psychoses in children, psychotherapy. M

LEITE, Dr. Dante Moreira. Rua da Consolação 3552, apt. 33, São Paulo. b. 22 Oct 1927 Promissão. PH.D '54 Univ. of São Paulo, Brazil. ASST. PROF. of PSYCH, Fac. of Philos, Sci. and Letters, Univ. of São Paulo, Rua Maria Antonia 194, São Paulo. Member: BPA, São Paulo Psych. Socy. Teaching, research, student; prejudice, national character, social perception. M

LEONE BICUDO, Virginia. Rua Guarará 86, São Paulo. b. 21 Nov 1915 São Paulo. MA '45 Univ. of São Paulo, Brazil. PSYCHOLOGIST, Mental Hygiene Clinic, Rua Epitacio Pessoa 57, São Paulo; TRAINING ANALYST, Brazilian Assn. for Psychoanal, Rua Araujo 165, andar 5, São Paulo. Member: BPA, Brazilian Psychoanal. Socy, São Paulo Psych. Socy. Psychotherapy, teaching, research; psychoanalysis as research and therapeutic method, social psychology, personality and attitude studies. F

LETAYF, Prof. Sonia. Alameda Santos 2450, apt. 72, São Paulo. b. 29 Apr 1927 Beirut Lebanon. Lic. '51 Sorbonne, France. ASSISTANT, Inst. of Exper. Psych, Catholic Univ. of São Paulo, Monte Alegre 984, São Paulo; PROF. of EDUC. PSYCH, Fac. of Campinas. Research, teaching, testing, clinical analysis; measurement of attitudes, projective tests. F

LINS DE ALBUQUERQUE, Prof. Therezinha. Rua Marques de Abrantes 115, apt. 501, Rio de Janeiro. b. 2 Feb 1926 Recife. Lic. '49 Univ. of Recife, Brazil. EDUC. TECH, Cen. for Juvenile Guid, Ave. Rui Barbosa 716, Rio de Janeiro. Consulting, guidance, educational psychology, testing; educational guidance, projective techniques, intelligence tests, psychotherapy. F

LIPPMANN, Prof. Hanns Ludwig. Rua Barão de Oliveira Castro 3, apt. 201, Jardim Botânico, Rio de Janeiro. b. 22 Apr 1921. Master of Social Work, Catholic Univ. of São Paulo, Brazil. DIRECTOR, Inst. of Appl. Psych, Cath. Univ. of Rio de Janeiro, Rua Marquês de São Vicente 263, Rio de Janeiro; PROF. of EDUC. PSYCH, Fac.

Fluminense de Filosofia, Niterói; EDITOR, Psychopathol. Sect, *Brasil-Médico.* Teaching, testing, clinical analysis, research; learning theory, projective techniques, logical foundations of scientific psychology. M

LOURENÇAO, Prof. Odette. Rua Rosa e Silva 158, São Paulo. b. 15 June 1923 Barra Bonita. Specialist '48 Univ. of São Paulo, Brazil. ASST. PROF. of EDUC. PSYCH, Univ. of São Paulo, Rua Maria Antonia 258, São Paulo; PROF. of PSYCH, Inst. of Educ. "Caetano de Campos," São Paulo. Member: AIPA, SIP, BAAP, São Paulo Psych. Socy, Paulista Assn. of Ment. Hyg. and Child Psychiat. Teaching, testing, research, psychotherapy; projective techniques, attitude measurement, psychotherapeutic techniques, group process, psychology of adolescence. F

LOURENÇO-FILHO, Dr. Manoel Bergström. Rua Pedro Guedes 56, Rio de Janeiro. b. 10 Mar 1897 Porto Ferreira. PH.D '34 Univ. of São Paulo, Brazil. PROF. of EDUC. PSYCH. and CHMN, Dept. of Educ, Natl. Fac. of Philos, Univ. of Brazil, Ave. Presidente Antonio Carlos 40, Rio de Janeiro; EDITORIAL DIR, *Biblioteca de Educaçao.* Member: SFP, AIPA, BAAP, Amer. Educ. Res. Assn. Teaching, educational psychology, research; learning theory, achievement tests. M

LUCENA, Prof. José. Rua Alfonso Batista 67 Recife. b. 20 Feb 1908 Nazaré. MD '29 Univ. of Brazil. PROF. of PSYCHIAT, Fac. of Med, Univ. of Recife, Praça do Derby, Recife; DIRECTOR, Psychiat. Clinic, Hôpital d'Alienées, Recife. Member: Brazilian Socy. of Psychiat, Neur, and Mental Hygiene, Brazilian Assn. for the Advanc. of Sci. Teaching, research, consulting, clinical practice; projective techniques, research on the psychology of organic and toxic psychoses. M

MACEDO, Prof. Gilberto de. Rua Senador Mendança 180, Maceió, Alagoas. b. 28 Aug 1923 Penêdo. MD '48 Univ. of Recife. Brazil. PROF. of PSYCH, Fac. of Philos. of Alagoas, Rua Bento Junior 56, Maceió. Member: SIP. Psychotherapy, research, teaching; social perception, learning theory, group process. M

MACEDO DE QUEIROZ, Miss Aidyl. Rua Peixoto Gomide 1830, apt. 12, São Paulo. b. 14 Mar 1925 Ribeirao Bonito. Bacharel '46 Univ. of São Paulo, Brazil. PSYCHOLOGIST, Psych. Clinic, Pestalozzi Socy. of São Paulo, Rua Luis Coelho 103, São Paulo; PSYCHOLOGIST, Children's Mental Hyg. Serv, Pediat. Clinic, Hospital das Clínicas, Univ. of São Paulo. Member: AIPA. Testing, clinical analysis, psychotherapy, consulting, guidance, teaching;

50

BRAZIL

projective techniques, play therapy, personality tests. F

MACHADO, Miss Carmen Villas-Bôas. Edificio Capimirim, Apt. 12, Alamêda Capimirim 1, Salvador, Bahia. b. 16 Dec 1913 Salvador. Lic. '49 Univ. of Bahia, Brazil. ASST. in EDUC. PSYCH, Fac. of Philos, Univ. of Bahia, Ave. Joana Angélica 183, Salvador; INSTR. in PSYCH, Inst. Normal of Bahia. Teaching, testing, educational guidance; projective techniques, learning theory, achievement tests. F

MACHADO VIEIRA, Prof. Dahyl Marina. Rua Dona Delfina 11, Rio de Janeiro. b. 13 Apr 1927 Rio de Janeiro. Lic. '46 Univ. of the Fed. Dist, Brazil. ADMIN. ASST, C.I.S, Ministry of Labor, Industry and Commerce, Ave. Antonio Carlos 251, Rio de Janeiro. Member: BAAP, SIP, São Paulo Rorschach Socy. Testing, industrial psychology, personnel selection and guidance, research; projective techniques, achievement and intelligence tests. F

MACHADO VIEIRA, Prof. Marcus Vinicius. Rua Dona Delfina 11, Rio de Janeiro. b. 18 Apr 1918 Rio de Janeiro. Lic. en droit '44 Univ. of Brazil. PSYCH. TEACHER; STATISTICIAN, Dept. Nacional de Endemias Rurais, Ave. Pedro II, 283, São Cristovão, Rio de Janeiro. Member: BAAP, SIP, São Paulo Rorschach Socy. Teaching, applied psychology, testing; projective techniques, achievement and intelligence tests, social psychology. M

MARANHÃO, Dr. Odon Ramos. Rua São Carlos do Pinhal 485, apt. 36, São Paulo. b. 23 Mar 1924 São Paulo. MD '53 Univ. of São Paulo, Brazil. ASST. PROF. of FORENSIC MED, Univ. of São Paulo; PSYCHIATRIST, São Paulo Penitentiary. Member: São Paulo Psych. Socy, São Paulo Socy. of Legal Med. and Criminol. Forensic psychiatry, teaching, clinical practice; psychotherapy, criminal psychology and psychopathic personalities. M

MARCONDES, Prof. Dr. Durval Bellegarde. Rua Siqueira Campos 42, São Paulo. b. 27 Nov 1899 São Paulo. MD '25 Univ. of São Paulo, Brazil. DIRECTOR, Dept. of Student Mental Hygiene, Rua Epitácio Pessoa 57, São Paulo; PSYCHOANALYST, priv. prac; VIS. PROF. of CLIN. PSYCH, Univ. of São Paulo. Member: Brazilian Psychoanal. Socy, São Paulo Psych. Socy. Psychotherapy, administration, teaching; child guidance, psychosomatic medicine. M

MARTINELLI, Prof. Adolpho. Ave. da Liberdade 65, São Paulo. b. 31 Mar 1915 São Paulo. PH.B, Univ. of São Paulo, Brazil. LEGAL and RES. PSYCH'T, independent research. Member: São Paulo Psych. Socy. Legal practice, research, teaching; research on thinking, perception,

and intelligence, philosophic foundations of psychology. M

MARTINS, Dr. Joel. Domingos de Morais 1293, apt. 23, São Paulo. b. 27 Mar 1920 Santos. PH.D '53 Univ. of São Paulo, Brazil. ASST. PROF. of PSYCH, Univ. of São Paulo, Rua Maria Antonia, São Paulo. Member: BPA. Teaching, research; learning theory, theory construction, experiments in animal psychology, physiological psychology. M

MATTOS, Prof. Cecília Sincorá Orlandi. Rua Frei Vicente do Salvador 303, São Paulo. b. 3 May 1930 São Paulo. Lic. '52 Univ. of São Paulo, Brazil. PERSONNEL ADMIN, Dept. of Public Admin, Rua Florêncio de Abreu 848, andar 5, São Paulo. Member: São Paulo Psych. Socy. Administration, personnel selection, research; achievement, intelligence, personality and attitude tests. F

MEIRA, Prof. Luiz Antonio. Rua Riachuelo 731, Palegre. b. 9 June 1930 Porto Alegre. Cours Supérieur de Philos. '52 Catholic Univ. of Rio Grande do Sul, Brazil. PSYCHOLOGIST, Juvenile Court, Ave. Independencia 190, Porto Alegre. Analysis, psychotherapy and rehabilitation of juvenile delinquents, testing, guidance; projective techniques, psychology of child delinquency, psychological process of social readjustment. M

MENEZES, Mrs. Cinira Miranda de. Praia do Flamengo 172, apt. 2, Rio de Janeiro. b. 3 Oct 1915 Salvador. Superior grade '35 Univ. of the Fed. Dist, Brazil. CHIEF, Serv. of Psych. and Mental Disorders, Inst. of Educ. Res, Rua Almirante Barroso 81, andar 7, Rio de Janeiro. Member: BAAP. Consulting, guidance, testing, teaching; intelligence and personality tests, child psychotherapy. F

MIRA Y LOPEZ, Prof. Dr. Emilio. Rodolfo Dantas 16, apt. 603, Rio de Janeiro. b. 24 Oct 1896 Santiago, Cuba. Prof. '31 Univ. of Barcelona, Spain. DIRECTOR, Inst. de Seleção e Orientação Profissional (ISOP), Fundação Getúlio Vargas, Rua da Candelária 6, Rio de Janeiro; EDITOR, *Arquivos Brasileiros de Psicotecnica*. Member: APA, AIPA, BAAP, SIP, Amer. Psychiat. Assn. Research, teaching, applied psychology, professional writing; development of expressive techniques for study of personality, myokinetic psychodiagnosis, attitude measurement, mental hygiene. M

MONDEGO PORTO, Eglantina. Rua Pedroso de Alvarenga 1285, São Paulo. b. 3 Aug 1905 São Paulo. PSYCHOLOGIST, Ment. Hyg. Sect, Serv. of Student Hlth, Epitacio Pessoa 57, São Paulo. Member: São Paulo Psych. Socy. Testing, guidance, research;

intelligence tests, projective techniques, child psychotherapy. F

MORAES, Raul de. Dept. Estadual de Administração, Rua Florêncio de Abreu 848, andar 4, São Paulo. b. 4 Dec 1907 São Paulo. Lic. '34 Univ. of São Paulo, Brazil. DIR. of ORGANIZA. DIV, Dept. Estadual de Administração; RES. WRKR, Inst. of Admin, Univ. of São Paulo. Member: BPA, São Paulo Psych. Socy. Administration, industrial psychology, research on scientific management; measurement of aptitudes and personality traits, work conditions and efficiency. M

MORAES DE ANDRADE, Miss Eugênia. Rua Atlântica 694, São Paulo. b. 22 Mar 1911 Campanha. Lic. '37 Univ. of São Paulo, Brazil. DIRECTOR, Selection Div, Dept. of Public Admin, Florêncio de Abreu 848, andar 5, São Paulo. Member: São Paulo Psych. Socy, Brazilian Assn. for the Advanc. of Sci. Applied psychology, administration of personnel selection program, research; aptitude, achievement, intelligence and personality tests. F

MOREIRA, Maria Helena Mattoso. Rua Leopoldo Miguez 25, apt. 801, Rio de Janeiro. b. 24 Sept 1921 São Paulo. Lic. '42 Univ. of São Paulo, Brazil. GUIDANCE TECH, Inst. de Seleção e Orientação Profissional (ISOP), Rua da Candelária 6, andar 3, Rio de Janeiro. Member: BAAP. Applied and educational psychology, professional guidance; intelligence tests, guidance and counseling, psychology of adolescence. F

NAVA, Dr. José. 778 Rua Padre Rolim, Belo Horizonte. b. 4 Apr 1906 Juiz de Fóra. MD '36 Univ. of Minas Gerais, Brazil. DIRECTOR, Psychotech. Lab, Dept. Estadual de Trânsito, Ave. João Pinheiro 417, Belo Horizonte; TCHR. of APPL. PSYCH, Escola Superior de Educação Física. Member: BAAP. Applied psychology, testing, teaching; vocational guidance and psychodiagnosis. M

NEDER, Prof. Mathilde. Rua Peixoto Gomide 1830, apt. 31, São Paulo. b. 30 Nov 1923 São Paulo. Especialista '54 Catholic Univ. of São Paulo, Brazil. PSYCHOLOGIST, Psych. Clinic, Pestalozzi Socy. of São Paulo, Rua Luiz Coelho 103, São Paulo; STATE INSPECTOR, Normal Sch; TCHR. of PSYCH, Mackenzie Inst. Member: São Paulo Psych. Socy, Pestalozzi Socy. of São Paulo, Paulista Assn. of Psychiat. and Ment. Hyg. Testing and clinical analysis, clinical practice, guidance, psychotherapy; individual and group play therapy, projective techniques, attitude measurement, human relations. F

NÉRICI, Prof. Imideo Giuseppe. Ave. Macedo Soares 353, Campos de Jordão, São Paulo.

b. 15 Mar 1915 Lucca, Italy. Lic. '54 Univ. of Brazil. PROF. of EDUC. PSYCH, Fac. of Philos, Sci. and Arts, Univ. of the Fed. Dist, Haddock Lobo 269, Rio de Janeiro; EDITOR, Escola Nova. Teaching, administration, educational psychology; personality, psychology of adolescence, learning. M

NOVAES, Miss Maria Helena da Silva. Praia do Flamengo 392, andar 9, Rio de Janeiro. b. 13 July 1926 Rio de Janeiro. BA '46 Santa Ursula Univ, Brazil. PSYCHOLOGIST, Inst. de Seleção e Orientação Profissional (ISOP), Rua da Candelária 6, Rio de Janeiro. Member: BAAP. Counseling, testing, teaching; projective techniques, social perception, group dynamics, group psychotherapy, phenomenological psychology, existential analysis. F

OLIVEIRA, Prof. Esmeralda C. Rua Marques de S. Vicente 316, Gavea, Rio de Janeiro. b. 8 Dec 1912 Rio Branco. MA '41 Escola de Aperfeiçoamento, Brazil. TECH. ASST. in EDUC, Ministry of Justice, Rua Real Grandeza 255, Rio de Janeiro. Testing, educational psychology, research. F

OLIVEIRA, Mrs. María Alves Pinto de. Rua da Bahia 1265, apt. 510, Belo Horizonte. b. 21 Oct 1923 Martinho Campos. Social Assistant '49 Cath. Univ. of Minas Gerais, Brazil. SOC. ASST, Guid. and Sel. Cen. of Minas Gerais, Rua Pernambuco, Belo Horizonte; PSYCHOTECHNICIAN, Dept. Estadual de Trânsito, Ave. João Pinheiro, Belo Horizonte. Member: BAAP. Testing, research; projective techniques, vocational guidance. F

PAIS BARRETO, Prof. Annita. Rua do Cupim 37, Recife. b. 3 June 1907 Recife. Lic. '50 Univ. of Recife, Brazil. PROF. of EDUC. PSYCH, Escola de Belas Artes, Rua Benfica 50, Recife; PSYCHOLOGIST, Clínica de Conduta, Fac. of Philos. of Recife, Rua Conde da Boa Vista 921, Recife; DIRECTOR, Escola Ulisses Pernambucano. Teaching, consulting and guidance, testing, clinical analysis; projective techniques, intelligence tests, child and adolescent psychology. F

PAIVA MARCUCCI, Dr. Yolanda. Rua Cândido Espinheira 612, São Paulo. b. 21 Nov 1916 São Paulo. B.SC '39 Univ. of São Paulo, Brazil. TEACHER, Inst. of Educ. "Caetano de Campos," Praça da Republica 53, São Paulo. Member: São Paulo Psych. Socy. Educational psychology, teaching, guidance; psychology of adolescence, learning. F

PATERNOSTRO, Prof. José Novaes. Rua Riachuelo 275, andar 9, São Paulo. b. 16 Jan 1918 São Paulo. Bacharel '46 Univ. of São Paulo, Brazil. CHIEF, Personnel Selection Division, Estrada de Ferro

Sorocabana, Alameda Cleveland 20, São Paulo. Member: BAAP, São Paulo Psych. Socy, São Paulo Rorschach Socy. Applied, industrial psychology, teaching, testing; aptitude and intelligence tests, projective techniques, selection and vocational guidance processes. M

PENNA, Prof. Antonio Gomes. Inst. of Psych, Ave. Nilo Peçanha 155, andar 6, Rio de Janeiro. b. 13 May 1917 Rio de Janeiro. BA '48 Univ. of Brazil. ASST. PROF, Natl. Coll. of Philos, Univ. of Brazil; ASST. RES. WRKR, Inst. of Psych, Univ. of Brazil. Member: BPA. Teaching, professional writing, student, research; systems of psychology, social perception. M

PEREIRA, Ruth. Rua 18 de Outubro 78, Tijuca, Rio de Janeiro. b. 17 June 1913 Rio de Janeiro. Lic. '41 Univ. of Fed. Dist, Brazil. DIRECTOR, Inst. Brasileiro de Reeducação Motora, Rua Desembargador Isidro 89, Tijuca, Rio de Janeiro; SPEECH THERAPIST, Pestalozzi Socy. of Brazil. Member: BAAP. Guidance, teaching, testing, speech therapy; child psychology, therapy for cerebral palsy victims. F

PEREIRA DA SILVA, Prof. Estella Tinoco. Rua Lacerda Coutinho 46, Rio de Janeiro. b. 15 Dec 1905 Rio de Janeiro. Lic. '41 Univ. of Brazil. CHIEF, Setor de Orientação Pré-vocacional e Assistência Social (SOPVAS) Praça Floriano 55, andar 11, Rio de Janeiro. Member: BAAP. Consulting, guidance, testing, teaching, research; psychotechnics, tests of personality, manual aptitude and intelligence. F

PERESTRELLO, Dr. Mrs. Marialzira. Praia do Russel 694, andar 6, Rio de Janeiro. b. 5 Mar 1916 Rio de Janeiro. MD '39 Univ. of Brazil. PSYCHOANALYST. Member: Socy. of Psychiat, Neur. and Legal Med, Brazilian Socy. of Psychother, Argentine Psychoanal. Assn. Psychoanalysis, consulting, guidance, professional writing. F

PIMENTEL, Prof. Dr. Iago. Inst. Raul Soares, Belo Horizonte. b. 23 Mar 1890 São João del Rei. MD '12 Natl. Univ. of the Fed. Dist, Brazil. PROF. of PSYCH, Fac. of Economic Sci, Rua Curitiba 832, Belo Horizonte; PROF. of EDUC. PSYCH, Inst. of Educ. of Minas Gerais; PSYCHIATRIST, Inst. Raul Soares. Teaching individual and social psychology, educational psychology, tests, individual differences. M

PONTUAL, Prof. José da Silveira. Rua Aires Saldanha 72, apt. 101, Rio de Janeiro. b. 21 Aug 1908 Pernambuco. Bacharel '31 Univ. of Recife, Brazil. PROF. and GUID. SERV. DIR, Brazilian School of Pub. Admin, Fundação Getúlio Vargas, Praia de Botafogo 186, Rio de Janeiro. Member: AIPA, BAAP. Applied psychology, student,

guidance, testing, teaching; psychodiagnosis, personnel psychology, counseling. M

PONTUAL, Marcos. Rua São Luiz 1291, São Paulo. b. 17 Apr 1922 São Paulo. Lic. '46 Univ. of São Paulo, Brazil. ADMINISTRATOR, Comissão Brasileiro-Americana de Educação Industrial (CBAI), Rua Xavier de Toledo 280, andar 8, São Paulo; PROF. of COMPARATIVE PSYCH, Catholic Univ. of São Paulo. Member: BPA, São Paulo Psych. Socy. Administration of industrial training program, consulting, teaching; industrial psychology, training and personnel selection, guidance. M

POPPOVIC, Mrs. Ana Maria. Caixa Postal 3888, São Paulo. b. 22 Mar 1928 Rosario, Argentina. Lic. '49 Catholic Univ. of São Paulo, Brazil. PSYCHOLOGIST, Pestalozzi Socy. Clinic, Rua Luiz Coelho 103, São Paulo. Psychotherapy, clinical practice, play therapy, testing; projective techniques, use of drama in educational guidance. F

QUEIROZ, Prof. Carlos Sanchez. Ave. Atlantica 3916, apt. 1104, Rio de Janeiro. b. 31 July 1907 Rio de Janeiro. Docteur '32 Univ. of Brazil. PROFESSOR, Escola Nacional de Educação Física, Ave. Wenceslau Braz, Rio de Janeiro. Member: BPA. Teaching, research, educational psychology; memory and learning, attitude measurement. M

QUINTELA, Prof. Glória Fernandina. Fundação Getúlio Vargas, Rua da Candelária 6, andar 2, Rio de Janeiro. b. 30 May 1909 Juiz de Fora. PSYCHOLOGIST, Inst. de Seleção e Orientação Profissional (ISOP), Fundação Getúlio Vargas; DIRECTOR, Div. of Publications, Federal Senate. Member: BAAP. Applied psychology, testing, student, research; projective techniques. F

RABELLO, Prof. Sylvio. Rua José Clementino 34, Recife. b. 29 Nov 1899 Aliança. Bacharel, Univ. of Recife, Brazil. PROF. of PSYCH, Fac. of Philos. of Pernambuco, Rua Nunes Machado 42, Recife; DIRECTOR, Serviço Nacional de Aprendizagem Comercial (SENAC), Pernambuco. Teaching, applied psychology, professional writing; personality, perception, memory. M

RAINHO, Dr. Otacílio. Cen. for Appl. Psych, Rua Senador Dantas 118, andar 9, Rio de Janeiro. b. 5 Apr 1905 Niterói. MD '27 Univ. of Brazil. DIRECTOR, Dept. of Res, Cen. for Appl. Psych. (CEPA). Member: BPA. Applied psychology, testing, teaching; intelligence tests, projective techniques, attitude measurement. M

RIBEIRO, Athayde. Rua Humaitá 77, apt. 601, Rio de Janeiro. b. 30 Jan 1915 Uberlândia. Bacharel em Direito. LAWYER, Inst. de Aposentaduria e Pensões dos

Industriarios, Rua Marechal Câmara 310, Rio de Janeiro; CHIEF, Serviço de Emprêgo, Inst. de Seleção e Orientação Profissional (ISOP). Member: BAAP. Applied psychology, testing, administration professional writing; aptitude tests, projective and expressive techniques. M

RIBEIRO, Prof. Emília de Mello. Rua Lopo Gonçalves 278, Porto Alegre. b. 4 Sept 1913 Pelotas. Lic. '47 School of Philos, Porto Alegre, Brazil. DIRECTOR, Tech. Div, Secretariat of Educ. and Culture, Rua Sarmento Leite 425, Porto Alegre; PROF. of PSYCH, Fac. of Political Sci. and Economics, Univ. of Rio Grande do Sul. Member: BAAP, Psych. Socy. of Rio Grando de Sul. Psychotherapy, guidance, administration, teaching; dynamics of human adjustment, projective techniques, psychotherapy of behavior disorders in children and adolescents. F

RIBEIRO DA SILVA, Prof. Jason. Companhia Municipal de Transportes Coletivos, Rua Martins Fontes 230, andar 3, São Paulo. b. 3 Jan 1915 Salto. Superior '34 Univ. of São Paulo, Brazil. ASST. to the CHIEF, Personnel Dept, Companhia Municipal de Transportes Coletivos. Member: BAAP, São Paulo Psych. Socy. Administration, applied psychology, testing; study of personality, intelligence tests, learning theory. M

ROCHA, Prof. Gabriel Munhoz da. Rua Lamenha Lins 918, Curitiba. b. 18 Mar 1915 Curitiba. Bacharel em Direito '34 Univ. of Paraná, Brazil. PROF. of PSYCH, Fac. of Philos, Univ. of Paraná. Member: Paraná Psych. Socy. Teaching; general psychology, depth psychology. M

ROMANO BARRETO, Prof. Antenor. Rua Itajobi 80, São Paulo. b. 11 Apr 1893 São Paulo. Advogado, Univ. of São Paulo, Brazil. PROF. of SOCIOL, Escola Normal "N. D. de Sion," Ave. Higienopolis, São Paulo; LAWYER; EDITOR, Revista Sociologia. Member: São Paulo Psych. Socy, Socy. of Legal Med. and Criminol. Teaching, research, professional writing; panic, suggestion, group process. M

SÁ CARVALHO, Prof. Irinéa. Fundação Getúlio Vargas, Rua da Candelária 6, andar 2, Rio de Janeiro. b. 2 Dec. 1922 Mato Grosso. PSYCHOLOGIST, Inst. de Seleção e Orientação Profissional (ISOP), Fundação Getúlio Vargas. Member: BAAP, Brazilian Assn. for the Advanc. of Sci. Counseling, teaching, testing; rehabilitation and group process. F

SANTOS SOUTO, Maria do Carmo dos. Rua da Saudade 48, Recife. b. 14 July 1928 Recife. Lic. '50 Univ. of Recife, Brazil. PSYCHOLOGIST, Clínica de Conduta, Fac. of Philos. of Recife, Rua Conde da Boa Vista 921, Recife; PSYCHOTECHNICIAN, Escola Ulisses Pernambucano. Child psychotherapy, educational psychology, teaching, research, testing; projective techniques, achievement tests. F

SATACRUZ LIMA, Miss Maria. Fundação Getúlio Vargas, Rua da Candelária 6, Rio de Janeiro. b. 19 Nov 1898 Goiás. PSYCHOLOGIST, Fundação Getúlio Vargas. Member: BAAP. Testing, clinical analysis, teaching, research; learning theory, social perception, projective techniques. F

SCHEEFFER, Mrs. Ruth. Fundação Getúlio Vargas, Rua da Candelária 6, andar 2, Rio de Janeiro. b. 8 Apr 1923 Recife. MA '51 Columbia Univ, USA. PSYCHOLOGIST, Fundação Getúlio Vargas. Member: AIPA, BAAP. Counseling, guidance, clinical analysis, testing, teaching; projective techniques, psychotherapy, social psychology.F

SCHNEIDER, Prof. Eliezer. Inst. of Psych, Ave. Nilo Peçanha 155, andar 6, Rio de Janeiro. b. 18 Oct 1916 Rio de Janeiro. MA '47 Univ. of Iowa, USA. HEAD, Div. of Appl. Res, Inst. of Psych, Univ. of Brazil. Member: BPA, BAAP. Research in applied psychology and clinical analysis, testing for psychiatric diagnoses, teaching systematic and applied psychology; achievement tests, motivation and personality development. M

SEGUIN, Roger Gustave. Rua Constante Ramos 34, apt. 202, Rio de Janeiro. b. 28 Mar 1921 Paris, France. Lic. '49 Univ. of Paris, France. PSYCHOLOGIST, Natl. Serv. for Mental Illness, Ave. Pasteur 296, Rio de Janeiro; PSYCHOLOGIST, Sel. and Pers. Serv. of the Navy, Ave. Presidente Vargas 290, Rio de Janeiro; PROF. of PSYCH, Inst. of Appl. Psych, Catholic Univ. of Rio de Janeiro. Member: BAAP. Testing, clinical analysis, applied and industrial psychology, teaching; vocational guidance and selection, projective techniques, diagnosis. M

SILVA, Prof. Mario Geraldo. Escola Prática de Agricultura "Fernando Costa," Pirassununga. b. 19 Nov 1910 Sorocaba. Professor '30 Univ. of São Paulo, Brazil. DIR. of GUID, Escola Prática de Agricultura "Fernando Costa." Member: São Paulo Psych. Socy. Educational and vocational guidance, testing, applied psychology; learning theory, attitude measurement, psychotechnics. M

SILVEIRA, Prof. Dr. Aníbal. Marconi 53, andar 8, 808, São Paulo. b. 17 Mar 1902 São Roque. Lecturer '41 Univ. of São Paulo, Brazil; MD '30 Fac. of Med, Univ. of São Paulo, Brazil. VISITING PROF. of PSYCHOPATHOL. and PROJECTIVE TECHNIQUES, Univ. of São Paulo, Rua Maria Antonia 294, São Paulo; HEAD, Ment. Hyg.

Serv, São Paulo Dept. of Hlth; LECT. in PSYCHIAT, Fac. of Med, Univ. of São Paulo. Member: Amer. Orthopsychiat. Assn, Amer. Group Psychother. Assn, São Paulo Psych. Socy, São Paulo Rorschach Socy. Psychotherapy, family counseling, teaching projective techniques, genetic dynamics of mental symptoms and patterns. M

SILVEIRA, Paulo Guaracy. Dept. do Ensino Profissional, Rua Formosa 51, São Paulo. b. 14 Feb 1923 São Paulo. M.ED '56 Southern Methodist Univ, USA. EDUC. TECH, Dept. do Ensino Profissional. Member: BAAP, São Paulo Psych. Socy. School administration, educational psychology, guidance; counseling, industrial psychology. M

SOARES DOS ANJOS, Dr. Edgard. Rua México 21, andar 2, Rio de Janeiro. b. 24 Apr 1912 Caxias. MD '48 Univ. of Brazil. ASST. in PSYCHIAT, Inst. des Pensions Industriaires, Rua Henrique Valadares 147, Rio de Janeiro. Research, industrial psychology, psychotherapy; attitude measurement, intelligence tests. M

SOARES VAZ, Dr. Vasco. Ave. Sete de Setembro 288, Niterói. b. 18 Jan 1912 Astolfo Dutra. MD '35 Fluminense Fac. of Med, Brazil. PSYCHOPEDIATRICIAN, priv. prac, Rua Santa Luzia 799, Rio de Janeiro; CHIEF of CHILD GUID. SECT, Inst. de Seleção e Orientação Profissional (ISOP), Rua da Candelária 6, andar 2, Rio de Janeiro. Psychotherapy, research, teaching; juvenile delinquency, parapsychology. M

SOUZA, Francisco Pedro Estrazulas Pereira de. Andradas 1646, S. 61, Porto Alegre. b. 7 May 1927 São Gabriel. Lic. '50 Univ. of Rio Grande do Sul, Brazil. CLIN. PSYCH'T, Inst. Pedagógico, Rua Ipanema, s/n, Porto Alegre, and priv. prac; TCHR. of CLIN. PSYCH, Catholic Univ. of Porto Alegre. Member: APA, BPA, Psych. Socy. of Rio Grande do Sul. Guidance, psychotherapy, clinical analysis; projective techniques, play therapy, research on diagnosis and psychotherapy. M

SOUZA BITTENCOURT, Dr. Roberto de. Inst. of Psych, Univ. of Brazil, Ave. Nilo Peçanha 155, andar 6, Rio de Janeiro. b. 30 June 1927 Porto Alegre. MD '52 Univ. of Brazil. ASST. PROF, Fac. of Med. Sciences, Univ. of the Fed. Dist, Rua Fonseca Telles 121, Rio de Janeiro; RES. ASST. in PSYCH, Inst. of Psych, Univ. of Brazil. Teaching, clinical practice, research; clinical guidance, projective techniques, intelligence tests. M

TCHAICOVSKY, Prof. Fany Malin. Rua General Glicério 326, apt. 604, Rio de Janeiro. b. 20 Mar 1924 Rio de Janeiro. MA '45 Univ. of Brazil. CHIEF, Educ. and Vocat. Guid. Sect, Brazilian-Amer. Comm.

on Indus. Educ. (CBAI), Ave. Marechal Câmara 350, andar 8, Rio de Janeiro; EDITOR, Series of CBAI Guidance Bulletins. Member: BPA, BAAP, Natl. Vocat. Guid. Assn. Research, administration, teaching, planning guidance service programs and training programs for guidance counselors; aptitude and achievement tests, group process, case study techniques. F

TOMCHINSKY, Dr. Roberto. Rua Valerio Giuli 12, São Paulo. b. 1 Apr 1922 São Paulo. MD '49 Fac. of Med. of São Paulo, Brazil. PSYCHIATRIST, Hosp. de Juqueri, Franco da Rocha, São Paulo. Member: São Paulo Psych. Socy, São Paulo Rorschach Socy, Paulista Med. Assn. Clinical practice, psychotherapy, clinical analysis; projective techniques, psychiatry. M

TRENCH, Prof. Guaraciaba. Rua Conde de Irajá 166, São Paulo. b. 30 June 1898 Avaré. Diploma, Escola Normal. PSYCHOLOGIST, Companhia Municipal de Transportes Colectivos de São Paulo, Ave. Brigadeiro Luiz Antonio 1367, São Paulo. Member: BAAP, São Paulo Psych. Socy. Applied, educational and industrial psychology, testing, personnel selection and training; learning theory, projective techniques, aptitude measurement. M

VEIT, Dr. Robert. Rua José Maria Lisboa 860, São Paulo. b. 10 Mar 1896 Offenburg, Germany. MD '22 Univ. of Freiburg, Germany. PSYCHOTHERAPIST. Member: São Paulo Psych. Socy. Psychotherapy, clinical analysis, applied psychology; use of graphology and the Rorschach test in psychopathology. M

VELLOSO, Miss Elisa Dias. Juvenile Guid. Cen, Ave. Rui Barbosa 716, andar 3, Rio de Janeiro. b. 16 Feb 1912 Belo Horizonte. CHIEF, Juvenile Guid. Cen, Brazilian Children's Bureau. Member: BAAP, WFMH, Brazilian Educ. Assn. Testing, clinical analysis, child guidance, consulting, psychotherapy; intelligence tests, projective techniques, child behavior and the nature-nurture problem. F

VIEIRA DA CUNHA, Mrs. Raquel. Rua Dr. Vila Nova 268, São Paulo. b. 18 Jan 1918 Berlin, Germany. MA '45 Univ. of Chicago, USA. CO-DIRECTOR, Vocat. Guid. Cen, Inst. de Organização Racional do Trabalho (IDORT), Praça Dom José Gaspar 30, andar 10, São Paulo. Member: APA, São Paulo Psych. Socy. Diagnostic testing, counseling, group work; human development and child psychology, group process, projective techniques. F

VILLALVA DE ARAUJO, Prof. Zenaide. Rua das Rosas 139, Vila Mariana, São Paulo. b. 14 Dec 1912 São Paulo. Diplome, Univ. of São Paulo, Brazil. DIRECTOR, Psychopedagogical Lab, Inst. Feminino de

Educação "Padre Anchieta," Rua Visconde de Abaeté 154, São Paulo. Member: São Paulo Psych. Socy. Educational psychology, teaching, psychotherapy; learning, personality, projective and other tests. F

VILLAS-BÓAS, Miss Maria Constança Calmon. Rua Princesa Isabel 84, apt. 101, Salvador. b. 15 Feb 1934 Salvador. BA '54 Univ. of Bahia, Brazil. PSYCHOLOGIST, Psychiat. Clin, Hosp. das Clinicas, Sch. of Med, Univ. of Bahia. Member: BAAP. Testing, clinical guidance, applied psychology, student; projective techniques, social perception, aptitude measurement, psychotherapeutic techniques. F

VILLEMOR AMARAL, Fernando de. Rua 7 de Abril 404, São Paulo. b. 13 July 1920 Rio de Janeiro. CLIN. PSYCH'T, Psych. Clinic, Pestalozzi Socy. of São Paulo, Rua Luiz Coelho 103, São Paulo. Member: BAAP, Groupement Français du Rorschach, São Paulo Rorschach Socy, São Paulo Psych. Socy. Testing, clinical analysis, consulting, guidance, psychotherapy; projective techniques, intelligence tests, educational guidance. M

VITA, Prof. Luis Washington. Rua Francisco J. Azevedo 133, São Paulo. b. 23 Mar 1921 São Paulo. Lic, Univ. of São Paulo, Brazil. PROF. of PSYCH, Colégio Estadual Brasílio Machado, Rua D. Júlia 37, São Paulo; BIBLIOGRAPHIC RES. WRKR, Secção de Filosofia, Biblioteca Municipal de São Paulo; BIBLIOGRAPHIC ED, *Revista Brasileira*

de Filosofia. Member: Paulista Psych. Socy. Teaching, editorial, library; social perception, group process, psychology of esthetics. M

WEIL, Prof. Pierre Gilles. Rua Emilio Berla 118, apt. 202, Rio de Janeiro. b. 16 Apr 1924 Strasbourg, France. Diplôme '46 Univ. of Lyon, France. CHIEF, Educ. and Profes. Guid. Sect, Serviço Nacional de Aprendizagem Comercial (SENAC), Rua da Candelária 9, andar 8, Rio de Janeiro. Member: BAAP, AIPA. Research, teaching, applied psychology, testing; intelligence tests, projective and personality tests, human relations. M

YAHN, Dr. Mário. Instituto Aché, Ave. Lacerda Franco 527, São Paulo. b. 4 July 1908 Campinas. MD '32 Univ. of São Paulo, Brazil. DIRECTOR, Inst. Aché; PSYCHIATRIC CONSULT. in PUBLIC HEALTH, Public Health Centers, São Paulo. Member: Brazilian Socy. of Psychoanal, São Paulo Psych. Socy, Socy. of Mental Hygiene and Child Psychiat. Psychotherapy, consulting, clinical practice, administration; group process, psychoanalysis, social psychology, individual psychotherapy. M

ZAUSMER, Mrs. Anny. Caixa Postal 755, São Paulo. b. 8 Dec 1902 Vienna, Austria. VOLUNTEER WRKR, Serviço de Assistencia dos Menores do Estado, Ave. Celso Garcia 2231, São Paulo. Member: São Paulo Psych. Socy. Guidance and research with juvenile delinquents; projective techniques, research on drawing tests. F

BRITISH WEST INDIES

BEDELL, Dr. Benjamin John. 7 Third Ave, Cascade, St. Anns, Port-of-Spain, Trinidad. b. 31 Jan 1899 Bristol, Eng. PH.D '50 Univ. of Edinburgh, Scot. EDUCATION OFFICER Port-of-Spain, Trinidad. Member: BPS. Teaching, research; mental testing, factor analysis. M

BISSESSAR, Miss Elodie Sarah. 23 Taylor St, Woodbrook, Port-of-Spain, Trinidad. b. 30 Mar 1912 Claxton Bay, Trinidad. BA '42 Mount Allison Univ, Canada, ED.B '46 Univ. of Edinburgh, Scot. EDUC. OFF. and LECT. in PSYCH, Govt. Teachter Training Coll, 105 Saint Vincent St, Port-of-Spain. Teaching, educational psychology, testing; learning theory, mental tests, social perception. F

MANLEY, Douglas Ralph. 48 College Common, Univ. Coll. of the West Indies, Mona P.O, Jamaica. b. 30 May 1923 London, Eng. MA '51 Univ. of London, Eng. LECTURER, Dept. of Educ, Univ. Coll. of the West Indies. Teaching, research; mental testing, migration. M

MEREDITH, Mrs. Ruby Wilhelmina. Shortwood College, Constant Spring, Jamaica. b. 19 July 1897 Jamaica. BS '29 Teachers Coll, Columbia Univ, USA; Diploma, Univ. of London, Eng. PRINCIPAL, Shortwood Training Coll; EDUC. CONSULT, Secondary and Vocat. Schools, Dept. of Educ. Administration, testing, teaching; child psychology. F

PEGGS, Dr. A. Deans. Government High School, Nassau, Bahamas. b. 16 Dec 1915 Ashington, Eng. PH.D '51 Univ. of Edinburgh, Scot. HEAD MASTER, Govt. High School. Member: BPS, Natl. Inst. of Indus. Psych, Royal Stat. Socy. Administration, teaching, research; aptitude and achievement tests. M

WALTERS, Dr. Elsie Hopkins. Univ. Coll. of the West Indies, Mona, St. Andrew, Jamaica. b. 16 Nov 1894 London, Eng. PH.D '29 Univ. of London, Eng. SR. LECT, Cen. for the Study of Educ, Univ. Coll. of the West Indies. Member: BPS. Research, teaching, educational psychology, consulting. F

UNION OF BURMA

BU, Prof. Dr. Hla. Univ. of Rangoon, Rangoon. b. 21 Apr 1897 Padigon. PH.D '34 Univ. of London, Eng. PROF. and DIR, Psychology Lab, Univ. of Rangoon. Member: BPS. Teaching, administration, translating and editing psychological books and articles; intelligence testing, projective techniques. **M**

CHAN, Miss Kathleen. 23 Ady Road, Rangoon. b. 14 June 1929 Rangoon.

MA '55 Bryn Mawr Coll, USA. STUDENT, Pennsylvania State Univ, USA. Conceptual processes, learning, motivation and emotion. **F**

TU, U Sein. Dept. of Psych, Univ. of Rangoon, Rangoon. b. 4 June 1929 Maymyo. MA '52 Columbia Univ, USA. ASST. LECT, Univ. of Rangoon. Teaching, research, testing; personality testing, attitude measurement, methodology. **M**

CAMEROUN (FRENCH)

STOERCKEL, Paul Charles. P.O. Box 4, Douala. b. 6 Sept 1909 Paris, Fr. Conseiller '42 Inst. Natl. d'Orientation Professionnelle, Paris Fr. HEAD, Psych. Serv. for Profes. Guid. and Selectn, Cameroun.

Member: AIPA, APPD, Groupement Français du Rorschach. Consulting, guidance, testing, applied psychology, administration; morphopsychology, study of group aptitudes and geographical environment. **M**

CANADA

ABRAHAM, Nelson William. 2842 Robinson St, Regina, Sask. b. 7 Feb 1916 Indore, Madhya-Bharat, India. MA '44 Nagpur Univ, India. DIR. of PERS, Dept. of Mineral Resources, Govt, Admin. Bldg, Regina. Member: CPA, Can. Ment. Hlth. Assn. Administration, personnel testing, selection and training, teaching; retarded children, psychotherapy, projective techniques, group process. **M**

AGNEW, John Neil McKinnon. Dept. of Psych, Univ. of Toronto, Toronto 5, Ont. b. 4 Apr 1924 Weyburn. MA '50 Univ. of Toronto, Can. INSTRUCTOR, Univ. of Toronto. Member: APA. Teaching, research, student; clinical research, evaluation of therapy and experimental psychopathohology, learning theory, social perception. **M**

AHARAN, Charles H. Alcoholism Res. Found, 287 Queens Ave, London, Ont. b. 19 Apr 1923 Moncton. MA '52 Univ. of Western Ontario, Can. EXEC. SECY, Alcoholism Res. Found. Member: CPA. Psychotherapy, administration, clinical analysis; psychology of addictions. **M**

ALDERDICE, Dr. Ernest Terence. Ont. Hosp, 999 Queen St. W, Toronto, Ont. b. 11 Nov 1924 Vancouver. PH.D '55 Univ. of Toronto, Can. SR. PSYCH'T, Ont. Hosp; TCHNG. FELLOW, Dept. of Psych, Univ. of Toronto. Member: CPA, APA. Testing, clinical analysis, research, administration, teaching; perception, personality theory, learning theory. **M**

ALDRIDGE, Athelstan Arnold. 11622-88 St Edmonton Alta. b. 26 Aug 1902 Fort Sask.

ED.M '53 Oregon State Univ, USA. SUPERV. of GUID, Alta. Dept. of Educ, Edmonton. Member: Amer. Pers. and Guid. Assn, Amer. Sch. Counselors Assn, Natl. Vocat. Guid. Assn, Int. Counc. for Except. Child. Guidance, consulting, testing, educational psychology; intelligence and achievement testing, preparation of occupational information. **M**

ALLEN, Miss Barbara Mary. Apt. 221, 3787 Côte des Neiges Rd, Montreal, P.Q. b. 7 Jan 1925 Montreal. MA '48 Teachers Coll, Columbia Univ, USA. CLIN. PSYCH'T, Allan Memor. Inst. of Psychiat, 1025 Pine Ave. W, Montreal. Member: CPA, APA, SPT, ICWP. Testing, consulting, clinical analysis, teaching; personality theory, projective techniques, intelligence measurements applied to psychiatric syndromes. **F**

ANDREWS, Mrs. Eva. 43 Meadowland Dr, Brampton, Ont. b. 8 May 1928 Toronto. MA '51 Univ. of Toronto, Can. Member: Ont. Psych. Assn. Consulting, research; child guidance, mental health, research on childhood schizophrenia. **F**

APRIL, Regis. Med. Soc. Cen. for Children, Inc, 565 St. Jean St, Que. b. Rivière du Loup. L.PS '55 Univ. of Montreal, Can. CLIN. PSYCH'T, Med. Soc. Cn. for Children, Inc. Member: Que. Assn. of Psych'ts. Diagnostic testing and analysis, psychotherapy, consulting; projective techniques, child psychotherapy, play therapy. **M**

AUCLAIR, Gilles A. 433 Vine St, W. LaFayette, Indiana, USA. b. 12 Apr 1930 Fall River, Massachusetts, USA. L.PS '54 Univ. of Montreal, Can. STUDENT, Purdue

Univ, USA. Member: CPA. Industrial psychology, research; attitude measurement, group dynamics, test construction in the veld of industrial psychology. M

AULT, Dr. Orvill E. 643 Echo Dr, Ottawa. b. 17 Dec 1899 Ottawa. PH.D '35 Univ. of Edinburg, Scot. DIR. of PLANNING and DEVEL, Civil Serv. Comm, Bank St, Ottawa; ED. COMM, *Public Personnel Review*. Member: CPA. Administration, personnel selection methods, staff training; group process, personality measurement, projective techniques, test development. M

AUSTIN, Miss Nancy Marie. 3528 Lorne Ave, Apt. 7, Montreal, P.Q. b. 18 Oct 1928 Toronto. BA '51 Univ. of Toronto, Can. TRAINER, Assn. for Help to Retarded Children, 630 Dorchester St. W, Montreal. Member: CPA. Teaching and training retarded children, research, student. F

AYERS, Dr. John Douglas. Can. Teacher's Fed, 444 Maclaren St, Ottawa 4, Ont. b. 30 Oct 1917 Redvers. PH.D '51 Univ. of Toronto, Can. RES. DIR, Can. Teacher's Fed; TCHR. of PSYCH, Carleton Coll, Ottawa. Member: CPA, APA. Applied, educational psychology, research, professional writing; measurement, applications of research. M

BABARIK, Paul. 831 Mary St, Oshawa, Ont. b. 30 June 1929 Oshawa. MA '53 Univ. of Toronto, Can. SUPERVISOR, Pers. Eval. and Deval, Genl. Motors of Can, Oshawa. Member: APA, Ont. Psych. Assn. Industrial psychology, testing, administration; interpersonal relations, human development, personality analysis. M

BAKER, Dr. Chester Hamilton. Def. Res. Med. Labs, Box 62, Postal Sta. K, Toronto, Ont. b. 13 May 1919 Victoria. PH.D '51 Univ. of Toronto, Can. RES. SCI, Med. Res. Counc. of Great Britain, Appl. Psych. Res. Unit, 15 Chaucer Rd, Cambridge, Eng. Member: CPA, APA, Exper. Psych. Grp. of Great Britain. Research; psycho-physiology of vision, visual presentation of information, human engineering. M

BAKER, Miss Nancy L. Sunnybrook Hosp, Toronto. b. 31 Dec 1927 Toronto. MA '53 Univ. of Toronto, Can. CLIN. PSYCH'T, Sunnybrook Hosp. Member: CPA. Testing, psychotherapy; projective techniques. F

BAMPTON, Miss Virginia Fox. Youth Couns. Serv. for British Columbia, 955 Burrard St, Vancouver 1. b. 12 Nov 1925 Seattle, Washington, USA. BA '47 Univ. of British Columbia, Can. PSYCHOMET. and SECY, Youth Couns. Serv. for B.C. Member: B.C. Psych. Assn. Administration and scoring of tests for vocational guidance purposes. F

BARBEAU, Dr. Gérard L. 10554 Chambord, Montreal. b. 8 Nov 1920 Montreal. PH.D '46 Univ. of Montreal, Can. DIR. of SPEC. EDUC, Comm. of Catholic Schools, 117-0 St.

Catharine, Montreal; PROF. AGRÉGÉ, Univ. of Montreal. Member: Amer. Assn. for Ment. Defic, Psych. Assn. of P.Q. Applied and educational psychology, research, teaching; special education, intelligence testing, vocational guidance. M

BARROWS, Dr. Gordon Arthur. Can. Bank of Commerce, 25 King St. W, Toronto, Ont. b. 3 May 1916 Rochester, New York, USA. PH.D '52 Western Reserve Univ, USA. CHIEF PSYCH'T, Pers. Eval. Sect, Can. Bank of Commerce. Member: CPA, APA. Personnel psychology, testing, administration; vocational guidance, personnel administration. M

BARRY, William Frederick. 7503 Sherbrooke St. W, Apt. 14, Montreal, P.Q. b. 21 May 1928 Montreal. BA '51 Loyola Coll, Can. INTERNE in PSYCH, Ontario Hosp, Kingston, Ont. Member: CPA. Clinical analysis, research, guidance, student; projective techniques, psychoanalysis, play therapy, psychodrama. M

BATES, Alphonsus James. 1815 College St, Ville St. Laurent, Montreal, P.Q. b. 25 Apr 1922 New Waterford. MA '47 Columbia Univ, USA. RES. SUPERV, Can. Natl. Railways, 355 McGill St, Montreal. Member: CPA. Personnel psychology, administration, research; vocational guidance, achievement tests, attitude measurement. M

BATES, Dr. F. Lester. Sask. Trng. Sch, Moose Jaw, Sask. b. 31 Dec 1909 Loveland, Colorado, USA. ED.D '47 Univ. of California, USA. DIR. of TRNG, Sask. Trng. Sch. Member: Sask. Psych. Assn. Administration, applied and educational psychology, teaching; learning, achievement tests, mental deficiency. M

BEACH, Dr. Horace D. 28 Raleigh St, St. John's, Newf. b. 12 Mar 1919 Ernfold. PH.D '55 Mc Gill Univ, Can. CLIN. PSYCH'T, Hosp. for Ment. and Nerv. Diseases, Waterford Rd, St. John's. Member: CPA, APA. Testing, clinical analysis, research, teaching; learning, personality, intelligence and personality tests. M

BEAUCHEMIN, C. H. Guy. 3245 W. Gouin Blvd, Montreal 9, P.Q. b. 16 Apr 1923 Montreal. L.PS '45 Univ. of Montreal, Can. PERS. TECH, City of Montreal, Hotel De Ville. Member: Psych. Assn. of P.Q. Applied and personnel psychology, teaching; use of aptitude and achievement tests for personnel selection. M

BEAUCHEMIN, Mrs. Françoise. 10793 Esplanade, Montreal 12, P.Q. b. 23 Sept 1923 Montreal. L.PS '48 Univ. of Montreal, Can. CLIN. PSYCH'T, priv. prac. Member: Psych. Assn. of P.Q. Clinical practice, consulting, psychotherapy, testing; projective techniques, guidance. F

BEAUCHEMIN, Jean M. 10793 Esplanade, Montreal 12, P.Q. b. 2 July 1920 Trois Pistoles. L.PS '48 Univ. of Montreal, Can. RES. DIR, Féd. de Collèges Classiques, 625 Ste Croix Blvd, Ville St. Laurent, Montreal; CONSULT. PSYCH'T, Child Guid. and Vocat. Guid. Clin. Member: CPA, SPT, Amer. Cath. Psych. Assn. Research in educational psychology, guidance, consulting, testing; projective techniques, nondirective psychotherapy, vocational psychology. M

BEAUDRY, Prof. Gérard. 5982 Mount St. Michel, Montreal 36, P.Q. b. 13 Dec 1909 Montreal. Licence '38 Univ. of Montreal, Can. PROF. of MATH, Jacques Cartier Normal· Sch, 1301 Sherbrooke St. E, Montreal; ED. CONSULT, Publications of Cen. of Educ. Psych. Member: CPA. Teaching, professional writing, editorial; causes of deficiency in mathematics.M

BEAUDRY, Philippe E. 184 Osgoode St, Ottawa 2, Ont. b. 24 Apr 1929 Aylmer. B.SC '53 Univ. of Ottawa, Can. CHILD PSYCH'T, Ottawa Genl. Hosp, Bruyère St. Member: CPA. Testing, clinical analysis, play therapy; testing the brain injured child, projective techniques with children.M

BÉCHARD-DESLANDES, Dr. Monique. 4207 Marquette St, Montreal, P.Q. b. 7 Nov 1922 Sault-au-Récollet. D.PS '47 Univ. of Montreal, Can. Member: CPA. Applied and educational psychology, professional writing; child and adolescent psychology, parent-child relationship, psychology of women. F

BÉLANGER, David. 5609 Westminster Ave, Ville Côte, St. Luc, Montreal 29. b. 4 June 1921 St. Fabien. L.PS '50 Univ. of Montreal, Can. ASSOC. PROF. Inst. of Psych, Univ. of Montreal. Member: CPA, APA. Teaching, research, administration; motor, thought and verbal responses, perceptual processes. M

BELL, Robert John Rice. 350 Broadway Ave, Toronto 12, Ont. b. 27 Nov 1914 Toronto. MA '44 Univ. of Toronto, Can. SUPERV. of LABOR RELATIONS, Imperial Oil Ltd, 56 Church St, Toronto. Member: CPA. Industrial psychology; personnel practices, labor relations. M

BELL, Stanley Edward. Ontario Hosp, Kingston, Ont. b. 23 July 1929 Smiths Falls. MA '55 Univ. of Toronto, Can. PSYCHOLOGIST, Ont. Hosp. Member: Ont. Psych. Assn. Testing, interviewing, guidance, research; projective techniques, psychotherapy, attitude measurement. M

BELYEA, Prof. Edwin Stephens Waycott. Dept. of Philos. and Psych, Univ. of British Columbia, Vancouver 8. b. 29 May 1917 Fredericton. MA '41 Univ. of Toronto, Can. ASSOC. PROF. of PSYCH, Univ. of B.C; PERS.

CONSULT, Royal Can. Navy; CONSULT. ED, *Canadian Journal of Psychology*. Member: CPA, APA, BPS. Teaching, educational and personnel psychology; industrial selection techniques, small group interaction, preschool development and education. M

BERGERON, Côme. 142 Notre Dame E, Box 235 Victoriaville, P.Q. b. 30 Dec 1931 Drummondville. B.PS '55 Univ. of Ottawa, Can. DIR. and SOC. WRKR, Victoriaville Off, Soc. Serv. Diocese, 29 St. Augustin St, Victoriaville. Member: CPA. Applied psychology, testing, consulting, guidance; feebleminded children, characteristics of neurosis. M

BERMAN, Miss Isadora. Jewish Vocat. Serv, 493 Sherbrooke St. W, Montreal, P.Q. b. 21 May 1923 New York City, USA. MA '46 Tchrs. Coll, Columbia Univ, USA. SUPERVISOR, Couns. Dept, Jewish Vocat. Serv. Member: APA, Psych. Assn. of P.Q. Training counselors, vocational and educational guidance, testing; perception, learning theory, attitude formation. F

BERNHARDT, Prof. Karl S. Dept. of Psych, Univ. of Toronto, Toronto 5. b. 14 Oct 1901 Toronto. PH.D '33 Univ. of Chicago, USA. PROFESSOR, Univ. of Toronto; ASST. DIR, Inst. of Child Study, Univ. of Toronto; EDITOR, *Bulletin of the Institute of Child Study*. Member: CPA, APA, Amer. Pers. and Guid. Assn. Teaching, administration, editorial, research; learning, teaching methods, developmental psychology. M

BERRY, Raymond Grant. Civic Hosp, Peterborough, Ont. b. 15 May 1925 Oshawa. MA '52 Univ. of Western Ontario Can. PSYCHOLOGIST, Dept. of Health, Parliament Bldgs, Toronto. Member: CPA. Testing, psychotherapy, research; attitude measurement, color perception. M

BETTSCHEN, Miss Virginia. Prince Albert Hlth. Region, Prince Albert, Sask. b. 5 Mar 1907 Regina. BA '48, B.ED '49 Univ. of Saskatchewan, Can. TCHR. PSYCH'T, Prince Albert Hlth. Region. Member: Sask. Psych. Assn. Teacher training in mental health, educational consulting, testing; special education, grading systems, remedial teaching. F

BINDRA, Dr. Dalbir. Dept. of Psych, McGill Univ, Montreal 2, P.Q. b. 11 June 1922 Rawalpindi, Pakistan. PH.D '48 Harvard Univ, USA. ASSOC. PROF, McGill Univ. Member: APA, CPA. Teaching, research, professional writing; motivation, personality and contemporary psychological theory. M

BISHOP, John Scott. Provincial Hosp, P.O. Drawer 20, Lancaster, N.B. b. 7 Dec 1931 Fredericton. MA '56 Delhousie Univ, Can. CLIN. PSYCH'T, Dept. of Hlth. and Soc. Serv, Province of N.B, Fredericton. Member:

CPA. Testing, clinical analysis, psychotherapy, projective techniques, abnormal psychology, vocational counseling. M

BLACK, James Elmo Lennox. 1 Prince Albert, Ottawa Ont. b. 2 Apr 1902 Sintaluta. MA '37 Univ. of Chicago, USA. CONSULT. PSYCH'T, Civil Serv. Health Div, Dept. of Health and Welf, Ottawa. Member: CPA. Consulting, testing, clinical analysis, applied psychology; learning theory, achievement tests, attitude measurement, personnel selection. M

BLACK, Wallace William. Box 481, Weyburn, Sask. b. 26 Oct 1909 Gull Lake. B.ED '40 Univ. of Saskatchewan, Can. TCHR. PSYCH'T, Dept. of Pub. Health, Province of Sask, Regina. Member: Sask. Psych. Assn. Educational consulting, guidance, teacher training in mental health, testing; attitude measurement, educational guidance and counseling. M

BLACKBURN, Dr. Julian Murray. Queen's Univ, Kingston, Ont. b. 5 Dec 1903 Hove, Eng. PH.D '33 Univ. of Cambridge, Eng. HEAD, Dept. of Psych, Queen's Univ; ED. BD, *Canadian Journal of Psychology.* Member: CPA, BPS. Teaching, administration, research; inter-ethnic relations in Canada, experience factor and role perception in old age, personality constellations of alcoholics. M

BLACKWELL, Dr. Harold Neil. Ontario Hosp, London, Ont. b. 25 Mar 1924 London. PH.D '55 Univ. of Toronto, Can. SR. PSYCH'T, London Area, Ont. Hosp. Serv. Member: Ont. Psych. Assn. Testing, research, psychotherapy teaching; projective techniques, empathy and communication, learning theory. M

BLAIR, Lt. Col. William Robert Nelson. 462 Melbourne Ave, Ottawa, Ont. b. 22 Mar 1915 Millbank. MA '49 Univ. of Alberta, Can. DIRECTOR, Pers. Sel. Serv, Can. Army, Dept. of Natl. Def, Ottawa. Member: CPA. Administration, personnel psychology, research; military delinquency, measurement of abilities and attitudes. M

BLATZ, Prof. William E. Univ. of Toronto, 45 Walmer Rd, Toronto. b. 30 June 1895 Hamilton. PH.D '24 Univ. of Chicago, USA; MB '21 Univ. of Toronto, Can. PROF. of PSYCH, Univ. of Toronto; DIRECTOR, Inst. of Child Study, Univ. of Toronto; ASSOCIATE, Toronto Psychiat. Hosp. Member: CPA, APA, Can. Psychiat. Assn, Natl. Assn. of Nursery Educ. (USA). Research, teaching, consulting; marital relations, measurement of security in children, ideational development in children. M

BLEWETT, Dr. Duncan Bassett. Munroe Wing, Genl. Hosp, Regina, Sask. b. 28 Oct 1920 Edmonton. PH.D '53 Univ. of London, Eng. SUPERVISING PSYCH'T, Psychiat.

Serv. Br, Dept. of Pub. Health, Provincial Health Bldg, Regina. Member: CPA. Research, consulting, clinical testing and diagnosis; intelligence, mental disorders, projective techniques. M

BLOOM, Gerald Moyse. Psych. Dept, Ontario Hosp. Sch, Smiths Falls, Ont. b. 8 May 1929 Montreal. MA '54 Univ. of Toronto, Can. PSYCHOLOGIST, Ont. Hosp. Sch. Member: CPA. Testing, educational and vocational guidance and training of mental defectives, psychotherapy; physiological stigmata in mental deficiency, psychological effects of stress. M

BOCK, John Carson. Dept. of Veterans Affairs, Lancaster Hosp, Prince St, Lancaster, N.B. b. 25 Sept 1925 Spring Bay. MA '49 Univ. of Toronto, Can. PSYCHOLOGIST, Dept. of Vets. Affairs, Lancaster Hosp. Testing, psychotherapy, research; projective techniques, group dynamics and group process, measurement of deterioration in organic processes. M

BOIS, Dr. J. Samuel. Bois and Howard, 1509 Sherbrooke W, Montreal 25, P.Q. b. 21 Apr 1892 Stratford Cen. PH.D '36 McGill Univ, Can. INDUS. PSYCH'T, Bois and Howard. Member: CPA, APA. Industrial and management consulting, administration; social perception, group process, communication. M

BOISVERT, Dr. Marcel. 400 Ave. Outremont, Montreal, P.Q. b. 13 Dec 1922 La Sarre. MD '55 McGill Univ, Can. CHILD PSYCHIATRIST, Montreal Children's Hosp, 2337 Dorchester W, Montreal; CONSULTANT, Sacred Heart Hosp, Cartierville; ASSISTANT, Inst. of Psychother, Montreal. Member: Assn. of Psychiatrists of P.Q. Research, psychotherapy, consulting; projective techniques, attitude measurement, interpersonal relations. M

BOND, Lt. James Manson. H.M.C.S. Tecumseh, Calgary, Alta. b. 11 May 1926 Regina. BA '50 Univ. of Alberta, Can. STAFF. OFF, Royal Can. Navy, Natl. Def. Hq, Ottawa, Ont. Member: CPA. Administration, personnel selection; placement and personnel problems. M

BOULANGER, Prof. Jean Baptiste. 4050 Chemin de la Côte Ste. Catharine, Montreal 26, P.Q. b. 24 Aug 1922 Edmonton. MD '48 Univ. of Montreal, Can. ASST. PROF. of PSYCHIAT, Fac. of Med, Univ. of Montreal; PSYCHIATRIST and NEUROLOGIST, Notre Dame Hosp; PSYCHOANALYST, priv. prac; MED. DIR, Coll. of St. Denis; ED. ASST, *Canadian Medical Association Journal.* Member: SFP, Psych. Assn. of P.Q, Int. Rorschach Socy, Can. Psychoanal. Socy, Can. Psychiat. Assn. Psychoanalysis, teaching, consulting, clinical practice; social psychology, projective techniques. M

BOULARD, Hugh Marcel. 8280 Chambord St, Montreal 35, P.Q. b. 29 Sept 1914 Montreal. Orienteur '44 Univ. of Montreal, Can. SCH. INSPECTOR, Dept. of Pub. Instr, Govt. of P.Q. Member: CPA. Administration, educational and personnel psychology, teaching; aptitude and achievement tests. M

BOURDEAU, Guy. 4680 Notre Dame E, Montreal, P.Q. b. 7 Oct 1922 Lachine. Licence '49 Univ. of Montreal, Can. DIR. and PSYCH'T, Vocat. Guid. Bur, Bur. d'Orientation de l'Aide à la Jeunesse, 35 Notre Dame W; COUNSELOR, priv. prac. Member: CPA. Administration, guidance, consulting research; aptitude tests, selection of students for technical schools. M

BOVARD, Jr. Dr. Everett Warner. Dept. of Psych, Univ. of Toronto, Toronto 5, Ont. b. 11 Nov 1916 Port Chester, New York, USA. PH.D '49 Univ. of Michigan, USA. ASSOC. PROF, Univ. of Toronto; RES. CONSULT, Natl. Film Bd. of Can. Member: CPA, APA. Research, teaching; interpersonal relations, neurophysiology, research methodology. M

BOYD, John Baldwin. R.R. 1, Highland Creek, Ont. b. 29 Apr 1907 Kutien, China. MA '32 Univ. of Toronto, Can. PERS. RES. SUPERV, Hydro Elec. Power Comm. of Ont, 620 Univ. Ave, Toronto. Member: CPA. Research, industrial psychology; personnel selection, work-man adaptation, development methods. M

BRACHMAN, Howard Melvin. Ste. 17 Stadacona Apts, Moose Jaw, Sask. b. 2 Aug 1925 Swift Current. MA '52 Univ. of Manitoba, Can. PSYCHOLOGIST, Sask. Trng. Sch, Moose Jaw. Member: Sask. Psych. Assn. Testing, teaching, psychotherapy; achievement tests, projective techniques. M

BRAY, Miss Ruth Marie. 25 Main St, Toronto 13, Ont. b. 25 June 1929 Toronto. BA '53 Univ. of Toronto, Can. PSYCHOLOGIST, Cath. Children's Aid Socy, 67 Bond St, Toronto. Member: CPA. Testing, clinical analysis, consulting, research; projective techniques, maternal deprivation, childhood psychosis. F

BREEN, Dr. Harold John. Carleton Coll, Ottawa. b. 16 June 1925 London. PH.D '53 Univ. of Western Ontario, Can. ASST. PROF. of PSYCH, Carleton Coll. Member:CPA. Teaching, research; group dynamics in teaching, projective drawing, psychotherapy. M

BRIDGES, Prof. James Winfred. Sir George Williams Coll, 1441 Drummond St, Montreal. b. 13 Sept 1885 Prince Edward Island. PH.D '15 Harvard Univ, USA. SR PROF, Sir George Williams Coll. Member: CPA, APA, Amer. Anthrop. Assn. Teaching, administration, professional writing; measurement of mental ability, social learning, analysis of temperament. M

BROMILEY, Dr. Reg B. Def. Res. Med. Labs, P.O. Box 62, Postal Sta. K, Toronto. Ont. b. 22 May 1911 Edmonton. PH.D '47 Johns Hopkins Univ, USA. CHIEF, Appl. Exper. Psych. Sect, Def. Res. Med. Labs; ED. CONSULT, *Canadian Journal of Psychology.* Member: CPA, APA. Research, administration; visual indicators, dials, scales. M

BROUGHAM, Miss Norma Isabella. 441 King St, London, Ont. b. 5 Feb 1915 Woodstock. MA '50 McGill Univ, Can. STUDENT, Inst. of Psychiat, Univ. of London, Eng. Member: CPA, SPT, Amer. Assn. for Ment. Defic. Research, clinical testing; physiological psychology, attitude measurement, learning theory. F

BROWN, Arthur Edwin. Apt. 18, Joseph Ct, 16 St. Joseph St, Toronto, Ont. b. 2 Jan 1930 Winnipeg. MA '53 Univ. of Manitoba, Can. PSYCHOLOGIST, Child Adjustment Serv, Toronto Bd. of Educ, 151 College St. Member: CPA. Testing, student, research; learning theory, projective techniques, attitude measurement. M

BROWN, Maj. Frederick Thorburn. HQ Western Cmd, Can. Army, Kingsway Ave, Edmonton, Alta. b. 18 May 1910 Brant. M.SC '50 McGill Univ, Can. PERS. OFF, HQ Western Cmd, Can. Army. Member: CPA. Administration, personnel psychology, consulting. M

BROWN, Flight Lt. Jack McDougall. Selectn. and Trng. Anal. Unit, Royal Can. Air Force, 1107 Ave. Rd, Toronto, Ont. b. 19 July 1921 Belleville. MA '50 Univ. of Toronto, Can. OFF. in CHARGE, Aircrew Trng. Res, Royal Can. Air Force. Member: APA, CPA. Personnel and aviation psychology, research; learning theory, achievement tests, attitude measurement. M

BROWN, Miss Jean. Toronto Psychiat. Hosp, 2 Surrey Pl, Toronto, Ont. b. 20 Oct 1901 Toronto. MA '27 Univ. of Toronto, Can. SR. PSYCH'T, Toronto Psychiat. Hosp. Member: CPA. Diagnostic testing, consulting, teaching, research; projective techniques, testing for organic deficits. F

BRUCE, Richard R. Shellburn Refinery, Shell Oil of Can. Ltd, Box 69, Vancouver 1, B.C. b. 25 July 1931 Calgary. MA '54 Univ. of Oregon, USA. PERS. PSYCH'T, Shell Oil of Can. Ltd. Member: CPA. Industrial psychology, consulting, testing; selection techniques, conference leadership training. M

BRYAN, Jackson Ross. Chanticleer Farm, R.R. 4, Welland, Ont. b. 26 Oct 1914 Port Arthur. MA '50 Univ. of Toronto, Can. SUPERINTENDENT, Welland County Genl. Hosp, 224 Bald St, Welland. Member.

CPA, APA. Administration, industrial psychology, consulting; aptitude and attitude measurement, group process. M

BRYENTON, Gordon A. M. 2971 W. 28th Ave, Vancouver 10, B.C. b. 13 June 1918 Hazenmore. MA '51 Univ. of Toronto, Can. DIRECTOR, Marriage Couns. Serv, Can. Ment. Hlth. Assn, B.C. Div, Ste. 5, 5 E. Broadway, Vancouver 10. Member: CPA. Psychotherapy, consulting, guidance, administration, teaching; attitude change, development of social perception, learning, projective techniques. M

BURNETT, Dr. Alastair. Hosp. for Ment. and Nerv. Diseases, St. John's, Newf. b. 26 Nov 1922 Blantyre, Br. Central Africa. PH.D '55 McGill Univ, Can. SR. PSYCH'T, Hosp. for Ment, and Nerv. Diseases. Member: CPA, APA. Diagnostic testing, research, professional writing, teaching; learning theory, projective techniques, statistical methods and test construction. M

BURWELL, Mrs. Elinor J. 479 Richardson Ave, Ottawa 3, Ont. b. 11 Apr 1925 Toronto. BA '46 Univ. of Toronto, Can. SCI. INFO. OFF, Def. Res. Bd, Dept. of Natl. Def, Elgin St, Ottawa. Member: CPA, APA. Professional writing, student; military psychology, projective techniques, learning. F

BUTLER, Dr. Alfred James. The Training School, Vineland, New Jersey, USA. b. 23 Mar 1923 Goderich. PH.D '54 Univ. of Toronto, Can. PSYCHOLOGIST, The Trng. Sch. Member: CPA, APA. Research, testing, clinical analysis; genetics of abilities. M

BUTLER, Miss Bernice Marjorie. 202 Scarboro Crescent, Toronto 13, Ont. b. 8 Feb 1924 Brantford. MA '51 Univ. of Toronto, Can. PSYCHOLOGIST, Res. Div, Inst. of Child Study, Univ. of Toronto. Member: CPA. Research, testing, teaching, child guidance; play therapy, sensory discrimination, mental organization and mental health. F

CADWELL, Miss Dorothy Helen Belle. Apt. 1, 265 Elgin St, Ottawa, Ont. b. 15 Jan 1910 Saskatoon. MA '48 Columbia Univ, USA. PERS. SEL. OFF, Civil Serv. Comm. of Can, Jackson Bldg, Bank and Slater Sts, Ottawa. Member: CPA, ICWP. Test construction, personnel psychology, research; intelligence, aptitude and achievement testing. F

CALLAGAN, Dr. John Edwin. Juv. and Fam. Court of Metrop. Toronto, Albert St, Toronto, Ont. b. 25 Feb 1920 Manchester, Eng. PH.D '52 Univ. of London, Eng. PSYCH'T. and ASST. DIR, Psychiat. Cen, Juv. and Fam. Ct. Member: BPS, CPA, APA. Testing, clinical analysis, administration, consulting; projective techniques, attitude measurement, social perception, juvenile delinquency. M

CAMPBELL, Edgar Harper. St. Catherines Genl. Hosp, 142 Queenston, St. Catherines, Ont. b. 28 Dec 1918 Toronto. MA '52 Univ. of Toronto, Can. PSYCHOLOGIST, St. Catherines Genl. Hosp. Member: CPA. Diagnostic testing, personality assessment, psychotherapy, teaching; social perception, projective techniques. M

CAPRIOLI-FISHER, Dr. Adèle. Apt. 11, 4330 Sherbrooke W, Montreal. b. 22 May 1914 Naples, Italy. PH.D '38 Naples Univ, Italy. DIR. of SCHOOLS, Assn. for Help of Retarded Children, Inc, 251 Percival Ave, Montreal. Member: CPA. Educational psychology, personnel selection and training, research with retarded and disturbed children, consulting; projective techniques, educational and ability tests. F

CARMENT, David William. 663 Lawrence Ave. W, Toronto 10, Ont. b. 28 Oct 1928 Winnipeg. MA '54 Univ. of Toronto, Can. PSYCHOLOGIST, Dept. of Vets. Affairs, Sunnybrook Hosp, Bayview Ave, Toronto. Member: CPA. Clinical testing and analysis, research, student; group process, application of behavior theory to social phenomena, psychotherapy. M

CARSON, John J. Ontario Hydro Elec. Power Comm, 620 Univ. Ave, Toronto, Ont. b. 11 Oct 1919 Vancouver. MA '48 Univ. of Toronto, Can. DIR. of EMPLOYEE RELAT, Ont. Hydro Elec. Power Comm. Member: CPA. Administration, personnel psychology, consulting; industrial psychology. M

CARSON, Miss Marjorie E. C. Child Care Dept, Children's Aid and Infants' Homes of Toronto, 33 Charles St. E, Toronto, Ont. b. Ontario. MA '38 Univ. of Toronto, Can. SR. PSYCH'T, Child Care Dept, Children's Aid and Infants' Homes of Toronto. Member: CPA, SPT. Testing, consulting, supervising student training; projective techniques, longitudinal study of neglected children. F

CELLARD, Maurice. 2290 18th St, Que. b. 1 Sept 1924 St. Jean L'Evangéliste. L.PS '52 Laval Univ, Can. CLIN. PSYCH'T, St. Michel Archange Hosp, Mastai, Que. Member: CPA. Diagnostic testing and clinical analysis; aptitude measurement, projective tests. M

CELOVSKY, Dr. Angelika. 71 a William St. W, Smiths Falls, Ont. b. 11 Nov 1928 Memel, Lithuania. PH.D '54 Univ. of Heidelberg, Germany. CLIN. PSYCH'T, Ontario Hosp. Sch, Smiths Falls. Member: CPA, APA. Diagnostic testing, clinical analysis, vocational guidance, counseling; projective techniques, child development, theory of personality. F

CERVINKA, Dr. Vladimir Bohdan. 105 Yorkville Ave, Toronto. b. 12 Mar 1914 Petersburg, Russia. PH.D '48 Charles' Univ.

Czech. RES. ASSOC, Dept. of Psych, Univ. of Toronto, 102 St. George St, Toronto Member: CPA. Research in group dynamics, professional writing, teaching; testing, mathematical models in group processes, learning and personality theory.   M

CHAGNON, Gilles Joseph. 54 Hastey, Apt. 2, Ottawa, Ont. b. 8 Sept 1927 Ottawa. BA '48 Univ. of Ottawa, Can. PSYCHOLOGIST, Psychiat. Serv, Ottawa Civic Hosp, Dept. of Hlth. of Ont, Carling Ave, Ottawa; LECT. in PSYCH, Univ. of Ottawa. Member: CPA. Testing, clinical analysis, child therapy, teaching, research; projective techniques, personality theory, diagnostic testing.   M

CHALMERS, Dr. John West. 9851 86th Ave, Edmonton, Alta. b. 18 Apr 1910 Winnipeg. ED.D Stanford Univ, USA. INSPECTOR of HIGH SCHOOLS, Alberta Dept. of Educ, Edmonton; EDITOR, *Curriculum News Letter*. Member: CPA, Can. Ment. Hlth. Assn. Supervision of secondary school teaching, professional writing, educational psychology; achievement tests.   M

CHANT, Prof. Sperrin N. F. 1650 Wesbrook, Crescent, Vancouver. b. 31 Oct 1896 St. Thomas. MA '24 Univ. of Toronto, Can. DEAN of ARTS and SCI, PROF. and HEAD, Dept. of Philos. and Psych, Univ. of British Columbia, Vancouver. Member: CPA. Administration, teaching, professional writing; psychology of thinking, attitude measurement, morale studies.   M

CHÉNÉ, Hubert. 370 Chemin Ste. Foy, Apt. 7, Quebec. b. 15 Apr 1926 Oka. lic. '49 Laval Univ. Can. DIRECTOR, Service d'Hygiène Mentale and d'Orientation, 197 Rue St. Jean, Quebec 4; PROFESSOR, Laval Univ. and l'Escole des Infirmières, St. Michel Archange Hosp. Member: Psych. Assn. of P.Q. Administration, research in mental hygiene, teaching; intelligence tests, attitude measurement.   M

CHEVRIER, Dr. Jean-Marc. 10560 St. Urbain, Montreal, P.Q. b. 2 Mar 1916 Chénéville. D.PS '49 Univ. of Montreal, Can. CHIEF, Dept. of Psych, Rehab. Inst. of Montreal, 6265 Hudson Rd, Montreal; CONSULT. PSYCH'T, priv. prac. Member: CPA, APA, Amer. Cath. Psych. Assn. Counseling, guidance and consulting, teaching; diagnostic methods in psychology, prediction of rehabilitation success of the handicapped.   M

CHIDLEY, Mrs. Erma Nadine. 318 Winchester St, Winnipeg 12, Man. b. 13 Jan 1911 Winnipeg. M.ED '56 Univ. of Manitoba, Can. HEAD of PSYCH. DEPT, Child Guid. Clin. of Greater Winnipeg, Sch. Dist. of Winnipeg No. 1, William and Ellen Sts, Winnipeg. Member: CPA. Administration, consulting; psychology of exceptional

children, educational psychology, intelligence and achievement tests.   F

CHILDERHOSE, Keith Donald. 127 Metcalfe St, Ottawa, Ont. b. 24 Nov 1925 North Bay. MA '51 Univ. of Toronto, Can. TRAINEE, Indus. Relat. Div, E. B. Eddy Co, Hull. Member: CPA. Industrial psychology, testing, interviewing, administration; achievement tests, projective techniques, morale surveys.   M

CHURCH, Dr. Edward John Maxwell. 436 Carpenter Way, Ottawa 2, Ont. b. 10 Dec 1915 Toronto. PH.D '50 Univ. of Toronto, Can. ADVIS. to CHIEF of TRNG, Royal Can. Air Force, Def. Res. Bd, Natl. Def. Hq, Cartier Square, Ottawa. Member: Ottawa Assn. of Psych'ts. Personnel psychology, administration, operational research; learning theory, achievement tests, personnel selection and training method.   M

CIMON, S. J., Rev. Conrad. Sudbury Coll, 261 Notre Dame St, Sudbury, Ont. b. 26 Apr 1910 Biddeford, Maine, USA. L.PS '52 Univ. of Montreal, Can. JESUIT PRIEST; DEAN of STUDIES, Sacred Heart Coll. and Sudbury Coll. Member: CPA. Administration, educational psychology, consulting; analysis, testing.   M

CLAKE, John. 36 Van Stassen Blvd, Toronto, Ont. b. 9 Feb 1922 Winnipeg. BA '50 Univ. of Manitoba, Can. STUDENT, Univ. of Toronto. Member: CPA, APA. Student, consulting in industrial psychology, teaching; accident liability, social perception, group process.   M

CLARK, Miss Barbara Ainsley. Staff Dept, Head Off, Bank of Montreal, 119 St. James St, Montreal, P.Q. b. 25 July 1929 Montreal. BA '50 McGill Univ, Can. ASST. to PERS. ADVIS, Bank of Montreal. Employment testing and interviewing; vocational guidance.   F

CLARK, Charles Augustus Fordyce. P.O. Box 21, Ottawa, Ont. b. 4 Oct 1900 Binghamton, New York, USA. MA '51 Univ. of British Columbia, Can. EDUC. SURVEYS OFF, Dept. of Citizenship and Immigration, Indian Affairs, 294 Albert St, Ottawa; PERS. SEL. OFF, Army Reserve; EDITOR, *Indian School Bulletin*. Member: CPA. Administration of Indian Schools, testing, editorial; intelligence and aptitude testing, personality inventories.   M

CLARKE, Dr. Stanley C. T. Fac. of Educ, Div. of Educ. Psych, Univ. of Alberta, Edmonton. b. 13 Feb 1912 Scrooby, Eng. ED.D '48 Stanford Univ, USA. ASSOC. PROF, Univ. of Alberta. Member: CPA, Amer. Pers. and Guid. Assn. Teaching and research in teacher education, testing; child psychotherapy, emotional adjustment of children, educational guidance and testing.   M

CLELAND, John Franklin. Sask. Hosp, Box 1056, Weyburn, Sask. b. 15 June 1925 Weyburn. MA '53 Montana State Univ, Montana, USA. CLIN. PSYCH'T, Sask. Hosp. Member: Sask. Psych. Assn. Testing, clinical analysis, teaching, psychotherapy; personality theory and dynamics, projective techniques. M

CLERK, Dr. Gabrielle. Inst. of Psych, Univ. of Montreal, Montreal, P.Q. b. 30 June 1923 Ottawa. PH.D '53 Univ. of Montreal, Can. PROF. AGRÉGÉ, Univ. of Montreal; CLIN. PSYCH'T, Montreal Children's Hosp. Member: CPA, APA, SPT. Teaching, psychotherapy, testing; child psychotherapy, projective techniques. F

COHEN, Miss Clarice. 122 Noble Ave, Winnipeg, Man. b. 8 July 1929 Granam. BA '49 Univ. of Manitoba, Can. PSYCHOLOGIST, Deer Lodge Hosp, Dept. of Vets. Affairs, Portage Ave, Winnipeg. Member: CPA, Man. Med. Assn. Testing, clinical analysis, counseling, teaching; projective techniques, group therapy, individual counseling. F

COLLETT, Dean William John. Mount Royal Coll, 7th Ave. and 11ht St. W, Calgary, Alta. b. 6 Mar 1910 Hilperton, Eng. MA '37 Columbia Univ, USA. DEAN, Mount Royal Coll. Member: CPA. Administration, student counseling, teaching; achievement tests, group dynamics. M

CONGER, D. Stuart. 1672 Bayview Ave, Willowdale P.O. Ont. b. 30 Jan 1926 Ottawa. BA '49 Univ. of British Columbia, Can. PERS. RES. ASST, Ont. Hydro Elect. Power Comm, 620 Univ. Ave, Toronto. Member: CPA. Research in industrial and personnel psychology, testing; relation between abilities and personality, group process in industry, statistical methods in analysis of tests. M

CONWAY, Dr. Clifford Bruce. Dept. of Educ, Parliament Bldgs, Victoria, B.C. b. 6 Dec 1909 Miniota. D.PED '37 Univ. of Toronto, Can. DIRECTOR, Div. of Tests, Standards and Res, B.C. Dept. of Educ. Member: CPA. Testing, administration, research; achievement and intelligence testing, educational statistics. M

COONS, Dr. Wesley H. Ontario Hosp, Hamilton, Ont. b. 29 June 1924 Lamont. PH.D '55 Univ. of Toronto, Can. SR. PSYCH'T, Ont. Hosp; EDITOR, *Psychology Bulletin* of Ont. Dept. of Hlth. Member: CPA, APA. Psychotherapy, research, testing, administration; social perception, group process. M

CORMIER, Gérard. 47 Ave. Lefurgey, Moncton, N.B. b. 16 Jan 1926 Moncton. MA '51 Univ. of Montreal, Can. CLIN. PSYCH'T, Ment. Health Clin, North King St, Moncton. Member: CPA. Testing, clinical

analysis, psychotherapy, teaching; projective techniques, psychometrics. M

COSGRAVE, Dr. Gerald Pelton. YMCA Couns. Serv, 40 College St, Toronto. b. 22 Jan 1904 Winnipeg. PH.D '28 Univ. of Toronto, Can. DIRECTOR, YMCA Couns. Serv. Member: CPA. Marriage and retirement counseling, administration, educational and personnel psychology; aptitude tests, remedial reading, counseling techniques. M

COSTELLO, John Martin. 6222 Loran St, St. Louis 9, Missouri, USA. b. 31 Aug 1921 Bounty. MA '47 Univ. of Toronto, Can. INSTR. in PSYCH, St. Louis Univ, 221 N. Grand Blvd, St. Louis 3, Missouri, USA; FIELD PSYCH'T, Geo. Fry and Assoc, Chicago, Illinois, USA. Member: CPA, APA. Teaching, research, student counseling, student; labor-management relations, motivation research, learning theory. M

COULTER, Dr. Thelma T. Psych. Dept, S 4, Shaughnessy Hosp, Vancouver, B.C. b. 30 Sept 1916 New Westminster. PH.D '54 Inst. of Psychiat, Maudsley Hosp, London, Eng. CLIN. PSYCH'T, Dept. of Vets. Affairs, Shaughnessy Hosp. Member: CPA, APA, Amer. Cath. Psych. Assn, Amer. Assn. for Ment. Defic. Testing, psychotherapy, research; projective techniques, research on phenylpyruvic acid in mental deficiency. F

COURVAL, Jean. 5242 St. Denis, Montreal. b. 3 June 1921 Montreal. L.PS '48 Univ. of Montreal, Can. SUPERV. of TECH. SERV, Civil Serv. Comm, Hôtel de Ville, Montreal; VOCAT. GUID. COUNS, priv. prac. Member: CPA. Personnel psychology, research, administration; intelligence, aptitude and interest measurement. M

COX, Albert Ernest. 4343 West 14th Ave, Vancouver, B.C. b. 23 Nov 1921 Prestatyn, Wales. MA '50 Univ. of Toronto, Can. STUD. COUNS. and LECT. in PSYCH, Univ. of British Columbia, Vancouver. Member: CPA. Educational psychology, teaching, counseling; social organization and interaction, perception, personality theory and evaluation. M

CRADDICK, Ray Albert. Regina Gaol, Regina, Sask. b. 3 Mar 1927 Innisfail. MA '55 Univ. of Alberta, Can. PSYCHOLOGIST, Correctn. Br, Dept. of Soc. Welf, and Rehab, Regina. Member: APA, Sask. Psych. Assn. Diagnostic testing and classification, consulting, psychotherapy; projective techniques, penal psychology. M

CRAIG, William John. Psychiat. Res, Dept. of Pub. Health, Univ. Hosp, Univ. of Sask, Saskatoon. b. 23 Feb 1923 Sault Ste. Marie. MA '50 Queen's Univ. Can. RES. PSYCH'T, Univ. Hosp, Univ. of Sask. Member: APA. Research, testing, clinical observation and consulting; objective and projective techniques and their correlation with physiological and biochemical measures. M

CRAMER-AZIMA, Fern J. Allan Memor. Inst. of Psychiat, McGill Univ, 1025 Pine Ave. W, Montreal, P.Q. b. 3 Jan 1928 Kingston. MA '49 Cornell Univ, USA. LECTURER, Dept. of Psychiat, McGill Univ. Member: CPA, APA, SPT. Student, teaching, testing, research; projective techniques, psychoanalysis, research in schizophrenia. F

CROFTS, Miss Irene. 134 Traverse Ave, Norwood, Man. b. 25 Feb 1926 Winnipeg. M.ED '56 Univ. of Manitoba, Can. EDUC. PSYCH'T, Child Guid. Clin. of Greater Winnipeg, Ellen and Bannatyne Sts, Winnipeg 2, Man. Intelligence testing in schools, educational psychology, research; intelligence and vocational testing. F

CROWE, Major Herman Albert. HQ Central Cmd, Oakville, Ont. b. 1 Sept 1919 Moose Jaw. MA '50 Univ. of Michigan, USA. MILIT. PSYCH'T, Dept. of Natl. Def, Can. Army, Ottawa, Ont. Member: CPA. Applied and personnel psychology, consulting, research; attitude measurement, group dynamics. M

CUSHING, Travis W. 1 Hazen Ave, St. John, N.B. b. 28 July 1915 St. John. M.ED '49 Boston Univ, USA. SUPERV. of GUID, Bd. of Sch. Trustees, St. John. Member: Amer. Pers. and Guid. Assn. Educational psychology, administration, guidance; learning theory, achievement tests, group process. M

DAIGLE, Renald J. P. 29 Ave. 32. Edmundston, N.B. b. 16 June 1928 Edmundston. L.PS '53 Univ. of Montreal, Can. TRAINEE, Dept. of Psych, Children's Memor. Hosp, Montreal, P.Q. Member: CPA. Student, testing, psychotherapy; projective techniques, diagnostic interviews. M

DAVIDSON, Miss Marjorie Élaine. 123 Tompkins Hall, North Carolina State Coll, Raleigh, North Carolina, USA. b. 12 Dec 1926 Wetaskiwin. MA '50 Univ. of Alberta, Can. INSTRUCTOR, North Carolina State Coll. Member: CPA, APA. Student, teaching; projective techniques, group process, attitude measurement. F

DAVIS, Miss Inez Adeline. P.O. Dunrobin, Ont. b. 7 Sept 1918 Dunrobin. MA '50 Univ. of Toronto, Can. Member: CPA. Personality and intelligence tests for clinical and guidance purposes, projective techniques. F

DAWE, John Frederick. 111 Glenview Ave, Ottawa 1, Ont. b. 13 May 1912 Stoughton. AM '47 Columbia Univ, USA. TEST. RES. ADVIS, Civil Serv. Comm. of Can, Ottawa. Member: CPA. Personnel psychology, research, testing; achievement tests, rating scales and attitude surveys, interviewing. M

DAWKINS, Peter Bradley Harold. Rm. 308, Sutton Hall, Univ. of Texas, Austin, Texas, USA. b. 22 Nov 1920 Birmingham,

Eng. MA '52 Univ. of Toronto, Can. STUD. and COUNS. TRAINEE, Testing and Guid. Bur, Univ. of Texas. Member: CPA. Counseling and test interpretation, research, teaching; self theory and measurement, counseling and human development. M

DAYHAW, Prof. Lawrence T. Univ. of Ottawa, Ont. b. 1 Nov 1902 Ottawa. PH.D '34 Catholic Univ. of Louvain, Belgium. ASSOC. PROF, Univ. of Ottawa. Member: CPA, APA, APSLF. Teaching, research, industrial psychology; statistics, test construction, personnel evaluation. M

DÉCARIE, Prof. Thérèse Gouin. 5584 Canterbury, Montreal 26, P.Q. b. 30 Sept 1923 Montreal. L.PS '47 Univ. of Montreal, Can. PROF. AGRÉGÉ, Inst. of Psych, Univ. of Montreal. Member: SPT, Psych. Assn. of P.Q. Teaching, research, applied psychology; infant nurture, educational methods, development of religious feelings in the child. F

DELLI-COLLI, Pascal Joseph. 125 Laurier St, Apt. 11, Hull, Que. b. 18 Mar 1930 Montreal. BA '54 St. Michael's Coll, Vermont, USA. GUID. COUNS, Guid. Cen, Univ. of Ottawa, 1 Stewart St, Ottawa. Member: CPA. Testing, vocational guidance, counseling, research, student; projective techniques, intelligence and aptitude tests. M

DESJARDINS, Mrs. Thérèse. 6675 St. Dominique St, Montreal, P.Q. b. 16 Dec 1910 Montreal. Licence '51 Laval Univ, Can. VOCAT. GUID. COUNS, Can. Inst. of Vocat. Guid, 4327 St. Hubert St, Montreal. Member: Psych. Assn. of P.Q. Assn. of Guid. Couns. Guidance, applied psychology, testing; aptitude testing. F

DESJARLAIS, Dr. Lionel. 630 Cumberland St, Ottawa, Ont. b. 21 June 1920 Providence, Rhode Island, USA. PH.D '53 Univ. of Ottawa, Can. PROF. of EDUC, Univ. of Ottawa. Member: CPA, Can. Educ. Assn. Teaching, educational psychology, research; bilingualism, learning theory. M

DETTMER, Miss Ruth. 434 Maitland St, London, Ont. b. 30 Nov 1925 Kitchener. BA '49 Univ. of Western Ontario, Can. PSYCHOLOGIST, Ment. Hlth. Clin, Ont. Hosp, London. Member: CPA. Testing, counseling, psychotherapy; intellectual and educational measures, projective techniques. F

DEVEREAUX, Ralph Spence. Teachers' Coll, Elmwood Ave, London, Ont. b. 19 Oct 1915 Ridgetown. MA '48 Univ. of Western Ontario, Can. HEAD, Psych. Dept, Ont. Dept. of Educ. Member: CPA. Teaching educational psychology, guidance; child development, learning theory, mental health, group process. M

DEVERELL, Dr. Alfred Frederick. Coll. of Educ, Univ. of Sask, Saskatoon, Sask. b. 23 Aug 1908 Province of Alta. ED.D '50 Stanford Univ, USA. ASSOC. PROF. of EDUC, Univ. of Sask; DIRECTOR, John Dolan Sch. for Ment. Ret. Child. Member: CPA, Can. Educ. Assn, Can. Ment. Hlth. Assn. Teaching, administration, educational psychology; learning theory applied to reading, teaching the exceptional child, counseling techniques. M

DICKIE, Capt. Robert Daniel. HQ Cen. Cmd, Can. Army, Oakville, Ont. b. 29 Sept 1918 Preston. MA '50 McGill Univ, Can. PERS. OFF, Can. Army. Member: CPA. Administration, personnel selection, research; psytration, personnel selection, research; psychometrics, military psychology, operational research. M

DIDUCH, Mrs. Joyce Alice. Ste. 614 Med. Cen. Apts, 765 Notre Dame Ave, Winnipeg 3, Man. b. 16 Mar 1931 Toronto. BA '53 Univ. of Manitoba, Can. CLIN. PSYCHOMET, Winnipeg Psychopathic Hosp, Emily and Bannatyne Sts, Winnipeg. Member: CPA. Testing, teaching, consulting; projective techniques. F

DIGGORY, Mrs. Elsinore. Psych. Dept, Ont. Hosp, London, Ont. b. 23 June 1924 London. BA '47 Univ. of Western Ontario, Can. CLIN. PSYCH'T, Ont. Hosp. Member: Ont. Psych. Assn. Testing, clinical analysis, consulting, psychotherapy; personality testing, projective techniques. F

DINSDALE, Prof. Walter Gilbert. 562 23 St, Brandon, Man. b. 3 Apr 1916 Brandon. MA '51 Univ. of Toronto, Can. MEMBER of PARLIAMENT, House of Commons, Govt. of Canada, Ottawa. Member: CPA. Human relations, applied psychology, consulting, teaching; guidance, counseling. M

DIXON, Miss Jean Linse. 9932 105 St, Edmonton, Alta. b. 14 Oct 1922 Scott. MA '48 Univ. of Alberta, Can. CLIN. PSYCH'T Provincial Guid. Clin, 10523 100 Ave, Edmonton. Member: CPA. Testing, psychotherapy, parent interviews, teaching; play therapy, projective techniques, intelligence testing. F

DOIG, David Norman Watson. Psych. Dept, Ont. Hosp, Hamilton, Ont. b. 29 Sept 1922 Halifax. MA '51 Univ. of Ottawa, Can. CLIN. PSYCH'T, Ont. Hosp. Member: CPA. Testing, diagnosis, psychotherapy, research; projective techniques, social perception. M

DOLMAGE, Prof. Miss Grace L. Univ. of Manitoba, Winnipeg 9. b. 20 Mar 1903 Souris. M.SC.ED '40 Northwestern Univ, USA. ASST. PROF, Fac. of Educ, Univ. of Man. Member: CPA, WFMH. Teaching, testing, educational psychology; child development, mental measurement, social

perception, group process, mental health. F

DÖRKEN, Dr. Herbert O. Verdun Protestant Hosp, P.O. Box 6034, Montreal, P.Q. b. 7 July 1925 Montreal. PH.D '51 Univ. of Montreal, Can. PSYCH'T in CHARGE, Dept. of Psych, Verdun Protestant Hosp; LECT. in PSYCH, McGill Univ; STUD. COUNS, Sir George Williams Coll. Member: CPA, APA, SPT. Research, administration, teaching; projective techniques, human experimental research using psychophysical measures. M

DOUYON, Emerson. 3100 Maplewood, Apt. 7, Montreal, P.Q. b. 16 June 1929 Cayes, Haiti, West Indies. L.PS '55 Univ. of Montreal, Can. PSYCHOMET. RES. ASST, Univ. of Montreal. Member: CPA. Research, testing, student; projective techniques, intelligence tests for children, mental processes in schizophrenia. M

DOUYON, Mrs. Louise Gamache. 3100 Maplewood, Montreal. b. 21 Mar 1931 St. Jean. L.PH '55 Univ. of Montreal, Can. PSYCHOMET. RES. ASST, Univ. of Montreal. Research, student; projective techniques, child psychology, education. F

DOWNEY, Richard Harold. Psych. Dept, Univ. of British Columbia, Vancouver. b. 15 June 1928 Vancouver. MA '56 Univ. of British Columbia, Can. PRISON PSYCH'T, Oakalla Prison Farm, Drawer O, South Burnaby. Member: CPA, B.C. Probat. and Correctn. Socy. Applied and personnel psychology, testing, consulting, research; projective techniques, aptitude tests, employee morale and public relations. M

DRAPER, William Arthur. Stud. Guid. and Placement Off, Marquette Univ, Milwaukee, Wisconsin, USA. b. 27 Sept 1928 Toronto. MA '53 Univ. of Toronto, Can. CLIN. PSYCH'T, Stud. Guid. and Placement Off, Marquette Univ. Member: CPA. Teaching, testing, consulting, therapy; projective techniques, personality theory and psychoanalytical techniques. M

DUBOIS, Miss Suzanne. 17 Rue Peel, Sherbrooke, P.Q. b. 11 Dec 1926 Sherbrooke. Licence '52 Laval Univ, Can. PLACEMENT OFF, Natl. Placement Serv, 357 W. Rue King, Sherbrooke; LECTURER, Fac. of Arts, Univ. of Sherbrooke. Member: Psych. Assn. of P.Q, Assn. of Guid. Couns. of P.Q. Guidance and placement of the mentally and physically handicapped, testing, teaching; aptitude tests, interviewing. F

DUBREUIL, Guy. Inst. of Psych, P.O. Box 6128, Univ. of Montreal, Montreal, P.Q. b. 15 May 1925 Montreal. MA '51 Univ. of Montreal, Can. ASST. PROF, Univ. of Montreal. Member: CPA. Teaching, research, administration; social perception, minority problems, comparative study of class and race relations. M

DUFRESNE, Dr. Georges. 49 Spring Grove

Crescent, Montreal. b. 25 Jan 1917 Montreal. D.PS '48 Univ. of Montreal, Can. DIR. of PSYCH, SERV, Dept. of Vets. Affairs, 4565 Chemin Queen Mary, Montreal. Member: CPA, APA, SPT. Testing, administration, teaching, research; projective techniques, psychology in art and literature.M

DUNLAP, Prof. Dr. George Murray. Univ. of Alberta, Edmonton. b. Carleton Place. PH.D '51 Columbia Univ, USA. PROF. and CHMN, Dept. of Educ. Psych, Univ. of Alberta. Member: CPA, APA. Administration, research, teaching; psychology of learning, child and adolescent, psychology, educational achievement. M

DUNSTON, Miss Anne Jeanette. 1246 York St, London, Ont. b. 28 Sept 1894 London, Eng. MA '33 Columbia Univ, USA. TEACHER, Lord Roberts Pub. Sch, Bd. of Educ, London. Member: CPA. Teaching oral class for hard of hearing, guidance of parents and children, audiometric testing. F

DUVAL, Roch. Ecole de Pédagogie et d'Orientation, Laval Univ, 71 Rue d'Auteuil, Quebec. b. 22 Dec 1916 Quebec. Licence '49 Univ. of Quebec, Can. DIR. of RES, Guid. Sect, Ecole de Pédagogie et d'Orientation; DIRECTOR, Laval Inst. for Vocat. Guid; EDITOR, Etudes Psychopédagogiques de Laval. Member: Psych. Assn. of P.Q, Assn. of Guid. Couns. of P.Q. Teaching, consulting, guidance, administration; counseling methods, vocational problems. M

EARLE, Dr. Jeffrey B. 333 Redfern Ave, Westmount, Que. b. 2 Apr 1920 Montreal. PH.D '56 Univ. of Ottawa, Can. CONSULT. CLIN. PSYCH'T, priv. prac. Member: CPA, BPS, APA. Consulting, clinical practice, psychotherapy, teaching, research; personality testing, therapeutic processes. M

EASTERBROOK, James Arthur. Box 72, Hubbards, N.S. b. 10 Apr 1923 Spooner, Minnesota, USA. MA '51 Queen's Univ, Can. SCI. OFF, Def. Res. Bd, Dept. of Natl. Def, Ottawa. Member: CPA, Operational Res. Socy. of Amer. Operational research, administration, teaching; stress, motivation, emotion. M

EGENER, Mrs. Katheline Margaret. 296 Victoria St, London, Ont. b. 3 Sept 1910 St. Catherines. MA '53 Univ. of Western Ontario, Can. RES. ASST, Dept. of Psychiat. and Preven. Med, Univ. of Western Ontario, London. Member: CPA. Research, testing; alcoholism, mental health. F

ELART, Miss Alice Jean. Crease Clin. of Psych. Med, Essondale, B.C. b. 19 Apr 1927 New Westminster. BA '48 Univ. of British Columbia, Can. CLIN. PSYCH'T, B.C. Ment. Hlth. Serv, Essondale. Member: CPA. Testing, teaching, administration; projective techniques, group therapy. F

ESSERT, Gene. 333 Simcoe St, Apt. 2, London, Ont. b. 26 Nov 1917 Riga, Latvia. MA '54 Univ. of Western Ontario, Can. PSYCHOLOGIST, Ont. Hosp, Dundas St, East London, Ont. Testing, interviewing, teaching, psychotherapy; motivational theories, stress studies, psychosomatic medicine, projective techniques. M

ETHIER, Dr. Wilfrid. Can. Inst. of Vocat. Guid, 4327 St. Hubert St, Montreal, P.Q. b. 8 Oct 1905 Ste. Victoire. PH.D '40 Univ. of Montreal, Can. DIRECTOR, Can. Inst. of Vocat. Guid. Member: CPA, APA, Amer. Pers. and Guid. Assn. Consulting, guidance, teaching, professional writing; counseling, religious guidance, psychological theory. M

FAHRIG, Lt. (W) Marjorie W. Box 270, Rural Route 1, Westboro, Ont. b. 3 Sept 1922 Ochre River. MA '51 Dalhousie Univ, Can. STAFF OFF, Naval Job Anal. Comm, Personnel Br, Royal Can. Navy, Ottawa. Member: CPA. Military personnel psychology, research, vocational counseling; job analysis and evaluation, juvenile delinquency. F

FEINTUCH, Dr. Alfred. 2000 Norway Rd, Mt. Royal, Que. b. 31 July 1915 New York City, USA. PH.D '54 New York Univ, USA. EXEC. DIR, Jewish Vocat. Serv, 493 Sherbrooke St. W, Montreal. Member: APA, Psych. Assn. of P.Q, Amer. Pers. and Guid. Assn. Administration, guidance, consulting, educational psychology; sheltered workshops, vocational counseling, group guidance. M

FERGUSON, Allan Brent. J. H. McQuaig and Co, 330 Bay St, Toronto, Ont. b. 2 July 1924 Bowanville. MA '50 Univ. of Toronto, Can. ASST. MGR, J. H. McQuaig and Co, Indus. Consultants. Member: CPA. Industrial psychology, testing, consulting; industrial selection of executives and salesmen, projective techniques, guidance. M

FERGUSON, Donald Gordon. P.O. Box 800, Transcona, Man. b. 22 June 1925 St. Boniface. BA '48 Univ. of Manitoba, Can. PERS. ASST, Hudson's Bay Co, Fur Trade Dept, Hudson's Bay Hse, Winnipeg. Member: CPA. Personnel psychology, interviewing, testing; measurement of intelligence. M

FERGUSON, Prof. George Andrew. Dept. of Psych, McGill Univ, 3600 Mc Tavish St, Montreal, P.Q. b. 23 July 1914 New Glasgow. PH.D '40 Univ. of Edinburgh, Scot. PROFESSOR, McGill Univ. Member: CPA. Teaching, research; psychological test theory, learning theory, factor analysis. M

FERGUSON, Kingsley George. Psych. Dept, Westminster Hosp, London, Ont. b. 13 Apr 1921 Newcastle-on-Tyne, Eng. MA '50 Univ. of Toronto, Can. SR. PSYCH'T, Westminster Hosp. Member: APA, SPT,

Ont. Psych. Assn. Psychotherapy, consulting, administration, research, teaching; projective techniques, psychosomatics. M

FINKEL, Philip Harold. Prep School, 4240 Girouard Ave, Montreal 28, P.Q. b. 29 July 1914 London, Eng. B.SC '50 Sir George Williams Coll, Can. ASST. PRIN. and DIR. of SPEC. EDUC, Prep. Sch. Member: CPA. Teaching, psychotherapy, administration; effect of character attitudes on learning. M

FISHER, Dean Edward Joseph. Coll. of Optometry, 140 St. George St, Toronto, Ont. b. 25 Nov 1913 Winnipeg. MA '48 Univ. of Toronto, Can. DEAN, Coll. of Optom. Member: CPA. Administration, teaching, research; experimental psychology applied to visual perception. M

FLINT, Mrs. Betty M. 188 Redpath Ave Toronto, Ont. b. 20 Aug 1920 Toronto. MA '48 Univ. of Toronto, Can. RES. ASSOC, Inst. of Child Study, Univ. of Toronto, 45 Walmer Rd, Toronto. Member: CPA, Ont. Nursery Educ. Assn. Research, teaching, infant testing and consulting; mental health of infant. F

FOLEY, Patrick Joseph. Def. Res. Med. Labs, Postal Sta. K, Box 62, Toronto, Ont. b. 25 July 1926 Stirling, Scot. MA '52 Univ. of Glasgow, Scot. DEF. SCI. SERV. OFF, Def. Res. Med. Labs. Research in psychophysiology of visual perception; color vision. M

FORGUES, Roland Gérard. Hôtel Dieu Hosp, 109 W. Pine Ave, Montreal, P.Q. b. 21 Aug 1924 Lewiston, Maine, USA. PH.D '46 Univ. of Ottawa, Can. CLIN. PSYCH'T, Hôtel Dieu Hosp; CONSULTANT, priv. prac. Member: CPA. Testing, clinical analysis, consulting, teaching; child psychology, organic patterns on French adaptation of intelligence tests, epileptoid patterns on electroencephalographs. M

FORTIER, J. Théo. 275 St. Thomas St, Longueuil, P.Q. b. 13 Apr 1916 Quebec. MA '48 Laval Univ, Can. GUID. COUNS, P.Q. Ministry of Child and Soc. Welf, 32 Notre Dame W, Montreal. Member: CPA. Guidance, testing, research; aptitude measurement, social perception, rehabilitation of the physically handicapped. M

FOURNIER, Guy E. 157 Plateau Ouimet, P.O. Box 296, Ste. Rose, P.Q. b. 12 Oct 1925 Outremont. L.PS '51 Univ. of Montreal, Can. CLIN. PSYCH'T, Inst. Albert Prévost, 6555 Blvd. Gouin W, Cartierville, Montreal. Member: APA, Psych. Assn. of P.Q. Testing, clinical analysis, psychotherapy, research; projective techniques, fatigue, predisposition to accidents. M

FRANCOEUR, Dr. Thomas Alexander. 1070 Crevier Ave, Ville St. Laurent, P.Q. b. 3 Dec 1921 London, Eng. PH.D '51 Univ. of Montreal, Can. PROF. of PSYCH, St. Joseph

Teachers' Coll, 5360 Côte St. Antoine, Montreal, P.Q; PROF. of EXPER. PSYCH, Seminary of Philosophy, Montreal, and St. George Inst, Univ. of Montreal. Member: CPA, SPT. Teaching, consulting, research; marital guidance, psychodynamics of religious vocation, projective techniques. M

FRANKS, Dr. Mrs. Ruth MacLachlan. 71 Crescent Rd, Toronto 5, Ont. b. 31 May 1898 Toronto. PH.D '36 Univ. of Toronto, Can; MD. PSYCHIATRIST, priv. prac. Member: Ont. Psych. Assn. Psychotherapy, clinical practice, testing; student counseling, behavior problems in children.F

FRASER, Allon Winfield. 9939 83 St, Edmonton, Alta. b. 26 Aug 1916 Consort. MA '49 Univ. of Alberta, Can. DIR. of TREATMENT, Alcoholism Found. of Alta, 9910 103 St, Edmonton. Member: CPA. Administration, psychotherapy, counseling, consulting; group process, alcoholism, mental deficiency. M

FRÉCHET, Prof. Arthur. 2488 Mathieu St, Ste. Foy, Quebec 10. b. 14 May 1919 Ottawa. MA '50 Laval Univ, Can. VOCAT. COUNS, Laval Univ, 71 Rue D'Auteuil, Quebec. Member: Psych. Assn. of P.Q, Assn. of Guid. Couns of P.Q. Guidance, teaching, educational and industrial psychology; aptitude measurement, achievement tests. M

FRIESEN, Dr. Edward Peter. Stevenson and Kellogg, Ltd, 810 Royal Bank Bldg, Vancouver 2, B.C. b. 4 Aug 1917 Leader. PH.D '51 Columbia Univ, USA. CONSULT. PSYCH'T, Stevenson and Kellogg, Ltd. Member: CPA, APA. Personnel psychology, consulting, vocational guidance, research; theory and practice of counseling, attitude measurement, learning and personality theory. M

FRY, Miss Lois Margaret. Manitoba Sch. for Ment. Defective Persons, Box 1190, Portage La Prairie, Man. b. 22 Feb 1915 Guelph. MA '51 Univ. of Manitoba, Can. PSYCHOLOGIST, Man. Sch. for Ment. Defective Persons. Member: CPA, Man. Psychiat. Assn, Amer. Assn. of Ment. Defic. Diagnostic testing, teaching, research; learning process, group relations, vocational rehabilitation. F

GADDES, Dr. William Henry. Victoria Coll, Richmond Rd, Victoria, B.C. b. 10 Oct 1912 Kelowna. PH.D '55 Claremont Coll, USA. ASSOC. PROF. of PSYCH, Victoria Coll; CLIN. PSYCH'T, Dept. of Vets. Affairs. Member: CPA, APA. Teaching, clinical testing, consulting, vocational psychology; projective techniques, personality and learning theory. M

GADOURY, Prof. Louis D. 4849 Fabre St, Apt. 4, Montreal 34, Que. b. 23 Aug 1901 Montreal. Licence '45 Univ. of Montreal

Can. DIR. of GUID, Montreal Catholic Sch. Comm, 117 St. Catherine St. West, Montreal 18. Member: CPA, Amer. Pers. and Guid. Assn, Assn. of Guid. Couns. of P.Q. Guidance, administration, teaching; educational and vocational guidance. M

GAGE, Mrs. Onalee June. Chapleau, Ont. b. 8 June 1927 Kitchener. MA '50 Univ. of Toronto, Can. Member: CPA. Vocational counseling, testing children and parental counseling in Child Guidance Clinic. F

GAGNON, Major Joseph Alphonse Aurèle. Directorate of Manning, Can. Army HQ, B. Bldg, Ottawa. b. 19 Sept 1914 Limoges. MA '42 McGill Univ, Can. CMD. PERS. OFF, Directorate of Manning, Can. Army. Member: CPA. Research, administration, personnel psychology, student; personality inventories, intelligence tests for selection purposes, interviewing, techniques. M

GAGNON, Jean Joseph Jules. 197 St. Jean, Que. b. 24 Sept 1925 Chicoutimi. Licence, Laval Univ, Can. GUID. COUNS, Ment. Hyg. and Guid. Serv. for Children, Dept. of Psychiat, Laval Univ, P.Q. Member: Assn. of Guid. Couns. of P.Q. Research, testing, consulting, guidance; clinical testing, personality tests for children. M

GANDER, Mrs. Elizabeth Mary. 9205 95 St, Edmonton, Alta. b. 25 July 1917 Calgary. MA '42 Univ. of Alberta, Can. Member: CPA. Achievement tests, eugenics, learning processes. F

GARNEAU, Dr. Jean. 640 Laurentian Blvd, Apt. 12, Ville St. Laurent, P.Q. b. 5 Apr 1922 Montreal. PH.D '51 Univ. of Montreal, Can. CHIEF PSYCH'T, Ste. Anne's Vets. Hosp, Ste. Anne de Bellevue, P.Q; CO-EDITOR, *The Canadian Psychologist*. Member: CPA, Psych. Assn. of P.Q. Diagnostic testing, psychotherapy, administration, teaching; projective techniques, army selection procedures. M

GAUDREAU, Guy. 8042 Blvd. St. Michel, Montreal 38, P.Q. b. 19 Aug 1926 Montreal. Licence '53 Univ. of Montreal, Can. PSYCHOLOGIST, Social Serv. of Nicolet, Nicolet, P.Q. Member: CPA. Educational psychology applied to problem children, interviewing; learning, projective techniques. M

GAUTHIER, Dr. Gaston. 1645 Rue Guertin, Ville St. Laurent, Montreal, P.Q. b. 25 Sept 1920 Montreal. Doctorat '47 Univ. of Montreal, Can. DIRECTOR, Clinique d'Aide à l'Enfance, 294 Carré St. Louis, Montreal. Member: CPA. Clinical practice, psychotherapy, testing, clinical analysis; projective techniques, vocational guidance. M

GÉDÉON, Frère, S. C. Mont Sacré Coeur, Granby, Que. b. 30 Apr 1911 Ste. Rose, Temiscouata. D.PED '44 Univ. of Montreal, Can. DIRECTOR, Junior High School, Mont

Sacré Coeur. Member: Psych. Assn. of P.Q, Assn. of Guid. Couns. of P.Q. School administration, teaching, testing, counseling; vocational and professional guidance, test construction. M

GELFAND, Leonard. Dept. of Psychiat, Univ. of Toronto, 2 Surrey Pl, Toronto 5, Ont. b. 26 Apr 1923 Winnipeg. MA '49 Univ. of Toronto, Can. RES. ASST, Univ. of Toronto. Member: CPA, APA. Research; learning, measurement, projective techniques. M

GERSTEIN, Dr. Reva. 35 Glen Oak Dr, Toronto, Ont. b. 27 Mar 1917 Toronto. PH.D '45 Univ. of Toronto, Can. DIR. of PROG. PLNG, Can. Ment. Health Assn, 732 Spadina Ave, Toronto; PRESIDENT, Natl. Council of Jewish Women of Can, 152 Beverley St, Toronto. Member: CPA,APA. Administration, program consultant on mental health; geriatrics, problems related to women. F

GIBSON, David. Ontario Hosp. Sch, Smiths Falls, Ont. b. 6 Apr 1926 Galt. MA '52 Univ. of Toronto, Can. SR. PSYCH'T, Ont. Hosp. Sch. Member: CPA, APA, Amer. Assn. for Ment. Defic. Testing, administration, research; theoretical and applied work in mental deficiency, genetics of behavior. M

GILES, Harvey Alfred. 87 Brucewood Crescent, Toronto 10, Ont. b. 25 May 1912 Saskatoon. M.SOC. Work '49 Univ. of Toronto, Can. PERS. DIR, United Co-operatives of Ont, 28 Duke St, Toronto. Member: Ont. Psych. Assn. Industrial and personnel psychology, administration, testing; employment interviewing and testing, non-directive counseling. M

GILL, Charles. 1368 Rue Notre Dame, Trois-Rivières, P.Q. b. 16 Aug 1920 Montreal. L.PS '45 Univ. of Montreal, Can. EDUC. PSYCH, Comm. of Cath. Schools of Trois-Rivières, Rue Hart, Trois-Rivières. Consulting, educational and family guidance, testing, psychotherapy; psychometry, projective techniques, juvenile delinquency. M

GODFREY, Maurice Lachlin. 20 Lozoway Dr, Scarborough, Ont. b. 5 Apr 1912 Toronto. BA '46 Univ. of Toronto, Can. REMED. TCHR. and SCH. PSYCH'T, East York Bd. of Educ, 670 Cosburn Ave, Toronto 6. Member: Ont. Psych. Assn, Int. Counc. for Exep. Child. Remedial teaching, testing, diagnosis and treatment, psychotherapy; attitude measurement, achievement tests, learning theory. M

GOGUEN, Roger. Provincial Hosp, P.O. Drawer 20, Lancaster, N.B. b. 2 June 1926 Moncton. Licenciate '51 Univ. of Montreal, Can. CLIN. PSYCH'T, Dept. of Hlth. and Soc. Serv, Province of N.B. Fredericton. Member: CPA. Testing, clinical analysis, psychotherapy, teaching; projective techniques, social psychology. M

GOLICK, Mrs. Margaret. 944 Dunlop, Outremont, Que. b. 11 July 1928 Yarmouth. M.SC, McGill Univ, Can. CLIN. PSYCH'T, Montreal Children's Hosp, Cedar. Ave, Montreal. Member: SPT, Psych. Assn. of P.Q. Testing, teaching, research; projective and psychometric techniques, evaluation of handicapped children, developmental psychology. F

GOOD, John Atkins. 40 Harwood Rd, Toronto 7, Ont. b. 24 Sept 1931 Toronto. MA '55 Univ. of Toronto, Can. PSYCHOLOGIST, Pers. Br, Hydro-Elect. Power Comm. of Ont, 620 Univ. Ave, Toronto 2. Member: CPA. Personnel psychology, testing; group process, educational disabilities. M

GOODFELLOW, H. D. L. Ontario Hosp. School, Orillia, Ont. b. 14 May 1910 Ontario. BA '34 Queen's Univ, Can. PSYCH'T. and DIR. of EDUC, Ont. Hosp. Sch, Orillia. Member: CPA, Amer. Assn. for Ment. Defic. Administration of training program, educational psychology, testing; child psychology, achievement tests, learning. M

GORMAN, Ivan Lloyd. Delong Dr, Rothwell Hgts, Ottawa, Ont. b. 4 Mar 1921 Merrickville. BA '49 Queen's Univ, Can. PSYCHOLOGIST, Govt. of Can, Dept. of Natl. Def, Ottawa. Member: CPA. Research, applied psychology, consulting; projective techniques. M

GRAHAM, David Murray. 100 St. George St, Toronto, Ont. b. 2 Sept 1929 Walkerville. MA '53 Univ. of Toronto, Can. STUDENT. Member: Maritime Psych. Assn, Ont. Psych. Assn. Student, school consultant; diagnosis and play therapy with disturbed children, perceptual difficulties in brain injury, group process. M

GRAPKO, Dr. Michael Frederic. Inst. of Child Study, Univ. of Toronto, 45 Walmer Rd, Toronto, Ont. b. 4 Feb 1921 Stuartburn. PH.D '53 Univ. of Toronto, Can. RES. ASSOC, Inst. of Child Study. Member: CPA, APA. Research, teaching, testing; mental health measurement, personality evaluation, test construction, learning theory. M

GRATTON, Rev. Prof. Henri, o.m.i. Oblate Ave, Ottawa-East, Ont. b. 30 June 1915 Eastview. PH.D '50 Univ. of Ottawa, Can. PROFESSOR, Fac. of Philos, Univ. of Ottawa, Laurier St, Ottawa. Member: CPA, American Cath. Psych. Assn. Teaching, guidance, research, testing, pastoral work; relation between philosophical and empirical psychology, psychoanalysis, empirical research on moral and religious attitudes. M

GRATTON, Hubert. 149 Carleton Ave, Ottawa 3, Ont. b. 5 Sept 1930 Ottawa.

PH.L '51 Univ. of Ottawa, Can. ASST. ADMIN, Can. Civil Serv, Ottawa. Member: CPA, Can. Guid. and Placement Assn. Administration, research, applied and personnel psychology; projective techniques, aptitude tests, personality. M

GRENON, Léopold. P.O. Box 43, Alma, P.Q. b. 17 Dec 1920 St. Aimé. Licence '50 Laval Univ, Can. DIRECTOR, Vocat. Guid. Cen, Sch. Comm. of Alma. Member: Assn. of Guid. Couns. of P.Q, Natl. Vocat. Guid. Assn. (USA), Amer. Pers. and Guid. Assn. Vocational guidance, consulting, testing, psychotherapy, teaching; achievement and aptitude tests, projective techniques. M

GRIFFIN, Dr. John Douglas. Can. Ment. Hlth. Assn, 732 Spadina Ave, Toronto 4, Ont. b. 3 June 1906 Hamilton. MD '32 Univ. of Toronto, Can. GENL. DIR, Can. Ment. Hlth. Assn; CONSULTANT, Can. Broadcasting Corp; LECTURER, Sch. of Soc. Work, Univ. of Toronto. Member: CPA. Administration, applied psychology, consulting;community mental health programs, preventive programs in schools and industry. M

GRIMM, Noel F. 3015 Queen St. E, Apt C 12, Toronto, Ont. b. 18 Apr 1920 Barberton, Ohio, USA. MA '53 Univ. of Akron, USA. STAFF PSYCH'T, Can. Bank of Commerce, 25 King St, Toronto. Member: CPA. Clinical testing, research, personnel psychology; perception and personality, projective techniques, personnel selection. M

GROLEAU, Miss Thérèse. 135 Rue Ste. Anne, Apt. 4, Quebec. b. 13 Sept 1933 St. Zacharie. Licence '55 Laval Univ, Can. EDUC. PSYCH'T, Medico-Soc. Cen. for Children, 565 Rue St. Jean, Quebec. Member: Assn. of Guid. Couns. of P.Q. Educational psychology, testing, guidance; vocational adjustment of physically handicapped. F

GUINDON, Miss Jeannine. Cen. d'Orientation, 39 Blvd. Gouin W, Montreal 12, P.Q. b. 3 Sept 1919 Montreal. L.PS '48 Univ. of Montreal, Can. DIRECTOR, Cen. d'Orientation; DIR. of EDUC. PSYCH, courses on Maladjusted Children, Inst. of Psych, Univ. of Montreal. Member: CPA, APA. Teaching, psychotherapy, testing, administration; projective techniques, reeducation of juvenile delinquents. F

GULUTSAN, Metro. Dept. of Pub. Hlth, 53 Stadacona W, Moose Jaw, Sask. b. 25 Nov. 1925 Buchanan. BA '47 Univ. of Saskatchewan, Can. PSYCH'T. and TCHR, Dept. of Pub. Hlth. Member: Sask. Psych. Assn. Educational psychology, guidance, testing; mental health problems of school children. M

HALLBERG, Miss Margaret Charlotte. Box 307, Edmonton, Alta. b. 12 Sept 1926

Nanaimo. MA '55 Univ. of Alberta, Can. CLIN. PSYCH'T, Provincial Ment. Ints, Edmonton. Member: CPA. Testing, clinical analysis, research, teaching, psychotherapy; projective techniques, research with mentally competent offenders. F

HALPERN, Miss Ester. 3570 Ridgewood, Apt. 208, Montreal, P.Q. b. 6 Nov 1929 Brăila, Rumania. M.PS.SC '54 McGill Univ, Can. CLIN. PSYCH'T, Montreal Children's Hosp, 2337 Dorchester W, Montreal. Member: CPA, SPT. Diagnostic testing, rehabilitation, consulting, guidance; testing children with physical or emotional handicaps, projective and achievement tests. F

HAMELIN, Rev. Brother Roger. Ecole Supérieure Beaudet, 685 Blvd. Décarie, Montreal 9, P.Q. b. 22 Feb 1915 Montreal. Licence '45 Univ. of Montreal, Can. PROFESSOR, Ecole Supérieure Beaudet; STUD. COUNS, Coll. St. André, St. Césaire, Co. Rouville, P.Q. Teaching, counseling and guidance, testing; delinquency, intelligence tests. M

HARDER, Miss Jean. 486 Strathcona Ave, Montreal 6, P.Q. b. 5 Dec 1922 Philadelphia, Pennsylvania, USA. MA '50 Tchrs. Coll, Columbia Univ, USA. ASST. STUD. COUNS, Sir George Williams Coll, 1435 Drummond St, Montreal 25. Member: Psych. Assn. of P.Q. Testing, counseling, administration; educational and vocational testing and counseling. F

HARPER, Frank Berryman Wilson. Psych. Dept, Provincial Ment. Hosp, Ponoka, Alta. b. 29 Mar 1927 Greenock, Scot. MA '52 Univ. of Glasgow, Scot. CLIN. PSYCH'T, Provincial Ment. Hosp. Member: BPS. Testing and diagnosis of mentally ill, psychotherapy, teaching; projective and psychometric testing, group psychotherapy, psychiatric nursing as psychotherapy. M

HARPER, Robert Johnston Craig. Div. of Psych, Fac. of Educ, Univ. of Alberta, Edmonton. b. 29 Mar 1927 Edmonton. MA '53 Univ. of Edinburgh, Scot. DIRECTOR, Educ. Clin. and ASST. PROF, Univ. of Alta; ASST. ED, *Alberta Journal of Educational Research.* Teaching, consulting, editorial; testing, counseling, projective techniques, play therapy. M

HARRIS, Miss Rilda Catherine. 87 Victoria Rd, Apt. 1, Halifax, N.S. b. 17 Jan 1934 Pictou. MA '56 Dalhousie Univ, Can. PSYCHOLOGIST, Nova Scotia Hosp, Dartmouth. Member: CPA. Testing, clinical analysis; personality theory. F

HAYES, Herbert Orville. 5625 Toronto Rd, Vancouver 8, B.C. b. 27 Jan 1910 Winnipeg. MA '49 Univ. of British Columbia, Can. ASST. in PERS. and RES, Vancouver Sch. Bd,

1595 W. 10 Ave, Vancouver 9. Member: CPA, Pacific Northwest Pers. Management Assn. Personnel psychology, educational research, testing, counseling; mental tests and measurements, personnel classification and placement. M

HEBB, Prof. Donald Olding. Dept. of Psych, McGill Univ, Montreal 2. b. 22 July 1904 Chester. PH.D '36 Harvard Univ, USA. PROFESSOR, McGill Univ; CONSULT. ED, *Canadian Journal of Psychology, Psychological Review.* Member: CPA, APA, BPS. Teaching, administration, professional writing; theory of behavior, comparative psychology, relation of physiological to psychological method. M

HENLEY, Dr. Gordon H. Ment. Health Div, Dept. of Hlth. and Soc. Serv, 658 Queen St, Fredericton, N.B. b. 26 Apr 1922 Toronto. PH.D '55 Ohio State Univ, USA. SR. PSYCH'T, Ment. Hlth. Div, Dept. of Hlth. and Soc. Serv. Member: CPA, APA, Amer. Pers. and Guid. Assn. Consulting administration of in-service clinical training, teaching; personality theory; psychotherapy, counseling. M

HERBERT, Bernard L. P.O. Box 614, Digby, N.S. b. 6 May 1919 Berthierville. B.PS '48 Univ. of Montreal, Can. CLIN. PSYCH'T, Digby Psychiat. Clin, Box 448, Digby. Member: CPA, SPT. Diagnostic testing, research, child guidance; projective techniques, diagnosis and reeducation of maladjusted children. M

HERON, Dr. Woodburn. Dept. of Psych, McGill Univ, Montreal 2. b. 3 July 1926 Mandeville, Jamaica, B.W.I. PH.D '53 McGill Univ, Can. RES. ASSOC, McGill Univ. Member: CPA, APA. Research, teaching; sensory and thought processes, perception. M

HEWSON, Dr. John Cecil. Stevenson and Kellogg, Ltd, 810 Royal Bank Bldg, Vancouver 2, B.C. b. 20 Nov 1907 Barrie. PH.D '42 Univ. of California, USA. SR. CONSULT. PSYCH'T, Stevenson and Kellogg, Ltd. Member: CPA, APA. Industrial psychology, testing, administration; test development for industrial purposes. M

HICKLING, James Frederick. Can. Pers. Consultants, 134 Bloor St. W, Toronto, Ont. b. 20 Feb 1921 Welland. MA '49 Univ. of Toronto, Can. DIRECTOR, Can. Pers. Consultants. Member: CPA. Industrial psychology, testing, consulting, vocational guidance; group process, projective techniques, learning theory. M

HIRSCH, Morris. Dalhousie Pub. Hlth. Clin, Univ. Ave, Halifax, N.S. b. 1 Sept 1927 Sydney. MA '52 Univ. of Toronto, Can. PSYCHOLOGIST, Dept. of Hlth. and Welf, City of Halifax. Member: CPA, APA. Consulting, child guidance, teaching, testing, therapy, research. M

HODDINOTT, Bernard Arthur. 3 Hubbard Blvd, Toronto, Ont. b. 2 Feb 1933 Toronto. MA '56 Univ. of Ottawa, Can. CLIN. PSYCH'T, Sunnybrook Hosp, Bayview Ave, Toronto; PERS. SEL. OFF, Can. Army. Member: CPA. Testing, clinical analysis, psychotherapy, research. M

HOFFMAN, Irving James. 881 Ave. Rd, Toronto, Ont. b. 8 Aug 1908 Lublin, Poland. MA '46 Univ. of Toronto, Can. RETIRED. Member: CPA. Private guidance and personnel work; projective techniques and other testing. M

HOGUE, Prof. J. Pierre. 8407 Rue Drolet, Montreal 10, P.Q. b. 24 Nov 1927 Montreal. L.PS '52 Univ. of Montreal, Can. STUDENT. Member: CPA. Student, consulting, teaching; industrial psychology, publicity, market research. M

HOLDSWORTH, Benjamin Herbert. Hillside Ave, Hudson Heights, P.Q. b. 25 Apr 1920 Toronto. BA '44 Univ. of Toronto, Can. INDUS. PSYCH'T, B. H. Holdsworth Co, Hudson Heights. Member: CPA. Research in industrial psychology, public relations and advertising; human motivation, personnel consulting and placement techniques, attitude measurement. M

HOPKINS, Albert William. Psych. Dept, Ontario Hosp, Hamilton, Ont. b. 7 June 1921 Winnipeg. MA '53 Univ. of Toronto, Can. PSYCHOLOGIST, Ont. Hosp. Member: CPA. Diagnostic testing, psychotherapy, research; teaching methods, group process. M

HOSHIKO, Michael S. Speech and Hearing Clin, Purdue Univ, Lafayette, Indiana, USA. b. Canada. AM '49 Bowling Green State Univ, USA. RES. FELLOW, Purdue Univ. Member: CPA, APA, Amer. Speech and Hrng. Assn. Student, diagnostic and audiological testing, research, speech therapy; electromyographic research, psychotherapy, audition. M

HOUGH, Rev. Arthur John Bates. Stud. Advisory Serv, Univ. of Alberta, Edmonton. b. 25 Jan 1912 Beausejour. MA '55 Univ. of Western Ontario, Can. STUD. COUNS. and LECT. in PSYCHOMET, Univ. of Alta. Student counseling, teaching, research, testing; personality theory, experimental design, child development. M

HOWARD, Dr. James Willis. 1509 Sherbrooke St. W, Montreal, P.Q. b. 29 June 1899 Orangeville. PH.D, Cornell Univ, USA. CONSULT. PSYCH'T, priv. prac. Member: BPS, CPA. Clinical practice, testing and clinical analysis, research; projective techniques. M

HOWARD, Kenneth Gilbert. 66 Ruttan Bay, Fort Garry, Winnipeg 9, Man. b. 30 May 1925 Selkirk. MA '52 Univ. of Western Ontario, Can. CLIN. PSYCH'T, Child Guid. Clin. of Greater Winnipeg, Sch. Dist. of Winnipeg No. 1, William and Ellen Sts, Winnipeg. Member: CPA. Testing, clinical analysis, psychotherapy, research on juvenile delinquency, industrial consulting; projective techniques, group process. M

HOWE, John Lyman. Marian Wing, St. Joseph's Hosp, Richmond St, London, Ont. b. 21 June 1920 Toronto. MA '53 Univ. of Western Ontario, Can. CLIN. PSYCH'T, St. Joseph's Hosp. Member: CPA. Testing, consulting, teaching; projective techniques, group and music therapy. M

HOWLETT, Major John Marcus. Pers. Selectn. Serv, HQ CDN Base Units Europe, CDN Regular Army, CAPO 5050, Montreal, P.Q. b. 30 Oct 1908 Bournemouth, Eng. MA '51 Univ. of Alberta, Can. ARMY PERS. OFF, Dept. of Natl. Def, CDN Army, Ottawa. Member: CPA. Personnel selection and placement, testing and clinical analysis of maladjusted personnel, administration; evaluation of adjustment in Army and the use of projective, diagnostic and achievement tests. M

HOWSON, Rev. James Donald L. Dept. of Natl. Def, HQ, Quebec Cmd, 3530 Atwater Ave, Montreal. b. 14 Oct 1914 Peterborough. MA '47 Univ. of Toronto, Can. STAFF CHAPLAIN, Dept. of Natl. Def, HQ, Que. Cmd. Member: CPA. Consulting, guidance, applied psychology, administration, parish work; projective techniques, psychology of religion, abnormal psychology. M

HOYT, Dr. Ruth. 655 Rideau St, Ottawa, Ont. b. 9 June 1914 Methuen, USA. PH.D '52 McGill Univ, Can. SR. STAFF OFF, Def. Res. Bd, Elgin St, Ottawa. Member: CPA, APA. Research in human resources, administration; physiological psychology, human engineering. F

HUBERMAN, Dr. Jur. John. Western Plywood Co, Ltd, 900 E. Kent Ave, Vancouver, B.C. b. 27 Feb 1911 Vienna, Austria. Dr. Jur. '32 Univ. of Budapest, Hungary. DIR. of INDUS. RELATIONS, Western Plywood Co, Ltd. Member: CPA. Administration, industrial psychology, personnel testing and selection, counseling; projective techniques, achievement tests, personality theory. M

HUGHES, Kenneth Russell. 871 Garwood Ave, Winnipeg 9, Man. b. 7 May 1933 Winnipeg. MA '56 Univ. of Manitoba, Can. RES. ASSOC, Univ. of Man, Winnipeg. Member: CPA. Research, student; biochemical influences on learning, comparative psychology, physiological psychology. M

HUGHES, Miss Mona Athol. Bell Telephone Co. of Can, 1050 Beaver Hall Hill, Montreal.

b. 1 Feb 1921 Toronto. MA '47 Univ. of Toronto, Can. ASST. in EDUC. ACTIV, Bell Telephone Co. of Can. Member: CPA. Educational and personnel psychology, teaching, research in training methods; learning theory, group process, use of psychotherapeutic methods in industry. F

HUMPHRIES, Michael. 383 Spadina Rd, Toronto, Ont. b. 25 May 1923 Birmingham, Eng. MA '53 Univ. of Toronto, Can. LECTURER, Univ. of Toronto; CONSULT. ED, *Canadian Journal of Psychology.* Member: APA, CPA. Research, teaching, professional writing, consulting; learning theory, motor learning and human engineering, research methods.   M

HUTCHISON, Harry Clinch. 7 Kentucky Ave, Toronto 9, Ont. b. 22 May 1921 Dundee, Scot. MA '52 Univ. of Toronto, Can. PSYCHOLOGIST, Forensic Clin, Toronto Psychiat. Hosp, 2 Surrey Pl, Toronto. Member: APA. Psychometric and projective testing, research; personality characteristics of stutterers, lie detection with forensic patients.   M

HUTSON, R. Leighton. Lab. for Psych. Studies, Allan Memor. Inst. of Psychiat, 1025 Pine Ave. W, Montreal, P.Q. b. 23 Dec 1925 Barbados, B.W.I. MA '53 Univ. of Montreal, Can. CLIN. PSYCH'T, Allan Memor. Inst. of Psychiat. Member: CPA, APA, SPT. Clinical analysis, teaching, research; projective techniques, learning theory, interpersonal studies.   M

IRVINE, Mrs. Lucille. 3440 Peel St, Apt. 34, Montreal, P.Q. b. 14 Feb 1900 Montreal. MA '48 McGill Univ, Can. SPEC. LECT, McGill Sch. of Soc. Work, 3600 Univ. St, Montreal; LECTURER, Ment. Hygiene Inst, Montreal. Member: CPA. Teaching, psychotherapy, consulting; developmental psychology, mental hygiene, application of psychoanalytic theory to social work, child guidance and personality problems.   F

JACKSON, Prof. Robert William Brierley. Ontario Coll. of Educ. Univ. of Toronto, 371 Bloor St. W, Toronto 5, Ont. b. 26 Sept 1909 Seven Persons. PH.D '37 Univ. of London, Eng. PROF. and ASST. DIR, Dept. of Educ. Res, Ont. Coll. of Educ. Member: CPA. Research, teaching, administration; intelligence and achievement tests, statistics, measurement.   M

JENSEN, Mrs. H. Elizabeth. c/o Dr. McCullough, 4742 55 St, Red Deer, Alta. b. 11 July 1924 Ponoka. MA '48 Univ. of Toronto, Can. Member: CPA. Projective techniques, vocational counseling, attitude measurement.   F

JILLINGS, Charles R. 3323 McCallum Ave, Regina, Sask. b. 11 Dec 1923 Saskatoon. MA '51 Univ. of British Columbia, Can.

ADMIN. SUPERV, Psychiat. Serv, Dept. of Pub. Hlth, College Ave, Regina; EDITOR, *Saskatchewan Psychologist.* Member: CPA. Administration, personnel psychology, testing; diagnosis, psychotherapy, projective techniques.   M

JOHNSON, Lt. James Arthur. H.M.C.S. "Stadacona," Halifax, N.S. b. 4 May 1923 Lancaster. MA '52 Dalhousie Univ, Can. ASST. TRNG. COMMANDER, Dept. of Natl. Def. Member: CPA. Training junior officers, administration.   M

JOHNSTON, Mrs. Nancy Mary Elizabeth. Ontario Hosp, St. Thomas, Ont. b. 7 Aug 1927 Toronto. MA '50 Univ. of Toronto, Can. CLIN. PSYCH'T, Ont. Hosp, 999 Queen St. W, Toronto. Member: CPA. Diagnostic testing, research, psychotherapy, teaching; rigidity of self-definition and its effect on interpersonal relationships, confused laterality, group therapy.   F

JOLIN, Louis. 289 Principale, Waterloo, Que. b. 29 Dec 1922 Waterloo. BA '43 Univ. of Montreal, Can. LAW STUDENT, Univ. of Montreal. Member: Psych. Assn. of P.Q. Student; juvenile delinquency.   M

JONES, Douglas William. 40 Braeside Rd, Toronto. b. 14 Nov 1918 St. Catharines. MA '52 Univ. of Toronto, Can. STAFF PSYCH'T, J. B. Fraser and Assoc. Ltd, 185 Bloor St. E, Toronto. Member: CPA. Projective testing for selection of executives, management consulting, interviewing, guidance, psychotherapy; projective techniques, group dynamics, prefrontal leucotomy, research.   M

JONES, Elvet Glyn. Univ. of Minnesota, Minneapolis, Minnesota, USA. b. 20 May 1922 Victoria. MA '49 Univ. of British Columbia, Can. INSTRUCTOR, Univ. of Minn. Member: CPA, APA. Administration, guidance, teaching; personality, psychotherapy.   M

JONES, W. Caron. Med. Serv. Div, Ontario Hydro Elec. Power Comm, 620 Univ. Ave, Toronto. b. 28 Nov 1913 Detroit, Michigan, USA. MA '51 Univ. of Toronto, Can. STAFF PSYCH'T, Ont. Hydro Elec. Power Comm; LECT. in PSYCH, Univ. of Toronto. Member: Ont. Psych. Assn. Vocational and personal guidance and counseling, testing; dynamics of therapy process, immobilizing restrictions of self-image, motivation.   M

JOSEPH-OVIDE, Sister. St. Mary's Hosp, Sch. of Nrsng, Timmins, Ont. b. 20 Apr 1916 St. Tite. MA '54 Fordham Univ, USA. DIRECTOR, Sch. of Nrsng, St. Mary's Hosp. Member: Psych. Assn. of P.Q. Testing, teaching, administration; achievement tests, learning theory, group process.   F

JOYNER, Dr. Robert Campbell. Dept. of Psych, Univ. of Toronto, 98 St. George St,

Toronto, Ont. b. 25 July 1921 Kingston. PH.D '53 Univ. of Toronto, Can. LECTURER, Univ. of Toronto; EDITOR, *Newsletter* of Ont. Psych. Assn. Member: CPA, APA. Teaching, research, industrial psychology; group process, action research, human relations in industry. M

KAMIN, Dr. Leon J. Dept. of Psych, Queen's Univ, Kingston, Ont. b. 29 Dec 1927 Taunton, Massachusetts, USA. PH.D '54 Harvard Univ, USA. RES. ASSOC, Queen's Univ. Member: APA. Research, teaching, professional writing; learning and personality theory, individual differences. M

KARAL, Mrs. Pearl. 501 Hillsdale Ave. E, Toronto. b. 16 Aug 1925 Winnipeg. MA '49 Univ. of Toronto, Can. RES. ASST, Inst. of Child Study, 45 Walmer Rd, Toronto. Member: CPA. Research, testing, consulting, student; personality theory, projective techniques, child study. F

KEELEY, Mrs. Faith Elizabeth. Rural Route 3, Chatham, Ont. b. 29 Aug 1917 Hastings, Eng. MA '42 Univ. of Western Ontario, Can. Member: CPA. F

KELLY, Mrs. Gwynedd Hartwell. 1105 First St. E, Saskatoon, Sask. b. 10 Nov 1925 London. BA '47 Univ. of Western Ontario, Can. PSYCHOLOGIST, MacNeill Clinic, 514 Queen St, Saskatoon. Member: CPA. Testing, play therapy, consulting; achievement and projective tests. F

KENNY, Dr. Douglas Timothy. Dept. of Psych, Univ. of British Columbia, Vancouver. b. 20 Oct 1923 Victoria. PH.D '52 Univ. of Washington, USA. ASST. PROF, Univ. of B.C. Member: CPA, APA. Teaching, research, professional writing; theory of humor, learning and personality theory. M

KESCHNER, Miss Dorothee Ann. 9 Cottingham Rd, Toronto. b. 12 May 1924 Solingen, Germany. MA '48 Univ. of Toronto, Can. PSYCHOLOGIST, Bd. of Educ, 155 College St, Toronto. Member: CPA. Testing, interviewing, consulting, educational psychology; play therapy, intelligence and projective testing of children. F

KETCHUM, Prof. John Davidson. Dept. of Psych, Univ. of Toronto, Toronto 5, Ont. b. 10 June 1893 Cobourg. MA '25 Univ. of Toronto, Can. PROFESSOR, Univ. of Toronto; EDITOR, *Canadian Journal of Psychology*. Member: CPA. Teaching, editorial, research; theory of social psychology, research on social behavior, group dynamics. M

KIBBLEWHITE, Edward James. 7915 119 St, Edmonton, Alta. b. 13 July 1895 Alton. MA '31 Univ. of Alberta, Can. CHIEF CLIN. PSYCH'T, Provincial Guid. Clinics, Dept. of Pub. Hlth, Admin. Bldg, Edmonton. Member: CPA. Clinical practice, testing,

administration, psychotherapy; general ability measurement, learning theory, preventive work in mental health. M

KING, Herbert Baxter. 104 Strathcona Ave, Ottawa. b. 1 Jan 1879 Dorking. PH.D '36 Univ. of Washington, USA. Retired. M

KING, Dr. Mrs. Margery Rean. 421 St. Clair Ave. E, Toronto. b. 30 Dec 1913 Woodstock. PH.D '50 Univ. of Toronto, Can. EXEC. DIR, Toronto Br, Can. Ment. Hlth. Assn, 111 St. George St, Toronto; CONSULT. PSYCH'T, Dept. of Vets. Affairs. Member: CPA. Administration, research, teaching, consulting; social adjustment of school children, mental health training of teachers. F

KIRBY, Hugh Wride. 2011 Mansfield St, Apt. 37, Montreal, P.Q. b. 20 June 1926 Sarnia. MA '56 Univ. of Toronto, Can. PERS. SEL. OFF, Canadian Army, 3530 Atwater St, Montreal. Member: CPA. Personnel psychology, student, research, teaching; learning theory, social psychology and group dynamics, personality scale construction. M

KIRK, William R. 724 Coxwell Ave, Apt. B, Toronto 6, Ont. b. 27 May 1920 Toronto. MA '49 Univ. of Toronto, Can. ASST. DIR, Dept. of Univ. Extension, Univ. of Toronto, Simcoe Hall, Toronto. Member: CPA. Administration of business and industrial education program, educational psychology. M

KLIMAN, Earl M. 244 Highland Rd. W, Apt. 8, Kitchener, Ont. b. 23 Sept 1925 Regina. MA '50 Univ. of Toronto, Can. PSYCHOLOGIST, Ont. Dept. of Hlth, Ment. Hlth. Clin, K-W Hosp, Kitchener. Member: CPA. Diagnostic testing, psychotherapy, teaching; projective techniques, psychotherapeutic process, social perception. M

KLONOFF, Dr. Harry. 936 W. 18 Ave, Vancouver 9, B.C. b. 29 July 1924 Winnipeg. PH.D '54 Univ. of Washington, USA. SR. PSYCH'T, Shaughnessy Vets, Hosp, 30 and Laurel St, Vancouver. Member: CPA, APA. Clinical practice, consulting, testing, research; projective techniques, group psychotherapy, attitude measurement. M

KOERBER, Dr. Walter F. 24 Kappele Ave, Toronto 12, Ont. b. 2 Dec 1909 Tavistock. D.PAED '47 Univ. of Toronto, Can. CHIEF SUPERV. of SPEC. EDUC. Scarborough Bd. of Educ, 1650 Kingston Rd, Toronto 13. Member: CPA. Administration, testing, consulting; educational psychology applied to physically and mentally deviant children, testing of intellectual potential. M

LACHANCE, Rev. Jean-Marie. 3 de l'Université, Que. b. 2 Dec 1921 Quebec. Licence '55 Univ. of Montreal, Can. TEACHER, Sch. of Educ. and Guid, 71 d'Auteuil, Quebec. Member: APA, Psych. Assn. of P.Q. Teaching, psychotherapy, guidance, consulting; psychology of personality and of adolescence. M

LACOMBE, Prof. André. 2897 Pl. Harper, Trois-Rivières, Que. b. 2 May 1924 Grand 'Mere. M.ED '50 Univ. of Montreal, Can. GUID. COUNS, Soc. Serv. Cen, 1337 Blvd. du Carmel, Trois-Rivières. Member: CPA. Guidance, teaching, educational and personnel psychology; educational guidance and counseling. M

LAIDLAW, Dr. Robert Gordon Nicholas. Inst. of Child Study, 45 Walmer Rd, Toronto. b. 11 Apr 1916 Toronto. PH.D '54 Univ. of Toronto, Can. RES. ASST, Inst. of Child Study. Member: CPA, APA. Research, educational psychology, teaching; interpersonal perception, group process, personality testing. M

LAIRD, Prof. Isabel Margaret. Psych. Dept. Queen's Univ, Kingston, Ont. b. 29 June 1905 Edinburgh, Scot. B.ED '29 Univ. of Edinburgh, Scot. ASST. PROF, Queen's Univ. Member: BPS, CPA. Teaching, educational psychology, research; hospitalization and institutionalization of children, religious training of children. F

LAMBERT, Dr. Wallace E. Psych. Dept, McGill Univ, Montreal, P.Q. b. 31 Dec 1922 Amherst. PH.D '53 Univ. of North Carolina, USA. ASST. PROF, McGill Univ. Member: APA, CPA. Teaching, research; learning theory, social perception, attitude measurement, bilingual behavior. M

LAMOND, Conrad MacDonald. Employee Appraisal and Devel. Serv, 939 Hornby St, Vancouver 1, B.C. b. 20 Feb 1923 Oak Lake. CONSULT. PSYCH'T, Employee Appraisal and Dev. Serv. Member: CPA, APA, Amer. Pers. Guid. Assn. Industrial and personnel psychology, guidance, testing, teaching; aptitude testing and counseling, projective techniques, human relations, training of supervisors. M

LAMPARD, Miss Dorothy Mary. Fac. of Educ, Univ. of Alberta, Edmonton. b. 16 Sept 1911 Calgary. MA '46 Univ. of Chicago, USA. ASST. PROF, Univ. of Alta; ED. BD, *The Reading Teacher*. Member: CPA, BPS. Teaching, educational psychology, research, reading consultant; reading clinics, group process, achievement tests. F

LANDRY, Miss Lydia. 534 Rue Sherbrooke E, Montreal, P.Q. b. 16 Sept 1919 Pockmouche. Licence '53 Univ. of Montreal, Can. PSYCHOLOGIST, Guid. Cen, 39 Blvd. Gouin W, Montreal. Member: CPA. Diagnostic testing, guidance, psychotherapy; projective techniques, achievement tests, social perception. F

LANGLOIS, J. H. Robert. 2348 Madison Ave, N.D.G., Montreal, P.Q. b. 12 May 1921

Estcourt. MA '50 Laval Univ, Can. GUID. COUNS, Can. Inst. of Vocat. Guid, 4327 St. Hubert St, Montreal. Member: CPA, Assn. of Guid. Couns. of P.Q. Consulting, guidance, testing, interviewing, research; group verbal intelligence tests, attitude measurement, personality questionnaires, methods of follow-up. M

L'ARCHEVÊQUE, Dr. Paul. 45 d'Artigny St, Que. b. 7 May 1910 Montreal. Doctor '44 Univ. of Montreal, Can. PROFESSOR, Sch. of Educ. and Guid, Laval Univ, 71 Rue d'Auteuil, Que. Member: CPA, Amer. Cath. Psych. Assn. Teaching, research, psychotherapy; clinical and diagnostic uses of personality measurement. M

LA RIVIÈRE, André. 3426 Marcil Ave, N.D.G. Montreal. b. 11 Nov 1919 Montreal. MA '46 Univ. of Montreal, Can. PSYCHOTHERAPIST, priv. prac. Member: BPS, HPS, DGP. Psychotherapy, clinical practice, testing; psychoanalysis. M

LA ROCHE, Jean. 10395 Verville, Montreal. b. 23 May 1919 Que. MA '51 Laval Univ, Can. PSYCH. CONSULT, priv. prac. Member: CPA, Assn. of Guid. Couns. of P.Q. Consulting, guidance, testing, applied psychology; achievement and aptitude tests, family guidance. M

LATOUR, Jean Paul. 2665 Pie IX, Apt. 4, Montreal. b. 30 Sept 1924 Montreal. Licence '53 Univ. of Montreal, Can. PSYCHOLOGIST, Vocat. Guid. Bur, 35 Notre Dame W, Montreal. Member: CPA. Guidance, testing; vocational counseling. M

LAURENDEAU, Prof. Monique. Inst. of Psych, Univ. of Montreal, 2900 Blvd. Mont Royal, Montreal. b. 11 Mar 1930 Montreal. MA '52 Univ. of Montreal, Can. ASST. PROF, Inst. of Psych, Univ. of Montreal. Member: CPA. Teaching, research, administration; theory, development and measurement of intelligence, learning theory, test construction. F

LAURIER, Brother Blaise V. The Clerics of St. Viateur, 1145 West St. Viateur St, Outremont, Montreal 8, P.Q. b. 7 Jan 1910 Lachenaie. PH.D '48 Cath. Univ. of America, USA. DIR. OF STUDIES, The Clerics of St. Viateur; LECTURER, Univ. of Montreal. Member: CPA, APA, Amer. Cath. Psych. Assn. Administration, consulting, teaching; assessment of good teachers and their personality development in training. M

LAURIN, Miss Gaëtane. 870 Rockland, Montreal, P.Q. b. 15 Feb 1926 Montreal. L.PS '51 Univ. of Montreal, Can. DIRECTOR, Maternelle de St. Hippolyte, 1055 Tassé, Ville St. Laurent, Montreal. Member: CPA. Educational psychology, counseling, testing, teaching; projective techniques, learning theory, preventive psychiatry, play therapy. F

LAVER, Major A. Bryan. 1987 Alta Vista Dr, Ottawa 1, Ont. b. 11 Dec 1918 Regina. MA '55 Queen's Univ. Can. PERS. OFF, Pers. Sel. Serv, Army HQ, Dept. of Natl. Def, Lisgar St, Ottawa 4. Member: Ottawa Psych. Assn. Writing, personnel selection and classification manuals, administration, research; group personality tests, interview techniques, attitude measurement. M

LAVOIE, Guy. Inst. of Psych, Univ. of Montreal, 2900 Blvd. Mont Royal, Montreal. b. 2 Oct 1925 Montreal. L.PS '50 Univ. of Montreal, Can. TEACHER, Univ. of Montreal. Member: APA, CPA. Teaching, research; experimental psychology, psychometry, statistics, factor analysis. M

LAVOIE, Brother Stanislas, c.s.v. Ecole Supérieure St. Michel, Rouyn, Que. b. 15 Feb 1902 Worcester, Massachusetts, USA. Diplôme '44 Univ. of Montreal, Can. PRINCIPAL, Ecole Supérieure St. Michel, Cath. Sch. Bd, Rouyn. Member: Psych. Assn of P.Q, Assn. of Guid. Couns. of P.Q, Natl. Vocat. Guid. Assn. Administration, teaching, testing, counseling students; achievement tests, attitude measurement.M

LAWRENCE, William John. 89 Charles St. W, Toronto 5, Ont. b. 3 Mar 1930 Manville. BA '53 Univ. of British Columbia, Can. STUDENT, Univ. of Toronto. Member: Ont. Psych. Assn. Teaching, research; nondirective psychotherapy, group process, social perception. M

LAYCOCK, Dr. Samuel Ralph. Univ. of Saskatchewan, Saskatoon, Sask. b. 7 Mar 1891 Marmora. PH.D '27 Univ. of London, Eng. DEAN EMER, Univ. of Sask; ASSOC. ED, *Understanding the Child*; ADVIS. ED, *Parents Magazine.* Member: BPS, CPA, Socy. for Res. in Child Devel. (USA). Retired, professional writing, lecturing, consulting; mental testing, adjustments of exceptional children, psychology of learning, child development. M

LEBLANC, Alphee Gerard. 4610 Linton Ave, Apt. 1, Montreal, P.Q. b. 24 Sept 1922 Green River. L.PS '52 Univ. of Montreal, Can. SR. PSYCH'T, Queen Mary Vets. Hosp, Queen Mary Rd, Montreal. Member: APA, CPA, SPT. Consulting, guidance, research, testing, diagnostic interviewing; employability assessment, psychomotor and social adaptation tests, gerontology. M

LEFEBVRE, Prof. Brother Joseph Paul Edgar, c.s.v. Juvénat des Saints-Anges, Bertierville, Que. b. 2 Jan 1915 Ste. Elisabeth. L.PAED '50 Univ. of Montreal, Can. PRINCIPAL, Juvénat des Saints-Anges; DIRECTOR, Vocat. Guid. Bur, St. Joseph High School, Bertierville. Member: Psych. Assn. of P.Q, Assn. of Guid. Couns. of P.Q. Administration, applied and educational psychology, guidance, teaching; a-

chievement tests, projective techniques. M

LEGARE, Pierre. 34 Ste. Julie, Apt. 3, Quebec. b. 24 Oct 1929 Beauce, St. Joseph. MA '56 Laval Univ, Can. GUID. COUNS, and STUDENT. Guidance, interviewing, testing; guidance counseling. M

LEHMANN, Dr. Heinz Edgar. 6603 Lasalle Blvd, Montreal, P.Q. b. 17 July 1911 Berlin, Germany. MD '35 Univ. of Berlin, Germany. CLIN. DIR, Verdun Protestant Hosp, 6875 Lasalle Blvd, Montreal; ASST. PROF. in PSYCHIAT, McGill Univ, Montreal; ASSOC ED, *Canadian Journal of Psychiatry.* Member: SPT, Psych. Assn. of P.Q. Clinical supervision, psychotherapy, teaching, research; projective techniques, psychophysiological perceptual tests. M

LEONARD, Robert P. 10730 Olympia Blvd, Montreal, P.Q. b. 12 Oct 1930 Hamilton. MA '54 Univ. of Montreal, Can. PERS. ASST, Employee Relat. Dept, Canadian Industries Ltd, 1253 McGill College St, Montreal. Member: CPA. Applied and industrial psychology, interviewing, testing, student; industrial selection and placement methods, use of psychological methods in classification, social perception and process in small industrial groups. M

LESSARD, Jean-Charles. Psycho-Social Cen, Rehab. Socy, Box 996, Sherbrooke. b. 2 Sept 1922 Ste. Ursule. L.PS '48 Univ. of Montreal, Can. CLIN. PSYCH'T, Psycho-Soc. Cen, Rehab. Socy; LECT. in PSYCH. and EDUC, Laval Univ. and Univ. of Sherbrooke. Member: CPA, Amer. Cath. Psych. Assn. Consulting, clinical practice, educational psychology, teaching; child psychology, diagnosis and education of the mentally deficient, social maturation and social training. M

LEVEY, Archie. Suite 45, Community Apts, Saskatoon, Sask. b. 4 Dec 1924 Kamloops. MA '52 Univ. of British Columbia, Can. CLIN. PSYCH'T, Univ. Hosp, Dept. of Psychiat, Saskatoon; ASSISTANT, Schizophrenic Res. Unit, Dept. of Pub. Hlth, Sask. Member: CPA. Testing, child psychotherapy, research; projective techniques, prognosis in choice and outcome of play therapies, behavior theory. M

LEVINSON, Mrs. Toby Ferne. 232 Glenholme Ave, Toronto, Ont. b. 31 May 1924 Toronto. MA '50 Univ. of Toronto, Can. PSYCHOLOGIST, Toronto Psychiat. Hosp, 2 Surrey Pl, Toronto. Member: CPA, WFMH. Diagnostic testing, vocational counseling, research, teaching; projective techniques, organic impairment test, vocational aptitude studies. F

LEWIS, Mrs. Hanna. Alcoholism Foundation of Alberta, 9910 103 St, Edmonton. b. 2 June 1918 Brant. BA, Univ. of Alberta, Can. PSYCH. COUNS, Alcoholism Found. of

Alta. Member: CPA. Counseling; group therapy, counseling techniques, social perception.   F.

LINN, John R. 303 Cunningham Ave, Ottawa, Ont. b. 20 Oct 1910 Canada.: D.PAED '55 Univ. of Toronto, Can. ASST. PSYCH'T, Ottawa Pub. Sch. Bd, 330 Gilmour St, Ottawa. Member: Ont. Psych. Assn. Educational psychology, testing, consulting, guidance.   M

LIVINGSTON, Prof. Kenneth Charles. 319 Ridelle Ave, Toronto, Ont. b. 17 Feb 1923 Toronto. M.A.SC '47 Univ. of Toronto, Can. ASST. PROF, Inst. of Bus. Admin, Univ. of Toronto, 273 Bloor St. W, Toronto. Member: CPA. Teaching, research, industrial psychology, consulting; learning theory, group process.   M

LOBB, Harold O. Dept. of Pub. Hlth, Province of Sask, Regina. b. 1 Sept 1920 Stoughton. M.ED '50 Univ. of Saskatchewan, Can. TCHR. PSYCH'T, Dept. of Pub. Hlth; CONSULTANT, Bd. of Directors, Regina Sch. for Mentally Retarded Children. Member: Sask. Psych. Assn. Applied and educational psychology, consulting, counseling teachers in mental health, testing; developmental psychology, learning and adjustment theory, intelligence testing.   M

LOCKWOOD, Richard David. 2850 Keele St, Apt. 3, Downsview, Ont. b. 22 Apr 1925 Lachine. MA '50 Queen's Univ, Can. PERS. OFF, Hydro Elec. Power Comm. of Ont, 620 Univ. Ave, Toronto. Member: CPA. Personnel psychology and administration; social perception, attitude measurement, group process.   M

LONG, James Alan. 50 Hollywood Crescent, Toronto 8, Ont. b. 1 Jan 1925 Toronto. MA '52 Univ. of Toronto, Can. FELLOW in CLIN. PSYCH, Southeast Louisiana Hosp, Dept. of Institutions, Mandeville, Louisiana USA. Member: CPA. Student, testing, research; psychodynamic function of delusions, group psychotherapy, projective techniques.   M

LOOMER, Miss Alice. 123 Waverly Pl, New York 11, New York, USA. b. Falmouth. MA '39 Univ. of Toronto, Can. REHAB. PSYCH'T, Inst. of Physical Med. and Rehab, New York Univ, Bellevue Med. Cen, 400 E. 34 St, New York. Member: CPA, APA. Testing, vocational and personal counseling; psychotherapy, projective testing, vocational guidance.   F

LOTT, Capt. Walter John. HQ Western Cmd, Kingsway Ave, Edmonton, Alta. b. 29 Dec 1921 Moose Jaw. MA '55 Univ. of Alberta, Can. PERS. OFF, HQ Western Cmd, Can. Army. Member: CPA. Personnel selection and placement, testing, counseling.   M

LUKE, Brother, F. S. C. Inst. St. Georges, Mont-La-Salle, Montreal. b. 22 Sept 1892 St. Isidore. PH.D '36 Univ. of Ottawa, Can. DEAN, Inst. St. Georges. Member: CPA, Can. Educ. Assn. Administration, teaching, testing; tests and measurements, experimental psychology.   M

LUSSIER, Mrs. Monique Lortie. 5761 Rue Déom, Montreal, P.Q. b. 19 Dec 1928 Paris, France. MA '52 Univ. of Montreal, Can. RES. ASST. in SOC. PSYCH, Human Relat. Res. Cen, 2765 Ch. Ste. Catherine, Montreal; ASST. PROF, of PSYCH, Univ. of Montreal. Member: CPA. Research, teaching; intergroup cultural relations, group dynamics. F

LUTHE, Dr. Wolfgang. Inst. of Psych, Univ. of Montreal, Blvd. Mont Royal, Montreal. b. 27 Oct 1922 Pansdorf/Holstein, Germany. MD '48 Univ. of Hamburg, Germany. ASST. PROF. of PSYCHOPHYSIOL, Inst. of Psych, Univ. of Montreal. Member: CPA. Teaching, research, consulting; neurohumoral organization, personality theory, graphomotor organization.   M

LUYENDYK, Walter Rigby. 113 Alice Ave, Apt. 2, Ottawa 2, Ont. b. 11 June 1923 Calgary. MA '52 Univ. of British Columbia, Can. PERS. SEL. OFF, Can. Civil Serv. Comm, Jackson Bldg, Ottawa. Member: CPA. Research in selection methods, applied and personnel psychology, testing; examination techniques, aptitude and achievement tests.   M

MacARTHUR, Dr. Russell Stuart. Fac. of Educ, Univ. of Alberta, Edmonton. b. 7 Jan 1918 Trochu. PH.D '51 Univ. of London, Eng. ASSOC. PROF. of EDUC, Univ. of Alta. Member: CPA, Can. Educ. Assn, Amer. Assn. of School Admin. Teaching, research, educational psychology, consulting; tests and measurements, personality, learning theory.   M

MacCARA, Mrs. Anne Elizabeth. P.O. Box 31, Barrington, N.S. b. 15 June 1930 Halifax. MA '53 Dalhousie Univ, Can. Member: CPA. Projective techniques.   F

MacDONALD, Dr. D. Stewart. Knox Reeves Adv, Inc, 600 First Natl.-Soo Line Bldg, Minneapolis, Minnesota, USA. b. 16 Jan 1916 Toronto. PH.D '50 Univ. of Toronto, Can. RES. ASST, Knox Reeves Adv. Inc. Member: CPA, SPT, Amer. Marketing Assn. Research, applied and industrial psychology; projective techniques, psychotherapy, advertising research.   M

MacEACHRAN, John Malcolm. 11619 Saskatchewan Dr, Edmonton, Alta. b. 16 Jan 1877 Glencoe. PH.D '06 Queens Univ, Can. PROF. EMER. of PHILOS, Univ. of Alberta; CHAIRMAN, Eugenics Bd, Province of Alta. Member: CPA. Retired.   M

MacGREGOR, Miss Mary Geraldine. Child Guid. Clin, 263 Bridge Ave, Windsor, Ont.

b. 6 Dec 1920 Winnipeg. BA '41 Univ. of Saskatchewan, Can. PSYCHOLOGIST, Child Guid. Clin. Member: CPA. Testing, psychotherapy, research; intelligence testing, projective techniques, individual and group therapy. F

MacKAY, Dr. Donald Copeland Gibson. Dept. of Psych, Univ. of British Columbia, Vancouver 8. b. 5 Dec 1905 Barrie. PH.D '34 Stanford Univ. USA. ASSOC. PROF, Univ. of B.C. Member: B.C. Psych. Assn. Teaching, research, supervising psychology library; animal behavior. M

MACKAY, Edward Arthur. 49 Norden Crescent, Don Mills, Ont. b. 6 Mar 1921 Calgary. MA '51 Univ. of Alberta, Can. ASSOC. DIR, Canadian Pers. Consultants, 134 Bloor St. W, Toronto. Member: CPA. Industrial psychology, testing, consulting, vocational guidance; industrial training. M

MacKINNON, Frederick Ashcroft. School Board Offices, Saskatoon, Sask. b. 22 Oct 1912 Saskatoon. M.ED '48 Univ. of Saskatchewan, Can. SCH. PSYCH'T, Saskatoon Pub. Schools, 211 4 Ave. S, Saskatoon; LECTURER, Coll. of Educ, Univ. of Sask. Member: CPA. Educational psychology, testing, teaching; mental and achievement testing, developmental psychology. M

MacLACHLAN, Rev. Archibald James. Dundas Baptist Church, 104 Park St, Dundas, Ont. b. 12 Apr 1907 Sault Ste. Marie, Michigan, USA. MA '54 Harvard Univ, USA. MINISTER, Dundas Baptist Church; DIRECTOR, Clin. Trng for Ministers, McMaster Univ, Hamilton, Ont. Member: CPA, Natl. Counc. on Fam. Relat. Psychotherapy, teaching, testing, marriage counseling; projective techniques, relation of personality factors to choice of ministry for a profession. M

MacLEAN, James Duncan. St. John Vocat. Sch, Douglas Ave, St. John, N.B. b. 21 Oct 1894 East Apple River. MA '15 Mt. Allison Univ, Can. ASST. DIR. and GUID. COUNS, St. John Vocat. Sch. Member: CPA, Natl. Vocat. Guid. Assn. Guidance, testing, educational psychology, school administration; placement, public relations. M

MacMILLAN, Lt. Col. Allister Myles. 110 N. Quarry St, Ithaca, New York, USA. b. 20 June 1909 Boiestown. PH.D '54 Cornell Univ, USA. RES. ASSOC, Dept. of Sociol. and Anthrop, Cornell Univ, 230 Morrill Hall, Ithaca, New York. Member: CPA. Research on mental health, administration, professional writing; rural community studies, validation and standardization of psychological screening test, sub-cultural differences in social perception. M

MacMILLAN, Dr. John Walker. 178 Balmoral Ave, Toronto, Ont. b. 29 Aug 1908 Toronto. PH.D '39 Cornell Univ, USA.

DIRECTOR, Indus. Psych. Div, Business Plng. Assoc, 330 Univ. Ave, Toronto. Member: CPA, APA. Psychology applied to business and industry, research, consulting; selection and classification, group process, evaluation of performance, management development. M

MacNEIL, Malcolm. Apt. 4, 152 Hilton Ave, Toronto, Ont. b. 16 Jan 1920 Glace Bay. MA '52 Univ. of Ottawa, Can. TECH. OFF, Dept. of Natl. Def, RCAF, 1107 Avenue Rd, Toronto. Member: Ont. Psych. Assn. Personnel psychology, research, testing, statistical analysis; personnel and placement, vocational guidance, attitude measurement. M

MacTAVISH, Donald Argyll. 26 Balmoral Ave, Apt. 108, Toronto, Ont. b. 4 Mar 1920 Seaforth. MA '53 Univ. of Toronto, Can. SPEC. SERV. INSPECTOR, Dept. of Educ, Queen's Park, Toronto. Administration and supervision of special education, edudational psychology, consulting, guidance. M

MAHONEY, Dr. Gerald Maurice. 6657 Viau St, Montreal, P.Q. b. 5 Oct 1912 Montreal. PH.D '49 McGill Univ, Can. PSYCHOLOGIST, Bois and Howard, 1509 Sherbrooke St. W, Montreal; TCHR. of PSYCH. and VOCAT. GUID, Sir George Williams Coll, Montreal. Member: APA, Psych. Assn. of P.Q. Personnel psychology, vocational guidance, teaching; projective and objective measures in personnel work, group process, attitude measurement. M

MAILHIOT, Dr. Claude. 10455 Laverdure, Montreal, P.Q. b. 13 Dec 1917 Montreal. PH.D '45 Univ. of Montreal, Can. DIRECTOR, Clinique d'Aide à l'Enfance, Carré St. Louis, Montreal. Member: CPA. Psychotherapy, clinical practice, consulting, teaching, research; research on juvenile delinquency. M

MAILLOUX, Prof. Noël. Inst. of Psych, Univ. of Montreal, 2900 Blvd. Mont Royal, Montreal, P.Q. b. 25 Dec 1909 Napierville. PH.D '34 Angelicum Univ, Rome, Italy. PROF. and HEAD, Psych. Dept, Univ. of Montreal; DIRECTOR, Human Relat. Res. Cen; CLIN. DIR, Guidance Center; CHIEF ED, Contributions à l'Etude des Sciences de l'Homme; ED. CONSULT, Canadian Journal of Psychology. Teaching, administration, editorial, research; personality theory, religious psychology, delinquency. M

MAKEPEACE, Roy. 957 E. 31 Ave, Vancouver 10, B.C. b. 8 June 1926 Port Elizabeth, Union of South Africa. B.SC '49 Rhodes Univ, South Africa. PERS. TECH, City of Vancouver, City Hall, 453 W. 12 Ave, Vancouver. Member: SAPA, Pacific Northwest Pers. Management Assn. Personnel selection, counseling, job evaluation, testing, administration; mental ability theory and psychometrics, perception, learning.   M

MALLINSON, Dr. Thomas J. Dept. of Psychiat, Univ. of Toronto, 2 Surrey Pl, Toronto, Ont. b. 27 May 1919 Calgary. PH.D '54 Univ. of Toronto, Can. RES. ASSOC, Dept. of Psychiat, Univ. of Toronto. Member: CPA, APA. Research, teaching; group process, evaluation of psychotherapeutic process and effects, statistical methods.   M

MALMO, Dr. Robert B. Lab. for Psych. Studies, Allan Memor. Inst. of Psychiat, McGill Univ, 1025 Pine Ave. W, Montreal 2, P.Q. b. 24 Oct 1912 Canal Zone, Panama. PH.D '40 Yale Univ, USA. DIRECTOR, Lab. for Psych. Studies, Allan Memor. Inst. of Psychiat; ED. BD, *Canadian Journal of Psychology.* Member: CPA, APA, Assn. for for Res. in Nerv. and Ment. Diseases. Research, professional writing, administration, teaching; physiological studies of personality.   M

MANN, William Graves. Head Office, Bank of Montreal, Montreal, P.Q. b. 28 Feb 1901 Surrey, Eng. B.SC '26 Univ. of London, Eng. PERS. ADVIS, Bank of Montreal. Member: CPA. Personnel selection, testing, consulting, administration, vocational guidance; projective techniques, achievement tests, attitude measurement. M

MANN, Wilburn Raymond. 290 Kennedy Pl, Windsor, Ont. b. 30 Mar 1925 Moorecroft, Wyoming, USA. MA '53 Catholic Univ. of America, USA. ACTING HEAD, Dept. of Psych, Assumption Coll, Huron Line, Windsor. Member: CPA, APA, Amer. Cath. Psych. Assn. Teaching, research, administration, guidance; systematic psychology, physiological psychology, experimental psychology.   M

MANUGE, Mrs. Elizabeth Starr. 4851 Cote St. Luc, Apt. 409, Montreal, P.Q. b. 18 July 1925 Hamilton. MA '51 Univ. of Toronto, Can. STAFF ASST, Aluminium Co. of Canada, Ltd, Sun Life Bldg, 1700 Metcalfe St, Montreal. Member: CPA, SPT. Administration, testing, research; projective techniques, evaluation of courses in human relations.   F

MANUILOW, Mrs. Tatiana. 16 Cote St. Catherine Rd, Montreal, P.Q. b. 8 Dec 1918 Sarapul, Russia. MA '52 Univ. of Montreal, Can. RES. ASST, Queen Mary Vets. Hosp, Queen Mary Rd, Montreal. Member: CPA, APA, SPT. Research, testing, student; projective techniques, personality and culture, juvenile delinquency.   F

MARCOTTE, Dr. J. E. Alexandre. 2165 Mont Royal, Montreal, P.Q. b. 2 Nov 1899 Sorel. MD '25 Univ. of Montreal, Can. CHIEF PSYCHIATRIST, Hlth. Serv. of Montreal, Rue Craig, Montreal; PROF. AGRÉGÉ of

MENT. HYG, Inst. of Psych, Univ. of Montreal. Member: Psych. Assn. of P.Q. Testing, teaching, psychotherapy.   M

MARCOTTE, Yves. 9201 Ave. de Chateaubriand, Montreal, P.Q. b. 19 Oct 1925 Montreal. Licence '53 Univ. of Montreal, Can. CLINICIAN in PSYCHIAT, Hosp. Notre Dame, Rue Sherbrooke, Montreal. Member: CPA. Testing, clinical analysis, consulting, psychotherapy; intelligence and personality tests, psychology of delinquency, dynamics.   M

MARSHMAN, Cameron Stanley. Apt. 1, 88 Carlton St, Toronto, Ont. b. 6 Mar 1915 London. MA '42 Univ. of Toronto, Can. EXEC. SECY, Toronto Comm, RCAF Benevolent Fund, 14 Cawthra Sq, Toronto. Member: CPA. Administration; learning theory, industrial personnel activities. M

MARTYN, Ian Dale. 7785 McEachran Ave, Montreal, P.Q. b. 16 Dec 1923 North Bay. MA '51 Univ. of Western Ontario, Can. PERS. ASST, DuPont Co. of Canada, 1135 Beaver Hall Hill St, Montreal. Member: CPA. Personnel psychology, testing, administration; interest, ability and personality tests, attitude measurement.   M

MASON, Geoffrey Pliny. 5227 Delmonte Ave, Royal Oak, V.I, B.C. b. 19 Apr 1920 London, Eng. MA '55 Univ. of British Columbia, Can. SCH. COUNS, Greater Victoria Sch. Bd, Victoria, B.C; CONSULTANT, priv. prac. Member: CPA. Educational psychology, counseling, testing, clinical analysis, psychology applied to teaching; reading and spelling, projective techniques, perception.   M

MASON, Robert Joseph. 1333 Dundas St. E, London, Ont. b. 10 Oct 1927 Toronto. MA '52 Univ. of Western Ontario, Can. MED. STUD, Univ. of Western Ont, London; CLIN. PSYCH'T, Ontario Hosp, Dundas St, London. Member: CPA. Student, testing, teaching; projective techniques, social perception.   M

MASSON, Louis I. Can. Army, No. 4 Pers. Depot, Montreal, P.Q. b. 25 Nov 1923 Winnipeg. B.ED '53 Univ. of Manitoba, Can. SR. PERS. OFF, Can. Army. Member: Psych. Assn. of P.Q. Administration, research, personnel psychology; achievement tests, personality inventories.   M

McALLISTER, Robert Vernon. 1933 W. Third Ave, Vancouver 9, B.C. b. 13 Apr 1918 Victoria. BA '48 Univ. of British Columbia, Can. PRISON PSYCH'T, Inspector of Gaols, Court House, Vancouver. Member: CPA. Testing, applied psychology, consulting; use of tests for inmate classification, personal counseling for prisoners.   M

McBAIN, William Norseworthy. Dept. of Psych, McGill Univ, Montreal 2, P.Q.

b. 19 Apr 1918 Orillia. PH.D '53 Univ. of California, USA. ASST. PROF, McGill Univ; EDITOR, *Directory of Members of CPA*. Member: CPA, APA. Teaching, research, industrial consulting, vocational counseling; human relations in industry, personnel testing and selection, relation between stimulus variability and efficiency. M

McCALLUM, Jason Walker. Toronto Ment. Health Clin, 34 Isabella St, Toronto, Ont. b. 7 Jan 1929 Milden. MA '54 Univ. of Toronto, Can. PSYCHOLOGIST, Toronto Ment. Hlth. Clin. Member: CPA. Testing, clinical analysis, psychotherapy, research; group process, personality theory and appraisal. M

McCLELLAN, Miss Grace. 678 Anderson Ave, Winnipeg 4, Man. b. 12 Apr 1911 Selkirk. BA '33 Univ. of Manitoba, Can. EDUC. PSYCH'T, Child Guid. Clin. of Greater Winnipeg, Bannatyne and Ellen Sts, Winnipeg. Member: CPA. Psychiat. Div. of Man. Med. Assn. Educational psychology, testing, consulting, psychotherapy; reading difficulties and their relation to emotional problems. F

McCREARY, Dr. John Kenneth. Dept. of Psych, Bates Coll, Lewiston, Maine, USA. b. 17 Sept 1907 Toronto. PH.D '44 Univ. of. Toronto, Can. ASSOC. PROF, Bates Coll. Member: CPA, APA. Teaching, administration, professional writing, student guidance; child and adolescent development, mental hygiene and abnormal psychology, learning theory. M

McFARLANE, Arthur Hardisty. 5088 Beaconsfield Ave, Montreal 29, P.Q. b. 26 Sept 1917 Montreal. MA '46 McGill Univ., Can. PERS. SUPERV, Canadian Industries Ltd, 1253 McGill College Ave, Montreal. Member: CPA, APA. Administration, personnel psychology, testing; aptitude and attitude measurement. M

McINTOSH, Dr. John Ranton. Univ. of British Columbia, Vancouver. b. 9 May 1910 Morden. PH.D '42 Columbia Univ, USA. DIRECTOR, Sch. of Educ, Univ. of B.C; ED. BD, *The Reading Teacher*. Member: APA, Can. Ment. Hlth. Assn. Administration, teaching, editorial; psychology of reading, learning theory, tests and measurements. M

McKENZIE, William John. Box 829, Weyburn, Sask. b. 12 Oct 1917 Tate. B.ED '41 Univ. of Saskatchewan, Can. PERS. OFF. and EDUC. CONSULT, Sask. Hosp, Weyburn. Member: CPA, BPS. Educational and personnel psychology, administration; motivation, learning theory applied to teaching methods, perception. M

McLEOD, Dr. Hugh N. Dept. of Psych, Toronto Psychiat. Hosp, 2 Surrey Pl, Toronto, Ont. b. 7 Nov 1923 Wolseley.

PH.D '54 Univ. of London, Eng. RES. PSYCH'T, Toronto Psychiat. Hosp. Member: Ont. Psych. Assn. Research; personality structure. M

McMURRAY, Dr. Gordon Aylmer. Dept. of Psych, Univ. of Saskatchewan, Saskatoon. b. 19 Oct 1913 Lennoxville. PH.D '49 McGill Univ, Can. HEAD, Dept. of Psych, Univ. of Sask. Member: CPA, APA. Teaching, research, administration; perception, assessment of reaction to pain, motivation theory. M

McMURRAY, J. Grant. North York Bd. of Educ, 7 Kenneth St, Willowdale, Ont. b. 31 July 1924 St. Marys. MA '52 Univ. of Western Ontario, Can. SCH. PSYCH'T, North York Bd. of Educ. Member: APA, CPA, Amer. Assn. for Ment. Defic, Amer. Orthopsychiat. Assn, Can. Ment. Hlth. Assn. Clinical consulting, administration, educational psychology, research in human genetics; mental deficiency, social perception, learning theory. M

McRAE, Mrs. Opal Eulala. 1160 Sinclair St, West Vancouver, B.C. b. 4 Apr 1927 Vernon. BA '49 Univ. of British Columbia, Can. CLIN. PSYCH'T, Child Guid. Clin, Willingdon and Grandview Highway, Burnaby, B.C. Member: CPA. Consulting, testing, clinical analysis, psychotherapy; projective techniques, play therapy, interviewing adolescents, preschool education. F

MEHMEL, Philip Vincent. Ment. Hlth. Clin, Regina Genl. Hosp, Regina, Sask. b. 16 Sept 1927 Winnipeg. MA '50 Univ. of Manitoba, Can. PSYCHOLOGIST, Regina Ment. Hlth. Clin, Dept. of Pub. Hlth, Regina. Member: CPA, APA. Clinical practice, testing, psychotherapy, consulting guidance, student; early childhood development, group process, personality theory. M

MELZACK, Dr. Ronald. Univ. of Oregon Med. Sch, 3181 S.W. Sam Jackson Park Rd, Portland, Oregon, USA. b. 19 July 1929 Montreal. PH.D '54 McGill Univ, Can. RES. ASSOC, Univ. of Oregon Med. Sch. Member: CPA, APA. Research; physiological and comparative psychology. M

MIGNAULT, O. P., Rev. Father Richard. Coll. des Dominicains, 96 Ave. Empress, Ottawa, Ont. b. 3 Sept 1914 St. Anselme. PH.D '53 Univ. of Montreal, Can. PROF. of METAPHYSICS, Coll. des Dominicains; ED. CHIEF, *Parents et Instituteurs*. Teaching, psychotherapy, editorial, consulting; psychology of adolescence, vocational guidance. M

MILLICHAMP, Prof. Dorothy Akers. Inst. of Child Study, Univ. of Toronto, 45 Walmer Rd, Toronto, Ont. b. 8 Nov 1907 Toronto. MA '32 Univ. of Toronto, Can. ASST. DIR, Inst. of Child Study; ASST. PROF. of CHILD

STUDY, Univ. of Toronto. Member: CPA. Administration of research division, parent education, and elementary school laboratory, teaching, research; mental health, developmental assessment of the well child, longitudinal study of personality development. F

MIVILLE, Dean Roméo. Ecole de Pédagogie et d'Orientation Professionnelle, 71 Rue d'Auteuil, Quebec. b. 26 Sept 1912 St. Paul. L.PS, Univ. of Montreal, Can. DEAN, Fac. of Arts, Laval Univ; DIRECTOR, Ecole de Pédagogie et d'Orientation Professionnelle. Member: Psych. Assn. of P.Q. Educational psychology, psychotherapy, administration; experimental psychology, human dynamics, psychology of personality. M

MOONEY, Dr. Craig McDonald. 20 Gregory St, Brampton, Ont. b. 17 Apr 1913 Lloydminster. PH.D '55 McGill Univ, Can. HEAD, Pers. Res. Sect, Def. Res. Med. Labs, Def. Res. Bd, Dept. of Natl. Def, Ottawa. Member: CPA. Administration, research, editorial; perceptual processes, learning theory, operational research. M

MOORE, Dr. Herbert. 140 Highbourne Rd, Toronto, Ont. b. 18 Jan 1894 Blackhead. PH.D '31 Harvard Univ, USA. DIR. and INDUS. CONSULT, Psych. Serv. Cen, 200 St. Clair Ave, Toronto. Member: CPA, APA. Industrial psychology, consulting, testing; maladjustment, interpersonal relations and organization in industry. M

MOREAU, Dr. Gilles-Yvon. Coll. Saint-Denis, 4152 Rue Ste. Denis, Montreal, P.Q. b. 22 June 1916 Iberville. D.PS '64 Univ. of Montreal, Can. DIRECTOR, Psycho-Educ. Cen, Coll. Saint-Denis. Member: CPA, APA. Educational psychology, consulting, administration; educational and psychological guidance. M

MORF, Dr. Gustav. P.O. Box 6034, Montreal. b. 11 Jan 1900 Winterthur, Switz. MD '39 Univ. of Bern, Switz; PH.D '30 Univ. of Neuchatel, Switz. SR. PSYCHIATRIST, Verdun Protestant Hosp, Verdun, Que. Member: SPT, Psych. Assn. of P.Q. Psychotherapy, applied psychology, teaching, professional writing; mental health, Jungian psychotherapy. M

MUNN, William Walter. Personnel Off, Saskatchewan Hosp, Weyburn, Sask. b. 17 Oct 1929 Virden. BA '50 Univ. of Saskatchewan, Can. PERS. PSYCH'T, Sask. Hosp. Member: Sask. Psych. Assn. Personnel psychology, administration, research. M

MUNRO, Miss Marjory Helen. 3338 Granville St, Vancouver, B.C. b. 21 July 1908 Huntly, Scot. MA '46 Univ. of British Columbia, Can. CHIEF PSYCH'T, Child Guid. Clinics, Provincial Ment. Hlth. Serv,

Essondale, B.C. Member: CPA. Administration, consulting, guidance, psychotherapy, testing; personality development, perception, learning theory. F

MURRAY, Kenneth Hemsley. Jr. High Sch, Westmount, P.Q. b. 11 Jan 1902 Stratford. M.ED '35 Springfield Coll, USA. GUID. SUPERV, Westmount Protestant Schools, Sch. Commissioners, City of Westmount. Member: CPA. Educational psychology, consulting, guidance, testing; learning theory, mental health of school children. M

MYERS, Prof. C. Roger. 100 St. George St, Toronto, Ont. b. 12 Feb 1906 Calgary. PH.D '37 Univ. of Toronto, Can. PROF. of PSYCH, Univ. of Toronto. Member: CAP, APA, Amer. Assn. for Ment. Defic. Administration, teaching, research; aptitude measurement, interview therapy. M

NAKAMURA, George Kan. 11204 70 Ave, Edmonton, Alta. b. Sept 1919 Edmonton. BA '55 Univ. of Alberta, Can. PSYCHOLOGIST, Provincial Guid. Clin, 134 8 Ave E, Calgary, Alta. Testing, psychotherapy, guidance; projective techniques, psychometrics, social perception. M

NASH, Dr. John Charles. Provincial Hosp, Lancaster, N.B. b. 21 Apr 1920 London, Eng. PH.D '54 Univ. of Edinburgh, Scot. CHIEF PSYCH'T, Dept. of Hlth. and Soc. Serv, Province of New Brunswick, Fredericton. Member: CPA, APA. Testing, research, consulting; developmental psychology, personality assessment, social anthropology. M

NEAL, Dr. Leola. Univ. of Western Ontario, London. b. 7 Sept 1911 Merlin. PH.D '42 Univ. of Toronto, Can. ASSOC. PROF. of PSYCH, DEAN of WOMEN, Univ. of Western Ont. Member: CPA, APA. Teaching, applied and educational psychology, consulting, guidance; clinical methods. F

NEIGER, Dr. Stephen. 110 Baldwin St, Toronto. b. 7 June 1924 Budapest, Hungary. PH.D '52, MD '54 Univ. of Innsbruck, Austria. CLIN. PSYCH'T, Toronto Psychiat. Hosp, 2 Surrey Pl, Toronto; CO-EDITOR, *International Journal of Sexology.* Teaching, testing, clinical analysis, clinical practice, consulting, editorial; projective techniques, sexology, schizophrenia. M

NETHERCOTT, J. Pliny S. Bd. of Educ, City Hall, London, Ont. b. 8 July 1890 Parkhill. MA, Teachers' Coll, Columbia Univ, USA. DIR. of GUID, Bd. of Educ, London. Member: Natl. Vocat. Guid. Assn, Can. Pers. and Guid. Assn. Educational and vocational guidance, training counselors, testing; learning theory, placement. M

NEWBIGGING, Prof. P. Lynn. McMaster Univ, Hamilton, Ont. b. 14 Apr 1925 Davidson. PH.D '52 Univ. Coll. of London,

Eng. ASST. PROF. of PSYCH, McMaster Univ; ED. CONSULT, *Canadian Journal of Psychology*. Member:CPA,APA.Teaching, administration, research; social perception, research methods and experimental design, personality theory. M

NEWELL, David Stowell. 42 Jubilee Rd, Bridgewater, N.S. b. 24 Nov 1932 Springvale, Maine, USA. BA '54 Acadia Univ, Can. PSYCH. FIELD WRKR, Cornell Prog. for Commun. Res, Cornell Univ, Ithaca, New York, USA. Member: CPA. Testing, student, research; individual differences in perception and level of aspiration, learning theory, group process. M

NEWTON, Donald Grant Seburn. Dept. of Psych, Ontario Hosp, Toronto, Ont. b. 23 Jan 1927 St. John. MA '55 Univ. of Toronto Can. PSYCHOLOGIST, Dept. of Hlth, Province of Ont. Member: Ont. Psych. Assn. Testing, diagnosis, research, psychotherapy; projective techniques, emotional stress, interpersonal relations. M

NICHOLS, Dr. Edward George. Nova Scotia Hosp, Dartmouth, N.S. b. 12 Feb 1929 Halifax. PH.D '56 Univ. of London, Eng. CHIEF PSYCH'T, Nova Scotia Hosp, Dept. of Hlth, Province of Nova Scotia, Halifax. Member: CPA, BPS, APA. Clinical analysis, testing, teaching, research; perception and personality, psychophysiology, personality appraisal in clinical setting. M

NICHOLS, Dr. Marie-Ange. 3750 Cote des Neiges Rd, Montreal, P.Q. b. 8 Sept 1901 St. Hyacinthe. PH.D '44 Columbia Univ, USA. TEACHER, Montreal Catholic Sch. Comm, 117 Rue Ste. Catherine West, Montreal. Member: CPA, APA. Teaching consulting, psychotherapy, testing; educational and vocational guidance. F

NICHOLSON, Ralph Hugh. 27 Otter Crescent, Toronto 12, Ont. b. 20 Sept 1919 Montreal. MA '49 Univ. of Toronto, Can. SUPERVISOR, Manpower Devel. Dept, Hydro Elec. Power Comm. of Ont, 620 Univ. Ave, Toronto. Member: CPA. Personnel psychology, administration, teaching; group process, learning theory, personality theory. M

NICKERSON, Kenneth Stanford. Clin. Psych. Div, Dept. of Psychiat, Duke Hosp. Annex, 2204 Erwin Rd, Durham, North Carolina, USA. b. 11 Sept 1930 Halifax, Canada. MA '52 Dalhousie Univ, Can. PSYCH. INTERN, Dept. of Psychiat, Duke Hosp. Member: CPA. Testing, clinical analysis, research, student, psychotherapy; perception and personality, therapeutic process, projective techniques. M

NORRIS, Dr. Kenneth E. Sir George Williams Coll, 1441 Drummond St, Montreal. b. 15 Mar 1903 Perth. PH.D '39 McGill Univ, Can. PRINCIPAL, Sir George Williams Coll.

Member: CPA, APA. Administration, testing, teaching; educational psychology. M

NORTH, Dr. Sidney L. Dept. of Psych, Ontario Hosp, St. Thomas, Ont. b. 11 Mar 1923 London, Eng. PH.D '53 Univ. of Western Ontario, Can. CHIEF PSYCH'T, Ont. Hosp. Member: CPA. Testing, clinical analysis, research, teaching, psychotherapy; visual-motor projective techniques, experimental studies in hypnosis, mental health measurement. M

NORTHEY, Lt. Commander William Herbert. H.M.C.S. Naden, Esquimalt, B.C. b. 28 Apr 1924 Vancouver. BA '49 Univ. of British Columbia, Can. CMD. PERS. SEL. OFF, Royal Can. Navy, Dept. of Natl. Def, Ottawa, Ont. Member: CPA. Applied and personnel psychology, consulting, testing, research; psychometric and projective testing, naval personnel selection and training programs. M

NORTHWAY, Prof. Mary Louise. Inst. of Child Study, Univ. of Toronto. b. 28 May 1909 Toronto. PH.D '38 Univ. of Toronto, Can. RES. SUPERV, Inst. of Child Study; CHAIRMAN, Publications Comm, Inst. of Child Study. Member: CPA, APA. Research in mental health, editorial; sociometric studies of children. F

NOTKIN, Miss Joan Carol. 4752 Upper Roslyn Ave, Montreal, P.Q. b. 6 Aug 1931 Montreal. MA '54 McGill Univ, Can. EMPL. COUNS, Jewish Vocat. Serv, 493 Sherbrooke St. West, Montreal. Member: CPA, Montreal Socy. of Projective Techniques. Personnel psychology, job placement and adjustment counseling, testing; counseling techniques, vocational adjustment of the handicapped, projective techniques. F

OGILVIE, Dr. John Charles. Def. Res. Med. Labs, Box 62, Postal Sta. K, Toronto, Ont. b. 25 July 1925 Hyderabad, Deccan, India. PH.D '55 Univ. of Toronto, Can. RES. PSYCH'T, Def. Res. Med. Labs. Member: CPA, APA. Pure and applied experimental research in visual problems; psychophysiology of vision, psychophysical methods, statistical methods in experimental design. M

PAGE, Prof. Francis Hilton. Dept. of Psych, Dalhousie Univ, Halifax, N.S. b. 11 Apr 1905 Toronto. MA '27 Univ. of Toronto, Can. HEAD, Dept. of Psych, Dalhousie Univ; LECT. in PSYCH. and PHILOS. of RELIG, Pine Hill Divinity Hall, Halifax. Member: CPA. Teaching, administration; psychology of religion, philosophy of mind, thought processes. M

PAITICH, Daniel. 3884 Bathurst St, Apt. 207, Downsview, Ont. b. 3 Nov 1929 Hamilton. MA '54 Univ. of Western Ontario, Can. GRAD. STUDENT, Dept. of Psych, Univ. of Toronto; REGIONAL ED,

Ontario Psychological Association Newsletter.
Teaching, motor skills research; projective
techniques, social perception, learning
theory.   M
PANABAKER, Harold Edward. 1416 9 St.
N.W, Calgary, Alta.   b. 19 July 1898
Hespeler. MA '53 Univ. of Alberta, Can.
DIR. of JR. HIGH SCHOOLS and GUID. SUPERV.
Calgary Sch. Bd, 4 Ave. and 6 St. West,
Calgary. Member: CPA.   Administration
and supervision; tests and measurements,
counseling, guidance.   M
PAP, Miss Margaret Dorothy. Ontario Hosp,
Hamilton, Ont. b. 16 Dec 1929 Brantford.
MA '55 Univ. of Ottawa, Can.   CLIN.
PSYCH'T, Ont. Hosp.   Member: CPA.
Testing, psychotherapy, research, teaching;
projective techniques.   F
PAPLAUSKAS RAMUNAS, Prof. Dr. Antoine.
309 Nicholas, Ottawa, Ont. b. 31 Dec 1910
Komenka, Lithuania. PH.D '44 Univ. of
Vienna, Austria. PROF. TITULAR, Grad.
Sch. of Psych. and Educ, Univ. of Ottawa;
DIRECTOR, Cen. of Comparative Educ; ED.
CONSULT, *Revue Internationale de Pédagogie.*
Member: CPA, BPS. Teaching, educational
psychology, research; memory, con-
ceptualization, socialization of the child. M
PARENT, Rolland.   58 Ouest des Saules,
Quebec.   b. 9 July 1909 St. Camille.
Licence '51 Laval Univ, Can.   EDUC.
PSYCH'T, Catholic Sch. Comm. of Quebec,
20 Rue Richelieu, Que. Member: Psych.
Assn. of P.Q, Assn. of Guid. Couns. of P.Q.
Research, consulting, guidance, testing;
research in achievement, vocational
guidance.   M
PARMENTER, Prof. Morgan Dewart. 56
Glencairn Ave, Toronto, Ont. b. 28 June
1904 Toronto. MA '33 Univ. of Toronto,
Can. PROF. of GUID. and DIR. of GUID. CEN,
Ont. Coll. of Educ, Univ. of Toronto, 371
Bloor St. West, Toronto; EDITOR, *The
School Guidance Worker.* Member: CPA,
Amer. Pers. and Guid. Assn. Administ-
ration, teaching, editorial; educational and
vocational guidance.   M
PATTON, Dr. Joseph Alexander. 898 Eglinton
Ave. East, Toronto, Ont. b. 4 July 1920
Owen Sound. PH.D '55 Univ. of Michigan,
USA. RES. ASSOC, Bur. of Audience Res,
Canadian Broadcasting Corp, 354 Jarvis
St, Toronto.   Member: CPA.   Research,
administration; social perception, group
process, attitude measurement.   M
PAUL, John. 555 Russell Hill Rd, Toronto,
Ont. b. 11 Feb 1918 Budapest, Hungary.
MA '54 Univ. of Toronto, Can. INSTRUCTOR
Dept. of Psych, Univ. of Toronto, 100 St.
George St, Toronto; INSTR. in PSYCH,
Ryerson Inst, Gould St, Toronto. Member:
CPA. Research, teaching, student; industrial
and social psychology, gerontology, mass

communication.   M
PAULSON, Morris James. Psych. Clin, Dept.
of Psych, Univ. of Kansas, Lawrence,
Kansas, USA. b. 10 Jan 1921 Medicine Hat.
PH.D '56 Univ. of Kansas, USA.   ASST.
INSTR, Dept. of Psych, Univ. of Kansas.
Member: CPA, APA.   Testing, teaching,
psychotherapy; projective techniques, atti-
tude measurement, educational psycholo-
gy.   M
PENFOLD, Douglas John.   Ontario Trng.
Cen, Ont. Dept. of Reform Institutions,
Brampton, Ont. b. 24 Dec 1919 Guelph.
MA '51 Univ. of Western Ontario, Can.
PSYCHOLOGIST, Ont. Trng. Cen. Member:
CPA, APA. Applied psychology, consulting,
guidance, testing, classification; a-
chievement tests, group process and
attitude measurement in reform insti-
tutions.   M
PENTLAND, Mrs. Mary A.   Lundberg
Explorations Ltd, 96 Eglinton Ave. E,
Toronto 12, Ont. b. 19 Aug 1929 Ed-
monton. MA '52 Univ. of Alberta, Can.
Member: CPA. Testing, consulting.   F
PÉPIN, Prof. Jean-Guy.   Jacques Cartier
Teacher's Coll, 1301 Sherbrooke St. East,
Montreal, P.Q. b. 12 Jan 1922 Montreal.
Licence '52 Univ. of Montreal, Can. MENT.
HYG. TCHR, Jacques Cartier Teacher's Coll.
Member: Socy of. Pedagogy of Montreal.
Teaching, professional writing, educational
psychology; study of teacher's behavior
and adjustment of school children.   M
PÉRUSSE, Mrs. Françoise. 10140 Waverly,
Montreal, P.Q. b. 27 Nov 1924 Montreal.
MA '54 Univ. of Montreal, Can.   PSY-
CHOLOGIST, priv. prac. Member: Psych.
Assn. of P.Q. Clinical practice, consulting,
research; depth psychology.   F
PHILIP, Dr. B. Roger.   323 Annette St,
Toronto, Ont. b. 29 Apr 1892 Toronto.
PH.D '28 Catholic Univ. of America, USA.
PROF. AGRÉGÉ, Fac. of Commerce, Laval
Univ, Que; CONSULT. PSYCH'T, St. John's
Trng. Sch, Toronto. Member: APA, CPA,
Psychomet. Socy. Teaching, research,
administration; psychometrics, perception,
learning.   M
PIERCE, Lt. Col. Harry Feltus. Suite 2, 141
Frontenac St, Sherbrooke, Que. b. Beebe,
P.Q. D. Psych. '47 Univ. of Oxford, Eng.
PSYCHOLOGIST, priv. prac. Member: BPS,
DGP.   Clinical practice, consulting in
alcoholism rehabilitation, applied psy-
chology, research; military psychology,
attitude measurement.   M
PILON, Miss Marguerite. 89 Maisonneuve,
Hull, P.Q. b. 18 Nov 1916 Verner. M.PS '56
Univ. of Ottawa, Can. CONSULT, PSYCH'T,
Guid. Cen, Univ. of Ottawa, 1 Stewart St,
Ottawa. Member: CPA, Amer. Cath. Psych.
Assn.   Consulting, guidance, testing,

psychotherapy; projective techniques, a-chievement tests, counseling methods, personality.   F

PIMM, June Barbara. 556 Westminster Ave, Ottawa, Ont. b. 8 June 1927 Ottawa. M.PS.SC '52 McGill Univ, Can. PSY-CHOLOGIST, priv. prac; TCHR. of PSYCH. TESTING, Carleton Coll, Ottawa. Member: CPA. Administration and analysis of tests, consulting, teaching; projective tech-niques, intelligence and aptitude testing. F

PINARD, Rev. Adrien. Inst. of Psych, Univ. of Montreal, Montreal, P.Q. b. 14 Feb 1916 Montreal. PH.D '54 Univ. of Montreal, Can. PROFESSOR, Inst. of Psych, Univ. of Montreal. Member: CPA, APA. Teaching, research, administration; sensation and perception, learning theory, intelligence test construction.   M

PINKNEY, Mrs. M. June. Box 153, Thedford, Ont. b. 11 July 1933 London. BA '54 Univ. of Western Ontario, Can. CLIN. PSYCH'T, Ontario Hosp, Dundas St. E, London. Testing, clinical analysis, re-search, teaching; group process, projective techniques, achievement tests.   F

PINSONNEAULT, Roger. 624 Kind Edward, Ottawa, Ont. b. 5 Nov 1927 Montreal. ED.B '54 Univ. of Montreal, Can. STUDENT, Univ. of Ottawa; ASSISTANT, Guid. Cen, Univ. of Ottawa. Student, guidance, psy-chotherapy; projective techniques, re-search.   M

PITT, Prof. Clifford C. V. 15 Glen Robert Dr, Toronto, Ont. b. 15 Apr 1915 London, Eng. MA '49 Teachers Coll, Columbia Univ, USA. ASSOC. PROF. of EDUC, Ont. Coll. of Educ, Univ. of Toronto, 371 Bloor St. W, To-ronto. Member: CPA. Teaching edu-cational psychology, research; achievement and intelligence tests, learning theory, psychology of adolescence.   M

PIUZE, Louis Roland. 5697 Levesque Blvd, St. Vincent de Paul, Montreal 12, P.Q. b. 24 July 1908 St. Paul du Nord. Licence '38 Univ. of Montreal, Can. CLASSIF. OFF, St. Vincent de Paul Penit, 160 St. François St, St. Vincent de Paul, P.Q. Member: Psych. Assn. of P.Q. Testing, guidance, teaching; psychometry, projective tech-niques, group process.   M

PLÉCHATY, Michel. 925 Ave. Marguerite Bourgeoys, Apt. 7, Que. b. 28 May 1927 Kopisty, Czech. MA '53 Univ. of Montreal, Can. CHIEF CLIN. PSYCH'T, Medico-Social Cen. for Children, 565 Rue St. Jean, Que. Member: Psych. Assn. of P.Q. Psycho-therapy, testing, teaching; projective tech-niques, child and adolescent psycho-therapy.   M

PLOURD, Prof. Albert A. St. John's Coll, 492 St. John St, Que. b. 11 Sept 1909 Albertine. MA '37 St. Joseph's Coll, Can.

PROF. of PSYCH, St. John's Coll. Member: CPA, Amer. Catholic Psych. Assn. Teaching, industrial psychology, consulting; mental hygiene, personality, industrial and com-mercial psychology.   M

POIRIER, Rolland. Psychiat. Serv, Maison-neuve Hosp, 5415 Blvd. L'Assomption, Montreal, P.Q. b. 3 Feb. 1928 Valleyfield. L.PH '53 Univ. of Montreal, Can. CLIN. PSYCH'T, Psychiat. Serv, Maisonneuve Hosp. Member: CPA. Testing, psycho-therapy, consulting; studies of patho-logical personality, projective techniques. M

PORTER, Mrs. Helen Margaret. 90 Parklea Dr, Toronto 17, Ont. b. 29 Dec 1909 Toronto. MA '51 Univ. of Toronto, Can. SR. PSYCH'T, Dept. of Vets. Affairs, Govt. of Canada, Bayview Ave, Toronto. Member: CPA. Testing, administration, teaching; projective techniques, interview methods.   F

POSER, Dr. Ernest George. 3600 McTavish St, Montreal, P.Q. b. 2 Mar 1921 Vienna, Austria. PH.D '52 Univ. of London, Eng. ASST. PROF, McGill Univ, Montreal; CHIEF PSYCH'T, Montreal Rehab. Cen; CO-EDITOR, *Canadian Psychologist.* Member: CPA, APA, SPT. Teaching, consulting, clinical practice, guidance, research; psychosomatic re-search, genetic and constitutional aspects of personality, objective behavior tests.   M

POTASHIN, Miss Reva. Apt. 7, 3851 W. Fourth Ave, Vancouver 8, B.C. b. 13 Sept 1921 Toronto. PH.D '51 Univ. of Toronto, Can. ASST. PROF. of PSYCH, Univ. of British Columbia, Vancouver 8. Member: CPA, APA. Teaching, consulting, behavior problems in children, group process, pro-jective techniques.   F

PROCUNIER, David James. 663 Lawrence Ave. W, Toronto 10, Ont. b. 21 Feb 1925 Chicago, Illinois, USA. BA '50 Univ. of Toronto, Can. PERS. APPRAISAL SPEC, Can. General Elcctric Co, 212 King St. W, Toronto. Member: CPA. Industrial and personnel psychology, vocational guidance; personality appraisal, attitude measure-ment.   M

QUARRINGTON, Prof. Bruce Joseph. 32 Langbourne Pl, Don Mills, Ont. b. 28 May 1923 Toronto. PH.D '53 Univ. of Toronto, Can. ASST. PROF. of PSYCH, TCHR. of CLIN. PSYCHIAT, Univ. of Toronto, 241 Elizabeth St, Toronto, Ont. Member: CPA. Research, testing, clinical analysis, teaching; cyclical clinical phenomena, lateral organization problems, stuttering.   M

QUIRK, Douglas Arthur. 3 Tanvalley Ct, Don Mills, Ont. b. 11 July 1931 Pitha-puram, India. MA '55 Univ. of Toronto, Can. PSYCHOLOGIST, East York-Leaside Child Guid. Clin, 1273 Pape Ave, Toronto, Ont. Member: CPA. Consulting, guidance, parent interviews, testing, play therapy; projective techniques, cerebral structural abnormalities, individual abnormal processes. **M**

QUIRK, Mrs. Eve Lyn Anne May. 3 Tanvalley Ct, Don Mills, Ont. b. 2 July 1932 Toronto. MA'55 Univ. of Toronto, Can. PSYCHOLOGIST, Ontario Hosp, 999 Queen St. W, Toronto. Clinical testing, research, psychotherapy; projective techniques, perception, abnormal linguistic processes. **F**

RABINOVITCH, Dr. M. Sam. Dept. of Psych, Montreal Children's Hosp, Montreal 25, P.Q. b. 27 May 1927 Montreal. PH.D '52 Purdue Univ, USA. DIRECTOR, Dept. of Psych, Montreal Children's Hosp; PROF. of PSYCH, McGill Univ. Member: CPA, APA, SPT. Psychodiagnostic testing, teaching, administration; child development, tests for physically handicapped children. **M**

RANDS, Stanley. 3630 Argyle Rd, Regina, Sask. b. 20 July 1909 Ft. Macleod. MA '37 Univ. of Alberta, Can. DEPUTY DIR, Psychiat. Serv, Sask. Dept. of Pub. Hlth, Provincial Hlth. Bldg, Regina. Administration, teaching, research coordination; adult education, mental health, child training. **M**

RANKIN, Winston Bertram. St. Anne's Milit. Infirmary, St. Anne's Hosp, Ste. Anne de Bellevue, Que. b. 3 Mar 1923 Georgetown, British Guiana. MA '49 McGill Univ, Can. PSYCHOLOGIST, St. Anne's Milit. Infirmary. Member: SPT, Psych. Assn. of P.Q. Testing, clinical-analysis, consulting, psychotherapy; projective techniques, group dynamics, therapy. **M**

READ, Lea MacLean. 154 Sunnyside Ave, Montreal 33, P.Q. b. 12 Feb 1912 Moncton. BA '47 Sir George Williams Coll, Can. PERS. SEL. SUPERV, Bell Tel. Co. of Can, 1050 Beaver Hall Hill, Montreal; LECTURER, Sir George Williams Coll, Montreal. Member: CPA. Personnel psychology, teaching, research and administration of employee selection methods, aptitude and achievement tests for business and industry, reading techniques for supervisors, personnel management. **M**

READ, William H. Dept. of Psych, Univ. of Michigan, Ann Arbor, Michigan, USA. b. 2 Sept 1923 Winnipeg. MA '53 Univ. of Toronto, Can. TEACHING FELLOW, Univ. of Michigan. Member: Ont. Psych. Assn. Teaching human relations in industry, research, student; industrial, personnel, and social psychology, group process. **M**

RECORD, Father Maurice Adrian. Assumption Coll, Windsor, Ont. b. 18 Jan 1913 Owen Sound. MA '50 Univ. of Toronto, Can. CHAIRMAN, Psych. Dept., Assumption Coll. Member: CPA, APA,

Amer. Cath. Psych. Assn, Int. Counc. for Excep. Child. Teaching, testing, guidance, consulting; educational and clinical psychology. **M**

RENAUD, Rev. Father Philippe-André, O.M.I. Univ. of Ottawa, Laurier Ave. E, Ottawa, Ont. b. 25 Jan 1920 Montreal. M.ED '54 Univ. of Toronto, Can. GENL. SUPT, Native Commun. Devel. Bur, Univ. of Ottawa; CONSULT. in FUNDAMENTAL EDUC, UNESCO. Member: CPA, Amer. Cath. Psych. Assn. Research, student, educational psychology, testing, teaching; acculturation, group process, attitude measurement. **M**

RHEAULT, Georges Michel. 20 Perreault, Victoriaville, Que. MA '56 Univ. of Ottawa, Can. STUDENT, Univ. of Ottawa, Ont. Guidance, testing, student; adaptation, interests and preferences, pathology. **M**

RITCHIE, Robinson Lyndhurst Wadmore. 289 Kerwood Ave, Victoria, B.C. b. 24 Oct 1914 Lethbridge. BA '36 Univ. of Alberta, Can. CHIEF PERS. OFF, British Columbia Civil Serv. Comm, 544 Michigan St, Victoria. Member: CPA. Personnel psychology, administration, testing; aptitude and achievement test development, personality measurement, management training.M

RIVARD, Rev. Father Reynald. Psycho-Social Inst, 1337 Blvd. du Carmel, Trois-Rivières, P.Q. b. 10 Aug 1919 Trois-Rivières. PH.D '55 Univ. of Ottawa, Can. TECH. DIR, Psycho-Soc. Inst. Member: CPA, Int. Socy. for Spec. Educ, Assn. of Guid. Couns. of P.Q. Administration, consulting, educational psychology, teaching; measurement of emotional instability, developmental psychology, audiovisual techniques in learning. **M**

ROBERTS, Dennis F. 237 Wembley Dr, Sudbury, Ont. b. 16 Feb 1915 London, Eng. MA '48 Univ. of Toronto, Can. SR. PSYCH'T, Psychiat. Unit, Sudbury Genl. Hosp, Paris St, Sudbury. Member: CPA. Testing, psychotherapy, teaching; projective techniques, vocational guidance. **M**

ROBSON, Prof. Clifford Joseph. 228 Brock St, Winnipeg 9, Man. b. 15 Aug 1915 Kenora. MA '49 Univ. of Minnesota, USA. ASSOC. PROF. of PSYCH, United Coll, Winnipeg 2. Member: CPA. Teaching, testing, counseling administration; critical incidents of behavioral success and failure, achievement testing. **M**

ROGERS, Mrs. Elizabeth June. 161 Maple Lane, Rockcliffe, Ottawa, Ont. b. 5 June 1926 Toronto. MA '50 George Washington Univ, USA. Member: CPA. Diagnostic testing with children, clinical and child psychology, nursery schools. **F**

ROGERS, Dr. Kenneth Herbert. 3473 University St, Montreal 2, P.Q. b. 3 May 1902 Tewkesbury, Eng. PH.D '33 Univ. of

Toronto, Can. WARDEN and PROF. of PASTORAL THEOLOGY, Montreal Diocesan Theological Coll; LECTURER, Fac. of Divinity, McGill Univ. Member: CPA, APA. Teaching, counseling, administration, pastoral work; teaching methods, personnel selection, counseling process and techniques. M

ROOS, Robert Charles. Paris, Ont. b. 16 Dec 1923 Weston. MA '48 Univ. of Toronto, Can. TEACHER, Paris Dist. High Sch. Bd. Member: CPA. Teaching, guidance, educational psychology; interviewing and counseling students, testing, psychotherapy. M

ROSS, Miss Constance. 360 Russell Hill Rd, Toronto, Ont. b. 12 May 1923 Toronto. MA '50 Univ. of Minnesota, USA. STUDENT. Member: Ont. Psych. Assn. Student, testing; clinical work with children. F

ROSS, Dr Murray G. Sch. of Soc. Work, Univ. of Toronto, Toronto. b. 12 Apr 1911 Sydney. ED.D '50 Columbia Univ, USA. ASSOC. PROF, Univ. of Toronto. Member: CPA. Teaching, professional writing, research; social therapy, community organization, group process, leadership. M

ROSS, Robert Robertson. 18 Lorindale Ave, Toronto, Ont. b. 22 Feb 1933 Edinburgh, Scot. BA '53 Univ. of Toronto, Can. STUDENT, Dept. of Psych, Univ. of Toronto, Research on sexual perversion, testing; forensic psychology, projective techniques, alcoholism. M

ROSS, Roy W. Toronto Genl. Hosp, Toronto 2, Ont. b. 9 Mar 1920 Sydney. MA '50 Univ. of Toronto, Can. PSYCHOLOGIST, Toronto Genl. Hosp; TEACHING FELLOW Univ. of Toronto. Member: CPA, APA. Testing, clinical diagnosis, teaching, rehabilitation, student; braininjury assessment, aptitude and attitude measurement. M

ROSS, Dr. Verity Mitchell. School of Soc. Work, McGill Univ, 3600 Univ. St, Montreal, P.Q. b. Sherbrooke. PH.D '52 McGill Univ, Can. ASST. PROF. of SOC. WORK, McGill Univ. Member: CPA, APA. Research, teaching, student guidance, consulting. F

ROSS, Dr. W. Donald. Dept. of Psychiat, Cincinnati Genl. Hosp, Cincinnati 29, Ohio, USA. b. 13 Sept 1913 Hamilton. Fellow of the Royal Coll. of Physicians of Canada '48; MD '38 Univ. of Manitoba, Can. ASSOC. PROF. of PSYCHIAT. and ASST. PROF. of INDUS. MED, Coll. of Med, Univ. of Cincinnati; PSYCHOTHERAPIST, priv. prac. Member: CPA, APA, SPT. Teaching, administration, research, testing, psychotherapy; projective techniques, group process, group psychotherapy, industrial psychiatry. M

ROSSITER, Miss Maryellen. Perry Secretarial

Agency, 985 Sherbrooke St. W, Montreal, P.Q. b. 10 June 1919 East Angus. MA '42 McGill Univ, Can. PERS. MGR, Perry Secretarial Agency. Member: CPA. Personnel psychology, testing, placement; vocational guidance and counseling. F

ROWCLIFFE, Rev. Robert Gay. 21 Salem St, Sackville, N.B. b. 15 June 1905 St. Peter Port, Guernsey, Channel Islands. BA '31 Univ. of Bishop's Coll, Can. CLASSIF. OFF, Dorchester Penit, Fed. Dept. of Justice, Penitentiaries Br, Ottawa. Member: CPA. Testing, compiling case histories, counseling, administration, research; projective techniques, social maladjustment, group therapy. M

ROWE, Miss M. Florence. 568 Connaught Ave, Apt. 3, Sudbury, Ont. b. 3 May 1913 North Bay. MA '52 Columbia Univ, USA. DIR. of GUID, Sudbury Pub. Schools, 296 Van Horne St, Sudbury. Testing, counseling, consulting, educational psychology, learning theory, achievement tests, remedial techniques. F

RUEL, Prof. Pierre H. 931 Rue Appollon, St, Vincent de Paul, Laval, P.Q. b. 12 Oct 1923 Quebec. L.PH '54 Univ. of Montreal, Can. PROF. of PSYCH, Jacques Cartier Normal Sch, 1301 E. Sherbrooke, Montreal; LECTURER, Laval Univ, and Montreal Univ; DIRECTOR, Psych. Cen, St. Denis Coll. Member: CPA. Teaching, professional writing, consulting, guidance; psychogenesis of the normal personality, educational diagnostics and corrective teaching, projective techniques and personality questionnaires. M

SAFRAN, Dr Carl. 3207 26 St. S.W, Calgary, Alta. b. 12 July 1917 Calgary. ED.D '51 Univ. of Colorado, USA. PSYCH'T. and ASST. SUPERV. of GUID, Calgary Pub. Sch. Bd, McDougall Sch, 4 Ave. and 6 St. W, Calgary. Administration, testing, guidance, consulting; intelligence and personality tests, statistical research. M

SAGE, Miss Flora Margaret. 4687 W. Fourth Ave, Vancouver, B.C. b. 12 May 1919 Vancouver. MA '51 Western Reserve Univ, USA. READING THERAPIST and INSTR, Psych. Dept, Couns. Serv, Univ. of British Columbia, Vancouver 8. Member: CPA, APA, ICWP. Administration, teaching, counseling; diagnostic problems in reading, comparison of methods of reading instruction. F

ST. PIERRE, Lionel. 1305 Elisabeth St, Ville St. Laurent, Montreal, P.Q. b. 17 Aug 1916 Windsor. MA '49 Univ. of Montreal, Can. EMPL. MGR, Steinberg's Ltd, 5400 Hochelaga St, Montreal. Member: CPA. Personnel selection and training, testing, administration, vocational guidance; achievement and attitude measurement. M

SALISBURY, Mrs. Mary Roseborough. 65 C Dana St, Cambridge 38, Massachusetts, USA. b. 17 Feb 1926 Toronto. MA '49 Univ of Toronto, Can. INSTR. in SOCIOL, Tufts Univ, Medford 55, Massachusetts, USA. Member: CPA. Teaching, research, professional writing; small group research, family and the socialization of the child, social perception. F

SALK, Dr. Lee. Allan Memor. Inst. of Psychiat, McGill Univ, 1025 Pine Ave. W, Montreal, P.Q. b. 27 Dec 1926 New York, USA. PH.D '54 Univ. of Michigan, USA. RES. ASSOC, Dept. of Psychiat, McGill Univ. Member: CPA, APA. Research, consulting, teaching; personality theory, psychoendocrinology, social perception. M

SALMON, Donald Leslie. 544 Normandie St, Arvida, Que. b. 29 Sept 1929 Montreal. M.PS.SC '52 McGill Univ, Can. ASST. to INDUS. RELAT. OFF, Aluminum Co. of Can, Ltd. Member: CPA. Industrial psychology, testing, consulting; group process, social perception, communication. M

SAMSON, Dr. G. Henri. 2150 W. Sherbrooke, Montreal, P.Q. b. 23 Sept 1907 Quebec. MD, Laval Univ, Can. DIRECTOR, Inst. of Psychother, Laval Univ, 77 Rue Ste. Anne, Que. Member: Int. Assn. of Cath. Psychotherapists. Teaching, psychotherapy; techniques employed in adult psychotherapy. M

SASLOW, Harry Lewis. Staunton Clin, 3601 Fifth Ave, Pittsburgh 13, Pennsylvania, USA. b. 21 June 1929 Edmonton. MS '54 Univ. of Oregon, USA. JR. FELLOW in PSYCH, Dept. of Psychiat, Sch. of Med, Staunton Clin; LECT. in EDUC. PSYCH, Univ. of Pittsburgh. Clinical testing and research, teaching, student; tests and measurement, learning theory applied to personality assessment, psychosomatic medicine. M

SAWATSKY, Prof. John C. Univ. of Toronto, Toronto, Ont. b. 6 Oct 1918 Russia. PH.D '49 Univ. of Toronto, Can. ASST. PROF. of ADMIN, Univ. of Toronto. Member: CPA. Teaching, industrial psychology, research; group process, social learning. M

SAYONS, Prof. Dr. Karol M. Dept. of Psych, Univ. of Manitoba, Winnipeg. b. 19 May 1913 Zakopane, Poland. PH.D '55 Oxon, Eng. ASSOC. PROF, Univ. of Man. Member: BPS, CPA. Teaching, research, testing; perception and thinking, personality, research methods. M

SCHECTER, Mrs. Véra. 3800 Dupuis Ave, Montreal, P.Q. b. 23 Feb 1912 Dnieprepetrovsk, USSR. Diplôme '37 Univ. of Geneva, Switz. EMPL. COUNS, Jewish Vocat. Serv, 493 Sherbrooke W, Montreal. Member: Psych. Assn. of P.Q. Personnel and applied psychology, testing, vocational counseling;

projective techniques, memory, attitude measurement. F

SCHNORE, M. Morris. 2005 Patricia Ave, Apt. 1, Montreal, P.Q. b. 21 Sept 1925 Rezekne, Latvia. MA '54 Univ. of Western Ontario, Can. RES. ASST, Allan Memor. Inst. of Psychiat, Lab. for Psych. Studies, 1025 Pine Ave. W, Montreal 2. Member: CPA. Testing and research in experimental physiological psychology, student; personality tests, projective techniques, psychopathology. M

SCHULTE-GIESKE, Dipl. Psych. Leo William. Box 600, Dept. of Psych, Ontario Reformatory, Guelph, Ont. b. 28 June 1918 Boen, Germany. Dipl. Psych. '49 Univ. of Goettingen, Germany. STAFF PSYCH'T. and HEAD, Dept. of Psych, Ont. Reformatory; LECT. in PSYCHOPATHOL, Waterloo Coll. Member: BDP. Consulting, psychotherapy, testing and classification of prisoners, teaching; attitude measurement, projective techniques, human behavior under stress and punishment, mass communication. M

SCOTT, Dr. William Clifford Munroe. 1025 Pine Ave. W, Montreal, P.Q. b. 11 Mar 1903 Ontario. MB '27 Univ. of Toronto, Can. ASSOC. PROF. of PSYCHIAT, McGill Univ, Montreal; PSYCHOANALYST, priv. prac; ASST. ED, *International Journal of Psychoanalysis*. Member: BPS, Can. Psychoanal. Socy, Br. Psychoanal. Socy. Teaching, psychotherapy, research; development of speech, body scheme, psychoanalytic techniques. M

SCOTT, William George. 128 Oxford St, Kitchener, Ont. b. 6 Dec 1919 Windsor. MA '50 Univ. of Toronto, Can. DIR. of INDUS. and PUB. RELAT, Dominion Electrohome Industries Ltd, 39 Edward St, Kitchener; LECTURER, Waterloo Coll, Univ. of Western Ontario. Member: CPA. Personnel administration, labor and public relations, testing; aptitude testing, attitude measurement, group dynamics. M

SHANE, S. Gerald. 4571 Sherbrooke St. W, Westmount, Montreal, P.Q. b. 22 Sept 1919 Montreal. MA '42 McGill Univ, Can. CONSULT. PSYCH'T, priv. prac. Member: CPA, APA, SPT. Consulting, applied and industrial psychology, testing; projective techniques, group therapy, industrial counseling. M

SHEPHARD, Prof. Alfred Henry. Dept. of Psych, Univ. of Toronto, Toronto 5, Ont. b. 4 Mar 1917 Vancouver. PH.D '50 State Univ. of Iowa, USA. PROFESSOR, Univ. of Toronto. Member: CPA, APA. Teaching, research, administration; perceptual motor learning. M

SHEVENELL, Prof. Raymond Henry. Univ. of Ottawa, Ottawa, Ont. b. 20 Apr 1908

Rollinsford, New Hampshire, USA. PH.D '49 Univ. of Ottawa, Can. DIRECTOR, Sch. of Psych, Univ. of Ottawa; DIRECTOR, Guid. Cen. and Child Guid. Cen, Univ. of Ottawa. Member: CPA, APA, Amer. Cath. Psych. Assn. Teaching, administration, guidance, consulting, research; epistemology of psychologies, personality theories. M

SHIRRAN, Alexander Forrester. 3008 W. 31 Ave, Vancouver, B.C. b. 1 Sept 1920 Strome. MA '50 Univ. of British Columbia, Can. PSYCH'T, and DIR. of YOUTH COUNS. SERV, Univ. of B.C. Member: CPA. Counseling, teaching, educational and personnel psychology; therapeutic counseling, use of psychometrics in educational and vocational guidance. M

SIDLAUSKAS, Prof. Agatha Elizabeth. 157 Nicholas St, Ottawa 2, Ont. b. 5 Feb 1914 Lithuania. PH.D '42 Cath. Univ. of the Sacred Heart, Italy. PROFESSOR, Sch. of Educ. and Psych, Ottawa Univ, Laurier Ave, Ottawa. Member: CPA, APA. Teaching, guidance, testing. F

SIGAL, John Jacob. Verdun Protestant Hosp, Box 6034, Montreal, P.Q. b. 27 Nov 1927 Kerrobert. MA '53 Univ. of Montreal, Can. RES. FELLOW, Verdun Protestant Hosp. Member: CPA. Clinical research, psychotherapy, testing; personality theory, content analysis of group discussion. M

SIGNORI, Dr. Edro I. Dept. of Psych, Univ. of British Columbia, Vancouver 8. b. 29 July 1915 Calgary. PH.D '47 Univ. of Toronto, Can. ASSOC. PROF, Univ. of B.C. Member: CPA, APA, Amer. Cath. Psych. Assn. Teaching, industrial and vocational consulting, research; selection tests, psychotherapy, personality theory, mental hygiene. M

SIMMONS, Mrs. Roberta Blodwyn. Norfolk Ment. Hyg. Cen, 746 Graydon Ave, Norfolk 7, Virginia, USA. b. 23 July 1914 Drumheller. M.ED '50 Univ. of Alberta, Can. CLIN. PSYCH'T, Norfolk Ment. Hyg. Cen. Member: CPA, APA. Testing, clinical analysis, consulting, psychotherapy; psychodiagnosis with standardized intellectual tests and projective techniques. F

SLATER, Prof. Eddy. 2777 Des-Quatre-Bourgeois, Quebec 10, Ste. Foy, P.Q. b. 25 Aug 1924 St. Romuald. Licence '50 Laval Univ, Can. ADMIN. SECY, Sch. of Educ. and Guid, Laval Univ, 71 Rue D'Auteuil, Quebec 4. Member: CPA, AIPA, Assn. of Guid. Couns. of P.Q. Administration, teaching, guidance; psychometrics, industrial selection, economic factors in vocational guidance. M

SLEMON, Alan Gray. 10 Grenadier Heights, Toronto 3, Ont. b. 9 May 1928 Winnipeg. MA '52 Univ. of Western Ontario, Can.

STUDENT, Dept. of Psych, Univ. of Toronto. Member: CPA, Amer. Assn. on Ment. Defic. Student; projective techniques, social perception, mental deficiency. M

SLOAN, Squadron Leader Emmett Patrick. RCAF Sel. and Trng. Analysis Unit, 1107 Avenue Rd, Toronto, Ont. b. 25 Sept 1920 Ottawa. MA '49 McGill Univ, Can. COMMANDING OFF, RCAF Sel. and Trng. Anal. Unit. Member: CPA, APA. Personnel psychology, selection and training research, aviation psychology; psychometrics, learning. M

SMITH, Dr. Albert Henry. 285 Westdale Ave, Kingston, Ont. b. 1 Nov 1907 Ilkeston, Derbyshire, Eng. PH.D '50 Univ. of Toronto, Can. ASSOC. PROF, Queen's Univ, Kingston. Member: CPA, APA. Teaching, research, professional writing; visual perception, learning theory, aptitude tests. M

SMITH, Prof. Clarence Ebblewhite. Dept. of Educ, McGill Univ, Montreal, P.Q. b. 12 Feb 1906 Nottingham, Eng. D.PAED '35 Univ. of Toronto, Can. PROF. of EDUC, McGill Univ; DEPUTY DIR, Inst. of Educ, McGill Univ. Member: CPA, BPS. Teaching, administration, testing, guidance; intelligence and achievement testing, child guidance and development. M

SMITH, David Duncan. 37 Hillcrest Ave, Pointe Claire, Montreal 33, P.Q. b. 8 July 1927 Montreal. MA '50 Univ. of Minnesota, USA. STUD. COUNS. and LECT. in PSYCH, Sir George Williams Coll, 1441 Drummond St, Montreal 25. Member: CPA, Amer. Pers. and Guid. Assn. Administration of counseling service, guidance, teaching; relationships between measured ability and interest, counseling and therapeutic techniques, theory of mental measurement. M

SMITH, Miss M. Roberta. Ment. Hlth. Clin, Ontario Hosp, Brockville, Ont. b. 27 Nov 1904 St. John. MA '29 Univ. of Toronto, CPA. Clinical practice, psychotherapy, testing; teaching; child guidance, psychological testing. F

SNODGRASS, Prof. Florence Thompson. Dept. of Psych, Univ. of New Brunswick, Fredericton. b. 8 Apr 1902 Young's Cove. PH.D '49 Yale Univ, USA. PROF. and HEAD, Dept. of Psych. and Sociol, Univ. of N.B. Member: CPA, APA. Teaching, administration, research; intelligence tests, profiles and learning theory. F

SOPER, Harry Hubert. Ment. Hlth. Clin, Ontario Hosp, Hamilton, Ont. b. 12 May 1923 Durham. MA '54 Univ. of Toronto, Can. PSYCHOLOGIST, Ont. Hosp; CONSULT. PSYCH'T. and PSYCHOTHERAPIST, Lynwood Hall Children's Cen, Hamilton. Member: CPA, APA. Testing, clinical analysis, psychotherapy, teaching; child psychotherapy, diagnostic testing, personality appraisal. M

SPEED, Richard Henry. Western Socy. for Rehab, 900 W. 27 Ave, Vancouver, B.C. b. 2 Sept 1924 Wilton, Eng. MA '52 Univ. of British Columbia, Can. VOCAT. COUNS, Western Socy. for Rehab. Member: CPA. Counseling, personnel psychology, testing; aptitude and ability testing, counseling and psychotherapy, motivation. M

SPIRES, Alan M. Ment. Hlth. Clin, 5 Hazen Ave, St. John, N.B. b. 13 June 1924 Montreal. BA '49 McGill Univ, Can. SR. CLIN. PSYCH'T, Ment. Hlth. Clin. Member: CPA, APA, SPT. Clinical testing and analysis psychotherapy, consulting; projective techniques, personality and intelligence testing, anxiety and cognition. M

SPRINGBETT, Dr. Bruce MacQueen. Univ. of Manitoba, Winnipeg. b. 10 Apr 1907 Red Deer. PH.D '54 McGill Univ, Can. ASSOC. PROF, Univ. of Man. Member: CPA. Teaching, research, industrial psychology; thinking, personnel selection techniques. M

SPROULE, John Alexander. 99 Elgin Ave, Valois, Que. b. 4 May 1925 Hamilton. M.PS.SC '53 McGill Univ, Can. ASST. STUD. COUNS, Sir George Williams Coll, 1441 Drummond St, Montreal. Member: CPA. Guidance, testing, teaching; vocational and educational counseling, reading techniques. M

STAPLEFORD, Miss Elsie Maude. 4 Silverwood Ave, Toronto 10, Ont. b. Vancouver. MA '32 Univ. of Toronto, Can. PSYCHOLOGIST, Ont. Dept. of Pub. Welf. and DIR. of DAY NURSERIES BR, Queen's Park, Toronto 2; LECT. in PSYCH, Univ. of Toronto. Member: CPA. Administration, consulting, teaching; child psychology, mental testing, parent education and nursery schools, psychology of old age. F

STEFANIUK, Walter Bennie. Saskatchewan Hosp, Weyburn. b. 5 Nov 1927 Raeburn. BA '51 Univ. of Manitoba, Can. RES. ASSOC, Sask. Comm. for Schizophrenia Res, Sask. Hosp. Member: Sask. Psych. Assn. Research on hallucinogenic drugs, testing, consulting; assessment of therapeutic change, drug effects on vision and perception. M

STEHELIN, Mrs. Mary Elizabeth. East York Collegiate Inst, Coxwell and Cosburn Aves, Toronto, Ont. b. 18 Mar 1908 Londonderry. MA '40 Univ. of Toronto, Can. PSYCH. CONSULT, East York Bd. of Educ, Cosburn Ave, Toronto. Member: CPA. Educational counseling and guidance, testing, teaching, research; motivation, relationship between abstract vocabulary and intelligence, remedial mathematics. F

STEIN, Dr. Harry L. Univ. of Manitoba, Fort Garry. b. 29 Dec 1902 London, Eng. PH.D '42 Univ. of Minnesota, USA. PROF. of EDUC. PSYCH, Univ. of Man; EDUC. and VOCAT. COUNS, priv. prac. Member: CPA, APA. Teaching, research, consulting; mental and achievement tests, statistics, counseling. M

STENNETT, Richard Gene. 1360 Decarie Blvd, Apt. 34, Ville St. Laurent, P.Q. b. 4 Mar 1930 Ridgetown. MA '53 Univ. of Western Ontario, Can. STUDENT, McGill Univ, Montreal. Member: CPA, APA. Doctoral research, consulting; physiological recording, quantitative methods, projective techniques. M

STEPHENSON, Gordon Earl. 10041 155 St, Edmonton, Alta. b. 28 July 1933 Westlock. BA '53 Univ. of Alberta, Can. STAFF PSYCH'T, Alcoholism Found. of Alberta, 9910 103 St, Edmonton. Counseling, testing, psychotherapy; projective techniques, group psychotherapy, personality dynamics and diagnosis. M

STEVENS, Vernon Stanley. 339 Annette St, Toronto 9, Ont. b. 2 July 1892 Strathroy. MA '37 Univ. of Toronto, Can. TCHR. and CLINICIAN, Bd. of Educ, Western Tech.-Commercial Sch, Evelyn Crescent, Toronto 9; LECT. in PSYCH, McMaster Univ, Hamilton, Ont; CONSULT. PSYCH'T, priv. prac. Member: CPA, APA, Natl. Vocat. Guid. Assn. Teaching, educational psychology, consulting, vocational guidance; attitude measurement, test construction, industrial psychology. M

STEWART, Dr. David A. Bell Clin, 15 Horsham Ave, Willowdale, Toronto, Ont. b. 31 Aug 1911 Campbellton. PH.D '39 Univ. of Toronto, Can. CHIEF PSYCH'T, Bell Clin; WRITER of ABSTRACTS in NEUR. and PSYCHIAT, *Excerpta Medica*, Amsterdam. Member: CPA. Psychotherapy, clinical practice, research; social perception, group process, thinking. M

STEWART, Miss Joan Chalmers. 94 Crescent Rd, Apt. 305, Toronto 5, Ont. b. 27 Aug 1928 Toronto. MA '51 Univ. of Toronto, Can. STUDENT, Univ. of Toronto. Member: CPA. Testing, research. F

STOCKER, Mrs. Amalia Maria. 114 Richardson Ave, Toronto, Ont. b. 20 Apr 1913 Nowy Bytom, Poland. MA '48 Univ. of Edinburgh, Scot. PRINCIPAL, York Township Sch. for Retarded Children, 64 Hany, Toronto. Member: Ont. Psych. Assn. Administration, testing, teaching; learning theory, education and social adaptation of the retarded child.. F

STOKES, Miss Rosemary. 5612 Trafalgar St, Vancouver 13, B.C. b. 23 Aug 1929 Vancouver. MA '54 Univ. of British Columbia, Can. PSYCHOLOGIST, Provincial Child Guid. Clin, 455 W. 13 Ave, Vancouver 10. Member: CPA. Testing, clinical analysis, psychotherapy, adult education; individual

diagnosis, group dynamics.   F
STOTHERS, Dr. Carman Edmund.   22
Princeton Rd, Toronto 18, Ont. b. 11 June
1896 Canada. D.PAED '34 Univ. of Toronto,
Can. DIR. of SPEC. SERV, Ont. Dept. of
Educ; INSTRUCTOR, Ont. Coll. of Educ,
371 Bloor St. W, Toronto; EDITOR, *Year-
book*, Res. Comm. of Ont. Sch. Inspectors'
Assn. Member: CPA, Int. Counc. for
Excep. Child, Amer. Assn. on Ment. Defic.
Consulting, educational psychology,
teaching, administration; special education,
intelligence test construction, vocabulary
research.   M
STRUCKETT, Miss Pauline Bryant A.   416
English St, Apt. 8, London, Ont. b. 7 June
1926 Montreal. MA '51 Univ. of Western
Ontario, Can. PSYCHOLOGIST, Victoria
Hosp, South St, London. Member: CPA.
Consulting, testing, clinical analysis,
teaching; personality appraisals, autism in
children.   F
STYMEST, Ralph Crawford. Can. Industries
Ltd, Box 10, Montreal, P.Q. b. 24 Feb 1931
Rexton. MA '52 Univ. of Edinburgh, Scot.
PERS. ASST, Employee Relat. Dept, Can.
Indus. Ltd. Member: CPA, APA. Personnel
psychology, testing, consulting; projective
techniques, personnel relations, psycho-
therapy, counseling.   M
SUNDE, John Alfred. Box 33, Burwash, Ont.
b. 1 June 1919 Flekkefjord, Norway.
MA '50 Univ. of Manitoba, Can. PSY-
CHOLOGIST, Indus. Farm, Ont. Dept. of
Reform Institutions, Burwash. Member:
CPA, APA. Consulting, psychotherapy,
testing; personality theory, psychology
of criminal behavior, psychotherapy
methods.   M
SUTHERLAND, James Shannon. Box 188,
Ontario Hosp, Kingston, Ont. b. 19 Feb
1927 Guelph. MA '51 Univ. of Toronto,
Can. SR. PSYCH'T, Ont. Hosp; PSY-
CHOLOGIST, Child Guid. Clin. Member:
CPA. Child guidance, psychotherapy,
diagnostic testing, teaching; childhood
behavior disorders, personality develop-
ment, perception of self.   M
SYDIAHA, Daniel. 921 Athabasca St. W,
Moose Jaw, Sask. b. 29 Dec 1927 Buttress.
BE '49 Univ. of Saskatchewan, Can. RES.
and TCHNG. ASST, McGill Univ, 3600
McTavish St, Montreal 2, P.Q. Member:
CPA. Research, student, teaching; social
perception, vocational guidance, evaluation
of human relations training.   M
SZYRYNSKI, Prof. Victor. 297 Laurier Ave.
East, Ottawa. b. 10 Oct 1913 St. Peters-
burg, Russia. PH.D '49 Univ. of Ottawa,
Can; MD '38 Univ. of Warsaw, Poland.
ASSOC. PROF. of PSYCHOTHER. and PSYCHO-
PHYSIOLOGY, Univ. of Ottawa; NEUROLO-
GIST, Ottawa Civic Hosp; CONSULT.

NEUROLOGIST and PSYCHIATRIST, R.C.A.F.
Rockcliffe Hosp. Member: BPS, CPA, APA,
Amer. Psychiat. Assn, Can. Psychiat. Assn.
Teaching, psychotherapy, electroence-
phalography, clinical practice, consulting;
psychotherapy with adolescents, dynamic
psychology.   M
TAYLOR, Frank W. R. 96 St. George St,
Toronto, Ont. b. 24 Apr 1919 Cochrane.
MA '52 Univ. of Toronto, Can. STUDENT,
Univ. of Toronto. Member: CPA. Re-
search, teaching; learning theory, per-
ception, emotion.   M
TEGHTSOONIAN, Robert. Dept. of Psych,
Memorial Hall, Harvard Univ, Cambridge
38, Massachusetts, USA. b. 4 Feb 1932
Toronto. MA '55 Univ. of Toronto, Can.
STUDENT, Harvard Univ. Member: CPA.
Learning theory, motor skills, group
process.   M
THIBERT, Clément T. Jacques Cartier
Normal Sch, 1301 Sherbrooke St. E,
Montreal, P.Q. b. 1 Nov 1925 St. Constant.
Licence '52 Univ. of Montreal, Can.
PROFESSOR, Jacques Cartier Normal Sch.
Member: Psych. Assn. of P.Q. Amer. Assn.
on Ment. Defic. Teaching, educational
psychology, research; mental deficiency,
psychological development of exceptional
children.   M
THOMAS, Rev. Theodore Elia. Box 536,
Athabasca, Alta. b. 27 Oct 1927 Smoky
Lake. MA '51 Univ. of Alberta, Can.
MINISTER, The United Church of Can,
Athabasca. Member: CPA. Pastoral work,
counseling, guidance; socio-psychological
research in treatment of juvenile delinquency, projective techniques, learning
theory.   M
THOMPSON, Miss Winnifred Estelle.   339
Maplewood Ave, Winnipeg 13, Man.
b. 19 Dec 1913 Winnipeg. B.ED '55 Univ.
of Manitoba, Can. EDUC. PSYCH'T, Child
Guid. Clin, Ellen and Bannatyne St,
Winnipeg. Consulting and diagnostic
testing of reading problems, administration; achievement and psychometric
tests, survey testing procedures.   F
THOMPSON, Dr. William Robert. Dept. of
Psych, Queens Univ, Kingston, Ont.
b. 10 July 1924 Toulon, France. PH.D '51
Univ. of Chicago, USA. LECTURER, Queens
Univ. Member: CPA, APA. Teaching, re-
search, administration; prenatal influences,
inheritance of behavior, psychology of
knowledge and curiosity.   M
THOMSON, Miss Zillah. Maple Lane Sch,
Box 300, Route 1, Centralia, Washington,
USA. b. 7 Oct 1920 Winnipeg. MA '49 State
Coll. of Washingotn, USA. CLIN. PSYCH'T,
Maple Lane Sch. Member: CPA. Con-
sulting, testing, administration.   F
THURLOW, Mrs. Jean Kathleen. 40 Hemlock

St, St. Thomas, Ont. b. 4 July 1900 Keewatin. MA '41 Univ. of Toronto, Can. GUID. DIR. and REGISTRAR, Alma Coll, St. Thomas. Member: CPA. Teaching, guidance, testing; learning theory, group process, personality adjustment. F

TOYE, Miss Elizabeth Jane. 344 Roselawn Ave, Toronto 12, Ont. b. 1 June 1931 Toronto. BA '53 Univ. of Toronto, Can. SCH. PSYCH'T, Toronto Bd. of Educ, 155 Coll. St, Toronto. Member: CPA. Testing, educational psychology, child guidance, psychotherapy; intelligence tests, play therapy, projective techniques. F

TRATCH, Roman. Munroe Wing, Genl. Hosp, Regina, Sask. b. 9 Apr 1927 Kolomyja, Ukraine. Licentiate '52 Catholic Univ. of Louvain, Belgium. ASSOC. SOC. WRKR, Dept. of Pub. Hlth. Bldg, Regina. Member: CPA. Psychiatric social work, psychotherapy; personality theory, phenomenological psychology. M

TREMBLAY, Prof. Arthur. Laval Univ, 71 Rue D'Auteuil, Quebec. b. 18 June 1917 St. Bruno. M.ED '45 Harvard Univ, USA. ASST. DIR. and PROF, Sch. of Educ. and Guid, Laval Univ. Member: CPA, APA. Teaching, research, administration; educational psychology. M

TUCK, Prof. James Albert. Mt. Allison Univ, Sackville, N.B. b. 13 Nov 1922 Toronto. MA '50 Univ. of Toronto, Can. HEAD, Dept. of Psych, Mt. Allison Univ; SR. PSYCH'T, Sunnybrook Hosp. Member: CPA. Teaching, consulting, research; psychotherapy; social factors in academic performance. M

TURGEON, Jean. Laval Inst. of Vocat. Guid, 71 D'Auteuil, Quebec. b. 6 Dec 1931 St. Leonard. Licence '56 Laval Univ, Can. GUID. COUNS, Laval Inst. of Vocat. Guid. Counseling, testing, applied psychology; projective techniques, aptitude measurement, industrial psychology, achievement tests. M

TURNER, Prof. Gordon Haslam. Dept. of Psych, Univ. of Western Ontario, London, Ont. b. 15 June 1912 Montreal. PH.D '39 Univ. of Toronto, Can. PROF. and HEAD, Dept. of Psych, Univ. of Western Ont; CONSULT. ED, Canadian Journal of Psychology. Member: CPA, APA. Teaching, administration, research; personality theory, human relations, group process. M

TYLER, Dr. Earl John. 2239 Van Horne Ave, Brandon, Man. b. 22 Dec 1913 Moose Jaw. PH.D '54 Univ. of Utah, USA. PROF. of PSYCH, Brandon Coll. Inc, 18 St, Brandon. Member: CPA. Teaching, administration, educational psychology, consulting; learning theory, group process, attitude measurement. M

VAILLANCOURT, Jean-Paul. 2576 Rue Ménard, St. Foy, Quebec 6. b. 3 Aug 1915

Bonaventure. MA '49 Laval Univ, Can. PSYCHOLOGIST, Ste. Foy Hosp, 2705 Blvd. Laurier, Ste. Foy. Member: CPA, Amer. Cath. Psych. Assn. Testing, psychotherapy, consulting; achievement tests, problems of personnel adaptation. M

VALADE, L. Roger. 2411 Prefontaine St. Cité Jacques Cartier, Montreal 23. b. 13 Nov 1914 Montreal. BA '36 Univ. of Montreal, Can. SUPERVISOR, Soc. Welf. Dept, Dept. of Vets. Affairs, 35 Mc Gill St, Montreal. Member: Psych. ASSN. of P.Q. Administration, applied psychology, teaching. M

VAN LEIGHT FRANK, Mrs. Margit. 2 W. 67 St, New York City 23, USA. b 9 Jan 1898 Berlin, Germany. MA '54 McGill Univ, Can. PSYCHOTHERAPIST, priv. prac. Member: CPA, Socy. of Analytical Psych'ts. of New York. Psychotherapy; research in gerontology, dream analysis. F

VERNON, William Henry Dalton. c/o Dept. of Sociol. and Anthrop, Cornell Univ, Ithaca, New York, USA. b. 7 May 1908 Kingston, Jamaica, B.W.I. PH.D '56 Harvard Univ, USA. SR. PSYCH'T, Digby Psychiat. Clin; RES. ASSOC, Cornell Univ. Member: CPA, APA. Research; clinical and social psychology, testing, psychotherapy, mental health education. M

VINCENT, Mrs. Margaret Anne. Camp Hill Hosp, Halifax, N.S. b. 11 Nov 1923 Tacoma, Washington, USA. MA '51 Dalhousie Univ, Can. PSYCHOLOGIST, Camp Hill Hosp, Can. Member: Maritime Psych. Assn. Testing, clinical analysis, research, psychotherapy; projective techniques, aptitude tests. F

VINETTE, Dr. Roland. 840 Sir Adolphe Routhier, Quebec, P.Q. b. 4 July 1913 Montreal. D.PAED '43 Univ. of Montreal, Can. DIR. GENL. of NORMAL SCH, Dept. of Pub. Instr, Hotel du Gouvernement, Que. Member: CPA. Administration. M

WAINWRIGHT, John Anderson. 842 Wellington St, London, Ont. b. 7 Mar 1927 Tillsonburg. MA '51 Univ. of Western Ontario, Can. INSTR. in PSYCH, Univ. of Western Ontario. Member: CPA. Teaching, personnel psychology, research; group process, testing, attitude measurement. M

WAKE, Dr. Frank Robert. 123 Powell Ave, Ottawa, Ont. b. 14 Sept 1941 Knoxville, Tennessee, USA. PH.D '50 McGill Univ, Can. CHAIRMAN, Dept. of Psych, Carleton Coll, First Ave, Ottawa; CONSULTANT, Ment. Hlth. Div, Dept. of Natl. Hlth. and Welf. Member: CPA, APA. Teaching, administration, research; theories of criteria for maturity, expressive movement, fatigue. M

WALBY, Miss Grace Solveig. 293 Polson Ave, Winnipeg, Man. b. 28 Mar 1918 Winnipeg.

MA '52 Univ. of Chicago, USA. HEAD, Reading Dept, Child Guid. Clin. of Greater Winnipeg, Ellen and Bannatyne, Winnipeg. Member: CPA. Testing and remedial work, administration, student; achievement and diagnostic tests related to reading. F

WALKER, Charles Bertram. 155 Hopewell Ave, Ottawa, Ont. b. 25 Sept 1918 Toronto. BA '39 Univ. of Toronto, Can. STATISTICIAN, Biostatistics Sect, Res. and Stat. Div, Dept. of Natl. Hlth. and Welf, Jackson Bldg, Bank and Slater Sts, Ottawa. Member: Ont. Psych. Assn. Health research, administration, teaching; community organizations. M

WAND, Mrs. Barbara Bews. Educ. Testing Serv, 20 Nassau St, Princeton, New Jersey, USA. b. 2 Dec 1926 Port Hope. MA '52 Cornell Univ, USA. ASSOC. in RES, Educ. Tstng. Serv. Member: CPA. Research, testing, professional writing; achievement tests, social perception, motivation. F

WAY, Dr. Harrison Hedley. Central State Coll, Edmond, Oklahoma, USA. b. 12 Feb 1920 Bonavista. ED.D '53 Indiana Univ, USA. ASSOC. PROF. of PSYCH, Central State Coll. Member: CPA, APA. Teaching, testing, research; vocational and personal guidance, child and adolescent development, testing and analysis. M

WEES, Dr. Wilfred Rusk. Rural Route 3, Stouffville, Ont. b. 24 Nov 1899 Bracebridge. PH.D '35 Univ. of Toronto, Can. VICE PRES. and MGR, Textbook Div, W. J. Gage and Co. Ltd, 82 Spadina Ave, Toronto. Member: CPA. Educational psychology, editorial, administration; learning theory, memory cognition. M

WEININGER, Dr. Otto. Dept. of Psych, Univ. of Western Ontario, London, Ont. b. 19 Mar 1929 Montreal. PH.D '54 Univ. of Toronto, Can. INSTRUCTOR, Univ. of Western Ont; CLIN. PSYCH'T, Ont. Hosp, St. Thomas; EDITOR, Ontario Psychological Bulletin. Member: CPA, APA. Teaching, research, psychotherapy, testing; effect of infant experiences in adult personality, play therapy, perception. M

WELCH, Dr. Louise Marjorie. Dept. of Psych, Dalhousie Univ, Halifax, N.S. b. 14 Feb 1916 St. John. PH.D '44 Yale Univ, USA. PROF. of CLIN. PSYCH, Dalhousie Univ. Member: CPA. Teaching, consulting, research; learning theory, vocational guidance, personality theory. F

WELDON, Dr. Richard Chapman. Child Guid. Clin, Winnipeg 2, Man. b. 31 Aug 1908 Calgary. PH.D '51 Univ. of California, USA. EDUC. PSYCH'T, Winnipeg Sch. Bd, William and Ellen Sts, Winnipeg 2. Member: CPA. Diagnostic testing and consultations on reading problems, group therapy; attitude measurement, learning theory applied to reading, emotionally disturbed children. M

WENDT, Major Russell Allan. 86 Rita Ave, City View P.O, Ottawa, Ont. b. 15 Mar 1917 Edberg. MA '48 Univ. of Alberta, Can. PSYCHOLOGIST, Pers. Sel. Serv, Can. Army, Natl. Def. Hq, Ottawa; LECTURER, Carleton Coll, Ottawa. Member: CPA. Research, in test development, applied psychology, teaching; test construction, learning, systematic psychology. M

WERNER, Dr. Ingeborg Edith. 45 Bernard Ave, Toronto, Ont. b. 10 July 1924 Vienna, Austria. PH.D '49 Univ. of Vienna, Austria. PSYCHOLOGIST, Bd. of Educ, 155 College St, Toronto. Member: BOP. Diagnostic testing, educational and clinical psychology; projective techniques. F

WESTCOTT, James William. Apt. 5, 200 Mt. Vernon Ave, Montreal W. 28, P.Q. b. 16 June 1928 Saskatoon. MA '50 McGill Univ, Can. INDUS. ENGR, Noranda Copper and Brass Ltd, Sherbrooke and Durocher Sts, Montreal E. Member: CPA. Industrial and personnel psychology; selection methods, attitude measurement, training. M

WHITE, Paul Owen. Toronto Psychiat. Hosp, 2 Surrey Pl, Toronto, Ont. b. 23 Dec 1929 Toronto. BA '55 Univ. of Toronto, Can. PSYCH. ASST, Toronto Psychiat. Hosp. Member: CPA. Research, student; learning theory, experimental method, etiology of mental illness. M

WHITNEY, Mrs. Marjorie. 203 The Elms, 12 Elm Grove Ave, Toronto 3, Ont. b. 17 Jan 1932 Toronto. MA '55 Univ. of Toronto, Can. PSYCHOLOGIST, Ont. Dept. of Hlth. Member: Ont. Psych. Assn. Testing, clinical analysis, research; projective techniques, group dynamics, social development in children. F

WHITNEY, Raymond Cyril. 203 The Elms, 12 Elm Grove Ave, Toronto 3, Ont. b. 16 July 1929 Prescott. BA '53 Queen's Univ, Can. ASST. PERS. OFF, Hydro Elect. Power Comm. of Ont, 620 Univ. Ave, Toronto. Member: CPA. Industrial psychology, administration, personnel guidance and counseling; learning theory, industrial group dynamics, personnel training. M

WHITWORTH, Dr. Frederick Edward. 1221 Heron Rd, Ottawa. b. 12 May 1903 Winnipeg. PH.D '36 Univ. of California, USA. CHIEF, Res. Sect, Educ. Div, Dominion Bur. of Stat, Ottawa; LECTURER, Carleton Coll, Ottawa. Member: CPA. Research, teaching, educational psychology, vocational guidance. M

WIDEMAN, Dr. Harley Roy. 67 Pleasant Blvd, Toronto 7, Ont. b. 30 June 1917 Toronto. PH.D '53 Univ. of Toronto, Can. PSYCHOLOGIST, Toronto Genl. Hosp, Wellesley Div, Homewood Pl, Toronto;

PSYCHOTHERAPIST, priv. prac. Member: CPA, APA. Testing, clinical analysis, psychotherapy, research; projective techniques, hypnotherapeutic techniques, etiology of childhood schizophrenia. M

WIGDOR, Dr. Blossom T. 5580 Gatineau Ave, Apr. 15, Montreal, P.Q. b. 13 June 1924 Montreal. PH.D '52 McGill Univ, Can. PSYCHOLOGIST, Queen Mary Vets. Hosp, 4565 Queen Mary Rd, Montreal. Diagnostic testing, personality and geriatric research, teaching. F

WILKIN, Miss Eileen. 791 Hellmuth Ave, London, Ont. b. 9 Sept 1930 London, Eng. B.SC '52 Bedford Coll, Eng. INSTRUCTOR, Univ. of Western Ontario, London. Member: BPS, CPA. Teaching, research; role theory, stereotypes, projective techniques. F

WILKINS, Miss Muriel Faye. Ontario Hosp, King St. W, Kingston, Ont. b. 16 July 1930 Campbellton. BA '54 Queen's Univ, Can. PSYCHOLOGIST, Ont. Hosp. Member: CPA. Testing, student; projective techniques, achievement tests, group process. F

WILLIAMS, Prof. David Carlton. Dept. of Psych, Univ. of Toronto, 102 St. George St, Toronto. b. 7 July 1912 Winnipeg. PH.D '40 Univ. of Toronto, Can. PROFESSOR, Univ. of Toronto; CONSULTANT, Toronto Fam. Ct; CHAIRMAN, Human Resources Res. Comm, Def. Res. Bd. Member: CPA, APA. Teaching, research, administration; juvenile delinquency, mass communications, social perception. M

WILSON, Frederick Stewart. Hosp. for Ment. Diseases, Selkirk, Man. b. 20 Dec 1924 Winnipeg. B.SC '49 Univ. of Man, Can. PSYCHOMETRIST, Hosp. for Ment. Diseases. Member: CPA. Clinical testing, teaching, administration, student; intelligence testing, projective techniques. M

WILSON, Prof. Lolita. Stud. Advis. Serv, Univ. of Alberta, Edmonton, Alta. b. 6 Oct 1913 Lethbridge. MA '52 Univ. of British Columbia, Can. ASST. PROF. of PSYCH, and ASST. DIR, Stud. Advis. Serv, Univ. of Alta. Member: CPA. Student counseling, teaching, student; objective tests, industrial psychology, counseling. F

WITTKOWER, Prof. Eric David. Allan Memor. Inst, 1025 Pine Ave. W, Montreal, P.Q. b. 4 Apr 1899 Berlin, Germany. MD '24 Univ. of Berlin, Germany. ASSOC. PROF. of PSYCHIAT, Allan Memor. Inst; ASSOC. PSYCHIATRIST, Royal Victoria Hosp. and Montreal Genl. Hosp; ASSOC. ED, *American Journal of Psychosomatic Medicine.* Member: BPS, Br. Psychoanal. Socy, Royal Socy. of Med, Can. Psychoanal. Socy, Amer. Psychiat. Assn. Teaching, research, psychotherapy, consulting, clinical practice; psychosomatic medicine. M

WOLFE, Mrs. Shawna Warren. 48 Nina Ave, Toronto, Ont. b. 5 Sept 1931 Halifax. MA '53 Dalhousie Univ, Can. Member: CPA. Projective techniques, self assessment. F

WRIGHT, Prof. Henry Wilkes. 112 Church St, Kitchener, Ont. b. 16 Aug 1878 St. James, Michigan, USA. PH.D '03 Cornell Univ, USA. EMER. PROF. of PSYCH, Univ. of Manitoba; LECT. in PSYCH, Waterloo Coll, Waterloo, Ont. Member: CPA. Teaching, research, retired; psychological field theory, personality, communication. M

WRIGHT, Dr. Mary Jean. Dept. of Psych, Univ. of Western Ontario, London, Ont. b. 20 May 1915 Strathroy. PH.D '49 Univ. of Toronto, Can. ASSOC. PROF, Univ. of Western Ont; CONSULTANT, Children's Aid Socy. Member: CPA, APA. Teaching, research, testing; child development, family relationships, education of the gifted. F

WRIGHT, Dr. Morgan Wilkes. 711 E. 18 Ave, Regina, Sask. b. 18 Mar 1921 Winnipeg. PH.D '52 Univ. of Toronto, Can. CLIN. PSYCH'T, Med. Arts Clin, 2125 11 Ave, Regina; CONSULTANT, Cerebral Palsy Cen. Member: CPA. Clinical practice, psychotherapy, testing; clinical evaluation, teaching. M

YEATS, Lewis Clifford. 250 Oakwood Ave, Toronto. b. 15 Aug 1922 Port Colborne. MA '52 Univ. of Western Ontario, Can. STUDENT, Univ. of Toronto. Member: Ont. Psych. Assn. Psychotherapy with psychotic patients, projective techniques, learning theory. M

YOUNG, Ira L. 317 McLeod Bldg, Edmonton, Alta. b. 14 Oct 1926 Edmonton. MA '50 Univ. of Alberta, Can. PSYCHOLOGIST, priv. prac. Member: CPA, APA. Research, professional writing; psychoanalytic theory, psychology of creative activity. M

YOUNG, Prof. John Ernest McKim. Macdonald Coll, P.Q. b. 31 Mar 1913 Hamiota. PH.D '52 Univ. of Toronto, Can. ASST. PROF. of EDUC, McGill Univ, Montreal. Member: CPA, APA. Teaching, educational psychology, guidance; achievement and intelligence tests, attitude measurement. M

ZUBEK, Prof. John P. Dept. of Psych, Univ. of Manitoba, Winnipeg. b. 10 Mar 1925 Czechoslovakia. PH.D '50 Johns Hopkins Univ, USA. PROF. and CHMN, Dept. of Psych, Univ. of Man; CONSULT. ED, *Canadian Journal of Psychology.* Member: CPA, APA. Research, professional writing, administration; somesthesis, biochemical basis of learning, intellectual and sensory change in the aged. M

ZWEIG, Joseph Philip. 7944 Querbes Ave, Montreal 15, P.Q. b. 12 July 1914 Montreal. MA '52 McGill Univ, Can. LECTURER, Sir George Williams Coll, Drummond St,

Montreal; PRINCIPAL, Secular Dept, Rabbinical Coll. of Can. Member: CPA, APA. Teaching, administration, guidance; vo-

cational and educational counseling, learning theory, achievement tests, perception. **M**

CEYLON

COREA, James Clifford Aelian. Ramanathan Hall, Univ. of Ceylon, Peradeniya. b. 17 June 1904 Chilaw. MA '39 Univ. of London, Eng. WARDEN, Ramanathan Hall; EXAM. and LECT. in EDUC. and PSYCH, Univ. of Ceylon. Member: BPS. Educational psychology, testing, guidance, teaching; aptitude measurement, personality, psychoanalytic theory and mental hygiene. **M**

GREEN, Prof. Thomas Leslie. Univ. of Ceylon, Colombo. b. 17 Feb 1904 Hereford, Eng. MA '40 Univ. of Bristol, Eng. PROF. and HEAD, Dept. of Teacher Trng, Univ. of Ceylon. Teaching, research, administration, consultant to government and UNESCO; cultural determination of behavior, intergroup relations, adolescence and childhood. **M**

JAYASURIYA, Dharamasoka Laksiri. Dept. of Soc, Univ, of Ceylon, Peradeniya. b. 27 Oct 1931 Kandy. BA '54 Univ. of Sydney,

Austl. ASST. LECT, Univ. of Ceylon. Member: BPS-A. Teaching, research; culture and personality, psychometrics and mental testing, small group process. **M**

JAYASURIYA, John Ernest. Univ. of Ceylon, Colombo 3. b. 14 Feb 1918 Colombo. MA '49 Univ. of London, Eng. LECTURER, Univ. of Ceylon; EDITOR, *Journal of the National Education Society of Ceylon*. Teaching, research, educational psychology; intelligence and achievement testing. **M**

PIERIS, Miss Hilda Evelyn. Govt. Training Coll, Maharagama. b. 1 Oct 1906 Moratuwa MA '49 Univ. of London, Eng. LECT. in EDUC. and EDUC. PSYCH, Govt. Trng. Coll. Member: BPS. Teaching, practice teaching, supervision, research, student guidance; intelligence and interest measurement, learning theory, teaching methods, sociometry, backwardness, delinquency, mental health. **F**

CHILE

AGUIRRE G., Alfonso. Inst. of Educ. Res, Santa Isabel 478, Santiago. b. 20 Mar 1908 Rancagua. DIRECTOR, Inst. of Educ.Res; PSYCHOLOGIST, Serv. of Child Psychopathol Olivos 831, Santiago. Member: Chilean Psych. Socy. Research, testing children, teaching; attitude measurement, learning theory. **M**

ALVAREZ P., Prof. Alfonso. Casilla 3103, Santiago. b. 15 Oct 1915 Santiago. Professor, Inst. Pedagogico, Univ. of Chile. PSYCHOTECHNICIAN, Central Inst. of Psychotechnics, Providencia 1649, Santiago; ASSISTANT, Dept. of Psychotechnics, Ministry of Natl. Defense. Member: Chilean Psych. Socy. Testing, guidance, research in professional guidance; vocational guidance, aptitude tests. **M**

GANZARAIN, Prof. Dr. Ramón. Ave. Paraguay 461, andar 1, C, Santiago. b. 18 Apr 1923 Iquique. MD '47 Univ. of Chile. AUXILIARY PROF. of PSYCHIAT, Univ. of Chile, Santos Dumont 835, Santiago; LECT. and TRNG. ANALYST, Chilean Psychoanal. Inst; ED. BD, *Revista de Psiquiatria y Disciplinas Conexas*, Univ. of Chile. Member: Chilean Psychiat. Assn, Chilean Psychoanal. Assn, Int. Group Psychother. Assn. Psychotherapy, teaching, research; group process, Rorschach test. **M**

GÓMEZ SÁEZ, Emilio Ignacio. Bandera 236,

Oficina 410, Santiago. b. 22 May 1929 Santiago. Psychologist '53 Univ. of Chile. CLIN. PSYCH'T, Hosp. Salvador, Ave. Salvador 364, Santiago; PSYCHOLOGIST, Central Inst. of Psychotech. and Guid. Member: Chilean Assn. of Psych'ts, Chilean Psych. Socy. Testing, consulting, guidance, clinical practice, applied psychology; projective techniques, aptitude measurements. **M**

JÜNEMANN, Dr. Georgina. Casilla 2598, Santiago. b. 26 May 1925 Santiago. PH.D '54 Univ. of Montreal, Canada. PROFESSOR, Catholic Univ, Ave. Bernardo O'Higgins 340, Santiago; PSYCHOLOGIST, Hosp. San Juan de Dios, Santiago. Member: SIP, APA, CPA, Chilean Psych. Socy, Spanish Psych. Assn. Psychotherapy, teaching, testing, clinical analysis; projective techniques, personality, group and individual therapy. **F**

KERNBERG FRIEDMANN, Dr. Otto. Huérfanos 878, dpto. 802, Santiago. b. 10 Sept 1928 Vienna, Austria. MD '53 Univ. of Chile. ASST. PHYSICIAN, Pyschiatric Clinic, Univ. of Chile, Ave. Santos Dumont 835, Santiago; PROF. of PSYCHOPATHOL, School of Soc. Serv, Natl. Health Serv. Psychotherapy, consulting, clinical practice, guidance, teaching; psychoanalysis, group psychotherapy, projective techniques. **M**

KIBEDI, Dr. Jorge. Lira 1067, Santiago. b. 14 May 1920 Budapest, Hungary. Diploma '44 Univ. József Nádor, Hungary. INDUS. ADVIS, Personnel Dept, ENDESA, Moneda 921, Santiago. Applied, industrial psychology, research, human relations training; measurement of attitudes, group process.   M

LECLERC, Dr. Claude Pierre. Gasilla 9280, Santiago. b. 26 May 1928 Paris, France. MD '54 Univ. of Santiago, Chile. ASST. in PSYCHIAT, Univ. of Chile, Santos Dumont 825, Santiago; CLIN. ASST, Univ. Psychiat. Clinic. Group psychotherapy, clinical practice, teaching; child psychoanalysis, psychosomatic medicine, psychological problems of students.   M

MATTE-BLANCO, Prof. Dr. Ignacio. Univ. Psychiat. Clin, Casilla 6507, Santiago. b. 3 Oct 1908 Santiago. MD '30 Univ. of Chile. PROF. and HEAD, Dept. of Psychiat, Univ. of Chile, Santiago; PSYCHOANAL. and PSYCHIATRIST, priv. prac; ED. DIR, *Revista de Psiquiatria*, Univ. of Chile. Member: APA, Amer. Psychiat. Assn, Int. Psychoanal. Assn. Research, teaching, administration; research on methodology for the study of psychical processes.   M

NASSAR, Prof. Carlos. Casilla 9319, Santiago. b. 27 Apr 1912 San Fernando. MD '40 Univ. of Chile. DIRECTOR, Child Psychiat. Clin, Natl. Hlth. Serv, Ave de la Paz 850, Santiago; PROF. of ABN. PSYCH. and MENT. HYG, Univ. of Chile. Member: SIP, APA, Amer. Orthopsychiat. Assn, Chilean Psych. Socy. Teaching, consulting, clinical practice, guidance, psychotherapy; projective techniques, group process.   M

ORBE KRUZ, Gastón. (Gastón Lagos Orbeta). Casilla 28, San Bernardo. b. 31 July 1915 Victoria. INSPECTOR and PROF, Liceo de Hombres y Liceo Nocturno, A. Prat 435, San Bernardo. Teaching, administration, research; general and educational psychology, psychopathology.   M

PLOCH, Dipl. Psych. Dr. phil. Joachim. Casilla 1978, Santiago. b. 23 July 1922 Hindenburg, Ger. PH.D '54 Univ. of Würzburg, Ger. PROFESSOR, Colegio Alemán, Ave. Antonio Varas 666, Santiago. Teaching, testing, child guidance; youth group relationships, sociometry, projective techniques.   M

POBLETE BADAL, Manuel. Siglo Veinte 245, Santiago. b. 1 Oct 1929 Santiago. Egresado '54 Univ. of Chile. PSYCHOLOGIST, Inst. of Criminol, Penitenciaría de Santiago de Chile, Ave. Pedro Montt 1902, Santiago. Member: Chilean Psych. Socy. Research on the psychology of criminals, diagnosis and guidance; intelligence tests, aptitude measurement, projective techniques.   M

SANDOVAL CARRASCO, Prof. Juan. Bernardo de Amasa 626, Santiago. b. 4 Nov 1904 Buin. Professor, Escuela Normal Superior, Chile. TECHNICAL ADVISOR, Schools for the Mentally Deficient; PROF. of THERAPEUTIC EDUC, Escuelas de Temporado, Univ. of Chile. Member: Chilean Psych. Socy. Teaching, research, professional writing, testing; psychology of the mentally deficient.   M

SOLARI CANESSA, Dr. Guido. Andrés de Fuenzalida 144, dpto. 35, Santiago. b. 12 July 1926 Valparaíso. MD '51 Univ. of Chile. ASSISTANT, Cátedra Titular de Psiquiatría, School of Med, Univ. of Chile, Santiago. Clinical practice, teaching, research; neuropsychiatry, psychoses related to alcoholism.   M

VALDERRAMA DE LA CRUZ, Dr. Genoveva. Casilla 9280, Santiago. b. 11 Dec 1929 Santiago. MD '54 Univ. of Chile. ASST. to the CHAIR of PSYCHIAT, Univ. of Chile, Univ. Psychiat. Clinic, Santos Dumont 825, Santiago. Psychotherapy, teaching, research; group psychotherapy, child psychoanalysis, problems of adolescence. F

VIVANCO, Prof. Santiago. La Fetra 115, Santiago. b. 16 Apr 1921 Rancagua. PH.M '55 Catholic Univ. of Chile. PROFESSOR, Catholic Univ. of Chile. Member: Chilean Psych. Socy. Teaching, applied psychology, student; industrial psychology, human relations, educational and vocational guidance.   M

ZAPATA BARRA, Prof. Alberto. Inst. Científico de Lebu, Ave. Latorre 607, Lebu. b. 23 Aug 1913 Lebu. DIRECTOR, Inst. Científico de Lebu. Member: Latin Amer. Coordinating Comm. of Psych. (Montevideo). Teaching, applied psychology, professional writing; intelligence and personality tests, memory and learning.   M

CHINA MAINLAND

BAO, Prof. Dji-Lih. Dept. of Educ, Teachers Coll, Nanking. b. 22 Feb 1902 Chekiang. PH.D '33 Univ. of Michigan, USA. PROF. of PSYCH, Nanking teachers Coll. Member: CH.PA. Teaching, research; psychology of perception and memory, child psychology.   F

CHAN, Prof. Ying. Tientsin Teachers Coll, Tientsin. b. 16 May 1916 Liao-cheng. ED.D, Columbia Univ, Teachers Coll, USA. ASSOC. PROF, Tientsin Teachers Coll, Ma-chang Tao, Tientsin. Member: CH.PA. Teaching, research, educational and industrial psychology; reading, achievement tests.   M

CHANG, Shao-ying. Szechuan Univ, Chengtu, Szechuan. b. 17 Sept 1917 Szechuan. PH.D '50 Boston Univ, USA. ASSOC. PROF, Szechuan Univ. Member: CH.PA. Teaching, research; projective techniques, group therapy. M

CHANG, Miss Tsun-sung. Shantung Teachers Coll, Tsinan. b. 2 Oct 1919 Peking. MA '50 Columbia Univ, Teachers Coll, USA. INSTRUCTOR, Shantung Teachers Coll. Teaching, research, educational psychology. F

CHANG, Prof. Yao-chiang. Eastern China Normal Univ, Shanghai. b. 9 Apr 1893 Hankow. MA '19 Columbia Univ, USA. PROF. and HEAD, Dept. of Psych. and Educ, Eastern China Normal Univ. Member: CH.PA. Teaching. research, educational psychology; Chinese contributions to psychology, study of genius, psychology of safety. M

CHEN, Prof. Dr. Han-Piao. Southern China Teachers Coll, Canton. b. 6 Apr 1906 China. PH.D '46 State Univ. of Iowa, USA. PROF. of PSYCH, Southern China Teachers Coll. Member: CH.PA. Teaching, research, administration; child development, memory and learning, theoretical psychology. M

CHEN, Prof. Ho-chin. Nanking Teachers Coll, 122 Ninghai Rd, Nanking. b. 1 Mar 1892 Shang-yu. MA '19 Columbia Univ, Teachers Coll, USA. PRES. and PROF. of PRESCHOOL CHILDREN'S EDUC, Nanking teachers Coll. Member: CH.PA. Administration, teaching; infant and child psychological development, children's toys. M

CHEN, Dr. Hsuan-shan. Ministry of Educ, Peking. b. 13 May 1903 Hangchow. PH.D '28 Columbia Univ, USA. VICE DIRECTOR, Dept. of High Normal Educ, Ministry of Educ; ED. BD, Peoples Education. Member: CH.PA. Administration, editorial; educational psychology. M

CHEN, Dr. Lih. Chekiang Pedagogical Inst, Hangchow. b. 22 July 1906 Pingkiang. PH.D '33 Univ. of London, Eng. VICE PRES. and PROF. of PSYCH, Chekiang Pedagogical Inst. Member: CH.PA, Psychomet. Socy. (USA). Administration, teaching, research; experimental psychology. M

CHEN, Prof. Shu. Chekiang Teachers Coll, Hangchow. b. 3 Nov 1910 Hinghwa, Kiangsu. MA '48 Colorado State Coll. of Educ, USA. PROF. of PSYCH, Chekiang Teachers Coll. Member: CH.PA. Teaching, research, professional writing; learning theory, Pavlov's theories of higher nervous activities. M

CHENG, Prof. Dr. Nai-yi. Peking Univ, Peking. b. Dec 1900 China. PH.D, Univ. of Chicago, USA. PROF. of PSYCH, Peking Univ. Member: CH.PA. Teaching, research; psychology of learning and thinking. M

CHENG, Yung-Fu. Kunming Teachers Coll, Kunming. b. 23 Oct 1917 Kunming. MA '50 George Peabody Coll. for Teachers, USA. ASSOC. PROF, Kunming Teachers Coll. Member: CH.PA. Teaching, research, testing; learning theory, achievement tests, group process. M

CHING, Prof. Yuen-King. South China Teachers Coll, Canton. b. 30 July 1905 Kwangtung. BA '32 Sun Yat-sen Univ, China. VICE PRES. and PROF, S. China Teachers Coll. Member: CH.PA. Administration, teaching, research; personality, learning. M

CHOU, Prof. Li-chiu. Szechuan Normal Coll, East Gate, Chengtu City, Szechuan. b. 21 Jan 1903 Changsha. MS '30 Yenching Univ, China. PROF. of PSYCH, Szechuan Normal Coll. Member: CH.PA. Teaching, research, educational psychology; projective techniques, learning theory, social perception. F

CHOU, Prof. Siegen K. Psych. Lab, Univ. of Peking. b. 10 Aug 1903 Anhwei. PH.D '30 Stanford Univ, USA. PROF. of PSYCH, Dept. of Philos, Univ. of Peking; DIR. of STUD. RES, Peking Inst. of Physical Educ. Member: CH.PA, APA. Research, teaching, applied psychology of athletics; experimental design for research, emotion and will, subvocal conditioning in psychogalvanic reflex. M

CHOW, Prof. Shih-boo. Southwest Teachers Coll, Chungking. b. 29 Jan 1907 Yochih, Szechuan. BA '33 Wuhan Univ, China. PROF. of PSYCH. Southwest Teachers Coll. Member: CH.PA. Teaching, research; thinking, memory, learning. M

CHU, Chih-hsien. Dept. of Psych, Peking Normal Univ, Peking. b. 9 Jan 1909 China. BA '34 Natl. Cen. Univ, China. PROF. and HEAD, Dept. of Psych, Peking Normal Univ. Member: CH.PA. Teaching, research, administration; modern psychological theories, child psychology. M

CHU, Prof. Hsi-Liang. Psych. Div, Dept. of Educ, Hua-Chung Teachers Coll, Wuchang. b. 4 May 1900 Lin-Chuan, Kiangsi. MA '28 Univ. of Wisconsin, MS '30 Yale, USA. PROF. and CHMN, Psych. Div, Hua-Chung Teachers Coll. Member: CH.PA. Teaching, research, administration; memory, association theory, development of concepts by children, functions of make-believe in mental life of children. M

CHU, Si-Hou. Kunming Med. Coll, Yunnan. b. 1 Mar 1914 Kirin. Docteur ès sciences '42 Univ. of Lyon, Fr. PROF. and DIR, Physiol. Sect, Kunming Med. Coll. Member: CH.PA, Chinese Physiol. Socy. Teaching, research, administration; activity of higher nervous system, psychophysiology of sensations, affective activity and emotions. M

FENG, Prof. Pan-yang. Fukien Teachers Coll, Foochow. b. 11 May 1909 Foochow. MA '32 Munic. Univ. of Wichita, USA. PROF. of EDUC, Fukien Teachers Coll. Member: CH.PA. Teaching, research, administration; learning theory, psychological traits of middle school students, inheritance, environment and education. M

FONG, Prof. Ting-Yuen. Dept. of Educ, East China Teachers Coll, Shanghai. b. 12 June 1898 Shanghai. PH.D '45 Univ. of Pennsylvania, USA. PROFESSOR, East China Teachers Coll. Member: CH.PA. Teaching, research. M

FOO, Prof. Thoong-sien. Shantung Teachers Coll, Tsi-nan, Shantung. b. Jan 1910 Hu-nan. PH.D '50 Columbia Univ, USA. PROF. and HEAD, Dept. of Educ. and Psych, Shantung Teachers Coll. Member: CH.PA. Teaching, research, educational psychology; personality, thought and language, learning theory. M

FU, Prof. Jen-fang. Kweiyang Teachers Coll, Kweichow. b. 10 Sept 1915 Wanhsien, Szechuan. MS '48 Cen. Missouri State Coll, USA. ASSOC. PROF. of PSYCH, Kweiyang Teachers Coll. Member: CH.PA. Teaching, research, educational psychology; learning theory, personality and adjustment, achievement tests. M

HAO, Prof. Yao-tung. Sian Teachers Coll, Sian, Shensi. b. 10 Dec 1891 Shensi. MA '23 Stanford Univ, USA. PROF. of EDUC, Sian Teachers Coll. Member: CH.PA. Teaching, research, administration; developmental, physiological and experimental psychology. M

HO, Assoc. Prof. Chi-kai. Southwestern Teachers Trng. Coll, Chunking. b. 3 Oct 1914 Kiangsu. BA, Szechuan Univ, China. ASSOC. PROF, Dept. of Educ, Southwestern Teachers Trng. Coll. Member: CH.PA. Teaching, administration, research; projective techniques. M

HSIAO, Prof. Hsiao-hung. No. 4, 1293, rd Lane, Yu-yuen Rd, Shanghai. b. 25 Nov 1896 Hengyang. PH.D '30 Univ. of California, USA. PROFESSOR, Eastern China Teachers Coll, N. Chung-Shan Rd, Shanghai; EDITOR, Psych. Series for Teachers. Member: CH.PA, Chinese Sci. Socy. Teaching, research, administration; Pavlov's theory of higher nervous activities, stages of language, development studies of personality. M

HSIEH, Prof. Hsuin-chu. 236, Lane 25, S. Shensi, Shanghai. b. 20 May 1895 Dang-doo. MA '22 Univ. of Chicago, USA PROF. of PSYCH, East China Normal Univ. Shanghai. Member: CH.PA. Teaching, research, administration; learning theory, process of thinking. M

HUANG, Prof. Yu-chi. Hunan Med. Coll,

Changsha, Hunan. b. 1 Feb 1906 Foochow. PROFESSOR, Dept. of Neur. and Psychiat, Hunan Med. Coll. Member: CH.PA, Chinese Med. Assn. Teaching, research, clinical practice, educational psychology. M

HSÜ, Dr. F. H. Inst. of Psych, Academia Sinica, Peking. b. 22 Mar 1911 Peking. PH.D '42 Cath. Univ. of America, USA. RES. PROF, Academia Sinica. Member: CH.PA. Research; research design, social perception, statistics. M

HU, Prof. Chi-Nan. Eastern China Normal Univ, 3663 N. Chung Shan Rd, Shanghai. b. 22 Nov 1905 Shanghai. PH.D '34 Univ. of Chicago, USA. PROFESSOR, Eastern China Normal Univ. Member: CH.PA. Teaching, administration, research; general, physiological and experimental psychology. M

HU, Prof. I. Hopei Teachers Coll, Tientsin. b. 3 Mar 1904 Changsha PH.D '28 Univ. of Chicago, USA. VICE PRESIDENT, Hopei Teachers Coll. Member: CH.PA. Administration, research, teaching; psychology of learning, reading. M

HU, Assoc. Prof. Shih-hsiang. Psych. Br, Tientsin Normal Coll, Ma-chang-Tao, Tientsin. b. 22 Feb 1920 Changsha, Hunan. MS '49 Central Missouri State Coll, USA. ASSOC. PROF. and HEAD, Psych. Br, Tientsin Normal Coll. Member: CH.PA. Teaching, administration, research; personality and motivation, thinking, perception. M

HU, Tsu-ying. Shanghai Second Teachers Coll, Kwe-lin Rd, Shanghai. b. 7 May 1908 Hangchow. MA '38 Univ. of Michigan, USA. ASST. HEAD, Educ. and Psych. Dept, Shanghai Second Teachers Coll. Member: CH.PA. Teaching, research, administration; mental characteristics of adolescence, learning theory. M

KAO, Prof. Chuo-foo. Nanking Teachers Coll, Nanking. b. 5 Nov 1896 Wenchow. BA '23 Hongkong Univ, China. VICE PRES, Nanking Teachers Coll; PROF. of PSYCH, Educ. Dept, Nanking Teachers Coll. Member: CH.PA. Teaching, research, administration; projective techniques, learning theory, social perception. M

KAO, Prof. Wen-yuan. Dept. of Educ, Nanking Teachers Coll, Nanking. b. 7 July 1905 Sian. MS '30 Univ. of Michigan, USA. PROF. of PSYCH, Nanking Teachers Coll. Member: CH.PA. Teaching, research; memory, psychology of speech, child psychology. M

KOWH, Prof. Yu-yu. Kiangsu Teachers Coll Soochow. b. 5 May 1900 Luchowfu Anwhei. PH.D '34 Univ. of Kentucky, USA PROF. of EDUC, Kiangsu Teachers Coll Member: CH.PA. Research, administration teaching; child and educational psychology. M

KUO, Chao-yee. Nanking Teachers Coll

Ning Hai Rd, Nanking. b. 8 Jan 1921 Shanghai. MA '50 New York Sch. of Soc. Work, Columbia Univ, USA. TEACHER, Nanking Teachers Coll. Member: CH.PA. Teaching, research; child psychology. F

KUO, Prof. Dr. Itzen. Peking Normal Univ, Peking. b. 6 Sept 1894 Wantsai. PH.D '28 Univ. of Tübingen, Ger. PROF. of PSYCH, Educ. Dept. Peking Normal Univ. Member: CH.PA, Gesellschaft für Experimentelle Psych. Research, teaching, professional writing; Chinese history of psychology, space perception, typology of personality. M

LI, Assoc. Prof. Djoh-i. 33 Paak Hok Tung, Canton. b. 16 Sept 1908 Canton. BA '30 Ginling Coll, China; BA '34 Univ. of California, USA. ASSOC. PROF, South China Teachers Coll, Canton. Teaching, research, student. M

LI, Prof. Kwang-wu. South China Teachers Coll, Canton. b. 22 Dec 1916 Canton. PH.D '52 Univ. of Wisconsin, USA. PROFESSOR, Dept. of Educ. South China Teachers Coll. Member: CH.PA. Research, administration, professional writing; thinking. M

LI, Prof. Tsing-song. Shanghai Second Teachers Coll, Shanghai. b. 25 Jan 1903 Nanking. BA '26 Natl. Southeastern Univ, Nanking, China. PROFESSOR, Shanghai Second Teachers Coll. Member: CH.PA. Teaching, research, professional writing; thought and language, higher nervous activity, learning theory. M

LIAO, Dr. Sze-Chen. First Normal Coll, Pao-Shing Rd, Shanghai. b. 16 June 1892 Kating. PH.D '21 Brown Univ, USA. PRESIDENT, First Normal Coll. Member: CH.PA. Administration, teaching, research; achievement tests, learning theory, attitude measurement. M

LIN, Prof. Chuan-ting. Peking Pedagogical Inst, Peking. b. 1 Oct 1913 Foochow. Docteur en Psych. Appliquée '49 Univ. of Louvain, Bel. DIR. of STUDIES, Peking Pedagogical Inst. Member: CH.PA. Administration, research, teaching; emotional expression, perceptual process in reading Chinese, age differences in mental traits. M

LIU, Dr. Ching-ho. Psych. Inst, Academia Sinica, Peking. b. 1 May 1911 Shanghai. PH.D, Columbia Univ, USA. RES. WRKR, Psych. Inst, Academia Sinica. Member: CH.PA. Research; development of speech and thought in children. F

LU, Prof. Chun. Kunming Teachers Coll, Kunming. b. 21 Oct 1916 Lusi. MA '44 Natl. Cen. Univ, China. PROF. of PSYCH, Kunming Teachers Coll; EDITOR, *Ai Wei*. Member: CH.PA. Teaching, student; child and educational psychology. M

NI, Prof. Dr. Chung-fang Sect. of Educ,

Kunming Normal Coll, Kunming. b. 5 Oct 1903 Yungien Hsian. PH.D '34 Univ. of Chicago, USA. PROF. of PSYCH. and DEAN, Sect. of Educ, Kunming Normal Coll. Member: CH.PA. Teaching, research, administration; sensation and perception, psychological teaching methods, psychological theory. M

PAN, Prof. Shuh Inst. of Psych, Academia Sinica, Peking. b. 13 July 1897 Ihing. PH.D, Univ. of Chicago, USA. DIRECTOR, Inst. of Psych, Academia Sinica. Member: CH.PA. Administration, research, professional writing; visual perception literature and arts, theory of consciousness. M

PAN, Prof. Dr. Yuen. 10 Tankao Lung, Shaohing, Chekiang. b. 22 Jan 1892 Chekiang. PH.D '30 Univ. of London, Eng. PROF. of PSYCH, Shangting Normal Coll, Tsinan. Member: CH.PA, BPS. Retired, research, testing; relation of feeling and cognition, sensation and perception, mental activity from the standpoint of dialectical materialism. M

PEN, Prof. Fei. Fac. of Educ, Peking Normal Univ, Peking. b. 19 July 1914 Tang Shan. Peking Normal Univ, China. DEAN, Fac. of Educ, Peking Normal Univ. Member: CH.PA. Teaching, administration, research; personality, psychology of thinking and language. M

SANG, Prof. Tshan-han. Peking Univ, Peking. b. 31 July 1909 Changsu. BA '30 Fuh Tan Univ, China. PROF. of PSYCH, Peking Univ. Member: CH.PA. Teaching, research, industrial psychology; personality, thinking. M

SHEN, Prof. Nai-Chang. Peking Univ, Peking. b. 24 Nov 1915 Huchow. MS '36 Tsing Hua Univ, China. PROF. of PSYCH, Div. of Psych, Dept. of Philos, Peking Univ. Member: CH.PA. Teaching, research, administration; sensory-perceptive processes, physiology of higher nervous activity, animal discrimination. M

SHOU, Jui-Chen. Dept. of Educ, Eastern China Normal Univ, Hwatung. b. 15 Jan 1916 Kunsha, Kiangsu. BS, Univ. of Chekiang, China. LECT. in PSYCH, Dept. of Educ, Eastern China Normal Univ. Member: CH.PA. Teaching, research, editorial. F

SUN, Edith Chia-ying. 25 Sha-shih-tao, Tientsin. b. 9 Sept 1908 Tientsin. MS '37 Oregon State Univ, USA. LECT. in PSYCH, Tientsin Normal Coll, Race Course Rd, Tientsin. Member: CH.PA. Teaching, research, student; age and psychological development, experimental psychology, child psychology. F

TAAI, Prof. Dr. Wal-king. Hua-chung Teachers Coll, Wuchang, Hupeh. b. 15 Jan 1896 Canton. PH.D '39 New York

Univ, USA. PROFESSOR, Huachung Teachers Coll. Teaching, research, student; learning theory.   F

T'AN, Prof. Dr. TienKai L. East China Normal Univ, N. Chung-shan Rd, Shanghai. b. 26 June 1904 Weihsin. PH.D '29 Stanford Univ, USA. PROFESSOR, East China Normal Univ. Member: CH.PA. Psychological research, professional writing; projective techniques.   M

TANG, Prof. Ming-sin. Dept. of Educ, Fukien Teachers Coll, Foochow, Fukien. b. 15 Sept 1905 Kiukiang. MA '33 Vanderbilt Univ, USA. TEACHER, Fukien Teachers Coll; ADVISER, Dept. of Neuropsychiat, Prov. Foochow's Psychopathic Hosp, Foochow. Member: CH.PA. Teaching, research, guidance; psychological traits among different age groups in children, psychological development and behavior guidance for children, preventive psychiatry.   F

TANG, Prof. Yüeh. Dept. of Psych, Peking Univ, Peking. b. 7 Jan 1891 Foochow. PH.D '20 Harvard Univ, USA. PROFESSOR, Peking Univ. Member: CH.PA. Research, teaching; history of psychology, criticism of contemporary psychological schools, psychological study of classical Chinese literature.   M

TAO, Dr. Kuo-tai. Nanking Neuropsychiatric Inst, Nanking. b. 18 May 1916 Wusih, Kiangsu. MD '41 Chengtu Med. Coll, China. MED. DIR, Nanking Neuropsychiatric Inst; PROF. of PSYCHIAT, Kiangsu Med. Coll. Member: CH.PA. Clinical practice, teaching, psychotherapy; child psychiatry, preventive psychiatry.   M

TENG, Prof. Dr. Ta-chun M. Hopei Tientsin Teachers Coll, 2 Tien-wei Rd, Tientsin. b. 13 Nov 1908 Peking. ED.D '50 Univ. of Colorado, USA. PROF. of EDUC, Hopei Tientsin Teachers Coll. Teaching, research; history of education, learning theory.   M

TSAI, Miss Chun-nien. 22 Yea-chiu-nung, Fung-Meng, Suchow. b. 29 Aug 1924 Shanghai. MA '51 Stanford Univ, USA. INSTRUCTOR, Chiang-Su Teachers Coll, Suchow. Member: CH.PA. Teaching.   F

TSANG, Prof. Yü-Ch'üan. Anatomy Dept, Peking Med. Coll, Peking. b. 10 May 1901 Wanshien, Hopei. PH.D '34 Univ. of Chicago, USA. PROF. of ANATOMY, Peking Med. Coll. Member: CH.PA. Research, teaching.M

TSANG, Prof. Y. Y. Shantung Teachers Coll, Tsinan, Shantung. b. 6 May 1901 Chuchow. MA '26 Univ. of Washington, USA. HEAD, Dept. of Psych, Shantung Teachers Coll. Member: CH.PA. Teaching, research, professional writing; application of psychological findings to teaching process, character measurement, popularization of psychological principles.   M

TSAO, Prof. Fei. Inst. of Psych, Academia Sinica, Peking. b. 21 Apr 1908 Sungkiang, Kiangsu. PH.D '42 Univ. of Toronto, Can. RES. FELLOW, Inst. of Psych, Academia Sinica. Member: CH.PA. Research; memory and learning, statistical methods, projective techniques, factor analysis.   M

TSAO, Prof. Dr. Jih-chang. Academia Sinica, Peking. b. 11 Jan 1911 Hopei. PH.D '48 Cambridge Univ, Eng. VICE DIRECTOR, Inst. of Psych, Academia Sinica; EDITOR, *Journal of Psychology*. Member: CH.PA. Teaching, research, administration; visual perception, higher nervous activity, learning and memory.   M

TSENG, Prof. Tso-chung. Hunan Teachers Coll, Changsha. b. 27 Mar 1894 Kweilin. PH.D '32 Univ. of Washington, USA. PROF. of PSYCH. and HEAD, Educ. Dept, Hunan Teachers Coll. Member: CH.PA. Teaching, research, educational psychology, professional writing; animal and human conditioned reflexes.   M

TSO, Prof. Cheng-en. Eastern China Normal Univ, Shanghai. b. 28 Nov 1903 Wuchang. Docteur ès lettres '31 Univ. of Montpellier, Fr. PROF. of PSYCH, Eastern China Normal Univ. Member: CH.PA. Teaching, research; projective techniques, learning theory, achievement tests.   M

TSO, Prof. Hsue-Li. No. 6, 3rd. Hutung, Shi-pan-fang, Peking. b. 4 July 1917 Canton. BA, Sun-Yat-Sen Univ, China. PROFESSOR, Peking Normal Univ, Peking. Member: CH.PA. Teaching, research; learning theory.   F

TWAN, Prof. Tsen. Teachers Coll. of Chekiang, Hangchow. b. 20 Aug 1903 Poyang, Kiangsi. MA, Univ. of Paris, Fr. PROF. of PSYCH. and HEAD, Fac. of Psych, Teachers Coll. of Chekiang. Member: CH.PA. Teaching, research, child psychology; sensation, character and temperament.   M

WANG, Prof. Dr. Feng-gang Honan Teachers Coll, Kaifeng, Honan. b. 10 Nov 1901 Siping, Honan. PH.D '31 Stanford Univ, USA. PROF. of PSYCH, Honan Teachers Coll. Member: CH.PA. Teaching research, professional writing; general and child psychology, psychology of learning. M

WANG, Prof. Pei-tsu. Shih-chia-chuang Teachers Coll, Shih-chia-chuang, Hopei. b. 24 Nov 1909 Shantung. ED.D '50 Univ. of Colorado, USA. PROF. of PSYCH. and HEAD, Dept. of Psych. Res, Shih-chiachuang Teachers Coll; DIRECTOR, Bur. of Educ. Res, Shih-chia-chuang. Teaching research, administration; learning theory, critical study of behaviorism and Gestalt psychology.   M

WONG, Hop-Wo. West-North Teachers Coll Lanchow. b. 4 Nov 1915 Canton. BA '4?

Sun Yat Sen Univ, China. TEACHER, West-North Teachers Coll. Member: CH.PA. Teaching, research; projective techniques, learning theory. M

WOO, Prof. Dr. Chiang-Lin. Inst. of Psych, Academia Sinica, Peking. b. 3 Feb 1914 Chuanchow. PH.D '48 Syracuse Univ, USA. RES. FELLOW, Inst. of Psych, Academia Sinica; EDITOR, The Translated Journal of Psychology; ED. COMM, Chinese Journal of Psychology. Member: CH.PA. Research, editorial, teaching; experimental study of thinking and learning, theory of psychology. M

WU, Prof. Hwei-ling. Hopei Peking Teachers Coll, Peking. b. Jan 1912 China. MA '37 State Univ. of Iowa, USA. ASSOC. PROF, Hopei Peking Teachers Coll. Member: CH.PA. Teaching, research, administration; development of children's mental life. F

WU, Asst. Prof. Tzi-chiang Fukien Normal Coll. b. 17 Nov 1901 Kiangsi. Graduated, Tokyo Art and Science Univ, Japan. ASST. PROF. of EDUC. and HEAD, Dept. of Educ, Fukien Normal Coll, Foochow. Member: CH.PA. Teaching, research, administration; learning theory, achievement tests, group process. M

YEH, Prof. Ling. Dept. of Educ, Southwestern Normal Coll, Chungking, Szechuan. b. 12 Dec 1893 Kuson. Docteur ès lettres '29 Univ. of Lyon, Fr. PROF. of PSYCH. and DIR, Psych. Sect, Southwestern Normal Coll. Member: CH.PA. Teaching, administration, research, educational psychology; psychology of interest, psychology of art, language and thought of children. M

YEH, Prof. Pei-hua. South China Teachers Coll, Sheh-pai, Canton. b. 18 Apr 1912 Hu-peh. MA '46 Univ. of Minnesota, USA. DEAN of STUDY, South China Teachers Coll. Research, administration, teaching; experimental design, learning theory, achievement tests, statistics. M

YOUNG, Prof. Dr. Chen-wha. Honan Teachers Coll, Kaifeng, Honan. b. 20 Feb 1893 An-young, Honan. PH.D '31 Univ. of Paris, Fr. PROF. of PSYCH. and ASST. DEAN, Dept. of Educ, Honan Teachers Coll; DIRECTOR, Tchng. and Sci. Res. in Psych. and Educ, Honan Teachers Coll. Member: CH.PA. Research, teaching, administration; learning theory, general and child psychology. M

CHINA TAIWAN

CHANG, Miss Shing-hwa. 18, Lane 105, Sect. 1, N. Chung Shang Rd, Taipei, Taiwan. b. 21 Apr 1930 Mu-san-Taipei. B.SC '53 Natl. Taiwan Univ, China. ASSISTANT, Dept. of Psych, Natl. Taiwan Univ, Taipei; COUNSELOR, Classif. Cen. of Vocat. Assistance Comm. of Retired Servicemen, Nan-nan, Keelung, Taiwan. Member: Chinese Assn. of Psych. Testing, Chinese Assn. of Ment. Hyg. Student, testing, teaching; projective techniques, intelligence tests. F

CHEN, Prof. Hsueh-ping. Dept. of Psych, Natl. Taiwan Univ, Taipei, Taiwan. b. 1 Nov 1901 Kiangsu. MA '27 Columbia Univ, USA. PROFESSOR, Natl. Taiwan Univ. Member: Chinese Assn. of Psych. Teaching, administration, research; personality, social perception, group process. M

CHENG, Prof. Fai-mi. Ministry of Exam. and Selectn, Exam. Yuan, Taipei, Taiwan. b. 9 May 1914 Pao-ying. BA '40 Natl. Cen. Univ, Nanking. TECH. CONSULT, Ministry of Exam. and Selectn; PROF. of PERS. PSYCH, Chinese Local Govt. Correspondence Sch; ASSOC. PROF. of PSYCH. and EDUC MEASUREMENT, Taiwan Normal Univ. Member: Chinese Assn. of Psych. Testing. Research, test construction and analysis, teaching; occupational guidance, psychological warfare. M

CHENG, Assoc. Prof. Fa-yu. Dept. of Psych, Natl. Taiwan Univ, Taipei. b. 16 Oct 1916 Taiwan. ASSOC. PROF, Natl. Taiwan Univ; EDITOR, China Anthropology Assn. Member: Chinese Assn. of Psych. Testing. Teaching, research, testing; depth perception, learning theory, race character and cultural background. M

CHENG-WEN, Miss Hsu. No. 2, Lane 169, Chien Kuo (S) Rd, Taipei, Taiwan. b. 10 Jan 1917 Tungshan, Kwangsu. BA, Natl. Cen. Univ, Nanking, China. RES. WRKR, First Bur, Chinese Army Hq, Taipei, Taiwan. Member: Chinese Assn. of Psych. Testing, Chinese Assn. of Ment. Hyg, Chinese Educ. Assn. Research, teaching, testing; aptitude and achievement tests, attitude measurement. F

CHIEN, Prof. Ping. Taiwan Normal Univ, Taipei, Taiwan. b. 5 Dec 1911 Wutsin, Kiangsu. MA '39 Natl. Chungshan Univ, China. PROFESSOR, Taiwan Normal Univ. Member: Chinese Assn. of Psych. Testing, Chinese Assn. of Ment. Hyg. Teaching, research, professional writing; mental health, child guidance. F

CHING WAN, Miss Sun. No. 7, Lane 140, Sung Chiang Rd, Taipei, Taiwan. b. 26 Sept 1923 Nanking. BS '47 Natl. Cen. Univ, Nanking, China. TESTING PSYCH'T, Classif. Cen. of Vocat. Assistance Comm. of Retired Servicemen, NanNan, Keelung, Taiwan. Member: Chinese Assn. of Psych. Testing,

Chinese Assn. of Ment. Hyg. Testing, teaching, research; testing techniques. F

DJANG, Prof. Siao-sung. No. 6, Lane 16, Hsin-seng S. Rd, III, Taipei, Taiwan. b. 14 July 1901 Hankow, Hupeh. PH.D '35 Univ. of Michigan, USA. PROF. of PSYCH, Natl. Taiwan Univ, Roosevelt Rd, Sect. 4, Taipei, Taiwan; SUPERVISOR, Separation Cen. for Retired Servicemen. Member: Chinese Assn. of Ment. Hyg, Chinese Assn. of Psych. Testing. Teaching, research, supervising; learning theory, personnel research, mental hygiene. F

HER-SHENG, Chyau. Taiwan Normal Univ, Taipei, Taiwan. b. 4 Apr 1925 Kiangsu. B.SC '55 Natl. Taiwan Univ, Taiwan. ASSISTANT, Dept. of Educ, Taiwan Normal Univ. Member: Chinese Assn. of Psych. Testing. Research, laboratory work; visual perception, learning theory. M

HWANG, Chien-hou. 190 Chao Chow St, Taipei, Taiwan. b. 25 Sept 1920 Changsha, Hunan. MA, Teachers Coll, Columbia Univ, USA. CHIEF, Ment. Hyg. Div, Natl. Inst. of Hlth, 22 S. Chungking Rd, Sect. 3, Taipei, Taiwan; ASSOC. PROF, Dept. of Psych, Natl. Taiwan Univ; CHIEF, Testing Sect, Classif. Cen, Vocat. Assistance Comm. for Retired Servicemen, Taipei; EDITOR, *Mental Hygiene Booklet Series.* Member: Chinese Assn. of Ment. Hyg, Chinese Assn. of Psych. Testing. Testing, teaching, consulting; child guidance, mental hygiene in schools, projective techniques. M

KAO, Mrs. Yung-huo L. 40 S. Westmore Ave, Lombard, Illinois, USA. b. 30 June 1913 Foochow. MA '38 Mills Coll, USA. IN-STRUCTOR, Elmhurst Coll, Elmhurst, Ill, USA. Member: Chinese Educ. Assn, Chinese Assn. of Psych. Testing. Teaching, research; culture and personality, psycholinguistic studies, social ideology. F

KUAN-YING, Tang. Dept. of Psych, Natl. Taiwan Univ, Taipei, Taiwan. b. 10 Oct 1908 Haining. BA '32 Natl. Chekiang Univ, China. INSTRUCTOR, Natl. Taiwan Univ; CHIEF COUNS, Classif. Separation Cen. for Retired Servicemen. Teaching, guidance, research; industrial psychology, projective techniques, learning theory. M

LEE, Hsing-Tang. Natl. Police Admin, Ministry of Interior, Taipei, Taiwan. b. 6 Mar 1918 Mukden. B.SC '45 Natl. Cen. Univ, Chungking, China. SR. INSPECTOR, Natl. Police Admin. Member: Chinese Assn. of Psych. Testing, Chinese Assn. of Mental Hyg, Chinese Police Assn. Research, teaching, administration; psychological testing, police education. M

LIAN, Prof. Ni. Dept. of Psych, Natl. Taiwan Univ, Taipei, Taiwan. b. 12 July 1902 Nanking. Docteur ès Lettres '31 Univ. of Paris, Fr. PROFESSOR, Natl. Taiwan Univ;

SUPERVISOR, Ment. Testing Sect, Servicemen's Classif. Cen; EXAMINER, Natl. High Exam, Examination Yuan. Member: Chinese Assn. of Psych. Testing, Chinese Assn. of Ment. Hyg. Teaching, testing, administration, direction of student research; projective techniques, aptitude testing, statistical study of reliabilities. F

LIN, Yi-guang. 611 Church St, Ann Arbor Michigan, USA. b. 15 Sept 1931 Fukian. B.SC '54 Natl. Taiwan Univ, China. GRAD. STUDENT, Univ. of Michigan, Ann Arbor, Michigan, USA. Learning theory, motivation, personality theory. M

LU, Chun-yo. No. 19, Lane 161, Tsin-sun (s) Rd, Sect. 1, Taipei, Taiwan. b. 28 Dec 1914 Chucheng, Shantung. BA, Natl. Cen. Univ, Nanking, China. TECH. CONSULT, Pers. Bur, Chinese Navy, Taipei, Taiwan; PROF. of MILIT. PSYCH. and PSYCH. WARFARE, Naval Acad, Naval Cmd, Staff Coll. Member: Chinese Assn. of Psych. Testing, Chinese Assn. of Ment. Hyg, Chinese Educ. Assn. Research, personnel psychology, testing, teaching; military psychology, group process, aptitude and achievement tests. M

LUI, Mrs. Chia-Yu. No. 4, Lane 6, Chao-An St, Taipei, Taiwan. b. 13 Nov 1924 Peiping. BS '47 Natl. Cen. Univ, China. PSY-CHOLOGIST, G-1 Ministry of Natl. Def. of China, North Chungking Rd, Taipei, Taiwan. Member: Chinese Assn. of Psych. Testing, Chinese Educ. Assn. Military personnel selection, testing, teaching, research; job analysis, theory of testing, aptitude measurement. F

PAO, Miss Sophia Chung-ling. 4, Lane 9, Chang-chow St, Taipei, Taiwan. b. 10 Sept 1929 Chengkiang, China. B.C. '55 Natl. Taiwan Univ, Taiwan. TCHING. ASST, Dept. of Educ, Natl. Chengchi Univ, Mu-sen, Taipei; PLACEMENT COUNS, Vocat. Classif. Cen. for Retired Servicemen, Nan-nan, Keelung. Member: Chinese Assn. of Psych. Testing, Chinese Assn. of Ment. Hyg. Guidance, testing, research; vocational guidance, projective techniques, personality. F

SHIH, Yao-Hsun. Factory No. 6, Taiwan Fertilizer Co, Ltd, Nanking, Taiwan. b. 111 May 1930 Taipei, Taiwan. B.SC '53 Natl. Taiwan Univ, China. ASSISTANT, Pers. Div, Taiwan Fertilizer Co, Ltd. Member: Chinese Assn. of Psych. Testing, Chinese Assn. of Ment. Hyg. Industrial psychology, testing; intelligence tests, attitude measurement, projective techniques. M

SU, Prof. Hsiang-Yu. Dept. of Psych, Coll. of Sci, Natl. Taiwan Univ, Taipei, Taiwan. b. 9 Nov 1901 Hsin-Chu, Taiwan. PROF. and HEAD, Dept. of Psych, Natl. Taiwan Univ; DIRECTOR, Natl. Taiwan Univ. Lib.

Member: Chinese Assn. of Psych. Testing, Chinese Assn. of Ment. Hyg. Administration, teaching, research; psychoanalysis, personality development, projective techniques. M

TSENG, Mrs. Elizabeth Yeo-hsien. Taiwan Normal Univ, Taipei, Taiwan. b. 19 Jan 1925 Hankow, Hupeh. B.SC '48 Natl. Cen. Univ, Nanking, China. !NSTRUCTOR, Taiwan Normal Univ. Member: Chinese Assn. of Psych. Testing, Chinese Assn. of Ment. Hyg. Teaching, research, testing; learning

theory, achievement tests. F

WANG, Fung-Chiai. Natl. Inst. for Compilation and Translation, 245 Third Sect, Keelung Rd, Taipei, Taiwan. b. 14 Nov 1896 Siangtan, Hunan. PH.D, Univ. of Chicago, USA. DIRECTOR, Natl. Inst. for Compilation and Translation. Member: Chinese Assn. of Psych. Testing, Chinese Educ. Assn. Administration, professional writing, teaching, research; learning theory, psychology of reading, theory of mental testing. M

COLOMBIA

AMADOR-BARRIGA, Dr. Ernesto Mario. Psychometric Lab, Carrera 4, 19-04, Bogotá. b. 17 Sept 1909 Bogotá. PH.D, Univ. of Chicago, USA. DIRECTOR, Psychomet. Lab; PROFESSOR, Natl. Univ. and Univ. Javeriana, Bogotá; ADMIN. ED, *Revista de Psicología,* Inst. of Psych, Natl. Univ. Testing, clinical analysis, applied psychology, guidance, teaching; projective techniques, aptitude measurement, intelligence tests. M

CAMERO, Prof. Raquel. Carrera 16 A, 47-25, Bogotá. b. 31 Oct 1929 Bogotá. Licence '54 Natl. Univ. of Colombia. EDUC. PSYCH'T, Univ. de los Andes, Liceo de Pereira, Apartado 17, Bogotá. Member: Colombian Fed. of Psych'ts. Testing, psychotherapy, educational psychology; projective techniques, aptitude measurement, processes of learning. F

CONVERS VERGARA, Miss Josefina. Carrera 9, 58-07, Bogotá. b. 30 Apr 1934 Bogotá. Bachillerato Superior '52 Inst. Alice Block, Colombia. STUDENT, Inst. of Psych, Natl. Univ, Bogotá. Member: Colombian Fed. of Psych'ts. Student; child psychology, application of tests, clinical analysis. F

CURREA, Inés de. Carrera 18, 57-25, Bogotá. b. 14 Nov 1921 Cudinamarea. Licence '56 Natl. Univ. of Bogotá, Colombia. TCHR. of SPANISH, Inst. Distrilalde Comercio, Calle 57, 14-36, Bogotá. Member: Colombian Fed. of Psych'ts. Student, teaching, applied psychology; projective techniques, social perception. F

GIRALDO ANGEL, Dr. Jorge. Inst. of Psych, Natl. Univ, Bogotá. b. 24 Oct 1924 Bogotá. MD '53 Univ. Pontificia Javeriana, Colombia. PROF. of MED. PSYCH, Univ. Javeriana, Bogotá; PROF. of PSYCHOPHYSIOL, Natl. Univ; ED. BD, *Revista de Psicología,* Inst.of Psych, Natl. Univ. Psychotherapy, teaching, research; medical psychology, psychotherapy, characterology and personality. M

MANKELIUNAS, Prof. Mateo-Vytautas. Inst. of Psych, Natl. Univ, Bogotá. b. 27 July

1912 Jeznas, Lithuania. PH.D, Univ. Pontificia Javeriana, Colombia. PROFESSOR, Inst. of Psych, Natl. Univ; ED. BD, *Revista de Psicología,* Inst. of Psych, Natl. Univ. Teaching, editorial, educational psychology; psychology of religion. M

MARQUEZ PINZON, Dr. Campo Elias. Calle 25 A, 25-88 A, Bogotá. b. 4 Aug 1920 Ramiriquí. Dr. Educ. Sci. '55 Univ. of Tunya, Colombia. ASST. DIR, Psychomet. Lab, K 4 a, 19-04, Bogotá; PROF. of INDUS. PSYCH, Inst. of Psych, Natl. Univ, Bogotá. Member: Colombian Fed. of Psych'ts. Industrial psychology, teaching, testing; personnel selection, voactional guidance, quantitative tests. M

PEDRAZA, Dr. Fanny Gómez de. 1618 Wheeler, Houston 4, Texas, USA. b. 21 Feb 1931 Ibagué, Colombia. Lic. '54 Natl. Univ. of Bogotá, Colombia. STUDENT, Psych. Dept. Univ. of Houston, Texas, USA. Member: Colombian Fed. of Psych'ts. Projective techniques, attitude measurement. F

RODRIGUEZ VALDERRAMA, José M. Calle 71, 10-47, Bogotá. b. 28 Mar 1933 Bogotá. MD '56 Natl. Univ, Colombia, L.PS '56 Inst. of Psych, Natl. Univ, Colombia. SPEC. CONSULT. IN PSYCHOMET, Inst. Médico-Pedagógico de la Costa, Ave. Central del Bosque 51-56, Cartagena. Member: Colombian Fed. of Psych'ts. Student, testing; projective techniques, psychophysiology, dynamic psychology. M

SARMIENTO, Ligia. Carrera 13, 21-02, Bogotá. b. 10 Sept 1927 Bogotá. Lic. '56 Natl. Univ, Colombia. TEACHER, Colegio de las Esclavas del Sagrado Corazón, Diagonal 47, 15-68, Bogotá. Member: Colombian Fed. of Psych'ts. Teaching, student, educational psychology; psychometric techniques, projective techniques, memory and learning. F

SERPA-FLOREZ, Prof. Dr. Robert. Calle 54, 6-38, Bogotá. b. 1 Nov 1925 Bucaramanga. Prof. Titular '55 Univ. Libre, Colombia; MD '50 Natl. Univ, Colombia. SCI. DIR,

Psychopedagogic Inst. of Bogotá; PSY-CHIATRIST, priv. prac. Member: SIP, Socy. of Psychopathol, Neur. and Legal Med. of Colombia. Consulting, clinical practice, teaching, testing; projective techniques, learning theory, child psychology, intelligence tests.   M

ULLOA, Lic. Gabriel. Carrera 28, 70-84, Bogotá. b. 3 Jan 1928 Bogotá. Lic. '52 Natl. Univ, Colombia. PSYCH. CONSULT, Radio Nacional de Colombia, Transversal 17, 25-65, Bogotá; PERSONNEL CONSULT, priv. prac. Testing, professional writing; projective techniques, radio programs on psychological subjects.   M

VEGA, Miss Beatriz de la. Cen. of Psych, Calle 77, 11-91, Bogotá. b. 8 June 1925 Caracas, Venezuela. Lic. '52 Natl. Univ, Colombia. STAFF MEMBER, Cen. of Psych. Testing, clinical analysis, child guidance, applied and educational psychology; pro-

jective tests for children.   F

VILLAR GAVIRIA, Dr. Alvaro. Carrera 12, 20-69, Unidia, Bogotá. b. 31 Dec 1921 Bogotá. MD '50 Natl. Univ. of Colombia. PROFESSOR, Inst. of Psych, Natl. Univ. of Colombia, Bogotá; PSYCHIATRIST, Clínica Montserrat, Inst. Colombiano del Sistema Nervioso; CHIEF, Servicio del Frenocomio de Mujeres. Member: SIP, Socy. of Psychosomatic Med. Teaching qualitative techniques, consulting, testing; qualitative tests, child psychology, psychotherapy. M

ZACHMANN, Mrs. Esther. Apartado Aéreo 40-84, Bogotá. b. 17 Mar 1926 Nova Sulita, Rumania. Lic. '57 Natl. Univ, Colombia. STUDENT, Natl. Univ. of Colombia, Bogotá; CLIN. PSYCH'T, Women's Asylum, Bogotá. Member: Colombian Fed. of Psych'ts. Student, testing, clinical analysis, consulting; projective techniques, psychotherapy, vocational guidance.   F

COSTA RICA

QUIROS M., Prof. Dr. Fernando A. Apartado 1738, San José. b. 12 Aug 1907 San José. MD '35 Univ. of Bonn, Germany. DIR. GEN, Neuropsychiat. Hosp. Asilo Chapui, Paseo Colón, San José; DIRECTOR, Dept. of Ment. Hyg, Ministry of Public Hlth, San José;

PROF. of PSYCHIAT, Univ. of Costa Rica. Member: Amer. Psychiat. Assn, Cuban Socy. of Neur. and Psychiat, Psychiat; Assn. of Central Amer. and Panama. Clinical practice, administration, teaching; individual and group psychotherapy.   M

CUBA

AGRAMONTE, Dr. Roberto. Calle 4 No. 106, Vedado, Havana. b. 3 May 1904 Santa Clara. PH.D '25 Univ. of Havana, Cuba. PROF. of SOCIOL, Univ. of Havana; ED. DIR, Revista, Univ. of Havana. Teaching, research, editorial; social perception, group process.   M

ALOMÁ MARTÍNEZ, Dr. Ana del Carmen. Apartado 3266, Havana. b. 1 June 1925 Ranchuelo. PH.D '47 Univ. of Havana, Cuba. DIRECTOR, Dept. of Psychomet, "Miss Helen's Studio," Calle 27 No. 2611, La Sierra, Havana; DIR. of PSYCH. STUDIES, Cuban Inst. of Humanities, Havana; EDITOR, Revista del Instituto Cubano de Humanidades, Boletín, Sociedad Cubana de Estudios Psicosociológicos. Member: Cuban Socy. of Psycho-sociol. Studies. Teaching, research, testing, guidance; social psychology, collective behavior, folk customs.   F

BERNAL DEL RIESGO, Prof. Dr. Alfonso. Univ. of Havana, Dihigo Building, Calle G y Zapata, Havana. b. 23 Jan 1903 Havana. PH.D '27 Univ. of Havana, Cuba. PROF. of PSYCH, Univ. of Havana; CLIN. PSYCH'T, priv. prac. Member: APA, AAAS, Assn. for the Advanc. of Psychother,

Cuban Socy. of Psych. Consulting, clinical practice, teaching, industrial psychology; personality tests, projective techniques, non-directive psychotherapy.   M

BUSTAMANTE, Dr. Segura. Ave. del Rio 2206 entre Avé. de Europa y Ave. de América, Alturas de Miramar, Havana, b. 18 Mar 1911 Havana. PH.D '34 Univ. of Havana, Cuba. PROF. TITULAR of PSYCH. Univ. of Havana, G y Zapata, Vedado, Havana. Research, teaching, professional writing; child psychology and psychotherapy, guidance.   F

FERNÁNDEZ DE CASAL, Dr. Elvira J. 20 de Mayo 570, Havana. b. 18 Nov 1923 Havana. PH.D '53 Univ. of Havana, Cuba. ASST. PROF. of PSYCH, Univ. of Havana, G y Zapata, Havana. Member: APA. Teaching, consulting, testing, clinical analysis; learning theory, personality testing of children.   F

GARCÍA HERRERA, Dr. Aurora. Fac. of Educ, Univ. of Havana, Havana. b. 5 Feb 1893 Tangier, Morocco. ED.D '22 Univ. of Havana, Cuba. PROF. EMER, Univ. of Havana. Member: Latin Amer. Coordinating Comm. of Psych. Professional writing, educational psychology, testing;

mental hygiene, projective techniques. F
GUEVARA, Dr. Juan J. Orientación Psiquiátrica Infantil, Calle G 305 entre 13 y 15,ᵗHavana. b. 28 May 1927 Havana. PH.D '53 Univ. of Havana, Cuba. PSYCHOLOGIST, Orientación Psiquiátrica Infantil. Testing, clinical analysis, educational psychology, teaching; projective techniques, research in educational psychology, educational tests, aptitude measurement. M
GUTIÉRREZ, Prof. José M. Strampes 408, Havana. b. 25 Sept 1901 Consolacion Sur. ED.D, Univ. of Havana, Cuba. DEAN and PROF, Fac. of Educ, Univ. of Havana. Member: Cuban Socy. of Psych, Biometric Socy, Amer. Stat. Assn. Teaching, consulting, guidance, testing; vocational and child guidance, children with educational difficulties. M
LASAGA, Dr. José I. Calle 9 No. 407, Vedado, Havana. b. 25 Oct 1913 Havana. PH.D '40 Univ. of Havana, Cuba. DIRECTOR, Sch. of Psych, Univ. of Villanueva, Reparto Biltmore, Havana; CLIN. PSYCH'T, priv. prac. Member: APA, Cuban Socy. of Psych. Testing, clinical analysis, teaching, administration, research; projective techniques. M
PÉREZ-VALDÉS, Dr. Noemí Eulalia. Orientación Psiquiátrica Infantil (OPI), Calle G No. 305 entre 13 y 15, Vedado, Havana. b. 10 Dec 1926 Havana. PH.D '54 Univ. of Havana, Cuba. CLIN. PSYCH'T, Orientación Psiquiátrica Infantil (OPI). Testing, clinical analysis, teaching; pro-

jective techniques, intelligence and achievement tests. F
TORROELLA, Dr. Gustavo. Natl. Inst. of Applied Psych, Ave. 35 No. 3013 entre 30 y 34, Marianao, Havana. b. 20 May 1918 Havana. PH.D '45 Univ. of Havana, Cuba. DIRECTOR, Natl. Inst. of Applied Psych. Member: APA, Cuban Socy. of Psych. Consulting, guidance, applied psychology, teaching; projective techniques, measurement of public opinion, consumer motivation research. M
VEGA-VEGA, Dr. René. Linea 906 entre 6 y 8, Vedado, Havana. b. 20 Sept 1926 Havana. MD '52 Univ. of Havana, Cuba. CHILD PSYCHIATRIST, Orientación Psiquiátrica Infantil, Calle G 305 entre 13 y 15, Havana. Psychotherapy, research, teaching; projective techniques, aptitude measurement, research in industrial psychology. M
VELILLA DE SOLÓRZANO, Dr. Martín. Apartado 3266, Havana. b. 23 Nov 1923 Havana. Dr. of Soc. Sci, Univ. of Havana, Cuba. DIR. of RES, Sterling Products International, Inc, Edif. Radiocentro, Havana; EDITOR, *Revista del Instituto Cubano de Humanidades, Boletín,* Sociedad Cubana de Estudios Psico-sociológicos. Member: Cuban Inst. of Humanities, Cuban Socy. of Psycho-sociol. Studies. Applied psychology, research, teaching; social persuasion, social change, methods of public opinion research, psycho-political elements in human interaction. M

CZECHOSLOVAKIA

CHMELAŘ, Prof. Dr. Vilém. Inst. of Psych, Fac. of Letters, Masaryk Univ, Grohova 7, Brno. b. 19 Nov 1892 Podolí u Přerova. PH.D '25 Charles Univ, Czech. PROF. of PSYCH, Masaryk Univ; DIRECTOR, Inst. of Psych, Masaryk Univ; EDITOR, *Journal,* Fac. of Letters, Univ. of Brno. Member: Czech. Psych. Socy. Teaching, research, editorial; visual and aural perception. M
DOLEŽAL, Prof. Dr. Jan. Půlkruhová 34, Prague 6. b. 30 Mar 1902 Vnorovy. PH.D '26 Karl Marx Univ, Leipzig, Ger. PROFESSOR, Dept. of Psych, Charles Univ, Hradčanské nám 5, Prague IV. Member: Comm. for Psych, Czech. Acad. of Sci. Research, industrial psychology, teaching; psychology of labor, ᵥpsychological method. M
JUROVSKÝ, Prof. Dr. Anton. Mamatejova 2, Bratislava. b. 26 Mar 1908 Uľanka. PH.D '33 Komenský Univ. of Bratislava, Czech. PROF. of PSYCH. and RES. DIR, Fac. of Philos, Komensky Univ, Šafárikovo nám 12, Bratislava; RES. DIR, Czech. Acad. of Sci; ED. COMM, *Československá Psycho-*

logie. Member: Comm. for Psych, Czech. Acad. of Sci. Educational psychology, research, administration; social factors in personality development, educational problems in collective institutions. M
LINHART, Prof. Dr. Josef. Kamenická 1, Prague VII. b. 1 Dec 1917 Rtyně. Univ. Prof. '54 Univ. of Prague, Czech. PROF. of PSYCH, Vysoka Pedagogická Škola, M.D. Rettigové c 4, Prague. Member: Comm. for Psych, Czech. Acad. of Sci. Research, teaching, educational psychology; genetic psychology, learning theory, typology. M
PŘÍHODA, Dr. Václav. Kübišova ulice 26, Prague 8. b. 7 Sept 1889 Sány, Bohemia. PH.D '16 Charles Univ, Czech. PROFESSOR, Dept. of Psych, Charles Univ, Toskánský palác, Prague IV. Textbook writing, teaching, research, consulting; developmental psychology, phylogenesis and ontogenesis, educational psychology, learning.M
STAVEL, Prof. Dr. Josef. Nad Šárkou 58, Prague 6. b. 12 Mar 1901 Znojmo. PH.D '24 Charles Univ, Czech. PROF. of PSYCH,

Charles Univ, Hradčanské nám, Toskáns. palác, Prague IV. Research, teaching, textbook writing; motivation, personality traits.   M
TARDY, Prof. Dr. Vladimir. Cukrovarnická 34, Prague V. b. 18 Sept 1906 Louny. RN.DR '31 Charles Univ, Czech; PH.D '36

Charles Univ, Czech. PORFESSOR, Vysoká Škola Pedagogická, M.D. Rettigové 4, Prague II; ED. COMM, *Československá Psychologie*. Member: Comm. for Psych, Czech. Acad. of Sci. Teaching, research; personality, philosophical psychology, history of psychology.   M

DENMARK

AGERSTED, Maj. Fin. Kochsvej 19, Copenhagen V. b. 10 May 1922 Copenhagen. Cand. Psych. '55 Univ. of Copenhagen, Den. MAJOR. Member: DP. Military psychology.   M

AKHÖJ NIELSEN, Mrs. Karen. Godthaabshave 8, Copenhagen F. b. 9 Apr 1923 Holböl. Cand. Psych. '54 Univ. of Copenhagen, Den. MILIT. PSYCH'T, Inst. of Milit. Psych, Frederiksberg Slot, Copenhagen. Member: DP. Testing, personnel selection, guidance, research; education of military personnel.   F

ALBRECHTSEN, Connie. Sdr. Fasanvej 35, Copenhagen F. b. 31 July 1930 Copenhagen. Cand. Psych. '53 Univ. of Copenhagen, Den. CLIN. PSYCH'T, Sundby Hosp, Italiensvej, Copenhagen S; TEACHER, Elem. and Evening Sch. Member: DP, Danish Assn. for Ment. Health. Clinical analysis, consulting, teaching; achievement tests, projective techniques, group process.   F

ANDERSEN, Ellen. Søborgtorv 8/843, Søborg. b. 18 July 1917 Copenhagen. Cand. Psych. '52 Univ. of Copenhagen, Den. SCH. PSYCH'T, Gladsaxe Kommune. Member: DP. Educational psychology, teaching.   F

ANDERSEN, Erik Nørgaard. Kobbelvænget 17, Brønshøj. b. 26 Mar 1917 Copenhagen. Cand. Psych. '52 Univ. of Copenhagen, Den. SCH. PSYCH'T, Skolepsykologisk Kontor, Krausesvej 3, Copenhagen. Member: DP. Teaching, research.   M

ANDERSEN, Erling. Ulrikkenborg Plads 5/I, Kgs. Lyngby. b. 20 Oct 1916 Calcutta, India. Cand. Psych. '56 Univ. of Copenhagen, Den. SCH. PSYCH'T. Skolepsykologisk Kontor, Krausesvej 3, Copenhagen. Member: DP, Assn. for Psych. and Philos. Teaching, testing.   M

ANDERSEN, Gunnar. Nebs Møllegård, Jystrup. b. 11 Apr 1912 Døstrup. Cand. Psych. '51 Univ. of Copenhagen, Den. DIRECTOR, Inst. for Maladjusted Children, Nebs Møllegård. Member: DP. Guidance, administration, teaching; group and individual psychotherapy for children, parent guidance.   M

ANDERSEN, Jørgen. Jernstøbervænget 5, Køge. b. 29 Nov 1921 Copenhagen. Cand. Psych. '48 Univ. of Copenhagen, Den.

SCHOOL PSYCH'T, Communal Sch. of Køge, Bur. of Sch. Psych, Brochmands Skole, Køge. Member: DP, Danish Assn. of Sch. Psych'ts. Educational psychology, testing, administration.   M

ANDREASEN, Kjeld. Sorgenfridal, Kgs. Lyngby. b. 26 May 1921 Copenhagen. Cand. Psych. '50 Univ. of Copenhagen, Den. CLIN. PSYCH'T, Overførstergarden, Jægersborg alle 139, Jægersborg; CLIN. PSYCH'T Kommunehospitalet, Øster Farimagsgade 5, Copenhagen. Member: DP. Consulting, group psychotherapy, testing; social perception and group process, projective techniques, alcoholism.   M

BENTSEN, Peder Vilhelm. Egevænget 7, Lyngby. b. 27 Feb 1924 Copenhagen. Cand. Psych. '50 Univ. of Copenhagen, Den. SCH. PSYCH'T, Skolepsykologisk Rådgivning, Buddinge Skole, Søborg. Member: DP, Assn. for Psych. and Philos. Guidance, teaching, phenomenological and educational research; learning theory, social perception.   M

BERNTH, Mrs. Inger. Nørregade 18, Copenhagen K. b. 27 Mar 1926 Frederiksberg. Cand. Psych. '47 Univ. of Copenhagen, Den. MA '48 Vassar Coll, USA. LECT. in CHILD PSYCH, Univ. of Copenhagen, Frue Plads, Copenhagen K. Member: DP. Teaching, testing, psychotherapy, personality development, projective techniques, depth psychology.   F

BERNTSEN, Karen Ingrid. Duntzfeltsalle 27, Hellerup, Copenhagen. b. 14 June 1914 Copenhagen. Cand. Psych. '48 Univ. of Copenhagen, Den. PSYCH'T, The Prisons of Copenhagen, Vigerslevalle 1, Copenhagen. Member: DP. Consulting and guidance, research, testing; rehabilitation, criminology.   F

BICHEL, Preben. Individualskolen, Henningsens alle 68, Hellerup. b. 26 July 1918 Egedesminde, Greenland. Cand. Psych. '51 Univ. of Copenhagen, Den. PSYCHOTHER. and LEADER, Individualskolen. Member: DP, Assn. for Child Psychiat. and Clin. Child Psych. Group psychotherapy, educational psychology, clinical analysis; learning process, psychoanalysis.   M

BICHEL, Mrs. Ruth. Individualskolen, Henningsens alle 68, Hellerup. b. 31 Aug

1917 Copenhagen. Cand. Psych. '51 Univ. of Copenhagen, Den. LEADER, Individual-skolen. Member: DP, Assn. for Child Psychiat. and Clin. Child Psych. Psychotherapy, applied and educational psychology, clinical analysis; group dynamics, school psychology.	F

BINGER, Mrs. Birte. Torvegade 12, Esbjerg. b. 27 Sept 1920 Copenhagen. Cand. Psych. '52 Univ. of Copenhagen, Den. SCH. PSYCH'T, Skolepsykologisk Kontor, Kronprinsensgade 33, Esbjerg; TEACHER, Tchr. Trng. Coll, Esbjerg. Member: DP. Educational psychology, testing, guidance, teaching, research; school maturity problems, reading process.	F

BLEGVAD, Mogens. Voldmestergade 9, Copenhagen Ø. b. 25 June 1917 Copenhagen. Mag. art. '42 Univ. of Copenhagen, Den. LIBRARIAN, Royal Lib, Christians Brygge 8, Copenhagen; HEAD, Dept. of Philos. and Psych, Univ. Ext, Univ. of Copenhagen. Member: DP, APA, Assn. for Psych. and Philos. Library, research, teaching; social psychology of values and norms, vocational guidance.	M

BOHM, Ewald Bernhard. Statholdervej 7, Copenhagen N.V. b. 24 June 1903 Graudenz, Ger. Dr. phil. '53 Univ. of Zurich, Switz. PSYCHOLOGIST, priv. prac; CO-EDITOR, *International Journal of Sex Sciences*; *Zeitschrift für Diagnostische Psychologie und Persönlichkeitsforschung.* Member: Int. Rorschach Socy. Testing, clinical analysis, research, teaching; projective techniques, pedagogy, psychology of sex.	M

BREUM, Erik K. Torsvang 77, Kgs. Lyngby. b. 8 Nov 1921 Copenhagen. Cand. Psych. '53 Univ. of Copenhagen, Den. SCH. PSYCH'T, Skolepsykologisk Kontor, Hyldegaardskolen, Charlottenlund. Member: DP, Danish Assn. of Sch. Psych'ts. Teaching testing, guidance; learning theory, maturation, projective techniques.	M

BUCH-OHLSEN, Mrs. Karen. Vagtelvej 64, Copenhagen, F. b. 26 Mar 1913 Aarhus. Cand. Psych. '50 Univ. of Copenhagen, Den. CLIN. PSYCH'T, Børnehospitalet på Fuglebakken, Drosselvej 57, Copenhagen F. Member: DP. Testing, clinical practice, psychotherapy; projective techniques, social perception.	F

CASTENSKIOLD, Maj. Christian Erik. Rigensgade 9 D, Copenhagen K. b. 10 Jan 1921 Copenhagen. Cand. Psych. '53 Univ. of Copenhagen, Den. CHIEF, Dept. of Milit. Psych, Frederiksberg Slot, Copenhagen F. Member: DP, Assn. for Psych. and Philos. Administration, testing, teaching; group process, officer selection procedures, achievement and aptitude tests.	M

CHRISTENSEN, Svend Emil. Sapalyst-

parken 36, Højbjerg. b. 14 July 1921 Hals. Cand. Psych. '51 Univ. of Copenhagen, Den. SCH. PSYCH T, Skolepsykologisk Kontor, Mejlgade 8, Aarhus. Member: DP, Danish Assn. of Sch. Psych'ts. Guidance, testing, teaching; backward children, learning theory, projective techniques.	M

CHRISTOPHERSEN, Kurt Edvard. Årøsundvej 85, Haderslev. b. 10 Apr 1921 Copenhagen. Cand. Psych. '52 Univ. of Copenhagen, Den. COUNTY SCH. PSYCH'T, Haderslev Amts Skoledirektion, Storegade 88, Haderslev. Member: DP. Consulting, testing; intelligence and achievement tests.	M

CLAUSEN, Mrs. Merete. Flakholmen 20 St, Copenhagen, Vanløse. b. 22 Feb. 1915 Copenhagen. Cand. Psych. '50 Univ. of Copenhagen, Den. CHILD PSYCH'T, Dept. of Child Psychiat, Rigshospitalet, Blegdamsvej, Copenhagen Ø. Member: DP, Danish Assn. for Ment. Health, Assn. for Child Psychiat. and Clin. Child Psych. Child psychotherapy, clinical testing, consulting; psychotherapy of borderline cases, Rorschach testing, testing and differentiating between organic psychotic and mentally defective children.	F

DAEHNERT, Hugo Walter. Rud. Wulffsgade 13, Aarhus. b. 12 Mar 1913 Aabenraa. Cand. Psych. '49 Univ. of Copenhagen, Den. CHIEF SCH. PSYCH'T, Skolepsykolgisk Kontor, Mejlgade 8, Aarhus. Member: DP, Danish Assn. of Sch. Psych'ts. Administration, educational psychology, testing; psychology of reading and arithmetic, learning theory, projective techniques, achievement tests.	M

DALSJÖ, Ib Erik Lennart. Frederiksdalsalle 76a, Skive. b. 23 Feb 1920 Copenhagen. Cand. Psych. '50 Univ. of Copenhagen, Den. TEACHER, Skive Seminarium, Skive; CLIN. PSYCH'T, Hosp. for Ment. Diseases, Viborg. Member: DP. Teaching, testing, clinical analysis; projective techniques.	M

DALSJÖ, Mrs. Karen Kirstine. Frederiksdalalle 76a, Skive. b. 3 Mar 1924 Lemvig. Cand. Psych. '50 Univ. of Copenhagen, Den. TEACHER, Skive Seminarium, Skive. Member: DP, Assn. for Child Psychiat. and Clin. Child Psych. Psychotherapy, teaching clinical treatment of children with emotional disturbances.	F

DANIELSEN, Martin. Rosenlunden 6, Odense. b. 10 Sept. 1902 Asp. Cand. Psych. '47 Univ. of Copenhagen, Den. CHIEF SCH. PSYCH'T, Rådhuset, Odense. Member: DP. Administration, guidance, teaching; handicapped children.	M

DIEMER, Aage Frederik. Villa Helle, Hindholm Højskole pr. Fuglebjerg. b. 5 June 1914 Stockholm, Swed. Cand. Psych.

'47 Univ. of Copenhagen, Den. TEACHER, Hindholm Højskole, Hindholm pr. Fuglebjerg; Member: DP. Teaching, applied and educational psychology, psychotherapy; cultural psychology. M

DOHN, Sigfrid. Havsgaardsvej 8, Hellerup, Copenhagen. b. 13 Feb 1908 Copenhagen. Mag. art '47 Univ. of Copenhagen, Den. DIRECTOR, State Res. and Guid. Clin. for Deaf and Hard of Hearing Children, Vendersgade 29, Copenhagen; LECTURER Univ. of Copenhagen. Member: DP. Administration, research, clinical analysis and testing; psychology of the deaf, achievement tests, psychology of religion. M

ELLEHAMMER, Mogens F. Ejderstedgade 14, Copenhagen V. b. 10 Jan 1907 Damsholte Mön. Cand. Psych. '46 Univ. of Copenhagen, Den. DIR, Reading Classes of Copenhagen, Sch. Psych. Bur, Krausesvej 3, Copenhagen Ø; LECTURER, Teachers' Coll. Member: DP, Danish Assn. of Sch. Psych'ts. Administration, teaching; research; psychology and teaching of reading, social factors in educational situations. M

ENEVOLDSEN, Lavra. Lindegårdsvej 7, Frederikshavn. b. 6 Mar 1904 Pandrup. Cand. Psych. '48 Univ. of Copenhagen, Den. SCH. PSYCH'T, Frederikshavn Kommunale Skolevæsen, Ørnevej, Frederikshavn. Member: DP. Teaching, testing, guidance; educational psychology.F

EPLOV, Helge. Ejderstedgade 14, Copenhagen. b. 17 Oct 1911 Copenhagen. Cand. Psych. '56 Univ. of Copenhagen, Den. CONSULTANT, County League of Free Kindergartens, Buen No. 6, Copenhagen V; EDUC. DIR, General Study Assn, Ejderstedgade 14. Member: DP, Danish Milit. Psych. Socy. Teaching, educational and industrial psychology, administration; learning theory, group process, selection procedure.F

ERIKSEN, Erik. Borgvold 18, Vejle. b. 7 Jan 1914 Gudum. Cand. Psych. '53 Univ. of Copenhagen, Den. SCH. PSYCH'T, Vejle Kommunale Skolevæsen, priv. prac. Member: DP. Testing, applied and educational psychology, administration. M

FÆRGEMANN, Svend. Aakjaers alle 16, Søborg. b. 2 Mar 1908 Bælum. Cand. Psych. '49 Univ. of Copenhagen, Den. CHIEF SCH. PSYCH'T, Skolepsykologisk Rådgivning, Buddinge Hovedgade 81, Søborg. Member: DP. Administration, testing, research; psychology of arithmetic, learning methods for dyslectics, educational selection. M

FARUP, Bodil. Maglekildevej 10, Copenhagen V. b. 2 Jan 1906 Ribe. Cand. Psych. '45 Univ. of Copenhagen, Den. DIRECTOR, Child Guid. Clin., Univ. of Copenhagen, Gl. Kongevej 10, Copenhagen V., LECTURER, Dept. of Psych., Univ. of Copenhagen. Member: DP, Dan. Assn. for Child Psychiat.

and Clin. Child Psych. Psychoanalysis, psychotherapy, lecturing and supervision.F

FELDMAN, Wulff. Holbergsgade 19/V, Copenhagen. b. 13 Sept 1926 Copenhagen. Cand. Psych. '53 Univ. of Copenhagen, Den. PSYCH'T, Inst. for Psychopathic Criminals, Herstedvester, Glostrup. Member: DP. Psychotherapy, research, teaching; group psychotherapy with psychopathic criminals, learning theory, projective techniques. M

FISKER, Peter Børge. Hasselvej 34, Copenhagen Vanløse. b. 28 July 1912 Als. Cand. Psych. '54 Univ. of Copenhagen, Den. SCH. PSYCH'T Skolepsykologisk Kontor, Krausesvej 3, Copenhagen H. Member: DP, Danish Assn. of Sch. Psych'ts, Danish Assn. for Ment. Health. Teaching, testing, educational psychology. M

FLORANDER, Jesper B. Emdrup Banke 63, Copenhagen Ø. b. 10 Sept 1918 Astrup. Cand. Psych. '47 Univ. of Copenhagen, Den. DEPT. HEAD, Natl. Inst. for Educ. Res, Emdrupvej 101, Copenhagen. Member: DP. Educational psychology, research, administration; experimental education, educational and communication research. M

FREDERIKSEN, Lis. Nørrebrogade 22, Copenhagen. b. 13 July 1928 Copenhagen. Cand. Psych. '55 Univ. of Copenhagen Den. CLIN. PSYCH'T Bispebjerg Hosp, Tagensvej, Copenhagen. Member: DP. Clinical analysis and testing, teaching; projective techniques, intelligence testing, mental diseases, psychotherapy. F

FRIDERICHSEN, Mrs. Marchen. Classensgade 61/IV, Østerbro, Copenhagen. b. 19 Nov 1933 Madras, India. Cand. Psych. '56 Univ. of Copenhagen, Den. CLIN. STUD, Child Guid. Clin, Univ. of Copenhagen, Gamme Kongevej 10, Copenhagen. Member: DP. Testing; projective techniques, child psychology and therapy. F

FRISTED, Leo Nissen. Ymersvej 44, Randers. b. 2 Mar 1917 Glud. Cand. Psych. '50 Univ. of Copenhagen, Den. COUNTY SCH. PSYCH'T, Randers Amts Skoledirektion, Sandgade 12, Randers. Member: DP, Danish Assn. of Sch. Psych'ts. Educational psychology, administration, guidance; dyslexia, feeblemindedness, psychosomatic reactions in children. M

FROM, Prof. Franz. Gustav. Azaleavej 28, Copenhagen, Valby. b. 14 Feb 1914 Agerskov. Dr. phil. '53 Univ. of Copenhagen, Den. PROF. of PSYCH, Univ. of Copenhagen. CHAIRMAN, Humanistic Res. Committee of the Ministry of Greenland. Member: DP, Assn. for Psych. and Philos. Research, teaching, administration; psychology of direct experience, social perception, culture and personality. M

GIØRTZ-LAURSEN, Kai Linde. Skolepsy-kologisk Kontor, Kildegade 46, Horsens. b. 23 Aug 1920 Klovborg. Cand. Psych. '56 Univ. of Copenhagen, Den. SCH. PSYCH'T, Kommunale Skolevæsen, Horsens. Member DP. Educational psychology, adminis-tration, teaching. M

GLARBORG, Ib. Rosenhaven 14, Valby, Copenhagen. b. 3 Nov 1919 Randers. Cand. Psych. '55 Univ. of Copenhagen, Den. SCH. PSYCH'T, Krausesvej 3, Copenhagen Ø; PSYCHOLOGIST, Inst. of Child Welf. Member: DP. Teaching, testing, guidance.M

GLARBORG, Mrs. Kirsten. Rosenhaven 14, Valby, Copenhagen. b. 1 May 1930 Copen-hagen. Cand. Psych. '55 Univ. of Copen-hagen, Den. CHILD PSYCH'T, Child Guid. Clin, Univ. of Copenhagen, Gammel-kongevej 10, Copenhagen. Member: DP. Clinical analysis, guidance, child psycho-therapy. F

GREEN, Mogens. Strandboulevarden 29/3, Copenhagen Ø. b. 27 Sept 1928 Copen-hagen. Cand. Psych. '53 Univ. of Copen-hagen, Den. Member: DP, Danish Assn. for Ment. Health. Film production; per-ception, film time and space, audiovisual aids in education. M

GRODE, John. Lyngparken 53, Lyngby. b. 28 Oct 1919 Svaneke. Cand. Psych. '53 Univ. of Copenhagen, Den. SCH. PSYCH'T, Copenhagen Skolevæsen, Krausesvej 3, Copenhagen. Educational psychology, teaching, testing; achievement tests, learning theory, educational deficiencies, dyslexia. M

GRUE-SØRENSEN, Prof. Knud. Univ. of Copenhagen, Frue Plads, Copenhagen. b. 21 Jan 1904 Hee. Dr. phil. '50 Univ. of Copenhagen, Den. PROF. of EDUC, Univ. of Copenhagen; ADVIS. BD, Nat. Inst. of Educ. Res.; CO-EDITOR, *Leksikon for Opdragere.* Member: DP, Assn. for Psych. and Philos. Teaching, professional writing, research; learning theory, personality formation, social class psychology. M

GRUNDÉN, Mrs. Esther. Løvsangervej 7, Hellerup. b. 25 June 1913 Copenhagen. Cand. Psych. '53 Univ. of Copenhagen, Den. CHILD PSYCH'T, Nebs Møllegaard, Jystrup Midtsjælland. Member: DP, Assn. for Child Psychiat. and Clin. Child Psych. Psychotherapy, student, clinical analysis; Rorschach testing, group process, in-stitutional therapy for children. F

GYLLING, Mrs. Eli. Høje Skodsborgvej 10, Skodsborg. b. 13 Dec 1897 Frederiksberg. Cand. Psych. '53 Univ. of Copenhagen, Den. Member: DP. Teaching, research, guidance; remedial teaching, learning theory, parent guidance. F

HAMBORG, Arne Oskar Ege. Køgevej 9, Haslev. b. 24 July 1922 Copenhagen.

Cand. Psych. '50 Univ. of Copenhagen, Den. LECTURER, Haslev Seminarium, Søndergade, Haslev. Member: DP. Teaching; learning theory, intelligence tests, topology. M

HANSEN, Axel. Hectors alle 3, Hvidovre, Valby. b. 7 Nov 1916 Slangerup. Cand. Psych. Univ. of Copenhagen, Den. SCH. PSYCH'T, Kommunale Skolevæsen, Hvi-dovre. Member: DP. Testing, adminis-tration, teaching; achievement tests, pro-jective techniques. M

HANSEN, Birgitte Willum. Taffelbays alle 10, Hellerup. b. 12 Apr 1916 Holbæk. Cand. Psych. '53 Univ. of Copenhagen, Den. CHILD PSYCH'T, priv. prac. Member: DP. Consulting, testing, guidance. F

HANSEN, Ernst. Havnevej 50, Holbæk. b. 5 Nov 1915 Helsinge. Cand. Psych. '52 Univ. of Copenhagen, Den. COUNTY SCH. PSYCH'T, Holbæk Amts Skoledirektion, Amtskentoret, Holbæk. Member: DP. Testing, consulting, administration; education for retarded and disturbed children. M

HANSEN, Gunner. Skovbrynet 6, Bagsværd. b. 23 Sept 1923 Tranderup, Aerø. Cand. Psych. '54 Univ. of Copenhagen, Den. PSYCH'T, Vadgård Skole, Kong Hans alle 34, Søborg. Member: DP, Assn. for Psych. and Philos. Testing, guidance, adminis-tration; achievement tests, learning theory, projective techniques. M

HARLANG, Inge Merete. Lille Kirkestræde 8. Copenhagen. b. 5 July 1925 Kolping, Cand. Psych. '51 Univ. of Copenhagen, Den. CHILD PSYCH'T, Univ. Clin. of Pädiatrics, Blegdamsvej, Copenhagen. Member: DP, Assn. for Child Psychiat. and Clin. Child Psych. Clinical analysis and testing, child guidance, psychotherapy; developmental diagnosis of infants, pro-jective techniques in clinical studies of children. F

HASLUND, Lise. V. Ringgade 214, Aarhus. b. 25 Nov 1918 Sneslev. Cand. Psych. '50 Univ. of Copenhagen, Den. CLIN. PSYCH'T, Børnepsykiatriske Konsultationer, Kom-munehospital, Aarhus. Member: DP, Assn. for Child Psychiat. and Clin. Child Psych. Clinical practice, child psychotherapy, testing; achievement tests, projective tech-niques, spastic children. F

HEGELER, Sten. Kastrupvej 247, Kastrup. b. 28 Apr 1923 Copenhagen. Cand. Psych. '53 Univ. of Copenhagen, Den. PSY-CHOLOGIST, Dept. of Milit. Psych, Frede-riksberg Slot, Copenhagen; EDITOR, *Mental hygiejne.* Member: DP. Educational psy-chology, military officer selection, psycho-therapy, professional writing; sex edu-cation, achievement tests, psychoanalysis.M

HEGELSKOV, Sven. Saltværksvej 159,

Kastrup. b. 2 June 1904 Ajstrup, Malling. Cand. Psych. '54 Univ. of Copenhagen, Den. LAWYER, priv. prac. Member: DP. Consulting; criminal sociology, group process. M

HEGELUND, Helge. Næstved. b. 27 Apr 1914 Østerby. Cand. Psych. '55 Univ. of Copenhagen, Den. SCH. PSYCH'T, Næstved Skolevæsen, Jernbanegade, Næstved. Member: DP. Teaching, testing, guidance; learning theory, social perception, psychology of religion. M

HEGNBY, Karl. Nr. Søby. b. 14 Apr 1924 Alborg. Cand. Psych. '49 Univ. of Copenhagen, Den. HEADMASTER, Søbysøgård Juv. Prison, Nr. Søby. Member: DP. Administration, teaching, guidance; vocational guidance, group psychotherapy, group reactions, criminology. M

HEISE, Commander Vilhelm Preben. Østervoldgade 42, Copenhagen K. b. 8 Apr 1919 Slagelse. Cand. Psych. '56 Univ. of Copenhagen, Den. COMMANDER, Inst. for Milit. Psych, Rigensgade 11, Copenhagen; LECT. in PSYCH. and EDUC, Danish Naval Acad, Copenhagen. Military psychology, teaching administration; psychological tests and interviewing for personnel selection, social psychology, learning theory. M

HELWEG-NIELSEN, Kalis. Hummeltoften 37, Lyngby. b. 11 Aug 1921 Sønderborg. Cand. Psych. '47 Univ. of Copenhagen, Den. CLIN. PSYCH'T, Kindergartens; PSYCH. TCHR, Coll. for Kindergarten Tchrs; CLIN. PSYCH'T, priv. prac. Member: DP. Consulting, teaching, psychotherapy; social psychology, personality, clinical psychology for preschool children. F

HENRIKSEN, Flora Charlotte Beyer. Ved Kagså 21, Herlev, Copenhagen. b. 5 Aug 1925 Bergen, Nor. Cand. Psych. '50 Univ. of Copenhagen, Den. CLIN. PSYCH'T, "Baunegården," Lille Værløse. Member: DP, Assn. for Child Psychiat. and Clin. Child Psych, Danish Assn. for Ment. Health. Psychotherapy, research, clinical analysis; diagnosis and therapy of children with mental, social and criminal disorders, parent guidance, military psychology. F

HENRIKSEN, Ove. Hegnsvej 123, Nærum. b. 28 Apr 1924 Copenhagen. Cand. Psych. '49 Univ. of Copenhagen, Den. PSYCH'T, Div. of Vocat. Guid, Labor Dept, Nyropsgade 28/IV, Copenhagen. Member: DP. Vocational testing, research; readjustment of criminals. M

HERLAK, Miss Ester. Rygårds alle 25, Hellerup. b. 30 Apr 1922 Copenhagen. Cand. Psych. '48 Univ. of Copenhagen, Den. SCH. PSYCH'T, Kommunale Skolevæsen, Gentofte. Member: DP, Danish Assn. of Sch. Psych'ts. Teaching, testing, consulting, guidance. F

HESS, Miss Grethe. Refsnæsgade 48, Copenhagen N. b. 21 Nov. 1918 Copenhagen. Cand. Psych. '54 Univ. of Copenhagen, Den. EEG ASST, Rigshospitalet, Blegdamsvej, Copenhagen. Member: DP. Electroencephalography, teaching; correlation between psychology and electroencephalography. F

HJELHOLT, Gunnar. Marsk Stigs alle 2, Søborg. b. 30 Apr 1920 Copenhagen. Cand. Psych. '51 Univ. of Copenhagen, Den. CIVIL PSYCH'T, Dept. of Milit. Psych, Frederiksberg slot, Copenhagen F. Member DP. Personnel psychology, research, psychotherapy; group structure and change in adolescent groups, Rorschach testing, supervision of psychological training. M

HOECK-GRADENWITZ, Erik. Vanløsealle 54, Copenhagen, Vanløse. b. 2 May 1906 Breslau, Ger. CHIEF PSYCH'T, Inst. for Psychopathic Criminals, Herstedvester per Glostrup. Member: DP, Dansk Kriminalistforening. Psychotherapy, research, teaching, consulting; Criminal psychology, social perception, social learning, group process. M

HØJLUND, Mrs. Louise. Aggersvej 6, Skodsborg. b. 10 Nov 1917 Den. Cand. Psych. '53 Univ. of Copenhagen, Den. PSYCHOLOGIST, Controlled Fam. Care of the Feebleminded, Nyropsgade 28, Copenhagen. Member: DP, Assn. for Child Psychiat. and Clin. Child Psych. Educational psychology, clinical analysis, psychotherapy with the feebleminded; learning theory, brain injuries. F

HØJSTEEN, Niels Frederik. Ejbygade 59, Odense. b. 23 Sept 1928 Copenhagen. Cand. Psych. '51 Univ. of Copenhagen, Den. SCH. PSYCH'T, Bur. of Sch. Psych, Townhall, Odense. Member: DP, Danish Assn. of Sch. Psych'ts. Clinical analysis, guidance, psychotherapy; mental disorders, anomalies, perception. M

HOLM, Miss Ester Elisabeth. Rosenvængets alle 40 B, Copenhagen. b. 4 Aug 1913 Odense. Cand. Psych. '47, Univ. of Copenhagen, Den. COUNSELOR, Ministry of Educ, Frederiksholms Kanal 21, Copenhagen. Member: DP. Consulting, teaching. F

HOLT HANSEN, Kristian. Schæffergården, Ermelundsvej 105, Gentofte. b. Denmark. Dr. phil., Univ. of Copenhagen, Den. PSYCHOLOGIST, priv. prac. Member: Assn. for Psych. and Philos. Research, teaching, educational psychology; social perception, learning theory, group process, behavior. M

HVIDMARK, Miss Inge. Ringtoften 5, Skovlunde. b. 7 Mar 1923 Gentofte. Cand. Psych. 50 Univ. of Copenhagen, Den. SCH. PSYCH'T, Aalborg Kommunale Skole-

væsen. Member: DP, Danish Assn. of Sch. Psych'ts. Educational psychology, teaching, administration. F
HVOLBY, Robert Viggo. Stumpedal 20, Herlev. b. 10 Aug 1926 Nørresundby. Cand. Psych. '56 Univ. of Copenhagen, Den. TCHR. and SECY, Danmarks Lærerforening, Jernbanegade 3, Copenhagen. Administration, teaching, student. M
INGELS, Gerd. Rosenvængets Sidealle 3, Copenhagen Ø. b. 22 May 1922 Strinda, Nor. Cand. Psych. '50 Univ. of Oslo, Nor. PSYCHOTHERAPIST, priv. prac. Member: DP. Psychotherapy; psychology and treatment of alcoholics, parapsychology. F
IRGENS-MØLLER, Ole. Børnehjemmet, Baunegård, L. Værløse. b. 22 Mar 1923 Copenhagen. Cand. psych. Univ. of Copenhagen, Den. DIRECTOR, Home for Maladjusted Children. Member: DP. Administration, guidance, psychotherapy, teaching; educational and social psychology therapy. M
IVERSEN, Ruth. Frederikssundsvej 199. V.7.v, Copenhagen Brh. b. 4 June 1922 Copenhagen. Cand. Psych. '54 Univ. of Copenhagen, Den. PSYCH'T, Dept. of Milit. Psych., Frederiksberg Slot, Copenhagen. Member: DP, Assn. for Psych. and Philos, Danish Milit. Psych. Socy. Testing, consulting, teaching. F
JAKOBSEN, Maj. Bent Oluf. Rigensgade 9 D, Copenhagen K. b. 20 May 1916 Sindal. Cand. Psych. '50 Univ. of Copenhagen, Den. BATTALION COMMANDER, 2 Trainafdeling, Svenemøllens Kaserne, Copenhagen; INSTR. in PSYCH. and PEDAGOGY, Army and Air Force Officers Sch. Member: Danish Milit. Psych. Socy, Finnish Milit. Psych. Socy. Administration, educational and personnel psychology, testing, clinical analysis; learning theory, instructional practice. M
JAKOBSEN, Rasmus. Tværvangen 2 Brh, Copenhagen. b. 8 May 1906 Rynkeby. Cand. Psych. '47 Univ. of Copenhagen, Den. CHIEF SCH. PSYCH'T, Skolepsykologisk Kontor, Krausesvej 3, Copenhagen; EDITOR, Gyldendals Pædagogiske Bibliotek. Member: DP, Danish Assn. of Sch. Psych'ts. Administration, consulting, psychotherapy; educational psychology. M
JENSEN, Ejvind. Bagsværdvej 246 B, Bagsværd. b. 1 June 1918 Boeslunde. Cand. Psych. '47 Univ. of Copenhagen, Den. SCH. PSYCH'T, Emdrupborg Exper. Sch, Emdrupvej 101, Copenhagen NV. Member: DP, Danish Ass. of Sch. Psych'ts. Educational research and psychology, teaching; research in reading and arithmetic, test construction. M
JENSEN, Miss Else V. Teisensvej 14, Odense. b. 18 Mar 1906 Aalborg. Cand. Psych. '52

Univ. of Copenhagen, Den. SCH. PSYCH'T, Odense Skolevæsen, Radhuset, Flakhaven, Odense. Member: DP, Danish Assn. of Sch. Psych'ts. Consulting, guidance, testing, educational psychology; relations between child and parents, school and leisure time. F
JENSEN, Henrik Christian. Livøgade 9 st tv, Copenhagen. b. 25 Oct 1919 Copenhagen. Cand. Psych. '52 Univ. of Copenhagen, Den. KOMMUNELÆRER, Seminarioskolen på Kapelvej, Kapelvej, Copenhagen. Teaching; education of children, children's homes, juvenile courts, tests. M
JENSEN, Reimer. Borups Alle 173, Copenhagen N.V. b. 6 Dec 1918 Copenhagen. Cand. Psych. '47 Univ. of Copenhagen, Den. CLIN. PSYCH'T, Child Guid. Clin, Univ. of Copenhagen, Gamle Kongevej 10, Copenhagen V; TEACHER, N. Zahle's Tchrs. Coll, Copenhagen. Member: DP. Guidance, psychotherapy, teaching; psychoanalysis, child-parent relationships. M
JESPERSEN, Andreas. Kollegiehaven 27, Charlottenlund. b. 2 Nov 1916 Nykøbing Sj. Cand. Psych, Univ. of Copenhagen, Den. SCH. PSYCH'T, Gentofte Komm. Skolepsykologiske Kontor, Hyldegårdsvej 22, Charlottenlund; TEACHER, Tchrs. Coll, K.F.U.M, Hellerup. Member: DP, Danish Assn. of Sch. Psych'ts. Testing, educational psychology, consulting, teaching; motivation, projective techniques. M
JESPERSEN, Miss Inger. Agerkær 15/XII, Valby. b. 16 Aug 1927 Copenhagen. Cand. Psych. Univ. of Copenhagen, Den. CLIN. PSYCH'T, Child. Dept, Rigshospitalet, Blegdamsvej, Copenhagen Ø. Member: DP. Consulting, clinical practice, guidance, testing, teaching; psychosomatic medicine. F
JESSEN, Mrs. Nanna. Snaregade 5/II, Copenhagen K. b. 17 Sept 1927 Copenhagen. Cand. Psych. '53 Univ. of Copenhagen, Den. CHILD PSYCH'T, Samfundet og Hjemmet for Vanføre, Hans Knudsens Plads 3, Copenhagen Ø. Member: DP. Testing, guidance, research; treatment, research and education for children with cerebral palsy. F
JESSEN, Ove G. Guldborgvej 30, Copenhagen F. b. 24 Feb 1921 Copenhagen. Cand. Psych. '51 Univ. of Copenhagen, Den. CLIN. PSYCH'T, Kommunehosp, Øster Farimagsgade, Copenhagen. Member: DP. Diagnostic testing, research, teaching; projective techniques, perception, personality theory, learning, Gestalt psychology.M
JØRGENSEN, Ingvard Skov. P. B. Lundsvej, Skanderborg. b. 11 Nov 1915 Ryslinge. Cand. Psych. '47 Univ. of Copenhagen, Den. COUNTY SCH. PSYCH'T. Skanderborg. Member: DP. Administration, educational

psychology, testing; learning theory, intelligence tests, social behavior of backward children.   M

JOHANSEN, Martin Volodja. Blidahpark 17, Hellerup, Copenhagen. b. 13 Nov 1920 Copenhagen. Mag. art. '50 Univ. of Copenhagen, Den. ASST. PROF. Psych. Lab, Univ. of Copenhagen, Studiestræde 6, Copenhagen; CONSULTANT, Royal Acad. of Arts, Architectural Sch, Copenhagen. Member: DP. Research, teaching, professional writing, testing; perception of three dimensional forms, spatial perception tests, personality.   M

JOHANSEN, Paul B. Hummeltoften 37, Lyngby. b. 13 Nov 1919 Fårevejle. Cand. Psych. '47 Univ. of Copenhagen, Den. PSYCHOTHERAPIST, priv. prac; CONSULT. PSYCH'T, Danish Air Force. Member: DP. Teaching, psychotherapy, applied psychology; psychoanalysis, personality.   M

JORDAN, Rasmus. Rørtangvej 7, Snekkersten. b. 2 Jan 1924 Aalborg. Cand. Psych, Univ. of Copenhagen, Den. CLIN. PSYCH'T, Nervesanatorium, Montebello, Helsingør. Member: DP. Testing, psychotherapy, clinical practice and analysis.   M

JØRGENSEN, Arne Søgård. Torvestien 39, Glostrup. b. 8 Nov 1918 Viborg. Cand. Psych. '48 Univ. of Copenhagen, Den. VOCAT. ADVIS. and HEAD, Vocat. Guid. Dept, State Empl. Serv, Nørregade 49, Copenhagen; SUPERVISOR, Munic. Child. Welf. Serv. Member: DP. Administration, industrial psychology, consulting; vocational and youth psychology.   M

JØRGENSEN, Mrs. Edith G. K. Tingskrivervej 1, Copenhagen N.V. b. 4 July 1927 Charlottenlund. Cand. Psych. '52 Univ. of Copenhagen, Den. CHILD PSYCH'T, Child Guid. Clin, Univ. of Copenhagen, Gl. Kongevej 10, Copenhagen V. Member: DP. Psychotherapy, testing, clinical analysis, research.   F

JUEL-CHRISTIANSEN, Eyvind. Jægersvinget 3, Gentofte. b. 14 June 1910 Starupsogn. Cand. Psych. '49 Univ. of Copenhagen, Den. SCH. PSYCH'T. and ASST. INSPECTOR, Pub. Schools of Gentofte, Hyldegaardsvej 22, Charlottenlund;PSYCH. TCHR, Teachers Coll. Member: DP. Educational psychology, teaching, administration.   M

KLEVEN, Mogens. Spurvegården 12, Hvidovre. b. 5 May 1926 Roskilde. Cand. Psych. '53 Univ. of Copenhagen, Den. PSYCHOLOGIST, Psykoteknisk Inst, Borgergade 18, Copenhagen. Member: DP. Testing, applied and industrial psychology, vocational guidance; projective techniques, personality and perception, opinion and attitude measurement, human relations.   M

KOELLER, Nina. Ermelundsvej 117, Gentofte. b. 26 Nov 1927 Copenhagen. Cand. Psych. '51 Univ. of Copenhagen, Den. PSYCHOLOGIST, Dron. Louises Børnehosp., Copenhagen. Member: DP. Testing, guidance, teaching; group process, intelligence measurement.   F

KONGSTAD, Mrs. Gunvor. Taarbækdalsvej 3 C, Klampenborg. b. 31 Oct 1927 Odense. Cand. Psych. '54 Univ. of Copenhagen, Den. PSYCHOLOGIST, Mødrehjælpen, Copenhagen. Member: DP. Testing, child psychotherapy, teaching children's nurses; diagnosis of mental disorders by projective techniques.   F

KOSELEFF, Paul. Holsteinsgade 7, Copenhagen Ø. b. 15 Feb 1911 Dresden, Ger. Mag. art. '46 Univ. of Copenhagen, Den. Member: DP. Research, psychotherapy; perception of weight, psychoanalysis.   M

KRAGH-MÜLLER, Carl Christian. Henningsens alle 2 A, Hellerup, Copenhagen. b. 12 June 1914 Copenhagen. Cand. Psych, '47 Univ. of Copenhagen, Den. HEADMASTER, The Int. Sch. in Denmark, Hellerupvej 11, Copenhagen. Member: DP. Administration, educational psychology, professional writing; intelligence research, social perception in childhood, pseudofeeblemindedness.   M

KÜHL, Poul-Heinrich. Strødamvej 32, Copenhagen. b. 12 Nov 1913 Copenhagen. Cand. Psych. 51 Univ. of Copenhagen, Den. PSYCH T, State Prison, Vridsløse; TEACHER, Sch. for Social Wrkrs. Member: DP, Danish Sociol. Assn, Danish Criminol. Assn. Consulting, research, teaching; group and individual psychotherapy; psychological pathogenesis of criminal behavior.   M

KYNDRUP, Niels Erik. Saltværksvej 167, Kastrup. b. 4 June 1919 Hadsund. Cand. Psych, Univ. of Copenhagen, Den. TEACHER, K.F.U.M. Seminarium, Nyelandsvej 27, Copenhagen. Member: DP. Teaching; child psychology, problem children, learning theory, social perception, educational psychology.   M

KYNG, Birthe. Nordkrog 6, Hellerup. b. 5 Jan 1925, Copenhagen. Cand. Psych. 47 Univ. of Copenhagen, Den. CLIN. PSYCH'T, Child Guid. Clinic, Univ. of Copenhagen, Gammel Kongevej 10, Copenhagen V. Member: DP, Dan. Assn. for Child Psychiat. and Clin. Child Psych. Child psychology, psychotherapy.   F

KYNG, Mogens. Nordkrog 6, Hellerup. b. 13 Jan 1916, Copenhagen. Cand. Psych. 47 Univ. of Copenhagen, Den. CLIN. PSYCH T., Sct Hans hospital, Roskilde, priv. pract. Member: DP, Dan. Assn. for Child Psychiat. and Clin. Child Psych. Psychotherapy, research.   M

LAMBERT, Finn. Kornagervej 97, Lyngby. b. 5 Feb 1922 Sarpsborg, Norway. Cand. Psych. 55 Univ. of Copenhagen, Den. SCH. PSYCH'T, Sch. Psych. Off, Krausesvej 3, Copenhagen; TEACHER, Pub. Sch. for Backward Child. Member: DP. Educational psychology, testing, teaching; vocational counseling for backward youth. M

LANGER, Inger Margrethe. Sindssyge-hospitalet ved Aarhus, pr. Risskov. b. 7 Dec 1925 Den. Cand. Psych. '53 Univ. of Copenhagen, Den. CLIN. PSYCH'T, Sinds-sygehospitalet. Member: DP. Research, testing, teaching, guidance; social psychology, criminology. F

LANGKJÆR, Asger. Fiolstræde 23, Copenhagen K. b. 9 Apr 1905 Frederikssted St. Croix, Virgin Islands. Mag. art. 37 Univ. of Copenhagen, Den. LECTURER, Commercial High School, Julius Thomsens Plads 10, Copenhagen V. Member: DP. Research, teaching; theory of needs, motivation. M

LARSEN, Carl Åge. Fragariavej 1, Hellerup. b. 3 Feb 1915 Vantinge. Cand. Psych. '45 Univ. of Copenhagen, Den. DEPT. HEAD, Natl. Inst. for Educ. Res., Emdrupvej 101, Copenhagen. Member: DP. Didactic problems, child development, research. M

LARSEN, Carl Aage Høeg. Hattensensalle 14/3, Copenhagen F. b. 16 June 1911 Odense. Cand. Psych. '49 Univ. of Copenhagen, Den. SCH. PSYCH'T, Frederiksberg Kommunes Skolevæsen, Frederiksberg Rådhus, Frederiksberg; PROG. SPEC, UNRWA UNESCO, P.O.B. 149, Jerusalem, H.K. Jordan. Member: DP, Danish Assn. of Sch. Psych'ts. Educational psychology, psychotherapy, teaching; ability and achievement tests, projective techniques. M

LARSEN, Miss Gerda O. Uss. Kongevej 143, Kokkedal. b. 17 Aug 1912 Karlebo. Cand. Psych. '54 Univ. of Copenhagen, Den. TEACHER, Rungsted Skole, Rungsted Kyst. Member: DP. Teaching, educational psychology, testing; elementary reading, reading readiness and difficulties, parent-teacher relationship. F

LARSEN, Mrs. Ingeborg Paulin. Børne-hjemmet Fagerlund, Svaneke, Bornholm. b. 30 Mar 1909 Copenhagen. Cand. Psych. '50 Univ. of Copenhagen, Den. DIRECTOR Children's Home Fagerlund. Member: DP. Psychotherapy, educational psychology, administration; case studies, child psychology, neuroses. F

LAURITZEN, Bente. Lindealle 54, Vanløse. b. 29 May 1929 Frederiksberg. Cand. Psych. '56 Univ. of Copenhagen, Den. TCHR. and SCH. PSYCH'T, Frederiksberg Skolevæsen, Frederiksberg Rådhus, Copenhagen F. Member: DP. Teaching, testing, research. F

LAURITZEN, Svend. Martensens alle 8, Copenhagen V. b. 3 Nov 1902 Horsens. Cand. Psych. '52 Univ. of Copenhagen, Den. PSYCHOLOGIST, Dept. of Milit. Psych. Frederiksberg Slot, Copenhagen. Member: DP, Danish Milit. Psych. Socy. Selection of military personnel, testing, teaching; a-chievement tests, interviewing group process. M

LAUSTSEN, Arne Mølgard. Ribevej 32, Skærbæk. b. 20 Sept 1917 Rønbjerg. Cand. Psych. '52 Univ. of Copenhagen, Den. COUNTY SCH. PSYCH'T, County of Tønder. Member: DP, Danish Assn. of Sch. Psych'ts. Testing, consulting, teaching; learning theory, achievement tests, reading difficulties. M

LETH, Mrs. Grete Mygind. Lindholmsvej 31, Brønshøj. b. 29 Mar 1925 Copenhagen. Cand. Psych. '52 Univ. of Copenhagen, Den. SCH. PSYCH'T, Skolepsykologisk Kontor, Krausesvej 3, Copenhagen Ø. Member: DP. Educational psychology, teaching, testing. F

LEUNBACH, Mrs. Budda. Viadukt alle 11, Hellerup. b. 9 June 1918 Svendborg. Cand. Psych. '48 Univ. of Copenhagen, Den. CLIN. PSYCH'T, Østifternes Ånds-svageforsorg, Nyrospgade 28, Copenhagen; PSYCHOTHERAPIST, priv. prac. Member: DP. Psychotherapy, testing, lecturing, re-search; psychology of sex, projective tests, character analysis, vegetotherapy. F

LEVY-AHLBERG, Mrs. Elisabeth. Holbergs-gade 26, Copenhagen. b. 14 June 1922 Copenhagen. Cand. Psych. '54 Univ. of Copenhagen, Den. PSYCHOLOGIST, Rya-gårdens Yrkesskola, Örkelljunga, Sweden. Member: DP. Testing, applied psychology, psychotherapy; projective techniques, group therapy, social perception. F

LILBAEK, Grete. Godthaabsvej 94, Copen-hagen F. b. 4 Nov 1927 Copenhagen. Cand. Psych. '53 Univ. of Copenhagen, Den. CLIN. PSYCH'T, Finsen Inst, Strand Blvd. 43, Copenhagen. Member: DP, Assn. for Child Psychiat. and Clin. Child Psych. Testing, clinical analysis, guidance, psycho-therapy. F

LORENTZEN, Verner Henrik. Spurvegården 22, Valby. b. 4 Feb. 1924 Ribe. Cand. Psych. '52 Univ. of Copenhagen, Den. SCH. PSYCH'T, Hvidovre Skolevæsen, Hvidovre. Member: DP, Danish Assn. of Sch. Psych'ts. Testing, consulting, psycho-therapy; learning theory, projective tech-niques, clinical analysis. M

LUDVIGSEN, Mrs. Linda Grete Helene. Elstedvej 18, Rødovre pr. Vanløse. b. 29 Nov 1912 Frederiksberg. Cand. Psych. '55 Univ. of Copenhagen, Den. TEACHER, Copenhagen Skoledirektion, Nyropsgade 21, Copenhagen V. Member: DP. Teaching and testing children in a psychiatric hospital, psychotherapy; children's difficulties and parental neuroses, somatic and psychological aspects of neurosis, development of criminal tendencies. F

LUNDBERG, Mrs. Ellen Margrethe. Jyllandsvej 22, Copenhagen F. b. 9 Oct 1921 Copenhagen. Cand. Psych. '52 Univ. of Copenhagen, Den. SCH. PSYCH'T, Tårnby Kommunes Skolevæsen, Saltværksvej 63, Kastrup. Member: DP. Testing, consulting, guidance, administration; social perception, attitude measurement, retarded children. F

MADSEN, Kristen Bent. Kærdals alle 14, pr. Vanløse, Copenhagen. b. 5 June 1922 Kalundborg. Cand. Psych. '50 Univ. of Copenhagen, Den. LECTURER, State Tchr. Trng. Coll, Emdrupborg, Emdrupvej 101, Copenhagen; RES. ASST, Nat. Inst. for Educ. Res. Member: DP. Teaching, research, professional writing; theoretical psychology, motivation, educational psychology. M

MARCKMANN, Wilhelm O. L. Kildegaardsvænget 23, Hellerup. b. 5 Mar 1919 Vordingborg. Cand. Psych. '50 Univ. of Copenhagen, Den. SCH. PSYCH'T, Emdrupborg Exper. Sch, Emdrupvej 101, Copenhagen. Member: DP, Danish Assn. of Sch. Psych'ts. Research, educational psychology; sociometry, social attitudes and school structure, school readiness. M

MARKUS, Rudolf. Haraldsgade 49, Copenhagen N. b. 24 Aug 1908 Saarbrücken, Ger. Cand. Psych. '56 Univ. of Copenhagen, Den. PSYCH'T, Inst. for Psychopathic Criminals. Statsfängslet, Horsens. Member: DP, Danish Milit. Psych. Socy. Psychotherapy, guidance, testing; group therapy for psychopathic criminals, achievement tests for selection of military radio operators. M

MATTHIESSEN, Erik. Amagervej 14, Esbjerg. b. 1 Mar 1918 Copenhagen. Cand. Psych. '49 Univ. of Copenhagen, Den. CHIEF SCH. PSYCH'T, Esbjerg City Sch. System, Kronprinsensgade 33, Esbjerg; LECTURER, Esbjerg Tchr. Trng. Coll. Member: DP, Danish Assn. of Sch. Psych'ts. Administration, testing, guidance; psychology of reading, achievement and scholastic tests, anthropological psychology. M

MEYER, Henning. Hattensensalle 4/III, Copenhagen F. b. 1 Mar 1885 Copenhagen. Mag. art. '24 Univ. of Copenhagen, Den. TCHR. of PEDAGOGICAL PSYCH, Dan. Tchrs. High School. Member: DP (Honorary member), Danish Assn. of Sch. Psych'ts. Retired, teaching, educational psychology, guidance; memory, achievement and educational tests. M

MOGENSEN, Alan. Frederiksberg alle 20/2, Copenhagen V. b. 13 Nov 1927 Copenhagen. Cand. Psych. '53 Univ. of Copenhagen, Den. CLIN. PSYCH'T, Copenhagen Kommunehosp, Øster Farimagsgade, Copenhagen. Member: DP. Clinical analysis, research; projective techniques, mental functioning and achievement tests, studies of twins. M

MOGENSEN, Ib Borg. Brøndbyøstervej 136, Glostrup. b. 17 Aug 1922 Copenhagen. Cand. Psych. '53 Univ. of Copenhagen, Den. PERS. PSYCH'T, Mutual Insurance Co. of Denmark, Niels Brocksgade 1, Copenhagen V. Member: DP. Personnel and educational psychology, psychotherapy; social psychology, achievement and projective tests. M

MØHL, Miss Marianne. Frydenlundsvej 7, Skodsborg. b. 25 Aug 1930 Copenhagen. Cand. Psych. '55 Univ. of Copenhagen, Den. TCHR. and PSYCH'T, Himmelev Børnehjem, Frederiksborgvej, Roskilde. Member: DP. Teaching, educational psychology, testing; evaluation of foster homes, group dynamics, treatment of autism. F

MØLLER-HOLST, Mrs. Inge Ullstad. Rude Vang 20, Holte. b. 23 Oct 1920 Copenhagen. Cand. Psych. '52 Univ. of Copenhagen, Den. CLIN. PSYCH'T, Dr. Louise's Børnehosp, Ø Farimagsgade 34, Copenhagen. Member: DP, Assn. for Child Psychiat. and Clin. Child Psych. Clinical practice, testing, psychotherapy. F

MØLLER-HOLST, Mrs. Tove. Frederiksberg alle 26, Copenhagen V. b. 8 Jan 1907 Copenhagen. Cand. Psych. '47 Univ. of Copenhagen, Den. CLIN. PSYCH'T, Child Guidance Clin, Univ. of Copenhagen, Gammel Kongevej 10, Copenhagen V. Member: DP, Assn. for Child Psychiat. and Clin. Child Psych, Assn. for Psych. and Philos. Child psychotherapy, consulting, testing; psychoanalysis, counseling. F

MØNSTER, Karl. Aarup, Snedstad. b. 31 Oct 1919 Sejet. Cand. Psych. '50 Univ. of Copenhagen, Den. COUNTY SCH. PSYCH'T. Thisted Amt, Skovgade, Thisted. Member: DP, Danish Assn. of Sch. Psych'ts. Testing, administration, educational psychology. M

MOSEGAARD, Mrs. Ester. Rosenørnsalle 58/II Copenhagen V. b. 9 June 1921 Copenhagen. Cand. Psych. '54 Univ. of Copenhagen, Den. PSYCHOLOGIST, Arbejdsdirektoratet, Nyropsgade 28, Copenhagen. Member: DP. Testing, research. F

MUNCK, Mrs. Kirsten. Ordruphøjvej 17, Charlottenlund. b. 26 May 1926 Copenhagen. Cand. Psych. Univ. of Copenhagen, Den. TEACHER, School for Retarded Readers, Reventlowsgade 16, Copenhagen. Member: DP. Teaching, testing, guidance; word blindness. F

MUNK, Miss Yrsa. Lundely 6, Hellerup. b. 13 Aug 1931 Vedersø. Cand. Psych. '55 Univ. of Copenhagen, Den. EXCHANGE STUD, Columbia Univ, New York 27, N.Y., USA. Member: DP. Research, testing, guidance; group process, psychodrama. F

NERUP, Hans J. Cæciliavej 16, Valby, Copenhagen. b. 19 Dec 1910 Hobro. Cand. Psych. '51 Univ. of Copenhagen, Den. SCH. PSYCH'T, Frederiksberg Munic. Sch. Dept, Town Hall, Frederiksberg, Copenhagen. Member: DP. Testing, educational psychology, teaching. M

NIELSEN, Anker. Jägersborg alle 225, Gentofte. b. 12 June 1918 Nöbbet. Cand. Psych. '49 Univ. of Copenhagen, Den. SCH. PSYCH'T, Gentofte Skoleväsen, Bernstorffsvej, Gentofte. Member: DP. Educational psychology, testing, teaching; reading and writing difficulties of school children. M

NIELSEN, Bøgill. Hendriksholms Blvd. 23, Valby, Copenhagen. b. 10 Sept 1914 Den. Cand. Psych. '47 Univ. of Copenhagen, Den. HEADMASTER, Frederiksgård Skole, Frederiksgårds alle 13, Copenhagen; CONSULT. PSYCH'T, Child Welf. Inst, Copenhagen. Member: DP. Administration, teaching, testing; backward children, children with behavior disturbances. M

NIELSEN, Mrs. Gerda Karen. Vestergade 18, Silkeborg. b. 8 Nov 1919 Aarhus. Cand. Psych. '51 Univ. of Copenhagen, Den. CLIN. PSYCH'T, Child Psychiat. Clin, Kommunehospitalet, Aarhus. Member: DP. Testing, guidance, teaching; projective techniques, psychotherapy, group process.F

NIELSEN, Mrs. Karen Akhøj. Røntoftevej 37, Søborg. b. 9 Apr 1923 Holböl. Cand. Psych. '54 Univ. of Copenhagen, Den. PSYCH'T, Dept. of Milit. Psych, Frederiksberg Slot, Copenhagen. Member: DP. Testing, personnel selection, guidance, research; education of military personnel. F

NIELSEN, Poul. Toftekærsvej 112, Søborg, Copenhagen. b. 11 Apr 1915 Copenhagen. Cand. Psych. '47 Univ. of Copenhagen, Den. SCH. PSYCH'T, Skolepsykologisk Kontor, Krausesvej 3, Copenhagen. Member: DP, Danish Assn. of Sch. Psych'ts. Guidance, testing, teaching; educational psychology. M

NØRVIG, Mrs. Anne Marie. Emdrupvej 105, Copenhagen NV. b. 24 Dec. 1898 Hårmark. Samsø. Cand. Psych. '47 Univ. of Copenhagen, Den. HEADMASTER, Emdrupborg Exper. Sch, Emdrupvej 101, Copenhagen. Member: DP, ICWP, Danish Assn. of Sch. Psych'ts, Assn. for Child Psychiat. and Clin. Child Psych. Teaching, educational psychology, administration; group process, attitude measurement, cooperative projects

in educational administration. F

ÖHRSTRÖM, Sigurd. Egeløvsvej 15, Virum. b. 2 Mar 1922 Copenhagen. Cand. Psych. '53 Univ. of Copenhagen, Den. SCH. PSYCH'T, Søllerød Kommune, Rådhuset, Holte. Member: DP, Danish Assn. of Sch. Psych'ts. Educational psychology, teaching, consulting; learning theory, teaching retarded children, testing school maturity, guidance of teachers and parents. M

OLSEN, Mrs. Beate-Maria. 36-38, Store Kongensgade, Copenhagen K. b. 1 Mar 1921 Berlin, Ger. Cand. Psych. '51 Univ. of Copenhagen, Den. PSYCHOLOGIST, Psychotech. Inst, Borgergade 18, Copenhagen. Member: DP. Testing, educational psychology, psychotherapy; child psychology, play therapy. F

ØSTERGAARD, Lise. Islandsvej 12 B, Lyngby. b. 18 Nov 1924 Odense. Cand. Psych. '47 Univ. of Copenhagen, Den. CLIN. PSYCH'T, Rigshospitalet, Blegdamsvej, Copenhagen. Member: DP. Testing, clinical analysis, consulting, guidance; projective techniques. F

PALSVIG, Kurt. Nørre Søgade 45, Copenhagen K. b. 21 May 1924 Copenhagen. Cand. Psych. '54 Univ. of Copenhagen, Den. RES. ASST, Inst. for Psychopathic Criminals, Herstedvester. Member: DP, Danish Milit. Psych. Socy, Assn. for Psych. and Philos. Applied psychology, research, diagnosis, psychotherapy; social perception, role, adjustment, criminology. M

PEDERSEN, Anker. Nordbyvej 27, Vanløse. b. 22 Feb 1906 Copenhagen. Cand. Psych. '47 Univ. of Copenhagen, Den. SCH. PSYCH'T, Off. of Sch. Psych, Krausesvej 3, Copenhagen. Member: DP, Danish Assn. of Sch. Psych'ts, Assn. for Psych. and Philos. Consulting, testing; school psychology. M

PEDERSEN, Richard. P. Bangsvej 159, Copenhagen F. b. 24 Nov 1911 Skaarup. Cand. Psych. '47 Univ. of Copenhagen, Den. SCH. PSYCH'T, Frederiksberg Munic. Sch. Dept, Town Hall, Copenhagen F. Member: DP. Consulting and guidance, psychotherapy, testing, teaching; educational problems. M

PEDERSEN-LIPTAKOVA, Mrs. Edita. Sindssygehospitalet, Risskov. b. 28 Apr 1925 Kosice, Czech. Cand. Psych. '51 Univ. of Oslo, Nor. CLIN. PSYCH'T, Sindssygehospitalet. Member: DP, Danish Assn. for Ment. Health. Clinical diagnosis, teaching; projective techniques, personality theory, learning theory, psychoanalysis, social norms. F

PERCH, Poul Werner. Buddingevej 21 B, Lyngby. b. 11 May 1911 Copenhagen. Cand. Psych. '47 Univ. of Copenhagen, Den. EDUC. ADVIS, Danish Ministry of Soc.

Affairs, Slotsholmsgade 6, Copenhagen. LECTURER, Dept. of Psych., Univ. of Copenhagen. Member: DP, Assn. for Psych. and Philos., Assn. for Psychiat. and Clin. Child Psych. Educational psychology, testing, ment. deficiency, administration. M

PETERSEN, Henry Holmgaard. Hornemannsgade 21, Copenhagen Ø. b. 3 Nov 1912 Ullerød. Cand. Psych. '50 Univ. of Copenhagen, Den. CLIN. PSYCH'T, priv. prac. Member: DP. Clinical analysis and practice, teaching; sexual behavior, social behavior, personality inventory. M

PETERSEN, Jørgen. Statsungdomshjemmet, Sølager, Hundested. b. 19 Dec 1923 Copenhagen. Cand. Psych. '53 Univ. of Copenhagen, Den. TEACHER, State Home for young Delinquents; CLIN. PSYCH'T, Children's Home, Frederiksværk, N. Sealand. Member: DP. Teaching, educational psychology, guidance, psychotherapy; group dynamics, group and individual therapy, reeducation of young criminals. M

POULSEN, Jørgen Egedal. Nøkkerosevej 44, Copenhagen NV. b. 11 May 1921 Roskilde. Cand. Psych. '49 Univ. of Copenhagen, Den. SCH. PSYCH'T, Emdrupborg Exper. Sch, Emdrupvej 101, Copenhagen NV; Res. Ass Nat. Inst. for Educ. Res., Emdrupborg, Copenhagen NV. Member: DP. Research, teaching, vocational guidance, testing; achievement tests, educational experiments. M

POULSEN, Ulla. Gl. Kongevej 70/5, Copenhagen V. b. 24 Feb 1926 Copenhagen. Cand. Psych. '52 Univ. of Copenhagen, Den. PSYCH'T, Dept. of Milit. Psych, Frederiksberg Slot, Copenhagen F. Member: DP, Danish Milit. Psych. Socy. Applied psychology, testing, military personnel selection. F

RASMUSSEN, Prof. Edgar Tranckjær. Skovtoftebakken 13, Kgs. Lyngby. b. 21 July 1900 Copenhagen. Mag. scient. '30 Univ. of Copenhagen, Den. PROF. and DIR, Psych. Lab, Univ. of Copenhagen, Studiestræde 3, Copenhagen K; PSYCH. ADVIS, Nat. Inst. for Educ. Res; PSYCH. ADVIS, Dept. of Milit. Psych. Member: DP, Assn. for Psych. and Philos. Administration, teaching, research; perception, psychological theories, personality. M

RASMUSSEN, Hans Christian. Tværbommen 13, Gentofte. b. 19 Nov 1921 Løgten. Cand. Psych. '51 Univ. of Copenhagen, Den. INSPECTOR, Overinspektionen for Børneforsorg, Rosenvængets alle 18; RES. ASST, Nat. Inst. for Ed. Res; ED. in CHIEF, *Nordisk Psykologi*; ED. COMM, *Acta Psychologica*. Member: DP. Administration, research, editorial, teaching; group process. M

RASMUSSEN, Harald. Aegirs alle 5, Esbjerg.

b. 6 Jan 1925 Copenhagen. Cand. Psych. '50 Univ. of Copenhagen, Den. SCH. PSYCH'T, Esbjerg Skolevæsen; TEACHER, Tchr. Trng. Coll. Member: DP, Danish Assn. of Sch. Psych'ts. Educational psychology; psychology of reading. M

RASMUSSEN, Henry. Dalhøjgård, Lumsas. b. 29 May 1916 Mern. Cand. Psych. '53 Univ. of Copenhagen, Den. DIRECTOR, Kolonien Dalhøjgård. Member: DP. Applied psychology, administration, teaching. M

RASMUSSEN, Ib. Kirkebjerg alle 93, Glostrup. b. 13 July 1913 Copenhagen. Cand. Psych. '53 Univ. of Copenhagen, Den. SCH. PSYCH'T, Sch. System of Rødovre, Rødovre Parkvej 150, Vanløse; ED. COMM, *Læsepædagogen*. Member: DP. Educational psychology, testing, teaching; reading difficulties. M

RASMUSSEN, Knud J. Åhavevej 74, Silkeborg. b. 15 Jan 1922 Løjtofte. Cand. Psych. '50 Univ. of Copenhagen, Den. SCH. PSYCH'T, Off. of Educ. Psych, Markedsgade, Silkeborg; TEACHER, Tchr. Trng. Coll. Silkeborg. Member: DP, Danish Assn. of Sch. Psych'ts. Teaching, educational psychology; education of retarded children. M

RASMUSSEN, Mrs. Liss. Tværbommen 13, Gentofte. b. 23 Feb 1925 Thyrsting. Cand. Psych. '54 Univ. of Copenhagen, Den. RES. ASST, Nat. Inst. for Educ. Res. Emdrupborg. Member: DP. Teaching, research, testing; psychology of fashion. F

RASMUSSEN, Ove. W. H. Roskildevej 260, Copenhagen. b. 16 Dec 1916 Copenhagen. Cand. Psych. '49 Univ. of Copenhagen, Den. SCH. PSYCH'T, Skolepsykologisk Kontor, Krausesvej 3, Copenhagen. Member: DP. Testing, educational psychology, psychotherapy. M

RAVNMARK, Anker Nielsen. Syrenvej 21, Ringsted. b. 6 May 1918 Jennum. Cand. Psych. '49 Univ. of Copenhagen, Den. COUNTY SCH. PSYCH'T, Sorø Amts Skoledirektion, Amtskontoret Sorø. Member: DP. Testing, consulting, administration; achievement and intelligence tests, school adjustment, special education in public schools. M

REVENTLOW, Iven E. R. Hørsholmvej 43 A, Rungsted Kyst. b. 2 June 1926 Tillitze. Mag. art. '54 Univ. of Copenhagen, Den. RES. ASST. Psych. Lab, Univ. of Copenhagen, Studiestrade 6, Copenhagen. Member: DP, Assn. for Psych. and Philos. Research, testing, teaching; animal psychology, perception. M

RINDOM, Per. Ved Volden 8, Copenhagen V. b. 26 June 1927 Copenhagen. Cand. Psych, Univ, of Copenhagen, Den. CONSULT. PSYCH'T, Mothers' Aid Inst, Svendborggade, Copenhagen. Member: DP, Assn. for Psych. and Philos. Teaching, research, testing, consulting; measurement of racial attitudes. M

ROBINSOHN, Miss Susanne Birgitte. Lille Strandvej 1A, Hellerup, Copenhagen. b. 18 June 1927 Hamburg, Ger. Cand. Psych. '56 Univ. of Copenhagen, Den. KINDERGARTEN TCHR. Member: DP. Teaching, clinical child psychology. F

ROBINSON, Arthur Hedley. Fængsels-afdelingen ved Nørre Snede, Jylland. b. 22 Nov 1922 Manchester, Eng. Cand. Psych. '55 Univ. of Copenhagen, Den. PSYCH'T, Open Inst. for First Offenders, Nørre Snede, Jylland. Member: DP. Testing, clinical analysis, consulting; criminology. M

ROSS, Strange. Frederikssundsvej 119 V 7v, Copenhagen Brh. b. 10 Oct 1928 Copenhagen. Mag. art. '56 Univ. of Copenhagen, Den. VOLUNTEER LAB. ASST, Psych. Lab. Univ. of Copenhagen, Studiestræde 6, Copenhagen. Member: DP, Assn. for Psych. and Philos. Research, professional writing, applied psychology; psychoacoustics, theory and practice of psychological measurements, theoretical psychology. M

ROTHE, Mrs. Wenja. Ramløsevej 17/II, Copenhagen. b. 11 Mar 1916 Oslo, Nor. Cand. Psych. '48 Univ. of Copenhagen, Den. CLIN. PSYCH'T, Child Guid. Clin, Univ. of Copenhagen, Gl. Kongevej 10, Copenhagen. Member: DP, Danish Assn. for Child Psychiat. and Clin. Child Psych. Testing, child guidance and psychotherapy, teaching; projective techniques. F

SADDERUP, Ellen Ruth. Lyngvigvej 5, Vnl. b. 19 Dec 1915 Odense. Cand. Psych. '49 Univ. of Copenhagen, Den. SCH. PSYCH'T, Skolepsykologisk Kontor, Krausesvej 3, Copenhagen. Member: DP. Educational psychology, guidance, teaching, testing. F

SCHIÖLER, Grete. Maria Kirkeplads 2, Copenhagen V. b. 2 Feb 1910 Lögstör. Cand. Psych. '53 Univ. of Copenhagen, Den. PSYCH'T, Dept. of Milit. Psych. Frederiksberg Slot, Copenhagen F., priv. consult. Member: DP. Testing, applied psychology, research; officer assessment. F

SCHRØDER, Mrs. Birgit. Hostrups Have 46, Copenhagen. b. 25 July 1921 Copenhagen. Cand. Psych. '50 Univ. of Copenhagen, Den. PSYCH'T, Dept. of Milit. Psych, Frederiksberg Slot, Copenhagen F. Member: DP, Danish Milit. Psych. Socy. Personnel psychology, consulting. F

SCHULSINGER, Mrs. Hanne. Sindssyge-hospitalet, Nykøbing Sjælland. b. 19 May 1927 Copenhagen. Cand. Psych. '55 Univ. of Copenhagen, Den. CLIN. PSYCH'T, State Ment. Hosp. Member: DP. Testing, clinical analysis, psychotherapy; cognitive

testing, projective techniques. F

SIGSGAARD, Jens. Holte. b. 14 Aug 1910 Kaas. Cand. Psych. '45 Univ. of Copenhagen, Den. DIRECTOR, Froebel Trng. Coll, Ryesgade 101, Copenhagen. Member: DP. Teaching, administration; writing children's books. M

SIGSGÅRD, Thomas. Elmevej 14, Holte. b. 8 Sept 1909 Jetsmark. Cand. Psych. '46 Univ. of Copenhagen, Den. SCH. PSYCH'T, Skolepsykologisk Kontor, Krausesvej 3, Copenhagen; LECTURER, Psych. Dept, Univ. of Copenhagen. Member: DP, Danish Assn. of Sch. Psych'ts. Consulting, teaching, administration; achievement tests, school psychology. M

SJALLUNG, Grunddal. Himmerlandsvej 22, Copenhagen F. b. 22 Sept 1895 Odense. PH.D '29 Emerson Univ, USA; Mag. art. '31 Univ. of Copenhagen, Den. PSYCH. CONSULT, Univ. Lib, Copenhagen; PRESES, Socy. of Heraldry, Copenhagen. Library, consulting, applied psychology; psychological basis of heraldry, characterological tests, aptitude tests, epistemological principles of psychology. M

SKINHØJ, Kirsten. Øster Søgade 18, Copenhagen K. b. 14 May 1921 Copenhagen. Cand. Psych. '53 Univ. of Copenhagen, Den. PSYCHOLOGIST, Børneafdelingen Blegdamshosp, Blegdamsvej, Copenhagen. Member: DP, Assn. for Child Psychiat. and Clin. Child Psych. Testing, psychotherapy, research; intelligence tests, projective techniques, psychosomatic diagnosis, psychotherapy, parent guidance. F

SKJÖLDBYE, Verner. Ved Kløvermarken 7/II, Copenhagen. b. Copenhagen. Cand. Psych, Univ. of Copenhagen, Den. SCH. PSYCH'T, Sch. Psych. Off, Krausesvej 3, Copenhagen Ø; CONSULT. PSYCH'T, Milit. Forces; LEADER, Adult Evening Sch. Member: DP, Danish Assn. of Sch. Psych'ts. Educational psychology, consulting, guidance, teaching; projective techniques, achievement tests, social perception, group process. M

SKOVGAARD-PETERSEN, Kirsten. Moltkes-vej 39, Copenhagen. b. 11 Dec 1913 Copenhagen. Cand. Psych. '47 Univ. of Copenhagen, Den. SOC. CONSULT, Bethesda, Rømersgade 17, Copenhagen. Member: DP. Psychotherapy, guidance, teaching psychology to nurses. F

SLOTH, Otto. Ejnarsvej 94, Lyngby. b. 15 June 1918 Korinth. Cand. Psych. '51 Univ. of Copenhagen, Den. SCH. PSYCH'T, Community of Gentofte. Member: DP. Educational psychology, teaching, testing. M

SLOTH, Mrs. Tove. Ejnarsvej 94, Lyngby. b. 11 Apr 1923 Copenhagen. Cand. Psych. '50 Univ. of Copenhagen, Den.

TEACHER, Community of Gladsaxe, Søborg. Teaching. F

SØEGÅRD, Arne. Hybenvej 84, Virum. b. 27 Sept 1912 Næstved. Cand. Psych. '48 Univ. of Copenhagen, Den. SCH. PSYCH'T, Skolepsykologisk Kontor, Sorgenfriskolen, Kongevejen 55, Lyngby. Member: DP. Testing, clinical analysis, educational guidance. M

SÖRENSEN, Otto. Lindebugten 27, Copenhagen, Valby. b. 19 May 1911 Sejlflod. Cand. Psych. '53 Univ. of Copenhagen, Den. HEADMASTER, Frederiksberg Kommune, Frederiksberg Rådhus, Copenhagen F. Member: DP, Bansk Lærerforening. Teaching, testing, psychotherapy, guidance; projective techniques, social perception, attitude measurement. M

SPELLING, Kaj Aage. Maj alle 80, Herlev. b. 6 Dec 1915 Rønne. Cand. Psych. '47 Univ. of Copenhagen, Den. SCH. PSYCH'T, Copenhagen Kommune, Skolepsykologisk Kontor, Krausesvej 3, Copenhagen Ø. Member: DP, Danish Assn. of Sch. Psych'ts, Assn. for Psych. and Philos. Educational psychology, testing, teaching; non-verbal intelligence testing, child guidance, administration. M

SPIES, Simon. Skt. Olaigade 2, Elsinore. b. 9 Jan 1921 Elsinore. Can. Psych. '50 Univ. of Copenhagen, Den. PSYCHO-THERAPIST, priv. prac. Member: DP. Psychotherapy, professional writing, applied psychology. M

STEINOV, Kristian. Henrik Hertzvej 12, Odense. b. 12 Oct 1921 Ålesund, Norway. Cand. Psych. '51 Univ. of Copenhagen, Den. COUNTY SCH. PSYCH'T, Odense amt. TEACHER, Tchr's Trng. Coll, Odense; PSYCHOLOGIST, Ment. Hlth. Guid. Clin. Member: DP. Educational psychology, teaching, guidance and consulting; special education for retarded children. M

STENBAEK, Arne. Toftekærsvej 98, Søborg. b. 17 May 1918 Vordingborg. Cand. Psych. '53 Univ. of Copenhagen, Den. SCH. PSYCH'T, Skolepsykologisk Kontor, Krausesvej 3, Copenhagen. Member: DP. Teaching, testing, educational psychology; learning theory, reading, social perception. M

STENKILDE, Mrs. Astrid Solveig. Ulrik Birch's alle 14/4, Copenhagen S. b. 7 May 1926 Oslo, Nor. Cand. Psych. '52 Univ. of Copenhagen, Den. Member: DP. Testing, consulting, research; achievement tests, projective techniques, interviewing. F

STRUNGE, Miss Kirsten. Strynøgade 13, Aalborg. b. 25 Oct 1915 Viborg Amt. Cand. Psych. '49 Univ. of Copenhagen, Den. SCH. PSYCH'T, Skolepsykologisk Kontor, Vejgård Rådhus, Aalborg. Member: DP. Applied and educational psychology, testing, clinical analysis, teaching. F

STÜRUP, Dr. Georg K. Vingårds alle 36, Hellerup. b. 3 Mar 1905 Odense. MD '40 Univ. of Copenhagen, Den. DIRECTOR, Inst. for Psychopathic Criminals, Herstedvester, pr. Glostrup; PSYCHIAT. ADV, Ministry of Justice, Dept. of Prisons. Member: Assn. for Psych. and Philos. Administration, psychotherapy, research. M

SUHR-JESSEN, Hans J. F. Sct. Thomas alle 4, Copenhagen V. b. 25 July 1925 Frederiksberg. Cand. Psych. '56 Univ. of Copenhagen, Den. MAJOR, Dept. of Milit. Psych., Frederiksberg Slot, Copenhagen F. Member: DP, Milit. Psych. Socy. Administration, military psychology, educational psych., personnel management. M

TANGHØJ, Johs. Nordvestpassagen 63, Århus. b. 5 Nov 1920 Struer. Cand. Psych. '48 Univ. of Copenhagen, Den. SCH. PSYCH'T, Sch. Psych. Off, Meilgade 8, Århus. Member: DP, Danish Assn. of Sch. Psych'ts. Testing, psychotherapy, guidance; school maturity problems. M

THEILGAARD, Mrs. Alice. Solkrogen 2. Glostrup. b. 29 Dec 1926 Copenhagen. Cand. Psych. '51 Univ. of Copenhagen, Den. CLIN. PSYCH'T, Rigshospitalet, Blegdamsvej, Copenhagen. Member: DP. Testing, clinical analysis, psychotherapy, applied psychology; projective techniques, psychosomatic medicine. F

THOMSEN, Erik. Ordrupvej 75 A, Charlottenlund. b. 14 May 1909 Boestrup. Mag. art. '41 Univ. of Copenhagen, Den. DIRECTOR, Natl. Inst. for Educ. Res, Emdrupvej 101, Copenhagen NV; TEACHER, Univ. of Copenhagen. Administration, educational research, teaching; learning theory, educational tests. M

THUNE-STEPHENSEN, Asker. Furesøkolonien, Bistrupvej 137, Birkerød. b. 6 Oct 1919 Aalborg. Cand. Psych. '50 Univ. of Copenhagen, Den. DIRECTOR Furesøkolonien. Member: DP. Educational psychology, administration, teaching; pedagogical and psychological differential diagnosis. M

THYREGOD, Mrs. Any. Hovedgaden 23, Bagsværd. b. 29 July 1921 Copenhagen. Cand. Psych. '47 Univ. of Copenhagen, Den. SCH. PSYCH'T, Skolepsykologisk Kontor, Krausesvej 3, Copenhagen. Member: DP. Guidance, testing; educational psychology. F

TORPE, Harald. Ved Renden 35, Søborg. b. 11 Jan 1910 Stege. Mag. art, Univ. of Copenhagen, Den. CHIEF SCH. PSYCH'T, Sch. Psych. Off, Town Hall of Frederiksberg, Copenhagen F; LECTURER, Univ. of Copenhagen. Member: DP. Educational psychology, testing, consulting, teaching; test psychology. M

TOTTEY, Edward Revill. Christiansholmsvej

26, Klampenborg. b. 27 Mar 1928 Wirral, UK. Mag. art. '56 Univ. of Copenhagen, Den. RES. PSYCH'T, Rigshospitalets, Neuromed. Div, Militærhosp, Tagensvej, Copenhagen. Member: DP, Assn. for Psych. and Philos. Research, clinical analysis, teaching; brain injuries, physiology of learning, attention.   M

VEILEBORG, Mrs. Elisabeth Ingrid. Josteinsvej 15B, Bagsværd. b. 19 Mar 1920 Hemmed. Cand. Psych. '54 Univ. of Copenhagen, Den. PSYCHOLOGIST. Member: DP. Applied and educational psychology, testing, consulting; projective techniques, individual psychotherapy.   F

VELSING-RASMUSSEN, Gunnar. Søllerødvej 53, Holte. b. 11 Aug 1914 Vindehelsinge. Cand. Psych. '47 Univ. of Copenhagen, Den. SCH. PSYCH'T, Skolepsykologisk Kontor, Krausesvej 3, Copenhagen Ø. Member: DP. Educational psychology, testing, consulting.   M

VESTERGAARD-BOGIND, Mrs. Jytte. Lundtoftevej 182, Lyngby. b. 10 Feb 1928 Aerøskøbing. Cand. Psych. '55 Univ. of Copenhagen, Den. CLIN. PSYCH'T, Rigshospitalet, Blegdamsvej, Copenhagen. Member: DP. Testing, educational psychology, psychotherapy; projective techniques, achievement tests.   F

VIDRIKSEN, Poul. Ved Bellahøj 1 vest 3th, Copenhagen Brh. b. 17 Jan 1926 Copenhagen. Cand. Psych, Univ. of Copenhagen, Den. PSYCH'T, Psychotechnical Inst., Copenhagen K; ED. COMM, Nordisk Erhvervsvejledning. Member: DP, APA. Testing, administration, research; job

analysis, accident proneness, measurements of vocational maturity.   M

VOLQVARTZ, Miss Rigborg Margrethe. Sindssygehospitalet, Vordingborg. b. 14 June 1900 Copenhagen. Mag. art. '47 Univ. of Copenhagen, Den. CLIN. PSYCH'T, Sindssygehospitalet. Member: DP, Assn. for Psych. and Philos. Testing, clinical analysis; visual perception, psychology of esthetics, projective techniques.   F

WHITTA-JØRGENSEN, Poul. Joachim Rønnowsvej 22, Virum. b. 29 Jan 1921 Copenhagen. Cand. Psych. '55 Univ. of Copenhagen, Den. SCH. PSYCH'T, Frederiksberg Sch. System, Frederiksberg Rådhus, Copenhagen F; RES. ASST, Nat. Inst. of Educ. Res. Member: DP. Research, educational psychology, testing; attitude measurement.   M

WILLANGER, Rolf. Ved Bella høj 30, Copenhagen. b. 6 Sept 1927 Bergen, Nor. Cand. Psych. '52 Univ. of Oslo, Nor. PSYCH'T, Dept. for Milit. Psych, Frederiksberg Slot, Copenhagen. Member: DP. Applied and industrial psychology, testing, guidance; character structure, human relations in industry and administration.   M

WILTRUP, Mrs. Jonna. Havnegade 47, Copenhagen K. b. 2 Feb 1921 Copenhagen. Cand. Psych. '51 Univ. of Copenhagen, Den. CLIN. PSYCH'T, Child Psychiat. Dept, Bispebjerg Hosp, Copenhagen. Member: DP, ICWP, Assn. for Child Psychiat. and Clin. Child Psych. Child psychotherapy, testing, parent guidance; projective techniques.   F

ECUADOR

BACA, Max Raymond. Inst. of Inter-Amer. Affairs, c/o U.S. Embassy, Quito. b. 5 Aug 1922 Albuquerque, New Mexico, USA. M.ED '54 Univ. of California, USA. EDUC. TECH, Inst. of Inter-Amer. Affairs; EDITORIAL DIR, Reports of Dept. of Educ. of Quito. Testing, clinical analysis, administration, research, training teachers in testing and counseling methods; psychometrics, remedial psychology in schools, educational counseling for children and parents.   M

BOSSANO, Dr. Prof. Luis. Apartado postal 94, Quito. b. 19 Apr 1906 Quito. LL.D, Central Univ. of Ecuador. PROF. of SOCIOL, Central Univ. of Ecuador, Ciudad Universitaria, Quito. Teaching; social psychology, international law.   M

CARBO, Dr. Edmundo. Apartado 675, Quito. b. 16 Nov 1910 Jipijapa. PH.D '55 Central Univ. of Ecuador. PROF. of PSYCH, Central Univ. of Ecuador; PROJECT ADMIN,

Inst. of Inter-Amer. Affairs, Servicio Cooperativo de Educacíon, Quito. Member: Psych. Socy. of Ecuador, Casa de la Cultura Ecuatoriana. Teaching, research, administration, testing; aptitude, achievement and personality tests.   M

ENDARA, Prof. Dr. Julio. Casilla 185, Quito. b. 19 June 1899 Quito. MD, Central Univ. of Ecuador. PROF. of NEUROPSYCHIAT, Central Univ. of Ecuador; EDITOR, Archivos de Criminología, Neuropsiquiatría y dsiciplinas conexas. Member: Socy. of Psych. and Neuropsychiat. of Quito, Casa de la Cultura Ecuatoriana. Teaching, research, editorial, psychotherapy, testing; projective tests.   M

JACOME, Dr. Gustavo Alfredo. Fac. de Filosofía, Letras y Ciencias de la Educacíon, Univ. Central, Calle Chile, Quito. b. 12 Oct 1912 Otavalo. Doctor, Univ. Central, Ecuador. UNIV. PROF, Univ. Central; PROFESSOR, Colegio Americano,

Quito; EDITOR, *Revista de Educacion.*
Teaching, educational psychology, professional writing; inferiority complex,
social problems, social psychology.   M
OLMEDO BOADA, Prof. Hector Rodrigo.
Colegio Municipal "Salcedo," Calle Sucre,

Salcedo. b. 15 Jan 1929 Quito. Psychologist '54 Central Univ. of Ecuador.
PROF. of PSYCH, Colegio Municipal "Salcedo." Testing, clinical analysis, teaching,
psychotherapy; intelligence tests, study and
treatment of asocial conduct in children. M

EGYPT

ABDEL-SALAM Ahmed, Dr. Mohamed.
44 Omar Ebn El-Khattab St, Heliopolis,
Cairo.   b. 9 Feb 1909 Cairo. PH.D '51
Columbia Univ, USA.   ASSOC. PROF. of
PSYCH, Inst. of Educ. for Women, Heliopolis Univ, Cairo.   Member: Egyptian
Psych. Assn. Teaching, research, testing;
aptitude tests, achievement tests, learning
theory, mental hygiene.   M
BARAKAT, Dr. Mohamed Khalifa. Ministry
of Educ, El Falaky St, Cairo. b. 21 Apr
1914 Fowa. PH.D '50 Univ. of London, Eng.
DEPUTY DIR, Dept. of Res, Ministry of
Educ;   EDITOR, *Egyptian Educational
Bulletin.*   Member: BPS, APA, Egyptian
Psych. Assn. Research, testing, teaching;
intelligence and achievement testing, educational research, counseling.   M
CHAFAI, Dr. Abou-Madian. 23 Rue Amin
Pacha-Sami, Mounira, Cairo. b. 17 July
1917 Tlemcen, Algeria. PH.D '47 Univ. of
Cairo, Egypt.   PSYCHOTHERAPIST, priv.
prac. Member: Assn. for Psychic Studies.
Psychotherapy, testing, consulting, research; will, effort, psychic energy and
attention.   M
EL-BAHAY, Dr. Fouad.   Inst. of Educ,
Mounira, Cairo. b. 21 Sept 1915 Cairo.
PH.D '51 Univ. of Reading, Eng. SR. LECT.
in PSYCH, Inst. of Educ; RES. ADVIS,
UNESCO; RES. ADVIS, Point IV; RES. ADVIS,
Ministry of Soc. Affairs. Member: BPS,
Egyptian Psych. Assn. Research, testing,
lecturing; factor analysis, attitude measurement, test analysis and construction.   M
EL-KOUSSY, Prof. Abd-El-Aziz.   Inst. of
Educ, Mounira, Cairo. b. 14 Apr 1906
Assuit. PH.D '34 Univ. of London, Eng.
TECH. COUNS, Ministry of Educ, Falaky St,
Cairo;   EDITOR, *Journal of Education.*
Member: BPS, Egyptian Psych. Assn,
Egyptian Assn. for Ment. Hlth. Research,
educational psychology, teaching; test
construction, psychotherapy, factor
analysis.   M
EL-MELIGI, Dr. Abdel Moneim Abdel Aziz.
Fac. of Arts, Ein Shams Univ, Cairo.
b. 2 Nov 1923 Gharbieh. PH.D '54 Inst. of
Psychiat, Univ. of London, Eng. LECT. in
CLIN. PSYCH, Psych. Dept, Ein Shams Univ.
Member: BPS, Egyptian Assn. for Psych.
Res, Egyptian Assn. of Integrative Psych.
Teaching, clinical practice, consulting,

professional writing; projective techniques,
learning theory, social perception.   M
FAHMY, Prof. Mostafa.   Higher Inst. of
Educ, Mounira, Cairo. b. 23 Aug 1909
Cairo. PH.D '49 Univ. of Cambridge, Eng.
PROF. of MENT. HYG, Higher Inst. of Educ;
DIRECTOR, Psych. Clin, Inst. of Educ.
Teaching, psychotherapy, research; psychotherapy,   child   development,   speech
problems.   M
FAHMY, Dr. Sumaya Ahmad. 23 Yehia Pasha
Ibrahim, Zamalek, Cairo. b. 1 Oct 1910
Mansurah. PH.D '53 Univ. of Indiana, USA.
ASSOC. PROF. of PSYCH, Inst. of Educ, Ein
Shams Univ, 27 Ismail Mohamed, Zamalek,
Cairo.   Member: APA, BPS.   Teaching,
clinical practice, research; learning theory,
educational psychology, psychotherapy. F
FAYEK, Ahmed Fouad. 5, Latif Hegazy St,
Manial Rodah, Cairo. b. 8 Aug 1936
Alexandria. MA '56 Ein Shams Univ, Cairo.
PSYCHOLOGIST, Psych. Clin, Ministry of
Educ. Research, testing, consulting; projective techniques, personality theories,
psychotherapy.   M
HAFEZ, Abdelhalim, Dr. Ibrahim.   Inst. of
Educ, Bacos-Ramleh, Alexandria. b. 21
Oct 1916 Alexandria. PH.D '54 Univ. of
London, Eng. SR. LECT. in PSYCH, Inst. of
Educ; CONSULT. PSYCH'T, Alexandria Child
Welf. Cen; CONSULT. PSYCH'T, Alexandria
Soc. Serv. Bur. for Students. Teaching,
testing, consulting, guidance; mental
testing, attitude measurement, delinquency.   M
HAMZA, Dr. Mukhtar. Higher Inst. of Educ.
for Women Teachers, Zamalek, Cairo.
b. 3 Mar 1919 Cairo. PH.D '51 Leeds Univ,
Eng. SR. LECT. in PSYCH, Higher Inst. of
Educ. for Women Tchrs; PSYCHOLOGIST,
Rehab. Cen, Kasr-El Eine, Cairo; Referral
Unit for Secondary Pupils, Dept. of Soc.
Activ, Ministry of Educ, Cairo. Member:
BPS. Teaching, testing, consulting; projective techniques, mental testing, statistical psychology.   M
HANA, Dr. Attia Mahmoud. 9 Saad Zagloul
St, Kasr El Aini, Cairo. b. 22 Apr 1918
Cairo.   PH.D '54 Columbia Univ, USA.
HEAD, Educ. and Psych. Dept, Cairo
Teachers Coll, Abbasia, Cairo. Member:
APA, American Pers. and Guid. Assn,
Egyptian Psych. Assn. Teaching, research,

educational psychology; psychological and
vocational testing, educational and vo-
cational guidance, psychotherapy.　M
IBRAHIM, Dr. Naguib Iskander. Inst. of
Educ, Ein Shams Univ, Kasr El-Einy,
Mounira, Cairo.　b. 2 Aug 1919 Cairo.
PH.D '55 Ohio State Univ, USA. TEACHER,
Dept. of Philosophical and Soc. Foundations
of Educ, Inst. of Educ; ED. STAFF, *Scientific
Committee for Humanistic Studies.* Member:
Egyptian Assn. for Psych. Res. Teaching,
research, professional writing; learning
theory, social perception, methodology and
history of psychology.　M
ISMAIL, Dr. Mohamed E. Inst. of Educ,
Mounira, Cairo. b. 6 Feb 1918 Cairo.
ED.D '54 Columbia Univ, USA. INSTRUCTOR,
Inst. of Educ. Member: APA, Egyptian
Psych. Assn. Teaching, research, edu-
cational psychology; learning theory,
social perception, psychotherapy.　M
MANSOUR, Dr. Roshdy Fam. c/o Maurice
Bishay, 2 Omar El-Seyouty, Boulak, Cairo.
b. 14 Nov 1921 Fayoum. PH.D '55 Univ.
of North Carolina, USA. ASST. PROF,
Higher Inst. of Educ, Shotse, Raml,
Alexandria. Teaching, educational psy-
chology, research; attitude measurement,
group process, educational and psycho-
logical statistics.　M
MOURAD, Prof. Youssef. Rue Fadia,
Medinet al-Awkof, Agouza, Cairo. b. 28
Dec 1902 Cairo. Docteur ès lettres, Sor-
bonne, Fr. PROF. of PSYCH. and CHIEF,
Sect. of Philos. and Sociol, Fac. of Letters,
Univ. of Cairo, Guizeh, Cairo. Member:
AIPA, Egyptian Assn. of Integrative Psych,
Egyptian Assn. for Psych. Res. Teaching,
professional writing, consulting; psycho-
therapy, origins of psychology.　M
MOURST, Dr. Elsayed Mohamed Khairy.
115 Shubra St, Cairo.. b. 14 Jan 1917
Alexandria. PH.D, Univ. of London, Eng.
LECTURER, Fac. of Arts, Ein Shams Univ,
Cairo; CONSULTANT, Dept. of Selection and
Recruitment, Civil Serv. Comm. Member:
BPS. Teaching, applied psychology, re-
search; aptitude testing, vocational se-
lection, factor analysis, statistical psy-
chology.　M
NAGATY, Dr. Mohamed Osman. Fac. of Arts,
Univ. of Cairo, Cairo. b. 31 July 1914
Khartoum, Sudan. PH.D '51 Yale Univ,

USA. ASST. PROF. of PSYCH, Fac. of Arts,
Univ. of Cairo; SUPERV. of TECH. WORK,
Pub. Opinion Admin, Ministry of Guid;
PSYCHOTHERAPIST, priv. prac. Member:
APA, Egyptian Psych. Assn, Egyptian Assn.
of Psychother. Psychotherapy, research,
teaching; attitude measurement, learning
theory.　M
RAGEH, Prof. Ahmed Ezzat. Fac. of Arts,
Alexandria Univ, Alexandria. b. 24 Sept
1908 Damietta. Docteur ès lettres '38
Univ. of Paris, Fr. PROF. of PSYCH,
Alexandria Univ; LECTURER, Higher Inst.
of Educ; LECTURER, Higher Inst. of Nrsng,
Alexandria. Member: Egyptian Psych.
Assn. Teaching, research, testing; problem
children, adolescent counseling, motor
tests.　M
RAMZIA, Dr. El Gareib. Inst. of Educ. for
Women Teachers, 27 Ismail Pasha
Mohamed, Zamalek, Cairo. b. 28 July 1917
Cairo. PH.D '49 Univ. of Edinburgh, Scot.
ASST. PROF. of PSYCH, Inst. of Educ, Ein
Shams Univ. Member: Egyptian Assn.
for Psych. Res. Teaching, research,
testing; learning theory, educational and
vocational guidance, child development. F
SALEH, Dr. A. I. Inst. of Educ, Mounira,
Cairo. b. 10 Jan 1920 Cairo. PH.D '48
Univ. of London, Eng. ASST. PROF. of
PSYCH, Inst. of Educ; PSYCHOLOGIST
Egyptian Armed Forces. Member: BPS,
Egyptian Assn. for Psych. Res. Teaching,
research, applied psychology; educational
and military psychology.　M
TAWADROS, Dr. Samuel Magarius. Ein
Shams Univ, Inst. of Educ, Mounira, Cairo.
b. 7 Feb 1923 Cairo. PH.D '52 Univ. of
London, Eng. SR. LECT. in PSYCH, Ein
Shams Univ; PSYCHOTHERAPIST, Clin. of
Inst. of Educ. Member: BPS. Teaching,
psychotherapy, research; group psycho-
therapy, sociometry, group dynamics.　M
ZIWAR, Prof. Dr. Moustafa. 1 Soliman Racha
St, Cairo. b. 1 Sept 1907 Cairo. MD '41
Univ. of Paris. Fr. CHAIRMAN, Dept. of
Psych. and Soc. Sci; PROF. of ABN. PSYCH,
Fac. of Arts, Ein Shams Univ, 108 Choubra
St, Cairo; EDITOR, *Egyptian Journal of
Psychology*; *Egyptian Journal of Mental
Hygiene.* Teaching, research, psycho-
therapy; psychosomatics, social psy-
chiatry, social process.　M

FINLAND

AHLA, Mervi. Wecksellintie 2 A 3, Helsinki.
b. 29 Oct 1917 Helsinki. Mag. phil. '38
Univ. of Helsinki, Finland. TCHR. of SOC.
CASEWORK, Sairaanhoitaien Jatko-opisto,
Tukholmankatu 10, Helsinki. Member:
SPS. Teaching.　F

AHMAVAARA, Dr. Yrjö Arvi. Koroistentie
15 A 8, Helsinki. b. 7 Aug 1929 Oulu.
PH.D '54 Univ. of Helsinki, Finland.
Member: Psychomet. Socy. (USA). Research, theoretical psychometrics; factor
theory of mind, physiology of the brain,

sociological factor analysis. M
AIRAS, Dr. Erkki. Pohjoisniementie 3, Lauttasaari. b. 24 July 1908 Raahe. Cand. phil. '47 Univ. of Helsinki, Finland. Member: SPS. Research; sources and reactions of guilt, interviewing, projective techniques. M
ALLARDT, Dr. Erik Anders. Unionsgatan 45 B 40, Helsinki. b. 9 Aug. 1925 Helsinki. PH.D '52 Univ. of Helsinki, Finland. ACTING PROF. of SOCIOL, Univ. of Helsinki, Fabianinkatu 33, Helsinki; DIRECTOR, Res. Inst, Helsinki Sch. of Soc. Sci. Member: SPS. Small group research, teaching; social perception, attitude measurement, social psychology. M
BORG, Jaakko Gabriel. Tunturikatu 5 A, Helsinki. b. 29 Aug 1927 Pori. Phil. lic. '53 Univ. of Helsinki, Finland. PSYCHOLOGIST, Lastensuojeluvirasto, Unioninkatu 27, Helsinki. Member: SPS, Suomen Kasvatusneuvolain Liitto. Research, testing, clinical analysis, psychotherapy; projective techniques. M
BRUHN, Prof. Dr. Karl. Åggelby. b. 28 Jan 1894 Kotka. PH.D '21 Univ. of Helsinki, Finland. PROFESSOR, Univ. of Helsinki. Member: SPS. Teaching, administration; projective techniques, child psychology. M
CAVONIUS, Dr. Gösta Edvin. Runebergsgatan 58, Helsinki. b. 14 Apr 1905 Tusby. PH.D '43 Univ. of Helsinki, Finland. ADMIN. DIR, Swedish Sch. in Finland, Skolstyrelsen, Bangatan 2, Helsinki; LECT. in PEDAGOGY and PSYCH, Univ. of Helsinki, Svenska Medborgarhögskolan i Helsinki. Member: SPS. Administration, teaching, research. M
EERIKÄINEN, Ella Maria. Apollonkatu 3 C 19, Helsinki. b. 6 Mar 1906 Sulkava. Mag. phil. '49 Univ. of Helsinki, Finland. CLIN. PSYCH'T, Hosp. Kivelä, Kammionkatu 12-14, Helsinki. Member: SPS. Testing and clinical analysis; principal dimensions of personality, cognitive testing, psychopathology of mental disorders. F
FIEANDT, Prof. Kai von. Elisabetsg. 16 A, Helsinki. b. 24 Aug 1909 Helsinki. PH.D '38 Univ. of Helsinki, Finland. PROF. and HEAD, Inst. of Psych, Univ. of Helsinki, Fabianink. 33, Helsinki. Member: SPS, APA, AIPA. Teaching, research, administration; perception, neurophysiology of brain functions, psychophysiology of the aging. M
GRÖNROOS, Mrs. Pirkko-Liisa. Pitkäniemi. b. 27 Nov 1928 Tampere. Mag. phil. '52 Univ. of Helsinki, Finland. CLIN. PSYCH'T, Pitkäniemi Ment. Hosp, Pitkäniemi. Member: SPS, Suomen Kasvatusneuvolain Liitto. Clinical analysis, guidance, psychotherapy; projective techniques, educational and child psychology. F

HAGMAN, Harriet. Kaptensg. 20, Helsinki, b. 13 Mar 1927 Helsinki. Mag. phil. '54 Univ. of Helsinki, Finland. PSYCHOLOGIST, Lastenlinna, Lastenlinnant 2, Helsinki. Member: SPS, Suomen Kasvatusneuvolain Liitto. Psychotherapy, testing and clinical analysis, teaching; personality in normal and disturbed young children. F
HÄKKINEN, Sauli. Koskelantie 23 A 3, Helsinki. b. 31 Jan 1921 Lappee. Dipl. Engr. '50 Tech. Univ, Finland. ASST. DIR, Psych. Dept, Inst. of Occupat. Hlth, Haartmaninkatu 1, Helsinki. Member: SPS. Research, industrial psychology, testing; traffic accident research, aptitude tests, selection procedure. M
HÄKKINEN, Uuno Ossian. Konnevesi Hytölä. b. 25 June 1916 Rautalampi. Mag. phil. '51 Univ. of Helsinki, Finland. TEACHER, Continued Elem. Sch, Jatkokoulu, Kemijärvi. Member: SPS. Teaching; psychology of sex, animal psychology, learning theory. M
HAVU, Laila Marjatta. Arkadiankatu 35 B 27, Helsinki. b. 12 Feb 1930 Helsinki. Mag. phil. '53 Univ. of Helsinki, Finland. HOSP. PSYCH'T, Lapinlahti Psychiat. Clin, Univ. of Helsinki, Lapinlahden Sairaala, Helsinki. Member: SPS, ICWP, Finnish Socy. for Promotion of Psychoanal. Testing, psychotherapy; projective techniques, psychotherapy, sociometric methods in psychology. F
HEIKKILÄ, Mrs. Aira. Pikonlinna. b. 3 Dec 1922 Utajärvi. Mag. ped. '53 Inst. of Pedagogy, Finland. HEAD PSYCH'T, Child Guid. Clin. Otavalankatu 8 B 15,Tampere. Member: SPS. Testing, psychotherapy consulting; projective techniques, achievement tests, learning theory. F
HEIKKINEN, Dr. Väinö Juhani. Linnank 28 B 24, Turku. b. 12 June 1924 Hyrynsalmi. PH.D '52 Univ. of Turku, Finland. INSTRUCTOR, Inst. of Educ, Univ. of Helsinki, Fabianinkatu 33, Helsinki. Teaching, research, educational psychology; school learning and its correlates. M
HINTIKKA, Heikki Elias. Oulunkyläntie 12, Helsinki. b. 21 May 1923 Helsinki. Mag. phil. '53 Univ. of Helsinki, Finland. CHILD Guid. PSYCH'T, Child Guid. Clin. of Helsinki, II linja 16, Helsinki. Member: SPS, Suomen Kasvatusneuvolain Liitto. Testing, psychotherapy, teaching; projective techniques, social perception, achievement tests. M
HIRVAS, Simo Juhani. Unioninkatu 20 B 6, krs, Helsinki. b. 4 May 1933 Helsinki. Mag. phil. '57 Univ. of Helsinki, Finland. VOCAT. GUID. ASST, Vocat. Guid. Bur. Munic. Empl. Office, Helsinki. Member: SPS. Testing, guidance; projective techniques, psychotherapy. M
IKONEN, Pentti Pekka Juhani. Ryyti-

maantie 1 A 10, Huopalahti. b. 25 Oct 1924
Jääski. Mag. phil. '51 Univ. of Helsinki,
Finland. PSYCHOANALYST, priv. prac.
Member: SPS, Swedish Psychoanal. Socy.
Psychotherapy, research; psychoanalysis,
projective techniques, epistemological
problems in psychology. M
JOHANSSON, Erik Bertil. Ohjaajantie 6 A 6,
Helsinki. b. 31 Jan 1928 Jyväskylä.
Mag. phil. '54 Univ. of Helsinki, Finland.
EDUC. PSYCH'T, Osuuskassojen Keskus-
liitto, Arkadiankatu 23, Helsinki. Member:
SPS. Administration, teaching, testing;
group process, selection methods, occu-
pational analysis. M
KÄÄRIÄINEN, Risto Tapio. Nononpelto.
b. 23 May 1930 Pieksämäki. Mag. phil. '55
Univ. of Helsinki, Finland. INST. PSYCH'T,
Innermission Socy. of Finnish Church,
Inst. for Ment. Defective Child. Member:
SPS. Testing and clinical analysis, guidance,
psychotherapy; factor analysis, clinical
testing and education of the mentally
defective. M
KAILA, Mrs. Helmi Lea. Kellokoski, Sairaala.
b. 1 May 1925 Karttula. Mag. phil, Univ.
of Helsinki, Finland. HOSP. PSYCH'T,
Kellokoski Hosp. Member: SPS. Clinical
testing, psychotherapy, teaching; projective techniques, achievement tests,
attitude measurement. F
KAMU, Sirkka Tuulikki. Koskelantie 40 A 2,
Helsinki-Käpylä. b. 5 Nov 1916 Helsinki.
MA '53 Univ. of Minnesota, USA. SOC.
PSYCH'T, Vocat. Guid. Bur. Munic. Empl.
Office, Helsinki. Member: SPS. Guidance,
educational and industrial psychology,
testing and clinical analysis; vocational
testing, counseling and interviewing. F
KARSTEN, Miss Anitra L. C. Kaserngatan
14 A, Helsinki. b. 12 Dec 1902 Åbo. PH.D
'28 Univ. of Giessen, Ger. ASST. PROF,
Swed. Sch. of Econ, Arkadiangatan 22,
Helsinki, ASSISTANT, Univ. of Helsinki;
LECT. in SOC. PSYCH, Soc. Inst, Helsinki;
ED. in CHIEF, Geron. Member: SPS, APA,
AIPA, ICWP. Research, teaching, editorial;
mental fatigue, social psychology, gerontology, prejudice. F
KASURINEN, Miss Martta. Järvenpää.
b. 14 July 1904 Kuopio. Mag. phil, Univ.
of Helsinki, Finland. LECT. in PEDAGOGY,
Tchrs. Coll. of Home Econ, Järvenpää.
Member: SPS. Educational psychology,
teaching, library; sociometry, family edu-
cation, teaching methods. F
KERAVUORI, Raili Elisabet. Puutarhakatu
7 b B 13, Turku. b. 19 Sept 1927 Heinola.
Mag. phil. '49 Univ. of Turku, Finland.
ASST. PSYCH'T, Child Psych. Clin, Sairas-
huoneeenkatu 6-8, Turku. Member: SPS,
Suomen Kasvatusneuvolain Liitto. Testing
psychotherapy, teaching; projective tech-

niques. F
KIURU, Veikko. Näätätie 18 A, Helsinki.
b. 4 Oct 1926 Vuoksenranta. Mag. phil. '53
Univ. of Helsinki, Finland. SUPERV. of
VOCAT. GUID, Ministry of Communic. and
Pub. Works, Vocat. Guid. Bur, Manner-
heimintie 9 A, Helsinki; MILIT. PSYCH'T,
Hq. of the Finnish Def. Forces. Member:
SPS, Finnish Socy. of Milit. Psych. Ad-
ministration, educational psychology,
teaching; curriculum planning, socio-
metric measurement. M
KOSKENNIEMI, Prof. Matti. Runebergink.
56 B 20, Helsinki-Töölö. b. 19 Dec 1908
Iida, Japan. PH.D '36 Univ. of Helsinki,
Finland. PROF. of EDUC, Dept. of Educ,
Univ. of Helsinki, Fabianink. 33, Helsinki.
Member: SPS. Educational psychology,
teaching, research; social psychology of
school life. M
LAHTINEN, Miss Pirkko Maija-Leena.
Hyrylä. b. 20 Jan 1930 Tampere. Mag.
phil. '53 Univ. of Helsinki, Finland.
PSYCHOLOGIST, Child Guid. Clin., Hyrylä.
Member: SPS, Suomen Kasvatusneuvolain
Liitto, Finnish Socy. for Promotion of
Psychoanal. Clinical analysis, psycho-
therapy, guidance; projective techniques,
psychotherapeutic procedure, social per-
ception. F
LAPPALAINEN, Mrs. Ann Sigrid Aline.
Honkatie 4 A 4, Helsinki. b. 6 Dec 1931
Helsinki. Mag. phil. '54 Univ. of Helsinki,
Finland. CHILD GUID. PSYCH'T, Child
Guid. Clin. of Helsinki, II linja 14, Helsinki.
Member: SPS, Suomen Kasvatusneuvolain
Liitto. Testing, child psychotherapy; pro-
jective techniques, achievement tests. F
LAPPALAINEN, Mailis. Oulunkyläntie 19,
Helsinki. b. 7 May 1928 Helsinki. Mag.
phil. '54 Univ. of Helsinki, Finland.
SPEECH THER. and TCHR, Finnish Inst. of
Speech, Topeliuksenkatu 15, Helsinki.
Member: SPS. Consulting and clinical
practice, professional writing, teaching;
psychology of speech and language. F
LEHTI, Yrjö A. Harakka, Lepinkäisentie 4.
b. 8 June 1921 Eura. Phil. lic. '55 Univ. of
Helsinki, Finland. PSYCHOLOGIST, Inst. of
Occupat. Hlth. Member: SPS. Industrial
psychology, testing; graphology. M
LEHTONEN, Risto Rauno. Majavatie 10 A 9,
Helsinki-Herttoniemi. b. 8 Apr 1923
P-Pirkkala. Mag. phil. '55 Univ. of
Helsinki, Finland. Clin. PSYCH'T, Inst. of
Brain Injury, Mäntytie 8, Helsinki.
Member: SPS. Testing, research, student;
neuropsychology, perceptual processes,
projective techniques. M
LEHTOVAARA, Prof. Dr. Arvo Johannes.
Maneesikatu 2 a C 47, Helsinki. b. 29 Dec
1905. PH.D, Univ. of Helsinki, Finland.
PROF. of PSYCH, Univ. of Helsinki, Fabian-

inkatu 33, Helsinki; ACTING PROF. of PSYCH, Univ. of Turku. Member: SPS, APA, Suomen Kasvatusneuvolain Liitto. Teaching, research, educational psychology; developmental and genetic psychology. M

LEPPO, Dr. Kaisa H. E. Pihlajatie 23, Helsinki. b. 22 June 1911 Vikti. MD '45 Univ. of Helsinki, Finland. PSYCHIATRIST, Dist. Ment. Clin, Sülinjärvi. Member: SPS, WFMH, AIPA, Finnish Socy. of Neuropsychiat. Psychotherapy, clinical practice, research, translation of foreign professional works; child psychiatry. F

LUOMA, Matti Albert. Kavallintie 4, Kauniainen. b. 10 July 1925 Tampere. Mag. phil. '50 Turun Yliopisto, Finland. VOCAT. GUID. INSPECTOR, Vocat. Guid. Bur, Ministry of Labor, Mannerheimintie 9 A, Helsinki. Member: SPS. Industrial psychology, editorial, research; job analysis, personnel selection, vocational guidance. M

LYYTIKÄINEN, Mrs. Kyllikki. Pajalahdentie 27 A 11, Helsinki. b. 1 Sept 1930 Vaasa. Mag. ped. '52 Inst. of Pedagogics Jyväskylä, Finland. CHILD PSYCHOTHERAPIST, Lapinlahti Hosp, Helsinki; Child Guid. Clin. of Helsinki. Member: SPS, Suomen Kasvatusneuvolain Liitto. Psychotherapy, testing, guidance; projective techniques. F

MÄKELÄ, Jouko Vihtori. The Invalid Foundation, Tenholantie 10, Helsinki-Töölö. b. 26 Mar 1930 Vaasa. Mag. phil. '55 Univ. of Helsinki, Finland. PSYCHOLOGIST, The Invalid Foundation. Member: SPS. Testing, research, consulting, guidance; differential testing of abilities, psychology of the physically handicapped, factor analysis. M

MANTILA, Miss Liisa Maria. Kulmavuorenkatu 6 A 7, Helsinki. b. 22 Oct 1921 Helsinki. Mag. phil. '48 Univ. of Helsinki, Finland. PSYCHOLOGIST, Child Guid. Clin. of Helsinki, II Linja 16, Helsinki. Member: SPS. Testing, psychotherapy, administration; projective techniques, child psychotherapy. F

MÄNTYOJA, Helka. Oksasenk 4 b B 21, Helsinki. b. 31 Oct 1909 Oulu. Mag. phil. '53 Univ. of Helsinki, Finland. PSYCHOLOGIST, Bur. of Child Welf, Psychiat. Off, Unionink. 27 B, Helsinki. Member: SPS. Testing and clinical analysis, consulting, guidance; projective techniques, social perception. F

MARKKANEN, Touko Aatos. Vuorimiehenkatu 33 B 51, Helsinki. b. 1 May 1922 Helsinki. RES. SECY, Finnish Found. for Alcohol Studies, Itämerenkatu 51, Helsinki; PSYCH. TCHR, State Police Sch. Research, teaching, administration; factor analysis in sociological studies and personality studies, alcoholism. M

MATIKAINEN, Rauno Heikki. Teollisuuden Työnjohto-opisto, Pohjoiskaari 34, Lauttasaari, Helsinki. b. 21 Mar 1929 Tampere. Mag. phil. '54 Univ. of Helsinki, Finland. PSYCHOLOGIST, Inst. of Indus. Superv. Member: SPS. Testing, teaching, industrial psychology; analysis of leadership qualities through psychological testing. M

MERI, Miss Sirkka-Liisa. Museokatu 9 B 20, Helsinki. b. 16 Dec 1918 Helsinki. Phil. lic. '55 Helsingin Yliopisto, Finland. LIB. and CHIEF, Hosp. Libraries in Helsinki, Pub. Lib. of Helsinki, Rikhardinkatu 3, Helsinki. Member: SPS. Library, research teaching; bibliotherapy, adult education, psychology of alcoholism. F

MERILUOTO, Sirkka L. K. Jääkärink. 15 A 8, Helsinki. b. 8 Nov 1920 Pieksämäki. Mag. phil. '55 Univ. of Helsinki, Finland. ASSISTANT, Ministry of Communic. and Pub. Works, Bur. of Vocat. Guid, Mannerheimintie 9 A, Helsinki. Member: SPS. Statistical research, testing, industrial psychology; projective techniques, achievement tests. F

MIELONEN, Erkki Olavi. Pohjoiskaari 34, Lauttasaari, Helsinki. b. 25 Feb 1920 Kuopio. Mag. phil. '46 Univ. of Helsinki, Finland. VICE RECTOR, Inst. of Indus. Superv. Member: SPS. Teaching, educational and industrial psychology, consulting. M

MIETTINEN, Allan. Roihuvuorentie 18 C 149, Herttoniemi. b. 5 Dec 1919 Kuopio. Mag. ped. '50 Inst. of Pedagogy, Finland. SUPERV. of VOCAT. GUID, Ministry of Communic. and Pub. Works, Mannerheimintie 9 A III, Helsinki. Member: SPS. Research, administration, industrial psychologie; projective techniques, achievement tests, factor analysis. M

MULTIMÄKI, Kaarlo Valio. Sammonk. 6 B 35, Helsinki. b. 23 Apr 1923 Kivijärvi. Mag. ped, Inst. of Pedagogy, Finland. PSYCHOLOGIST, Inst. of Occupat. Guid, Unionink. 20 B, Helsinki. Member: SPS. Testing, guidance, teaching; psychological theory of occupational choice, projective techniques. M

NOUSIAINEN, Tapio. Pihlajatie 39, Helsinki. b. 28 May 1922 Pielavesi. Mag. phil. '48 Univ. of Helsinki, Finland. PSYCHOANALYST, priv. prac. Member: SPS, Swedish Psychoanal. Socy. Psychoanalytic practice; projective techniques, psychology of arts. M

NUMMENMAA, Tapio. Jyväskylän Kasvatusopillinen Korkeakoulu, Jyväskylä. b. 9 Nov 1931 Helsinki. Mag. phil. '56 Univ. of Helsinki, Finland. ASSISTANT, Inst. of Pedagogy, Dept. of Psych, Jyväskylä. Educational psychology, research, teaching; achievement tests, mental test theory, attitude measurement. M

OKSALA, Prof. Ohto Antero Kaarle. Apollonkatu 4 A 3, Helsinki. b. 5 Oct 1905 Jyvaskyla. Mag. Phil. '31 Univ. of Helsinki, Finland. PROFESSOR, Technological Univ, Abrahaminkatu 1-5, Helsinki; CHIEF of PSYCH. DEPT, Inst. of Occupat. Health, Helsinki. Member: SPS, APA. Teaching, industrial and personnel psychology, research; field theory, psychology of work, job evaluation. M

OSANEN, Mrs. Helvi Kaarina. Vapaudentie 15 C 75, Lahti. b. 25 Oct 1928 Suojärvi. Mag. phil. '53 Univ. of Helsinki, Finland. PSYCHOLOGIST, Child Guid. Clin, Välikatu 4, Lahti. Clinical analysis, psychotherapy; child psychology. F

PALMEN, Miss Anne Marie. Högbergsgatan 1 B, Helsinki. b. 1 Feb 1925 Helsinki. Mag. phil. '53 Univ. of Helsinki, Finland. VOCAT. COUNS, Vocat. Guid Bur. Munic. Empl. Office, Helsinki. Member: SPS, Nordiskt Yrkesvägledarförbund. Testing, educational and industrial psychology, guidance; test analysis, psychological statistics. F

PALOHEIMO, Mrs. Anna Sinikka. Haartmanink. 1, Helsinki. b. 18 May 1919 Jaakkima. Mag. phil. '54 Univ. of Helsinki, Finland. PSYCHOLOGIST, Työterveyslaitos. Member: SPS. Educational psychology, testing, research; psychology of music, aptitude tests, learning theory. F

PALOMÄKI, Erkki Kalervo. Sofianlehdonkatu 7 F 53, Käpylä. b. 16 May 1917 Rauma. Mag. phil. '42 Univ. of Helsinki, Finland. TEACHER, Business and Adv. Sch, Messuhalli, Helsinki-Töölö; MANAGER, Psych. Consult. Co, Valintakoe Oy, Helsinki. Member: SPS. Industrial psychology, testing, teaching. M

PENNANEN, Jyrki Heikki Ylermi. Lyseokatu 4 A 13, Tempere. b. 13 Feb 1933 Pori. Mag. phil. '53 Univ. of Helsinki, Finland. PSYCHOLOGIST, Educ. Guid. Off. of Tampere, Otavalankatu 8 B 15, Tampere. Member: SPS, Suomen Kasvatusneuvolain Liitto. Testing, educational psychology, psychotherapy; graphology, Rorschach. M

PENTTI, Lauri Johannes. Aurorankatu 13 B 24, Helsinki. b. 4 Apr 1931 Helsinki. Mag. phil. '56 Univ. of Helsinki, Finland. MILIT. PSYCH'T, Finnish Army Hq, Dept. of Trng, Punanothonkatu 4 F, Helsinki; VOLUNTEER ASST, Psych. Inst, Univ. of Helsinki. Member: SPS, Suomen Sotilaspsykologinen Seura. Research, personnel psychology, military psychology; psychology of perception, testing and measurement apparatus, aviation psychology. M

PIIROINEN, Esteri. Porrassalmenkatu 8, Mikkeli. b. 25 Oct 1930 Liperi. Mag. phil. '53 Univ. of Helsinki, Finland. CHILD PSYCH'T, Child Guid. Clin. Member: SPS.

Testing, educational psychology, teaching, consulting; psychometric and projective techniques, vocational aptitude measurement. F

PIISINEN, Irja. Munkkiniemen Puistotie 7 as 7, Helsinki. b. 23 Feb 1913 Kuopio. Mag. phil. '49 Univ. of Helsinki, Finland. PSYCHOLOGIST, Kindergarten Tchrs. Coll, Helsinginkatu 3-5, Helsinki. Member: SPS. Teaching, testing, guidance; projective techniques, performance tests, interview, ability tests for pedagogical professions. F

POIKONEN, Pirkko. Pietari Hannikaisentie 2 R 89, Pohj-Haaga. b. 27 Aug 1927 Helsinki. Mag. phil. '51 Univ. of Helsinki, Finland. SCH. PSYCH'T, Helsingin Kaupungin Kansakoulujen Kasvatuaneuvola, I linja 5, Helsinki. Member: SPS, Suomen Kasvatusneuvolain Liitto. Teaching, consulting and guidance of school children. F

RAINIO, Dr. Kullervo. Rauhankatu 9 B 37, Helsinki. b. 10 Aug 1924 Jyväskylä. PH.D '55 Univ. of Helsinki, Finland. RES. PSYCH'T, and TCHR, Inst. of Indus. Superv, Pohjoiskaari 34, Lauttasaari, Helsinki. Member: SPS, AIPA. Research, testing, teaching; theory of leadership, group dynamics, factor analysis, general theory of force concept in psychology. M

RAIVIO, Yrjö Albert. Riihimäki VR. b. 8 May 1915 Virrat. Phil. lic. '52 Univ. of Helsinki, Finland. CHAPLAIN, Army of Finland; CHAPLAIN, Finnish State Prison. Member: SPS. Research, testing, guidance, teaching; projective techniques, intelligence measurement, psychology of sex. M

RAUHALA, Lauri Matias. Psych. Dept, Inst. of Occupat. Hlth, Helsinki. b. 13 Sept 1914 Sievi. Phil. lic. '53 Univ. of Helsinki, Finland. SR. PSYCH'T, Clin. Sect, Psych. Dept, Inst. of Occupat. Hlth; SUMMER LECT, Univ. of Helsinki. Member: SPS, Finnish Neuropsychiat. Assn. Clinical analysis, testing, research, teaching; family behavior, rehabilitation of institutionalized mental patients, mental health. M

ROSSI-JÄÄSKELÄINEN, Mrs. Kerttu. Meritullink. 14 A 1, Helsinki. b. 19 Aug 1910 Terijoki. Mag. phil. '37 Univ. of Helsinki, Finland. PSYCHOTHERAPIST, priv. prac. Member: SPS, Finnish Socy. for Promotion of Psychoanal. Child psychotherapy, professional writing, research; therapeutic methods, psychoanalysis, psychodrama and catharsis. F

ROUTIO, Mrs. Liisa Marjatta. Roihuvuorentie 9 B, Helsinki-Herttoniemi. b. 12 Apr 1927 Viipuri. Mag. phil. '55 Univ. of Helsinki, Finland. ASST. PSYCH'T, Vocat. Guid. Bur. Munic. Empl. Office Helsinki, Unioninkatu 20 B, Helsinki. Member: SPS. Vocational guidance, testing, applied and educational psychology; interviewing methods, test construction, achievement tests. F

SAARI, Dr. Erkki. Leppävesi. b. 7 July 1916 Tampere. PH.D '51 Univ. of Helsinki, Finland. DIRECTOR, Receiving Cen. for Maladjusted Boys, Järvilinnan Vastaanottokoti, Leppävesi. Member: SPS, Suomen Kasvatusneuvolain Liitto. Guidance, administration, criminological research; diagnostic methods in research on juvenile delinquency. M

SAARINEN, Miss Pirkko Annikki. Koskelantie 28 C 12, Helsinki. b. 12 Mar 1924 Vilppula. Phil. lic. '56 Univ. of Turku, Finland. PSYCH. ASST, Sch. of Soc. Sci, Franzenik. 13, Helsinki; TEACHER, Coll. of Nrsng, Helsinki. Member: SPS. Teaching, research, administration; child psychology, developmental studies. F

SAARINEN, Mrs. Raija Ainamo. Meritullinkatu 4 B, Helsinki. b. 31 Jan 1930 Hämeenlinna. Mag. phil. '55 Univ. of Helsinki, Finland. Member: SPS. Research, editing a psychological dictionary. F

SALONEN, Mirja Astrid. Hevostorinkatu 7, Savonlinna. b. 18 Mar 1925 Savonlinna. SECRETARY, Kirjeopisto Via. Member: SPS. Teaching, research, educational psychology; psychology of thinking, mental hygiene. F

SAMOOJA, Martti Veikko Tapio. Ainonkatu 4 C 45, Helsinki. b. 7 June 1926 Turku. Mag. phil, Univ. of Turku, Finland. CHIEF, Vocat. Guid. Bur, Munic. Employment Off. of Helsinki, Unioninkatu 20 B, Helsinki; PSYCHOLOGIST, priv. prac. Member: SPS. Consulting and guidance, testing, teaching; interviewing methods, projective techniques, test construction, psychotherapy. M

SCHALIN, Lars-Johan. Lotsg. 16, Helsinki. b. 21 Mar 1931 Helsinki. Mag. phil. '54 Univ. of Helsinki, Finland. ASST. in VOCAT. GUID, Vocat. Guid. Bur. Munic. Empl. Office, Helsinki. Member: SPS, Finnish Socy. for Promotion of Psychoanal. Guidance, testing, psychotherapy; vocational guidance. M

SIRO, Eljas. Männikkötie 5 G 39, Helsinki. b. 4 May 1917 Helsinki. Mag. phil. '53 Univ. of Helsinki, Finland. PSYCH. ASST, Univ. of Helsinki, Fabianinkatu 33, Helsinki. Member: SPS. Teaching, administration, research; projective techniques, intelligence measurement, typology. M

SVEDLIN, Miss Christel. Rönnvägen 40 A 32, Helsinki. b. 17 Sept 1926 Helsinki. Mag. phil. '51 Univ. of Helsinki, Finland. CHILD PSYCH'T, Aurora Hosp, Helsinki. Member: SPS, Finnish Socy. for Promotion of Psychoanal. Psychotherapy, clinical analysis, research; projective techniques. F

SYSIHARJU, Mrs. Anna-Liisa. Pohjaiskaari 14 A 14, Helsinki- Lauttassari. b. 7 June 1919 Kajaani. Phil. lic. '56 Univ. of Helsinki, Finland. LECT. in PSYCH. and PEDAGOGY, Coll. of Home Econ. Tchrs, Sturenkatu 2 b, Helsinki. Member: SPS, APA. Teaching, research; social roles, attitude research, personality tests for teachers. F

TAKALA, Dr. Annika Maria. Vapaudenkatu 33, Jyväskylä. b. 3 Oct 1921 Sortavala. PH.D. '53 Univ. of Helsinki, Finland. ASST. in PSYCH, Dept. of Psych, Inst. of Pedagogy, Jyväskylä. Member: SPS. Teaching, research; relations between parents' attitudes and child development, frustration tolerance, child diagnostic techniques. F

TAKALA, Kalevi. Tuhkimotie 10-14 b, J 112, Helsinki. b. 30 Dec 1925 Jyväskylä. ASST. PSYCH'T. Vocat. Guid. Bur. Munic. Empl. Office, Helsinki. Member: SPS. Student, testing and clinical analysis, guidance; projective techniques, psychoanalysis, psychology of art. M

TAKALA, Mrs. Lea Mirjam. Tuhkimotie 10-14b, J 112, Helsinki. b. 20 Feb 1918 Valkeala. Mag. phil. '49 Univ. of Turku, Finland. PUB. SCH. TCHR, H:gin Kaupungin Kansakoulut, Helsinki. Member: SPS. Educational psychology, testing, guidance; child psychology, projective techniques. F

TAKALA, Prof. Martti Ilmari. Vapaudenkatu 33, Jyväskylä. b. 20 Dec 1924 Helsinki. PH.D '51 Univ. of Helsinki, Finland. PROF. of PSYCH, Dept. of Psych, Inst. of Pedagogy, Jyväskylä. Member: SPS, APA. Research, teaching; motor expressions and personality, objective personality tests, relations between perception and motor reactions. M

TAMMINEN, Antti J. Koroistentie 6 B C, Helsinki-T. b. 1 Sept 1917 Ikaalinen. Mag. phil. '44 Univ. of Helsinki, Finland. VOCAT. COUNS, Inst. of Occupat. Hlth, Haartmaninkatu 1, Helsinki; LECTURER, Sch. of Soc. Sci, Helsinki. Member: SPS. Guidance, applied and industrial psychology, teaching; achievement tests, projective techniques, problems of disability and rehabilitation. M

TAMMINEN, Kerttu Maria. Paasikivenkatu 16 A 27, Lahti. b. 6 Apr 1913 Helsinki. Mag. ped. '48 Inst. of Pedagogy, Finland. CHIEF. PSYCH'T, Child Guid. Clin, Välikatu 4, Lahti. Clinical analysis, child guidance, administration. F

TANNER, Timo Unto. Betaniank. 10 A 2 Turku. b. 8 Feb 1926 Helsinki. Mag. phil. '53 Univ. of Helsinki, Finland. CHIEF of TRNG, Sampo Insurance Co, Yliopistonkatu 27, Turku. Member: SPS. Personnel psychology, teaching, research; projective techniques, learning theory, selection of insurance agents. M

TENNY, Mrs. Marja Wallasvaara. Palisades, New York, USA. b. 26 Dec 1921 Turku, Finland. MA '53 Univ. of Helsinki, Finland. SCH. PSYCH'T, Vocat. Educ. and Ext. Bd. of Rockland County, New City, New York, USA. Member: SPS. Testing, educational psychology, guidance; projective techniques, perception, psychology of color, psycholinguistics. F

TOIVAINEN, Yrjö Johannes. Hämeentie 42 A 9, Helsinki. b. 23 Apr 1928 Säynätsalo. Mag. phil. '55 Univ. of Helsinki, Finland. MANAGER,Educ. Div, Ossuutukkukauppa, Hämeentie 19, Helsinki. Member: SPS. Applied and industrial psychology, research, teaching, administration; aptitude and attitude measurement, merit rating procedures. M

TONI, Pirkko Liisa. Koroistentie 9 A 1, Helsinki. b. 4 Mar 1927 Teisko. Mag. phil. '52 Univ. of Helsinki, Finland. CHILD PSYCH'T, Aurora Hosp, Helsinki. Member: SPS, Suomen Kasvatusneuvolain Liitto, Finnish Socy. for Promotion of Psychoanal. Testing, psychotherapy, consulting, teaching; projective techniques, play therapy, casework. F

TROIL, Ulla Maria von. Norra Hesperiagatan 5, Helsinki. b. 12 Oct 1930 Helsinki. Mag. phil. '54 Univ. of Helsinki, Finland. CHILD PSYCHOTHERAPIST, priv. prac; TCHR. of CHILD PSYCH, Nurses' Sch, Helsinki. Member: SPS, Finnish Socy. for Promotion of Psychoanal. Psychotherapy, clinical analysis, teaching; child psychotherapy, personality, children's drawings. F

TUOMPO, Prof. Aarre Aatos. Rauhankatu 11 A 17, Helsinki. b. 11 May 1908 Jaakkima. PH.D '42 Univ. of Turku, Finland. PROF. of PSYCH. High Sch. of Soc. Sc., DOCENT of PSYCH, Univ. of Helsinki, Fabianinkatu 33, Helsinki; DOCENT, Univ. of Turku. Member: SPS, APA, AIPA, Int. Rorschach Socy. Teaching, research, testing; projective techniques, psychodiagnostics, personnel psychology. M

VEPSÄLÄINEN, Martti Antero. Käpyläntie 4 E 51, Käpylä. b. 11 Feb 1923 Kemi. MILIT. PSYCH'T, Finnish Army Hq, Dept. of Trng, Punanotkonkatu 4 F, Helsinki. Member: SPS, Suomen Sotilaspsykologinen Seura. Military psychology, research, student; perception, achievement tests, leadership. M

VIRKKI, Irma Kyllikki. Gyldenintie 3 B 24, Helsinki. b. 14 Aug 1918 Sakkola. Mag. phil. '55 Univ. of Helsinki, Finland. CLIN. PSYCH'T, Lapinlahti Hosp, Helsinki;CHILD PSYCH'T, Kivelä Hosp, Helsinki; CHILD PSYCH'T, Child Guid. Clin. of Helsinki. Member: SPS, Suomen Kasvatusneuvolain Liitto. Clinical testing, psychotherapy, guidance; intelligence testing, projective

techniques, child therapy. F

VIRTA, Impi. Child Guid. Clin, Uppsalatalo, Hämeenlinna. b. 21 July 1907 Turku. Mag. phil. '46 Univ. of Turku, Finland. PSYCHOLOGIST, Child Guid. Clin. Member: SPS, Suomen Kasvastusneuvolain Liitto. Testing, applied psychology, psychotherapy; projective techniques, group process. F

VUORINEN, Voitto. Savilinnantie 1 C 28, Tampere. b. 16 Jan 1919 Turku. Mag. phil. '45 Univ. of Turku, Finland. VOCAT. GUID. PRIN, Ammatinvalinnan Ohjaus, Kouluk. 8, Tempere. Member: SPS. Vocational guidance; achievement tests, attitude measurement, projective techniques. M

WECKROTH, Johan Elias. Aino Ackténtie 3 F 55, Pohj. Haaga, Helsinki. b. 29 Dec 1924 Helsinki. Mag. phil. '54 Univ. of Helsinki, Finland. PSYCHOLOGIST, Inst. of Occupat. Hlth, Haartmaninkatu 1, Helsinki; PSYCH. LECT, Prison Div, Ministry of Justice. Applied and industrial psychology, research, teaching; objective characterogical tests, small group studies and rating methods. M

WEGELIUS, Miss Eva Bergliot Anita. Storsvängen 13, Drumsö, Helsinki. b. 11 July 1917 Hattula. Mag. phil. '52 Univ. of Helsinki, Finland. PSYCHOLOGIST, Child Guid. Clin, Samfundet Folkhälsan, Tavaststjernagatan 7, Helsinki. Member: SPS, Suomen Kasvatusneuvolain Liitto, Finnish Socy. for Promotion of Psychoanal. Testing, teaching, clinical practice; intelligence tests, projective techniques, training nurses. F

WICKSTRÖM, Mrs. Kristina. Kommunala Sjukhuset, Turku. b. 20 Nov 1915 Helsinki. Mag. phil. '38 Univ. of Helsinki, Finland. PSYCHOLOGIST, Child Guid. Clin, Föreningen Folkhälsan i Åboland, Kaskisg 13, Turku. Member: SPS. Testing, guidance, teaching; intelligence tests, child psychology, school failure as a psychological and social problem. F

WIHERHEIMO, Dr. Onni. Mellunkylä, Bredbacka. b. 19 Apr 1904 Helsinki. PH.D '50 Univ. of Helsinki, Finland. AUDITOR and COMPTROLLER of INDUS. WORKS and TRAFFIC, City of Helsinki, Unionink. 20, Helsinki. Member: SPS. Administration, industrial psychology; social psychological and group dynamic problems of industrial units. M

WRIGHT, Dr. Johan Magnus von. Rievägen 17A, Munksnäs, Helsinki. b. 31 Mar 1924 Helsinki. Dr. Phil. '55 Oxford Univ, Eng. SR. ASST. in PSYCH, Univ. of Helsinki, Fabiansgatan 33, Helsinki; FINNISH ED, *Nordisk Psykologi*, *Acta Psychologica*. Member: SPS. (Chairman). Research, teaching, administration; human learning and remembering, perception. M

FRANCE

ABADIE, René Jean. Cen. d'Orientation, Cité Blanqui, Limoges. b. 30 Oct 1927 Algiers, Algeria. Diplôme d'état '53 Univ. of Paris, Fr. GUID. COUNS, Cen. d'Orientation. Consulting and guidance; characterology, morphopsychology, family relations. M

ABRAHAM, Louis. Inspection de l'Orientation Professionnelle, 25 Pl. de la Madeleine, Paris 8. b. 29 July 1914 Pleubian. VOCAT. GUID. INSPECTOR, Inspection de l'Orientation Professionnelle. Member: AIOP, ACOF, Fr. Assn. for the Devel. of Educ. Methods. Vocational guidance, administration; memory and learning, achievement tests, educational psychology.M

AJURIAGUERRA, Dr. Julian de. 150 Rue de Rennes, Paris 6. b. 7 Jan 1911 Bilbao, Spain. MD, Univ. of Paris, Fr. RES. WRKR, Henri-Rouselle Hosp, 1 Rue Cabanis, Paris; EDITOR, L'encéphale. Member: SFP. Research, clinical practice, editorial; genetic psycholpathology. M

ALBOU, Paul. 25 Ave. de Laumière, Paris 19. b. 13 Feb 1926 Paris. Diplôme d'études supérieures '54 Sorbonne, Fr. TECH. ADVIS. and ADMIN, Instituts de Recherches en Sciences Humaines, Ministère des Affaires Economiques, 41 Quai Branly, Paris. Member: Fr. Assn. of Soc. Psych. Administration, research; inter-ethnic contacts, acculturation, professional training. M

AMADO LEVY-VALENSI, Prof. Elaine. 42 Ave. Herbillon, St. Mandé. b. 11 May 1919 Marseille. Agrégation '50 Univ. of Paris, Fr. RES. WRKR, Natl. Cen. for Sci. Res. (CNRS), 13 Quai Anatole France, Paris; PSYCHOTHERAPIST, Centre de l'Elan Retrouvé. Member: Fr. Psychoanal. Socy. Research, psychotherapy, educational psychology; inter-subjective rapport in psychoanalysis, intercommunication, adolescent student behavior. F

AMOYEL, Mrs. Geneviève. 68 Rue Stanislas, Nancy. b. 3 Sept 1928 Toulouse. Diplôme '53 Univ. of Paris, Fr. VOCAT. GUID. COUNS, Cen. Public d'Orientation Professionnelle, 16 Rue de Glacis, Nancy. Member: ACOF, Rorschach Study Grp. of Nancy. Guidance, testing, applied psychology; aptitude and achievement tests, projective techniques. F

ANDREETI, Paul. 80 Rue Breteuil, Marseille. b. 15 Mar 1905 Banon. Conseiller '47 Inst. de Biométrie Humaine et Orientation Professionnelle, Fr. GUID. COUNS, Cen. Public d'Orientation Professionnelle, 11 Rue Mission de France, Marseille. Member: ACOF. Testing, vocational and educational guidance; memory and learning, achievement, personality, intelligence tests. M

ANDREY, Bernard Michel. Ecole de Garçons, 11 Cours Jean Jaurès, Grenoble. b. 22 Aug 1919 Chalindrey. Licence '50 Univ. of Paris, Fr. DIRECTOR, Service de Psychologie-Scolaire de l'Isère, Ecole de Garçons. Member: SNPPD. Educational psychology, testing and guidance of retarded students, student orientation; tests of intelligence, memory and learning.M

ANDRIEUX, Miss Cécile. 14 Rue des Ecoles, Paris 5. b. 19 July 1919 Paris. Diplôme d'études supérieures '49 Sorbonne, Fr. RES. ASST, Natl. Cen. for Sci. Res. (CNRS), 13 Quai Anatole France, Paris 7; BOOK REVIEWER, l'Année Psychologique (personality section). Member: SFP, APSLF, Groupement Français du Rorschach. Research; differential psychology of the sexes, attitude measurement, spatial perception. F

ANSELME, Miss Michèle Marie Pauline. 25 Ave. de Marinville, St. Maur. b. 17 May 1931 Paris. Licence '53 Univ. of Paris, Fr. TECH. AIDE, Natl. Cen. for Sci. Res. (CNRS) Cen. for Sociol. Studies, 54 Rue de Varenne, Paris 7. Research, clinical analysis, student; emotional psychopathology, personality measurement. F

ANTHONY, Miss Geneviève. Inspection de l'Orientation Professionnelle, 2 Rue Paul Cabet, Dijon. b. 3 July 1927 Urcerey. Licence '54 Fac. of Letters, Univ. of Dijon, Fr. VOCAT. GUID. COUNS, Inspection de l'Orientation Professionnelle. Member: ACOF, AIOP. Guidance, testing, personnel psychology; achievement and aptitude testing. F

ANZIEU, Prof. Didier. 7 bis Rue Laromiguière, Paris 5. b. 8 July 1923 Melun. Agrégation '48 Univ. of Paris, Fr. HEAD, Dept. of Psych, Fac. of Letters, Inst. of Psych, 1 Rue Goethe, Strasbourg; ED. in CHIEF, Bulletin du Groupement français du Rorschach. Member: SFP, SNPPD, Natl. Assn. of Psychoanal. Psych'ts. Teaching, psychotherapy, consulting, guidance; projective techniques, psychodrama and roleplaying, psychoanalysis and group psychotherapy. M

APELLANIZ-OGER, René. 21 Rue Jean Jaurès, L'Hay-les-Roses. b. 6 Sept 1921 St. Jean-de-Luz. Licence '51 Univ. of Paris, Fr. PSYCHOLOGIST, Cen. d'Observation Public d'Educ. Surveillée de Paris, Ministry of Justice, Savigny-sur-Orge. Member: SNPPD. Testing, clinical analysis, applied psychology; psycho-criminology of children and adolescents, projective techniques. M

APELLANIZ-RIKKERS, Mrs. Rassa Elisabeth. 21 Rue Jean Jaurès, L'Hay-les-Roses.

b. 3 Feb 1914 Wilno, Russia. Diplôme d'études supérieures '41 Univ. of Paris, Fr. PSYCH'T. and CHIEF of SERV, Cen. d'Observation Public d'Educ. Surveillée de Paris, Ministry of Justice, 4 Pl. Vendôme, Paris. Member: SNPPD. Testing, clinical analysis, psychotherapy, applied psychology; diagnostic psycho-criminology of children and adolescents, adolescent psychotherapy; projective techniques.   F

ARDOINO, Jacques Bernard. 2 Rue Chauchat, Paris 9. b. 6 Mar 1927 Paris. Diplôme d'études supérieures '51 Univ. of Rennes, Fr. ASSISTANT, Fac. of Letters, Univ. of Bordeaux. Member: SNPPD, Natl. Assn. for Devel. of Appl. Human Sci. Teaching, research, testing, educational psychology; projective techniques, characterology, group process.   M

ASSENMACHER, Dr. Ivan André. Lab. d'Histophysiologie, Collège de France, 4 Ave. Gordon Bennett, Paris 16. b. 17 May 1927 Erstein. MD '51 Univ. of Strasbourg, Fr. ASST. RES. DIR, l'Ecole Pratique des Hautes Etudes, Lab. d'Histophysiologie, Collège de France. Member: SFP. Research, teaching, professional writing; sexual behavior and its relation to endocrine glands and nervous centers.   M

AUDIBERT-BERGEY, Mrs. Anny. 153 Rue Mondenard, Bordeaux. b. 3 Mar 1921 Bordeaux. GUID. COUNS, Cen. d'Orientation 30 Rue Casteja, Bordeaux. Consulting, guidance; achievement tests, projective techniques.   F

AUDOUARD, Xavier. 74 Rue Lauriston, Paris 16. b. 6 Feb 1924 Sanelonis. Diplôme d'études supérieures '51 Univ. of Paris, Fr. PSYCHOTHERAPIST, Cen. Claude Bernard, Paris. Member: SNPPD, Fr. Psychoanal. Socy, Syndicat Natl. des Psychologues Psychanalystes. Psychotherapy, testing, clinical analysis, research; psychoanalysis, projective techniques.   M

AVENATI, Philippe-Louis. Villa des Chevau-Légers, 27 Rue de Satory, Versailles. b. 15 Aug 1916 Angers. Diplôme '48 Inst. of Psych, Univ. of Paris, Fr. DIVISION CHIEF, Cen. for Appl. Psych, 15 Rue Henri Heine, Paris 16. Member: APPD. Applied psychology; human relations in industry, personnel selection.   M

AVRIL, Miss Anne-Marie. 16 Rue de Romainville, Montreuil s/Bois. b. 8 Feb 1913 Paris. Diplôme d'études supérieures '36 Univ. of Paris, Fr. PSYCHOLOGIST, Medico-pedagogical Cen, Natl. Socy. of Fr. Railroads, 20 Blvd. Diderot, Paris 12. Member: SNPPD, Rorschach Socy. Educational psychology, testing, teaching; projective techniques, interviewing techniques.   F

BACHER, Miss Françoise. 6 Square de Port-Royal, Paris 13. b. 6 July 1928 Paris.

Licence '50 Sorbonne, Fr. RES. WRKR, Natl. Cen. for Sci. Res. (CNRS), Natl. Inst. for Vocat. Guid, 41 Rue Gay-Lussac, Paris 5. Research, statistics, testing; structure of intelligence, memory, learning.   F

BACQUELIN, Mrs. Geneviève. Rue du Petit St. Germain, Brive. b. 27 Oct 1909 Nevers. Conseiller '46 Univ. of Paris. Fr. GUID. COUNS, Cen. Départemental d'Orientation Professionnelle, Pl. Molière, Brive. Guidance, applied psychology, testing.   F

BANCAREL, Dr. Jeanne. Rue du Petit St. Germain, Brive. b. 23 Jan 1907 Decazeville. Conseiller '39 Univ. of Paris, Fr. DIRECTOR, Cen. d'Orientation Professionnelle, Pl. Molière, Brive. Applied psychology.   F

BARIOUX, Max. Serv. de Sondages et Statistiques, 18 Rue Quentin Bauchart, Paris. b. 5 Mar 1905 Braila, Rumania. Licence ès sciences, Univ. of Paris, Fr. DIRECTOR, Serv. de Sondages et Statistiques. Research, applied psychology; opinion measurement, projective techniques.   M

BARNET, Mrs. Marthe. 7 Blvd. Jean Jaurès, Aurillac. b. 19 Nov 1919 Tiviers. Diplôme d'état '46 Univ. of Paris, Fr. DIRECTOR, Cen. d'Orientation Professionnelle du Departement du Cantal. Member: ACOF. Guidance, testing; testing techniques, educational psychology, mental deficiency.   F

BARTHES, Noel. Cen. d'Orientation Professionnelle, 1 Pl. d'Italie, Paris 13. b. 2 Mar 1924 Montpezat. Licence ès lettres '48 Univ. of Paris, Fr. GUID. COUNS, Cen. d'Orientation Professionnelle. Member: ACOF. Guidance, testing, applied psychology; educational and vocational guidance.   M

BARTHES-LALA, Mrs. Jeannette. 288 Rue de Vaugirard, Paris 15. b. 28 July 1923 L'Isle sur Tarn. Diplôme d'état Univ. of Paris, Fr. VOCAT. GUID. COUNS, Cen. Départemental d'Orientation Professionnelle de la Seine, 25 Pl. de la Madeleine, Paris. Member: ACOF. Guidance, testing, applied psychology; achievement tests, child psychology, evaluation of children's books.   F

BAUMGARDT, Dr. Ernest. Lab. de Physiologie Générale, 1 Rue Victor Cousin, Paris 5. b. 23 Nov 1904 Frankfurt, Germany. Docteur ès sciences '48 Sorbonne, Fr. RES. DIR, Natl. Cen. for Sci. Res. (CNRS), 13 Quai Anatole France, Paris 12. Member: SFP, APSLF. Research; psychophysiology of vision, peripheral sensory mechanisms.   M

BAYER, Prof. Raymond. 51 Ave. Georges-Mandel, Paris 16. b. 2 Sept 1898 Paris. Doctorat '33 Univ. of Paris, Fr. PROFESSOR, Sorbonne, Rue des Ecoles, Paris. Member: SFP. Teaching, research, professional writing; genetic psychology, intelligence tests. M

BAYLE, Dominique Jean-Claude Edmond. 9 bis Rue Boileau, Paris 16. b. 20 Aug 1923 Paris. Licence '47 Univ. of Paris, Fr. LIBRARIAN, Ecole Normale Supérieure, Ave. du Palais, St. Cloud; ASST. ED, *Revue Internationale d'Ethnopsychologie Normale et Pathologique.* Member: Int. Soc. for Normal and Abnormal Ethnopsych. Library work, research, editorial; cultural factors in personality development, psychophysiology. M

BEAUSSIER, Jean. Centre d'Orientation, 11 Rue des Réservoirs, Versailles. b. Beauvais. Licence ès lettres, Univ. of Paris, Fr. DIRECTOR, Centre Départemental d'Orientation. Member: SFP, AIOP. Administration, guidance, applied psychology; adjustment of the adolescent to professional and social life. M

BÉJARANO ,Angélo. 32 Rue La Fontaine, Paris 16. b. 1 Sept 1909 Vigny, Diplôme '29 Ecole Nationale d'Agriculture de Grignon, Fr. PSYCHOANALYST, priv. prac. Member: APPD, Société Française du Rorschach, Société Française de Psychoanalyse, Syndicat National des Psychologues-Psychoanalystes. Psychotherapy, testing, clinical analysis, consulting; psychoanalytic problems and techniques, projective techniques, vocational and educational guidance. M

BELLEGY, Miss Denise Marie Françoise. Assn. pour l'Education des Jeunes Mères, 7 Rue César Franck, Paris 15. b. 18 Dec 1922 Peyrat-la-Noniere. Licence, Univ. of Clermont-Ferrand, Fr. PSYCHOLOGIST, Assn. pour l'Education des Jeunes Mères. Member: SNPPD. Testing, clinical analysis, applied and educational psychology, teaching; projective techniques, achievement tests. F

BÉNASSY, Dr. Maurice. 4 Rue de l'Odéon, Paris 6. b. 16 Oct 1904 Paris. Docteur '30 Univ. of Paris, Fr. PSYCHOANALYST, priv. prac; ASST. LECT, Inst. of Psych, Univ. of Paris. Member: SFP, APSLF. Psychotherapy, teaching; psychoanalytic theory and practive, psychophysiology. M

BÉNASSY-CHAUFFARD, Mrs. Colette. 4 Rue de l'Odéon, Paris 6. b. 7 Oct 1914 Neuilly-sur-Seine. Licence ès lettres, Univ. of Paris, Fr. SECY. GENL, Inst. Natl. d'Orientation Professionnelle, 41 Rue Gay-Lussac, Paris. Member: SFP, APSLF, APPD. Administration, research, teaching; psychological tests, vocational adjustment. F

BENOIT, Dr. Jean-Claude. 15 Rue Thiboumèry, Paris 15. b. 27 Feb 1928 Lille. Interne '53 Fac. of Med, Univ. of Paris, Fr. PSYCHIAT. INTERNE, Ste. Anne Psychiat. Hosp, 1 Rue Cabanis, Paris 13. Clinical practice and analysis, consulting, testing, psychotherapy; biological psychiatry, projective techniques, psychology of language. M

BENOIT, Prof. Paul M. Lab. of Genl. Physiol, Fac. of Sci, Pl. Victor Hugo, Marseille 3. b. 7 July 1912 Asnières. Docteur ès sciences '47 Sorbonne, Fr. PROF. and DIR, Lab. of Genl. Physiol; DIRECTOR, Inst. de Biométrie Humaine et d'Orientation Professionnelle, 11 Rue Mission de France, Marseille. Member: SFP. Teaching, research, administration; physiology of sensations and sense organs, vision, hearing. M

BENOIT-LEVI, Miss Renée. 59 Rue Froidevaux, Paris 14. b. 23 July 1901 Paris. Diplôme, Univ. of Paris, Fr. INDUS. PSYCH'T, Dept. of Human Problems and Indus. Psych, O.T.I.A.C.-B. Dorizon, 13 Rue Beudant, Paris 17. Member: AIPA, APPD, Groupement Français du Rorschach. Applied and industrial psychology, consulting, guidance, research; personnel evaluation, job analysis, projective techniques. F

BENUSIGLIO, Dany. Commission Générale d'Organisation Scientifique, 33 Rue Jean-Goujon, Paris. b. 11 Sept 1931 Paris. Licence '53 Univ. of Paris, Fr. SOCIAL PSYCHOLOGIST, Comm. Générale d'Organisation Scientifique. Industrial consulting, research, student; communication in organizations, group dynamics, human relations in industry. M

BENUSIGLIO, Mrs. Lucienne. 41 Rue de Maubeuge, Paris 9. b. 2 Jan 1927 Liège, Bel. Licence '53 Univ. of Paris, Fr. Applied psychology, testing, motivation research; group interviews and individual non-directive interviews in marketing and motivation research. F

BERGER, Prof. Gaston Louis Constant. 173 Blvd. Saint-Germain, Paris 6. b. 1 Oct 1896 Saint-Louis, Sénégal. Doctorat ès lettres '41 Aix-Marseille Univ, Fr. DIR. GENL. of HIGHER EDUC, Ministry of Natl. Educ, 110 Rue de Grenelle, Paris 7; DIR. GENL, *l'Encyclopédie Française.* Member: SFP. Teaching, research, administration; psychology of personality, characterology.M

BERGERON, Dr. Marcel. Hôpital Psychiatrique, 54 bis Ave. de la République, Villejuif. b. 11 Feb 1905 Nantes. MD, Univ. of Paris, Fr. PSYCHIATRIST, Hôpital Psychiatrique. Member: SFP, APSLF, Société Médico-Psychologique. Clinical practice, research on child psychology, professional writing; psychopathology. M

BERLIOZ, Louis. 112 Rue St. Denis, Colombes. b. 2 Mar 1915 Rumilly. Diplôme d'état '56 Univ. of Paris, Fr. DIR. of PSYCHOTECH. RES, Direction des Services de Sélection, 13 Rue Paul Chautard, Paris 15. Member: APSLF, APPD. Research, applied and personnel psychology, testing; conditioning, achievement tests, educability. M

BERLY, René. Centre d'Orientation Professionnelle, Cité Blanqui, Limoges. b. 12 Nov 1913 Leboutin. Diplôme d'état '45 Univ. of Paris, Fr. DIRECTOR, Cen. d'Orientation Professionnelle. Vocational guidance, counseling. M

BERNARD, Marc. 78 Blvd. Barbes, Paris. b. 13 Mar 1900 Tavaux. Diplôme d'état '56 Univ. of Paris, Fr. DIRECTOR, Laboratoires Psychotechniques des Transports Parisiens, 118 bis Rue du Mont Cenis, Paris. Member: APPD. Applied and industrial psychology, professional writing, administration; vocational aptitude measurement. M

BERNYER, Mrs. Germaine Suzanne. 11 Square Albin Cachot, Paris 13. b. 2 Jan 1907 Arvert. Licence ès sciences '29 Univ. of Bordeaux, Fr. RES. DIR, Natl. Cen. of Sci. Res. (CNRS), 13 Quai Anatole France, Paris 7. Member: SFP, AIPA, APSLF. Research, professional writing, teaching; statistics, factor analysis, aptitude tests. F

BERTHOLOM, André. 51 Ave. de Ségur, Paris 7. b. 14 Feb 1922 Paris. Diplôme, Inst. of Psych, Univ. of Paris, Fr. PSYCHO-TECHNICIAN, Cen. d'Etudes et Recherches Psychotechniques, 13 Rue Paul Chautard, Paris 15; on duty at Cen. Natl. d'Orientation, Prisons de Fresnes, Ministry of Justice. Member: SFP, APPD, Fr. League of Ment. Hyg. Applied psychology, consulting, guidance, research; vocational aptitudes, training and rehabilitation of prisoners. M

BESSON, Abbé Jean. Ecole de Psychologues Praticiens, 21 Rue d'Assas, Paris 6. b. 6 Oct 1913 Clermont-Ferrand. Diplôme d'études supérieures' 34 Sorbonne, Fr. DIRECTOR, Ecole de Psychologues Praticiens; PROF. of GENL. and EXPER. PSYCH, Faculté Libre des Lettres, Paris. Teaching, administration, research; psychology of guidance. M

BEUCHET, Prof. Jean-François. Faculté des Lettres, 7 Pl. Hoche, Rennes. b. 27 Mar 1914 Nantes. Diplôme d'études supérieures '48 Univ. of Rennes, Fr. DIR. of PSYCH. STUDIES, Lab. of Psych, Faculté des Lettres. Member: SFP. Teaching, directing research in experimental psychology, administration; memory, imagination, perception. M

BIZE, Prof. Dr. René. 60 Ave. de la Bourdonnais, Paris 7. b. 3 Feb 1901 Paris. MD '30; Prof. '48 Conservatoire National des Arts et Métiers, Fr. PROFESSOR, Conservatoire National des Arts et Métiers, 292 Rue Saint-Martin, Paris 3; PSYCHIATRIC PRAC. Member: Int. Socy. of Criminol.

Teaching, research, clinical practice, guidance; psychomotor tests, projective tests in industry, criminology. M

BLANC, Dr. Claude. 15 Rue Emilio Castelar, Paris 12. b. 2 July 1928 Poitiers. MD '54 Hôpitaux Psychiatriques, Fr. MED. ASST, Ste. Anne Psychiat. Cen, 1 Rue Cabanis, Paris 14; CHIEF, EEG Lab, Hérold Hosp, Paris. Member: SFP. Clinical practice and electroencephalography; general psychopathology, phenomenology. M

BLANCARD, René. 40 Blvd. Magenta, Rennes. b. 29 Aug 1924 Algiers, Algeria. L.PS '49 Univ. of Paris, Fr. DIRECTOR, Sel. Cen. of Rennes, Ministry of Labor, 13 Rue Paul Chautard, Paris 15. Administration, personnel psychology, guidance; vocational selection, aptitude tests, reclassification of the physically handicapped. M

BLIQUE, Claude. 17 Rue de Saverne, Nancy. b. 23 Jan 1921 France. Conseiller '44 Univ. of Paris, Fr. INDUS. PSYCH'T, priv. prac. and Usines Sidérurgiques, Région de Nancy. Member: AIPA, APPD. Industrial psychology, consulting, teaching; vocational selection and guidance. M

BLOCH, Vincent. 16 Rue Maurice Berteaux, Sèvres. b. 2 Aug 1925 Sèvres. Licence ès lettres '47 Univ. of Paris. Fr. RES. ASST, Natl. Cen. for Sci. Res. (CNRS), Lab. of Comp. and Exper. Psych, Univ. of Paris; EXEC. ED, *L'Année Psychologique*. Member: SFP, APSLF. Research, editorial, teaching; emotion and levels of activity, physiological recording in man, brain stimulation in animals. M

BOCKSTAELE, Jacques van. 5 Rue Michel-Chasles, Paris 12. b. 20 Aug 1924 Roubaix. Licence '44 Fac. of Letters, Sorbonne, Fr. RES. ASSOC, Natl. Cen. for Sci. Res. (CNRS), Lab. of Social Psych, 16 Rue de la Sorbonne, Paris 5; TECH. ASSOC, Fr. Productivity Cen. Research, applied and industrial psychology, industrial training in human relations; group dynamics, social perception, learning theory, attitude surveys. M

BOCKSTAELE, Mrs. Maria van. 5 Rue Michel-Chasles, Paris 12. b. 8 June 1927 Montgeron. Licence '49 Fac. of Letters, Sorbonne, Fr. CONSULTANT, Conseil Supérieur de la Recherche Scientifique et du Progrès Technique, 68 Rue de Bellechasse, Paris 7; LECT. in SOC. PSYCH, Inst. for the Trng. of Business Admin, Univ. of Toulouse. Research, teaching, administration; organization structure, decision process, social perception. F

BOISSELIER, Mrs. Françoise. 87 bis Ave. du Général Leclerc, Paris 14. b. 14 Apr 1915 Paris. Diplôme '54 Inst. Natl. d'Orientation Professionnelle, Fr. VOCAT. GUID. COUNS, Inst. Natl. d'Orientation Professionnelle, 41 Rue Gay-Lussac, Paris 5. Consulting, guidance, testing, clinical analysis. F

BONNAIRE, Jean Pierre. 9 Rue Borghèse, Neuilly sur Seine. b. 16 Dec 1919 Paris. Chef de Travaux '54 Inst. of Psych, Univ. of Paris, Fr. DIRECTOR, Psychotech. Serv, Regie Nationale des Usines Renault, 10 Ave. Emile Zola, Billancourt; DIR. of PRACTICAL TRNG, Inst. of Psych, Univ. of Paris. Member: AIPA, APPD. Industrial psychology, testing, teaching; work accidents, social status and choice of profession, methods of apprentice training. M

BONNARDEL, Prof. Raymond Georges. 41 Rue Gay-Lussac, Paris 5. b. 17 May 1901 Limay. MD, Univ. of Paris, Fr. DIRECTOR, Lab. of Appl. Psych, Ecole des Hautes Etudes, Sorbonne; PROFESSOR, Inst. of Psych, Univ. of Paris; DIRECTOR, Le Travail Humain; EDITOR, Bulletin de l'Association Internationale de Psychologie Appliquée. Member: AIPA, APSLF. Research, teaching, applied psychology; psychometric methods, statistical methods in applied psychology, human problems in industry. M

BONNEAU-MAGNANT, Mrs. Georgine Eliane. Centre d'Orientation Professionnelle, 36 Rue Raspail, St. Quentin. b. 23 Oct 1914 Availles sur Chize. Licence ès lettres '48 Univ. of Poitiers, Fr. VOCAT. GUID. COUNS, Cen. d'Orientation Professionnelle. Member: ACOF. Testing, consulting, guidance, educational psychology; achievement tests, memory and learning, manual aptitudes. F

BOUCHET, Elisée. Cen. d'Etudes et d'Instruction Psychologique de l'Armée de l'Air (CEIPAA), Caserne Denfert, Versailles. b. 7 Apr 1927 St. Julien de Maurienne. Licence ès lettres '50 Univ. of Grenoble, Fr. PSYCHOTECH. and CHIEF of INSTR. DIV, CEIPAA. Member: APPD. Teaching, applied and educational psychology; methodology, statistics and learning theory. M

BOUÊT, Miss Marie-Odile. 35 Rue Célestin Port, Angers. b. 9 Feb 1921 Cholet. Diplôme d'état '53 Inst. Natl. d'Orientation Professionnelle, Fr. GUID. COUNS, Off. d'Orientation Scolaire et Professionnelle, 79 Rue Desjardins, Angers. Member: ACOF. Educational psychology, testing, consulting, guidance; retardation and maladjustment of students, educational guidance, vocational guidance of young girls. F

BOUILLUT, Jean. 2 Square La Fontaine, Paris 16. b. 24 Nov 1929 Lille. Licence '53 Univ. of Paris, Fr. DOCUMENTARY RES. WRKR, Documentation Serv, Inst. des Sciences Humaines Appliquées, 5 Rond-point Bugeaud, Paris 16. Research, professional writing, documentation; social

psychology, communication, information, language. M

BOURDON, Marcel René Henri. 4 Pl. Saintin, Montlhéry. b. 6 July 1922 Paris. Licence ès lettres '46 Univ. of Paris, Fr. INDUS. PSYCH'T, Syndicat Général des Fondeurs de France, 2 Rue de Bassano, Paris 16. Member: SFP. APPD. Applied and industrial psychology, testing, guidance; human relations. M

BOURDON, Paul. 13 bis Ave. des Quinze Arbres, Rodez. b. 22 Nov 1913 Auvillers. Diplôme d'état '46 Inst. Nat. d'Etude du Travail et d'Orientation Professionnelle, Fr. VOCAT. and EDUC. GUID. COUNS, Cen. Public d'Orientation & Professionnelle, Caserue Ste. Catherine, Rodez. Member: ACOF. Consulting, guidance, testing, administration; achievement, aptitude and character testing. M

BOURNONVILLE, Jean-Jacques. Ave. H. Delecaux, Lambersart. b. 8 Dec 1927 Calais. Diplôme '54 Inst. of Psych, Univ. of Paris, Fr. PSYCHOLOGIST, Centre d'Observation Mineurs Delinquents, 2 Ave. Foch, Lambersart. Member: SNPPD. Testing, clinical analysis, educational psychology, research; projective techniques. M

BOYER, Miss Simone. 19 Rue d'Aubeterre, Montpellier. b. 12 Feb 1920 Ginestas. Certificate '53 Univ. of Montpellier, Fr. ASST. PSYCH'T, Clinic for Ment. and Nerv. Diseases, Fac. of Med, Montpellier. Member: SNPPD. Research, consulting, student; projective techniques, achievement tests, tests for mental deterioration. F

BRABANT, Mrs. Valentine. Centre Public d'Orientation Professionnelle, 2 Blvd. Montauriol, Montauban. b. 11 Aug 1921 Grisolles. Licence ès lettres '43 Univ. of Toulouse, Fr. DIRECTOR, Cen. Public d'Orientation Professionnelle. Member: ACOF. Guidance, administration; educational and vocational guidance of adolescents, aptitude, psychomotor and achievement tests. F

BRAUNER, Dr. Alfred. 13 Blvd. de Neuilly, Paris 12. b. 3 July 1910 St. Mandé. Docteur ès lettres '47 Univ. of Paris, Fr. DIRECTOR, Sect. for Mentally Retarded Children, Groupement de Recherches Pratiques pour l'Enfance, 50 Rue Ste. Anne, Paris 2. Teaching, research; special teaching techniques for mentally retarded children and maladjusted bi-lingual children. M

BRESSON, François. 133 Rue Lamarck, Paris 18. b. 4 Mar 1921 Paris. Agrégé, Univ. of Paris, Fr. RES. WRKR, Natl. Cen. for Sci. Res. (CNRS), Paris; PROF. of PSYCH, Natl. Inst. for Vocat. Guid, Paris. Member SFP, APSLF. Research, teaching; stochastic models in perception theory, language and symbolic processes. M

BREYTON, Miss Madeleine. 81 Blvd. Brune, Paris 14. b. 6 Feb 1921 Grenoble. Diplôme d'études supérieures '55 Univ. of Paris, Fr. PSYCHOLOGIST, Cen. of Appl. Psych. (CPA), 15 Rue Henri Heine, Paris 16. Member: APPD, Groupement Français du Rorschach. Applied psychology, testing, clinical analysis, psychotherapy; projective techniques, re-education of children with reading difficulties, child psychotherapy.   F

BRIED, Charles Joseph. 3 Rue de Dôle, Besançon. b. 16 Jan 1922 Besançon. Licence ès lettres '46 Univ. of Besançon, Fr. PROF. of PSYCHOPEDAGOGY, Ecole Normale d'Instituteurs, 6 Rue de la Madeleine, Besançon. Teaching, research, educational psychology; development of esthetic values, aspiration level, sex differences.   M

BRISSON, Georges Henri. Inspection Régionale d'Orientation, 2 Rue Paul Cabet, Dijon. b. Parsac. Doctorat '53 Univ. of Dijon, Fr. VOCAT. GUID. SUPERV, Inspection Régionale d'Orientation. Member: ACOF, AIOP. Consulting, educational and vocational guidance, teaching; achievement tests, academic success, social adaptation. M

BROUSSEAU, Miss Françoise. 109 Ave. Henri Martin, Paris 16. b. 29 June 1928 Quebec, Canada. Diplôme '54 Univ. of Paris, Fr. RES. WRKR, Natl. Cen. for Sci. Res. (CNRS), 13 Quai Anatole France, Paris; PSYCHOLOGIST, Hérold Hosp, Salpétrière, Paris. Member: SFP. Testing, consulting, research; infant testing, psychology of the school child.   F

BRUNET, Mrs. Odette. 11 Rue de la Vérité, Montmorency. b. 21 May 1922 Paris. Licence '43 Univ. of Paris, Fr. RES. WRKR, Natl. Cen. for Sci. Res. (CNRS), Lab. of Psych, Henri Rousselle Hosp, 1 Rue Cabanis, Paris. Member: SFP, APSLF. Research, testing, consulting and guidance; infant psychology, relation between development of intelligence and social environment, language.   F

BUFFARD, Denis. 41 Rue d'Assas, Paris 6. b. 13 Oct 1932 Paris. L.PS '56 Sorbonne, Fr. STUDENT, Sorbonne, Paris 5. Communication, psychopathology, social psychology.   M

BUSER, Prof. Pierre-Albert. 4 Ave. Gordon Bennett, Paris 16. b. 19 Aug 1921 Strasbourg. PH.D '53 Univ. of Paris, Fr. PROFESSOR, Univ. of Paris, Rue Victor Cousin, Paris. Member: SFP. Research, teaching; experimental neurophysiology and psychophysiology.   M

CAHN, Miss Paulette. 3 Rue Friesé, Strasbourg. b. 17 Feb 1914 Mutzig. Diplôme d'études supérieures, Univ. of Strasbourg, Fr. RES. WRKR, Natl. Cen. for Sci. Res. (CNRS), 13 Quai Anatole France, Paris 7.

Member: SFP. Research, teaching, testing; sibling relationships, sociometric techniques, films as a method of psychological investigation.   F

CAILLE, Dr. Emile J. P. La Solitude, Le Pradet. b. 31 May 1921 Rennes. MD '45 Univ. of Bordeaux, Fr. DIRECTOR, Serv. de Sélection et d'Orientation de la Marine, Arsenal de la Marine, Toulon. Member: AIPA. Personnel psychology, guidance, testing, research teaching; psychometry, validation studies, achievement tests, projective techniques.   M

CAILLOT, Pierre. Route de Saligny. Sens. b. 12 May 1921 Persan. Diplôme d'état '53 Univ. of Paris, Fr. VOCAT. GUID. COUNS, Cen. d'Orientation Professionnelle, 22 Rue de Lyon, Sens. Member: ACOF. Educational and vocational guidance; aptitude measurement.   M

CAILLOU, Michel. 12 Rue Paul Deroulède, Jarny. b. 27 Feb 1932 Bar-le-Duc. Licence '55 Univ. of Strasbourg, Fr. INDUS. PSYCH'T, Société Lorraine-Escaut, Division de Thionville, Thionville. Industrial psychology, research, student; industrial accidents, selection and vocational guidance of personnel in industry.   M

CAMBON, Mrs. Jacqueline. 8 Rue Monttessuy, Paris 7. b. 22 Nov 1920 Paris. Licence '51 Sorbonne, Fr. VOCAT. GUID. COUNS, Natl. Inst. for Vocat. Guid, 41 Rue Gay-Lussac, Paris 5. Member: SFP, AIPA. Research, testing, teaching; vocational guidance, occupational adjustment.   M

CANIVET, Mrs. Nella. 4 Rue Duvivier, Paris 7. b. 30 Oct 1893 Alexandria, Egypt. Diplôme Général '31 Univ. of Geneva, Switz. PSYCH. ASST, priv. prac. of Dr. A. Morali-Daninos, 7 Ave. Trudaine, Paris 9. Member: SNPPD, APPD, Groupement française du Rorschach. Testing, clinical analysis, applied psychology; projective tests.   F

CARDINET, Dr. Jean Maurice. 9 Rue du Sergent Bauchat, Paris 12. b. 18 Jan 1927 Paris. PH.D '52 Univ. of Chicago, USA. CHIEF of RES. DEPT, Cen. for Appl. Psych, 15 Rue Henri Heine, Paris 16. Member: SFP, APPD. Research, teaching, applied psychology; classification of personnel, objective tests of personality, factor theory.   M

CARDO, Bernard. Psych. Lab, Faculté des Lettres, 20 Cours Pasteur, Bordeaux. b. 27 Feb 1925 Thiviers. Diplôme d'études supérieures '52 Univ. of Bordeaux, Fr. RES. WRKR, Psych. Lab. Member: SFP, APSLF. Research; psychology of space perception, relation between space perception and personality traits.   M

CARPENTIER, Raymond. 1 Rue des Carmes, Paris 5. b. 31 Aug 1919 Paris. Certificat d'études supérieures '50 Univ. of Paris, Fr. CHIEF, Bur. of Res, Psychotech. Lab, Régie Autonome des Transports Parisiens, 43 Quai des Grands-augustins, Paris 6; TCHR. of PERS. and GUID. METHODS, Conservatoire National des Arts et Métiers. Member: SFP, AIPA, APPD. Applied and industrial psychology, teaching; accident prevention, dynamics of the man-job relationship. M

CARRON, René. 2 Rue Mélingue, Paris 19. b. 8 Jan 1928 Paris. Licence ès lettres '54 Univ. of Paris, Fr. RES. DIR, Centre d'Etudes de Radio-Télévision de la Radiodiffusion Télévision Française, 37 Rue de l'Université, Paris 7. Research, applied social psychology, professional writing; communication, perception, acoustical psychophysiology, music and emotion, methodology of the social sciences. M

CARSUZAA, Henri Gabriel. Centre d'Orientation Professionnelle, Parc Wilson, Blvd. Carnot, Montlucon. b. 19 Jan 1910 Ustaritz. Conseiller '51 Inst. Natl. d'Orientation Professionnelle, Fr. VOCAT. GUID. COUNS, Cen. d'Orientation Professionnelle. Member: ACOF. Guidance, consulting, testing; child and adolescent psychology. M

CARTAL, Mrs. Simone. 6 Villa Pasteur, St. Gratien. b. 3 May 1924 St. Gratien. Diplôme d'état '50 Univ. of Paris, Fr. VOCAT. GUID. COUNS, Centre d'Orientation Professionnelle, 2 Blvd. Robespierre, Poissy Member: ACOF. Testing, consulting, vocational guidance; achievement tests, memory, learning, child psychology. F

CASALIS, Jean-Pierre. 5 Rue Macornet, Chambéry. b. 16 Dec 1929 Chambon-sur-Lignon. Diplôme, Inst. of Psych, Univ. of Paris, Fr. CONSULT. PSYCH'T, priv. prac. Member: SNPPD. Applied psychology, consulting, guidance, testing; personality study, social and vocational adaptation, psychology of the family, educational guidance. M

CAULLIER, Jacques André Gabriel. Cen. d'Orientation de Lyon, Palais du Commerce, Pl. des Cordeliers, Lyon. b. 18 Nov 1921 Posieres. Diplôme '43 Univ. of Paris, Fr. DIRECTOR, Cen. d'Orientation de Lyon. Member: Fédération Régionale Rhône-Alpes des Psychologues Praticiens. Educational psychology, testing, research, producing vocational guidance films; educational adjustment problems and teaching techniques, vocational preparation of children. M

CAVOZZI, Jean Louis. 160 Rue du Temple, Paris 3. b. 16 Oct 1921 Paris. Diplôme '48 Univ. of Paris, Fr. DIR. of INDUS. RELAT, Electricité et Gaz de France, 68 Faubourg St. Honoré, Paris; INDUS. COUNSULT, priv. prac; DIR. of RES. in PERS. SEL. and GUID, Conservatoire Natl. des Arts et Métiers,

Paris. Member: SFP, AIPA, APPD, SNPPD, Groupement Français du Rorschach. Industrial psychology, personnel selection and training, testing, research; group dynamics, attitude measurement, merit ratings, job analysis, projective techniques. M

CHABRERIE, André. Centre d'Orientation Professionnelle, 4 Rue du Ménil, Asnieres. b. 12 Dec 1914 France. Diplôme d'état '45 Inst. Natl. d'Orientation Professionnelle, Fr. DIRECTOR, Cen.d 'Orientation Professionnelle. Member: AIOP, ACOF. Vocational guidance, applied psychology. M

CHABRIER, Dr. Alphonse. 155 Blvd. de la Liberté, Lille. b. 6 June 1910 Roubaix. MD '39 Univ. of Lille, Fr. Member: APPD. Testing, clinical analysis, consulting, clinical practice, guidance, applied and industrial psychology; vocational selection, educational maladjustment. M

CHALMET-SAINT JUST, Mrs. Rolande. 9 Rue Fessart, Boulogne-Billancourt. b. 11 July 1926 Le Châtelet. L.PS '50 Univ. of Paris, Fr. RES. DIR, Sel. Serv. of the Ministry of Labor, 13 Rue Paul Chautard, Paris. Member: APPD. Research, applied and personnel psychology, consulting, student; learning, guidance, work adjustment. F

CHAMBON, André-Roger. 4 Rue Marmontel, Clermont-Ferrand. b. 30 Aug 1923 Clermont-Ferrand. Licence '50 Univ. of Paris, Fr. DIRECTOR, Centre Public d'Orientation Professionnelle du Puy-de-Dôme, Cité Administrative, Rue Pélissier, Clermont-Ferrand. Member: SNPPD, ACOF. Consulting, testing, administration; juvenile delinquency, vocational information interviews. M

CHAMBOULANT, Mrs. Simone Marie Geneviève. 3 Ave. Jean Jaurès, Athis-Mons. b. 8 May 1911 Lonzac. Diplôme d'état, Univ. of Paris, Fr. HEAD, Stud. Guid. Serv. of B.U.S., 5 Place St. Michel, Paris 5; PROF. of APPL. PSYCH, Ecole des Surintendantes d'Usine, 5 Rue Las Case, Paris 7. Member: AIOP, ACOF, Assn. Française de Psychotechnique, Assn. Int. de Psychotechnique. Consulting, educational guidance, research, teaching; research on the establishment of criteria of student guidance, analysis of educational success and failure, personality. F

CHANDESSAIS, Lt. Col. Charles. 28 Rue d'Assas Paris 6. b. 7 May 1904 Versailles. Diplôme d'état '56 Univ. of Paris Fr. DIR. of HUMAN SCIENCES, Secrétariat Permanent du Comité d'Action Scientifique de Défense Nationale, 3 Rue de Liège, Paris 9. Member: SFP, AIPA, WAPOR, APPD. Research, administration, editorial; military psychology, morale, factor analysis. M

CHARALIER, Gaston. La Lézardière, Chemin de Montmaurt, Rte. de Mende, Montpellier. b. 4 July 1919 Langogne. Licence ès lettres, Univ. of Montpellier, France. CLIN. PSYCH'T, Clinique Rech, Ave. Charles Flahaut, Montpellier; EDITOR, *Revue*, Assn. Régionale pour la Sauvegarde de l'Enfance et de l'Adolescence. Testing, clinical analysis, psychotherapy, teaching; projective techniques, perceptive structure tests. M

CHARLIN, Miss Paulette. S.N.C.F., 20 Blvd, Diderot, Paris 12. b. 7 Sept 1913 Morez. Diplôme d'études supérieures '32 Univ. of Besançon, Fr. DIRECTOR, Vocat. Guid. Off, S.N.C.F. Consulting, guidance, testing, teaching; achievement and personality tests, attitude measurement. F

CHARPENTIER, Dr. René. 27 Ave. de la Costa, Monte Carlo, Monaco. b. 7 Apr 1881 Anet. MD; Chef de Clinique '07 Univ. of Paris, Fr. EDITOR-in-CHIEF, *Annales Médico-Psychologiques*, Librairie Masson, 120 Blvd. Saint-Germain, Paris. Member: SFP, Société Médico-Psychologique, Société Clinique de Médecine Mentale. Editorial, retired. M

CHASTAING, Prof. Dr. Maxime. Fac. of Letters, Rue Chabot-Charny, Dijon. b. 7 May 1913 Paris. Agrégé '36 Sorbonne, Fr. PROF. of PSYCH, Fac. of Letters. Member: SFP. Teaching, research, professional writing; language, understanding others, publicity. M

CHATEAU, Prof. Jean Yves. Faculté des Lettres, 20 Cours Pasteur, Bordeaux. b. 17 July 1908 St. Quentin de Chabanais. Doctorat ès lettres '47 Univ. of Paris, Fr. PROFESSOR, Faculté des Lettres. Member: SFP, APSLF, Bordeaux Psych. Socy. Research, teaching, educational psychology; child psychology, differential psychology, general pedagogy. M

CHAUBET, Gaston. 47 Route de Morieres, Avignon. b. 11 Nov 1921 Aix en Provence. Diplôme d'état. VOCAT. GUID. COUNS, Centre Départemental d'Orientation Professionnelle, 1 bis Rue Victor Hugo, Avignon. Consulting, guidance, testing, applied psychology; achievement tests. M

CHAUCHARD, Dr. Paul Albert. 57 Ave. Division Leclerc, Chatillon-sous-Bagneux. b. 14 June 1912 Paris. MD '39 Univ. of Paris, Fr. ASSOC. DIR. of LAB, Ecole pratique des Hautes Etudes, Sorbonne, 1 Rue V. Cousin, Paris; PROF. of PSYCHOPHYSIOL, Ecole de Psychologues Praticiens, 21 Rue d'Assas, Paris; MEMBER, Comm. for Fr. Edition, *Revue des questions Scientifiques*. Member: SFP. Research, professional writing, teaching; psychosomatics, conditioned reflexes, psychophysiology of consciousness. M

CHAUMIEN, Miss Jeanne-Françoise. 12 Rue Lacretelle, Paris 15. b. 3 Jan 1899 Saulieu. Licence ès lettres '52 Sorbonne, Fr. VOCAT. GUID. COUNS, Caisse Centrale d'Allocations Familiales, 10 Rue Viala, Paris 15. Research, testing, clinical analysis, guidance; characterology, projective techniques, achievement tests. F

CHAUVIN, Prof. Dr. Rémy. Station de Recherches Apicoles, Bures sur Yvette. b. 10 Oct 1913 Toulon. Doctorat '41 Univ. of Paris, Fr. DIRECTOR, Bures Apicultural Station. Member: SFP, APSLF. Research; psychophysiology of insects. M

CHOCHOLLE, René. 161 Ave. de Neuilly, Neuilly-sur-Seine. b. 2 Apr 1915 Villers-Bretonneux. Docteur '47 Univ. of Paris, Fr. RES. DIR, Natl. Cen. for Sci Res. (CNRS), Collège de France, Pl. Marcellin Berthelot, Paris 5. Member: SFP, APSLF. Research, psychophysiology of hearing. M

CHOMBART DE LAUWE, Paul. 10 Rue de Chateaudun, Ivry. b. 8 Apr 1913 Cambrai. Docteur ès lettres, Univ. of Paris, Fr. DIR. of RES, Cen. for Sociol. Studies, Natl. Cen. for Sci. Res. (CNRS), 13 Quai Anatole France, Paris; ASST. LECT, Inst. of Ethnology, Univ. of Paris. Member: SFP, Ligue Française d'Hygiène Mentale. Research, teaching; study of relation between social environment and behavior, psychosociology of familial groups. M

CLAUZIER, Marc. Centre d'Orientation Professionnelle, 2 Pl. Adelbert, Privas. b. 15 July 1927 Desaignes. Diplôme d'état '53 Univ. of Paris, Fr. VOCAT. GUID. COUNS, Cen. d'Orientation. Member: ACOF. Consulting, guidance, applied psychology, testing; achievement tests, aptitude measurement, child and adolescent psychology, reclassification of the physically handicapped. M

CLAVEIROLE, Guy. Pl. des Cordeliers, Montferrand. b. 1 Aug 1922 St. Etienne. Licence '45 Univ. of Clermont-Ferrand, Dr. PSYCH. ASST, Cen. Médico-Psychologique Infantil, 1 Pl. A. Varenne, Clermont-Ferrand. Member: SNPPD. Testing, clinical analysis, consulting, guidance, teaching, research; achievement and personality tests, projective techniques. M

COLIN, Mrs. Régine. Quai St. Dominique, Troyes. b. 14 Mar 1914 Romans. Diplôme '46 Inst. Natl. d'Etudes du Travail et d'Orientation Professionnelle, Fr. PSYCH. COUNSELOR, Guid. Cen, Pl. St. Pierre, Troyes. Member: ACOF. Applied psychology, testing, consulting and guidance; aptitude measurement, projective techniques, study of personality. F

COLIN, Roger. Quai St. Dominique, Troyes. b. 7 June 1909 Vichy. Diplôme '45 Inst. Natl. d'Etudes du Travail et d'Orientation

Professionnelle, Fr. DIRECTOR, Guid. Services, Dept. of l'Aube, Troyes; PSYCHO-TECHNICIAN, priv. prac. Member: ACOF. Industrial psychology, testing, guidance; aptitude measurement, projective techniques, study of personality, psychotherapy. M

COLLIGNON, Miss Marcelle. 8 Rue Michelet-Issy, Les Moulineaux. b. 29 Sept 1930 Longwy. Licence '53 Sorbonne, Fr. ASST. in RES, Natl. Cen. of Sci. Res. (CNRS), 13 Quai Anatole France, Paris 7. Member: SNPPD. Research, consulting; psychology of adolescence, social psychology. F

COLUMELLI, Fulbert Antoine. 133 Rue Championnet, Paris 18. b. 1 Aug 1921 Paris. Licence '53 Univ. of Paris, Fr. PSYCHOTECHNICIAN, Cen. d'Etudes et Recherches Psychotechniques, 13 Rue Paul Chautard, Paris. Research in industrial psychology, counseling, vocational guidance, student; social perception, attitude measurement, motivation. M

COMMUNIER, Mrs. Simone. 1 Rue de Montfort, Rennes. b. 24 Apr 1924 Perpignan. Diplôme '51 Univ. of Rennes, Fr. INDUS. PSYCH'T and PSYCHOTECHNICIAN. Member: APPD. Industrial psychology, testing, teaching; achievement tests, personnel selection, reeducation of maladjusted children. F

CONSTANT, Miss Marie-Paule. 15 Rue des Orphelins, Strasbourg. b. 12 Jan 1923 Strasbourg. Licence ès lettres '49 Univ. of Strasbourg, Fr. PSYCHOLOGIST, Hospices Civils, Station 91, Pl. de l'Hôpital, Strasbourg. Testing, clinical analysis, teaching, administration; achievement tests, projective techniques, social psychology, orphans, education of problem children. F

CORNE, Pierre. 3 Rue Grenéta, Paris. b. 27 Dec 1920 Conflans-Jarny. Licence '44 Fac. of Nancy, Fr. PSYCHOTECHNICIAN, Psychotech. Serv. of S.N.C.F., 88 Rue St. Lazare, Paris. Member: APPD. Applied psychology, testing, research; aptitude measurement, vocational selection, statistical techniques. M

COTELLE, Micheline Renée Germaine. 14 Grande Rue Nogent-sur-Marne. b. 16 Feb 1927 Boulogne-sur-mer. Diplôme d'état '50 Univ. of Paris, Fr. VOCAT, GUID. COUNS, Cen. Départemental d'Orientation Professionnelle, 2 Pl. de la Madeleine, Paris. Member: ACOF. Consulting, guidance, testing; achievement tests, projective techniques, aptitude measurement. F

COUMÉTOU, Dr. Maurice-Louis. 101 Blvd. Arago, Paris 14. b. 21 May 1904 Paris. MD '30 Univ. of Paris, Fr. PROFESSOR, Inst. of Psych, Sorbonne, Paris; RES. DIR, Inst. Natl. d'Etude du Travail et d'Orientation Professionnelle, 41 Rue Gay-Lussac,

Paris 5; ASSOC. DIR, Psych. Sect, Inst. de Médecine du Travail, Univ. of Paris; ED. DIR, *L'Encyclopédie Médico-Chirurgicale.* Member: AIPA, APSLF, Société de Médecine du Travail. Teaching, editorial, professional writing; sensory functions, psychophysiology, statistics. M

COUPRIE, Henry. Centre Départemental d'Orientation Professionnelle du Jura, 59 Rue Lecourbe, Lons de Saunier. b. 19 Nov 1904 Brussels, Belgium. DIRECTOR, Cen. Départemental d'Orientation Professionnelle du Jura. Member: ACOF. Consulting, vocational guidance, administration, research; projective techniques, achievement tests, social perception, juvenile delinquency. M

COURBIN, Jean Pierre. 37 Rue Froidevaux, Paris 14. b. 13 Apr 1908 Salles. Diplôme '48 Univ. of Paris, Fr. DIR. of RES, Cen. d'Etudes et Recherches Psychotechniques, 13 Rue Paul Chautard, Paris 15. Member: APPD. Teaching, research, administration; educational psychology, vocational counseling. M

COURTHIAL, Dr. Andrée. 1 Rue Léon Séché, Paris 15. b. 28 Oct 1889 Pont St. Esprit. PH.D '32 Columbia Univ, USA. DIR. of PSYCH. and GUIDANCE, Caisse Centrale d'Allocations Familiales, 10 Rue Viala, Paris 15; CONSULT. PSYCH'T, Centre d'Etudes et d'Organisation, 16 Ave. de la Mayes, Versailles. Member: SFP, AIPA, APSLF, AIOP. Psychological consultation and vocational guidance, applied, industrial psychology, research; aptitude and interest tests, projective techniques, personality measurement. F

COUSINET, Prof. Roger. 29 Blvd. de Ménilmontant, Paris 11. b. 30 Nov 1881 Arcueil. Licence ès lettres '03 Univ. of Paris, Fr. PROF. of PEDAGOGY, Univ. of Paris; EDITOR, *l'Ecole Nouvelle Française.* Member: SFP. Research, educational psychology, teaching; child psychology, psychopedagogy. M

COUVREUR, Albert. Cen. d'Orientation Professionnelle, 6 Rue Puits du Temple, Montpellier. b. 29 Mar 1925 Pavant. Diplôme d'état '54 Univ. of Paris, Fr. GUID. COUNS, Cen. d'Orientation Professionnelle. Member: ACOF. Testing, educational and vocational counseling and guidance; achievement tests, aptitude measurement, projective techniques. M

CREMIEUX, Dr. Albert. 255 Rue Paradis, Marseille 6. b. 18 May 1895 Marseille. MD; Prof. Agrégé '52 Univ. of Aix-Marseille, Fr. PROF. of PSYCHIAT, Fac. of Med. and Fac. of Letters, Le Pharo, Marseille; PSYCHIATRIST. Member: Société Médico-Psychologique. Teaching psychiatry, clinical practice, professional writing;

psychiatry, psychopathology. M

CROZIER, Dr. Michel Jean. 10 Rue Yves Toudic, Paris. b. 6 Nov 1922 Ste. Menehould. Docteur '50 Univ. of Lille, Fr. STUDY DIR, Natl. Cen. for Sci. Res. (CNRS), 27 Rue de Fleurus, Paris. Research in industrial and human relations; attitude measurement, group process. M

CURTIS, Harry François-Michel. 25 Rue de Vaugirard, Paris 6. b. 1 Jan 1922 Paris. Diplôme '50 Univ. of Paris, Fr. INDUS. PSYCH'T, I.B.M. Co. of France,, 5 Pl. Vendôme, Paris 1. Member: APPD. Testing, applied and industrial psychology, consulting, guidance; projective techniques, attitude measurement, characterology. M

DAMET, Michel Georges. 23 bis Rue de Constantinople, Paris 8. b. 3 Feb 1928 Bourg. Licence '56 Univ. of Paris, Fr. APPL. PSYCH'T, Cen. for Appl. Psych. (CPA), 15 Rue Heine, Paris 16. Industrial psychology; psychology of work, projective techniques. M

DANGER, Miss Daniele. 68 Blvd. Soult, Paris 12. b. 12 Jan 1914 Paris. Diplôme '39 Univ. of Paris, Fr. ENGINEER, Dept. of Indus. Psych, Compagnie d'Organisation Rationnelle du Travail, 65 Ave. Kléber, Paris 16; DIRECTOR, Psychotech. Cen. for the Prevention of Accidents, Toulouse. Member: AIPA, APPD. Applied and industrial psychology, testing, consulting; study of gestures, prevention of accidents, projective techniques. F

DARCHEN, Dr. Roger-Jean. La Mancelière par Brezolles. b. 16 Mar 1921 Paris. RES. WRKR, Natl. Inst. for Agronomic Res, Bures/Yvette. Research; animal psychology, instinct in insect societies. M

D'AUTHEVILLE, Miss Geneviève. 63 bis Rue Boursault, Paris 17. b. 16 Aug 1904 Chambéry. Diplôme d'état, Inst. Nat. d'Orientation Professionnelle, Fr. DIRECTOR Cen. for Vocat. Guid, Société Nationale des Chemins de Fer Français, 20 Rue de Rome, Paris 8, Member: ACOF. Administration, consulting, guidance, clinical analysis; attitude measurement, achievement and projective tests. F

DAVOST, Dr. Paul-Henri. 2 Rue de Rohan Rennes. b. 17 Dec 1924 Paris. MD '53 Univ. of Paris, Fr. ASST. in PSYCH, Fac. of Letters, Univ. of Rennes; DIRECTOR, Clin. of the Fac. of Med; SECY. GENL, Cen. for Psychotech. Studies. Member: Biotypology Socy, Anthrop. Socy. of Paris. Teaching, research, consulting; psychology of alcoholics, psychodiagnostic use of the Rorschach test for feeblemindedness, electroencephalography and behavior. M

DE BRISSON DE LAROCHE, Dr. Joseph-Alexis. Air Force Cen. for Psych. Studies and Instruction, 29 Rue Marechal Joffre, Versailles. b. 3 July 1916 Royat. MD '43 Univ. of Lyon, Fr; Licence ès lettres '53 Univ. of Paris, Fr. DIRECTOR, Serv. for Psych. Studies of Navigation Pers, Air Force Cen. for Psych. Studies and Instruction. Direction of research, testing, adminsitration; psychological problems of piloting, selection techniques. M

DEG, Miss Eve. 11 bis Rue Dulong, Paris 17. b. 31 Jan 1931 Paris. Diplôme d'études supérieures '53 Sorbonne, Fr. STUDY DIR, Cen. for Psychotech. Res. and Studies, 13 Rue Paul Chautard, Paris 15; PSYCHOLOGIST, Cen. for Educ. Guid. Member: APPD. Research, consulting; genesis of delinquency, industrial change and worker attitudes, psychology of the working woman. F

DEJEAN, Marcel Gabriel. 12 bis Rue Louis Eydoux, Toulouse. b. 22 June 1923 Bordeaux. Licence ès lettres '45 Univ. of Toulouse, Fr. REGIONAL DIR, Bureau Universitaire de Statistique et de Documentation Scolaires et Professionnelles, Acad. of Toulouse, 2 Rue d'Alsace-Lorraine, Toulouse. Member: SFP. Administration, guidance, applied and educational psychology, testing, clinical analysis; psychical processes in education, language and thought. M

DELAY, Prof. Jean. Ste. Anne Psychiat. Cen, 1 Rue Cabanis, Paris 14. b. 14 Nov 1907 Bayonne. Docteur ès lettres '42 and MD '35 Univ. of Paris, Fr. PROF. of CLIN. PSYCHIAT, Fac. of Med. of Paris, Rue de l'Ecole de Médecine, Paris 5; Director, Inst. of Psych, Univ. of Paris; DIRECTOR, *L'Encéphale.* Member: SFP. Teaching, research, editorial; pathological psychophysiology, literary and esthetic psychology. M

DELCHET, Jean Pierre Richard. 89 Rue Andre Bollier, Lyon 7. b. 22 Nov 1914 Mauriac. L.PS '53 Univ. of Lyon, Fr. LAB. DIRECTOR, Ecole Practique de Psych, 164 bis Rue P. Corneille, Lyon; RES. DIR, Cen. Regional de Documentation Pédagogique, Académie de Lyon, 47 Rue Ph. de Lamatte, Lyon 4. Research, teaching, administration, educational psychology, testing; educational psychology, experimental education. M

DELCOURT, Maurice. 155C Rue Antoine Durafour, St. Etienne. b. 26 Feb 1924 Levallois-Perret. Diplôme '49 Sorbonne, Fr. CHILD PSYCH'T, Serv. d'Hygiène Scolaire, Bureau Municipal d'Hygiène, Ville de St. Etienne, 1 bis Rue Blanqui. Member: SNPPD. Testing, consulting, guidance, research, psychotherapy; achievement tests, study of children's emotions. M

DELEURANCE, Dr. Edouard Philippe. Lab.

of Evolution, 105 Blvd. Raspail, Paris 6.
b. 13 Jan 1918 Saigon, Vietnam. Docteur
ès sciences '55 Univ. of Paris, Fr. DIR. of
RES, Natl. Cen. for Sci. Res. (CNRS), Lab.
of Evolution. Member: Int. Union for
Study of Social Insects. Research,
teaching; animal behavior. M
DELPECH, Prof. Léon. 47 Blvd. Grignan,
Le Mourillon, Toulon. b. 3 Mar 1908
Algiers, Algeria. Diplôme d'études supérieures '32 Fac. of Letters, Aix-en-Pro-
vence, Fr. DIRECTOR, Cen. Public d'Orien-
tation Professionnelle du Varenne, Palais
du Soleil, St. Roch, Toulon. Member: Fr.
Socy. for Study of the Szondi Test, Socy.
of the South-East, Fr. Socy. for Cybernetic
Res. Consulting, guidance, testing,
teaching; projective techniques, group
process, study of theoretical models. M
DEMARET, Pierre Michel. Secretariat of
Vocat. Guid, Acad. of Paris, 11 Rue
Tronchet, Paris. b. 29 July 1913 Stains.
Diplôme '42 Univ. of Caen, Fr. VOCAT.
GUID. INSPECTOR, Acad. of Paris. Member:
AIOP, ACOF. Guidance, administration,
applied and educational psychology;
guidance and education. M
DENIS-KELLER, Mrs. Gisèle. 4 Rue Bois-
sonade, Paris 14. b. 15 Mar 1927 Bourgla-
Reine. Diplôme '53 Univ. of Paris, Fr.
PSYCHOLOGIST, Bur. of Appl. Psych. and
Sociol, Compagnie française d'Organisation,
37 Rue de Bassano, Paris 8; CHILD GUID.
COUNS, priv. prac. Member: APPD. Testing,
consulting, guidance, applied and industrial psychology; achievement tests,
projective techniques, attitude measurement. F
DENNER, Alfred. 15 Rue Froidevaux, Paris
14. b. 4 July 1924 Tarnow, Poland.
Licence, Sorbonne, Fr; Diplôme, Inst. of
Psych, Paris, Fr. CONSULT. PSYCH'T, priv.
prac. Member: SFP, WAPOR, APPD. Market
research; attitude measurement, projection and symbolism, spread of communication and culture diffusion. M
DESCARGUES, Miss Marie Antoinette. 79
Ave. Franklin, Villemomble. b. 2 Nov 1932
Fontenay sous Bois. L.PS '56 Univ. of
Paris, Fr. VOCAT. GUID. COUNS, Caisse
d'Allocation Familiale, 27 Rue des Vignes,
Paris 16. Consulting, guidance, testing,
student; projective techniques, drawings,
personality tests, questionnaires. F
DESCOMBES, André. 8 Rue des Deux Portes,
Versailles. b. 21 July 1924 Valence. Elève
Diplômé '54 Univ. of Paris, Fr. MILIT.
PSYCH'T, Psychotech. Lab, S.T.A., 5 Rue
Carnot, Versailles. Member: APPD. Applied
psychology, research on the use of mental
tests in recruits' orientation; aptitude and
intelligence tests. M
DEUTSCH, Emeric. 3 Rue Tournus, Paris 15.

b. 10 Apr 1924 Budapest, Hungary.
Diplôme, Univ. of Paris, Fr. DIR. of
SERVICE, Societé O.R.I.C., 3 Ave. de l'Opéra,
Paris; PSYCHIAT. CONSULT, A.P.A.S. Dispensary, 31 Rue Lamarck, Paris 18.
Member: SFP. Applied psychology,
motivation research, consulting, testing;
research on deformation perceptives, group
dynamics, attitude measurement, psy-
chology of publicity. M
DIEL, Paul. 7 Impasse de Rouet, Paris 14.
b. 11 July 1893 Vienna, Austria. RES. DIR,
Natl. Cen. for Sci. Res. (CNRS), Lab. of
Child Psychobiol, 41 Rue Gay-Lussac,
Paris 5. Member: SFP, APSLF, Educational
psychology, consulting and research on the
re-education of maladjusted children; depth
psychology, unconscious symbolism. M
DIVERREZ, Jean. 17 Ave. des Bruyères,
La Garenne. b. 15 June 1919 Brest.
PROFESSOR, Cen. de Formation et de Per-
fectionnement des Cadres et de la Maîtrise,
90 Rue d'Amsterdam, Paris 9. Member:
APPD. Industrial psychology, teaching,
testing; public relations, personnel manage-
ment, group process, job evaluation. M
DORON, Dr. Roland. 4 Rue Général André,
Talence. b. 12 Sept 1921 Le Mans. MD '56
Univ. of Bordeaux, Fr. PROFESSOR, Inst.
of Psych. and Psychosociol. Studies, 20
Cours Pasteur, Bordeaux. Member: SFP,
Psych. Socy. of Bordeaux. Teaching, research; genetic psychology, educational
psychology, psychomotor tests. M
DORRA-NAGGAR, Mrs. Huguette. Etude du
Travail et Applications Psychotechniques,
27 Rue Pierre Demours, Paris 17. b. 13 Jan
1926 Alexandria, Egypt. Licence '48 Univ.
of Paris, Fr. CO-DIRECTOR, Etude du
Travail et Applications Psychotechniques.
Member: SNPPD, Groupement Français du
Rorschach. Industrial psychology, testing,
vocational guidance, consulting, professional writing; projective techniques, group
dynamics, group process, directed interviews, counseling. F
DOUARD, Henri. 16 Rue Bayard à Colombes.
b. 22 Jan 1922 Paris. Licence ès lettres '46
Univ. of Paris, Fr. ADVIS. in INDUS.
PSYCH, André Vidal and Co, 51 Rue Henri
Heine, Paris 16. Member: Assn. de Psychologues Praticiens Diplômés. Industrial
psychology, testing, research; projective
techniques, group process. M
DREVILLON, Jean. 65 Rue de la Polle,
Cherbourg. b. 4 Sept 1927 Brest. Diplôme
d'état '50 Univ. of Paris, Fr. DIRECTOR,
Centre Public d'Orientation Profession-
nelle, 12 Rue Guillaume Fouace, Cherbourg;
EDITOR, *Bulletin de l'Institut National
d'Orientation Professionnelle.* Member:
ACOF. Vocational guidance and counseling,
testing, applied psychology; aptitude tests,

learning techniques, methodology. M

DRILLET, Maurice. La Résidence, Ave. Victor Hugo, Montfermeil. b. 4 Apr 1921 Paris. Diplôme, Univ. of Paris, Fr. PERS. DIR, Thomson Houston Co, 78 Ave. S. Bolivar, Paris 19. Member: APPD. Personnel selection and administration; aptitude tests, character evaluation, merit ratings. M

DROUAN, Chef de Bataillon Robert. 38 Ave. Théophile Gautier, Paris 16. b. 17 Dec 1914 Baria, Indo-China. Baccalauréat en droit '49 Univ. of Paris, Fr. ADMIN. ASST. in PROPAGANDA and RECRUITMENT, Sect. d'Etudes et d'Informations des Troupes Coloniales, Caserne Clignancourt, Paris 18. Member: APPD. Administration, coordination of research on personnel selection and training; achievement tests, non-verbal tests for non-occidental and illiterate adults. M

DUBUISSON, Mrs. Paulette. 49 Rue de Flandre, Paris 19. b. 27 May 1920 Paris. Licence ès lettres '42 Univ. of Paris, Fr. PSYCHOTHERAPIST, Cen. Psycho-Pédagogique, 1 Ave. du Parc des Princes, Paris 16. Member: Syndicat Natl. des Psychologues Psychanalystes. Psychotherapy, consulting, clinical practice, research; child psychotherapy, group psychotherapy, psychodrama. F

DUCHAPT-MICHEL, Mrs. Henriette Denise. 17 Rue Dinant, Clamart. b. 13 Apr 1905 Paris. Diplôme '41 Univ. of Paris, Fr. DIRECTOR, Centres Publics d'Orientation Professionnelle d'Eure et Loir, 6 Rue de Beauvais, Chartres; ED. BD, *Bulletin de l'Association des Conseillers d'Orientation de France.* Member: AIPA, ACOF. Educational and vocational guidance, administration; guidance and vocational adjustment of farm youths in urban areas, intelligence and aptitude tests for the mentally and educationally retarded. F

DUGAS, Prof. Guy. 20 Ave. Ambroise Rendu, Paris 19. b. 13 July 1907 Genneteil. Certificat '41 Univ. of Paris, Fr. SECY. GENL, Cen. d'Etudes Techniques des Industries de l'Habillement (CETIH), 29 Rue des Pyramides, Paris 1. Applied and industrial psychology, teaching, research; aptitude measurement, learning theory, scientific organization of work, job evaluation. M

DUMONTET, Albert. 7 Rue Loyson de Chastelus, Villefranche. b. 23 Jan 1894 Villefranche. DIRECTOR, Office d'Orientation Professionnelle, Blvd. Gambetta, Hôtel de la Chambre de Commerce, Villefranche. Member: ACOF. Vocational consulting and guidance; achievement tests, memory and learning. M

DUPUIS, Daniel Marcel Louis. 42 Blvd. St. Germain, Paris 5. b. 28 June 1910 Vendôme

Diplôme '51 Univ. of Paris, Fr. DIRECTOR, Centre Sélection Psychotechnique, 1-S, 3 bis, Blvd. Kellermann, Paris 13. Member: APPD. Applied psychology, consulting, guidance, testing. M

DURANDIN, Guy Charles. 81 Rue de Bagneux, Montrouge. b. 1 June 1916 Paris. Agrégé '45 Univ. of Paris, Fr. ASST. in PSYCH, Fac. of Letters and Inst. of Psych, Univ. of Paris, 17 Rue de la Sorbonne, Paris. Member: SFP, APSLF, Syndicat National des Psychologues Psychoanalystes. Teaching, research, psychotherapy; psychology of lying, propaganda, prejudive. M

DURUP, Gustave Ernest. Collège de France, Paris 5. b. 10 May 1900 Paris. Diplôme '30 Ecole Pratique des Hautes Etudes, Sorbonne, Fr. ASST. DIR. of LAB, Collège de France. Member: SPF, APSLF. Research, professional writing, educational psychology; vision, psychological vocabulary, general pedagogy. M

DUVERGE, Mrs. Hélène. 3 Rue Louis, Antony. b. 31 May 1919 St. Cloud. Diplôme '41 Univ. of Paris, Fr. CHIEF, Guid. Bur, Office for Overseas Students, 27 Rue Oudinot, Paris. Member: ACOF, SNPPD. Educational and vocational guidance of African youths, testing, administration, research; achievement tests adapted for African school children, research in educational adjustment of African children, memory and learning. F

ENRIQUEZ, Eugène. 6 Rue Juliette Lamber, Paris 17. b. 30 July 1931 La Goulette, Tunisia. Diplôme d'études supérieures '54 Univ. of Paris, Fr. DIR. of RES, Assn. Française d'Accroissement de la Productivité, Rue du Faubourg St. Honoré, Paris. Applied, industrial psychology, student; industrial studies, group dynamics, communication. M

ENRIQUEZ, Mrs. Micheline. 6 Rue Juliette Lamber, Paris 17. b. 11 Sept 1931 Chalons. Diplôme '54 Inst. of Psych, Univ. of Paris, Fr. PSYCHOLOGIST, St. Anne Psychiat. Cen, 1 Rue Cabanis, Paris 14. Member: SNPPD. Testing, clinical analysis, student; projective techniques, psychometrics, tests of hysteria. F

ESPINASSE, René. 19 Ave. de Chambéry, Annecy. b. 25 Jan 1907 Mirecourt. Conseiller '41 Inst. d'Orientation Professionnelle, Annecy, Fr. DIRECTOR, Centre d'Orientation de la Haute-Savoie, 11 Ave. d'Aléry, Annecy. Member: ACOF. Consulting, guidance, testing, applied psychology; aptitude measurement, achievement tests, study of temperament. M

FAISAN, Michel. 3 Rue de Nevers, Paris 6. b. 11 Feb 1931 Paris. Licence '52 Univ. of Poitiers, Fr. RES. DIR, Centre d'Etudes et Recherches Psychotechniques, 13 Rue Paul

Chautard, Paris 15. Research, applied psychology; human engineering, group process. M

FANCHON, Miss Lisette Marie-Louise Pâquerette. 2 Rue Alice, Courbevoie. b. 23 Apr 1916 Agnewz, California, USA. Diplôme d'études supérieures, Univ. of Aix-Marseille, Fr. LECT in SOC. PSYCH, Ecole de Psychologues Praticiens, 21 Rue d'Assas, Paris, 6. Member: SFP, SNPPD, Assn. Professionelle des Psychologues Praticiens Diplômés de l'Inst. Catholique de Paris. Teaching, research, applied and industrial psychology; study of groups, attitude measurement, industrial social psychology. F.

FAUCHEUX, Claude. 4 Rue de Braque, Paris 3. b. 22 Apr 1929 Chateau du Loir. Diplôme d'études supérieures, Univ. of Paris, Fr. RES. WRKR, Natl. Cen. for Sci. Res. (CNRS), Lab. of Soc. Psych. of the Sorbonne, 16 Rue de la Sorbonne, Paris 5. Research; group dynamics, measurement of cultural attitudes. M.

FAVERGE, Prof. Jean-Marie. 4 Ave. de la Porte du Point du Jour, Paris 16. b. 18 July 1912 Balanod. Agrégation '36 Univ. of Paris, Fr. DIR. of RES, Cen. for Psychotech. Studies and Res, 13 Rue Paul Chautard, Paris 15; PROFESSOR, Inst. of Psych. Univ. of Paris. Member: SFP. Research, teaching; psychometrics. M

FAVEZ-BOUTONIER, Prof. Mrs. Juliette. 2 Rue de la Montagne, St. Geneviève, Paris 5. b. 24 Jan 1903 Roquefort-les-Pins. Doctorat '45 Univ. of Paris, Fr. PROFESSOR, Sorbonne, Rue des Ecoles, Paris. Member: SFP, Fr. Psychoanal. Socy. Teaching, psychotherapy, research; maladjusted children, juvenile delinquency. F

FAVRE, Francisque. Centre d'Orientation Professionnelle, Rue St. Just, Romans sur Isère. b. 16 July 1927 Thoiry. Diplôme d'état '55, France. DIRECTOR, Cen. d'Orientation Professionnelle de Romans sur Isère. Member: ACOF. Vocational and educational consulting and guidance, testing, research; achievement tests, tests of factor G, projective techniques. M

FEILLOUCAT, Miss Janine. 32 Rue des Jacobins, Beauvais. b. 21 July 1920 Bordeaux. Licence ès lettres '42 Univ. of Aix-Marseille, Fr. DIRECTOR, Centre Départemental d'Orientation Professionnelle, Ministère de l'Education Nationale, Pl. du Jeu de Paume, Beauvais. Member: ACOF. Educational and vocational consulting and guidance, testing, administration; learning theory, achievement tests, motivation. F

FERRY, Prof. Gilles. Clairbois, Rond Point du Petit Clamart, Clamart. b. 4 Jan 1917 Paris. Diplôme d'études supérieures, Univ. of Paris, Fr. PROF. of PSYCH,

Ecole Normale Supérieure d'Education Physique des Jeunes Filles, Chatenay-Malabray; PROFESSOR, Natl. Cen. of Special Educ, Beaumont. Member: SFP. Teaching, research; educational psychology applied to physical education, social psychology of employed adolescents. M

FESSARD, Prof. Alfred. 4 Ave. Gordon Bennett, Paris 16. b. 28 Apr 1900 Paris. Docteur ès sciences '36 Univ. of Paris, Fr. PROF. of NEUROPHYSIOL, Collège de France, 1 Pl. Marcelin Berthelot, Paris 5; CO-EDITOR *L'année Psychologique.* Member: SFP, APSLF, Société de Biotypologie. Teaching, administration, research; brain waves and their psychological correlates, proprioception, motor activity. M

FICHELET, Raymond. 88 bis Rue Michel-Ange, Paris 16. b. 5 June 1931 Le Havre. Diplôme, Inst. of Psych, Univ. of Paris, Fr. RES. DIR, Commissariat Général à la Productivité, 41 Quai Branly, Paris 7. Industrial and social psychology, research, testing, clinical analysis, administration; application of social psychological techniques to group psychotherapy, communication in discussion groups. M

FLACHOT, Guy. 54 Blvd. Exelmans, Paris 16. b. 10 Dec 1918 Paris. PSYCHTECHNICIAN Centre de Synthèse, 93 Blvd. Péreire, Paris 17; ED. COMM, *Travail Social.* Industrial psychology, testing, consulting; aptitude tests, characterology and personality studies, human relations in industry, vocational adaptation and training. M

FLAMENT, Claude. 180 Blvd. de Stalingrad, Champigny s/Marne. b. 9 May 1930 Paris. Licence '56 Univ. of Paris, Fr. RES. WRKR, Natl. Cen. for Sci. Res. (CNRS), Lab. of Exper. and Comp. Psych, Sorbonne, Paris. Research; group dynamics, systems of communication, attitude change. M

FLAMENT, Mrs. Fanny. 180 Blvd. de Stalingrad, Champigny s/Marne. b. 26 Apr 1928 Paris. Licence '50 Univ. of Paris, Fr. PSYCHOLOGIST, Hôpital Psychiatrique de Prèmontré, Aisne. Testing, education of the retarded; intelligence tests for the feebleminded, psychology and education of infants. F

FLORES, César. Lab. of Exper. and Comparative Psych. of the Sorbonne, 46 Rue St. Jacques, Paris 5. b. 1 Mar 1922 St. Nazaire. Diplôme, Univ. of Paris, Fr. RES. WRKR, Natl. Cen. for Sci. Res. (CNRS), 13 Quai Anatole France, Paris 7; ED. SECY, *l'Année Psychologique.* Member: SFP, APSLF. Research, editorial; memory and verbal learning. M

FONDU, Roger. Castel-Azur, 4 Rue Lange, Nice. b. 25 Sept 1913 St. Amand. Diplôme d'état '50 Inst. Natl. d'Orientation Professionnelle, Fr. VOCAT. GUID. COUNS,

Centre d'Orientation Professionnelle, 16 Blvd. Carabacel, Nice. Member: ACOF. Consulting, guidance; achievement, intelligence and motor tests. M

FOUILHE, Pierre. 48 Blvd. de Glatigny, Versailles. b. 5 Oct. 1923 Sète. Licence ès lettres '47 Univ. of Paris, Fr. RES. WRKR, Natl. Cen. for Sci. Res. (CNRS), 13 Quai Anatole France, Paris 7; EDITOR, *Recherches Sociologiques*. Research, teaching, editorial; attitude measurement, mass medias, acculturation of the child. M

FOURMENT, Miss Claude. 46 Rue Cortambert, Paris 16. b. 5 Feb 1925 Paris. Licence ès sciences '49 Univ. of Paris, Fr. PSYCH. ASST, Assistance Publique, Paris; ASST. in PSYCH, Inst. Médico-Psychologique Edouard Claparède, Paris. Member: SNPPD, Groupement Français du Rorschach. Testing, clinical analysis, consulting, guidance, applied psychology; projective and mental achievement tests. F

FRAISSE, Prof. Paul. 19 Rue d'Antony, Chateny-Malabry. b. 20 Mar 1911 St. Etienne. PH.D '45 Univ. of Louvain, Belgium. PROF. EXP. PS. Fac of Letters; DIRECTOR, Ecole des Hautes Etudes, Sorbonne, 47 Rue des Ecoles, Paris; ASST. DIR, Inst. of Psych; CO-DIRECTOR, *Année Psychologique*. Member: SFP, APSLF. Research, teaching, administration; perception, motor reaction, time and rhythm. M

FRANCES, Robert. 39 Rue de Jussieu, Paris 5. b. 12 Apr 1919 Brousse, Turkey. Agrégé '47 Univ. of Paris, Fr. RES. WRKR, Natl. Cen. for Sci. Res. (CNRS), 13 Quai Anatole France, Paris. Member: SFP, APSLF. Experimental research on the psychology of music, professional writing; perception of musical sound, psychology of esthetic experience, evolution of cultural perception. M

FRANCES, Simone. 39 Rue de Jussieu, Paris 5. b. 24 Aug 1926 Rabat, Morocco. Certificat '47 Univ. of Paris, Fr. RES. ASST, Natl. Cen. for Sci. Res. (CNRS), 13 Quai Anatole France, Paris. Member: SFP. Research; attitude measurement. F

FRANDEMICHE, Robert. 67 Blvd. Félix Grat, Laval. b. 28 Jan 1909 Laval. Bachelier '28 Univ. of Rennes, Fr. DIRECTOR, Cen. Départemental d'Orientation Professionnelle, Rue de Bretagne, Laval. Member: ACOF. Testing, consulting, guidance, applied psychology. M

FREY, Louis-Georges. Bibèmus, Chemin de Bibèmus, Aix en Provence. b. 26 Juni 1924 Tunis, Tunisia. Diplôme d'études supérieures '51 Univ. of Aix-Marseille, Fr. RES. WRKR, Inst. des Sciences Humaines Appliquées, 5 Rond Point Bugeaud, Paris. Member: SNPPD. Research, teaching, industrial psychology; social psychology,

field theory, small groups. M

FUKUI, Mrs. Noëlle Marie. 45 Rue du Ranelagh, Paris 16. b. 24 Dec 1929 St. Nazaire. Diplôme '54 Inst. of Psych. Univ. of Paris, Fr. PSYCHOLOGIST, S.N.C.F., E. Region Social Serv, 9 Rue du Chateau Landon, Paris; Hôpital St. Joseph, 1 Rue Pierre Larousse, Paris. Member: SNPPD. Testing, clinical analysis, guidance; achievement tests, projective techniques. F

FUSSWERK. Dr. Joseph. 14 bis Rue Olier, Paris 15. b. 9 Apr 1905 Varsovie, Poland. MD, Univ. of Paris, Fr. PSYCHOTHERAPIST, St. Anne Hosp, 1 Rue de Cabanis, Paris, PSYCHIATRIST, priv. prac. Member: SFP, Société Médico-Psychologique. Clinical practice, psychotherapy, clinical analysis; narcoanalysis, Rorschach test, pathography. M

GALIBERT, René Jean. Boussorp, La Croix-Blanche. b. 28 May 1909 Cauzac. Certificat '43 Inst. Natl. d'Orientation Professionnelle, Fr. TEACHER, Ecole Publique, La Croix-Blanche; EDITOR, *La Voix Laïque*. Member: ACOF. Teaching, editorial; educational information and counseling for parents. M

GASTAUT, Prof. Henri. 149 Promenade de la Corniche, Marseille. b. 5 Apr 1915 Monaco. Prof. '49 Fac. of Med, Univ. of Marseille, Fr. HEAD, Lab. of Neurobiology, Fac. of Med. Univ. of Marseille; HEAD, Lab. of Electrophysiol, Hosp. of Marseille. Member: SFP, APSLF, RMPA, Socy. of Psychosomatic Med. Research, teaching, consulting; electroencephalographic and neurophysiologic studies of pathological behavior, conditioning, and learning. M

GATIER, Gérard. 7 Rue Mercière, Lyon. b. 17 May 1926 Boën-sur-Lignon. '49 Univ. of Geneva, Switzerland. PSYCH. ADVISOR, priv. prac; CONSULT. PSYCH'T, Assistance à l'Enfance, Département du Rhône, Lyon and Sauvegarde de l'Enfance, 25 Pl. Bellecour, Lyon. Member: AIPA, Groupement Français du Rorschach. Clinical practice, consulting, testing, clinical analysis, research; projective techniques for children, maturation of perception in learning to read. M

GAUCHET, François. 25 Rue Jean Goujon, Paris 8. b. 2 Mar 1921 Paris. Diplôme d'études supérieures, Univ. of Paris, Fr. PSYCHOLOGIST, Assn. française pour l'Accroissement de la Productivité, 11 Rue du Faubourg St. Honoré, Paris 8. Member: AIPA, APPD. Testing, industrial psychology, research; projective techniques, intelligence tests, social perception. M

GAUTHERON, Pierre. 137 Rue du Lt. Col. Montbrison, Rueil-Malmaison. b. 10 Sept 1913 Paris. DIRECTOR, Indus. Psych. Cen, Société Nationale Etude et Construction Moteurs d'Aviation, 68 Quai du Point du Jour, Boulogne-Billancourt. Member: AIPA, APPD, SNPPD. Applied, industrial psychology, testing, administration; projective techniques, intelligence tests. M

GAVINI, Miss Hélène Marie Brigitte. 91 Rue St. Jacques, Marseille. b. 3 Nov 1903 Bourges. Diplôme d'études supérieures '28 Montpellier Univ, Fr. DIRECTOR, Lab. of Psycho-Acoustics, Natl. Cen. for Sci. Res. (CNRS), 66 Rue St. Sébastien, Marseille. Member: SFP, APSLF, APPD. Research, teaching, applied psychology; auditory perception, sensory experiments, occupational selection. F

GAYRARD, Mrs. Hélène Marie. 14 Allée Voltaire, Villeneuve le Roi. b. 10 Sept 1906 Aubin. Diplôme d'état '46 Univ. of Paris, Fr. PSYCHOPHYSIOLOGIST, Cen. Natl. d'Etudes des Télécommunications, 24 Rue Bertrand, Paris 7. Member: AIPA, APPD, ACOF, Groupement des Acousticiens de Langue Française. Research in audiometry, industrial psychology, administration; tests of fatigue, memory, hearing, study of noise. F

GAZEL, Mrs. Laure. Cen. Public D'Orientation Professionnelle, Privas. b. 22 May 1908 Lyon. Diplôme d'état '52 Univ. of Paris, Fr. VOCAT. GUID. COUNS, Cen. d'Orientation Professionnelle. Member: ACOF. Consulting, guidance, applied psychology, testing; achievement tests, aptitude measurement, child and adolescent psychology, reclassification of the physically handicapped. F

GENEST, Marc Jean Henri. A.N.I.F.R.M.O., 13 Rue Paul Chautard, Paris, 15. b. 22 June 1926 Issoire. Licence ès sciences '46 Univ. of Rennes, Fr. PSYCHOTECHNICIAN, Cen. d'Etudes et Recherches Psychotechniques, A.N.I.F.R.M.O. Research on the techniques of psychological tests; psychobiology of work, vocational education and selection. M

GESSAIN, Dr. Robert. 80 Ave. de Versailles. Paris 16. b. 11 Apr 1907 Clermont. MD '32 Univ. of Paris, Fr. RES. WRKR, Lab. of Anthrop, Musée de l'Homme, Pl. du Trocadéro, Paris. Member: Fr. Psychoanal. Socy. Research, consulting; relation between cultural anthropology and analytic psychology. M

GIACCHETTI, Mrs. Edith. 9 Rue Milton, Paris, 9 b. 2 Nov 1924 Paris. Diplôme d'état '46 Natl. Inst. of Vocat. Guid, Fr. PSYCHOTECHNICIAN, Cen. for Appl. Psych. 14 Rue Henner, Paris 9. Member: APPD. Industrial psychology, testing. F

GILLE, Maxime Jean Laurent. 1 Rue Aristide

Briand, Gentilly. b. 23 Dec 1917 La Chartre-sur-le-Loir. Diplôme d'état, Univ. of Paris, Fr. INDUS. PSYCH'T, Cen. for Productivity in the Jute Industry, 33 Rue de Miromesnil, Paris 8. Member: SNPPD. Industrial psychology, teaching, organizational methods, research; group dynamics, group process, opinion studies, work incentives. M

GIRARD, Alain. 58 Rue de la Faisanderie, Paris 16. b. 13 Mar 1914 Paris. Diplôme d'études supérieures, Univ. of Paris, Fr. DEPT. HEAD, Natl. Inst. for Demographic Studies, 23 Ave. Franklin D. Roosevelt, Paris 8; SECY. GENL, Sondages. Member: SFP. Research; social psychology, public opinion. M

GIRERD-CHANEL, André. 6 Rue Leon Dalloz, Tarbes. b. 15 Feb 1922 Lyon. Diplôme d'état '47 Inst. Natl. d'Orientation Professionnelle, Fr. DIRECTOR, Gen. d'Orientation Professionnelle, 31 Rue Georges Clémenceau, Tarbes. Administration, applied and educational psychology testing, clinical analysis, guidance; achievement tests, aptitude, behavior. M

GIRERD-CHANEL, Mrs. Fernande. 6 Rue Leon Dalloz, Tarbes. b. 6 Aug 1913 Oran, Algeria. Diplôme d'état, Inst. Natl. d'Orientation Professionnelle, Fr. VOCAT. and EDUC. GUID. COONS, Cen. d'Orientation, 31 Rue Georges Clémenceau, Tarbes. Teaching, applied and educational psychology, testing, consulting, guidance; achievement tests, aptitudes, behavior. F

GISCARD, Pierre. 27 Rue de Tocqueville, Paris 17. b. 14 July 1929 Curemonte. L.PS '54 Univ. of Aix-Marseille, Fr. RES. DIR, Cen. d'Expérimentation et de Recherche pour l'Amélioraton de Méthodes de Perfectionnement du Pers. d'Encadrement, 81 Rue de Mirosmenil, Paris 8. Research, applied and industrial psychology; group dynamics, training of industrial excutives, use of statistics in psychology, operational research. M

GLUGE, Miss Marianne. 5 Ave. du Général Balfourier, Paris 16. b. 8 Apr 1930 Nice. L.PS '51 Univ. of Paris, Fr. RES. WRKR, Natl. Cen. for Sci. Res. (CNRS), Lab. of Social Psych, 16 Rue de la Sorbonne, Paris 5. Research, testing, clinical analysis; opinion studies. F

GOGUELIN, Pierre Louis Georges. 9 Rue des Marais, Viroflay. b. 2 July 1922 Cherbourg. Diplôme '47 Inst. of Psych, Univ. of Paris, Fr. DIRECTOR, Management Trng. Prog. Electricité de France, 68 Rue du Faubourg St. Honoré, Paris; DIRECTOR, Société française d'étude du travail, 21 Rue du Cardinal Lemoine, Paris. Member: APPD, ACOF,

Assn. Libre des Professionnels de la Psychologie et de la Psychosociologie Appliquées, Assn. Internationale de Psychotechnique. Industrial psychology, personnel training, research, teaching.　M

GOUSTARD, Dr. Michel. 13 Ave. de la Gare, Limours. b. 30 Mar 1920 Fontanay-aux-Roses. Doctorat ès lettres '55 Univ. of Paris, Fr. RES. DIR, Natl. Cen.for Sci. Res, (CNRS), 13 Quai Anatole France, Paris 7. Member: SFP, APSLF. Research; learning theory, zoopsychology, psychology of affectivity.　M

GOZLAN, Miss Alice. 53 bis Quai des Grands Augustins, Paris 6. b. 29 Oct 1922 Constantine, Algeria. L.PS '52 Univ. of Paris, Fr. CLIN. PSYCH'T, Préfecture de la Seine, 9 Pl. de l'Hôtel de Ville, Paris. Member: SNPPD. Testing, clinical analysis, consulting clinical practice, guidance; projective techniques, achievement tests.　F

GRANJON-GALIFRET, Mrs. Nadine Janine. 7 Rue de l'Industrie, Paris 13. b. 26 Apr 1918 Nice. Licence ès lettres '41 Univ. of Grenoble, Fr. RES. WRKR, Natl. Cen. for Sci. Res. (CNRS), 13 Quai Anatole France, Paris 7; PSYCH. LAB. ASST, Hôpital Henri Rouselle. Member: SFP, APSLF. Research, testing, student; educational psychology, development of language, left handedness, typology.　F

GRASSÉ, Prof. Pierre-Paul. 105 Blvd. Raspail, Paris 6. b. 27 Nov 1895 Périgueux. Docteur ès sciences, Univ. of Paris, Fr. PROFESSOR, Fac. of Sciences, Univ. of Paris; DIRECTOR, Laboratoire d'Evolution des Etres organisés, Paris. Member: SFP. Research, professional writing, editorial: animal behavior, animal sociology.　M

GRISEZ, Jean. 52 Ave. Henri Corvol, Choisy-le-Roi. b. 27 Oct 1928 Paris, Diplôme '54 Univ. of Paris, Fr. PSYCHO-TECHNICIAN, Cen. d'Etudes et Recherches Psychotech, 13 Rue Paul Chautard, Paris 15. Research, applied psychology, testing: psychological aspects of industrial accidents, intelligence, personality.　M

GROGNOU, Guy. 9 Rue Guillemin Tarayre, Toulouse. b. 11 May 1928 Versailles. Diplôme '54 Inst. Natl. d'Orientation Professionnelle, Fr. VOCAT. GUID. COUNS, Cen. d'Orientation Professionnelle, 32 Rue de la Dalbade, Toulouse. Member: ACOF. Guidance, testing, applied psychology; intellectual aptitude and motivation tests, achievement and character tests, projective techniques, behavior.　M

GROUSSET, Dr. Christian. Centre d'Examen Médical du Personnel de l'Aéronautique Navale, Hôpital St. Anne, Toulon. b. 16 Dec 1921 Caussade. MD '47 Univ. of

Bordeaux, Fr; Licence '54 Univ. of Rennes, Fr. DIRECTOR, Appl. Psych. Sect. of Naval Aeronautics, Hôpital Maritime de St. Anne; CLIN. PSYCH'T, Neuropsychiat. Serv, Hôpital St. Anne. Member: APPD. Testing, clinical practice, applied psychology; projective techniques, learning, group process.　M

GUETTA, Pierre. 7 Rue Gay-Lussac, Paris 5. b. 31 Oct 1930 Algiers, Algeria. Licence '51 Univ. of Paris, Fr. RES. DIR, Inst. for Indus. Soc. Sci, 6 Rue de Tournon, Paris 6. Member: APPD. Applied psychology; industrial relations, attitude measurements, social perception.　M

GUIGUET, Bernard. 24 Rue Banes, Meudon. b. 4 Feb 1929 Paris 16. Diplôme '53 Inst. of Psych, Univ. of Paris, Fr. RES. DIR, Cen. d'Etudes et Recherches Psychotech, 13 Rue Paul Chautard, Paris 15. Member: SFP. Research, applied psychology; adaptation of the machine to man, physiology of work.　M

HANOT, Marc. 2 Ave. de Versailles, Paris 16. b. 31 Mar 1925 Paris. Diplôme '55 Univ. of Paris, Fr. PSYCHOTECHNICIAN, Société Française de Psychotechnique, 117 Rue Réaumur, Paris 2. Member: APPD. Vocational guidance, testing, applied psychology; projective techniques, sociometry.　M

HEIDET, Michel. 4 Villa Stendhal, Paris 20. b. 1 Apr 1930 Sceaux. L.PS '56 Sorbonne, Fr. PSYCHOTECHNICIAN, Régie Autonome des Transports Parisiens, 53 Quai des Grands Augustins, Paris. Member: APPD. Applied psychology, student; accident prevention, development of aptitudes, management training.　M

HELMAN, Mrs. Zena. 8 Rue Cochin, Paris 5. b. 20 Aug 1914 Galati, Rumania. Doctorat d'état '56 Univ. of Paris, Fr. RES. WRKR, Natl. Cen. for Sci. Res. (CNRS), 13 Quai Anatole France, Paris 7. Member: Groupement Français du Rorschach. Research, applied psychology, clinical analysis, professional writing; electroencephalography, Rorschach and drawing in psychopathology and in child psychology.　F

HENRI, Pierre. 1 Impasse des Champs Garreau, Le Mans. b. 2 May 1921 Le Mans. Conseiller '41 Inst. Natl. d'Orientation Professionnelle, Fr. DIRECTOR, Cen. Public d'Orientation de la Sarthe, Le Mans. Consulting, guidance, administration, testing; projective techniques, characterology.　M

HENRIOT, Jacques. Ecole Normale Supérieure, St. Cloud. b. 28 Apr 1923 St. Mandé. Agrégation '49 Univ. of Paris, Fr. DIRECTOR Lab. of Psychopedagogy, Ecole Normale Supérieure. Teaching, research, educational psychology; formation and structure of the aesthetic and moral conscience in the child. **M**

HERMITTE, Léon. Inst. de Biométrie Humaine et d'Orientation Professionnelle, 11 Rue Mission de France, Marseille 1. b. 8 July 1911 Basses Alpes. RES. DIR, Inst. de Biométrie Humaine; DIRECTOR, Cen. Public d'Orientation Professionnelle. Member: ACOF. Teaching, administration, applied and educational psychology, consulting, guidance; vocational guidance. **M**

HEUYER, Prof. Georges. 1 Ave. Emile Deschanel, Paris 7. b. 30 Jan 1884 Pacy sur Eure. PROF. of PSYCHIAT, Fac. of Med, Univ. of Paris, 47 Blvd. de l'Hôpital, Paris 13; EDITOR, *Revue de Neuro-psychiatrie infantile et d'Hygiène Mentale de l'Enfant.* Member: SFP, Société Médico-Psychologique. Teaching, research, clinical practice; child psychology. **M**

HIRIARTBORDE, Edmond. 366 bis Rue de Vaugirard, Paris 15. b. 18 Apr 1925 St. Palais. Licence '49 Sorbonne, Fr. DIR. of RES, Ecole Normale Supérieure d'Education Physique et Sportive, Place Voltaire, Chatenay-Malabry. Member: SFP, APSLF. Research, applied educational psychology, teaching; motor learning, genetic psychology. **M**

HUGELIN, André. 4 Rue Théodore de Banville, Paris 17. b. Dec 1923 Paris. MD '54 Univ. of Paris, Fr. RES. WRKR, Inst. Natl. d'Hygiène, Lab. of Neurophysiology, Hôpital Henri Rousselle, Paris 14. Member: SFP. Research; conscience. **M**

HUGONNIER, René. 131 Ave. St. Simond, Aix-les-Bains. b. 5 Jan 1921 Lyon. TECHNICIAN, Genl. Comm. for Productivity, 41 Quai Branly, Paris. Member: APPD. Industrial psychology; human relations, organization. **M**

HUMBERT, Miss Claudine. 5 Rue de Nice, Paris 11. b. 6 June 1932 Paris. Licence ès lettres '56. Univ. of Paris, Fr. TECHNICIAN, Lab. of Social Psych, Univ. of Paris, 16 Rue de la Sorbonne, Paris 5. Research; collective process, attitude measurement. **F**

HURTIG, Michel. 106 Rue Cardinet, Paris 17. b. 6 May 1931 Bucharest, Rumania. L.PS '55 Univ. of Paris, Fr. RES. ASST, Natl. Cen. for Sci. Res. (CNRS), Paris. Research, testing, applied psychology; child psychology, learning abilities. **M**

HUSSON, Prof. Léon Alphonse. Fort St. Irénée, Lyon 5. b. 19 Apr 1897 St. Etienne. Docteur ès lettres '47 Sorbonne, Fr. PROF. of PSYCH, Fac. of Letters, 72 Rue Pasteur, Lyon; DIRECTOR, Ecole Pratique de Psychologie et de Pédagogie, Univ. of Lyon, 164 bis Rue Pierre Corneille, Lyon; EDITOR, *Bulletin* de l'Ecole Pratique de Psychologie et de Pédagogie. Member: AIPA, APSLF,

SFP. Teaching, administration, historical analysis and criticism of the major psychological theories; psychology of law. **M**

HYRIEN, Claude. 15 bis Rue du Pot de Fer, Paris 5. b. 16 Aug 1930 Henvic. L.PS '53 Univ. of Rennes, Fr. PSYCHOLOGIST, Cen. d'Observation Public d'Education Surveillée de Paris, Ferme de Champagne, Savigny-sur-Orge. Member: SNPPD. Applied psychology, testing, clinical analysis, psychotherapy, student; familial, social and individual attitude measurement, role playing, conflicts, character structure. **M**

IMBERT, Raymond. Cen. d'Orientation Professionnelle, 28 Rue Victor Hugo, Mont de Marsan. b. 27 Oct. 1919 Cagnac les Mines. Conseiller '49 Inst. Natl. d'Orientation Professionnelle, Fr. DIRECTOR, Cen. d'Orientation Professionnelle. Member: ACOF. Consulting, guidance, testing, administration; achievement tests, collective process, child psychology. **M**

JALLAS, Miss Anne Marie. 1 Rue Gabriel Peri, Grenoble. b. 25 Aug 1925 La Tronche. Diplôme '48 Inst. of Psych. Univ. of Paris, Fr. SCH. PSYCH'T, Ecole de Filles, 11 bis Cours Jean Jaurès, Grenoble. Member: SNPPD. Educational psychology, consulting guidance, testing, clinical analysis; achievement tests, projective techniques, observations of behavior. **F**

JAMPOLSKY, Pierre. 8 Rue du Four, Paris 6. b. 16 Aug 1918 Paris. Diplôme d'études supérieures, Univ. of Paris, Fr. DIR. of RES, Natl. Cen. for Sci. Res. (CNRS), 13 Quai Anatole France, Paris 7; DIR. of PSYCH. LAB, Child Psychiat. Clinic, Fac. of Med, Univ. of Paris. Member: SFP, APSLF, Groupement d'étude de Neuro-psychopathologie Infantile. Research, clinical analysis, teaching; personality development projective tests, neuroses, social attitudes. **M**

JANIW, Prof. Dr. Wolodymyr. 27 Rue des Bauves, Sarcelles. b. 21 Nov 1908 Lviv, Ukraine. PH.D '44 Friedrich-Wilhelms Univ, Germany. PROF. of PSYCH. and SOCIOL, Ukrainian Free Univ, Ernst Reuterstr. 4, Munich, Germany; SECY. GENL, Société Scientifique Ševčenko, Sarcelles. Member: DGP, BDP. Research, teaching, administration; psychology of imprisonment, ethnopsychology, social psychology. **M**

JAUR, Dr. Jeanne-Marie. 102 Rue Marengo, Marseille 6. b. 22 Dec 1910 Marseille. Docteur en Droit '41 Univ. of Aix-Marseille, Fr. DIRECTOR, Tech. Cen. for Documentation and Profes. Guid, 171 Rue de Rome, Marseille 6; PROF. of GENL, PHYCH, Sch.

of Soc. Work, Marseille. Member: AIPA, APPD, AIOP, ACOF. Applied psychology, guidance, teaching, research, administration; projective techniques, learning theory, achievement tests, social perception group process. F

JOLY DE BRESILLON, Miss Jeannine Marguerite Antoinette. 28 Rue de Montreuil, Pantin. b. 25 Nov 1927 Paris. Diplôme d'état '51 Sorbonne, Fr. PSYCHOTECHNICIAN, Société française de Psychotechnique, 117 Rue Réaumur, Paris 2. Member: APPD. Applied psychology, personnel selection, testing, vocational guidance; intelligence and aptitude tests, personality tests. F

JOUBLIN, Mrs. Claude. 6 Rue du Débarcadère, Paris 17. b. 21 Jan 1927 Paris. Diplôme '49 Univ. of Paris, Fr. DIR. of PUBLICATIONS, Cen. for Appl. Psych. 15 Rue Henri Heine, Paris 16. Member: APPD. Editorial work, administration, testing; publication of psychological tests in French and other languages. F

JOUSSE, Michel. 90 Rue de la Jonquière, Paris 17. b. 30 Mar 1930 Mayenne. L.PS Univ. of Paris, Fr. DIR. of RES, Inst. for Econ. and Soc. Res. (IRES), 12 Rue Soufflot, Paris 5. Research, applied psychology; consumer motivation, market research, group dynamics, job analysis. M

JOUVET, Dr. Michel. Lab. of Physiol, Fac. of Med, Lyon. b. 16 Nov 1925 Lons-le-Saunier. MD '56 Univ. of Lyon, Fr. RES. ASST, Lab. of Physiol; HEAD, Neuropsychiat. Clin, Hôpital E. Herriot, Lyon. Member: SFP. Research, clinical practice; neurophysiological mechanisms concerning conditioning and learning. M

JUSTET, Lucien. 79 Ave. de Villiers, Paris 17. b. 26 Apr 1925 Givors. Diplôme, Inst. of Psych, Univ. of Paris, Fr. DIR. GENL, Société Française de Psychotechnique, 117 Rue de Réaumur, Paris 2. Member: APPD. Applied and industrial psychology, administration, testing, clinical analysis; vocational guidance, group process. M

KOMORNICKA, Miss Christiane de. 19 Rue de la Croix, Avignon. b. 17 Mar 1924 Baden, Austria. Licence en Droit '45 Univ. of Montpellier, Fr. VOCAT. GUID. COUNS, Cen. Départemental d'Orientation Professionnelle, Rue Victor Hugo, Avignon. Member: ACOF. Consulting, guidance, testing; achievement tests, aptitude measurement, characterology. F

KOUPERNIK, Cyrille. 37 Rue Erlanger, Paris 16. b. 13 Mar 1917 Petrograd, Russia. MD. HEAD, Child Neuropsychiat. Clin, Univ. of Paris; ASSISTANT, Hôpital de la Salpêtrière, Assistance Publique, 47 Blvd. de l'Hôpital, Paris; LECTURER, Inst. of Psych, Sorbonne, Paris; EDITOR, Psychiatrie Sociale de l'Enfant. Member: SFP.

Consulting, clinical practice, teaching, professional writing; infant psychology, brain injuries, mental hygiene. M

KULTSCHYTZKYI, Prof. Dr. Alexandre. Sarcelles. b. 8 Feb 1895 Skalet, Poland. PH.D '30 Univ. of Lemberg, Poland. RES. WRKR, Natl. Cen. for Sci. Res. (CNRS), 13 Quai Anatole France, Paris. Research, teaching, professional writing; ethnopsychology, social psychology, characterology. F

LABORDE, Paul Henri. 20 Ave. Moutier, Livry-Gargan. b. 13 Nov 1921 Paris. Diplôme '52 Univ. of Paris, Fr. INSPECTOR, P.T.T. Services, 140 Blvd. Montparnasse, Paris. Member: APPD. Testing, guidance, research; test development, factor analysis. M

LACROZE, Prof. Dr. René Henri. 9 Rue Jean Mermoz, Le Bouscat. b. 5 Aug 1894 Lujan, Argentina. Docteur ès lettres, Sorbonne, Fr. PROFESSOR, Fac. of letters, Univ. of Bordeaux; DIRECTOR, Inst. of Psych. and Psycho-social Res, Univ. of Bordeaux. Member: SFP. Teaching, administration; phenomenological psychology. M

LAFAYE, Jean. 7 Rue du Fort St. Irénée, Lyon 5. b. 27 Oct 1921 Dompierre. Diplôme '43 Inst. Natl. d'Orientation Professionnelle, Fr. DIRECTOR, Cen. Public d'Orientation Professionnelle, 9 Pl. de la Libération, Villeurbanne. Member: ACOF. Vocational guidance, administration, research; use of group motor and visualization tests in vocational guidance. MF

LAFON, Prof. Dr. Pierre Louis Robert. 2 Rue Ancien Courrier, Montpellier. b. 14 May 1905 Marseillan. MD '34 Univ. of Montpellier, Fr. PROFESSOR, Clinic of Mental and Nervous Disorders, Fac. of Med, Univ. of Montpellier; DIRECTOR, Inst. de Psycho-Pédagogie Médico-Sociale, Univ. of Montpellier; EDITOR, Revue Sauvegarde de l'Enfance. Member: SFP, Société Médico-Psychologique. Teaching, research, clinical practice; psychopathology, projective techniques, tests of deterioration, psychobiology pharmacodynamics. M

LAGACHE, Prof. Daniel. 240 bis Blvd. St. Germain, Paris, 7. b. 3 Dec 1903 Paris. MD, PHD, Univ. of Paris, Fr. PROF. of PATHOLOGICAL PSYCH. and DIRECTOR of INST. of PSYCH, Fac. of Letters, Univ. of Paris. Member: SFP, Société Française de Psychoanalyse, Société Médico-Psychologique. Teaching, psychotherapy, research; verbal hallucinations, jealousy, group dynamics, transference, Oedipus complex.M

LAIRY, Dr. Mrs. Gabrielle-Catherine. 55 Ave. de Versailles, Paris 16. b. 27 Aug 1923 Lagrave. MD '49 Univ. of Paris, Fr. RES. DIR, Inst. Natl. d'Hygiène, Henri Rousselle Hosp, I Rue Cabanis, Paris; EEG CONSULT,

Bonneval Psychiat. Hosp. Member: SFP. Consulting, clinical practice, electroencephalography research; application of electroencephalography to theoretical problems of psychopathology. F

LALANDE, Prof. André. 28 Ave. Casimir, Asnières. b. 19 July 1867 Dijon. Docteur ès lettres '99 Sorbonne, Fr. PROF. EMER, Sorbonne, Paris. Member: SFP, Société Française de Philosophie. Editorial, professional writing, retired; normative psychology, psychology of language, relationship between logic and psychology. M

LALANDE, Miss Hélène Geneviève Marie de. Cen. for Observation of Juvenile Delinquents, Chevilly-Larue. b. 5 Feb 1922 Paris. Diplôme '56 Univ. of Paris, Fr. VOCAT. GUID. COUNS, Cen. for Observation of Juvenile Delinquents. Member: SNPPD. Vocational guidance; emotional problems of maladjusted adolescents, general factors in social maladjustment, projective techniques. F

LALLAU, Raymond. 4 Rue du Pont Rouge, Frelinghien. b. 24 Mar 1903 Lille. Certificat '35 Inst. Natl. d'Orientation Professionnelle, Fr. ADMIN. DIR, Mairie, Lille; HONORARY DIR, Cen. d'Orientation Professionnelle de Lille. Member: ACOF. Administration, consulting, retired; vocational guidance. M

LAMBERT, Dominique. 24 Rue Desbordes-Valmore, Paris 16. b. 30 sept 1910 Versailles. Licence '48 Univ. of Paris, Fr. PSYCHOTECHNICIAN, Natl. Cen. for Sci. Res. (CNRS), 13 Quai Anatole France, Paris 7; ASST. in PSYCH. Policlinique Ney, 118 Blvd. Ney, Paris 18. Member: SFP, Fr. Psychoanal. Socy. Testing, clinical analysis research, psychotherapy; achievement tests, projective techniques, child psychotherapy. F

LAMBERT, Roger Marcel. 4 Rue René Véziel, Clichy. b. 30 Aug 1918 Clichy. Diplôme '46 Univ. of Paris, Fr. RES. WRKR, Natl. Cen. for Sci. Res. (CNRS), 13 Quai Anatole France, Paris 7. Member: SFP. Research; group dynamics, attitude measurement. M

LAROCHE, Miss Denise. 44 Rue d'Ypres, Strasbourg. b. 26 Jan 1926 Strasbourg. Licence '49 Univ. of Strasbourg, Fr. CHIEF of PSYCH. SERV, Cen. Psycho-Pédagogique, 1 Rue de l'Université, Strasbourg; PROF. of PSYCH, L'Ecole d'Educateurs, Strasbourg; PSYCHOLOGIST, Psychiat. Clin. Hôpital Civil, Strasbourg. Member: APSLF, SNPPD. Testing, clinical analysis, applied and educational psychology, teaching, research; projective techniques, family relations, group process. F

LAURENT, Louis. 71 Rue Oudinot, Nancy. b. 22 Jan 1921 Lutry, Switz. L.PS '45 Univ. of Geneva, Switz. PSYCHOANALYST, Cen. for Observation of Juvenile Delinquents,

Nancy; PSYCHOANALYST, priv. prac. Member: SNPPD. Psychotherapy, consulting, guidance, testing, clinical analysis; psychoanalysis projective tests, emotional difficulties. M

LE BEAU, Dr. Jacques. 107 Rue de l'Université, Paris 7. b. 5 Dec 1908 Bellac. MD. CHIEF of SERVICE, Hôpital Lariboisière, 2 Rue Ambroise Paré, Paris; DIRECTOR, Lab. of Physiol. and Neurosurgical Psych, Ecole Pratique des Hautes Etudes. Member: SFP, Société Médico-Psychologique. Research, testing, clinical analysis, consulting, neurosurgery; objective tests, factorial analysis of personality, conditioning. M

LEBEAU, Miss Marie-Laure. 34 Rue Poncelet, Paris 17. b. 14 Aug 1932 Boulogne-Billancourt. L.PS '55 Univ. of Paris, Fr. PSYCHOTECHNICIAN, Natl. Inst. for the Deaf-Mute, 254 Rue St. Jacques, Paris. Research, industrial psychology, testing; psychology of the deaf-mute, projective techniques, personality tests. F

LEBOUTET, Mrs. Lucie. 24 Rue des Près-Aubry, Chaville. b. 24 Apr 1912 Argenteuil. Professorat '36 Univ. of Paris, Fr. PROF. and RES. DIR, Cen. Natl. de Documentation Pédagogique, 29 Rue d'Ulm, Paris; LAB. ASST, Inst. of Psych, Paris. Member: SFP, APSLF. Research, teaching, applied and educational psychology; experimental psychology, audio-visual techniques in teaching. F

LECHEVALLIER, Miss Marguerite. 8 Ave. Philippe Le Boucher, Neuilly sur Seine. b. 20 Mar 1914 Pirou. Diplôme '49 Univ. of Paris, Fr. TEACHER, Maison Familiale E.D.F., la Haye Bérou, Guichainville. Member: ACOF. Teaching, testing, student; achievement tests, group process, attitude measurement, morphopsychology. F

LECLERC, Marcel Louis. 10 Rue Félicien David, St. Germain en Laye. b. 20 Aug 1920 Paris. Diplôme '54 Inst. of Psych, Fr. ENGINEER, Ste. Quillery Matières Plastiques, 52 Rue Venue Lacroix, La Garenne. Member: APPD. Personnel psychology, testing, guidance, teaching; group process, memory and learning, job analysis, group dynamics. M

LECOMPTE, Miss Thérèse Marguerite Gilberte. Cen. d'Orientation Professionnelle, 29 Pl. du Trichon, Roubaix. b. 6 Feb 1924 Roubaix. Conseiller '54 Inst. Natl. d'Orientation Professionnelle, Fr. VOCAT. GUID. COUNS, Cen. d'Orientation Professionnelle. Member: ACOF. Vocational and educational guidance, testing, student; achievement tests, projective techniques, psychology of the group. F

LECOMTE, Jacques. Station de Recherches Apicoles, Bures S/Yvette. b. 28 Nov 1924 Paris. Licence ès sciences, Univ. of Paris,

Fr. RES. ASST, Inst. Natl. de la Recherche Agronomique, Station de Recherches Apicoles. Member: APSLF. Research; study of innate and instinctive behavior. M

LEDOUX, Miss Violette Madeleine. 80 Rue du Rocher, Paris 8. b. 20 July 1925 Paris. Licence ès lettres '50 Univ. of Paris, Fr. RES. WRKR, Natl. Cen. for Sci. Res. (CNRS), 6 Quai Anatole France, Paris 7. Member: SFP, Société Française de Biotypologie. Research, testing, clinical analysis, teaching, adaptation to work environment, social perception, success. F

LEFETZ, Michel. Société Nationale des Chemins de Fer Français, 51 Rue de la Chapelle, Paris 18. b. 10 July 1921 Amiens. Diplôme '53 Ecole Pratique des Hautes Etudes, Fr. INDUS. PSYCH'T, Psychotech. Lab, Société Natl. des Chemins de Fer Français. Member: AIPA, SFP, APPD. Applied industrial psychology, research, testing; aptitude and personality tests, selection and guidance of personnel, industrial safety. M

LE GAT, Andrè. 3 Rue de Lorgues, Toulon. b. 7 Sept 1922 Lambézellec. Diplôme d'état '51 Inst. Natl. d'Orientation Professionnelle, Fr. GUID. COUNS, Cen. Public d'Orientation du Var, Palais du Soleil, St. Roch, Toulon. Member: ACOF. Consulting, guidance, testing, applied psychology; projective techniques, morphopsychology, graphology. M

LE GRAND, Miss Jacqueline. 1 bis Ave. des Rosiers, Villeneuve-le-Roi. b. 26 Feb 1924 Tours. Brevet Supérieur '43 Univ. of Paris, Fr. VOCAT. GUID. COUNS, Service des Jeunes, 16 Rue de l'Abbays, Paris 6. Member: ACOF. Vocational guidance, testing, research. F

LE GRAND, Prof. Yves. Lab. of Appl. Physics, Natl. Museum of Natural History, 57 Rue Cuvier, Paris 5. b. 31 Mar 1908 Paris. Docteur ès sciences, Univ. of Paris, Fr. PROF. and DIR, Lab. of Appl. Physics; PROFESSOR, Inst. of Optics, Paris. Member: SFP. Research, teaching; physiological optics, perception of light, color and space. M

LE MAGNEN, Jacques. 51 Rue Claude Bernard, Paris 5. b. 30 July 1916 Le Havre. Docteur ès sciences naturelles, Univ. of Paris, Fr. DIR. of RES, Natl. Cen. for Sci. Res. (CNRS), Collège de France, Place M. Berthelot, Paris. Member: SFP. Research; sensory psychophysiology, hunger, thirst, taste and smell. M

LEMAINE, Gérard. 8 Rue Scipion, Paris 5. b. 2 Oct 1931 Carsix. L.PS, Univ. of Paris, Fr. DOCUMENTARY RES. WRKR, Inst. des Sciences Humaines Appliquées, 4 Rue Maréchal Joffre, Bordeaux. Research, administration, library; group dynamics, social communication, learning. M

LEMAINE, Jean-Marie. 20 Ave. du Parc Montsouris, Paris 14. b. 1 Jan 1924 Carsix. Licence '45 Univ. of Paris, Fr. RES. ASST, Natl. Cen. for Sci. Res. (CNRS), 13 Quai Anatole France, Paris. Research; social perception, group dynamics. M

LE MEN, Jean. 17 Rue Marcel Peretto, Grenoble. b. 25 Apr 1920 Versailles. Licence '49 Univ. of Grenoble, Fr. EDUC. PSYCH'T, Service de Psychologie-Scolaire, 11 Cours Jean Jaurès, Grenoble. Member: SNPPD. Applied and educational psychology, consulting, guidance, research; drawing as a projective technique, intelligence and aptitude tests. M

LEMPÉRIÈRE, Dr. Thérèse. 42 Rue Henri Barbusse, Paris 5. b. 29 June 1925 Cherbourg. RES. WRKR, Natl. Cen. for Sci. Res. (CNRS), 13 Quai Anatole France, Paris. Member: SFP. Research, teaching, clinical practice; projective techniques in clinical psychology. F

LENCLOS, Miss Liliane. 12 Rue Edmond Roger, Paris 15. b. 6 Dec. 1919 Paris. Licence en Droit '40 Univ. of Paris, Fr. DIRECTOR, Cen. d'Orientation des Jeunes, Société Nationale des Chemins de Fer Français, Région Nord, 173 Rue du Faubourg St. Denis, Paris 10. Member: SNPPD, Groupement Français du Rorschach. Consulting, guidance, testing, clinical analysis, administration, teaching; aptitude tests, choice of profession. F

LE NY, Jean François. 9 Rue Girardot, Montreuil-sous-Bois. b. 17 May 1924 Le Faouët. Diplôme d'études supérieures, Univ. of Paris, Fr. RES. WRKR, Natl. Cen. for Sci. Res. (CNRS), 13 Quai Anatole France, Paris. Member: SFP, APPD, APSLF. Research, applied and industrial psychology; learning theory, experimental psychology and psycho-sociology of work. M

LÉON, Antoine. 5 Rue Louis Dumas, Vaujours. b. 1 Oct 1921 Algiers, Algeria. Diplôme d'études supérieures '51 Univ. of Paris, Fr. VOCAT. GUID. COUNS, Natl. Inst. of Vocat. Guid, 41 Rue Gay-Lussac, Paris 5. Member: SFP, ACOF. Research, applied psychology, teaching; psycho-pedagogy of vocational guidance, vocational choice, training methods. M

LEPEZ, Robert. 9 Rue Bausset, Paris 15. b. 3 June 1920 St. Valéry-sur-Somme. Licence '45 Univ. of Paris, Fr. EDUC. PSYCH'T, Lycée Chaptal, 45 Blvd. des Batignolles, Paris 8. Member: SFP. Educational psychology, testing, guidance; research on psychology of attention, intelligence tests, theory of test construction. M

LEPLAT, Jacques. 12 Ave. Parmentier, Paris 11. b. 19 Oct 1921 Paris. Licence '50 Univ. of Paris, Fr. DIR. of RES, Centre d'Etudes et Recherches Psychotechniques, 13 Rue Paul Chautard, Paris 15; LECTURER, Univ. of Paris. Member: SFP. Research, teaching; human engineering, motor learning. M

LÉRIDON-TESTOR, Mrs. Simone. Centre de Sélection Psychotechnique, 3 bis Blvd. Kellermann, Paris 13. b. 15 Jan 1921 Rosny-sous-Bois. Diplôme '52 Inst. of Psych. Fr. PSYCHOTECHNICIAN, Cen. de Selection Psychotechnique. Member: APPD. Applied psychology, testing, guidance; learning, social psychology. F

LEROY, Miss Louise Angiolina. 16 Blvd. Jules Verne, Amiens. b. 27 Jan 1910 Breteuil-Oise. Diplôme '51 Inst. of Psych, Fr. PSYCHOTECHNICIAN, Services Médicaux et Sociaux du Textile, 18 Rue Lamartine, Amiens. Member: APPD. Industrial psychology, testing personnel selection; achievement tests, learning. F

LEROY-BOUSSION, Mrs. Alice Marie Jeanne. 62 Ancien Chemin de Mazargues, Marseille. b. 24 May 1923 Paris. Diplôme d'études supérieures, Univ. of Paris, Fr. RES. WRKR, Natl. Cen. for Sci. Res. (CNRS), 66 Rue St. Sebastien, Marseille. Research in child psychology; effects of motion pictures on the young child, children's drawings, study of laughter. F

LESAGE, Prof. Honoré. Les Poulardières, St. Cyr sur Loire. b. 29 Mar 1887 Angoulème. Agrégation '14 Univ. of Paris, Fr. PROF. of PSYCH, Univ. Catholique de l'Ouest, Pl. Andrè-Leroy, Angers. Member: SFP. Teaching, translation of American psychological works; projective techniques. M

LESÈVRE, Mrs. Nicole. 127 Blvd. St. Michel, Paris 5. b. 12 Mar 1924 Paris. Licence ès lettres '50; L.PS '52 Univ. of Aix-Marseille, Fr. RES. WRKR, Lab. of EEG and Appl. Neurophysiol, Hôpital de la Salpêtrière, Paris. Member: SFP, Groupement Français du Rorschach. Research. testing, clinical analysis; psychological and electroencephalographical typology, projective tests, epileptics. F

LE THUIT-RUELLAN, Mrs. Annie. 56 Rue Madame, Paris 6. b. 10 July 1926 Paris. Diplôme '47 Univ. of Paris, Fr. PSYCHO-TECHNICIAN, Service Psychotechnique des Tabacs et Allumettes, 53 Quai d'Orsay, Paris. Member: APPD. Applied psychology, testing; achievement tests, projective techniques, questionnaire construction. F

LEURET, Dr. Miss Simonne. 38 Rue Lacépède, Paris 5. b. 28 Jan 1896 Paris. MD '38 Univ. of Paris, Fr. NEURO-PSYCHIATRIST, priv. prac; VOCAT. GUID. CONSULT, Chair of Hyg, Fac. of Med. Univ. of Paris. Member: Société Médico-Psychologique, Assn. des Médecins d'Orientation Professionnelle.

Psychotherapy, consulting, clinical practice, guidance, testing, teaching; personality analysis, motivation, retarded students. F

LEVINE, Jacques. 34 Rue Vieille du Temple, Paris 4. b. 4 June 1923 Eu. Diplôme d'études supérieures '47 Univ. of Paris, Fr. RES. WRKR, Natl. Cen. for Sci. Res. (CNRS), 13 Quai Anatole France, Paris 7. Member: SFP. Research, consulting, guidance, teaching; memory and learning, development of self-awareness in the child, academic motivation. M

LÉVY-LEBOYER, Mrs. Claude. 1 Rue Savorgnan de Brazza, Paris. b. 16 June 1928 Paris. Licence '48 Sorbonne, Fr. STUDY DIR, l'Ecole Pratique des Hautes Etudes; STUDY DIR, Inst. of Psych, Sorbonne, Paris. Member: AIPA, SFP, APPD. Research, teaching, applied psychology; leaderless group test, social adaptation to work environment. F

LÉVY-SCHOEN, Mrs. Ariane. 6 Rue Armand Moisant, Paris 15. b. 10 Sept 1927 Strasbourg. Licence '48 Sorbonne, Fr. RES. WRKR, Natl. Cen. for Sci. Res. (CNRS), 13 Quai Anatole France, Paris 7. Member: SFP, APSLF. Research, testing, teaching; developmental psychology, social perception, affective tone. F

LÉZINE, Mrs. Irène. 43 Rue Rémy, Dumoncel, Paris 14. b. 12 Sept 1909 Moscow, Russia. Diplôme d'études supérieures, Univ. of Paris, Fr. RES. DIR, Natl. Cen. for Sci. Res. (CNRS), 13 Quai Anatole France, Paris. Member: SFP, APPD, APSLF. Research, professional writing, guidance; guidance of adolescents, testing of infants, psychology of infancy. F

LHERMITTE, Prof. Jean. 9 Rue Marbeuf, Paris 8. b. 20 Jan 1877 Mont Saint-Père. PROF. EMER, Fac. of Med, Univ. of Paris, Fr; EDITORIAL BD, l'Encéphale, Journal de Psychiatrie et de Psychosomatique. Member: SFP. Editorial, consulting on neuro-psychiatry, retired; abnormal psychology. M

LIÉNART, Miss Suzanne. 32 Rue Gambetta, Dijon. b. 5 Mar 1932 Besançon. Licence '55 Univ. of Paris, Fr. PSYCHOTECHNICIAN, Cen. de Sélection Psychotechnique, 2 Rue Hoche, Dijon. Applied psychology, testing, research; psychology of vocational learning, conditioning. F

LIÉVOIS, Louis-Pierre. 10 Rue Félicien David, St. Germain en Laye. b. 28 May 1918 Chatellerault. ASST. ADMIN. DIR, Compagnie de Construction Electro-Mécanique, 37 Rue du Rocher, Paris 8. Member: APPD. Administration, industrial psychology, research on group rewards; opinion research, human relations in industry. M

LONG, Jean. Cen. Départemental d'Orientation Professionnelle, Palais Jacques Coeur,

Bourges. b. 9 July 1918 Geneva, Switz. Licence en droit and Diplôme d'état '45 Univ. of Paris, Fr. DIRECTOR, Cen. Départemental d'Orientation Professionnelle, Education Nationale, Inspection Académique, Bourges. Member: AIOP, ACOF. Guidance, applied psychology, testing, career interviews; research on vocational aptitudes, technique of adaptation, learning theory. M

LUCAS, Mr. 221 Cité de la Plaine, Clamart. b. 28 Jan 1926 Le Faouët. Licence '51 Univ. of Paris, Fr. RES. WRKR, Régie Renault, 8 Ave. Emile Zola, Billancourt. Research, industrial psychology, administration; research on conditions of industrial work. M

LUCAS-FONTAINE, Mrs. Yvette. Cité du Port-Garaud, Pavillon B, Toulouse. b. 20 Sept 1928 Châteauneuf. Diplôme d'études supérieures '51 Univ. of Paris, Fr. PSYCHO-TECHNICIAN, Cen. de Sélection Psychotechnique, Ministry of Labor, 16 Blvd. de la Gare, Toulouse; CLIN. PSYCH'T, Psychiat. Hosp. of Montauban. Member: SFP, SNPPD, APPD. Industrial psychology, testing, consulting, guidance; aptitudes, learning semi-automatic skills in industry, clinical diagnosis of mental deterioration. F

MAFFRE, Mrs. Colette. 7 Ave. des Ternes, Paris 17. b. 13 Oct 1914 Lille. Bachelier '34 Univ. of Paris, Fr. DIRECTOR, Sect. d'Orientation Professionnelle, Service d'Orientation et de Placement des Jeunes, 16 Rue de l'Abbaye, Paris 6. Member: ACOF. Guidance, research. F

MAISONNEUVE, Prof. Jean. 25 Rue Montparnasse, Paris 6. b. 17 Feb 1918 Paris. Agrégé '45 Univ. of Paris, Fr. RES. WRKR, Cen. for Sociol. Studies, 54 Rue de Varenne, Paris 7. Member: SFP. Research, teaching, applied psychology; interpersonal relations, socio-affective group patterns. M

MALÉFANT, Jann Célestin. 1 Rue d'Estrées, Rennes. b. 10 May 1924 Plouagat. L.PS '50 Univ. of Paris, Fr. PSYCHOLOGIST, Cen. d'Observation, La Prevalaye, Rennes. Member: SNPPD. Testing, clinical analysis, consulting, guidance, applied psychology; social maladjustment in children and adolescents, mental achievement tests, environment. M

MARLIEU, Prof. Philippe. 12 Rue Bonamy, Toulouse. b. 19 May 1912 Carcallonne. Docteur ès lettres '50 Univ. of Paris, Fr. PROF. OF PSYCH. and PEDAGOGY, Fac. of Letters, Univ. of Toulouse, 4 Rue Albert Lautman, Toulouse. Member: SFP, APSLF. Teaching, research, applied and educational psychology; emotion in children, adolescent personality. M

MARCONNÈS, Denise. 15 Rue Arsène Vermenouze, Aurillac. b. 21 Apr 1929 St.

Haon. Diplôme d'état '54 Univ. of Paris, Fr. VOCAT. GUID. COUNS, Cen. d'Orientation Professionnelle, 4 Blvd. Jean Jaurès Aurillac. Member: ACOF. Guidance, testing: achievement and aptitude tests, memory and learning, projective techniques. , F

MARCUS, Joachim. 24 Rue de la Faisanderie, Paris 16. b. 8 Jan 1928 Berlin, Germany. Diplôme d'études supérieures '49 Univ. of Paris, Fr. RES. DIR, C.E.R.A.M.P.P.E., 81 Rue de Miromesnil, Paris 8. Research, applied psychology; group dynamics. M

MARENCO, Mrs. Claudine. 21 Rue Général Colonieux, Rueil Malmaison. b. 15 May 1931 Paris. Certificat '52 Univ. of Aix, Fr; Certificat '54 Univ. of Paris, Fr. RES. WRKR, Inst. de Filmologie, Fac. of Letters, Univ. of Paris. Member: SNPPD. Research, testing, administration; films psychology, typology. F

MARTIN, Dr. Jacques Yves. 137 Blvd. de la Reine, Versailles, b. 28 Mar 1917 St. Maixent. MD '43 Univ. of Paris, Fr. CHIEF, Human Relations Dept, S.N.E.C.M.A., 150 Blvd. Haussmann, Paris 8. Member: SFP, APPD, Fr. Psychoanal. Socy. Medical and psychological practice in industry, psychotherapy, administration; projective techniques, group dynamics, personality and psychotherapy. M

MAUCO, Georges. 1 Square Alfred Capus, Paris 16. b. 16 Apr 1899 Paris. Docteur ès lettres. DIRECTOR, Cen. Psycho-Pédagogique Claude Bernard, 1 Ave. du Parc des Princes, Paris 15; EDITOR, Psychologie. Member: Syndicat Natl. des Psychologues Psychanalystes. Educational psychology, psychotherapy, consulting, clinical practice, guidance; psychoanalysis, educational methods. M

MAUCORPS, Paul Hassan Louis. Moulin de Flagy, Champeaux. b. 11 Jan 1911 Constantinople, Turkey. MA, MSC. '46 Sorbonne, Fr. STUDY DIR, Cen. for Sociol. Studies, Natl. Cen. for Sci. Res. (CNRS), 13 Quai Anatole France, Paris. Member: APPD, AIPA. Research, professional writing, educational psychology; group dynamics, social attitude surveys, child and adolescent psychology. M

MAUPERTUIS, Miss Gilberte Augustine. 2 Rue du Languedoc, Toulouse. b. 15 Aug 1922 Dorceau. Baccalauréat '43 Univ. of Caen, Fr. VOCAT. GUID. COUNS, Centre d'Orientation, 39 Rue de la Dalbade, Toulouse. Member: ACOF. Testing, clinical analysis, consulting, guidance, applied psychology; studies of drawing tests. F

MÉDIONI, Jean. Lab. of Animal Psych, 12 Rue de l'Université, Strasbourg. b. 14 Oct 1926 Paris. Licence '48 Univ. of Paris, Fr. TCHNG. ASST. in PSYCHOPHYSIOL, Fac. of Sciences, Lab. of Animal Psych. Member:

SFP, APSLF. Student, teaching, research; physiology of vision in animals, animal phototropism, hereditary behavior. M

MERCADIER, Miss Jacqueline. 24 Rue Cardinet, Paris 17. b. 18 Apr 1923 Chartres. Diplôme '52 Sorbonne, Fr. CONSULT. CHILD. PSYCH'T, priv. prac; PSYCH. COUNSELOR, Inst. Féminin de Paris, 14 Rue Clapeyron, Paris 9. Member: APPD. Testing, clinical analysis, consulting, guidance, educational psychology; projective techniques, achievement tests, psychotherapy, Freudian psychoanalysis. F

MERCIER, Miss Paulette. 7 Ave. du Général de Gaulle, Croix. b. 27 Mar 1925 Paris. Licence ès lettres '53 Univ. of Aix-en-Provence, Fr. PROFESSOR, Ecole des Psychologues Praticiens, 21 Rue d'Assas, Paris 6. Teaching, research, testing; achievement and aptitude tests, projective techniques. F

MÉRIEL, Jacques Emile Clément. 7 Rue Maurice Rechsteiner, Argenteuil. b. 27 Jan 1919 Livarot. Diplôme d'état '43 Univ. of Caen, Fr. COUNSELOR, Centre Départemental Obligatoire d'Orientation Professionnelle de la Seine, Section d'Asnières, 4 Rue du Ménil, Asnieres. Member: ACOF. Applied psychology, consulting, guidance, documentation. M

MESSIMY, Mrs. Madeleine. 3 Quai Saint Michel, Paris 5. b. 24 Nov 1902 , Paris. Diplôme '46 I.N.F.R.C., Fr. PSYCHOTECHNICIAN, Service du Reclassement, Ministry of Labor, 113 Rue Cardinet, Paris 17. Testing, clinical analysis, guidance, applied and industrial psychology, research; achievement tests, attitude measurement, learning. F

MÉTRAUX, Mrs. Ruth Watt. 81 Rue de l'Université, Paris 7. b. 24 July 1913 Charleston, West Virginia, USA. MA '41 Univ. of Michigan, USA. EDUC. COUNS, United Nations Nursery School, 35 Rue Boulainvilliers, Paris 16. Member: Int. Rorschach Socy, Groupement Français du Rorschach. Consulting, guidance, research, testing; child development, Rorschach test, speech and hearing therapy. F

MEUNIER, Georges. 29 Rue Faidherbes, St. Mandé. b. 12 Mar 1909 Bourges. Diplôme '49 Univ. of Paris, Fr. DIRECTOR, Dept. of Indiv. Diagnosis, Cen. for Appl. Psych. 14 Rue Henner, Paris 9. Member: APPD. Applied psychology, research, consulting; projective techniques. M

MEYER, Paul Joseph. 54 Rue Gabriel Mouilleron, Nancy. b. 6 Aug 1926 Puttelange. Licence '49 Univ. of Strasbourg, Fr. PSYCHOTECHNICIAN, A.N.I.F.R.M.O., Sel. Serv. Dept, Psychotech. Cen, Blvd. Foch, Nancy. Member: Groupement des Psychologues Praticiens de la Région de l'Est. Consult-

ing, guidance, testing, student: reclassification of the physically handicapped, accident prevention, general problems of vocational adaption. M

MEYERSON, Prof. Ignace. 60 Rue Montcalm, Paris 18. b. 27 Feb 1888 Warsaw, Poland. Docteur ès lettres '47 Univ. of Paris, Fr. DIR. of STUDIES, Ecole Pratique des Hautes Etudes, Sorbonne, Paris 5; DIRECTOR, Res. Cen. for Comp. Psych, 54 Rue de Varenne, Paris 7; PROF. HONORAIRE, Fac. of Letters, Univ. of Toulouse; DIRECTOR, *Journal de Psychologie normale et pathologique*; ASSOC. ED, *British Journal of Educational Psychology*. Member: SFP, Société d'Etudes psychologiques de Toulouse. Research, teaching, editing; comparative history of psychology. M

MIALARET, Prof. Gaston Georges. 14 Rue Gaston Labouche, St. Cloud. b. 10 Oct 1918 Paris. Diplôme '48 Univ. of Paris, Fr. ASST. LECT. in PSYCH, Fac. of Letters, Paris and Caen; PROF. of PSYCH. and PEDAGOGY, Ecole normale supérieure de Fontenay. Member: SFP, APSLF. Teaching, educational psychology, research; selection and training of teachers, experimental didactics. M

MIAULT, Mrs. Alice. 36 Rue de la Paix, Bois-Colombes. b. 10 July 1919 Paris. Baccalauréat '37 Univ. of Paris, Fr. VOCAT. GUID. COUNS, Direction des Services Postaux, 140 Blvd. du Montparnasse Paris 14. Member: APPD, ACOF. Personnel psychology, vocational guidance, testing, administration; aptitudes and learning, adaptation to vocational duties. F

MICHAUD, Edmond. Ecole Normale, Périgueux. b. 2 Aug 1901 Châtelneuf. Docteur ès lettres '47 Univ. of Paris, Fr. DIRECTOR, Ecole Normale. Administration, teaching, research; development of intelligence between the ages of 6 and 14, retarded students, maladjusted children. M

MICHELAT, Guy. 80 Ave. Gabriel Péri, St. Ouen. b. 11 Nov 1933 Paris. Diplôme '56 Inst. of Psych, Fr. RES. ASST, Lab. of Social Psych, Sorbonne, 16 Rue de la Sorbonne, Paris 5; RES. WRKR, Cen. for Sociol. Studies, Paris. Research, student, applied psychology; group dynamics, social psychology of children's books. M

MILLARDET, Gabrielle. 15 Rue Pierre Nicole, Paris 5. b. 2 Oct 1901 Mont de Marsan. Diplôme '43 Inst. of Psych, Sorbonne, Fr. PSYCHOLOGIST, Caisse Primaire Centrale de la Securité Sociale, 69 bis Rue de Dunkerque, Paris 9. Member: APPD. Consulting, guidance and testing of the mentally deficient, clinical analysis; aptitude measurement, social applications. F

MILLET, Gilbert Henri. Etude du Travail et Applications Psychotechniques, 27 Rue Pierre Demours, Paris 17. b. 15

Aug 1920 Divonne. Licence '48 Univ. of Paris, Fr. CO-DIRECTOR, Etude du Travail et Applications Psychotechniques. Member. SNPPD, Groupement Français du Rorschach. Industrial psychology, testing, consulting, guidance, staff selection and training; projective techniques, group dynamics, group process, directed interviews, counseling. M

MINKOWSKI, Dr. Eugène. 68 Rue de Babylone, Paris 7. b. 17 Apr 1885 Petrograd, Russia. MD, Univ. of Paris, Fr. CHIEF PHYSICIAN, Dispensaire Française Minkowska, 11 Rue Saulnier, Paris 9; EDITOR, *Evolution Psychiatrique.* Member: SFP, Société Médico-Psychologique, Groupement Français du Rorschach. Clinical practice, psychotherapy, research, editorial; psychopathology, phenomenology, problems of time and space. M

MIREUX, Miss Andrée. 15 Rue de Monttessuy, Paris 7. b. 16 Sept 1907 Puiseaux. Diplôme, Inst. Natl. d'Orientation Professionnelle, Fr. GUID. COUNS, Cen. Départemental d'Orientation de la Seine, 116 Rue de Grenelle, Paris. Consulting, educational and vocational guidance, testing, administration; achievement tests, aptitude measurement, educational psychology. F

MIROGLIO, Abel. Boîte Postale 258, Le Havre. b. 7 Feb 1895 Cherbourg. Agrégé, Univ. of Paris, Fr. DIRECTOR, Inst. Havrais de Sociologie Economique et de Psychologie des Peuples, 56 Rue Anatole France, Le Havre: EDITOR, *Revue de psychologie des peuples.* Editorial, administration, research; cultural anthropology, psychology of ethnic and regional groups. M

MONAVON, Mrs. Anne Marie. 3 Rue de Banville, Nice. b. 9 May 1923 Bois-Colombes. LPS '50 Univ. of Paris, Fr. Member: APPD. Testing, clinical analysis, private consultations; projective techniques, learning theory, achievement tests. F

MONNIER, Prof. Alexandre Marcel. Lab. of Physiol, Sorbonne, 1 Rue Victor Cousin, Paris 5. b. 25 Aug 1904 Jeurre. Docteur ès sciences '34 Univ. of Paris, Fr. PROFESSOR, Univ. of Paris. Member: SFP. Research, teaching; sensory physiology. M

MONOD, Miss Mireille. 4 bis Rue Pleyel, Paris 12. b. 10 July 1919 Enghien-les-Bains. Licence '44 Univ. of Strasbourg, Fr. ASST. in PSYCHOTHER, Sanatorium d' Enfants, Le Roc-des-Fiz. Member: APSLF, APA, Socy. of Biotypology, Int. Rorschach Socy. Psychotherapy, testing, clinical analysis, consulting, clinical practice, guidance, research; projective techniques, child psychopathology, clinical psychology, group and individual psychotherapy. F

MONTIFROY, Berthin. 39 bis Rue de Général

Leclerc, Bois-Colombes. b. 26 Aug 1905 Allogny. Conseiller '33 Inst. Natl. d'Orientation Professionnelle, Fr. DIRECTOR, Serv. d'Orientation Professionnelle, 94 Rue P. Déroulède, Bois-Colombes. Guidance; vocational guidance. M

MONTMOLLIN, Mrs. Germaine de. 10 Ave. du Parc, Vanves. b. 2 Apr 1923 Beauvais. Diplôme d'études supérieures '46 Sorbonne, Fr. RES. WRKR, Lab. of Exper. and Comp. Psych, Natl. Cen. for Sci. Res. (CNRS), 46 Rue St. Jacques, Paris: TEACHER, Inst. of Psych, Sorbonne. Member: SFP. Research, teaching, professional writing; social psychology, group dynamics. F

MONTMOLLIN, Maurice de. 10 Ave. du Parc, Vanves. b. 17 Mar 1926 Neuchâtel, Switz. Docteur ès sciences '47 Univ. of Paris, Fr. PSYCHOLOGIST, Cen. for Appl. Psych. (CPA), 15 Rue Henri Heine, Paris 16; SECRETARY, *Revue de Psychologie Appliquée.* Member: APPD. Applied psychology, research, editorial; selection of personnel. M

MOOR, Dr. Lisette. 4 Rue Verdi, Paris 16. b. 18 Jan 1927 Vienna, Austria. MD '52 Univ. of Paris, Fr. ASST. PSYCH'T, Cen. Psychiat. Sainte Anne, Paris. Member: SFP, APSLF, Groupement Français de Neuro-Psychopathol. Infantile, Groupement Français du Rorschach. Testing, clinical analysis, consulting, guidance; application of intelligence tests for child and adult psychiatry. F

MORALI-DANINOS, Dr. André. 7 Ave. Trudaine, Paris 9. b. 14 Feb 1909 Algiers, Algeria. MD '36 Univ. of Algiers, Algeria. MED. CONSULT, Surgical Orthopedic Clin, Fac. of Paris, Hôpital Cochin: PSYCHIATRIST, priv. prac. Member: APPD, Groupement Français du Rorschach. Psychotherapy, consulting, clinical practice, research; projective tests, psychosomatic medicine, psychology of occupational accident.s. M

MORGAUT, Marc Edmond. 25 Rue Galilée, Paris 16. b. 12 May 1911 Orléans. Doctorat '37 Univ. of Paris, Fr. RES. COORD, Pechiney, 23 Rue Balzac, Paris 8. Member: ACOF. Applied psychology, journalism, testing; intelligence tests, social attitudes, personnel selection, African psychosociology. M

MORGOULIS, Mrs. Jeanne. 17 Rue de Lisbonne, Paris 8. b. 29 Aug 1913 Cairo, Egypt. Diplôme '47 Inst. of Psych, Sorbonne, Fr. RES. WRKR, Lab. de Psychobiologie de l'Enfant, 41 Rue Gay Lussac, Paris. Member: SFP, Groupement Français du Rorschach. Research, testing, clinical child psychology, group behavior of children, social relations among children. F

MORRIS, Miss Suzanne. 34 Ancien Chemin de Castelnau, Montpellier. b. 10 May 1916 Montpellier. Diplôme '53 Inst. Jean

Jacques Rousseau, Switz. PSYCH. ASST, Assn. Régionale de Sauvegarde de l'Enfance, Ave. Prof. Flahault, Montpellier. Member: SNPPD. Testing, clinical analysis, research; achievement tests, projective techniques, study of behavior. F

MOSCOVICI, Serge. 27 Rue Ballu, Paris 9. b. 14 July 1925 Braila, Rumania. L.PS '50 Univ. of Paris, Fr. RES. WRKR. Natl. Cen. for Sci. Res. (CNRS), 13 Quai Anatole France, Paris 5. Member: SFP, APSLF. Research, writing, applied psychology; theory and measurement of attitudes, sociology of knowledge, communication in large groups, sociometry. M

NACHT, Dr. Sacha. 80 Rue Spontini, Paris 16. b. 23 Sept 1901 Bacav, Rumania. DIRECTOR Inst. of Psychoanal, 187 Rue St. Jacques, Paris; ED. DIR, L'Actualité Psychanalytique. Member: SFP. Psychotherapy, teaching, editorial; theories and practice of psycho-analysis. M

NAHOUM, Charles. 32 Rue Raymond Marcheron, Vanves. b. 30 Nov 1917 Tunis, Tunisia. Diplôme d'études supérieures, Sorbonne, Fr. PSYCHOTECHNICIAN, Caisse de Securité Sociale, Vocat. Rehab. Ser, 21 Rue Octave Feuillet, Paris 16. Member: APPD. Consultation, guidance, teaching; clinical interviewing, psychology of the disabled, vocational rehabilitation of the handicapped. M

NAVILLE, Pierre. 164 Quai Louis Blériot, Paris 16. b. 1 Feb 1904 Paris. Doctorat '56 Univ. of Paris, Fr. RES. DIR, Natl. Cen. for Sci. Res. (CNRS), 13 Quai Anatole France, Paris. Member: SFP, APSLF. Research, teaching, professional writing; behavior, vocational guidance. M

NEPVEU, Miss Anne. 24 bis Rue Tournefort, Paris 5. b. 17 July 1909 Saumur. Certificat d'études supérieures '34 Univ. of Paris, Fr. DIRECTOR, Cen. d'Application, Inst. Natl. d'Orientation Professionnelle, 41 Rue Gay-Lussac, Paris 5. Member: SFP, AIPA, Groupement Français du Rorschach. Guidance, teaching; psychological problems of social and vocational adjustment of adolescents. F

NICOLAS, Miss Simonne. 11 Rue Ferdinand Duval, Paris 4. b. 20 Apr 1923 Paris. Diplôme d'état. VOCAT. GUID. COUNS, Centre Obligatoire d'Orientation Professionnelle, 25 Pl. de la Madeleine, Paris 8. Member: ACOF. Guidance, testing, clinical analysis; achievement tests, aptitude measurement, projective techniques. F

NOËL, Mrs. Janine Madeleine Marguerite. 211 bis Rue de Bercy, Paris 12. b. 17 Mar 1922 Langres. VOCAT. GUID. COUNS, S.N.C.F., 20 Blvd. Diderot, Paris 12. Member: ACOF. Guidance, testing; achievement tests, attitude measurement. F

NUSSBAUM-FREY, Mrs. Michèle. Bibèmus, Chemin de Bibèmus, Aix en Provence. b. 29 Sept 1929 Arles. Licence ès lettres '53 Univ. of Aix-Marseille, Fr. RES. WRKR, Inst. des Sciences Humaines Appliquées, 5 Rond Point Bugeaud, Paris; TCHR. of SOCIAL PSYCH, Inst. d'Administration des Enterprises, Aix en Provence. Field theory in social psychology, social organization of small groups. F

OBERLÉ, René. 3 Rue Edouard Teutsch, Strasbourg. b. 2 Feb 1927 Sarreguemines. L.PS '53 Univ. of Strasbourg, Fr. PSYCHOLOGIST, Cen. d'Observation pour Garçons, Chateau d'Angleterre, Strasbourg-Bischheim. Member: SNPPD. Testing, clinical analysis, educational psychology, research; projective techniques, group dynamics, reeducational methods. M

OLÉRON, Mrs. Geneviève Thérèse. 24 Rue Olivier de Serres, Paris 5. b. 4 Oct 1922 Angers. L.PS, Licence ès sciences, Univ. of Paris, Fr. LAB. ASST, Lab. of Exper. and Comp. Psych, Ecole Pratique des Hautes Etudes, Sorbonne, 66 Rue St. Jacques, Paris 5. Member: SFP, APSLF. Research, administration, teaching; rhythm and motor responses, memory. F

OLÉRON, Prof. Pierre André. 24 Rue Olivier de Serres, Paris 15. b. 4 Oct 1915 Belfort. Agrégé '39 Univ. of Paris, Fr. DIR. of RES, Natl. Cen. for Sci. Res, (CNRS), 13 Quai Anatole France, Paris; LECTURER, Inst. of Psych, Univ. of Paris. Member: SFP, APSLF. Research, teaching; intelligence, language and mental development, psychology of deaf children. M

OLIVÈRES, Mr. Marguerite Marie Agnès. 5 Allée des Soupirs, Toulouse. b. 7 Apr 1907 St. André. Licence ès lettres '43 Univ. of Caen, Fr. EDUC. and VOCAT. GUID. COUNS. Cen. d'Orientation Professionnelle, 32 Rue de la Dalbade, Toulouse. Member: ACOF. Guidance, testing, applied and educational psychology; characterology, projective techniques, graphology. F

ORMEZZANO, Jean Denis. Cen. de Réadaptation Professionnelle et Sociale, Hôpital-Hospice, St. Martin de Ré. b. 17 Apr 1925 Lyon. Licence ès lettres '47 Univ. of Grenoble, Fr. DIRECTOR, Cen. de Réadaptation. Member: SNPPD, Groupement Français du Rorschach. Testing, clinical analysis, administration, research; psychotechnical check of pharmaceutical dynamic experiments, Rorschach test, psychopedagogy. M

ORSINI, Miss Francine. 89 Rue St. Charles, Paris 15. b. 29 July 1928 Marseille. Licence ès lettres '52 Univ. of Paris, Fr. RES. WRKR, Lab. for Exper. and Comp. Psych, Natl. Cen. for Sci. Res (CNRS), 46 Rue St. Jacques, Paris 5. Member: SFP, APSLF.

Resarch; time perception, motivation.   F

PACAUD, Suzanne. 17 Rue Méchain, Paris 14. b. 10 Aug 1902 Krakow, Poland. PH.D '27 Univ. of Krakow, Poland. DIR. of RES, Natl. Cen. for Sci. Res (CNRS), Paris; ASSOC. DIR, l'Ecole Pratique des Hautes Etudes, 41 Rue Gay-Lussac, Paris 5. Member: SFP, APPD, Soc. of Biotypology. Research, testing, applied and industrial psychology; vocational guidance for adults, accident prevention, gerontology, methodology in applied psychology.   F

PAGÈS, Max. 8 Martins-Pêcheurs, La Celle St. Cloud. b. 26 Jan 1926 Istanbul, Turkey. L.PS '50 Univ. of Paris, Fr. PRIN. ENGR, Human Rel. Div, C.E.G.O.S., 33 Rue Jean Goujon, Paris. Member: APPD. Applied and industrial psychology, research, consulting, guidance; process of social consultation, training in social relations, group dynamics.   M

PAGÈS, Robert. 3 Rue Rambukau, Paris 4. 25 Aug 1919 Belmontet. Diplôme d'études supérieures '42 Univ. of Toulouse, Fr. RES. WRKR, Natl. Cen. for Sci. Res (CNRS), 16 Rue de la Sorbonne, Paris 5; DIRECTOR, lab. of Social Psych, Sorbonne. Member: SFP, APSLF. Research, teaching, administration; emotion in interpersonal relations, social perception, group dynamics.   M

PAGNAC, André Albert. 4 bis Rue d'Ulm, Paris 5. b. 26 Nov 1925 Fr. Licence '53 Univ. of Paris, Fr. ASST. LECT, Univ. of Angers, Pl. Andrè-Leroy, Angers. Teaching, research, testing; child guidance, juvenile delinquency, differential anthropology. M

PAILLARD, Dr. Jacques René. 42 Rue du Bac, Paris 7. b. 5 Mar 1920 Nemours. Docteur ès sciences, Univ. of Paris, Fr. RES. DIR, Natl. Cen. for Sci. Res, 13 Quai Anatole France, Paris 7; PROFESSOR, Inst. for Profes. Guid. Member: SFP, APSLF. Research, teaching, professional writing; neurophysiology, psychophysiology of motor functions.   M

PALMADE, Guy Henri. 2 Sq. H. Delormel, Paris 14. b. 10 July 1920 Paris. Docteur '52 Univ. of Paris, Fr. HEAD, Psychotech. Mission, Fr. Gas and Electric Co, 68 Rue du Faubourg St. Honoré, Paris; CONSULTANT, Comm. Française d'Organisation (CO.FR. OR.), 37 Rue de Battano, Paris. Applied psychology, teaching, research; group dynamics, characterology, character tests, psychosociology of work.   M

PAOLETTI, Miss Ophelia. 8 bis Rue des Gobelins, Paris 13. b. 26 May 1923 Zignago, Italy. L.PS '50 Univ. of Paris, Fr. CLIN. PSYCH'T, Inst. Psycho-Pédagogique, 11 Rue Molière, Paris. Member: SNPPD. Testing, clinical analysis, educational psychology, psychotherapy; projective techniques, group process, psychoanalysis. F

PATIN, Jacques Charles. 55 Rue de Nantes, Mitry-le-Neuf. b. 25 July 1923 Bourron-Marlotte. L.PS '48 Univ. of Paris, Fr. RES. DIR, Cen. d'Etudes et Recherches Psychotechniques (CERP), 13 Rue Paul Chautard, Paris. Member: APPD. Applied psychology, administration, research; construction of tests, vocational training, professional evaluation.   M

PÉCHOUX, Raymond Joseph Alexandre. 12 Allée des Tilleuls, Caluire. b. 7 Jan 1908 Bourg-en-Bresse. MD '32 Univ. of Lyon, Fr. TECH. CONSULT, Army Genl. Staff, Ministry of Natl. Defense, Blvd. St. Germain 231, Paris; ASST. LECT, Ecole Pratique de Psychologie et Pédagogie, and Inst. de Méd. du Travail, Univ. of Lyon. Member: Société Médico-Psychologique, Groupement Français du Rorschach. Selection of recruits, teaching, research; projective techniques, intelligence tests, social psychology.   M

PELLISSIER, Miss Marguerite. 8 Rue Barthelemy Ramier, St. Etienne. b. 8 June 1927 Lyon. Diplôme d'état '55 Inst. Natl. d'Orientation Professionnelle, Fr. VOCAT. GUID. COUNS, Cen. d'Orientation Professionnelle, Quartier Péraudy, Metz. Member: ACOF. Testing, guidance, applied psychology; aptitude and achievement tests, psychotechnical selction.   F

PELTIER, Jean-René. 10 Rue de Copenhague, Paris 8. b. 24 Feb 1931 Paris. Docteur ès sciences '55 Univ. of Paris, Fr. RES. DIR, Cen. d'Etudes et d'Instruction Psychologiques de l'Armée de l'Air, 29 Rue du Maréchal Joffre, Versailles. Teaching, research, student, testing; opinion surveys, attitudes and motivation.   M

PERNIN, Daniel. Société CALOR, 142 Ave. des Frères Lumière, Lyon. b. 15 Oct 1925 Paris. Licence '46 Univ. of Paris, Fr. HEAD, Psychotech. Serv, Société CALOR. Member: APPD. Industrial psychology, testing; learning theory, job evaluation, group dynamics, projective techniques.   M

PERRON, Roger. Lab. of Psych, Hôpital Henri Rousselle, 1 Rue Cabanis, Paris 14. b. 25 Mar 1926 St. Maur. L.PS '51 Univ. of Paris, Fr. RES. WRKR, Natl. Cen. for Sci. Res. (CNRS), 13 Quai Anatole France, Paris. Member: SFP. Research, testing, teaching; motivation in test situations, auto-estimation of voluntary control.   M

PERSE, Jacques. 4 Ave. Pasteur, Gentilly. b. 26 Dec. 1923 Vincennes. Diplôme '50 Inst. of Psych, Univ. of Paris, Fr. HEAD, Psych. Lab, Clin. for Ment. Diseases, 1 Rue Cabanis, Paris 14; LAB. ASST, Inst. of Psych, Univ. of Paris. Member: SFP. Research, testing, clinical analysis, teaching; projective techniques, standardization and validation of mental tests, application to psychopathological diagnosis. M

PÉTIN, Mrs. Monique. 45 Rue du Cardinal Lemoine, Paris 5. b. 12 June 1914 Remiremont. Licence, Univ. of Paris, Fr. ADVISOR, Res. Serv, Inst. Natl. d'Orientation Professionnelle, 41 Rue Gay Lussac, Paris 5. Member: SFP. Research, guidance, industrial psychology; occupational apprenticeship for women, vocational guidance for girls. F

PICARD, Mrs. Andrée Lise. 2 Ave. de la Porte Brancion, Paris 15. b. 11 Mar 1903 Boulogne. Diplôme, Inst. Natl. d'Orientation Professionnelle, Fr. RES. WRKR, Inst. of Pub. Opinion, 20 Rue d'Aumale, Paris 18. Member: SNPPD. Research on Szondi test, testing, clinical analysis, consulting; projective techniques, characterology, normal and pathological human behavior. F

PICHOT, Prof. Pierre Jean. Clinique de la Faculté, Hôpital Psychiatrique Sainte Anne, 1 Rue Cabanis, Paris 5. b. 3 Oct 1918 La Roche sur Yon. MD '48 Univ. of Paris, Fr. ASSOC. PROF. Fac. of Med, Univ. of Paris, Rue de l'Ecole de Médecine; Paris 5; PROFESSOR, Inst. of Psych, Sorbonne; TECH. ADVIS, Cen. for Appl. Psych. (CPA), Paris; EDITOR, *Encéphale*; DIRECTOR, *Revue de Psychologie Appliquée*. Member: SFP, BPS. Teaching, research, editing; diagnostic psychological testing. M

PIEGAY, André. Ensemble, Le Rond Point, St. Etienne. b. 21 May 1924 St. Martin en Haut. L.PS '50 Univ. of Paris, Fr. VOCAT. GUID. COUNS, Cen. d'Orientation Professionnelle de St. Etienne-Loire, 14 Rue Elisée Reclus, St. Etienne; ED. COMM. CHMN, *Cahiers d'Orientation Humaine*. Consulting, guidance, applied and educational psychology, teaching; achievement and aptitude tests, personality prognosis, psychological problems of manual workers. M

PIÉRON, Prof. Henri. 52 route de la Plaine, Le Vésinet. b. 18 July 1881 Paris. Docteur ès sciences, Univ. of Paris, Fr. PROFESSOR, Coll. de France, Paris; DIRECTOR, Inst. Natl. d'Orientation Professionnelle, Paris; EDITOR, *Année Psychologique*. Member: SFP, APSLF, AIPA. Teaching; physiological psychology. M

PIN, Patrice. 20 Ave. de Friedland, Paris 8. b. 15 Nov 1928 Toulouse. L.PS '51 Univ. of Paris, Fr. DIRECTOR, Selection Cen, Cen. d'Etudes et Recherches Psychotechniques, 13 Paul Chautard, Paris 8. Research; industrial accidents, work rhythm. M

PLETTENER, Louis. 11 Rue Ursulines, Paris. b. 27 Oct 1927 Lagarenne. L.PS '54 Univ. of Paris, Fr. DIRECTOR, A.O.F. Mission in Abidjan, Fr. W. Africa, Inst. des Sci. Humaines Appliquées, 5 Rond Point

Bugeaud, Paris. Member: SNPPD. Research, applied and industrial psychology, testing, clinical analysis; social psychology, industrial psychosociology, psychotechnics. M

POINAT, Charles Maurice Marie Joseph. 2 Ave. Constance, Athis-Mons. b. 21 Sept 1912 Toulon. Licence ès lettres '50 Univ. of Aix-Marseille, Fr. SOC. RELATIONS ENGR, Co. Electro-Mécanique, 37 Rue du Rocher, Paris 8. Testing, clinical analysis, applied and industrial psychology; selection and guidance of engineers and workers by individual tests, clinical projective tests, morphopsychology. M

POLGE, Mrs. Marguerite. 27 Rue St. Ferdinand, Paris 17. b. 27 July 1912 Aigues-Vives. Licence ès lettres '33 Univ. of Montpellier, Fr. GUID. COUNS, Inst. de Psych. Industrielle et Commerciale, 6 Ave. Léon Heuzey, Paris 16. Member: APPD. Applied and industrial psychology, testing, clinical analysis, guidance; character tests, intellectual achievement and vocational aptitudes, psychoanalysis. F

PORC'HER, Dr. Yves. Hôpital Henri Rousselle, 1 Rue Cabanis, Paris 14. b. 24 June 1887 Rouen. MD '23 Univ. of Paris, Fr. CHIEF PHYS, Hôpital Henri Rousselle; DIRECTOR, Inst. of Social Biol. and Ment. Hyg. Member: SFP, Fr. League of Ment. Hyg. Administration, consulting, clinical practice, guidance, educational psychology. M

POURQUÉ, Mrs. Odette Marie Claire. Cen. d'Observation Médico-Psychologique, Domaine Saint Denis, Ambares. b. 21 Mar 1926 Osse-en-Aspe. L.PS '49 Univ. of Paris, Fr. APPL. PSYCH'T, Cen. d'Observation Médico-Psych. Member: SNPPD. Testing, guidance, research; projective techniques, achievement tests, visual and motor tests. F

PROT, Marcel. 21 Blvd. Lefebvre, Paris 15. b. 3 July 1892 Chateauroux. Docteur ès lettres '40 Univ. of Paris, Fr. INSPECTOR GENL, Ministry of Pub. Works, 244 Blvd. St. Germain, Paris 2. Member: SFP. Administration, research, applied psychology; psychology of language, international relations. M

PRUSCHY-BEJARANO, Mrs. Ruth. 5 Rue Delambre, Paris 14. b. 27 Mar 1913 Basel, Switz. Conseiller '33 Inst. Natl. d'Orientation Professionnelle, Fr. PSYCH. CONSULT, Editions Techniques, 18 Rue Seguier, Paris. Member: SNPPD, Syndicat Natl. des Psych. Psychanalystes, Groupement Français du Rorschach. Applied psychology, personnel selection, psychotherapy; depth psychology aided by psychoanalysis, projective techniques. F

QUANTIN, Marc-Henri Jean. Société CALOR, 142 Ave. des Frères Lumière, Lyon. b. 4 Aug 1926 Meximieux. Diplôme, Inst.

Catholique, Fr. PSYCHOTECHNICIAN, Société CALOR. Applied psychology, testing, consulting, guidance; achievement tests, projective techniques. M

QUESNEL, Louis. 12 Ave. du Parc, Vanves. b. 23 Feb 1928 Balleroy-Calvados. Diplôme d'état '55 Univ. of Paris, Fr. RES. DIR, Inst. des Sci. Sociales du Travail, 6 Rue Picot, Paris. Research, applied, industrial and commercial psychology; psycho-economic attitudes, market research.M

RAGUENEAU, Mrs. Eliane. 101 Ave. J.B. Clément, Boulogne. b. 24 July 1922 Gourin. Diplôme, Inst. of Psych, Univ. of Paris, Fr. PSYCHOTECHNICIAN, Cen. for Appl. Psych. (CPA), 14 Rue Henner, Paris 9. Applied psychology, testing, research; reasons for vocational choice among nurses and social workers. F

RAUSCH DE TRAUBENBERG, Miss Nina. 64 Rue Brancion, Paris 15. b. 2 Sept 1920 Tavastehus, Finland. Diplôme '46 Univ. of Paris, Fr. CLIN. PSYCH'T, Child Neuropsychiat. Clin, Fac. of Med. of Paris, Hôpital de la Salpêtrière, 47 Blvd. de l'Hôpital, Paris 13. Member: SFP, APA, Groupement Français du Rorschach. Testing, clinical analysis, research, consulting, clinical practice, professional writing; projective techniques, pathology of perception in children. F

RÉMY, Marcel. 10 Rue de la Victoire, Soissons. b. 29 Jan 1913 Paris. Diplôme '48 Inst. Natl. d'Etude du Travail et d'Orientation Professionnelle, Fr. DIRECTOR, Cen. Pub. d'Orientation Professionnelle, 3 Rue de Braine, Soissons. Member: ACOF. Consulting, guidance, testing, administration. M

RENAUD, Miss Monique Marie Colette. Cen. d'Etudes et d'Instruction Psych. de l'Armée de l'Air (C.E.I.P.A.A.), 29 Rue du Maréchal Joffre, Versailles. b. 31 Aug 1925 Asnières. Licence ès lettres '48 Univ. of Paris, Fr. PSYCHOTECHNICIAN, C.E.I.P.A.A. Member: APPD. Research, teaching, student; achievement tests, educational and vocational guidance, evaluation. F

RENNES, Pierre. 3 Villa Blaise Pascal, Neuilly. b. 26 May 1914 Champigny. Diplôme '42 Inst. of Psych, Univ. of Paris, Fr. CHIEF, Res. Dept, Cen. for Appl. Psych. (CPA), 15 Rue Henri Heine, Paris; INSTRUCTOR, Inst. of Psych, Univ. of Paris; CO-EDITOR, *Revue de Psychologie Appliquée*. Member: SFP, AIPA, APPD. Applied and industrial psychology, teaching, editorial; publication of psychological tests. M

RÉRAT, Gabriel. 3 Rue Anatole France, Chaville. b. 10 May 1929 Besançon. Diplôme '52 Univ. of Paris, Fr. INDUS. PSYCH'T, Otiac B-Dorizon, 13 Rue Beudant, Paris 17; RES. DIR, Cen. d'Etudes et Re-

cherches Psychotechnique. Member: APPD. Research, industrial psychology, testing, consulting; attitude measurement, job analysis, management and executive selection. M

REUCHLIN, Maurice. 41 Rue Gay Lussac, Paris 5. b. 15 Sept 1920 Marseille. L.PS '47 Univ. of Paris, Fr. CHIEF of RES. SERV. and ED. in CHIEF, Inst. Natl. d'Etudes du Travail et d'Orientation Professionnelle; ASST. LECT, Inst. of Psych, Univ. of Paris. Member: SFP, APPD, APSLF. Research, teaching, editorial; factor analysis, tests, epistomology. M

REY-HERME, Dr. Philippe Alexandre. 6 Rue Jean Ferrandi, Paris 6. b. 17 Aug 1914 St. Etienne. Doctorat '44 Sorbonne, Fr. PROFESSOR, Inst. de Psycho-Pédagogie Appliquée, 9 Rue Anatole France, Paris. Teaching, research, professional writing; group dynamics, influence of adult social structure on children, psychosociology. M

RIBAUCOURT, Miss Blanche de. 86 Blvd. Port Royal, Paris 5. b. 19 Nov. 1925 Paris. Diplôme Inst. of Psych, Univ. of Paris, Fr. SPEECH CORRECTIONIST, Salpêtrière, Neur. Clin, Blvd. de l'Hôpital, Paris; DIRECTOR, Pierre Marie Speech Cen. Member: SFP, Syndicat des Psychologues Cliniciens. Testing, clinical analysis, research; problems of speech and language. F

RICOSSAY, Georges Marcel. 15 Rue de la République, Charenton. b. 23 Apr 1906 Lavernat. PSYCHOTECHNICIAN, priv. prac. Member: ACOF. Applied psychology, testing, clinical analysis, test construction; study of types of employment, evaluation of functions, group dynamics. M

RIEGERT, Claude Pierre. 4 bis Rue Giradet, Nancy. b. 5 May 1930 Belfort. L.PS '56 Univ. of Strasbourg, Fr. PSYCHOTECHNICIAN, Cen. Lorrain de Psychotechnique, 25 Rue de la Source, Nancy. Member: APPD, SNPPD. Industrial psychology, research, teaching; testing, study of industrial employment, non-projective techniques of personality, industrial social psychology. M

RIORTEAU, Mrs. Hélène. 114 Ave. Jean Jaurès, Maubeuge. b. 29 Sept 1910 Nantes. Conseiller '43 Univ. of Caen, Fr. EDUC. and VOCAT. GUID. COUNS, Cen. d'Orientation Professionnelle, Pl. du Marché aux Herbes, Maubeuge. Member: ACOF. Consulting, guidance, applied psychology, testing; achievement, aptitude and projective tests. F

RIORTEAU, Henri. 114 Ave. Jean Jaurès, Maubeuge. b. 22 May 1919 Caen. Conseiller '43 Univ. of Caen, Fr. EDUC. and VOCAT. GUID. COUNS, Cen. d'Orientation Professionnelle, Pl. du Marché aux Herbes,

Maubeuge. Member: ACOF, AIOP. Consulting, guidance, applied psychology, testing; achievement, aptitude and projective tests, industrial selection. M

RIQUIER, Mrs. Marthe Manon Henriette. 55 Blvd. Beaumarchais, Paris 3. b. 9 Mar 1918 Paris. L.PS '50 Univ. of Paris, Fr. PSYCH. CONSULT, Bur. Universitaire des Stat, 29 Rue d'Ulm, Paris. Member: SFP, ACOF. Educational psychology, testing clinical analysis, consulting, guidance; projective techniques, vocational and academic guidance. F

ROCHE, Michel. 107 Ave. du Maine, Paris 14. b. 19 Jan 1923 Baudement. Diplôme '47 Inst. of Psych, Univ. of Paris, Fr. DIRECTOR, Lab. de Recherches Psychotechniques de la Prévention Routière, 35 Rue Cugnet, Colombes. Member: SFP, APPD, AIPA. Research, applied psychology, testing; psychology of motorists, prevention of traffic accidents. M

ROCHEBLAVE-SPENLÉ, Mrs. 8 Sq. Georges Contenot, Paris 12. b. 22 Aug 1923 Colmar. Diplôme d'études supérieures '50 Univ. of Paris, Fr. RES. WRKR, Natl. Cen. for Sci. Res. (CNRS), 13 Quai Anatole France, Paris 7. Member: Groupement Français du Rorschach. Research, testing, clinical analysis, psychotherapy; social roles, psychodrama, psychology of sex. F

RODRIGUEZ, Raymond. 80 Rue de Paris, Massy. b. 6 June 1931 Paris. L.PS '53 Univ. of Paris, Fr. PSYCHOLOGIST, Ministry of Justice, Paris. Member: SNPPD. Testing, consulting, guidance, administration; delinquency prevention, projective techniques. M

ROLLINDE DE BEAUMONT, Guy. 10 Rue Georges Berger, Paris 17. b. 29 July 1900 Tunis, Tunisia. Diplôme, Inst. Natl. d'Orientation Professionnelle. MANAGER, Société Française de Psychotechnique, 117 Rue Réaumur, Paris 2. Applied psychology, research, testing; projective techniques, test construction, psychomorphology in industry. M

ROMIER, Pierre. 19 Beaulieu Le Rond Point, St. Etienne. b. 28 Sept 1926 Firminy. Diplôme d'études supérieures '50 Univ. of Paris, Fr. PSYCHOTECHNICIAN, Compagnie des Ateliers et Forges de la Loire, 16 Rue de la Résistance, St. Etienne. Member: APPD. Testing, industrial psychology, teaching; written personality tests, industrial relations, selection of management personnel. M

ROUX, Mrs. Camille Baldit. 6 Ave. Cantini, Marseille. b. 3 Feb 1912 Lyon. Diplôme d'état '43, Fr. VOCAT. GUID. COUNS, Cen. Pub. d'Orientation Professionnelle, 66 Rue St. Sebastien, Marseille. Member: ACOF. Applied and educational psychology, testing, clinical analysis, guidance. F

ROY, Pierre. Cen. Pub. d'Orientation, 36 Rue Raspail, St. Quentin. b. 4 Feb 1909 Amiens. Diplôme d'état '47 Inst. Natl. d'Etude du Travail et d'Orientation Professionnelle, Fr. DIRECTOR, Cen. Pub. d'Orientation Professionnelle. Member: AIOP, ACOF. Consulting, guidance, testing, applied psychology; aptitude measurement, achievement tests, projective techniques. M

ROYER, Miss Jacqueline. 116 Blvd. Notre Dame, Marseille. b. 16 Apr 1913 Vosges, Conseiller, Inst. Natl. d'Orientation Professionnelle, Fr. GUID. COUNS, Cen. for Appl. Psych. (CPA), 171 Rue de Rouse, Marseille. Consulting, applied psychology, professional writing, research; projective techniques. F

RUIZ, Mrs. Ingeborg Rompel. 22 Rue Jean Hermann, Strasbourg. b. 30 Apr 1929 Strasbourg. L.PS '49 Univ. of Strasbourg, Fr. Member: SNPPD. Achievement tests, projective techniques. F

SAINT-LAURENT, Miss Marguerite de. 148 Rue de Fougères, Rennes. b. 2 Feb 1919 Versailles. L.PS '53 Univ. of Rennes, Fr. PSYCHOTECHNICIAN, Cen. de Selectn. Psychtechnique, 40 Blvd, Magenta, Rennes. Member: SNPPD. Applied psychology, testing; industrial psychology. F

SAINT-MARC, Mrs. Claude. H. L. H., Tête de Pont, Beaumont sur Oise. b. 31 Oct 1926 Brest. L.PS, Sorbonne, Fr. EDUC. PSYCH'T, Ecole de Garçons, Beaumont sur Oise. Applied and educational psychology, testing, research, teaching; adaptation of the young child to school life, education of retarded children. F

SALIGNON, Emile Claude. 11 Rue Ernest Cresson, Paris 14. b. 23 Feb 1910 Toulon. Licence ès lettres, Univ. of Grenoble, Fr. PSYCHOTECHNICIAN, Co. des Freins et Signaux, Westinghouse, 18 Rue Volney, Paris 2. Member: SFP, APPD. Industrial psychology, testing, clinical analysis, consulting, clinical practice, guidance; analysis of work, vocational training, psychosociology of organizations. M

SALLES, Mrs. Odette. 1 Rue de Navarre, Paris 5. b. 26 Apr. 1897 Coutre-Vèrac. Diplôme d'études supérieures, Sorbonne, Fr. DIRECTOR, Cen. d'Orientation Professionnelle, 5 Rue d'Alifre, Paris 12. Member: AIOP, ACOF. Consulting, guidance, testing, applied psychology; guidance. F

SALMONA, Gérard. 60 Rue de Seine, Paris 6. b. 9 Oct 1928 Paris. L.PS, Inst. of Psych Univ. of Paris, Fr. SOC. PSYCH'T, Electricité de France, Gaz de France, 25 Rue Cambon, Paris. Industrial psychology, research, teaching, editorial; cybernetics, automation, group dynamics, attitude measurement, market research, statistics. M

SAUTELET, Marc. 5 Rue du Général Lanrezac, Neuilly. b. 12 Jan 1922 Paris. Conseiller '46 Univ. of Paris, Fr. VOCAT. GUID. COUNS, Secrétariat d'Orientation Professionnelle de l'Académie de Paris, 11 Rue Tronchet, Paris. Consulting, guidance, applied psychology; aptitude tests, learning, achievement tests. M

SAVOUREY, Jacques. 5 Rue St. Jean, Senlis. b. 7 Apr 1926 Belfort. L.PS '50 Sorbonne, Fr. RES. ASSOC, Société Française de Psychotechnique de Paris, 117 Rue Réamur, Paris 9. Applied psychology, testing, consulting, guidance; psychosociological research among tribes of French Equatorial Africa, mental hygiene. M

SAVY, Miss Jacqueline. 12 Rue Consolat, Marseille. b. 27 Apr 1932 Marseille. Diplôme d'état '55 Inst. Natl. d'Orientation Professionnelle, Fr. VOCAT. GUID. COUNS, Cen. d'Orientation, Quartier Féraudy, Metz. Member: ACOF. Testing, guidance, applied psychology; aptitude and achievement tests, psychotechnical selection. F

SCHMITT, Fernand. 7 Promenade Leclerc, Thionville. b. 24 Sept 1926 Forbach. Diplôme d'état '50 Inst. Natl. d'Orientation Professionnelle, Fr. INDUS. PSYCH'T. and HEAD, Cen. Psychotechnique, Société Lorraine de Laminage Continu, Seremange. Member: APPD. Applied psychology, clinical analysis, guidance; intelligence tests, projective techniques, job evaluation. M

SCHUHL, Prof. Pierre-Maxime. 17 Rue de la Sorbonne, Paris. b. 28 June 1902 Paris. Docteur ès lettres '34 Sorbonne, Fr. PROFESSOR, Fac. of Letters, Sorbonne, Paris: DIRECTOR, *Revue Philosophique.* Member: SFP. Teaching research, editorial; psychology of imagination, mental functions throughout history history of thought, philosophy. M

SCHUTZENBERGER-ANCELIN, Mrs. Anne. 14 Ave. Paul Appell, Paris 14. b. 29 Mar 1919 Moscow, Russia. Licence ès lettres '48 Sorbonne, Fr. RES. DIR, Cen. d'Etudes et Recherches Psychotechniques, Ministry of Labor; RES. DIR, Natl. Cen. for Sci. Res. (CNRS), 13 Rue Paul Chautard, Paris 15. Member: SFP, APPD, AIPA, Int. Sociometric Socy, APA, Adult Educ. Assn. (USA). Training of adults in human relations, research, applied psychology; group dynamics, communication in groups, psychodrama. F

SICARD, Pierre. 38 Route de Bry, Villiers sur Marne. b. 18 Apr 1926 Nice. Diplôme '50 Univ. of Paris, Fr. INDUS. PSYCH'T, Co. de Machines BULL, 94 Ave. Gambetta, Paris. Member: APPD. Industrial psychology; learning theory, achievement tests. M

SILLAMY, Norbert. Direction Départementale de la Santé, Cité Sanitaire, Toulon. b. 3 Nov 1926 Algiers, Algeria. L.PS '52 Univ. of Strasbourg, Fr. PSYCHOLOGIST, Direction Départmentale de la Santé. Member: SNPPD. Consulting, guidance, psychotherapy, testing, clinical analysis; projective techniques, achievement tests, child psychology. M

SIMON, Prof. Jean René. 8 Rue Changarnier, Paris 12. b. 21 Feb 1920 Charenton le Pont. Licence '49 Univ. of Paris, Fr. PROF. of FRENCH, Cours Complémentaire, Rue Bignon, Paris 12. Member: SFP. Teaching, educational psychology; genetic psychology applied to the learning of reading, writing, spelling. M

SIVADON, Dr. Paul Daniel. Hôpital Psychiatrique de Ville-Evrard, 2 Ave. Jean Jaurès, Neuilly sur Marne. b. 10 Jan 1907 Moncoutant. MD '33 Univ. of Paris, Fr. MED. CHIEF, Cen. for Treatment and Soc. Rehab, Hôpital de Ville-Evrard. Member: SFP, AIPA, APSLF, APPD, Fr. League for Ment. Hyg. Consulting, clinical practice, guidance, psychotherapy, industrial psychology; collective process, social and vocational adaptation, psychopathology in industry. M

SOLOMONIDIS, Virgile. (André Kédros) 9 Quai aux Fleurs, Paris 4. b. 1 Jan 1917 Bucharest, Rumania. Docteur ès lettres '38 Caroline Univ, Czech. RES. WRKR, Lab. of Child Psychobiol, 41 Rue Gay Lussac, Paris 5. Research, applied psychology; statistics, writing, psychology of the rural child. psychology of leisure. M

SOULAIRAC, Prof. André. Sorbonne, 1 Rue Victor Cousin, Paris 5. b. 17 June 1913 Maubeuge. MD '47 Univ. of Paris, Fr. PROF. and DIR, Lab. of Psychophysiol, Sorbonne; ED. SECY, *Annales d'Endocrinologie.* Member: SFP, Société Médico-Psychologique. Teaching, research, psychiatry; hormones and behavior, physiology of central nervous system, pharmacology of behavior. M

STAMBAK, Mrs. Mira. 12 Rue Thouin, Paris 5. b. 31 Aug 1923 Novisad, Yugoslavia. L.PS, Sorbonne, Fr. RES. WRKR, Nat. Cen. for Sci. Res. (CNRS), Paris; CLIN. PSYCH'T, Psych. Lab, Hôpital Henri Rousselle, 1 Rue Cabanis, Paris. Member: SFP. Research, consulting, guidance, testing; motor development, general development of the child from birth to 2 years. F

STOETZEL, Prof. Jean. 9 Rue Casimir Périer, Paris 7. b. 23 Apr 1910 Saint Dié. Docteur ès lettres '43 Sorbonne, Fr. PROF. of SOC. PSYCH, Sorbonne, Paris; PRESIDENT, Fr. Inst. of Pub. Opinion, 20 Rue d'Aumale, Paris 9. Member: SFP, WAPOR. Teaching, research, administration; individual and public opinion, social psychology of economic behavior, social psychology applied to ethnology. M

STORA, Renée. 16 Rue Ranelagh, Paris 16. b. 1 Dec 1912 Paris. Licence ès lettres, Univ. of Paris, Fr. RES. WRKR, Natl. Cen. for Sci. Res. (CNRS), Paris. Member: SFP, Groupement Français du Rorschach. Research, psychoanalysis, pofessional writing; projective techniques, personality research. F

SUARÈS, Dr. Nadine. 15 Ave. de la Bourdonnais, Paris 7. b. 3 July 1893 Alexandria, Egypt. MD '21 Univ. of Rome, Italy. HEAD MISTRESS, Lycée Française, Alexandria, Egypt; TCHR, St. Antoine Hosp, Paris. Member: Swiss Rorschach Socy. Psychotherapy, teaching, testing; projective techniques. F

TAILLE, Jean de. 6 Rue Frédéric Clavel, Suresnes. b. 4 Dec 1928 Suresnes. Diplôme, Cath. Univ. of Paris, Fr. CLIN. PSYCH'T, Hôpital Laemec, 42 Rue de Sèvres, Paris 7; PROFESSOR, Cath. Inst. of Paris, 21 Rue d'Assas, Paris. Consulting, clinical practice, research, teaching; projective techniques, mental hygiene. M

TENENBAUM, Max. 4 Rue du Vert Bois, Paris 3. b. 13 Feb 1927 Paris. Licence ès lettres '51 Univ. of Paris, Fr. PSYCHO-TECHNICIAN, Société Nationale des Chemins de Fer Français (SNCF), Service Psychotechnique, 61 Rue de la Chapelle, Paris. Member: APPD. Testing, clinical analysis, applied psychology, consulting, guidance; achievement tests, social perception, vocational guidance. M

TERRIER, Gilbert. Inst. Molière, 11 Rue Molière, Paris 1. b. 26 June 1921 Pantin. L.PS '50 Univ. of Paris, Fr. DIRECTOR, Psychopedagogical Cen, Inst. Molière. Member: SNPPD. Educational psychology, psychotherapy, clinical practice; learning theory, perceptive and affective difficulties in educational maladjustment, familial and social causes of maladjustment. M

THIERCELIN, Jean Jacques. 8 Rue Boutarel, Paris 4. b. 2 July 1929 Paris. Diplôme, Inst. of Psych, Univ. of Paris, Fr. VOCAT. GUID. COUNS, Cen. Pub. Départemental d'Orientation Professionnelle de l'Oise, Pl. du Jeu de Paume, Beauvais. Member: ACOF. Vocational and educational consultations and guidance; learning theory, achievement and motor tests. M

THURIOT-METZGER, Francette Madeleine. 272 Ave. Jean Jaurès, Belfort. b. 25 June 1916 Belfort. Conseiller '50 Inst. Natl. d'Orientation Professionnelle, Fr. VOCAT. GUID. COUNS, Cen. d'Orientation Professionnelle, Belfort. Member: ACOF. Testing, consulting, guidance, applied psychology; aptitude tests. F

TISSERAND-PERRIER, Dr. Mrs. Marie. 42

Rue Henri Barbusse, Paris 5. b. 24 Feb 1897 Bourges. Doctorat '22 Fac. of Med, Univ. of Paris, Fr. RES. WRKR, Cen. for Stat, Med, and Soc. Studies, Fac. of Med; RES. PSYCH'T, Cen. for Anthropometric Studies; CONSULTANT, Children's Hosp, Paris. Member: SFP. Groupement Français du Rorschach. Research, consultation; behavior of twins, projective techniques, statistics, genetics. F

TOURNAY, Dr. Auguste. 58 Rue de Vaugirard, Paris 6. b. 6 Dec 1878 Maray. MD, Univ. of Paris, Fr. RES. DIR, Fondation Aide Aux Enfants Paralysés, 1 Rue Croix Faubin, Paris 11; DIRECTOR, Lab. Physiopathologie Nerveuse, Ecole des Hautes Etudes. Member: SFP, Fr. Neur. Socy, Société d'Electroencephalographie de Langue Française. Teaching, research; electroencephalographic techniques and psychophysiology. M

TRANCART, Jean. 13 Rue de Joinville, Paris 19. b. 29 Oct 1929 Douai. L.PS, Univ. of Paris, Fr. PSYCHOTECHNICIAN, Radiotechnique, S.A.R.L., 51 Rue Carnot, Suresnes. Member: APPD. Applied psychology, testing, clinical analysis, consulting, guidance; projective techniques, industrial psychology. M

TREMBELLAND, Guy. 71 Rue Jean Compadieu, Montolivet, Marseille 12. b. 14 Aug 1923 Pailly, Switz. Diplôme '45, Inst. of Psych, Univ. of Paris, Fr. DIR. of PSYCH. SERV, Cen. d'Observation, Les Chutes Lavie, Marseille 13. Member: SNPPD. Applied and educational psychology, testing, clinical analysis, research; criminology, juvenile delinquency, personality, social and familial maladjustment. M

URBAIN, Achille. 57 Rue Cuvier, Paris 5. b. 9 May 1884 Le Havre. Docteur ès sciences, Univ. of Paris, Fr. PROF. and HONORARY DIR, Natl. Museum of Natural History, Paris. Member: Paris Psychological Society. Retired; animal psychology. M

VALABREGA, Jean-Paul. 4 Sq. Desnouettes, Paris. 15. b. 21 June 1922 St. Claude. Diplôme d'études supérieures '43 Univ. of Toulouse, Fr. RES. WRKR, Natl. Cen. for Sci. Res. (CNRS), 13 Quai Anatole France, Paris 7. Member: SNPPD. Research, psychotherapy, professional writing; clinical and social psychology, patient-doctor relationships, psychoanalysis. M

VALIN, Emile Jean-Pierre. 13 Allée des Potagers, St. Michel sur Orge. b. 17 July 1920 Evin-Malmaison. L.PS '50 Univ. of Paris, Fr. VOCAT. GUID. COUNS, Inst. Natl. d'Orientation Professionnelle, 41 Rue Gay Lussac, Paris 5. Member: SFP. Research applied psychology, teaching; intelligence and achievement tests, selection of candi-

dates for technical institutions.   M
VALLÈS, Prosper Francois André.   7 Pl.
Sainte-Claire, Grenoble.   b. 12 Jan 1903
Montreuil.   Conseiller   '43 Inst. Natl.
d'Orientation Professionnelle.   VOCAT.
GUID. INSPECTOR, l'Académie de Grenoble,
Cité Administrative, Rue Joseph Chanrion,
Grenoble. Member: AIPA, ACOF. Adminis-
tration, consulting, guidance, applied
psychology;   tests   of   mathematical
knowledge, management training.   M
VAN ELSUWE, Albert. 3 Rue Théodore de
Banville, Paris 17. b. 27 Jan 1916 Brussels,
Bel.   Diplôme, Inst. of Psych., Univ. of
Paris, Fr.   DIRECTOR, A.P.A.S. du Batiment
et des Travaux Publics, 20 Pl. Vendôme,
Paris 1.   Member: APPD.   Consulting,
guidance, applied and industrial psycholo-
gy, administration; achievement and apti-
tude tests, vocational guidance.   M
VASSEUR, Paul.   2 Chemin de Roucourt,
Dechy. b. 3 Oct 1917 Calais.   Diplôme
d'état. INSPECTOR, Houillères du Bassin,
Nord-Pas de Calais, Aniche.   Member:
AIPA, ACOF. Industrial psychology, personal
relations, testing, consulting, guidance,
collective process.   M
VEIL, Dr. Claude Frédéric. 55 Rue de Passy,
Paris 16. b. 19 Oct 1920 Paris.   Lauréat,
'52 Fac. of Med, Univ. of Paris, Fr.
PSYCHIAT. CONSULT, Reclassement Pro-
fessionnel,   113   Rue   Cardinet,   Paris.
Member: AIPA, SFP, APPD.   Consultation,
psychotherapy, teaching; adjustment to
professional work, industrial psychiatry. M
VERMEERSCH, Miss Mireille. 10 Rue Cré-
mieux, Paris 12. b. 26 Sept 1922 Lille.
Diplôme '50 Inst. of Psych., Univ. of
Paris, Fr.   PSYCHOLOGIST, Soc. Welf.
Agency, 69 bis Rue de Dunkerque, Paris 9.
Member: Assn. Profes. Psychotech. Di-
plomés.   Consulting, guidance, research,
vocational guidance for the physically
handicapped, interview, achievement tests,
attitude measurement.   F
VERNANT, Jean-Pierre.   112 Grande Rue,
Sèvres. b. 4 Jan 1914 Provins. Agrégé '37,
Fr. RES. DIR, Natl. Cen. for Sci. Res (CNRS),
13 Quai Anatole France, Paris; ED. SECY,
*Journal de Psychologie Normale et Patholo-
gique*; EDITOR, *Bulletin Analytique*.   Research, editorial, administration; historial
psychology, religious and social thought in
ancient Greece, psychological aspects of
labor in the ancient world.   M
VIAUD, Prof. Dr. Jean Gaston.   39 Rue
Erckmann Chatrian, Strasbourg.   b. 3
Nov. 1899 Nantes.   Doctorat ès sciences
'50 Univ. of Strasbourg, Fr.   PROF. of
PSYCHOPHYSIOL, Fac. of Sci, Univ. of
Strasbourg, 12 Rue de l'Université, Strasbourg. Member: SFP, APSLF, Int. Union
for the Study of Soc. Insects.   Teaching,

research, professional writing; tropisms
and tactisms, psychology, of the lower
animals.   M
VIBERT, Paul. 8 Rue Sainte Beuve, Paris 6.
b. 29 Aug 1927 St. Martin-de-Belleville.
Diplôme d'état '55 Univ. of Paris, Fr.
RES. DIR, Cen. d'Etudes et Recherches
Psychotechniques, 13 Paul Rue Chautard,
Paris 15.   Research; measurement of
attitudes of industrial personnel toward
reconversion and decentralization.   M
VILMINOT, Jean. 8 Rue Charles Divry, Paris
14. b. 2 June 1910 Joeuf. Certificat '55
Univ. of Paris, Fr.   DIRECTOR, Sect.
Technique de l'Armée, 1 Pl. St. Thomas
d'Aquin, Paris 7. Member: APPD. Writing,
teaching, research; classification of personnel, projective techniques, psychometrics.M
VINDRAS, Jean. 6 Ave. Lamarck, Paris 18.
b. 6 Jan 1933 Mortagne. Diplôme '53 Inst.
of Psych, Univ. of Paris, Fr. PSYCHOTECH-
NICIAN, SNECMA, 18 Ave. Pierre Grenier,
Boulogne.   Member: APPD.   Applied and
personnel psychology, research, student;
occupational analysis, attitude and motivation in occupational tests, motor tests,
adolescent psychology.   M
VINDRAS, Mrs. Suzanne Solange.   6 Ave.
Lamarck, Paris 18. b. 22 Oct 1933 Paris.
Diplôme '53 Inst. of Psych, Univ. of Paris,
Fr. APPL. PSYCH'T, Radiotechnique, 51
Rue Carnot, Suresnes. Member: Assn. des
Psychologues Praticiens Diplômés. Applied
psychology, research, student; projective
techniques, adolescent psychology, rural
psychology.   F
VOUTSINAS, Dimitri. 9 Rue Victor Cousin,
Paris 5.   b. 20 Jan 1921 Constantinople,
Turkey. Diplôme d'études supérieures '52
Sorbonne, Fr.   DIRECTOR, *Bulletin de
Psychologie*, Groupe d'Etudes de Psych,
Univ. of Paris, 17 Rue de la Sorbonne,
Paris 5.   Member: APSLF.   Editorial,
student; depth psychology.   M
VUILLAUME, Dr. Maurice. La Guyonnerie,
Bures sur Yvette. b. 21 Nov 1924 Jaillon.
Docteur ès sciences '53 Univ. of Paris,
France. LAB. ASST, Fac. of Sci, Univ. of
Rennes.   Teaching, research; behavior,
social insects.   M
VURPILLOT, Miss Eliane.   101 Ave. de
Versailles, Paris 14. b. 12 June 1914 Jougne
Licence ès Lettres '54 Sorbonne, Fr. RES.
WRKR, Natl. Cen. for Sci. Res. (CNRS),
Lab. of Exper. and Comp. Psych, Sor-
bonne, 46 Rue Saint Jacques, Paris 5;
ED. SECY, *Psychologie Française*; ADMIN.
SECY, SFP. Member: APSLF, SFP. Research,
editorial; visual perception.   F
WALLON, Prof. Henri. 19 Rue de la Tour,
Paris 16. b. 15 June 1879 Paris. MD, Univ.
of Paris, Fr. RES. WRKR, Natl. Cen. for
Sci. Res, (CNRS), Lab. of Child Psych,

41 Rue Gay Lussac, Paris; HONORARY PROF, Coll. de France. Member: SFP, Int. Union of Sci. Psych. Research, editorial; biopsychic development of the child, achievement tests, projective techniques. M

WARSCHAVSKY-MORANDO, Mrs. Marie-Thérèse. Cen. d'Orientation Professionnelle, 11 Ave. d'Aléry, Annecy. b. 17 Jan 1913 Modane. Conseiller '51 Univ. of Paris, Fr. EDUC. and VOCAT. GUID. COUNS, Cen. d'Orientation Professionnelle. Member: ACOF. Constulting, child guidance, testing, applied psychology; educational maladjustments. F

WEILL, Denise. 8 Blvd. Poissonnière, Paris 9, b. 6 Oct 1926 Paris. Diplôme '47 Inst. of Psych, Univ. of Paris, Fr. PSYCH. CONSULT, Hôpital des Enfants Assistés, 74 Ave. Denfert-Rochereau, Paris. Member: SNPPD, APPD, Groupement Français du Rorschach. Clinical analysis, educational psychology, research; projective techniques, achievement tests for maladjusted children. F

WISLER, Mr. Jacques Emile. 5 Rue du Doubs, Mulhouse-Riedisheim. b. 19 Jan 1929 Sarralbe. Licence ès lettres '53 Univ. of Strasbourg, Fr. EDUC. PSYCH'T, Service Municipal d'Hygiène Scolaire, 10 bis Porte du Miroir, Mulhouse. Member: SNPPD. Testing, clinical analysis; achievement tests, projective techniques. M

WISNER, Dr. Alain. 22 Rue de l'Est, Boulogne. b. 2 Nov 1923 Paris. MD '52 Univ. of Paris, Fr. DIRECTOR, Lab. of Physiol, Régie Renault, 8 Ave. Emile Zola, Boulogne. Member: AIPA, SFP, Ergonomic Res. Socy. Human engineering, research, applied psychology; sensory fatigue, tests of nervous fatigue, color perception. M

XYDIAS, Miss Nelly. 75 Rue Madame, Paris 6. b. 8 June 1908 Odessa, USSR. Diplôme, Inst. of Psych, Univ. of Paris, Fr. INDUS. PSYCH'T, priv. prac. Member: APPD, AIPA, APSLF, SFP. Industrial psychology, testing,

clinical analysis, guidance; personnel orientation and selection, job evaluation, sociological research. F

ZAIDENBERG-SOLOMONIDIS, Mrs. Dorothée. 85 Rue Daguerre, Paris 14. b. 8 June 1918 Bucharest, Rumania. PH.D '45 Univ. of Geneva, Switz. RES. DIR, Cen. d'Etudes et Recherches Psychotechniques, 13 Rue Paul Chautard, Paris 15. Member: SFP, APPD. Research, applied educational and industrial psychology; methodology, readjustment of psychopaths, learning. F

ZAZZO, Prof. René. 79 Blvd. St. Michel, Paris 5. b. 10 Oct 1927 Paris. Diplôme '33 Sorbonne, Fr. DIRECTOR, Ecole des Hautes Etudes, Sorbonne, 46 Rue St. Jacques, Paris 5; PROFESSOR, Inst. of Psych, Sorbonne; LAB. DIR, Lab. of Clin. Psych, Hôpital Henri Rousselle, Paris. Member: SFP, APSLF. Research, teaching, consulting, clinical practice; heredity and social class, mental deficiencies, psychology of motion pictures, child psychobiology. M

ZISSMAN, Miss Hélène. 12 Ave. Pierre Premier de Serbie, Paris 16. b. 8 Nov 1920 Geneva, Switz. L.PS '51 Univ. of Paris, Fr. PSYCHOTECHNICIAN, Cen. d'Etudes et Recherches Psychotechniques, 13 Rue Paul Chautard, Paris 15; EDITOR, Bulletin, Cen. d'Etudes et Recherches Psychotechniques. Member: AIPA. Applied psychology, research; psychology of disabled persons. attitude measurement, achievement test. F

ZURFLUH, Jean. 59 bis Rue de Romainville, Paris 19. b. 4 Oct 1927 Paris. Diplôme, Inst. of Psych, Univ. of Paris, Fr. RES. DIR, Cen. d'Expérimentation et de Recherches pour l'Amélioration des Méthodes de Perfectionnement du Personnel d'Encadrement (C.E.R.A.M.P.P.E.), 81 Rue de Miromesnil, Paris 8. Research, industrial psychology, professional writing; social perception, attitude measurement, industrial accidents, decision process. M

FRENCH EQUATORIAL AFRICA

DORMEAU, Mrs. Gisèle. B. P. 940, Brazzaville. b. 25 Apr 1920 Froideville, Fr. Licence ès lettres '47 Univ. of Paris, Fr. INDUS. PSYCH'T, Cen. d'Etude des Problèmes du Travail, Brazzaville. Member: APPD. Applied psychology, research, testing; psychological and social evolution of the African populations, vocational adaptation. F

LATOUCHE, Dr. Guy Louis Marcel. P.O. Box 940, Brazzaville. b. 3 Oct 1910 Lorient, Fr. MD '34 Univ. of Bordeaux, Fr. HEAD, Cen. d'Etudes des Problèmes du Travail, Brazzaville; INSPECTOR GENL, Ministère de la France d'Outre Mer, Rue Oudinot, Paris, Fr. Industrial psychology, research, testing, psychology of African populations, professional adaptation, industrial medicine, human relations. M

FRENCH WEST AFRICA

BARDET-GIRAUDON, Dr. Mrs. Christiane. Direction Fédérale des Mines, Dakar-Fann, Senegal. b. 12 Sept 1920 Toulouse, Fr. Médicin-Chef '52 Ministry of Health, Paris, Fr. NEUROPSYCHIATRIST, Pediat. Serv, Sch. of Med, Dakar. Testing, consulting, clinical practice, guidance, research; intellectual, affective or social difficulties in school, achievement tests, projective techniques. F

DURAND, Raoul. 14 Rue Descartes, Dakar-Fann. b. 20 Jan 1914 Poissy, Fr. Diplôme d'état '56 Univ. of Paris, Fr. HEAD, Mission d'Etudes des Problèmes du Travail, Inspection Générale du Travail, Dakar. Member: AIPA, APPD. Applied and industrial psychology, research, testing; evolution of social attitudes in Africa, acculturation. M

LÈQUES, Raymond Louis. IFAN, BP 206, Dakar. b. 15 Jan 1915. Licence ès lettres '41 Aix au Provence, Fr. EDITOR, IFAN, Dakar. Member: Int. Socy. of Normal and Pathol. Ethnopsych. (Paris). Administration, research, testing; projective techniques, social perception, group process. M

ROLLAND, Jean. Mission d'Etudes des Problèmes du Travail, Route de Ouakam Km. 4, Dakar. b. 29 Jan 1929 Morlaix, Fr. Diplôme '53 Inst. of Psych, Univ. of Paris, Fr. ASSISTANT, Mission d'Etudes des Problèmes du Travail. Applied and industrial psychology, testing, clinical analysis, research; study of racial attitudes, problems of perceptive structure among Africans, achievement tests. M

THOMAS, Louis. Inst. des Hautes Etudes, Dakar. b. 20 June 1922 Paris, Fr. Diplôme d'études supérieures, Univ. of Paris, Fr. PROFESSOR, Inst. des Hautes Etudes. Teaching, research, testing, professional writing; psychology of the Senegalese. M

GERMANY

ABELS, Dr. Dietrich Meno. Börnestr. 39, Hamburg 23. b. 22 Dec 1901 Saratow, Russia. PH.D '42 Univ. of Poznan, Poland. CRIM. PSYCH'T, Gefängnisbehörde, Holstenglacis 3, Hamburg. Member: BDP. Criminal psychology, guidance of juvenile delinquents, testing, teaching; psychology of adolescents, social psychology, vocational and aptitude tests. M

ABT, Ernst Georg. Johannistr. 144, Osnabrück. b. 19 Dec 1921 Hannover. Dipl. '49 Univ. of Göttingen, Ger. ASST. PHYSICIAN, priv. prac. Consulting, medicine; internal medicine, psychiatry. M

AHLERS, Dr. Phil. Otto W.G. Alter Postweg, Horst über Winsen/Luhe. b. 10 Jan 1915 Hamburg. PH.D '45 Univ. of Kiel, Ger. PERS. MGR, Deutsche Shell AG, Alsterufer 4-5, Hamburg. Member: BDP. Administration, personnel management, industrial relations, testing; industrial psychology, psychology of work, human relations. M

AHRENS, Dr. med. Dr. phil. Rolf. Herzbergerlandstr. 70, Göttingen. b. 29 Nov 1920 Dt. Krone. Dipl. Psych. '51 Univ. of Göttingen, Ger. ASST. PHYSICIAN, Univ. Nerv. Clin, von Sieboldstr, Göttingen. Research, clinical practice, clinical analysis; brain psychopathology, testing organic and endogenous psychosis, psychotherapy. M

ALBRECHT, Mrs. Margrit Rose. Stetten/Remstal, Württ. b. 6 Feb 1929 Stuttgart. Dipl. Psych. '54 Univ. of Tübingen, Ger. DIPL. PSYCH, Heil und Pflegeanstalt, Stetten/Remstal. Member: BDP. Consulting and guidance, teaching, psychotherapy; projective techniques, psychology of religion, psychotherapy. F

ALDER, Mrs. Gisela Ursel. Blucherstr. 40, Berlin s.w. 29. b. 5 Feb 1920 Berlin. Dipl. Psych. '55 Free Univ. of Berlin, Ger. EDUC. COUNS. Luisenstiftung Internat, Podbielskiallee 78, Berlin; EDUC. COUNS, Erziehungsberatungsstelle, City of Berlin, Tempelhof. Student, psychotherapy, testing; psychotherapy, neopsychoanalysis, testing of interests, educational consultation. F

ALEFELDER, Dipl. Psych. Alfons. Olpener Str. 918, Cologne. b. 8 Apr 1921 Engelskirchen. Dipl. Psych. '53 Univ. of Bonn, Ger. DEPT. PSYCH'T, Deutschen Bundesbahn, Arnulfstrasse 32, Munich. Industrial psychology, test construction, testing, guidance; achievement and personality tests, group process. M

ALLROGGEN, Dipl. Psych. Heribert. Rembergstr. 31, Hagen/Westf. b. 1 Apr 1926 Warburg/Westf. Dipl. Psych. '51 Univ. of Marburg/L, Ger. HOME DIR, Caritas Verband Hagen e.V, Potthofstr. 17, Hagen/Westf. Applied and educational psychology, guidance, marriage counselor; pedagogical psychology, educational guidance, child and adolescent psychology. M

ALTGASSEN, Mrs. Maria Cäcilie. Weissenburgstr. 59, Bamberg. b. 6 Apr 1930 Bamberg. Dipl. Psych. '54 Univ. of Würzburg, Ger. JOURNALIST, „Fränkischer Tag,"

Fleischstr. 17, Bamberg. Member: BDP. Applied and educational psychology, professional writing, testing; family guidance, psychology of work.　F

ALTMANN, Dr. phil. Mrs. Ruth. Branichstr. 5, Schriesheim/Bergstr. b. 1 Sept 1908 Gleiwitz, o/s. PH.D '36 Univ. of Marburg/L, Ger. EXEC. SECY, Beratungs und Forschungsinst. für Menschliche Beziehungen F2, 4a/II, Mannheim. Member: BDP, Studiengesellschaft für Praktische Psychologie. Educational psychology, psychotherapy.　F

AMBERG-DAUBRESSE, Mrs. Yvonne. Blankenheimerstr. 18, Cologne. b. 1 Mar 1903 Charleroi, Belgium. Lic. Sci. Pédagogiques '38 Univ. of Brussels, Belgium. PSYCHOLOGIST, Vocat. Guid. Off, Hasselbergstr, Cologne. Member: BDP. Testing, clinical practice, research; projective techniques, tests of intelligence and social behavior.　F

AMTHAUER, Dipl. Psych. Ingeborg. Merziger Weg 4, Frankfurt/M Schwanheim. b. 7 Apr 1923 Zwickau. Dipl. Psych. '45 Univ. of Leipzig, Ger. PSYCHOLOGIST, priv. prac. Member: BDP. Industrial psychology, teaching, research; personnel methods, measurement of vocational aptitudes and attitudes.　F

AMTHAUER, Dr. Rudolf. Merziger Weg 4, Frankfurt/M Schwanheim. b. 19 Dec 1920 Iserlohn. Dr. rer. nat. '52 Univ. of Göttingen, Ger. INDUS. PSYCH'T, priv. prac. Member: BDP. Industrial psychology, testing, research; intelligence and aptitude testing, vocational placement.　M

ANDRESEN, Dr. phil. Hertha. Meerweinstr. 13, Hamburg 39. b. 3 Jan 1911 Hamburg. PH.D '39 Univ. of Hamburg, Ger. DEPT. PSYCH'T, Hamburg Employment Off, Besenbinderhof 15, Hamburg. Member: BDP. Testing, vocational aptitude research; vocational psychology, psychotherapy.　F

ANDRIESSENS, Dr. Elsa. Leopoldstr. 30, Braunschweig. b. 8 Sept 1912 Berlin-Charlottenburg. Dipl. Psych, Dr. rer. nat. EDUC. CONSULT, priv. prac; EDITOR, *Kinderpsychologie*. Member: BDP. Educational psychology, guidance, research; family counseling, group psychotherapy, achievement tests.　F

ANDRIESSENS, Dr. phil. Pola. Dahlmannstr. 21, Göttingen. b. 26 Nov 1919 Mannheim. PH.D '51 Georg-August-Univ, Ger. DOZENT, Paedagogische Hochschule, Herzberger Landstr. 25, Göttingen. Member: BDP. Teaching, testing, guidance; educational psychology, work with problem children, intelligence and school readiness tests.　F

ANGER, Dr. phil. Hans Horst. Feuerleinstr.

12, Stuttgart. b. 13 June 1920 Essen. MD '47, PH.D '50 Univ. of Marburg, Ger. FIRST ASST, Institut für Vergleichende Sozialwissenschaften, Charlottenplatz 17, Stuttgart; LECT. in SOC. and INDUS. PSYCH, Tech. Univ. of Stuttgart. Research, industrial psychology, testing, social psychology.　M

ANSLINGER, Heinrich. Meister Ekkehartstr. 1, Cologne. b. 10 July '25 Maikammer/ Rheinpfalz. Dipl. Psych. '53 Univ. of Munich, Ger. INDUS. PSYCH'T, Knapsack Griesheim AG, Knapsack/Cologne. Industrial and applied psychology; educational guidance, industrial psychology, diagnosis, graphology.　M

ARENSMEYER, Dr. med. Ernst. Warendorferstr. 19, Telgte/Westf. b. 12 Jan 1925 Buer-Erle. MD '54 Univ. of Münster/W, Ger. ASST. PHYS, St. Josef Hosp, Tom Hövel 4, Gelsenkirchen-Horst. Clinical practice, clinical analysis, psychotherapy; psychosomatic medicine, parapsychology.M

ARNOLD, Prof. Dr. Wilhelm. Meyer-Olbersleben Str. 7, Würzburg. b. 14 Oct 1911 Nuremberg. Prof. '53 Univ. of Würzburg; CHIEF PSYCH'T, Nuremberg Employment Off; EDITOR, *Psychologie und Praxis*. Member: DGP, AIPA. Teaching, applied psychology, research; aptitude tests, group process, personality theory.　M

ARNTZEN, Dr. Friedrich. Wuellnerstr. 6, Münster. b. 1 Mar 1914 Dortmund. PH.D '48 Univ. of Münster, Ger. LECTURER, Univ. of Münster; DIRECTOR, Inst. for Legal Psych. Member: DGP, BDP. Research, teaching, testing; aptitude tests, forensic and educational psychology.　M

ASCHENHEIM, Dr. phil. Eva-Brigitte. Buschingstr. 24, Munich 27. b. 29 June 1923 Remscheid. PH.D '52 Univ. of Munich, Ger. PSYCHOTHERAPIST, priv. prac. Member: BDP. Psychotherapy, clinical analysis, guidance; criminal psychology, child guidance.　F

AURIN, Dipl. Psych. Kurt. Wilhelmsaue 133, Berlin-Wilmersdorf. b. 5 Aug 1923 Nordhausen/Harz. Dipl. Psych. '54 Free Univ. of Berlin, Ger. DOZENT, Pestalozzi-Fröbel-Haus, Karl-Schrader-str. 7/8, Berlin W30. Member: BDP. Educational psychology, teaching; group processes, clinical treatment.　M

BAACKE, Dpl. Psych. Hans. Schlosserstr. 26, Stuttgart S. b. 10 July 1923 Berlin. Dipl. Psych, Univ. of Freiburg, Ger. ASSISTANT, Wirtschaftskontor Dr. Schleip, Danneikerstr. 14, Stuttgart. Psychotherapy, consulting, clinical analysis; child, adolescent and developmental psychology, diagnostic psychology, graphology, psychotherapeutic research.　M

BACH, Heinz. Heinrichstr. 37, Braunschweig.

b. 5 Sept 1923 Berlin. Lehrerprüfung '51
Pädagogische Hochschule of Braunschweig,
Ger. TEACHER, Admin. District of Braunschweig, Bohlweg, Braunschweig. Teaching,
guidance; projective techniques, education-
ally difficult children.   M
BACH, Dipl. Psych. Wilfried. Frankfurter
Str. 23, Weilburg/L. b. 14 June 1924
Chemnitz. Dipl. Psych. '53 Humboldt
Univ. of Berlin, Ger. PSYCHOLOGIST, priv.
prac. Member: BDP. Educational psy-
chology, teaching, testing, psychotherapy;
learning theory, group process, non-
directive therapy.   M
BAHLE, Dozent Dr. phil. Julius. Landhaus,
Hemmenhofen am Bodensee. b. 9 Jan 1903
Tettnang. Dr. phil. Univ. of Würzburg,
Ger. PRIVATGELEHRTER, priv. prac.
Member: BDP. Psychotherapy, research;
psychiatry and psychology of productive
intellectual activity.   M
BALSER, Dr. phil. Max. Arndtstr. 16, Offen-
bach/M. b. 8 Sept. 1913 Offenbach/M.
PH.D '51 Johannes Gutenberg Univ, Ger.
CONSULT. PSYCH'T, priv. prac. Member:
BDP. Industrial psychology, consulting,
optical perception, aptitude tests, methods
of self-analysis.   M
BARCK, Wolfgang. Tullastr. 10, Mannheim.
b. 8 Jan 1928 Bofsheim-Baden. Dipl.
Psych. '54 Univ. of Freiburg, Ger. Gestalt
psychology, depth psychology, psycho-
therapy, psychosomatic medicine, re-
ligious psychology.   M
BARDORFF, Dipl Psych. Dr. Wilhelm. Inst.
für Lehrerfortbildung, Burnitzstr. 65,
Frankfurt/M.S. 10. b. 17 Mar 1893 Frank-
furt/M. Dipl. Psych. Univ. of Frankfurt/M,
Ger. DIRECTOR, Inst. for Tchr. Trng.
Member: BDP. Teaching; aptitude tests,
projective techniques, graphology.   M
BÄRSCH, Dr. phil. Walter. Alsterkrugchaus-
see 304, Hamburg 20. b. 10 Oct 1914
Weinböhlab, Dresden. PH.D '43 Univ. of
Prague, Czech. DOZENT, Volkshochschule,
Schulbehörde, Dammtorstr, Hamburg.
Member: BDP. Teaching, psychotherapy,
educational psychology; lecturing, depth
psychology, disturbances in children's
development.   M
BASIEN, Dipl. Psych. Karl Amadeus Martin.
Brand Post Eschenau Mittelfranken Nr. 88.
b. 22 Mar 1922 Chemnitz. Dipl. Psych.
'54 Univ. of Erlangen, Ger. ELEM. SCH.
TCHR, Regierung von Mittelfranken, Ans-
bach/Bavaria. Teaching, student, guidance;
projective techniques, achievement tests,
social perception, small group process. M
BASTEN, Dipl. Psych. Mrs. Gerda. Mozartstr.
15, Bonn. b. 18 Nov 1919 Berlin-Schöneberg. Dipl. Psych. '51 Univ. of Bonn, Ger.
PSYCHOLOGIST, priv. prac. Consulting,
guidance, testing, psychotherapy; social

perception, psychology of juvenile delinquency, educational guidance.   F
BATEN, Wilhelm. Schlebuschweg 25, Hamburg-Bergedorf. b. 29 Jan 1925 Bocholt/
Westf. Dipl. Psych. '51 Univ. of Münster,
Ger. DIRECTOR, Priv. Commercial Sch.
Teaching; learning theory, group process,
sociometry.   M
BATHELT, Dipl. Psych. Helmut. Breitestr.
20, Mössingen bei Tübingen. b. 23 Jan
1928 Mössingen/Würtemberg. Dipl. Psych.
'54 Univ. of Munich, Ger. STUDENT.
Student, testing, applied psychology;
testing and projective techniques.   M
BATTES, Dr. phil. Alexander. Kopernikus-
str. 13, Offenbach/M. b. 28 Apr 1903
Frankfurt/M. PH.D, Univ. of Frankfurt/M,
Ger. TCHR. and LECT, Berufsschule für
Gestaltende Gewerbe (Kunst-), Hamburger
Allee 23, Frankfurt/M. Member: BDP.
Teaching, educational psychology, re-
search; cultural psychology, social psy-
chology.   M
BAUER, Dipl. Psych. Berthold. Otto Devrient
Str. 16, Jena. b. 31 Dec 1925 Essen. Dipl.
Psych. '51 Humboldt Univ, Berlin, Ger.
DIPL. PSYCH, Medizinische Universitäts-
poliklinik für Innere und Nervenkrank-
heiten, Bachstr, Jena. Member: BDP.
Psychotherapy, clinical analysis, psycho-
therapeutic and projective techniques;
achievement tests, psychogalvanic reflex,
association techniques.   M
BAUER, Mrs. Genoveva. Walchenseeplatz
3/4, Munich 9. b. 30 Nov 1906 Munich.
Dipl. Psych. '55 Univ. of Munich, Ger.
TEACHER, Volksschule Munich, Weissen-
seestr. Munich. Member: BDP. Teaching,
testing, guidance; learning theory.   F
BAUER, Dipl. Psych. Helmut. Hartmannstr.
9, Hannover. b. 4 July 1920 Mannheim.
Dipl. Psych. '53 Braunschweig Tech.
Coll, Ger. INDUS. PSYCH'T, Nordmende,
Bremen-Hemelingen, Diedrich Wilkens Str.
Member: BDP. Industrial and personnel
psychology; psychology of work, aptitude
tests, professional writing.   M
BAUER, Dr. phil. Joseph Ignaz. Schwepper-
mannstr. 6/I, Amberg/Oberpfalz. b. 16
May 1899 Munich. PROFESSOR, Inst. für
Lehrerbildung, Kaiser Wilhelm Ring 7,
Amberg/Oberpfalz. Member: BDP. Teaching,
administration, guidance; child and youth
psychology, psychopathology, criminal
psychology.   M
BÄUERLE, Dipl. Psych. Wolfgang. Lüdmoor
12, Hamburg-Bramfeld. b. 8 June 1925
Ulm. Dipl. Psych. '53 Univ. of Tübingen,
Ger. DIR. of PSYCHOTHERAPEUTIC DIV,
Hamburg Children's Home, Knabeweg 40,
Hamburg-Osdorf. Member: BDP. Guidance,
psychotherapy, psychodiagnostics, edu-
cational psychology; social perception,

group process, play therapy.　M

BAUERMEISTER, Dipl. Psych. Gerhard. Ekkebertstr. 29, Freiburg. b. 5 Nov 1928 Kronach/Ofr. Dipl. Psych. '55 Albert Ludwigs Univ, Freiburg, Ger. Research, professional writing, testing; general semantics, language and „Denkformen" applied to psychology, „situative Ganzheit", color psychology.　M

BAUMGART, Dipl. Psych. Helmut. Kant Hochschule, Konstantin Uhde 16, Braunschweig. b. 24 Oct 1919 Berlin. Dipl. Psych. '54 Free Univ. of Berlin, Ger. DOZENT, Kant Hochschule. Teaching, research, consulting and guidance; personality theory, group process, educational psychology.　M

BÄUMLER, Friedrich. Brunsstr. 35, Tübingen. b. 7 Jan 1916 Feldstetten. Dipl. Psych, Univ. of Tübingen, Ger. STUDIENRAT, Klinisches Jugendheim der Nervenklinik, Frondsbergstr. 16, Tübingen. Teaching, applied and educational psychology, testing; pedagogical psychology, psychological tests, sociology.　M

BAUS, Miss Magdalene. Kantstr. 33, Dudweiler, Saar. b. 1 Dec 1923 Dudweiler, Ger. Dipl. Psych. '55 Univ. of Saarbrücken, Ger. RES. WRKR, Univ. of Saarland, Saarbrücken 15; TEACHER, Tchr's. Coll. Research, teaching, guidance; vocational aptitudes, educational psychology, projective techniques.　F

BECKER, Bernhard. Kaiserplatz 7/III, Munich. b. 28 Sept 1929 St. Wendel. Dipl. Psych. '54 Univ. of Munich, Ger. EDUC. CONSULT, Psychosomatische Beratungsstelle für Kinder, Univ. Kinderpoliklinik, Pettenkoferstr. 8a, Munich 15. Member: BDP. Testing, clinical practice, consulting, educational psychology; projective tests, intelligence tests.　M

BECKER, Dr. Egon. Wilhelm Buschstr. 25, Frankfurt/M. b. 16 Dec 1923 Frankfurt/M. Dr. rer. nat. '54 Univ. of Frankfurt, Ger. SCIENTIFIC ASST, Inst. for Soc. Res, Senckenberg-Anlage 26, Frankfurt/M. Research, teaching; industrial psychology, group process, statistical methods.　M

BECKER, Dr. Friedebert. Freihausweg 42 1/12, Bad Wiessee, Upper Bavaria. b. 17 June 1907 Cologne. PH.D '30 German Univ. of Prague, Czech. Member: DGP. MAGAZINE CORRESPONDENT. Professional writing on psychological subjects; theoretical psychology, animal psychology.　M

BECKER, Dr. Horst. Buschingstr. 39/II, Munich 27. b. 3 Jan 1928 Altena/Westf. PH.D '53 Univ. of Bonn, Ger. INDUS. PSYCH'T, Siemens and Halske AG, Wittelsbacherplatz 4, Munich. Industrial psychology, testing, research, teaching; social perception, personnel management.　M

BECKER, Dr. Ing. Immanuel. Gerichtstr. 12, Berlin-Lichterfelde. b. 28 Dec 1899 Stuttgart. Dr. Ingenieur '32 Tech. Hochschule of Stuttgart, Ger. DIR, Berlin Seminars for Vocat. Training, Arbeitsstelle für Betriebliche Berufsausbildung, Schillerstr. 3, Berlin-Charlottenburg; DIR. of VOCAT. GUID, Berlin-Brandenburg. Member: BDP. Industrial psychology, testing, administration, teaching; industrial and management psychology, vocational aptitudes, leadership.　M

BECKER, Dr. Josef. Moritzbergstr. 61, Nuremberg/Laufamholz. b. 29 July 1911 Trier. Dr. phil. '35 Univ. of Bonn, Ger. GOVT. ADVIS, Psych. Dept, Nuremberg Employment Off, Nuremberg; DOZENT of PSYCH, Volkshochschule, Nuremberg. Member: BDP. Personnel psychology, testing, teaching; industrial psychology, projective techniques, achievement tests. M

BECKER, Dr. phil. nat. Joseph. Bergstr. 4, Ellwangen-Jagst, Würtemberg. b. 24 Feb 1894 Camberg, Hessen. Dr. phil. nat. '35 Univ. of Frankfurt/M, Ger. TEACHER, Marienpflege-Ellwangen-Jagst, Dalkingerstr. Ellwangen-Jagst. Teaching, research, retired; psychology of perception.　M

BECKER, Wilhelm. Evang. Kinderheim, Wolf/Mosel. b. 8 Feb 1922 Bornich. Dipl. Psych. '51 Joh. Wolfg. Goethe Univ, Frankfurt/M, Ger. EDUC. SUPERV, Evang. Kinder und Jugendheim, Wolf/Mosel. Educational psychology, guidance, teaching; child guidance, group process, learning theory.　M

BECKERATH-KASTEN, Dipl. Psych. Mrs. Dorothea von. Kurfürstenstr. 5, Godesberg/ Rhein. b. 11 Mar 1900 Leipzig. Dipl. Psych. '53 Univ. of Bonn, Ger. PSYCHOTHER. and LECT. Psych. Inst, Frederic William Univ, Hofgarten, Bonn; PSYCHOTHERAPIST, priv. prac. Psychotherapy, consulting and guidance, teaching, research; psychology of expression.　F

BEER, Dr. Ulrich. Hirschau bei Tübingen. b. 2 Nov 1932 Langlingen Kr. Celle. Dipl. Psych. '54 Univ. of Erlangen, Ger. EDUCATOR, Jugendsozialwerk Tübingen, Gartenstr. 51, Tübingen. Member: BDP. Educational psychology, testing, research; psychology of expression, graphology. M

BEHN, Prof. Siegfried. Postfach 406, Bonn. b. 3 June 1884 Hamburg. o. Prof, Univ. of Bonn, Ger. RES. O. PROF. EMER, Univ. of Bonn. Member: BDP. Retired, research, teaching; aesthetics, expert judgment, industrial psychology.　M

BEHREND, Dr. phil. Oda. Viktoriastr. 7. Mannheim. b. 17 Nov 1909 Mannheim. PH.D, Univ. of Heidelberg, Ger. PROFES. COUNS, Employment Off, Kaiserstr. 69, Heidelberg. Member: BDP. Vocational guidance, industrial psychology; learning theory, achievement tests. F

BELTZ, Wolfgang. Quellenweg 13, Hamburg 26. b. 9 Jan 1921 Remscheid. Dipl. Psych, Univ. of Hamburg, Ger. HEAD, Inst. for Motivation Res, Lintas G.m.b.h. (Unilever), Burchardtr. 14, Hamburg. Member: BDP. Applied psychology, testing, psychotherapy consulting; depth psychology, projective tests, psychology of advertising. M

BENDER, Prof. Dr. Hans. Eichhalde 12, Freiburg. b. 2 May 1907 Freiburg. PROF. of PSYCH, Freiburg Univ; HEAD, Inst. für Grenzgebiete der Psychologie und Psychohygiene; EDITOR, *Grenzgebiete der Psychologie.* Teaching, research, psychotherapy; depth psychology, parapsychology. M

BENDZIULA, Albrecht. Vereinigte Glanzstoff Fabriken AG, Kelsterbach/Main. b. 8 Nov 1925 Heilsberg. Dipl. Psych. '56 Free Univ. of Berlin, Ger. ASST. MANAGER, Vereinigte Glanzstoff Fabriken AG. Industrial psychology, administration, testing; personnel selection, aptitude tests. M

BENESCH, Dr. Hellmuth. Gillestr. 3, Jena. b. 24 Dec 1924 Dux, Czech. PH.D '53 Univ. of Jena, Ger. LECTURER, Dept. of Psych, Friedrich Schiller Univ, Kahleische Str. 1, Jena; EDITOR, *Wissenschaftliche Zeitschrift der Universität Jena.* Member: BDP. Teaching, research; psychophysical problems, psychology of knowledge. M

BENING, Mrs. Luise. Lothringerstr. 73, Bremen. b. 12 Sept 1913 Hannover. Dipl. Psych. '49 Univ. of Göttingen, Ger. PSYCHOLOGIST, Employment Off, Bürenstr. 19, Bremen. Member: BDP. Applied psychology, testing; aptitude tests, social psychology of women in industry. F

BERGER, Dr. Ernst. Viktoriastr. 29, Bad Godesberg. b. 14 Apr 1915 Gera. Dr. rer. nat. '38 Univ. of Jena, Ger. DIR, Staff Dept, Wirtschaftsberatung Aktiengesellschaft, Achenbachstr. 43, Dusseldorf. Member: BDP. Guidance, testing, industrial psychology; characterology. M

BERGIUS, Dr. Rudolf. Klingsorstr. 54, Berlin-Steglitz. b. 22 Apr 1914 Carlshof. PH.D '39 Friedrich Wilhelms Univ, Ger. DOZENT of PSYCH, Psych. Inst, Free Univ. of Berlin, Gelfertstr. 36, Berlin-Dahlem. Member: DGP, BDP. Teaching, research, consulting; psychology of thinking, time perspective, prejudice, pharmaco-psychology, aptitude tests. M

BERGLER, Dr. phil. Reinhold. Leubenfingstr. 111, Nuremberg. b. 24 Jan 1929 Nuremberg. PH.D '54 Univ. of Erlangen, Ger. SCI. ASST, Psych. Inst, Univ. of Würzburg, Domerschulstr. 13, Würzburg. Research, applied psychology, teaching; juvenile psychology, motivation research, psychology of public opinion. M

BERNHARD, Dr. phil. Wolfgang. Selzen/ Kreis Mainz. b. 1 Feb 1923 Friesenheim/ Krs. Mainz. PH.D '48 Univ. of Heidelberg, Ger. PASTORAL CANDIDATE, Evangelische Kirche in Hessen und Nassau, Adelungstr. 38, Darmstadt. Theology, guidance; psychotherapy, typology, psychology of nations. M

BESOLD, Dr. med. Friedrich. Dr. Besold Clin, Schillerplatz 7, Kaiserslautern. b. 28 July 1905 Speyer. Staats exam. '29 Univ. of Munich, Ger. CLIN. DIR, Dr. Besold Clin. Member: Deutsche Psychoanalytische Vereinigung. Clinical practice, psychotherapy, research; psychosomatic medicine, element of transference, metapsychology of self. M

BETHSOLD, Werner. Bismarckstr. 61, Berlin-Charlottenburg. b. 11 Oct 1925 Berlin. GRAPHOLOGIST, priv. prac. Member: BDP. Consulting, applied psychology, research; projective techniques, psychological problems in modern art and literature, problems of cooperation in partnership. M

BEYER, Dr. phil. Dr. med. Georg. Pirkheimerstr. 33, Nuremberg. b. 11 May 1920 Nuremberg. PH.D '52 Univ. of Erlangen, Ger; MD '47. PHYSICIAN, priv. prac. Member: Allgemeine Ärztliche Gesellschaft für Psychotherapie. Psychotherapy, clinical practice; mental hygiene, gerontology, geriatrics. M

BEYERLE, Piet. Soderstr. 115, Darmstadt. b. 17 Feb 1914 Heidelberg. SOC. PEDAGOGUE, SCI. ASST, REFA, Inst. für Arbeitswissenschaft, Holzhofallee 33a, Darmstadt. Member: BDP. Industrial psychology, teaching; group process, sensory involvement in performing manual operations, industrial training. M

BICHEL, Dr. phil. Ingeborg. Knooper Weg 135, Kiel. b. 6 Sept 1924 Schwalenberg/ Lippe. PH.D '54 Univ. of Kiel, Ger. LEGAL ADVIS, Tech. Superv. Assn. of Hamburg, Julius Leber Str, Hamburg-Altona. Industrial psychology; communications, educational psychology, aptitudes and achievement. F

BICHEL, Dr. Ulf. Knooper Weg 135, Kiel. b. 9 Apr 1925 Kiel. Dr. '54 Univ. of Kiel, Ger. ASSISTANT, Inst. for Pedagogy and Psych, Univ. of Kiel, Westring, Kiel. Administration, research, educational psychology; psychology of performance, communications, educational psychology. M

BIEBRICHER, Dipl. Psych. Hildegard A.G. Landeskrankenhaus für Hirn-, Rückenmark- und Nervenverletzte, Meisenheim/ Glan. b. 9 Mar 1909 Gleiwitz/Oberschlesien. Dipl. Psych. '51 Univ. of Göttingen, Ger. CONSULT. PSYCH'T, Landeskrankenhaus für Hirn-, Rückenmark- und Nervenverletzte.

Member: BDP. Clinical electroencephalography, testing, consulting; social rehabilitation of brain injured patients, psychosomatics, non-directive therapy. F

BIERNERT, Dipl. Psych. Rosemarie. An St. Severin Nr. 3, Frechen b. Cologne. b. 25 Mar 1928 Guben. Dipl. Psych. '53 Univ. of Göttingen, Ger. STUDENT, Psych. Inst, Meister Ekkehartstr, Cologne. Educational psychology; developmental psychology, school failure, memory and learning. F

BIGLMAIER, Dipl. Psych. Franz. Whistlerweg 17, Munich-Solln. b. 11 June 1926 Pforzen/Allgäu. Dipl. Psych. '55 Univ. of Munich, Ger. TEACHER and SCH. COUNS, Govt. of Upper Bavaria, Maximilianstr, Munich; GUID. COUNS. Inst. of Psych, Munich Teacher's Assn. Member: BDP. Teaching, research, guidance; testing; diagnostic and therapeutic methods for reading difficulties, projective techniques, group process in the classroom. M

BIRUKOW, Prof. Dr. Georg. Zoological Inst, Univ. of Freiburg, Katharinenstr. 20, Freiburg. b. 25 Sept 1910 St. Petersburg, Russia. Dr. rer. nat; Prof. '55 Univ. of Freiburg, Ger. SCIENTIFIC ASST, Zoological Inst, Univ. of Freiburg. Research, teaching, administration; animal physiology, learning, analysis of fixed behavior patterns. M

BITTER, Dr. med. Dr. phil. Wilhelm. Gustav Siegle Str. 43, Stuttgart W. b. 18 Mar 1893 Langenberg. PH.D '20 Univ. of Heidelberg, Ger; MD '40 Univ. of Berlin, Ger. PSYCHIATRIST, priv. prac; EDITOR, *Mitteilungsblatt* der Gemeinschaft Arzt und Seelsorger. Member: Deutsche Gesellschaft für Psychotherapie und Tiefenpsychologie, Gemeinschaft Arzt und Seelsorger. Research, teaching, psychotherapy; analytical psychotherapy. M

BITTNER, Miss Ursula. Guntzelstr. 60, Berlin-Wilmersdorf. b. 23 Oct 1927 Wolfen. Dipl. Psych. '54 Free Univ. of Berlin, Ger. MED. STUD, Free Univ, Boltzmennstr. 3, Berlin; TEACHER, Grundschule, Berlin-Neukölln. Student, teaching, guidance; projective techniques, achievement tests, attitude measurement. F

BLIND, Dipl. Psych. Robert. Ötztalerstr. 30, Stuttgart-Untertürkheim. b. 23 Sept 1919 Stuttgart. Dipl. Psych. '55 Univ. of Freiburg, Ger. PSYCH'T. and HANDWRITING EXPERT, Polizeipräsidium Stuttgart, Kriminaltechnische Anstalt, Dorotheestr. 10, Stuttgart. Member: BDP. Criminal psychology and legal handwriting comparison; psychological diagnosis, graphology, criminal psychology. M

BOECHER, Dr. med. Heinz-Wolfgang. Moltkestr. 9, Heidelberg. b. 5 Jan 1923 Nieder-Bessingen. MD '54 Univ. of Heidelberg,

Ger. ASST. PHYSICIAN, Medizinische Universitätsklinik, Bergheimerstr. 58, Heidelberg. Clinical practice, clinical analysis, testing, industrial psychology; national character, projective techniques, psychology of expression. M

BOESCH, Prof. Dr. Ernest. Inst. of Psychology, Univ. of the Saar, Saarbrücken. b. 26 Dec 1916 St. Gallen, Switzerland. PH.D '46 Univ. of Geneva, Switz. PROF. and DIR, Dept. of Psych, Univ. of the Saar; UNESCO CONSULT, DIRECTOR, Int. Inst. for Child Study, Bangkok, Thailand. Member: SSP, DGP, APSLF, Swiss Psychoanal. Socy. Teaching, research, guidance; child psychology. M

BOESENBERG (née Beetz), Dr. phil. Hulda. Hofweg 57 Ir, Hamburg 21. b. 7 Nov 1897 Nordhausen/Harz. PH.D '30 Univ. of Greifswald, Ger. TEACHER and CONSULT. PSYCH'T, School BD, City of Hamburg, Dammtorstr. 25, Hamburg 36. Member: BDP. Teaching, applied and educational psychology, consulting, guidance; intelligence tests, social perception. F

BOG, Dipl. Psych. Rudolf. Hedwigstr. 1a, Braunschweig. b. 10 Oct 1918 Munich. Dipl. Psych. '54 Univ. of Munich, Ger. DEPUTY PERS. DIR, J. A. Schmalbach Blechwarenwerke AG, Hamburgerstr. 37-41, Braunschweig. Member: BDP. Industrial psychology, testing, writing; psychological anthropology, psychological diagnosis through mimicry, speech, walk and gestures, cultural psychology. M

BÖHM, Dr. phil. Wolfgang E. Reuterstr. 18, Bonn. b. 9 June 1920 Teplitz, Czech. PH.D '54 Univ. of Vienna, Austria. ASSISTANT, Psych. Inst, Univ. of Bonn. Member: DGP. Teaching, research, applied psychology; Gestalt psychology, test theory, visual aids. M

BOHNENBERGER, Dipl. Psych. Hans. Rheindorfer Str. 53, Bonn. b. 11 Sept 1919 Wittlich, Mosel. Dipl. Psych. '51 Univ. of Bonn, Ger. VOCAT. CONSULT, Employment Off, Kaiser Karl Ring 9, Bonn. Member: BDP. Consulting, applied psychology; aptitude diagnosis, industrial psychology. M

BOLL, Dr. phil. Oberkirchenrat a.D. Karl Friedrich. Steilshooper Str. 158a, Hamburg 33. b. 30 June 1898 Lübeck. PH.D '24 Univ. of Rostock, Ger. EXEC. SECY, Berufsverband Deutscher Psychologen, Hamburg. Research, administration; psychology of knowledge, psychology of administration. M

BOLTEN, Dr. phil. Karl Hubert. Grafenberger Allee 99, Düsseldorf. b. 20 Dec 1911 Aachen. PH.D; Dipl. Psych. '50 Univ. of Munich, Ger. PSYCHIATRIST, priv. prac. Member: BDP. Psychotherapy, testing, clinical analysis, consulting; psychoanalysis. M

3OLTZ, Dr. Vera. Francke Str. 25, Kiel. b. 23 Sept 1920 Berlin. Dipl. '53 Univ. of Munich, Ger. TEACHER, Kindergärtnerinnen Seminar, Arkonastr. 3, Kiel. Member: BDP. Teaching, educational psychology. F

3ONDY, Prof. Dr. phil. Curt Werner. Psych. Inst, Univ. of Hamburg, Bornplatz 2, Hamburg 13. b. 3 Apr 1894 Hamburg. PH.D '21 Univ. of Hamburg, Ger. PROF. of PSYCH. and SOC. PEDAGOGY, Univ. of Hamburg; DIRECTOR, Psych. Inst, Univ. of Hamburg. Member: APA, DGP, BDP. Teaching, administration, research, educational psychology; adolescent psychology, social psychology, social pedagogy. M

3ORELLI, Dozent Dr. med. Dr. phil. Siegfried. Dermatology Clinic, Univ. of Munich, Frauenlobstr. 9, Munich 15. b. 2 June 1924 Berlin-Wilmersdorf. MD '48; PH.D '50 Univ. of Hamburg, Ger. DOZENT, Dermatology Clin, Univ. of Munich. Member: Allgemeine Ärztliche Gesellschaft für Psychotherapie. Research, psychotherapy, clinical analysis; psychosomatic research in medicine, psychodiagnostics, characterology. M

3ORN, Dr. phil. Johannes Georg. Berrenrather Str. 74, Efferen bei Cologne. b. 21 Apr 1910 Johannsdorf Wpr. PH.D '39 Albertus Univ. of Königsberg, Ger. TCHR. and PSYCH'T, Realschule Hürth-Hermülheim bei Cologne, Krankenhausstr 95/97, Hermülheim bei Cologne. Member: BDP, Bund Deutscher Kunsterzieher. Educational psychology, teaching, research; child and youth work, educational evaluation, the homeless youth. M

3ORNEMANN, Dr. Mrs. Anne Maria. Vödestr. 58, Bochum. b. 17 Apr 1910 Berleburg. PH.D '34 Univ. of Munich, Ger. Member: BDP. Teaching, guidance, testing; social psychology, group process, educational psychology. F

3ORNEMANN, Dozent Dr. phil Ernest. Vödestr. 58, Bochum. b. 21 May 1912 Aachen. Dr. phil. habil. '45 Univ. of Münster, Ger. HEAD, Advis. Bd. for Parents and Children, Pestalozzi Haus, Westhofstr, Bochum; LECTURER, Tech. Coll, Aachen; LECTURER, Univ. of Münster. Member: DGP, BDP, AIPA, Gesellschaft für Arbeitswissenschaftliche Forschung. Research, clinical practice, guidance, teaching; group process, motivation in industry, educational psychology. M

3OSKAMP, Dr. Ingeborg. Geisselerstr. 34, Saarbrücken 3. b. 29 Apr 1926 Steinfeld. Dr. '56 Univ. of Saarbrücken, Ger. SCI. ASST, Psych. Inst, Univ. of the Saar, Saarbrücken. Guidance, testing, teaching; child guidance, group therapy, projective

techniques. F

BÖTCHER, Dipl. Psych. Elmar. Mühlenstr. 11, Hamburg-Wandsbek. b. 21 Aug 1919 Celle. Dipl. Psych. '52 Univ of Göttingen, Ger. INDUS. PSYCH'T, Esso AG, Neuer Jungfernstieg 21, Hamburg. Member: BDP. Industrial psychology, testing, personnel research; rating methods, attitude measurement, aptitude tests. M

BOTHE, Dipl. Psych. Hans Werner. Rodigallee 131, Hamburg-Wandsbek. b. 19 Oct 1919 Hamburg. Dipl. Psych. '44 Univ. of Hamburg, Ger. SECTION HEAD, Employment Off, Besenbinderhof 16, Hamburg. Member: BDP, Deutsche Gesellschaft für Personalwesen. Administration, personnel psychology, testing; industrial training, aptitude problems. M

BOURWIEG, Dr. phil. Hans. Neuengrodener Weg 14, Wilhelmshaven. b. 2 Oct 1911 Leer. PH.D '36 Univ. of Göttingen, Ger. PSYCHOLOGIST, Bundesanstalt für Arbeitsvermittlung und Arbeitslosenversicherung, Nuremberg. Member: BDP. Testing, applied psychology, administration, aptitude tests, psychology of adolescence, vocational psychology. M

BRACKEN, Prof. Dr. Helmut August Richard von. Rollwiesenweg 12, Marburg. b. 21 May 1899 Muhlheim-Ruhr. PH.D '25 Univ. of Jena, Ger; MD '40 Univ. of Bonn, Ger. PROFESSOR, Lehrgange zur Ausbildung von Sonderschullehrern, Rollwiesenweg 12, Marburg; ASST. PROF. of PSYCH. and EDUC, Tech. Coll. of Braunschweig; CO-EDITOR, *Psychologische Beiträge.* Member: DGP, BDP, APA, Studiengesellschaft für praktische Psychologie. Teaching, research, medical practice; psychology of personality, psychophysiology of fatigue, education of abnormal children. M

BRANDT, Anny. Strassburgerstr. 27, Bremen. b. 15 Apr 1912 Bremen. Dipl. Psych. '49 Univ. of Munich, Ger. PSYCHOLOGIST, priv. prac. Member: BDP. Psychological guidance. F

BRAUN, Dr. phil. Michael. Aicherstr. 32, Munich-Pasing. b. 1 Jan 1912 Munich. PH.D '36 Univ. of Munich, Ger; Medizinisches Staatsexamen. PHYSICIAN, Dept. of Pub. Hlth. and Welf, Govt. of Upper Bavaria. Member: BDP. Medical practice; medical psychology, youth psychology. M

BRAUNSCHWEIG, Dr. med. Dr. phil. Wolfgang. Kreiskrankenhaus, Geislingen/Steige. b. 7 July 1923 Mannheim. PH.D '51; MD '52 Univ. of Heidelberg, Ger. ASST. PHYSICIAN, Kreiskrankenhaus. Psychotherapy, clinical practice, consulting, testing, teaching; problems of Gestalt psychology. M

BRÄUTIGAM, Dr. Georg. Am Hostbleek 38, Braunschweig. b. 6 Oct 1921 Arnstadt/ Thuringen. Dr. rer. nat. '44 Univ. of Jena,

Ger. PERS. DIR, Voigtländer AG, Berliner Str, Braunschweig. Member: BDP. Industrial psychology, administration, research; psychological diagnosis, adolescent psychology, personnel management. M

BRENIG, Ruth. Am Goldgraben 11, Göttingen. b. 7 June 1929 Nordhausen. Dipl, Univ. of Göttingen, Ger. STUDENT, Univ. of Göttingen. Guidance, applied and educational psychology, teaching; psychology of learning, social perception, child guidance. F

BRENNER, Dr. Anton. 24359 Union, Dearborn 8, Michigan, USA. b. 2 Dec 1910 Aalen, Ger. PH.D '37 Univ. of Tübingen, Ger. PROJECT. DIR, Dept. of Psych, The Merrill-Palmer School, 71 E. Ferry, Detroit 2, Michigan, USA. Member: BDP, Natl. Educ. Assn. (USA). Research, teaching, consulting; dynamics of human development, learning, philosophy and psychology of education. M

BRENNIG, Walter. Siegfriedstr. 47, Weinheim/Baden. b. 3 May 1923 Lampertheim/Hessen. SCH. PSYCH'T, City School Bd, Q7, 1-7, Mannheim/Baden. Consulting and guidance, testing, teaching; educational guidance, school readiness testing, instruction observation. M

BRENSCHEIDT, Miss Irmengard. Le Chatelard, Vennes s/Lausanne, Switz. b. 7 May 1925 Bremen, Ger. Dipl. Psych. '53 Univ. of Munich, Ger. GOVERNESS, Le Chatelard. Curative educational psychology, testing; achievement tests, play therapy, occupational therapy, testing maladjusted children, education of feebleminded children. F

BRESSER, Dr. med. Dr. phil. Paul. Ehringhausen 14, Remscheid. b. 23 Mar 1921 Düsseldorf. MD '46, PH.D '50 Univ. of Munich, Ger. SCI. ASST, Univ. Nerve Clin, Joseph Stelzmannstr. 9, Cologne. Member: BDP, DGP, Ärztliche Gesellschaft für Psychotherapie. Clinical practice, legal advisor; clinical psychology. M

BRETSCHNEIDER, Kraft. Kiesstr. 17, Frankfurt/M. b. 21 Sept 1920 Dresden. Dipl. Psych. '56 Johann Wolfgang Goethe Univ. of Frankfurt/M, Ger. STUDENT. Student; psychology of films, psychology of language, culture and personality. M

BRINCKMANN, Dr. Ilse. Sonnenwall 55, Duisburg. b. 20 Apr 1911 Leipzig. Dr, Univ. of Leipzig, Ger. PSYCHOLOGIST, priv. prac. Educational psychology, testing, psychotherapy. F

BRINKMANN, Dipl. Psych. Eva-Maria. Lüerstr. 14, Hannover. b. 10 June 1917 Berlin. Dipl. Psych. '50 Univ. of Göttingen, Ger. PSYCH. COUNS, priv. prac; LECTURER, Volkshochschule; LECTURER, Landeskriminalamt. Member: BDP. Guidance, consulting, teaching, testing; group process,

child development, educational psychology. F

BROCHER, Dr. med. Tobias. Promenade 5, Ulm/Donau. b. 21 Apr 1917 Danzig. MD '42 Univ. of Berlin, Ger. HEAD, Familien- und Elternberatung der Stadt und des Landkreises Ulm, Olgastr. 143, Ulm/Donau. Member: WFMH, Deutsche Gesellschaft für Tiefenpsychologie und Psychotherapie, Deutsche Gesellschaft für Neurologie und Psychiatrie. Psychotherapy, guidance, clinical analysis; group process, projective techniques, psychoanalysis, psychosomatic treatment of criminals. M

BROCK, Prof. Dr. Friedrich Richard Carl. Magdalenenstr. 66, Hamburg 13. b. 26 Jan 1898 Leipzig. Prof. '43 Univ. of Hamburg, Ger. DIRECTOR, Inst. für Umweltforschung der Universität Hamburg, Gurlittstr. 37, Hamburg 1; DOZENT, Volkshochschule. Member: DGP, Deutsche Zoologische Gesellschaft. Research, educational psychology, teaching; social research, behaviorism, sensory physiology. M

BROCK, Dr. phil. Rustan. Lessingstr. 36, Heidelberg. b. 8 Sept 1927 Dorpat. PH.D '54 Univ. of Heidelberg, Ger. ASSISTANT, Med. Cen, Heidelberg. Clinical analysis, and practice, psychotherapy; psychosomatic medicine. M

BROCKMEIER, Dipl. Psych. Hans Otto. Veldhauser Str. 88, Nordhorn (Kreis Bentheim). b. 16 Dec 1925 Münster/Westf. Dipl. Psych. '52 Univ. of Göttingen, Ger. INDUS. PSYCH'T, B. RAWE and Co, Nordhorn, Kr. Bentheim; PSYCHOLOGIST, priv. prac. Member: BDP, AIPA. Industrial psychology, testing; aptitude tests, learning and developmental methods, social psychology and group process. M

BRORS, Hans. Am Heidberg 225, Duisburg-Serm. b. 7 Mar 1927 Düsseldorf. Dipl. Psych. '55 Univ. of Munich, Ger. LEGAL ADV, Duisburg Court. Administration, law; psychology in juvenile courts. M

BROSCH, Dipl. Psych. Heinrich. Dahlmannstr. 19, Göttingen. b. 21 Apr 1916 Garzweiler. Dipl. Psych. '45 Univ. of Göttingen, Ger. HEAD of VOCAT. GUID. DIV, Employment Off, Baurat Gerber Str. 4-6, Göttingen. Member: BDP. Applied psychology, administration; youth psychology, testing, depth psychology. M

BRUCKNER, Mrs. Erika Johanna. Kappenberger Damm 172, Münster/Westf. b. 9 Sept 1927 Leipzig. Dipl. '49 Univ. of Leipzig, Ger. Teaching, child psychology, clinical practice; projective techniques. F

BRÜCKNER, Dr. phil. Gustav Heinrich. Mobil Oil AG, Steinstr. 5, Hamburg 1. b. 26 Aug 1901 Feldberg. PH.D '31 Univ. of Rostock, Ger. PERS. CONSULT, Mobil Oil AG. Member: BDP. Industrial and personnel psychology, administration, testing; social group structure of animals, social tensions. **M**

BRUCKNER, Peter. Kappenberger 172, Münster/Westf. b. 13 May 1922 Dresden. Dipl. '53 Univ. of Münster, Ger. Clinical practice, testing, pharmacological psychology; projective techniques, child psychology, behavior disorders. **M**

BUBLITZ, Dipl. Psych. Dr. phil. Gerhard. Georgstr. 42a, Bremerhaven. b. 13 Apr 1924 Stettin. PH.D '54 Univ. of Würzburg, Ger. INDUS. PSYCH'T, and DIR. of VOCAT. GUID, Employment Off, Friedrich-Ebert Str, Bremerhaven. Industrial psychology, guidance, research; cultural psychology, social psychology. **M**

BUCHMANN, Dr. Heinz. Recklinghausen i Westf. b. 26 Nov 1915 Recklinghausen. Dr. phil; Dipl. Psych. '42 Univ. of Bonn, Ger. HEAD, Profes. Couns. Serv, Employment Off, Recklinghausen. Consulting, testing, industrial psychology. **M**

BULLINGER, Dr. phil. Dipl. Psych. Elisabeth. Vordersteig 14, Ettlingen/Baden. b. 27 Oct 1925 Ettlingen. PH.D '56 Leopold Franzen Univ, Austria. PSYCHOLOGIST, Inst. für Menschenkunde, Josephinenstr. 25, Munich-Solln. Member: BDP. Applied psychology, diagnostic analysis of test results and graphology, research; hypnosis, relations between colors and the psyche. **F**

BULLINGER, Dr. phil. Hermann Joseph Albert. Vordersteig 14, Ettlingen/Baden. b. 22 Mar 1929 Ettlingen, Baden. PH.D '56 Univ. of Innsbruck, Austria. STUDENT. Member: BDP. Student, professional writing, applied psychology; group process. **M**

BUNSMANN, Miss Margarete. Schillerstr. 33, Heidelberg. b. 11 May 1916 Bochum. Dipl. Psych. '49 Univ. of Heidelberg, Ger. PSYCHOLOGIST, Heilpädogogische Beratungsstelle an der Psychiat. und Neur. Klinik, Blumenstr. 8, Heidelberg; TCHR. of PSYCH. and PEDAGOGY, Soziale Frauenschule, Heidelberg. Testing, consulting, teaching; projective techniques, diagnostics, developmental psychology. **F**

BURGER, Dr. phil. Robert. Hiltenspergerstr. 107/II, Munich 13. b. 23 July 1920 Munich. PH.D '55 Univ. of Munich, Ger. STUDIENRAT, Deutsches Gymnasium mit Inst. für Lehrerbildung, Domberg 24, Freising, Bavaria. Teaching, educational psychology, guidance; college aptitude tests, projective tests, methods of teaching science. **M**

BURKARDT, Dipl. Psych. Friedhelm. Waterloostr. 8, Dortmund-Nette. b. 8 Apr 1929 Castrop Rauxel. Dipl. Psych, Univ. of Cologne, Ger. INDUS. PSYCH'T, Braunkohlen und Briketwerke, Roddergrube AG, Comesstr, Brühl. Industrial psychology, testing, research; human factors in acci-

dents, accident proneness, individual and group changes in adolescent boys, measurement of occupation abilities. **M**

BUSEMANN, Prof. Dr. phil. Adolf. Wehra über Marburg/L. b. 15 May 1887 Emden. PH.D '25 Univ. of Göttingen, Ger. DOZENT, Lehrgänge zur Ausbildung von Sonderschullehrern, Rollwiesenweg 12, Marburg/L; CO-EDITOR, *Schule und Psychologie*. Member: DGP, Deutsche Vereinigung für Jugendpsychiatrie. Research, teaching, consulting; psychology of childhood and adulthood, speech and intelligence defects, psychological theory. **M**

BUSING, Edgar. Dreilindenstr. 30, Berlin-Wannsee. b. 19 May 1927 Bremen. Dipl. Psych. '53 Free Univ. of Berlin, Ger. GRAPHOLOGIST, priv. prac. Member: BDP. Consulting, guidance; social perception, group process, graphology. **M**

BUSSCHE-IPPENBURG, Dr. Helga Freifrau von dem. c/o DIVO GmbH, Wiesenhüttenplatz 32, Frankfurt/M. b. 12 Jan 1927 Stolp/Pommern. Dipl. Psych. '51 Univ. of Göttingen, Ger. SPEC. in MOTIVATION RES, DIVO, Markt und Meinungsforschungs-GmbH. Public opinion and market research, testing, applied psychology; projective techniques, group studies, clinical studies, advertising research. **F**

BÜTTNER, Dr. phil. Hans S.H. Laüfen, Salzach, Oberbayern. b. 18 Nov 1909 Günzenhausen. PH.D '33 Univ. of Munich, Ger. DIRECTOR, Youth Correctl. Inst, Bavarian Dept. of Justice, Laüfen-Lebenau, Laüfen, Oberbayern. Member: BDP. Educational psychology, editorial, guidance, administration; characterology, cultural psychology, criminal psychology. **M**

BUTZMANN, Dr. Kurt. Schlüterstr. 56, Hamburg 13. b. 8 Dec 1909 Dessau. Dr. Exam. '49 Univ. of Jena, Ger. GOVT. ADMIN, Landesarbeitsamt Hamburg, 18, Neuer Jungfernstieg, Hamburg. Member: BDP. Administration, industrial psychology, psychology of expression; mimicry, motor skills, gestures. **M**

CANDERS, Dipl. Psych. Franz-Josef Leo Steinbrecherstr. 13/III, Braunschweig. b. 10 Apr 1929 Oberhausen-Osterfeld. Dipl. Psych. '54 Technische Hochschule Braunschweig, Ger. Member: BDP. Research, German translation of American psychological works, student; projective techniques, social psychology, personality theory. **M**

CAPRIVI, Dipl. Psych. Marianne von. Akademiestr. 23, Munich 13. b. Harmelsdorf, Krs. Dt. Krone. Dipl. Psych. '53 Univ. of Munich, Ger. PSYCHOLOGIST, priv. prac. Consulting, student; social perception, social psychology, graphology. **F**

CASPAR, Dipl. Psych. Rudolf. Osannstr. 38,

Darmstadt. b. 27 May 1928 Zützer Kr.
d.-Krone. Dipl. Psych. '55 Univ. of Mar-
burg/L, Ger. CONSULTANT, Berater für
Jugendwohnheime, Immenhof, Hützel Kr.
Sultan. Member: BDP. Consulting, testing,
educational psychology; childhood development in foster homes, projective techniques,
play therapy.   M
CAUER-KLINGELHÖFFER, Dr. phil. Luise-
Charlotte. Klappacher Str. 92, Darmstadt.
b. 17 Feb 1916 Kiel. PH.D '44 Univ. of
Frankfurt, Ger. INDUS. PSYCH'T, Chem.
Fabrik E. Merck AG, Frankfurter Str 250,
Darmstadt. Member: BDP. Industrial
psychology, testing, teaching, consulting;
human relations in industry, test con-
struction.   F
CAUSEMANN, Dr. med. Hans Josef. Cranger-
str. 220, Gelsenkirchen-Buer. b. 25 June 1925
Radevormwald. MD '51 Univ. of Göttingen,
Ger. ASSISTANT, St. Vincenz Hosp, Datteln.
Member: BDP, Ärztliche Gesellschaft für
Psychotherapie. Clinical practice, student,
testing; projective techniques, intelligence
tests, psychotherapy.   M
CEHAK, Dr. phil Gerd. Bonifatiusplatz I/II,
Hannover. b. 1 Apr 1910 Segeberg. PH.D
'36 Univ. of Munich, Ger. PSYCHOLOGIST,
Inst. für Empirische Soziologie, Bismarck
Str. 35, Hannover. Member: BDP. Teaching,
educational psychology, research; social
perception, group process, family relations.   M
CHRISTIANSEN, Ewald R. Carlo Mierendorffstr. 22, Mainz-Gonsenheim. b. 12 May
1928 Schweinfurt. Dipl. '56 Univ. of Mainz,
Ger. PSYCHOLOGIST, Fürst zu Ysenburg
und Büdingen, Schloss Büdingen, Ober-
hessen. Teaching, industrial psychology,
testing; projective techniques, achievement
tests, human relations.   M
CLASSEN, Dipl. Psych. Heinz. Bahnhofstr.
52, Dremmen, Bezirk Aachen. b. 26 June
1929 Dremmen. Dipl. '55 Univ. of Bonn,
Ger. STUDENT. Student, psychotherapy,
guidance; psychotherapy in theory and
practice, social psychology.   M
CLAUSS, Prof. Dr. Ludwig Ferdinand. Postfach 5, Oberursel, Taunus. b. 8 Feb 1892
Offenburg/Baden. Hon. Prof. '34 Tech.
Univ. of Danzig, Ger. RETIRED. Member:
DGP. Retired, professional writing, research;
ethnological psychology, philosophical
anthropology.   M
CLOD, Dipl. Psych. Mrs. Gisela. Meyerfeld 9,
Bielefeld. b. 20 Oct 1921 Bad-Nauheim.
Dipl. Psych. '53 Univ. of Freiburg/Br, Ger.
DIRECTOR, Welf. Sch. of Bielefeld, Land-
schaftsverband Westfalen-Lippe, Landes-
haus, Münster/Westf. Member: BDP.
Teaching, educational psychology, child
guidance; group process, social psychology,
child guidance.   F

CLOSTERMANN, Dr. phil. Gerhard. Hermann-
Lönsstr. 13, Gelsenkirchen-Buer. b. 10 May
1892 Dortmund, Westf. PH.D. SCI. DIR,
Städtisches Forschungsinst. für Psycho-
logie der Arbeit und Bildung, Josefstr. 26,
Gelsenkirchen; EDITOR, Veröffentlichungen
des Städt. Forschungsinstituts, Archiv für
Psychologie der Arbeit und Bildung,
Praktische Arbeits- und Bildungspsycho-
logie. Member: BDP, Studiengesellschaft
für Praktische Psychologie. Applied
psychology, research, editorial; psychology
of work, educational psychology.   M
CONZE, Miss Dorothea. Am Sonnenhang 2,
Langenberg/Rhein. b. 17 Jan 1927
Langenberg. Dipl. Psych. '55 Univ. of
Freiburg, Ger. PSYCHOLOGIST, Univ.
Children's Hosp, Lindenburg Cologne.
Testing, guidance, applied psychology;
clinical testing.   F
DACH, Oberregierungsrat Dr. phil Johann-
Sebastian. Hohenzellernstr. 6, Bonn.
b. 6 Oct. 1909 Breslau. PH.D '36 Univ. of
Heidelberg, Ger. OBERREGIERUNGSRAT,
Bundesverkehrsministerium, Kaufmannstr.
58, Bonn. Member: BDP. Administration,
professional writing, traffic psychology;
applied psychology.   M
DAEUMLING, Dr. Adolf Martin. Bieder-
steiner Str. 9, Munich 23. b. 12 Feb 1917
Munich. Privatdozent '53 Univ. of Munich,
Ger. PRIVATDOZENT and CURATOR, Dept. of
Psych, Univ. of Munich, Geschwister
Scholl Platz 1, Munich; EDITOR, Ment. Hyg.
Sect, Psychologie und Praxis. Member:
BDP, DGP, Deutsche Gesellschaft für Psycho-
therapie und Tiefenpsychologie. Teaching,
research, consulting, editorial; mental
hygiene, psychotherapy, case work.   M
DAHMER, Dr. Jürgen. Jasperallee 23,
Braunschweig. b. 10 May 1927 Danzig.
PH.D, Inst. of Tech, Braunschweig, Ger.
SCHOOL DIR, Kaufm. Privatschule Oskar
Kämmer, Breite Herzogstr. 13, Wolfen-
büttel. Member: BDP. Teaching, educational
psychology, administration; learning theory,
social perception, group process, school
psychology and sociology.   M
DAMBACH, Dr. Karl. Am Schönen Rain 53,
Esslingen a.N. b. 10 Dec. 1890 Satteldorf
Württemberg. PH.D '29 Univ. of Tübingen,
Ger. STUDIENRAT i.R., Staatliche Ingenieur-
schule Esslingen, Kanalstrasse, Esslingen
Württemberg. Member: BDP. Teaching
educational psychology, retired; science of
character, mental constitution, disposition,
guidance, graphology.   M
DAMM, Dipl. Psych. Heinz. Thune 24,
Braunschweig-Land. b. 23 Mar 1920 Duis-
burg. Dipl. Psych. '53 Inst. of Tech,
Braunschweig, Ger. ASSISTANT, Hochsch.
für Internat. Päd. Forschung, Schloss-
Strasse 29, Frankfurt/M. Member: BDP.

Educational psychology, testing, research; learning theory, achievement tests, child guidance, bioclimatic measurement. M

DANCKWORTT, Dieter. Muthesiusweg 2, Hannover-Kirchrode. b. 27 Sept 1925 Hannover. Dipl. Psych. '53 Univ. of Göttingen, Ger. RES. ASST, Internationale Jugendgemeinschaftsdienste, Maschstr. 22, Hannover. Member: BDP. Research; group process, attitude measurement, cultural change. M

DANKER, Mrs. Gertrud. Moritzstr. 6, Wiesbaden. b. 22 Oct 1913 Ouro-Fino, Brazil. Dipl. Psych. '55 Johannes Gutenberg Univ. of Mainz, Ger. Teaching, educational and industrial psychology, guidance, student; school psychology, graphology, characterology. F

DARNIEDER, Mrs. Hildegard Maria Elfriede. Hansteinstr. 36, Kassel. b. 26 May 1931 Hanau. Dipl. Psych. '54 Univ. of Marburg/L, Ger. Student, applied psychology; projective techniques, child guidance. F

DATAN, Dipl. Psych. Hans Henning. Planckstr. 5, Hannover. b. 20 Jan 1929 Halberstadt. Dipl. Psych. '55 Univ. of Göttingen, Ger. VOLUNTEER WRKR, Deutsche Gesellschaft für Personalwesen, Frankfurt/M. Research, industrial psychology, student; interview techniques, work samples, general personnel selection. M

DAUELSBERG, Dr. phil. Ernst. Bremer Str. 30, Oldenburg. b. 9 May 1907 Delmenhorst. PH.D '34 Univ. of Marburg, Ger. VOCAT. GUID. COUNS, Oldenburg Employment Off, Oldenburg. Member: BDP. Vocational guidance, personnel psychology, testing; aptitude tests, vocational placement of the physically handicapped. M

DAUTEL, Dipl. Psych. Mrs. Mathilde. Oberwiesenstr. 70, Stuttgart-Sillenbuch. b. 2 Nov 1906 Geislingen-Altenstadt. Dipl. Psych. '51 Univ. of Tübingen, Ger. PERS. PSYCH'T, Employment Off, Neckarstr. 155, Stuttgart. Member: BDP. Testing, applied psychology, consulting, guidance; human relations, social research, projective techniques. F

DAWO, Dr. phil. Dipl. Psych. Adelheid. Im Wiesengrund, Rheinbach bei Bonn. b. Rhaunen/Hunsrück. Dr. phil. '52 Univ. of Mainz, Ger. HEAD, Kinderheim Dr. Dawo. Member: Assn. Int. des Educateurs de Jeunes Inadaptés. Applied and educational psychology, educational counseling; psychology of human development, education of maladjusted children. F

DAWO, Dr. med. Alfons. Im Wiesengrund, Rheinbach bei Bonn. b. 14 June 1923 St. Ingbert, Saar. MD '50 Univ. of Mainz, Ger. MED. DIR, Kinderheim Dr. Dawo. Member: Assn. Int. des Educateurs des Jeunes Inadaptés. Applied and educational

psychology, educational counseling; psychology of human development. M

DEICHMANN, Miss Christa. Klueterstr. 29, Detmold. b. 21 June 1924 Kiel. Dipl. Clin. Psych. '54 Univ. of Hamburg, Ger. POST GRAD. TRAINEE, Child Guid. Cen, 201 Desoto St, Pittsburgh 13, Pennsylvania, USA. Psychiatric case work, guidance, applied psychology; projective techniques, group and individual therapy and individual therapy. F

DENK, Dipl. Psych. Karl. Am Südpark 11, Cologne-Marienburg. b. 7 Oct 1926 Sokolka. Dipl. Psych. '54 Univ. of Göttingen, Ger. TEACHER, City School Bd, Cologne-Dischhaus. Educational psychology, consulting and guidance; learning theory, achievement tests. M

DESSAUER, Mathilde. Ottostr. 9/0, Munich 2. b. 11 Dec 1912 Bonn. LICENSED GRAPHOLOGIST, priv. prac. Member: BDP. Graphologischen Gesellschaft (Munich). Graphology consultant for industry and the courts, research, teaching; judgment of children's handwriting, comparison of hand writings. F

DEUSSING, Dr. phil nat. Hans. Ferd. Wallbrecht Str. 21, Hannover. b. 18 Mar 1900 Stuetzerbach, Thueringen. Dr. phil. nat. '26 Univ. of Jena, Ger. INDUS. PSYCH'T, Hackethal Draht und Kabel Werke AG, Hannover. Member: BDP. Industrial psychology, testing, guidance; aptitude testing, evaluation of achievement. M

DEUTSCHMANN, Manfred Joachim. Kirchstr. 30, Weende bei Göttingen. b. 15 Mar 1926 Breslau. Dipl. Psych. '55 Univ. of Göttingen, Ger. STUDENT, Psych. Inst. Univ. of Göttingen, Hoher Weg 15 Göttingen. Social perception, attitude measurement, human relations. M

DIESEL, Mrs. Eleonore. Apartado 2078, Embajada De Alemania, Caracas, Venezuela. b. 6 Oct 1930 Koblenz, Ger. Dipl. Psych. '54 Univ. of Freiburg, Ger. CONSULTANT, priv. prac. Applied psychology, testing, consulting; projective techniques, achievement tests, graphology. F

DIESING, Dr. med. Ulrich R. Universitäts-Kinderklinik, Homburg, Saar. b. 24 Aug 1927 Magdeburg, Ger. MD '51 Univ. of Hamburg, Ger; Dipl. Psych. '53 Joh. Gutenberg Univ. Mainz. Ger. CHAIRMAN, Dept. of Psychopediatrics, Universitäts-Kinderklinik. Member: BDP. Psychotherapy, clinical practice, testing; psychodiagnostics, child guidance, hypnosis, projective techniques, group therapy. M

DIETERLE, Dipl. Psych. Detlef. Hausener Weg 41, Frankfurt/M. b. 26 May 1927 Breslau. Dipl. Psych. '54 Univ. of Mainz, Ger. INDUS. PSYCH'T, Deutsche Gold und Silber Scheideanstalt, Frankfurt/M. Industrial psychology, testing. M

DIETRICH, Dr. phil. Werner. Adelheidstr. 14, Hannover. b. 13 Nov 1908 Oelsnitz. PH.D '37 Univ. of Leipzig, Ger. OBER-REGIERUNGSRAT, Dept. of Educ. of Lower Saxony, Schiffgraben 7-9, Hannover. Member: BDP. Administration, teaching, educational psychology; characterology, educational counseling, graphology. M

DIETZ, Dr. med. Hermann. Uhlandstr. 5, Mainz/Rh. b. 15 Feb 1925 Kaiserlautern. MD '53 Univ. of Mainz, Ger. RES. ASST, Deutsche Forschungsgemeinschaft, Franken graben 40, Bad Godesberg, Rhein. Member: DGP. Research, surgery, applied psychology DGP. Research, surgery, applied psychology, psychotherapy; influence of weather, psychology of traffic. M

DIRKS, Dr. phil. Heinz. Office for Psych. in Industry, Hansaplatz 7, Dragass. b. 25 Nov 1906 Dragass. PH.D '31 Univ. of Königsberg, Ger. INDUS. PSYCH'T, priv. prac. Member: DGP, BDP. Industrial psychology, teaching, research; training in industrial management. M

DIRR, Lothar. Eppendorferweg 256/IV, Hamburg 20. b. 18 Sept 1926 Stammheim. Dipl. Psych, Univ. of Tübingen, Ger. PSYCH'T, Lintas, Ltd, Advertising Serv, Burchardstr. 14, Hamburg. Member: BDP. Student, industrial psychology, motivation research; group process, graphology, depth psychology. M

DÖHL, Dr. phil. Miss Ilse. Erlenstr. 29, Mannheim. b. 26 May 1895 Berlin. PH.D '33 Univ. of Heidelberg, Ger. Member: BDP. Teaching, research, retired; psychology of Leibniz, historical studies in psychology and philosophy. F

DOLCH, Prof. Dr. Josef. Orffstr. 6, Munich 19, b. 11 Mar 1899 Munich. Dr. phil. habil. '42 Univ. of Munich, Ger. PROF. of PEDA-GOGY, Univ. of Munich, Ludwigstr., Munich; EDITOR, *Zeitschrift für Pädagogik*; *Welt der Schule*. Member: DGP, BDP. Research, teaching, educational psychology; learning theory, mental development, curriculum. M

DOMBROWSKY, Dr. phil. Hans Louis. Osterdeich 70, Bremen. b. Bremen. PH.D '34 Julius Maximilian Univ. of Würzburg, Ger. MANAGER, Bohm and Kruse, Machine Factory, Osenbruckstr. 16-20, Bremen-Hemelingen. Administration, industrial psychology; psychology of accidents, traffic, and apprentice training. M

DORNER, Dr. phil. Ernst. Uhlandstr. 26, Nuremberg. b. 20 Apr 1914 Nuremberg. PH.D '46 Univ. of Erlangen, Ger. TEACHER, Blindenanstalt Nuremberg, Kobergerstr. 34. Teaching, research, professional writing; psychology of the blind, psychology of vocal expression. M

DREY-FUCHS, Dr. phil. Christel. Mecken-heimerallee 117/I, Bonn. b. 24 Mar 1915 Cologne. PH.D '39 Univ. of Cologne, Ger. LECTURER, Psych. Inst., Univ. of Bonn, Am Hof, Bonn. Member: BDP, Int. Rorschach Socy. Teaching, testing, consulting; projective techniques, the psychic effect of colors, psychotherapy. F

DÜBEL, Siegfried. Haus Siegblick, Stein über Hennef/Sieg. b. 8 May 1924 Magdeburg. Dipl. Psych. '51 Free Univ. of Berlin, Ger. CONSULTANT, Bundesministerium f. Gesamtdeutschefragen, Bottlerplatz 3, Bonn. Administration; developmental psychology. M

DUHM, Dr. phil. Erna. Hoher Weg 15, Göttingen. b. 25 Mar 1923 Meseberg/Altmark. PH.D '49 Univ. of Göttingen, Ger. LECT. and ASSISTANT, Psych. Inst. Univ. of Göttingen. Member: DGP, BDP. Teaching, research guidance, forensic psychology; projective techniques, learning theory. F

DÜKER, Prof. Dr. phil. Heinrich. Bantzerstr. 11, Marburg/L. b. 24 Nov 1898 Dassel, Krs. Einbeck. PH.D '25 Univ. of Göttingen, Ger. PROF. and DIR, Inst. of Psych, Univ. of Marburg/L, Gutenbergstr. 18, Marburg/L. Member: DGP, BDP. Research, teaching, professional writing; theory of will, pharmacopsychological research, learning theory. M

DURMEYER, Dr. phil. Friederike. Hohenzollernstr. 93/2, Munich 13. b. 11 Aug 1917 Kempten/Allgäu. PH.D '44 Univ. of Munich, Ger. PSYCHOTHERAPIST, priv. prac. Member: Deutsche Gesellschaft für Psychotherapie und Tiefenpsychologie. Psychotherapy, applied psychology, guidance; character analysis, child guidance. F

DURMEYER, Dr. Siefgried. Hohenzollernstr. 93, Munich. b. 4 Mar 1917 Griesbach/Rottal. Dr. med. vet. '50 Univ. of Munich, Ger. PSYCHOTHERAPIST, priv. prac. Member: Deutsche Gesellschaft für Psychotherapie und Tiefenpsychologie. Psychotherapy, child guidance, character analysis; psychoanalysis. M

DZIATZKO Dipl. Psych. Annemarie. Schellingstr. 55, Munich 13. b. 26 Nov 1928 Wriezen an der Oder. Dipl. Psych. '54 Ludwig Maximilian Univ. of Munich, Ger. STUDENT; STAFF MEMBER, Workcamp Organization. Research, guidance; group process and therapy. F

EBEL, Dipl. Psych. Hans. Tidoweg 30, Wilhelmshaven. b. 26 Aug 1924 Gumbinnen. Dipl. Psych. '54 Univ. of Göttingen, Ger. VOCAT. GUID. COUNS, Bundesanstalt für Arbeitsvermittlung und Arbeitslosen Versicherung, Nuremberg; GUID. COUNS, Wilhelmshaven Employment Off. Member: BDP. Personnel psychology, testing, guidance; interviewing and counseling techniques, intelligence tests. M

EBEL, Dr. phil. Martin Ernst August. Paulusweg 6, Ludwigsburg/Neckar. b. 18 Mar 1908 Wittenberge. PH.D '51 Univ. of Bonn, Ger. DOZENT, Diakonieanstalt Ludwigsburg, Evangelische Wohlfahrtsschule Ludwigsburg, Evangelische Diakonie-Seminar Denkendorf b/Esslingen, Ludwigsburg. Teaching, educational psychology, consulting; psychology of religion, psychology of medicine. M

ECKARDT, Dr. Hans-Henning. Frankenwarte 4a, Würzburg. b. 8 Mar 1927 Berlin. PH.D '52 Univ. of Würzburg, Ger. PSYCHOLOGIST, Employment Off, Ludwigskai 2-3, Würzburg. Member: BDP. Testing, vocational guidance; achievement tests, projective techniques, psychology of professions. M

ECKSTEIN, Dr. phil. habil. Ludwig Gotthold. Löwenstein Kreis Heilbronn/Württ. b. 26 Oct 1904 Löwenstein. Dr. phil. habil. '42 Univ. of Erlangen, Ger. DIRECTOR, Erziehungsberatungsstelle Heilbronn, Stadtverwaltung Heilbronn, Gartenstrasse, Heilbronn. Member: BDP. Guidance, consulting, educational psychology, testing; adolescent psychology, developmental and educational psychology, psychology of expression. M

EDIG, Mrs. Maria van. Rückerstr. 6/II, Berlin-Steglitz. b. 4 Apr 1908 Brambauer, Kreis Dortmund. Dipl. Psych. '52, Germany. OFFICE DIR, Stadtverwaltung Wedding, Volksbildung. Member: BDP. Educational psychology, library, guidance, research; projective techniques, children's books. F

EHLERS, Gesi. Inst. für Jugendkunde e.V. Lübeckerstr. 2a, Bremen. b. 25 Nov 1901 Bremen. ACTING HEAD, Inst. für Jugendkunde e.V. Member: BDP. Educational psychology, testing, teaching; retarded and problem children, educational and vocational tests. F

EHRENSTEIN, Prof. Dr. Walter. Goebenstr. 45, Bonn. b. 10 Oct 1899 Altenkirchen. Dr. phil. nat, Univ. of Frankfurt/M, Ger; Dr. phil. habil, Giessen Univ, Ger. RES. WRKR, Deutsche Forschungsgemeinschaft. Member: DGP. Research, professional writing; visual perception, typology, fundamental emotions. M

EHRMANN, Dr. phil. Barbara. Dennerstr. 4b, Hamburg 33. b. 26 Aug 1918 Leipzig. Dr. phil. '43 Univ. of Leipzig, Ger. PSYCHOLOGIST, Employment Off, Besenbinderhof, Hamburg. Member: BDP. Aptitude testing for vocational guidance; educational counseling, depth psychology. F

EIKEL, Dipl. Psych. Amalie. Silberbornstr 21, Frankfurt/M. b. 2 June 1927 Frankfurt/M. Dipl. '54 Joh. Wolfgang Goethe Univ, Frankfurt/M. Ger. EDUCATOR, Home for Retarded and Difficult Children. Educational psychology, testing, research; intelligence and development tests, therapy for difficult children, educational guidance. F

EIKENBERG, Hellmut. Wilhelmstr. 38-41, Braunschweig. b. 23 Apr 1924 Wilhelmshaven. Dipl. Psych. '53 Univ. of Göttingen, Ger. SCI. CO-WRKR, Forschungsinstitut für Arbeitspsychologie (FORFA), Garküche 3, Braunschweig, Member: BDP. Industrial psychology, research, testing; achievement tests, attitude measurement, social perception. M

EILKS, Dr. phil. Hans. Ahlmannstr 12, Kiel. b. 1 July 1910 Berlin. PH.D '35 Univ. of Marburg, Ger. GOVT. ADMIN, DIR. of VOCAT. GUID, Employment Off, Wilhelm Platz, Kiel. Member: BDP. Testing, guidance, administration; industrial psychology, intelligence tests, psychology of management. M

EISNACH, Dipl. Psych. Mrs. Herta. Regina Str. 1, Kassel. b. 2 Aug 1914 Modersitz Kr. Gera Thür. Dipl. Psych. '52 Georgia Augusta Univ. of Göttingen, Ger. EDUC. PSYCH'T, Nordhessische Vereinigung für Erziehungshilfe, Ständeplatz, Kassel. Member: BDP. Consulting, educational psychology, testing, teaching; developmental psychology, learning theory, achievement tests. F

EISTEL, Dipl. Psych. Achim V.R. Grossheidestr 21, Hamburg 39. b. 5 May 1929 Berlin. Dipl. Psych. '53 Free Univ. of Berlin, Ger. ASST. to the TRNG. OFF, Margarine-Union AG, Esplanade 6, Hamburg 36. Member: BDP. Industrial psychology, research, criminal psychology; personnel selection and education, psychology of expression. M

ELL, Dipl. Psych. Ernst. Strahlenburgweg 16, Karlsruhe. b. 9 Apr 1915 Friesenheim/Lahr. Dipl. Psych. '48 Univ. of Freiburg, Ger. DIR. of SCH. PSYCH. GUID. OFF, City School Bd, Kreuzstr 12, Karlsruhe. Applied and educational psychology, consulting, guidance; pedagogical psychology, developmental psychology, tests.M

ELLER, Miss Carmen. Mauspfad 303, Cologne Dellbrück. b. 1 Jan 1929 Malaga, Spain. Dipl. Psych. '52 Univ. of Cologne, Ger. ASSISTANT, Psych. Inst, Univ. of Cologne, Meister Ekkehart Str. 11, Cologne. Testing student, guidance; child guidance, psychotherapy, achievement and personality tests. M

ELLWANGER, Wolfram. Staufenbergstr 14a, Baden-Baden. b. 19 Feb 1928 Baden-Baden. Dipl. Psych. '54 Univ. of Freiburg, Ger. PSYCHOLOGIST, Stulz-Schriever's Orphanage, Eckbergstr 10, Baden-Baden. Educational psychology, testing, research; projective techniques, case work. M

ELSÄSSER, Prof. Dr. med. Günter. Kölnstr. 208a, Bonn. b. 24 Apr 1907 Halle. Prof; MD, Univ. of Bonn, Ger. PROF. DR. MED, Landesheilanstalt; LECT. for PSYCHOTHER, Univ. of Bonn; EDITOR, *Psychiatrie und Psychotherapie*. Member: Deutsche Gesellschaft für Psychotherapie und Tiefenpsychologie, Allgemeine Ärtztliche Gesellschaft für Psychotherapie, Deutsche Gesellschaft für Psychiatrie und Nervenheilkunde. Psychotherapy. M

EMGE, Dr. phil. Richard Martinus. Hans Wolfsbrunn, Post Kirchzell über Amorbach. b. 20 Jan 1921 Giessen. PH.D '50 Univ. of Heidelberg, Ger. PRESS and PUB. RELAT. OFF, Auswärtiges Amt, Koblenzerstr, Bonn. Applied psychology, professional writing, research; group psychology, public opinion, psychology of nations. M

EMUNDS, Dr. phil. Heinz. Kaiserplatz 1, Düren/Rheinland. b. 21 Aug 1922 Düren. PH.D '51 Univ. of Cologne, Ger. SCI. LIB. ASST, Städtische Volksbüchereien, Johannisstr, Cologne. Library, research, teaching; metaphysical foundations of psychology, history of psychology, phenomenological analysis. M

ENDRES, Dr. phil. habil. Hans. Schnellbachstr. 27, Neckargemünd/Heidelberg. b. 26 Feb 1911 Stuttgart. Dr. phil. habil. '42 Univ. of Tübingen, Ger. PSYCHOLOGIST, Inst. of Social Psych, Krehlstr. 39, Stuttgart-Vaihingen; EDITOR, *Volkstümliche Darstellung Wissenschaftlicher Forschungsergebnisse und deren Anwendung im Täglichen Leben*. Member: BDP. Consulting and guidance, applied psychology, social pedagogy, research; social reform, characterology, religious psychology. M

ENDRES, Dozent Dr. Nikelaus. St. Wolfgangsplatz 10, Munich 11. b. 10 Dec 1904 Limbach/Saar. Dr. Psych. '50 Univ. of Munich, Ger. LECTURER, Landesverband der Katholisch-caritativen Erziehungsheim in Bayern e V, Liebigstr. 10, Munich 22; LECTURER, Theological Sch, Benediktbeuern, Bavaria. Teaching, educational psychology, editorial; group process, psychology of human development, depth psychology. M

ENGELHARDT, Erich. Furtherstr. 4a, Nuremberg. b. 9 June 1907 Nuremberg. GRAPHOLOGIST, LEGAL HANDWRITING EXPERT, Institut für Menschenkenntnis. Member: Physiognomische Gesellschaft of Nuremberg. Research, testing, teaching; learning theory. M

ENGELKE, Heinz. Scharnhorstr 186, Bremen. b. 18 Aug 1907 Bremen. GRAPHOLOGIST, LEGAL HANDWRITING EXPERT, priv. prac. Member: DBP. Personnel psychology, consulting; characterology, psychological theories, vocational aptitudes. M

ENGELMANN, Dr. Elsbeth. Kyllburgerstr. 18, Cologne. b. 4 Feb 1925 Eltville. Dr. rer. nat. '55 Univ. of Cologne, Ger. VOLUNTEER WRKR, Gertrudisheim, Ulmenstr, Dusseldorf; GUID. COUNS, Nachbarschaftsheim, Cologne. Member: BDP. Teaching, psychotherapy; projective techniques, group process, depth psychology. F

ENGELMANN, Dr. phil. Waldemar. Cäcilienstr. 11, Hamburg 39. b. 23 Jan 1905 Sulzbach/Saar. PH.D '27 Univ. of Rostock, Ger. OBERREGIERUNGSRAT z.Wv, Hamburg Employment Off, Besenbinderhof 16, Hamburg 1. Member: BDP. Consulting, applied psychology, administration; social psychology, vocational aptitudes, consumer attitudes, psychology of advertising. M

ENGELMANN, Dr. phil. Wolfhard. Waldschule, Schönberg/Taunus. b. 12 June 1923 Mannheim. PH.D '55 Univ. of Heidelberg, Ger. HEAD, Waldschule Boys' Home. Member: BDP. Educational psychology, research, professional writing; child training educational work with juvenile delinquents, educational counseling. M

ENGELMAYER, Dr. phil. Otto A. C. M. v. Weberstr. 30, Bayreuth. b. 21 July 1901 Memmingen. PH.D '32 Univ. of Munich, Ger. DOZENT and OBERSTUDIENRAT, Inst. für Lehrerbildung, Königsallee 17, Bayreuth. Member: DGP. Teaching, research; sociometry, group dynamics, learning theory, personnel selection. M

ENGLERT, Dr. Othmar. Rüdesheimerstr. 19, Wiesbaden. b. 12 Nov 1910 Esslingen a.N. Doctorat '41 Univ. of Fribourg, Switz. OBERREGIERUNGSRAT, DIRECTOR, Dept. of Youth Welf, Hessisches Innenministerium, Luisenstr. 13, Wiesbaden; PROF. of SOC. PEDAGOGY, Univ. of Marburg; EDITOR, *Beiträge zur praktischen Jugendhilfe in Hessen*. Member: BDP, Deutscher Verband der Sozialarbeiter. Administration, teaching, editorial, research; social psychology and social pedagogy, group education and therapy. M

ENKE, Dr. med. Dipl. Psych. Helmut J. Sickingenstr. 1, Freiburg/Br. b. 4 Dec 1927 Marburg/L. MD '52 Philipps Univ. of Marburg/L, Ger. RES. FELLOW, Deutsche Forschungsgemeinschaft, Frankengraben, Bad Godesberg. Psychotherapy, testing, research; psychosomatics, projective techniques. M

ERETIER-COERPER, Mrs. AnneLiese. Krautstr. 74, Wuppertal-Barmen. b. 15 May 1923 Düsseldorf. Dipl. Psych. '53 Univ. of Bonn, Ger. DIRECTOR, Child Guid. Clin, Wupperstr. 80, Solingen. Member: Assn. of Child Guid. of Rheinland/Westf. Research, consulting and guidance, testing; group process, attitude measurement, projective techniques. F

ERFMANN, Dr. phil. Irmgard. Gerresheimer-str. 23, Hilden, Rhl. b. 16 July 1926 Solingen. Dipl. Psych. '54 Univ. of Bonn, Ger. MED. STUDENT, Univ. of Erlangen; PSYCHOLOGIST, priv. prac. Consulting, psychotherapy; projective techniques, achievement tests, attitude measurement. F

ERPELT, Wolfgang. Heilpädagogisches Kinderheim „Martinsberg," Martinsberg1, Naila/Ofr. b. 9 June 1919 Düsseldorf. Dipl. Psych. '52 Univ. of Munich, Ger. PSYCH. DIR, Heilpädagogisches Kinderheim „Martinsberg"; LECTURER, Volkshochschule. Member: BDP. Psychotherapy, consulting, administration, teaching; expression theory, depth psychology, national, cultural and artistic psychology. M

ERPELT-SAUER, Mrs. Margarete. Heilpädagogisches Kinderheim „Martinsberg," Martinsberg 1, Naila/Ofr. b. 25 Nov 1920 Augsburg. Dipl. Psych. '49 Univ. of Erlangen, Ger. CLIN. PSYCH'T, Heilpädagogisches Kinderheim „Martinsberg." Member: BDP, ICWP. Clinical practice, psychodiagnosis, teaching; projective techniques in child therapy, group therapy, developmental psychology. L

ESLEBEN, Ben. Ostfalenstr. 14, Dortmund-Hörde. b. 9 Apr 1924 Hörde. Dipl. Psych. '51 Univ. of Bonn, Ger. INDUS. PSYCH'T, Vereinigte Aluminium-Werke AG, Am Nordbahnhof, Bonn. Member: BDP. Industrial psychology, testing; aptitude testing, supervisory training, job evaluation. M

EWERT, Dr. phil. Otto Maximilian. Erbacherstr. 77, Darmstadt. b. 23 May 1928 Wiesbaden. PH.D '53 Univ. of Mainz, Ger. SCI. ASST, Johann Gutenberg Univ, Saarstr. 21, Mainz. Member: DGP. Teaching, research, testing; phantasy and thought, achievement motivation, projective tests.M

EWERT, Mrs. Ursula Martha. Erbacherstr. 77, Darmstadt. b. 21 May 1929 Nassau. Dipl. Psych. '53 Univ. of Mainz, Ger. PERS. MGR, Kaufhof AG, Ernst Ludwigs Platz 1, Darmstadt. Applied and industrial psychology, personnel training, testing, consulting, guidance; achievement tests, projective techniques, learning theory, group work. F

FÄHRMANN, Dr. phil. Rudolf. Vogelsangstr. 157, Stuttgart W. b. 24 Nov 1921 Leipzig. Dipl. Psych. '49 Univ. of Tübingen, Ger. VOLUNTEER SCI. WRKR, Wissenschaftl. Arbeitsgemeinschaft für Jugendkunde, Bundesgesundheitsamt im Innenministerium, Bonn. Member: BDP. Testing, guidance, research; child and adolescent psychology, anthropology, consitutional types. M

FALT, Dr. Theodor. Anstalten Hephata, Troysa, Bez. Kassel. b. 15 Nov 1911 Herrnhut. Dr. '55 Univ. of Kiel, Ger. HEAD, Heimerzieherschule und der Erziehungsabteilung für Kinder, Anstalten Hephata. Teaching, consulting, testing; youth psychology, sex research and education group process. M

FECHNER-MAHN, Dr. phil. Annelise. Hallstattstr. 38, Tübingen. b. 13 Mar 1914 Antwerp, Bel. PH.D '48 Univ. of Tübingen, Ger. CLIN. and CONSULT. PSYCH'T, Kreis-Jugendamt, Tübingen; TEACHER, Büchereischule, Stuttgart. Member: BDP, Pestallozzi-Fröbel Verband. Teaching, testing, psychotherapy, guidance; developmental psychology, psychotherapy. F

FEHLAUER, Dr. rer. nat. Rudolf. Gabelsbergerstr. 9, Braunschweig. b. 1 Apr 1922 Hannover. Dipl. Psych. '53 Technische Hochschule Braunschweig, Ger. INDUS. PSYCH'T, Huttenwerk Salzgitter AG. Member: BDP. Industrial psychology, research, graphological analysis; industrial aptitude testing, psychology of accident prevention, human relations. M

FERENBACH, Dr. phil. Magda. L. Nelson Str. 33, Göttingen. b. 6 May 1915 Aachen. PH.D '41 Univ. of Bonn, Ger. DRILLMASTER, Univ. of Göttingen. Student, research, teaching; educational psychology, psychology of expression, speech therapy. F

FERVERS, Prof. Dr. med. Dr. phil. Carl. Psychotherapeutisches Inst, Stiftsplatz 5, Bonn. b. 7 Jan 1898 Mühlheim-Koblenz. PROFESSOR, Psychother. Inst; CHAIRMAN, Dept. of Med. Psych, Univ. of Bonn. Member: Gesellschaft für Psychiatrie und Psychotherapie, Gesellschaft Deutscher Naturforscher und Ärzte. Psychotherapy, teaching, clinical analysis; suggestion and hypnosis, psychotherapeutic treatment of pain, use of drugs in psychoanalysis. M

FICHTBAUER, Dipl. Psych. Siegfried. Cherubinistr. 2, Munich 23. b. 10 Feb 1927 Berlin. Dipl. Psych. '50 Univ. of Munich, Ger. STUDENT. Member: BDP. Relationship between personality and accidents, measuring driver attitudes, projective techniques. M

FIGOY, Walter Herman A. J. Zimmerstr. 21, Hamburg 21. b. 10 Oct 1912 Hamburg. Dipl. Psych, Univ. of Hamburg, Ger. CONSULTANT, Firma Hans Schwarzkopf, Hohenzollernring 127-129, Hamburg-Altona. Member: BDP. Testing, personnel selection, consulting guidance; projective techniques, graphology, achievement tests, characterology, visual perception. M

FINCKE, Miss Barbara Ruth. Freiwaldauer Weg 28, Berlin-Lichterfelde. b. 2 Sept 1929 Berlin. Dipl. Psych. '53 Free Univ. of Berlin, Ger. VOCAT. CONSULT, Employment Off, Schlosstr. 1, Berlin-Charlottenburg. Member: BDP. Student, vocational guidance; personnel selection, educational

research.   F
FINCKENSTEIN, Fedor Hans Karl Graf von.
Haus Elbroich, Düsseldorf-Holthausen.
b. 18 Sept 1914 Dresden. Dipl. Psych.
'54 Univ. of Göttingen, Ger. HEAD, Cath.
Child Guid. Clin, German Caritas-Verband,
Benratherstr. 11, Düsseldof. Member:
BDP. Testing, consulting, teaching; pro-
jective techniques, attitude measurement,
group process.   M
FINK, Dipl. Psych. Käthe. Rambergstr.
810, Munich 13. b. 17 May 1922 Leipzig.
Dipl. Psych. '46 Univ. of Munich, Ger.
EDUC. COUNS, Psych. Inst, Univ. of
Munich. Member: BDP. Administration,
testing, teaching and research; problems
of industrial psychology, intelligence
testing, guidance.   F
FINKENSTAEDT, Dr. phil. Ernst. Kleistweg
16, Marburg/L. b. 25 Mar 1915 Lohre.
PH.D '39 Philipps Univ. of Marburg/L, Ger.
EDUC. PSYCH'T, Staatsdienst des Landes
Hessen, Marburg/L. Member: BDP. Edu-
cational psychology, teaching, guidance;
psychology of adolescence, intelligence
testing, graphology.   M
**FIRGAU, Dozent Dr. phil. habil. Reg. Rat z.
Wv. Hans-Joachim.** Von Erckerstr. 51,
Munich 59. b. 21 Feb 1906 Marienwerder.
Dozent '37 Friedrich Wilhelm Univ, Ger;
PSYCH'T and VOCAT. ADVIS, Employment
Off, Nikola Str, Lanshut/Isar; VIS. DOZENT,
Technische Hochschule, Stuttgart. Member
DGP, BDP. Testing, consulting, teaching,
research; research methods, perception,
educational counseling.   M
FISCHEL, Prof. Dr. phil. habil. Werner.
Inst. for Psych, Otto Schillstr. 1, Leipzig
Cl. b. 21 Oct 1900 Saarburg. Prof. '54
Univ. of Leipzig, Ger. COMMISSIONED DIR,
Inst. for Psych. Research, teaching,
administration; animal behavior.   M
FISCHER, Prof. Dr. Gert Heinz. Calvinstr.
2, Marburg/L. b. 19 Mar 1909 Krotoschin,
Poland. Dr. phil. habil. '36 Univ. of Mar-
burg, Ger. OBERSTUDIENRAT, State Hessen.
Member: BDP. Teacher training, research,
educational psychology, psychotherapy;
learning theory, social perception.   M
FISCHER, Hermann. Bergstr. 73, Heidel-
berg. b. 11 Mar 1923 Hamburg. Dipl.
Psych. '56 Univ. of Heidelberg, Ger.
INDUS. PSYCH'T, priv. prac; EDITOR,
Ausdruckskunde. Industrial and personnel
psychology, editorial; graphology, projective techniques, social perception.   M
FISCHER, Dipl. Psych. Horst. Graf Spee Str.
57, Duisburg-Huckingen. b. 15 Sept 1922
Bielefeld. Dipl. Psych. '51 Univ. of Münster, Ger. INDUS. PSYCH'T, Mannesmann-
Hüttenwerke AG, Ehinger Str. 506, Duis-
burg-Wanheim. Member: BDP. Industrial
psychology, testing, consulting; testing

of technical abilities, accident prevention,
group process.   M
FISCHLE, Dr. phil. Willy H. Höhenbuhlweg
37, Esslingen/Neckar. b. 2 Oct 1915 Ulm/
Donau. PH.D '48 Univ. of Tübingen, Ger.
EDUC. and VOCAT. GUID. COUNS, priv.
prac. Member: Deutsche Gesellschaft für
Psychotherapie und Tiefenpsychology.
Psychotherapy, educational and industrial
psychology, testing; depth psychology,
developmental psychology, Rorschach.   M
FISCHLE-CARL, Dr. phil. Hildegund. Dann-
eckerstr. 7/6, Stuttgart-S. b. 7 Nov 1920
Stuttgart. PH.D '47 Univ. of Tübingen, Ger.
EDUC. and VOCAT. GUID. COUNS, priv. prac.
Member: Deutsche Gesellschaft für Psycho-
ther. und Tiefenpsych. Psychotherapy,
educational psychology, testing; group
therapy, clinical psychology, intelligence
and Rorschach tests.   F
**FLIK, Oberregierungsrat Dr. phil. habil.
Gotthilf.** Personnel Office, Ministry of
Defence, Bonn. b. 6 Jan 1901 Württem-
berg-Magstadt. Dr. phil. habil. '42 Univ.
of Prague, Czech. CHIEF of MILIT. PSYCH,
Pers. Off, Ministry of Defence; LECT. in
APPL. PSYCH, Univ. of Erlangen, Bavaria.
Member: BDP, Int. Assn. of Criminol.
Administration, research, teaching; attitude
measurement, sensory perception, criminal
psychology.   M
FLOEGEL, Dr. phil. Herbert. Gaussstr. 3,
Frankfurt/M. b. 3 Mar 1926 Oderberg,
Czech. PH.D '55 Univ. of Munich, Ger.
MARKET RES. DIR, H.K. McCann Co. Ltd,
Mainzer Landstr. 48, Frankfurt/M. Member
BDP. Teaching, social and industrial re-
search; achievement tests, social perception,
group process.   M
FLOSDORF, Dipl. Psych. Peter Paul. Trau-
bengasse 19, Würzburg. b. 7 Oct 1928
Siegen. Dipl. Psych. '53 Univ. of Munich,
Ger. PSYCHOLOGIST, Psychotherapeutischer
Beratungsdienst und Heilpädagog. Psycho-
therap. Abtlg, Frankfurterstr. 24, Würz-
burg. Guidance, testing, psychotherapy;
child therapy, projective techniques.   M
FLÜGGE, Gerd. Kottwitzstr. 58, Hamburg
20. b. 17 Oct 1922 Berlin. Dipl. Psych.
'53 Free Univ. of Berlin, Ger. PERS. MGR,
Prüfungsamt für den Offentlichen Dienst,
Senate of the City of Hamburg, Steckel-
hörn 12, Hamburg 11. Member: BDP.
Industrial and applied psychology,
guidance; personality diagnosis, psychology of prejudice and expression.   M
FLÜGGE, Mrs. Ingrid. Kottwitzstr. 58,
Hamburg 20. b. 13 Nov 1928 Berlin. Dipl.
Psych. '53 Free Univ. of Berlin, Ger.
PSYCHOLOGIST, priv. prac. Member: BDP.
Consulting, translations of psychological
and educational literature; social factors
in learning, formation of judgement,

theories of development. F
FOERSTER, Dr. phil. Joachim-Friedrich von.
Mörikestr. 9, Hamburg-Blankenese. b.
10 June 1897 Rädnitz-Brandenburg. PH.D
'22 Univ. of Berlin, Ger. VOCAT. CONSULT,
Employment Off, Besenbinderhof, Hamburg. Member: BDP. Testing, consulting,
personnel psychology, research; graphology,
vocational aptitude testing, projective
techniques. M
FÖRSTER, Miss Claire. Am Pferdeteich 19,
Duderstadt. b. 4 Nov 1921 Duderstadt.
Dipl. Psych. '55 Univ. of Würzburg, Ger.
PSYCHOLOGIST, Psychiat. Dept. Univ.
Children's Hosp, Josef Schneiderstr, Würzburg. Testing, clinical analysis, student;
social psychology, anthropology, intelligence and motor tests, projective techniques. F
FÖRSTER, Reg. Rat z. Wv. Dr. phil. Herbert.
Eugen Richterstr. 11, Worms/Rhein. b.
15 Dec. 1911 Kiel. PH.D '39 Univ. of
Marburg/L, Ger. TCHR. and REGIERUNGS-
RAT z. Wv, Bezirksregierung für Rheinhessen, Worms. Member: BDP. Teaching,
psychotherapy, educational advisor; child
and adolescent psychology, psychological
diagnosis, psychotherapy. M
FRANKE, Dipl. Psych. Joachim. Theodor
Francke Str. 5, Templehof, Berlin. b. 10
Apr 1926 Swinemünde. Dipl. Psych. '54
Free Univ. of Berlin, Ger. SCI. CO-WORKER,
Inst. for Psych. Res, Free Univ. of Berlin,
Altensteinstr. 44a, Dahlem, Berlin. Member
BDP. Applied psychology, research, testing;
expression, psychology of partnership,
human relations. M
FRANKE, Dipl. Psych. Martin. Frhr. v.
Steinstr. 4, Mainz. b. 2 May 1927 Breslau.
Dipl. Psych. '55 Univ. of Munich, Ger.
STUDENT. Psychotherapy, consulting,
testing, educational psychology; educational guidance, characterology, projective techniques, learning theory, a-
chievement tests. M
FRANKE, Wolfgang. Böningerstr. 36, Duisburg. b. 2 Aug 1922 Quedlinburg. Dipl.
Psych. '55 Univ. of Göttingen, Ger. SUPERV.
of EDUC. GUID, Erziehungsberatung des
Caritasverbandes, City of Duisburg. Consulting, educational psychology; learning
theory, methods of psychological
treatment. M
FREIDEBURG, Dr. phil. Ludwig von. Rubens-
str. 23, Frankfurt/M. b. 21 May 1924
Wilhelmshaven. PH.D '52 Albert Ludwigs
Univ. of Freiburg, Ger. RES. DIR, Inst. for
Soc. Res, Johann Wolfgang Goethe Univ,
Senckenberg Anlage 26, Frankfurt/M.
Research, teaching, administration; attitude measurement, group process, projective techniques. M
FRENZEL, Dipl. Psych. Mrs. Renate. Frauen-

steinstr. 21, Frankfurt/M. b. 1 Apr 1923
Bielefeld. Dipl. Psych. '50 Univ. of
Göttingen, Ger. SCI. ASST, Agrar Soziale
Gesellschaft, Kurze Geismarstr. 23, Göttingen; TUTOR. Sociological research,
applied psychology, consulting; learning,
memory, developmental psychology, research on the psychology of sex. F
FREYBERG, Dr. phil. Herbert. Luisen Str.
20/22, Aachen. b. 22 Nov 1907 Halle/Saale.
PH.D '32 Univ. of Halle, Ger. PSYCHOLOGIST,
Employment Off, An den Frauenbrüdern,
Aachen; DIRECTOR, Dept. of Educ. Guid,
Aachen; Educational psychology, guidance,
research, testing; aptitude measurement,
psychology of the talented. M
FRIEDRICH, Werner. Potsdamer Chaussee
52, Berlin-Nikolassee. b. 4 Aug 1926 Aue
Kr. Schwarzenberg. Dipl. Psych. '52 Free
Univ. of Berling, Ger. PLAY GRP. LEADER,
Bezirksamt Spandau v. Berlin, Carl
Schurz Str. 2-7, Berlin-Spandau. Member:
BDP. Guidance, testing, teaching; nondirective group and play therapy, psychology of expression in child therapy. M
FRIEDRICHS, Dr. phil. Hans. Blumenstr. 13,
Hagen/Westf. b. 22 May 1914 Krefeld.
PH.D '40 Univ. of Bonn, Ger. CONSULT.
PSYCH'T, priv. prac. Member: BDP. Applied
and forensic psychology, consulting; credibility of legal testimony, sexual behavior,
juvenile delinquency. M
FRISCH, Prof. Dr. Karl von. Zoological Inst,
Univ. of Munich, Luisenstr. 14, Munich 2.
b. 2 Nov 1886 Vienna, Austria. Prof. '21
Univ. of Rostock, Ger. DIRECTOR, Zoological Inst; EDITOR, *Verständliche Wissenschaft*; CO-EDITOR, *Berichte über die Wissenschaftliche Biologie*. Research, teaching,
administration, editorial; psychology of
insect societies, communication in bee
swarms, psychology of schools of fish. M
FRITZ, Miss Magdalena. Friedrichstr. 34,
Stuttgart-Korntal. b. 18 Sept 1921
Stuttgart. Dipl. Psych. '52 Univ. of
Tübingen, Ger. ASST. WARDEN, Bethesda,
Mainzerstr. 8, Boppard/Rh. Teaching,
educational psychology, testing; teacher
training, learning theory, group process. F
FUCHS, Dr. Rainer. Inst. for Psych, Gutenbergstr. 18, Marburg. b. 20 Oct 1915 Strasbourg, Fr. Dr. habil. '53 Univ. of Marburg,
Ger; Dr. rer. nat. '41 Univ. of Göttingen,
Ger. DOZENT, Inst. for Psych; PSYCH.
TCHR. Univ. of Marburg. Member: DGP,
BDP. Teaching, research; clinical and
experimental research on motivation, cognitive process, learning theory. M
FUHR, Miss Irmgard. Sachsentor 19, Hamburg-Bergedorf. b. 25 July 1922 Hamburg.
Dipl. Psych. '50 Univ. of Hamburg, Ger.
SOCIAL CASE WRKR, BP Benzin und Petroleum Gesellschaft mit Beschränkter

Haftung, Steinstr. 5, Hamburg. Member:
BDP. Personnel psychology, adminis-
tration. F
FÜRST, Dr. phil. Dr. rer. nat. Josef. Wildtal
bei Freiburg. b. 12 Nov 1913 Tauber-
bischofsheim. PH.D '39 Univ. of Freiburg,
Ger; Dr. rer. nat. '40 Univ. of Freiburg,
Ger. GOVT. COUNS. and SECT. HEAD,
Employment Off, Wilhelmstr, Freiburg.
Member: BDP. Administration, applied
psychology; intelligence testing, vocational
psychology. M
GAGERN, Dr. med. Friedrich Ernst, Freiherr
von. Widenmayerstr. 5, Munich 22. b. 2
Oct 1914 Melsungen, Regierungsbez. Kassel
MD '41 Univ. of Munich, Ger. PSYCHIATRIST,
priv. prac. Member: Deutsche Ärztliche
Gesellschaft für Psychotherapie, Assn.
Catholique Int. pour l'Etude sur le Rapport
entre la Psych. Normale et Pathologique.
Psychotherapy, consulting, professional
writing; relation of psychopathological
phenomena to theological practices,
anthropology. M
GALLE, Dr. phil. Gerhard Willi. Lindemann-
str. 23, Dortmund. b. 22 Dec 1910 Pirna/
Sachsen. PH.D '42 Univ. of Leipzig, Ger.
INDUS. PSYCH'T, Dortmund-Hörder Hüt-
tenunion AG, Rheinische Str. 173, Dortmund; SCH. PSYCH'T, City of Dortmund.
Member: BDP, Gesellschaft für Arbeitswissenschaftliche Forschung. Industrial
psychology, testing, teaching; personnel
psychology, educational psychology, aptitude testing. M
GALLMEIER, Regierungsrat Dr. phil. Michael. Aussere Passauerstr. 26A, Straubing,
Bavaria. b. 30 May 1903 Schierling, Bavaria. PH.D '34 Univ. of Munich, Ger.
REGIERUNGSRAT APPL. PSYCH'T, Straubing
Penitentiary. Member: BDP. Criminal
psychology, educational psychology, research, teaching; characterology, rehabilitation of criminals, depth-psychology. M
GARBSCH, Mrs. Ilse. Gruenewaldstr. 12,
Braunschweig. b. 6 Sept 1919 Breslau/
Silesia. Dipl. Psych. '54 Univ. of Munich,
Ger. DOZENT, Sch. of Soc. Work, Niedersächsische Landeswohlfahrtsschule, Gruenewaldstr. 12. Member: BDP. Applied
and educational psychology, guidance,
teaching, case work; projective techniques,
group process, play therapy. F
GAUHL, Dr. phil. Werner. Bodenstedtstr. 12,
Frankfurt/M. b. 29 Feb 1908 Frankfurt/M.
PH.D '39 Univ. of Marburg, Ger. PSYCHO-
THERAPIST, priv. prac. Member: BDP,
Gewerkschaftsbund Erziehung und Wissenschaft, Int. Montessori Assn. Child psychotherapy, clinical analysis, child guidance;
play therapy, projective techniques, theory
of learning and training. M
GAUPP, Prof. Dr. phil. Albrecht. Landes-

anstalt für Erziehung und Unterricht,
Abteilung für Jugendkunde, Hegelplatz 1,
Stuttgart-N. b. 25 Jan 1910 Freiburg.
PH.D, Univ. of Greifswald, Ger. DIRECTOR,
Abteilung für Jugendkunde; LECTURER,
Sch. for Adults. Member: BDP, Vereinigung
Deutscher Psychagogen. Applied and
educational psychology, research, testing,
clinical analysis; adult education, student
selection. M
GECK, Dr. phil. Werner. Stubenrauchstr. 34,
Mönkeberg über Kiel. b. 11 Dec 1921
Lüdenscheid. P.HD '53 Univ. of Kiel, Ger.
STUDIENASSESSOR, Kulturministerium des
Landes Schleswig-Holstein, Kiel. Teaching;
juvenile psychology, group process, Gestalt
psychology. M
GENESCHEN, Miss Margarete. Gereonstr. 42,
Viersen. b. 31 July 1929 Viersen. Dipl.
Psych. '55 Univ. of Bonn, Ger. Consulting,
testing, student; social perception, child
psychology, group process. F
GERBERT, Dr. phil. Karl. Maschstr. 11,
Braunschweig. b. 5 Jan 1924 Mannheim.
PH.D '51 Univ. of Würzburg, Ger. RES.
WRKR, Forschungsinst. für Arbeitspsy-
chologie und Personalwesen, Garküche 3,
Braunschweig. Member: DGP. Applied
psychology, testing, motivation and adver-
tising research, criminal psychology; pro-
jective techniques, psychology of ex-
pression. M
GERHARDT, Dr. phil. Ursula. Sächsische
Str. 66, Berlin W. 15. b. 15 June 1925
Berlin. Dipl. Psych, Dr. phil. '51 Free
Univ. of Berlin, Ger. CLIN. PSYCH'T,
Psychiat. Clin, Free Univ. of Berlin,
Nussbaumallee 38, Berlin-Charlottenburg.
Psychotherapy, clinical practice, testing;
social perception, group process, develop-
ment of neurosis. F
GERHARTZ, Dr. phil. Ingrid Nana Luise.
Teutonenstr. 16, Berlin-Nikolassee. b. 31
Dec 1922 Hildesheim. PH.D '49 Univ. of
Berlin, Ger. RES. WRKR, Free Univ. of
Berlin; DOZENT of PSYCH, Kranken-
schwestern und Lehrer Kursen. Student,
research, teaching; film psychology, edu-
cational psychology. F
GERHOLD, Dipl. Psych. Herbert. Inst. für
Werbepsychologie und Markterkundung,
Rathensuplatz 2-8, Frankfurt. b. 24 Feb
1926 Bottrop/Westf. Dipl. Psych, Univ.
of Frankfurt, Ger. APPL. PSYCH'T, priv.
prac. Applied psychology, market research; psychology of advertising, research
on theories of perception and motivation. M
GERLOFF, Dipl. Psych. Otfried. Jennerstr.
25, Göttingen. b. 19 Aug 1925 Göttingen.
Dipl. Psych. '55 Univ. of Göttingen, Ger.
PSYCHOLOGIST, priv. prac. Applied psychology, market and opinion research;

psychology of films, attitude measurement, interviewing.   M
GILEN, Prof. Dr. Leonhard, S. J. Hochschule St. Georgen, Offenbacher Landstr. 224, Frankfurt/M. b. 22 June 1900 Ehlenz/Rh. Dr. theol. '29 Ignatiuskolleg, Ger; Dr. phil. '49 Univ. of Mainz, Ger. PROF. of PSYCH, Hochschule St. Georgen. Member: DGP. Teaching empirical and philosophical psychology, research, spiritual guidance; psychology of adolescence, matter and spirit in man, structural psychology.   M
GODERBAUER, Dipl. Psych. Max. Salacherstr. 33, Stuttgart-Wangen. b. 3 July 1919 Landshut. Dipl. Psych. '49 Univ. of Munich, Ger. EDUC. CONSULT, City of Stuttgart, Wilhelmsplatz 8, Stuttgart. Member: BDP. Consulting, testing, research; forensic psychology.   M
COERRES, Privatdozent Dr. med. Dr. phil. Albert. Wilhelm-Beerweg 169, Frankfurt/M b. 13 Sept 1918 Berlin. Privatdozent '55 Univ. of Mainz, Ger. DOZENT, Johannes Gutenberg Univ, Mainz. Member: DGP, Deutsche Gesellschaft für Tiefenpsychologie und Psychotherapie. Research, psychotherapy, teaching; depth psychology, methods of psychoanalysis, personality development and disorders.   M
GORIWODA, Dipl. Psych. Katrin. Dientzenhoferstr. 24, Bamberg. b. 1 Nov 1921 Sohrau. Dipl. Psych. '45 Univ. of Leipzig, Ger. CHILD PSYCH'T, Nervenklinik St-Getreu Bamberg, St-Getreu Str. 14, Bamberg. Member: BDP. Testing, clinical analysis, guidance, psychotherapy; projective and intelligence tests, graphology, forensic psychology, child psychotherapy. F
GÖTTE, Martin. Social Res. Center, Univ. of Münster, Rheinlanddamm 199, Dortmund. b. 24 Mar 1928 Eissen. Dipl. Psych. '55 Univ. of Göttingen, Ger. SCI. ASST, Soc. Res. Cen, Univ. of Münster. Research, applied and industrial psychology, sociological research; field theory, non-directive counseling, social engineering, social forces, vocational training methods.M
GÖTTING, Hans Georg. Tiestestr. 16-18/III, Hannover. b. 25 June 1920 Hamburg. Dipl. Psych. '56 Univ. of Hamburg, Ger. VOLUNTEER ASST, Med. Psych, Inst. for Industry, Bergbau und Verkehr beim TÜV, Hannover. Member: BDP. Communication, industrial psychology, guidance; projective techniques, intelligence tests, social adaptation.   M
GOTTSCHALDT, Prof. Dr. Kurt. Oranienburger Str. 18, Berlin C 2. b. 25 Apr 1902 Dresden. Prof. '38 Univ. of Berlin, Ger. PROF. and DIR, Inst. for Psych, Humboldt Univ, Unter den Linden 6, Berlin. DIRECTOR, Cen. for Exper. and Appl. Psych, German Acad. of Sci; EDITOR, *Zeitschrift*

für Psychologie; *Schriftenreihe zur Entwicklungspsychologie.* Member: DGP. Research, teaching, editorial; personality, experimental social psychology, industrial psychology.   M
GRAEFE, Dr. phil. Oskar. Gertrüdenstr. 12, Münster/Westf. b. Nov 1913 Bochum. PH.D '50 Univ. of Münster, Ger. SCI. ASST, Psych. Inst, Univ. of Münster. Member: DGP. Teaching, research, consulting; perception, personality development.   M
GRAF, Prof. Dr. med. Otto. Max Planck Inst. for Indus. Physiol, Dortmund. b. 29 July 1893 Patersdorf. A.O. Prof, Univ. of Münster, Ger. DIRECTOR, Dept. of Psych, Max Planck Inst. for Indus. Physiol; DOZENT, Socialakademie, Dortmund. Member: Deutsche Gesellschaft für Arbeitswissenschaft. Applied and industrial psychology, research, teaching; psychology of travel, mental fatigue, psychiatry.   M
GRAF, Studienrat Dr. phil. Otto. Calvorder Str. I/II, Magdeburg. b. 22 Aug 1889 Calbe. PH.D '14 Univ. of Jena, Ger. Member: BDP. Retired; psychotherapy, educational psychology.   M
GRAMS, Dipl. Psych. Günter. Geygerstr. 11, Berlin-Neuköln. b. 4 Aug 1921 Berlin. Dipl. Psych. '55 Free Univ. of Berlin, Ger. EDUC. CONSULT, Bezirksamt Wedding, Pankstr. 28-30, Berlin N 20. Member: BDP. Educational psychology, testing, guidance; psychology of human development, social psychology.   M
GRASSL, Dipl. Psych. Mrs. Elisabeth. Widenmayerstr. 26, Munich. b. 11 Mar 1924 Munich. Dipl. Psych. '50 Univ. of Munich, Ger. CHILD GUID. COUNS, priv. prac. Member: BDP. Testing, clinical analysis, guidance, psychotherapy; research in child guidance and psychotherapy, projective testing.   F
GRASSL, Dr. med. Dr. phil. Erich. Boschetsriederstr. 56/II, Munich 25. b. 30 Aug 1913 Kaiserlautern. PH.D '36 Univ. of Munich, Ger. Dr. med. '45 Univ. of Innsbruck, Austria. PHYSICIAN, priv. prac. Member: BDP. Clinical analysis, psychotherapy, professional writing; psychology of will and illness, psychology of abnormal children, characterology.   M
GRAUMANN, Dr. phil. Carl-Friedrich. Hardstr. 11, Cologne-Klettenberg. b. 31 Mar 1923 Cologne. PH.D '52 Univ. of Cologne, Ger. RES. ASST, Psych. Inst, Univ. of Bonn, Am Hof 1e, Bonn. Member: DGP, Wissenschaftliche Arbeitsgemeinschaft für Jugendkunde. Research, teaching, consulting; cognition, relationship between psychology and phenomenology, social perception.   M
GRAUMANN, Dipl. Psych. Hannah. Hardstr. 11, Cologne-Klettenberg. b. 15 Aug

1924 Kiel. Dipl. Psych. '54 Univ. of Cologne, Ger. PSYCH. FIELD WRKR, Wissenschaftliche Arbeitsgemeinschaft für Jugendkunde, Kreisgesundheitsamt, Grevenbroich. Member: Wissenschaftliche Arbeitsgemeinschaft für Jugendkunde. Applied psychology, testing, research; child psychology, sex difference.   F

GRAVE, Egon. Taubenstr. 9, Münster. b. 11 July 1928 Münster. Dipl. Psych. '55 Univ. of Munich, Ger. SCULPTOR, Akademie der Bildenden Künste, Akademie Str, Munich. Testing, psychotherapy, consulting, art student; clinical psychology, breathing therapy, psychology of art.   M

GREVE, Dipl. Psych. Hans Georg. Biefangstr. 106, Oberhausen-Sterkrade. b. 30 July 1923 Magdeburg. Dipl. Psych. '50 Martin Luther Univ, Ger. PSYCHOLOGIST, Employment Off, Oberhausen/Rhld; INDUS. PSYCH'T, Bundesanstalt für Arbeitsvermittlung und Arbeitslosenversicherung, Nuremberg. Member: BDP. Testing, industrial psychology, administration; intelligence and performance tests, characterology, observation of behavior.   M

GRIES, Dr. phil. Ulrich. Lichtstr. 4, Dieringhausen. b. 23 May 1925 Gummersbach. PH.D '55 Univ. of Bonn, Ger. INDUS. PSYCH'T, Hackethal Draht- und Kabelwerke AG. Stader Landstr. 1, Hannover. Member: BDP. Industrial psychology, testing, research; theory of personality, diagnostics, medical psychology, social psychology.   M

GRIESBACH, Dr. phil. Ernst. Talblick 7, Fürth/By. b. 10 June 1911 Gotha/Thür. PH.D '50, Ger. DIR. of SCH. and EDUC. GUID, Amtshaus am Kohlenmarkt, Fürth/By. Member: BDP, Gewerkschaft Erziehung und Wissenschaft. Guidance, psychotherapy, testing, teaching; developmental and educational psychology, group therapy, social psychological research.   M

GRIMM, Dr. Kurt. Buchgasse 7, Frankfurt/M. b. 22 Aug 1910 Fambach. Dr. phil. nat. '33 Univ. of Jena, Ger. PSYCHOLOGIST, REGIERUNGSRAT z.Wv. Wiesbaden Employment Off, Boseplatz 1, Wiesbaden. Testing, consulting, teaching; aptitude testing, professional counseling, vocational psychology, human development.   M

GROETENHERDT, Landesverwaltungsrat Dr. Karl Max. Grimmstr. 8, Münster. b. 29 Dec 1901 Erfurt. Dr. phil. nat, Univ. of Jena, Ger. LANDESVERWALTUNGSRAT, Landschaftsverband Westfalen-Lippe Landeshaus, Fürstenbergstr, Münster. Member: BDP. Applied psychology, vocational testing of the handicapped; achievement tests.   M

GROFFMANN, Dr. phil. Karl Josef. Inst. for Psych. and Characterology, Univ. of Freiburg, Bertoldstr. 17, Freiburg. b. 27

May 1926 Saarbrücken. PH.D '53 Univ. of Freiburg, Ger. SCI. ASST, Inst. for Psych. and Characterology. Member: DGP. Consulting, teaching, research, social psychology; projective techniques, personality theory, child psychology.   M

GROSSE HARTLAGE, Dr. Walter. Parzivalstr. 3A, Munich. b. 12 Apr 1926 Schwege bei Osnabrück. PH.D '54 Univ. of Munich, Ger. RES. ASST, Heckscher Clin, Munich; PSYCH'T, Board of Trade, State of Bavaria. Member: BDP, Bund Deutscher Ärzte, Hartmannbund. Research, testing, applied psychology, psychotherapy; psychoanalysis social perception, group process.   M

GRUHLE-STOLZ, Dr. phil. Ilse. Sitzbuchweg 27, Ziegelhausen bei Heidelberg. b. 17 Nov 1924 Düsseldorf. PH.D '50 Univ. of Bonn, Ger. INDUS. PSYCH'T, Farbenfabriken Bayer, Leverkusen. Industrial psychology, testing, psychotherapy, consulting; projective techniques.   F

GRUNERT, Dr. Johannes. Denningerstr. 5, Munich 27. b. 23 Sept 1921 Lautawerk. PH.D '53 Univ. of Munich, Ger. INDUS. PSYCH'T, Med. Psych. Res. Cen, TÜV, Kaiserstr. 14-16, Munich 23. Member: BDP. Industrial psychology, consulting, research; social perception, group process.   M

GRUNERT (née Wiehen), Dr. Ursula. Denningerstr. 5/III, Munich 27. b. 11 Aug 1926 Wüstegiersdorf. PH.D '53 Univ. of Munich, Ger. CHILD GUID. COUNS, priv. prac. Member: BDP. Consulting, guidance, clinical practice, testing; projective techniques, group therapy, learning theory, national character.   F

GRÜNEWALD, Dr. phil. Dipl. Psych. Gerhard. Schubertstr. 24, Freiburg. b. 1 Sept 1922 Siegen/Westf. PH.D '48 Univ. of Bonn, Ger. RES. ASST, Inst. for Psych, Univ. of Freiburg, Member: BDP. Research, applied psychology, professional writing; learning theory, pharmacological psychology, personality measurement, psychophysiology.   M

GRÜTTNER, Dr. Reinhold. Düsseldorfer Landstr. 33, Duisburg-Buchholz. b. 12 Feb 1902 Berlin. Dr. rer. nat. '38 Univ. of Göttingen, Ger. PSYCHOLOGIST, Duisburg Employment Off. Member: BDP. Testing, industrial psychology, research; projective techniques, performance tests, psychophysics, psychology of will.   M

GÜNDLICH, Dipl. Psych. Germanus. Beuerbergerstr. 3, Munich-Solln. b. 12 Sept 1923 Deggendorf, Niederbayern. Dipl. Psych. '55 Univ. of Munich, Ger. DIRECTOR, Priv. Psych. Inst. Munich-Schwabing, Cristoph-Schmidstr. 28, Munich. Member: BDP. Industrial and educational psychology, testing, clinical practice, guidance; attitude measurement, achievement tests, graphology, psychotherapy.   M

GÜNZEL-HAUBOLD, Dr. phil. Mrs. Marianne Ahornstr. 10, Lochham/Munich. b. 24 July 1898 Leipzig. PH.D '32 Univ. of Leipzig, Ger. DOZENT, Sozialen Frauenschule, Neuberghauserstr, Munich. Member: BDP. Teaching, educational psychology, group work; social perception, group process. F

GÜRTLER, Dipl. Psych. Heinz. Odenaldstr. 80, Cologne-Kalk. b. 20 June 1929 Zehrensdorf, Teltow. Dipl. Psych. '53 Free Univ. of Berlin, Ger. PSYCHOLOGIST, Gesellschaft für Soziale Betriebspraxis, Friedrich Ebert Str. 31-33, Düsseldorf; INDUS. SOCIOL. CONSULT, priv. prac; EDITOR, *Fachberichte.* Member: BDP. Research, industrial psychology, consulting, editorial; interview design, industrial accident prevention, training on the job, job and employment planning, industrial relations. M

GÜSSEFELDT, Dipl. Psych. Horst. Rottfeldstr. 5, Strümp, Post Osterath. b. 11 Mar 1921 Ratingen. Dipl. Psych. '51 Univ. of Bonn, Ger. PSYCHOLOGIST, Kinder- und Jugendheime Neu-Düsselthal, Wittlaer, Post Düsseldorf-Kaiserwerth. Member: BDP. Testing, educational psychology, psychotherapy; personality and achievement tests, characterology, educational prognosis, psychological instruction and counseling for educators. M

HAAS, Dr. Irmgard. Poschingerstr. 12, Munich 27. b. 6 Aug 1917 Hamburg. PH.D '53 Univ. of Munich, Ger. PSYCHOTHERAPIST, priv. prac. Member: BDP, ICWP. Psychotherapy, clinical practice, testing; projective techniques, play therapy, psychology of religion. F

HABERKORN, Hans. Oberschwaigstr. 10, Sulzbach-Rosenberg Hütte. b. 21 Oct 1912 Nuremberg. Staatsprüfung, Univ. of Würzburg, Ger. INDUS. PSYCH'T, DEPT. SUPERV, Eisenwerkgesellschaft Maximilians hütte, Sulzbach-Rosenberg Hütte; TEACHER, Industrie und Handelskammer Bayreuth. Educational and industrial psychology, teaching, administration; pedagogy, social perception, accident prevention. M

HACKBARTH, Mrs. Gisela. Messeweg 38, Braunschweig. b. 18 June 1924 Gladbeck. Dipl. Psych. '53 Tech. Univ. of Braunschweig, Ger. TEACHER, Kindergärtnerinnen und Hortnerinnen Seminar, Pestalozzistiftung, Grossburgwedel bei Hannover. Teaching, educational psychology, research; social perception, group process, diagnostic problems, projective techniques. F

HAGER, Dr. phil. Wilhelm. Viktoriastr. 11/III, Munich 23. b. 19 May 1886 Miesbach. PH.D, Dipl. Psych, Univ. of Munich, Ger. GRAPHOLOGIST, priv. prac. Member BDP, Graphologische Gesellschaft. Applied

and industrial psychology, teaching; theory of knowledge, characterology, cultural psychology. M

HAHN, Dr. phil. Wolfgang Dietrich. Carlo Mierendorffstrr. 16, Mainz-Gonsenheim. b. 18 Jan 1929 Bebra. PH.D '55 Univ. of Mainz, Ger. CRIM. PSYCH'T, Strafanstalt, Limburgerstr. 122, Diez/Lahn. Member: BPD. Administration, testing, research, psychotherapy, consulting; criminal relapse prognosis, resocialization. M

HALTAUFDERHEIDE, Dipl. Psych. Günther. Facherstr. 4, Dortmund. b. 12 Dec 1922 Dortmund. Dipl Psych. '50 Univ. of Münster, Ger. DIRECTOR, Psych. Dept, Dortmund Employment Off, Rheinlanddamm, Dortmund. Member: DGP. Testing, consulting, applied psychology; child psychology, educational guidance. M

HAMM, Karl Ernst. Am Lindenbaum 67/II, Frankfurt/M. b. 14 Nov 1920 Frankfurt/M. Dipl. Psych. '51 Johann Wolfgang Goethe Univ. of Frankfurt/M Ger. ASST. SUPERV, Opekta Gesellschaft Ltd, Xantenerstr. 99, Cologne; ASSISTANT, Inst. für Werbepsychologie und Marketkundung, Rathenauplatz 2-8, Frankfurt/M. Applied and industrial psychology, administration, testing; opinion research, group psychology, psychology of advertising. M

HAMPEL, Dr. phil. Hans-Jürgen Rosenstr. 30, Düsseldorf. b. 20 Apr 1927 Berlin. PH.D, Dipl. Psych, Free Univ. of Berlin, Ger. ACCOUNT EXEC, MacCann Erickson Co, Immermannstr. 40, Düsseldorf. Member: BDP. Applied psychology, research, teaching; psychology of advertising, marketing and motivation reserach, scientific method. M

HANSEN, Prof. Dr. phil. Wilhelm. Vechta in Oldb. b. 8 Nov. 1899 Gladbach. PH.D '27 Univ. of Kiel, Ger. PROFESSOR, Pädagogische Hochschule, Vechta in Oldb. Member: BDP. Teaching, research, educational psychology; child and adolescent psychology, character development. M

HARDE, Dr. phil. Otto. Elsa Brandstroem Str. 7, Holzwickede. b. 13 Apr 1914 Dortmund. PH.D '40 Univ. of Göttingen, Ger. RECTOR, Gemeindeverwaltung, Rathaus, Holzwickede. Member: BDP. Teaching research; educational psychology. M

HARTHERZ, Wolf Dieter. Schumannstr. 69, Frankfurt/M. b. 13 Aug 1927 Frankfurt/M. Dipl. Psych. '55 J. W. Goethe Univ. of Frankfurt/M. Ger. PSYCHOLOGIST, priv. prac. Medical student, educational psychology, psychotherapy; pedagogy, psychoanalysis, projective techniques, autogenous training. M

HARTMANN, Klaus-Dieter. Hindenburgstr. 78, Remscheid. b. 21 Nov 1929 Magdeburg.

Dipl. Psych. '54 Free Univ. of Berlin, Ger. PSYCHOLOGIST, Wissenschaftliche Arbeitsgemeinschaft für Jugendkunde, Remscheid. Member: BDP. Research, educational psychology, testing; child and youth development, psychology of perception, political psychology, psychology in advertising. M

HASE, Dr. phil. Wolfgang. Herdweg 79, Stuttgart-N. b. 16 Oct. 1922 Einbeck/Hannover. PH.D '51 Univ. of Würzburg, Ger. TRAFFIC PSYCH'T, Medizinisch-Psychologisches Inst. für Verkehrssicherheit e.V, Bebelstr. 58, Stuttgart. Member: BDP. Testing, research, teaching; characterology, depth psychology, aptitude measurement. M

HASEMANN, Dipl. Psych. Klaus. Hildastr.12, Freiburg. b. 24 Sept 1929 Ströbitz Kreis Kottbus. Dipl. Psych. '54 Univ. of Freiburg, Ger. Member: BDP. Industrial psychology, testing, student; industrial education, personnel management, projective techniques, economics. M

HAU, Dipl. Psych. Elisabeth M. Friedländerweg 10, Göttingen. b. 28 Dec 1927 Hildesheim. Dipl. Psych. '52 Georg-August Univ. of Göttingen, Ger. PSYCHOTHERAPIST, priv. prac. Member: BDP, Studiengesellschaft für Praktische Psychologie. Psychotherapy, clinical practice, testing; psychoanalysis, child guidance, projective techniques. F

HAU, Dipl. Psych. Dr. Theodor F. Friedländerweg 10, Göttingen. b. 29 Jan 1924 Essen. Dipl. Psych. '53 Georg-August Univ. of Göttingen, Ger. VOLUNTEER PHYSICIAN, Niedersächsisches Landeskrankenhaus, Tiefenbrunn bei Göttingen. Member: BDP, Studiengesellschaft für Praktische Psychologie. Psychotherapy, clinical practice, testing; psychoanalysis, structure of neurotic personality, psychosomatic medicine.M

HAUFF, Bundesverwaltungsrat Dr. Eberhard v. Gänsheide 95, Stuttgart. b. 22 Feb 1914 Berlin. Dr. '36 Univ. of Jena, Ger. BUNDESVERWALTUNGSRAT, VOCAT. CONSULT, Stuttgart Employment Off, Neckarstr, Stuttgart; VOCAT. GUID. COUNS, priv. prac. Member: BDP. Guidance, testing, psychotherapy; graphology, characterology, astrology. M

HAUFF-POHLACK, Dr. Leoni v. Gänsheide 95, Stuttgart. b. 12 Apr 1912 Elsaft, Saar. Dr. '38 Univ. of Jena, Ger. GRAPHOLOGIST and GUID. COUNS, priv. prac. Consulting, guidance, psychotherapy, teaching; projective techniques, psychology of the adolescent girl, graphology. F

HAUPT, Dr. Klaus. Rathsbergerstr. 11 1/2, Erlangen. b. 30 June 1931 Wiesbaden. Dipl. Psych. '55 Univ. of Erlangen, Ger. SCI. ASST, Pädagogisches Seminar der Univ, Kollegienhaus, Erlangen. Consulting, research, applied psychology; social per-

ception, group process, industrial relations. M

HAUSMANN, Prof. Dr. Gottfried. Mainz, Breslauerstr. 9, Mainz. b. 18 Sept 1906 Düren. A.O. Prof. '53 Univ. of Mainz, Ger. GUEST. PROF. of PEDAGOGY and PSYCH, Dil ve Tarih-Gografya Fakültesi, Atatürk Bolvari, Ankara, Turkey; EDIT. STAFF, Die Deutsche Schule. Member: DGP. Teaching, research, editorial; developmental psychology, social psychology. M

HAUSS, Dr. Kurt. Moltkestr. 37, Kiel. b. 18 Oct 1921 Duisburg. Dr. rer. nat. '54 Univ. of Göttingen, Ger. CLIN. PSYCH'T, Univ. Nervenklinik, Kiel. Member: BDP. Testing, psychotherapy, clinical practice, child guidance; psychology of human development, projective tests, achievement test. M

HECHT, Dr. phil. Karl. Alterdorferstr. 108, Hamburg. b. 11 July 1904 Hamburg. PH.D '37 Univ. of Hamburg, Ger. TEACHER, Schulbehörde, Dammtorstr. 25, Hamburg. Member: BDP. Teacher education, testing; personality development, intelligence testing. M

HECKHAUSEN, Dr. phil. Heinz. Psych. Inst, Univ. of Münster, Rosenstr. 9, Münster/Westf. b. 24 Mar 1926 Wuppertal. PHD '54 Univ. of Münster, Ger. SCI. ASST, Psych. Inst, Univ. of Münster. Research, teaching, testing; psychology of motivation, projective techniques, child psychology. M

HECKHAUSEN, Werner. Zweibrücker Str. 73, Berlin-Spandau. b. 13 Apr 1916 Krefeld. Dipl. Psych. '53 Free Univ. of Berlin, Ger. Member: BDP. Retired. M

HECTOR, Dr. phil. Heinz. Pfalz Str. 47, Düsseldorf. -b. 18 July 1922 Herleshausen. PH.D '47 Univ. of Freiburg, Ger. Research, professional writing; design preferences as personality projection, history and theory of mosaic tests. M

HEDICKE, Dr. phil. Helmut. Kielerstr. 17, Schacht-Audorf bei Rendsburg. b. 9 Jan 1910 Leisnig, Saxony. PH.D '40 Univ. of Greifswald, Ger. TEACHER, Kreisberufsschule Rendsburg, Neue Kieler Landstrasse, Rendsburg. Member: BDP. Teaching, educational psychology, guidance, religious psychology; personality development, forms of Christian existence. M

HEHLGANS, Dipl. Handelslehrer Hans. Lönsweg 21, Verden, Aller. b. 3 June 1921 Peine. Dipl Handelslehrer '49 Univ. of Nuremberg, Ger. HANDELSSTUDIENRAT, Kaufmännische Bildungsanstalten Bremen, Block D, Buerenstr, Bremen. Member: BDP. Teaching, educational psychology; talents and performance, aptitude and educational tests. M

HEIN, Dipl. Psych. Clara. Gehlengraben 3b, Hamburg-La 1. b. 5 June 1910 Hamburg.

Dipl. Psych. '54 Univ. of Hamburg, Ger. HEAD, Dept. for Sci. Asst, Psych. Inst, Univ. of Hamburg, Bornplatz 2/IV, Beratungsstelle, Hamburg 13. Member: BDP. Teaching, testing, social work. F

HEINELT, Dr. Gottfried. Tengstr. 32, Munich 13. b. 17 June 1923 Jauernick. Dr. '52 Univ. of Freiburg, Ger. SCI. ASST, Psych. Inst. of the Univ, Geschwister-Scholl-Pl. 1, Munich. Member: DGP, BDP. Teaching, testing, research; projective tests, psychology of testing, social psychology. M

HEINEN, Dr. phil. Anny. Karl Jacobstr. 25, Hamburg-Nienstedten. b. 31 Jan 1904 Bremen. PH.D '38 Univ. of Hamburg, Ger. DIR. of VOCAT. GUID. for WOMEN, Employment Off, Besenbinderhof 16, Hamburg 1. Member: BDP. Vocational guidance, administration; professional work of women and its problems, vocational psychological problems. F

HEISS, Prof. Dr. Robert. Roteweg 3, Freiburg. b. 22 Jan 1903 Munich. o.ö. Prof. '43 Univ. of Freiburg, Ger. DIRECTOR, Inst. for Psych. and Characterology, Univ. of Freiburg; EDITOR, *Zeitschrift für Diagnostische Psychologie und Persönlichkeitsforschung*. Member: DGP, BDP, Int. Rorschach Socy. Teaching, research, applied psychology, testing; projective techniques, graphology, depth psychology, personality. M

HEISS-KRACHENFELS, Dr. Leo. Stitzenburgstr. 18, Stuttgart S. b. 14 Jan 1921 Weizen. Dr. rer. nat. '51 Univ. of Tübingen, Ger. INDUS. PSYCH. CONSULT, priv. prac. Industrial psychology, research, testing; graphology, projective techniques, social psychology. M

HEITBAUM, Dr. Heinrich. Rosental 47, Bonn b. 18 Dec 1911 Ratingen. Dr. '39 Univ. of Bonn, Ger. CONSULTANT, Wirtschaftswissenschaftliches Inst. der Gewerkschaften, Domkloster 3, Cologne. Member: BDP, AIPA. Research, applied psychology; scientific labor management, group work, social psychology. M

HELBIG, Miss Rita. Schiersteinerstr. 29, Wiesbaden. b. 15 Jan 1923 Dortmund/West. ASST. TEACHER, Volksschule, Eltville/Rheingau; EDUC. GUID. COUNS, Rüdesheim/Rheingau. Teaching, testing, guidance; projective techniques, learning theory, achievement tests, social perception. M

HELFENBERGER, Dipl. Psych. Otto Hans Adalbertstr. 86, Munich 13. b. 19 Dec 1921 Munich. Dipl. Psych. '51 Univ. of Munich, Ger. SUPERINTENDENT, Verein Lehrlingschutz Munich, Morassistr 14, Munich 5. Guidance, administration, educational psychology; social perception, group process, test theory. M

HELFERICH, Miss Hildegard. Bonner Talweg 66, Bonn. b. 20 Aug 1930 Leipzig.

Dipl. Psych. '55 Univ. of Munich, Ger. PERS. PSYCH'T, Farbenfabrieken Bayer, Leverkusen. Testing, industrial psychology, guidance; projective techniques, characterology, aptitude testing. F

HEMPEL, Dieter. Seldeneckstr. 11, Munich. b. 1 July 1930 Chemnitz. Dipl. Psych. '55 Univ. of Munich, Ger. PERS. PSYCH'T Siemens and Halske AG, Wittelsbacherplatz, Munich. Member: BDP. Industrial psychology, consulting and guidance; group process, social perception. M

HEMSING, Dr. Walter. Martinstr. 6, Aachen. b. 24 Sept 1921 Mülheim. Dr, Univ. of Leipzig, Ger. Member: Assn. Int. des Educateurs de Jeunes Inadaptés. Industrial psychology, personnel testing, psychotherapy, child guidance; graphology, educational psychology. M

HENN, Dipl. Psych. Rainer Heinz Eberhard. Auf der Vogelstang 28, Mannheim-Käfertal. b. 25 Sept 1928 Mannheim. Dipl. Psych. '53 Univ. of Heidelberg, Ger. PSYCH. ASST; EDUC. GUID. OFF, Caritas-Verband, Mannheim. Research, clinical analysis, psychotherapy; educational guidance, psychological diagnosis of brain injuries and their treatment. M

HENNICKER, Dr. Rolf. Inst. für Flugmedizin, Kölnerstr. 70, Bad Godesberg. b. 15 July 1925 Flensburg. Dr. 49 Univ. of Kiel, Ger. PSYCHOLOGIST, Inst. für Flugmedizin. Member: BDP. Aviation psychology, educational guidance, forensic psychology. M

HENNING, Dipl. Psych. Mrs. Grete. Kaiser Sigmundstr. 79, Frankfurt/M. b. 6 Nov 1911 Leinefelde. Dipl. Psych. '49 Univ. of Frankfurt, Ger. PERS. PSYCH'T, Deutsche Gesellschaft für Personalwesen, Feldbergstr. 38, Frankfurt/M. Member: Gesellschaft für Menschenkunde. Industrial psychology, personnel selection, testing; personality scales, achievement tests, graphology, test construction, job analysis. F

HENSLER, Dipl. Psych. Arnold. Neckarstaden 16, Heidelberg. b. 25 Mar 1930 Dresden. Dipl. Psych. '54 Univ. of Heidelberg, Ger. Applied psychology, testing, student; child guidance, psychotherapy, clinical testing. M

HENZ, Dr. phil. Hubert. Inst. für Lehrerbildung, Passau-Freudenhain. b. 9 May 1926 Bad Kissingen. PH.D '52 Univ. of of Würzburg, Ger. STUDIENRAT, DOZENT, Inst. für Lehrerbildung. Teaching, educational psychology, testing; anthropology. M

HERMANN, Dr. Erich. Pfarrgasse 12a, Heilsbronn bei Ansbach, Bavaria. b. 19 Apr. 1909 Dresden. Dr. rer. cult. '39 Tech. Hoch. Dresden, Ger. SCHULRAT, Evangelical

Lutheran Church, Bavaria. Member: BDP. Teaching, guidance; pedagogical psychology. M

HERMANN, Dr. Max. S.W.F., Spezialfabrik für Autozubehör, Bietigheim, Württ. b. 3 Dec 1918 Friedrichshafen, Bodensee. Dr. '55 Univ. of Freiburg, Ger. INDUS. PSYCH'T, S.W.F., Spezialfabrik für Autozubehör. Industrial psychology, personnel work, testing, consulting; projective techniques, graphology, achievement testing. M

HERRIG, Dipl. Psych. Dr. Gerhard Hans Werner. Piusalle 23, Münster. b. 2 Feb 1920 Braunschweig. Dr. rer. nat. '55 Georg-August Univ. of Göttingen, Ger. CO-WORKER, German Inst. for Sci. Pedagogy, Neustr. 3, Münster. Member: BDP. Research, educational psychology, guidance; psychology of juvenile delinquents, social psychology. M

HERRIG, Dipl. Psych. Ingeborg Margarethe. Piusalle 23, Münster/Westf. b. 31 Oct 1920 Bremen. Dipl. Psych. '51 Univ. of Göttingen, Ger. PSYCH. TCHR, Kindergärtnerinnen Seminar. Supervising social group workers, educational psychology, teaching; group process, learning theory, projective techniques. F

HERRMANN, Dr. phil. Theo. Carlo Mierendorffstr. 22, Mainz-Gonsenheim. b. 24 May 1929 Bochum. Dipl. Psych. '54 Univ. of Mainz, Ger. ASSISTANT, Psych. Inst. of the Univ, Saarstr., Mainz. Member: DGP. Research, teaching, applied and industrial psychology; thinking and memory, social psychology in industry, personnel selection. M

HERTER, Dr. Benedikt. Bismarckstr. 62, Tübingen. b. 17 Sept 1923 Hayingen. Dr. rer. nat. '52 Univ. of Tübingen, Ger. CLIN. PSYCH'T, Versorgungskrankenhaus für Hirnverletzte, Tübingen. Member: BDP. Clinical, social and industrial psychology, vocational guidance, clinical practice; social perception, group process, projective techniques. M

HERTER, Dipl. Psych. Karl Mathias. Hoherklosterweg 8, Boppard/Rhein. b. 8 June 1928 Langstadt, Hessen. Dipl. Psych. '55 Univ. of Bonn, Ger. Member: BDP. Student, research; diagnosis, perception, communications. M

HERWIG, Prof. Dr. phil. Gustav Heinrich Bernhard. Abt. Jerusalem Str. 8, Braunschweig. b. 9 Sept 1983 Berlin. PH.D '19 Univ. of Marburg, Ger. PROF. of PSYCH, Technische Hochschule, Pockelsstr. 4, Braunschweig; DIRECTOR, FORFA-Forschungsinst. für Arbeitspsych. und Personalwesen, Garküche 3, Braunschweig. Member: BDP, DGP. Teaching, industrial psychology, research, editorial; human relations, management education, psycho-

logical diagnosis, psychology of communications. M

HERZOG Dr. phil. Edgar. Südl. Schlossrondell 23, Munich 38. b. Dec 1891 Berlin. PH.D, Univ. of Leipzig, Ger. PSYCHOTHERAPIST, priv. prac; PROF. and HEAD, Instruction Dept, Inst. of Psych. Res. and Psychother. Member: BDP, Deutsche Gesellschaft für Psychother. und Tiefenpsych. Psychotherapy, research, teaching; depth psychology, adult and child psychotherapy. M

HERZOG-DÜRCK, Dr. phil. Johanna. Südl. Schlossrondell 23, Munich 38. b. 19 Feb 1902 Leverkusen. PH.D, Univ. of Bern, Switz. PSYCHOTHERAPIST, priv. prac; DOZENT, Inst. of Psych. Res. and Psychother. Member: Deutsche Gesellschaft für Psychother. und Tiefenpsych. Psychotherapy, research, teaching, professional writing; fundamental problems of depth psychology in religion and philosophy. F

HERZOG-GMELIN, Mrs. M. Wyk/Föhr Wiesenhaus Lerchenweg Südstrand Schleswig-Holstein. b. 25 Apr 1895 Stuttgart. Psychotherapy, teaching; learning theory, special psychotherapy for children suffering from effects of disaster or war. F

HESELHAUS, Dipl. Psych. Karl. Employment Off, Stühmeyer Str, Bochum. b. 9 Mar 1922 Dorsten/Westf. Dipl. Psych. '51 Univ. of Münster, Ger. APPL. PSYCH'T, Employment Off. Industrial psychology, testing and clinical analysis, research; vocational and professional psychology, educational guidance, pedagogical and clinical psychology. M

HETZER, Prof. Dr. phil. Hildegard. Danzigerstr. 4, Weilburg/L. b. 9 June 1899 Vienna, Austria. PH.D '27 Univ. of Vienna, Austria. PROF. of PSYCH. Pädagogisches Inst, Frankfurterstr. 40, Weilburg/L. Member: BDP, DGP. Teaching, research, guidance; child and adolescent psychology, development tests, remedial education. F

HILBIG, Dipl. Psych. Otto. Kant Hochschule, Konstantin Uhde Str, Braunschweig. b. 25 Nov 1924 Ahlhorn/Oldenburg. Dipl. Psych. '55 Univ. of Hamburg, Ger. ASSISTANT, Kant Hochschule. Teaching, administration, guidance; school psychology, psychodiagnosis. M

HILD, Dipl. Psych. Theodor. Junkernstr. 15, Herzberg am Harz. b. 10 Dec 1903 Berlin. Dipl. Psych. '49 Univ. of Göttingen, Ger. MITTELSCHULLEHRER, Ernst-Moritz-Arndt-Schule, Heidestr. 10, Herzberg am Harz. Member: BDP, Studiengesellschaft für praktische Psychologie. Teaching, educational psychology, guidance; depth psychology and its philosophical foundations, problems of art and science in psychology. M

HILDEBRANDT, Dr. phil. Friedrich. Garbeweg 37, Hannover-Buchholz. b. 31 Dec 1909 Frankfurt/M. PH.D, Volks und Staatswissenschaft Univ. of Marburg, Ger. CRIM. PSYCH'T, Strafgefängnis und Untersuchungshaftanstalt, Hannover. Criminal psychology and criminology; adolescent and cultural psychology. M

HILLEBRAND, Prof. Dr. Max Josef. Hausdorffstr. 84, Bonn. b. 7 Dec 1896 Wehrden/Weser. Dr. '30 Univ. of Prague, Czech. RECTOR and DOZENT, Pedagogical Acad. and Univ, Bonn. Member: DGP. Student, educational psychology, teaching, research; pedagogical psychology, child and adolescent psychology, psychology of corrective education. M

HILLER, Dr. phil. Anne. Nienburger Str. 11, Hannover. b. 23 Sept 1927 Zittau. PH.D '55 Univ. of Freiburg, Ger. HEAD, Fachschule für Kindergärtnerinnen, Münster; DEACONESS, Diakonissen Mutterhaus, Münster. Teaching, educational psychology; social perception, problems of institutions for maladjusted children, projective techniques, social work education. F

HILLERS, Dr. Friedrich. Nervenklinik, Ilten über Hannover. b. 16 Aug 1916 Velen/Westf. Med. Staatsexam. '46 Univ. of Münster, Ger. PSYCHIATRIST, Wahrendorffsche Krankenanstalten; INSTRUCTOR, Sch. for Occupat. Therapy. Clinical practice, testing, teaching; feeblemindedness, intelligence testing. M

HILLERS, Mrs. Ilse. Nervenklinik, Ilten über Hannover. b. 4 Apr 1921 Hildesheim. Dipl. Psych. '49 Univ. of Göttingen, Ger. Teaching, educational psychology, guidance; child psychology, social psychology. F

HISCHER, Dipl. Psych. Erhard Norbert. Kaisheim 87, bei Donauwörth. b. 1 June 1925 Neustadt, Upper Silesia. Dipl. Psych. '55 Univ. of Munich, Ger. TCHR. of CRIM. and EDUC. PSYCH, Abteilung Strafvollzug, Bavarian Dept. of Justice, Munich. Applied and educational psychology, consulting, guidance, research, testing; group process, psychology of sex and personality development, projective techniques. M

HOBERG, Mrs. Doris. Ludwig Thomaweg 16/1, Starnberg/Obb. b. 7 Oct 1928 Münster/Westf. Dipl. Psych. '54 Univ. of Munich, Ger. Student, testing; the study of twins, criminal psychology. F

HOCHHEIMER, Prof. Dr. Wolfgang. Königin Luisestr. 76, Berlin-Dahlem. b. 4 Mar 1906 Berlin. Dr. phil. nat. '30 Univ. of Frankfurt, Ger. PROFESSOR, Pädagogische Hochschule Berlin, Marienfelderstr. 74-100, Berlin-Lankwitz; EDITOR, Psyche. Member: DGP, BDP, Deutsche Gesellschaft für

Psychotherapie und Tiefenpsychologie. Teaching, research, educational psychology, psychotherapy, editorial; field research, human relations, depth psychology. M

HOEFER, Diakonisse Liese. Diakonissen Mutterhaus Sarepta, Bethel/Bielefeld. b. 28 Mar 1920 Wuppertal. Dr. '50 Univ. of Bonn, Ger. DEACONESS, Mutterhaus Sarepta, Bethel. Educational psychology, teaching; child and adolescent psychology, pastoral psychology. F

HOFFMANN, Dr. phil. Carl. Zugspitzstr. 1, Gauting bei Munich. b. 28 May 1889 Geisenhausen, Bavaria. PH.D '21 Univ. of Munich, Ger. HEAD, Akademische Studienberatung, Studentenwerk Munich, Veterinaerstr. 1; EDITOR, Höhere Schule und Beruf. Member: BDP. Applied psychology, teaching, editorial, professional guidance. M

HOFFMANN, Dipl. Psych. Eva Charlotte. Zesenstr. 15, Hamburg 39. b. 8 Mar 1930 Leipzig. Dipl. Psych. '56 Tech. Hochschule Braunschweig, Ger. SCI. ASST, Psych. Inst. of the Univ., Bornplatz 2, Hamburg 13. Assisting in teaching, applied psychology, consulting; opinion research, personality theories, cultural psychology. F

HOFFMANN, Dipl. Psych. Wolfhart. Melbacher Str. 13, Dorheim, Weterau, Kreis Friedberg/Hessen. b. 22 Apr. 1928 Dresden. Dipl. Psych. '55 Univ. of Frankfurt/M, Ger. Psychotherapy, clinical analysis, applied and educational psychology, testing; projective techniques, marriage counseling, vocational guidance, clinical analysis. M

HOFMARKSRICHTER, Dr. phil. Karl. Regensburgerstr. 36, Straubing, Bavaria. b. 4 Apr 1900 Munich. PH.D '31 Univ. of Munich, Ger. DIRECTOR, Inst. for Deaf and Hard of Hearing Child., Straubing; TCHR. of PSYCH, Univ. of Munich. Member: BDP. Teaching, research, testing, administration; psychology of speech, psychology of deaf and hard of hearing children. M

HOFSCHNEIDER, Dr. phil. Dr. med. Peter Hans. Hausmannstr. 40 Haus 3, Stuttgart. b. 14 Feb 1929 Stuttgart. PH.D '54 Univ. of Heidelberg, Ger; MD '54 Univ. of Tübingen, Ger. ASST. PHYSICIAN, Medizinische Poliklinik, Univ. of Freiburg, Hermann-Herderstr. 6, Freiburg. Member: BDP. Clinical medicine, clinical analysis, psychotherapy; social perception, projective techniques. M

HOFSTAETTER, Prof. Dr. Peter R. Hochschule für Sozialwissenschaften, Wilhelmshaven-Ruestersiel. b. 20 Oct 1913 Vienna, Austria. Dr. phil. habil. '41 Univ. of Vienna, Austria. PROF. and HEAD, Dept. of Psych, Hochschule für Sozialwissenschaften; CO-EDITOR, Psychologie und Praxis. Member: DGP, APA, Amer. Stat. Assn, Amer. Acad. Polit. and Soc. Sci. Research, teaching, testing; attitude research, learning theory, probability models. M

HOGREFE, Dr. Dipl. Psych. Carl Jürgen. Hoher Weg 15, Göttingen. b. 29 Jan 1924 Hellental. Dr. '50 Univ. of Göttingen, Ger. ASSISTANT, Psych. Inst, Univ. of Göttingen; EDITOR and PUBLISHER, *Psychologisches Rundschau, Zeitschrift für Experimentelle und Angewandte Psychologie.* Member: BDP, DGP. Research, editorial, publishing; research on hypnosis and memory. M

HÖHN, Dr. phil. Elfriede. Schaffhausenstr. 27, Tübingen. b. 1 Apr 1915 Freudenstadt. PH.D '47 Univ. of Tübingen, Ger. LECTURER, Psych. Inst. of the Univ, Münzgasse 11, Tübingen. Member: DGP, BDP, ICWP. Teaching, research, testing, educational psychology, child guidance; projective techniques, learning theory, sociometry. F

HOLFTER, Dipl. Psych. Hans Georg. Gladbacher Str. 1, Cologne. b. 29 Apr 1927 Neisse. Dipl. Psych. '52 Univ. of Göttingen, Ger. ADMIN. PSYCH'T, City of Cologne, Rathaus, Unter Goldschmied. Member: BDP. Administration, research, testing and evaluation of personnel, intelligence tests, job analysis, human relations. M

HOLTMEIER, Dr. med. Otto Friedrich. Freiburg. b. 24 Dec 1925 Münster. MD '55 Univ. of Freiburg, Ger. Internal medicine, psychotherapy, research, clinical analysis; projective techniques, aesthetics, psychoanalysis. M

HOLZKAMP, Dipl. Psych. Klaus. Birkbuschgarten 8/III, Berlin-Steglitz. b. 30 Nov 1927 Schöneiche bei Berlin. SCI. CO-WRKR, Dr. K. S. Sodhi Inst. für Psych. Forschung, Altensteinstr. 44a, Berlin-Dahlem. Member: BDP. Research, applied psychology, clinical analysis; social perception, national prejudice. M

HOLZSCHUHER, Ludwig, Freiherr von. Gmünd am Tegernsee. b. 30 Jan 1897 Munich. OWNER, Adv. Agency Werbestudio von Holzschuher, Pegnitz Str. 5, Munich. Member: BDP. Applied psychology, professional writing; psychology of advertising. M

HÖRMANN, Dr. Hans. Goetheallee 12, Göttingen. b. 23 Oct 1924 Ulm/Donau. Dr. rer. nat. '53 Univ. of Göttingen, Ger. SCI. ASST, PSYCH. INST. of the Univ, Hoher Weg 15, Göttingen. Member: BDP. Administration, research; personality dynamics, projective techniques, social perception. M

HÖRMANN (née Ries), Mrs. Hildegard. Goetheallee 12, Göttingen. b. 25 May 1928 Westerstede/Oldb. Dipl. Psych. '52 Univ. of Göttingen, Ger. SCI. ASST, Psych. Inst. of the Univ, Göttingen. Member: BDP. Administration, student; aptitude and attitude measurement. F

HORN, Hartmut. Im Vegelsang 2, Butzbach/ Hessen. b. 1 Mar 1930 Oldenburg. Dipl. Psych. '56 Univ. of Marburg, Ger. Member: BDP. Student, research, industrial psychology; rehabilitation of the disabled, differential psychology. M

HORN, Dipl. Psych. Wolfgang. Taunusstr. 18, Butzbach. b. 20 Mar 1919 Oppeln. Dipl. Psych. '47 Univ. of Marburg, Ger. CRIM. PSYCH'T, Strafanstalt Butzbach, Kleebergerstr. 23, Butzbach. Member: BDP. Testing, guidance, research; tests for primary mental ability, mental stability, criminal tendencies. M

HORNEY, Dr. rer. nat. Heinz-Ludwig. Kühlwetterstr. 5/III, Düsseldorf. b. 10 May 1927 Braunschweig. Dr. rer. nat. '51 Tech. Hochschule of Braunschweig, Ger. INDUS. PSYCH'T, FORFA-Forschungsinst. für Arbeitspsych. und Personalwesen, Friedrichstr. 9, Düsssldorf. Member: BDP. Industrial psychology, research, testing; studies of fatigue, psychology of accidents, studies of time and motion. R

HÖRNING, Dr. phil. Richard. Wotanstr. 29, Munich 39. b. 21 July 1910 Dresden. PH.D '47 Univ. of Dresden, Ger. ASST. DIR, Städtische Abendmittelschule für Berufstätige, Deroystr. 1, Munich 2. Member: BDP. Teaching, administration, educational psychology; graphology, social and political perception. M

HOTZ, Dipl. Psych. Kurt. Hagellachstr. 32, Heidelberg-Kirchheim. b. 18 Sept 1927 Meersburg. Dipl. Psych. '53 Univ. of Heidelberg, Ger. VOCAT. GUID. COUNS, Employment Off. Schwäbisch Hall. Member: BDP. Vocational guidance, testing, teaching; thinking, motivation, personality. M

HOYER, Dipl. Psych. Harro. Friedländer Weg 9, Göttingen. b. 26 July 1928 Eisdorf/ Hannover. Dipl. Psych. '55 Univ. of Göttingen, Ger. Student, research; learning theory, emotion and expression, counseling. M

HOYOS, Dr. phil. Karl Alois, Graf. Hallerstr. 48, Hamburg 13. b. 6 May 1923 Baumgarten. PH.D '54 Univ. of Hamburg, Ger. SCI. ASST, Univ. of Hamburg, Edmund Siemers Allee, Hamburg. Member: DGP, BDP. Teaching, research, educational psychology; perception, validation studies, industrial psychology. M

HRUSCHKA, Erna. Hohenheimerstr. 89, Stuttgart-Birkach. b. 18 Dec 1912 Hindenburg. Dipl. Psych. '56 Univ. of Tübingen, Ger. ASSISTANT, Inst. für Landwirtsch. Beratung, Landw. Hochschule Hohenheim, Stuttgart. Applied psychology, research; social and general psychology. F

HUCK, Dr. phil. Wolfgang. Spitzwegstr. 24, Braunschweig. b. 16 Apr 1908 Zörbig/

Bitterfeld. PH.D '34 Univ. of Marburg/L, Ger. CHIEF PSYCH'T, Forschungs Inst. für Arbeitspsych. und Personalwesen, Garküche 3, Braunschweig. Member: BDP. Industrial psychology, testing, administration, research, teaching; human relations in industry, training programs, group process. M

HUENNIGER, Miss Edith. Rotenberg 50, Marburg/L. b. 13 Mar 1926 Frankfurt/M. Dipl. Psych. '52 Univ. of Frankfurt/M, Ger. INDUS. PSYCH'T, Farbwerke Hoedist, Brüningstr, Frankfurt/M. Industrial psychology, testing, research; achievement tests, standardization of intelligence tests, group process, family structure. F

HUG, Miss Hildegard. Scharnhorststr. 21, Münster/Westf. b. 8 Jan 1929 Berlin. Dipl. Psych. '54 Free Univ. of Berlin, Ger. HEILPÄDAGOGIN, Psych. Inst. Univ. of Münster, Rosenstr. 9, Münster. Member: BDP. Guidance, testing, psychotherapy; test development. F

HUTH, Prof. Dr. phil. Albert. Haberlstr.8, Gräfeling bei Munich. b. 9 Oct 1892 Hamburg. PH.D '23 Univ. of Munich, Ger. PROFESSOR, Univ. of Munich, Geschwister Scholl Platz, Munich. Member: BDP, DGP. Teaching, educational psychology, testing; studies of personality, psychohygiene, professional guidance. M

IHNE, Dr. phil. Wilhelm. Adolfstr. 39, Kassel. b. 8 Feb 1905 Duisburg. PH.D '50 Univ. of Münster, Ger. APPL. PSYCH'T, priv. prac. Applied industrial psychology, testing; personnel instruction, aptitude investigation, psychology of selling. M

INGENKAMP, Studienrat Dipl. Psych. Karlheinz. Briesingstr. 1, Berlin-Lichtenrade. b. 20 Dec 1925 Berlin. Dipl. Psych. '56 Free Univ. of Berlin, Ger. TEACHER, Ulrich von Hutten High Sch. Moltkestr. 40-44, Berlin-Lichtenrade. Teaching, educational psychology, research; teaching and learning theory, achievement tests, group process. M

IRLE, Dr. rer. nat. Martin. Böheimstr. 93, Stuttgart-S. b. 26 Jan 1927 Witten/Ruhr. Dipl. Psych. '52 Univ. of Göttingen, Ger; Dr. rer. nat. '55 Univ. of Göttingen, Ger. ASSISTANT, Inst. of Comp. Social Sci, Charlottenplatz 17, Stuttgart. Member: BDP. Research, industrial psychology, teaching, industrial morale, groupdynamics, field theory. M

IWERT, Dipl. Psych. Hans August Ernst. Diesterwegplatz 52, Frankfurt/M. b. 3 Mar 1925 Braunschweig. Dipl. Psych. '56 Technische Hochschule Braunschweig, Ger. VOLUNTEER WRKR, Frankfurter Versicherungs AG; Allian 2 Versicherungs AG, Taunusanlage 20, Frankfurt/M. Member: BDP. Applied psychology, testing, administration; projective tests, achievement

tests, intelligence tests. M

JABLINSKI, Dipl. Psych. Alfred. Isestr. 73, Hamburg 13. b. 25 Apr 1926 Berlin. Dipl. Psych. '55 Univ. of Berlin, Ger. Member: BDP. Industrial psychology, testing, guidance; personnel management, industrial relations, projective techniques, child and youth guidance. M

JACOBS, Victor. Schloenbachstr. 4, Bad Rothenfelde/TW. b. 17 Oct 1919 Erbringen/Saar. Dipl. '50 Univ. of Münster, Ger. SPEECH THER, Landschaftsverband Westfalen-Lippe, Fürstenbergstr., Münster. Clinical practice, psychotherapy, testing; play and activity group therapy, nondirective therapy, projective techniques. M

JACOBSEN, Dr. phil. Walter. Baumschul Allee 3/I, Bonn. b. 12 Jan 1895 Altona. PH.D '33 Univ. of Hamburg, Ger. OBERREGIERUNGSRAT, Bundeszentrale für Heimatdienst, Königstr. 85, Bonn. Member: BDP, AIPA. Applied and industrial psychology, testing, consulting, political psychology; human relations, prejudices, human rights, social psychology. M

JAENNSCH, Dipl. Psych. Christa. Martin-Lutherstr. 3, Würzburg. b. 19 Oct 1919 Freiberg. Dipl. Psych. '52 Univ. of Würzburg, Ger. DIRECTOR, Diözesan Filmstelle, Herrenstr., Würzburg. Administration, teaching, editorial, research; psychological influence of films. F

JÄGER, Dipl. Psych. Adolf-Otto. Beethovenstr. 58, Göttingen. b. 25 June 1920 Usseln Dipl. Psych. '54 Univ. of Göttingen, Ger. PSYCHOLOGIST, Deutsche Gesellschaft für Personalwesen, Feldbergstr. 38, Frankfurt/M. Member: BDP. Personnel psychology, testing, research, guidance; diagnosis, personality theory, learning, psychotherapy. M

JAIDE, Dr. phil. Walter. Bismarckstr. 35, Hannover. b. 10 May 1911 Berlin. PH.D '37 Univ. of Berlin, Ger. DOZENT of PSYCH, Pädagogische Hochschule. Member: BDP. Teaching, research, guidance; child development, professional choice and guidance, professional groups. M

JÄNISCH, Dipl. Psych. Günter. Egerländerstr. 23, Ludwigsburg. b. 10 Jan 1924 Breslau. Dipl. Psych. '55 Univ. of Tübingen Ger. TEACHER, Oberschulamt Nordwürtemburg, Rotebühlstr. 30, Stuttgart. Teaching, psychotherapy; learning theory, projective techniques, characterology. M

JANSEN, Dr. phil. Elsbeth. Welschstr. 18, Mainz. b. 26 June 1919 Düsseldorf. PH.D, Univ. of Mainz, Ger. SCI. ASST, Inst. for Legal Med. and Criminol, Univ. Clin, Mainz. Testing, clinical analysis, forensic psychology, teaching; clinical psychology. F

JASPERS, Dr. med. Siegfried. Hammer Str. 147, Münster/Westf. b. 8 Aug 1924

Hopsten/Westf. Dipl. Psych. '51 Univ. of Münster, Ger. SCI. CO-WRKR, Schering AG. Mullerstr. 170-172, Berlin. Research, applied psychology, consulting; characterology, graphology. M

JEBSEN, Dr. phil. Rolf H.P. Hammerichstr. 22, Hamburg-Othmarschen. b. 2 Apr 1912 Hamburg. PH.D '39 Univ. of Leipzig, Ger. DOZENT, Werbefachschule, Hamburg; DOZENT, Akademie der Volkswirtschaftlichen Gesellschaft, Hamburg. Member: BDP. Applied psychology, teaching, research; psychology of advertising, market research, human relations in industry. M

JENSSEN, Dipl. Psych. Horst. Sülldorfer Brooksweg 114b, Hamburg-Rissen. b. 31 May 1922 Hamburg. Dipl. Psych. '53 Univ. of Hamburg, Ger. CRIM. PSYCH'T, Jugendstrafanstalt Hahnöfersand der Gefängnisbehörde Hamburg, Post Jork/Elbe. Member: BDP. Applied psychology, guidance, clinical analysis; projective techniques, achievement tests in criminal psychology, juvenile delinquency, forensic psychology. M

JENTSCH, Hans-Joachim. Grafenstr. 25, München-Gladbach. b. 16 Oct 1927 Saarau. Dipl. Psych. '54 Univ. of Mainz, Ger. HOME DIR, Caritas Verband, Kaiserstr. 58, München-Gladbach. Applied and educational psychology, psychotherapy, administration, testing; characterology, projective techniques, social perception. M

JOHN, Dr. jur. Dipl. Psych. Peter. Höhenweg 13, Werdohl/Westf. b. 20 Apr 1912 Brüx, Czech. Dr. jur. '35 German Univ. of Prague, Czech; Dipl. Psych. '55 Technische Hochschule Braunschweig, Ger. PERS. MGR, Vereinigte Deutsche Metallwerke AG, Zweigniederlassung Carl Berg, Plattenbergerstr. 1, Werdohl/Westf. Member: BDP. Industrial psychology, graphology; test techniques. M

JOLAS, Dr. phil. Guenther. Toplerstr. 30, Nuremberg. b. 12 Sept 1920 Bremen. PH.D '53 Univ. of Freiburg, Ger. DIRECTOR, Indus. Psych. Div, Siemens Schuckertwerke AG, Landgrabenstr. 100, Nuremberg. Member: BDP. Personnel psychology, testing, consulting; aptitude tests, projective techniques, group process. M

JOPPE, Miss Luise Ernestine. Fritz-Hellerstr. 3, Nienburg-Weser. b. 15 Nov 1921 Bethel bei Bielefeld. Dipl. Psych. '52 Univ. of Munich, Ger. VOCAT. PSYCH'T, Bundesanstalt für Arbeitsvermittlung und Arbeitslosenversicherung, Frauentorgraben 33/35, Nuremberg. Member: BDP. Testing, applied psychology, research, administration; child and youth psychology, ethnic psychology, group processes. F

JORSWIECK, Dr. med. Eduard. Stindestr. 16, Berlin-Steglitz. b. 23 Sept 1919 Rohrheim.

MD '50 Univ. of Berlin, Ger. DOZENT of PSYCH, Pädagogische Hochschule, Berlin-Laukwitz; PSYCHOTHERAPIST, Krankenversicherungsanstalt, Berlin; PSYCHOTHERAPIST, priv. prac. Member: Deutsche Gesellschaft für Tiefenpsych, Ärztliche Gesellschaft für Psychother. Teaching, psychotherapy, educational psychology; developmental psychology in psychopathology, psychoanalysis. M

JUCKNAT, Prof. Dr. phil. Margarete. Dornbluthweg 15, Jena. b. 28 Jan 1904 Gumbinnen. PH.D '36 Univ. of Berlin, Ger. PROF. of PSYCH, Univ. of Jena, Goetheallee, Jena. Member: DGP, BDP. Teaching, research, administration; group dynamics, field theory, personality. F

JÜLICH, Dipl. Psych. Anneliese. Königstr. 7, Bonn. b. 3 Jan 1914 Berlin. Dipl. Psych. '48 Univ. of Bonn, Ger. Testing and clinical analysis; folklore, graphology, Gestalt psychology. F

JUNGKUNZ, Andreas. Clockengasse 6, Regensburg, Bavaria. b. 19 Oct 1923 Gössheinstein, Bavaria. Dipl. Psych. '53 Univ. of Erlangen, Ger. CHIEF PSYCH'T, Employment Off, Minoritenweg 10, Regensburg. Member: BDP. Vocational and child guidance, testing, applied and industrial psychology, research; projective techniques, achievement tests, group process. M

JUNK, Dr. phil. Margarete. Mozartstr. 45, Stuttgart-Süd. b. 10 June 1898 Erfurt. PH.D '33 Univ. of Munich, Ger. DIRECTOR, Sch. of Soc. Work, Johannsstr. 60, Stuttgart-W. Member: BDP. Teaching, educational psychology, psychotherapy, guidance; social work, professional guidance. F

JUNKER, Dipl. Psych. Erika. Stockheimerstr. 18, Frankfurt/M. b. 3 Feb 1926 Giessen/L. Dipl. Psych. '54 Univ. of Frankfurt/M, Ger. GRAD. STUD, Psych. Inst, Mertonstr. 17, Frankfurt/M. Research, clinical analysis; motivation research, statistics. F

JUNNE, Dr. Erich Otto. Sophienstr. 32, Frankfurt/M. b. 15 July 1916 Nordhausen. Dr. rer. pol. '40 Univ. of Munich, Ger. PSYCHOANALYST, priv. prac. Member: Deutsche Gesellschaft für Psychother. und Psych. Forschung. Psychotherapy, research; psychology of religion, projective techniques, psychoanalysis. M

JUSTIN, Dr. rer. nat. Eva. Braubachstr. 18-22, Frankfurt/M. b. 23 Aug 1909 Dresden. Dr. '43 Univ. of Berlin, Ger. EDUC. ADVIS, Hlth. Dept, City of Frankfurt/M. Criminal psychology, guidance, testing; attitude measurement, group process, social perception, projective techniques. F

KAENGER, Maria. Braamkamp 43, Hamburg 39. b. 12 June 1909 Hamburg. TEACHER,

Schulbehörde Hamburg, Dammtorstr. 26, Hamburg. Member: BDP. Teaching, applied and educational psychology, graphology; child and school psychology, characterology. F

KAHRS, Dr. phil. Ernst Wilhelm. Hattingerstr. 279, Bochum. b. 7 Oct 1916 Bochum. PH.D '47 Univ. of Münster, Ger. PRINCIPAL, Waldschule, Buscheystr. 91, Bochum. Teaching, administration, research; educational and developmental psychology. M

KALBITZER, Dr. phil. Roderich. Lönsberg 28, Essen. b. 11 Aug 1911 Essen. PH.D '36 Univ. of Bonn, Ger. INDUS. PSYCH'T, priv. prac. Member: BDP. Testing, clinical analysis, applied psychology, teaching; psychotherapy, group processes. M

KAMINSKI, Dipl. Psych. Gerhard. Weimarsche Str. 5, Berlin-Wilmersdorf. b. 19 Sept 1925 Steinau/Oder. Dipl. Psych. '52 Free Univ. of Berlin, Ger. SCI. ASST, Inst. for Psych. Res, Free Univ. of Berlin, Altensteinstr. 44a, Berlin-Dahlem. Member: BDP. Teaching, research, administration; psychological method, diagnosis, consulting, guidance. M

KARL, Dr. phil. Helmut. Moltkestr. 14, Emmendingen. b. 3 July 1923 Emmendingen. PH.D '54 Univ. of Freiburg, Ger. LECTURER, Inst. für Psych. und Charakterologie, Univ. of Freiburg, Bertholdstr. 17, Freiburg. Research, teaching, testing, educational psychology; study of personality, testing techniques. M

KEMMLER, Dr. phil. Lilly. Neustr. 48, Bottrop/Westf. b. 19 Nov. 1924 Bottrop. PH.D '55 Univ. of Münster, Ger. ASSISTANT, Psych. Inst. Univ. of Münster, Rosenstr. 9, Münster. Child guidance, clinical practice, testing, teaching, research; psychology of ego, will and motivation in early childhood, neurotic and maladjusted children, projective techniques. F

KEMPF, Dipl. Psych. Elsbeth. Eckenheimer Landstr. 47, Frankfurt/M. b. 27 Feb 1929 Marburg/L. Dipl. Psych. '55 Univ. of Heidelberg, Ger. RES. PSYCH'T, Heumann Werbe Ltd. Eysseneckstr. 12, Frankfurt/M. Market research; projective techniques, social perception, psychoanalysis, achievement tests. F

KERN, Artur. Pädagogisches Inst, Keplerstr. 85, Heidelberg. b. 7 Mar 1902 Hartheim OBERSTUDIENRAT, Pädagogisches Inst. Member: BDP. Teaching, educational psychology, research; theory of learning, school readiness tests, attitude measurements. M

KERSCHBAUM, Dr. phil. Peter. Rheinische Klinik für Hirnverletzte, Rheindorferstr. 147, Bonn. b. 6 Aug 1908 Holzminden/Weser. PH.D '33 Univ. of Hamburg, Ger. APPL. PSYCH'T, Rheinische Landesklinik für Hirnverletzte. Member: BDP. Testing,

clinical analysis, guidance, research; deterioration and personality alteration after cerebral injury, projective techniques, rehabilitation. M

KESSELRING, Prof. Michael. Friedrichstr. 15, Kaiserlautern. b. 27 Mar 1889 Marksteft/M. Lehrambtsprüfung '23 Univ. of Munich, Ger. PROFESSOR, Bezirksseminar f. d. Höhere Lehramt, Martin Lutherstr. 2, Kaiserlautern. Member: BDP, DGP. Educational psychology, teaching, research; youth psychology, testing, studies of memory. M

KIEBACK, Günter. Noorstr. 23, Eckernforde. b. 3 Apr. 1925 Albersdorf. Dipl. Psych. '54 Univ. of Kiel, Ger. VOCAT. GUID. COUNS, and PSYCH'T, Employment Off, Wittendorfer Str. Neumünster; TEACHER, Volksschule. Member: BDP. Industrial psychology and guidance, aptitude testing, projective techniques, technical aptitudes. M

KIENER, Dr. Franz. Neuburgerstr. 90, Passau. b. 17 Apr 1910 Krandorf. Dr. '36 Univ. of Munich, Ger. STUDIENRAT, Städtische Wirtschaftsaufbauschule, Heiligen Geist Gasse 9, Passau. Member: BDP. Teaching, research; psychology of expression, dress, gestures, speech. M

KIENZLE, Prof. Dr. Richard. Moltkestr. 62, Esslingen. b. 4 Mar 1898 Pforzheim. Dr. habil. '43 Univ. of Tübingen, Ger. PROFESSOR, Univ. of Tübingen. Member: DGP. Teaching, research, psychotherapy; studies of mimicry, analysis of speech, graphology. M

KIETZ, Dr. phil. Gertraud. Brackstr. 47, Oberhausen-Osterfeld. b. 31 Mar 1913 Leipzig. PH.D '42 Univ. of Leipzig, Ger. PSYCHOLOGIST, städt. Fachschulen und Berufsfachschulen, Oberhausen. Member: DGP, BDP. Teaching, professional writing; educational psychology; developmental psychology, social pedagogy, psychology of expression, characterology. F

KIRCHHOFF, Dr. phil. Hans. Alte Landstrasse 112, Hamburg-Hummelsbüttel. b. 2 Mar 1914 Hamburg. PH.D '46 Univ. of Hamburg, Ger. SCH. PSYCH'T, Dienststelle Schülerhilfe der Schulbehörde Hamburg, Bundesstr. 88; DOZENT, Inst. für Lehrerfortbildung, Hamburg; CO-EDITOR, *Schule und Psychologie.* Member: BDP. Teaching, research, editorial, testing, consulting; anthropology. M

KIRCHHOFF, Dr. Robert. Bahnhofstr. 6, Neulussheim/Baden. b. 4 May 1920 Bad-Hall, Austria. Dr. phil. habil. '56 Univ. of Heidelberg, Ger. DOZENT, Psych. Inst, Univ. of Heidelberg, Hauptstr. 126, Heidelberg. Member: BDP, DGP. Teaching, research, testing; psychology of thinking, language, and expression, psychodiagnosis. M

KIRSCH, Helmut. Bahnhöfsstr, Gemünden/M
b. 29 Oct 1924 Würzburg. Dipl. Psych. '55
Univ. of Würzburg, Ger. INDUS. PSYCH'T,
Frankfurter Allianz, Versicherungs AG,
Frankfurt/M. Industrial psychology, motivation research, testing; social psychology,
projective techniques, graphology.   M

KIRSTEN, Dr. phil. Hans. Maria Louisen
Stieg 6a, Hamburg 39.   b. 25 Apr 1914
Berlin. PUBLICITY DIR, Hamburg Mann-
heimer Versicherungs AG, Alsterufer 1,
Hamburg. Member: BDP. Applied psychology, editorial, professional writing;
social psychology, psychology of advertising.   M

KISKER, Dr. phil. Dr. med. Karl Peter.
Psychiatr. Neurolog. Klinik, Vosstr. 4,
Heidelberg.   b. 25 Sept 1926 Mülheim.
PH.D, Univ. of Heidelberg, Ger. PSYCHIA-
TRIST, Psychiatr. Neurolog. Universitäts-
klinik. Psychotherapy, clinical practice,
testing, research; psychology of perception,
group psychology.   M

KITTLER, Dr. phil. Hermann. Am Homburg
5, Saarbrücken 3.   b. 18 Dec 1896 Krefeld.
PH.D '34 Univ. of Bonn, Ger. REGIERUNGS-
RAT, Employment Off., Allestr. 17-19, Saarbrücken. Member: BDP. Applied psychology,
testing, consulting; vocational psychology,
social education, academic guidance.   M

KLAUSMEIER, Mrs. Ruth Gisela. Neuer
Trassweg 12, Refrath/Cologne.   b. 2 June
1922 Dortmund. Dipl. Psych. '53 Univ. of
Bonn, Ger. EDUC. CONSULT, Kölnerstr,
Euskirchen/Rhl. Guidance, psychotherapy,
research; child psychology, children's
books, psychology of nations.   F

KLEIN, Dr. phil. Adolf. Gottfried Daniels
Str. 9, Cologne-Ehrenfeld.   b. 14 Nov 1925
Krefeld. PH.D '51 Univ. of Cologne, Ger.
RES. ASST, Deutsche Forschungsgemein-
schaft, Frankengraben, Bad-Godesberg.
Research, administration; time perception,
individual differences in the reproduction
of temporal intervals.   M

KLEINER, Fritz. Schellingstr. 33/II, Munich
13.   b. 24 Feb 1913 Mindelheim, Bavaria.
Dipl. Psych. '47 Univ. of Munich, Ger.
GRAD. STUD, Psych. Inst, Univ. of Munich.
Research; systematization of the psy-
chology of personality.   M

KLEINER (née Moosdiele), Dipl. Psych. Ina.
Am Klarenberg 8, Schwäbisch Gmünd.
b. 7 Sept 1916 Munich. Dipl. Psych. '49
Univ. of Munich, Ger. EDUC. CONSULT,
Erziehungsberatungsstelle, Schulpsycholo-
gischer Dienst, Schillerstr. 14, Göppingen;
EDITOR, *Göppinger Schulreifetest*. Member:
BDP. Educational psychology, testing,
guidance, editorial; problems of school
maturity.   F

KLEINHANS, Dipl. Psych. Walter. Breiten-
bach, Krs. Schlüchtern.   b. 5 Sept 1927

Bruchhausen-Vilsen.   Dipl. Psych. '55
Univ. of Marburg, Ger. SONDERSCHUL-
LEHRER, Govt. of Hessen, Humboltstr. 6,
Wiesbaden.   Educational psychology,
guidance, teaching; learning and the
teacher, social control in groups, personality
tests.   M

**KLENNER, Dipl. Psych. Karl Robert Wolf-
gang.**   Eckardtsheim über Bielefeld.
b. 6 Feb 1921 Berlin. Dipl. Psych. '50 Univ.
of Göttingen, Ger. YOUTH PSYCH'T, Von
Bodelschwingische Anstalten Bethel bei
Bielefeld,   Zweiganstalt   Eckardtsheim,
Bethel. Member: BDP. Clinical analysis,
administration, guidance, teaching; attitude measurement, group process, Gestalt
theory.   M

KLIEMKE; Dr. phil. Ewalt. Prinz Friedrich
Leopoldstr. 28, Berlin-Nikolassee.   b. 27
Sept 1898 Berlin. PH.D '25 Univ. of Königsberg, Ger. PSYCHOLOGIST, Dienststelle für
Schwerbeschädigte der Berliner Arbeits-
ämter, Potsdamer Str. 180, Berlin. Member.
BDP. Testing, clinical analysis, guidance,
teaching;   psychophysiology,   psychopathology, psychology of the physically
handicapped.   M

KLINGHAMMER, Dipl. Psych. Hans Dietrich.
Langenhorst   über   Burgsteinfurt/Westf.
b. 23 Apr 1919 Erfurt. Dipl. Psych. '55
Univ. of Heidelberg, Ger. TCHR. of DEAF
CHILDREN, Landschaftsverband Westfalen-
Lippe, Landeshaus, Münster/Westf; CHILD.
GUID. COUNS, Klinik für Jugendpsychiat,
Gütersloh/Westf. Member: BDP. Applied
psychology, testing, student, guidance;
psychology of the deaf and dumb, psycho-
logical and physiological research in
affectivity, forensic psychology.   M

KLIX, Dr. phil. Gudrun. Martin Luther Str.
40, Bad Neustadt/Saale.   b. 24 Nov 1917
Blankenhagen. Dr. '43 Univ. of Munich,
Ger. Member: BDP. Guidance, testing,
teaching, retired; social perception, group
process.   F

KLOCKMANN, Dr. phil. Egon. Haselhain 12,
Hamburg-Harburg. b. 1 Jan 1920 Harburg/
Elbe. PH.D '51 Univ. of Hamburg, Ger.
MANAGER, BAWI-Bekleidungswerke, Ebert-
str. 58, Wilhelmshaven. Member: BDP.
Industrial psychology, personnel management, testing, research; psychological research on film, theatre, broadcasting, and
television.   M

KLÜWER, Dr. phil. Rolf. Holzstr. 12,
Munich 5.   b. 19 May 1925 Cologne. PH.D
'53 Univ. of Cologne, Ger. ASSISTANT,
Psychosomatische Beratungsstelle für Er-
wachsene, Mediz. Poliklinik, Pettenkoferstr.
8a, Munich.   Psychotherapy, clinical
practice; psychoanalysis, psychosomatic
medicine.   M

KNEHR, Dr. phil. Edeltraut. Im Langen Hau

6, Stuttgart-Rohr. PH.D '44 Univ. of Tübingen, Ger. PSYCHODIAGNOSTICIAN, Inst. of Psychother, Neue Weinsteige 16, Stuttgart. Child psychotherapy, educational psychology, testing; projective techniques, achievement tests. F

KNÖFEL, Dr. phil. Gerhart Helmut Ingo. Hochstr. 8a, Munich 8. b. 27 Sept 1910 Berlin. PH.D, Univ. of Würzburg, Ger. DIRECTOR, Jugendwohnheim Rädda Barnen I, Hochstr. 8a. Member: BDP. Educational psychology, testing, teaching, administration; social perception, group process. M

KNOHSALLA, Dipl. Psych. Josef Herbert Viktor. Siemensstr. 18, Nuremberg. b. 2 Nov 1926 Hindenburg. Dipl. Psych. '54 Julius Maximilians Univ. of Würzburg, Ger. MED. STUD, Univ. of Erlangen, Schlossplatz, Erlangen; EDUC. and VOCAT. CONSULT, priv. prac. Member: BDP. Applied psychology, testing, clinical analysis, consulting; statistical methods, diagnostics. M

KOCH, Dr. phil. Manfred. Quick Verlag, Brienner Str. 46, Munich. b. 20 Oct 1928 Düsseldorf. PH.D '54 Univ. of Tübingen, Ger. PSYCHOLOGIST, Quick Magazine, Verlag Th. Martens und Co. Member: DGP. Applied psychology, editorial, opinion and market research; communications, motivation, typology. M

KOEBERLE, Dipl. Psych. Fidelio. Höhscheider Str. 2, Düsseldorf-Wersten. b. 12 May 1915 Düsseldorf. Dipl. Psych. '50 Univ. of Bonn, Ger. PSYCH'T. and GRAPHOLOGIST, priv. prac. Graphology, psychotherapy, consulting, testing; individual therapy, guidance. M

KOEHLER, Prof. Dr. Otto. Zoologisches Inst, Katharinenstr. 20, Freiburg. b. 20 Dec 1889 Insterburg. PROF. and DIR, Zoologisches Inst; CO-EDITOR, Zeitschrift für Tierpsychologie, CO-EDITOR, Behaviour. Research, teaching, professional writing; animal behavior, ethology. M

KOHL, Dr. Kurt. Inst. für Leibesübungen, Kettenhofweg 139, Frankfurt/M. b. 15 Nov 1918 Frankfurt/M. Dr. phil. nat. '55 Univ. of Frankfurt/M., Ger. SCI. ASST, Inst. für Leibesübungen, Univ. of Frankfurt. Teaching, student; learning theory, sensory-motor development. M

KOHLRAUSCH, Dipl. Psych. Helmut. Walter vom Rathstr. 23, Frankfurt/M. b. 1 May 1924 Berlin. Dipl. Psych. '53 Technische Hochschule Braunschweig, Ger. HEAD, Cen. Employment and Pers. Off, Frankfurter Versicherungs AG, Taunusanlage 20, Frankfurt/M. Member: BDP. Personnel psychology, guidance, teaching, testing; social psychology. M

KOHLSCHEEN, Dr. phil. Günther. Am Botanischen Garten 72, Cologne. b. 19 Apr 1923 Wimmersbull. PH.D '53 Univ. of

Cologne, Ger. HEAD, Evangelical Beratungsstelle für Erziehungs- und Ehefragen, Boltensternstr. 2, Cologne. Member: BDP. Psychotherapy, applied and educational psychology, consulting; child guidance, probation, social work. M

KÖNIG, Dipl. Psych. Günter. Schlessstr. 54, Berlin-Steglitz. b. 13 Sept 1924 Berlin. Dipl Psych. '56 Free Univ. of Berlin, Ger. Member: BDP. Psychology of perception. M

KÖNIG, Helmut Hans Hermann. Massmannstr. 4/1, Munich 2. b. 1 July 1927 Barnstorf. Dipl. Psych. '53 Univ. of Tübingen, Ger. INDUS. PSYCH'T, Technischer Überwachungsverein Munich, Kaiserstr. 14-16, Munich. Industrial psychology, testing, counseling, professional writing; field theory, perception, projective techniques, achievement tests, group process and therapy. M

KÖNIG, Prof. Dr. phil. René. Nietzschestr. 1, Cologne. b. 5 July 1906, Magdeburg. PH.D '30 Univ. of Berlin, Ger. PROFESSOR, Univ. of Cologne, Albertus Magnus Platz, Cologne; EDITOR, Kölner Zeitschrift für Soziologie und Sozialpsychologie. Teaching, research, editorial; social psychology. M

KONRAD, Dipl. Psych. Günther. Theodor Körnerstr. 10/IV, Würzburg. b. 30 Nov 1927 Uttigsdorf, Czech. Dipl Psych '54 Univ. of Würzburg, Ger. PSYCHOLOGIST, Employment Off, Ludwigskai, Würzburg. Member: BDP. Student, testing, applied and educational psychology; achievement tests, psycho-diagnostics, factor analysis. M

KONRAD, Dr. phil. Klaus. Specklinplatz 35, Munich 25. b. 5 Dec 1904 Würzburg. PH.D, Univ. of Würzburg, Ger. TEACHER, Stadtschulamt, Munich. Member: BDP. Educational and industrial psychology, teaching, testing, guidance; professional aptitude tests, rehabilitation of criminals. M

KORB, Dr. rer. nat. Marianne Bertha. Mädchenheime, Diakonissenhaus, Düsseldorf/Kaiserswerth. b. 30 May 1922 Halle/Saale. Dipl Psych. '45 Georg August Univ. of Göttingen, Ger. GUID. COUNS, Diakonissenanstalt. Member: BDP. Testing, consulting and guidance for young girls, teaching; diagnostic testing, learning theory, group work, case work. F

KORFF, Dipl. Psych. Ernst. Holzhofallee 35, Darmstadt. b. 30 Oct 1902 Wuppertal Elberfeld. Dipl Psych '51 Univ. of Freiburg, Ger. INDUS. PSYCH'T, priv. prac; LECT. in APPL. PSYCH: EDITOR, Psychologische Hefte. Personnel psychology, editorial, consulting; graphology, testing, projective techniques, group process, management training. M

KORFF, Dr. phil. Wilhelm A. Gustav. Hindenburgstr. 24, Erlangen. b. 23 Sept

1901 Worms/Rhein. PH.D '41 Univ. of Erlangen, Ger. Member: BDP. Testing, administration, research; aptitude tests, educational and child psychology.   M

KORN, Miss Sigrid Erna. Ottweilerstr. 85, Saarbrücken II. b. 6 Sept 1926 Leipzig. Dipl. Psych. '53 Free Univ. of Berlin, Ger. RES. WRKR, Univ. of Saarland, Saarbrücken 15 Research, guidance, student; motivation research, attitude measurement, adaptation of audio-visual materials for educational use in underdeveloped areas.   F

KORNADT, Dr. phil. Hans Joachim. Inst. of Psych, Gutenbergstr. 18, Marburg/L. b. 16 June 1927 Stargard. PH.D '56 Phillips Univ. of Marburg/L. Ger. RES. ASST, Inst. of Psych. Research, consulting and guidance, clinical analysis; personality, social and cultural processes, relations of psychology and physiology, memory, projective techniques.   M

KÖRNER, Dr. med. Otto. Adolf Vorwerkstr. 31, Wuppertal-Barmen. b. 7 Oct 1886 Dresden. MD '13 Univ. of Freiburg, Ger. PSYCHIATRIST, priv. prac; LECTURER, Volkshochschule. Member: Allgemeine Ärztliche Gesellschaft für Psychother, Studiengesellschaft für Praktische Psych. Psychotherapy, clinical practice; Jungian therapy, the collective unconscious, psychotherapy and Indian philosophy.   M

KOSCHITKI, Karl. Zwinger 32½, Würzburg. b. 31 Aug 1924 Ohrawalde, Poland. Dipl. Psych. '55 Univ. of Würzburg, Ger. SCH. PSYCH'T, Oberrealschule, Sanderring 8, Würzburg. Member: BDP. Teaching, educational psychology, guidance; school psychology, sociology, group investigation, diagnosis, projective techniques.   M

KOSTKA, Dr. Fritz. Schellenstr. 16, Bad Pyrmont. b. 8 Nov 1921 Berlin. Dipl. Psych. '51 Univ. of Mainz, Ger. ASST. PHYSICIAN, County Hosp, Hitzacker/Elbe. Psychotherapy, consulting, clinical practice; medical psychology, psychotherapy, hypnosis.   M

KOTTE, Mrs. Ursula. Eschholzstr. 62, Freiburg. b. 9 May 1924 Freiburg. Dipl. Psych. '53 Univ. of Freiburg, Ger. DOZENT of PSYCH, Evangelisches Seminar für Wohlfahrtspflege, Goethestr. 2, Freiburg. Teaching, consulting, applied and educational psychology; human growth and development, child guidance, group process.   F

KRAAK, Dr. phil. Bernhard. Gminderstr. 6, Reutlingen. b. 30 Oct 1922 Rostock. PH.D '56 Free Univ. of Berlin, Ger. DIRECTOR, Evangelische Schule für Heimerziehung, Gustav Werner Str. 8, Reutlingen. Member: BDP. Educational psychology, guidance, research; play therapy, test construction.   M

KRAFT, Hans. Luitpoldstr. 43, Ottobeuren/

Allgäu. b. 21 Feb 1915 Ottobeuren/Allg. Dipl. Psych. '44 Univ. of Munich, Ger. PSYCHOLOGIST, Erziehungsberatungsstelle Memmingen, Kramerstr. 15/11, Memmingen/Allgäu. Member: BDP. Guidance, testing, applied and educational psychology; projective techniques, child therapy.   M

KRAFT, Werner. Wilhelmstr. 61, Dossenheim über Heidelberg. b. 14 Nov 1924 Dossenheim/Hdlbg. Dipl. Psych. '54 Univ. of Heidelberg, Ger. STUDENT, Univ. of Tübingen, Psych. Inst. Münzgasse 11, Tübingen. Applied and industrial psychology, research; performance tests, factor analysis, general psychology, perception. M

KRAMER, Dr. phil. Peter. Kurhausstr. 32, Bad Segeberg, Holstein. b. 19 Oct 1918 Rothenkrug. PH.D '53 Univ. of Kiel, Ger. TEACHER, Oberschule zum Dom, Musterbahn, Lübeck. Applied and educational psychology, research, student; university placement tests, character typology, psychology of advertising.   M

KRAUSE, Dr. Erwin Karl Hermann. Coburgerstr. 21, Bonn. b. 7 Apr 1908 Neufährdorf. Dr. Ing. '34 Techn. Hochschule Berlin, Ger. MANAGER, Arbeitsstelle für Betriebliche Berufsausbildung, Markt 37, Bonn. Member: BDP. Industrial psychology; industrial education.   M

KRAUSE, Ludwig. Braystr. 18, Munich 8. b. 22 May 1929 Martinau Kr. Benthen. Dipl. Psych. '55 Univ. of Munich, Ger. EDUC. ADVIS, Catholic Youth Welf. Assn, Liebigstr. 10, Munich. Member: BDP. Consulting, testing, research; test psychology, psychology of children in educational homes.   M

KRECKL, Fridolin. Lichtenau bei Ansbach. b. 16 Apr 1919 Gabersee, Bavaria. Dipl. Psych. '47 Univ. of Munich, Ger. DIRECTOR, Bavarian State Sch; YOUTH SPEC, Local Juv. Ct. Member: BDP. Clinical guidance, testing, administration; group psychology, group therapy, psychodrama. M

KREISSLER, Dr. phil. Hellmut Fritz. Wilhelm Busch-Str. 4, Braunschweig. b. 31 Oct 1099 Neuhausen. PH.D '40 Univ. of Leipzig, Ger. INDUS. PSYCH'T, priv. prac. Member: BDP. Testing, vocational counseling, editorial; projective techniques, achievement tests, attitude measurement. M

KRENN, Dr. phil. Stephanie. Roentgenstr. 21, Bad Godesberg. b. 21 Dec 1919 Leibnitz, Austria. PH.D '45 Univ. of Graz, Austria. ENGLISH LANGUAGE SPEC, American Embassy, Nehlener Ave, Bonn/Mehlem. Preparation of English teaching material, teaching, research; attitude measurement, achievement tests, professional adaptation tests.   F

KRETSCHMANN, Dr. rer. nat. Oskar. Friedr. Engelsstr. 16, Gera. b. 31 Oct 1899 Thüringen. Dr. rer. nat. '41 Univ. of Jena, Ger. PSYCHOLOGIST, Landeskrankenhaus Tannenfeld bei Schmölln, Bezirk Leipzig. Member: Berufsverband der im Gesundheitswesen der DDR tätigen Psychologen. Clinical analysis, psychotherapy, clinical practice; handwriting, effect of illness on personality, Gestalt psychology. M

KRETSCHMER, Dr. Wolfgang. Nervenklinik Tübingen. b. 14 Feb 1918 Mergentheim. DOZENT, Univ. of Tübingen, Ger. CLIN. DIR, Universität Nervenklinik, Tübingen. Member: Gesellschaft für Ärztliche Psychotherapie. Teaching, psychotherapy, clinical practice; neuroses, individual maturation, national character, psychology of religion. M

KREUSCH, Wolfdieter. Bleichenbrücke 6/IV Hamburg 36. b. 16 Oct 1924 Berlin. |Dipl. Psych. '52 Free Univ. of Berlin, Ger. PERS. ADVIS, Senat der Freien und Hansestadt Hamburg Prüfungsamt f.d. Öffentlichen Dienst, Steckelhörn 12, Hamburg 11. Member: BDP. Applied and personnel psychology, testing, guidance; personnel selection, aptitude tests, criminal psychology. M

KRIEGSMANN, Günter. Bergstr. 71, Cologne. b. 22 Sept 1927 Cologne. Dipl. Psych. '53 Univ. of Bonn, Ger. RELIG. TCHR, Cologne Trng. Sch. for Professions, Rathaus, Cologne. Teaching, student, consulting; psychoanalysis, testing methods, educational and vocational counseling. M

KRIEN, Dipl. Psych. Johannes Paul Otto. Steinheilpfad 8, Berlin-Lichterfelde. b. 7 Mar 1924 Bütow. Dipl. Psych. '54 Free Univ. of Berlin, Ger. Member: BDP. Student, applied psychology, guidance; projective techniques, achievement tests, clinical tests. M

KROEBER, Dr. phil. Walter. Kolpingstr. 18, Beuel-Bonn. b. 17 Mar 1906 Leipzig. Dr, '38 Univ. of Leipzig, Ger. REGIERUNGS-RAT, Employment Off, Kaiser Karl Ring 9, Bonn. Member: BDP. Testing, applied psychology, administration; mechanics of intellectual work, achievement tests, learning theory. M

KRUDEWIG, Priv. Doz. Dr. phil. Maria. Wolfgang Müllerstr. 22, Cologne. b. 28 May 1897 Siegburg. PH.D '28 Univ. of Cologne, Ger. PRIVAT DOZENT, Psych. Inst. Univ. of Cologne, Meister Ekkehartstr. 11, Cologne. Member: DGP, BDP. Teaching, research, professional writing; thinking, character development, visual perception. F

KRÜGER, Dipl. Psych. Ulrich. Martin Luther Str. 30, Berlin-Schöneberg 1. b. 6 May 1924 Jastrow. Dipl. Psych. '52 Free Univ. of Berlin, Ger. GUID. COUNS, Verein zur Förderung der Wiedervereinigung Deutschlands, Poppelsdorfer Allee 19,

Bonn. Member: BDP. Consulting, applied psychology, testing; political behaviour, cultural and social psychology, group process, educational counseling. M

KRUMBHOLZ, Dr. phil. Carl. Worringerstr. 77, Wuppertal-Elberfeld. b. 24 Feb 1910 Essen. PH.D '35 Univ. of Münster, Ger. VOCAT. GUID. COUNS, Employment Off, Wuppertal. Member: BDP. Consulting, guidance, testing, applied psychology; projective techniques, attitude measurement. M

KÜCHENHOFF, Dr. phil. Werner. Schloss-Str. 29, Frankfurt/M. b. 18 July 1910 Bleicherode. PH.D '39 Univ. of Marburg, Ger. ASST. PROF. and SCI. RES. WRKR, Inst. for Int. Educ. Res; EDITOR, Mitteilungen und Nachrichten. Member: BDP. Research, professional writing, educational psychology; attitude measurement, problem children, clinical guidance. M

KÜCHLE, Erwin. Seutterweg 10, Ulm/Donau. b. 22 Oct 1927 Ulm/D. Dipl. Psych. '55 Univ. of Munich, Ger. INDUS. PSYCH'T, Siemens-Schuckertwerke AG, Traunreut und Traunstein/Obb. Member: BDP. Industrial psychology, research, psychotherapy; projective techniques, social perception, personnel management. M

KUDERA, Hans-Wolfgang. Bäckerstr. 32, Munich-Pasing. b. 10 July 1925 Beuthen O./S. Dipl. Psych. '54 Univ. of Munich, Ger. INDUS. PSYCH'T, Psychologisch-medizinische Untersuchungsstelle beim Technischen Überwachungsverein, Kaiserstr. 14/16, Munich. Member: BDP. Industrial psychology, guidance; projective techniques, group process, expressive movement and related techniques, mental hygiene. M

KUELL, Dr. phil. Gisela. Junkerstrasse 7, Solingen-Ohligs. b. 14 Oct 1926 Solingen-Ohligs. PH.D '55 Univ. of Cologne, Ger. ADV. PSYCH'T, Troost Werbeagentur, Immermannstr. 40, Düsseldorf. Market and opinion research, applied psychology; motivation research, attitude measurement, non-directive methods in social research. F

KUENBURG, Dr. Marcellina-Georgina, Gräfin von. Agnesstr. 2, Munich 13. b. 19 Jan 1893 Dresden. Dr. Univ. of Munich, Ger. CLIN. PSYCH'T Heckscher Clinic, Heckscherstr. 9, Munich; CLIN. PSYCH'T, Hirnverletzen Clinic, Tristanstr. 20, Munich. Member: BDP. Consulting, clinical analysis and practice, research; speech therapy. F

KUFNER, Dr. phil. Mrs. Lore. Herzogstr. 10, Munich 23. b. 1 Jan 1920 Munich. PH.D '56 Univ. of Munich, Ger. SCH. PSYCH'T and TCHR, Regierung von Oberbayern, Maximilianstr. 14, Munich 22. Educational psychology, consulting, guidance; child psychology. F

KUGELGEN, Mrs. Gertrud von. Schubertstr. 16, Constance-Petershausen. b. 18 Feb 1886 Breslau. GRAPHOLOGIST, priv. prac. Member: BDP, Fachverband für Gerichtliche Sachverständige. Consulting, guidance, teaching; analysis of handwriting, marriage and vocational counseling.   F

KÜGLER, Dr. phil. Ernst Hermann Emil. Weserstr. 75, Wilhemshaven. b. 3 Nov 1912 Berlin. PH.D '54 Univ. of Göttingen, Ger. TEACHER, Niedersächsischer Verwaltungsbezirk, Oldenburg i.o. Teaching, psychotherapy, educational psychology; psychoanalysis, social perception.   M

KUHN, Miss Annemarie. Markusstr. 5, Bamberg. b. 12 May 1930 Bamberg. Dipl. Psych. '53 Univ. of Erlangen, Ger. VOCAT. GUID. CONSULT, Employment Off, Sedanstr. 17, Hof/Saale. Testing, applied and industrial psychology, administration; child development, projective techniques, psychology of personality.   F

KUHN, Dr. Hermenegild-Josef. Goethestr. 10, Aachen. b. 8 Apr 1904 Würtemberg. Dr, Univ. of Tübingen, Ger. PROF. OF PSYCH, Pädag. Akademie, Beeckstr. 26, Aachen. Member: DGP. Teaching, educational psychology, research; psychology of teaching, child and adolescent psychology.   M

KULLER, Dipl. Psych. Erich Christian. Augartenstr. 2, Mannheim. b. 10 Dec 1930 Breslau. Dipl Psych. '55 Johan Wolfgang Goethe Univ. of Frankfurt, Ger. SCI. ASST, Inst. für Werbewissenschaftliche Untersuchungen, Augusta Anlage 34, Mannheim. Applied psychology, research; general psychology, research; general psychological methods, advertising psychology. M

KUNKEL, Dipl. Psych. Eberhard Theodor. Schiersteinerstr. 122, Martinstal/Rhg. b. 10 Apr 1931 Limburg/L. Dipl. Psych. '55 Univ. of Mainz, Ger. EDUC. CONSULT, Zentrale für Private Fürsorge, Beethovenstr. 61, Frankfurt/M. Research, educational psychology, psychotherapy, child guidance; stereotypes.   M

KUNKEL, Dipl. Psych. Waltraut. Kaulbach Str. 49, Munich. b. 8 Jan 1923 Würzburg. Dipl. Psych. '54 Univ. of Munich, Ger. LEADER, Studentinnenheim, Studentwerk Munich, Veterinaerstr. 11, Munich. Member: BDP. Psychotherapy, clinical analysis; analysis of the human voice, psychotherapy and physical environment.   F

KÜPPERS, Dr. phil. Mrs. Waltraut. Jugendheim a.d. Bergstrasse, Tannenstrasse. b. 14 Feb 1915 Wanfried/Werra. PH.D '46 Univ. of Göttingen, Ger. DOZENTIN, Pädagogisches Inst. Darmstadt. Member: BDP. Teaching, research, testing, psychotherapy; human development, educational psychology.   F

KURZ, Dipl. Psych. Rolf. Buerklinstr. 52, Lahr/Baden. b. 7 Apr 1922 Unteraichen/ Stuttgart. Dipl. Psych. '51 Univ. of Tübingen, Ger. HEAD, Erziehungs Beratungsstelle Lahr, Waldstr. 10, Lahr/Baden. Member: BDP. Consulting, testing, applied and educational psychology; projective techniques, child development, social perception.   M

LACHENMEIR, Dipl. Psych. Irmingard. Agnes Bernauer Str. 158/II, Munich 40. b 24 July 1920 Munich. Dipl. Psych. '50 Univ. of Munich, Ger. EDUC. PSYCH'T, priv. prac. Member: BDP. Teaching, educational psychology, guidance; child psychology, educational and general counseling, achievement tests.   F

LADE, Hildegard. Röderbergweg 207, Frankfurt/M. b. 21 June 1913 Spremberg/Lausitz. Dipl. Psych. '50 Univ. of Göttingen, Ger. DOZENT, Seminar für Soziale Berufsarbeit, Schaumainkai 29, Frankfurt/M. Member: BDP Teaching social workers; developmental psychology, educational and industrial psychology.   F

LAEMMERMAN, Dozent Dr. Hans. Schillerstr. 8, Gengenbach, Baden. b. 31 Jan 1891 Nuremberg. Dr, '30 Univ. of Jena, Ger. STUDIENRAT, Paedagogische Akademie, Genenbach. Member: BDP. Teaching, educational psychology, testing; mental tests, talent selection, student examinations.   M

LAEPPLE, Dr. phil. Ernst. Honoldweg 6, Stuttgart-W. b. 11 Mar 1902 Flacht/Stuttgart. Dr, Univ. of Munich, Ger. BUNDESVERWALTUNGSOBERRAT, Employment Off, Baden Württemberg in Stuttgart, Hölderlinstr. 36, Stuttgart. Member: BDP. Administration, guidance; adolescent psychology, aptitude psychology.   M

LAKASCHUS (née Brever), Dipl. Psych. Mrs. Carmen. Scheidswaldstr. 60, Frankfurt/M. b. 1 June 1931 Bevel/Bonn. Dipl. Psych. '55 Univ. of Cologne, Ger. INDUS. PSYCH'T, McCann Co, Neue Mainzer Str. 60, Frankfurt/M. Market research, industrial psychology, consulting; motivation research, psychotherapy, projective techniques.   F

LAKASCHUS, Erwin E. A. Scheidswaldstr. 60, Frankfurt/M. b. 17 Dec 1926 Düsseldorf. Dipl. Psych. '55 Univ. of Cologne Ger. RES. DIR, Laux Studios, Hauptwache 10, Frankfurt/M. Research, industrial psychology, psychotherapy; psychoanalytical dynamic theories in social psychology, group psychology, psychotherapy.   M

LAMBRECHT, Mrs. Anni. Waitzstr. 8/II Hamburg. b. 21 Oct 1898 Hamburg GRAPHOLOGIST, priv. prac. Member: BDP Research, teaching, consulting; characterology, depth psychology.   I

LAMM, Stud. Prof. Theodor. Regensburger Str. 25, Straubing, Bavaria. b. 28 Sept 1900 Würzburg. PH.D '30 Univ. of Würzburg, Ger. STUDIENPROFESSOR, Priv. Teachers' College, Seminargasse 8, Straubing. Member: BDP. Teaching, educational psychology; aptitude measurement, sociology of development. M

LANG, Miss Erika. Bremerhaven Child Guid. Clin, Anton Schumacherstr. 13, Bremerhaven. b. 28 Jan 1923 Jesten/Tilsit. Dipl. Psych. '51 Univ. of Göttingen, Ger. CHIEF PSYCH'T, Bremerhaven Child Guid. Clin. Member: BDP. Testing,consulting, teaching; projective techniques, social perception, children's treatment. F

LANGE, Dipl. Psych. Anneliese. Zillestr. 104, Berlin-Charlottenburg 5. b. 30 Apr 1931 Berlin. Dipl. Psych. '55 Free Univ. of Berlin, Ger. SCI. CO-WRKR, Inst. for Psych. Res, Free Univ. of Berlin, Altensteinstr. 44a, Berlin, Dahlem. Member: BDP. Consulting, testing, educational psychology; child therapy, psychology of imperssion and expression. F

LANGE, Dipl. Psych. Friedrich. Langestr. 42, Schleswig. b. 5 Apr 1929 Schleswig. Dipl. Psych. '55 Univ. of Göttingen, Ger. STUDENT, Psych. Inst, Univ. of Göttingen, Hoher Weg 15, Göttingen. Research; motivation and learning theory, animal psychology, attitude measurement, group process. M

LANGE, Dipl. Psych. Hans Hermann. Zillestr. 104, Berlin-Charlottenburg 5. b. 20 May 1913 Berlin. Dipl. Psych. '51 Humboldt Univ. of Berlin, Ger. EDUC. GUID. COUNS, Senator für Jugend und Sport, Am Karlsbad 8, Berlin. Testing, psychotherapy, guidance. M

LANGER, Dr. med. Dieter. Wallmodenstr. 40, Hannover-Kleefeld. b. 22 Apr 1931 Brieg/Breslau. MD '56 Univ. of Göttingen, Ger. CLIN. PSYCH'T, Niedersächsisches Landeskrankenhaus, Göttingen. Clinical practice, research; personality, neurosis and psychotherapy, psychopathology. M

LANGHANS, Dr. phil. Siegfried. Schellingstr. 85, Munich 13. b. 19 Apr 1915 Berlin. PH.D '55 Univ. of Munich, Ger. PSYCHOLOGIST, Technischer Überwachungsverein, Kaiserstr. 14-16, Munich. Member: BDP. Applied psychology, guidance, clinical analysis; psychoanalysis, traffic psychology. M

LANKES, Dr. phil. Marianne. Isartorplatz 4/V, Munich 22. b. 11 Aug 1923 Munich. PH.D '51 Ludwig Maximilian Univ. of Munich, Ger. CONSULT. PSYCH'T, Widenmayerstr. 31/o, Munich 22. Consulting, child psychology, testing, guidance of criminal youth; projective tests, intelligence tests, achievement tests. F

LATTKE, Dr. phil. Herbert. Rheinstr. 31,

Beuel bei Bonn. b. 11 Nov 1909 Langenbielau. PH.D '35 Univ. of Bonn, Ger. DIRECTOR, Seminar für Wohlfahrts und Jugendpfleger,Georgstr. 5,Cologne; EDITOR, *Die Soziale Arbeit.* Member: BDP. Teaching, administration, educational psychology, methods of social work; graphology, human relations. M

LAUBE, Dr. phil. Horst. Weichelstr. 2, Nuremberg. b. 3 July 1912 Dresden. PH.D '41 Tech. Hochschule Dresden, Ger. STUDIENRAT, Berufsoberschule, Adam Kraft Str. 2, Nuremberg; DOZENT, Ohm-Polytechnikum, Kessler Platz, Nuremberg; TEACHER, Rationalisierungs Kuratorium der Deutschen Wirtschaft. Member: BDP. Industrial psychology, teaching; human relations in industry, training of foremen. M

LAUX, Dipl. Psych. Irmgard. Humboldtstr. 105, Düsseldorf. b. 2 Feb 1919 Kempen. Dipl. Psych. '54 Univ. of Bonn, Ger. CRIM. PSYCH'T, Polizeipräsident, Dürgensplatz, Düsseldorf. Member: BDP. Applied psychology, graphology, professional writing; handwriting analysis of children, juvenile criminals. F

LEBENDER, Eberhard. Vereinigte Glanzstoff Fabriken Werk Obernburg, Obernburg/M. b. 7 July 1929 Stettin. Dipl. Psych. '56 Free Univ. of Berlin, Ger. INDUS. PSYCH'T, Vereinigte Glanzstoff Fabriken, Laurentiusplatz, Wuppertal-Elberveld. Member: BDP. Industrial psychology, testing, guidance; diagnostic psychology, psychology of civilization. M

LEBER, Dr. phil. Aloys. Birkenwaldstr. 130, Stuttgart-N. b. 6 Nov 1921 Fehlheim, Hessen. PH.D '51 Univ. of Mainz, Ger. PSYCH. COUNS, Caritas Verband für Württemberg, Weissenburgstr. 13, Stuttgart. Member: BDP. Guidance, psychotherapy, consulting; characterology, projective techniques, psychoanalysis. M

LEBER, Gabriele. Birkenwaldstr. 130, Stuttgart-N. b. 13 July 1930 Warendorf/ Westf. Dipl. Psych. '55 Univ. of Mainz, Ger. VOLUNTEER PSYCH. CONSULT, Caritasverband, Weissenburgstr. 13, Stuttgart. Consulting, testing; child guidance, anthropological research. F

LEDIG, Dipl. Psych. Hans Manfred. Lortzingstr. 10, Berlin-Lichtenrade. b. 10 Mar 1921 Berlin. Dipl. Psych. '53 Free Univ. of Berlin, Ger. RES. ASST, Pädagogische Hochschule, Marienfelder Str. 74-100, Berlin-Lankwitz. Member: BDP. Research, teaching, testing; school psychology, achievement and intelligence tests, educational guidance. M

LEHMANN, Dr. phil. Harry. Querstr. 21, Dortmund. b. 29 June 1912 Cologne-Deutz. PH.D '35 Univ. of Innsbruck, Austria. DIR. of VOCAT. GUID. and BUNDESVER-

WALTUNGSRAT, Employment Off, Rhein-landdamm, Dortmund. Industrial psychology, administration, guidance; social psychology, aptitudes, psychotherapy.   M

LEHMANN-WAFFENSCHMIDT, Dipl. Psych. Felicitas. Bergstr. 55, Heidelberg. b. 30 May 1930 Karlsruhe. Dipl. Psych. '55 Univ. of Heidelberg, Ger. Student, industrial psychology, testing; human relations, industrial aptitude research, projective test methods, reeducation of maladjusted children.   F

LEHR, Dr. Ursula. Reuterstr. 68, Bonn. b. 5 June 1930 Frankfurt/M. Dr. '54 Univ. of Bonn, Ger. RES. ASST, Psych. Inst, Rhein. Friedr. Wilh. Univ, Bonn; ASSISTANT, Univ. of Erlangen. Educational and industrial psychology, research, professional writing; child psychology, characterology.   F

LENNEPER, Dipl. Psych. Peter. Oppenhoff-Allee 115, Aachen. b. 26 Dec 1906 Cologne. Dipl. Psych. '48 Univ. of Bonn, Ger. DIV. DIR, Handwerkskammer, Couvenstr. 18, Aachen; DOZENT, Werkkunstschule der Stadt Aachen. Member: BDP. Teaching, research, administration; psychological development and research in Belgium, Holland, France.   M

LEOPOLD, Dipl. Psych. Rosemarie. Bauerstr. 19, Munich 13. b. 19 Dec 1928 Dresden. Dipl. '55 Univ. of Munich, Ger. Member: BDP. Student, educational psychology; educational consulting.   F

LERSCH, Dipl. Psych. Brigitte. Dreschstr. 5, Munich 23. b. 24 Nov 1932 Dresden. Dipl. Psych. '55 Univ. of Munich, Ger. Student; educational guidance.   F

LERSCH, Prof. Dr. phil. Philipp. Dreschstr. 5, Munich. b. 4 Apr 1898 Munich. PH.D '22 Univ. of Munich, Ger. PROF. and DIR, Psych. Inst., Univ. of Munich, Ludwigstr. 17, Munich; CO-EDITOR, *Zeitshrift für Experimentele und Angewandte Psychologie.* Member: BDP, DGP, Int. Psych. Assn. Teaching, research, guidance; personality theory, aspiration and motivation, mimicry.   M

LEYER, Dr. Kurt. Frankfurter Str. 82, Salzgitter-Thiede. b. 6 Jan 1914 Bergfeld. Dipl. Psych. '38 Univ. of Marburg, Ger. SECONDARY SCH. TCHR, Mittelschule, Panscheberg, Salzgitter. Member: BDP. Teaching, educational psychology, graphology.   M

LEYHAUSEN, Dr. Paul. Auf dem Hagen 28, Göttingen. b. 10 Nov 1916 Bonn. Dr. rer. nat. '48 Univ. of Freiburg, Ger. DIRECTOR, Dept. of Biol. and Psych. Res. Inst. für Wissenschaftlichen Film, Bunsenstr. 10, Göttingen. Member: Deutsche Gesellschaft für Anthropologie. Direction of research and educational films, research; comparative psychology, ontogeny, phylogeny and physiology of behavior, group process.   M

LIENERT, Dr. med. Dr. phil. Gustav Adolf. Gutenbergstr. 18, Marburg. b. 13 Dec 1920 Michelsdorf, Czech. MD '50 Univ. of Vienna, Austria; PH.D '51 Univ. of Marburg, Ger. SCI. ASST, Psych. Inst, Univ. of Marburg; TCHR. of CHILD PSYCH, Lehrgänge für Ausbildung von Sonderschullehrern. Member: DGP. Teaching, research, testing; test construction, effect of drugs on achievement, experimental design.   M

LILLER, Miss Beate. Kunigundenstr. 56, Munich 23. b. 5 Apr 1926 Berlin. Dipl. Psych. '54 Ludwig Maximilian Univ. of Munich, Ger. Student, testing, psychotherapy, guidance; projective techniques, child guidance, individual psychotherapy.   F

LILLIG, Dipl. Psych. Marianne. Dietlinden-str. 16, Munich 23. b. 14 July 1927 Osnabrück. Dipl. '52 Univ. of Munich, Ger. PSYCH. COUNS, priv. prac. Member: BDP. Educational psychology, testing, consulting, guidance; social psychology.   F

LINDENBLATT, Dr. phil. Wolfgang. Bushing Str. 25/I, Munich 27. b. 28 Apr 1919 Wartenburg. PH.D '52 Univ. of Munich, Ger. SECY. GENL, Landesverband Bayern des „Gesamtdeutscher Block-BHE", Pacellistr. 8/III, Munich 2. Member: BDP. Applied psychology, administration; cultural psychology, social perception, achievement tests.   M

LIPPERT, Dr. med. Herbert. Kobellstr. 6, Munich 15. b. 28 July 1930 Horaschdowitz, Czech. MD '53 Univ. of Munich, Ger. Research, industrial psychology, pharmaco-psychology, factor analysis, projective techniques in psychiatry.   M

LÖBERT, Dipl. Psych. Werner Willi. Reinsburgstr. 77 A I, Stuttgart W. b. 25 Feb 1925 Wilhelma, Palestine. Dipl. Psych.'51 Univ. of Tübingen, Ger. PSYCHOLOGIST, Haftanstalt Stuttgart, Urbanstr. 18A, Stuttgart-Ost. Guidance, administration, research.   M

LOHR, Dipl. Psych. Winfried. Psych. Inst, Univ. of Tübingen, Münzgasse 11, Tübingen b. 12 June 1926 Gelsenkirchen. Dipl. Psych. '54 Univ. of Heidelberg, Ger. ASSISTANT, Psych. Inst. Univ. of Tübingen. Research, guidance, counseling, teaching; motor movements, coordination, constancy of performance, child development.   M

LOHSE, Mrs. Martha Bertha Christine. Frenssenstr. 46, Hamburg-Blankenese. b. 13 Dec 1906 Kiel. GRAPHOLOGIST, priv. prac. Member: BDP. Graphology; characterology, psychology of expression.   F

LOOFS, Dr. phil. Sigrid Maria Johanna. Adalbert Stifter Str. 22, Freiburg. b. 26 May 1916 Freiburg. Dipl. Psych, PH.D, Univ. of Freiburg, Ger. DIRECTOR, Heilpädagogischen Beratungsstelle Stadtjugend-amt Freiburg; DOZENT in PSYCH, Deutscher Caritasverband Freiburg, Werthmannhaus, Freiburg. Member: BDP, Kath. Lehrerin-nenverein, Berufsverband Kath. Für-sorgerinnen. Clinical practice, teaching, research; diagnosis and therapy for problem children, social case and group work.　F

LOOFS-RASSOW, Mrs. Elisabeth. Alte Romerstr. 29, Wilhelmsfeld/Heidelberg. b. 18 July 1890 Witzenhausen, Werra. LECT. for SCI. GRAPHOLOGY, Psych. Inst, Univ. of Heidelberg, Hauptstr. 186, Heidelberg; GRAPHOLOGIST, priv. prac. Member: BDP. Applied psychology, teaching, research.　F

LORENZ, Dipl. Psych. Herbert. Arp Snitger Stieg 19a, Hamburg-Neuenfelde. b. 13 Apr 1923 Harta, Czech. Dipl. Psych. '52 Univ. of Freiburg, Ger. TEACHER, Schulbehörde Hamburg, Dammtorstr. 25, Hamburg 36. Teaching, research, educational psychology; child psychology, projective tests, grapho-logy.　M

LORENZ, Dipl. Psych. Hiltrud. Arp Snitger Stieg 19a, Hamburg-Neuenfelde. b. 1 June 1928 Ulm. Dipl. Psych. '52 Univ. of Frei-burg, Ger. Testing, research; graphology. F

LORSBÄCHER, Hans Werner. Opladen Im Kreuzbruch. b. 3 Nov 1923 Niederjosbach. INDUS. PSYCH'T, Farbenfabriken Bayer, Leverkusen. Industrial psychology, re-search, testing; industrial aptitude research, graphology, psychotherapy, psychology of thought.　M

LOSSEN, Dr. phil. Heinz. Dottendorferstr. 99, Bonn-Süd. b. 16 Dec 1913 Landau/Pfalz. PH.D '47 Univ. of Freiburg, Ger. REGIE-RUNGSRAT, Bundesministerium für Wirt-schaft, Lengsdorferstr, Bonn11; VOLUNTEER TCHR, Evangelische Akademie für Arbeiter-fragen, Bad Boll, Württemberg. Member: DGP. Testing, public relations, research, teaching; projective techniques, social psychology, industrial psychology.　M

LÖSSL, Dipl. Psych. Eberhard. Pfalzgraf Otto Str. 1, Mosbach/Baden. b. 6 Oct 1929 Hötensleben. Dipl. Psych. '55 Univ. of Heidelberg, Ger. ASSISTANT, Wirtschafts-hochschule, Mannheim Schloss, Mannheim; TCHR. in ADULT EVENING SCH, Abend-akademie, Mannheim; TEACHER, Abend-akademie, Volkshochschule, Ludwigshafen. Industrial psychology, teaching, student; attitude measurement, market analysis, diagnostics, social perception.　M

LUCASSEN, Mrs. Magdalene. Maschstr. 22, Braunschweig. b. W5 Apr 1909 Bückeburg. Dipl. Psych. '55 Tech. Hochschule Braun-schweig, Ger. SPEC. SCH. TCHR, Kielhorn-schule, Reichsstr. 22, Braunschweig; PSYCHOLOGIST, priv. prac; PSYCHOTHERA-PIST, Child Guid. Clin, Hannover. Teaching,

applied and educational psychology, con-sulting and guidance; special school problems, selection, guidance and treatment of children.　F

LUCIUS, Helmut. Schlierbergstr. 8b, Frei-burg. b. 27 Oct 1919 Nuremberg. MD, Univ. of Erlangen, Ger; Dipl. Psych, Univ. of Freiburg, Ger. PSYCHOTHERAPIST, priv. prac. Psychotherapy, clinical analysis; psychotherapy of neuroses and psychoses.M

LUCKE, Prof. Dr. phil. Victor. Kettwig Ruhr/Düsseldorf. b. 17 Mar 1894 Franken-berg/Eder. P.HD '26 Univ. of Marburg/L, Ger. PROFESSOR, Pädagogische Akademie, Brederbachstr. M, Kettwig. Member: DGP. Teaching, research; developmental psy-chology, characterology, typology.　M

LUCKER, Dr. phil. Elisabeth Maria. Peter-platz 8, Oberhausen/Rh. b. 18 Sept 1914 Friedenshütte. PH.D '44 Friedrich Wilhelms Univ. of Berlin. DOZENT in PSYCH, Päda-gogische Akademie, Schwermannstr, Essen-Kupferdreh. Member: BDP. Teaching, educational psychology, research; edu-cational problems, guidance, psychological sex differences.　F

LÜDERS, Dipl. Psych. Helmut. Amselweg 74, Tübingen/N. b. 25 Sept 1924 Doelitz, Krs. Pyritz. Dipl. Psych. '52 Univ. of Tübingen, Ger. STUDENT, Univ. of Tübingen. Industrial psychology, student; public relations, group process, communications, advertising.　M

LÜDERS, Dr. phil. Wolfram. Dernbergstr. 25c, Berlin-Charlottenburg. b. 23 Apr 1922 Drawehn. PH.D '56 Free Univ. of Berlin, Ger. PSYCHOLOGIST, Employment Off, Schlossstr. 1, Berlin-Charlottenburg. Member: BDP. Industrial psychology, testing; social motivation, methodology, marketing psychology.　M

LUKASCZYK, Dr. phil. Kurt F. R. Seinsheim-str. 12, Munich-Pasing. b. 30 Nov 1923 Dortmund-Hoerde. SCI. ASST, Psych. Inst. Univ. of Munich, Geschwister Scholl Platz 1, Munich 22. Member: DGP, BDP. Teaching, research, applied and industrial psychology; social psychological theory, group process, attitude and prejudice research.　M

LUNDBERG, Dipl. Psych. Harry. Beyerstr. 32, Göttingen. b. 17 Dec 1929 Riga Latvia. Dipl. Psych. '55 Univ. of Göttingen, Ger. PUBLICATIONS ASST, Verlag für Psych, Dr. C. J. Hogrefe, Brentanoweg 10, Göttingen. Editorial, research, student; forensic psychology, psychopathology, psycho-therapy.　M

LÜNEBERG, Dr. phil. Theodor. Strasse: Qu 7, 9, Mannheim. b. 31 Aug 1901 Eichendorf. PH.D '38 Univ. of Graz, Austria. PSYCHOLOGIST, Employment Off, M3a, Mannheim; EDITOR, *Archivs für Religionspsychologie*. Member: BDP. Applied and educational psychology, editorial, research; psychology of religion. M

LUNGWITZ, Dr. med. Dr. phil. Hans. Württembergallee 8, Berlin-Charlottenburg. b. 19 Oct 1881 Gössnitz Thüringen. PH.D '05; MD '07 Univ. of Halle, Ger. NEUROTHERAPIST, priv. prac. Member: Psychobiologischen Gesellschaft. Psychotherapy, applied psychology, research; problems of body and mind, neurosis, diagnostic therapy. M

LUTZE, Dr. Erich. Parkallee 103, Bremen. b. 8 Nov 1900 Göttingen. Dr. phil. nat. '31 Univ. of Frankfurt/M, Ger. CHIEF PSYCH'T, Employment Off, Bürenstr. 19, Bremen; TCHR. of APPL. PSYCH, Univ. of Göttingen. Member: BDP. Industrial psychology, testing, teaching; aptitude testing, vocational psychology, human relations in industry. M

LÜTZELER, Dipl. Psych. Joseph. Alfterstr. 16, Cologne-Zollstock. b. 11 Sept 1915 Cologne. Dr. phil. '49 Univ. of Bonn, Ger. PSYCHOLOGIST, Employment Off, Siegen. Member: BDP. Personnel psychology, testing. guidance; aptitude test, educational counseling, psychotherapy. M

LYSINSKI, Prof. Dr. phil. Edmund. Kleinschmidtstr. 44, Heidelberg. b. 4 Feb 1889 Kolmar/Posen. PH.D '11 Univ. of Leipzig, Ger. PROF. and DIR, Inst. for Econ. Psych. Wirtschaftshochschule, Mannheim. Member: BDP. Teaching, research; psychology of work, advertising and selling, psychophysics. M

MAGIN, Philipp. St. Nikolausheim, Dürrlauingen über Günzburg. b. 24 July 1920 Neu-Ulm-Donau. Dipl. Psych. '55 Univ. of Munich, Ger. PSYCHOLOGIST, Kath. Jugendfürsorgeverein, Schaezlerstr. 34, Augsburg. Clinical analysis, testing, applied and educational psychology, guidance; influences of heredity and environment, vocational guidance for the feebleminded. M

MAHRENHOLZ, Mrs. Lotte. Kaiser Wilhelmstr. 22, Hannover-Kirchrode. b. 7 June 1928 Bielefeld. Dipl. Psych. '52 Univ. of Göttingen, Ger. PSYCHOLOGIST, Employment Off, Clevertor 2, Hannover. Member: BDP. Personnel selection, aptitude testing, guidance. F

MAIER, Otto Heinrich. Hiltenspergerstr. 34/IV, Munich 13. b. 19 Apr 1925 Waldsee. Dipl. Psych. '53 Univ. of Tübingen, Ger. INDUS. PSYCH'T, Technischer Überwachungsverein Kaiserstr. 16, Munich 13. Member: BDP. Applied and industrial psychology, testing; characterology, projective techniques, traffic and industrial counseling. M

MALETZKE, Dr. phil. Gerhard. Sievekingsallee 92, Hamburg 26. b. 6 Jan 1922 Neustettin. Dr. phil. '50 Univ. of Hamburg, Ger. REFERENT, Hans Bredow Inst. für

Rundfunk und Fernsehen, Univ. of Hamburg, Rothenbaumchaussee 5, Hamburg; CHIEF ED, *Rundfunk und Fernsehen.* Member: BDP. Teaching, research, administration, editorial; social psychology, mass communications, public opinion, propaganda. M

MALETZKE, Mrs. Ursula. Sievekingsallee 92, Hamburg 26. b. 27 Apr 1928 Danzig. Dipl. Psych. '54 Univ. of Marburg, Ger. RES. ASST, Lintas, Burchardstr. 14, Hamburg. Member: BDP. Motivation research, advertising psychology; public opinion, projective techniques. F

MALL, Prof. Dr. med. Dr. phil. Gerhard. Nervenklinik Landeck über Landau. b. 23 Feb 1909 Codacal, India. Prof, Univ. of Tübingen, Ger. SUPERINTENDENT, Ment. Hosp, Landeck. Member: DGP, Deutsche Gesellschaft für Psychiatrie, Deutsche Gesellschaft für Endocrinologie. Clinical practice, psychotherapy, clinical analysis; instinct, emotion, psychogalvanic reflex. M

MARCH, Dr. med. Hans. Hohenzollerndamm 83, Berlin-Grünewald. b. 14 June 1895 Berlin-Charlottenburg. MD, Humboldt Univ. of Berlin, Ger. CHIEF PHYS, Neurological Div, Auguste Viktoria Hosp, Canovastr. 9, Berlin-Friedenau; TEACHER, German Psych. Inst, Berlin. Member: Deutsche Psychoanalytische Vereinigung, Deutsche Gesellschaft für Neur. und Psychiat. Clinial practice, psychotherapy, teaching; psychosomatic medine, clinical and applied psychology. M

MARSCHNER, Dr. Günter. Lindenaststr. 6, Nuremberg. b. 8 Aug 1923 Düsseldorf. Dr, '53 Univ. of Göttingen, Ger. INDUS. PSYCH'T, Grundig Radio-Werke Ltd, Kurgartenstr. 37, Fürth. Member: BDP. Industrial psychology, testing, guidance; aptitude tests, fatigue, human relations. M

MARTIN, Privat. Dozent Dr. Johann. Prinz Friedrich Leopold Str. 7, Berlin-Nikolassee. b. 11 June 1891 Braunschweig. Dr. phil. habil. '52 Free Univ. of Berlin, Ger. PRIV. DOZENT, Free Univ. of Berlin, Gelferstr, Berlin-Dahlem. Member: BDP. Teaching, research, educational psychology; psychology of impression formation. M

MARTINY, Dr. phil. Dozent Margarete. Sültenweg 53, Lüneburg. b. 18 Oct 1909 Lüneburg. PH.D '49 Univ. of Göttingen, Ger. DOZENT, Pädagogische Hochschule, Wilscheubrucherweg 84, Lüneburg. Teaching; school psychology. F

MARX, Dipl. Psych. Richard. Widenmayerstr. 26, Munich. b. 29 Dec 1924 Munich. Dipl. Psych. '50 Univ. of Munich, Ger. PSYCHOTHERAPIST, priv. prac; COURT PSYCH'T, Munich Probation Off. Member BDP. Psychotherapy, clinical practice testing, clinical analysis; projective testing child guidance, therapy for criminals. M

MATHEIS, Dr. phil. Hermann. Haupt Str. 30, Clausen/Pirmasens. b. 12 Aug 1924 Rodalben. PH.D '51 Univ. of Mainz, Ger. ASSISTANT, Neur. Inst, Univ. of Frankfurt, Gartenstr. 229, Frankfurt/M. Member: BDP. Research; neurology and psychology, physiological psychology, neuropathology, comparative psychology. M

MATHEY, Dr. phil. Dipl. Psych. Franz Josef. Psych. Inst, Univ. of Erlangen, Kollegienhaus, Erlangen. b. 16 Jan 1926 Euskirchen. PH.D '55 Univ. of Erlangen, Ger. PSYCH. CO-WRKR, Wissenschaftliche Arbeitsgemeinschaft für Jugendkunde. Member: DGP. Research, testing, teaching; longitudinal research, traffic psychology, graphology. M

MATZUTT, Dr. phil. Marianne. Mannsfelder Str. 59, Cologne-Raderberg. b. 9 Nov 1919 Erkelenz. PH.D '48 Univ. of Bonn, Ger. DIRECTOR, Cath. Child Guid. Clin, Archbishopry Cologne, Weissenburgstr. 14, Cologne. Member: BDP. Child guidance, psychotherapy, testing, teaching; achievement tests, social perception, group process. F

MAUSSHARDT, Dipl. Psych. Martin. Föhrstr. 21, Rentlingen/Württ. b. 18 Aug 1927 Württemberg. Dipl. Psych. '53 Albert Ludwigs Univ. of Freiburg, Ger. PSYCHOLOGIST, Landesverband der Inneren Mission in Württemberg, Reinsburgstr. 46, Stuttgart. Member: BDP. Testing, educational psychology, consulting; projective techniques, counseling, techniques and therapy, group studies. M

MAYER, Prof. Dr. Arthur. Nietzschestr. 32, Mannheim. b. 8 Dec 1911 Ottenbach. Prof. '54: Dr. phil. habil. '51 Univ. of Mannheim, Ger. PROF. of PSYCH, Wirtschaftshochschule, Schloss, Mannheim. Member: DGP, BDP. Teaching and research, industrial psychology, testing; social relations in industry, man in industrial society. M

MAYER, Dipl. Psych. Erich. Lohhof 5/III, Hamburg 26. b. 9 Sept. 1920 Coburg. Dipl. Psych. '53 Univ. of Erlangen, Ger. PERS. CHIEF, Frankfurter Versicherung, Mönckerbergstr. 5, Hamburg 1. Industrial psychology, testing; social perception, graphology, projective techniques. M

MAYER, Dr. phil. Klaus. Rossstr. 148, Düsseldorf. b. 6 Sept 1926 Düsseldorf. PH.D '56 Univ. of Bonn, Ger. SCI. ASST, Forschungsinst.f ür Arbeitspsychologie und Personalwesen, Friedrichstr. 9, Düsseldorf. Member: BDP. Clinical analysis, psychotherapy, applied psychology; projective techniques, pathogenesis and psychogenesis of psychoses, experimental methods. M

MAYR, Dr. phil. Georg. Sämannstr. 10,

Lockham/Munich. b. 21 Jan 1910 Bad Aibling. PH.D, Univ. of Munich, Ger. PSYCHOTHERAPIST, priv. prac. Member: Münchener Gesellschaft für Tiefenpsychologie und Lebenshilfe. Psychotherapy, research; synthesis between the theories of Freud and Jung. M

MEIMBERG, Mrs. Hildegard. Brommstr. 3, Frankfurt/M. b. 28 Feb 1914 Prüm/Eifel. Dipl. Psych. '45 Univ. of Marburg, Ger. PSYCHOLOGIST, Heilpädagogische Beratungsstelle, Braubachstr. 18-22, Frankfurt/M. Member: BDP. Child guidance, testing, psychotherapy; diagnosis, projective techniques, achievement tests, group therapy. F

MEINECKE, Dr. phil. Georg. Kieler Str. 148/I, Hamburg-Altona. b. 28 June 1911 Hannover. PH.D '38 Univ. of Bonn, Ger. SCI. OFF, Lehranstalt für Allgemeine und Sozialhygiene, Hyg. Inst, City of Hamburg, Gorch Fock Wall 15/17. Member: BDP, DGP, Studiengesellschaft für Psychologie. Teaching, research; social psychology, group pedagogy, psychology of productive thinking, group dynamics. M

MENTE, Dr. Arnold. Papendelle 9, Duisburg. b. 14 May 1914 Vechta/Oldenburg. PH.D '50 Univ. of Münster, Ger. STUDIENRAT, Landfermann Gymnasium, Mainstr, Duisburg. Teaching, psychotherapy, guidance; sentiments, striving, social contact. M

MENZ, Dr. med. Heinrich. Pfafferode 105, Muehlhausen/Thür. b. 10 Sept 1919 Kreuzburg O.S. MD '44 Univ. of Tübingen, Ger. CHIEF PHYS. and VICE DIR, Krankenanstalten Pfafferode, Muehlhausen. Member: BDP. Psychiatry and neurology, clinical practice, administration; psychotherapy, test psychology. M

MERTENS, Dipl. Psych. Annemarie. Laubenheimer Str. 4, Berlin-Wilmersdorf. b. 11 Feb 1929 Dombrowka, Poland. Dipl. Psych. '53 Free Univ. of Berlin, Ger. PSYCH, ASST, Radio Free Berlin. Member: BDP, AIPA. Applied psychology, characterology, intelligence testing, casework, child guidance clinics, group therapy. F

MERTENS, Dipl. Psych. Dieter. Laubenheimer Str. 4, Berlin-Wilmersdorf. b. 14 May 1922 Berlin. Dipl. Psych. '52 Free Univ. of Berlin, Ger. DIR. and EDUC. COUNS. OFF, Bezirksamt Berlin-Wilmersdorf, Fehrbelliner Platz 4, Berlin; DOZENT, Rahmen Westberliner Volkshochschulen; Pädagogischen Arbeitsstelle Berlin. Member: BDP, AIPA. Guidance, administration, educational psychology, testing; intelligence testing, characterology, child guidance clinics, individual and group therapy. M

MERTENS, Mrs. Elsbeth von. Worpsswede 6, Bremen. b. 27 June 1894 Coblenz/Rh. GRAPHOLOGIST, priv. prac. Member: BDP.

Handwriting analysis; graphology, characterology, depth psychology.   F

MERTENS, Senta Maria. Marktstr. 30, Rheydt. b. 15 Nov 1930 Würzburg. Dipl. Psych. '54 Univ. of Würzburg, Ger. TCHR. of PSYCH. and EDUC, Staatliche Handels und Gewerbeschule, Peltzerstr. 20-30, Rheydt. Teaching, educational psychology; child and adolescent psychology, social perception, projective techniques, graphology.   F

MERZ, Dr. Ferdinand K.R. Domerschulgasse 13, Würzburg. b. 16 May 1924 Chicago, USA. Dr. '51 Univ. of Würzburg, Ger. SCI. ASST, Univ. of Würzburg, Sanderring 2, Würzburg. Member: DGP. Teaching, research, testing; attitude measurement, motor activities, criminal investigation. M

MESCHEDE, Dipl. Psych. Ilse. Eversberg/Ruhr, Kreis Meschede. b. 20 Mar 1929 Düsseldorf. Dipl. Psych. '54 Univ. of Freiburg, Ger. STUDENT, Pädagogisches Akademie, Freiburg. Member: BDP. Educational psychology, testing, teaching; projective techniques, child guidance. F

METZGER, Prof. Dr. phil. Wolfgang. Habichtshöhe 26, Münster/Westf. b. 22 July 1899 Heidelberg. PH.D '26 Univ. of Berlin, Ger. PROF. of PSYCH, Univ. of Münster; DIRECTOR, Psych. Inst, Westfälische Wilhelms Universität, Schlossplatz, Münster; EDITOR, *Psychologia Universalis, Psychologische Forschung.* Member: DGP, APSLF. Teaching, research, editorial; perception, thought, criminology, developmental psychology.   M

MEUMANN, Dr. phil. Ingeborg. Parkallee 4, Hamburg 13. b. 29 May 1905 Oelle. PH.D '34 Univ. of Hamburg, Ger. PSYCHOLOGIST, Employment Off, Besenbinderhof 16, Hamburg. Member: BDP. Aptitude testing; intelligence tests, projective techniques, social behavior.   F

MEY, Hans Georg. Rombergstr. 30, Vechta/O. b. 12 Dec. 1924 Insterburg. Dipl. Psych. '51 Tech. Hochschule of Braunschweig, Ger. CRIM. PSYCH'T. and DEPT. DIR, Juvenile Court, Willostr, Vechta. Member: BDP. Testing, adolescent psychology, guidance; criminal psychology, projective techniques, social rehabilitation of juvenile delinquents.   M

MEYER, Dipl. Psych. Günter Georg. Alsterdorferstr. 189, Hamburg 39. b. 29 Nov 1921 Hamburg. Dipl. Psych. '54 Univ. of Hamburg, Ger. SCI. ASST, Psych. Inst, Univ. of Hamburg, Bornplatz 2, Hamburg. Member: BDP. Consulting, testing, guidance; projective techniques, child psychology, aptitude testing.   M

MEYER (née Hahn), Dipl. Psych. Mrs. Ursula. Rathenaustr. 12, Worms. b. 15 July 1923. Stuttgart. Dipl. Psych. '46 Univ. of Munich, Gr. Member: BDP. Child psy-

chology, psychopathology, criminal psychology.   F

MEYERHOFF, Dr. Horst. Ferd. Rhode Str. 16, Leipzig C 1. b. 13 Jan 1920 Naumburg/S Dr. rer. nat. '45 Univ. of Jena, Ger. SCI. ASST, Inst. für Gerichtl. Medizin und Kriminalistik, Univ. of Leipzig, Johannisallee 28, Leipzig. Member: BDP. Testing, professional writing, research, teaching; personality testing, criminal psychology, heredity.   M

MICHEL, Dipl. Psych. Lothar. Tonndorfer Hauptstr. 98, Hamburg-Wandsbek. b. 6 Oct 1929 Hamburg. Dipl. Psych. '55 Albert Ludwigs Univ. of Freiburg, Ger. DIRECTOR, Guid. Dept, Inst. für Psych. und Characterologie, Univ. of Freiburg, Bertoldstr. 17, Freiburg. Student, testing, handwriting analysis research; projective techniques.   M

MIERKE, Prof. Dr. phil. habil. Karl. Diesterwegstr. 24, Kiel. b. 4 Mar 1896 Zellerfeld. Prof. '53 Univ. of Kiel, Ger. PROF. and DIR, Inst. for Pedagogy and Psych, Univ. of Kiel, Ohlshausenstr, Kiel; DIRECTOR, Pädagogischen Hochschule, Diesterwegstr, Kiel. Member: BDP, DGP. Research, teaching; experimental, educational and social psychology.   M

MIESKES, Prof. Dr. Hans. Volkshochschule, Heselberg über Wassertrüdingen. b. 17 Feb 1915 Zeiden, Rumania. Dr. habil. '46 Univ. of Jena, Ger. PROF. and HEAD, Wissenschaftlichen Erziehungsberatung und Pädagogischen Therapie, Univ. of Jena, Grietgasse 17a, Jena. Member: DGP. Teaching, educational psychology, psychotherapy; psychology of problem children, social psychology.   M

MILLER, Anton. Piusheim, Post Glonn, Obb. b. 21 Aug 1930 Ulm/Do. Dipl. Psych. '55 Univ. of Tübingen, Ger. PSYCH'T. and EDUC. DIR, Piusheim. Member: BDP. Consulting, psychotherapy, testing; child play, group process, adoption.   M

MITSCHERLICH, Prof. Dr. med. Alexander. Dept. of Psychosomatic Med, Klinischen Universitätsanstalten, Vossstr. 2, Heidelberg. b. 20 Sept 1908 Munich. Prof. '52 Univ. of Heidelberg, Ger. DIRECTOR, Dept. of Psychosomatic Med, Klinische Universitäts-Anstalten Heidelberg; CO-EDITOR, *Psyche.* Member: Int. Psychoanal. Assn, Deutsche Gesellschaft für Psychother. und Tiefenpsych. Psychotherapy, research, teaching, editorial; psychoanalysis, theory of psychosomatic medicine, group process.   M

MITZE, Dr. phil. Wilhelm. Vörwärtsstr. 20, Dortmund. b. 20 Sept 1912 Möltenort/Kiel. PH.D '37 Univ. of Marburg, Ger. VERWALTUNGSRAT and PSYCH'T, Stadtverwaltung Dortmund,   Erziehungsberatungsstelle,

Landgrafenstr. 77, Dortmund. Member: BDP. Industrial psychology, child guidance, research; projective techniques, social perception, group process, attitude measurement. M

MOERING, Miss Gesina. Moevenstr. 7, Hamburg 39. b. 21 June 1924 Hamburg. Dipl. '56 Univ. of Bonn, Ger. MED. ASST, Univ. Hosp. „Eppendorf", Martinistr. 52, Hamburg 20. Clinical practice, research, student; anthropology and ethnology, social sciences, testing. F

MOERS, Dr. phil. Dorith. Argelanderstr. 22, Bonn. b. 21 July 1900 Langenberg/Rhld. Dipl. Psych. '48 Univ. of Bonn, Ger. PSYCH. CO-WRKR, Dr. Alfred Schröder, Kaiserplatz 16, Bonn. Testing, psychotherapy, clinical practice; achievement tests, social perception, attitude measurement. F

MOERS, Prof. Dr. phil. Martha. Godesberger Str. 25, Bonn. b. 25 July 1877 Düsseldorf. PH.D '18 Univ. of Bonn, Ger. PROF. of APPL. PSYCH, Univ. of Bonn. Member: DGP, BDP. Industrial and applied psychology, testing, clinical analysis, teaching; juvenile delinquency, vocational problems of women, research on brain injuries. F

MOERS-MESSMER, Dr. phil. Dr. med. Wolfgang von. Gaisbergstr. 35, Heidelberg. b. 7 Dec 1921 Heidelberg. Dipl. Psych.'51 Univ. of Heidelberg, Ger. TRAINEE in PSYCHIAT, Psychiatrisches Landes Krankenhaus, Wiesloch/Heidelberg. Member: BDP. Psychotherapy, clinical practice, research; perception, intelligence, feeling, typology, pathological psychology. M

MÖLLER, Günter. Spohrstr. 62, Frankfurt/M. b. 28 Jan 1928 Bochum-Langendreer. Dipl. Psych. '55 Free Univ. of Berlin, Ger. PSYCHOLOGIST, Int. Bund für Sozialarbeit, Jug. Sozialwerk, Untermainkai 27-28, Frankfurt/M. Educational and applied psychology, psychotherapy; education and psychotherapy for backward children and refugee adolescents. M

MOOSMANN, Harald. Karl Kuppingerstr. 33, Pfullingen. b. Oct 1925 Germany. Dipl. Psych. '55 Univ. of Tübingen, Ger. PRIMARY SCH. TCHR, Wolfgangschule, Pfullingen. Teaching, student, testing; educational and test psychology. M

MOSMANN, Dr. phil. Werner. Göbenstr. 13, Saarbrücken 1. b. 12 Jan 1928 Illingen. PH.D '55 Univ. of Saarbrücken, Saar. SCI. ASST, Psych. Inst, Univ. of the Saar, Saarbrücken 15. Member: DGP. Association Internationale des Educateurs des Jeunes Inadaptés. Research, teaching, testing; statistics, achievement tests, attitude measurement. M

MÜCHER, Dipl. Psych. Eri. Ubbelohdestr. 1, Marburg/L. b. 27 Apr 1927 Gelnhausen,

Hessen. Dipl. Psych. '50 Philipps Univ. of Marburg, Ger. PSYCHOLOGIST, priv. prac. Consulting, guidance, applied and educational psychology, psychotherapy; social group behavior of children, educational problems in the family, marriage problems. F

MÜCHER, Dipl. Psych. Hans. Ubbelohdestr. 1, Marburg/L. b. 5 May 1926 Nordrhein/Westf. Dipl. Psych. '50 Philipps Univ. of Marburg, Ger. SCI. ASST, Forschungsgemeinschaft für Arbeitsmedizin, Prof. Dr. Borgard, Wurzerstr. 17, Munich. Research, industrial psychology, teaching; experimental performance and motivation research, learning theory, psychological and physiological parallel processes. M

MUCHOW, Dr. phil. Brigitte. Oesterleystr. 13, Hannover. b. 1 May 1922 Schlawe/Pom. PH.D '48 Univ. of Freiburg, Ger. PSYCHOLOGIST, Psychotherapeutic Inst, Wiesenstrasse 24/25, Hannover. Member: BDP. Psychotherapy, clinical practice, clinical analysis, teaching; child psychology, projective techniques. F

MUELLER, Dr. med. Dieter. Treitschke Str. 18, Nuremberg. b. 4 Nov 1920 Würzburg. Dipl. Psych, Univ. of Würzburg, Ger. HEAD PHYS, City Women's Hosp, Flurstr. 7, Nuremberg. Clinical practice, psychotherapy, clinical analysis; sexual psychology, comparative developmental psychology. M

MÜHLE, Dr. phil. Günther Wolfgang. Wallstr. 16, Mainz. b. 9 Feb 1916 Ludwigshafen/Rh. Privatdozent '53 Univ. of Mainz, Ger. CHIEF ASST. and PRIVATDOZENT, Psych. Inst, Univ. of Mainz, Saarstr. 21. Member: DGP, Studiengesellschaft fur Praktische Psychologie. Teaching, research, educational psychology; developmental psychology, learning theory, psychology of art and expression, social psychology, cultural anthropology. M

MÜLLER, Mrs. Anna Luise. Hessenplatz 6, Frankfurt/M. b. 19 May 1931 Giessen. Dipl. Psych. '54 Univ. of Göttingen, Ger. ASST. PSYCH'T, Frankfurter/Allianz. Taunusanlage 20, Frankfurt/M. Member: BDP. Testing, industrial psychology, research; intelligence and achievement tests, projective techniques, learning theory, psychology of expression. F

MÜLLER, Dr. phil. Hans A. Dorenberg 4, Bad Salzdetfurth. b. 18 Nov 1913 Nienburg. PH.D '39 Univ. of Leipzig, Ger. Member: BDP. Educational psychology, guidance, teaching; depth psychology, communication. M

MÜLLER, Dipl. Psych. Horst. Hochstr. 12, H. M. Waldbröl/Rhld. b. 1 July 1926 Kohlfurt/Silesia. Dipl. Psych. '54 Univ. of Bonn, Ger. STUDENT, Univ. of Bonn; ASST.

PHYSICAL EDUC. ATHLETIC TCHR, Univ. of
Bonn. Guidance, research; group process,
social sciences, analytical psychotherapy. M
MÜLLER, Dr. Kurt. In der Witz 13, Mainz-
Kastel. b. 23 Aug 1921 Mainz. Dr. rer. nat.
'54 Univ. of Frankfurt, Ger. SCI. ASST,
Psych. Inst, Univ. of Frankfurt, Mertonstr.
17, Frankfurt/M. Research, teaching, ad-
ministration; perception, child psycholo-
gy.   M
MÜLLER, Dr. rer. nat. Richard G. E. Moor-
ende 16, Hamburg 26. b. 9 Aug 1910
Dortmund. Dipl. Psych. '51 Technische
Hochschule Braunschweig, Ger. LEADER,
Sonderschule Bülaustrasse, Bülaustr. 38,
Hamburg; FORENSIC PSYCH'T, Juv. Ct;
LECTURER, Tchr. Trng. Inst. Member:
BDP. Administration, testing, clinical
practice, guidance, teaching; child de-
velopment, maladjusted children and ado-
lescents, intelligence, learning.   M
MÜLLER, Dr. Rolf-Gerhard. Amalienstr. 12,
Braunschweig.   b. 19 Mar 1920 Berlin.
Dr. rer. nat. '50 Technische Hochschule
Braunschweig, Ger. PSYCH. CONSULT,
Hauptverband der gewerblichen Berufs-
genossenschaften, Reuterstr. 157-161, Boon;
DOZENT in PSYCH. and PEDAGOGY. Member:
DGP, BDP. Industrial psychology, testing,
administration; projective techniques,
forensic psychology, accident prevention. M
MÜLLER-BRAUNSCHWEIG, Dr. phil. Carl.
Sulzaer Str. 3, Berlin-Schmargendorf.
b. 8 Apr 1881 Braunschweig. PH.D '13
Univ. of Giessen, Ger. PRESIDENT, German
Psychoanal. Inst; LECTURER, Free Univ. of
Berlin. Member: BDP, German Psychoanal.
Assn, Int. Psychoanal. Assn, Deutsche
Gesellschaft für Psychotherapie und Tiefen-
psychologie.   Psychotherapy,   research,
teaching; psychoanalytic anthropology,
theory of neurosis, psychoanalytic tech-
niques, depth psychology.   M
MÜLLER-BRAUNSCHWEIG, Hans. Argen-
tinische Allee 10, Berlin-Zehlendorf. b. 6
July 1926 Berlin. Dipl. Psych. '54 Free
Univ. of Berlin, Ger. ASST. in EDUC. GUID,
Erziehungsberatung Charlottenburg, Nie-
buhrstr. 60, Berlin. Member; BDP. Testing,
guidance; projective techniques, psychodrama, psychotherapy.   M
MÜLLER-LUCKMANN, Dr. Elisabeth. Amalienstr. 12, Braunschweig. b. 16 Oct 1920
Braunschweig.   Privatdozent '55 Tech.
Hochschule Braunschweig, Ger. PRIVAT-
DOZENT for PSYCH, Tech. Hochschule
Braunschweig, Mühlenpfordtstr. 23, Braun-
schweig. Member: DGP, BDP. Teaching,
research, educational psychology; female
criminals, projective techniques, psychology
of culture.   F
MÜLLER-SUUR, Prof. Dr. med. Hemmo.
Rosdorfer Weg 70, Göttingen. b. 11 Nov

1911 Königsberg. MEDIZINALRAT and
CHIEF PHYS, Landeskrankenhaus und
Universitätsklinik für Psychische und
Nervenkrankheiten, Göttingen; CON-
SULTANT, Staatliches Gesundheitsamt, Göt-
tingen. Member: DGP, Deutsche Gesellschaft
für Psychiatrie und Nervenheilkunde.
Psychotherapy, consulting, clinical practice,
research; general and special psycho-
pathology, psychotherapy.   M
MÜNCH, Dipl. Psych. Hermann. Kaiserstr.
36, Munich 23. b. 14 Nov 1922 Fürth. Dipl.
Psych. '52 Univ. of Munich, Ger. GRA-
PHOLOGIST, priv. prac.   Member: BDP.
Research, applied psychology, consulting;
personality, achievement tests, criminal
psychology.   M
**MUNSCH, Regierungsrat a.D. Dr. phil.
Gerhard.** Kaiser Str. 16, Munich 23. b. 22
June 1911 Posen. PH.D '39 Univ. of Breslau,
Ger. DIRECTOR, Psych. Med. Res. Cen,
Technische Ueberwachungs Verein, Kaiser
Str. 14-16, Munich 23. Member: BDP.
Testing, industrial psychology, research;
aptitude investigation for industry, manage-
ment and traffic.   M
**MUTHIG, Dipl. Psych, Dr. rer. nat, Dipl. Ing.
Januarius.** Bismarckstr. 55, Krefeld.
b. 18 Sept 1889 Burgsinn, Unterfranken.
Dipl. Psych. '56 Univ. of Bonn, Ger.
CHIEF ENGR, Rhein. Westfäl. Eltwerk,
Rellinghause Str, Essen; CO-WRKR, VDE
Vorschriften.   Member: BDP, Arbeits-
gemeinschaft für Soziale Betriebsgestaltung.
Industrial psychology, testing, accident
prevention; psychology of work, intelligence
tests, projective techniques, Gestalt and
animal psychology.   M
NACHTWEIJ, Dr. phil. Hermann Josef. Am
Brambusch 12, Düsseldorf-Lohansen. b. 5
Feb 1911 Dortmund. PH.D '36 Univ. of
Münster, Ger. MINISTERIALRAT, Ministry
of Interior, Elisabethstr. 6-10, Düsseldorf.
Member: BDP. Teaching, testing, adminis-
tration; social perception.   M
NAEGELSBACH, Dr. phil. Hans. Heckerdamm 8b, Berlin-Plötzensee. b. 6 Mar 1903
Schömberg, Württ. PH.D '27 Univ. of
Munich, Ger. DIRECTOR, Jugendstraf-
anstalt Plötzensee, Heckerdamm 7, Berlin-
Charlottenburg. Member: BDP. Applied
psychology; vocational and criminal psychology.   M
NAFFIN, Dr. phil. Paul Bernhard. Bischof
Str. 6, Homberg, Bez. Kassel, b. 26 Sept
1899 Kleingartz. PH.D '35 Univ. of Königsberg, Ger. DIRECTOR, State Inst. for the
Deaf and Mute. Educational psychology,
testing, teaching, audiometry; achievement
tests, social perception, group process. M
NASS, Gustav. Klinikstr. 7, Kassel-Ha.
b. 1 July 1901 Stargard. Dr. phil. '32 Univ.
of Bonn, Ger. CRIM. PSYCH'T, Hessisches

Justizministerium Wiesbaden; LECTURER, Musikadademie Kassel. Member: BDP. Testing, research, teaching; criminal psychology, pedagogy, social psychology, psychology of culture. M

NEULANDT, Rolf Günter. Jugendstrafanstalt, Rockenberg/Oberhessen. b. 4 May 1927 Gotha/Thür. Dipl. Psych. '53 Univ. of Marburg, Ger. PSYCHOLOGIST, Jugendstrafanstalt Rockenberg. Member: BDP. Applied psychology, guidance, testing; causes of adolescent criminal behavior, group process, social value, projective techniques. M

NEUMANN-KERN, Dr. med. Dipl. Psych. Viktoria. Lichtentalerstr. 6, Baden. b. 11 Mar 1915 Frankfurt/M. MD '44 Univ. of Jena, Ger. PHYS. and PSYCH'T, priv. prac; DIRECTOR, Erziehungsberatungsstelle, Stefanien Str. 6, Baden. Member: BDP, Ärztliche Gesellschaft für Psychother. Psychotherapy, clinical practice, testing; projective techniques, developmental psychology. F

NIEDERHOFFER, Dr. rer. nat. Egon von. Diefenbachstr. 8, Munich-Solln. b. 11 Aug 1904 Bad Reichenhall. Dr. rer. nat. '40 Friedr. Schiller Univ. of Jena, Ger. CO-WORKER, Inst. für Menschenkunde, Josephinenstr. 25, Munich-Solln. Member: BDP. Applied psychology, research, professional writing; projective techniques, graphology. M

NITZSCHE, Manfred. Psych. Inst. Univ. of Saarbrücken, Saarbrücken. b. 4 June 1920 Falkenberg. Dipl. Psych, Univ. of Berlin, Ger. SCI. WRKR, Psych. Inst, Univ. of Saarbrücken. Research, testing, clinical practice, guidance, student; sociometry, structure of the family, projective techniques, children's drawings. M

NOLTE, Dozent Dr. phil. Erwin. Moelling Str. 28, Kiel. b. 11 Aug 1912 Hannover. PH.D '32 Univ. of Göttingen, Ger. DOZENT for PSYCH, Pädagogische Hochschule, Kelm Str. 14, Flensburg-Muer Wik; PSYCHOLOGIST, Staatsanwaltschaft. Member: DGP. Teaching, research, guidance, professional writing; school selection tests, activity measurement, pharmacological and psychological research. M

NOLTE, Dr. phil. Wilhelm Friedrich. Rehmstr. 1/B, Osnabrück. b. 28 Apr 1911 Leipzig. PH.D '38 Univ. of Leipzig, Ger. PSYCHOLOGIST, Bundesanstalt für Arbeitsvermittlung und Arbeitslosenversicherung, Employment Off, Osnabrück. Member: BDP. Applied and industrial psychology; communications; aptitude measurement, educational an child psychology. M

NUTZHORN, Dr. Horst. Ootmarsumer Weg 47, Nordhorn. b. 8 May 1921 Rüstringen. Dr. rer. nat, Technische Hochschule

Braunschweig, Ger. INDUS. PSYCH'T, Niehues and Dütting, Nordhorn-Nino-Werke, Nordhorn. Member: BDP, Studiengesellschaft für Praktische Psychologie. Industrial psychology, testing, research; left-handedness, human relations. M

OBERHOFF, Dr. phil. Eugen. Obermain-Anlage 20, Frankfurt/M. b. 7 Mar 1902 Wuppertal-B. PH.D '28 Univ. of Cologne, Ger. SYNDIC, Gesamtverband d. Deutschen Textilindustrie, Schaumainkai 87, Frankfurt/M. Member: BDP. Industrial psychology, research, testing, time and motion studies; human relations in industry. M

OBST, Dipl. Psych. Günter Helmut. Günthersbuhlerstr. 55, Nuremberg-Erlenstegen. b. 2 June 1928 Berlin. Dipl Psych. '52 Univ. of Göttingen, Ger. INDUS. PSYCH'T, Siemens Schuckert Werke AG, Werner v. Siemens Str. 50, Erlangen. Industrial psychology, testing, teaching; vocational testing, group dynamics, selection and instruction of personnel. M

OBST, Prof. Dr. phil. Josef Amandus. Seminarstr. 26, Alfeld/Leine 20a. b. 7 July 1906 Trebisch/Warthe, Grenzmark. PH.D '36 Univ. of Rostock, Ger. PROF. of PSYCH, Pädagogische Hochschule Alfeld/Leine, Seminarstr. 27, Alfeld. Member: BDP. Teaching, educational psychology, research; learning, thinking, psychohygiene, character judgement, role of suggestion and the unconscious. M

OEHMICHEN, Werner. Jaguarstieg 26, Hamburg-Stellingen. b. 16 Apr. 1916 Hamburg. Tech. Hochschule Braunschweig, Ger. GRAPHOLOGIST, priv. prac. Member: BDP. Industrial psychology; characterology, depth psychology, expression. M

OHDE, Hans-Jürgen. Griesstr. 97, Hamburg 26. b. 1 Jan 1927 Hamburg. Dipl. Psych. '52 Univ. of Hamburg, Ger. DIR. of MARKET RES, Brinkmann Ltd, Dötlingerstr. 4, Bremen. Member: BDP. Market research, industrial and applied psychology; projective techniques, depth interviews, motivation research. M

OSTWALD (née Goeschel), Dr. Marianne. Braamkamp 24, Hamburg 39. b. 5 July 1908 Vecauce, Latvia. Dr. '43 Univ. of Hamburg, Ger. PSYCH. CONSULT, priv. prac. Member: BDP. Guidance, counseling, testing; testing methods, progressive techniques, structural testing, genetic theory of sex. F

PATZKE, Kurt Lothar. 1397 S. 3rd St, Louisville, Kentucky, USA. b. 30 Oct 1928 Danzig. Dipl Psych. '55 Univ. of Tübingen, Ger. RES. PSYCH'T, Enro Shirt Co, 1010 S. Preston, Louisville, Ky. Industrial psychology, market research, psychotherapy; change of frame of reference, production, group process, speech correction, play therapy. M

PAULUS, Studienrat Dr. phil. Stefan. Peter Lippert Str. 8, Amberg/Oberpf. b. 18 June 1913 Tauberrettersheim. PH.D '41 Univ. of Würzburg, Ger. STUDIENRAT, Inst. für Lehrerbildung, Kaiser Wilhelm Ring 7, Amberg/Oberpf. Teaching, educational psychology, testing; learning theory, psychology of personality.   M

PELZING, Mrs. Elfriede Rosemarie. Waldhörnlestr. 26, Tübingen-Derendingen. b. 25 Oct 1923 Dinkelsbühl. Dipl Psych. '52 Univ. of Tübingen, Ger. PSYCHOLOGIST, Educ. Advis. Bd, Regional Youth off, Württemberg. Member: BDP. Testing, educational guidance, consulting; diagnosis, projective techniques, social perception.   F

PERGANDE, Armin. Gutenberstr. 18, Marburg/L. b. 7 Nov 1925 Berlin. Dipl. Psych. '55 Univ. of the Saar, Ger. PSYCH. ASST. Heilpädagogisches Kinderheim Martinsberg, Naila im Frankenwald. Member: BDP. Testing, psychotherapy, consulting; projective techniques, achievement tests, cultural determinants in personality.   M

PETERS, Prof. Dr. phil. Wilhelm. Leistenstr. 27, Würzburg. b. 11 Nov 1880 Vienna, Austria. PH.D '40 Univ. of Leipzig, Ger. PROF. and DIR. EMER, Inst. of Psych, Univ. of Jena; PROF. EMER. of EXPER. and EDUC. PSYCH, Univ. of Istanbul, Turkey. Member: BPS, Gesellschaft für Arbeitswissenschaftliche Forschung. Research, professional writing, retired; perception, heredity, mental growth, personality.   M

PETRILOWITSCH, Dr. med. Dr. phil. Nikolaus. Univ. Nerve Clin, Mainz/Rh. b. b. 30 Oct 1924 Heideschütz, Yugoslavia. MD. PH.D '50 Univ. of Frankfurt, Ger. SCI. ASST, Univ. Nerve Clin, Mainz. Member: Ger. Psychiat. Socy. Clinical practice, research, psychotherapy; clinical psychology, theoretical psychology.   M

PETRY, Hans Joachim. Hauptstr. 24, Heidelberg/Neckar. b. 15 Mar 1928 Wiesbaden. Dipl. Psych. '55 Univ. of Mainz, Ger. MED. STUD. Univ. of Heidelberg. Clinical psychology.   M

PFAFFENBERGER, Hans G. Rheinvillenstr. 11, Mannheim. b. 27 May 1922 Nuremberg. Dipl. Psych. '48 Univ. of Münster, Ger. ASST. DIR, Seminar für Sozialberufe, Lindenhofplatz 7, Mannheim. Member: BDP, APA. Teaching, administration. research; child development, personality, group dynamics.   M

PFAHLER, Prof. Dr. Gerhard. Christofstr. 2, Tübingen. b. 8 Dec 1897 Freudenstadt. PROF. EMER, Psych. Inst, Eberhard-Karls-Univ. Tübingen. Member: DGP. Psychotherapy, teaching, research; depth psychology, inherited character, genetic psychology.   M

PFEFFERKORN, Friedrichkarl. Melanch-

thonstr. 16, Tübingen. b. 9 Sept 1914 Württemberg. GRAPHOLOGIST and INDUS. ADVIS, priv. prac. Member: BDP. Applied and industrial psychology, consulting; psychological expression, personatity, social and national psychology.   M

PFISTNER, Dipl. Psych. Hans Jürgen. Plöck 35, Heidelberg. b. 25 Aug 1930 Rastatt. Dipl. Psych. '55 Univ. of Heidelberg, Ger. GRAD. STUD, Univ. of Heidelberg. Research, educational psychology, testing; projective techniques, learning theory, attitude measurement.   M

PFITZER, Dipl. Psych. Rosemarie. Fichtestr. 24, Stuttgart W. b. 16 July 1929 Stuttgart. Dipl. Psych. '54 Univ. of Freiburg, Ger. Testing, child guidance, graphology; projective techniques, psychotherapy, graphotherapy, parent guidance.   F

PFLANZ, Dr. Manfred. Medizinische Poliklinik, Frankfurter Str. 63, Giesen/Lahn. b. 23 Sept 1923 Berlin. MD '48 Univ. of Munich, Ger. SCI. ASST, Medizinische Poliklinik. Member: Deutsche Vereinigung für Jugendpsychiat. Research, clinical analysis, psychotherapy; pharmacological psychology, suggestion, psychosocial medicine.   M

PFORTNER, Dr. Gerhard. Meuschel 69/I, Nuremberg. b. 7 May 1910 Merseburg. Dr. rer. nat. '40 Univ. of Jena, Ger. Member: BDP. Consulting, industrial psychology, professional writing; psychology of the handicapped.   M

PHILIP, Dr. phil. Franz Heinrich. Heinrich Heine Str. 9, Marburg/L. 16. b. 25 Nov 1887 Königsberg. Member: BDP. Retired; psychology of thought, character, typology.   M

PICHOTTKA, Dr. phil. Ilse. Rambergstr. 8. Munich 13. b. 4 May 1909 Berlin. PH.D '46 Ludwig Maximilian Univ. of Munich, Ger. HEAD, Child Guid. Clin, Stern Inst; LECTURER, Univ. of Munich. Member: BDP. Guidance, testing, teaching, research; psychology of human development, projective techniques, child psychology.   F

PIEPER, Heinz. Schüttorf/Bentheim. b. 15 Jan 1923 Schüttorf. Dipl. '55 Univ. of Göttingen, Ger. GRAD. STUD, Psych. Inst, Hoher Weg 15, Göttingen. Teaching, educational psychology, consulting and guidance; projective techniques, learning theory, attitude measurement.   M

PIETROWICZ, Dipl. Psych. Bernhard. Auf dem Draun 92, Münster/Westf. b. 20 Jan 1923 Hildesheim/Han. Dipl. Psych. '48 Univ. of Braunschweig, Ger. DOZENT, Soziales Seminar, Domplatz, Münster; EDITOR, *Erbe und Entscheidung*; VOCAT. and CHILD GUID. CONSULT, priv. prac. Member: BDP, AIPA, Studiengesellschaft für Praktische Psychologie. Educational psychology, teaching, editorial, psychotherapy;

occupational therapy, diagnosis of retarded children. M

PIRKL, Dr. phil. Friedrich Johannes. Herbartstr. 49, Nuremberg. b. 13 Aug 1925 Sulzbach. PH.D '52 Univ. of Erlangen, Ger. HEAD PSYCH'T Employment Off. for Northern Bavaria, Karl Brögerstr. 9, Nuremberg. Teaching, industrial psychology, administration; personality, factor analysis. M

PLÄTZER, Dr. phil. Oskar. Unter den Ulmen 49, Gütersloh. b. 3 Mar 1910 Leipzig. PH.D '43 Univ. of Leipzig, Ger. LANDESVERWALTUNGSRAT, Westfälische Klinik für Jugendpsychiat, Hermann Simon Str. 7, Gütersloh. Member: BDP. Clinical analysis and practice, educational psychology, psychotherapy; group therapy, child development, brain injured children, social perception. M

PLERSCH, Charlotte Josefa. Imhofstr. 57, Augsburg. b. 3 Sept 1921 Illertissen/Schw. Dipl. '52 Univ. of Munich, Ger. PSYCHOLOGIST, Child Guid. Clin, Psych. Consult. Center, Metzgplatz 1, Augsburg. Applied and educational psychology, testing, clinical analysis, psychotherapy; projective techniques, psychology of expression, graphology. F

POERTNER, Dr. phil. Dipl. Psych. Rudolf. Ferdinand Koch Str. 16, Landau/Pfalz. b. 23 Mar 1913 Berlin. PH.D '40 Univ. of Bonn, Ger. DOZENT, Pädagogische Akademie, Nordring 4, Landau/Pfalz. Member: BDP. Teaching, educational psychology, psychotherapy, testing; psychology of human development, forensic psychology, psychopathology, social research. M

POPP, Dipl. Psych. Irene Louise. Innere Wienerstr. 4/VI, Munich. 8. b. 4 Dec 1925 Bamberg. Dipl. Psych. '55 Univ. of Munich Ger. HEAD, Psychologische Beratungsstelle am Gasteig, Munich. Member: BDP. Educational counseling, consulting, psychotherapy; projective techniques. F

POSCHLOD, Dr. phil. Dipl Psych. Manfred. Spielfeldstr. 4, Haunstetton bei Augsburg. b. 17 Jan 1929 Gleiwitz. PH.D '55 Univ. of Munich, Ger. INDUS. PSYCH'T, Farbwerke Hoechst AG, Adolf von Baeyerstr, Gersthofen bei Augsburg. Member: BDP. Personnel psychology, testing, administration; aptitude tests, social perception, attitude measurements, projective techniques. M

POSENENSKE, Miss Rosemarie. Bahnstr. 27, Schneidhain über Königstein. b. 13 Oct 1930 Breslau. Dipl. Psych. '56 Philipps Univ. of Marburg/L, Ger. SCI. ASST, Hochschule für Int. Pädagogische Forschung, Schlosstr. 29, Frankfurt/M. Psychological statistics, testing, guidance; child guidance, non-directive play therapy. F

POTEMPA, Prof. Dr. phil. Dipl. Psych. Father Rudolf, O.F.M. Nr. 430 Dettelbach/M. b. 30 Sept 1910 Zalenze Kr. Kattowitz.

PROF. of PSYCH. of RELIG. and PERSONALITY, Univ. of Würzburg. Member: DGP, BDP, Studiengesellschaft für Praktische Psych. Teaching, research, guidance; metaphysical psychology. M

POTT, Friedrich. Kölnerstr. 20a, Opladen/ Cologne. b. 25 May 1931 Opladen. Dipl. Psych, Univ. of Erlangen, Ger. Student; psychotherapy, educational psychology, problems of social perception. M

POTT, Dr. phil. Heinz Herbert. Grenzweg 87, Herne/Westf. b. 2 Apr 1915 Herne/Westf. PH.D '48 Univ. of Münster, Ger. SCH. PRINCIPAL, Evangelische Volksschule III, Städtische Erziehungsberatungsstelle, Mörikestr. 1, Herne/Westf. Guidance, testing, educational psychology; diagnostical psychology. M

PREISS, Dipl. Psych. Helmut. Kahlaische Str. 27, Jena. b. 1 May 1920 Leipzig. Dipl. Psych. '51 Univ. of Leipzig, Ger. CHIEF ASST. and INSTR, Friedrich Schiller Univ, Inst. of Pedagogy, Jena. Member: BDP. Teaching, research; psychology of examinations, sex education. M

PREUSCHHOF, Eckhard. Drennhausen über Winsen/Luhe. b. 12 Dec 1930 Königsberg. Dipl. Psych. '54 Univ. of Hamburg, Ger. TEACHER, Primary Sch. Marxen über Winsen/Luhe. Member: BDP. Teaching, educational psychology, testing; educational guidance, social pedagogy. M

PRIESTER, Dipl. Psych. Hans Joachim, Hummelsbuetteler, Kirchenweg 51, Hamburg. b. 4 Oct 1924 Leipzig. Dipl. Psych. '54 Univ. of Hamburg, Ger. SCI. ASST, Psych. Inst, Univ. of Hamburg, Bornplatz 2, Hamburg 13. Teaching, testing, guidance; psychometrics, psychological testing Rorschach. M

PROKOP, Karl Ludwig. Am Weissen Stein 18, Göttingen. b. 11 Jan 1927 Krumau, Czech. Dr. phil. '55 Univ. of Graz, Austria. INSTRUCTOR, Max Planck Gymnasium, Theaterplatz, Göttingen. Teaching, research, student; psychology of speech, muteness. M

PTASNIK, Mrs. Irene Ingeborg. Grünstr. 29 Bielefeld. b. 6 Apr 1926 Danzig. Dipl. '52 Univ. of Frankfurt/M, Ger. TEAM MEMBER, Child Guid. Clin, Erziehungsberatung, Koblenzerstr. 7, Bielefeld. Psychological testing, psychotherapy, guidance; projective techniques, psychoanalysis, achievement tests. F

PUFAHL, Ursula. Kussmaulstr. 3, Mannheim. b. 7 Jan 1915 Danzig. Dipl. Psych. '51 Univ. of Heidelberg, Ger. DIR. of EDUC. GUID, Beratung für Familie und Erziehung Innere Mission, Trailbeurstr. 48, Mannheim; OFFICER, Juv. Ct. Member: BDP. Guidance, testing, teaching; anthropological psychology, psychotherapy. F

QUAISSER, Wolfgang. Schillerstr. 31, Göttingen. b. 8 Apr 1927 Reichenberg, Czech. Dipl. Psych. '53 Univ. of Göttingen, Ger. GRAD. STUD, Psych. Inst, Univ. of Göttingen. Member: BDP. Testing, clinical practice; clinical psychology, projective techniques, psychological treatment methods. M

QUEDNAU, Dr. Horst Wilhelm Rudolf. 39 Sharia Muhamed Mazhar Pasha, Zamalek, Cairo, Egypt. b. 23 Oct 1914 Tilsit, Ger. Dr. Ing. '40 Technische Hochschule Berlin, Ger. VOCAT. TRNG. EXPERT, United Nations Tech. Assistance Prog, Productivity and Vocat. Trng. Cen, Nozha/Abou-Bakr El-Siddik St, Heliopolis, Cairo, Egypt. Member: BDP. Industrial psychology, testing; technical education, vocational aptitude testing, industrial sociology. M

QUINT, Dr. med. Dr. phil. Hans. Niedersächsische Landeskrankenhaus, Göttingen- Tiefenbrunn. b. 9 May 1922 Essen. MD '51, PH.D '52 Univ. of Bonn, Ger. DOCTOR'S ASST, Niedersächsische Landeskrankenhaus. Member: BDP, Deutsche Gesellschaft für Psychother. Psychotherapy, clinical analysis, consulting; the neurotic personality. M

RABITZ, Dr. Miss Johanna. Landeskrankenhaus, Königslutter/Braunschweig. b. 1 Mar 1924 Sondershausen/Thür. Dr. '54 Univ. of Göttingen, Ger. PSYCHOLOGIST, Psychiat. Clin, Landeskrankenhaus. Clinical analysis, consulting; projective techniques, intelligence tests, attitude measurement. F

RADBRUCH, Mrs. Maria Luise. Eidhampsweg 62, Hamburg-Fuhlsbüttel. b. 14 Apr 1915 Ditmarschen/Albersdorf. Dipl. Psych. '50 Univ. of Hamburg, Ger. Educational psychology, testing; educational matters, juvenile court. F

RADESPIEL, Mrs. Hella Mathilde. Schottmüllerstr. 30/III, Hamburg 20. b. 27 Jan 1920 Flensburg. Dipl. Psych. '51 Univ. of Göttingen, Ger. SCI. CLERK, Prüfungsamt für den Öffentlichen Dienst, Steckelhörn 12, Hamburg. Member: BDP. Aptitude research, consulting, testing; social attitudes, projective techniques, performance tests. F

RAETHER-GOETZE, Mrs. Lore Melitta. Luisenstr. 32, Bad Godesberg. b. 13 Sept 1927 Landesberg/Warthe. Dipl. Psych. '54 Univ. of Bonn, Ger. PSYCHOLOGIST, Wissenschaftliche Arbeitsgemeinschaft für Jugendkunde Arbeitsstelle, Gesundheitsamt, Engeltalstr, Bonn. Member: BDP. Research, testing, guidance; child and developmental psychology, Gestalt psychology, drawing tests. F

RAHMEL, Rosemarie. Voltastr. 34, Nuremberg. b. 22 Jan 1930 Berlin. Dipl. Psych. '54 Univ. of Würzburg, Ger. INDUS. PSYCH'T, Firma Henkel Ltd, Henkelstr. 67,

Düsseldorf-Holthausen. Member: BDP. Industrial psychology, testing, psychological statistics; aptitude testing. F

RAHN, Dr. phil. Gottfried. Kanonenwall 1/II, Hannover. b. 12 Apr 1909 Costewitz. PH.D '34 Univ. of Leipzig, Ger. DOZENT, for Sch. Pedagogy, Pädagogische Hochschule, Bismarckstr. 35, Hannover; DIRECTOR, Zentralstelle des Forschungskreises für die Sprechspur. Member: BDP. Teaching, research, editorial; psychology of writing, developmental psychology. M

RANKE, Prof. Dr. Otto F. Physiologisches Inst, Universitätsstr. 17, Erlangen. b. 17 Aug 1899 Munich/Thalkirchen. Prof. '47 Univ. of Erlangen, Ger. PROF. and DIR, Physiologisches Inst; CO-EDITOR, Internationalen Zeitschrift für Angewandte Physiologie, Einschliesslich Arbeitsphysiologie. Teaching, research, editorial. M

RASCH, Dipl. Psych. Wolf Dietrich. Tivolistr. 26, Freiburg. b. 25 Sept 1923 Bremen. Dipl. Psych. '52 Univ. of Freiburg, Ger. DIRECTOR, Guid. Dept, Inst. für Psych. und Characterologie, Univ. of Freiburg, Bertoldstr. 17, Freiburg. Industrial psychology, research, teaching; parapsychology, the possibilities and limitations of graphology, verification of psychodiagnostic findings. M

RASSMANN, Dipl. Psych. Walter. Feuerbachstr. 2, Braunschweig. b. 29 Dec 1907 Stralsund. Dipl. Psych. '55 Univ. of Braunschweig, Ger. OBERSTUDIENRAT and DIR, Braunschweig Kolleg. Teaching, educational and forensic psychology, administration; psychological selection for high school aptitude, juvenile court testimony. M

RAUCH, Dr. phil. Bernhard. Kaulbachstr. 32, Nuremberg. b. 1 Mar 1926 Nuremberg. PH.D '49 Univ. of Bonn, Ger. PSYCHOLOGIST, Bayerische Jugendhilfe, Blumenthalstr. 5/I, Nuremberg. Member: BDP. Psychotherapy, consulting, educational psychology; educational and developmental disturbances, psychosomatic problems, traffic psychology. M

RAUSCH, Prof. Dr. Dr. Edwin. Melsunger Str. 14, Frankfurt/M. b. 1 Feb 1906 Baumholder. Dr. habil. '41 Univ. of Frankfurt/M, Ger. PROF. of PSYCH. and DIR, Psych. Inst, Univ. of Frankfurt, Merton Str. 17, Frankfurt/M. Member: DGP, BDP, APSLF. Teaching, research, administration; perception, thinking, categorical analysis. M

RECHE (née Ackermann), Mrs. Hildegard. Lessingplatz 3, Wolfenbüttel. b. 5 Oct 1923 Wolfenbüttel. Dipl. Psych. '48 Technische Hochschule Braunschweig, Ger. TEACHER, Hilfschule Jasperstr. 11, Wolfenbüttel. Member: BDP. Teaching, educational psychology, testing; personality development. F

REESE, Ilsabe. Kinderheim, Güldene Sonne, Rehburg/Stadt, Kr. Nienburg. b. 22 Apr 1926 Celle. Dipl. Psych. '55 Univ. of Göttingen, Ger. CLIN. PSYCH'T, Evan. Luth. Wichemstift, Adelheide bei Delmenhorst. Member: BDP. Educational psychology, clinical analysis, consulting, psychotherapy; non-directive therapy, developmental psychology, group structures. F

REHM, Dipl. Psych. Rolf. Berglehrlingsheim Westende, Schlachtenstr. 1, Duisburg-Meiderich. b. 21 Dec 1923 Rastatt/Baden. Dipl. Psych. '50 Univ. of Freiburg, Ger. SOC. PSYCH'T, Berglehrlingsheim Westende. Member: BDP. Educational psychology, testing, administration; educational guidance, adolescent and child psychology. M

REICHARDT, Dr. rer. nat. Karl-Wilhelm. Gustav Tweer Str. 29, Osnabrück. b. 22 Sept 1913 Jlmenau/Thür. Dr. rer. nat. '40 Univ. of Jena, Ger. Teaching, applied psychology; school psychology, character, social psychology. M

REINEKE, Dr. rer. nat. Helmuth Heinrich Friedrich. Postschliessfach 1090, Stuttgart 1. b. 13 Feb 1914 Hamersleben. Dr. rer. nat. '42 Univ. of Göttingen, Ger. CONSULT. PSYCH'T, priv. prac. Member: BDP. Educational and industrial psychology, graphology, testing; diagnosis of talent, psychology of marriage. M

REINERT, Gunther R. M. Schusterstr. 27, Freiburg. b. 2 Jan 1928 Saarbrücken. Dipl. Psych. '55 Univ. of Freiburg, Ger. RES. FELLOW, Psych. Inst, Univ. of Freiburg, Bertoldstr, Freiburg. Research, testing, psychotherapy; projective techniques, child psychotherapy, school psychology. M

REINHARD, Dipl. Psych. Walter. Allacherstr. 254, Munich-Allach. b. 24 Feb 1925 Kaufbeuren/Allgäu. Dipl. Psych. '54 Univ. of Munich, Ger. TCHR. and SCH. PSYCH'T, State of Bavaria, Maximilianstr. 14, Munich. Teaching, guidance, applied and educational psychology; diagnostics of graphic expression, writing difficulties. M

REITBERGER, Dipl. Psych. Georg. Bernsteinweg 21, Munich 45. b. 1 June 1920 Schöllnach/Ndb. Dipl. Psych. '54 Univ. of Munich, Ger. CLIN. PSYCH'T, Amorc, Promenadeplatz 13/III, München. Member: BDP. Guidance, administration; parapsychology, mental hygiene, group therapy. M

REMPLEIN, Dr. Heinz. Liebigstr. 12/III, Munich 22. b. 23 July 1914 Munich. Dr. '40 Univ. of Munich, Ger. TEACHER, Berufspädagogisches Inst, Lothstr. 17, Munich. Professional writing, teaching, educational psychology; psychology of character, human development, projective techniques.

RENTHE-FINK, Dr. phil. Leonhard von. Kommando der Grenzschutz-Schulen, Luebeck-St. Hubertus. b. 21 Mar 1907 Berlin. PH.D '33 Univ. of Bonn, Ger. REGIERUNGSRAT, Kommando der Grenzschutz-Schulen. Member: BDP. Applied and educational psychology, teaching, research; army personnel selection, psychology of religion, graphology. M

RESAG, Prof. Dr. phil. Kurt. Wilhelmstr. 9, Weilburg/L. 16. b. 16 Jan 1896 Kirchheim-Teck. PH.D '41 Univ. of Tübingen, Ger. PROF. of EDUC, Pedagogical Inst, Frankfurterstr. 40, Weilburg. Member: DGP. Teaching, educational psychology; learning theory. M

RETZ, Käthe. Hohenzollernstr. 101, Siegburg/Bonn. b. 11 Aug. 1928 Honnef/Rh. Dipl. Psych. '55 Univ. of Bonn, Ger. PSYCHOLOGIST, Child. Guid. Clin, Erziehungsberatung, Hauptgebäude Am Hof 1, Bonn. Guidance, testing, applied psychology. F

REVERS, Dr. phil. Wilhelm Josef. Schiesshaus Str. 21, Würzburg. b. 18 Aug 1918 Mülheim/Cologne. PH.D '41 Univ. of Bonn, Ger. DOZENT for PSYCH, Univ. of Würzburg, Sauderring 2, Würzburg; EDITOR, Jahrbuch für Psychologie und Psychotherapie. Member: BDP, DGP. Educational and industrial psychology, testing, consulting, editorial, teaching, research; social and cultural psychology, history of psychology, motivation. M

RICHARZ, Dr. phil. Elisabeth. Wittelbachstr. 26, Ludwigshafen. b. 13 Sept 1919 Greifswald. PH.D '47 Univ. of Heidelberg, Ger. TEACHER, Town of Ludwigshafen, Jubiläumsplatz, Ludwigshafen. Member: BDP. Teaching, testing, educational psychology; child psychology, learning theory, projective techniques. F

RICHTER, Dr. phil. Horst-Eberhard. Westendallee 99 b, Berlin-Charlottenburg 9. b. 28 Apr 1923 Berlin. PH.D '48 Univ. of Berlin, Ger. DIRECTOR, Consult. and Res. Cen. for Ment. Disturbances in Children, Child Hosp, Berlin-Wedding, Reinickendorferstr, Berlin N. 65; ASSISTANT, Univ. Nerv. Clin, Berlin; PSYCHOTHERAPIST, priv. prac. Member: Ger. Psychoanal. Socy. Research, psychotherapy, guidance; psychopathology, medical child psychology, methodological research, psychology of perception. M

RICHTER, Rudolf Georg. Krehlstr. 39, Stuttgart-Vaihingen. b. 4 Apr 1900 Stuttgart. FACHSCHULOBERLEHRER, Gewerbliche Beruf- und Fachschule, Weimarstr. 26, Stuttgart S.W. Member: BDP, Ger. Graphology Socy. Teaching, educational and industrial psychology, testing; psychodiagnostic tests, graphology, industrial human relations. M

RIECHERT, Dr. phil. Johannes. Seebachstr. 27, Dresden. b. 20 Dec 1903 Chemnitz. PH.D '43 Univ. of Prague, Czech. Member: BDP. Applied psychology, handwriting, psychotherapy; technique and efficiency in intellectual work.   M

RIECKE, Mrs. Ursula. Wittenbergskamp 20, Salzgiller-Bad. b. 21 Sept 1920 Berlin. Dipl. Psych. '48 Tech. Hochschule Braunschweig, Ger. TEACHER, Land Niedersachsen, Hannover. Testing, guidance, teaching; school maturity tests.   F

RIEDEL, Dr. phil. Gerhard. Schwartauer Allee 1, Lübeck. b. 4 Sept 1911 Sachsen. PH.D '36 Univ. of Leipzig, Ger. DIR. of VOCAT. GUID, Employment Off, Fackenburger Allee, Lübeck. Member: BDP. Educational and industrial psychology, guidance, research; vocational aptitudes, characterology, psychopathology.   M

RIEDEN, Dipl. Psych. Charlotte. Gossler Str. 32, Göttingen. b. 16 Dec 1916 Berlin. Dipl. '55 Georg August Univ. of Göttingen, Ger. GRAD. STUD, Psych. Inst, Univ. of Göttingen, Hoher Weg 15, Göttingen. Testing, teaching, guidance; psychology of memory, non-directive therapy, play therapy.   F

RIEDLBERGER, Dr. phil. Anton. Baumannstr. 67, Bernau-Chiemsee. b. 11 May 1909 Ingolstadt. PH.D '36 Univ. of Munich, Ger. REGIERUNGSRAT, Prison of Bernau, Bahnhofstr. 136, Bernau-Chiemsee. Member: BDP. Testing, applied psychology, administration; achievement tests, criminology, sociology.   M

RIEGEL, Dipl. Psych. Georg. Gut Gstor-Post: Zollhaus, Allgäu. b. 25 May 1902 Nuremberg. Dipl. Psych. of Munich, Ger. CHILD GUID. CONSULT, Erziehungs Beratungs Stelle des Kreis Jugend Amtes Kempten, Residenzplatz, Kempten/Allgäu. Member: BDP, Deutsche Gesellschaft für Personalwesen. Educational guidance, lecturing; child and social psychology, projective methods.   M

RIEGEL, Klaus F. K. Grindelhof 57, Hamburg 13. b. 6 Nov 1925 Berlin. MA '55 Univ. of Minnesota, USA. RES. WRKR, Psych. Inst. Univ. of Hamburg, Bornplatz 2, Hamburg 13. Research, teaching; statistics, psychometrics, gerontology.   M

RIES, Miss Gerhild. Frankfurterstr. 3, Michelstadt. b. 28 Sept 1924 Landsberg/Warthe. Dipl. Psych. 53 John Gutenberg Univ. of Mainz, Ger. Member: BDP. Student, teaching, administration; educational, developmental and school psychology.   F

RITTER, Dr. phil. Gerhard Reinhard. Schliessfach 7265, Bremen 7. b. 14 Mar 1903 Berlin. PH.D, Univ. of Bonn, Ger. VOCAT. GUID. COUNS, Employment Off,

Burenstr. 79, Bremen; CHIEF ED, *Jugend und Alter.* Member: BDP. Educational and industrial psychology, psychotherapy; developmental psychology, criminology, medical psychology, marriage.   M

RÖBER, Dipl. Psych. Johannes. Feuerbachstr. 14/III, Frankfurt/M. b. 7 Aug 1929 Nossen. Dipl. Psych. '55 Univ. of Marburg, Ger. PERS. PSYCH'T, Deutsche Gesellschaft für Personalwesen, Feldbergstr. 38, Frankfurt/M. Applied and industrial psychology, testing, research; mechanical tests, personnel psychology, mental growth of children, job analysis, test construction.   M

ROEMER, Dr. med. Georg A. Psychomedizinisches Inst. Tutzing, Kurhaus Hauptstr. 36, Tutzing. b. 19 July 1892 Stuttgart. MD '17 Univ. of Tübingen, Ger. DIRECTOR, Psychomed. Inst. Tutzing. Member: Med. Assn. of Bavaria. Research, testing, psychotherapy, clinical practice; test evaluation, personality.   M

ROGGENKÄMPER, Dipl. Psych. Albrecht. Argelanderstr. 46, Bonn. b. 21 Jan 1928 Dortmund. Dipl. Psych. '54 Univ. of Bonn, Ger. CLIN. PSYCH'T, priv. prac, Schönebeckstr. 27c, Wuppertal-Barmen. Research, psychotherapy, guidance; parapsychology, hypnotherapy, guidance of criminals.   M

ROHÉ, Dr. phil. Carl. Hopfelderstr. 282, Hess.-Lichtenau 16, b. 4 Feb 1896 Cologne-Mülheim. PH.D '24 Univ. of Cologne, Ger. SCH. PSYCH'T, City School, Heinrichstr, Hessisch-Lichtenau. Member: BDP. Administration, educational psychology, testing; school readiness, efficiency and vocational testing.   M

ROHR, Dr. phil. Leonhard Wilhelm. Hechtsheimer-Landstr. 8, Mainz. b. 14 Jan 1921 Mainz. Dipl. Psych. '53 Univ. of Mainz, Ger. EDUC. ADVIS, Erziehungsberatung des Caritas Verbandes, Wilhelmiterstr. 1 Mainz. Testing, applied and educational psychology, consulting and guidance; projective tests, personality tests, graphology.   M

ROON-KÜHNECK, Anneliese von. Lahnstr. 78, Wiesbaden. b. 15 Mar 1921 Danzig. Dipl. Psych. '46 Univ. of Innsbruck, Austria. EDUC. GUID. COUNS, priv. prac. Member: BDP. Guidance, educational psychology, testing; statistics, achievement tests, test construction.   F

ROSBITZKI, Dipl. Psych. Lia von. Shillerstr. 33, Heidelberg. b. 2 June 1923 M. Neustadt, Czech. Dipl. '47 Univ. of Heidelberg, Ger. GROUP PSYCHOTHERAPIST, Erziehungsberatung der Psychiatrischen und Neurologischen Klinik, Heidelberg. Member: BDP. Educational psychology, testing, clinical analysis, consulting, clinical practice; educational guidance, mentally disturbed children.   M

ROSEN, Dr. phil. Helmut. Theoderichstr. 5, Cologne-Kalk. b. 30 Aug 1920 Cologne. PH.D '50 Friedrich Wilhelm Univ. of Bonn, Ger. INDUS. PSYCH'T, priv. prac. Member: BDP. Educational and industrial psychology, testing, clinical practice, consulting; aptitude research, industrial counseling, medical psychology, educational guidance. M

ROST, Mrs. Thea. Sonnenbergerstr. 20, Wiesbaden. b. 15 Jan 1882 Wiesbaden. GRAPHOLOGIST, priv. prac. Member: BDP. Graphology, teaching, applied psychology; personnel selection, child and adult problems. F

ROTH, Dipl. Psych. Erwin A. Enheimer Str. 487, Marktbreit/Main. b. 29 May 1926 Marktbreit. Dipl. Psych. '54 Univ. of Würzburg, Ger. Member: BDP. Student, testing, educational psychology; achievement tests, projective techniques. M

ROTH, Prof. Dr. Heinrich. Inst. for Int. Educ. Res, Frankfurt/M. b. 3 Mar 1906 Gerstetten. Dr. '33 Univ. of Tübingen, Ger. PROFESSOR, Inst. for Int. Educ. Res, Schloss Str. 29, Frankfurt/M; CO-EDITOR, *Die Deutsche Schule.* Member: BDP, DGP. Teaching, research, educational psychology; learning theory, attitude measurement, group process. M

ROYL, Wolfgang. Westendstr. 79, Frankfurt/M. b. 26 Apr 1929 Kassel. Dipl. Psych. '56 Johann Wolfgang Goethe Univ. of Frankfurt, Ger. TEACHER, Regierungspräsident des Regierungsbezirks Wiesbaden, Humboldtstr. 6, Wiesbaden. Member: BDP. Teaching, testing, student; Rorschach diagnostics, student counseling and guidance. M

RÜDIGER, Dr. Jutta. Grunerstr. 39, Düsseldorf. b. 14 June 1910 Berlin. Dr. '33 Univ. of Würzburg, Ger. APPL. PSYCH'T, priv. prac. Member: BDP. Educational guidance, industrial consulting, testing; aptitude testing, vocational guidance. F

RÜFNER, Prof. Dr. phil. Vinzenz. Philosophisches Seminar B, Univ. of Bonn, Rhein. b. 17 Sept 1899 Dettingen/Main. PH.D '24 Univ. of Würzburg, Ger. PROF. of PHIL. Univ. of Bonn. Member: DGP. Research, teaching, administration; animal behavior, comparative psychology, juvenile psychology. M

RULFS, Dr. Ilse. Ernst August Str. 25, Bad Rothenfelde TW. b. 10 Feb 1923 Duisburg/Rh. Dipl. Psych. '54 Univ. of Münster/Westf, Ger. SPEECH THERAPIST, Landschaftsverband Westfalen-Lippe, Fürstenbergstr, Münster/Westf. Clinical practice, psychotherapy, teaching; play group therapy, non-directive therapy, learning theory. F

RUPPELT-SCHEEL, Mrs. Rosemaria. Feilitzschstr. 14/II, Munich 23. b. 21 Oct 1912

Neustadt. GRAPHOLOGIST, priv. prac. Member: BDP. Handwriting expert; teaching graphology. F

RÜSSEL, Prof. Dr. phil. Arnulf. Lachmannstr. 8, Braunschweig. b. 25 May 1902 Zörbig. PH.D '30 Univ. of Leipzig, Ger. DIR. of RES, Forschungsinst. für Arbeitspsych, Garküche 3, Braunschweig. Member: BDP, DGP. Industrial psychology, teaching; accidents, play, motor reactions. M

SAAR, Mrs. Ursula. Sprungschanzenweg 6/8, Berling-Zehlendorf. b. 10 Feb 1924 Berlin. Dipl. Psych. '53 Free Univ. of Berlin, Ger. Member: BDP. Consulting, applied psychology, translating; graphology. F

SACHER, Dr. phil. Horst. Univ. Nervenklinik, Erlangen. b. 5 Oct 1916 Seidenberg. PH.D '51 Univ. of Erlangen, Ger. CLIN. PSYCH'T, Univ. of Erlangen. Research, testing, teaching; methodological criticism of test techniques, theory of personality. M

SACHERL, Dr. Karl. Beckstr. 80, Darmstadt. b. 10 Feb 1916 Zweibrücken. Habil. '54 Johannes Gutenberg Univ. of Mainz, Ger. DOZENT of PSYCH, Technische Hochschule, Darmstadt. Member: DGP. Research, teaching, testing; psychology and sociology of bureaucracy, middle class social psychology, social pathology. M

SACHTELEBEN, Friedhelm. Karlstr. 25, Lingen-Ems 23. b. 22 Aug 1929 Barmen. Dipl. '55 Free Univ. of Berlin, Ger. INDUS. PSYCH. ASST, Vereinigte Glanzstoff Fabriken Werk AG, Obernburg/Uffr. Industrial psychology, testing; projective techniques, achievement tests, graphology. M

SADER, Manfred. Weckmarkt 15, Frankfurt/M. b. 5 Mar 1928 Koeslin/Pom. Dipl. Psych. '54 Univ. of Frankfurt/M, Ger. SCI. ASST, Psych. Inst, Mertonstr. 17-25, Frankfurt/M. Student, projective tests, achievement tests, traffic psychology. M

SALBER, Dr. phil. Wilhelm. Memelstr. 24, Erlangen. b. 9 Mar 1928 Aachen. PH.D '52 Univ. of Bonn, Ger. SCI. ASST, Inst. for Psych, Univ. of Erlangen. Member: BDP, DGP. Research, teaching, applied psychology; classification, behavioral patterns, advertising art. M

SALBER-ROERICHT, Dipl. Psych. Christa. Memel Str. 24, Erlangen. b. 7 Oct 1928 Slönkirch, Silesia. Dipl. Psych. '53 Univ. of Bonn, Ger. Applied psychology; child development, psychology of movies. F

SANDER, Prof. Dr. phil. Friedrich. Psych. Inst, Univ. of Bonn, Am Hof I, Bonn. b. 19 Nov 1889 Greiz. PH.D '13 Univ. of Leipzig, Ger. DIRECTOR, Psych. Inst, Univ. of Bonn. Member: DGP, BDP. Teaching, research, editorial, applied psychology; testing; personality, psychology of art, morphotypology, psychology of movement. M

208 GERMANY

SAUL, Ortwin. Aussere Wiener Str. 32/III, Munich. b. 30 Jan 1928 Rathenow. Dipl. Psych. '54 Univ. of Munich, Ger. co-worker, Inst. für Psych. Beratung, Parzivalstr. 3a, Munich. Member: bdp. Consulting, testing, applied psychology; occupational psychology, psychology of advertising, analytical psychotherapy. M

SCHAAF, Kurt. Rothenbaumchaussee 158, Hamburg 13. b. 12 May 1902 Berlin. Member: bdp. Graphology. M

SCHABER, Dozent Dr. phil. Georg. Kopernikusstr. 23, Karlsruhe. b. 19 June 1906 Reicholzried. ph.d '38 Univ. of Munich, Ger. dozent, Pädagogisches Inst. und Technische Hochschule, Gartenstr. 5a, Karlsruhe, Baden. Member: bdp. Educational psychology, teaching; developmental psychology, test psychology, character, vocational psychology. M

SCHACHT, Dr. Joachim. Uhlandstr. 6, Ilvesheim bei Mannheim. b. 11 Nov 1903 Berlin. Dr. '56 Univ. of Munich, Ger. psychotherapist, priv. prac. Member: Deutsche Gesellschaft für Psychother. und Tiefenpsych, Arbeitsgemeinschaft für soziale Betriebsgestaltung. Psychotherapy, consulting, applied psychology; social perception, industrial human relations. M

SCHAEFER, Joachim. Seehofstr. 49, Siegburg/Rhld. b. 2 Feb 1920 Coburg. Dipl. Psych. '52 Technische Hochschule Dresden, Ger. vocat. guid. counc. Employment Off, Wilhelmstr, Siegburg. Member: bdp. Applied psychology, testing, administration; vocational guidance, group psychology. M

SCHÄFERS, Dr. phil. Franz. Feldstr. 116, Kiel. b. 13 Feb 1910 Holzminden. ph.d '39 Friedr. Wilhelms Univ. of Bonn, Ger. bundesverwaltunsrat, Employment Off, Wilhelmsplatz 12/13, Kiel; dozent in psych, Landeswohlfahrtsschule. Member: bdp. Consulting, teaching, administration; theory of learning, social perception. M

SCHAPER, Friedrich. Zeppelinstr. 1. Braunschweig. b. 18 Sept 1916 Braunschweig. Dipl. Psych. '54 Technische Hochschule Braunschweig, Ger. teacher, Niedersächsische Erziehungsstätte, Grünewaldstr. 10-12, Braunschweig. Member: bdp. Educational psychology, research, testing; achievement tests, social perception group process. M

SCHARGE, Dr. rer. nat. Hermann. Herzogstr. 18-22, Düsseldorf. b. 13 May 1919 Hehlen/Weser. Dr. '54 Univ. of Göttingen, Ger. inst. dir, Forschungsinst. für Arbeitspsych. und Personalwesen (forfa), Garkuche 3, Braunschweig; Zweiginst. Düsseldorf, Friedrichstr. 9, Düsseldorf. Member: bdp. Industrial psychology, research, guidance; accident prevention,

forensic psychology, industrial management training. M

SCHARMANN, Dr. phil. Dorothea Luise. Hittorf Str. 4, Bonn. b. 21 Sept 1915 Berlin. ph.d '54 Univ. of Bonn, Ger. indus. psych't, priv. prac. Applied psychology, consulting, testing; industrial psychology, vocational guidance, graphology. F

SCHARMANN, Dr. phil. Theodor. Hittorf Str. 4, Bonn. b. 12 July 1907 Kreuzlingen. ph.d '35 Univ. of Frankfurt/M, Ger. oberregierunsrat, State Dept. of Labor, Bonn; prof. of sociol. and soc. psych, Univ. of Bonn. Member: dgp, aipa, Deutsche Gesellschaft fur Soziologie. Administration, teaching, industrial social psychology; group process, sociology of work. M

SCHAUER, Hans. Neur. Clin, Medizinischen Akademie, Moorenstr, 5, Düsseldorf. b. 24 Dec 1928 Kassel. Dipl. Psych. '53 Univ. of Göttingen, Ger. clin. psych't, Neur. Clin. Member: bdp. Clinical practice, testing, clinical analysis, research; achievement testing of aphasic and demented patients, diagnosis of neurotic tendencies, psychotherapeutic methods. M

SCHEIDER, Dipl. Psych. Jürgen. Friedländer Weg 31, Göttingen. b. 2 Apr 1928 Berlin. Dipl. Psych. '55 Univ. of Göttingen, Ger. res. stud, Psych. Inst, Univ. of Göttingen, Hoher Weg 15, Göttingen. Research; objective personality research, perception, motivation, test construction, opinion research. M

SCHELLER, Arthur. Schaffnerstr. 14, Regensburg. b. 28 Oct 1920 Regensburg. Cand. phil. '55 Univ. of Munich, Ger. psychologist, Erziehungsberatungsstelle, Regensburg. Member: bdp. Guidance, testing; projective techniques, group process, psychoanalysis. M

SCHELLER, Dipl. Psych. Nikolaus W. Wildfängerweg 21, Duisburg-Rahm. b. 28 Mar 1924 Prenzlau. Dipl. Psych. '53 Univ. of Münster, Ger. dept. head, Bd. of Youth, Stadthaus, Duisburg. Administration, applied psychology, consulting; theoretical research, structure, dynamic relations and functions of personality. M

SCHENKEL, Dr. phil. Dipl. Psych. Rose Maria. Hölderlingweg 31, Esslingen. b. 26 Apr 1929 Stuttgart. ph.d '54 Univ. of Tübingen, Ger. Member: bdp. Trainee in psychotherapy, consulting, educational guidance; psychodiagnosis, projective techniques, depth psychology, child therapy. F

SCHERKE, Prof. Dr. phil. Felix. Steinplattenweg 130, Nuremberg. b. 1 Feb 1892 Cottbus. ph.d '21 Univ. of Halle-Wittenberg, Ger. prof. of psych. and pedagogy, Hochschule für Wirtschafts und Socialwissenschaften, Findelgasse 7, Nuremberg. Member: bdp, Deutsche Gesellschaft für

Psychother. und Tiefenpsych. Teaching, research, educational psychology, vocational guidance; achievement tests, social perception, group process. M
SCHEUBER, Dr. Franz. Kreuzwehr Str. 4, Coburg. b. 2 Apr 1904 Coburg. Dr. phil. nat. '34 Univ. of Jena, Ger. STUDIENRAT, High School, Coburg. Member: BDP. Consulting, guidance, teaching; pedagocical and medical psychology. M
SCHEUNERT, Dr. med. Gerhart. Wilskistr. 58, Berlin-Zehlendorf. b. 11 Jan 1906 Leipzig. MD '30 Univ. of Leipzig, Ger. PSYCHIAT. DIR, Family Guid. Clin, Pestalozzi-Fröbel Haus, Karl Schrader Str. 7/8, Berlin; PSYCHOTHERAPIST, priv. prac. Member: German Psychoanal. Assn, Gesellschaft für Psychother. und Tiefenpsych. Psychotherapy, consulting, guidance, teaching; psychoanalysis. M
SCHEURMANN, Bundesverwaltungsoberrat Dr. phil. Rudolf. Heinrichstr. 25, Düsseldorf. b. 18 Dec 1898 Wuppertal-Elberfeld. PH.D '22 Univ. of Bonn, Ger. BUNDESVERWALTUNGSOBERRAT, Employment Off, Fritz Roeber Str. 3, Düsseldorf. Member: BDP. Administration, testing, industrial psychology; vocational guidance. M
SCHEWE, Walter. Westfälische Wohlfahrtsschule, Domplatz 23, Münster. b. 14 Aug 1919 Ginderich, Krs. Moers. Dipl. Psych. '55 Univ. of Bonn, Ger. DOZENT, Westfälische Wohlfartsschule. Teaching, research, industrial psychology; industrial research, group process, case work. M
SCHILLING, Dipl. Psych. Dr. med. Helmuth. Evangelisches Kinder und Jugendheim, Wolf an der Mosel. b. 5 Aug 1922 Chemnitz. MD '51 Univ. of Göttingen, Ger. DIRECTOR, Inst. for Educ. of Children, Innere Mission Rheinland, Bonsfelder Str, Langenberg. Member: BDP. Clinical practice, guidance, testing, teaching; child psychology, psychodiagnosis, psychotherapy. M
SCHILLING, Raimar. Schulze-Delitzschstr. 10, Lörrach. b. 15 Sept 1929 Lorräch. Dipl. Psych. '53 Univ. of Freiburg, Ger. Ger. MED. STUD, Univ. of Freiburg. Industrial psychology, testing; psychiatry, projective techniques, psychotherapy. M
SCHIÖBERG, Dipl. Ing. Eberhard. Forstweg, Elsenfeld/M. b. 4 Sept 1906 Pritzerbe. Dipl. Ing. '30 Technische Hochschule Darmstadt, Ger. INDUS. PSYCH'T, Vereinigte Glanzstoff Fabriken, Werk Obemburg/M. Member: BDP. Industrial psychology, testing; achievement tests, group process, social perception. M
SCHIRM, Rolf. W. Am Kirchberg 34, Frankfurt/M. b. 3 Jan 1918 Nuremberg. MANAGEMENT CONSULT, priv. prac; EDITOR, *Informationen für Führungskräfte.* Industrial psychology, editorial; psychology

and sociology of the work group. M
SCHITTIG, Heinz. Winterleitenweg 65c, Würzburg. b. 17 June 1929 Würzburg. Dipl. '55 Univ. of Würzburg, Ger. SCI. ASST, Psych. Inst, Univ. of Würzburg, Domerschulstr. 13, Würzburg. Applied psychology, testing, consulting; motivation research, psychology of advertising. M
SCHLEIER, Dr. Richard. Stuettekofenerstr. 5, Leverkusen-Schlebusch. b. 22 Oct 1913 Marburg. Dr. '39 Univ. of Marburg, Ger. PSYCHOLOGIST, Farbenfabriken Bayer, Bayerwerk, Leverkusen. Member: BDP. Industrial psychology; vocational tests, human relations. M
SCHLESIGER, Norbert. Psych. Inst, Domerschulgasse 13, Würzburg. b. 10 Mar 1929 Stettin. Dipl. Psych. '55 Univ. of Würzburg, Ger. SCI. ASST, Psych. Inst. Würzburg. Reseach, applied psychology, psychotherapy, testing; group process, projective techniques, motivation research, psychology of advertising, graphology. M
SCHLIE, Dipl. Psych. Eberhard. Bergisches Kindersanatorium, Aprath/Rhld. b. 20 Sept 1927 Duisburg. Dipl. Psych. '53 Free Univ. of Berlin, Ger. PSYCHOLOGIST, Bergisches Kindersanatorium. Member: BDP. Guidance, testing, clinical analysis, psychotherapy; child guidance, special education for neurotic children, child development. M
SCHLIEBE, Prof. Dr. phil. Georg. Taunusstr. 77, Wiesbaden. b. 29 Dec 1901 Zschopau. PH.D '30 Univ. of Giessen, Ger. BUNDESVERWALTUNGSRAT, Employment Off, Feuerbachstr. 50, Frankfurt/M. Member: DGP. Editorial, teaching, industrial psychology; audio-visual aids. M
SCHLIEBE-LIPPERT, Dr. habil. Elisabeth. Taunusstr. 77, Wiesbaden. b. 22 Nov 1898 Kaiserslautern. Dr. habil. '32 Univ. of Giessen, Ger. OBERSCHULRAT, Ministerum für Erziehung und Volksbildung, Luisenplatz 10, Wiesbaden. Member: DGP. Administration, educational psychology, research; psychological research on child victums of war. F
SCHLOSSER, Hans. Walter Oertel Str. 63, Karl Marx Stadt. b. 6 Mar 1911 Chemnitz. Dipl. Psych. '43 Deutsche Karls Univ. of Prague, Czech. PSYCHOTHERAPIST, Hosp. Zeisigwald, Karl Marx Stadt. Member: BDP. Clinical analysis, psychotherapy, applied psychology; connection between character and illness. M
SCHLÜTER, Johannes. Untere Maschstr. 13A, Göttingen. b. 26 Dec 1922 Gr. Giesen. Dipl. Psych. '54 Univ. of Göttingen, Ger. TEACHER, Regierung, Domhof, Hildesheim. Member: BDP. Teaching, educational psychology; development of expression in children. M

SCHMALTZ, Prof. Dr. Ing. Dr. med. h.c. Gustav. Kettenhofweg 137, Frankfurt/M b. 25 May 1884 Offenbach/M. Prof., Technische Hochschule Hannover; Dr. Ing. Technische Hochschule Darmstadt; MD, Univ. of Frankfurt, Ger. PSYCHOANALYST, priv. prac; EDITOR, *Theorie und Praxis der Psychotherapie*. Member: Deutsche Gesellschaft für Psychother. und Tiefenpsych. Psychotherapy, research, editorial.   M

SCHMELCHER, Dr. Grid Yvonne. Brachtstr. 6, Essen-Bredeney. b. 15 Dec 1923 Essen. Dr. '55 Univ. of Freiburg, Ger. ASST. and PROBATIONER, Employment Off, Essen. Member: BDP. Guidance. applied psychology, testing, student; projective techniques, learning theory, women's professional problems.   F

SCHMIDT, Arthur. Cellerstr. 93, Braunschweig. b. 12 Apr 1913 Auerbach/Vogtl. Dipl. Psych. '53 Technische Hochschule Braunschweig, Ger. TEACHER, Mittelschule, Sidonienstr, Braunschweig. Teaching, testing; projective techniques, achievement tests, attitude measurement.   M

SCHMIDT, Carl H. Südenstr. 15, Berlin-Steglitz. b. 8 May 1925 Glogau. Dipl. Psych. '52 Univ. of Hamburg, Ger. PSYCHOTHERAPIST, priv. prac. Member: BDP. Teaching, psychotherapy, radio; projective techniques, juvenile psychology, psychology of delinquency.   M

SCHMIDT, Dipl. Psych. Herbert. Lutzstr. 90, Munich 42. b. 18 July 1927 Munich. Dipl. Psych. '54 Univ. of Munich, Ger. PRIV. PRAC. Member: BDP. Educational guidance, consulting, research; psychology of expression, personality diagnosis.   M

SCHMIDT, Dr. phil. Wolfgang. Ostanlage 17, Worms. b. 6 Aug 1912 Kraschewo. PH.D '47 Univ. of Königsberg. DOZENT, Pädagogische Akademie, Nibelungenplatz 3, Worms. Teaching, applied, educational and industrial psychology, research; psychology of expression, developmental psychology.   M

SCHMIDT-HIEBER, Dr. phil. Klaus. Feuerbacher Heide 16, Stuttgart N. b. 29 Feb 1920 Stuttgart. PH.D, Univ. of Tübingen, Ger. PSYCH. CONSULT, priv. prac. Member: BDP. Industrial psychology, testing; aptitude measurement.   M

SCHMIDTKE, Dr. rer. nat. Heinz. Oberbrucherstr. 76, Heinsgerg/Rhld. b. 6 Aug 1925 Goslar. D.SC '49 Technische Hochschule Braunschweig, Ger. ASST. PERS. MGR, Vereinigte Glanzstofffabriken AG, Oberbruch, Aachen. Member: BDP, Gesellschaft für arbeitswissenschaftliche Forschung. Industrial psychology, research, teaching; human relations, achievement tests, group process, fatigue, industrial management.   M

SCHMIDT-SCHERF, Dr. phil. Wilhelm. Uhlbergstr. 17, Stuttgart 13. b. 13 Mar 1904 Dortmund. PH.D '39 Univ. of Erlangen, Ger. PSYCHOTHERAPIST, priv. prac. Member: BDP. Applied psychology, psychotherapy, testing.   M

SCHMOLKE, Dr. phil. Herbert. 5-7 West 91 St, Apt 5B, New York 24, N.Y. USA. b. 22 Oct 1899 Xions, Ger. PH.D, Free Univ. of Berlin, Ger. ADMIN. ACCOUNTANT, Oppenheimer Vanden Broeck and Co, 120 Broadway, New York. Member: BDP, APA. Administration, testing, consulting; achievement tests, social perception, industrial psychology.   M

SCHNAITH, Wolfgang. Mühlstr. 3, Tübingen. b. 31 Mar 1927 Tübingen. Dipl. Psych. '54 Univ. of Tübingen, Ger. STUDENT, Psych. Inst, Univ. of Kiel. Applied psychology, testing, consulting; projective techniques, performance and motivation.   M

SCHNEHAGE, Dr. Hans-Joachim. Bockenheimer Landstr. 113, Frankfurt/M. b. 16 Jan 1910 Graudenz. Dr. rer. nat. '37 J. W. Goethe Univ. of Frankfurt, Ger. HEAD, Vocat. Guid. Dept, Employment Off, Gartenstr. 138, Frankfurt/M. Member: BDP. Administration, testing, vocational guidance; projective techniques, achievement tests, attitude measurement, industrial psychology.   M

SCHNEIDER, Dipl. Psych. Elfriede Gertrud. Niederramstädterstr. 158, Darmstadt. b. 7 Feb 1926 Braunschweig. Dipl. Psych. '51 Univ. of Göttingen, Ger. Member: BDP. Applied and educational psychology, psychotherapy, consulting; social psychology, child guidance.   F

SCHNEIDER, Friedrich. Ringstr. 46, Berlin-Lichterfelde. b. 8 Mar 1909 Siegen/Westf. GRAPHOLOGIST, priv. prac. Member: BDP. Applied psychology, graphology; criminal psychology, social and occupational psychology.   M

SCHNEIDER, Dr. med. Dr. phil. Karl. Am Hof 30, Cologne, ·b. 21 Dec 1913 Aschaffenburg. MD '41 Univ. of Innsbruck, Austria. DIRECTOR, Sch. Hlth. Serv. Neumarkt 15-19, Cologne; TEACHER, Soc. Welf. Sch. for Nurses; TEACHER, Acad. for Tchr. Educ. Educational psychology, psychotherapy, child guidance, administration; child development, school psychology, child psychiatry.   M

SCHNEIDER, Miss Ortrun. Klenzestr. 103, Munich. b. 19 Dec 1924 Munich. Dipl. Psych. '52 Univ. of Munich, Ger. MED. STUD, Univ. of Munich. Consulting, testing, clinical analysis; psychology of expression, characterology, psychosomatics, psychiatry.   F

SCHNORR, Dr. Friedrich. Schleswigerstr. 16, Frankfurt/M. b. 26 May 1910 Karlsruhe.

Dr. '37 Univ. of Göttingen, Ger. APPL. PSYCH'T, Employment Off, Gartenstr. 138, Frankfurt/M. Member: BDP. Testing, applied and industrial psychology; projective techniques, aptitude and intelligence tests. M

SCHOCH, Helmut. c/o Potas, Schadowstr. 2, Cologne-Ehrenfeld. b. 16 Sept 1918 Berlin. Dipl. Psych. '54 Univ. of Munich, Ger. PSYCHOLOGIST, Med. Psych. Inst. für Verkehrs und Betriebssicherheit, Lukasstr. 90, Cologne. Member: BDP. Industrial psychology, research; selection and training of personnel, psychological problems of traffic regulation. M

SCHOLL, Dr. phil. Robert. Krämerstr. 19, Stuttgart. b. 27 Mar 1897 Neckarwestheim Kr. Heilbronn. PH.D Univ. of Tübingen, Ger. DIRECTOR, Jugendamt, Wilhelmplatz 8, Stuttgart. Member: BDP. Educational psychology, administration, teaching; juvenile psychology, conscience, child and youth welfare. M

SCHOLZ, Dr. phil. Herbert. Rheinlanddamm 201, Dortmund. b. 11 July 1912 Berlin. PH.D '51 Univ. of Kiel, Ger. SCI. ASST, Max Planck Inst. für Arbeitspsychologie. Member: BDP. Industrial psychology, research; physiology of work. M

SCHOMBURG, Prof. Dr. phil. Eberhard Hugo. Freytagstr. 7, Hannover. b. 13 July 1904 Boffzen Kr. Holzminden. PH.D '41 Technische Hochschule Braunschweig, Ger. PROF. of SPEC. EDUC, Pädagogische Hochschule Hannover, Bismarck Str. 35, Hannover. Member: BDP, DGP, Verband Freiberuflicher Gerichtsschriftsachverständiger. Teaching, educational psychology, administration, research; achievement tests, learning theory, handicapped children, child guidance. M

SCHÖN, Joseph. Schlossberg 21 bei Giese Heidelberg. b. 23 Apr 1924 Ludwigshafen/Rh. Dipl. Psych. '54 Univ. of Heidelberg, Ger. SCI. RES. ASST, Psych. Inst, Univ. of Heidelberg, Hauptstr. 126, Heidelberg. Research, technician in electro-acoustics; psychology of hearing and the human voice. M

SCHÖNBERGER, Dr. phil. Konrad. Flandernweg 24, Korbach/Waldeck. b. 7 Jan 1905 Etzgersrierth. PH.D '33 Univ. of Freiburg, Ger. VOAT. GUID. COUNS, Employment Off, Louis Peter Str, Korbach/Waldeck. Member: BDP. Administration, vocational guidance, industrial psychology; testing. M

SCHORN, Prof. Dr. phil. Maria. Sophie Charlottestr. 5, Berlin-Zehlendorf. b. 13 Oct 1894 Cologne. Prof. '53 Free Univ. of Berlin, Ger. PROFESSOR, Psych. Inst, Free Univ. of Berlin, Gelfertstr. 36, Berlin-Dahlem. Member: DGP, BDP. Applied, industrial and educational psychology,

teaching, research; social work, forensic psychology. F

SCHOTT, Dr. phil. Günter. Stauffenbergstr. 101, Esslingen/Neckar. b. 5 Apr 1917 Ulm/Donau. PH.D '52 Univ. of Freiburg, Ger. PSYCH. CONSULT, Employment Off, Ebershaldenstr. 14, Esslingen. Member: BDP. Vocational guidance, applied industrial psychology, consulting; graphology, psychotherapy, psychology and medicine. M

SCHOTT, Dr. Karl-Heinz. Blücherstr. 12, Bonn/Rh. b. 17 Mar 1916 Wuppertal. Dipl. Psych. '49 Univ. of Bonn, Ger. TEACHER, Michael Schule, Friesdorfer Str, Bad Godesberg. Member: BDP. Teaching, guidance; educational psychology, school psychology, counseling. M

SCHOTTMAYER, Dipl. Psych. Georg. Burmesterstr. 25, Hamburg 33. b. 19 Dec 1924 Hamburg. Dipl. Psych. '56 Univ. of Hamburg, Ger. TEACHER, Sch. Bd, Dammtorstr 25, Hamburg; TCHR. in THEMATIC TECHNIQUES, Univ. of Hamburg. Teaching, applied and educational psychology, testing, clinical analysis; film psychology, school psychology. M

SCHRAML, Dr. Walter Josef. Nietzschestr. 4, Mannheim. b. 12 May 1922 Munich. PH.D '47, MD '48 Univ. of Munich, Ger. CLIN. DIR, Inst. für Psychohyg. und Soziale Beratung, Mittelstr. 42, Mannheim; LECT. in MENT. HYG, Univ. of Würzburg; PSYCHOTHERAPIST, priv. prac; ED. BD, *Psychologie und Praxis*. Member: BDP, DGP, Deutsche Gesellschaft für Psychother. und Tiefenpsych, Allgemeine ärztliche Gesellschaft für Psychother. Psychotherapy, consulting, teaching, research; intelligence and emotional disturbances, attitudes in the psychotherapeutic process. M

SCHREIBER, Dr. Peter Alfred. Auf der Steinrausch 19, Trier/Mosel. b. 21 Jan 1925 Kapfenberg, Austria. Dr. '51 Univ. of Bonn, Ger. PSYCH'T and DOZENT, Stadt Trier Tourist Off, Simeonstr, Trier; PARENT GUID. COUNS, priv. prac. Administration, public relations, teaching, applied and educational psychology; problem children, personnel selection, potentialities of public relations. M

SCHREIBER, Mrs. Sibylle. Edlingerstr. 1, Munich 9. b. 30 Oct 1928 Berlin. Dipl. Psych. '54 Ludwig Maximilian Univ. of Munich, Ger. Group training and work therapy, projective techniques, graphology. F

SCHREINER, Dipl. Psych. Helmut. Kirchstr. 17, Trier/Mosel. b. 8 Sept 1926 Edesheim-Pfalz. Dipl. Psych. '51 Univ. of Mainz, Ger. APPL. PSYCH'T, Employment Off, Trier. Testing, guidance, industrial psychology; projective techniques, psychoanalysis, vocational guidance. M

SCHRIEVER, Bernt. Heinskamp 9, Hamburg 21. b. 19 July 1921 Hagenow. Dipl. Psych. '53 Univ. of Hamburg, Ger. PSYCHOLOGIST, Technischer Überwachungs Verein, Julius Leber Str. 10, Hamburg-Altona. Member: BDP. Testing, applied psychology, consulting; child guidance, intelligence measurement, traffic, psychology.   M

SCHRÖDER, Dr. phil. Hans. Fritz Tarnow Str. 13, Frankfurt/M. b. 30 July 1904 Altenkirchen. PH.D '33 Friedrich Wilhelm Univ. of Bonn, Ger. BUNDESVERWALTUNGSOBERRAT, Employment Off, Feuerbachstr. 50, Frankfurt/M. Member: BDP. Vocational guidance, consulting, testing, administration; developmental psychology, vocational aptitude research.   M

SCHROEDER, Dr. phil. Lisa. Blumenstr. 59/I, Hamburg 39. b. 24 Dec 1916 New York, USA. PH.D, Dipl. Psych. '50 Univ. of Hamburg, Ger. PSYCHOTHERAPIST, priv. prac. Member: BDP. Child guidance, psychotherapy, teaching.   F

SCHRÖER, Dipl. Psych. Heinz. Krayerstr. 227, Essen-Kray. b. 20 Feb 1929 Essen. Dipl. Psych. '54 Univ. of Hamburg, Ger. LAW STUD, Univ. of Hamburg. Consulting, testing; anthropology, criminology, social perception.   M

SCHROFF, Dr. phil. Erwin. Kussmaulstr. 5, Heidelberg. b. 19 Aug 1896 Ludwigshafen/Rh. PH.D '28 Univ. of Heidelberg, Ger. SCH. PSYCH'T, City Sch. Bd, Theaterstr. 9, Heidelberg. Member: BDP. Educational psychology, testing, clinical analysis, consulting, guidance; learning theory, intelligence and achievement tests.   M

SCHUBART, Dr. phil. Maximilian. Friedrich Karlstr. 14, Mannheim. b. 12 Dec 1919 Munich. PH.D '53 Univ. of Heidelberg, Ger. Member: BDP. Industrial and applied psychology; personnel problems, projective techniques, Gestalt theory.   M

SCHUH, Dr. phil. Wilhelm. Postfach 30, Gröbenzell vor Munich. b. 15 June 1910 Elversberg, Saar. PH.D '35 Univ. of Munich, Ger. GRAPHOLOGIST, priv. prac. Member: BDP. Industrial psychology, advertising, graphology; characterology, social adjustment, youth and family problems. M

SCHUHMANN, Dr. phil. Helmut. Erzbergerstr. 22, Karlsruhe. b. 11 May 1915 Würzburg. PH.D '46 Univ. of Würzburg, Ger. TEACHER, Speech Correctn. Sch, Kapellenstr. 1, Karlsruhe. Member: BDP. Teaching, educational psychology, guidance; group therapy, public opinion, problems of social adaption.   M

SCHULZ, Dipl. Psych. Dr. med. Christof Friedrich. Heil- und Pflegeanstalt, Lohr/M, Bavaria. b. 24 Jan 1925 Berlin. Dipl. Psych. '49, MD '53 Univ. of Würzburg, Ger.

PHYS. and APPL. PSYCH'T, Heil- und Pflegeanstalt, Lohr/M. Member: BDP. Clinical practice, psychotherapy, testing; psychodiagnostic tests, psychosomatic medicine, lie detection, psychotherapy of psychosis and neurosis.   M

SCHUMACHER, Dipl. Psych. Helene. Scheven b. Kall/Eifel. b. 27 Feb 1915 Scheven/Eifel. Dipl. '52 Univ. of Cologne, Ger. Educational psychology.   F

SCHUMACHER, Dr. med. Dr. rer. nat. Willy. Röcklingen bei Herchen am Sieg. b. 30 Mar 1928 Röcklingen. MD '52; Dr. rer. nat. '55 Univ. of Cologne, Ger. SCI. COWRKR, Psych. Inst. Univ. of Cologne, Meister Ekkehardstr. 11, Cologne. Research; psychosomatic medicine, neurophysiology, psychoanalysis,.   M

SCHUMANN, Wolfgang. Friedrich Naumann Str. 7, Kassel W. b. 20 Feb 1919 Siegen. Dipl. Psych. '50 Augusta Victoria Univ. of Göttingen, Ger. INDUS. PSYCH'T, Spinnfaser AG, Wohnstr. 1, Kassel B. Member: BDP. Industrial psychology, testing, teaching; leadership, personnel counseling.   M

SCHUSTER, Georg. Wallmerstr. 23, Stuttgart-Untertürkheim. b. 30 Mar 1901 Rosenheim. GRAPHOLOGIST, priv. prac. Member: BDP. Industrial counseling, graphology; personality, psychology of expression.   M

SCHWAB, Dipl. Psych. Rudolf. Weingärten 91, Geislingen. b. 12 Mar 1923 Plauen. Dipl. Psych. '51 Univ. of Leipzig, Ger. TEACHER, Sonderschule, Platzgasse, Ulm/Donau. Teaching, educational psychology; theoretical basis of psychology, social psychology, heredity.   M

SCHWADORF, Miss Marianne. Richard Wagnerstr. 2, Bonn. b. 9 Oct 1930 Bonn. Dipl. Psych. '55 Friedr. Wilh. Univ. of Bonn, Ger. PSYCHOLOGIST, Inst. für Personalauslese im öffentlichen Dienst, Rathaus, Cologne. Administration; achievement tests, projective techniques, social perception.   F

SCHWEIGER, Valentin. Bertastr. 59, Nuremberg. b. 16 Aug 1920 Hassfurt. Dipl. '53 Univ. of Würzburg, Ger. EDUC. CONSULT, Städt. Aufbauheim/Stadtjugendamt, Grossweidenmühlstr. 37, Nuremberg. Educational psychology; depth psychology, social and cultural psychology.   M

SCHWEIGER-SCHMITZDORFF, Mrs. Gertrud. Bertastr. 59, Nuremberg. b. 14 Feb 1924 Berlin. Dipl. '51 Univ. of Würzburg, Ger. COUNSELOR, Eheberatungsstelle/Kath. Volksbüro, Georg Strobel Str. 43, Nuremberg. Consulting, guidance; depth psychology, characterology.   F

SCHWEIGHÖFER, Dr. Jürgen. Rudolf Troost Str. 20, Neuwied. b. 22 June 1921

Allenstein. Dipl. Psych. '51 Johannes Gutenberg Univ. of Mainz, Ger. PSYCHOLOGIST, Employment Off, Hermannstr. 41, Neuwied. Testing, vocational guidance, applied psychology; achievement tests, projective techniques, social perception. M

SCHWINCK, Dr. rer. nat. Ilse. Dept. of Pharmacology, New York Univ. Med. Sch, 550 First Ave, New York 16, N.Y. USA. b. 23 May 1923 Hamburg, Ger. Dr. rer. nat. '50 Univ. of Tübingen, Ger. RES. FELLOW, New York Univ. Med. Sch. Research; physiological and chemical basic reactions of psychology, biochemical genetics. F

SCHWUNG, Dr. Henriette. Sternbergweg 17, Hamburg. b. 4 Apr 1904 Bocholt/W. Dr. '31 Univ. of Hamburg, Ger. GRAPHOLOGIST, priv. prac; DOZENT, Hamburg Volkshochschule. Member: BDP. Applied psychology, consulting, guidance; psychology of expression, graphology, depth psychology. F

SEEBERGER, Dr. med. Hans Jürgen Paul. Voss Str. 2, Heidelberg. b. 8 Apr 1918 Dölzig. PSYCHIATRIST, Psychosomatic Div, Univ. Clin, Heidelberg. Member: German Psychoanal. Assn. Clinical psychotherapy, testing, consulting; social perception, mental hygiene. M

SEELBACH, Dr. Hans. Hochstr. 91/III, Hagen/Westf. b. 2 Aug 1900 Wuppertal-Elberfeld. Dr. '33 Friedrich Wilhelms Univ. of Bonn, Ger. PSYCHOTHERAPIST, priv. prac; PRINCIPAL, Volksschule, Gevelsberg. Member: BDP. Psychotherapy, educational psychology, testing, clinical analysis; depth psychology, psychology of human development. M

SEGNER, Mrs. Elfriede. Kolonnenstr. 10-11, Berlin-Schöneberg. b. 14 May 1919 Berlin. Dipl. Psych. '55 Free Univ. of Berlin, Ger. PSYCHOLOGIST, Erziehungsberatung, Fehrbelliner Platz, Berlin-Wilmersdorf. Member BDP. Consulting, psychotherapy, diagnosis; psychological lectures for parents, school and educational problems. F

SEHRINGER, Dr. phil. Wolfgang. Hebelstr. 32, Schopfheim/Baden. b. 21 May 1929 Mannheim. PH.D '56 Univ. of Freiburg, Ger. STUDENT, Univ. of Freiburg. Research testing; children's drawings, national character. M

SEIFERT, Prof. Dr. Friedrich Karl. Schellingstr. 40, Munich 13. b. 1 Jan 1891 Würzburg. Prof. '27 Univ. of Munich, Ger. PROF. of PSYCH. and PHILOS, Univ. of Munich; Technische Hochschule Munich; PSYCHOTHERAPIST, priv. prac. Member: Deutsche Gesellschaft für Psychother. und Tiefenpsych. Psychotherapy, professional writing, teaching; psychology of the unconscious, theory of neuroses, interpretation of dreams. M

SEIFERT, Dr. phil. Harald Gerhard Ernst. Helenenstr. 7a, Leverkusen. b. 31 Oct 1919 Lugau/Erzgeb. PH.D '56 Univ. of Bonn, Ger. INDUS. EDUC. EXPERT, Theodor Wuppermann Ltd, Friedrichstr. 38, Leverkusen. Member: BDP. Educational and industrial psychology, testing, teaching; learning theory, psychological statistics, psychometric methods, social and group psychology. M

SEIFERT, Karl Heinz. Hauptstr. 218, Heidelberg. b. 2 July 1928 Ilsenburg/Harz. Dipl. Psych. '51 Univ. of Heidelberg, Ger. TRNG. PROF. SUPERV, Arbeitsgemeinschaft für soziale Betriebsgestaltung; TCHR. in DIFFERENTIAL PSYCH, Psych. Inst, Univ. of Heidelberg. Research, teaching, applied and industrial psychology; training and personnel selection tests, non-verbal tests for the deaf and dumb, dreams and reality. M

SENNEWALD, Dr. Helmut. Schultze Delitzsch Str. 17, Erfurt. b. 19 Mar 1927 Sömmerda. LECTURER, Div. of Psych, Kahlaische Str. 1, Jena; EDITOR, *Wissenschaftliche Zeitschrift*, Univ. of Jena. Member: BDP. Research. teaching; group process, projective techniques. M

SICKEL, Wilhelm. Am Waldschlösschen 17, Werdohl-Eveking/Westf. b. 18 Aug 1922 Gotha/Thur. Dipl. Psych. '53 Tech. Acad. Braunschweig, Ger. PERS. MGR, Vereinigte Deutsche Metallwerke AG, Zweigniederlassung Carl Berg, Werdohl. Member: BDP. Industrial psychology, testing, personnel management; projective techniques, group process. M

SIEMES, Dr. Wolfgang. Neue Ansbacherstr. 7A/II, Berlin-Schöneberg. b. 3 May 1926 Moers. Dr. rer. nat. '53 Univ. of Göttingen, Ger. PHYSICIST, Borsig AG, Berlinerstr, Berlin-Tegel; PHYSICIST, Tech. Chem. Inst. D. TW, Hardenberstr, Berlin-Charlottenburg. Retired; statistical methods, industrial psychology, characterology. M

SIEMS, Dr. phil. Gerd. Sternplatz 10, Uelzen/Hann. b. 21 Nov 1924 Uelzen. PH.D '56 Univ. of Innsbruck, Austria. Member: BDP. Research, consulting, testing; theory of changes of memory, social behavior, methods of empiric psychology, social psychology. M

SIGGEMANN, Claus. Gaisbergstr. 87, Heidelberg. b. 29 Apr 1924 Mannheim. Dipl. Psych. '52 Univ. of Heidelberg, Ger. COLL. TCHR, Pädagogisches Inst, Keplerstr. 87, Heidelberg. Teaching, research, testing; symbolism, learning theory, Gestalt theory. M

SIMMERDING, Dr. phil. Dipl. Psych. Gertrud Maria. Von der Tann Str. 5, Munich 22. b. 30 Sept 1919 Vienna, Austria. PH.D '50

Univ. of Munich, Ger. TV PRODUCER, Bayerischer Rundfunk, Rundfunkplatz 1, Munich 2. Applied and educational psychology; achievement tests, blind children, psychological background of television for children. F

SIMONEIT, Ministerialrat a.D. Dr. phil. habil. Max. Seeblick 13, Kiel. b. 17 Oct 1896 Arys. Dr. phil. habil, Univ. of Königsberg, Ger. Member: BDP, DGP. Teaching, applied psychology, retired; psychology of advertising. M

SIX (née Mende), Mrs. Maria Theresia. Liebigstr. 18/VI, Munich 22. b. 3 June 1914 Fraustadt/Silesia. Dipl. Psych, Univ. of Munich, Ger. PSYCH'T and SOC. WRK. DIR, Psychosomatic Guid. Cen. for Children, Univ. Child. Hosp, Pettenkofer Str. 8a, Munich 15. Member: BDP. Testing, guidance, child psychotherapy; social perception, character, psychology of thought. F

SODHI, Prof. Dr. phil. Kripal Singh. Schmarjestr. 12, Berlin-Zehlendorf. b. 15 Apr 1911 Roorkee, India. PH.D '41 Friedrich Wilhelms Univ. of Berlin, Ger. PROF. of PSYCH, Free Univ. of Berlin, Boltzmannstr. 3, Berlin-Dahlem. Member: DGP. Research, teaching; perception, group process, social prejudice. M

SONDERGELD, Dr. phil. Walter. Ludwig Bruns Str. 19, Hannover. b. 18 Feb 1907 Hannover. PH.D '34 Univ. of Göttingen, Ger. CO-WRKR, Forschungsinst. für Arbeitspsych. und Personalwesen, Garkuche 3, Braunschweig. Member: BDP. Industrial psychology, testing, advertising, traffic psychology; projective techniques, achievement tests, social perception, group process. M

SORGE, Dipl. Psych. Helmut. Lornsenstr. 8, Kiel. b. 26 Dec 1929 Kiel. Dipl. Psych. '55 Univ. of Kiel, Ger. GRAD. STD, Psych. Inst, Univ. of Kiel. Member: BDP. Applied psychology, testing, administration; projective techniques, graphology, personnel selection. M

SOYKA, Mrs. Elisabeth F. Ch. Gertrudenstr. 5, Flensburg. b. 1 June 1928 Flensburg. Dipl. '54 Univ. of Göttingen, Ger. TEACHER, Landesfachschule für Frauenberufe, Bahnhofsstr. 6, Flensburg. Member: BDP. Teaching, student; educational and developmental psychology, social perception, attitude. F

SPENGLER, Dr. phil. Gustav Rudolf Andreas. Westfalenweg 280, Wuppertal-Elberfeld. b. 18 Jan 1913 Rübeland. PH.D '38 Univ. of Marburg, Ger. INDUS. PSYCH'T, Vereinigte Glanzstoff Fabriken AG, Am Laurentiusplatz, Wuppertal-Elberfeld. Member: BDP. DGP. Industrial psychology, teaching, testing; achievement

tests, learning theory, industrial training. M

SPIEGEL, Dr. Bernt. Augusta Anlage 34, Mannheim. b. 20 Apr 1926 Heidelberg. Dr. '52 Univ. of Heidelberg, Ger. SCI. ASST, Wirtschafts Hochschule, Schloss, Mannheim; SCI. DIR, Fachinst. für werbwissenschaftliche Untersuchungen, Mannheim. Member: BDP, DGP. Research, industrial psychology, teaching; traffic psychology. M

SPIELER, Prof. Dr. phil. Josef. Südendstr. 6, Karlsruhe. b. 5 Aug 1900 Walldürn. PH.D '25 Univ. of Würzburg, Ger. DIR. and PROF, Pädagogisches Institut, Karlsruhe; LECTURER, Univ. of Freiburg. Member: DGP. Teaching, research, editorial; educational psychology, remedial education. M

SPITZNAGEL, Dr. phil. Albert. Schubertstr. 24, Freiburg. b. 27 Oct 1929 Grussen. PH.D '55 Univ. of Freiburg, Ger. RES. FELLOW, Inst. of Psych, Bertholdstr. 17, Freiburg. Member: BDP. Research, industrial psychology, student; experimental psychology, social psychology. M

SPRANGER, Prof. Dr. phil. h.c., Dr. iur. h.c. Eduard. 12 Rumelinstr, Tübingen. PH.D '05 Univ. of Berlin, Ger. PROF. EMER. of PSYCH, Univ. of Tübingen. Member: DGP. Research, educational psychology; personality, developmental psychology. M

SPREEN, Dr. phil. Otfried. Städtische Nervenklinik, Osterholzer Landstr. 51, Bremen. b. 7 Nov 1926 Bochum. PH.D '52 Univ. of Freiburg, Ger. CLIN. PSYCH'T, Städtische Nervenklinik. Member: BDP, DGP. Testing, consulting, psychotherapy, research; projective techniques, brain disease, theory of neuroses. M

STAHL, Dr. phil. Dipl. Psych. Minnie. Rauenthalerstr. 9, Wiesbaden. b. 26 Sept 1921 Hallein, Austria. PH.D, Univ. of Graz, Austria. DIRECTOR, Inst. für Erziehungshilfe, Adolfsallee 31, Wiesbaden. Member: BDP. Child guidance, teaching, research; child growth and development, social perception, group process. F

STANGL, Dr. phil. Anton G. Birkachstr. 1, Stuttgart-Degerloch. b. 31 May 1917 Würzburg. PH.D '49 Univ. of Würzburg, Ger. GRAPHOLOGIST, priv. prac. Member: BDP. Industrial psychology, graphology, teaching; graphology, personnel psychology, psychology of advertising. M

STANNEK, Dipl. Psych. Bernhard. Elisenstr. 11, Wuppertal-Elberfeld. b. 3 Feb 1927 Breslau. Dipl. Psych. '52 Univ. of Göttingen, Ger. INDUS. PSYCH'T, Vereinigte Glanzstoff Fabriken AG, Am Laurentiusplatz, Wuppertal-Elberfeld; DIR. of INDUS. PSYCH. DIV, Glanzstoff Werkes Oberbruch/Rhld. Member: BDP. Industrial psychology, testing, teaching; test methods, supervisory training, group process, youth leadership. M

STAPFF, Dipl. Psych. Wolfram. Widenmayerstr. 31, Munich 22. b. 22 May 1925 Hamm/Westf. Dipl. Psych. '55 Ludwig Maximilian Univ. of Munich, Ger. PSYCH. CONSULT, priv. prac. Consulting, testing, guidance; projective techniques, intelligence and developmental tests, child psychology.   M

STARCK, Dipl. Psych. Dr. phil. Willy. Oelckersallee 34, Hamburg-Altona. b. 21 Feb 1923 Hamburg. PH.D '56 Univ. of Munich, Ger. CONSULT. PSYCH'T, priv. prac. Member: BDP. Research, testing; causes of asociality, treatment of asocial persons. M

STÄRKE, Dr. Hermann. Schwarzwaldstr. 22, Mannheim-Lindenhof. b. 1 Apr 1920 Wittstock. Dr. rer. nat. '54 Georg August Univ. of Göttingen, Ger. INDUS. PSYCH'T, Heinrich Lanz AG, Mannheim-Lindenhof. Member: BDP. Industrial psychology, testing, guidance; diagnosis, vocational and economic psychology.   M

STEFFEN, Dipl. Psych. Gerhard Johannes Julius. Stoeckhardtstr. 13, Hamburg 26. b. 21 Jan 1925 Hamburg. Dipl. Psych. '55 Christian Albrechts Univ. of Kiel, Ger. Consulting, applied, educational and industrial psychology, teaching; adult and child guidance, emotional psychological problems, human relations.   M

STEGLITZ, Dipl. Psych. Günter. Dantestr. 25, Heidelberg. b. 15 Dec 1922 Halle/Saale. Dipl. Psych. '53 Univ. of Heidelberg, Ger. VOCAT. GUID. COUNS, Employment Off, Turmstr. 13, Neustadt/Pfalz. Industrial psychology, testing, guidance; vocational counseling and testing.   M

STEIN, Freimut Friedrich Burkhard. Am Mazfeld 95, Nuremberg. b. 16 June 1924 Nuremberg. Dipl. Psych. '52 Univ. of Erlangen, Ger. Professional writing, applied psychology, consulting; psychology of expression and thought, psychology of sport.   M

STEIN, Mrs. Herta Regina. Am Mazfeld 95, Nuremberg. b. 20 Mar 1925 Rochau/Krs. Angerburg. Dipl. Psych. '52 Univ. of Erlangen, Ger. Educational and applied psychology, consulting; educational guidance, psychology of expression, special instruction for the retarded children.   F

STEINEMANN, Dr. phil. Käthe Ph. M. Durlacherstr. 2, Berlin-Schöneberg. b. 9 May 1920 Berlin. PH.D '54 Ludw. Maxim. Univ. of Munich, Ger. PSYCHOLOGIST, Jugendstrafanstalt Berlin-Plötzensee, Heckerdam 7, Berlin. Member: BDP. Research, administration, testing; criminal psychology, social psychology, attitude measurement. M

STEINHAUSEN, Dr. phil. Mrs. Margrit. Thumbstr. 66, Cologne. b. 18 June 1924 Cologne. PH.D '55 Univ. of Cologne, Ger.

Educational psychology; adolescent psychology.   F

STEINIGER, Dr. Alexander Rudolf. Inheidener Str. 27, Frankfurt/M. b. 23 June 1908 Schleiz/Thur. Dr. rer. nat. '34 Univ. of Jena, Ger. VOCAT. GUID. COUNS, Employment Off, Gartenstr. 138, Frankfurt/M. Member: BDP. Guidance, industrial psychology, administration; social psychology, vocational testing, youth psychology. M

STEINIGER, Dr. phil. Konrad. Moorreye 43, Hamburg-Langenhorn 1. b. 14 July 1921 Ammenberg. PH.D '54 Univ. of Bonn, Ger. CHIEF SUPERV. PSYCH'T, Deutsche Versuchsanstalt für Luftfahrt, Inst. für Flugmedizin und Fliegeruntersuchungsstelle, Airport Halle Nord B II, Hamburg. Guidance, applied psychology, teaching; aviation psychology.   M

STEINWACHS, Dr. phil. Friedrich. Hornschuchstr. 6, Tübingen. b. 31 Jan 1911 Hannover. ASSISTANT, Psych. Lab, Univ. Psych. Hosp, Forschungsstelle für Konstitutions und Arbeitspsych, Univ. of Tübingen, Osianderstr. 22, Tübingen. Member: BDP. Industrial psychology, teaching, research; psychology of work, motor skills.   M

STENDER, Dr. Berthold. Kühlwetter Str. 16a, DSsseldorf 10. b. 3 June 1923 Hannover. Dr. rer. nat. '55 Technische Hochschule Braunschweig, Ger. INDUS. PSYCH'T, Forschungsinst. für Arbeitspsych. und Personalwesen (FORFA), Friedrichstr. 9, Düsseldorf. Member: BDP. Research, industrial psychology, testing; projective techniques, accident psychology.   M

STENGER, Prof. Father Hermann. Kirchplatz 65, Gars am Inn. b. 29 Aug 1920 Munich. Dipl. Psych. '54 Univ. of Munich, Ger. PROF. of PSYCH, Ordenshochschule der Redemptoristen. Research, teaching, psychotherapy; psychology and education of theologians and members of religious orders.   M

STERNEGGER, Benedikt. Adelsried/Augsburg. b. 6 Aug 1904 Meitingen/Wertingen. RECTOR, Adelsried Parish, Bischöfliches Ordinariat, Augsburg. Parish priest, research, professional writing; nuclear psychology.   M

STEVER, Dr. rer. nat. Johannes. Eltmannshausen über Eschwege, Kassel. b. 27 Nov 1912 Heygendorf. Dr. rer. nat. '40 Friedrich Schiller Univ. of Jena, Ger. STUD. ASST, Hochschule für Int. Paedagogische Forschung, Schlossstr. 29, Frankfurt/M. Member: BDP. Research, teaching, testing; learning theory, educational psychology, guidance, Gestalt psychology.   M

STIEBITZ, Dipl. Psych. Gerhard. Genfer Str. 125, Berlin-Reinickendorf 1. b. 11 Apr 1926 Berlin. Dipl. Psych. '55 Free Univ.

of Berlin, Ger. INDUS. PSYCH'T, Allgemeine Elektrizitäts Gesellschaft, Holländerstr, Berlin; TEACHER, Volkshochschule. Member: BDP. Personnel psychology, testing, research; ability testing, industrial group process, apprentice training.　M

STILLER-REINECKE, Dr. med. Margot. Sertürnerstr. 14, Göttingen. b. 4 Nov 1926 Göttingen, Ger. MD '55 Univ. of Göttingen, Ger. VOLUTEER PHYS, Niedersächsisches Landeskrankenhaus, Rosdorferweg 70, Göttingen. Member: Studiengesellschaft für praktische Psych. Psychotherapy, clinical analysis, psychiatry; personality adjustment, diagnosis and treatment of the disturbed mind.　F

STING, Albert Eugen. Vogelsangstr. 16, Waiblingen. b. 7 May 1924 Ludwigsburg. Dipl. Psych. '55 Univ. of Tübingen, Ger. PASTOR, Evangelische Landeskirche in Württemberg, Gerokstr. 21-29, Stuttgart. Consulting, guidance, testing; developmental psychology, psychology of religion.　M

STÖHR, Adolf. Christoph Schmid Str. 28, Munich 13. b. 10 Apr 1916 Bayreuth. Dipl. Psych, Univ. of Munich, GER. TEACHER, Hilfsschule an der Simmernstr, Munich; PSYCHOLOGIST, Psych. Inst, Munich. Member: BDP. Teaching, educational and industrial psychology, testing, consulting, guidance; psychology of learning, child therapy, graphology.　M

STRAUCH, Dr. phil. Hans. Stefansiedlung 29, Passau. b. 9 July 1903 Erfurt. PH.D '34 Univ. of Erlangen, Ger. STUDIEN PROF, Städt. Wirtschaftsaufbauschule Passau, Heiligengeist Gasse 10, Passau. Teaching; psychoanalysis, characterology, Gestalt psychology.　M

STRICKMANN, Dipl. Psych. Dr. phil. Renate. Wilhelmstr. 34, Tübingen. b. 11 May 1930 Melle/Osnabrück. PH.D '56 Univ. of Erlangen, Ger. SCI. ASST, Forschungsstelle der Universitätsnervenklinik, Osianderstr, Tübingen. Research, student; mental and pshysical development, student aptitude measurement.　F

STRIEFLER-WUSTERHAUSEN, Mrs. Helga. Hohe Str. 34, Bad Godesberg. b. 25 July 1925 Potsdam. Dipl. Psych. '55 Univ. of Bonn, Ger. TEACHER, Evangelische Schule, Meckenheimerstr, Mehlem/Rh. Teaching, educational psychology; child psychology, educational guidance, developmental psychology, school readiness tests.　F

STRÜBER, Hans Joachim. Psych. Inst, Munzgasse 11, Tübingen. b. 18 Sept 1927 Mexico City, Mexico. Vordiplom '52 Univ. of Hamburg, Ger. STUDENT, Psych. Inst, Univ. of Tübingen. Research; psychological epistemology, general psychology.　M

STRÜBING, Dietrich. Krausenstr. 33, Han-

nover. b. 2 July 1926 Waren, Mecklenburg. Dipl. Psych. '54 Univ. of Hamburg, Ger. SCI. ASST, Med. Psych. Inst. für Indus, Bergbau und Verkehr beim TÜV Hannover, Tiestestr. 16-18, Hannover. Member: BDP. Traffic psychology, industrial psychology, guidance; projective techniques, intelligence measurement, social adjustment.　M

STRUNZ, Prof. Dr. Kurt. Spessart Str. 25a, Würzburg. b. 21 Sept 1898 Adorf/Vogtl. Dr. phil. habil. '52 Univ. of Würzburg, Ger. EDUC. PSYCH'T, Psych. Inst, Univ. of Würzburg, Domerschulgasse 13, Würzburg. Member: BDP, DGP. Teaching, research, educational psychology; high school teaching, typology.　M

STUMPF, Dr. phil. Manfred. Dillisstr. 1, Munich 23. b. 16 Sept 1919 Dresden. PH.D '45 Univ. of Munich, Ger. PSYCHOTHERAPIST, priv. prac; LECTURER, Volkshochschule, Munich. Member: Munich Gesellschaft für Tiefenpsych. und Lebenshilfe. Psychotherapy, teaching, research; nervous diseases, psychoanalytic theory and Christian philosophy.　M

STURM, Dr. Hertha. Glümerstr. 5, Freiburg. b. 22 Jan 1925 Nuremberg. Dr, Univ. of Freiburg, Ger. HEAD, Sch. and Youth Programs, Südwestfunk, Kyburg, Freiburg. Editorial; youth problems.　F

STUTZ, Dr. Wilhelm. Goethestr. 24, Recklinghausen. b. 18 Aug 1908 Düsseldorf. REGIERUNGSRAT, Employment Off, Hertenerstr. 74, Recklinghausen. Member: BDP. Testing, administration, applied psychology; character, vocational aptitude, perception.　M

SÜLLWOLD, Dr. Fritz. Bertheaustr. 9, Göttingen. b. 6 Aug 1927 Herne/Westf. Dr. rer. nat. '53 Univ. of Göttingen, Ger. RES. ASST, Deutsche Forschungsgemeinschaft, Frankengraben 40, Bad Godesberg. Member: BDP. Research, teaching; psychology of thought ,attention, memory.　M

SUTTINGER, Dr. Günter. Bundesring 42, Berlin-Tempelhof. b. 24 Sept 1913 Strassburg. Dr. rer. nat. '41 Univ. of Berlin, Ger. DIR. of CRIMINOL. RES, Strafvollzugsamt Berlin, Lehrter Str. 58, Berlin NW 40. Member: BDP. Consulting, research, teaching; criminal psychology, learning theory, anthropology, relation of psychology, psychiatry and psychoanalysis.　M

TÄGERT, Dr. phil. Ilse. Sudendstr. 59, Berlin-Steglitz. b. 30 May 1913 Osnabrück. PH.D '51 Univ. of Göttingen, Ger. LECTURER, Pestalozzi-Froebel-Haus, Barbarossastr, Berlin W 30. Member: BDP, DGP, ICWP. Teaching, guidance, testing; marriage guidance, characterology, projective techniques.　F

TAMBORINI, Dipl. Psych. Albert. Potsdamer

Chaussee 87, Berlin-Schlachtensee. b. 14 Sept 1927 Berlin. PSYCHOLOGIST, Senator für Jugend und Sport, Berlin, Am Karlsbad 8, Berlin W. Member: BDP, Assn. of German Soc. Wrkrs. Testing, research, teaching, psychotherapy, educational psychology; social diseases, anthropology, sociology, clinical psychology, heredity, delinquency. M

TAUSCH, Dr. Anne-Marie. Windhof, Weilberg/L. b. 7 May 1925 Berlin. Dr. '53 Univ. of Göttingen, Ger. SCI. CO-WRKR, Psych. Inst, Univ. of Marburg, Gutenbergstr. 18, Marburg/L. Ecudational psychology, teaching, psychotherapy; social perception. F

TAUSCH, Dozent Dr. Reinhard. Gutenbergstr. 18, Malburg/L. b. 11 June 1921 Braunschweig. Dr. '51 Univ. of Göttingen, Ger. DOZENT, Päd. Inst. Weilburg/L; INSTR. of EDUC. PSYCH, Univ. of Marburg/L. Member: BDP, DGP. Teaching, research, psychotherapy; perception, psychotherapy. M

TEUFFEL, Mrs. Inge. Birkenwaldstr. 90, Stuttgart. b. 6 Jan 1920 Tübingen. Dipl. Psych. '53 Univ. of Tübingen, Ger. EDUC. CONSULT, Jugendamt Stuttgart, Wilhelmsplatz 11, Stuttgart. Member: BDP. Consulting, guidance, testing, clinical analysis, graphology; test psychology. F

THEOBALD, Adolf. Hans Thomastr. 21, Frankfurt/M. b. 23 May 1927 Frankfurt. Dipl. Psych. '52 Univ. of Frankfurt, Ger. INDUS. PSYCH'T, priv. prac. Industrial psychology; perception, physiological theories of cortical reactions. M

THIELITZ, Hans Friedrich. Pestalozzistr. 10, Braunschweig. b. 11 Feb 1926 Wanne-Eickel/L. Dipl. Psych. '53 Technische Hochschule, Braunschweig, Ger. ASSISTANT Dept. of Indus. Sci. and Pers, Ilseder Hütte, Gerhardstr. 10, Peine bei Hannover. Member: BDP. Applied and industrial psychology, testing, research; fatigue, projective research methods. M

THOLE, Dipl. Psych. Maria. Fa. C. A. Thole, Mühlenstr. 6, Cloppenburg/Oldbg. b. 7 Dec 1928 Oldenburg. Dipl. Psych. '52 Univ. of Bonn, Ger. PERS. PSYCH'T, Fa. C. A. Thole. Testing, personnel selection; projective techniques, social perception. F

THOMAE, Prof. Dr. Hans. Jordanweg 2, Erlangen. b. 31 July 1915 Winkl. Dr. phil. habil. '42 Univ. of Leipzig, Ger. PROF. of PSYCH. and DIR, Inst. of Psych, Univ. of Erlangen, Schloss, Erlangen. Member: BDP, DGP. Teaching, research, guidance; personality, motivation, longitudinal studies in children, juveniles and adults. M

THOMAS, Dipl. Psych. Sigrid Marion. Petristr. 20, Braunschweig. b. 28 July 1929

Dresden. Dipl. Psych. '54 Technische Hochschule Braunschweig. MEMBER, Forschungsinst. für Arbeitspsych. und Personalwesen (FORFA), Garküche 3, Braunschweig; EDITOR, FORFA-Briefe zur Arbeitspsychologischen Information. Editorial, industrial psychology, research; projective techniques, child psychology, achievement testing. F

THOST, Dr. phil. Werner. Bergmoserstr. 18, Gauting bei Munich. b. 26 Sept 1916 Dresden. PH.D '52 Univ. of Munich, Ger. INDUS. PSYCH'T. and GRAPHOLOGIST, priv. prac. Member: BDP. Industrial psychology, graphology, testing, consulting; graphological aptitude testing, projective techniques, group process in industry. M

THOST-CARNAP, Mrs. Hanna. Bergmoserstr. 18, Gauting bei Munich. b. 2 June 1920 Freiburg. State Exam. '42 Inst. for Physical Ther, Univ. of Munich, Ger. GRAPHOLOGIST, priv. prac. Member: BDP. Industrial psychology, testing, consulting, graphology; aptitude tests, marriage, educational and general counseling, group work. F

THURN, Dipl. Psych. Dr. Lic. Hubertus. Stolzestr. 1a, Cologne. b. 6 Mar 1908 Oberhausen. Dr, Univ. of Bonn, Ger. PSYCHOLOGIST, Canisius Haus, Cologne. Teaching, testing, psychotherapy, guidance; graphology, characterology. M

TILLMANN, Karl Georg. Eckertstr. 6, Cologne-Lindenthal. b. 24 Oct 1928 Blankenheim/Eifel. Dipl. Psych. '50 Univ. of Bonn, Ger. ADV. ASST, Kraft Ltd, Bockenheimer Landstr. 20, Frankfurt/M. Industrial psychology, advertising; advertising psychology, propaganda, ethnology. M

TIMMERMANN, Prof. Dr. phil. Henry. Thälmannsiedlung 1, Lehnitz-Nordbahnhof bei Berlin. b. 11 Jan 1894 Hamburg. PH.D '39 Univ. of Hamburg, Ger. PROFESSOR, Humbolt Univ, Unter den Linden, Berlin. Member: BDP. Teaching, industrial psychology; psychology of music. M

TIPPELS, Dr. Hans. Hildastr. 4, Heidelberg. b. 14 Feb 1924 Schetzler, Czech. Dipl. Psych, Univ. of Heidelberg, Ger. Research, testing, teaching, student; projective techniques. M

TITTMANN, Dipl. Psych. Susanne. Riegelerstr. 8, Bonn. b. 14 Sept 1928 Cologne. Dipl. Psych. '52 Univ. of Bonn, Ger. VOLUNTEER ASST, Psych. Inst, Univ. of Bonn, Am Hofe 1e, Bonn. Applied psychology, testing, guidance; forensic psychology, personality, motivation, individual guidance, social development. F

TITZ, Dr. Bernhard. Altewiekring 21, Braunschweig. b. 26 Jan 1923 Braunschweig. Dr. rer. nat. '53 Technische Hochschule, Braunschweig, Ger. HEAD, Adv. Dept, Senkingwerk, Hildesheim. Research, applied psychology, publicity and advertising; psychology of advertising, aptitude analysis, clinical psychology.　M

TÖGEL, Dr. phil. Fritz. Poetenweg 43, Leipzig N 22. b. 25 Dec 1888 Leipzig. PH.D, Staatsexamen, Univ. of Leipzig Ger. GRAPHOLOGIST, priv. prac. Member: BDP. Educational consulting, research, teaching, psychotherapy; graphology.　M

TÖNNESMANN, Miss Gisela. Waldsaum 60, Essen-Stadtwald. b. 15 July 1927 Bochum. Dipl. Psych. '54 Univ. of Freiburg, Ger. TCHR. in PSYCH, EDUC. and SOCIOL, Bildungsanstalt für Frauenberufe, Westfalenstr. 311, Essen-Stelle. Applied, educational and industrial psychology, teaching, testing; social work, group process, vocational pedagogy.　F

TORMIN, Miss Erika. Lessingstr. 1, Lueneburg. b. 3 Sept 1928 Luebeck. Dipl. Psych. '53 Univ. of Hamburg, Ger. EDUC. ASST, Päd. Hochschule, Wilschenbrucherweg 84, Lueneburg. Member: BDP. Teaching, educational psychology, testing, guidance; projective techniques, psychology of childhood and youth, social work.　F

TRÄNKLE, Dr. med. Wolfgang A. E. Speyererstr. 120, Mannheim. b. 17 Nov 1923 Mannheim. MD, Univ. of Tübingen, Ger. ASSISTANT, Kantonale Heil- und Pflegeanstalt, Waldhaus/CHUR, Switz. Member: Allgemeine ärztliche Gesellschaft für Psychother. Clinical analysis, research, psychotherapy, consulting; projective techniques, attitude measurement in clinical research on heart patients, physiological psychology, psychosomatic medicine.　M

TRAPP, Prof. Dr. phil. Georg. Pullach bei Munich. b. 21 June 1915 Regensburg. PH.D '49 Univ. of Munich, Ger. PROF. of PSYCH, Berchmanskolleg, Wolfratshauser Str. 30, Pullach. Teaching, administration; the problem of body and soul, psychology of expression.　M

TRAXEL, Dr. phil. Werner. Körnerstr. 27, Marburg/L. b. 6 Dec 1924 Hanau. PH.D '52 Univ. of Munich, Ger. SCI. ASST, Psych. Inst, Univ. of Marburg, Gutenbergstr. 18, Marburg/L. Member: BDP. Research, teaching, applied psychology; experimental psychology, personality, emotional processes.　M

TREBECK, Dr. Richard. Friedrich-Karlstr. 71, Cologne-Weidenpesch. b. 21 Jan 1906 Oberhausen/Rhld. Dr. rer. nat. '39 Univ. of Jena, Ger. INDUS. PSYCH'T, Glanzstoff-Courtaulds Ltd, Neusser Landstr. 2, Cologne-Weidenpesch. Member: BDP. Industrial psychology, teaching; aptitude diagnosis, personality development.　M

TREIBER, Dr. med. Albin. Pleydenwurffstr.

11, Nuremberg. b. 15 May 1927 Nuremberg. Dipl. Psych. '53 Univ. of Erlangen, Ger. Testing, clinical practice, psychotherapy; psychological diagnostics, characterology, anthropology.　M

TROEBST, Mrs. Elsbeth. Theresienstr. 461 V, Munich. b. 9 Sept 1901 Cologne. Dipl. Psych. '54 Univ. of Munich, Ger. COUNSELOR, Landratsamt, Mariahilfpl. 17a, Munich. Member: BDP. Educational psychology, teaching, research, psychotherapy, guidance; child and adolescent psychology, psychology of women.　F

TRÖGER, Dipl. Psych. Iris. Wulfsbrook 10, Kiel-Hassee. b. 9 Dec 1928 Hamburg. Dipl. Psych, Univ. of Kiel, Ger. VOCAT. GUID. COUNS, Employment Off, Wilhelmplatz 12-13, Kiel. Guidance, testing, research, administration; projective techniques, social perception, youth work.　F

TRUMPLER, Dr. phil. Hans-Joachim. Rottmannstr. 8, Heidelberg. b. 1 July 1928 Merseburg/Saale. PH.D '53 Univ. of Heidelberg, Ger. TRAFFIC PSYCH'T, Psych. med. Inst. für Verkehrssicherheit beim TÜV Mannheim, Richard-Wagnerstr. 2, Mannheim. Member: BDP. Testing of drivers, traffic psychology, research; projective techniques, perception.　M

TSCHERPEL, Dipl. Psych. Rudolf. Pfadstr. 2, Hofingen, Kr. Leonberg bei Stuttgart. b. 20 Jan 1921 Schluckenan, Czech. Dipl. Psych. '50 Univ. of Marburg, Ger. EDUC. PSYCH'T, priv. prac. Member: BDP. Educational psychology, testing, research; memory and learning, attitude measurement, achievement tests, cultural psychology.　M

TUBBESING, Mrs. Jutta. Reinhäuserlandstr. 51, Göttingen. b. 19 July 1928 Göttingen. Dipl. Psych. '52 Univ. of Göttingen, Ger. PSYCHOLOGIST, Beratungs und Betreuungsstelle, Psych. Inst, Univ. of Göttingen, Hoher Weg 15, Göttingen. Member: BDP. Testing, guidance, play and work therapy; problems of children, psychology of thinking.　F

TUMBRÄGEL, Miss Margret. Am Homburg 39, Saarbrücken 3. b. 21 Apr 1926 Vechta/ Oldenburg. Dipl. Psych. '54 Univ. of Bonn, Ger. RES. WRKR, Univ. of Saarland, Saarbrücken 15. Research, guidance, student; social attitudes, child guidance, educational pscyhology.　F

UHRIG, Gertrud. Kaiserstr. 99, Lahr/Baden. b. 14 Feb 1922 Marburg/L. Dipl. Psych. '48 Alb. Ludw. Univ. of Freiburg, Ger. HEILPÄDAGOGIN, Evangelical Home for Girls, Offenburgerstr 11, Lahr-Dinglingen. Applied and educational psychology, testing; child and adolescent psychology, play therapy, individual and group therapy, psychotherapy, graphology.　F

ULICH, Dr. phil. Eberhard H. J. Rheinland-damm 201, Dortmund. b. 29 Nov 1929 Greifswald. PH.D '54 Univ. of Munich, Ger. RES. WRKR, Max Planck Inst. for Indus. Psych. Member: BDP. Industrial psychology, research, consulting; shift operations in industry, group process, industrial relations. M

ULLMANN, Dipl. Psych. Hans. Pestalozzistr. 7a, Bobingen bei Augsburg. b. 4 Oct 1927 Hindenburg. Dipl. Psych. '55 Univ. of Würzburg. Ger. LAW STUDENT, Psych. Inst, Univ. of Munich. Member: BDP. Research, industrial psychology; use of films in applied psychology. M

UMBACH, Dr. phil. Rolf. Buchenring 7, Wpt.-Barmen. b. 19 Aug 1926 Leverkusen. PH.D, Univ. of Munich, Ger. INSTR. for PSYCH, State Police Sch, Norbertstr. 165, Essen. Member: BDP. Teaching, applied psychology. M

UNDEUTSCH, Prof. Dr. rer. nat. Udo. Meister Ekkehart Str. 7, Cologne-Lindenthal. b. 22 Dec 1917 Weimar. Dr. rer. nat. '40 Friedrich Schiller Univ. of Jena, Ger. PROF. of PSYCH. and DIR, Psych. Inst, Univ. of Cologne. Member: BDP, DGP. Research, teaching, applied psychology; adolescent and youth psychology, test theory, psychology of testimony. M

URLAUB, Mrs. Margret. Mannheim R. 7, 12. b. 27 Feb 1927 Schweinfurt. Dipl. Psych. '50 Univ. of Munich, Ger. PSYCHOLOGIST, Child Guid. Clin, Erziehungs-beratungsstelle des Caritasverbandes Mann-heim. Member: BDP. Applied psychology, testing, guidance, social work; achievement tests, group process. F

VALENTINER, Bertha. Sophienstr. 70, Bremen. b. 10 Nov 1881 Delmenhorst/O. PSYCH. ADVIS, Inst. für Jugendkunde, Lübeckerstr. 2a, Bremen. Member: BDP. Applied and educational psychology, testing, consulting, research; test evalu-ation, statistics. F

VALENTINER, Dr. phil. Bernhard Wilhelm Theodor. Sophienstr. 70, Bremen. b. 26 Jan 1878 Mannheim. PH.D '06 Univ. of Leipzig, Ger. DIRECTOR, Inst. für Jugend-kunde und Jugendbildung, Lübeckerstr. 2a, Bremen. Member: BDP, DGP, AIPA. Applied psychology, testing, guidance, editorial; examination of apprentices; retarded and problem children. M

VETTER, Prof. Dr. August. Münsing vor Munich. b. 19 Feb 1887 Wuppertal. Prof. '47 Univ. of Munich, Ger. PROFESSOR, Psych. Inst, Univ. of Munich, Geschwister Scholl Platz, Munich; CO-EDITOR, *Der Zeit-schrift für Menschenkunde.* Member: DGP. Industrial psychology, psychotherapy, teaching; character theory, psychology of expression. M

VIEWEG, Dr. phil. Gottwalt Adolf Johannes. Neusurenland 164, Hamburg-Farmsen. b. 8 Feb 1891 Leipzig. PH.D '18 Univ. of Leipzig, Ger. Member: BDP. Retired, consulting, industrial, applied and edu-cational psychology; educational and vocational guidance. M

VOGL, Günter. Grolandstr. 14, Nuremberg. b. 26 Mar 1929 Munich. Dipl. Psych. '54 Univ. of Munich, Ger. PSYCHOLOGIST, Soc. Counseling Cen, Marienstr. 15, Nurem-berg. Member: BDP. Guidance, consulting, testing; psychology of expression, pro-jective tests. M

VOIGT, Dr. rer. nat. Johannes. Campestr. 8, Braunschweig. b. 29 Mar 1902 Altenburg. Privatdozent '45 Univ. of Jena, Ger. RES. WRKR, Deutsche Forschungsgemein-schaft, Bad Godesberg. Member: DGP. Research, teaching, applied psychology; psychology of thought, psychophysical problems. M

VOIGT, Martin. Luisenstr. 9, Frankfurt/M. b. 13 Feb 1921 Wermdorf. Dipl. Psych. '52 Univ. of Frankfurt, Ger. Student; learning theory. M

VOIGTLÄNDER, Hans Joachim Bruno. Kühle-bornweg 2, Berlin-Steglitz. b. 22 July 1925 Halle/Saale. Dipl. Psych. '54 Free Univ. of Berlin, Ger. EDUC. ADVIS, Jugendamt des Bezirkes Wedding, Pankstr. 28-30, Berlin. STUDENT, Inst. für Psychother, Berlin. Member: BDP. Consulting, guidance. M

VOLKELT, Prof. Dr. Hans. Austr. 103, Bietigheim/Wrttbg. b. 4 June 1886 Basel, Switz. Prof. '30 Univ. of Leipzig, Ger. Member: DGP. Research, editorial; de-velopmental, theoretical and educational psychology. M

VONESSEN, Dr. phil. Franz K. Winterstr. 67, Freiburg. b. 8 Mar 1923 Cologne. PH.D '52 Albert Ludwig Univ. of Freiburg, Ger. Retired, psychotherapy; depth psychology, psychology and philosophical anthropolo-gy. M

VOSSMANN, Dr. phil. Johannes. Beisinger Weg 12, Rechlinghausen. b. 20 Sept 1925 Werl. PH.D '53 Univ. of Bonn, Ger. DI-RECTOR, Priv. Child Guid. Clin, Hause Carl Sonnerschein. Member: BDP. Applied and educational psychology, testing, child guidance; personality tests, juvenile court testimony. M

VOSSMANN-BUTZ, Dr. phil. Marie Therese. Beisinger Weg 12, Rechlinghausen. b. 14 Feb 1923 Gelsenkirchen. PH. D '52 Univ. of Bonn, Ger. TEAM MEMBER, Child Guid. Clin. Caritasverband, Borster Weg 11-13, Rechlinghausen; PSYCHOLOGIST, priv. Child Guid. Clin. Member: BDP. Teaching, applied and educational psychology, child guidance; personality tests, group thera-py. F

WAGNER, Dr. phil. Elisabeth. Kaskadenweg 12, Munich-Obermenzing. b. 29 May 1896 Altenkirchen/Rhld. PH.D '24 Univ. of Marburg/L, Ger. GRAPHOLOGIST, priv. prac. Member: BDP, Graphologische Gesellschaft. Graphological analysis, psychotherapy. F

WAGNER, Dipl. Psych. Hermann Josef. Finkensteig 6, Hof/Saale. b. 9 Jan 1928 Kitzingen/M. Dipl. Psych. '52 Univ. of Würzburg, Ger. VOCAT. GUID. COUNS, Employment Off, Sedanstr. 17, Hof/Saale. Industrial psychology, testing, guidance; human relations, personnel management. M

WAGNER, Johanna. Münzgasse 14, Tübingen. b. 24 July 1926 Kiel. Dipl. Psych. '51 Univ. of Mainz, Ger. RES. PSYCH'T, Philos. Inst, Univ. of Tübingen, Münzgasse 24, Tübingen. Student; characterology, problems of philosophical anthropology, educational psychology. F

WAGNER, Dr. phil. Lutz. Kaskadenweg 12, Munich-Obermenzing. b. 18 Oct 1896 Marienwerder. PH.D '24 Univ. of Freiburg, Ger. GRAPHOLOGY INSTR, Univ. of Munich, Geschwister Scholl Platz 1, Munich. Member: BDP, Graphologische Gesellschaft. Research, teaching, graphological analysis; theory of expression. M

WAIDNER, Dipl. Psych. Günther. Bruchspitze 7, Mainz-Gonsenheim. b. 14 Mar 1923 Nothweiler. Dipl. Psych. '50 Univ. of Mainz, Ger. PSYCHOLOGIST, Employment Off, Schiessgartenstr, Mainz. Member: BDP. Testing, applied psychology, consulting; achievement tests, projective techniques, graphology, educational guidance. M

WALCH, Dr. phil. Dipl. Psych. Max. Burgpflegerstr. 10, Augsburg 11. b. 16 Sept 1917 Grunertshofen bei Munich. PH.D '54 Univ. of Munich, Ger. PSYCHOLOGIST, Augsburg Vocat. Guid. Cen, Karolinenstr. 28, III, Augsburg. Member: BDP. Applied psychology, testing; test psychology, factor analysis, expression, school psychology. M

WALDECK, Dipl. Psych. Manfred. Kurkinderheim Ebenöde, Vlotho/Weser. b. 10 Nov 1929 Klodnitz O/S. Dipl. Psych. '53 Free Univ. of Berlin, Ger. PSYCHOLOGIST, Home for psychoneurotic Children, Kreisverwaltung des Landkreises Herford. Testing, clinical analysis, psychotherapy, consulting; psychotherapeutic work and research with psychoneurotic children and delinquent youths. M

WALLAU, Dr. Johanna. Alte Römerstr. 122, Wilhelmsfeld/Heidelberg. b. 2 Dec 1884 Wittlich. Dr. rer. pol. '25 Univ. of Cologne, Ger. Member: BDP. Retired, industrial psychology, testing, teaching; achievement tests. F

WALLIS, Dipl. Psych. Ingeborg. Sophie Charlottestr. 5, Berlin-Zehlendorf. b.

17 July 1908 Küstrin. Dipl. Psych. '53 Free Univ. of Berlin, Ger. DIRECTOR, Oberlin-Seminar, Berufsfachschule für Kindergärtnerinnen und Hortnerinnen, Am Sandwerder 21, Berlin-Wannsee. Member: BDP. Guidance, teaching; projective techniques, criminology, forensic psychology, child development, therapy. F

WALTHER-FISCHER, Dipl. Psych. Dr. rer. nat. Mrs. Maria Elisabeth. Tübingen Str. 13, Cologne. b. 4 July 1926 Dresden. Dr. rer. nat. '54 Georg August Univ. of Göttingen, Ger. ASST. PERS. DIR, Allianz Versicherungs AG, Kaiser Wilhelm Ring 31-41, Cologne. Member: BDP. Personnel psychology, testing, consulting; examination of salesmen and trainees. F

WAMBACH-PRESTEL, Dipl. Psych. Mrs. Ursula. Sandreuthstr. 19, Nuremberg. b. 4 Oct 1927 Nuremberg. Dipl. Psych. '52 Univ. of Erlangen, Ger. PSYCHOLOGIST, Child Guid. Clin, Sozialer Beratungsdienst, Marienstr. 15, Nuremberg. Member: BDP. Guidance, psychotherapy, testing; test methods, group and individual psychotherapy, social work, developmental psychology. F

WARTEGG, Dr. phil. Ehrig. Lienhardweg 50, Berlin Köpenick Wendenschloss. b. 7 July 1897 Dresden. PH.D, Univ. of Leipzig, Ger. PSYCHOTHERAPIST, Haus der Gesundheit, Leninallee 23-27, Berlin C 2. Member: BDP, DGP. Testing, clinical analysis, psychotherapy, research; experimental psychodiagnosis, projective test methods, depth psychology. M

WASNER, Dr. phil. Ruth. Riemannstr. 6, Göttingen. b. 9 July 1911 Hirschberg/Riesengebirge. PH.D '56 Univ. of Göttingen, Ger. Educational psychology, learning theories. F

WASKEWITZ, Dr. phil. Bernhard. Inst. für Menschenkunde, Josephinenstr. 25, Munich. b. 27 May 1926 Schleswig. PH.D '52 Univ. of Kiel, Ger. PSYCHOLOGIST, Inst. für Menschenkunde. Member: BDP. Testing, graphological analysis; psychology of expression, graphology, vocational psychology. M

WEBER, Dipl. Psych. Charlotte. Psych. Inst, Univ. of Bonn, Am Hof 1, Bonn. b. 2 Aug 1924 Nordhausen/Harz. Dipl. Psych. '53 Univ. of Bonn, Ger. SCI. ASST, Psych. Inst, Univ. of Bonn. Guidance, educational psychology, testing; social and developmental psychology. F

WEDEL, Dr. Adolf. Schröterstr. 5, Jena. b. 19 Aug 1916 Brotterode. Dr. rer. nat. '42 Univ. of Jena, Ger. DOZENT, Dept. of Educ. Psych, Friedrich Schiller Univ, Kahlaische Str. 1, Jena. Member: BDP. Teaching, research; child psychology, psychology of work. M

WEGENER, Dr. med. Dr. phil. Hermann.
Wilhelmshavenerstr. 23, Kiel. b. 6 June
1921 Kiel. PH.D '49 Univ. of Kiel, Ger.
Member: BDP, DGP. Research, teaching,
guidance, educational retardation, motivation, psychology of legal testimony. M

WEGNER, Dipl. Psych. Klaus. Gosslerstr. 13,
Akademische Burse, Göttingen. b. 23 Jan
1926 Hannover. Dipl. Psych. Georg
August Univ. of Göttingen, Ger. SCI. ASST,
Psych. Inst, Georg August Univ. of Göttingen, Hoher Weg 15, Göttingen. Administration, research; general psychology,
perception. M

WEHNER, Dipl. Psych. Ernst G. J. Löhrstr.
42, Fulda. b. 15 Feb 1931 Fulda. Dipl.
Psych. '55 Univ. of Würzburg, Ger.
STUDENT, Psych. Inst, Univ. of Würzburg.
Research, industrial psychology; psychology of expression and its applicaton to art,
theory of management. M

WEHNES, Dr. phil. Franz-Josef. Hauptstr.
48, Urfeld bei Bonn. b. 22 July 1926
Recklinghausen. PH.D '53 Univ. of Bonn,
Ger. TEACHER, Ministry of Educ, State of
Nordrhein-Westfalen, Düsseldorf. Teaching
research; educational psychology, psychology of human development, characterology. M

WEICKERT, Dipl. Psych. Monika. Mittelstr.
11a, Oberbieber bei Neuwied/Rh. b. 14
June 1929 Dresden. Dipl. Psych. '54 Free
Univ. of Berlin, Ger. PSYCHOLOGIST, Evangelisches Kinder und Jugendheim, Au-
bachstr. 12, Oberbieber bei Neuwied.
Member: BDP. Guidance, testing; educational guidance, play therapy, projective
techniques, child psychotherapy, juvenile
delinquency. F

WEIDEMANN, Dr. med. Jürgen. Univ.
Child. Hosp, Mainz. b. 22 Oct 1923 Berlin.
Dipl. Psych. '53 Technische Hochschule
Braunschweig, Ger. SCI. ASST, Univ.
Child. Hosp, Univ. of Mainz; PSYCHOTHERA-
PIST, priv. prac. Child psychotherapy,
research, clinical analysis; projective tech-
niques in child psychology, psychopharma-
cology. M

WEIFFENBACH, Miss Doris. Tullastr. 56,
Karlsruhe. b. 3 June 1929 Karlsruhe.
Dipl. Psych. '55 Univ. of Freiburg, Ger.
VOCAT. GUID. COUNS, Employment Off,
Ruppurretstr. 29, Karlsruhe; TCHR. of
PEDAGOGY and PSYCH, Kindergärtnerinnen-
seminar. Guidance, testing, teaching;
projective techniques, aptitude research,
psychology of infancy. F

WEINERT, Dipl. Psych. Franz. Pfisterstr. 6,
Bamberg. b. 9 Sept 1920 Komotau, Czech.
Dipl. Psych. '55 Univ. of Erlangen, Ger.
TCHR. and EDUC. GUID. COUNS, Land
Bayern, Referat Volksschule, Bamberg.
Teaching, testing; learning theory, group

psychology, developmental tests. M

WEINGARDT, Oberstudiendirektor Erich;
Muhlenweg 167, Leverkusen. b. 5 Aug 1908
Wilhelmshaven. OBERSTUDIENDIREKTOR,
Stadtverwaltung, Leverkusen. Member:
BDP. Teaching, administration; learning
theory, social perception. M

WEINGARTEN, Dr. phil. Gertrud. Liebigstr.
46, Dortmund. b. 24 Dec 1911 Cologne.
PH.D '47 Friedrich Alexander Univ. of
Erlangen, Ger. DOZENT, Westfälische
Wohlfahrtsschule, Silberstr. 13, Dortmund.
Teaching, testing, applied and educational
psychology; social perception, group
process, child guidance. F

WEINSCHENK, Dr. phil. Dr. med. Curt.
Univ. Psychiat. Clin, Ortenbergstr. 8,
Marburg/L. b. 14 Sept 1905 Wachau bei
Leipzig. PH.D, Univ. of Berlin, Ger; MD,
Univ. of Marburg, Ger. SCI. ASST, Univ.
Psychiat. Clin. Member: DGP. Research,
psychotherapy; memory, consciousness,
delusion. M

WEISSKIRCHEN, Dr. Fritz. Bonngasse
10-12, Bonn. b. 16 May 1922 Bonn. Dr.
'51 Univ. of Bonn, Ger. STUDIENRAT,
Staatliches Beethoven Gymnasium, Koblenzerstr. 51-53, Bonn. Member: BDP.
Educational psychology, teaching, research; characterology, theory of will,
tests of attention. M

WEIZSÄCKER, Mrs. Lucy. Immenweg 19,
Berlin-Steglitz. b. 25 Dec 1892 Riga,
Latvia. GRAPHOLOGIST, priv. prac. Graphological analysis, consulting, guidance;
depth psychology. M

WELLEK, Prof. Dr. Albert. Friedrich von
Pfeiffer Weg 3, Mainz. b. 16 Oct 1904
Vienna, Austria. Dr. phil. habil. '38 Univ.
of Leipzig, Ger. PROF. and DIR, Inst. for
Psych, Univ. of Mainz, Saarstr. 21, Mainz;
CO-EDITOR, *Jahrbuch für Psychologie und
Psychotherapie*; *Zentralblatt für Verkehrs-
Medizin und Psychologie*. Member: BDP,
DGP, Int. Union of Sci. Psych. Research,
teaching, administration; personality
theory, projective and expressive methods,
psychology and esthetics of music and
musical talent. M

**WENCK, Dipl. Psych. Dr. phil. Miss Inge
Lina Alwine.** Friesenring 72, Münster/
Westf. b. 19 Aug. 1919 Ohligs/Rhld.
PH.D '45 Karl Franzens Reichs Univ. of
Graz, Austria. PSYCHOLOGIST, Landschafts-
verband Westfalen-Lippe, Wärendorferstr.
1, Münster; LECTURER, Volkshochschule.
Administration, teaching, guidance; social
perception, projective techniques. F

WENDT, Dr. phil. Hans-Werner. Psych. Inst,
Univ. of Mainz, Saarstr. 21, Mainz. b.
25 July 1923 Berlin. PH.D '52 Univ. of
Marburg, Ger. CHIEF INVES, Mainz and
Wesleyan Univ. Joint Psych. Proj, Univ.

of Mainz. Member: DGP. Research, experimental social psychology, teaching; measurement of motivation, effects of physiological and psychological stress variables on mental processes, design of experimental equipment. M

WENZL, Prof. Dr. phil. Alois. Bonnerstr. 24, Munich, b. 25 Jan 1887 Munich. Dr. phil; habil. '26 Univ. of Munich, Ger. PROFESSOR, Philosophisches Seminar II, Geschwister Schollplatz, Munich. Member: DGP. Teaching, research, administration; talent, memory, free will. M

WERNER, Dr. phil. Rudolf Hans. Rohrbacher Str. 142, Heidelberg. b. 23 Mar 1904 Leipzig. PH.D '32 Univ. of Leipzig, Ger. EXEC. DIR, Arbeitsgemeinschaft für Soziale Betriebsgestaltung, Ziegelhäuser Landstr. 69, Heidelberg. Member: BDP. Teaching, industrial psychology, administration; social perception, group process, attitude measurement. M

WESSLING, Miss Anna Thekla. Kunigundenstr. 56, Munich 23. b. 19 Jan 1916 Duelmen/Westf. Dipl. Psych. '55 Univ. of Munich, Ger. EDUC. ADVIS, Kreisjugendamt Ludwigstr. 16, Bad Tölz. Member: BDP. Testing, social work, guidance; play therapy vocational guidance, psychotherapy. F

WESTERMANN, Dr. phil. Dr. med. Hubert. Haager Weg 17, Bonn. b. 24 June 1916 Gelsenkirchen. PH.D '41 Univ. of Bonn, Ger. PSYCHIATRIST, priv. prac. Member: BDP. Psychotherapy, internal medicine, consulting. M

WESTERMANN, Dr. phil. Renate. Holler Allee 51, Bremen. b. 20 June 1913 Berlin. PH.D '42 Univ. of Jena, Ger. DIRECTOR, Sch. of Soc. work, Kirchbachstr. 212, Bremen. Member: BDP. Teaching, consulting, administration; social perception, social group work, social case work, psychoanalysis, child development. F

WESTRICH, Dipl. Psych. Edmund. Balbierstr. 5, Kaiserslautern. b. 1 Apr 1927 Landstuhl/Pfalz. Dipl. Psych. '53 Univ. of Mainz, Ger. VOCAT. GUID. COUNS, Arbeitsamt Kaiserslautern, Am Altenhof 5, Kaiserslautern. Industrial psychology, administration; developmental psychology, characterology, social psychology, psychology of religion. M

WETZEL, Dipl. Psych. Otto Guido. Neusser Str. 493, Cologne-Weidenpech. b. 30 May 1918 Bern, Switz. Dipl. Psych. '52 Univ. of Mainz, Ger. ASST. DIR, Fm. Rheinkabel, Amsterdamer Str, Cologne. Member: BDP. Applied psychology, editorial; psychology of advertising and sales, psychology of accidents, communication. M

WEWETZER, Dr. phil. Karl Hermann. Hans Sachs Str. 8, Marburg/L. b. 1 Dec 1926 Freyenstein, Ostprignitz. PH.D '52

Univ. of Freiburg, Ger. PSYCH. ASST, Inst. für ärztl. pädagog. Jugendhilfe, Univ. of Marburg/L. Member: DGP. Clinical practice, testing, research; projective techniques, intelligence tests, psychopathology of the brain-injured child. M

WIEDEMANN, Dr. phil. Albert. Martin Richter Str. 13, Nuremberg. b. 16 Mar 1908 Dresden. PH.D '31 Univ. of Erlangen, Ger. CHIEF PSYCH'T, Siemens Schuckertwerke AG, Cen. Works Admin, Werner von Siemensstr. 50, Erlangen. Member: BDP, DGP, AIPA. Industrial psychology, testing, consulting; personnel selection and placement, training of junior executives, group process. M

WIEDENHORN, Mrs. Ruth. Psych. Inst, Meister Ekkehart Str. 11, Cologne-Lindenthal. b. 16 Apr 1929 Baden-Baden. Dipl. Psych. '53 Univ. of Bonn, Ger. ASSISTANT, Inst. for Psych, Univ of Cologne. Research, forensic psychology, testing, consulting; personality theory, projective techniques, abnormal personality, attitudes. F

WIEGMANN, Dr. phil. Otto. Wunstorfer Str. 18, Hannover. b. 12 Feb 1888 Hannover. PH.D '28 Univ. of Hamburg, Ger. Member: BDP, Freie Forschungsgesellschaft für Psych. und Grenzgebiete des Wissens. Retired, research, educational psychology, testing; achievement tests, learning theory. M

WIESBROCK, Dr. phil. Heinz Georg. Neckarhalde 8a, Tübingen. b. 29 June 1924 Dortmund. PH.D '51 Univ. of Heidelberg, Ger. SCI. ASST, Psych. Inst, Univ. of Tübingen. Münzgasse, Tübingen. Member: BDP, DGP. Administration, teaching, research; psychology of motion group process, national differences and characteristics. M

WIESE, Dr. phil. Helmut. Tongrubenweg 22, Hamburg-Wandsbeck. b. 16 July 1902 Lübeck. PH.D '27 Univ. of Hamburg, Ger. DIRECTOR, Dienststelle Schülerhilfe der Schulbehörde Hamburg, Bundesstr. 88, Hamburg 13; DOZENT, Inst. für Lehrerfortbildung, Hamburg. Member: BDP. Educational psychology, teaching, guidance. M

WIESE, Dipl. Psych. Dr. Kurt. Hamburg-Glinde. b. 7 Dec 1919 Erfurt. Dipl. Psych. '55 Univ. of Hamburg, Ger. PSYCHOLOGIST, Psychotherapeutische Behandlungsstelle, Virchowstr. 50, Hamburg; DOZENT, Inst. für Lehrerfortbildung, Hamburg. Member: BDP. Psychotherapy, testing, clinical analysis, teaching. M

WIESE, Ulrich. Talgraben 2, Geislingen/Steige. b. 12 Aug 1923 Stuttgart. Dipl. Psych. '53 Univ. of Tübingen, Ger. PERS. MGR, Württembergische Metallwarenfabrik, Geislingen, Steige. Member: BDP. Industrial psychology, projective techniques. M

WIESEHOFF, Elisabeth. Adolfsallee 31, Wiesbaden. b. 26 Aug 1923 Münster. Dipl. Psych. '54 Univ. of Mainz, Ger. EDUC. GUID. COUNS, Inst. für Erziehungshilfe. Guidance, testing; projective techniques, learning theory, social control. F

WIETRZVCHOWSKI, Mrs. Elfriede. Gerberei 15, Erlangen. b. 18 July 1922 Leipzig. Dipl. Psych. '45 Univ. of Leipzig, Ger. CHILD GUID. COUNS, priv. prac. Member: BDP. Child guidance, psychotherapy, clinical analysis; child and youth psychology, social relations, depth pscyhology, social psychology. F

WILDE, Prof. Dr. phil. Kurt. Gosslerstr 19, Göttingen. b. 12 June 1909 Eldena. Prof. '52 Univ. of Göttingen, Ger. DIRECTOR, Psych. Inst, Univ. of Göttingen, Hoher Weg 15, Göttingen; EDITOR, *Diagnostica.* Member: BDP, DGP. Teaching, administration, research; perception, learning, personality and performance tests. M

WILDENHOF, Mrs. Dorothea. Ostwall 16, Dortmund. b. 19 Aug 1929 Breslau. Dipl. Psych. '54 Univ. of Göttingen, Ger. DIRECTOR, Zentrale des Kath. Fürsorge-Vereins für Mädchen, Frauen und Kinder. Guidance, testing, psychotherapy, teaching; intelligence tests, projective techniques. F

WILDFANG, Dipl. Psych. Walter. Goethestr. 6, Kiel. b. 13 Mar 1925 Quaal. Dipl. Psych. '54 Univ. of Kiel, Ger. Member: BDP. Industrial psychology, testing; educational consulting. M

WILHELM, Dr. Wolfgang. Bismarkstr. 19, Oldenburg. b. 23 Oct 1913 Tokyo, Japan. Dr. '39 Univ. of Leipzig, Ger. PSYCHOTHERAPIST, priv. prac; TEACHER, Volkshochschule Ofenerstr, Oldenburg. Member: BDP. Psychotherapy, consulting, testing, teaching; psychoanalysis, psychology of expression. M

WILLECKE, Friedrich-Wilhelm. Heimfelderstr. 73, Hamburg-Harburg. b. 16 May 1905 Halle. GRAPHOLOGIST, priv. prac. Member: BDP. Industrial psychology, testing, consulting, research; job analysis, personnel selection, character analysis, prognosis of behavior. M

WINKELMANN, Dipl. Psych. Gerhard. Sudl. Aüffahrtsallee 21, Munich. b. 9 May 1930 Munich. Dipl. Psych. '54 Univ. of Munich, Ger. MED. STUD, Univ. of Heidelberg. Psychosomatic medicine, pedagogy, sociology. M

WINKELMANN, Dipl. Psych. Richard. Zwehrenbühlstr. 48, Tübingen. b. 3 Feb 1932 Arpke/Hannover. Dipl. Psych. '56 Univ. of Tübingen, Ger. GRADSTUDENT, Psych. Inst, Univ. of Tübingen, Münzgasse 11, Tübingen. Research, industrial psychology, testing; projective and achievement tests, general psychology, motivation and market research. M

WINKLER, Dr. phil. Werner. Sallstr. 91, Hannover. b. 27 Aug 1924 Schönwald/Silesa. PH.D '52 Univ. of Tübingen, Ger. MANAGER, Medizinisch Psych. Inst. für Verkehr, Bergbau und Industrie, Tiestestr. 16/18, Hannover; INSTRUCTOR, Schule für Fahrlehrer. Member: BDP. Applied and industrial psychology of communications, perception. M

WINNEFELD, Prof. Dr. Friedrich. Franckeplatz 1, Haus 23, Halle/Saale. b. 14 Dec 1911 Jena. Dr. habil. '48 Univ. of Jena, Ger. PROFESSOR, Dept. of Psych, Univ. of Halle-Wittenberg. Member: BDP, DGP. Teaching, research, educational psychology, guidance; social psychology, personality. M

WINTER, Dr. phil. Ilselore. Hochschule für Int. Pädagogische Forschung, Schlosstr. 29, Frankfurt/M. b. 7 June 1927 Wiesbaden PH.D '55 Joh. Gutenberg Univ. of Mainz, Ger. SCI. ASST, Hochschule für Int. Pädagogische Forschung; PERS. PSYCH'T, German Air Force Branch, USAF-MDAP Prog. Member: DGP, Studiengesellschaft für praktische Psych. Testing, guidance, applied and educational psychology; learning theory, aptitude and intelligence tests, projective techniques, industrial psychology. F

WITTE, Prof. Dr. Wilhelm. Psych. Inst, Univ. of Tübingen, Münzgasse 11, Tübingen. b. 8 Jan 1915 Hattingen/Ruhr. Dr. phil. habil. '44 Univ. of Heidelberg, Ger. PROF. and HEAD, Psych. Inst, Univ. of Tübingen. Member: BDP. DGP. Research, teaching, editorial; experimental research on frames of reference, estimation of size and quantities. M

WITTIG, Prof. Dr. phil. Hans. Bismarkstr. 35, Hannover. b. 26 Oct 1910 Bremen. PH.D '37 Univ. of Hamburg, Ger. PROFESSOR Pädagogische Hochschule. Member: BDP. Teaching, research, educational psychology; basic psychological concepts, factor analysis, human development. M

WITTLICH, Dr. phil. Bernhard. Klosterhof 8, Preetz/Holstein. b. 12 Sept 1902 Tallin, Estonia. PH.D, Univ. of Berlin, Ger. STUDIENRAT, Gymnasium, Ihlsahl, Preetz; LECTURER, Univ. of Kiel. Member: BDP. Teaching, educational psychology, testing; graphology, characterology. M

WOBESER-WARNSTEDT, Dipl. Psych. Miss Maria-Gisella von. Pfeivestlstr. 31, Munich-Pasing. b. 23 July 1917 Heidelberg. Dipl. Psych. '49 Univ. of Munich, Ger. PSYCHOTHERAPIST, priv. prac. Member: BDP. Psychotherapy, testing, clinical analysis; psychoanalysis, personality theory. F

WOGATZKI, Rolf. Brehm Str. 62, Hannover. b. 3 Sept 1928 Hannover. Dipl. Psych. '55 Christian Albrechts Univ. of Kiel,

Ger. Stadtschaft für Niedersachsen, Schiffgraben 2, Hannover. Research, clinical analysis, practice; therapy, group psychology, psychology of rumor, motivation research, criminal psychology. M

WOHLFAHRT, Dr. Erich. Thielallee 93, Berlin-Zehlendorf. b. 6 Mar 1898 Leipzig. Dr, Univ. of Leipzig, Ger. PRESIDENT, Wissenschaftliches Landesprüfungsamt Berlin, Kufsteiner Str. 21, Berlin-Schöneberg. Member: BDP. Administration, applied psychology, consulting; methods of scholastic examination, interest, ability and achievement tests, projective techniques. M

WOLDRICH, Dipl. Psych. Carol. Rudolfstr. 5, Karlsruhe. b. 3 July 1918 Lublin, Poland. Dipl. Psych. '51 Univ. of Freiburg, Ger. GRAPHOLOGIST, priv. prac. Testing, research; graphology, psychotherapy. F

WOLF, Heinz E. Psych. Inst, Univ. of Saarland, Saarbrücken. b. 10 Mar 1920 Berlin, Ger. Dipl. Psych, Free Univ. of Berlin, Ger. RES. PSYCH'T, Psych. Inst, Univ. of Saarland. Member: BDP, Arbeitskreis Politische Psych. und Seelische Hyg. Attitude research, professional writing; political attitudes, developmental psychology. M

WOLF-DOETTINCHEM, Dipl. Psych. Heino Oskar Robert. Huttenstr. 3, Braunschweig. b. 28 Nov 1921 Braunschweig. Dipl. Psych. '53 Technische Hochschule Braunschweig, Ger. TEACHER, Präsident des Niedersächsischen Verwaltungsbezirks Braunschweig, Bohlweg, Regierung, Brunswick; PSYCHOLOGIST, priv. prac. Educational psychology, consulting, clinical practice. guidance, testing; psychological diagnosis, projective techniques, child and developmental psychology, guidance techniques for juvenile delinquents. M

WOLFF, Dr. phil. Wilhelm. Juvenellstr. 45, Nuremberg. b. 5 Mar 1901 Berlin. PH.D '35 Univ. of Berlin, Ger. MUNICIPAL OFFICER, Stadtjugendamt, Wetzendorfer Str. 58, Nuremberg. Educational psychology, consulting, research; group process, psychology of human development, acoustics. M

WOLFRUM, Dozent Dr. rer. nat. Erich. Beethovenstr. 9, Jena. b. 5 Sept 1912 Rauenstein/Thür. Dr. rer. nat. '40 Univ. of Jena, Ger. DOZENT, Univ. of Jena. Member: BDP, DGP. Teaching, educational psychology, learning theory, social perception, characterology. M

WÖLKER, Dr. phil. Herbert. Uttenreuther Str. 8, Nuremberg. b. 5 May 1923 Nuremberg. PH.D '55 Univ. of Erlangen, Ger. SCI. ASST, Forschungsinst. für Genossenschaftswesen, Univ. of Erlangen, Universitätsstr. 15, Erlangen. Research, psychology of ad-

vertising, social psychology. M

WÜBBE, Carlos. Gravensteinerweg 6, Hamburg 43. b. 21 Oct 1920 Hamburg. Dipl. '52 Univ. of Mainz, Ger. Member: BDP. Administration, applied psychology, testing. M

WURMBACH, Erdmute. St. Germanstr. 24, Speyer/Rh. b. 11 Apr 1929 Munich. Dipl. Psych. '56 Johann Gutenberg Univ. of Mainz, Ger. DOZENT, Landesverband für innere Mission, Ludwigstr. 6, Speyer/Rh. Teaching, administration; motivation research, psychopathology, human development. F

ZARNCKE, Dr. phil. Dr. theol. Lilly. Heidebrinkerstr. 13-15, Berlin N. 20. b. 5 Sept 1899 Hamburg. Prof. '51 Free Univ. of Berlin, Ger. DIRECTOR, Katholische Erziehungsberatung, Kolonnenstr. 38, Berlin-Schöneberg; LECTURER, Psych. Inst, Free Univ. of Berlin, Berlin-Dahlem; SCI. CONSULT, Deutscher Verein für öffentliche und private Fürsorge, Beethovenstr. 61, Frankfurt/M. Member: BDP. Applied and educational psychology, teaching, testing; art and dramatics as a means of psychodiagnosis, conscience development in children and adolescents. F

ZEHNER, Dr. rer. nat. Kurt. Reimann Str. 15, Kleinmachnow/Berlin. b. 15 Aug 1918 Leignitz. Dozent '52 Pädagogische Hochschule Potsdam, Ger. DIRECTOR, Inst. für Psych, Sanssouci, Potsdam. Teaching, research; educational psychology, developmental psychology, diagnostic methods. M

ZEIT, Hermann. Schwarzwaldstr. 9, Freiburg. b. 11 Mar 1925 Bonn/Rhein. Dipl. Psych. '55 Univ. of Freiburg, Ger. HEAD, Jugendhilfswerk, Fürstenbergstr. 21, Freiburg. Member: BDP. Group therapy, psychotherapy, child guidance; juvenile psychology, forensic psychology. M

ZELLINGER, Dr. Eduard. Psych. Inst. Univ. of Munich, Geschwister Scholl Platz 1, Munich. b. 23 Nov 1923 Munich. Dipl. Psych. '53 Univ. of Munich, Ger. SCI. ASST, Psych. Inst, Univ. of Munich. Member: BDP, DGP. Research, teaching, educational psychology; expression and film psychology, psychological diagnosis, psychopathology, psychology of art. M

ZIETZ, Prof. Dr. phil. Karl H.B. Jasperallee 35b, Braunschweig. b. 2 Mar 1903 Hamburg. PH.D '31 Univ. of Hamburg, Ger. PROFESSOR, Kant Hochschule, Konstantin Uhde Str, Braunschweig. Member: DGP. Teaching, research, clinical analysis, professional writing; child development. M

ZIFREUND, Dipl. Psych. Dr. Walther A.F. Inst. für Arbeitsmittel, Pädagogische Hochschule, Neuer Graben, Osnabrück. b. 18 Oct 1928 Wettern, Czech. PH.D '51

Univ. of Bonn, Ger. CO-WORKER, Inst. für Arbeitsmittel. Teaching, educational psychology, research; learning theory, characterology, anthropology. M

ZILLIG, Dr. phil. Maria. Friedrich Ebert Ring 26, Würzburg. b. 30 May 1896 Würzburg. PH.D '22 Univ. of Würzburg, Ger. LECTURER, Univ. of Würzburg. Member: DGP. Teaching, educational psychology; psychology of adolescent girls, expression, social psychology. F

ZILLMANN, Dipl. Psych. Charlotte. Agnesstr. 41, Munich 13. b. 9 Sept 1909 Berlin. Dipl. Psych, Univ. of Munich, Ger. CHILD PSYCH'T, Pädagogisch- Psychologische Beratungsstelle, Siegfriedstr. 22, Munich. Member: BDP. Educational psychology, testing, clinical analysis, child guidance; child psychology, achievement tests. F

ZIMMERMANN, Mila. Zehntscheuerstr. 18, Göttingen. b. 24 Feb 1930 Erfurt. Dipl.

Psych. '55 Univ. of Göttingen, Ger. STUDENT, Univ. of Innsbruck, Austria. Psychology of art, characterology; industrial psychology, advertising. F

ZOLLITSCH, Dietlinde. Hinterer Steingraben 14, Bad Hersfeld. b. 24 Sept 1930 Sonneberg/Thür. Dipl. Psych. '55 Univ. of Munich, Ger. EDUCATOR, Arbeiterwohlfahrt, Dottendorferstr. 168, Bonn. Member BDP. Educational psychology; social perception, projective techniques, group process. F

ZUBERBIER, Dr. phil. Dipl. Psych. Miss Erika Eva. Schubertstr. 24, Freiburg. b. 21 May 1926 Leipzig. PH.D '55 Univ. of Freiburg, Ger. RES. FELLOW and CONSULT, Inst. of Psych, Bertoldstr. 17, Freiburg. Member: BDP. Research, consulting, student; expressive movement, projective techniques, social psychology. F

GHANA

TAYLOR, Andrew. Univ. Coll. of the Gold Coast, Achimota. b. 27 Oct 1920 Glasgow, Scot. MA '48 Univ. of Wellington, New Zealand. SR. LECTURER, Univ. Coll. Member:

BPS. Teaching, research, educational psychology; child growth and development, personnel selection, achievement tests. M

GREECE

ASPIOTIS, Dr. Ar. A. 12 Rue Heraclite, Athens. b. 31 Mar 1910 Le Piree. MD, Univ. of Athens, Greece. DIRECTOR, Inst. of Med. Psych. and Ment. Hyg, Athens. Member: HPS. Professional writing, psychotherapy, consulting, clinical practice; depth psychology, analysis and synthesis of personality. M

BOCHLOGYROS, Dr. Nicolaos. 27 Artemissiou St, Athens. b. 18 May 1923 Athens. PH.D '54 Univ. of Munich, Germany. CHIEF PSYCH'T, Vocat. Guid. Bureau, Ministry of Labor, Athens. Member: HPS, DGP. Personnel and applied psychology, testing, vocational guidance; projective techniques, attitude measurement, learning theory. M

BOCHLOGYROS-ANASTASSAKI, Mrs. Chryssa. Greek Inst. of Psych, 27 Rue Artemissiou, Athens. b. 25 Dec 1926 Athens. Diplôme, Univ. of Athens, Greece. PSYCHOLOGIST, Greek Inst. of Psych. Teaching, applied psychology, testing; projective techniques, learning theory, attitude measurement. F

CALOUTSIS, Dr. A. Andrew. 39 Solonos St, Athens. b. 23 Nov 1910 Athens. MD '32 Univ. of Athens, Greece. DIRECTOR, Child Psychiat. Serv, Genl. Neuropsychiat. Hosp. of Athens, Daphni, Athens; DI-

RECTOR, Athenian Child Guid. Clin. Member: Psych. Socy. of Athens, Psychiat. Socy. of Athens, Ment. Hyg. Socy. of Athens. Clinical practice, child guidance, psychotherapy, testing; projective techniques, achievement tests. M

CARAPANOS, Mrs. Frosso. Ta Spourghitia, 35 i. Marasli, Athens. b. 13 Oct 1909 Athens. KINDERGARTEN TCHR, Ta Spourghitia; PSYCHOLOGIST, Medico-Pedagogic Cen, Athenian Polyclinic, Rue du Pirée, Athens. Teaching, testing, consulting, guidance; achievement tests, projective techniques. F

CHARVATIS, Dr. Miss Sultana-Nitsa. 7 Rue Marni, Athens. b. 23 Mar 1914 Ambélon. Doctorat '51 Univ. of Paris, France. EDUC. PSYCH'T, Protypon Lykion d'Athènes, Rue Prince Constantin, St. Démetre, Psychico, Athens; CLIN. PSYCH'T, Athenian Polyclinic. Member: HPS. Testing, clinical analysis, applied and educational psychology, teaching; achievement tests, projective techniques, attitude measurement, causes of dyslexia. F

CHOURDAKIS, Mrs. Marie. Emou 12, Nea Smyrni, Athens. b. 22 Dec 1918 Athens. Licence, Univ. of Athens, Greece. PSYCHOLOGIST, priv. prac, Leontos Sgourou 5, Athens. Member: HPS. Consulting, clinical practice, teaching; achievement, intelligence and aptitude tests.   F

CONSTANTINIDES, Prof. Constantin. 57 Stournara St, Athens. b. 1901 Parnassis. Prof, Univ. of Athens, Greece. DIRECTOR, Pub. Hosp. for Ment. Diseases, Dafni, Athens; PSYCHIATRIST, priv. prac. Member: HPS, Psychiat. Socy. of Athens. Teaching, research, clinical practice, student.   M

DEMETRIUS, Prof. Moraitis. 22 Monemvassias St, Athens. b. 15 Apr 1876 Skiathos. Diplôme, Univ. of Athens, Greece. Research, psychotherapy, retired; individual psychology by Adler.   M

DIMITROPULOS, Dr. Konstantin. Ajiu Alexandru 37, Palaion Phaleron, Athens. b. 9 Aug 1899 Ano Chorxnatpaktos. Docent '50 Univ. of Athens, Greece. SCH. INSPECTOR, Filekpedeftiki Heteria, 5D Pesmatzoglu, Athens. Member: Psych. Socy. of Athens. Teaching, professional writing, educational psychology; developmental psychology.   M

DRACOULIDES, Dr. Nicholas N. 27 Hipirou St, Athens. b. 24 May 1900 Athens. MD '20 Univ. of Athens, Greece. PSYCHOANALYST, priv. prac; MGR. DIR, *Chronicles*; CO-EDITOR, *Acta Psychotherapeutica*. Member: RMPA, WFMH, Fr. Medico-Psych. Socy, Belg. Psychoanal. Socy, Int. Socy. of Sexology, Hellenic Psycho-Biol. Assn. Psychotherapy professional writing, applied and educational psychology; psychoanalysis, psychopedagogy, art analysis, preventive mental hygiene.   M

EXARCHOPOULOS, Prof. Dr. Nicholas. 59 Skoufa St, Athens. b. 15 Dec 1874 Naxos. Prof. '12, PH.D '97 Univ. of Athens, Greece. ORDINARY MEMBER, Athens Acad. of Sciences, Eleftheriou Veniselou St, Athens; PROF. EMER, Univ. of Athens. Member: HPS. Retired, psychological and educational research and professional writing; measurement of intelligence, child psychology, psychograph.   M

GARMATI-THEODOROPOULOU, Dr. Anna. 3 Chersonos, Athens. b. 10 Oct 1910 Vrioula, Asia Minor. PH.D '52 Univ. of Athens, Greece. ASST. PROF. of PSYCH, Psych. Inst, Univ. of Athens, 57 Solonos, Athens; DIRECTOR, Night High Sch. of Christian Soc. Union, Athens. Member: HPS. Research, testing, consulting, teaching; social perception, attitude measurement diagnostic testing of abnormal schoo children.   F

HARITOS, Prof. John. 5 Laertou, Pagrati, Athens. b. 22 June 1909 Athens. Diplôme '29 Univ. of Athens, Greece. PROF. and PHILOLOGIST, Varvakios, Sch, 34 Koletti St, Athens. Member: Psych. Socy. of Athens. Teaching, educational psychology, professional writing; intelligence of school children, vocational guidance.   M

NOUAROS-MICHAELIDES, Dr. Andrew. 66 Phylis St, Athens. b. 21 Jan 1921 Smyrna. Turkey. PH.D '52 Univ. of Indiana, USA. INSTR. in CLASSICS, Orlinda Childs Pierce Coll, 5th Stop, Elleniko, Glyfada, Athens. Member: HPS. Teaching, research, professional writing; projective techniques, attitude measurement, achievement tests.   M

PAPACONSTANTINOU, Dr. Athanassios. 12 Katakouzinou St, Athens. b. 25 Dec 1909 Karpenissi. Doctor, Univ. of Salonica Greece. PERMANENT MEMBER, Supreme Board of Educ, Ministry of Educ, 2 Evangelistrias St, Athens; DIRECTOR, Vocat. Guid. Cen; DIRECTOR, *Educational Encyclopaedia*. Member: Hellenic Assn. of Ment. Hyg. Administration, testing, teaching, vocational guidance; test construction, testing and clinical analysis, educational psychology.   M

PARASKEVA, Dr. Sophia. Psych. Lab, Univ. of Athens, 57 Solonos, Athens. b. 8 Jan 1920 Arkadioupolis. PH.D '54 Univ. of Athens, Greece. ASSISTANT, Psych. Lab, Univ. of Athens; TEACHER, Sch. of Vocat. Guid, Athens. Member: HPS. Vocational guidance, testing, research; personality diagnosis, projective techniques.   F

PAVLIDES, Clio C. 27 Elefteriou Venizelou St, N. Psychico, Athens. b. 1907 Alexandrie. Graduate '34 Univ. of Athens, Greece. PROFESSOR, Trng. Coll. for Tchrs, Arsakion High Sch. for Girls, Psychico, Athens; CONSULTANT, Greek Broadcasting Serv. Member: HPS. Teaching, educational psychology, research; sociometry.   M

PHILIPPOPOULUS, Dr. George Spyros. 4 Monis Petraki St, Athens. b. 14 Nov 1911 Gymnon, Argos. MD '34 Univ. of Athens, Greece. CHIEF PSYCHIATRIST, Army Pensioner's Hosp, 10 Monis Petraki St, Athens; ASST. PROF. of PSYCHIAT, Univ. of Athens; CONSULT. PSYCHIATRIST, Higher Inst. for Soc. Wrkrs. and Child Guid. Clin, Athens. Member: Psychiat. Socy. of Athens, Greek Fed. for Ment. Hlth, Med. Assn. of Greece. Teaching, psychotherapy, consulting, clinical practice; intelligence tests, projective techniques.   M

PHYLACTOPOULOS, Prof. George S. P.O. Box 175, Athens Coll, Athens. b. 22 Apr 1905 Istanbul, Turkey. MA '32 Columbia Univ. USA. PROF. of PSYCH, Athens Coll. TCHR. of PSYCH, Pierce Coll, Athens. Member: HPS, Hellenic Psycho-Biol. Assn, Eugenics Socy. of Greece. Administration, teaching, testing, guidance; psychometric methods, psychological terminology in Greek, guidance.   M

PIPINELI, Mrs. Anna Potamianoy. Philothei, Rue Diadochoy Pavloy et Niovis, Athens.

b. Feb 1926 Pireus. Licence '49 Univ. of Athens, Greece. PSYCHOLOGIST, Medico-Pedagogic Cen, Amalias 6, Athens. Member: Socy. for the Prevention of Mental Diseases, Ment. Hyg. Socy. Psychotherapy, testing, teaching; achievement tests, projective techniques, psychotherapy. F

SAKELLARIOU, Prof. Dr. George. 14 Nereldon, Old Phaleron. b. 1 Dec 1887 Divritsa. PH.D '24 Univ. of Athens, Greece. PROF. of PSYCH. and PHILOS, Univ. of Athens; SCI. ADVIS, Royal Air Forces; DIRECTOR, *Prometheus*. Member: HPS, Int. Sociol. Socy. Teaching, research, applied psychology, professional writing; personality scales,

vocational guidance, measurement of intelligence. M

SPETSIERIS, Prof. Dr. Konstantin. 8 Odos Kallinikou, Athens. b. 30 Jan 1899 Kefallonia. Doctor '38 Univ. of Munich, Germany. Professional writing, retired; philosophical anthropology. M

VASSILAKIS, Dr. Constantine. 19B Yeraniou St, Athens. b. 4 Nov 1917 Naxos. PH.D '56 Univ. of Athens, Greece. PROFESSOR, Experimental Sch. of Athens Univ, 43 Skoufa St, Athens. Member: HPS. Teaching, research, educational psychology; Plato's psychology, projective techniques, free drawings of children. M

GUATEMALA

BARRIENTOS, Guido Allan. 940 Tennessee, Lawrence, Kansas. USA. b. 1 Dec 1931 Quetzaltenango. MA '57 Univ. of Kansas, USA. RES. ASST, Psych. Dept, Univ. of Kansas, Lawrence, Kansas, USA. Research, student, translation of statistical techniques into Spanish; learning theory, psychological statistics. M

BARRIOS PEÑA, Dr. Jaime. Fac. of Humanitas, Guatemala City. b. 20 Aug 1921 Guatemala City. PH.D, Natl. Autonomous Univ. of Mexico. CHIEF, Dept. of Psychopedagogic Res; DIR. GEN, Centers for Observation and Reeduc. of Juvenile Delinquents, San Pedrito, Guatemala City; PROFESSOR, Fac. of Humanities. Member: SIP, Guatemalan League of Ment. Hyg. Consulting, guidance, testing, teaching; projective tests, human relations, attitude measurement. M

CAHUEQUE M., Miss Rosa. 16 Ave. 13-33, Guatemala City 1. b. 5 Sept 1908 San Augustín Ac. Lic. '56 Univ. of Guatemala. PSYCH. TCHR, Fac. of Humanities of San

Carlos, 9 Ave. 13-39, Guatemala City. Teaching, educational guidance; achievement tests, attitude measurement. F

FERNÁNDEZ RIVAS, Prof. Elisa. 10 Ave. 12-18, Guatemala City 1. b. 30 Mar 1924 Guatemala City. Lic. '52 Univ. of San Carlos, Guatemala. PSYCHOLOGIST, Servicio Cooperativo Interamericano de Educacion (SCIDE), 12 Calle 10-27, Guatemala City 1; TEACHER, Fac. of Humanities, Univ. of San Carlos. Teaching, guidance, testing, psychotherapy; attitude measurement, educational psychology, psychometry. F

GILBERT, Otto. 16 Ave. 41-39 Zone 8, Guatemala City. b. 7 Aug 1928 Guatemala City. MA '53 Louisiana State Univ, USA. RES. PSYCH'T, Amer. Sch. of Guatemala, Finca las Conchas, apartado 83, Guatemala City; TEACHER, Fac. of Humanities, Univ. of San Carlos; VOCAT. GUID. COUNSELOR, Inst. Pre-Vocacional Adolfo V. Hall. Research on standardization of psychological tests for Guatemala, teaching, guidance; intelligence testing. M

HAITI

DOUYON, Chavannes. 242 Haut La Lue, Port-Au-Prince. b. 28 June 1925 Cayes. MA '57 Fisk Univ, USA. PROF. of PHILOS. and APPLIED PSYCH, Lycee National, Monseigneur Maurice, Cayes. Teaching,

research, applied and educational psychology; mentally and physically handicapped children, intelligence tests, mental illnesses. M

HONDURAS

DONAIRE FUNES, Dr. Victor. Dirección General de Educación Media, Tegucigalpa. b. 2 Jan 1926 Tegucigalpa. PSYCHOLOGIST '52 Univ. of Chile. HEAD, Central Serv. of Educ. and Vocat. Guid, Ministry of Educ, Tegucigalpa; PROF. of PSYCH,

Escuelas Normales and Escuela de Enfermeras. Member: SIP. Educational psychology, teaching, testing, guidance; learning theory, aptitude tests, projective techniques. M

HONG KONG

WRIGHT, Miss Beryl Robina. Univ. of Hong Kong, Hong Kong. b. 6 June 1911 Sydney, Austl. B.EC '34 Univ. of Sydney, Austl. LECT. in EDUC. PSYCH, Univ. of Hong Kong. Member: BPS-A. Teaching, guidance, testing; social perception and individual adjustment. F

HUNGARY

ARKOSI-UDVARDY, Mrs. Charlotte. Mester utca 33, Budapest IX. b. 7 June 1913 Budapest. Diploma '51 Univ. of Budapest, Hungary. ASST. RES. WRKR, Inst. for Child Psych, Hungarian Acad. of Sci, Szondy utca 83, Budapest VI. Administration; language development, clinical testing, guidance. F

BARANYAI, Dr. Elizabeth H. Váci ut 47c, Budapest XIII. b. 7 Jan 1894 Nagyszöllös. PH.D '32 Univ. of Szeged, Hungary. RES. WRKR, Inst. for Child Psych, Hungarian Acad. of Sci, Szondy utca 83, Budapest VI. Research, applied psychology; thought processes, learning, verbal expression. F

BARKÓCZI, Mrs. Ilona. Szondy u 45-47 I. em, Budapest VI. b. 22 Oct 1926 Budapest. Psych. Tchr. '50 Eötvös Loránd Univ, Hungary. ASSISTANT, Psych. Dept, Eötvös Loránd Univ, Pesti Barnabás u 1, Budapest. Teaching, research; development of motor skill in children. F

BIRÓ (née Emma Graber), Dr. Mrs. L. Fillér ucca 25, Budapest II. b. 5 July 1888 Budapest. Diplôme de Docteur '11 Univ. of Budapest, Hungary. Member: Hungarian Psych. Socy. Teaching, psychotherapy, school psychologist, retired; relations of characterology to education. F

BODA, Prof. Dr. Etienne. Buday László u. 5/b, Budapest II. b. 24 Oct 1894 Máramafossziget. Prof. Ordinaire '44 Ferenc Fószef Univ. of Kolozsvár, Hungary; PH.D. Research, applied and educational psychology, testing; general psychology, personality types, intelligence. M

CSIRSZKA, Dr. János. Baross u. 100, Budapest VI. b. 28 Sept 1916 Budapest. Doctorat '48 Univ. of Budapest, Hungary. PROFESSOR, M.T.H. Módszertani Intézet, Délibáb u. 21, Budapest VI. Applied and educational psychology, consulting, guidance, teaching; apprentice training and the power of suggestion, guidance in psychotherapy. M

ESZTERGOMI-MIKÓ, Dr. Eszter. Verpeléti ut 24, Budapest XI. b. 25 May 1909 Balassagyarmat. PH.D '37 Univ. of Pázmány, Hungary. RES. WRKR, Inst. for Res. in Spec. Educ, Gyógypedogógiai Tanárkepzö Föiskola, Bethlenö-tér, Budapest. Research, consulting, applied and educational psychology; special education, clinical psychology, achievement tests, social perception, psychopathology. M

FORRAI, Dr. Elizabeth. Rádai Str. 30, Budapest IX. b. 30 Nov. 1923 Moson megye. PH.D '47 Univ. of Budapest, Hungary. HIGH SCHOOL PROF, Fényes Elek közgazdasági technikum, Mezö utca 3, Budapest XI. Teaching, educational psychology, research; observational methods, intelligence tests for infants. F

GERÉB, Dr. Georges. Alföldi u. Szeged. b. 17 June 1923 Komárom. PH.D '47 Univ. of Szeged, Hungary. PROFESSOR, Pédagógiai Föiskola, Aprilis 4 utja 8, Szeged. Member: Psych. Comm. of the Hungarian Acad. of Sci. Teaching, research, applied psychology, psychotherapy; psychology of defects, psychology of fatigue, medical psychology. M.

GYÖRGY, Dr. Julia. Lenin Körut 14, Budapest VII. b. 29 June 1896 Szolnok. MD '22 Univ. of Budapest, Hungary. HEAD, Ambulatory Clinic for Child Guid, Trefort utca, Budapest VIII; CHILD PSYCHOTHERAPIST, priv. prac. Member: Hungarian Psych. Socy, Socy. for Ment. Hyg. Consulting, guidance, psychotherapy, educational psychology; criminal psychology, infantile neuroses, problems of community education. F

HALÁSZ, László. Sip-u. 6 faz. 7, Budapest VII. b. 7 Dec 1933 Budapest. Psych. Tchr. '56 Eötvös Lóránd Univ, Hungary. CHILD PSYCH'T, Med. Ambulatory Inst. for Children, 9 Nyar St, Budapest VII. Testing, clinical analysis, teaching, psychotherapy; characterology, psychological problems in literature. M

HERMANN, Dr. Imre. Lórántffy Zs. ut 5, Budapest II. b. 13 Nov 1889 Budapest. MD, Univ. of Budapest, Hungary. PSYCHOTHERAPIST, SZTK Rendelö Intézet, Maros u. 16, Budapest XII. Psychotherapy, research; psychology of thinking, comparative psychology, psychopathology of obsessional neurosis. M

HOFFMANN, Mrs. Gertrude. Bimbó ut 58, Budapest II. b. 28 Mar 1928 Budapest. Agrégation, Univ. of Eötvös Lóránd, Hungary. PROFESSOR, Lycée Michel Fazekas, Baross ut 62, Budapest VIII.

Teaching, research, student; social conduct, influence of emotions on the development of basic ideas and concepts in the child. F

KARDOS, Prof. Dr. phil. Ludwig. Szondy utca 54, Budapest VI. b. 14 Dec 1899 Rákospalota. PH.D '29 Univ. of Vienna, Austria. PROF. and HEAD, Dept. of Psych, Eötvös Lóránd Univ. of Budapest; DIRECTOR, Psych. Inst, Eötvös Lóránd Univ. of Budapest. Member: Psych. Comm. of the Hungarian Acad. of Sci. Research, teaching, psychotherapy; perception, learning theory, animal psychology, anthropogenesis. M

KATONA, Dr. phil. Klára. Királyi Pál u. 13/a, V. em. 2, Budapest V. b. 7 Aug 1911 Budapest. PH.D '36 Univ. of Budapest, Hungary. CHIEF LIBRARIAN, Pedagogical Sect, Budapest Municipal Library, Horváth Mihály-tér 8, Budapest VIII. Library work; educational psychology. F

KEMPELEN, Prof. Dr. Attila. Rózsa u. 3, Erdliget. b. 6 May 1898 Budapest. PH.D '23 Univ. of Pázmány, Hungary. TEACHER, Primary School of Ilkamajor, Erdliget. Member: Hungarian Psych. Socy, Hungarian Socy. for Child Study. Research, teaching, testing, professional writing; philosophic aspects of psychology, genetic psychology, adolescent psychology. M

KÉRI-JUST, Mrs. Hedvige. Benczur u. 39/b, Budapest VI. b. 27 Nov 1896 Komárom. RES. WRKR, Inst. for Child Psych, Hungarian Acad. of Sci, Szondy u. 83, Budapest VI. Research, applied psychology child psychotherapy; group process, aptitudes, child play. F

KERTÉSZ-ROTTER, Dr. Lily. Bródy Sandor u. 46, Budapest VIII. b. 5 May 1896 Budapest. MD '23 Univ. of Budapest, Hungary. EDUC. ADVIS, Child Guid. Centers; PSYCHOTHERAPIST, priv. prac, 1933-1948. Member: Hungarian Psychoanal. Socy. Psychotherapy, child and educational guidance; parent education, training of teachers, nursery staff, pediatricians. F

KIRÁLY, Joseph. Inst. of Pedagogy and Psych, Univ. of Szeged, Rue Tancsics 2, Szeged. b. 16 July 1925 Csongrád. Diplôme '51 Univ. of Budapest, Hungary. ASST. DIR, Inst. of Pedagogy and Psych, Univ. of Szeged. Member: Psych. Comm. of the Hungarian Acad. of Sci. Teaching, research, educational psychology; general psychology, characterology, parapsychology. M

KISS, Dr. Tihamér. Kálvin tér 19 I.e. 23, Debrecen. b. 28 Dec 1905 Diósgyör. Doctorat '36 Univ. of Debrecen, Hungary; Privat Docent '44 Univ. of Kolozsvar, Hungary. COMMITTEE SEC, Tudamányos Ismeretterjesztö Társulat, Société de la

Vulgarisation de Connaissances Scientifiques, Arany János utca 1/b, Debrecen. Applied and educational psychology, teaching, research; analysis and development of emotions, theory of knowledge, psychology of adult education. M

KÚTVÖLGYI, Prof. István. Alig utca 4 sz, Budapest XIII. b. 20 May 1909 Hódmezövásárhely. Prof. Diploma '50 Pázmány Peter Univ, Hungary. RES. WRKR, Capitol Psych. Inst, Budapest. Member: Hungarian Psych. Socy. Applied and educational psychology, testing, psychotherapy; learning theory, problems involved in professional choice, memory. M

LÁNYI, Mrs. Agnes. Bimbó ut. 23, Budapest II. b. 9 Feb 1930 Budapest. MA '52 Coll. of Health Education, Hungary. ASSISTANT, Dept. of Psych, Coll. of Hlth. Educ, Bethlen-tér 2, Budapest VII. Testing, teaching educational psychology; handicapped children. F

LÉNÁRD, Dr. Ferenc. Pengö u. 5, Budapest II. b. 1 Oct 1911 Fiume. Privat Docent '45 Univ. of Budapest, Hungary. RES. DIR, Sci. Inst. of Pedagogy, Szalay u. 10-14, Budapest V; EDITOR, *Magyar Psychologiai Szemle.* Member: Hungarian Psych. Socy, Swiss Socy. of Psych. and Appl. Psych. Research, teaching, editorial, educational psychology, testing; thinking, phases in thought processes, test analysis, expression and emotion. M

LÉNÁRT, Dr. Edith. Leninkörut 77, Budapest VI. b. 16 July 1890 Budapest. PH.D '23 Pázmány Péter Univ, Hungary. RES. WRKR, Inst. for Child Psych, Hungarian Acad. of Sci, Szondy utca 83, Budapest VI. Research, consulting; thought processes, learning, verbal expression. F

MAJOR, Mrs. Marguerite. Géza utca 7, Budapest V. b. 20 Jan 1886 Budapest. BA '04 Univ. of Budapest, Hungary. CHILD PSYCHOTHER, Polyclinique, Rue Trefort 3, Budapest VIII. Member: Hungarian Psychoanal. Socy. Psychotherapy, consulting; psychoanalysis, child psychology. F

MÁRTON (née Vázsonyi), Mrs. Ibolya Violette. Nyul utca 16, Budapest II. b. 13 Mar 1896 Budapest. TEACHER, Kindergarten; PSYCHOTHERAPIST, priv. prac. Member: Hungarian Psych. Socy. Teaching and research on projective techniques, testing, clinical practice, psychotherapy; planning of educational toys, clinical use of testing techniques. F

MÉREI, Ferenc. Pasaréti ut 36, Budapest II. b. 24 Nov 1909 Budapest. Licence ès lettres '34 Univ. of Paris, France. SCI. COLLABORATOR, Inst. of Psych, Univ. of Budapest, Pesti Barnabás ut 1, Budapest. V. Research, teaching; social behavior of children, pre-categorized thought in the child, interpretation of projective tests, psychological bases of contemporary education. M

MESTER BODA, Dr. Fiore. Krisztina körut 45, Budapest I. b. 13 July 1920 Lugos. PH.D '48 Univ. of Budapest, Hungary. RES. WRKR, Inst. for Child Psych, Hungarian Acad. of Sci, Szondi ut. 83, Budapest VI. Research, consulting, testing, clinical analysis, educational psychology, projective techniques, psychosomatic medicine. F

MEZEI, Árpád. Amerikai ut 77, Budapest XIV. b. 2 July 1902 Budapest. RES. ASSOC, Inst. of Child Psych, Hungarian Academy of Sci, 26 Ripple Rónai ucca, Budapest. Research, professional writing; psychosomatic research, theoretical foundations of psychology, experimental neuroses. M

MOLNÁR, Dr. Imre. Rippl Rónai utca 28, Budapest VI. b. 23 Jan 1909 Nagyvárad. PH.D '32 Univ. of Würzburg, Ger. DIRECTOR, Inst. for Child Psych, Hungarian Acad. of Sci, Szondy utca 83, Budapest VI. Member: Psych. Comm. of the Hungarian Acad. of Sci. Research, administration, consulting; transformation of habit, moral development in childhood and adolescence. M

MURÁNYI-KOVÁCS, Mrs. Suzanne. Sallai Imre u. 26, Budapest XIII. b. 4 Feb 1911 Budapest. Diplôme '50 Univ. of Budapest, Hungary. RES. WRKR, Inst. for Child Psych, Hungarian Acad. of Sci, Szondy u. 83, Budapest VI. Research in psychotherapeutic methods, psychotherapy; family environment and infant neurosis, psychology of habit, child development. F

NEMES, Lipót. Népszinház utca 31/111/3, Budapest VIII. b. 16 Oct 1886 Körmend. Member: Hungarian Psych. Socy; Hungarian Educ. Socy. Teaching, research, administration; social pedagogy, development of moral conscience in children. F

NEMES, Mrs. Livia. Rumbach Sebestyén u. 12, Budapest VII. b. 13 Aug 1919 Budapest. Prof. de Lycée '50 Univ. of Budapest, Hungary. RES. WRKR, Inst. of Pedagogy, Szalay u. 10, Budapest. Educational and industrial psychology, research, teaching; mental development of elementary school students. F

PERL-BALLA, Mrs. Lili. Bródi Sándor utca 23/a, Budapest VIII. b. 25 Dec 1891

Budapest. PSYCHOTHERAPIST, priv. prac. Member: Hungarian Psychoanal. Assn. F

PFEIFFER, Dr. Margit. Benczur utca 39/B, Budapest. b. 31 June 1897 Budapest. MD '31 Univ. of Budapest, Hungary. PSYCHIATRIST, Péterfy Sandor Hosp, Budapest. Psychotherapy, clinical practice, guidance, consulting; psychoanalysis. F

SCHNELL, Dr. János. Veres Pálné utca 30, Budapest V. b. 7 Mar 1893 Magyarszék. MD '24; Privat Docent '47 Fac. of Philos. of Szeged, Hungary. CHILD PSYCH'T. and HEAD, Ment. Hyg. Serv. for Children, Cen. Consult. Off. for the Budapest Schools, Nyár utca 9, Budapest VII. Member: Psych. Sect. of the Educ. Syndicat, Hungarian Psych. Socy, Socy. for the Study of Child Psych. Psychotherapy, applied psychology, administration; public education in the field of mental hygiene. M

SEVERINI, Dr. Elizabeth. Mátyás u. 11, Budapest IX. b. 20 Dec 1905 Lemberg, Poland. PH.D '41 Univ. of Budapest, Hungary; MA '35 Columbia Univ. USA. RES. WRKR, Dept. of Psych, Univ. of Budapest, Pesti B. u. 1. sz, Budapest V. Experimental research, educational psychology, psychology of work; will and action, learning theory, child development, group process. F

SZÉKELY, Dr. Ludwig. Szeberényi-u. 7, Fót. b. 22 June 1923, Fót. Doctor, Univ. of Pázmány, Hungary. DIR. of PSYCH. TESTING, Inst. für Arbeitsphysiologie, Baross-tér 9, Budapest VIII; LECT. and EDUC. ADVIS, Inst. for Nursery School Teachers. Educational guidance, testing, clinical diagnosis; tests for traffic ability, psychology of accidents. M

TÁNCZOS, Zsolt. Eszék u 20, Budapest XI. b. 15 Apr 1929 Iszkaszentgyörgy. Psych. Tchr. '52 Eötvös Lóránd Univ, Hungary. RES. WRKR, Tudomanyos Minosito Bizottság, Széchenyi rakpart 3, Budapest V. Research, student; physiological basis of perception, sensory-motor coordination, learning theory. M

TÖRÖK, Dr. Stephan Anton. Luther u. 3, Balassagyarmat. b. 22 Apr 1903 Teschen, Silesia. Diplôme '45 Univ. of Budapest, Hungary. LECTURER, Altalános iskola, Bajcsy-Zs. u. 7, Balassagyarmat. Research, applied and educational psychology; development of writing readiness, dynamics of the psyche, disturbances in mental development. M

ICELAND

BJÖRNSSON, Cand. Psych. Kristinn. Heil-suverndarstöd Reykjavikur, Reykjavik. b. 19 July 1922 Iceland. Cand. Psych. '53 Univ. of Oslo, Nor. VOCAT. PSYCH'T, Tryggingastofnun rikisins, Laugaveg 118, Reykjavik; CONSULT. PSYCH'T, Polyclinic for Alcoholics, Heilsuverndarstöd Reykjavikur. Member: Icelandic Psych. Assn. Vocational guidance of mentally and physically handicapped, applied psychology, testing; intelligence measurement, projective techniques, psychotherapy. M

GUNNARSSON, Cand. Psych. Ólafur. Mi-klubraut 60, Reykjavik. b. 30 Aug 1917 Stafafell í Lóni. PSYCHOLOGIST, Reykjavi-kurbaer, Hafnarstraeti 20, Reykjavik; ICELAND ED, *Norsk Allkunnebok.* Member: DP, Icelandic Psych. Assn. Vocational guidance, testing; achievement tests, reading and learning. M

JÓNASSON, Dr. phil. Matthías. Thinghóls-braut 3, Kopavogi, Reykjavik. b. 2 Sept 1902 Iceland. PH.D '36 Univ. of Leipzig, Ger. RES. PSYCH'T, Ministry of Pub. Educ. Reykjavik; LECT. in EDUC, Univ. of Iceland; EDITOR, *Hlaobúd; Mál og Menning;* Minis-try of Pub. Educ. Teaching, research, testing; intelligence measurement, psy-chological foundation of education, clinical treatment of maladjusted children. M

INDIA

ABDIN, Prof. Mohamed Zainul. Dept. of Psych, Patna Univ, Patna 5. b. 15 Dec 1910 Patna. BA '34 Univ. of London, Eng. HEAD, Dept. of Psych, Patna Univ. Teaching, administration, research; pro-jective techniques, group process, social conflicts, psychotherapy, crime and de-linquency. M

ACHAL, Ayodhya Prasad. Dept. of Philos. and Psych, S. Sinha Coll, Aurangabad, Bihar. b. 23 July 1924 Lucknow. MA '55 Banaras Hindu Univ, India. HEAD, Dept. of Philos. and Psych, Sachchidananda Sinha Coll; EDITOR, *Magadh Mahan.* Member: IPA. Teaching, research, editorial guidance, journalism; Yoga psychology, mental diseases in ancient Indian medical literature, caste prejudices in rural India. M

ADINARAYAN, Prof. Samuel P. Dept. of Psych, Madras Christian Coll, Tambaram, Madras. b. 23 Oct 1904 Madras. PH.D '53 Univ. of Madras, India. PROF. and HEAD, Dept. of Psych, Madras Christian Coll. Member: BPS, Madras Psych. Socy. Teaching, research, professional writing; attitude measurement, color prejudice, learning theory, effect of culture on memo-ry. M

ADISESHIAH, Dr. William Thomas Varanasi. 8 Tees January Marg, New Delhi. b. 1 Jan 1909 Madras. PH.D '51 Univ. of Cambridge, Eng. SR. SCI. in APPL. PSYCH, Def. Sci. Organiza, Ministry of Def, Govt. of India, New Delhi; PROFESSOR, Delhi Sch. of Soc. Work. Member: BPS, WFMH, Exper. Psych. Grp. (Eng). Teaching, research; studies in applied experimental psychology, group process. M

AGARWAL, Mrs. Sushila. c/o Dr. R. P. Agarwal, Math. Dept, Lucknow Univ, Lucknow. b. 28 Mar 1929 Aligarh. MA '56 Lucknow Univ, India. RES. ASST, Lucknow Univ. Member: Lucknow Psych. Assn. Research, applied psychology, student; attitude measurement, achievement tests, social prejudice. F

AGRAWAL, D. P. Pilot Cen. in Juv. De-linquency, Reformatory, Hazaribagh. b. 8 Jan 1934 Banaras. MA '53 Patna Univ, India. PROBAT. OFF, Pilot Cen. in Juv. Delinquency. After-care of discharged delinquent cases, research, testing; inter-viewing, counseling, intelligence and at-tainment tests, attitude measurement. M

AGRAWAL, Mrs. Vimla. 10 Havelock Rd, Lucknow, Uttar Pradesh. b. 21 July 1923 Meerut. MA '54 Lucknow Univ, India. RES. SUPERV, M.I.T. COMMUNIC PROJ, J. K. Inst, Lucknow Univ, Lucknow. Member: Lucknow Psych. Assn. Research, adminis-tration, teaching; student attitudes and values, dynamics of prejudice, communi-cation. F

AHMED, Syed Mashkoor. Dept. of Psych, Muslim Univ, Aligarh. b. 15 July 1929 Ajmer. MA '53 Muslim Univ, India. RES. SCHOLAR, Ministry of Educ, Govt of India, New Delhi. Research, teaching, profession-al writing; neurological correlates of consciousness, vocational choice, oper-ationalism. M

AKOLKAR, Prof. Vasant Vinayak. Gujarat Coll, Ellis Bridge, Ahmedabad 6. b. 6 July 1911 Nasik City. MA '37 Bombay Univ, India. HEAD, Philos. Dept; TCHR. of PSYCH, Gujarat Coll. Teaching, writing text books, research; social perception, attitude measurement. M

AMIN, Devenrdanath Laxmidas. Atira, Ahmedabad 9. b. 19 Nov 1923 Padra, Bombay. MA '47 Mysore Univ, India. SR. SCI. OFF, Ahmedabad Textile Industry's

Res. Assn, Navarangapura, Ahmedabad 9.
Member: ISCA. Applied industrial psychology, research, administration, counseling, guidance; group process, attitude survey, worker participation in industry. M

AMIN, Navnitlal Purushottamdas. Bunglow Wadi, Virsad, Bombay. b. 16 June 1925 Virsad. ED.M '56 M. S. Univ. of Baroda, India. PRINCIPAL, Ras High Sch, Bombay. Teaching, research, student; test construction and standardization, achievement tests, attitude measurement. M

ANAND, Kewal Krishan. Serv. Selectn. Bd, Ministry of Def, Govt. of India, Meerut Cantt. b. 3 Oct 1927 Gujranwala, Pakistan. MA '51 Punjab Univ, India. JR. PSYCH'T, Serv. Selectn. Bd. Member: IPA. Testing, personality assessment, personnel psychology, student; projective techniques, measurement of aptitude and personality qualities of school teachers. M

ANSARI, Dr. Anwar. Khalil Manzil, Marris Rd, Aligarh. b. 10 July 1922 Lucknow. PH.D '54 Univ. of London, Eng. READER in PSYCH, Muslim Univ, Aligarh; ED. BD, *Education and Psychology.* Member: ISCA. Teaching, research on social tensions, professional writing; social attitudes and values, group dynamics, culture and personality. M

ANSARI, Mrs. Ghazala. Women's Coll, Muslim Univ, Aligarh. b. 10 Aug 1924 Ghazipur. MA '53 Univ. of London, Eng. LECT. in EDUC, Women's Coll, Muslim Univ. Member: ISCA. Teaching, research, professional writing; social perception, group dynamics, attitudes and values. F

APPLACHARI, K. R. Teacher's Coll, Tuticorin, S. India. b. 27 Oct 1894 Nidamangalam, Tanjore. MA, Madras Univ, India. PRINCIPAL, Tchrs. Coll. Member: Madras Psych. Assn. Teaching, administration, professional writing; learning theory, achievement tests; social perception. M

ARANAYAKAM, Prof. Edwin Williams. Hindustani Talimi Sangh, Sevagram, Wardha. b. 5 May 1893 Vaddukoddai, Ceylon. ED.B '24 Univ. of Edinburgh, Scot. DIRECTOR, Hindustani Talimi Sangh. Member: BPS. Teaching, research, organizing and directing teacher training colleges; learning theory, social perception, group process. M

ARORA, Miss Chandrakala. Cen. Bur. of Educ. and Vocat. Guid, 33 Probyn Rd, Delhi 8. b. 29 July 1929 Kanpur. MA '53 Univ. of Banaras, India. COUNSELOR, Cen. Bur. of Educ. and Vocat. Guid; EDITOR, *Guidance News.* Member: IPA. Editorial, guidance, teaching; achievement tests, individual counseling, attitude measurement. F

ASTHANA, Bipin Chandrs. Psychomet.

Unit, Aligarh Univ, Aligarh. b. 27 June 1921 Hardoi. ED.M '50 Univ. of Edinburgh, Scot. SPEC. DUTY OFF, Exam. Res. Proj; EXEC. SECY, Psychometric Unit, Univ. of Aligarh; LECT. on Exper. EDUC, Univ. Trng. Coll, Aligarh. Member: BPS, APA, Indian Assn. of Sci. Wrkrs. Research, testing, teaching; factor analysis, achievement and aptitude testing, Rorschach. M

ASTHANA, Dr. Shanker Hari. 46 Sitla Prasad Rd, Rekabgunj, Lucknow. b. 27 Aug 1922 Hardoi. PH.D '50 Univ. of Lucknow, India. LECTURER, Univ. of Lucknow; EXEC. SECY, Univ. Psych. Clin, Lucknow; EDITOR, *Manasa: The Bulletin of Psychology,* Univ. of Lucknow. Member: APA, ISCA, Indian Psychiat. Socy, Indian Philos. Congress. Teaching, research, psychodiagnostics; personality theory, projective techniques, group dynamics. M

ATREYA, Prof. Dr. Bhikhan Lal. Atreya Niwas, P.O. Banaras Hindu Univ, Banaras 5. b. 24 Sept 1897 Judah, Saharanpur. DLitt '30 Banaras Hindu Univ, India. PROF. and HEAD, Dept. of Psych, Banaras Hindu Univ; DIRECTOR, Psychosocial Hlth. Serv, Banaras. Member: ISCA, Indian Socy. of Psychic and Yogic Res. Teaching, research in parapsychology, administration, psychotherapy; Yoga, psychoanalysis. M

ATREYA, Mrs. Induprabha. Govt. Girls Inter Coll, Bulandshahar. b. 4 May 1924 Aligarh. MA '52 Banaras Univ, India. LECT. in PSYCH. and EDUC, Govt. Girls Inter Coll. Teaching, guidance, student. F

ATREYA, Prof. Jagat Prakash. Dept. of Philos. and Psych, K.G.K. Coll, Agra Univ, Moradabad. b. 20 Jan 1930 Banaras. MA '52 Banaras Hindu Univ, India. PROF. and HEAD, Dept. of Philos. and Psych, K.G.K. Coll. Member: ISCA, Indian Philos. Congress, Indian Sociol. Assn. Teaching, research direction, educational psychology; measurement of social behavior and attitudes. M

ATREYA, Prof. Mrs. Prakash. Dept. of Psych, Gokuldas Hindu Girls' Degree Coll, Moradabad. b. 15 Feb 1929 Saharanpur. MA '56 Banaras Hindu Univ, India. PROF. and HEAD, Dept. of Psych, Gokuldas Hindu Girls' Degree Coll, Moradabad. Member: Indian Philos. Congress. Teaching, research, student; guidance, study of personality, Indian psychology. F

BAGCHI, Dr. Amalendu. P.O. Jalpaiguri, West Bengal. b. Aug 1914, Naogaon, Bengal. PH.D '51 Calcutta Univ, India. PROF. of SANSKRIT, A. C. Coll, Jalpaiguri, West Bengal. Member: IPA, ISCA. Teaching, research in Indian poetry, Yoga, and Nātyaśāstra; ancient Indian speculations on feelings and emotions, mind and behavior, psychology of art and poetry.   M

BAGH, Dhanapati. P. O. Sriniketon, District Birbhum, W. Bengal. b. 17 Sept 1918 Hooghli. M.SC '42 Calcutta Univ, India. LECT. in Soc. PSYCH. and EDUC, Visva-Bharati Univ, Shantiniketan, W. Bengal. Member: IPA, ISCA, Indian Psychoanal. Socy. Teaching, educational guidance, research; projective techniques, visual perception, social tensions.   M

BAKRE, Shri Ramchandra Pandurang. Govt. Training Coll, Khandwa Madhya Pradesh, Khandwa. b. 22 Oct 1909 Khandwa. MA '49 Univ. of Sagar, India. LECTURER, Govt. Training Coll. Teacher training, research, guidance; learning theory, achievement tests, attitude measurement. M

BANERJEE, Prof. Dr. Nikunja Vihari. Univ. of Delhi, Delhi 8. b. 26 Sept 1897 Punra, Bengal, PH.D '32 Univ. of London, Eng. PROF. of PHILOS, Univ. of Delhi; EDITOR, *The Philosophical Quarterly.* Member: IPA. Teaching, research, administration; method and techniques of psychological tests.   M

BASIT, Prof. Abdul. Delhi Coll, Ajmeri Gate, Delhi. b. 1 July 1929 Ghazipur City. MA '51 Aligarh Univ, India. PROFESSOR, Delhi Coll. Member: IPA. Teaching, psychotherapy, clinical practice; dreams, psychology of sex, psychology of fashion.   M

BEG, Moaziz Ali. Dpt of Psych, Muslim Univ, Aligarh. b. 17 Feb 1931 Agra. MA '52 Muslim Univ, India. LECTURER, Muslim Univ; EDITOR, Psych. Sect, *Nau Naslain.* Teaching, research; cultural determinants of personality, problem of social discontent, comparative study of caste prejudice in older and younger generations of Hindus. M

BHANDARI, Dr. Lalit. C. 2-B Pusa Rd, New Delhi. b. 3 June 1916 Amritsar. PH.D '50 Univ. of London, Eng. TEACHER, Punjab Univ; DIRECTOR, Child Guid, Ment. Hlth. and Personality Couns. Clin. Member: IPA, BPS, British Psychoanal. Socy.   Psychotherapy, teaching, child guidance, clinical practice; projective techniques, learning theory. ,   M

BHARADWAJ, S. B. L. Dist. Psych. Cen, Civil Lines, Bareilly. b. 2 Aug 1920 Lucknow. MA '42 Agra Univ, India. DIST. PSYCH'T, Dist. Psych. Cen, Bareilly, Allahabad. Member: Lucknow Counc. for Ment. Hyg. Educational, vocational and personal guidance, research; test construction, interest and intelligence measurement.   M

BHATIA, Prof. Baldev. Child Guid. Clin, Coll. of Nursing, 12 Jaswant Singh Rd, New Delhi. b. 17 Mar 1914 Sialkot. MA '43 Punjab Univ, India. DIRECTOR, Child Guid. Clin, Coll. of Nrsng. Member: IPA. Clinical practice, guidance, teaching, research; projective techniques, behavior and personality problems, child guidance techniques.   M

BHATT, Prof. L. J. Dept. of Psych. M.S. Univ, Baroda. b. 18 Sept 1913 Baroda. MA '37 Bombay Univ, India; MA '53 Leeds Univ, Eng. UNIV. LECT, Dept. of Psych, M.S. Univ; MANAGING ED, *Journal of Education and Psychology.* Member: IPA, ISCA. Baroda Psych. Socy. Teaching, research in job analysis and test standardization, guidance of graduate student research; social tensions, achievement and aptitude tests, attitude measurement.   M

BHATTACHARYA, Charu Chandra. 5/1 Suri Lane, Calcutta 14. b. 25 June 1917 India. M.SC '39 Univ. of Calcutta, India. INSTR. in APPL. PSYCH, Univ. of Calcutta, 92 Upper Circular Rd, Calcutta 9. Member: ISCA, IPA, Indian Ment. Hlth. Assn. Teaching, vocational, educational and clinical counseling, research; projective techniques, achievement and psychotechnical tests.   M

BIMALESWAR, Dr. De. L.S. Coll, Muzaffarpur, Bihar. b. 3 June 1919 Patna. PH.D Univ, of London, Eng. HEAD, Dept. of Psych, Bihar Univ. Member: IPA, ISCA. Teaching, research, administration, professional writing; projective techniques, attitude measurement, personality assessment.   M

BISI, Sunil Chandra. 20 Bepin Pal Rd, Calcutta 26. b. 1 Mar 1916 Calcutta. M.SC '42 Univ. of Calcutta, India. SUPT. PSYCH'T, Directorate Gen, Ordnance Factories, 6 Esplanade E, Calcutta 1. Member: IPA, Calcutta Assn. for Ment. Hlth, Bangiya Bignan Parishad. Applied industrial psychology, research, testing; test construction, treating and training the mentally handicapped.   M

BOAZ, Dr. G. D. Univ. of Madras, Madras. 2 b. 31 Mar 1908 S. Travanlore. PH.D '42 Oxford Univ, Eng. PROF. of PSYCH, Univ. Madras; DIRECTOR, Juv. Guid. Bur, Madras; PSYCHOTHERAPIST, priv. prac. Member: ISCA, Madras Psych. Socy. Teaching research direction, psychotherapy; dynamics of motivation, attitude measurement, projective techniques, mental hygiene.   M

BOSE, Miss Kshanika. Coll. of Nursing, Univ. of Delhi, New Delhi. b. June 1926 Dacca. MA '49 Univ. of Banaras, India. LECTURER, Coll. of Nrsng, Jaswant Singh Rd. 12, New Delhi. Member: IPA, ISCA. Teaching English, research, professional writing; translating education books into Bengali; projective techniques, studies in delinquency, diagnostic tests.   F

BOSE, Prof. Sudhir Kumar. Indian Inst. of Sci, Soc. Sci. Sect, Bangalore 3. b. 21

Aug 1902 Calcutta. M.SC '25 Univ. of Calcutta, India. ASST. PROF, Indian Inst. of Sci; ADVISOR, Vocat. Guid. Bur; READER in PSYCH, Calcutta Univ; EDITOR, *Indian Journal of Psychology*; ED. BD, *Journal of Genetic Psychology*, (USA). Member: IPA, ISCA. Research, editorial, teaching; attitude measurement, achievement tests, group process, industrial psychology, human relations.   M

CAUSHIC, Anant Rao. Jupiter Mills Ltd, P.O. Box 43, Ahmedabad. b. 27 May 1925 Mysore. MA '51 Mysore Univ, India. INDUS. PSYCH'T, Jupiter Mills. Member: ISCA, India Inst. of Vocat. and Educ. Guid. Training supervisors in industry, testing, research; achievement and intelligence tests, social perception, group process, attitude serveys, extra-sensory perception.   M

CHACKO, Miss Annamma K. Training Inst. for Women, Hawa Bagh, Jabalpur. b. 16 Oct 1929 Traraneore. MA '55 St. Johns Coll, Agra Univ, India. LECTURER, Training Inst. for Women. Teaching educational and experimental psychology; individual differences, learning theory, vocational guidance.   F

CHAUBE, Dr. Sarayu Prasad. Dept. of Educ. Lucknow Univ, Lucknow. b. 1 Feb 1919 Banaras. ED.D '52 Indiana Univ, USA. LECTURER, Dept. of Educ, Lucknow Univ; PSYCHOLOGIST, Lucknow Univ. Psych. Clin. Member: Lucknow Psych. Assn. Teaching, guidance, history of education, research; learning theory, guidance techniques, group process.   M

CHAUDHURV, Prof. K. P. Bur. of Educ. and Psych. Res. David Hare Trng. Coll, Calcutta 19. b. 1 Sept 1913 Sylhet, Pakistan. MA '46 Univ. of London, Eng. PROFESSOR, Bur. of Educ. and Psych. Res. Member: India Educ. and Vocat. Guid. Assn. Teaching, educational and vocational guidance, standardization of tests, training of guidance personnel; group tension, attitude measurement, teacher selection. M

CHOTHIA, Fali. Dhun-Abad, 106 Bhulabhai Desai Rd, Bombay 26. b. 28 Dec 1917 Bombay. MA '48 Univ. of London, Eng. VOCAT. GUID. OFF, Vocat. Guid. Bur, 3 Cruickshank Rd, Bombay 1. EDITOR, *Vocational Guidance News-Letter*. Member: India Educ. and Vocat. Guid. Assn, Bombay Psych. Assn. Guidance, teaching, administration; vocational guidance, testing, counseling.   M

CHOWDHRY, Dr. Kamla. Ahmedabad Textile Industry's Res. Assn, Navrangpura, Ahmedabad 9. b. 17 Dec 1920 Delhi. PH.D '49 Univ. of Michigan, USA. HEAD, Psych. Div, A.T.I.R.A. Research, industrial psychology, consulting; social perception,

group process, attitude measurement.   F

COELHO, Dr. George V. Dept. of Psych, Haverford Coll, Haverford, Pennsylvania, USA. b. 9 Nov 1918 Bombay India. PH.D '56 Harvard Univ, USA. ASST. PROF. of PSYCH, Haverford Coll. Member: IPA, APA. Teaching, research, professional writing; group conflict and prejudice, social perception, personality theory, experimental social psychology.   M

DANI, Shankar Krishna. Dept. of Psych, Prantiya Shikshen Mahevidyalaya, Jabalpur. b. 1 Apr 1923 Hinganghat. MA '47 Nagpur Univ, India. PROFESSOR, Dept. of Psych, Prantiya Shikshan Mahavidyalaya. Teaching, research, educational and vocational testing; intelligence testing, educational and vocational guidance, personality theory and measurement.   M

DAS, Barin. Selectn. Cen. N., Meerut Cantt. b. 12 Mar 1927 Patna Bihar. MA '49 Patna Univ, India. JR. PSYCH'T, Serv. Selectn. Bd, Meerut Cantt. Member: IPA, Meerut Psych. Socy, Calcutta Assn. of Ment. Hlth. Personnel psychology, research, testing, selection of officers for Indian army and navy; projective techniques, group process.   M

DAS, Dr. Radha Charan. R.N. Trng. Coll, Cuttack, Grissa. b. 7 Mar 1925 Aska. PH.D '50 Cornell Univ, USA. LECTURER, R.N. Trng. Coll; COUNSELOR, State Bur. of Educ. and Vocat. Guid. Teaching, testing, research in education, educational and vocational guidance; learning theory, achievement and aptitude tests, test construction.   M

DAS, Dr. Rames Chandra. 19 School Row, Bhowanipur, Calcutta 25. b. 19 Jan 1927 West Bengal. PH.D '55 Univ. of London, Eng. ASST. PROF. of PSYCH, Govt. Trng. Coll, Hooghly, W. Bengal. Member: BPS. Teaching, research, administration, professional writing; student selection, juvenile delinquency, measurement of interest. M

DAS, Dr. Rhea Stagner. Psychomet. Unit, Indian Stat. Inst, 203 Barrackpore Trunk Rd, Calcutta 35. b. 19 Dec 1929 Madison, Wisconsin, USA. PH.D '55 Univ. of Illinois, USA. INDUS. PSYCH'T, Indian Stat. Inst. Industrial selection, research, statistical design, personnel selection, attitude measurement.   F

DASGUPTA, Dr. Debendra Chandra. Univ. of Gauhati, Jhalakbari Campus, Quarter 56, Univ. P.O., Jhalakbari, Assam. b. June 1901 Binauti. ED.D '32 Univ. of California, USA. HEAD, Dept. of Educ. and Tchr. Trng. Dept, Gauhati Univ; ED. BD, *Gauhati University Journal*. Teaching, research, administration; educational psychology of ancient India.   F

DASTUR, Dr. Hormusji Pestonji. Tata Industries Priv. Ltd, Dept. of Indus. Hlth, Bombay House, Bruce St, Fort, Bombay 1. b. 12 Aug 1882 Broach. L.M. and S. '04 Univ. of Bombay, India. CHIEF INDUS. HLTH. OFF, Tata Industries Priv. Ltd. Member: Indian Inst. of Personnel Management. Administration, industrial health and welfare work, research; industrial psychology, group process, attitude measurement. M

DATTA, Anath Nath. Dept. of Psych, Univ. Coll. of Sci. and Tech, 92 Upper Circular Rd, Calcutta 9. b. 1 Feb 1909 Calcutta. M.SC '33 Calcutta Univ, India. LECTURER, Dept. of Psych, Univ. Coll. of Sci. and Tech. Member: IPA. Teaching, research; projective techniques. M

DATTA, Prof. H. M. Dept. of Educ, B. R. Coll, Agra. b. 1 Nov 1913 India. MA '36 Dacca Univ, Pakistan. PROFESSOR, B.R. Coll; DIRECTOR, Guid. Bur, B.R. Trng. Coll, Agra. Member: BPS, Indian Educ. and Vocat. Guid. Assn. Teaching, testing, guidance; intelligence and achievement tests. M

DAVAL, Ishwar. Alembic Chemical Works Co, Ltd, Alembic Rd, Baroda 3. b. 12 Nov 1924 Indore. MS '49 New York Univ, USA. HEAD, Res. Serv. Dept, Alembic Chemical Works. Member: IPA, Indian Psychiat. Socy. Direct and coordinate research, administration, industrial psychology; group process, social perception, attitude measurement. M

DEB, Asit Nath. Dept. of Psych, Ravenshaw Coll, Chowliagungj. Cuttack 3, Orissa. b. 23 Apr 1923 Balasore, Orissa. M.SC '50 Calcutta Univ, India. LECT. in PSYCH, Ravenshaw Coll. Member: IPA, ISCA. Teaching, research, testing; concept of crime, construction and standardization of tests, measurement of attitudes among industrial workers. M

DEB, Mrs. Maya. c/o P.K. Guha, Suite 9, 37 Syed Amir Ali Ave, Calcutta 19. b. 4 Aug 1926 Calcutta. M.SC '49 Calcutta Univ, India. HEAD MISTRESS, Indian Psychoanal. Socy, Bodhayana, 14 Parshibagan Lane, Calcutta 9. Member: IPA. Administration of the school, guiding mentally defective children, testing; vocational guidance, study of personality structure of mentally defective children. F

DESAI, Dr. Krishnakant G. A.G. Teachers Coll, Navrangpura, Ahmedabad 9. b. 22 May 1923 Surat. PH.D '54 Univ. of Bombay, India. LECT. in PSYCH. and EDUC, A.G. Tchrs. Coll. Teaching, research in psychometrics and education, testing, vocational counseling, guiding student research; intelligence and achievement tests. M

DESHMUKH, W. N. Psych. Res. Wing, Def.

Sci. Organiza, Ministry of Def, E Block, New Delhi 11. b. 1 Nov 1926 Rajura Manikgarh, Hydrabad. MA '49 Sangor Univ, India. JR. PSYCH'T, Psych. Res. Wing. Teaching, construction, standardization and revision of intelligence and aptitude tests, research on personnel selection methods in armed forces; projective techniques. M

DEVE GOWDA, Prof. A. C. Teachers' Coll, Mysore. b. 29 Apr 1908 Chikmagalur. MA '33 Columbia Univ, USA. DEAN, PRIN. and PROF. of EDUC, Faculty of Educ, Tchrs. Coll, Univ. of Mysore. Teaching, research, testing; achievement, intelligence and aptitude tests. M

DEVI, Miss Saradamani R. Cen. Inst. of Educ, 33 Probyn Rd, Delhi 8. b. 23 Sept 1926 Trivandrum, Travancore. MA '55 Univ. of Banaras, India. DEMONSTRATOR in PSYCH, Cen. Inst. of Educ. Member: IPA. Teaching, research, educational psychology; sociometrics, projective techniques, personality evaluation, aptitude testing. F

DHAR, Dr. Bansi. Asst. Labour Commr, Kanpur, Uttar Pradesh. b. July 1898 Kakori, Lucknow. PH.D '47 Univ. of Edinburgh, Scot. ASST. LABOUR COMMR, Labour Dept, Sampurnanand Indus. Psych. Lab, Kanpur. Member: BPS. Research, applied and industrial psychology, professional writing; intelligence, and personality testing, time and motion study, efficiency methods. M

DOSAJH, Nandlal. Dept. of Psych, Govt. Trng. Coll, Jullundur, Punjab. b. 15 May 1916 Lyallpur. MA '49 Punjab Univ, India. HEAD, Dept. of Psych, Govt. Trng. Coll; CLIN. PSYCH'T, priv. prac. Member: IPA, ISCA. Teaching, research, administration, clinical practice, psychotherapy; projective techniques, experimental and educational psychology. M

DUTT, Dr. Sunitee. Central Inst. of Educ, 33 Probyn Rd, Delhi. b. 20 Sept 1916 Rangoon, Burma. PH.D '55 Univ. of Delhi, India. LECT. in EDUC, Cen. Inst. of Educ; EDITOR, *C.I.E. Studies in Education and Psychology.* Member: IPA, ISCA. Teaching, research, editorial, translate books on education into Bengali; achievement tests, prognosis of different test scores. F

DUTTA, Miss Kalyani. 64 Mahanirban Rd, Calcutta 29. b. 26 Nov 1929 Calcutta. MA '55 Univ. of Calcutta, India. RES. SCHOLAR, Univ. Coll. of Sci, Psych. Dept, 92 Upper Circular Rd, Calcutta 9. Member: IPA. Research, testing; projective techniques, social perception, attitude measurement, psychology of the deaf-mute. F

DWIVEDI, Shanker Dutt. Bara Genesh,

Banaras.   b.   11 Sept 1932 Mirzapur. MA '54 Hindu Univ, India. ASST. PSYCH'T, Hosp. for Ment. Diseases, P.O. Kanke, Ranchi. Member: IPA. Testing, guidance, psychotherapy; projective techniques, attitude measurement, group process.   M

FRANKLIN, Eric Wilfred. Educ. Dept, Govt. of Madhya Pradesh, Nagpur. b. 11 Nov 1903 Bilaspur. MA '39 Univ. of Calcutta, India.   DIR. of PUB. INSTR, Govt. of Madhya Pradesh. Member: IPA. Teaching, administration, educational psychology; aptitude and achievement tests, learning theory.   M

GANGULI, Dr. Harish Chandra. Dept. of Humanities and Soc. Sci, Indian Inst. of Tech, Khargpur. b. 25 Nov 1924 Meerut. DLitt '56 Univ. of Calcutta, India. LECT. in INDUS. PSYCH, Indian Inst. of Tech. Member: IPA, ISCA. Research, teaching, research direction; attitude measurement, aptitude testing, industrial fatigue.   M

GANGULY, Dr. Dwijendralal. 21/1A Fern Rd, Calcutta 19. b. Oct 1903 Calcutta. M.SC '30 Univ. of Calcutta, India.   SR. LECT, Psych. Dept, Univ. of Calcutta, 92 Upper Circular Rd, Calcutta 9; ACTING ED, *Indian Journal of Psychology.* Member: IPA, ISCA. Teaching, research, editorial; projective techniques, achievement and psycho technical tests.   M

GANGULY, Onkarnath. DL. Nopany H.E. Sch, 2-D Nando Mullick Lane, Calcutta. b. 1 Nov 1931 W. Bengal. MA '55 Univ. of Calcutta, India.   SCH. PSYCH'T, DL Nopany H.E. Sch; SUPERINTENDENT, Hony at Bodhipeet, Calcutta. Member: IPA, Calcutta Assn. for Ment. Hlth. Testing, educational psychology, counseling, research; test construction, child guidance, clinical work, projective techniques.   M

GANGULY, Topodhan. 19 Nur Mahammad Lane, Calcutta 9. b. 2 May 1929 Calcutta. M.SC '52 Univ. of Calcutta, India.   ASST. RES. OFF, Indus. Hlth. Res. Unit, ICMR, All India Inst. of Hyg. and Pub. Hlth, 110 Chittaranjan Ave, Calcutta 12; JOINT ED, *Review of Occupational Health.* Member: IPA. Research on human relations in industry, teaching, administration; industrial tensions, attitude measurement, group process, achievement tests.   M

GARG, Pulin K. B.M. Inst. of Child Devel, Ellis Bridge, Ahmedabad. b. 4 Sept 1927 Dankaur. MA '52 Patna Univ, India. SOC. PSYCH'T, B.M. Inst. of Child Devel. Research, testing, applied psychology; social perception, group process, group dynamics, socialization and cultural processes of value transmission.   M

GAYEN, Dr. Anil Kumar. Indian Inst. of Tech, Kharagpur. b. 1 Feb 1919 Calcutta. PH.D '50 Cambridge Univ, Eng. PROF. of

STAT, Indian Inst. of Tech; EDITOR, *Indian Society for Quality Control Bulletin.* Member: Indian Stat. Inst. Research, teaching, applied psychology; psychometry, achievement tests, group process, attitude measurement.   M

GEORGE, Dr. E. I. University Coll, Trivandrum, Travancore-Cochin. b. 25 June 1925 Thumpamon. PH.D '54 Univ. of London, Eng. LECTURER, Univ. Coll; EXT. LECT. in CHILD PSYCH: DIRECTOR, Med. and Pub. Hlth, Travancore. Member: BPS. Teaching, applied and educational psychology, research, testing, clinical analysis, guidance; personality tests, social attitudes, interest measurements.   M

GHOSH, Miss Roma. Dept. of Humanities and Soc. Sci. Indian Inst. of Tech, Khargpur. b. 2 Oct 1932 Calcutta. M.SC '54 Calcutta Univ. Coll. of Sci, India.   JR. TECH. ASST, Indian Inst. of Tech. Member: IPA. Research and testing in industrial psychology, teaching, student; construction and validation of mechanical ability tests. F

GHOSH, Dr. Sachindra Prosad. Fac. of Art, Univ. of Delhi, Probyn Rd, Delhi 6. b. 1 Jan 1915 East Bengal. PH.D '51 Univ. of Calcutta, India.   LECT. in PSYCH, Univ. of Delhi. Member: IPA. Research, teaching, testing, social work; industrial personnel selection, vocational guidance, employer-employee relations.   M

GOSWAMI, Santimoy. Dept. of Humanities and Soc. Sci, Indian Inst. of Tech, Khargpur. b. 1 Feb 1927 Calcutta. M.SC '54 Calcutta Univ. Sci. Coll, India.   PSYCH. INVES, Indian Inst. of Tech. Conducting psychological interviews, attitude measurement, industrial relations research, teaching; intelligence tests, group process. M

GUPTA, Gian Chand. Cen. Bur. of Educ. and Vocat. Guid, 33 Probyn Rd, Delhi 8. b. 29 Sept 1929 India. MS.C '55 Calcutta Univ, India. RES. SCHOLAR, Cen. Bur. of Educ. and Vocat. Guid; PSYCH. TCHR, Punjab Univ. Coll, New Delhi. Member: IPA. Personality study, research, teaching; social perception, group process.   M

GUPTA, R. S. P. P.O. Belamegh, via Dalsingh-Sarai, Darbhanga, Bihar.   b. Jan 1936 Belamegh. MA '56 Banaras Hindu Univ, India. STUDENT, Banaras Hindu Univ, Banaras 5. Member: Banaras Hindu Univ. Philos. and Psych. Assn. Student, consulting; projective techniques, learning theory, attitude measurement.   M

GUPTA, S. C. Birkbeck Coll, Malet St, London W.C. 1, Eng. b. 18 Mar 1931 India. MA '55 Benares Univ, India. RES. STUD, Birkbeck Coll. Member: BPS. Research, applied psychology, testing; intelligence, attainment and personality testing.   M

GUPTA, Miss Vimla. B. M. Inst. of Child Devel, Ellis Bridge, Ahmedabad 6. b. 8 Aug 1931 Chin Hills, Falam, Burma. MA '52 Patna Univ, India. CLIN PSYCH'T, B.M. Inst. of Child Devel. Member: IPA. Testing and diagnosis of children and adults, psychotherapy; projective techniques, social perception. F

HAFEEZ, Abdul. Dept. of Psych, Univ. of Mysore, Maharaja's Coll, Mysore. MA '49 Univ. of Mysore, India. LECTURER, Univ. of Mysore; EDITOR, *Manasa Magazine.* Member: ISCA. Teaching, research and guiding student research, consulting; attitude measurement, psychology of values, sociometry. M

HORA, Dr. Rajni. c/o R.S. Hora, 9/10 Windsor Mansions, Queensway Lane, New Delhi. b. 1 Aug 1929 Peshawar. PH.D '56 Univ. Coll. of London, Eng. Member: BPS. Student, testing, lecturing in pychology; intelligence and attainment tests, projective techniques, nondirective play therapy. F

HUSAIN, Taqui Ali Khan. 1953 Akbar Rd, Mandi Mohalla, Mysore. b. 5 Aug 1932 Mysore. MA '55 Univ. of Mysore, India. LECT. in PSYCH, Univ. of Mysore. Teaching, research, educational psychology; achievement and intelligence testing, counseling, guidance. M

ISHAQ, S. M. Govt. Training Coll, Khandwa. b. 30 Dec 1924 Khamgaon. MA '49 Univ. of Sagar, India. LECTURER, Govt. Trng. Coll. Teaching educational psychology, testing, administration, guidance; learning theory, achievement tests, attitude measurement. M

JACOB, Miss Josephine Irene. Def. Sci. Organiza, Ministry of Def, E Block, New Delhi. b. 23 July 1923 Simla. MA '48 Lucknow Univ, India. JR. PSYCH'T, Psych. Res. Wing. Research, testing, applied psychology; construction and standardization of clerical, aptitude, performance, achievement and intelligence tests. F

JAHAGIRDAR, Prof. Keshao Tatyacharya. D. and H. Natl. Coll, Bandra, Bombay 20. b. 16 Apr 1914 Bijapur. MA '41 Allahabad Univ, India. PROF. of PHILOS. and PSYCH, D. and H. Natl. Coll; CO-EDITOR, *Manav.* Member: Socy. for Psych. Res, Bombay Philos. Socy, Bhandarkar Oriental Res. Inst. Teaching, research, editorial; psychotherapy. M

JAIN, N. R. 127 E Block, Ministry of Def, New Delhi. b. 6 May 1924 Bhadour. MA '46 Punjab Univ, India. JR. PSYCH'T, Ministry of Def. Member: IPA. Research, applied psychology, testing; projective techniques, interviewing, personality inventories. M

JAITLY, Kailash Nath. 511 Chaupatiyan,

Lucknow. b. 2 May 1929 Lucknow. MA '51 Lucknow Univ, India. RES. ASSOC, Psych. Dept, Univ. of Colorado, Boulder, Colorado, USA. Member: ISCA. Research, teaching, student; projective techniques, personality, attitude measurement. M

JALOTA, Dr. Shyam Swaroop. Banaras Hindu Univ, Banaras 5. b. 28 Jan 1904 Phagwara. PH.D '49 Calcutta Univ, India. READER in PSYCH, Banaras Hindu Univ; EDITOR, *Indian Journal of Psychology, Journal of Vocational and Educational Guidance.* Member: IPA, ISCA, Indian Philos. Congress Assn. Standardization of verbal group tests of general mental ability and personality, teaching, factor analysis, apparatus design; group psychometrics, experimental methods, industrial relations. M

JAMUAR, Krishna Kumar. B. N. Coll, Patna Univ, Patna 4. b. 16 Dec 1925 Mai. MA '49 Patna Univ, India. LECT. in PSYCH, Patna Univ, Patna 6. Member: B. N. Coll. Psych. Socy. Teaching, research, professional writing; dream analysis, projective techniques, juvenile delinquency. M

JAYASWAL, Dr. Sita Ram. Dept. of Educ, Lucknow Univ, Lucknow. b. 12 Sept 1920 Jaunpur. PH.D '55 Univ. of Michigan, USA. READER in EDUC, Lucknow Univ. Member: Socy. for Res. in Child Devel, Lucknow Psych. Assn. Teaching, educational psychology, professional writing; persistance and change in personality, psycholinguistics. M

JOSHI, Chandra Mohan. Lab. of Exper. Psych, Banaras Hindu Univ, Banaras 5. b. 27 Dec 1933 Almora. MA '54 Banaras Hindu Univ, India. RES. SCHOLAR, Dept. of Psych, Banaras Hindu Univ. Member: ISCA, IPA. Research on mental testing, teaching; clinical psychology. M

JOSHI, Miss Uma. Devi Niwas, Almora. b. 15 July 1936 Almora. MA '56 Univ. of Lucknow, India. STUDENT, Lucknow Univ. Member: Lucknow Psych. Assn. Testing, applied psychology; attitude measurement, group process, social perception. F

KAKKAR, Prof. Suraj Balram. Dept. of Psych, Govt. Trng. Coll. for Tchrs, Jullundur, Punjab. b. 5 Feb 1926 Khushab. MA '52 Univ. of Punjab, India. LECT. in EDUC. PSYCH. MENT. HYG, and CHILD GUID, Govt. Trng. Coll. for Tchrs. Member: IPA. Teaching, research, professional writing; personality tests, teacher attitudes, mental abnormalities. M

KANAL, Prof. Premlata S. Punjab Univ. Camp Coll, Reading Rd, New Delhi. b. 14 Jan 1914 Rawalpindi. MA '42 Univ. of Calcutta, India. HEAD, Dept. of Psych, Punjab Univ. Camp Coll. Member: IPA

Punjab Psych. Assn. Teaching, administration, educational psychology; learning theories, emotional development of children and adolescents.   F

KANUNGO, Rabindranath. Dept. of Psych, Ravenshaw Coll, Cuttack 3. b. 11 July 1935 Cuttack. MA '55 Patna Univ, India. LECT. in PSYCH, Ravenshaw Coll. Teaching, research, writing for popular periodicals; social perception, learning theory, projective techniques.   M

KANWAR, Miss Usha. 19-B Railway Colony, Kitchner Rd, New Delhi. b. 19 June 1934 Lahore. MA '55 Univ of Lucknow, India. RES. FELLOW, Central Inst. of Educ, Probyn Rd, Delhi. Member: IPA. Research, testing and statistical work; socialization, social perception, projective techniques.   F

KAPUR, R. L. All India Inst. of Ment. Hlth, Ment. Hosp, Bangalore 2. b. 15 Dec 1929 Peshawar, W. Pakistan. MA '52 Punjab Univ, India. GRAD. STUD, All India Inst. of Ment. Hlth. Member: IPA. Research and training in clinical psychology, testing; personality measurement with objective tests, projective techniques, learning theory.   M

KAR, Bhupendra Chandra. Staff Quarter 35, Jalukbari, P.O. Gauhati Univ, Assam. b. 1 Feb 1915 Mymensingh, Pakistan. MA '38 Univ. of Dacca, India. READER, Dept. of Educ. and Tchr. Trng, Gauhati Univ; ED. BD, *Teachers' Journal*, Gauhati Univ. Member: ISCA. Teaching, research, editorial; projective techniques, social perception, group process.   M

KHADKIKAR, Shri Shripao Dattatraya. Govt. Training Coll, Khandwa, Madhya Pradesh. b. 14 Mar 1920 Yeola. MA '49 Univ. of Saugar, India. LECTURER, Govt. Trng. Coll. Teaching, educational guidance, research, testing, administration; learning theory, achievement tests, attitude measurement.   M

KHANNA, Dr. Jawant Lal. 46 Dasya Gavj, Delhi 7. b. 5 July 1926 Lahore. PH.D '56 Univ. of Colorado, USA. ASSOC. PROF, Punjab Univ, India. Member: BPS, Delhi Psych. Socy. Teaching, research, student; social and personality psychology, industrial testing.   M

KHANNA, Mrs. Prabha. 871 24th St, Boulder, Colorado, USA. b. 20 July 1927 Amhala. PH.D '57 Univ. of Colorado, USA. TCHNG. FELLOW, Univ. of Colorado, Boulder, Colorado, USA. Teaching psychology, research, student; clinical diagnosis and therapy.   F

KHEMKA, Kailash C. Lohai Rd, Farrukhabad. b. 14 July 1930 Farrukhabad. MA '56 Lucknow Univ, India. RES. ASST, Dept. of Psych, Lucknow Univ. Research,

teaching, clinical practice; parapsychology, psychotherapy and clinical interviewing, national character.   M

KOTHANETH, Kunhunni Nair. Indian Air Force, Psych. Res. Wing, Ministry of Def, D.H.Q. Post Off, New Delhi. b. 15 May 1916 Madras. MB, BS '42 Univ. of Madras, India. PSYCHIATRIST, Indian Air Forces. Member: Indian Psychiat. Socy. Research, clinical practice, psychotherapy; projective techniques, play therapy.   M

KOTHURKAR, Vasudeo Krishna. Professors' Quarters, Univ. of Poona, Ganeshkhind, Poona 7. b. 2 Mar 1912 Kalvan. BA '40 Cambridge Univ, Eng. READER and HEAD, Dept. of Exper. Psych, Univ. of Poona; ED. BE, *Poona University Journal*. Member: ISCA, Indian Philos. Congress. Research, teaching, administration; verbal learning, social perception and group process.   M

KRISHNAMURTHY, Parthasarathy. Dept. of Psych, Maharaja's Coll, Mysore. b. 4 Dec 1926 Dharwar. MA '54 Univ. of Mysore, India. LECTURER, Maharaja's Coll, Univ. of Mysore. Teaching, research, testing; projective techniques, factor analysis, psychoanalysis.   M

KRISHNAN, Prof. Baliganahalli. Psych. Dept, Maharaja's Coll, Krishnaraja Rd, Mysore. b. 9 Oct 1917 Baliganahalli. MA '46 Univ. of Mysore, India. ASST. PROF, Univ. of Mysore. Member: ISCA, Madras Psych. Socy, All India Educ. and Vocat. Guid. Assn. Teaching, research, counseling; personality measurement, achievement and aptitude tests.   M

KUMAR, P. Hosp. for Ment. Diseases, Kanke P.O., Ranchi. b. 15 Jan 1928 Sasaram. MA '48 Patna Univ, India. ASST. PSYCH'T, Hosp. for Ment. Diseases. Member: Indian Psychiat. Socy. Individual and group psychotherapy, mental and personality testing, research, writing on psychology in Hindi; Rorschach test, guidance.   M

KUMAR, Miss Usha. Isbella Thoburn Coll, Lucknow. b. 22 Aug 1931 Lahore. MA '55 Lucknow Univ, India. LECT. in PSYCH, Isabella Thoburn Coll. Member: Lucknow Psych. Assn. Teaching psychology; social psychology, projective techniques.   F

KUMRIA, R. R. Govt. Training Coll, Jullundur, Punjab. b. 25 Sept 1902 Lahore. MA '25 Punjab Univ, India. PRINCIPAL, Govt. Trng. Coll, Punjab; EDITOR, *Punjab Educational Journal*. Member: IPA. Teaching, administration, research and writing.   M

KUNDU, Ramanath. Dept. of Psych, Univ. Coll. of Sci. and Tech, 92 Upper Circular Rd, Calcutta 9. b. 1 Jan 1931 Chandernagore. M.SC '55 Calcutta Univ, India. INSTR. in APPL. PSYCH, Calcutta Univ,

Coll. Square, Calcutat 7; ASST. ED, *Indian Journal of Psychology*. Member: IPA. Research, teaching, counseling, guidance; accident-prone personnel, construction and standardization of tests, vocational and educational counseling. M

KUPPUSWAMY, Dr. B. Univ. of Mysore, Mysore. b. 25 Feb 1907 Bangalore. DLitt '44 Univ. of Mysore, India. PROF. and HEAD, Dept. of Psych, Univ. of Mysore. Member: ISCA. Research, teaching, administration; attitude measurement, aptitude and achievement tests. M

LAHORI, Shamboo Nath. Cen. Bur. of Educ. and Vocat. Guid, Ministry of Educ, New Delhi. b. 15 Apr 1925 Shopian, Kashmir. MA '49 Lucknow Univ, India. TECH. ASST, Cen. Bur. of Educ. and Vocat. Guid. Teaching, testing and interviewing. M

LALL, Dr. Sohan. Def. Sci. Organiza, Psych. Res. Wing, Ministry of Def, New Delhi. b. 24 Oct 1902 Ferozepore. PH.D '45 Univ. of Edinburgh, Scot. CHIEF. PSYCH'T, Def. Sci. Organiza. Member: IPA. Research; projective techniques, intelligence and aptitude tests, group process. F

LELE, Trimbak Purushottam. Shastri's Pole, Baroda. b. 1 Dec 1909 Patan. ED.B '52 St. Andrews, Scot. SR. LECT, M.S. Univ, Camp Rd, Baroda. Member: ISCA, All India Assn. of Educ. and Vocat. Guid. Research, teaching, testing; learning theory, achievement tests, attitude measurement test construction. M

LOOMBA, Miss Krishna Priya. c/o Mr. A. L. Loomba, Model House, Lucknow. b. 18 Sept 1934 Lucknow. MA '55 Lucknow Univ, India. HONORARY ASST.PSYCH'T, Neuropsychiat. Clin, Noor Manzil, Lalbagh, Lucknow. Student, testing, research; projective tests, developmental psychology, concept formation, attitude measurement. F

LOOMBA, Ram Murti. Dept. of Philos. and Psych, Lucknow Univ, Badshah Bagh, Lucknow. b. 11 Aug 1913 Ujjain. MA '32 Lucknow Univ, India. LECTURER, Dept. of Philos. and Psych, Lucknow Univ; EDITOR, Educ. Psych. Sect, *Psychology News Bulletin*. Member: ISCA, IPA, Lucknow Psych. Assn. Teaching, testing, research, personal and educational guidance, editorial; psychology of interest, consciousness and its levels. M

MADAN, Dr. Shereen K. 72 Nair Rd, Bombay 8. b. 3 Nov 1927 Calcutta. PH.D '55 Univ. of London, Eng. PSYCHOLOGIST, Market Res. Dept, Lever Bros. Ltd, Ballard Estate, Bombay 1. Member: BPS, IPA. Applied psychology, motivation research, testing; projective techniques, social perception, attitude measurement. F

MAJUMDER, Miss Kanak. Hindi High Sch,

1 Moira St, Calcutta 16. b. 6 Oct 1925 Calcutta. M.SC '48 Univ. of Calcutta, India. SCH. PSYCH'T, Hindi High Sch; PSYCHOTHERAPIST, Lumbini Park Ment. Hosp. Member: IPA, Indian Psychoanal. Socy, Bodhipit. Counseling backward and difficult children, psychiatric social work, psychotherapy, testing; achievement tests, clinical studies and psychoanalysis. F

MALAVALLI, Yoganarasimhiah. Dept. of Psych, Maharaja's Coll, Univ. of Mysore, Mysore. b. 16 Oct 1926 Malavalli. MA '54 Teacher's Coll, Columbia Univ, USA. LECTURER, Maharaja's Coll, Univ. of Mysore. Member: ISCA. Research, applied psychology, testing, teaching; attitude measurement, achievement tests. M

MALHOTRA, Dr. Maharaj Krishen. c/o Ludenia Bergstr. 61, Berlin-Steglitz, Ger. b. 2 Nov 1926 Mirpur, India. PH.D '55 Free Univ. of Berlin, Ger. FES. STUD, Philosophisches Seminar, Gelferstr. 11, Berlin-Dahlem. Research, teaching; ethics in modern scientific psychology, figural aftereffects, experimental psychology. M

MARR, Miss Evelyn. Cen. Bur. of Educ. and Vocat. Guid, 33 Probyn Rd, Delhi 8. b. 8 July 1921 Gurdaspur. MA '53 Teacher's Coll, Columbia Univ, USA. COUNSELOR, Cen. Bur. of Educ. and Vocat. Guid. Guidance; teacher observation of pupils. F

MATHUR, Miss Krishna. Gulluji's St, Aligarh. b. 10 Sept 1933 Aligarh. MA '55 Muslim Univ. of Aligarh, India. INDIAN GOVT. RES. FELLOW, Muslim Univ, Aligarh. Teaching, research, administration; achievement tests, social behavior, educational psychology. F

MEDIRATTA, Lt. Col. Dr. H. C. Psych. Res. Wing, Def. Sci. Organiza, Ministry of Def, New Delhi 11. b. 12 July 1913 V. Trag. MB, BS '37 Punjab Univ, India. SR. PSYCHIATRIST, Def. Sci. Organiza. Testing, clinical practice, research; projective techniques, learning theory. M

MEHDI, Baqer Mirza. Cen. Bur. of Educ. and Vocat. Guid, 33 Probyn Rd, Delhi 8. b. 25 Jan 1930 Faizabad. MA '53 Aligarh Univ, India. COUNSELOR, Ministry of Educ, New Delhi. Member: IPA. Guidance, research, teaching; intelligence tests, aptitude tests, guidance aids. M

MEHROTRA, Dr. Shyam Narain. Bur. of Psych, U.P., Lowther Rd, Allahabad. b. 2 Jan 1920 Etawah. PH.D '54 Allahabad Univ, India. SR. RES. PSYCH'T, Bur. of Psych, U.P. Research, teaching, administration, guidance and selection; factor analysis, test construction and standardization, secondary school curriculum. M

MEHTA, Dr. Hoshang. c/o Mrs. F. S. Ginwalla, Khanpur Rd, Ahmedabad. b. 10 Nov 1914 Bombay. PH.D '44 Bombay

Univ, India. PSYCHOLOGIST, B.M. Inst. of Child Devel, Ellis Bridge, Ahmedabad; EDITOR, *Journal of Vocational and Educational Guidance.* Member: Indian Psychoanal. Socy, All India Educ. and Vocat. Guid. Assn. Research, editorial, psychotherapy, teaching; vocational counseling, play therapy, psychoanalysis. M

MEHTA, Prayag. c/o Jatan Raj Mehta, Jata Bas, Jodhpur. b. 22 Dec 1927 Jodhpur. MA '51 Univ. of Calcutta, India. VOCAT. GUID. OFF, Jeewan Bharati, Nanpura, Surat; CO-EDITOR, *Education and Psychology.* Member: ISCA, All India Educ. and Vocat. Guid. Assn. Consulting, testing, research, educational and vocational guidance; educational guidance for backward children, socio-economic differences and intelligence, factor analysis of school success. M

MEHTA, Prof. Miss Sushila V. Ramba Grad. Teachers Coll, Old Raj Mahal, Porbandar, Saurashtra. b. 17 Feb 1922 Saurashtra. MA, Bombay Univ, India; MA, Teachers Coll, Columbia Univ, USA. DIR. of EDUC. and VOCAT. GUID, Govt. of Saurashtra, Old Raj Mahal, Porbandar. Member: All India Assn. of Educ. and Vocat. Guid. Administration, test construction, guidance, teaching, writing on psychological topics in Gujarati; group intelligence tests, vocational interest inventory, pesonality assessment techniques. F

MENZEL, Dr. Emil Wolfgang. Civil Lines, Raipur M.P. b. 1 Mar 1897 Washington, D.C., USA. MA '34 Washington Univ, USA. STAFF ADVIS, Sch. of Amer. Evangelical Mission, Bd. of Int. Missions, 1505 Race St, Philadelphia, Pennsylvania, USA. Research, direction of education, testing, improvement of teaching methods, measurement in education and psychometrics. M

MISHRA, Prof. Ram Babu. Ranchi Coll, Ranchi, Bihar. b. 12 Nov 1927 Patna. MA '49 Patna Univ, India. HEAD, Dept. of Exper. Psych, Bihar Univ. Coll, Ranchi; CONSULT. PSYCH'T, Cen. Nursing Home. Member: IPA, ISCA. Teaching psychology and anthropology, psychotherapy, guidance, administration; psychosomatic disturbances, attitudinal factors in fecundity. M

MISRA, Dr. Damodar. S.K.C.G. Coll, Parlakimedi, Orissa. b. 1 May 1911 Cuttack. MA '35 Patna Univ, India. PRINCIPAL, S.K.C.G. Coll. Member: IPA, ISCA. Teaching, administration, research; learning theory, systematic psychology. M

MITRA, Prof. Suhrit Chandra. Psych. Dept, Calcutta Univ, 92 Upper Circular Rd, Calcutta 9. b. 28 Oct 1895 Calcutta. MA '19 Calcutta Univ, India. PROF. and HEAD, Psych. Dept, Calcutta Univ.

Member: IPA, ISCA, Indian Psychoanal. Socy, Mangiya Sahitya Parisad, Vignan Parisad. Teaching, research, administration, consulting; psychoanalysis, psychometry, social perception processes. M

MITRA, Dr. Shib Kumar. Psychomet. Res. and Serv. Unit, Indian Stat. Inst, 203 Barrackpore Trunk Rd, Calcutta 35. b. 7 Mar 1921 Calcutta. PH.D '54 Univ. of Chicago, USA. PSYCHOLOGIST, Indian Stat. Inst; EDITOR, Psychomet. Sect, *Psychology News Bulletin*; ED. BD, *Journal of Vocational and Educational Guidance.* Member: IPA, All India Vocat. and Educ. Guid. Assn. Administration, research in test theory and construction, personnel selection, student personnel work, editorial; projective techniques, measurement theory. M

MITTAL, Prof. Veerendra Kumar. 251 Noonia Mohalla, Meerut Cantt. b. 15 Sept 1927 Meerut. MA '50 Lucknow Univ, India. ASST. PROF. of PSYCH, Meerut Coll, Meerut. Member: Meerut Psych. Assn. Teaching, research on delinquency, educational psychology; attitude measurement. M

MODWEL, Miss Sudha. Suraj-Bhawan, Narayan Nagar, Banaras. b. 31 Jan 1932 Banaras. MA '53 Banaras Hindu Univ, India. VOCAT. GUID. COUNS, Dist. Psych. Cen, Bhadairi, Banaras. Teaching, testing, individual and vocational guidance, research; experimental education, memory and learning, achievement tests. F

MOGHNI, Dr. Shahabuddin Mohammad. Dept. of Philos. and Psych, Muslim Univ, Aligarh. b. 1 Jan 1925 Gaya, Bihar. PH.D '54 London Univ. Coll, Eng. READER in PSYCH, Aligarh Muslim Univ; DIRECTOR, Govt. Res. Proj, Ministry of Educ. Member: ISCA. Teaching, supervising research, warden of university hostel; experimental psychopathology, conflict and frustration behavior, learning theory, theory construction and methodology. M

MOHSIN, Dr. S. M. Educ. and Vocat. Guid. Bur, Patna, Bihar. b. 24 May 1912 Patna. PH.D '48 Edinburgh Univ, Scot. DIRECTOR, Educ. and Vocat. Guid. Bur. Member: IPA, ISCA. Guidance, training personnel, organizing educational guidance, teaching, research, construction and standardization of tests; achievement and intelligence tests, human motivation, experimental methodology. M

MOOKERJEE, Prof. Dr. Krishna Chandra. Bharadwaj Bhavan, Banerjeepara Lane, P.O. Dhakuria, Calcutta 31. b. 1 Dec 1914 Calcutta. PH.D '54 Univ. of Calcutta, India. ASST. PROF. in PSYCH, A.I.I.H.P.H., Calcutta 12; DIR. GENL, Health Services, Govt. of India, New Delhi; ASST. ED, *Indian Journal of Neurology and Psychiatry.*

Member: IPA, Indian Psychoanal. Socy, Indian Assn. of Neur. and Psychiat. Teaching, testing, research, editorial; projective techniques, attitude measurement, psychotherapy.   M

MUKERJI, Dr. Nirod. Educ. Dept, Gauhati Univ, Gauhati, Assam. b. 16 May 1912 Calcutta. PH.D '38 Univ. of London, Eng. READER in EDUC, Gauhati Univ; ED. BD, *Indian Journal of Psychology*. Member: IPA, ISCA. Teaching, research, editorial; perceptual theory, atittude and its genesis, normality.   M

MUKHERJEE, Bishwanath. Jakkanpur, G.P.O, Patna 1. b. 15 Oct 1933 Patna. MA '53 Univ. of Patna, India. PSYCHOLOGIST, B.M. Inst. of Child Devel, Ellis Bridge, Ahmedabad 6. Member: IPA, All India Assn. of Educ. and Vocat. Guid. Experimental study of cognitive processes, motivation, test construction and standardization, guidance, vocational counseling; learning theory, psychometry, factor analysis.   M

MUKHERJI, Kshirode G. Univ. Coll. of Sci, Psych. Dept, 92 Upper Circular Rd, Calcutta 9. b. 8 Feb 1898 Calcutta. LECT. in PSYCH, Calcutta Univ. Member: IPA, Natl. Inst. of Sci. of India, Asiatic Socy. of Bengal. Teaching, research, educational psychology; learning theory, social perception, group process.   M

MUKHTAR, Miss Ragia. c/o M. H. Ali, Mukhtar Manzil, Marris Rd, Aligarh. b. 14 Aug 1930 Barailley. MA '53 Muslim Univ. of Aligarh, India. DEMONSTRATOR, Muslim Univ, Aligarh. Teaching, laboratory work.   F

NAIDU, P. S. Vidya Bhavan Teachers' Coll, Udaipur. W. Ry. b. 30 July 1895 Aska. MA '24 Madras Univ, India. HEAD, Res. Dept, Vidya Bhavan Teachers' Coll; CHIEF ED, Educ. Sect, *Rajputana University Studies*. Member: ISCA. Research, guiding student research, teaching, testing, editorial; attitude measurement, learning, achievement tests.   M

NARAIN, Dr. Raj. Lab. of Psych, Lucknow Univ, Lucknow. b. 28 Aug 1913 Lakhimpur-Kheri. PH.D '50 Columbia Univ, USA. READER, Dept. of Philos, Lucknow Univ; EDITOR, *Manasi*; EDITOR, *Directory of Indian Psychologists*. Member: ISCA, Lucknow Psych. Assn. Teaching, supervision of research, professional writing, vocational guidance; leadership, psychology of religion, national character.   M

OJHA, Jagdish Chandra. c/o *Education and Psychology*, Hauz Kazi, Delhi 6. b. 4 July 1928 Halvad, Saurashtra. MA '50 Univ. of Calcutta, India. PSYCH'T in CHARGE, Manasayan Test Sect, 3438 Hauz Kazi, Delhi 6; ED. BD, *Education and Psychology*.

Member: IPA, ISCA. Editorial, research, consulting and guidance; psychological theory, personality assessment.   M

OJHA, Raj K. Sari Dube, Aligarh. b. 3 Nov 1934 Aligarh. M.SC, Muslim Univ. of Aligarh, India. ASST. ED, *The Indian Psychological Bulletin*. Student, editorial, research; Allport-Vernon study of values. M

PAL, Dr. Asim Kumar. ATIRA Ahmedabad 9. b. 14 May 1926 Calcutta. PH.D '53 Univ. of Birmingham, Eng. SR. PSYCH'T, Ahmedabad Textile Industry's Res. Assn; EDITOR, Indus. Psych. Sect, *Psychology News Bulletin*. Research, industrial psychology, testing; aptitude testing, intergroup relations in industry.   M

PAL, Dr. Gopeswar. 61 Hindusthan Park, Calcutta 29. b. 2 Feb 1894 Bolpur. D.SC '39 Univ. of Calcutta, India. EDUC. and VOCAT. GUID. COUNS, Calcutta Univ. Member: IPA, Indian Psychoanal. Socy. Retired, teaching, research, educational psychology; achievement tests, mental tests. M

PAREEK, Udai. c/o *Education and Psychology*, Hauz Kazi, Delhi 6. b. 21 Jan 1925 Jaipur. MA '50 Univ. of Calcutta, India. PSYCHOLOGIST, Nat. Cen. for Res. in Basic Educ, Govt. of India, Ministry of Educ, New Delhi; EDITOR, *Education and Psychology*. Member: ISCA, IPA. Teaching, research, testing; projective techniques, learning theory.   M

PARTHASARATHY, Major S. Presidency Coll, Madras, S. India. b. 19 Aug 1906 Madras. MA '29 Madras Univ, India. PROF. and HEAD, Dept. of Psych, Presidency Coll; ED. BD, Madras Psych. Socy, *Journal*. Member: Madras Psych. Socy, Regional Psych. Assn, Mysore. Teaching, research, administration; aptitude, achievement and intelligence testing, crime and delinquency, projective methods.   M

PASRICHA, Bal Rama. Natl. Def. Acad, P.O. Kharakvasla, Poona. b. 18 Apr 1917 Sialkot City, W. Pakistan. MA '49 Univ. of London, Eng. LECTURER, Natl. Def. Acad. Member: ISCA, Natl. Socy. for the Study of Educ. (USA), Bharata Ganita Parishad. Teaching, guidance, administration; personality assessment, educational administration, vocational and personal guidance.   M

PEREIRA, Dennyson Francis. Carmel View, 63 St. Sebastian's Colony, Bandra, Bombay 20. b. 15 May 1928 Bombay. MA '52 Bombay Univ, India. CLIN. PSYCH'T, Ment. Hyg. and Psychiat. Clin, Shri Sayaji Genl. Hosp, Baroda; SR. LECT, Fac. of Soc. Work, Maharaja Sayajirao Univ. of Baroda, Camp Rd, Baroda. Member: ISCA, IPA, All India Vocat. and Educ. Guid. Assn, Bombay Vocat. Guid. Assn. Clinical testing, research, guidance, consulting; projective techniques, aptitude testing. M

PILLAI, Prof. A. S. N. 510/10 College Lane, Trivandrum 1. b. Nagercoi. PH.D '51 Univ. of Madras, India. HEAD, Psych. Dept, Univ. of Travancore, Trivandrum. Member: BPS. Teaching, research, administration, student counseling; social perception, attitude measurement, aesthetics. M

PIRES, Dr. Edward Aloysius. Cen. Inst. of Educ, 33 Probyn Rd, Delhi 8. b. 13 Oct 1910 Nagoa, Goa. PH.D '39 Univ. of Bombay, India. VICE-PRINCIPAL, Cen. Inst. of Educ; ED. BD, *Educational Forum.* Member: IPA, New Education Fellowship. Administration, teaching, research; learning theory, achievement tests, personality measurement. M

PRABHU, Dr. Pandharinath. Vrindawan, 11/12 Turner Rd, Bandra, Bombay 20. b. 15 Nov 1911 Vengurla, Bombay. PH.D '37 Univ. of Bombay, India. SR. RES. OFFICER, UNESCO Res. Cen, P.O. Box 242, Calcutta; EDITOR, Soc. Psych. and Behavior Sect, *Psychology News Bulletin.* Member: IPA, APA, Int. Sociol. Assn. Research on social and psychological problems of industrialization and urbanization, administration, teaching; attitude measurement, group process, psychological factors in productivity and efficiency. M

PRAKASH, J. C. Dept. of Soc. Sci, Indian Inst. of Sci, Bangalore 3, Mysore. b. 25 May 1927 Mysore. P.G. '50 Univ. of Mysore, India. RES. ASST, Indian Inst. of Sci. Research, educational psychology, professional writing; psychometry, group process, social learning. M

PRASAD, Dr. Jamuna Srivastava. Bur. of Psych, Allahabad. b. 20 Mar 1915 Agra. PH.D '53 Allahabad Univ, India. PSYCHOLOGIST, Bur. of Psych. Educational, vocational and personal guidance, construction and standardization of tests, teaching, research, personnel selection; guidance and counseling, personality assessment, diagnostic testing. M

PRASAD, Prof. Kali. Dept. of Philos. and Psych, Lucknow Univ, Lucknow. b. Sept 1901 Sitapur. MA '24 Univ. of Allahabad, India. PROF. and HEAD, Dept. of Philos. and Psych, Lucknow Univ; ADVISOR, Pub. Serv. Comm, Govt. of India; ED. BD, *Journal of Social Psychology* (USA); *Indian Journal of Psychology*; ASSOC. ED, *Journal of Behavioral Research* (USA). Member: IPA, ISCA. Teaching, research, administration, editorial; social tensions, projective techniques, learning theory, social perception, group process. M

PRASAD, Ramchandra. Dept. of Psych, Patna Coll, Patna Univ. Patna 5. b. 2 Apr 1926 Champaran, Bihar. MA '51 Patna

Univ, India. LECT. in PSYCH, Patna Univ. Member: IPA. Teaching, student; history of psychology, social perception, group process, personality dynamics. M

PURI, Miss Snehlata. Cent. Inst. of Educ, 33 Probyn Rd, Delhi 8. b. 14 Mar 1927 Amritsar. ED.M '52 Univ. of Hawaii. PSYCHOLOGIST, Cent. Inst. of Educ. Educational psychology, research, teaching, test construction and standardization; intelligence and achievement tests, psychometrics. F

PUROHIT, Jayant. Ahmedabad Textile Industry's Res. Assn, Univ. Campus, Navrangpura, Ahmedabad 9. b. 16 Feb 1930 Bombay. MA '52 Bombay Univ, India; MA '56 Gujarat Univ, India. SR. SCI. OFF, Ahmedabad Textile Industry's Res. Assn. Research, experimentation on mill problems, student; group dynamics, human relations in technological change, communications studies. M

QADRI, A. Jamil. Dept. of Philos. and Psych, Muslim Univ. of Aligarh. b. 1 July 1929 Godhna, Buland Shahar. MA '52 Muslim Univ. of Aligarh, India. LECTURER, Dept. of Philos. and Psych, Muslim Univ; RES. PSYCH'T. in CHARGE, Lab. of Exper. and Appl. Psych. Member: ISCA, Assn. of Sci. Wrkrs. Teaching, research on causes and patterns of maladjustment among University students, administration; attitude measurement, learning theory, counseling, testing. M

RAJAN, Kannu V. Nur Manzil Psychiat. Cen, Lal Bagh, Lucknow. b. 9 Aug 1915 Travancore. MA, Harvard Univ, USA; Diploma, Washington Sch. of Psychiat, USA. PSYCHOTHERAPIST, Nur Manzil Psychiat. Cen. Member: IPA, Indian Psychiat. Socy. Psychotherapy, guidance. M

RAJU, Prof. Poolla Tirupati. Jaswant Coll. Bldgs, Joohpur, Rajarthan. b. 17 Aug 1905 Kottapalli. PH.D '35 Calcutta Univ, India. PROFESSOR of PHILOS. and PSYCH, Univ. of Rajpuhana, Jaswant Coll. Bldgs. Teaching, research, administration; social psychology, psychology and logic. M

RAMANUJACHARI, Prof. R. Faculty of Educ, Annamalai Univ, Annamalainagar. b. 6 Dec 1902 Nidamangalam. MA '24 Univ. of Madras, India. PROF. of PHILOS. and DEAN, Faculty of Educ, Annamalai Univ; EDITOR, *Journal of Annamalai University.* Member: Madras Psych. Assn. Teaching, testing, educational psychology; attitude measurement, diagnostic tests, child psychology. M

RANGACHAR, Prof. C. 2742 Vani Vilas Mohalla, Mysore. b. 18 May 1906 Kalkunte. B.SC '27 Univ. of Mysore, India. PROF. of EDUC, Teachers' Coll, Univ. of Mysore. Member: New Educ. Fellowship, All India

Educ. and Vocat. Guid. Assn. Teaching, research, administration; learning theory, achievement tests, interest and aptitude measurement, guidance and counseling. M

RAO, D. Gopal. Cen. Inst. of Educ, Probyn Rd, Delhi 8. b. 5 June 1926 Bangalore. ED.M '54 Univ. of Delhi, India. RES. FELLOW Cen. Inst. of Educ. Member: IPA. Teaching, research, testing; achievement tests, sociometric studies. M

RAO, Dr. K. Umamaheswara. Govt. Training Coll, Rajahmundry, Andhra. b. 10 Nov 1907 Aiyanampudi. PH.D '54 Univ. of London, Eng. PROF. of EDUC. and PSYCH, Govt. Trng. Coll. Member: Madras Psych. Socy. Teaching, research, administration, test construction and standardization; stress, achievement and intelligence tests, attitude measurement. M

RAO, Limbaji Narayan. Dept. of Psych, Maharaja's Coll, Univ. of Mysore, Mysore. b. 27 Nov 1927 Bangalore. MA '52 Univ. of Mysore, India. LECT. in PSYCH, Univ. of Mysore; EDITOR, *Manasa*. Member: IPA, ISCA. Research, teaching, testing, editorial; experimental parapsychology. M

RAO, Prof. Manthripragada Narasimha. All India Inst. of Hyg. and Pub. Hlth, 110 Chittaranjan Ave, Calcutta 12. b. 27 Aug 1912 Kakinada. Dr. P. H. '45 Harvard Univ, USA. OFF. in CHARGE, Indus. Hlth. Res. Unit, All India Inst. of Hyg. and Pub. Hlth. Direction of research in industrial psychology and hygiene, teaching, administration. M

RAO, Prof. N. C. Shankar Narayan. Vocat. Guid. Bur, Teachers' Trng. Coll, Jabalpore. b. 31 July 1917 Mysore. MA '40 Univ. of Mysore, India. DIRECTOR, Vocat. Guid. Bur, Tchr's. Trng. Coll. Member: ISCA, All India Educ. and Vocat. Guid. Assn. Guidance, teaching, research; attitude measurement, learning theory, emotion measurement, psychogalvanic reflex. M

RAO, Prof. S. K. Ramachandra. All India Inst. of Ment. Hlth, Ment. Hosp, Bangalore 2. b. 9 Feb 1926 Mysore. MA '48 Univ. of Mysore, India. ASST. PROF. of PSYCH, All India Inst. of Ment. Hlth. Guiding research, teaching, psychotherapy; mathematical theory, TAT, social problems, semantics, Yoga and Buddhism. M

RATH, Dr. Radhanath. Dept. of Psych, Ravenshaw Coll, Cuttack 3, Orissa. b. 20 Mar 1920 Cuttack. PH.D '48 Univ. of London, Eng. HEAD, Dept. of Psych, Ravenshaw Coll. Member: ISCA, IPA. Teaching, research, administration, writing popular books in psychology; attitude measurement, stereotypes, juvenile delinquency, criminal psychology, intelligence testing. M

RAWAT, K. S. District Psych. Cen, Meerut.

b. 1 May 1918 Garhwal. MA '43 Allahabad Univ, India. DIST. PSYCH'T, Dept. of Educ. Allahabad. Educational and vocational guidance, allocation, selection and handling of problem children; counseling, intelligence, interest and aptitude measurement. M

RAY-CHOWDHURV, Dr. Kartik. Aligarh Muslim Univ, Aligarh. b. 1 Mar 1925 Calcutta. PH.D '56 Univ. of London, Eng. LECT. in EXPER. and APPL. PSYCH, Aligarh Muslim Univ; EDITOR, *Indian Psychological Bulletin*. Member: ISCA, BPS. Teaching experimental and physiological psychology, vocational guidance, research in educational and vocational psychology; experimental study of imagery and its relation to abilities, attainment and intelligence tests, Allport-Vernon values scale. M

ROY, Pankaj Kumar. Dept. of Ext. Serv, Cen. Inst. of Educ, 33 Probyn Rd, Delhi 8. b. 1 Dec 1916 Benaras. ED.B '47 Univ. of Edinburgh, Scot. CO-ORDINATOR, Dept. of Ext. Serv, Cen. Inst. of Educ; MANAGING ED, *Educational Forum*. Member: IPA, BPS. Administration, editorial, teaching; learning theory, achievement and intelligence tests. M

ROY, Dr. S. N. Dept. of Appl. Psych, Univ. Coll. of Sci, 92 Upper Circular Rd, Calcutta 9. b. 28 Oct 1916 Calcutta. PH.D '52 Univ. of Calcutta, India. LECTURER, Dept. of Appl. Psych, Univ. Coll. of Sci, Calcutta Univ. Member: ISCA. Research direction, teaching, applied psychology, testing; vocational guidance, job analysis, personnel selection. M

ROZDON, Prof. Partap-narain. Teachers' Training Coll, Benares Hindu Univ, Benares 5. PH.D '32 Univ. of Edinburgh, Scot. PROF. and HEAD, Dept. of Educ, Benares Hindu Univ; PRINCIPAL, Teachers' Training Coll, Benares Hindu Univ; CHIEF ED, Journal of Teachers' College, Benares University. Administration, teaching, testing, educational and clinical guidance; color memory, intelligence and achievement tests, Eastern psychotherapeutic methods. M

SALAMATULLAH, Dr. Jamia Nagar P.O., New Delhi. b. 4 Aug 1913 Sahayal, Etawah. ED.D '48 Columbia Univ, USA. PROF. of EDUC. and DIR. of EDUC. RES, Jamia Millia Islamia; EDITOR, *Handbook for Teachers of Basic Schools*. Member: IPA, New Educ. Fellowship. Teaching, research, administration; test construction. M

SATHYAVATHI, Srimathi K. All India Inst. of Ment. Hlth, Bangalore 2. b. 1 Feb 1932 Mysore. MA '55 Univ. of Mysore, India. STUDENT, All India Inst. of Ment. Hlth. Research, testing; projective techniques, attitude measurement, achievement tests. M

SAXENA, Madhu Sudan Lall. Teachers' Training Sect, D.A.V. Coll, Dehra Dun. b. Tilhar, Shanjahanpur. MA '51 Banaras Hindu Univ, India. LECTURER, D.A.V. Coll. Teaching, research, educational psychology; construction of personality adjustment inventories and achievement tests. M

SEN, Dr. Indra. Sri Aurobindo Ashram, Pondicherry. b. 13 May 1903 Jhelum. PH.D '33 Univ. of Freiburg, Ger. PROF. of PSYCH, Sri Aurobindo Ashram, Sri Aurobindo Int. Univ. Cen, Pondicherry. Member: IPA. Teaching, research, educational psychology; psychological determination and exposition of Integral Yoga, integral education and human culture. M

SEN, Dr. Nripendra Nath. All India Inst. of Ment. Hlth, Ment. Hosp, Hosur Rd, Bangalore 2. b. 3 July 1924 Jaidevpur, Dacca. PH.D '53 London Univ. Inst. of Psychiat, Eng. ASST. PROF. of PSYCH, All India Inst. of Ment. Hlth. Member: ISCA, IPA. Research, teaching clinical psychology, psychotherapy, testing, clinical analysis; experimental psychopathology, conditioned response, objective and experimental behavioral tests in the clinical field. M

SEN GUPTA, Prof. Manjusree. Khurja A.K.P. Inter Coll, Bulandshahr. b. 16 Jan 1932 Calcutta. MA '53 Calcutta Univ, India. LECT. in PSYCH, A.K.P. Girls' Inter Coll. Member: IPA. Teaching, educational psychology, student. F

SEN MAZUMDAR, Deva Prasad. Nikhil Kutir, Yearpur Rd, Patna 1. b. 23 Dec 1933 Patna. MA '54 Patna Univ, India. LECT. in PSYCH, Patna Univ. Ashoke Rajrath, Patna. Member: IPA. Teaching, research, testing, administration; repression, mental and personality test construction, crime and delinquency. M

SHAMA, Irshad Begum. Dept. of Psych, Univ. of Lucknow, Badshah Bagh, Lucknow. b. 2 June 1933 Barrielly. MA '56 Lucknow Univ, India. RES. ASST, Lucknow Univ. Member: Lucknow Psych. Assn. Research in parapsychology. F

SHANKER, Prem. Dept. of Psych, Univ. of Lucknow, Lucknow. b. 7 Jan 1930 Benaras. M.SC '51 Patna Univ, India. LECT. in PSYCH, Univ. of Lucknow. Member: Lucknow Psych. Assn. Teaching, research; attitude measurement. M

SHANKER, Uday. Cen. Inst. of Educ, Probyn Rd, Delhi 8. b. 20 Jan 1914 U. Khairpur, Punjab. MA '50 Univ. of London, Eng. READER in PSYCH, Cen. Inst. of Educ. Member: ISCA. Teaching psychology, research, testing, child guidance; test construction, Rorschach, behavior problems, delinquency. M

SHANMUGAM, T. E. Univ. Exam. Hall, Marina, Madras 5. b. 8 Apr 1921 Madras. MLitt. '47 Univ. of Madras, India. SR. LECT, Dept. of Psych, Univ. of Madras, Triplicane, Madras 5; CHIEF TESTING OFF, Juv. Guid. Bur, Madras. Member: Indian Psychoanal. Socy, Madras Psych. Socy. Teaching psychology, research, guiding research, testing; studies in dynamics of adolescent adjustment, projective techniques. M

SHEOPURI, Miss Prakash. Cen. Inst. of Educ, 33 Probyn Rd, Delhi. b. 6 Feb 1928 Meerut. MA '52 Patna Univ, India. RES. WRKR, Cen. Inst. of Educ. Member: IPA. Educational psychology, testing school children, assisting research projects; personality and culture, sociology of education, individual and group interactions, guidance for adolescents. F

SHERJUNG, Mrs. Nirmala. Khyber Pass, Delhi 8. b. 8 Mar 1914 Lahore. MA '38 Punjab Univ, India. LECT. in PSYCH, Indraprastha Coll, Univ. of Delhi, Alipore Rd, Delhi 8. Member: IPA. Teaching, professional writing, educational psychology, broadcasting; projective techniques, attitude measurement. F

SHRIMATI, Chawla Vidya. 32 E/21 Patel Nagar, New Delhi 12. b. 1 Sept 1923 Dera Ghazi Khan. MA '56 Lucknow Univ, India. RES. SCHOLAR, Dept. of Psych, Lucknow Univ, Lucknow. Research, testing, guidance; projective techniques, attitude measurement. learning theory. F

SHUKLA, N. N. Fac. of Educ. and Psych, Maharaja Sayajirao Univ. of Baroda, Baroda. b. 1 June 1911 Bhuj, Cutch. ED.M '48 Bombay Univ, India. LECTURER, Maharaja Sayajirao Univ. of Baroda. Teaching, research, professional writing; standardization of intelligence, achievement and aptitude tests. M

SINGH, Baxish. II-K-21 Lajpat Nagar, New Delhi 14. b. 7 Apr 1912 Amritsar. MA '47 Punjab Univ, India. LECTURER, Punjab Univ. Camp Coll, New Delhi. Member: Delhi Psych. Assn. Teaching, psychotherapy, applied psychology; achievement tests, hypnotherapy. M

SINGH, Prof. B. N. Dept. of Psych, L.S. Coll, Bihar Univ, Muzaffarpur, Bihar. b. 24 May 1924 Champaran. MA '48 Patna Univ, India. ASST. PROF, L.S. Coll, Bihar Univ. Member: ISCA. Teaching, administration, research, testing; projective techniques, vocational guidance and selection. M

SINGH, Lieut. Nahar. Kuarsi, Aligarh. b. 16 June 1916 Kuarsi, Aligarh. MA '55 Muslim Univ. of Aligarh, India. SPEC. MAGISTRATE FIRST CLASS, Utter Pradesh Govt, Aligarh; EDITOR, *Udyog*, Natl.

Educ. and Tech. Inst. Member: Philos.
and Psych. Socy. of Muslim Univ. of
Aligarh. Research, administration, student;
educational maladjustments, social and
psychological consequences of judicial
decisions, psychology of testimony.   M
SINGH, Rameshwar. Pilot Res. Cen. in Juv.
Delinquency, Reform. Sch, Hazaribagh,
Bihar. b. 27 Mar 1918 Gaya, Bihar. MA
'53 Patna Univ, India.   JR. PSYCH'T,
Pilot Res. Cen. in Juv. Delinquency;
EDITOR, *Research Bulletin*, Res. Cen. in Juv.
Delinquency. Research, testing, consulting,
re-educating delinquent children; psy-
chological traits, interests, attitudes and
abilities of criminals, intelligence and
achievement tests, learning theory.   M
SINHA, Dr. Awadh Kishore Prasad. Dept.
of Psych, Patna Coll, Patna Univ, Patna 5,
Bihar. b. 6 June 1918 Tekanpura, Monghyr.
PH.D '51 Univ. of Michigan, USA. HEAD,
Dept. of Psych, Patna Coll. Member: IPA,
ISCA, APA. Teaching, research, adminis-
tration; learning theory, problems of
anxiety, attitude measurement.   M
SINHA, Durganand. Banaili Hse, Patna 1,
Bihar. b. 23 Sept 1922 Banaili, Purnea.
M.SC '49 Cambridge Univ, Eng. ACTING
DIR, Inst. of Psych. Res. and Serv, Patna
Univ, Patna 5. Member: ISCA, All India
Educ. and Vocat. Guid. Assn. Research,
teaching, testing, guiding student research,
test construction, vocational guidance;
public opinion, anxiety and perception,
leadership.   M
SINHA, Rajrajeshwari P.D. Dept. of Psych,
Langat Singh Coll, Muzapfarpur, Bihar.
b. 22 Nov 1932 Patna. MA '53 Parna Univ,
India. LECTURER, Langat Singh Coll.
Member: IPA. Teaching, research, testing;
juvenile delinquency, test construction,
child guidance.   M
SINHA, Dr. Suhridchandra. 15/1 Ramkanto
Bose St, Calcutta 3. b. 22 Mar 1903
Mymensingh. PH.D '50 Univ. of Graz,
Austria. LECTURER, Dept. of Psych. and
Appl. Psych, Calcutta Univ, Univ. Coll. of
Sci, 92 Upper Circular Rd, Calcutta 9;
CO-EDITOR, *Orient Review*. Member: IPA,
ISCA, APA. Teaching, research, adminis-
tration, applied and industrial psychology,
testing, guidance, counseling; projective
techniques, achievement tests, social per-
ception, group process, attitude measure-
ment, religious psychology, human re-
lations in industry.   M
SINHA, Dr. Tarun Chandra. 67 Jatindas Rd,
Calcutta 29. b. 25 Jan 1906 Shusung.
D.SC '55 Calcutta Univ, India. SUPER-
INTENDENT, Lumbini Park Ment. Hosp,
Bediadanga Rd, Calcutta 39; PSYCHO-
ANALYST, priv. prac. Member: IPA, Indian
Psychoanal. Socy. Psychotherapy, adminis-

tration, teaching, research in psychoanalysis; anthropology.   M
SIRCAR, Nimai Charan. Dept. of Psych,
Ravenshaw Coll, Cuttack 3. b. 29 July
1930 Cuttack. MA '53 Calcutta Univ, India.
SR. RES. SCHOLAR, Dept, of Psych, Ravenshaw Coll. Member: ISCA, IPA. Research, testing, clinical analysis, guidance,
professional writing; projective techniques,
attitude measurement, construction of
temperament tests.   M
SONI, B. J. Jr. Services Selection Bd, A.H.Q.,
Ministry of Def, Meerut Cantt. b. 22 May
1925 Hoshiarpur. MA, Punjab Univ; ED.M,
Univ. of Delhi, India. JR. PSYCH'T, Services
Sel. Bd. Member: IPA. Testing, assessment
of officer candidates, teaching; projective
techniques, educational and vocational
guidance.   M
SRINIVASIAH, Dr. Thonnur Venkatasubbiah.
Fac. of Educ. and Psych, Univ. of Baroda.
b. 20 Mar 1927 Pandavapura. PH.D '53
Univ. of London, Eng. SR. LECT, Fac. of
Educ. and Psych, Univ. of Baroda.
Member: ISCA, All India Vocat. and Educ.
Guid. Assn. Teaching, experimental, edu-
cational and statistical psychology, testing,
research; intelligence and achievement
tests, personality.   M
SUBBANNACHAR, N.V. 135 Town Planning
Area, Tirupathi, Andhra. b. 16 June 1927
Mysore. BA '51 Univ. of Mysore, India.
LECT. in PSYCH, Sri Venkateswara Arts
Coll, Tirupathi. Teaching, research, student;
social perception, group process, social
change.   M
TANDON, Prof. Ram Krishna. Psych. Dept,
Saket Degree Coll, Niyawan Rd, Faizabad.
b. 10 Mar 1920 Ayodhya. MA '51 Banaras
Hindu Univ, India. PROF. and HEAD,
Psych. Dept, Saket Degree Coll. Member:
Faizabad Psych. Assn. Teaching, research,
consulting; mental testing, construction
and standardization of intelligence tests,
personality testing, extra-sensory per-
ception.   M
TAYAL, Shanti S. B. 2720 Kinari Bazar,
Delhi 6. b. 18 Aug 1928 Delhi. MA '54,
ED.M '55 Univ. of Delhi, India. VIS. PROF,
Philippines. Member: IPA, Psych. Study
Circle (Delhi). Research, applied and
educational psychology, testing, teaching;
attitude measurement, projective tech-
niques, clinical interviewing.   M
TRIPATHI, Lal Bachan. Atreya Niwas,
Lanka, Banaras 5. b. 15 Sept 1935 Ballia.
MA '55 Banaras Hindu Univ, India. RES.
SCHOLAR in PSYCH, Banaras Hindu Univ,
Banaras 5. Member: Indian Philos.
Congress. Research, teaching, testing;
projective techniques, clinical analysis,
psycho-physical experiments.   M
TYAGI, Avanindra Kumar. 127 E-Block,

Ministry of Def, Psych. Res. Wing, D.H.Q, New Delhi. b. 19 June 1923 Guldher. MA '46 F.C. Coll. of Lahore, India. JR. PSYCH'T, Ministry of Def. Member: Delhi Psych. Assn. Research, testing, teaching; projective techniques, attitude measurement. M

VADEKAR, Prof. Devidas Dattatreya. Saraswati Prasad, 196/84A Sadashiv Peth, Tilak Rd, Poona 2. b. 25 May 1902 Satara. MA '26 Univ. of Bombay, India. PROF. and HEAD, Dept. of Philos. and Psych, Fergusson Coll, Fergusson Coll. Rd, Poona 4. Member: Indian Philos. Congress. Teaching. administration, research; psychological theories, psychological terminology. M

VAISHNAV, Maheshchandra. Sangam Ramba Grad. Teachers' Coll, Porbanda, Saurashtra. b. 28 July 1922 Junagadh. ED.M '56 M.S. Univ. of Baroda, India. LECT. in METHODOLOGY of SCI, Ramba Grad. Teachers' Coll. Teaching, research, testing, student; intelligence and achievement tests. M

VARMA, Manmohan. Univ. Training Coll, Nagpur. b. 1 July 1911 Indore. ED.B '39 Edinburgh Univ, Scot. PRINCIPAL, Univ. Trng. Coll; DEAN, Fac. of Educ, Nagpur Univ; EDITOR, The Educator. Member: Psychomet. Socy. (USA), Indian Stat. Inst. Teaching, research, administration, educational psychology, testing; test construction, factor analysis, attitude measurement, psychoanalytic theory. M

VASANTHARAJAIAH, H. D. Maharaja's Coll, Mysore. b. 27 June 1926 Mysore. MA '56 Univ. of Mysore, India. LECT. in PSYCH, Univ. of Mysore, Maharaja's Coll. Member: ISCA, Indian Philos. Congress. Teaching, research, educational psychology; attitude measurement, achievement and aptitude tests. M

VERMA, Ram Mohan. Melina Kutir, Machhuatoli, Patna 4, Bihar. b. 1 Aug 1928 Chapra. MA '53 Patna Univ, India. COUNSELOR, State Bur. of Educ. and Vocat. Guid, Patna. Guidance, counseling, testing, research; achievement tests, attitude measurement, social perception. M

VERMA, Prof. Shashilata. J. P. M. Maha Vidyalaya, Chapra, Saran, Bihar. b. 24 Oct 1950 Saran. MA '51 Patna Univ, India. LECT. in PSYCH, Jaya Prakash Mahila Maha Vidyalaya. Member: ISCA. Teaching, research, testing; projective techniques, test construction, personality. M

WADIA, Miss Khorshed Ardeshir. Cen. Bur. of Educ. and Vocat. Guid, 33 Probyn Rd, Delhi 8. b. 6 July 1922 Kanpur. MA '49 George Peabody Coll. for Teachers, USA. COUNSELOR, Cen. Bur. of Educ. and Vocat. Guid. Curriculum and vocational guidance of high school students, construction of aptitude tests; educational psychology, interviewing techniques, projective techniques. F

WARHADPANDE, N. R. P. R. W. E-Block, New Delhi. b. 25 Feb 1921 Raipur Madhya Pradesh. BLitt. '49 Oxford Univ. Eng. SR. PSYCH'T, Ministry of Def, Govt. of India, New Delhi. Research in selection methods, testing, professional writing; intelligence testing, pain and pleasure, psychology of mysticism. M

INDONESIA

LAMMERTS VAN BUEREN, Pier Hendrik. c/o B.P.M., Balikpapan, Kalimantan Timur Indonesia. b. 4 Dec 1926 Utrecht, Neth. Doctorandus Psych. '50 Univ. of Amsterdam, Neth. PERS. PSYCH'T, B.P.M. Member: NIPP. Applied psychology, personnel work. M

LIEM, Dr. Lie Pok. Dept. of Psychother, Med. Fac, Univ. of Indonesia, Salemba 6, Djakarta. b. 26 Nov 1921 Tjilatjap, Java. Doctor '54 Univ. of Leyden, Neth. CHIEF LECT. and COORD, Psych. Fac; HEAD, Dept. of Psychother, Med. Fac, Univ. of Indonesia. Member: NIPP. Teaching, psychotherapy, consulting, clinical practice, guidance; projective techniques, personality, dreams. M

NG, Po Kioen. Djalan Diponegoro 49, Djakarta. b. 21 Feb 1920 Pangkalpinang. Doctorandus '51 Univ. of Amsterdam, Neth. INDUS. PSYCH'T, priv. prac. Industrial psychology, testing; personnel selection and vocational guidance. M

OEI, Dr. Tjin San. Dj. Riau 93, Bandung. b. 5 July 1924 Padang. Doctoral '52 Univ. of Amsterdam, Neth. LECT. in PSYCH. and HEAD, Educ. Psych. Res. Cen, State Teacher's Coll, Bandung; LECT. in INDUS. PSYCH, Academy of State Railways. Research, teaching, industrial psychology, personnel selection; educational and industrial psychology. M

RODRIGUES, John Silva, Jr. Tjikini Raja 95 (Pav), Djakarta. b. 27 June 1924 Cambridge, Massachusetts, USA. MA '51 Harvard Univ, USA. BUS. MGR, Univ. of California, Univ. of Indonesia Project in Med. Educ. Member: APA. Administration, educational and applied psychology; social perception, dynamics of communication in a non-western society. M

SLAMET, Prof. Iman Santoso R. Dept. of Psychiat, Med. Fac, Univ. of Indonesia, Salemba 6, Djakarta. b. 7 Sept 1907

Wonosobo, Java. PROF. of PSYCHIAT. and NEUR, and CHMN, Psych. Fac, Univ. of Indonesia. Teaching, clinical practice,

consulting, guidance, psychotherapy; projective techniques, learning theory, achievement tests.   M

IRAN

ALBERTS, Mrs. Elizabeth. 4775 Sheridan Dr, Williamsville 21, New York, USA. b. 16 Sept 1925 Medina, New York, USA. MS '49 State Coll. of Washinton, USA. Psychological research in conjunction with rural development programs in the Middle East, administration, research, applied psychology; research in learning theory, construction of psychological tests in non-Western culture.   F

ARAM, Ahmad. Ziiaian House of Commerce, Nasser-Khosrow Ave, Teheran. b. 1916 Shiraz. B.SC '45 Univ. of Teheran, Iran. PERS. SPEC, Pers. Management and Res. Cen, Inst. for Admin. Affairs, Fac. of Law, Univ. of Teheran. Teaching, research, personnel psychology; test construction, translations, mental measurement, personnel evaluation.   M

ARDEBILI, Youssephe. Amole Ave. Koye' Shambayati, Teheran. b. Feb. 1927 Hamedan. Licence '49 Univ. of Teheran, Iran. MEMBER: Curricula and Res. Dept, Ministry of Educ, Akbatan, Teheran. Administration, teaching, testing; attitude measurement, achievement and intelligence tests.   M

AYMAN, Iraj. School. of Pub. Admin, Univ. of Southern California, Los Angeles 7, Calif, USA. b. 9 Feb 1928 Teheran. PH.D '57 Univ. of S. Calif. USA. CO-DIRECTOR, Pers. Management and Res. Cen, Inst. for Admin. Affairs, Univ. of Teheran; EDITOR, Pers. Management and Res. Cen. Member: Amer. Socy. for Pub. Admin. Research supervision, teaching, administration; psychological tests and testing, industrial psychology, youth leadership.   M

AYMAN-AHY, Mrs. Lily. School of Pub. Admin, Univ. of Southern California, Los Angeles 7, Calif, USA. b. 17 May 1929 Teheran. Certificate '52 Univ. of Edinburgh, Scot. CHILD SPEC, Salvation Army Day Nursery, Stanford Ave, Los Angeles; SUPERV. and INSTR, Trng. Prog, Pers. Mgmt. and Res. Cen, Univ. of Teheran. Teaching, educational psychology, administration, translation; psychological testing, growth, youth leadership.   F

BEHBAHANI, Zarin. c/o Mr. Malekpour, Shargh Ins. Co, Saadi Ave, Teheran. b. 25 Dec 1924 Shiraz. MA, New York Univ, USA. EDUCATOR, Ministry of Educ, Teheran. Teaching, testing, translation.   M

BEHZADI, Ghassem. 33 Rue Amin Dowleh. Ave. Cyrus, Teheran. b. May 1923 Teheran,

Certificat, Fac. of Med, Univ. of Paris, Fr. MED. CHIEF, Neuropsychiat. Serv, Milit. Hosp. No. 1, Pahlavie, Teheran; MED. CONSULT, Hosp. Rezai; Hosp. Tchehrazi. Consulting, clinical practice, guidance, psychotherapy, teaching; achievement tests, group process, projective techniques.   M

BEIJAN, Asa-dollah. Shah and Khah Ave, Teheran. b. 16 Mar 1900 Espahan. PH.D '28 Columbia Univ, USA. PROFESSOR, tchrs. Coll, Teheran Univ; TECH. ADVIS, Ministry of Educ, Teheran; HEAD, Educ. Res. Lab, Univ. of Teheran. Member: Ment. Hlth. Assn. Teaching, research, testing; psychology of adolescence, achievement tests, rural development.   M

DAHI, Mrs. Odette Micheline. 86 Ave. Vessal Chirazi, Teheran. b. 26 Aug 1925 Annecy, Fr. Licence ès lettres '50 Sorbonne, Fr. DIRECTOR, Lab. of Psych, Fac. of Letters, Univ. of Teheran. Member: APPD. Teaching, research, professional writing. F

DARGAHI, Mrs. Ghodsi. 3 Dargahi St, Sepah Ave, Teheran. b. 1 June 1923 Teheran. MA '51 Univ. of Denver, USA. PERS. SPEC, Inst. for Admin. Affairs, Fac. of Law, Univ. of Teheran. Research, personnel psychology, test construction, teaching; achievement tests, mental tests, child and adolescent psychology.   F

DAVIDIAN, Dr. Harutiun. Shahreza Ave, Sharoud St, Teheran. b. 21 Feb 1924 Teheran. MD '48 Univ. of Teheran, Iran. HEAD, Psychiat. Polyclin, Rouzbeh Mental Hosp, Simetri Ave, Teheran. Psychotherapy, clinical practice, research; social perception, social problems, development of personality.   M

GUILANI, Prof. Dr. Mohamad. Ave. Djami, Rue de la Chambre de Commerce 76, Teheran. b. 1 May 1909 Recht. Diplôme, Univ. of Lyon, Fr. PROF. AGRÉGÉ in PSYCHIAT, Hôpital Rouzbeh, Ave. Simetrie, Teheran; ASST. PROF, Fac. of Med. of Teheran; PSYCHIATRIST, priv. prac. Teaching, clinical practice.   M

HUSCHIAR, Prof. Dr. Schirazi. Ave. Pahlawi 1874, Teheran. b. 10 Feb 1903 Schiraz. PH.D '34 Univ. of Munich, Ger. PROFESSOR, Tchr. Trng. Coll, Univ. of Teheran. Teaching, educational psychology, professional writing; methods and results of personality diagnosis.   M

JALALI, Dr. Mehdi M. Villa Ave, Khosrow St, Teheran. b. 9 June 1912 Teheran. PH.D '38 Univ. of Pittsburgh, USA. PROF. of

EDUC. and CHILD PSYCH, Univ. of Teheran. Teaching, testing, consulting; theory of learning, intelligence and achievement tests.   M

MIR-SEPASSY, Dr. M. Abdol-Hossein. Carre-four Palavi Amirie, Teheran. b. 1 Oct 1907 Teheran. MD '35 Univ. of Lyon, Fr. PROFESSOR, Fac. of Med. of Teheran; DIRECTOR, Univ. Psychiat. Serv, Ment. Hosp. Rousbeh, Teheran; PSYCHIATRIST, priv. prac. Member: Iranian Socy. of Ment. Hlth. Teaching, psychotherapy, consulting, clinical practice, research, administration, professional writing.   M

MORTAZAVI, Miss Shamsi. Voice of America, Persian Serv, Washington 25, D.C., USA. b. 1 Mar 1928 Hamadan. MA '56 American Univ. Washington, D.C., USA. WRITER and ANNOUNCER, Voice of America. Student, professional writing.   F

NADJAHI, Dr. Mostafa. Baharestan 26 Rue Khadse-Nouri, Teheran. b. 12 Dec 1912 Teheran. Docteur ès lettres '51 Sorbonne, Fr. ASST. PROF, Fac. of Letters, Univ. of Teheran; ASST. DIR, Psych. Lab, Univ. of Teheran. Teaching, research, adminis-tration, testing, clinical analysis; attitude measurement, achievement tests, memory and learning.   M

RAD, Mrs. Parirokh M. 1748 Winona Blvd, Hollywood 27, California, USA. b. 27Apr 1924 Teheran. MA '54 Los Angeles State Coll, USA. Learning theory, achievement tests, attitude measurement.   F

REZAI, Prof. Hossein. Ave. Chah Reza, Teheran. b. 12 Apr 1904 Teheran. MD '35 Univ. of Toulouse, Fr. PROFESSOR, Fac. of Med, Hosp. Rousbeh, Ave. Simetrie,

Teheran. Member: Société Médico-Psy-chologique (Paris). Teaching psychiatry, professional writing, consulting; social perception.   M

SHAHAMIRI, Mr. Abdollah. Martin and Co, Agfa Agency, Esslambol Ave, Teheran. b. Dec 1927 Shiraz. Licence '51 Univ. of Teheran, Iran. RES. ASST, Ministry of Labor, Teheran. Personnel psychology, professional writing, research; construction and validation research on intelligence, achievement and temperament tests.   M

SHAPURIAN, Reza. Kaiserplatz 6, Bonn, Ger. b. 20 Sept 1926 Shiraz. Cand. phil, Univ. of Bonn, Ger. STUDENT, Inst. of Psych, Bonn, Ger. Projective techniques, learning theory, achievement tests.   M

SIASSI, Prof. Dr. Ali Akbar. Roosevelt Ave, Namdjou St, Teheran. b. 1896 Teheran. PH.D '31 Sorbonne, Fr. PRESIDENT and PROF, Fac. of Arts and Letters, Univ. of Teheran; SUPERV, Lab. of Psych, Univ. of Teheran. Administration, teaching, pro-fessional writing; learning theory, memory, personality.   M

SOBHANI, Farhad. Bachstr. 44, Benel b. Bonn, Ger. b. 28 Dec 1926 Teheran. Vordiplom '54 Univ. of Bonn, Ger. Psycho-therapy, clinical practice, teaching, student; graphology.   M

TCHEHRAZI, Ebrahim. Fac. of Med, Hosp. Tchehrazi, Ave. Chah Reza, Teheran. b. 15 Oct 1909 Ispahan. Doctorat '36 Univ. of Paris, Fr. PROF.of NEUROPSYCHIAT, Fac. of Med. Member: Société Médico-Psychological of Iran. Teaching, adminis-tration, psychotherapy, consulting; group process, alchoholism, drug addiction.   M

IRAQ

AKRAWI, Dr. Matta. Dept. of Educ, UNESCO, 19 Ave. Kléber, Paris 16. b. 9 Dec 1901 Mosul, Iraq. PH.D '34 Teachers Coll, Columbia Univ, USA. DEPUTY DIR, Dept. of Educ, UNESCO. Planning and directing

school education program of UNESCO, teaching, research, editorial, professional writing; tensions, prejudice, intolerance, educational psychology.   M

IRELAND (EIRE)

CASEY, Rev. Dermot M. 35 Lower Leeson St, Dublin. b. 2 June 1911 Dublin. PH.D '47 Univ. of Paris, Fr. DIRECTOR, Educ. Guid. Cen, 46 Lower Leeson St, Dublin; PROF. of PSYCH, St. Stanislaus Coll, Tulla-more. Member: BPS, APA. Child guidance, testing, teaching; projective techniques, personality development, vocational guidance, emotional and psychiatric problems of children.   M

DEMPSEY, Dr. Peter James R. St. Bonaven-ture's, Cork. b. 14 Sept 1914 Nenagh,

Tipperary. PH.D '49 Univ. of Montreal, Can. LECTURER, Univ. Coll, Cork. Member: BPS, APA. Teaching, professional writing, psychotherapy; personality group dynamics psychology of religion.   M

McKENNA, Dr. John. Foxrock Park, Fox-rock, Dublin. b. 19 Feb 1919 Glasgow, Scot. PH.D '55 Univ. of Montreal, Can. DIR. of PSYCH, St. John of God, Child Guid. Clin, 59 Orwell Rd, Rathgar, Dublin; RES. CONSULT, Natl. Child. Hosp, Dublin. Member: BPS. Testing, clinical analysis, diagnosis, teaching, research; learning theory, projective techniques, social perception. M

O'DOHERTY, Dr. Dominick John. 15 Fitzwilliam Square, Dublin. b. 21 June 1920 Clare. DPM '45 National Univ, Dublin, Eire. CONSULT. PSYCHOTHERAPIST, St. Michael's Hosp, Dun Laoghaire; PSYCHOTHERAPIST, priv. prac. Member: RMPA. Consulting, work in wards, running of psychiatric out-patient clinic, psycho-

therapy, research; psychiatry of neuroses. M

O'DOHERTY, Rev. Prof. Eamonn Feichin. 50 Whitehorn Rd, Clonskea, Dublin. b. 10 Feb 1918 Dublin. PH.D '45 Cambridge Univ, Eng. PROF. of LOGIC and PSYCH, Natl. Univ, Univ. Coll, Earlsfort Terr, Dublin. Member: BPS, WFMH. Teaching, consulting, research, psychotherapy; experimental studies of abstraction, psychology and religion, photobiology. M

ISRAEL

AKAVYA, Uriel. King Solomon St, Tel-Aviv. b. 19 Dec 1911 Warsaw, Poland. MA, New York Univ, USA. INSTR. in PSYCH, Levinsky's Tchr. Trng. Coll, Ben Yehouda St. 195, Tel-Aviv; INSTR. in PSYCH, Physical Culture Coll; INSTR. in PSYCH, Hadassah Sch. for Nurses. Member: IS.PA. Teaching, consulting, professional writing; guidance and counseling in schools, projective techniques, non-directive methods. M

ARNSTEIN, Dr. Ervin Eliezer. P.O. Box 1406, Jerusalem. b. 9 Dec 1899 Dobříš, Czech. PH.D '28 Univ. of Prague, Czech. DIRECTOR, Vocat. Guid. Bur. of Hadassah, 16 Rabbi Kook St, Jerusalem. Member: IS.PA, APA. Guidance, industrial psychology, research; occupational psychology. M

BEN-AARON, Mrs. Miriam. 29 Dereh Stella-Maris, German Colony, Haifa. b. 24 Mar 1923 Bialystok, Poland. Dipl. Psych. '53 Sorbonne, Fr. PSYCHOLOGIST, Youth Aliyah-Child Guid. Clin, 24 Heehalutz St, Haifa; INVESTIGATOR, Ministry of Justice. Member: IS.PA, AIPA. Testing, clinical analysis, guidance, psychotherapy; projective techniques, group process, achievement tests. F

BLUMENTHAL, Mrs. Ingeborg Chana. Nve Pagi Bayit V'Gan, Jerusalem. b. 17 Apr 1922 Berlin, Ger. BA '52 Univ. of Cape Town, South Africa. CLIN. PSYCH'T, Dept. of Psychiat, Hadassa-Rothschild Univ. Hosp, Jerusalem. Member: IS.PA. Clinical testing, psychotherapy, research; projective techniques, individual and group therapy, psychological and sociological factors in atherosclerosis. F

DAGONI-WEINBERG, Dr. Elise. Hameginim-str. 133, Haifa. b. 5 May 1917 Vienna, Austria. PH.D '44 Univ. of Zurich, Switz. CONSULTANT, Children's Hosp; CLIN. PSYCH'T, Ministry of Hlth, Haifa; CHILD GUID. COUNS, priv. prac. Member: Israeli Assn. of Clin. Psych'ts. Consulting, child guidance, psychotherapy, clinical analysis, educational psychology, testing, teaching; projective techniques. F

ELIZUR, Dr. Abraham. 6 Tel Hai St, Tel-Aviv. b. 8 Jan 1913 Tel-Aviv. PH.D '49 Columbia Univ, USA. CLIN. PSYCH'T, Kupath Holim, 29 Famenhof St, Tel-Aviv. Member: IS.PA, Israeli Assn. of Clin. Psych'ts. Psychotherapy, testing, clinical analysis, consulting; projective techniques, research. M

ELIZUR, Dov. 13 Marcus St, Talbiye, Jerusalem. b. 10 Feb 1922 Budapest, Hungary. MA '55 Hebrew Univ, Israel. CHIEF, Position Classif. Div, Israel Civil Serv. Comm, Silberstein Bldg, Koresh St, Jerusalem. Member: IS.PA. Industrial psychology, administration, testing; group dynamics, projective techniques. M

EPSTEIN, Dr. Yehuda. 5A Ahad Ha-am St, Haifa. b. 6 Apr 1903 Novodrodek, Russia. PH.D '49 Columbia Univ, USA. CLIN. PSYCH'T, Psych. Inst. and Child Guid. Clin; PSYCHOLOGIST, Dept. of Educ, City of Haifa; MEMBER, Advis. Comm, Marriage Couns. Bur, City of Haifa; LECTURER, Dept. of Culture, City of Haifa. Member: IS.PA. Testing, teaching, psychotherapy, guidance; projective techniques, psychological testing, learning theory, child guidance. M

FAIGAIN, Dr. Helen Hilda. 19 Metudella St, Rehavia, Jerusalem. b. 1 Mar 1925 Cleveland, Ohio, USA. PH.D '53 Harvard Univ, USA. RES. PSYCH'T, Inst. for Res. on Collective Educ, Oranim-Kiryar Amal; VIS. LECT, Dept. of Sociol, Hebrew Univ, Jerusalem. Member: IS.PA, APA, Israeli Assn. of Clin. Psych'ts, Israeli Anthrop. Assn. Research, teaching, professional writing; culture and personality, projective techniques, learning theory. F

FLUM, Dr. Yaël. 8 Bustenai St, Jerusalem. b. 8 Apr 1916 Usti u.L, Czech. PH.D '38 Univ. of Prague, Czech. DIRECTOR, Inst. for Vocat. Guid, Working Youth's Org, Psychotech. Inst. of the Near Ored, Hashmonaiu St, Jerusalem. Member: IS.PA. Applied psychology, guidance, research; projective techniques, interviewing, psychological research and vocational guidance of youth communal settlements.   F

FOA, Dr. Uriel G. Israel Inst. of Appl. Soc. Res, 1 King David St, Jerusalem. b. 25 Feb 1916 Parma, Italy. PH.D, Hebrew Univ, Israel. EXEC. DIR, Israel Inst. of Appl. Soc. Res; LECT. in SOC. RELAT, Tel-Aviv Sch. of Law and Econ. Member: IS.PA, WAPOR, Israel Soc. Sci. Assn, Amer. Sociol. Socy, Amer. Rural Sociol. Socy. Research, administration, teaching; small group process, social perception and communication, attitudes.   M

FRANKENSTEIN, Dr. Carl. Hebrew Univ, Jerusalem. b. 16 Feb 1905 Berlin, Ger. PH.D '27 Univ. of Erlangen, Ger. LECT. in SPEC. EDUC. and EDUC. RES, Hebrew Univ; EDITOR, *Megamoth*, Child Welfare Res. Quarterly. Member: Int. Assn. of Grp. Psychother. Teaching, professional writing, research; child psychopathology, special education.   M

GLUECKSOHN-WEISS, Mrs. Naomi. Harav Berlin Str, Kiriath Shmuel, Jerusalem. b. 24 Dec 1911 Odessa, Russia. MA '39 Univ. of London, Eng. CHIEF CLIN. PSYCH'T. and CHILD THERAPIST, Lasker Cen. of Ment. Hyg. and Child Guid, Hadassah Med. Org, Kovshei Katamon St, Jerusalem. Member: IS.PA, Israeli Assn. of Clin. Psych'ts. Psychotherapy, clinical analysis, research; screening techniques for immigrant children, psychotherapy, psychoanalysis.   F

GOLDMAN, Mrs. Hanna. 44 Rashi, Jerusalem. b. 12 Feb 1914 Krakow, Poland. MA '36 Univ. of Krakow, Poland. CLIN. PSYCH'T, Ment. Hyg. Clin, 11/52 Moshova Germamt, Jerusalem. Testing, clinical analysis, psychotherapy, consulting.   F

GOTTSTEIN, Mrs. Esther Rachel. 26 King George St, Jerusalem. b. 6 June 1928 Leipzig, Ger. GRAD. STUD, Univ. of London, Eng. Member: IS.PA, BPS, Israeli Clin. Psych. Socy. Research, testing, teaching; projective techniques, attitude measurement, cultural comparisons.   F

GRUNBERG, Mrs. Mirona. Dissimini House, Romema, Jerusalem. b. 10 Feb 1918 Safad. MA '51 Hebrew Univ, Israel. CHIEF PSYCH'T, Civil Serv. Comm, Israel, P.O. Box 291, Jerusalem. Member: IS.PA. Testing, personnel psychology, research, administration; psychological diagnosis, test construction, oral group tests.   F

GUTTMANN, Prof. Louis. Israel Inst. of Appl. Soc. Res, Rehow David, Hamelech 1, Jerusalem. b. 10 Feb 1916 New York, USA. PH.D '42 Univ. of Minnesota, USA. SCI. DIR, Israel Inst. of Appl. Soc. Res; PROF. of SOC. and PSYCH. MSMT, Hebrew Univ, Jerusalem. Member: IS.PA, Psychomet. Socy. Research, teaching, adminis-

tration; personnel psychology, achievement testing, social and attitude surveys.   M

HANDEL, Amos. Katamon, Bustenai 8, Jerusalem. b. 11 Dec 1925 Olomouc, Czech. MA '51 Hebrew Univ, Israel. VOCAT. GUID. COUNS, Y.L.O. Vocat. Guid. Cen, Melnor Baruch, Hashmonaim, Jerusalem. Member: IS.PA. Guidance, testing, research; adolescent psychology, group differences, verbal projective techniques.   M

HERMAN, Dr. Simon Nathan. Hebrew Univ, Jerusalem. b. 9 Apr 1912 Port Elizabeth, South Africa. PH.D '49 Univ. of Witwatersrand, South Africa. DIRECTOR, Cen. for Grp. Dynam, Hebrew Univ. Member: IS.PA. Teaching, research, administration; re-education, cross-cultural education, leadership and cultural background.   M

HOGAIN, Dr. Moshe. 78 Rehov Balfour, Bat Yam. b. 11 May 1903 Minsk, Russia. PH.D '34 Columbia Univ, USA. SCH. PSYCH'T, Bialik Govt. Sch, 95 Rehov Levinsky, Tel-Aviv; PSYCHOLOGIST, Munic. Child Guid. Clin, Tel-Aviv. Member: IS.PA. Educational psychology, guidance, research; achievement and mental tests, remedial teaching.   M

HUSS, Mrs. Chava. 45 B King George St, Jerusalem. b. 20 Sept 1928 Neubrandenburg, Ger. BA '52 Hebrew Univ, Israel. CLIN. PSYCH'T, Beith Habriut Strauss Hadassah, Strauss St, Jerusalem. Member: IS.PA. Diagnostic testing, clinical practice, student; projective techniques, group process, therapy.   F

ILAN, Elieser. 16/55 Baka, Jerusalem. b. 28 Jan 1915 Dresden, Ger. MA '53 Hebrew Univ, Israel. DIRECTOR, Child Guid. Clin, Ministry of Soc. Welf, Tachanah Letipul Bageled, Clisch St. 2 Katamon, Jerusalem. Member: IS.PA, Israeli Assn. of Clin, Psych'ts, Israeli Socy. for Psychoanal. Psychotherapy, guidance, testing; psychoanalysis, projective techniques.   M

KELLNER, Jacob. House Kellner, Shehunat Hapoalim, Herzlia. b. 4 Aug 1920 Cologne, Ger. BA '54 Hebrew Univ, Israel. DIST. PROBAT. OFF, Ministry of Welf, Juv. Probat. Off, Cen. Dist, Israel; TCHR. of PSYCH, The Govt. Tchrs. Coll, Nathanya. Member: IS.PA. Guidance, teaching, research; socialization process in re-education, diagnostic problems in juvenile delinquency, group process among neglected children. M

KOHEN, Dr. Reuven. 91 Jabotinski St, Ramat-Gan. b. 28 Apr 1921 Bukov, Czech. PH.D '53 Univ. of Zurich, Switz. EDUC. PSYCH'T, Dept. of Youth Aliah, 49 Aliah St, Tel-Aviv; RES. WRKR, Univ. of Jerusalem. Member: Israeli Assn. of Clin. Psych'ts. Consulting, testing, psychotherapy, research; achievement tests, therapy, group process.   M

KUGELMASS, Dr. Sol. 3 Shikun Amami, Kiryat Yovel, Jerusalem. b. 4 July 1926 New York, USA. PH.D '53 Columbia Univ, USA. RES. PSYCH'T, Psychophysiol. Lab, Hebrew Univ, Jerusalem. Member: IS.PA, APA. Research, teaching; perception, motivation, experimental abnormal. M

LEVY, Dr. Joshua. 6 Hagiz St, Zichran Moshe, Jerusalem. b. 18 Mar 1930 Jerusalem. PH.D '56 Hebrew Univ, Israel. ASSISTANT, Sch. of Educ, Hebrew Univ, Jerusalem. Member: IS.PA. Research, teaching; counseling, projective techniques, group process. M

LEWIN, Isaac. Israel Inst. of Appl. Soc. Res, David Hamelech 1, Jerusalem. b. 1 July 1924 Haifa. MA '41 Hebrew Univ, Israel. PROJ. DIR, Israel Inst. of Appl. Soc. Res; LECT. in RES. METHODS, Sch. for Soc. Work, Tel-Aviv. Member: IS.PA, Israel Soc. Sci. Assn. Research, teaching, testing; personality and attitude measurement, group process. M

MAHLER-FRANCK, Dr. Wera. 185 Dizengoff St, Tel-Aviv. b. 10 Dec 1899 Hamburg, Ger. PH.D '33 Univ. of Berlin, Ger. TEACHER, Trng. Colleges for Tchrs, Tel-Aviv; PSYCHOLOGIST, priv. prac. Member: IS.PA, Israeli Assn. of Clin. Psych'ts. Psychotherapy, teaching, consulting, guidance; home and institutional education, Adlerian psychotherapy. F

MALINOVSKY, Bertha-Batya. 19 Chissin St, Tel-Aviv. b. 27 July 1907 Moscow, Russia. Diplôme '33 Univ. of Geneva, Switz. VOCAT COUNS, Educ. and Vocat. Guid. Inst, 18 Rechov Gimel Hakirya, Tel-Aviv. Member: IS.PA. Guidance, testing, clinical analysis, research; rehabilitation, projective techniques. F

MALINOVSKY, Levy-Léon. 19 Chissin St, Tel-Aviv. b. 5 Jan 1907 Poltava, Russia. Diplôme '33 Univ. of Geneva, Switz. DIRECTOR, Educ. and Vocat. Inst, 18 Rechov Gimel Hakirya, Tel-Aviv. Member: IS.PA, AIPA. Administration, guidance, testing, research, teaching; attitude measurement, aptitude measurement. M

MENDELSOHN, Dr. Jakob. 23 Hameristr, Givataim. b. 25 Mar 1906 Posen, Pol. PH.D '32 Univ. of Berlin, Ger. PSYCHOTHERAPIST, Child. Home, Shekunat Zedor, Petah Tikva. Member: IS.PA. Psychotherapy, guidance, testing, teaching; depth psychology. M

MEROM, Dr. May Bere. 26 Dubnow St, Tel-Aviv. b. 14 Sept 1896 Winnipeg, Canada. PH.D '25 Columbia Univ, USA. LECT. in CHILD DEVEL, Sch. of Soc. Work, Tel-Aviv; LECTURER, Sch. of Educ, Hebrew Univ, Jerusalem; CLIN. PSYCH'T, priv. prac. Member: APA, ICWP. Teaching, clinical practice, research; cultural diversity and unity, projective techniques, child psychology. F

MONIN, Prof. Josef. 12 Iehuda Hanassi St, Kiriat-Amal. b. 16 Mar 1895 Kasanka, Russia. Prof. '23 Univ. of Buenos Aires, Argentina. DIRECTOR, Psychotech. Inst, 17/A Madregot Teman, Haifa. Member: IS.PA. Clinical analysis, guidance, teaching; psychology of drawing, reading difficulties. M

NARDI, Noah. Ministry of Educ. and Culture, Jerusalem. b. 4 Oct 1902. PH.D '35 Columbia Univ, Teachers Coll, USA. SCH. SUPT, Dist. of Jerusalem, Ministry of Educ. and Culture. Member: IS.PA, APA. Educational supervision, editorial, research; achievement and attitude tests, educational and child psychology, teaching methods. M

NAEDLER, Huga-Emanuel. 170 Rue Arlozoroff, Tel-Aviv. b. 7 July 1918 Bucharest, Rumania. Licence '44 Univ. of Bucharest, Rumania. VOCAT. GUID. COUNS, Psychotech. Inst, Dept. of Educ, Hakyrya, 18 Rue Ghimel, Tel-Aviv; EDITOR, Ministry of Educ. of Rumania. Member: IS.PA. Testing, consulting, guidance, teaching; achievement and projective tests, vocational guidance of students and the handicapped. M

ORMIAN, Dr. Haim Yosef. 16 Mitudela, Jerusalem-Rehavia. b. 10 Dec 1901 Tarnów, Poland. PH.D '25 Univ. of Vienna, Austria. EDITOR, *Educational Encyclopedia*; EDITOR, Psych. Sect, *Hebrew Encyclopedia*, Ministry of Educ. and Culture, P.O. Box 292, Jerusalem. Member: IS.PA, APA, AIPA. Editorial, research, teaching; vocational guidance, educational psychology, adolescent psychology. M

ORTAR, Mrs. Gina R. 5 Molho St, Jerusalem. b. 1 Dec 1912 Leningrad, Russia. MA, Hebrew Univ, Israel. INSPECTOR and PSYCH'T, Ministry of Educ. and Culture, Jerusalem; TEACHING FELLOW, Hebrew Univ; LECTURER, Inst. for Soc. Workers. Member: IS.PA. Research, teaching, administration; test construction, cultural differences, acculturation of new immigrants. F

PEKERIS, Mrs. Leah. Weizmann Inst, Rehovot. b. 3 Aug 1909 Grodno, Poland. BA '31 Radcliffe Coll, USA. CLIN. PSYCH'T, Ment. Hyg. Clin. of Kupat Holim, 29 Zamenhof St, Tel-Aviv. Member: IS.PA. Diagnostic testing, psychotherapy, teaching; projective techniques, group process and therapy. F

PERLBERGER, Dr. Klara. 19 Chissin St, Tel-Aviv. b. 4 Nov 1897 Kroscienko, Poland. PH.D '33 Univ. of Vienna, Austria. PSYCHOTHERAPIST, priv. prac. Member: IS.PA. Psychotherapy, consulting. F

PERTSCHONOK, Daniel. Dept. of Psych, Harvard Univ, Cambridge 38, Massachusetts, USA. b. 1925 Berlin, Ger. MA '56 Harvard Univ, USA. TCHNG. FELLOW in SOC. RELAT, Harvard Univ. Student; perception, thought processes, personality theory.   M

POKORNY, Dr. Richard Rafael. 4 Nes Ziona St, Tel-Aviv. b. 16 July 1894 Vienna, Austria. Dr. juris. '18 Univ. of Vienna, Austria. GRAPHOLOGIST, priv. prac. Member: IS.PA, Graphology Socy. (Paris). Consulting, testing, applied psychology, teaching, research.   M

RIEMERMANN, Jehuda. Gan-Rashal, Herzliah. b. 15 Sept 1913 Warsaw, Poland. Mag. phil. '39 Univ. of Warsaw, Poland. PROBAT. OFF, Ministry of Soc. Welf, Petach Tikwah. Member: IS.PA. Applied psychology, testing, guidance; projective techniques, achievement tests, problems of adjustment.   M

SCHUBERT, Josef. P.O. Box 610, Jerusalem. b. 24 Mar 1925 Berlin, Ger. MA '56 New York Univ, USA. DIRECTOR, Children's Home Bnei Brith, Bajith Wegan, Jerusalem; CLIN. PSYCH'T, priv. prac. Educational psychology, psychotherapy, testing; projective techniques, group psychotherapy, developmental psychology. M

SHAFIR, Avraham. 4 Bracha-Fuldst, Tel-Aviv. b. 3 Apr 1919 Leipzig, Ger. Dipl. '53 Inst. of Appl. Psych, Zurich, Switz. CLIN. PSYCH'T, Sick Fund Kupath-Cholim, 29 Samenhof, Tel-Aviv; PSYCHOTHERAPIST, priv. prac. Member: IS.PA, Israeli Assn. of Clin. Psych'ts. Testing, clinical analysis, psychotherapy, teaching; projective techniques, psychoanalysis.   M

SHUVAL, Dr. Judith. Israel Inst. of Appl. Soc. Res, 1 Julions Way, Jerusalem. b. 24 Aug 1925 New York, USA. PH.D '55 Radcliffe Coll, USA. SOC. RES. EXPERT, UNESCO, 19 Ave. Kléber, Paris, Fr. Member: IS.PA, Amer. Sociol. Socy. Research, teaching; intergroup relations, attitude research.   F

SLIOSBERG-SCHLOSSBERG, Dr. Mrs. Sarah. 3 Hillelst, Haifa. b. 13 July 1906 Grodno, Russia. PH.D '34 Univ. of Berlin, Ger. PSYCHOTHERAPIST, priv. prac; GUID. COUNS, Sch. for Mentally Disturbed Children. Member: IS.PA. Psychotherapy, guidance, teaching; social perception, projective techniques.   F

TAMARIN, Dr. Georges Raphael. Bizaron St, Blok 15, Tel-Aviv. b. 6 Sept 1920 Subotica, Yugoslavia. PH.D '48 Univ. of Zagreb, Yugoslavia. CHIEF PSYCH'T, Hosp. Tel Hashomer, Tel Litvinski, Tel-Aviv. Member: IS.PA, Israeli Assn. of Clin. Psych'ts. Psychotherapy, testing, clinical analysis, research; psychology of thought, organic deterioration of intelligence.   M

UCKO, Sinai. Hebrew Univ, Jerusalem. b. 11 July 1905 Gleiwitz, Ger. PH.D, Univ. of Koenigsberg, Ger. ASSOC. TCHR, Dept. of Educ, Hebrew Univ; CO-EDITOR, *Jyyun.* Teaching, educational psychology, administration; problems of psychology and philosophy.   M

WEISS, Dr. Avraham Artur. Harav Berlin St, Kiriath Shmuel, Jerusalem. b. 28 Jan 1912 Vienna, Austria. PH.D '37 Univ. of Vienna, Austria. CHIEF PSYCH'T, Keren Nechuth Psychiat. Hosp, Fac. of Med, Hebrew Univ, Disraeli St, Jerusalem; LECTURER, Dept. of Neur, Hadassah Univ. Hosp, Jerusalem. Member: IS.PA, Israeli Assn. of Clin. Psych'ts. Clinical analysis, teaching, research, resident training supervision; testing in clinical psychiatry, projective techniques.   M

YESHAYAHU, Dr. Rim. 39 Sea Rd, Haifa. b. 21 Apr 1922 Czernowitz, Rumania. PH.D '53 Univ. of London, Eng. INSTR. in Human RELAT, Israel Inst. of Tech, Haifa. Member: IS.PA. Teaching, research, industrial psychology; attitude surveys, industrial training and testing.   M

ITALY

AMLETO, Bassi. Lavezzola (Ravenna). b. 12 Dec 1913 Lavezzola. Lib. Doc. Member: It. Psych. Socy. Teaching, research, clinical analysis; projective techniques, group process.   M

ANCONA, Prof. Dr. Leonardo. Via Fontana 16, Milan. b. 2 May 1922 Milan. It. Lib. Doc. '55 Cath. Univ. of Milan, It. ASST. DIR, Inst. of Psych, Cath. Univ. of Milan, Piazza S. Ambrogio 9, Milan. Member: It. Psych. Socy, APSLF, APA. Teaching, research, psychotherapy; visual perception, group process, bioelectrical activity of brain.   M

BARONE, Pasquale. Via Cairoli 9, Bari. b. 11 Feb 1927 Bari. MB '53 Univ. of Bari, It. VOCAT. COUNS, Centro di Orientamento Professionale, Via Abbrescia 85, Bari. Member: It. Psych. Socy, AIOP. Vocational guidance, testing, student; attitude measurement, social adjustment of adolescents.   M

BATTACCHI, Dr. Marco Walter. Via Rialto 36, Bologna. b. 21 Dec 1930 Bologna. Laurea '54 Univ. of Bologna, It. UNIV. ASST, Inst. of Psych, Univ. of Bologna. Member: It. Psych. Socy. Research, teaching, guidance; learning, social perception, language, personality. M

BELLANOVA, Dr. Piero. Via Anneo Lucano 51, Rome. b. 5 Feb 1917 S. Agata d'Esaro (Cosenza). Laurea, Univ. of Rome, It. SCI. DIR, Cen. Psicotecnico, Polizia Italiana. Ministry of Interior, Rome; CONSULTANT, Indus. Psych. Cen, Bombrini-Parodi-Delfino. Member: It. Psych. Socy. Applied and industrial psychology, testing, psychotherapy; projective techniques, tests, attitude measurement. M

BERRINI, Dr. Maria Elvira. Via Sassetti 10, Milan. b. 7 July 1918 Luino (Varese). MD '43 Univ. of Milan, It. DIRECTOR, Child Guid. Clin. of the City of Milan, Via E. Muzio 3, Milan; PSYCHIATRIST, priv. prac. Member: It. Psychiat. Socy. Child psychotherapy, clinical practice, guidance, teaching, research. F

BOSINELLI, Dr. Marino. Via Zamboni 6, Bologna. b. 22 Mar 1927 Bologna. MD '51 Univ. of Bologna, It. CONSULTANT, Inst. Medico Psicopedagogico, Imola, Bologna; ASST. in PSYCH, Univ. of Bologna. Psychotherapy, clinical analysis, research; sociometry, perception, developmental psychology. M

BOZZI, Dr. Paolo. Largo Porta Nuova 1, Gorizia. b. 16 May 1930 Gorizia. Laurea '55 Univ. of Trieste, It. UNIV. ASST. Univ. of Trieste, Rue de l'Université 7, Trieste; TEACHER, Instituto Magistrale, Gorizia. Research, teaching, perception, psychology of music, thought processes. M

BUSNELLI, Prof. Dr. Claudio. Via Mura Gianicolensi 98, Rome. b. 7 July 1913 Milan. Lib. Doc. '56 Univ. of Rome, It. MED. PSYCH, Ente Nazionale Protezione Morale del Fanciullo Roma, Via degli Scipioni 287, Rome. Member: It. Psych. Socy, APSLF. Consulting, psychotherapy, applied psychology; personality diagnosis, child psychotherapy. M

CANESTRARI, Prof. Renzo. Via Ugo Foscolo 7, Bologna. b. 19 Aug 1924 Pesaro. Lib. Doc. '56 Univ. of Bologna, It. PROF. of PSYCH, Univ. of Bologna; DIR. and ED, Inst. of Psych, Univ. of Bologna. Member: It. Psych. Socy. Teaching, research, testing; learning theory, social perception, projective techniques. M

CANESTRELLI, Prof. Leandro. Via G. Baglivi 5/D, Rome. b. 5 Oct 1908 Rome. MD '36 Univ. of Rome, It. DIRECTOR, Inst. of Psych, Univ. of Rome; DIRECTOR, Natl. Inst. of Psych, Natl. Res. Counc. (CNR); ASSOC. DIR, *Rivista di Psicologia Generale e Clinica.* Member: It. Psych. Socy, It. Rorschach Socy, AIPA, APSLF. Teaching, research, administration, editorial; psychomotor measurements, cyclographic recording techniques, research on subjective processes. M

CANZIANI, Prof. Dr. Gastone. Viale Regina Margherita 9 bis, Palermo. b. 6 July 1904 Trieste. Prof. '50 Univ. of Palermo, It. DIRECTOR, Inst. of Psych, Univ. of Palermo, Policlinico Feliciuzze, Palermo; DIRECTOR, Centro de Psicologia del Lavoro dell 'E.N.P.I.; EDITOR, *Rassegna di Psicologia General e Clinica.* Member: It. Psych. Socy, AIPA, APSLF, It. Psychiat. Socy. Teaching, research, consulting; projective techniques, attitude measurement, psychiatric consulting. M

CATALANO, Dr. Renzo. Via Abate Gimma 15, Bari. b. 1 Sept 1929 Bari. MA '55 Univ. of Bari, It. PSYCHOLOGIST, Centro de Psicologia del Lavoro, Positano 6, Bari; INTERNE, Inst. of Psych, Univ. of Bari. Member: It. Psych. Socy. Applied psychology, research, teaching; projective techniques, attitude measurement, group process. M

CESA-BIANCHI, Prof. Dr. Marcello. Via Lanzone 2, Milan. b. 19 Mar 1926 Milan. MD, Lib. Doc, State Univ. of Milan, It. PROF. and HEAD of PSYCH, Fac. of Med, State Univ, Via S. Barnaba 8, Milan; ASSISTANT, Inst. of Psych, Cath. Univ. of Milan, Milan. Member: It. Psych. Socy, It. Psychiat. Socy. Teaching, research, consulting; perception and imagination, mental acitivites in old age, intelligence tests. M

CIMATTI, Prof. Dr. Leone. Via Archimede 23, Rome. b. 13 Aug 1899 Faenza. Lib. Doc, Univ. of Florence, It. DIR. of GUID. and RE-EDUC, Opera Nazionale per gli invalidi di guerra, Piazza Adriana 2, Rome; PRESIDENT, Istituto Statale di Tiflologia professionale, Via Antonio Cocchi 2, Florence; EDITOR, *Orientamento Professionale Differenziato e Normale.* Member: It. Psych. Socy. Administration, editorial. teaching; interviewing, psychomotor learning and vocational education for the physically handicapped. M

COSTA MINI, Dr. Mrs. Antonietta. Via F. Paolo Di Blasi 35, Palermo. b. 30 Aug 1924 S. Stefano Quisquina. Laurea '46 ,MD '52 Univ. of Palermo, It. ASSISTANT, Psych. Inst, Univ. of Palermo, Policlinico Filiciuzza, Palermo; Psychologist, Psych. Cen, Lavoro dell 'E.N.P.I.; PSYCHOLOGIST, Istituto Osservazione Minorenni, Ministero di Grazia e Guistizia; EDITOR, *Rassegna Psicologia Generale e Clinica.* Member: It. Psych. Socy. Research, applied psychology, consulting; attitude measurement, projective techniques, psychosociology. F

DALLA VOLTA, Prof. Amedeo. Via Angelo Orsini 1/14, Genoa. b. 23 Oct 1892 Mantua. MD '19 Univ. of Florence, It. DIRECTOR, Inst. of Psych, Fac. of Med, Univ. of Genoa, Via 5 Maggio 39, Genoa. Member:

It. Psych. Socy, AIPA, APSLF. Administration, research, teaching, consulting; psychological causality, child development, alcoholism.   M

DE GRADA, Dr. Eraldo. Via Borsieri 20, Rome. b. 15 Sept 1925 Gorizia. MD '53 Univ. of Rome, It. ASSISTANT, Natl. Inst. of Psych, Natl. Res. Counc. (CNR); ASSISTANT, Inst. of Psych, Univ. of Rome. Member: It. Psych. Socy, APSLF, AIPA. Research, applied psychology, testing; measurement of intelligence, personality assessment.   M

DERITA, Prof. Miss Lidia. Via Vittorio Veneto 70, Bari. b. 3 Aug 1926 Bari. Laurea '43 Cath. Univ, Milan. ASST. PROF. of PSYCH, Universita degli Studi, Palazzo Ateneo, Bari. Member: It. Psych. Socy, APSLF, AIPA, AIOP. Teaching, research, applied psychology; socialization and interaction processes, personality.   F

EMANUELE, Dr. Vittorio. Corso di Porta Nuova 4, Milan. b. 6 Feb 1909 Messina. MD '34 Univ. of Messina, It. MED. INSPECTOR, Istituto Nazionale Assistenza Malattie, Corso Italia 19, Milan; PSYCHOTHERAPIST, priv. prac. Member: It. Psych. Socy. Clinical practice, psychotherapy; psychoanalysis.   M

FALORNI, Prof. Dr. Maria Luisa. Via R. Lambruschini 28, Florence. b. 20 Mar 1921 Florence. Lib. Doc. '51. DOCENT PSYCH, Univ. of Pisa, Pisa; DIRECTOR, Sch. of Soc. Serv, Pisa; DIRECTOR, Psycho-Pedagogic Med. Cen, Pisa. Member: It. Socy, AIPA, AIOP. Teaching, research, consulting; psychology of personality, self concept, attitude and interest tests.   F

FERRIO, Prof. Dr. Carlo. Via Amedeo Peyron 38, Turin. b. 26 Dec 1898 Turin. MD '22 Univ. of Turin, It. PROF. of PSYCH, Univ. degli Studi di Turin, Via Po 18, Turin; PSYCHIATRIST, priv. prac. Member: It. Psych. Socy, It. Psychiat. Socy, It. Neur. Socy. Teaching, psychotherapy, consulting, research; developmental psychology, psychopathology, legal psychology.   M

FONZI, Dr. Ada. Corso Umberto 61, Turin. b. 29 Nov 1927 Rome. Laurea '49 Univ. of Rome, It. GUID. COUNS, Centro di Orientamento Professionale, Via Principe Amedeo 2, Turin; ASST. in PSYCH, Univ. of Turin; PSYCH. ADVIS, Opera Nazionale Maternità e Infanzia, Turin; ED. BD, *Rivista di Psicologia Sociale* and *Rivista di Psicologia Generale e Clinica.* Member: It. Psych. Socy, AIPA, AIOP. Guidance, teaching, testing; child psychology, social perception, attitude measurement.   F

FORNARI, Dr. Franco. Via Carroccio 18, Milan. b. 18 Apr 1921 Piacenza. MD '47 Univ. of Milan, It. LECTURER, Psych.

Inst, Univ. of Milan, Via Festa del Perdono 3, Milan; PSYCH. PHYSICIAN, Psychiat. Clin, Villa-Turro, Milan. Member: It. Psych. Socy. Teaching, clinical practice; psychopathology of schizophrenia.   M

FORTE, Dr. Rita T. Via Filippo Casini 6, Rome. b. 28 Dec 1919 New York City, USA. PH.D '46 Fordham Univ, USA. CONSULT. PSYCH'T, priv. prac. Member: APA, WFMH. Consulting, applied psychology, research; learning theory, motivational theory.   F

GALDO, Prof. Dr. Luca. Corso Vittorio Emanuele 121, Naples. b. Feb 1889 Naples. MD '14 Univ. of Naples, It. PROF. of PSYCH. and DIR, Psych. Inst, Univ. of Naples, Via Mezzocannone 8, Naples; TEACHER, Istituto Univ, Suor Orsola Beniucasa. Member: It. Psych. Socy. Teaching, research, administration; biology, personnel selection, physiological correlates of mental activity.   M

GEMELLI, Prof. Dr. Agostino. Piazza S. Ambrogio 9, Milan. b. 18 Jan 1878 Milan. MD; Prof. ord, Cath. Univ. of Milan, It. PROF. of PSYCH. and DIR, Inst. of Psych; RECTOR, Cath. Univ. of Milan; DIRECTOR, *Archivio di Psicologia Neurologia e Psichiatria.* Member: It. Psych. Socy, Academia pontificia scientiarum. Research, teaching, editorial, administration; general psychology, industrial psychology, psychology of perception.   M

IACONO, Prof. Dr. Gustavo. Via F. Ciampa 10, Piano di Sorrento, Naples. b. 4 Nov 1925 Naples. MD '48 Univ. of Naples, It. ASSISTANT, Inst. of Psych, Univ. of Naples, Via Universita 39, Naples; CONSULTANT, clin. prac. Member: It. Psych. Socy, AIPA, APSLF. Research, taeching, industrial psychology; perception, social and technological change, industrial maladjustment.   M

KANIZSA, Prof. Gaetano. Inst. of Psych, Univ. of Trieste, Trieste. b. 18 Aug 1913 Trieste. Laurea '37 Univ. of Padova, It. PROFESSOR, Univ. degli Studi di Trieste, Trieste; CO-DIR, *Rivista di Psicologia.* Member: It. Psych. Socy, APSLF. Teaching, research, editorial; visual perception, social perception, motivation.   M

MARZI, Prof. Alberto. Via della Colonna 17, Florence, b. 13 June 1907 Florence. Laurea '30 Univ. of Florence, It. PROF. of PSYCH, Univ. of Florence, Inst. of Psych, Via Cesare Battisti 4, Florence; DIRECTOR, *Collezione Psicologica.* Member: It. Psych. Socy, APA, IUSP. Teaching, research, editorial; attention, social perception, personality development.   M

MASSUCCO COSTA, Prof. Angiola. Via Principi d'Acaja 20, Turin. b. 13 Jan 1902 Brescia. Prof. '55 Univ. of Cagliari, It.

PROF. of PSYCH, and DIR, Inst. of Psych, Univ. of Cagliari, Via Corte d'Appello 87; DIRECTOR, Inst. of Social Psych, Turin; DIRECTOR, Cen. d'Orientation Professionnel, Turin; EDITOR, *Rivista di Psicologia Sociale*. Member: It. Psych. Socy, AIPA, AIOP. Research, teaching, industrial psychology, editorial, consulting; esthetic perception, collective processes, social tensions, mental rigidity, group dynamics. personality, characterology. F

MESCHIERI, Prof. Luigi. Istituto Nazionale di Psicologia. Consiglio Nazionale delle Ricerche, Piazzale delle Scienze 7, Bologna. b. 30 Jan 1919 Bologna. Lib. Doc. '50; MD '41 State Univ, Rome, It. RES. PSYCH'T. and VICE DIR, Istituto Nazionale di Psicologia; PROF. of PSYCH, Univ. of Rome; ED. STAFF, *Rassegna di Psicologia Generale e Clinica*. Member: It. Psych. Socy, AIPA, APA. Research, teaching, industrial psychology; test construction and validation, personality assessment, personnel selection, vocational guidance. M

MIGLIORINO, Prof. Dr. Giuseppe. Via Rome 19, Palermo. b. 6 Oct 1904 S. Agata Militello (Messina). MD; Prof. '54 Univ. of Palermo, It. PROFESSOR, Cen. of Psych. Stat, Univ. of Palermo, Via Marchese Ugo 56, Palermo; DIRECTOR, Laboratorio di Psicotecnica della Ferrovie dello Stato, Palermo; EDITOR, *Rivista di Psicologia Normale Patologica*. Member: It. Psych. Socy, AIPA. Research, teaching, testing; attitude measurement, group process, ability tests. M

MINGUZZI, Dr. Gian Franco. Via Matteotti 3, Bologna. b. 29 Aug 1927 Ravenna. MD '51 Univ. of Bologna, It. ASST. in PSYCH, Inst. of Psych, Univ. of Bologna. Member: It. Psych. Socy. Research, testing, teaching; perception, learning theory, projective techniques. M

MIOTTO, Prof. Antonio. Azzano di Mezzegra (Como). b. 9 Jan 1912 Split. Lib. Doc. '54 Univ. of Milan, It. PSYCH. WRITER, Garzanti-Rizzoli, Editors, Via Spiga 30, P. Erba 6, Milan. Member: It. Psych. Socy. Teaching, research, applied psychology; group process, propaganda, public opinion. M

MISITI, Dr. Raffaello. Via S. Marino 12, Rome. b. 25 Aug 1925 Reggio, Cal. MD '49 Univ. of Rome, It. ASSISTANT, Natl. Res. Counc, Pizzale delle Scienze 7, Rome; ASSISTANT, Inst. of Psych, Univ. of Rome. Member: AIPA, APSLF, It. Psych. Socy. Testing, research, teaching; achievement tests, attitude measurement, projective techniques, group process. M

MODIGLIANI, Dr. Claudio. Via Antonio Allegri da Correggio 11, Rome. b. 20 July 1916 Rome. Laurea '39 Univ. of Rome,

It. TRNG. ANAL, It. Psychoanal. Socy. Member: It. Psychoanal. Socy, Int. Psychoanal. Assn. Psychotherapy, teaching, consulting; learning theory, group process, psychoanalytic techniques.M

MORRA, Dr. Mauro. Via Veniero 38, Milan. b. 2 July 1922 Genoa. MD '48 Univ. of Milan, It. PSYCHOANALYST, priv. prac. Member: It. Psych. Socy. Psychotherapy, consulting; projective techniques, psychoanalysis, psychiatry. M

MURATORI, Dr. Anna Maria. Corso Rinascimento 52, Rome. b. 12 May 1925 Rome. CHIEF, Psychopedagogical Med. Cen, Ente Nazionale Protezione Morale del Fanciullo (E.N.P.M.F.), Via Segli Scipioni 287, Rome; DOCENT in CLIN. PSYCH. and PSYCHOPATHOL, Sch. of Soc. Serv. Member: APSLF. Psychotherapy, teaching, clinical analysis; genetic psychology, psychoanalysis. F

MUSATTI, Prof. Dr. Cesare. Corso di Porta Nuovo 22, Milan. b. 21 Sept 1897 Venice. Laurea '21 Univ. of Padua, It. PROF. of PSYCH. and DIR, Inst. of Psych, Univ. of Milan, Via Festa del Perdono 3, Milan; EDITOR, *Rivista di psicologia* and *Rivista di Psicoanalisi*; CO-EDITOR, *Archivio di psicologia, neurologia e psichiatri* and *Psicologia sociale*. Member: It. Psych. Socy, It. Psychoanal. Socy, Int. Psychoanal. Assn. Research, teaching, psychotherapy; perception of space, perception of color, psychoanalysis. M

NENCINI, Dr. Rodolfo. Via Sisco 7, Rome. b. 29 July 1925 Cecina, Leghorn. MD '50 Univ. of Pisa, It. ASSISTANT, Natl. Res. Counc, Piazzale delle Scienze 7, Rome. Member: It. Psych. Socy. Testing, research, teaching; projective techniques, achievement tests, group process. M

PASSUELLO, Dr. Edda. Via Lattuada 8, Milan. b. 19 June 1921 Bassano del Grappa, Vicenza. MD, Univ. of Milan, It. CHILD PSYCHIATRIST, Cen. of Med. Psychopedagogics, Prov. of Milan, Via Palermo 17, Milan. Member: It. Psych. Socy. Applied psychology, psychotherapy, conculting. F

PERROTTI, Prof. Dr. Nicola. Corso Trieste 146, Rome. b. 22 Dec 1897 Penne (Pescara). Lib. Doc, Univ. of Rome, It. TRNG. ANAL, It. Socy. of Psychoanal. Via Salaria 237, Rome. Member: It. Psych. Socy, Int. Psychoanal. Assn. Teaching, psychotherapy, consulting; psychoanalysis, social psychology. M

PERUGIA, Prof. Angelo. Piazza Vesuvio 23, Milan. b. 7 Aug 1913 Milan. Lib. Doc. '56 Univ. of Rome, It. PROFESSOR, Cath. Univ. of Milan, Piazza S. Ambrogio 9, Milan. Member: It. Psych. Socy. Teaching, research, applied and educational psychology; developmental psychology, mental activity, group relations.   **M**

PETTER, Dr. Guido. Via Cristoforo Colombo 12, Trieste. b. 20 Apr 1927 Agra (Varese). Laurea '52 Univ. of Milan, It. ASST. in PSYCH, Inst. of Psych, Univ. of Trieste, Trieste. ED. COMM, *Rivista di Psicologia*. Member: It. Psych. Socy. Teaching, research; intellectual development of the child, visual perception.   **M**

PONZO, Ezio. Via Poggio Moiano 55, Rome. b. 6 May 1923 Turin. MD '48 Univ. of Rome, It. ASSISTANT, Inst. of Psych, Univ. of Rome. Member: It. Psych. Socy, APSLF. Research, testing, teaching; child psychology, projective techniques. **M**

RESTA, Dr. Giorgio. Corso Firenze 95, Genoa. b. 13 Aug 1918 Rome. MD '42 Univ. of Genoa, Italy. ASSISTANT, Inst. of Psych, Univ. of Genoa, c/o Istituto Gaslini, Via 5 Maggio 39, Genoa. Member: It. Psych. Socy. Research; relationship between psychological and somatic development.   **M**

RICCOBONO-TERRANA, Dr. Mrs. Liliana. Via de Spuches 35, Palermo. b. 10 Mar 1920 Palermo. Laurea '50 Univ. of Palermo, It. ASSISTANT, Inst. of Psych, Univ. of Palermo; PSYCHOLOGIST, Psych. Cen, Lavoro dell 'E.N.P.I.; PSYCHOLOGIST, Med. Psycho-Pedagogical Cen. of E.N.P.M.F.; EDITOR, *Psicologia Generale e Clinica*. Member: It. Psych. Socy. Research, applied psychology; attitude measurement, projective techniques, diagnosis of abnormal children.   **F**

RIZZO, Dr. Giovanni Battista. Via Nomentana 60, Rome. b. 20 May 1928 Milan. MD '51 Univ. of Rome, It. ASSISTANT, Inst. of Psych, Univ. of Rome; PSYCH. CONSULT, Inst. Nazionale di Osservazione, Rebibbia, Rome. Member: It. Psych. Socy, APSLF. Testing, research, teaching; projective techniques, achievement tests, psychophysiology, psychology of criminality.   **M**

SABATELLI, Dr. Giuseppe. Via Putignani 211, Bari. b. 1 July 1922 Bari. Laurea '48 Univ. of Bari, It. UNIV. ASST, Inst. of Psych, Univ. of Bari, Palazzo dell 'Ateneo, Bari. Member: It. Psych. Socy. Research, applied psychology, journalism; social psychology, mass communications.   **M**

SARAVAL, Dr. Anteo. S. Croce 49, Venice. b. 11 June 1930 Venice. MD '54 Univ. of Padua, It. ASSISTANT, Clinica Neuropatologica, Univ. of Pavia, Via Palestro 3, Pavia. Clinical analysis, consulting, psychotherapy; projective techniques, psychoanalysis.   **M**

SERVADIO, Prof. Dr. Emilio. Via Annone 1, Rome. b. 14 Aug 1904 Genoa. Laurea '26 Univ. of Genoa, It. TRNG. and CONTROL

ANAL, It. Psychoanal. Socy. Member: It. Psych. Socy, It. Psychoanal. Socy, Int. Psychoanal. Assn. Psychotherapy, teaching, consulting; psychoanalysis, depth psychological approach to parapsychological problems.   **M**

SIGURTÀ, Dr. Renato. Corso Sempione 1, Milan. b. 4 Nov 1921 Milan. MD '46 Univ. of Milan, It. RES. WRKR, Inst. of Psych, Univ. of Milan, Via Festa del Perdono 3, Milan. Member: It. Psych. Socy, It. Socy. of Psychiat, It. Psychoanal Socy. Research, testing, psychotherapy; perception, projective techniques, psychoanalysis.   **M**

STOPPER, Dr. Alfredo. Via Stuparich 2, Trieste. b. 26 July 1917 Trieste. Laurea '40 Univ. of Padua, It. ASSISTANT, Inst. of Psych, Univ. of Trieste; TEACHER, Sch. for Social Serv, Trieste; CLIN. PSYCH'T, Inst. for the Blind, Trieste. Member: It. Psych. Socy. Research, teaching, testing, clinical analysis; group process, social perception, projective techniques, achievement testing.   **M**

STOPPER, Dr. Carolina. Via Stuparich 2, Trieste. b. 10 Feb 1922 Trieste. Laurea '50 Univ. of Trieste, It. ASST. in PSYCH, Univ. of Trieste. Member: It. Psych. Socy. Research, testing, consulting; achievement tests for children, projective techniques.   **F**

STROLOGO, Dr. Emilia. Rue P. Micca 15, Turin. b. 8 Feb 1932 Turin. Doctorat '56 Univ. of Turin, It. ADMIN. ASST, Inst. of Social Psych, Rue Principe Amedeo 2, Turin. Administration, student, research; aptitude measurement, conditioned reflex.   **F**

TAMPIERI, Prof. Giorgio. Piazza del Perugino 6, Trieste. b. 7 July 1925 Trieste. Laurea '47 Univ. of Trieste, It. PROF. of PSYCH, Univ. of Trieste, Via dell' Universita 7, Trieste; DIRECTOR, Vocat. Guid. Cen, Trieste. Member: It. Psych. Socy, AIPA. Research, teaching, guidance; visual perception, standardization of aptitude tests. **M**

TOMASI DI PALMA, Mrs. Alexandra. Via Butera 28, Palermo. b. 27 Nov 1896 Nice, Fr. VICE PRES, It. Sect, Int. Psychoanal. Assn; CO-EDITOR, *Rivista di Psicoanalisi*. Teaching, clinical analysis; psychoanalytic treatment of neurotic disturbances.   **F**

TRAMONTE, Dr. Anna. Matteotti 53, Bari. b. 13 July 1927 Ponte S. Pietro, Bergamo. Laurea, Univ. of Bari, It. PSYCHOLOGIST, Centro Medico Psicopedagogico dell 'E.N.P.M.F., Piazza Umberto 8, Bari. Testing; projective techniques, achievement tests.   **F**

TRAVERSA, Dr. Carlo. Corso Rinascimento 52, Rome. b. 24 Jan 1923 Rome. MD, Univ. of Rome, It. COORDINATOR, Ente Nazionale Protezione Morale del Fanciullo,

Via degli Scipioni 287, Rome; DOCENT in CLIN. PSYCH, Sch. of Soc. Work, Rome; PSYCHOTHERAPIST, priv. prac. Member: It. Psych. Socy, APSLF. Psychotherapy, applied, psychology teaching; genetic psychology, group dynamics, expressive movements. M

TURILLAZZI, Dr. Stefania. Inst. of Psych, Univ. of Rome. b. 20 June 1929 Grosseto. MD '52 Univ. of Rome, It. ASSISTANT, Inst. of Psych; CONSULT. PSYCH'T, Pediatric Clin, Univ. of Rome. Member: It. Psych. Socy, APSLF. Testing, clinical analysis, teaching; projective techniques, learning theory, clinical psychology. F

VALENTINI, Prof. Ernesto. Via di Porta Pinciana 1, Rome. b. 23 July 1907 Cosenza. Laurea '34 Univ. of Genoa, Italy. VICE DIR, Inst. of Psych, Univ. of Rome; PROF. of GENL. and CHILD PSYCH, Facoltà di Magistero. Member: It. Psych. Socy, APSLF, AIPA. Teaching, research, educational psychology; behavior of fantail pigeons, interference and rhythm, psychology of films. M

VELTRI, Dr. Pietro. Viale Lazie 9, Milan. b. 14 Jan 1904 Belmonte Calabro. Laurea '26 Univ. of Naples, It. MAGISTRATE, Court of Appeals of Milan, Via Freguglia, Milan; CO-DIRECTOR, *Rivista di Psicoanalisi.* Member: It. Psych. Socy, Int. Psychoanal. Socy. Judicial activities, research, editorial; criminology. M

ZAPPAROLI, Dr. Giovanni Carlo. Piazza della Republica 10, Milan. b. 13 Sept 1924 Omegna (Novara). MD '49 Univ. of Pavia, It. LECTURER, Inst. of Exper. Psych, Univ. of Milan, Via Festa del Perdono 3, Milan; CONSULTANT, Lab. of Exper. Psych, Ment. Hosp. of Mombello, Milan; PSYCHOTHERAPIST, priv. prac. Member: It. Psych. Socy, It. Psychoanal. Socy. Research, psychotherapy, consulting; perception in mental disease, memory and learning, psychotherapy. M

ZAVALLONI, Prof. Fr. Roberto. Pontificio Ateneo Antoniano, Via Merulana 124, Rome. b. 25 May 1920 Cervia. Maître Agrégé '51 Univ. of Louvain, Bel. PROF. of PSYCH, Pontificio Ateneo Antoniano; ASSISTANT, Inst. of Psych, Catholic Univ, Piazza S. Ambrogio 9, Milan. Member: It. Psych. Socy, APA. Teaching, research, psychotherapy; motor-perceptual development of moral and religious conduct, psychology of the cinema. M

ZECCA, Dr. Graziella. Inst. of Psych, Univ. of Genoa, Via 5 Maggio 39, Genoa. b. 13 Aug 1926 Parma. MD '51 Univ. of Genoa, It. ASSISTANT, Inst. of Psych, Univ. of Genoa. Member: It. Psych. Socy, APSLF. Research, clinical practice, teaching; developmental psychology, projective techniques. F

ZUNINI, Prof. Giorgio. Onno (Como). b. 7 May 1903 La Spezia. Laurea '28 Univ. of Milan, It. PROF. of PSYCH, and DIR, Psych. Lab, Univ. degli studi di Bari, Bari. Member: It. Psych. Socy, APSLF. Teaching, research, professional writing; animal learning, group process, personality. M

JAPAN

EXPLANATION OF JAPANESE ACADEMIC DEGREES

The academic degrees for Japan have been presented in Japanese. Degrees from four Faculties are found with some frequency in our entries. The greatest number are in the Faculty of Letters, and have the title of Bungakushi, granted after 16 or 17 years of education, including three or four years of university level training terminated by examinations and the presentation of a thesis. The advanced degree in Letters is the Bungakuhakushi, earned after special request to the Faculty of Letters and evidence of advanced scholarly attainment. A minimum requirement would be five years of graduate study and a thesis. An intermediate degree in Letters, the Bungakushushi, equivalent to the Master's degree in the United States, is granted after successful completion of two years of graduate study.

In the Faculty of Science, the first level degree is the Rigakushi and the advanced degree is the Rigakuhakushi. In the Faculty of Medicine, the first level degree is the Igakushi, equivalent to the MD. The advanced degree is the Igakuhakushi. In the Faculty of Law the first level degree is the Hogakushi. These eight degrees include most of the academic titles found in the Japanese entries.

ABBE, Prof. Magosiro. Dept. of Psych, Sin-ai Women's Coll, Wakayama. b. 14 Jan 1909 Yamagata. Bungakushi '36 Kyoto Univ, Japan. PROFESSOR, Sin-ai Women's Coll; DIRECTOR and EDITOR, Sociopsych. Lab, Suimon 45, Nara City. Member: JPA, JSAP, SCP, Kansai Psych. Assn, Nara Psych. Assn. Research, teaching experimental psychology; correlation of time and space perception, characterology, personality-symbol, topology of sociality. M

ABE, Prof. Junkichi. 116 Ohkuboyachi, Nagamachi, Sendai. b. 13 Feb 1915 Tokyo. Bungakushi '40 Tohoku Univ, Japan. ASST. PROF. of PSYCH, Coll. of Arts and Sciences, Tohoku Univ, Tomizawa, Sendai; RES. DIR, Tohoku Inst. for the Study and Trtmt. of Delinquency and Criminality. Member: JPA, JSAP, Tohoku Psych. Assn. Teaching, research; history of social psychology, value change in dynamics of personality, society and culture.   M

ABE, Prof. Kitao. 74 3-chome, Saginomiya, Nakano-ku, Tokyo. b. 3 Mar 1922 Tokyo. Bungakushi '47 Univ. of Tokyo, Japan. ASST. PROF. of PSYCH, Tokyo Coll. of Foreign Studies, Nishigahara, Tokyo; LECTURER, Aoyama-Gakuin Univ. Member: JPA, JSAP, SCP.   Research, teaching; memory and the effects of verbal suggestion.   M

ABE, Mitsukuni. Sendai Juvenile Classif. Cen, Kitarokubancho 301, Sendai. b. 1 Jan 1905 Tokyo. Bungakushi '32 Tohoku Univ, Japan. SUPERINTENDENT, Sendai Juv. Classif. Cen. Member: JSAP. Teaching, research, supervise guidance and treatment of juvenile delinquents; measurement of personality, genesis of character.   M

ABE, Dr. Saburō. Standing Committee for the Cabinet, House of Representatives, Nagata-cho, Tokyo. b. 6 June 1898 Yamada. Bungakuhakushi '39 Tohoku Univ, Japan. SPECIALIST, Standing Committee for the Cabinet, Hse. of Rep. Member: JPA. Teaching, research, administration; psychology of time.   M

ABE, Tadashi. 510-7 Koyama, Shinagawa-ku, Tokyo. b. 16 Sept 1913 Kanazawa. Igakushi '47 Keio Univ, Japan. ASST. in PSYCHIAT, Keio Univ, Shinanomachi, Tokyo; ASST. ED, *Seishin-Bunseki-Kenkyu*; PSYCHIATRIST, Okura Natl. Hosp. and Nippon Kokan Hosp. Member: JPA, JSAP, Japan Psychoanal. Socy. Psychotherapy, professional writing, testing, clinical analysis; projective techniques.   M

AIBA, Francis Hitoshi. 950 3-chome, Matsubaracho, Setagaya-ku, Tokyo. b. 5 Dec 1924 Utsunomiya. Bungakushi '50 Waseda Univ, Japan. ASSISTANT, Neuro-Psychiat. Clin, Keio Univ, Sch. of Med, Shinano-Machi, Tokyo. Member: JPA, JSAP. Research, testing, clinical analysis, clinical practice; galvanic skin response problems of constitution.   M

AIKAWA, Takao. Dept. of Psych, Aichi Univ. of Liberal Arts and Educ, Okazaki, Aichi. b. 25 June 1920 Fukuoka. Bunga-kushi '49 Tokyo Bunrika Univ, Japan. INSTR. in PSYCH, Aichi Univ. of Liberal Arts and Educ. Member: JPA, JSAP. Teaching developmental and clinical psychology; form and color response, person-

ality development, memory.   M

AIZAWA, Prof. Mutsuo. Tatada Branch, Niigata Univ, Nishishiricho, Takada. b. 25 June 1909 Iwate Ken. Bungakushi '32 Tohoku Univ, Japan. PROF. of PSYCH, Takada Branch, Niigata Univ. Member: JPA.   Teaching, consulting, research; auditory perception, aesthetic experience, psychology of music, attitude measurement.   M

AKAKURA, Prof. Takeshi. Dept. of Econ. and Polit. Sci, Meiji Univ, Kanda Chiyoda-Tokyo. b. 15 Dec 1904 Tokyo. Bungakushi '40 Hosei Univ, Japan. PROF. of PSYCH, Meiji Univ. Member: JPA. Teaching, research; group process and leadership, correlation between group attitudes and economic status.   M

AKAMATSU, Prof. Haruo. Dept. of Psych, Kagawa Univ, 121 Saiwai-cho, Takamatsu. b. 21 Nov 1907 Uwajima. Bungakushi '33 Univ. of Tokyo, Japan. PROFESSOR, Kagawa Univ. Member: JPA, JAEP. Teaching, research, testing; achievement and intelligence tests, learning theory.   M

AKAMATSU, Prof. Paul. Dept. of Psych, Waseda Univ, Totsuka, Tokyo. b. 14 Aug 1891 Shingu. Bungakushi '17 Waseda Univ, Japan. PROFESSOR, Waseda Univ. Member: JPA, JSAP. Teaching, research; learning theory.   M

AKATSUKA, Prof. Taizo. Dept. of Psych, Chuo Univ, Surugadai, Tokyo. b. 6 Mar 1907 Tokyo. Bungakushi '34 Tokyo Bunrika Univ, Japan. ASST. PROF, Chuo Univ. Member: JPA, JSAP. Teaching, research, testing; emotional and social factors in personality adjustment.   M

AKISHIGE, Dr. Yoshiharu. Kyushu Univ, Hakozaki, Fukuoka. b. 11 Oct 1904 Amagi. Bungakuhakushi '39 Kyushu Univ, Japan. PROF. and DIR, Dept. of Pysch, Kyushu Univ; ED. STAFF, *Japanese Journal of Psychology, Japanese Psychological Research*. Member: JPA, JSAP. Research, teaching, editorial; theory of perception and mental development.   M

AKIYAMA, Prof. Hiroshi. Osaka Tech. Coll, Kitanocho, Omiya, Asahiku, Osaka. b. 15 Mar 1909 Karatsu. Kogakushi '32 Univ. of Tokyo, Japan. ASST. PROF. in ELEC. ENGR, Osaka Tech. Coll. Member: JPA, Jap. Socy. for Animal Psych. Research, teaching; learning theory, conditioned reflex, electromagnetic theory. M

AKIYAMA, Prof. Seiichiro. Pre-Dental Course, Tokyo Dental Coll, Ichikawa, Chiba-ken. b. 12 Feb 1922 Ibaraki-ken. Bungakushi '48 Keio Univ, Japan. ASST. PROF. of PSYCH, Tokyo Dental Coll; LECT. in CLIN. PSYCH, Nihon Shakaijigyo Tanki Daigaku. Member: JPA, JSAP, Jap. Psychiat. and Neur. Assn. Teaching, research, consulting; abnormal aspects of thinking and emotion. **M**

AMANO, Prof. Makio. Inst. of Educ. Psych, Okayama Univ, Tsushima, Okayama. b. 8 Apr 1907 Okayama. Bungakushi '41 Hiroshima Univ, Japan. ASST. PROF. of PSYCH, Okayama Univ. Member: JPA, JSAP, JAEP. Teaching, educational research; psychological measurement and prediction. **M**

AMANO, Prof. Toshitake. Dept. of Psych, Fac. of Literature, Osaka Univ, Toyonaka, Osaka. b. 1 Jan 1904 Tokyo. Bungakuhakushi '43 Tokyo Univ, Japan. PROFESSOR, Osaka Univ; CHIEF LIBRARIAN, Osaka Univ. Lib. Member: JPA, JSAP. Teaching, library research; memory and thinking. **M**

AMO, Prof. Daihei. 73 6-chome Minamicho, Aoyama, Akasaka, Minatoku, Tokyo. b. 5 Feb 1922 Tokyo. Bungakushi '44 Keio Univ, Japan. ASST. PROF. of PSYCH, Musashino Women's Coll, 222 Kamihoya, Hoya, Kitatama-gun, Tokyo; CHIEF, Sect. of Couns. for Children, Musashino Educ. Comm; PSYCHOTHERAPIST, Sakuragaoka Ment. Hosp. Member: JPA, JSAP. Counseling, teaching educational psychology, psychotherapy; mathematical study of group dynamics, group psychotherapy, psychotherapeutic techniques. **M**

ANDO, Prof. Isao. Kogyokusha Jr. Coll, Nishioosaki, Shinagawa, Tokyo. b. 17 Feb 1887 Yamagata. Kogakushi '13 Univ. of Tokyo, Japan. PROF. of CIVIL ENGR, Kogyokusha Jr. Coll. Member: JSAP. Research, teaching, professional writing; theory of personal error in surveying. **M**

ANDO, Prof. Kohei. Dept. of Psych, Nihon Univ, Kanda, Tokyo. b. 15 Dec 1912 Gifu. Bungakushi '39 Nihon Univ, Japan. PROFESSOR, Nihon Univ. Member: JPA, JSAP, JAEP. Teaching, research; intelligence and scholastic aptitude tests. **M**

ANDŌ, Prof. Mizuo. 52 Eifukucho, Suginamiku, Tokyo. b. 26 Nov 1915 Tokyo. Bungakushi '40 Tohoku Univ, Japan. PROF. of PSYCH, Rikkyo Univ, Ikebukuro Toshimaku, Tokyo; LECTURER, St. Luke's Nursing Coll. and Shibaura Coll. of Indus. Tech; EDITOR, *Tohoku Journal of Psychology*. Member: JPA, JSAP. Teaching, research, professional writing; attitude measurement and employee evaluation. **M**

AOKI, Takao. Fukuoka Kyosei Kanku, Nagahama, Fukuoka. b. 25 Nov 1922 Tokyo. Bungakushi '44 Univ. of Tokyo, Japan. CHIEF, Health and Classif. Sect, Fukuoka Kyosei Kanku. Member: JPA. Consulting on health and classification problems in prison, testing, teaching; group dynamics, human relations. **M**

AOKI, Takayori. 836 3-chome, Nakmura,

Nerima, Tokyo. b. 8 Sept 1924 Koochi. Bungakushi '48 Tokyo Bunrika Univ, Japan. ASST. in PSYCH, Tokyo Univ. of Educ, Otsuka, Tokyo. Member: JPA, JSAP. Child guidance, research, teaching; psychological tests, evaluation. **M**

ARAI, Kōyū. Dept. of Psych, Fac. of Educ, Shinshu Univ, Nishi-Nagano, Nagano. b. 20 Feb 1928 Tochigi. Bungakushi '52 Tokyo Bunrika Univ, Japan. ASSISTANT, Shinshu Univ. Member: JPA, JSAP. Research, teaching, consulting; memory as related to retrograde amnesia after electro-shock. **M**

ARAI, Prof. Dr. Sadao. 241 Shoda, Gunge, Mikage-cho, Higashi-Nada-Ku, Kobe. b. 6 July 1899 Nagano-Ken. PH.D '33 Univ. of Chicago, USA. PROF. of EDUC, Kwansei Gakuin Univ, Uegahara, Nishinomiga; HEAD, Mikage Educ. Res. Inst. Member: JPA, Jap. Educ. Res. Assn. Teaching, research, student counseling; analytical study of moral situations, psychology of guidance, social psychology. **M**

ARAKAWA, Prof. Isamu. 863 Sekimae, Musashino-shi, Tokyo. b. 18 Dec 1918 Tokyo. Bungakushi '43 Univ. of Tokyo, Japan. ASST. PROF. of EDUC, Tokyo Univ. of Educ, Otsuka-Kubomachi, Tokyo. Member: JSAP. Research, teaching; psychology of the deaf. **M**

ASADA, Miss Mitsu. Dept. of Child Study, Osaka City Univ, Nishinagahori-Minamidori, Nishiku, Osaka. b. 5 Nov 1926 Osaka. Bungakushi '50 Ritsumeikan Univ, Japan. ASST. in CHILD EDUC, Osaka City Univ. Member: JPA, JSAP, Kansai Psych. Assn. Research, guidance; development of perception. **F**

ASAI, Prof. Asaichi. Dept. of Educ, Nara Women's Univ, Nara. b. 19 May 1908 Gosen. Bungakushi '38 Tokyo Bunrika Univ, Japan. PROF. of EDUC. and HEAD of HLTH. CEN, Nara Women's Univ; PRINCIPAL, Nara Women's Univ. Elem. Sch. Member: JSAP. Teaching, administration, research; social perception, group process, attitude measurement. **M**

ASAI, Kuniji. Dept. of Psych, Waseda Univ, Totsuka, Tokyo. b. 11 Aug 1924 Nagoya. Bungakushi '48 Waseda Univ, Japan. INSTRUCTOR, Waseda Univ. Member: JPA, JSAP. Teaching, research; perception, adaptation level. **M**

ASAKURA, Toshikage. Dentsu Advertising Co, Ginza-Nishi, Tokyo. b. 18 Oct 1922 Tokyo. Bungakushi '48 and Bungakushi '52 Univ. of Tokyo, Japan. ASST. DIR, Res. Dept, Dentsu Advertising Co. Member JPA, JSAP, WAPOR. Advertising and marketing research, applied psychology, testing; consumer attitude measurement, copy testing, motivation research. **M**

ASAMI, Miss Chizuko. 7430 Chigasaki, Chigasaki-shi, Kanagawa-ken. b. 16 Apr 1919 Hakodate. Bungakushi '49 Tokyo Bunrika Univ, Japan. ASST. in PSYCH, Tokyo Univ. of Educ, Otsuka Kubomachi, Tokyo. Member: JPA, JSAP, Jap. Socy. for Animal Psych. Child guidance, research, teaching; comparative and developmental approach to behavior theory and individual differences. F

ASANO, Tōru. 698 2-chome Matubara Setagaya, Tokyo. b. 5 Aug 1895 Ida. Bungakushi '36 Nihon Univ, Japan. HEAD, Res. Sect, Inst. of Illumination Engr, Tokyo. Member: JPA, JSAP. Research on vision and flourescent lighting. M

ASHIDA, Prof. Noboru. Dept. of Educ. Psych, Tokyo Univ. of Liberal Arts and Educ, Koganei, Tokyo. b. 25 Jan 1910 Taipei, Taiwan, China. Bungakushi '34 Univ. of Tokyo, Japan. ASST. PROF, Tokyo Univ. of Liberal Arts and Educ. Member: JPA, JSAP, JAEP. Teaching, research, educational psychology; perception and expression in children. M

ATAKA, Prof. Koji. Dept. of Genl. Educ, Kyushu Univ, Otsubo-Machi, Fukuoka. b. 2 Jan 1904 Wakayama-Ken. Bungakushi '29 Kyoto Univ, Japan. PROF. of PSYCH, Kyushu Univ. Member: JPA, Kyushu Psych. Assn. Research, teaching; adjustment, motivation, feeling and emotion. M

AYA, Prof. Tetsuichi. Dept. of Psych, Miyazaki Univ, Miyazaki. b. 28 Nov 1897 Kagawa. Bungakushi '32 Hiroshima Univ, Japan. PROFESSOR, Miyazaki Univ. Member: JPA, JAEP. Teaching, research; needs and personality based on sex differences. M

AZEGAMI, Prof. Hisao. Dept. of Educ, Niigata Univ, 2 Asahimachi, Niigatashi. b. 29 July 1896 Niigataken. Bungakushi '38 Tokyo Bunrika Univ, Japan. PROF. of VOCAT. GUID, Niigata Univ. Member: JPA, JSAP, Japan Vocat. Guid. Assn. Teaching, administration, guidance; industrial psychology, vocational guidance. M

AZUMA, Hiroshi. Dept. of Educ. Psych, Univ. of Tokyo, Bunkyo-ku, Tokyo. b. 3 Feb 1926 Tokyo. Bungakushi '49 Univ. of Tokyo, Japan. ASSISTANT, Univ. of Tokyo; LECT. in EDUC. PSYCH, Shirayuri Jr. Coll, Tokyo. Member: JPA, JAEP, Jap. Socy. for Animal Psych. Research, teaching, educational psychology; human learning and thinking, classical conditioning, relation of perception to experience, motivation, and personality variables. M

AZUMA, Mrs. Yasuko. 747 Nakano-Jutaku, Ekimaye-6, Nakanoku, Tokyo. b. 6 June 1923 Tokyo. Bungakushi '49 Univ. of Tokyo, Japan. LECT. in PSYCH, Tokyo Woman's Christian Coll, 3-124 Iogi, Sugi-

nami-ku, Tokyo. Member: JPA. Research, teaching, educational psychology; child's reactions to frustration, personality dynamics, projective techniques, psychotherapy. F

BEPPU, Dr. Akira. Dept. of Neuropsychiat, Kansai-Rosai Hosp, Imakita, Amagasaki, Hyogo. b. 4 Mar 1922 Osaka. Igakushi '43 Osaka Univ, Japan. DIRECTOR, Dept. of Neurpsychiat, Kansai-Rosai Hosp; DIRECTOR, Ment. Hyg. Clin, Kobe City. Member: JPA, SCP, JAP. Assn. of Psyciat. and Neur. Research, clinical analysis, consulting, clinical practice; visual perception, projective techniques, attitude measurement. M

CHIBA, Prof. Mochitaka. 1070 Uedajutaku, Morioka, Iwate. b. 1 Jan 1909 Esashi. Bungakushi '45 Nihon Univ, Japan. ASST. PROF, Iwate Univ, Ueda, Morioka. Member: JSAP. Teaching, applied and educational psychology; learning theory in plastic arts, perception of three dimensional forms, psychology of art. M

CHIBA, Prof. Tanenari. Dept. of Psych, Nihon Univ, Kanda, Tokyo. b. 21 Sept 1883 Miyagi. Bungakuhakushi '22 Kyoto Univ, Japan. PROFESSOR, Nihon Univ. Member: JPA, JSAP. Teaching, research; psychology of consciousness, „essence-intuition" as research method, Japanese art and Buddhism, *No, Zen, Yuishiki.* M

CHIWA, Prof. Hiroshi. Dept. of Educ, Aoyama-Gakuin Univ, Shibuya-ku, Tokyo. b. 29 June 1892 Okayama. Bungakushi '18 Univ. of Tokyo, Japan. PROF. of PSYCH, Aoyama-Gakuin Univ; LECTURER, Hosei Univ. Member: JPA.. Teaching, research; social perception, group process, learning theory. M

DOI, Aiji. Classif. and Parole Sect, Kanagawa Training Sch. for Boys, Sagamihara-shi, Kanagawa-Ken. b. 10 Feb 1919 Tokyo. Bungakushi, Keio Univ, Japan. CHIEF, Classif. and Parole Sect, Kanagawa Trng. Sch. for Boys. Member: JPA, JSAP. Administration, testing, applied psychology; projective techniques, vocational guidance. M

EGAMI, Prof. Hideo. 2-49 Kitayama-honmachi, Showa-ku, Nagoya. b. 19 July 1896 Suzuka City. Bungakushi '21 Univ. of Tokyo, Japan. PROF. of EDUC. and PSYCH, and DEAN of CHILD WELF. DEPT, Aichi Women's Coll, 3-28 Takada-cho, Nagoya. Member: JPA, JSAP. Teaching, administration, research; infant and adolescent psychology, achievement tests. M

ENDO, Prof. Ôkichi. Dept. of Psych, Doshisha Univ, Kyoto. b. 29 Sept 1905 Tokyo. Bungakushi '33 Kyoto Univ, Japan. PROF. and HEAD, Dept. of Psych, Doshisha Univ. Member: JPA, SCP, Kansai Psych.

Assn. Teaching, administration; personality, learning theory, attitude measurement. M

ENDO, Tatsuo. 45 Yukinoshita, Kamakura, Kanagawa. b. 1 Apr 1916 Asahikawa. Bungakushi '39 Univ. of Tokyo, Japan. CHIEF PSYCH'T, Correctn. Bur, Ministry of Justice, Kasumigaseki, Chiyoda-Ku, Tokyo. Member: JPA, JSAP. Administration, research, applied psychology; causes of delinquency or crime, group counseling, projective techniques. M

FUCHIGAMI, Takashi. Dept. of Educ, Kagoshima Univ, Kagoshima. b. 25 July 1909 Kagoshima. Bungakushi '31 Tokyo Bunrika Univ, Japan. PROF. of PSYCH, Kagoshima Univ. Member: JPA, JAEP. Teaching, research, educational psychology; social attitudes, group process. M

FUJIHIRA, Miss Kazuko. Sapporo Juvenile Court, Sapporo. b. 24 Feb 1924 Tokyo. Bungakushi '49 Univ. of Tokyo, Japan. PROBAT. OFF, Sapporo Juv. Ct. Member: JPA, Hokkaido Psych. Assn, Jap. Socy. for Animal Psych. Testing, research, case work with juvenile delinquents; learning theory. F

FUJII, Prof. Etsuo. 1425 Shimoshakujii Nerima-Ku, Tokyo. b. 29 Sept 1919 Tokyo. Bungakushi '42 Univ. of Tokyo, Japan. ASST. PROF. of PSYCH, Kanto Jr. Coll, Narushima, Tatebayashi-shi, Gunmaken. Member: JPA, JSAP, Jap. Educ. Assn. Teaching educational psychology and testing, research; relationship of aptitudes, education and achievement. M

FUJIMOTO, Prof. Kihachi. Dept. of Sociol, Rikkyo Univ, Ikebukuro, Tokyo. b. 20 Apr 1910 Kure. Bungakushi '34 Kyoto Univ, Japan. PROF. of VOCAT. GUID, Rikkyo Univ. Member: JPA, JSAP, Japan Socy. of Vocat. Guid. Industrial psychology, guidance, teaching; occupational information and vocational counseling. M

FUJINO, Fujitoshi. Dept. of Psych, Kumamoto Univ, Kurokami-machi, Kumamoto. b. 16 Apr 1921 Oita. Bungakushi '50 Tokyo Bunrika Univ, Japan. ASSISTANT, Kumamoto Univ. Member: JPA, JSAP, Kyushu Psych. Assn. Teaching, research, guidance; ridigity in personality. M

FUJINO, Prof. Takeshi. Dept. of Psych, Hokkaido Univ. of Liberal Arts and Educ, Sapporo City. b. 30 Mar 1912 Karafuto. Bungakushi '46 Hiroshima Bunrika Univ, Japan. ASST. PROF, Hokkaido Univ. of Liberal Arts and Educ. Member: JPA, JAEP. Teaching, research, psychotherapy; clinical psychology, mechanisms of anxiety. M

FUJISAWA, Prof. Shigeru. Dept. of Psych, Kyushu Univ, Hakozaki, Fukuoka. b. 25 Mar 1903 Nagano. Bungakushi '26

Univ. of Tokyo, Japan. PROFESSOR, Kyushu Univ. Member: JPA, Jap. Socy. of Ethnology. Teaching, research; personality tests. M

FUJISAWA, Shinshitchi. Hachioji Medical Prison, Koyasu-cho, Hachioji City, Tokyo. b. 22 Apr 1903 Oita Prefecture. Bungakushi '31 Nippon Univ, Japan. CHIEF, Classif. Sect, Hachioji Med. Prison. Member: JPA, JSAP, Jap. Assn. of Correctl. Med. Testing, psychological classification and rehabilitation of prisoners, research; psychometry in parole procedure. M

FUJISAWA, Taiichi. 303 Nitto Apt, Shimonakakita, Konakanomachi, Hachinoeshi, Aomoriken. b. 20 june 1923 Tokyo. Bungakushi '46 Univ. of Tokyo, Japan. MEMBER, Labor Sect, Nitto Kagaku Kogyo, Hachinoe Workshop, Aomoriken. Member: JPA. Industrial psychology, testing, research in labor policy; mental tests, personnel ratings, job analysis, morale surveys. M

FUJITA, Kakuya. Ground Self Defense Forces (GSDF), Kasumigaseki Chiyoda-ku, Tokyo. b. 15 June 1923 Gunma. Bungakushi '46 Nihon Univ, Japan. CHIEF of APTITUDE TSTNG, Adjutant General Sect, GSDF. Member: JSAP. Personnel psychology; research on personnel classification. M

FUJITA, Osamu. Dept. of Psych, Tokyo Univ. of Educ, 24 Otuka-kubōmachi, Bunkyo-ku, Tokyo. b. 1 Mar 1928 Kyoto. Bungaku-syushi '55 Tokyo Univ, Japan. GRAD. STD, Tokyo Univ. Member: JPA, Jap. Socy. for Animal Psych. Research; learning theory, perception, physiological bases of learning. M

FUJITA, Prof. Shōken. Liberal Arts Coll. of Wakayama Univ, Wakayama-shi. b. 4 Dec 1914 Wakayama-Ken. Bungakushi '37 Univ. of Tokyo, Japan. ASST. PROF. of EDUC. PSYCH, Wakayama Univ. Member: JPA. Teaching, research, consulting; personality disorders, home education in a rural community. M

FUJITA, Yasushi. 134 Minamisawa-gakuenmachi, Kurume-mura, Tokyo. b. 6 Sept 1911 Yokosuka. Rigakushi '36 Hokkaido Univ, Japan. TCHR. of SCI. and MATH, Kurume Middle Sch, Tokyo. Member: JPA, Jap. Socy. for Animal Psych. Teaching, research, testing; history of science, mathematical methods in scientific research. M

FUJITO, Mrs. Setsu. Neuropsychiat. Clinic, Osaka Univ. Hosp, Fukushima, Osaka. b. 5 May 1923 Kochi Prefecture. Igakushi '50 Osaka Med. Coll, Japan. ASST. in NEUROPSYCHIAT, Osaka Univ. Member: SCP. Research, psychotherapy, clinical practice; projective techniques. F

FUJIWARA, Kietsu. Noma Inst. of Educ, Otowa, Bunkyo, Tokyo. b. 24 June 1924 Tokyo. Bungakushi '50 Tokyo Bunrika Univ, Japan. RES. STAFF, Noma Inst. of Educ. Member: JPA, JSAP. Research, teaching, guidance; personality formation in adolescence. M

FUKUDA, Kosho. Shiga Br. of the Tokyo Inst. for Psychoanal, Kanaya Koracho, Takamiyakyoku. b. 23 Dec 1912 Shiga Prefecture. Bungakushi '37 Ryukoku Univ, Japan. DIRECTOR, Cen. Child Guid. Clin. of Shiga Prefecture, Higashiura Ichibancho, Ohtsu; LECTURER, Coll. of Shiga Prefecture; DIRECTOR, Children's Sect, Tokyo Inst. for Psychoanal. Member: JPA, JSAP, SCP. Psychotherapy, research, teaching; child psychoanalysis. M

FUKADA, Naohiko. 521 Fushoku Jyutaku, Horikawa-Kamichojyamachi, Kamigyoku, Kyoto. b. 4 June 1923 Osaka. Bungakushi '50 Doshisha Univ, Japan. CHIEF CLIN. PSYCH'T, Fushimi Child Guid. Clin, Butaicho, Fushimiku, Kyoto; CHIEF CLIN. PSYCH'T, Maizuru Child Guid. Clin, Kyoto. Member: JPA, SCP, Kansai Psych Assn. Psychological testing and diagnosis, research; drawing and painting as projective techniques. M

FUKUI, Mrs. Ikuko. Osaka Chu-o Jido Sodansho, 38 Ikutamamaecho, Tennoji, Osaka. b. 15 Sept 1927 Shizuoka. Igakushi '50 Kansai Med. Coll, Japan. STAFF PSYCHIATRIST, Child Guid. Clin, Osaka. Member: SCP, Kansai, Psych. Assn. Child guidance, psychotherapy, research; projective techniques. F

FUKUSHIMA, Prof. Masaji. Dept. of Psych, Hokkaido Univ. of Liberal Arts and Educ, Iwamizawa, Hokkaido. b. 1 Jan 1915 Sapporo. Bungakushi '48 Hiroshima Univ, Japan. ASST. PROF, Hokkaido Univ. of Liberal Arts and Educ. Member: JPA, JAEP. Research, teaching, educational psychology; child development in perception, attitude, intelligence. M

FUKUTOMI, Toshimitsu. Jono Medical Prison, Kokura City. b. 27 Apr 1925 Nagasaki. Bungakushi '50 Tokyo Bunrika Univ, Japan. CHIEF, First Med. Div, Jono Med. Prison; EDITOR, *Kyushu Correctional Education.* Member: JPA, Japan Socy. of Grp. Dynam, Jap. Assn. of Correctl. Med. Administration, clinical practice, research; psychotherapy and its application in correctional institutions, intensive counseling with personality disorders. M

FUNATSU, Takayuki. Dept. of Psych, Kyushu Univ, Fukuoka. b. 25 Feb 1925 Fukuoka. Bungakushi '48 Kyushu Univ, Japan. INSTRUCTOR, Kyushu Univ. Member: JPA. Research, teaching; comparison process in judgment of stimuli. M

FURU, Takeo. 952 Kichijyoji, Musashino City, Tokyo. b. 3 Mar 1907 Tokushima. Bungakushi '33 Kyoto Univ, Japan. RES. WRKR, Radio and TV Culture Res. Inst, NHK, Minato, Tokyo. Member: JPA, JSAP. Measuring educational value of radio and television, research, teaching; mass communication, audio -visual methods, attitude measurement. M

FURUHATA, Prof. Yasuyoshi. Dept. of Liberal Arts, Fukushima Univ, Fukushima. b. 24 Mar 1910 Fukushima. Bungakushi '42 Tokyo Bunrika Univ, Japan. PROF. of PSYCH, Fukushima Univ. Member: JPA, JSAP. Teaching, research; social status and attitudes, educational psychology. M

FUSE, Kuniyuki. Dept. of Psychiat, Kitano Hosp, Nishi-ogimachi, Kita-Ku, Osaka. b. 11 Apr 1926 Osaka. Igakushi '49 Kyoto Univ, Japan. STAFF PSYCHIATRIST, Kitano Hosp. Member: SCP, Jap. Psychiat. Assn. Consulting, clinical practice, clinical analysis, psychotherapy; psychodynamics of schizophrenia in childhood. M

GOTŌ, Prof. Kinjūrō. Osaka Univ. of Econ, Higashi-yodogawa, Osaka. b. 9 Sept 1922 Tokyo. Bungakushi '44 Kyoto Univ, Japan. PROF. of PSYCH, Osaka Univ. of Econ. Member- JPA. Research, teaching, testing; social psychology of adolescence. M

GOTO, Prof. Koki. Dept. of Psych, Kagoshima Univ, Kagoshima. b. 3 Mar 1894 Furukawa. Bungakushi '19 Univ. of Tokyo, Japan. PROFESSOR, Kagoshima Univ. Member: JPA. Teaching, research; psychology in everyday life. M

GOTO, Prof. Toyoharu. Dept. of Educ, Kokugakuin Univ, Shibuya, Tokyo. b. 1 Jan 1913 Kumamoto. Bungakushi '36 Univ. of Tokyo, Japan. PROF. of EDUC. PSYCH, Kokugakuin Univ. Member: JPA. Teaching, research, educational psychology; counseling techniques, aptitude tests, group process. M

GOTO, Prof. Yoichi. Dept. of Educ. Psych, Osaka Univ. of Liberal Arts and Educ, Tennoji, Osaka. b. 1 July 1912 Nara. Bungakushi '41 Univ. of Tokyo, Japan. ASST. PROF, Osaka Univ. of Liberal Arts and Educ. Member: JPA, JSAP. Teaching, research, administration; perceptual defense, dynamics of perception. M

HACHIYA, Prof. Kei. Dept. of Pedagogy, Osaka City Univ, Sumiyoshi, Osaka. b. 23 Jan 1920 Osaka. Bungakushi '41 Kyoto Univ, Japan. ASST. PROF, Osaka City Univ. Member: JPA, JAEP. Teaching, research, guidance; group dynamics in family and classroom. M

HAGINO, Prof. Genichi. Dept. of Psych, Hiroshima Univ, Higashisenda-machi, Hiroshima. b. 25 Apr 1913 Yahata. Bungakushi '36 Univ. of Tokyo, Japan. ASST. PROF, Hiroshima Univ. Member: JPA, JSAP. Research, taeching, applied psychology; depth perception, feeling and emotion. M

HAMANAKA, Miss Tadaka. 7 chome, Nishisuminoecho, Sumiyoshiku, Osaka. b. 19 Apr 1926 Wakayama. Igakushi '43 Osaka Univ, Japan. ASST. in NEUROPSYCHIAT, Osaka Univ. Member: JPA, SCP. Research, testing, psychotherapy; projective techniques. F

HAMANO, Rokuichiro. Hachimancho 24, Hachioji, Tokyo. b. 27 Nov 1908 Koriyama. Igakushi '32 Keio Univ, Japan. HEAD PHYS, Tamasogo Hosp, Tokyo. Member: JPA, Jap. Assn. of Psychiat. and Neur. Clinical practice, consulting, testing, psychotherapy. M

HARA, Keishiro. 500-6 Ujinamachi, Hiroshima. b. 9 June 1906 Tokyo. Bungakushi '33 Kyoto Univ, Japan. CHIEF, Hiroshima Juvenile Classif. Off, Ujinamachi 477, Hiroshima. Member: JPA, Kansai Psych. Assn, Hiroshima Clin. Psych. Assn. Testing and classification of juvenile delinquents; use of projective techniques for prevention of juvenile delinquency, and in guidance work with juvenile delinquents. M

HARA, Prof. Yoshio. Aichi Univ. of Liberal Arts and Educ, Daikocho, Nagoya. b. 4 Jan 1903 Yamaguchi. Bungakushi '33 Kyoto Univ, Japan. PROF. of PSYCH, Aichi Univ. of Liberal Arts and Educ. Member: JPA. Teaching; perception of time. M

HARADA, Dr. Kazuhiko. Kobe Family Court, 3 Aratacho, Hyogo-ku, Kobe. b. 5 Apr 1918. Igakuhakushi '53 Osaka Univ, Japan. PSYCHIATRIST, Kobe Family Court. Member: JPA, Jap. Assn. of Psychiat. and Neur. Medical consulting, psychotherapy, research; psychoneuroses.M

HASEGAWA, Prof. Mitsugi. Dept. of Psych, Nihon Univ, Kanda, Misaki-cho, Tokyo. b. 19 Sept 1897 Chigasaki. Bungakushi '32 Nihon Univ, Japan. PROFESSOR, Nihon Univ. Member: JPA, JSAP. Teaching, research, applied psychology; personality adjustment, human relations, human ecology. M

HASHIMOTO, Hitoshi. 1-22 Zoshigayamachi, Toshima-ku, Tokyo. b. 28 Nov Tokyo. Bungakushi '52 Waseda Univ, Japan. STUDENT, Waseda Univ, Tokyo; RES. FELLOW, Japan Color Res. Inst, 1 Akasaka, Fukuyoshi-cho, Minato-ku, Tokyo. Member: JPA, JSAP. Research; electrophysiological phenomena, classical conditioning, visual perception and sensation. M

HASHIMOTO, Prof. Juji. Yokohama Univ,

Kamakura, Kanagawa. b. 29 June 1908 Shimabara. Bungakushi '38 Tokyo Bunrika Univ, Japan. ASST. PROF. of EDUC. PSYCH, Yokohama Univ. Member: JPA, JSAP. Teaching, research; achievement tests and learning. M

HASUO, Prof. Chimato. Dept. of Psych, Ritsumeikan Univ, Kyoto. b. 10 Mar 1911 Kagoshima. Bungakushi '36 Kyoto Univ, Japan. PROFESSOR, Ritsumeikan Univ. Member: JPA. Teaching, research, industrial psychology; industrial fatigue, morale, accident prevention. M

HATANO, Prof. Isoko. 65 Otsuka-machi, Bunkyo-ku, Tokyo. b. 31 Mar 1906 Tokyo. RES. WRKR. in CHILD PSYCH, Aiiku Child Res. Inst, Morioka-cho, Tokyo. Member: JPA, JSAP. Professional writing, guidance, research; the relation between drawings of children and personality. F

HATANO, Prof. Dr. Kanji. Dept. of Educ. Psych, Ochanomizu Univ. for Women, Tokyo. b. 7 Feb 1905 Tokyo. D. Lit, Nihon Univ, Japan. PROFESSOR, Ochanomizu Univ; LECTURER, Tokyo Univ. Member: JPA. Research, teaching, professional writing; psychology of audiovisual materials. M

HATTORI, Kiyoshi. Dept. of Psych, Fukui Univ, Makinoshima, Fukui. b. 31 Aug 1926 Saitama. Bungakushi '48 Waseda Univ, Japan. INSTRUCTOR, Fukui Univ; ADVISOR, Child Guid. Clin, Turuga City. Member: JPA. Research, teaching, guidance; emotional maladjustment and delinquency. M

HAYASAKA, Prof. Taijiro. Dept. of Psych, Rikkyo Univ, Ikebukuro, Tokyo. b. 2 Feb 1923 Sendai. Bungakushi '48 Tohoku Univ, Japan. ASST. PROF, Rikkyo Univ; LECT. in EDUC. PSYCH, St. Lukes Nrsng. Coll; STAFF MEMBER, Rikkyo Psych. and Educ. Cen. Member: JPA. Research, teaching, guidance; social psychological survey, group work, counseling. M

HAYASHI, Prof. Chikio. Inst. of Stat. Math, 1 Azabu-Fujimicho, Minatoku, Tokyo. b. 7 June 1918 Tokyo. Rigakushi '42 Univ. of Tokyo, Japan. PROFESSOR, Inst. of Stat. Math; LECTURER, Tokyo Univ. and Hitotshashi Univ; EDITOR, *Annals and Proceedings, Inst. Stat. Math.* Member: JPA. Statistical research in sociology, psychology, and economics, teaching, consulting; group dynamics, attitude measurement, multivariate analysis. M

HAYASHI, Prof. Keizo. Dept. of Psych, Keio Univ, Mita, Tokyo. b. 19 Aug 1911 Nagoya. Bungakushi '36 Keio Univ, Japan. ASST. PROF, Keio Univ. Member: JPA, JSAP. Research, teaching, consulting, perception and feeling. M

HAYASHI, Prof. Masakuni. Dept. of Educ, Ibaraki Univ, Mito, Ibaraki-Ken. b. 6 Aug 1912 Nagoya. Bungakushi '45 Tokyo Bunrika Univ, Japan. ASST. PROF, Ibaraki Univ. Member: JPA, JSAP. Educational psychology, teaching; personality theory and measurement. M

HAYASHI, Prof. Mikio. Fac. of Educ, Hiroshima Univ, Hiroshima. b. 24 Nov 1914 Mihara. Bungakushi '43 Hiroshima Univ, Japan. ASST. PROF. of PSYCH, Hiroshima. Member: JPA, JAEP. Research, teaching, testing; psychology of aesthetic apperception and art. M

HAYASHI, Prof. Mitsuo. Fac. of Educ, Toyama Univ, Gotuku, Toyama. b. 4 Feb 1912 Uozu. Bungakushi '40 Keizyo Univ, Japan. ASST. PROF. of PSYCH, Toyama Univ. Member: JPA, JAEP. Teaching, research, consulting; educational psychology. M

HAYASHI, Prof. Shigemasa. Dept. of Psych, Hiroshima Univ, Hiroshima. b. 25 Nov 1921 Kobe. Bungakushi '48 Hiroshima Univ, Japan. ASST. PROF, Hiroshima Univ. Member: JPA, JAEP. Research, teaching, guidance; psychometric methods, factor analysis. M

HAYASHI, Dr. Shuzo. Kyoto Shonen Kanbetsusho, Yoshida, Sakyoku, Kyoto. b. 19 Nov 1917 Kobe. Igakuhakushi '55 Kyoto Univ, Japan. CHIEF, Kyoto Shonen Kanbetsusho. Member: JPA, Jap. Assn. of Psychiat. and Neur, Jap. Assn. of Correctl. Med, Jap. Assn. of Race Hyg. Classification of juvenile delinquents, administration, consulting, research; research on twins, projective techniques. M

HAYASHI, Tamotsu. Kyoto Univ. of Liberal Arts and Educ, Koyama, Ono, Kyoto. b. 7 Sept 1919 Kyoto. Bungakushi '47 Tokyo Bunrika Univ, Japan. INSTR. in PSYCH, Kyoto Univ. of Liberal Arts and Educ. Member: JPA, JSAP, Kansai Psych. Assn. Teaching, research, educational psychology; motor and verbal learning. M

HAYASHI, Yoshitoki. 1375 Kaneko-machi, Chofu-shi, Tokyo. b. 17 Nov 1896 Gunma Maebashi. HEAD TEACHER, Chuo Kyosei Kenkyujo, Daikan cho, Tokyo. Member: JPA, JSAP. Teaching; abnormal personality. M

HEMMI, Takemitsu. Psychiat. Clin. of Prison Hosp, Fuchu Prison, Fuchu, Tokyo. b. 8 Mar 1925 Kyoto. Igakushi '49 Kyoto Univ, Japan. PSYCHIAT. OFF, Bur. of Med. Affairs, Prison Hosp, Fuchu Prison; ASST. in PSYCHIAT, Kyoto Univ; EDITOR, *Japanese Journal of Correctional Medicine*. Psychiatric therapy, research, administration; criminal psychopathology, oligophrenia. M

HIDAKA, Hideyuki. Planning Staff Room,

Cen. Railway Training Inst, Jap. Natl. Railways, Ikebukuro, Tokyo. b. 7 Jan 1921 Tokyo. Bungakushi '43 Univ. of Tokyo, Japan. SENIOR LECT, Cen. Railway Trng. Inst. Member: JPA, JSAP, JAEP. Industrial psychology, research, teaching; morale surveys, human relations in industry. M

HIDANO, Prof. Tadashi. Dept. of Educ. Psych, Fac. of Educ, Univ. of Tokyo, Bunkyo-ku, Tokyo. b. 9 July 1920 Tokyo. Bungakushi '43 Univ. of Tokyo, Japan. ASST. PROF, Univ. of Tokyo. Member: JPA, JAEP, Jap. Socy. for Animal Psych. Educational psychology, teaching, research; theoretical foundations of psychological tests, validity of personality tests. M

HIGASHI, Sadao. Nishi Machi 124, Fukuyama. b. 18 Oct 1915 Hiroshima. Bungakushi '45 Hiroshima Bunrika Univ, Japan. INSTRUCTOR, Hiroshima Univ, Fukuyama. Member: JPA, JAEP. Teaching educational psychology, research, guidance; adolescent psychology, ego enhancement, attitude. M

HIGUCHI, Dr. Kokichi. 1076 Yoyogioyama-cho, Shibuya-ku, Tokyo. b. 1 July 1919 Niigata. Igakuhakushi '54 Univ. of Tokyo, Japan. CHIEF, Med. and Classif. Dept, Tokyo Med. Reform, Hatagaya, Tokyo; ASST. DIR, Med. and Classif. Sect, Correctl. Bur, Ministry of Justice; LECTURER, Tokyo Univ. of Educ; ED. in CHIEF, *Journal of Correctional Medicine*. Member: JSAP, Jap. Assn. of Psychiat. and Neur. Clinical and research work, teaching; juvenile delinquency, classification of criminals, group psychotherapy. M

HIGUCHI, Prof. Shingo. Dept. of Educ. Psych, Fac. of Educ, Tohoku Univ, Katahiracho, Sendai. b. 26 Oct 1920 Tokyo. Bungakushi '44 Univ. of Tokyo, Japan. ASST. PROF, Tohoku Univ. Member: JPA, JAEP. Research, teaching, educational psychology, testing; educational evaluation, vocational guidance. M

HIKAMI, Taisuke. Komuin Shikusha RA 47, 5-181, Kitaurawa, Urawa-shi. b. 25 Apr 1918 Okayama. Bungakushi '41 Univ. of Tokyo, Japan. INVESTIGATOR, Tokyo Family Court, Hibiya, Tokyo. Member: JPA, JSAP. Counseling, guidance, testing, research; human relations. M

HIRAI, Hisashi. Dept. of Psych, Waseda Univ, Totsuka-machi, Shinjuku-ku, Tokyo. b. 10 Aug 1928 Tokyo. Bungakushi '53, Bungakushushi '55 Waseda Univ, Japan. STUDENT and RES. WRKR, Waseda Univ. Member: JPA, Jap. Socy. for Animal Psych. Research, teaching; learning theory, comparative conditioned neuroses. M

HIRAI, Prof. Nobuyoshi. Dept. of Child Welfare, Ochanomizu Women's Univ, Bunkyo-ku, Tokyo. b. 30 Mar 1919

Tokyo. Bungakushi '41, Igakushi '44 Univ. of Tokyo, Japan. ASST. PROF. of CHILD WELF, Ochanomizu Women's Univ; PEDIATRICIAN, Pediatrics Clin, Aiiku Inst, Minatoku, Tokyo. Member: JPA, JSAP, Jap. Pediat. Socy, Jap. Assn. of Psychiat. and Neur. Teaching, research; child development, child mental health. M

HIRANUMA, Ryo. 133 Tsukimidai, Hodogayaku, Yokohama. b. 30 Jan 1899 Yokohama. Bungakushi '33 Tokyo Bunrika Univ, Japan. INSTR. in EDUC, Tokyo Univ. of Educ, Ostuka, Tokyo. EDITOR, *Educational Measurement* of the Appl. Educ. Inst. Member: JPA, JSAP. Education of exceptional children, teaching, research; educational measurement, achievement and intelligence tests. M

HIRAO, Yasushi. Obihiro Prison, Midorigaoka, Obihiro. b. 4 Dec 1911 Osaka. Bungakushi '36 Kyoto Univ, Japan. CHIEF of PRISON, Obihiro Prison. Member: JPA, SCP. Administration, research; criminal acts and their causes. M

HIRASAWA, Ryosuke. 484 Higashinaebocho, Sapporo, Hokkaido. b. 23 Oct 1919 Hokkaido. Bungakushi '46 Tokyo Bunrika Univ, Japan. HEAD, Dept. of Classif, Sapparo Prison, Hokkaido. Member: JPA, JSAP. Administration, testing, consulting; attitude measurement, projective techniques, group process. M

HIROHASHI, Prof. Satoshi. Yamaguchi Women's Coll, Miyano, Yamaguchi. b. 24 May 1903 Niigata. Bungakushi '26 Univ. of Tokyo, Japan. PROF. of PSYCH, Yamaguchi Women's Coll. Member: JPA. Administration, teaching, research; child psychology. M

HIROKAWA, Yasuo. Nerimaku Minamicho 4-6193, Tokyo. b. 2 May 1920 Niigata. Bungakushi '44 Hosei Univ, Japan. TECH. CONSULT, Tokyo Metrop. Central Child Welf. Center, Shinjukuku Kawadacho, Tokyo. Member: JPA, JSAP. Clinical practice, consulting, guidance. M

HIROTA, Prof. Kimiyoshi. Dept. of Psych, Saikyo Univ, Kyoto. b. 16 June 1925 Yokkaichi. Bungakushi '50 Kyoto Univ, Japan. ASST. PROF, Saikyo Univ. Member: JPA, Kansai Psych. Assn. Teaching, research, professional writing; group dynamics, communication, culture and personality. M

HIWATARI, Dr. Shiro. 203 Kamiokajutaku, Motoyama Cho, Higashinadaku, Kobe. b. 7 July 1918 Kagoshima. Igakuhakushi '54 Osaka Univ, Japan. ASST. PROF. of HLTH. EDUC, Kobe Univ, Sumiyoshi, Kobe. Member: JPA. Research, clinical practice, teaching; psychosomatic medicine. M

HOMMA, Hiromitsu. 2-453 Marukodori, Kawasaki. b. 30 Mar 1924 Tokyo. Bunga-

kushi '47 Waseda Univ, Japan. ASST. DIR, Res. Dept, Dentsu Adv. Ltd, 7-1 Nishi-Ginza, Tokyo; LECT. in SOC. PSYCH, Japan Women's Univ. Member: JPA. Administration, market research, teaching; attitude measurement, public opinion, market surveys. M

HONJÔ, Prof. Seiji. Child Study Course, Osaka Shoin Women's Coll, Fuse-shi, Osaka. b. 7 Jan 1879 Himeji. Bungakushi '07 Univ. of Tokyo, Japan. PROF. of PSYCH, Osaka Shoin Women's Coll. Member JPA, JAEP. Teaching, research; child development. M

HORI, Prof. Dr. Baiten. 89 Yamasato-machi, Nagasaki City. b. 12 May 1887 Yamagata. PH.D '16 Clark Univ, USA. PROF. of PSYCH, Kwassui Women's Jr. Coll, Higashiyamate, Nagasaki. Member: Kyushu Psych. Assn. Teaching; child psychology. M

HORI, Prof. Kaname. 5 3-chome, Siroki-cho, Chikusa-ku, Nagoya. b. 13 July 1907 Wakayama. Igakuhakushi '42 Nagoya Univ, Japan. ASST. PROF. of PSYCHIAT. and CHIEF, Child Div, Psychiat. Clin, Nagoya Univ. Sch. of Med, Tsurumaicho, Showa-ku, Nagoya; LECT. in MENT. HYG, Aichi Univ. of Liberal Arts and Educ. Member: Tokai Psych. Assn. Clinical practice, research, teaching; personality formation. M

HORI, Katsujiro. Higashino, Konan City, Aichi Prefecture. b. 3 Dec 1887 Osaka. Bungakushi '16 Univ. of Tokyo, Japan. LECT. in PSYCH, Aichi-Gakuin Coll, Kusumotocho Chikusa-ku, Nagoya. Member: JPA. Teaching, educational psychology, guidance. M

HORIBATA, Prof. Takaharu. Dept. of Psych, Aichi Univ. of Liberal Arts and Educ, Higashi, Nagoya. b. 16 Jan 1925 Kobe. Bungakushi '48 Hiroshima Bunrika Univ, Japan. ASST. PROF, Aichi Univ. of Liberal Arts and Educ. Member: JPA, Tokai Psych. Assn. Teaching, educational psychology, research, testing; concept formation in children. M

HORIIKE, Shinichi. Izumozi-Matunoshita-Cho 6, Kitaku, Kyoto. b. 16 July 1911 Kyoto. CHIEF, Kyoto Juv. Reform. Off, Kamikyo, Kyoto. Member: JPA, Kansai Psych. Assn. Testing and clinical analysis, guidance, research; projective techniques. M

HORIKAWA, Naoyoshi. Anal. and Res. Sect, The Asahi Press, Yurakucho, Tokyo. b. 5 May 1911 Kyoto. Bungakushi '35 Kyoto Univ, Japan. STAFF MEMBER, Anal. and Res. Sect, The Asahi Press; LECTURER, St. Paul Univ, Tokyo; LECTURER Sophia Univ, Tokyo. Member: JPA, JSAP. Research, teaching, professional writing; interviewing, mass communication, social psychology. M

HORIUCHI, Prof. Masazo. Dept. of Physical Educ, Hitotutsubashi Univ, Kodaira, Tokyo. b. 8 Oct 1917 Yamanashi. Bunkushi '46 Tokyo Bunrika Univ, Japan. ASST. PROF. in PHYSICAL EDUC, Hitotsubashi Univ. Member: JSAP. Psychological research in physical education, teaching; personality. M

HORIUCHI, Prof. Toshio. Dept. of Psych, Tokyo Univ. of Liberal Arts and Educ, Setagaya, Tokyo. b. 26 July 1911 Takaoka. Bungakushi '37 Univ. of Tokyo, Japan. ASST. PROF. in EDUC. PSYCH, Tokyo Univ. of Liberal Arts and Educ. Member: JPA, JSAP. Teaching, research in educational psychology, testing, consulting; adjustment in learning process, mental hygiene of the teacher. M

HORIUCHI, Prof. Yasuto. Dept. of Psych, Kumamoto Commercial Univ, Ooetoroku, Kumamoto. b. 20 Aug 1917 Okazaki. Bungakushi '41 Univ. of Tokyo, Japan. ASST. PROF. Kumamoto Commercial Univ. Member: JPA. Teaching; Pavlov's theory of conditioned reflex. M

HOZAWA, Prof. Ichiro. Dept. of Psych, Tsuda Coll, Kokubunji, Tokyo. b. 3 Sept 1917 Tokyo. Bungakushi '39 Univ. of Tokyo, Japan. ASST. PROF, Tsuda Coll. Member: JPA, JSAP. Teaching, research, student guidance, testing; personality tests. M

IBUKIYAMA, Taro. Inst. for Sci. of Labor, Soshigaya, Setagaya, Tokyo. b. 23 Oct 1904 Tokyo. Bungakushi '29 Kyoto Univ, Japan. RES. HEAD, Second Div. of Psych, Inst. for Sci. of Labor. Member: JPA, JSAP. Laboratory and field work in industrial psychology, testing; attitude measurement, group process, group dynamics. M

ICHIKAWA, Noriyoshi. Dept. of Psych, Aichi Univ. of Liberal Arts and Educ, Myodaigi, Okazaki. b. 24 Aug 1926 Toyokawa. Bungakushushi '56 Nagoya Univ, Japan. ASSISTANT, Aichi Univ. of Liberal Arts and Educ. Member: JPA, JSAP. Research, teaching, testing; shape perception, group dynamics. M

ICHIMURA, Kimimasa. 43 Shimoimamachi, Kanazawa. b. 14 Sept 1926 Kanazawa. Igakushi '49 Chiba Univ, Japan. PSYCHIASTRIST, Kanazawa Psychiat. Hosp, 15 Nagasakamachi, Kanazawa. Member: JSAP, Jap. Assn. of Psychiat. and Neur. Psychotherapy, testing, clinical analysis; projective techniques. M

IGARI, Ryo. Dept. of Educ, Ibaraki Univ, Mito. b. 20 Feb 1909 Fukushima. Bungakushi '39 Nihon Univ, Japan. ASST. PROF, Ibaraki Univ. Member: JPA, JSAP. Teaching, research, testing; effect of sound on animal growth. M

IHARA, Hodō. Shinjukuku Kikuicho 61, Tokyo. b. 11 Oct 1906 Saitama. Bungakushi '30 Hosei Univ, Japan. TECH. CONSULT, Tokyo Metrop. Central Child Welf. Center, Shinjukuku Kawadacho, Tokyo. Member: JPA. Clinical practice, consulting, testing; social perception. M

IIDA, Jun-o. Dept. of Psych, Otani Women's Coll, Kyoritsu Street, Abeno Ku, Osaka. b. 22 Sept 1902 Kamo. Bungakushi '28 Kyoto Univ, Japan. PROFESSOR, Otani Women's Coll. Member: JPA, Kansai Psych. Assn. Research, teaching; student interests and desires. M

IINUMA, Prof. Ryuon. 2 Nabeyacho, Higashiku, Nagoya. b. 22 June 1888 Gifu-ken. Bungakushi '16 Univ. of Tokyo, Japan. PROF. of PSYCH, Minobusan Univ, Minobusan, Yamanashi; LECTURER, Shizuoka Coll. of Pharmacy. Member: JPA, Tokai Psych. Assn. Teaching, research, administration; religious beliefs of the Japanese, Doppeler effect, mentality of the feral child of Formosa. M

IKEDA, Bunnosuke. Ryujo Kindergarten Teachers Coll, Meigetsu, Nagoya. b. 7 July 1902 Yokkaichi. Bungakushi '27 Univ. of Tokyo, Japan. INSTR. in PSYCH, Ryujo Kindergarten Teachers Coll. Member: JPA. Teaching, research, educational psychology; achievement tests, attitude measurement. M

IKEDA, Prof. Sadami. Dept. of Educ, Saga Univ, Akamatsumachi, Saga. b. 23 Oct 1927 Imari. Bungakushi '50 Hiroshima Bunrika Univ, Japan. ASST. PROF. in PSYCH, Saga Univ. Member: JPA, Kyushu Psych. Assn, Jap. Grp. Dynam. Assn. Teaching, child psychology, research, educational psychology; learning theory, attitude and emotion in learning. M

IKEDA, Miss Yoshiko. Dept. of Child Ment. Hlth, Natl. Inst. of Ment. Hlth, Konodai, Ichikawa, Chiba. b. 15 Oct 1924 Tokyo. Igakushi '46 Tokyo Women's Med. Coll, Japan. TECH. OFF, Ministry of Hlth. and Welf, Natl. Inst. of Ment. Hlth; CONSULT. in PEDIAT, Tokyo Saiseikai Cen. Hosp. Member: JPA. Research in child psychiatry, psychotherapy, consulting, clinical practice; play therapy, research on effects of maternal deprivation. F

IKEGAMI, Prof. Kihachiro. Dept. of Psych, Takada Branch Sch, Coll. of Educ, Niigata Univ, Takada City. b. 30 Sept 1918 Nagano. Bungakushi '42 Tokyo Bunrika Univ, Japan. ASST. PROF, Niigata Univ. Member: JPA, JSAP. Research, teaching educational psychology, guidance; psychology of arithmetic, achievement tests, development of exceptional children. M

IKEGUCHI, Hisao. 462 Kusugami-Cho, Takamatsu. b. 27 May 1899 Ijushi. Bungakushi '26 Univ. of Tokyo, Japan.

DIRECTOR, Correctn. and Rehab. Off., Takamatu Dist, 385 Nakano-Cho, Takamatu; DIRECTOR, Res. and Trng. Inst. for Correctn. and Rehab. Officials. Member: JPA. Administration, teaching; learning theory, social perception, group process. M

IKEMI, Dr. Takeshi. Res. Inst. for Racial Science, 2337 Kotaketyo, Nerima-Ku, Tokyo. b. 7 Dec 1907 Oita. Igakuhakushi '39 Nagoya Univ, Japan. PRESIDENT, Res. Inst. for Racial Sci. Member: JPA, JSAP. Administration, research. M

IKEEUCHI, Prof. Hajime. Kojimachi 5-7, Chiyodaku, Tokyo. b. 3 May 1920 Tokyo. Bungakushi '44 Univ. of Tokyo, Japan. ASST. PROF, Inst. of Journalism, Univ. of Tokyo, Bunkyoku, Tokyo. Member: JPA, Jap. Socy. for Animal Psych. Research, Teaching, professional writing; mass communication, public opinion. M

IKUZAWA, Masao. 50 Momoyama-Mizuno-sakon-Nishi-Cho, Fushimi-ku, Kyoto. b. 18 Sept 1927 Kyoto. Bungakushi '50 Kyoto Univ, Japan. INSTR. in PSYCH, Osaka City Univ, Awazanakadori, Nishi-ku, Osaka; LECT. in PSYCH, Kyoto Women's Coll. Member: JPA, Kwansai Psych. Assn. Teaching, research, testing; development of perception, child development, baby tests. M

IMADA, Prof. Megumi. Kwansei Gakuin Univ, Nishinomiya. b. 26 Aug 1894 Bofu. Bungakuhakushi '57 Univ. of Tokyo, Japan. PROF. and HEAD, Dept. of Psych, Kwansei Gakuin Univ; LECTURER, Kyoto Univ; EDITOR, *Japanese Journal of Psychology*; ED. BD, *Journal of General Psychology* (USA). Member: JPA, JSAP, SCP. Teaching, administration, research; personality and development, history of theoretical psychology. M

IMAJIMA, Hiroshi. Otaru Socy. of Appl. Psych, 53 Shiomidai, Otaru, Hokkaido. b. 7 Aug 1918 Otaru. Hogakushi '42 Nihon Univ, Japan. PRESIDENT, Otaru Socy. of Appl. Psych. Member: Hokkaido Psych. Assn, Otaru, Socy. of Appl. Psych. Administration, research, consulting. M

IMAMURA, Goro. Dept. of Psych, Univ. of Tokyo, Bunkyo-ku, Tokyo. b. 7 Nov 1930 Nagoya. Bungakushushi '55 Univ. of Tokyo, Japan. STUDENT, Univ. of Tokyo. Member: JPA, Jap. Socy. for Animal Psych. Research; learning theory, physiological mechanisms in learning and emotional behavior. M

IMAZAKI, Prof. Hideichi. Wakayama Univ, Wakayama City. b. 1 Nov 1903 Fukuoka. Bungakushi '27 Univ. of Tokyo, Japan. PROF. of SOCIOL, Wakayama Univ. Member: JPA. Teaching, research, consulting; friendship, conjugal relationship and character, personality. M

IMURA, Prof. Tsunero. Dept. of Psychiat, Nihon Univ, Itabashi, Tokyo. b. 17 Sept 1906 Choshi. Igakuhakushi '41 Univ. of Tokyo, Japan. PROFESSOR, Nihon Univ; LECT. in MENT. HLTH, Nippon Women's Univ. Member: Jap. Assn. of Psychiat. and Neur, JSAP. Research, teaching, administration, psychotherapy; psychopathology, psychodynamics of schizophrenia, psychoneurosis. M

INAURA. Yasutoshi. 64 Shinkoyo, Nishinomiya-shi, Hyogo-ken. b. 25 Apr 1920 Iga-Ueno. Bungakushi '48 Kyoto Univ, Japan. CHIEF of EXAM. SECT, Osaka Prefectural Central Child Guid. Clin, Ikutamamae-cho, Tennoji-ku, Osaka; LECTURER, Osaka Shoin Women's Univ. Member: JPA, SCP, Kansai Psych. Assn. Testing, consulting, teaching; intelligence tests, feeble-mindedness, projective techniques and the Draw-A-Person test. M

INDOW, Prof. Tarow. Dept. of Psych, Keio Univ, Mita, Shiba, Minato-ku, Tokyo. b. 22 Aug 1923 Tokyo. Bungakushi '45 Keio Univ, Japan. ASST. PROF, Keio Univ. Member: JPA, Psychomet. Socy, Japan Stat. Socy. Research, teaching, testing; mathematical analysis in perception, attitude and intelligence. M

INGU, Akio. 1065 Mihagino, Kokura. b. 28 Jan 1907 Karatsu. Bungakushi '29 Univ. of Tokyo, Japan. CHIEF, Fukuoka Pub. Vocat. Trng. Cen. for Handicapped, Mihagino, Kokura; LECT. in VOCAT. GUID, Higashitsukushi Coll, Kokura. Member: JPA. Administration, research, guidance; projective techniques. M

INOMATA, Prof. Satoru. Fac. of Liberal Arts and Educ, Shiga Univ, Zeze, Otsu. b. 19 Mar 1925 Shimane. Bungakushi '47 Kyoto Univ, Japan. ASST. PROF. of PSYCH, Shiga Univ. Member: JPA, Kansai Psych. Assn. Teaching, research; perception and time errors, personality tests. M

INOUE, Prof. Kazuyoshi. Dept. of Psych, Miyazaki Univ, Hanadono, Miyazaki. b. 21 Dec 1909 Nichinan. Bungakushi '44 Hiroshima Bunrika Univ, Japan. PROFESSOR Miyazaki Univ. Member: JPA, Kyushu Psych. Assn. Teaching, guidance, testing; social perception. M

INUI, Prof. Takasi. Dept. of Educ, Hosei Univ, Fujimi, Tokyo. b. 19 Aug 1911 Tokyo. Bungakushi '35 Hosei Univ, Japan. PROF. of PSYCH, Hosei Univ. Member: JPA, JSAP. Teaching, research, professional writing; mental development, facial expression, audience response. M

IRITANI, Prof. Tomosada. 824 Daitamachi, 2-chome, Setagaya, Tokyo. b. 7 July 1887 Kasugaishi. Bungakushi '16 Univ. of Tokyo, Japan. PROF. of PSYCH, Komazawa Univ, 1-chome, Setagaya, Tokyo. Member:

JPA, JSAP. Teaching, administration, editorial; psychology of adolescence, group process, perception of depth. M

ISAKA, Prof. Yukio. Dept. of Educ, Tokyo Univ. of Educ, Otska-Kubomachi, Bunkyo-Ku, Tokyo. b. 12 Oct 1913 Hitachi-Ohta. Bungakushi '38 Tokyo Bunrika Univ, Japan. ASST. PROF. in GUID. and COUNS, Tokyo Univ. of Educ. Member: JPA, JSAP. Teaching, guidance and counseling, research; clinical counseling for adolescents, remedial treatment of maladjusted children, group guidance. M

ISHIDA, Miss Noko. Kosaka Byoin Mental Hosp, 27 2-chome Eiwa, Fuse. b. 29 Apr 1925 Osaka. Igakushi '47 Osaka Women's Med. Coll, Japan. STAFF PSYCHIATRIST, Kosaka Byoin Ment. Hosp. Member: SCP. Therapy and testing, research, clinical practice; projective techniques. F

ISHIGE, Nagao. 1836 Kichijoji, Musashino City. b. 1 Aug 1922 Tokyo. Bungakushi '44 Univ. of Tokyo, Japan. INVESTIGATOR, Labor Sci. Res. Off, Jap. Natl. Railways, Tabatamachi Kitaku, Tokyo. Member: JPA, JSAP. Industrial and personnel psychology, testing, research on psychological problems of employees; aptitude tests, attitude survey, counseling. M

ISHIGURO, Sanji. 1 1-chome, Ikegami-cho, Nagoya. b. 26 July 1916 Aichi Prefecture. Bungakushi '46 Tokyo Bunrika Univ, Japan. INSTRUCTOR, Nagoya Univ. High Sch, Higashiyoshino-cho, Nagoya. Member: JPA, JSAP. Teaching, research, guidance; psychology of teaching, group learning process. M

ISHIGURO, Prof. Taigi. Maenami, 3-9 Maenami-cho, Higashi-ku, Nagoya. b. 10 Feb 1926 Yokohama. Bungakushi '50 Tokyo Bunrika Univ, Japan. ASST. PROF. of PSYCH, Chubu Soc. Work Jr. Coll, Takikawa-cho, Nagoya; RES. WRKR, Inst. of Human Relat. Member: JPA, JSAP, Tokyo Psych. Assn. Research, teaching, guidance; learning theory, parent-child relationship, personality formation. M

ISHII, Katsumi. Dept. of Psych, Kyushu Univ, Fukuoka. b. 14 Dec 1905 Tokyo. Bungakushi '30 Kyushu Univ, Japan. INSTRUCTOR, Kyushu Univ. Member: JPA. Research, teaching, testing; psychometric methods. M

ISHII, Oshie. Kanagawa Univ, Rokkaku-bashi, Yokohama. b. 28 May 1903 Tokyo. Bungakushi '32 Tokyo Bunrika Univ, Japan. LECT. in PSYCH, Kanagawa Univ. Member: JPA. Teaching, research; depth perception. M

ISHII, Prof. Shunzui. Dept. of Psych, Taisho Univ, Sugamo, Tokyo. b. 12 Apr 1894 Kyoto. Bungakushi '20 Univ. of Tokyo, Japan. PROFESSOR, Taisho Univ; PSYCH.

CONSULT, Tokyo Central Child Welf. Cen. Member: JPA, JSAP. Teaching, research, consulting and guidance, testing; clinical procedures in child guidance. M

ISHII, Sumio. Dept. of Educ. Psych, Okayama Univ, Tsushima, Okayama. b. 2 July 1924 Okayama. Bungakushi '47 Tokyo Bunrika Univ, Japan. ASSISTANT, Okayama Univ. Member: JPA. Teaching, special education, research; projective techniques, education and psychology of mentally handicapped children, frustration and personality. M

ISHII, Tetsuo. Japan Sch. of Soc. Work, Harajuku, Tokyo. b. 15 July 1927 Tokyo. Bungakushi '50 Univ. of Tokyo, Japan. INSTR. in PSYCH, Japan Sch. of Soc. Work. Member: JPA, JSAP. Research, teaching, testing; projective techniques for children. M

ISHIKAWA, Prof. Hideo. Tokyo Coll. of Econ, Kokubunji, Kitatamagun, Tokyo. b. 13 July 1922 Seoul, Korea. Bungakushi '44 Univ. of Tokyo, Japan. ASST. PROF. of PSYCH, Tokyo Coll. of Econ; LECTURER, St. Paul's Univ, Tokyo; INVESTIGATOR, Aiiku Child Welf. Inst, Azabu, Tokyo. Member: JPA, JSAP. Research, teaching, consulting; parent-child relationship, projective techniques, social behavior of young children. M

ISHIKAWA, Prof. Shimeji. Dept. of Psych, Yamanishi Univ, Kofu. Bungakushi '44 Tokyo Bunrika Univ, Japan. PROFESSOR, Yamanashi Univ. Member: JPA, JSAP. Research, teaching, testing; intelligence, personality and achievement tests. M

ISHIKAWA, Toru. Fac. of Educ, Shizuoka Univ, Oiwa, Shizuoka. b. 30 Jan 1919 Tokyo. Bungakushi '42 Tokyo Bunrika Univ, Japan. INSTR. in PSYCH, Shizuoka Univ. Member: JPA, JSAP. Research, teaching, guidance; psychology of adolescence, memory and the structure of stimuli. M

ISIHARA, Prof. Iwataro. Dept. of Psych, Kwansei Gakuin Univ, Uegahara, Nishinomiya. b. 13 Apr 1915 Osaka. Bungakushi '44 Tohoku Univ, Japan. ASST. PROF, Kwansei Gakuin Univ. Member: JPA, Kansai Psych. Assn. Teaching, research; verbal learning, psychology of language. M

ISOGAI, Prof. Nobutaro. Dept. of Educ, Ibaraki Univ, Mito. b. 15 Feb 1902 Gunma-Ken. Bungakushi '36 Tokyo Bunrika Univ, Japan. PROF. of PSYCH, Ibaraki Univ. Member: JPA, JSAP. Research, teaching; learning theory, educational psychology. M

ITAKURA, Yoshitaka. Dept. of Psych, Nihon Univ, Kanda-Misakicho, Tokyo. b. 29 Jan 1906 Tottori. Bungakushi '33 Nihon Univ, Japan. PSYCHOLOGIST, Labor Dept, Otemachi, Tokyo. Research, testing, guidance. M

ITO, Prof. Hiroshi. Osaka Coll. of Soc. Welf, Higasiku, Osaka. b. 15 Oct 1902 Toyohashi. Bungakushi '29 Univ. of Tokyo, Japan. PROF. of PSYCH, Osaka Coll. of Soc. Welf. Member: JPA, Kansai Assn. of Clin. Psych. Teaching, guidance, testing; vocational guidance, adjustment service after placement. M

ITO, Prof. Soemon. Dept. of Psych, Yamagata Univ, Yamagata. b. 20 Mar 1913 Yamagata. Bungakushi '43 Tokyo Bunrika Univ, Japan. ASST. PROF, Yamagata Univ. Member: JPA, JSAP. Teaching, research, testing; behavior and environment, psychology of occupations. M

ITO, Prof. Suketoki. Nakamachi 5-231 Urawa-shi, Saitama-Ken. b. 19 Mar 1911 Maebashi-shi. Bungakushi '38 Nihon Univ, Japan. PROF. of PSYCH, Nihon Univ, Misaki-cho, Tokyo; DIRECTOR, Nihon Vocat. Guid. Assn. Member: JPA, JSAP, Japan Vocat. Guid. Socy. Teaching, vocational guidance, professional writing. M

ITO, Prof. Yasuji. Dept. of Psych, Waseda Univ, Tokyo. b. 20 Mar 1901 Sakata. Bungakushi '27 Waseda Univ, Japan. PROFESSOR, Waseda Univ. Member: JPA, JSAP. Teaching social psychology, research; norms, attitudes, social distance. M

IWAHARA, Mrs. Kiyoko. c/o Ikuo, Sahogawa-Minamicho, Horen, Nara City. b. 5 Dec 1920 Tokyo. Bungakushi '46 Tokyo Bunrika Univ, Japan. LECT. in CHILD and EDUC. PSYCH, Tenri Jr. Coll, Tenri, Nara. Member: JPA, Japan Socy. of Pre-sch. Educ. Teaching, research, consulting; frustration in children, personality, pre-school education. F

IWAHARA, Prof. Shinkuro. Dept. of Psych, Nara Women's Univ. Nara. b. 2 Jan 1923 Toyohashi. PH.D '54 Univ. of Missouri, USA. ASST. PROF, Nara Women's Univ. Member: JPA, APA, Jap. Socy. for Animal Psych. Research, experimental design and statistics, teaching; learning theory, systematic psychology. M

IWATA, Prof. Shigeki. Fac. of Liberal Arts, Utsunomiya Univ, Mine, Utsunomiya. b. 31 Jan 1921 Nagano. Bungakushi '46 Tokyo Bunrika Univ, Japan. ASST. PROF. of EDUC. PSYCH, Utsunomiya Univ.Member: JPA, JSAP. Research, teaching; level of aspiration, factor analysis in studies of personality and abilities. M

IWAWAKI, Saburo. Dept. of Psych, Kyoto Univ, Sakyo, Kyoto. b. 10 Aug 1927 Nagoya. Bungakushi '52 Tohoku Univ, Japan. RES. WRKR, Nagoya Dentsu Co, Minamiotsudori, Nagoya. Member: JPA, Jap. Socy. for Animal Psych. Motivation and marketing research, testing; social and dynamic perception, intelligence tests. M

JIMBO, Prof. Kaku. Toyo Univ, Bunkyo-ku, Tokyo. b. 18 Apr 1883 Tokyo. Bungakushi '08 Univ. of Tokyo, Japan. PROF. of LINGUISTICS, Tokyo Univ. Member: JPA. Teaching, research; theoretical linguistics. M

JOHDAI, Prof. Koh. Dept. of Psych, Hiroshima Univ, Hiroshima. b. 26 Dec 1915 Matsue. Bungakushi '42 Hiroshima Univ, Japan. ASST. PROF, Hiroshima Univ. Member: JPA. Research, teaching, professional writing; construction of behavior theory, experimental extinction. M

KAGEYAMA, Saburo. 348 1-chome, Shimoochiai, Shinjiku-ku, Tokyo. b. 22 Nov 1911 Tokyo. Bungakushi '37 Univ. of Tokyo, Japan. ASST. ED. of CULTURAL SECT, The Asahi Press, Yurakucho, Tokyo. Member: JPA, JAEP. Research; mass communication. M

KAI, Prof. Hisao. Dept. of Psych, Nagoya Nursery Jr. Coll, Showa-ku, Nagoya. b. 30 July 1904 Takeda. Bungakushi '43 Hiroshima Bunrika Univ, Japan. ASST. PROF, Nagoya Nursery Jr. Coll. Member: JPA. Research, teaching child psychology, guidance; child development, language development in children. M

KAI, Tadayoshi. Dept. of Psych, Kumamoto Univ, Kurokami-machi, Kumamoto. b. 23 Mar 1919 Kumamoto. Bungakushi '46 Hiroshima Bunrika Univ, Japan. INSTRUCTOR, Kumamoto Univ. Member: Kyushu Psych. Assn. Teaching, research, guidance; personality tests and measurements. M

KAJIYAMA, Hisashi. 7 Niwakubocho, Kitakawachigun, Osaka-fu. b. 20 Aug 1926 Onomichi. Bungakushi '49 Doshisha Univ, Japan. STAFF MEMBER, Osaka Prefectural Vocat. Consult. Serv, Awabori, Osaka. Member: JPA, SCP, Kansai Psych. Assn. Vocational guidance; aptitude testing, occupational counseling. M

KAKETA, Prof. Katsumi. Dept. of Psychiat. and Neur, Juntendo Med. Coll, Ochanomizu, Tokyo. b. 30 Jan 1906 Sendai. Igakuhakushi '37 Tohoku Univ, Japan. PROF. of PSYCHIAT, Juntendo Med. Coll. Member: JPA, JSAP. Research, teaching, clinical practice; group process, projective techniques, psychoanalysis. M

KAKIZAKI, Prof. Sukeichi. Dept. of Psych, Kyoto Univ, Yoshida, Kyoto. b. 27 Aug 1915 Kobe. Bungakushi '41 Kyoto Univ, Japan. ASST. PROF, Kyoto Univ. Member: JPA, Kansai Psych. Assn. Teaching, research, administration; visual perception. M

KAMASE, Prof. Fujio. Dept. of Commerce, Kurume Univ, Miimachi, Kurume. b. 9 Apr 1903 Fukuoka. Bungakushi '26 Univ. of Tokyo, Japan. PROF. of PSYCH.

Kurume Univ. Member: JPA. Teaching, research, administration; personality theory, psychology of adolescence. M

KAMEDA, Prof. Hisashi. Dept. of Psych, Kagoshima Univ, Shimo-Ishiki, Kagoshima. b. 24 Jan 1921 Kumamoto. Bungakushi '44 Keijo Univ, Japan. ASST. PROF, Kagoshima Univ. Member: JPA, JAEP. Research, teaching, student; social behavior of child and adolescent. M

KAMEI, Kazutsuna. Sect. of Res, Editorial Dept, The Japan Newspaper Publishers and Editors Assn, 17-chome Nishi-Ginza, Chuo-ku, Tokyo. b. 16 Oct 1921 Tokyo. Bungakushi '44 Univ. of Tokyo, Japan. RES. WRKR, Res. Sect, The Japan Newspaper Publishers and Ed. Assn. Member: JPA, JSAP. Research, teaching, consulting; social psychology, the effects of personal and mass communication. M

KAMEI, Prof. Sadao. Dept. of Educ. Yamaguchi Univ, Yamaguchi. b. 1 Mar 1914 Iwakuni. Bungakushi '41 Tokyo Bunrika Univ, Japan. ASST. PROF. of PSYCH, Yamaguchi Univ. Member: JPA, JSAP. Teaching, research, educational psychology; adolescent personality. M

KAMITAKE, Prof. Masaji. Dept. of Psych, Tokyo Univ. of Educ, Otsuka, Tokyo. b. 13 Jan 1909 Nara. Bungakushi '35 Tokyo Bunrika Univ, Japan. PROFESSOR, Tokyo Bunrika Univ. Member: JPA, JSAP. Research, teaching, professional writing; heredity and environment in child development, leadership in children's groups. M

KANAI, Prof. Tatsuzo. Dept. of Psych, Yokohama Natl. Univ, Yukimoshita, Kamakura, Kanagawa-ken. b. 30 Sept 1917 Tokyo. Bungakuhsi '43 Tokyo Bunrika Univ, Japan. ASST. PROF, Yokohama Natl. Univ. Member: JPA, JSAP. Teaching, guidance, research; transfer of training in learning, evaluation and measurement in learning activities. M

KANEHIRA, Bunji. Exam. Res. Sect, Bur. of Recruitment, Natl. Pers. Authority, 1-2 Kasumigaseki, Chiyoda-ku, Tokyo. b. 6 Aug 1921 Fukuoka. Bungakushi '48 Kyushu Univ, Japan. CHIEF, Genl. Intelligence Unit, Natl. Pers. Authority. Member: JPA, JSAP. Construction of tests and analysis of results, research, administration; group processes, achievement tests. M

KANEKO, Prof. Jiro. Dept. of Psychiat, Nara Med. Coll, Kashihara, Nara. b. 12 Feb 1915 Nishinomiya. Igakuhakushi '49 Osaka Univ, Japan. PROFESSOR, Nara Med. Coll; CONSULTANT, Nara Family Count; LECT. in MENT. HYG, Nara Educ. Coll. Member: JPA, SCP. Teaching, research, consulting; psychology of the aged, projective techniques, intelligence tests. M

KANEKO, Prof. Hideaki. Dept. of Psych, Japan Women's Univ, Takada-Toyokawacho Bunkyoku, Tokyo. b. 10 Jan 1914 Tokyo. Bungakushi '37 Keio Univ, Japan. ASST. PROF, Japan Women's Univ; RES. MEMBER, Inst. for Hlth. of Mail Clerks. Member: JPA, JSAP. Research, teaching, industrial psychology; mental fatigue in industrial work. M

KANEKO, Prof. Hiroshi. Dept. of Psych, Hiroshima Univ, Higashisendacho, Hiroshima-shi. b. 26 Jan 1909 Tokyo. Bungakushi '31 Univ. of Tokyo, Japan. PROFESSOR, Hiroshima Univ; LECTURER, Tokyo Univ. of Educ; DIRECTCR, Assn. of Public Science. Member: JPA, JSAP. Teaching, research, administration; group process, social perception, attitude measurement. M

KANEKO, Takayoshi. 2-147 Tamagawa-yoga-machi, Setagaya-ku, Tokyo. b. 17 May 1928 Tokyo. MA '54 Univ. of Missouri, USA. STUDENT, Dept. of Psych, Tokyo Univ. of Educ, Tokyo; ED. BD, *Journal of Illuminating Engineering Institute.* Member: JPA. Research, editorial; illuminating engineering, psychology of vision as related to psychophysics and psychodynamis of color. M

KANEKO, Yuzo. Tokyo Metrop. Commercial and Indus. Guid. Off, Yurakucho 2-5, Chiyodaku, Tokyo. b. 20 Mar 1901 Numata. Bungakushi '24 Univ. of Tokyo, Japan. DIRECTOR, Tokyo Metrop. Commercial and Indus. Guid. Off. Member: JSAP. Guidance of small businesses, teaching, research; business psychology, market research. M

KANO, Hiroshi. Dept. of Psych, Inst. for Sci. of Labor, Setagaya, Tokyo. b. 24 Apr 1903 Shizuoka. Bungakushi '29 Univ. of Tokyo, Japan. RES. STAFF, Inst. for Sci. of Labor. Member: JPA, JSAP, Japan Assn. of Indus. Hyg. Research in industrial psychology; aptitude tests, industrial accidents. M

KASAMAKI, Prof. Kazuo. Dept. of Educ, Yamagata Univ, Midori-cho, Yamagata. b. 8 June 1915 Tokyo. Bungakushi '47 Tokyo Univ. of Educ, Japan. ASST. PROF, Yamagata Univ. Member: JPA. Teaching, guidance, testing; learning theory, achievement tests. M

KASHU, Kan. Dept. of Psych, Kwansei Gakuin Univ, Uegahara, Nishinomiya. b. 8 Nov 1928 Kobe. Bungakushushi '55 Kwansei Gakuin Univ, Japan. ASSISTANT, Kwansei Gakuin Univ. Member: JPA, Kwansei Psych. Assn. Research, teaching; verbal learning, psychology of language. M

KATAGUCHI, Yasufumi. Dept. of Psych, Natl. Inst. of Ment. Hlth, Konodai, Ichikawa, Chiba. b. 3 Nov 1927 Kanazawa.

Bungakushi '51 Tokyo Univ, Japan. TECH. OFF, Ministry of Welf, Natl. Inst. of Ment. Hlth. Member: JPA, JAEP. Testing, clinical practice, research; projective tests, Rorschach technique. M

KATO, Prof. Hitoshi. Chukyo Jr. Coll, Yagoto, Nagoya. b. 9 July 1926 Yokohama. Bungakushi '50 Keio Univ, Japan. ASST. PROF. of PSYCH, Chukyo Jr. Coll. Member: JPA. Research, teaching, consulting; perception, hypnosis. M

KATO, Prof. Ken. Dept. of Psych, Niigata Univ, Niigata. b. 10 Aug 1909 Tokyo. Bungakushi '40 Tohoku Univ, Japan. PROFESSOR, Niigata Univ. Member: JPA. Research, teaching educational psychology, administration; psychology of learning, thinking, problem-solving. M

KATO, Prof. Masahide. 81 2-chome Koshienguchi, Nishinomiya-shi, Hyogo-Ken. b. 29 July 1903 Kobe. Bungakushi '28 Kyoto Univ, Japan. PROF. of PSYCH, Univ. of Osaka Prefecture, Mozu, Sakai; PROF. of PSYCH, Nara Women's Univ. Member: JPA, JSAP, SCP, Kansai Psych. Assn. Teaching, research, administration; vocational guidance, aptitude tests, personality inventoryl. M

KATO, Prof. Masayasu. Dept. of Sociol, Chuo Univ, Kanda, Tokyo. b. 30 Dec 1918 Tokyo. Bungakushi '41 Univ. of Tokyo, Japan. ASST. PROF. of SOCIOL, Chuo Univ. Member: JPA. Study of broadcasting; social psychology, group dynamics. M

KATSURA, Prof. Hirosuke. Dept. of Psych, Tokyo Univ. of Educ, Otsuka, Tokyo. b. 13 Oct 1909 Oita. Bungakushi '34 Tokyo Bunrika Univ, Japan. PROFESSOR, Tokyo Univ. of Educ. Member: JPA, JSAP. Research, teaching adolescent psychology, editorial; moral development, projective techniques. M

KATSURAJIMA, Makio. Sendai Juv. Delinquent Detention and Classif. Off, Sendai. b. 5 Nov 1921 Sendai. Bungakushi '49 Tohoku Univ, Japan. CHIEF, Examination and Classif. Sect, Sendai Juv. Delinquent Detention and Classif. Off; STAFF MEMBER, Tohoku Res. Cen. of Correctnl. Sci. and Technique. Member: JPA, JSAP, Tohoku Psych. Assn. Testing and clinical analysis, administration, consulting, research; clinical use of projective techniques. M

KAWADA, Teijiro. Fujikuragakuen (Sch. for the Feebleminded), Ohshima, Tokyo. b. 3 Apr 1879 Shimodate. SUPERINTENDENT Fujikuragakuen. Member: JPA. Education and training of the feebleminded, research, guidance; abnormal psychology, educational psychology. M

KAWAGUCHI, Prof. Isamu. 58 Kawashima-Arisugawa-cho, Ukyo-ku, Kyoto. b. 7 Apr 1920 Osaka. Bungakushi '42 Univ. of Tokyo, Japan. ASST. PROF. of PSYCH, Kansai Univ, Senriyama, Suita; LECT. in ART EDUC, Aichi Teacher's Coll. Member: JPA, JAEP. Teaching, research, educational psychology; inter-group relations, psychology applied to art education. M

KAWAI, Satoru. Kagoshime-Ken Univ, Shimoshiki-machi, Kagoshimashi. b. 30 Sept 1926 Kobe. Bungakushi '50 Keio Univ, Japan. INSTR. in PSYCH, Kagoshima Prefectural Univ. Member: JPA. Research, teaching, testing; perception, hypnotism. M

KAWAMURA, Akira. Res. Dept, Futaba Co, Ltd, Inatsuke-machi, Kita-ku, Tokyo-to. b. 15 Aug 1901 Otsuki, Yamanashi-ken. CHIEF, Res. Dept, Futaba Co. Member: JSAP. Research on primary and secondary school text-books, testing, editorial; development of thinking in childhood. M

KAWAMURA, Hisato. Aichi Women's Coll, Takadacho, Mizuhoku, Nagoya. b. 5 Feb 1926 Nagoya. Bungakushi '51 Nagoya Univ, Japan. INSTR. in PSYCH, Aichi Women's Coll. Member: JPA, JSAP. Research, teaching, educational psychology; motivation. M

KAWAMURA, Prof. Shinichi. 33 Shimizu-cho, Muroran-Shi, Hokkai-Do. b. 9 Sept 1901 Tono-Shi. Bungakushi '38 Kyushu Univ, Japan. PROF. of PSYCH, Muroran Univ, Mizumoto-Cho, Muroran-Shi. Member: Hokkaido Psych. Assn. Teaching, research, educational psychology; learning theory, attitude measurement. M

KAWANAKA, Prof. Masaru. Dept. of Psych, Hiroshima Women's Jr. Coll, Uzina, Hiroshima. b. 2 Dec 1914 Miyazaki. Bungakushi '42 Hiroshima Bunrika Univ, Japan. ASST. PROF, Hiroshima Women's Jr. Coll. Member: JPA, SCP. Teaching educational psychology and mental hygiene, guidance, administration; problem of adjustment to frustration in study of personality, counseling. M

KAWASHIMA, Shinichi. Kawachi Shonenin, Ishikiricho, Hiraokashi, Osaka. b. 2 Apr 1912 Washinton, DC, USA. Bungakushi '37 Univ. of Tokyo, Japan. SUPERINTENDENT, Kawachi Trng. Sch. Member: JPA, Kansai Psych. Assn. Administration, applied psychology, testing, clinical analysis; group process, leadership. M

KIDA, Prof. Fumio. Nippon Med. Coll, 59 Sendagi, Bunkyo, Tokyo. b. 2 Dec 1908 Okayama. Igakyhakushi '40 Univ. of Tokyo, Japan. PROF. of CHILD MED. and PSYCH, Nippon Med. Coll. Member: JPA, JSAP. Teaching, consulting, research; psychosocial development of the child, clinical psychology, abnormal psychology. M

KIDA, Ichiji. 430 Imaicho, Chiba-shi. b. 30

Mar 1911 Tokyo. Bungakushi '35 St. Paul Univ, Japan. ASST. CHIEF, Child Protection Sect, Children's Bur, Ministry of Hlth. and Welf, 1 2-chome Kasumigaseki, Chiyoda Ward, Tokyo; EDITOR, *The Child*. Member: JPA, JSAP. Administration, guidance and testing of mentally handicapped children; intelligence tests, consulting techniques. M

KIDA, Shigeo. Shudo Coll, Mimanisenda, Hiroshima. b. 2 Sept 1925 Kure. Bungakushi '50 Hiroshima Univ, Japan. INSTR. in PSYCH, Shudo Coll. Member: JPA, JAEP. Teaching, educational psychology, research; attitude measurement. M

KIDO, Prof. Mantaro. Fac. of Educ, Hokkaido, Univ, Sapporo. b. 1 July 1893 Matuyama. Bungakushi '16 Univ. of Tokyo, Japan. DEAN, Fac. of Educ, Hokkaido Univ; EDITOR, *Japanese Journal of Educational Psychology*. Member: JPA, JAEP. Research, lecturing on science of education and educational psychology; cultural patterns and personality development. M

KIHARA, Takashi. Kashiwazaki Coll, Hisumi, Kashiwazaki. b. 21 Apr 1928 Tokyo. Bungakushushi '55 Tohoku Univ, Japan. INSTR. in PSYCH, Kashiwazaki Coll. Member JPA, JSAP, Tohoku Psych. Assn. Research, teaching; feeling and emotion, judgment facial expressions. M

KIKUCHI, Saburo. Nagasaki Juvenile Classif. Off, 243 Hashiguchi-cho, Nagasaki City. b. 19 June 1912 Shiroishi City. Bungakushi '37 Waseda Univ, Japan. CHIEF, Nagasaki Juvenile Classif. Off. Member: JPA. Guidance, research, administration; behavioristic research on delinquency and crime. M

KIKUCHI, Tetsuhiko. Lab. of Psych, Fac. of Letters, Tohoku Univ, Sendai. b. 16 Dec 1928 Shimodate. Bungakushi '53 Ibaragi Univ, Japan. STUDENT. Member: JPA, JSAP, Tohoku Psych. Assn. Research; motivation, learning theory, sign learning process in the blind. M

KIMORI, Shigeki. 14 Hashimoto-cho, Otsu, Shiga. b. 5 Feb 1909 Fukuoka. Bungakushi '32 Kyoto Univ, Japan. INSTR. in PSYCH, Osaka Univ. of Liberal Arts and Educ, Minami-kawahoricho, Tennoji-ku, Osaka. Member: JPA. Teaching, consulting; speech problems, stuttering. M

KIMOTO, Hideto. Dept. of Psych, Ibaraki Univ, Watari, Mito. b. 18 Apr 1922 Yamaguchi. Bungakushi '50 Tokyo Bunrika Univ, Japan. INSTRUCTOR, Ibaraki Univ. Member: JPA, JSAP. Teaching, research, professional writing; social perception, language, patterns of culture. M

KIMURA, Prof. Teiji. Dept. of Psych,

Nihon Univ, Misakicho, Kanda. Tokyo. b. 16 July 1901 Gunma. Bungakushi '29 Nihon Univ, Japan. PROFESSOR, Nihon Univ. Member: JPA, JSAP. Teaching educational psychology and history of psychology, research; use of attitude measurement in study of values and personality. M

KIMURA, Prof. Toshio. Dept. of Psych, Ibaraki Univ, Mito-shi, Ibaraki-ken. b. 11 July 1913 Hitachi. ¡Bungakushi '37 Kyoto Univ, Japan. ASST. PROF, Ibaraki Univ; LECTURER, Tohoku Univ. Member: JPA, JSAP. Research, teaching, color consulting; color perception, vision theory. M

KIRIHARA, Dr. Shigemi. Inst. for Sci. of Labor, Soshigaya-2, Setagaya-ku, Tokyo. b. 10 Nov 1892 Hiroshima. Bungakuhakushi '31 Univ. of Tokyo, Japan. DIRECTOR, Inst. for Sci. of Labor; EDITOR, *Journal of Medico-psychological Research of Labor*, Inst. for Sci. of Labor. Member: JPA, JSAP, Japan Socy. of Child Study. Administration, research, industrial psychology; working ability analysis, industrial fatigue. M

KISAKI, Prof. Fumiya. Dept. of Educ, Shizuoka Univ, Nagoricho, Hamamatsu. b. 11 Jan 1914 Kagoshima. Bungakushi '46 Tokyo Bunrika Univ, Japan. ASST. PROF. of EDUC. PSYCH, Shizuoka Univ. Member: JPA, JSAP. Teaching, testing, research; intelligence and projective tests, educational statistics. M

KISHIDA, Motomi. Dept. of Liberal Arts and Educ, Tokushima Univ, Josanjima, Tokushima. b. 14 Jan 1922 Ehime. Bungakushi '49 Hiroshima Bunrika Univ, Japan. INSTR. in PSYCH, Tokushima Univ. Member: JPA, JSAP, JAEP. Research, teaching, consulting; attitude measurement, group processes, teacher-child relations. M

KISHIDO, Prof. Mamoru. Dept. of Psych, Osaka City Univ, Sugimoto-cho, Osaka. b. 28 Mar 1910 Okayama. Bungakushi '41 Kyoto Univ, Japan. ASST. PROF, Osaka City Univ. Member: JPA, JSAP. Teaching and research in industrial psychology and vocational guidance; personnel management, job analysis, morale studies. M

KISHIMOTO, Prof. Kenichi. Inst. of Environmental Med, Nagoya Univ, Furocho Chikusaku, Nagoya. b. 12 July 1905 Nara. Igakuhakushi '36 Nagoya Univ, Japan. PROF. ofMED, Inst. of Environmental Med, Nahoya Univ; LECTURER, Aichi Jyoshi Coll. Member: JPA, JSPA. Psychotherapy, teaching, research; psychotherapy, *Daseinsanalyse*. M

KISHIMOTO, Prof. Suehiko. Inst. of Psych, Osaka Univ. of Liberal Arts and Educ, Tennoji, Osaka. b. 5 Oct 1909 Kumamoto.

Bungakushi '35 Kyushu Univ, Japan. PROFESSOR, Osaka Univ. of Liberal Arts and Educ. Member: JPA, Kansai Psych. Assn. Research, teaching; mental development, perception of space, time and movement. M

KITA, Shigetoshi. Tsu Juvenile Classif. Off, 109 Furukawa, Tsu, Mie-ken. b. 1 Nov 1902 Nara. Bungakushi '29 Kyoto Univ, Japan. DIRECTOR, Tsu Juvenile Classif. Off. Member: SCP, Kansai Psych. Assn, Tokai Psych. Assn. Teaching, administration, guidance; delinquency, case work, human relations. M

KITAGAWA, Kazutoshi. Ground Self Def. Forces (GSDF), Kasumigaseki Chiyoda-ku, Tokyo. b. 24 Aug 1925 Osaka. Bungakushi '48 Nihon Univ, Japan. ASST. CHIEF of TESTING, Adjutant General Sect, GSDF. Member: JSAP. Aptitude testing, applied and personnel psychology. M

KITAHARA, Chūsai, Child Welf. Cen, Yamanashi-ken, Kofu. b. 5 May 1922 Kyoto. CHIEF of GUID. CLIN, Child Welf. Cen. Member: JSAP. Family and child guidance, testing, clinical analysis, research; personality. M

KITAMURA, Prof. Seiro. Kita 6 bancho, Sendai. b. 21 Apr 1908 Sendai. Bungakushi '35 Tohoku Univ, Japan. ASST. PROF. of PSYCH, Tohoku Univ, Katahiracho, Sendai. Member: JPA, JAEP. Research, teaching, professional writing; personality, ego-involvement, self-derision. M

KITANO, Prof. Eimasa. Dept. of Psych, Hokkaido Univ. of Liberal Arts and Educ, Kushiro-shi. b. 18 Sept 1918 Komatsu. Bungakushi '50 Hiroshima Bunrika Univ, Univ, ASST. PROF, Hokkaido Univ. of Liberal Arts and Educ. Member: JPA, JAEP. Research, teaching, consulting; perception in relation to psychological need. M

KITAWAKI, Prof. Masao. Dept. of Vocat. Guid, Shizuoka Univ, Oiwa, Shizuoka. b. 1 Jan 1908 Shizuoka. Bungakushi '34 Nippon Univ, Japan. PROFESSOR, Shizuoka Univ; EDITOR, *Industrial Education and Vocational Guidance*. Member: JPA, JSAP. Research, teaching, educational psychology, editorial; vocational guidance and counseling, personnel psychology. M

KIYOMIYA, Eiichi. Kashiwagi 4-866, Shinjukuku, Tokyo. b. 21 Apr 1915 Urawa. Bungakushi '40 Univ. of Tokyo, Japan. INVESTIGATOR, Labor Sci. Res. Off, Hlth. Sect, Jap. Natl. Railways, Tabatamachi 806, Kitaku, Tokyo; LECTURER, Tokyo Inst. of Tech. Member: JPA, JSAP. Research on pyschological problems of employees, industrial psychology, teaching; aptitude tests, fatigue measurement, projective techniques. M

KIYOTŌ, Yutaka. Kushiro Juvenile Detention and Classif. Off, 110 Yayoi-cho, Kushiro-shi, Hokkaido. b. 6 Nov 1924 Kochi-ken. CHIEF, Classif. Dept, Kushiro Juv. Detention and Classif. Off. Member: JPA, Kushiro Socy. for the Study of Psych. Techniques. Testing and classification of juvenile delinquents, guidance, research; projective techniques, attitude measurement. M

KIYOHARA, Prof. Kenji. Dept. of Psych, Waseda Univ, Totsuka, Tokyo. b. 26 Apr 1918 Nagano. Bungakushi '42 Waseda Univ, Japan. ASST. PROF, Waseda Univ. Member: JPA, JSAP. Teaching, research, testing; psychomotor process. M

KOBAYASHI, Kiichiro. Dept. of Tech, Tokyo Metrop. Univ, Samezu, Tokyo. b. 2 Feb 1925 Tokyo. ASST. in TECH, Tokyo Metrop. Univ. Member: JPA. Student, research; psychology applied to architectural planning. M

KOBAYASHI, Ryota. 128 Kobiki, Hachioji, Tokyo. b. 27 Nov 1920 Osaka. Bungakushi '43 Kansei-Gakuin Univ, Japan. CHIEF, Classif. and Rehab. Sect, Tama Fraining School, Hachioji. Member: JPA. Testing, clinical analysis, psychotherapy, and guidance of delinquent youth; projective techniques. M

KOBAYASHI, Prof. Sae. Inst. of Psych, Jissen Women's Univ, 101 Tokiwamatsu, Shibuya-Ku, Tokyo. b. 21 July 1912 Hamamatsu. Bungakushi '37 Tokyo Univ, Japan. PROFESSOR, Jissen Women's Coll; LECT. in PSYCH, Chiba Univ. Member: JPA, JSAP. Research, teaching, consulting; group process, leadership. F

KOBAYASHI, Seiichiro. Yamagata Juv. Detention and Classif. Home, 1204 Koshirakawa-machi, Yamagata-shi. b. 7 Jan 1913 Niigata. Bungakushi '40 Univ. of Tokyo, Japan. DIRECTOR, Yamagata Juv. Detention and Classif. Home. Member: JPA. Administration, clinical research, guidance, testing; projective techniques, social perception, attitude measurement. M

KOBAYASHI, Tatsuo. Matayama Juv. Detention and Classif. Home, 484 Nishitachibana, Matsuyama. b. 26 Feb 1915 Hitachi. Bungakushi '39 Univ. of Tokyo, Japan. CHIEF, Matayama Juv. Detention and Classif. Home. Member: JPA, JSAP. Consulting, guidance, clinical analysis, testing, administration. M

KOBAYASHI, Prof. Toshinobu. Dept. of Psych, Hiroshima Women's Jr. Coll, Ujina-machi, Hiroshima. b. 1 June 1922 Hiroshima-Huchiu. Bungakushi '46 Hiroshima Bunrika Univ, Japan. ASST. PROF, Hiroshima Women's Jr. Coll. Member: JPA. Teaching, research, testing;

visual perception, testing, attitude measurement. M

KODA, Tadao. Osaka Prefectural Vocat. Consult. Serv, 51 1-chome, Awaboridori Nishiku, Osaka. b. 4 Sept 1910 Niigata. Bungakushi '38 Nihon Univ, Japan. DIRECTOR, Osaka Prefectural Vocat. Consult. Serv. Member: JPA, JSAP, Kansai Psych. Assn. Vocational counseling and selection, aptitude testing and analysis of results, research, administration; vocational guidance, occupational information. M

KODAKI, Prof. Nobuo. 789 Saika-cho, Matsue, Shimane-ken. b. 14 Sept 1921 Shimane. Bungakushi '49 Kyoto Univ, Japan. ASST. PROF, Shimane Univ, Nishi-kawatsu, Matsue. Member: JPA. Teaching, research, consulting; projective techniques. M

KODAMA, Prof. Habuku. Japan Women's Univ, Takata Toyokawa-cho, Bunkyo-ku, Tokyo. b. 2 Dec 1896 Ozu. PH.B '25 Univ. of Chicago, USA. PROF. of PSYCH. and CHMN, Dept. of Educ. and Child Study, Japan Women's Univ; LECTURER, Keio Univ; CO-EDITOR, *Series in Psychology,* Japan Socy. of Appl. Psych. Member: JPA, JSAP. Teaching, research, administration; Rorschach, test child and adolescent psychology. M

KOGA, Prof. Dr. Yoshiyuki. Tokyo Jikeikai Sch. of Med, Tokyo. b. 10 Nov 1902 Kumamoto. Igakuhakushi '36 Tokyo Jikeikai Sch. of Med, Japan. PROF. of INTERNAL MED, Tokyo Jikeikai Sch. of Med; CHAIRMAN, Koga Clinic. Member: JPA. Teaching, psychotherapy, research, clinical practice; research on psychoneurosis, psychosomatic medicine. M

KOGA, Prof. Yukiyoshi. Dept. of Psych, Hiroshima Univ, Hiroshima. b. 26 Nov 1891 Kumamoto. Bungakushi '14 Univ. of Tokyo, Japan. PROFESSOR, Hiroshima Univ; ED. STAFF, *Japanese Journal of Psychology.* Member: JPA, JSAP. Research, teaching, administration; psychometry, factoranalysis. M

KOGAWA, Prof. Chujiro. Dept. of Psych, Hirosaki Univ, Hirosaki, Aomori. b. 18 Feb 1909 Hiraka. Bungakushi '37 Hiroshima Bunrika Univ, Japan. PROFESSOR, Hirosaki Univ, Member: JPA. Teaching; history of educational psychology. M

KOJIMA, Kenshiro. Dept. of Psych, Waseda Univ, Totsuka-Machi, Tokyo. b. 28 Mar 1925 Ueda. Bungakushi '49 Waseda Univ. Japan. INSTRUCTOR, Kokushikan Jr. Coll, Setagaya, Tokyo. Member: JPA, JSAP. Research, teaching, guidance; educational psychology, personality theory, social perception, projective techniques. M

KOJIMA, Sotohiro. Dept. of Psych, Kago-

shima Univ, Kamoike-cho, Kagoshima. b. 17 Apr 1925 Kanazawa. Bungakushi '52 Nagoya Univ, Japan. INSTRUCTOR, Kagoshima Univ. Member: JPA. Research, teaching; perception. M

KOKADO, Kazunosuke. Merchant Marine Univ, Etchujima, Koto-Ku, Tokyo. b. 26 Jan 1895 Kishiwada. Bungakushi '29 Kyushu Univ, Japan. PROFESSOR, Merchant Marine Univ; MEMBER, Comm. on Maritime Labor Relations, Kanto District, and Maritime Cen. Empl. Security Council; ED. STAFF, *Journal of the Merchant Marine University.* Teaching, research, personnel psychology, marine policies on labor, safety and education; maritime labor-management relations, psychology of marine disasters. M

KOMATSU, Moriaki. 8 Hachihon-matsu Nagamachi, Sendai-shi, Miyagi-ken. b. 15 May 1916 Koti. Bungakushi '39 Univ. of Tokyo, Japan. CHIEF, Sendai Dist. Correctn. Hq, Nagamachi, Sendai-shi. Member: JPA, Jap. Educ. Assn. Administration, research; personality measurement, educational evaluation. M

KOMINE, Tomoichi. c/o Aikojoshigakuen, 1057 Koadachi, Komaemachi, Kitatamaguh, Tokyo. b. 7 Sept 1921 Tokyo. Bungakushi '46 Keio Univ, Japan. CHIEF, Classif. and Parole Sect, Aiko Trng. Sch. for Girls, Komae, Tokyo. Member: JPA, JSAP. Research, testing, clinical analysis, guidance; correction and rehabilitation. M

KOMIYAMA, Prof. Eiichi. Dept. of Psych, Tokyo Univ. of Educ, Bunkyoku, Tokyo. b. 12 Jan 1913 Nagano. Bungakushi '39 Tokyo Bunrika Univ, Japan. ASST. PROF, Tokyo Univ. of Educ; CO-EDITOR, *Child Study.* Member: JPA, JSAP. Research, teaching, educational psychology; testing.M

KOMURO, Prof. Shohachi. Dept. of Educ, Thoku Univ, Kita 7, Sendai. b. 19 June 1911 Miyagi Prefecture. Bungakushi '45 Tokyo Bunrika Univ, Japan. ASST. PROF, Tohoku Univ. Member: JPA, JAEP. Teaching, research, educational psychology; social behavior of children. M

KONDO, Prof. Hajime. Dept. of Psych, Hakodate Br, Hokkaido Univ. of Liberal Arts and Educ, Hokkaido. b. 3 Aug 1912 Hokkaido. Bungakushi '43 Hiroshima Bunrika Univ, Japan. PROFESSOR, Hakodate Br, Hokkaido Univ. of Liberal Arts and Educ; INSTR. in PSYCH, Hakodate Commercial Jr. Coll. Member: JPA, Hokkaido Psych. Assn, Hakodate Ment. Hyg. Assn. Teaching, consulting, research; educational and social psychology, family relations. M

KONDO, Prof. Koichiro. Sawabuchi, 3-1, Asahi-Cho, Okasaki, Aichi. b. 20 Apr 1919 Okasaki. Bungakushi '46 Keio Univ,

Japan. ASST. PROF. of PSYCH, Chubu Soc. Work Jr. Coll, Takikawa-Cho, Nagoya. Member: JPA, JSAP, Tokai Psych. Assn. Teaching developmental psychology, research, consulting; social and emotional development, feeble-mindedness, counseling in student personnel work. M

KONDO, Prof. Sadatsugu. Dept. of Educ. Psych, Nagoya Univ, Minamisotaborimachi, Nagoya. b. 21 Aug 1906 Sanjyo. Bungakushi '29 Univ. of Tokyo, Japan. PROFESSOR, Nagoya Univ. Member: JPA. Teaching, research, educational psychology; interpersonal process in teaching, social psychological determinants of industrial productivity. M

KONDO, Prof. Toshiyuki. Shinonome Br, Fac. of Educ, Hirshima Univ, Hiroshima. b. 20 Feb 1917 Tokushima. Bungakushi '46 Hiroshima Bunrika Univ, Japan. ASST. PROF. of PSYCH, Hiroshima Univ. Member: JPA, APA. Research, teaching, consulting; projective techniques, social perception. M

KONISHI, Prof. Katsuichiro. Dept. of Child Study, Osaka City Univ, Nishinagahori, Minamidori, Nishiku, Osaka. b. 16 July 1920 Tsuchima. Bungakushi '48 Kyoto Univ, Japan. ASST. PROF. of PEDAGOGY,, Osaka City Univ. Member: JPA, Kansai Psych. Assn. Teaching, research, educational psychology; projective techniques, attitude measurement. M

KONISHI, Teruo. Dept. of Psychiat, Osaka City Univ, Abeno, Osaka. b. 7 June 1927 Namerikawa. Igakushi '50 Osaka City Med. Coll, Japan. PSYCHIATRIST, Osaka City Univ. Member: SCP, Kinki Socy. of Psychiat. and Neur. Clinical practice and psychotherapy in child guidance clinic, research; non-directive psychotherapy of children. M

KONJIKI, Shudai. Med. Sect, Ground Self-Defense Forces (GSDF), Kasumigaseki, Chiyoda-ku, Tokyo. b. 7 Jan 1919 Tokyo. Bungakushi '47 Nihon Univ, Japan. CHIEF of RES, Med. Sect, GSDF. Applied psychology, consulting, administration. M

KORA, Prof. Takehisa. 3-1808 Shimo Ochiai, Shinjikuku, Tokyo. b. 18 Jan 1899 Kagoshimaken. MD, Kyushu Univ, Japan. PROF. of PSYCHIAT. and CLIN. PSYCH, Jikei Med. Univ, Atagocho Shiba Minatoku, Tokyo; PSYCHIATRIST, clin. prac. Member: JSAP, Japan Psychiat. Assn. Teaching, psychotherapy, research, clinical practice; theory and techniques of therapy in neuroses and neurasthenias. M

KORA, Mrs. Tomi Wada. 2-808 Shimo Ochiai, Shinjikuku, Tokyo. b. 1 July 1897 Takaoka PH.D '22 Columbia Univ, USA. MEMBER, Hse. of Councillors, Comm. on Educ. and

Welf, Natl. Parliament, Sangiin, Tokyo. Member: JPA, JSAP, ICWP. Legislative work, cultural activities in UNESCO, administration of international youth exchange programs; research on developmental psychology of children and youth, social psychology and culture characteristics of Asiatic races, use of educational and therapeutic techniques on juvenile social maladjustment. F

KOSAJI, Tomoo. Exam. Sect, Recruitment Bur, Natl. Personnel Authority, Chiyodaku, Tokyo. b. 10 Mar 1923 Tokyo. Bungakushi, '48 Univ. of Tokyo, Japan. CHIEF, Standard Control Unit, Natl. Pers. Authority. Member: JPA. Planning tests, applied psychology, administration; aptitude, personality and interest tests. M

KOSHIYAMA, Shizuo. Dept. of Psych, Kochi Univ. Asakura, Kochi. b. 31 Oct 1922 Kure. Bungakushi '48 Tokyo Bunrika Univ, Japan. INSTRUCTOR, Kochi Univ. Member: JPA. Teaching, research, testing; intellectual and social development in early childhood. M

KOTAKE, Prof. Yasho. Dept. of Psych, Kwansei Gakui Univ, Nishinomiya, Hyogo Ken. b. 19 Sept 1912 Osaka. Bungakushi '37 Kwansei Gakuin Univ, Japan. PROFESSOR, Kwansei Gakuin Univ; LECTURER, Sch. of Med, Osaka Univ. and Sch. of Educ, Okayama Univ. Member: JPA, JSAP, APA. Research, teaching, administration; conditioned reflex, experimental neurosis, animal learning. M

KOTANI, Prof. Zenichi. Dept. of Child Welf, Aichi Women's Jr. Coll, Takatacho, Mizuho-ku, Nagoya. b. 18 June 1913 Nagoya. Bungakushi '41 Hiroshima Bunrika Univ, Japan. ASST. PROF. of PSYCH, Aichi Women's Jr. Coll. Member: JPA, JSAP. Teaching developmental and educational psychology, research, consulting; development of affection and religious feeling. M

KOURA, Prof. Ichiro. Dept. of Psych, Hiroshima Univ, Hiroshima. b. 14 Jan 1913 Yonago. Bungakushi '36 Hiroshima Bunrika Univ, Japan. PROFESSOR, Hiroshima Univ. Member: JPA, JAEP. Teaching, research, consulting; language development. M

KOYANAGI, Kyoji. Inst. of Psych, Asahigawa Sch, Hokkaido Teachers Coll, Asahigawa, Hokkaido. b. 21 Apr 1929 Nayoro. Bungakushi '52 Tohoku Univ, Japan. INSTRUCTOR, Hokkaido Teachers. Coll; ED. STAFF, *Tohoku Journal of Experimental Psychology.* Member: JPA. Research, teaching, testing; spread of effect in learning, studies on blind children. M

KUBA, Prof. Tadatoshi. Dept. of Psych, Yamaguchi Univ, Yamaguchi. b. 20 Aug

1904 Iwakuni. Bungakushi '38 Hiroshima Bunrika Univ, Japan. ASST. PROF, Yamaguchi Univ. Member: JPA, JSAP. Teaching, educational psychology, testing; learning theory, achievement tests. M

KUBO, Shunichi. Natl. Inst. for Educ. Res, Kami-osaki, Shinagawaku, Tokyo. b. 9 Jan 1908 Tokyo. Bungakushi '31 Tokyo Univ, Japan. RES. WRKR, Natl. Inst. for Educ. Res. Research. M

KUBO, Prof. Yoshitoshi. Dept. of Psych, Hiroshima Univ, Higashisenda, Hiroshima. b. 23 Oct 1913 Tokyo. Bungakushi '36 Univ. of Tokyo, Japan. PROFESSOR, Hiroshima Univ. Member: JPA. Teaching, research; attitude and behavior of atomic bomb sufferers. M

KUMAKURA, Prof. Hiroshi. Fac. of Liberal Arts and Educ, Iwate Univ, Ueda, Morioka, Iwate. b. 27 Mar 1909 Niigata. Bungakushi '36 Nihon Univ, Japan. ASST. PROF. of VOCAT. GUID, Iwate Univ. Member: JSAP, JAEP. Teaching, research, guidance; vocational psychosis, attitude measurement. M

KUME, Prof. Kyoko. Dept. of Psych, Japan Women's Univ, Bunkyo-ku, Tokyo. b. 1 Jan 1906 Tokyo. ASST. PROF, Japan Women's Univ. Member: JPA. Teaching, research; perception and size constancy. F

KUNISAWA, Prof. Hiroshi. Fac. of Liberal Arts, Sci. and Educ, Gunma Univ, Seioji, Maebashi. b. 5 May 1901 Kochi. Bungakushi '26 Univ. of Tokyo, Japan. PROF. of PSYCH, Gunma Univ; HEADMASTER, kindergarten, primary and secondary schools of Gunma Univ. Member: JPA, JSAP, JAEP. Administration, teaching, consulting; socio-historical study of emotional perception, image (cinematic) thinking, child's perception of art. M

KUNITANI, Tsuguo. Hiroshima Fam. Court, Moto-machi, Hiroshima. b. 13 Oct 1912 Tottori. Bungakushi '47 Hiroshima Bunrika Univ, Japan. CHIEF PROBAT. OFF, Hiroshima Fam. Ct. Member: JPA, Chugoku Psych. Assn, Hiroshima Clin. Psych. Assn, Hiroshima Ment. Hyg, Assn. Investigation and guidance of delinquents, supervision of probation officers, teaching; projective techniques. M

KUNIYASU, Mrs. Kiyoka. Keisen Jr. Coll, Funahashi-cho, Setagaya-Ku, Tokyo. b. 14 Dec 1918 Yokohama. Bungakushi '50 Tokyo Bunrika Univ, Japan. ASST. PROF, Keisen Jr. Coll. Member: JPA, JSAP. Consulting, teaching, research; adolescent personality, mental hygiene, psychology of language. F

KURAHASHI, Masaru. Dept. of Educ. Psych, Kanazawa Univ, Otemachi, Kanazawa. b. 15 Nov 1918 Toyama. Bunga-

kushi '43 Univ. of Tokyo, Japan. INSTRUCTOR, Kanazawa Univ. Member: JPA. Teaching, research, testing; behavior, effects of electro-shock convulsions on behavior. M

KURAISHI, Prof. Seiichi. Fac. of Educ, Kyoto Univ, Yoshida, Kyoto. b. 21 Dec 1909 Takada. Bungakushi '32 Univ. of Tokyo, Japan. PROF. of EDUC. PSYCH, Kyoto Univ. Member: JPA, JSAP. Teaching, research, consulting; higher mental process, thinking, personality tests. M

KURIBAYASHI, Prof. Uichi. Dept. of Psych, Miyagi Gakuin Coll, Higashi San Bancho, Sendai. b. 14 Apr 1882 Sendai. Bungakuhakushi '48 Tohoku Univ, Japan. PROFESSOR, Miyagi Gakuin Coll. Member: JPA. Teaching, research, consulting; intelligence tests. M

KURODA, Prof. Jitsuo. Seiwa Jr. Coll, 1 Okadayama, Nishinomiya. b. 1 June 1928 Osaka. MA '52 Kwansei Gakuin Univ, Japan. ASST. PROF. of PSYCH, Seiwa Jr. Coll. Member: JPA. Research, teaching; conditioning, child development, projective techniques. M

KURODA, Prof. Masasuke. Dept. of Educ, Niigata Univ, Niigata. b. 29 Feb 1916 Sendai. Bungakushi '40 Tohoku Univ, Japan. PROF. of EDUC. PSYCH, Niigata Univ; ED. STAFF, *Report on Educational Psychology*, Niigata Univ. Member: JPA, JAEP, Japan Psychoanal. Socy. Teaching, research, professional writing; methodology, mental hygiene, handwriting. M

KUROHASHI, Kumeichi. Higashi-Hiratsu, Yoneda-cho, Innami-gun Hyogo-Ken. b. 22 Nov 1912 Hyogo-Ken. Bungakushi '42 Tokyo Bunrika Univ, Japan. CHIEF, Kobe Educ. Res. Inst, Kobe Bd. of Educ, Kobe. Member: JPA, JSAP. Research, consulting, educational psychology; achievement tests, attitude measurement. M

KUROKI, Soichiro. 761 Kamiuma 1, Setagaya, Tokyo. b. 18 Nov 1914 Kobe. Bungakushi '38 Univ. of Tokyo, Japan. CHIEF, Psycho-acoustic Res. Sect, Tech. Res. Lab, Broadcasting Corp. of Japan, Tokyo. Member: JPA. Directing research, applied psychology, teaching; perception, hearing. M

KUSHIDA, Toshihiko. Nagoya Juvenile Classif. Cen, Chikusaku, Nagoya. b. 12 Apr 1906 Nagoya. Bungakushi '31 Univ. of Tokyo, Japan. HEAD, Nagoya Juv. Classif. Cen. Member: JPA, JSAP. Personality classification of juvenile delinquents, consulting, guidance, administration; aptitude tests, personnel management, projective techniques. M

KUWADA, Prof. Yoshizo. Dept. of Psych, Univ. of Tokyo, Bunkyoku, Tokyo. b. 11 July 1882 Kurayoshi-shi. Bungakuhakushi '21 Univ. of Tokyo, Japan. PROF. EMER, Univ. of Tokyo; LECTURER, Chiba Univ, Chiba. Member: JPA. Research, teaching, retired; myth and religion in folk psychology, principles of social psychology, psychology of crowds. M

KUZUTANI, Prof. Takamasa. Dept. of Educ, Kumamoto Univ, Kurokami, Kumamoto. b. 1 Jan 1911 Gifu. Bungakushi '37 Tokyo Bunrika Univ, Japan. ASST. PROF. in PSYCH, Kumamoto Univ. Member: JSAP, JAEP, Kyushu Psych. Assn. Teaching, administration, educational psychology; attitude measurement. M

MACHII, Hikoshiro. 341 1-chome, Shiroyama machi, Nagasaki-shi. b. 16 June 1914 Fusan, Korea. Bungakushi '37 Keijo Univ, Korea. DIRECTOR, Tstng. and Clin. Prac. Room, Nagasaki Prefectural Inst. of Educ. Res, Tateyama, Nagasaki; LECTURER, Nagasaki Women's Jr. Coll; COUNSELOR, Nagasaki Prison. Member: JAEP, Kyushu Psych. Assn. Consulting, counseling, psychotherapy, testing; mental tests, projective techniques. M

MAEDA, Prof. Hisashi. Dept. of Psych, Kagoshima Univ, Kamojke, Kagoshima. b. 21 Jan 1917 Mijazaki. Bungakushi '41 Univ. of Tokyo, Japan. ASST. PROF, Kagoshima Univ. Member: JPA. Research, teaching experimental psychology; perception, group process. M

MAEDA, Prof. Saburo. Dept. of Psych, Osaka Univ. of Liberal Arts and Educ, Tennoji, Osaka. b. 17 Feb 1914 Nara. Bungakushi '42 Tokyo Bunrika Univ, Japan. ASST. PROF, Osaka Univ. of Liberal Arts and Educ. Member: JPA, JSAP, Kansai Psych. Assn. Research, teaching, testing; motor learning, mental hygiene. M

MAEDA, Teigoro. 13-1, 3-chome, Hataharadori, Kobe. b. 19 Jan 1902 Osaka. CHILD WELF. COUNS, Central Child Guidance Cen, Kusunoki-cho, Ikutaku, Kobe. Member: JPA. Research, testing, counseling, guidance; projective techniques, attitude measurement, personality of delinquents. M

MAEKAWA, Seiichi. Nagata Upper Secondary Sch, Nagata-ku, Kobe. b. 5 Apr 1901 Hygo Prefecture. Bungakushi '27 Kyoto Univ, Japan. PRINCIPAL, Nagata Upper Secondary Sch. Member: JPA. Administration, teaching, guidance; learning theory. M

MAKI, Yasuo. Inst. for Humanistic Sciences, Kyoto Univ, Yoshida, Sakyo-ku, Kyoto. b. 12 Feb 1925 Hukuchiyama. Bungakushi '49 Kyoto Univ, Japan. ASSISTANT, Inst. for Humanistic Sciences. Member: JPA. Research on Western culture, psychotherapy; self-analysis, semantics. M

MAKINO, Tatsuro. Dept. of Psych, Osaka

City Univ, Sumiyoshi-ku, Osaka. b. 15 Feb 1925 Fukui. Bungakushi '48 Univ. of Tokyo, Japan. INSTRUCTOR, Osaka City Univ. Member: JPA. Research, teaching experimental psychology; perception, size constancy. M

MAKITA, Hitoshi. Psych. Sect, Inst. for Psycho-Med. Res, Moro-Machi, Itabashi, Tokyo. b. 10 Apr 1926 Yamanashi-ken. Bungakushi '50 Keio Univ, Japan. STAFF MEMBER, Inst. for Psycho-Med. Res. Member: JPA, JSAP. Research, testing, consulting; personality theory, projective techniques. M

MAKITA, Minoru. Assn. of Pub. Opion Sci, 4-676 Sendagaya, Shibuyaku, Tokyo. b. 23 June 1919 Taikoku, Formosa. Bungakushi '42 Univ. of Tokyo, Japan. DIRECTOR, Assn. of Pub. Opinion Sci; LECT. in PSYCH, Waseda Univ. and Meiji Univ. Member: JPA, JSAP. Management, research, applied psychology, teaching; attitude measurement, prediction of social behavior, group process, use of statistics in psychology. M

MAMIYA, Prof. Takeshi. Dept. of Psych, Yokohama Natl. Univ, Kamakura, Kanagawa. b. 20 Oct 1915 Kanagawa. Bungakushi '41 Tokyo Bunrika Univ, Japan. ASST. PROF, Yokohama Natl. Univ. Member: JPA, JSAP, Japan Assn. of Aviat. Med. Teaching and research in adolescent psychology and clinical psychology; sex difference in development of reaction-time, intelligence, mental abilities. M

MANABE, Prof. Haruzo. Dept. of Psych, Osaka Univ, Toyonaka, Osaka. b. 2 Mar 1907 Niigata. Bungakushi '33 Univ. of Tokyo, Japan. ASST. PROF, Osaka Univ. Member: JPA. Research, teaching; visual perception and its application, industrial lighting. M

MANITA, Akira. Dept. of Psych, Tokyo Univ. of Educ, Kobumachi, Bunkyo-ku, Tokyo. b. 11 Jan 1927 Tokyo. Bungakushi '50 Tokyo Bunrika Univ, Japan. ASSISTANT Tokyo Univ. of Educ; LECTURER, Tokyotoritu Koto Hobogakuin; EDITOR: *Adolescent Psychology*. Member: JPA, JSAP. Research, teaching, testing; adolescent psychology and the formation of moral consciousness. M

MARUI, Fumio. Nagoya Univ, Minamisotoboricho, Nakaku, Nagoya. b. 29 Sept 1921 Nagano. Igakushi '47 Tohoku Univ, Japan. INSTR. in CLIN. PSYCH, Dept. of Educ, and LECT. in PSYCHIAT, Sch. of Med, Nagoya Univ. Member: JSAP, Japan Neuropsychiat. Assn, Int. Psychoanal. assn. Research, testing, teaching; projective techniques, culture and personality development, interdisciplinary research on human relations. M

MARUI, Prof. Sumiko. Lab. of Psych, Fac. of

Liberal Arts and Educ, Gifu Univ, Nagara, Gifu. b. 18 Dec 1924 Sendai. Bungakushi '46 Tohoku Univ, Japan. ASST. PROF. of PSYCH, Gifu Univ. and Hirosaki Univ. Member: JPA, Tohoku Psych. Assn, Int. Psychoanal. Assn. Research, teaching, consulting; projective techniques, experimental study of psychoanalytic phenomena.   F

MARUOKA, Tadashi. Matuyama Juvenile Classif. Off, Nishitachibana, Matuyama. b. 16 Nov 1924 Kagawa Prefecture. Bungakushi '49 Hiroshima Univ, Japan. CHIEF, Classif. Sect, Matuyama Juv. Classif. Off. Member: JPA, JSAP. Testing, clinical analysis of juvenile delinquents, consultant to juvenile court, teaching; projective techniques, group psychotherapy.   M

MASAKI, Prof. Masashi. Dept. of Educ. Psych, Kyoto Univ, Yoshida, Kyoto. b. 1 Jan 1905 Kumamoto. Bungakushi '29 Univ. of Tokyo, Japan. PROFESSOR, Kyoto Univ. Member: JPA, JAEP. Teaching educational psychology, research, guidance; adjustment, personality tests, counseling. M

MASATO, Shigeru. Dept. of Engr, Hiroshima Univ, Senda-Cho, Hiroshima. b. 11 Nov 1907 Kure. Bunakushi '43 Hiroshima Bunrika Univ, Japan. ASST. PROF. of INDUS. MANAGEMENT, Hiroshima Univ. Member: JPA, JSAP. Teaching, research, testing; industrial psychology, group process, attitude measurement.   M

MASUDA, Prof. Koichi. Teachers Coll, Kobe Univ, Sumiyoshi, Kobe. b. 14 Nov 1898 Tokyo. Bungakushi '23 Univ. of Tokyo, Japan. PROF. of PSYCH, Kobe Univ; LECTURER, Kwansei Gakuin Univ; CONSULT. in RES. MANAGEMENT, Osaka Inst. of Indus. Efficiency. Member: JPA, JSAP, SCP, AIPA, Kansai Psych. Assn, Amer. Pers. and Guid. Assn. Teaching, educational and industrial psychology, research; educational measurement and evaluation, vocational guidance, human relations in industry.   M

MATSUBARA, Keitaro. Dept. of Psych, Osaka Prefectural Univ, Sakai-shi, Osaka-fu. b. 1 Nov 1919 Shimonoseki. Bunga-kushi '50 Kwansei-Gakuin Univ, Japan. ASSISTANT, Osaka Prefectural Univ. Member: JPA, JSAP. Research, teaching, testing; psychological analysis of economic behavior.   M

MATSUDA, Prof. Iwao. Fac. of Physical Educ, Tokyo Univ. of Educ, 983 Yoyogi-nishihara, Shibuyaku, Tokyo. b. 22 Jan 1920 Toyooka. Bungakushi '45 Tokyo Bunrika Univ, Japan. ASST. PROF, Tokyo Univ. of Educ. Member: JPA, JSAP.

Teaching, research, tests and measurements in physical education; motor learning, physical fitness.   M

MATSUI, Mrs. Itoko. 60 1-chome, Mabashi, Suginami-ku, Tokyo. b. 30 Mar 1923 Kawasaki City. Bungakushi '43 Nihon Univ, Japan. COUNSELOR, Child Guid. Clin, Tokyo Metrop. Govt, Ogikubo, Suginami-ku, Tokyo. Member: JPA, JSAP. Counseling.   F

MATSUI, Prof. Mitsuo. Fac. of Educ, Univ. of Tokyo, Tokyo. b. 21 June 1898 Yamaguchi. Bungakushi '23 Univ. of Tokyo, Japan. PROFESSOR, Univ. of Tokyo. Member: JPA, JSAP. Teaching, research, editorial; motor fitness test, expressions in movement.   M

MATSUI, Shinjiro. Natl. Komei Inst. for the Blind, 60 1-chome, Mabashi, Suginami-ku, Tokyo. b. 28 Dec 1914 Kofu. Bungakush, '44 Nihon Univ, Japan. INSTRUCTOR, Natl. Komei Inst. for the Blind. Member JPA, JSAP. Teaching, administration, counseling; intelligence testing and vocational guidance of the blind.   M

MATSUMOTO, Prof. Kinju. Dept. of Educ. Psych, Fac. of Educ, Tohoku Univ. Kata-hiracho, Sendai. b. 21 July 1904 Tochigi-ken. Bungakushi '30 Univ. of Tokyo, Japan. PROFESSOR, Tohoku Univ; EDITOR, *Systematic Library in Contemporary Psychology*. Member: JPA, JSAP, Jap. Pedagocal Assn. Research, teaching, administration, editorial; developmental psychology, mental development and poverty.   M

MATSUMOTO, Shigetaka. 3-28 Kita-Ku, Tokyo. b. 31 Oct 1915 Tokyo. Bungakushi '41 Hosei Univ, Japan. PSYCH. TECH. EXPERT, Arakawa Child Welf. Cen, Arakawa, Tokyo; LECT. in PSYCH, Meiji Univ. Member: JPA, JSAP. Testing, clinical analysis, guidance, teaching; juvenile delinquency, retarded children.   M

MATSUMOTO, Prof. Yoshiyuki. Dept. of Psych, Tokyo Univ. of Fisheries, Shinagawa, Tokyo. b. 10 Feb 1895 Nagano-ken. Bungakushi '25 Univ. of Tokyo, Japan. ASST. PROF, Tokyo Univ. of Fisheries. Member: JPA. Teaching, research, administration; experimental study of educational methods.   M

MATSUMURA, Prof. Kohei. Dept. of Child Study and Psych, Ochanomizu Women's Univ, Otsuka, Tokyo. b. 17 June 1917 Tokyo. Bungakushi '41 Univ. of Tokyo, Japan. ASST. PROF. of PSYCH, Ochanomizu Women's Univ. Member: JPA, JSAP. Consulting, research, teaching; projective techniques.   M

MATSUMURA, Tomoyuki. Sakakibara Br.

Tsu Natl. Hosp, Mie-ken. b. 16 Apr 1909 Hiroshima. Igakushi '36 Kyoto Med. Coll, Japan. PHYSICIAN, Tsu Natl. Hosp. Member: JPA, Jap. Assn. of Psychiat. and Neur. Clinical practice, psychotherapy, clinical analysis; psychological characteristics of schizophrenia, retropsychotic amnesia. M

MATSUOKA, Takeshi. Dept. of Psych, Yamanashi Univ, Kofu, Yamanashi. b. 1 May 1924 Saitama. Bungakushi '50 Tokyo Bunrika Univ, Japan. INSTRUCTOR, Yamanashi Univ. Member: JPA. Research, teaching, testing; projective techniques, color symbolism personality test. M

MATSUSAKA, Prof. Suezo. Dept. of Educ, Osaka Prefectural Univ, Mozu, Sakai, Osaka. b. 15 Aug 1902 Wakayama. Bungakushi '40 Hiroshima Bunrika Univ, Japan. ASST. PROF. of EDUC. PSYCH, Osaka Prefectural Univ. Member: JPA, JSAP, Kansai Psych. Assn. Research, teaching, consulting; learning theory, projective techniques. M

MATSUURA, Prof. Tazuko. Dept. of Psych, Kawamura Jr. Coll, Mejiro, Toshima, Tokyo. b. 7 Oct 1922 Hiroshima. Bungakushi '48 Hiroshima Bunrika Univ, Japan. ASST. PROF, Kawamura Jr. Coll. Member: JPA, JSAP. Research, teaching child psychology, testing; psychological effects of atomic bombing. F

MATSUYAMA, Prof. Yoshinori. Dept. of Psych, Doshisha Univ, Kyoto. b. 5 Dec 1923 Kyoto. Bungakushi '45 Doshisha Univ, Japan. ASST. PROF, Doshisha Univ. Member: JPA, APA, Kansai Psych. Assn. Teaching, research; learning theory applied to study of personality. M

MATUURA, Kenji. 47 1-chome, Chohuminemati, Ota-ku, Tokyo. b. 24 Apr 1925 Kumamoto. Bungakushi '49 Nihon Univ, Japan. CHIEF of TESTING SECT, Natl. Pers. Authority, Kasumagaseki, Tokyo. Member: JPA, JSAP. Design and study of tests, research, editorial; principles of personnel testing. M

MIDZUNO, Hiroshi. Res. Sect, Bur. of Census, 95 Wakamatsucho, Shinjukuku, Tokyo. b. 5 Sept 1917 Tokyo. Rigakushi '41 Univ. of Tokyo, Japan. CHIEF, Res. Sect, Bur. of Census; INSTRUCTOR, Trng. Inst. of Stat. Pers. Member: JPA. Administration, consulting, research, editorial; survey methods, scaling, testing, attitude measurement, measurement theory. M

MIHAMA, Hisaharu. Dept. of Psych, Kwansei Gakuin Univ, Uegahara, Nishinomiya. b. 25 Jan 1928 Ashyia. Bungakushi '53 Kwansei Gakuin Univ, Japan. RES. WRKR, Kwansei Gakuin Univ. Member

JPA. Research; conditioned pupillary reflex. M

MIKI, Prof. Yasumasa. Dept. of Educ. Psych, Univ. of Tokyo, Hongo, Tokyo. b. 3 Dec 1911 Tokyo. Bungakushi '36 Univ. of Tokyo, Japan. PROFESSOR, Univ Tokyo; EDITOR, *Japanese Journal of Educational Psychology*; ED. in CHIEF, *Journal of Child Psychology and Mental Hygiene*. Member: JPA, JAEP. Research, administration. teaching; psychology and rehabilitation of the mentally retarded, psychology and education of pre-school children. M

MIMURA, Keiichi. Dept. of Physiology, Nagasaki Univ. Sch. of Med, Nagasaki. b. 11 Oct 1928 Tokyo. Bungakushi '53 Tokyo Bunrika Univ, Japan. ASST. in PHYSIOLOGY, Nagasaki Univ. Sch. of Med. Member: JPA. Research; physiological psychology, electroencephalograms. M

MINAMI, Prof. Hiroshi. Inst. for Soc. Psych, 25 Saneicho, Shinjuku-ku, Tokyo. b. 23 July 1914 Tokyo. PH.D, Cornell Univ, USA. ASST. PROF. of PSYCH, Hitotsubashi Univ, Kunitachi-cho, Kitatama-gun, Tokyo; DIRECTOR, Inst. for Soc. Psych. Member: JPA, JSAP, BPS, Jap. Socy. for Animal Psych, Japan Psychoanal. Socy. Research, teaching, professional writing; mass communication and mass entertainment in Japan, national character, social attitudes and psychology of the Japanese people. M

MISHIMA, Prof. Jiro. Dept. of Psych, Waseda Univ, Totsuka, Tokyo. b. 20 June 1919 Nagasaki. Bungakushi '42 Waseda Univ, Japan. ASST. PROF, Waseda Univ. Member: JPA, JSAP. Teaching, research, consulting; educational psychology. M

MISUMI, Prof. Jyuji. 1341 Minami, Yasumura, Asakuragun. Fukuoka-ken. b. 21 Mar 1924 Fukuoka. Bungakushi '47 Kyushu Univ, Japan. ASST. PROF. of EDUC. PSYCH, Kyushu Univ, Hakozaki, Fujuoka; EDITOR, *Studies of Group Dynamics*. Member: JPA, Jap. Socy. of Grp. Dynam; Research, teaching, educational psychology; group dynamics, perception. M

MITSUDA, Prof. Hisatoshi. Psychiat. Clin, Osaka Med. Sch, Osaka-Takatsuki. b. 15 June 1910 Osaka. Igakuhakushi '42 Kyototo Univ, Japan. PROF. of PSYCHIAT, Osaka Med. Sch. Member: Jap. Assn. of Psychiat. and Neur. Kansai Socy. of Clin. Psych. Clinical practice, teaching, tesearch; projective techniques. M

MIURA, Tadashi. Miyazaki Reformatory, Ichimanjyo, Miyakonojyo, Miyazaki. b. 5 Sept 1927 Miyazaki. CONSULTANT,

CONSULTANT, Miyazaki Reform. Member: JSAP. Research, testing, psychotherapy; projective techniques. M

MIURA, Prof. Takeshi. Dept. of Psych, Tokyo Metrop. Univ, Fusamacho, Megro-ku, Tokyo. b. 3 Sept 1919 Toyohashi. Bungakushi '44 Univ. of Tokyo, Japan. ASST. PROF, Tokyo Metrop. Univ. Member: JPA. Research, teaching, consulting; satiation, personality structure, psychology of kindergarten age children. M

MIURA, Prof. Yoshio. Dept. of Psych, Tokyo Univ. of Liberal Arts and Educ, Takehaya, Tokyo. b. 29 Jan 1901 Saitama. Bunga-kushi '32 Tokyo Bunrika Univ, Japan. PROFESSOR, Tokyo Univ. of Liberal Arts and Educ. Member: JPA, JSAP. Teaching, research, testing; intelligence and a-chievement tests, development of think-ing. M

MIYA, Prof. Koichi. Psych. Lab, Kanazawa Univ, Otemachi, Kanazawa. b. 12 May 1906 Niigata-ken. Bungakushi '31 Univ. of Tokyo, Japan. PROFESSOR, Kanazawa Univ; EDITOR, *Hokuriku Journal of Psy-chology, Studies in Philosophy and History.* Member: JPA, JSAP, Hokuriku Psych. Assn. Teaching, research, administration; comparative psychology, theories of brain functions. M

MIYABE, Isamu. Dept. of Educ, Yokohama City Off, Kanagawa, Yokohama. b. 6 Sept 1914 Kugenuma. Bungakushi '49 Tokyo Bunrika Univ, Japan. PSYCHOLO-GIST, Dept. of Educ. Yokohama City Off. Member: JPA, JSAP. M

MIYAGI, Prof. Otoya. 525 Yukigaya, Otaku, Tokyo. b. 8 Mar 1908 Tokyo. Igakuha-kushi '46 Keio Univ, Japan; Bungakushi '31 Kyoto Univ, Japan. PROF. of PSYCH, Tokyo Inst. of Tech, Ookayama, Tokyo; LECT. in PSYCH, Tokyo Univ; EDITOR, *Handbook of Psychology.* Member: JPA. Research, teaching, clinical social psycholo-gy; personality and its relation to abnormal psychology. M

MIYAKAWA, Prof. Tomoaki. Dept. of Educ. Psych, Fac. of Educ, Tohoku Univ, Katahiracho, Sendai. b. 15 Feb 1921 Fukui. Bungakushi '43 Univ. of Tokyo, Japan. ASST. PROF, Tohoku Univ. Member: JPA, JAEP, Jap. Pedagogical Assn. Re-search, teaching; development and per-ception. M

MIYAKE, Shuichi. Children's Bur, Ministry of Hlth. and Welf, Kasumigaseki, Chiyoda-ku, Tokyo. b. 20 Mar 1914 Hiroshima. Bungakushi '37 Univ. of Tokyo, Japan. ASST. CHIEF of PLANNING SECT, Children's Bur, Ministry of Hlth. and Welf; EDITOR, *Collection of Case work Records of Children.* Member: JPA, JSAP. Administration, re-search, teaching; projective techniques,

peripheral consciousness, social treatment of feebleminded children. M

MIYATA, Yoshio. Classif. Div, Fuchu Prison, Fujimi-cho, Fuchu, Tokyo. b. 18 Feb 1911 Tsuruga. Bungakushi '36 Waseda Univ, Japan. CHIEF, Classif. Div, Fuchu Prison; LECT. in PSYCH, Meiji Univ. Member: JPA, JSAP. Classification and correctional work, teaching, research; personality of recidivists. M

MIYAUTI, Miss Tamako. 100 Zosigaya, Bunkyoku, Tokyo. b. 1 Jan 1918 Tokyo. DIRECTOR, Acoustical Lab. for Jap. Language and Music, Meziro, Tokyo. Member: JPA. Acoustical research; ob-jective acoustical constructions of language and music and human experience. F

MIYAZAKI, Shozo. Ogikubo Primary Sch, 2-chome, Ogikubo, Suginami, Tokyo. b. 21 Nov 1926 Tokyo. Bungakushi '50 Keio Univ, Japan. TEACHER, Ogikubo Primary Sch. Member: JSPA. Teaching, research, testing; projective techniques, psychotherapy. M

MIYOSHI, Prof. Minoru. Dept. of Psych, Hiroshima Univ, Sendamachi, Hiroshima. b. 17 Oct 1906 Ehime. Bungakuhakushi '56 Hiroshima Univ, Japan. PROFESSOR, Hiroshima Univ; PRINCIPAL, Jr. and Sr. High Sch. of Hiroshima Univ; EDITOR, *Japanese Journal of Educational Psycholo-gy.* Member: JPA, JSAP. Research, teaching, professional writing; projective techniques, factor analysis of personality, inheritance in twins. M

MIZUGUCHI, Prof. Yoshiaki. Dept. of Psych, Kagawa Univ, Saiwai-cho, Taka-matsu. b. 18 July 1910 Takamatsu. Bungakushi '39 Kyushu Univ, Japan. ASST. PROF, Kagawa Univ. Member: JPA, JSAP, JAEP. Research, teaching; projective techniques, PGR, psychology of ado-lescence. M

MIZUHARA, Prof. Taisuke. Dept. of Child Study, Ochanomizu Women's Univ, Ot-suka, Tokyo. b. 14 July 1921 Hiroshima. Bungakushi '45 Univ. of Tokyo, Japan. ASST. PROF. of CHILD WELF, Ochanomizu Women's Univ. Member: JPA. Research, teaching educational psychology; group process, leadership. M

MIZUNO, Prof. Tsunekichi. Dept. of Educ, Tamagawa Univ, Machida Machi, Tokyo. b. 10 July 1880 Fukushima. MA '17 Univ. of Illinois, USA. PROF. of VOCAT. GUID. and EDUC. ADMIN, Tamagawa Univ. Member: JPA, JSAP. Teaching, administration; learning theory, attitude measurement. M

MIZUSHIMA, Keiichi. Tokyo-Shinagawa Child Guid. Clinics, Kita-Shinagawa, To-kyo. b. 3 Aug 1928 Tokyo. Hohgakushi '51 Univ. of Tokyo, Japan. COUNSELOR, Tokyo-Shinagawa Child Guid. Clin.

Member: JPA, JSAP, JAEP. Counseling, psychotherapy, research; diagnosis and treatment of socially pathological behavior.   M

MOCHIZUKI, Prof. Mamoru. Dept. of Psych, Chiba Univ, Konakadai-machi, Chiba. b. 4 Dec 1910 Tokyo. Bungakushi '33 Univ. of Tokyo, Japan. PROFESSOR, Chiba Univ. Member: JPA. Teaching, professional writing, research; social psychology, personality, inter-personal communication.   M

MONJI, Prof. Sansei. 3-187 Tamagawa Todoroki-Cho, Setagaya,-Ku, Tokyo. b. 26 June 1909 Nagano. Bungakushi '35 Hosei Univ, Japan. PROF. of PSYCH, Hosei Univ, Kizuki, Kawasaki; ASST. PRIN, Hosei Univ. Second High Sch. Member: JPA, JSAP. Applied psychology, testing, teaching; achievement tests.   M

MORI, Akira. Nara Juvenile Detention and Classif. Home, Hannyaderacho 3, Nara. b. 17 Aug 1922 Osaka. Bungakushi '44 Kwansei Gakuin Univ, Japan. CHIEF, Classif. Sect, Nara Juv. Detention and Classif. Home. Member: SCP, Kansai Psych. Assn. Testing and classification of juvenile delinquents, guidance, research; projective techniques.   M

MORI, Prof. Atsumaru. 154 Nagaracho, Otsu, Shiga Prefecture. b. 17 Dec 1907 Osaka. Bungakushi '31 Kyoto Univ, Japan. PROF. of PSYCH, Shiga Coll, Ikesu, Hikone. Member: JPA, Kansai Psych. Assn. Teaching, educational and child psychology; developmental psychology, the exceptional child.   M

MORI, Dr. Jiro. Bakuro Machi 14, Himeji, Hyogo-ken. b. 29 Jan 1916 Kobe. Igakuhakushi '55 Osaka Univ, Japan. PRESIDENT, Kakogawa Mental Hosp, Hiraoka Vil, Kagogawa City; PSYCH. ADVIS, Fuji Ironwork Camp, Hirohata; PSYCH. ADVIS, Himeji Jr. Prison. Member: SCP, Jap. Psychiat. Assn. Administration, clinical practice, psychotherapy, applied psychology; projective techniques, achievement tests.   M

MORI, Prof. Kiyoshi. Dept. of Psych, Kumamoto Univ, Kumamoto. b. 10 Sept 1910 Hondo. Bungakushi '35 Hiroshima Bunrika Univ, Japan. ASST. PROF, Kumamoto Univ. Member: JPA. Research, teaching developmental psychology and psychology of exceptional children; learning theory applied to feeblemindedness.   M

MORI, Prof. Shigetoshi. Dept. of Psych, Kagoshima Univ, Kagoshima. b. 18 Aug 1917 Oita. Bungakushi '45 Univ. of Tokyo, Japan. ASST. PROF, Kagoshima Univ. Member: JPA, JSAP. Research, teaching, professional writing; problem

solving behavior, exceptional children, social attitudes.   M

MŌRI, Prof. Shôzo. Dept. of Educ, Kumamoto Univ, Kurokami, Kumamoto. b. 24 July 1913 Tamana. Bungakushi '38 Univ. of Tokyo, Japan. ASST. PROF, Kumamoto Univ; RES. WRKR, Aeronautical Res. Lab, Univ. of Tokyo. Member: JPA, JAEP. Research, educational and aviation psychology, teaching; perception, rigidity in personality, attitude measurement.   M

MORI, Prof. Toshikichi. Dept. of Psych, Tokyo Woman's Christian Coll, Iogi, Suginami-ku, Tokyo. b. 26 July 1924 Ichinomiya. Bungakushi '48 Keio Univ, Japan. ASST. PROF, Tokyo Woman's Christian Coll. Member: JPA, Jap. Socy. for Animal Psych. Teaching, research; perception, figural after-effects and visual illusions, learning theory.   M

MORI, Prof. Yoshitaka. Dept. of Educ, Ehime Univ, Dogo, Matsuyama, Ehime-Ken. b. 8 Nov 1905 Ehime-Ken. Bungakushi '29 Univ. of Tokyo, Japan. PROF. of EDUC. PSYCH, Ehime Univ. Member: JPA, JAEP. Teaching, research, administration; growth and development of emotions.   M

MORIMOTO, Prof. Hiroshi. Dept. of Psych, Kobe Yamata Women's Jr. Coll, Futatabi-suji, Ikutaku, Kobe. b. 18 Oct 1920 Kobe. Bungakushi '44 Kwansei Gakuin Univ, Japan. ASST. PROF, Kobe Yamata Women's Jr. Coll. Member: JPA, Kansai Psych. Assn. Research, teaching, testing; learning, factor analysis of memory.   M

MORINAGA, Prof. Shiro. Psych. Lab, Chiba Univ, Konakadai, Chiba. b. 15 July 1908 Uozu. Bungakushi '31 Univ. of Tokyo, Japan. PROFESSOR, Chiba Univ. Member: JPA, JSAP. Teaching, research, administration; perception, optical illusion and figural after-effects, occupational therapy of victims of brain injury.   M

MORITA, Prof. Kiyoshi. Dept. of Psych, Aichi Univ. of Liberal Arts and Educ, Okazaki. b. 10 Oct 1908 Tokyo. Bungakushi '39 Tokyo Bunrika Univ, Japan. PROFESSOR, Aichi Univ. of Liberal Arts and Educ. Member: JPA, JSAP. Teaching, research; projective techniques.   M

MORIWAKI, Prof. Kaname. Dept. of Psych, St. Paul Univ, Toshimaku, Tokyo. b. 1 June 1910 Hashimoto. Bungakushi '36 St. Paul Univ, Japan. PROF. of PSYCH. and DEAN of STUDENTS, St. Paul Univ. Member: JPA. Teaching, psychotherapy, consulting; play and group therapy, development of personality.   M

MORIKAWI, Miss Taeko. Dept. of Child Psych, Ochanomizu Women's Univ, Otsuka Tokyo. b. 26 Apr 1931 Tokyo. Kaseigakushi '54 Ochanomizu Women's Univ, Japan. ASSISTANT, Ochanomizu Women's

Univ. Member: JSAP. Consulting, guidance, psychotherapy, research; doll therapy.	F

MORIYA, Prof. Mitsuo. Dept. of Psych, Himeji Univ. of Engr. and Tech, Himeji, Hyogo-ken. b. 6 Mar 1913 Tokyo. Bunga-kushi '36 Kyoto Univ, Japan. PROFESSOR, Himeji Univ. of Engr. and Tech. Member: JPA, Kansai Psych. Assn. Research, teaching, testing; projective techniques, experimental study of exceptional children, study of social climate.	M

MOTOAKI, Prof. Hiroshi. Dept. of Psych, Waseda Univ, Totsuka, Tokyo. b. 1 May 1918 Los Angeles, California, USA. Bunga-kushi '41 Waseda Univ, Japan. PROFESSOR, Waseda Univ. Member: JPA. Research, teaching, testing; projective techniques. M

MOTOKAWA, Prof. Koiti. Dept. of Physiolo-gy, Tohoku Univ, Sendai b. 17 Jan 1903 Kanazawa. Igakushi '29 Univ. of Tokyo, Japan. PROF. of PSYCHOLOGY, Tohoku Univ. Member: JPA. Teaching psychologi-cal physiology, research, editorial; psycholo-gy and physiology of visual perception, neurophysiology of the central nervous system.	M

MOTOMIYA, Prof. Isaac. Yahei. Doshisha Univ, Imadegawa, Kyoto. b. 3 June 1886 Sendai. MA '20 Yale Univ, USA. PROF. EMER, Doshisha Univ. Member: JPA, SCP. Teaching, research, consulting; structure of personality.	M

MOTOYOSHI, Ryoji. Dept. of Psych, Kyoto Univ, Sakyo-ku, Kyoto. b. 26 Dec 1921 Osaka. Bungakushi '45 Kyoto Univ, Japan. INSTRUCTOR, Kyoto Univ. Member: JPA, Kansai Psych. Assn. Re-search, teaching; learning theory, animal learning.	M

MURAI, Prof. Tyuichi. Dept. of Psych, Nagoya Inst. of Tech, Showa-ku, Nagoya. b. 30 Sept 1909 Tokushima. Bungakushi '33 Kyoto Univ, Japan. PROFESSOR, Nagoya Inst. of Tech; COMM. MEMBER, Labor Mediation Comm, Nagoya District. Member: JPA, JSAP. Teaching, research, industrial psychology; group process, atti-tude measurement, social perception.	M

MURAKAMI, Eiji. Motchu, Saori-cho, Amagun, Aichi-ken. b. 20 July 1924 Nagoya. Bungakushi '50 Univ. of Tokyo, Japan. INSTR. in PSYCH, Nagoya Univ, Mizuho-cho, Nagoya; CLIN. PSYCH'T, Dept. of Neuropsychiat, Sch. of Med, Nagoya Univ. Member: JPA, JSAP, SCP. Research, teaching, clinical testing and analysis; clinical psychology, Rorschach Test, edu-cational psychology.	M

MURAKAMI, Prof. Masashi. Dept. of Psy-chiat, Med. Coll, Kyoto Univ, Kawara-machi, Shogoin, Kyoto. b. 26 Jan 1910 Gifu. Igakuhakushi '40 Kyoto Univ, Japan. PROFESSOR, Kyoto Univ. Member:

JPA, Jap. Assn. of Psychiat. and Neur. Research, teaching and clinical practice in psychiatry; psychology of schizophrenics, psychotherapy.	M

MURAKAMI, Motohiko. Shirahata 118 Ura-wa. b. 6 Oct 1919 Saseho. Bungakushi '43 Univ. of Tokyo, Japan. ED. STAFF, Nihon Keizai, Nihonbashi, Tokyo. Member: JPA, Japan Socy. for Journalistic Studies. Editorial, research, applied psychology; mass communication by newspapers.	M

MURAKAMI, Prof. Sawako. Tohoku Univ, 86 Kitaichibancho, Sendai. b. 25 Sept 1909 Sendai. Bungakushi '49 Tohoku Univ, Japan. ASST. PROF. of PSYCH, Tohoku Univ. Member: JPA, JAEP. Teaching, educational psychology, re-search; development, learning, group process.	F

MURAKAMI, Yoshio. Ehime Educ. Res. Inst, Horinouchi, Matsuyama. b. 2 Dec 1913 Ehime. Bungakushi '43 Hiroshima Bunrika Univ, Japan. CHIEF, Ehime Educ. Res. Inst; LECT. in EDUC. PSYCH, Ehime Univ. Member: JPA. Research, teaching, consulting; learning theory, achievement tests.	M

MURAMATSU, Prof. Isao. Dept. of Psych, Sagami Women's Univ, Kamitsuruma Sagamihara. b. 25 June 1910 Kofu. Iga-kuhakushi '46 Keio Univ, Japan; Bunga-kushi '35 Nihon Univ, Japan. PROFESSOR, Sagami Women's Univ. Member: JPA, JSAP. Teaching, consulting, research; emotional reactions to pregnancy.	M

MURAMATSU, Prof. Tsuneo. Dept. of Neuropsychiat, Nagoya Natl. Univ. Sch. of Med, Showa-ku, Nagoya. b. 12 Apr 1900 Tokyo. Igakuhakushi '33 Univ. of Tokyo, Japan. PROF. of PSYCHIAT, Nagoya Natl. Univ; DIRECTOR, Res. Inst. of Human Relations, Nagoya; RES. CONSULT, Natl. Res. Inst. of Ment. Hlth, Ichikawa; ED. in CHIEF, *Mental Hygiene*; ED. STAFF, *Folia Psychiatrica et Neurologica Japonica*. Member: JPA, JSAP, Japan Assn. of Psy-chiat. and Neur. Research and teaching in neuropsychiatry, administration; group process, psychopathology of neuroses. M

MURANAKA, Kanematsu. Vocat. Trng. Sect, Ministry of Labor, Otemachi, Tokyo. b. 6 Nov 1908 Aomori. Bungakushi '39 Nihon Univ, Japan. DEPUTY CHIEF, Vocat. Trng. Sect, Ministry of Labor; LECT. in PSYCH, Nihon Univ. Member: JPA, JSAP. Research, teaching, adminis-tration; character tests, vocational training and guidance.	M

MURAO, Yoshinari. Dept. of Child Study, Osaka City Univ, Nishinagahori-Minami-Dori, Nishiku, Osaka. b. 3 Nov 1927 Sasebo. Bungakushi '50 Kyoto Univ, Japan. INSTR. in CHILD PSYCH, Osaka

City Univ; LECT. in CRIM. PSYCH, Ryukoku Univ, Kyoto. Member: JPA, Kansai Psych. Assn. Teaching, research, consulting; neuro-psychological study of child development, socio-psychological study of juvenile delinquency. M

MURASE, Prof. Ryuji. Fac. of Educ, Tohoku Univ, Kitashichibancho, Sendai. b. 22 Nov 1924 Asahikawa. Bungakushi '47 Univ. of Tokyo, Japan. ASST. PROF, Tohoku Univ. Member: JPA, Tohoku Psych. Assn. Teaching, research; psychology of adolescence. M

MURATA, Koji. Dept. of Psych, Osaka City Univ, Sugimotocho, Osaka. b. 28 July 1918 Tokyo. Bungakushi '49 Kyoto Univ. Japan. INSTRUCTOR, Osaka City Univ. Member: JPA, Kansai Psych. Assn. Research, teaching, professional writing-learning theory, problems of experimental neurosis. M

MURATA, Masatsugu. 86-23 Kejime, Nishi-. hirano, Mikage-cho, Higashinada-ku, Kobe b. 28 Dec 1924 Sakai. Bungakushi '49 Kwansei Gakuin Univ, Japan. DIRECTOR, Psych. Dept, Child Consultation Cen. of Hyogo Prefecture, Okurayama, Ikuta-ku, Kobe. Member: JPA, SCP, Kwansei Psych. Assn. Consulting, clinical practice, testing, research; projective techniques, color-effects in Rorschach Test. M

MURAYAMA, Hideo. 52 3-chome, Uwamachi, Yokosuka. b. 13 Jan 1913 Mito. Bungakushi '47 Tokyo Bunrika Univ, Japan. LECT. in PSYCH, Kanagawa Univ, Rokkakubashi, Yokohama. Member: JSAP. Consulting, educational psychology, research; structure of personality in the feebleminded. M

MURAYAMA, Mrs. Michiko. 947 Kasomachi, Kasoshi, Saitamaken. b. 1 May 1914 Hiroshima. Bungakushi '38 Hosei Univ, Japan. Member: JPA. Child psychology. F

NABESHIMA, Prof. Tomoki. Dept. of Psych, Kochi Univ, Asakura, Kochi. b. 15 Sept. 1909 Kochi. Bungakushi '33 Univ. of Tokyo, Japan. ASST. PROF, Kochi Univ. Member: JPA, JSAP. Teaching, research, counseling; feeblemindedness and delinquency, attitude measurement. M

NAGAMATSU, Ichiro. Kobe Juvenile Detention and Classif. Cen, Shimogioncho, Hyogoku, Kobe. b. 13 Jan 1904 Tokyo. Bungakushi '40 St. Paul Univ, Japan. CHIEF, Kobe Juv. Detention and Classif. Cen. Member: JPA. Administration, guidance, research. M

NAGAO, Prof. Tadashi. Wakamiyadori Yobai sageru, Kyoto. b. 28 Mar 1917 Kochi-shi. Bungakushi '41 Kyoto Univ, Japan. ASST. PROF, Ritsumeikan Univ, Kyoto. Member: JPA. Teaching, research;

projective techniques. M

NAGASAKA, Dr. Goro. Sakai Ment. Hosp, Sakai, Osaka. b. 13 June 1917 Hiroshima. Igakuhakushi '53 Osaka Univ, Japan. CHIEF of LAB, Sakai Ment. Hosp. Member: JPA, Jap. Assn. of Psychiat. and Neur. Psychotherapy, clinical analysis, testing, research; projective psychology. M

NAGASAWA, Koshichi. Dept. of Psych, Tokyo Univ. of Educ, 24 Otsuka-Kubomachi, Bunkyo-ku, Tokyo. b. 24 Mar 1913 Furukawa. Bungakushi '47 Tokyo Bunrika Univ, Japan. ASSISTANT, Tokyo Univ. of Educ; LECT. in PSYCH, Tokyo Women's Jr. Coll. and Fuji Jr. Coll. Member: JPA, JSAP. Research, teaching, testing; psychology of language, psychological study of learning English. M

NAGASHIMA, Prof. Sadao. Dept. of Psych, Tokyo Univ. of Educ, Bunkyo-ku, Tokyo. b. 2 May 1917 Nagano Prefecture. Bungakushi '42 Tokyo Univ. of Educ, Japan. ASST. PROF, Tokyo Univ. of Educ; RES. COMM. MEMBER, Jap. Natl. Commission for UNESCO; EDITOR, *Child Study*. Member: JPA, JSAP. Teaching, research, professional writing; parents' attitude toward children, personality tests, social determinants of personality. M

NAITŌ, Prof. Kōjirō. Dept. of Psych, Fac. of Literature, Ritsumeikan Univ, Kawaramachi-Hirokoji, Kamikyo-ku, Kyoto. b. 29 June 1901 Osaka. Bungakushi '26 Kyoto Univ, Japan. PROFESSOR, Ritsumeikan Univ. Member: JPA. Teaching, research; synaesthesia, logic in modern psychology, social movements. M

NAKAE, Prof. Kei. Dept. of Educ, Okayama Univ, Tsushima, Okayama. b. 25 Dec 1905 Kobe. Bungakushi '29 Univ. of Tokyo, Japan. PROF. of PSYCH, Okayama Univ. Member: JPA, JSAP, JAEP. Teaching educational psychology, research; projective techniques, personality theory, group process. M

NAKAGAWA, Prof. Dairin. Dept. of Psych, Fac. of Liberal Arts, Shinshu Univ, Agata, Matsumoto. b. 3 July Hawaii. Bungakushi '44 Univ. of Tokyo, Japan. ASST. PROF, Shinshu Univ. Member: JPA, JSAP, JAEP. Research, teaching, consulting; perception, mental hygiene. M

NAKAGAWA, Yaichi. Kinjo Coll, Omori, Nagoya. b. 8 Aug 1898 Kobe. Bungakushi '31 Taihoku Univ, Japan. ASST. PROF. of PSYCH, Kinjo Coll. Member: JPA. Psychotherapy, research, teaching educational psychology; structure of the family, social pathology, child development. M

NAKAGAWARA, Michiyuki. 187 Simorenjaku, Mitaka-shi, Tokyo. b. 15 Mar 1915 Tokyo. Bungakushi '37 Kei Univ, Japan. CHIEF, Genl. Affairs Dept, Kanto District

Comm, 1 Fujimi-cho Chiyoda-ku, Tokyo.
Member: JPA, JSAP. Administration, supervision of criminals; criminal psychology. M

NAKAHARA, Prof. Reizo. Dept. of Psych,
Kwansei-Gakuin Univ, Nishinomiya, Hyogo. b. 8 Sept 1922 Takarazuka. Bungakushi
'48 Kwansei-Gakuin Univ, Japan. ASST.
PROF, Kwansei-Gakuin Univ. Member: JPA.
Research, teaching developmental psychology, consulting; projective techniques. M

NAKAJIMA, Akiyoshi. Dept. of Psych,
Coll. of Genl. Educ, Univ. of Tokyo,
Komabamachi, Meguroku, Tokyo. b.
1 Apr 1927 Tokyo. Bungakushi '50 Univ.
of Tokyo, Japan. ASSISTANT, Univ. of
Tokyo. Member: JPA, JSAP. Research,
teaching; perception of obstacles by the
blind and the deaf-blind. M

NAKAJIMA, Sei. Dept. of Psych, Kyoto
Univ, Sakyo, Kyoto. b. 8 Oct 1924 Kochi.
Bungakushi '48 Kyoto Univ, Japan.
INSTRUCTOR, Kyoto Univ. Member: JPA,
Kansai Psych. Assn. Research, teaching,
consulting; perception. M

NAKAJIMA, Prof. Yoshiyuki. Dept. of
Psych, Gunma Univ, Seioji, Maebashi.
b. 4 Aug 1915 Maebashi. Bungakushi '39
Univ. of Tokyo, Japan. PROFESSOR, Gunma
Univ. Member: JPA, JSAP. Teaching, research, educational psychology, psychological tests and morale studies in
industry, acquisition of skill. M

NAKAMURA, Prof. Hiromichi. Dept. of
Psych, Coll. of Genl. Educ, Univ. of Tokyo,
Komabamachi, Meguroku, Tokyo. b. 12
Dec 1900 Kumamoto. Bungakushi
'27 Univ. of Tokyo, Japan. PROF. of
PSYCH, and DIR. of COUNSELING CEN, Univ.
of Tokyo. Member: JPA, JSAP. Teaching;
guidance, research, administration;
counseling. M

NAKAMURA, Prof. Hiroshi. Dept. of Literature, Seinangakuin Univ, Nishijinmachi,
Fukuoka. b. 6 May 1914 Fukuoka. Bungakushi '39 Kyushu Univ, Japan. PROF. of
PSYCH. and CHIEF LIBRARIAN, Seinangakuin
Univ. Member: JPA. Research, teaching,
psychoterapy; development of perception,
personality and perception. M

NAKAMURA, Prof. Hiyoshi. Dept. of Psych,
Tokyo Metrop. Univ, Fusuma-cho, Me-
guro-ku, Tokyo. b. 1 Aug 1925 Tokyo.
Bungakushi '47 Univ. of Tokyo, Japan.
ASST. PROF, Tokyo Metrop. Univ; LECTURER
Seisen Girl's Univ. Member: JPA, JSAP.
Teaching, research, applied psychology;
social psychology, group dynamics, human
relations in the family. M

NAKAMURA, Prof. Ikuta. Dept. of Psych,
Yamaguchi Univ, Yamaguchi-shi. b.
25 June 1904 Onoda. Bungakushi '33
Hiroshima Bunrika Univ, Japan. PRO-
FESSOR, Yamaguchi Univ. Member: JPA.

Research, teaching, professional writing;
attitude measurement, factor analysis, psychology applied to teaching mathematics. M

NAKAMURA, Prof. Shigeru. Dept. of Literature, Kobe Univ, Mikage, Kobe. b.
3 Feb 1912 Tokyo. Bungakushi '34 Univ.
of Tokyo, Japan. PROF. of PSYCH, Kobe
Univ. Member: JPA, JSAP. Research,
teaching, applied psychology; psychology
of the deaf, history of psychology. M

NAKANE, Fuyuo. Sugamo Prison, 3277
Nishisugamo, 1-chome, Toshima-ku, Tokyo.
b. 6 Aug 1922 Kyoto. Bungakushi '46
Doshisha Univ, Japan. CHIEF, Classif.
Sect, Tokyo Correctl. District, Aoyama-
Minamimachi, Tokyo. Member: JSAP.
Administration, research, testing and
classification of delinquents; attitude
measurement of adolescents. M

NAKANISHI, Prof. Noboru. Dept. of Child
Study, Osaka City Univ, Nishinagahori-
Minamidori, Nishiku, Osaka. b. 14 July
1911 Nagoya. Bungakushi '36 Kyoto
Univ, Japan. PROF. of CHILD PSYCH, Osaka
City Univ; EDITOR, *Reports of the Science
of Living.* Member: JPA, SCP, Kansai
Psych. Assn. Teaching, research, consulting; measurement of personality traits
in children, projective techniques, perception of the child. M

NAKANISHI, Shigemi. Dept. of Psych,
Osaka Univ. of Liberal Arts and Educ,
Tennoji, Osaka. b. 15 Apr 1928 Osaka.
Bungakushi '50 Kwansei-Gakuin Univ,
Japan. ASSISTANT, Osaka Univ. of Liberal
Arts and Educ. Member: JPA, JSAP, Jap.
Socy. for Animal Psych. Research,
teaching, applied psychology; learning
theory, conditioning. M

NAKANO, Kodo. Matsuyama Natl. Trng.
Sch. for Boys, Furumitsu, Matsuyama.
b. 1 May 1916 Matusyama. Bungakushi
'41 Komazawa Univ, Japan. CHIEF,
Classif. Sect, Matsuyama Natl. Trng. Sch.
for Boys. Member: JPA. Consulting, testing,
administration; psychology of Zen Buddhism. M

NAKANO, Prof. Sukezo. Dept. of Psych,
Tokyo Univ. of Educ, Otsuka, Bunkyo-ku
Tokyo. b. 25 Feb 1902 Kagawa Prefecture.
Bungakuhakushi '54 Tokyo Bunrika Univ,
Japan. PROFESSOR, Tokyo Univ. of Educ;
EDITOR, *Child Study.* Member: JPA, JSAP.
Research, teaching educational psychology,
consulting; learning theory, problem
solving. M

NAKANOWATARI, Nobuyuki. Dept. of
Econ. and Polit. Sci, Meiji Univ, Kanda
Chiyoda-ku, Tokyo. b. 9 Feb 1915 Aomori-
ken. Bungakushi '40 Hosei Univ, Japan.
INSTRUCTOR, Meiji Univ. Member: JPA,
JSAP. Teaching; attitude measurement,
correlation between group attitude and

economic life, psychology of Japanese fine arts.   M

NAKAYAMA, Shigeru. Ministry of Welf, Natl. Rehab. Cen. for the Physically Handicapped, 1 Toyama-cho, Shinjuku-ku, Tokyo. b. 2 July 1913 Tokyo. Bungakushi '38 Univ. of Tokyo, Japan. TECH. OFF, Ministry of Welf, Natl. Rehab. Cen. for the Physically Handicapped. Member: JPA, JSAP. Testing, consulting, applied psychology; intelligence tests.   M

NAKAZAWA, Prof. Shōju. Dept. of Educ, Shizuoka Univ, Oiwa, Shizuoka. b. 21 June 1915 Maebashi. Bungakushi '42 Tokyo Bunrika Univ, Japan. ASST. PROF. of PSYCH, Shizuoka Univ. Member: JPA, JSAP. Research, administration, teaching; learning theory.   M

NANJO, Prof. Masa-aki. Nagasaki Prefectural Sasebo Commercial Jr. Coll, Miura-machi, Sasebo City, Nagasaki Prefecture. b. 26 Nov 1913 Tokyo. Bungakushi '39 Kyoto Univ, Japan. PROF. of PSYCH, Nagasaki Prefectural Sasebo Commercial Jr. Coll; LECTURER, Nagasaki Prefectural Women's Jr. Coll. Member: JPA, JAEP, Kyushu Psych. Assn. Research, teaching educational psychology and measurement, consulting; formation of personality, sex difference and Masculinity-Femininity tests.   M

NARUSE, Gosaku. Dept. of Psych, Tokyo Univ. of Educ, 24 Kubomachi, Bunkyo, Tokyo. b. 5 June 1924 Gifu. Bungakushi '50 Tokyo Bunrika Univ, Japan. ASSISTANT, Tokyo Univ. of Educ. Member: JPA, JSAP. Research, testing, teaching; modification of memory image, study of motivation in abnormal psychology, perception, experimental hypnosis.   M

NIHAMA, Prof. Kunio. Dept. of Psych, Kwansei Gakuin Univ, Nishinomiya. b. 13 Jan 1925 Tientsin, China. Bungakushi '49 Kwansei Gakuin Univ, Japan. ASST. PROF, Kwansei Gakuin Univ. Member: JPA, JSAP. Research, teaching; learning theory, conditioning.   M

NIIMI, Katsunobu. 320 1-chome, Shimoumamachi, Setagaya-ku, Tokyo. b. 29 Aug 1917 Tokyo. Bungakushi '41 Waseda Univ, Japan. RES. WRKR, Iwanami Shoten, Kanda-Hitotsubashi, Tokyo. Member: JPA. Research, applied psychology; research for writers, publishers and readers.   M

NIIMI, Prof. Yosizumi. Dept. of Psych, Waseda Univ, Tozuka, Tokyo. b. 3 May 1923 Tokyo. Bungakushi '46 Waseda Univ, Japan. ASST. PROF, Waseda Univ. Member: JPA, JSAP. Research, teaching, consulting; galvanic skin response, electroencephalography, conditioning.   M

NIIZUMA, Tatsuo. 7-1 Higashidori Sakurazuka Toyonaka-shi, Osaka. b. 25 Feb 1927 Tokyo. Keizaigakushi '50 Kwansei Gakuin Univ, Japan. RES. WRKR, Kwansei Gakuin Univ, Uegahara, Nishinomiya. Member: JPA. Student, research; psychoanalysis.   M

NIKI, Kuniaki. 4 Minamisako-cho, 11-chome, Tokushima City, Tokushima Prefecture. b. 23 Nov 1921 Pusan, Korea. Bungakushi '45 Keijo Univ, Korea. CHIEF, Tokushima Prefecture Child Welf. Cen, 31 Shinkura-cho, 3-chome, Tokushima; LECTURER, Tokushima Univ. Member: JPA, SCP. Clinical analysis and guidance of maladjusted children, teaching, administration; psychotherapy research.   M

NISHI, Prof. Tokumichi. Dept. of Liberal Arts and Educ, Iwate Univ, Ueda, Morioka. b. 17 Oct 1886 Tokyo. Bungakushi '15 Univ. of Tokyo, Japan. PROF. of PSYCH, Iwate Univ. Member: JPA, Tohoku Psych. Assn. Teaching, research; visual space perception.   M

NISHIDA, Haruhiko. Dept. of Sociol, Wakayama Univ, Masago-cho, Wakyama. b. 13 Jan 1924 Kyoto. Bungakushi '48 Univ. of Tokyo, Japan. INSTRUCTOR, Wakayama Univ. Member: JPA. Research, teaching, testing; attitude measurement. M

NISHIHIRA, Naoki. Dept. of Psych, Yamanashi Univ, Kofuchu-machi, Kofu, Yamanashi. b. 13 Jan 1926 Tokyo, Bungakushi '50 Tokyo Bunrika Univ. Japan. INSTRUCTOR, Yamanashi Univ. Member: JPA. Research, teaching educational psychology, consulting; adolescent psychology.   M

NISHIJIMA, Prof. Yoshio. Dept. of Psych, Aichi Univ. of Liberal Arts and Educ, Okazaki. b. 3 Apr 1918 Kumamoto. Bungakushi '43 Kyoto Univ, Japan. ASST. PROF, Aichi Univ. of Liberal Arts and Educ. Member: JPA, JSAP. Research, teaching; learning theory, personality. M

NISHIKAWA, Dr. Yoshio. 389 4-chome, Kitazawa, Setagaya-ku, Tokyo. b. 12 Dec 1908 Tokyo. Bungakushi '35 Hosei Univ, Japan; Igakushi '32 Tokyo Jikeikai Med. Coll, Japan. ASST. CHIEF, Hlth. Superv. Sect, Welf. Bur, Jap. Natl. Railways, Marunouchi, Tokyo. Member: JPA. Administration, research, teaching; industrial safety, color conditioning. M

NISHIMOTO, Prof. Osamu. 111 Chausuyama-cho, Tennoji-ku, Osaka. b. 10 Mar 1924 Kobe. Bungakushi '47 Kwansei Gakuin Univ, Japan. ASST. PROF. of PSYCH, Child Guid. Clin, Shoei Jr. Coll. and Kindergarten, 36 6-chome, Nakayamate, Kobe. Member: JPA, JAEP. Research, teaching educational psychology, testing; child development, mental tests for infants and pre-school children, mental hygiene in early childhood.   M

NISHIMURA, Kanichi. Sapporo Juv. Classif. Hse, West-11 South-25, Sapporo, Hokkaido. b. 1 Nov 1900 Sakaiminato. Bungakushi '28 Nihon Univ, Japan. DIRECTOR, Sappore Juv. Classif. Hse. Member: JPA, JSAP, Hokkaido Psych. Assn. Administration, educational psychology, guidance; vocational guidance for juvenile delinquents. M

NISHIMURA, Tadayasu. Tsujido 7259, Fujisawa-shi. b. 3 Dec 1917 Kanazawa. Bungakushi '41 Univ. of Tokyo, Japan. PSYCH. ENGR, Dept. of Psych, Labor Sci. Res. Off, Jap. Natl. Railways, Tabata 608, Kita-ku, Tokyo. Member: JPA, Japan Assn. of Aviat. Med. and Psych. Personnel psychology, testing, research; aptitude tests. M

NISHINA, Yoshikazu. Chiba Prefecture Central Child. Consultat, Sakusabe, Chiba. b. 25 Aug 1929 Tokyo. Bungakushi '51 Nihon Univ, Japan. HEAD, Diagnosis and Guid. Sect, Chiba Prefecture Central Child Consultat. Member: JSAP. Guidance, clinical analysis, psychotherapy; social adjustment, adjustment of children in foster homes. M

NISHITANI, Prof. Kendo. Dept. of Educ, Keio Univ, Mita, Tokyo. b. 7 May 1899 Chiba. Bungakushi '24 Keio Univ, Japan. PROF. of EDUC. and DEVEL. PSYCH, Keio Univ. Member: JPA, JAEP. Teaching, research, professional writing; child and adolescent character. M

NISHITANI, Prof. Sanshiro. Dept. of Spec. Educ, Tokyo Univ. of Educ, Tokyo. b. 24 Aug 1914 Tokushima. Igakuhakushi '50 Kanazawa Med. Coll. Japan. ASST. PROF. of PSYCHIAT, Tokyo Univ. of Educ. Member: JPA, Jap. Assn. of Psychiat. and Neur. Teaching and research on the treatment of the mentally deficient, clinical practice; causes and diagnosis of mental deficiency. M

NISIHIRA, Sigeki. Inst. of Stat. Math, 1 Azabu Huzimi-cho, Minatoku, Tokyo. b. 4 Jan 1924 Tokyo. Rigakushi '47 Hokkaido Univ, Japan. DIR. of RES, Inst. of Stat. Math. Member: JPA. Statistical analysis of social-psychological problems, research, consulting, teaching; social conflicts, mass communication, social perception. M

NISIZAKI, Kiyoshi. Inst. for the Feebleminded, Okayama-ken, Yuga, Kotoura Kozima-shi, Okayama-ken. b. 2 June 1907 Okayama. Bungakushi '37 Hiroshima Bunrika Univ, Japan. HEAD, Inst. for the Feebleminded; PROFESSOR, Notre Dame Seishin Coll. Member: JPA. Administration, research, guidance; personality of the feebleminded, attitude measurement, learning theory. M

NITTA, Kenichi. 415 Koriyama, Ibaraki-shi. b. 18 Jan 1926 Tokyo. Bungakushi '53 Tohoku Univ, Japan. TEACHER, Naniwa Reformatory, Koriyama, Ibaraki. Member: JPA. Classification of juvenile delinquents, guidance, testing, research; group dynamics, criminology. M

NITTA, Noriyosi. Dept. of Educ. Psych, Natl. Inst. for Educ. Res, Chozyamaru, Sinagawa, Tokyo. b. 23 Nov 1924 Tokyo. Bungakushi '49 Univ. of Tokyo, Japan. RES. WRKR, Natl. Inst. for Educ. Res. Member: JPA, Jap. Socy. for Animal Psych. Psychological study of delinquents; juvenile delinquency. color constancy, visual perception in animals. M

NIWA, Prof. Yoshiko. Dept. of English, Toyoeiwa Women's Coll, Torrizaka-machi, Azabu, Minato-ku, Tokyo. b. 1 Aug 1913 Hiroshima. MA '52 George Peabody Coll. for Tchrs, USA. PROF. of ENGLISH, Toyoeiwa Women's Coll. Member: JPA, JSAP. Teaching adolescent psychology, research, educational psychology; counseling of adolescents, origins of social perception. F

NOBECHI, Prof. Masayuki. Dept. of Psych, Doshisha Univ, Karasuma-Imadegawa, Kyoto. b. 15 Aug 1921 Tokyo. Bungakushi '42 Doshisha Univ, Japan. ASST. PROF, Doshisha Univ. Member: JPA, Kansai Psych. Assn. Research, teaching; child and adolescent personality. M

NODA, Hirotaka. 741 Matsuzonocho, Hanamaki-shi, Iwate. b. 28 Mar. 1922 Hiroshima. Bungakushi '42 Risshoo Coll, Japan. COUNSELOR, Iwate-ken Child Welf. Cen, Uchimaru, Morioka. Member: JPA. Clinical diagnosis and counseling, psychotherapy; projective techniques, play therapy. M

NOGAMI, Prof. Toshio. 88 Zembu-cho, Shimo-Kaom, Sakyo-ku, Kyoto. b. 2 May 1882 Aikawa. Bungakuhakushi '18 Kyoto Univ, Japan. PROF. of PSYCH, Kyoto Women's Univ, Higashiyama-Shichijo, Kyoto. Member: JPA. Research, teaching; adolescent psychology. M

NOGUCHI, Dr. Shinji. Sakuragaoka Ment. Hosp, Tamamura, Minamitama-Gun, Tokyo. b. 19 Jan 1912 Tokyo. Igakuhakushi '51 Keio Univ, Japan. SUPERINTENDENT, Sakuragaoka Ment. Hosp; LECT. in CLIN. and MED. PSYCH, Keio Univ. Member: JPA, JSAP. Administration, research, clinical practice; projective techniques, group dynamics, criminal psychology. M

NOMI, Yoichi. Natl. Yokohama Juv. Classif. Home, Iwai-cho Hodogaya-ku, Yokohama. b. 15 May 1918 Hagi. Bungakushi 49 Tokyo Bunrika Univ, Japan. CHIEF, Clin. Sect, Yokohama Juv. Classif. Home. Member: JPA. Testing and classification of delinquents, guidance, research; projective techniques, electroencephalography. M

NOMURA, Prof. Nobukiyo. Dept. of the Sci. of Relig, Kyushu Univ, Hakozaki, Fukuoka. b. 1 Jan 1922 Kobe. Bungakushi '45 Univ. of Tokyo, Japan. ASST. PROF, Kyushu Univ. Member: JPA. Research, teaching the psychology of religion, testing; attitude measurement, projective techniques, religious personality. M

NONAKA, Minoru. Dept. of Psych, Kochi Univ, Kochi. b. 1 Feb 1920 Kochi. Bungakushi '46 Tokyo Bunrika Univ, Japan. INSTRUCTOR, Kochi Univ. Member: JPA. Teaching educational psychology, research, testing; projective techniques. M

NONISHI, Prof. Keizo. Dept. of Psych, Miyazaki Univ, Miyazaki. b. 10 May 1920 Hiroshima. Bungakushi '47 Hiroshima Bunrika Univ, Japan. ASST. PROF. Miyazaki Univ. Member: JPA. Teaching educational psychology, mental hygiene, and vocational guidance; human relations. M

NOZAWA, Shin. Dept. of Exper. Psych, Fac. of Letters, Hokkaido Univ, Sapporo, Hokkaido. b. 22 Feb 1923 Tokyo. Bungakushi '48 Univ. of Tokyo, Japan. INSTRUCTOR, Hokkaido Univ. Member: JPA, Hokkaido Psych. Assn, Jap. Socy. for Animal Psych. Teaching, research; perception, figural after-effects. M

NUKINA, Prof. Chikei. Dept. of Psych, Yokohama Natl. Univ, Yokohama. b. 20 Jan 1897 Saiki. Bungakushi '27 Univ. of Tokyo, Japan. PROFESSOR, Yokohama Nat. Univ. Member: JPA, JSAP. Research, teaching, consulting; study of personality through contemporary paintings. M

OBA, Mrs. Ayako. Women Workers' Sect, Women's and Minors' Bur, Labor Dept, Tokyo. b. 8 June 1912 Tokyo. CHIEF, Women workers' Sect, Women's and Minors' Bur. Member: JPA, JSAP. Administration, personnel psychology, psychological sex differences, occupational analysis and classification. F

OBA, Prof. Chiaki. Dept. of Psych, Ibaraki Univ, Mito. b. 18 Nov 1902 Hakodate. Bungakushi '28 Univ. of Tokyo, Japan. PROFESSOR, Ibaraki Univ; LECT. in CULTURAL ANTROP, Ibaraki Christian Coll, Omika, Hitachi. Member: JPA, JSAP. Teaching general and cultural psychology, research; psychological study of primitive education. M

OBIKA, Prof. Kazuo. Onomichi Coll, Onomichi-shi, Hirshima-ken. b. 3 Jan 1914 Mihara. Bungakushi '39 Hiroshima Univ, Japan. ASST. PROF, Onomichi Coll. Member: JPA. Teaching educational psychology and vocational guidance, research, administration; memory. M

OBONAI, Prof. Torao. Dept. of Psych, Tokyo Univ. of Educ, Otsuka, Tokyo. b. 24 Apr 1899 Fukuoka. Bungakuhakushi

'51 Univ. of Tokyo, Japan. PROFESSOR, Tokyo Univ. of Educ; EDITOR, *Japanese Journal of Psychology.* Member: JPA, JSAP, Jap. Assn. of Aviat. Med. and Psych. Research, teaching, administration; physiological psychology, visual sensation, perception, memory. M

OBUCHI, Tadao. Civil Aviat. Agency, Sapporo Off, 2-chome, Honcho, Chitose, Hokkaido. b. 17 Jan 1931 Sapporo. Bungakushi '54 Hokkaido Univ, Japan. AIR TRAFFIC CONTROLLER, Japan Civil Aviat. Agency, 1-chome Ohte-machi, Chiyoda, Tokyo. Member: Japan Assn. of Aviat. Med. and Psych. Radar operation, research, testing; aviation psychology, aptitude tests for airmen, emotions in flight. M

ODA, Prof. Kazuo. Dept. of Liberal Arts, Tottori Univ, Tottori. b. 4 Apr 1909 Kurayoshi. Bungakushi '37 Univ. of Tokyo, Japan. PROF. of PSYCH, Tottori Univ. Member: JPA, JAEP. Teaching, research, educational psychology; learning theory. M

ODA, Prof. Nobuo. Dept. of Psych, Tokushima Univ, Tokushima. b. 8 Aug 1899 Okayama. Bungakushi '33 Tokyo Bunrika Univ, Japan. PROFESSOR, Tokushima Univ. Member: JPA, JSAP. Research, teaching, guidance; field theory. M

ŌGA, Prof. Kazuo. Dept. of Psych, Fukuoka Univ. of Liberal Arts and Educ, Fukuokashi. b. 17 Sept 1913 Fukuoka Prefecture. Bungakushi '44 Hiroshima Bunrika Univ, Japan. ASST. PROF, Fukuoka Univ. of Liberal Arts and Educ. Member: JPA, Jap. Socy. of Grp. Dynam. Teaching, research, psychotherapy; play therapy, group psychotherapy, group process. M

OGASAWARA, Prof. Jiei. 611 Sekimachi 4-chome, Nerima, Tokyo. b. 2 Aug 1909 Gifu-ken. Bungakuhakushi '54 Univ. of Tokyo, Japan. ASST. PROF, Tokyo Univ. of Educ, Bunkyo-ku, Tokyo. Member: JPA. Teaching, research, illusions, constancy, theory of perception. M

OGAWA, Prof. Kazuo. Dept. of Psych, Teachers' Coll, Shimane Univ, Uchinakahara, Matsue. b. 6 Mar 1924 Miyazaki. Bungakushi '49 Hiroshima Univ, Japan. ASST. PROF, Teachers' Coll, Shimane Univ. Member: JPA, JAEP. Research, teaching, educational and child psychology; human relations, teachers' attitudes toward pupils. M

OGAWA, Saiji. Dept. of Spec. Educ, Tokyo Univ. of Educ, Bunkyo, Tokyo. b. 18 May 1926 Kyoto. Bungakushi '48 Univ. of Tokyo, Japan. ASSISTANT, Tokyo Univ. of Educ; LECTURER, Meiji Univ. Member: JPA, JSAP. Research, teaching; education of physically and mentally handicapped

children. M
OGAWA, Prof. Takashi. Dept. of Psych, Keio Univ, Mita, Tokyo. b. 16 Nov 1915 Tokyo. Bungakushi '38 Univ. of Tokyo, Japan. ASST. PROF, Keio Univ. Member: JPA, Jap. Socy. for Animal Psych. Teaching, research; perception, discrimination learning in comparatieve psychology. M
OGINO, Prof. Koichi. Dept. of Psych, Nanzan Univ, Showaku, Nagoya. b. 19 Jan 1921 Osaka. Igakuhakushi '44 Kyoto Univ, Japan. ASST. PROF, Nanzan Univ; LECT. in PSYCHIAT, Kyoto Univ. Member: JPA, SCP, Jap. Psychiat. Assn. Research, teaching, consulting; psychopathology, psychology of interpersonal relationships, religious psychology. M
OGISO, Prof. On. Fac. of Educ, Chiba Univ, Chiba. b. 20 Oct 1900 Ueda. Bungakushi '27 Univ. of Tokyo, Japan. PROF. of PSYCH, Chiba Univ. Member: JPA, JSAP. Teaching, research, educational psychology, testing; projective techniques. M
OGUMA, Prof. Toranosuke. Dept. of Psych, Meiji Univ, Kanda, Chiyodaku, Tokyo. b. 30 Mar 1888 Kasiwazaki. Bungakushi, '14 Univ. of Tokyo, Japan. PROFESSOR. Meiji Univ. Member: JPA, JSAP, Jap. Assn. of Criminol, Jap. Assn. of Psychiat. and Neur, Jap. Assn. of Psychoanal. Teaching, research, psychotherapy; psychological problems in testimony and court trials, dreams, treatment of neuroses. M
OGURA, Prof. Yoshihisa. Kobaranishi, Yamanashi-Shi, Yamanashi-ken. b. 2 Apr 1919 Tokyo. Bungakushi '42 Tokyo Bunrika Univ, Japan. ASST. PROF. of PSYCH, Yamanashi Univ, Kofuchu, Kofu. Member: JPA, JSAP. Teaching, research, educational psychology; learning theory, child development, audio-visual methods. M
OHBA, Katsumi. Dept. of Psych, Fac. of Letters, Hokkaido Univ, Sapporo, Hokkaido. b. 13 Sept 1926 Tokyo. Bungakushi '50 Univ. of Tokyo, Japan. ASSISTANT, Hokkaido Univ. Member: JPA, Hokkaido Psych. Assn, Jap. Socy. for Animal Psych. Research, teaching; comparative study of the social behavior of animals. M
OHINATA, Miss Satoko. Dept. of Psych, Keio Univ, Mita, Tokyo. b. 18 July 1929 Tokyo. Bungakushi '54 Keio Gijuku Univ, Japan. STUDENT. Member: JPA, Jap. Socy. for Animal Psych. Research; discrimination learning. F
OHIRA, Prof. Katsuma. Dept. of Educ, Kanazawa Univ, Otemachi, Kanazawa. b. 17 Sept 1907 Tokushima. Bungakushi '38 Nihon Univ, Japan. ASST. PROF. of PSYCH, Kanazawa Univ. Member: JPA, JSAP, JAEP. Research, teaching, testing; learning theory,

relationship between heredity and environment, physical maturation and mental development. M
OHKAWA, Prof. Nobuaki. Dept. of Psych, Tokyo Woman's Christian Coll, Iogi, Suginami-ku, Tokyo. b. 1 Jan 1921 Tokyo. Bungakushi '50 Univ. of Tokyo, Japan. ASST. PROF, Tokyo Woman's Christian Coll. Member: JPA, Jap. Socy. for Animal Psych. Research, teaching, consulting; constancy, contrast, and adaptation in perception. M
OHMIYA, Prof. Rokuro. Fac. of Liberal Arts, Ibaraki Univ, Mito. b. 30 June 1918 Tokyo. Bungakushi '43 Univ. of Tokyo, Japan. ASST. PROF. of PSYCH, Ibaraki Univ. Member: JPA. Research, teaching, guidance; personality types and cultural integration M
OHMURA, Masao. Dept. of Psych, Fac. of Letters, Nihon Univ, Kanda-Misaki-cho, Chiyoda-ku, Tokyo. b. 4 Oct 1925 Tokyo. Bungakushi '48 Nihon Univ, Japan. INSTRUCTOR, Nihon Univ; ASST. PROF, Nisho Gakusha Coll. Member: JPA, JSAP. Teaching, research, testing; personality adjustment, military psychology, sociometry. M
OHNISHI, Prof. Kenmei. Dept. of Psych, Osaka City Univ, Sugimotocho, Higashi-sumiyoshi-ku, Osaka. b. 6 Dec 1911 Takamatu. Bungakushi '36 Kyushu Univ, Japan. PROFESSOR, Osaka City Univ. Member: JPA, Kansai Psych. Assn, Kansai Socy. of Clin. Psych. Research, teaching, testing; personality, educational psychology. M
OHNO, Prof. Shinichi. 250 Hamada azasutokuin, Amagasaki-shi, Hyogo-ken. b. 3 June 1919 Matsuyama. Bungakushi '44 Kyushu Univ, Japan. ASST. PROF. of PSYCH, Osaka City Univ, Sugimoto-cho, Osaka. Member: JPA. Research, teaching, consulting; visual space perception. M
OHSHIO, Prof. Shunsuke. Dept. of Sociol, Tokyo Metrop. Univ, Meguro, Tokyo. b. 11 Dec 1923 Tokyo. Bungakushi '47 Univ. of Tokyo, Japan. ASST. PROF, Tokyo Metrop. Univ. Member: JPA. Research, teaching, testing; group dynamics. M
OHTA, Hideaki. Dept. of Psych, Hokkaido Univ, Sapporo. b. 21 Oct. 1930 Sapporo. Bungakushushi '55 Hokkaido Univ, Japan. STUDENT. Member: JPA, Hokkaido Psych. Assn. Research; group dynamics, decision process. M
OHTSUKA, Prof. Noboru. Psych. Inst, Konan Univ, Kobe. b. 16 Aug 1905 Tokushima. Bungakushi '37 Keio Univ, Japan. PROFESSOR, Konan Univ. Member: JPA, Jap. Socy. for Animal Psych. Teaching, research; genetics of behavior, symbolic behavior of animals. M
OHTSUKI, Kenji. Tokyo Inst. of Psychoanal,

Nishinasuno, Tochigi-ken. b. 2 Nov 1891 Japan. Bungakushi '18 Waseda Univ, Japan. DIRECTOR, Tokyo Inst. of Psychoanal; EDITOR, *Tokyo Journal of Psychoanalysis*. Clinical practice, psychotherapy, editorial; psychoanalysis. M

OHWAKI, Miss Sonoko. Saikyo Women's Coll, Katsura, Kyoto. b. 12 June 1928 Sendai. Bungakushi '51 Tohoku Univ, Japan. INSTR. in PSYCH, Saikyo Women's Coll. Member: JPA, JSAP. Research, teaching; visual perception, development of perception. F

OHWAKI, Prof. Yoshikazu. Kita 5 Bancho 15, Sendai. b. 7 Feb 1897 Kyoto. Bungakuhakushi '40 Tohoku Univ, Japan. PROF. of PSYCH, Tohoku Univ, Katahiracho, Sendai; LECTURER, Tenri Univ, Nara; EDITOR, *Tohoku Psychologyca Folia*; ED. BD, *Journal of Genetic Psychology* (USA), *Japanese Journal of Psychology*. Member: AIPA, JPA, JSAP. Teaching, research, editorial; eidetic and Bocci imagery, consciousness and behavior, environmental and racial differences. M

ŌI, Prof. Heiichiro. Dept. of Psych, Hokkaido Univ. of Liberal Arts and Educ, Asahigawa, Hokkaido. b. 20 Aug 1909 Hokkaido. Bungakushi '45 Hiroshima Bunrika Univ, Japan. PROFESSOR, Hokkaido Univ. of Liberal Arts and Educ; SCH. MASTER, Primary Sch. of Hokkaido Univ. of Liberal Arts and Educ. Member: JPA, JAEP. Teaching, research, administration; child development, learning theory, social prejudice, psychology of blind children. M

OIKAWA, Masao. 1307 Sakusabe-cho, Chiba. b. 17 June 1906 Chiba. Bungakushi '32 Univ. of Tokyo, Japan. CHIEF, Chiba Juv. Classif. Off, Sakusabe-cho, Chiba. Member: JPA. Administration, testing; social prognosis of the criminal. M

OIKAWA, Prof. Shingaku. Dept. of Psych, Rissho Univ, Osaki, Tokyo. b. 1 July 1907 Kyoto. Bungakushi '31 Rissho Univ, Japan. ASST. PROF, Rissho Univ. Member: JPA. Teaching, research; psychology of religion. M

OJIMA, Prof. Sekishin. Dept. of Spec. Educ, Tokyo Univ. of Educ, Bunkyo-ku, Tokyo. b. 3 Dec 1904 Tokyo. Bungakushi '31 Univ. of Tokyo, Japan. PROFESSOR, Tokyo Univ. of Educ. Member: JPA, JSAP. Administration, teaching, research; psychology of handicapped children. M

OKA, Prof. Dōko. Dept. of Psych, Osaka City Univ, Sugimotocho, Osaka. b. 5 Jan Wakayama. Bungakushi '22 Kyoto Univ, Japan. PROFESSOR, Osaka City Univ. Member: JPA, Kansai Psych. Assn. Teaching, research, administration; psychology of religion. M

OKA, Prof. Hiroko. Dept. of Psych, Seishin Univ, Miyashirocho Shibuya-ku, Tokyo. b. 20 July 1917 Saga. Bungakushi '42 Tokyo Bunrika Univ, Japan. PROF. and HEAD, Dept. of Psych, Seishin Univ. Member: JPA, JAEP. Research, teaching, consulting; dynamic processes of mental development. F

OKA, Prof. Naomichi. Dept. of Psych, Tokyo Univ. of Educ, Otsuka, Tokyo. b. 27 Jan 1909 Tokyo. Rigakush '33 Univ. of Tokyo, Japan. ASST. PROF, Tokyo Univ. of Educ; ED. BD, *The annual of Animal Psychology*. Member: JPA, Jap. Socy. for Animal Psych. Research, editorial, teaching; problem-solving, visual perception and innate behavior of animals. M

OKABAYASHI, Keio. 9 chome Ujinamachi, Hiroshima. b. 26 Apr 1926 Kumamoto. Bungakushi '50 Hiroshima Univ, Japan. SECT. CHIEF, Hiroshima Juv. Classif. Off, Ujinamachi, Hiroshima. Member: JPA, Hiroshima Clin. Psych. Assn. Testing, clinical analysis, guidance; projective techniques, juvenile delinquency. M

OKABE, Prof. Yatero. 1006 Yoyogi Nishihara-machi, Shibuya-ku, Tokyo. b. 20 June 1894 Ueda. Bungakushi '19 Univ. of Tokyo, Japan PROF of EDUC. PSYCH, Int. Christian Univ, 1500 Osawa, Mitakashi, Tokyo; CHMN. of ED. BD, *Japanese Journal of Educational Psychology*. Member: JPA, JSAP, JAEP. Teaching, research, guidance; character formation, educational evaluation, personality inventory. M

OKADA, Prof. Arisuke. Dept. of Psych, Chiba Univ, Chiba. b. 27 Nov 1909 Agano. Bungakushi '34 Univ. of Tokyo, Japan. PROFESSOR, Chiba Univ. Member: JPA, JSAP. Teaching, research, applied psychology; achievement tests, attitude measurement. M

OKAJI, Prof. Ichiro. Dept. of Psych, Hokkaido Univ. of Liberal Arts and Educ, Sapporo, Hokkaido. b. 11 Aug 1913 Sapporo. Bungakushi '46 Hiroshima Bunrika Univ, Japan. ASST. PROF, Hokkaido Univ. of Liberal Arts and Educ. Member: JPA, JAEP. Research, teaching; social attitudes, personality measurement. M

OKAMOTO, Prof. Eiichi. Kawamura Coll, Mejiro, Tokyo. b. 8 Apr 1929 Tokyo. Bungakushi '52 Univ. of Tokyo, Japan. ASST. PROF. of PSYCH, Kawamura Coll. Member: JPA, JSAP, Japan Electroencephalography Socy. Teaching, research, consulting; learning theory, perception, personality. M

OKAMOTO, Prof. Keiroku. Rissyo Gakuen Coll, Nishinakanobu, Shinagawa, Tokyo. b. 11 Feb 1925 Saitama. Bungakushi '48 Tokyo Bunrika Univ, Japan. ASST.

PROF, Rissyo Gakuen Coll. Member: JPA, JSAP. Teaching, clinical analysis, professional writing; intellectual development of children.   M

OKAMOTO, Prof. Shigeo. Dept. of Educ. Psych, Kobe Univ, Kobe. b. 20 Nov 1897 Tokyo. Bungakushi '22 Univ. of Tokyo, Japan. PROFESSOR, Kobe Univ. Member: JPA, JSAP. Teaching, research, guidance; personality and social adjustment, psychology of the adolescent, the middle-aged, and women.   M

OKAMOTO, Prof. Shun-ichi. Dept. of Psych, Fac. of Law and Literature, Okayama Univ, Tsushima, Okayama. b. 8 Apr 1898 Okayama. ASST. PROF, Okayama Univ. Member: JPA, Jap. Socy. for Animal Psych, Okayama Socy. for Animal Psych. Teaching, research, administration; visual sensation, comparative psychology, learning theory.   M

OKAMOTO, Yoshito. 6 Togocho, Nakano-ku, Tokyo. b. 1 Jan 1927 Tokyo. Bungakushi '50 Waseda Univ, Japan. HEAD, Market Survey and Pub. Opinion Res. Div, Pub. Opinion Sci. Assn, 676 4-chome, Sendayaga, Tokyo. Member: JPA. Planning and analysis of market surveys and public opinion research, teaching, editorial; study of consumer motivation using projective techniques, attitude measurement, evaluation of advertising.   M

OKAMURA, Niro. Dept. of Psych, Fukuoka Teachers Coll, Shiobaru, Fukuoka. b. 5 Dec 1926 Okayama. Bungakushi '50 Hiroshima Univ, Japan. ASSISTANT, Fukuoka Teachers Coll. Member: JPA, Kyushu Psych. Assn, Jap. Socy. of Grp. Dynam. Research, teaching; personality variables in social perception, group dynamics.   M

OKANO, Prof. Tsuneya. Dept. of Psych, Toyoko Jr. Coll, Todoroki, Tokyo. b. 2 Sept 1926 Tokyo. Bungakushi '50 Tokyo Bunrika Univ, Japan. ASST. PROF, Toyoko Jr. Coll. Member: JPA, Jap. Socy. for Animal Psych. Research, teaching, guidance; learning theory, discrimination learning and its transposition.   M

OKAYAMA, Takashi. Dept. of Educ. Psych, Ibaraki Univ, Mito, Ibaraki. b. 14 Nov 1916 Tokyo. Bungakushi '43 Keio Univ, Japan. INSTRUCTOR, Ibaraki Univ. Member: JPA, JSAP. Research, teaching, educational psychology; motivation.   M

OKI, Prof. Tadahiko. 2 Minatomachi, Otsu-shi, Shiga Prefecture. b. 16 Dec 1926 Tottori. Bungakushi '50 Kyoto Univ, Japan. ASST. PROF. Kyoto Women's Univ, 7 jiyo Imakumano, Kyoto; CHIEF, Clin. Psych. and Child Psychiat. Div, Minakuchi Ment. Hosp. Member: JPA, Jap. Assn. of Psychiat. and Neur.   Research, clinical analysis,

psychotherapy, teaching; emotional disorders of children.   M

OKINO, Horoshi. Osaka Child Guid. Cen, 38 Ikutamamaecho, Tennoji, Osaka. b. 3 June 1925 Hiroshima. Igakushi '48 Osaka Univ, Japan. STAFF PSYCHIATRIST, Osaka Child Guid. Cen. Member: SCP, Kansai Psych. Assn. Psychotherapy, child guidance, research; projective techniques.   M

OKUDA, Prof. Saburô. Fac. of Educ, Hokkaido Univ, Sapporo, Hokkaido. b. 27 Feb 1903 Asahikawa. Igakuhakushi '40 Univ. of Tokyo, Japan. PROF. of EDUC. PSYCH. and MENT. HYG, Hokkaido Univ; EDUC. ADVIS, Katei Gakko (Sch. for Problem Children). Member: JPA, JAEP, Jap. Assn. of Psychiat. and Neur. Teaching, research, educational consulting; behavior disorders, psychosomatics, psychotherapy.   M

OKUMURA, Kodo. Dept. of Psych, Doshisha Univ, Kyoto. b. 11 Nov 1920 Kyoto. Bungakushi '43 Doshisha Univ, Japan. INSTRUCTOR, Doshisha Univ. Member: JPA, JSAP, Japan Educ. Socy. Research, teaching, guidance; social perception.   M

OKUNO, Prof. Akira. Hokkaido Univ. of Liberal Arts and Educ, Kushiro. b. 8 July 1914 Hokkaido. Bungakushi '42 Hiroshima Bunrika Univ, Japan. PROFESSOR, Hokkaido Univ. of Liberal Arts and Educ; CONSULTANT, Kushiro Child Guid. Clin. Member: JPA, JAEP, Hokkaido Psych. Assn. Teaching, research, testing; personality, social tensions, group process.   M

ONDA, Prof. Akira. Dept. of Sociol, Toyo Univ, Bunkyo-ku, Tokyo. b. 26 Jan 1925 Tokyo. Bungakushi '48 Univ. of Tokyo, Japan. ASST. PROF, Toyo Univ. Member: JPA, JSAP. Research, educational and social psychology, teaching; psychodynamic theory of personality.   M

ONISHI, Prof. Seiichiro. Dept. of Psych, Nagoya Univ, Naka-ku, Nagoya. b. 25 Aug 1906 Kyoto. Bungakushi '38 Tokyo Bunrika Univ, Japan. ASST. PROF. Nagoya Univ. Member: JPA, JSAP. Research, teaching, guidance; group learning, social development of children.   M

ONIZAWA, Tadashi. Dept. of Psych, Tohoku Univ, Sendai. b. 14 Aug 1927 Mitao. Bungakushi '47 Tohoku Univ, Japan. Instructor, Shokei Women's Jr. Coll, 7 Nakajima-Cho, Sendai; LECTURER, Tohoku Univ. Member: JPA, JSAP, Tohoku Psych. Assn. Teaching, research, psychological measurement; visual perception.   M

ÔNO, Kei. Dept. of Spec. Educ, Chiba Prefectural Inst. for Educ, Azumacho, Chiba. b. 27 Sept 1912 Tokyo. Bungakushi '34 Univ. of Tokyo, Japan. HEAD, Dept.

of Spec. Educ, Chiba Prefectural Inst. for Educ. Member: JPA, JSAP. Research in clinical psychology and mental health, guidance, teaching; maladjusted and retarded children.　　　　　　　　　　M

ONO, Shigeru. Minami-bunko, Hiroshima Univ, Minami-cho, Hiroshima.　b. 27 Oct 1925 Okayama. Bungakushi '49 Univ. of Tokyo, Japan. INSTR. in PSYCH, Hiroshima Univ. Member: JPA, Jap. Socy. of Animal Psych. Research, teaching, guidance; animal behavior.　　　　　M

ONO, Prof. Yoshiaki. Biol. Lab, Fac. of Liberal Arts and Educ, Kagawa Univ, Takamatsu.　b. 27 Aug 1903 Takamatsu. Rigakuhakushi '55 Kyoto Univ, Japan. PROF. of BIOL, Kagawa Univ; ADVIS. ED, *The Annual of Animal Psychology*. Member: JPA, Jap. Socy. for Animal Psych. Research, teaching, administration; social behavior of animals.　　　　M

OSAKA, Prof. Ryoji. Dept. of Educ. Psych, Kyoto Univ, Sakyo-ku, Kyoto.　b. 28 June 1918 Kyoto. Bungakushi '43 Univ. of Tokyo, Japan. ASST. PROF. of EDUC, Kyoto Univ; LECT. in EXPER. PSYCH, Ritsumeikan Univ. Member: JPA, Japan Educ. Socy. Research, teaching, educational psychology; cognition.　　　M

OSAKI, Prof. Sachie. Dept. of Psych, Kumamoto Univ, Kurokami-mati, Kumamoto. b. 18 Oct 1904 Kumamoto. Bungakushi '34 Kyushu Univ, Japan. ASST. PROF, Kumamoto Univ. Member: JPA, JAEP. Teaching, research; speech, perception, child psychology.　　　　F

OSE, Akira. Takinogawa 7-45 Kitaku, Tokyo.　b. 12 Mar 1920 Tokyo. Bungakushi '43 Univ. of Tokyo, Japan. INVESTIGATOR, Labor Sci. Res. Off, Hlth. Superv. Sect, Jap. Natl. Railways, Tabatamachi 806 Kitaku, Tokyo. Member: JPA. Research in industrial psychology, testing; aptitude and intelligence tests.　　　　　M

OSUGA, Tetuo. Dept. of Labor Psych, Inst. for Sci. of Labor, Soshigaya II Setagaya, Tokyo. b. 27 Jan 1926 Fukuoka. Bungakushi '49 Univ. of Tokyo, Japan. RES. WRKR, Inst. for Sci. of Labor. Member: JPA, JSAP. Industrial psychology, testing, research, social attitudes and personality in industry.　　　　　　　　　　M

OSUGI, Takao. 620 Kashihara Nakagawachi, Osaka.　b. 2 Oct 1917 Osaka. Bungakushi '40 Rissho Univ. Japan. Lect. in Psych, Osaka. Prefectural Syutoku Reformatory, Kashihara, Osaka. Member: JPA, JSAP. Teaching, research, guidance; school friendships of children.　　M

OTA, Tetsuo. Dept. of Physical Educ, Tokyo Univ. of Educ, Shibuya, Tokyo.　b. 3 Dec 1922 Tokyo. Bungakushi '49 Tokyo Bunrika Univ, Japan. ASST. in PHYSICAL EDUC, Tokyo Univ. of Educ. Member: JPA, JSAP. Research, teaching, testing; motor performance in learning.　　M

OTAGAKI, Zuiichiro. Dept. of Labor Psych, Inst, for Sci. of Labor, Soshigaya II Setagaya, Tokyo.　b. 7 Nov 1915 Hyogo. Bungakushi '41 Keio Univ, Japan. RES. WRKR, Inst. for Sci. of Labor. Member: JPA, JSAP. Research, industrial psychology testing; motion study, industrial fatigue.　　　　　　　　　　M

OTAKE, Kiyoshi. Seibi Gakuen, 124 Maita Machi, Minami Ku, Yokohama.　b. 8 Dec 1884 Hamamatsu. PH.B '29 Univ. of Chicago, USA. PRESIDENT, Seibi Gakuen. Member: JPA. Teaching, administration, and research in a primary and secondary educational institution.　　　　　　M

OTAKE, Makoto. 134 Maitamachi, Minami-ku, Yokohama. b. 7 Oct 1915 Yokohama. Bungakushi '40 Tokyo Bunrika Univ, Japan. DEAN, Sibi Gakuen Girl's Senior High Sch, Maita, Yokohama. Member: JPA, JSAP, JAEP. Teaching, administration, student counseling; psychology of adolescent girls.　　　　　　　　M

OTANI, Dr. Shunji. 1209 Matsunoki-cho, Suginami-ku, Tokyo.　b. 8 July 1918 Yamaguchi. Igakushi '46 Okayama Coll, Japan. PEDIATRICIAN, priv. prac. Member: JSAP. Psychotherapy, clinical practice in internal medicine, research; psychosomatic medicine, child psychotherapy.　　　M

OTANI, Soji. Dept. of Psych, Chiba Univ, Chiba Shi. b. 8 Dec 1924 Chiba. Bungakushi '49 Univ. of Tokyo, Japan. ASSISTANT, Chiba Univ. Member: JPA. Research, teaching, consulting; size assimilation and contrast in perception.　　M

ŌTASHIRO, Prof. Motohiko. Dept. of Psych, Utsunomiya Univ, Utsunomiya, Tochigiken. b. 15 Mar 1908 Tokyo. Bungakushi '32 Tohoku Univ, Japan. PROFESSOR, Utsunomiya Univ. Member: JPA, JAEP. Research, teaching; mental development, history of psychological theory.　　M

OTOMO, Prof. Shigeru. Dept. of Educ, Kwansei-gakuin Univ, Nishinomiya.　b. 1 Mar 1892 Nara. PH.D '24 Univ. of Chicago, USA. PROFESSOR, Kwansei-gakuin Univ; DIRECTOR, Otomo Inst. for Educ. Res. Member: JPA, Japan Educ. Socy. Research, professional writing, teaching; intelligence and achievement tests, projective techniques.　　　　　　M

OUCHI, Shigeo. 683 5-chome, Zoshigaya-machi, Toshima-ku, Tokyo. b. 8 Jan 1921 Tokyo. Bungakushi '44 Tokyo Bunrika Univ, Japan. SPEC. in EDUC. PSYCH, Ministry of Educ, Kasumigaseki, Tokyo; ED. BD, *Adolescence, Educational Psychology*. Member: JPA, JSAP, JAEP. Training teachers in student guidance and audio-visual techniques, reaching, research; mass communication.   M

OYAMA, Tadasu. Dept. of Exper. Psych, Fac. of Letters, Hokkaido Univ, Hokkaido, Sapporo. b. 21 Jan 1928 Tokyo. Bungakushi '51 Univ. of Tokyo, Japan. INSTRUCTOR, Hokkaido Univ. Member: JPA, Jap. Socy. for Animal Psych. Teaching, research; figural after-effects and figureground reversal in visual perception.   M

OZAWA, Eikô. Shizuoka Juv. Classif. Off, Ojika, Shizuoka. b. 17 Sept 1911 Kyoto. Bungakushi '36 Kyoto Univ, Japan. DIRECTOR, Shizuoka Juv. Classif. Off. Member: JPA, JSAP, Jap. Assn. of Correctl. Med. Administration, guidance, testing and classification of juvenile delinquents; projective techniques, psychoanalysis, attitude measurement.   M

SABASHI, Shizuo. Correctn. Bur, Ministry of Justice, Kasumigaseki, Tokyo. b. 17 Feb 1922 Tokyo. Bungakushi '50 Tokyo Bunrika Univ, Japan. JUDICIAL EDUC. INSTR, Correctn. Bur, Ministry of Justice. Member: JSAP, Jap. Assn. of Correctl. Med. Educational planning for correctional institutions, administration, testing; projective techniques.   M

SAEKI, Katsu. Tokyo Juvenile Classif. Home Nerima-ku, Nakamachi, Tokyo. b. 17 Jan 1920 Tokyo. Bungakushi '46 Waseda Univ, Japan. CLASSIF. OFF, Tokyo Juv. Classif. Home; ASST. in PSYCHIAT, Dept. of Med, Nippon Univ. Member: JPA, JSAP. Guidance, psychotherapy, testing and classification of juvenile delinquents; psychological diagnostic testing, projective techniques.   M

SAGARA, Prof. Moriji. 5213 Kugenuma, Fujisawa-shi. b. 8 May 1903 Tsuruoka. Bungakuhakushi '52 Univ. of Tokyo, Japan. PROF. of PSYCH, Univ. of Tokyo, Bunkyo-ku, Tokyo; LECTURER, Waseda Univ; MANAGING ED, *Japanese Journal of Psychology*. Member: JPA, JSAP, Jap. Socy. for Animal Psych. Teaching, research, editorial; human learning, learning theory, motivation, social perception.   M

SAHARA, Prof. Rokuro. Dept. of Psych, Keio Univ, Mita, Tokyo. b. 24 Oct 1895 Tokyo. Bungakushi '21 Kyoto Univ, Japan. PROF. of SOC. PSYCH. and SOCIOL, Keio Univ. Member: JSAP. Research, teaching; group norms and group differences in behavior.   M

SAHEKI, Shigeo. Juvenile Sect, Crime Prevention Div, Metrop. Police Dept, Tokyo. b. 24 Mar 1922 Tokyo. Bungakushi '48 Nihon Univ, Japan. POLICE TECH, Metrop. Police Dept. Member: JPA, JSAP, Jap. Assn. of Criminol. Testing, clinical analysis, guidance and counseling, crime prevention and rehabilitation of juveniles; projective

techniques, criminal behavior.   M

SAITO, Kanjiro. Univ. Sect, Higher Educ. and Sci. Bur, Ministry of Educ, 4 3-chome, Kasumigaseki, Chiyoda-ku, Tokyo. b. 23 Sept 1922 Fukushima City. Bungakushi '50 Tokyo Univ. of Educ, Japan. GOVT. OFF, Ministry of Educ. Member: JPA, JSAP. Testing, research, administration of entrance exemaniations; scholastic and other aptitude tests.   M

SAITO, Prof. Kazushiro. Nagaoka Br, Dept. of Pedagogy, Niigata Univ, Gakkocho, Nagaoka. b. 2 Oct 1911 Hokkaido. Bungakushi '41 Tokyo Bunrika Univ, Japan. ASST. PROF. of EDUC. PSYCH, Nagaoka Br, Niigata Univ. Member: JPA, JAEP. Teaching, research; social development in rural districts, social behavior and family type.   M

SAITO, Koichiro. Dept. of Educ, Keio Univ, Mita, Tokyo. b. 7 Mar 1922 Sakata. Bungakushi '44 Keio Univ, Japan. INSTR. in EDUC. PSYCH, Keio Univ. Member: JPA, JSAP, JAEP. Research, teaching, educational psychology; developmental psychology, learning.   M

SAITO, Prof. Kunio. Fac. of Educ, Niigata Univ, Tokyo. b. 3 Oct 1914 Miyagi-ken. ASST. PROF. of EDUC. PSYCH, Niigata Univ, Asahimachi-2, Niigata. Member: JPA, JAEP, Jap. Stat. Sci. Socy. Research, teaching educational psychology and statistics; methodology, psychometry, social perception.   M

SAITO, Sadayoshi. Dept. of Psych, Univ. of Tokyo, Bunkyo, Tokyo. b. 31 July 1922 Uchigo. Bungakushi '49 Univ. of Tokyo, Japan. RES. DIR, Assn. of Public Opinion Sci, Sendagaya, Tokyo; INSTR. in PSYCH, Wayo Women's Univ. Member: JPA, JSAP. Social research, teaching, applied psychology; faddism, social learning and imitation, suggestion, rumor, social attitude.   M

SAITO, Yuichi. 62 Hayashi-cho, Bunkyo-ku, Tokyo. b. 31 Mar 1911 Tokyo. Bungakushi '34 Univ. of Tokyo, Japan. ADMIN. ASST. to PRES, Int. Christian Univ, 1500 Osawa, Mitaka-shi, Tokyo; LECT. in PSYCH, Nihon Univ, Misaki-cho, Chiyoda-ku, Tokyo. Member: JPA, JSAP. Administration, teaching, research; clinical, theoretical, and systematic psychology.   M

SAKAI, Kiyoshi. Tokyo Res. Inst. for Educ, Azabumorioka-cho 1, Minato-ku, Tokyo. b. 11 Aug 1910 Hikari. Bungakushi '41 Hiroshima Bunrika Univ, Japan. RES. WRKR, Tokyo Res. Inst. for Educ. Member: JPA. Psychological research in elementary and secondary school education, administration, teaching; personality, mental hygiene, psychology of learning.   M

SAKAI, Mitsuru. Nagoya Correctn. and

Rehab. Off, Dept. of Justice, 9-18 Oimatsu-cho, Naka-ku, Nagoya. b. 20 July 1917 Fushun, China. Bungakushi '42 Univ. of Tokyo, Japan. CHIEF, Third Div, Nagoya Correctn. and Rehab. Off. Member: JPA, Jap. Assn. of Correctl. Med. Administration of classification and education sections in prisons and reformatories, consulting, research; attitude measurement of prisoners and delinquents. M

SAKAI, Prof. Yukio. Dept. of Psych, Hiroshima Univ, Sendacho, Hiroshima. b. 5 July 1906 Hyogo Prefecture. Bungakushi '40 Hiroshima Bunrika Univ. Japan. ASST. PROF, Hiroshima Univ. Member: JPA, JAEP. Teaching, administration, research; group process, folk characteristics, decline of mental activity of the aged. M

SAKAKIBARA, Prof. Kiyoshi. Dept. of Psych, Tokyo Univ. of Educ, Otsuka, Bunkyo, Tokyo. b. 21 July 1900 Aichi. Bungakushi '18 Tokyo Bunrika Univ, Japan. ASST. PROF. of SPEC. EDUC, Tokyo Univ. of Educ. Member: JPA, JSAP. Teaching, research, testing; psychology and education of exceptional children, psychological tests. M

SAKAMOTO, Prof. Etsuro. 1353 Haramachi, Meguro-ku, Tokyo. b. 21 Jan 1906 Fukui. Bungakushi '30 Univ. of Tokyo, Japan. PROF. of PSYCH, Ochanomizu Women's Univ, Otsuka-Kubomachi, Tokyo. Member JPA. Teaching, educational psychology, professional writing; audio-visual method. M

SAKAMOTO, Prof. Hideo. Dept. of Educ, Shinshu Univ, Nishinagano, Nagano. b. 30 Mar 1910 Shizuoka-ken. Bungakushi '46 Tokyo Bunrika Univ, Japan. ASST. PROF. of PSYCH, Shinshu Univ; LECT. in EDUC. PSYCH, Nagano Prefectural Jr. Coll. Member: JPA, JSAP. Teaching, consulting; social perception, projective techniques. M

SAKAMOTO, Prof. Ichiro. K. 306 Kakino-kizaka, Meguroku, Tokyo. b. 1 July 1904 Nara-ken. Bungakushi '30 Tokyo Bunrika Univ, Japan. PROF. of EDUC. PSYCH, Tokyo Univ. of Liberal Arts and Educ, Setagaya, Tokyo; EDITOR, *Japanese Journal of Educational Psychology*, *Educational Psychology*. Member: JPA, JSAP, JAEP. Research, administration, teaching; psychology of language and reading. M

SAKATA, Prof. Hajime. Dept. of Psych, Saikyo Univ, Shimogamo, Sakyoku, Kyoto. b. 22 May 1909 Tokyo. Bungakushi '35 Kyoto Univ, Japan. ASST. PROF, Saikyo Univ. Member: JPA, JSAP. Teaching, research, professional writing; moral development in adolescence, counseling adolescents. M

SAKŌ, Prof. Eijirō. Kitamaegawa 2, Tokushima. b. 4 Feb 1904 Tokushima. Bungakushi '33 Tokyo Bunrika Univ, Japan.

PROF. of PSYCH, Okayama Women's Jr. Coll, Kamogata, Okayama. Member: JPA. Research, teaching, consulting; projective techniques, mental processes in retarded children. M

SAKUDA, Prof. Hoji. Dept. of Educ. Yamagata Univ, Midorimahi, Yamagata. b. 26 Apr 1899 Kanazawa. Bungakushi '29 Tokyo Higher Normal School, Japan. PROF. of PSYCH, Yamagata Univ. Member: JPA, JAEP. Teaching, research, consulting; psychology of arithmetic, achievement tests, psychology of thinking. M

SAKUMA, Akira. Fukuoka Univ. of Liberal Arts and Educ, 259 Arato-machi, Fukuoka. b. 10 Dec 1922 Tokyo. Bungakushi '48 Kyushu Univ, Japan. INSTR. in PSYCH, Fukuoka Univ. of Liberal Arts and Educ. Member: JPA. Research, teaching, educational psychology; language, psycholinguistic analysis of sign-process. M

SAKUMA, Prof. Kanae. 613 Narimune 2-chome, Suginami-ku, Tokyo. b. 7 Sept 1888 Togane. Bungakuhakushi '23 Univ. of Tokyo, Japan. PROF. of PSYCH. and LINGUISTICS, Tokyo Univ, 17 Haramachi, Bunkyo-ku, Tokyo. Member: JPA, Linguistic Socy. of Japan. Research, teaching, professional writing; structure of Japanese syntax. M

SAKURABAYASHI, Prof. Hitoshi. Psych. Lab, Tokyo Univ. of Arts, Ueno Park, Tokyo. b. 29 Aug 1916 Yokohama. Bungakushi '41 Taihoku Univ, Japan. ASST. PROF, Tokyo Univ. of Arts; LECTURER, Nihon Univ. and Tokyo Univ. of Educ. Member: JPA. Research, teaching educational psychology and psychology of music; perception. M

SAKURAI, Yoshiro. Funado Primary Sch. and Kindergarten, Kawaguchi, Saitama. b. 1 Jan 1929 Tokyo. Bungakushi '50 St. Paul Univ, Japan. RES. WRKR, Funado Primary Sch. Member: JSAP. Research, teaching, testing; development of social maturity in the child. M

SANO, Katsuo. Dept. of Psych, Keio Univ, Mita, Tokyo. b. 15 Feb 1923 Hokkaido. Bungakushi '49 Keio Univ, Japan. INSTR. in SOCIOL, Keio Univ; RES. ASSOC, Psych. Sect, Seishin-igaku Inst, Tokyo. Member: JPA, JSAP. Teaching, research, testing; personality, social roles, sociometry. M

SASE, Prof. Yasushi. Dept. of Psych, Kunitachi Coll. of Music, Kunitachi-machi, Tokyo. b. 24 Jan 1917 Tokyo. Bungakushi '41 Hosei Univ, Japan. ASST. PROF, Kunitachi Coll. of Music; LECT. in PSYCH, Hosei Univ. Member: JPA, JSAP. Teaching, research, educational psychology; mental development, cognition. M

SATAKE, Kiyomi. Classif. Dept, Kobe Detention House, Kikusuicho, Hyogoku,

Kobe. b. 16 Oct 1921 Osaka. Bungakushi '44 Kwansei Gakuin Univ, Japan. ASST. SECT. CHIEF, Kobe Detention House. Member: JPA, JSAP, GSP, Kwansei Psych. Assn. Testing and classification of prisoners applied psychology, research; personality, projective techniques, attitude measurement.   M

SATAKE, Dr. Ryuzo. Kanazawa Juvenile Classif. Center, 56 Kami-Yumino-Machi, Kanazawa. b. 18 Nov 1919 Uozu. Igakuhakushi '52 Kanazawa Univ, Japan. LECT. in PSYCH, Kanazawa Univ, Ote-Machi, Kanazawa. Member: JPA, JSAP, Jap. Assn. of Psychiat. and Neur. Clinical analysis, research, teaching psychopathology and clinical psychiatry; projective techniques.   M

SATO, Prof. Koji. Dept. of Psych, Kyoto Univ, Sakyo, Kyoto. b. 18 Mar 1905 Yamagata. Bungakuhakushi '56 Kyoto Univ; Japan. PROFESSOR, Kyoto Univ; GUEST PROF, Doshisha Univ; CO-EDITOR, *Journal of Social Psychology.* Member: JPA, JSAP, SCP, Kansai Psych. Assn. Teaching, research, administration; personality, discrimination and thought process.   M

SATO, Muneo. Central Child Guid. Clin. of Miyagi Prefecture, 207 Kitahachibancho, Sendai. b. 10 Oct 1927 Sendai. Bungakushi '51 Tohoku Univ, Japan. CLIN. PSYCH'T, Cen. Child Guid. Clin. of Miyagi Prefecture. Member: JPA, JSAP. Psychotherapy, guidance, testing, clinical analysis; child-centered play therapy, diagnosis of feeblemindedness.   M

SATO, Prof. Noriyuki. Dept. of Spec. Educ, Tokyo Univ. of Educ, Otsuka, Tokyo. b. 20 Apr 1910 Fukuyama. Bungakushi '35 Kyoto Univ, Japan. ASST. PROF, Tokyo Univ. of Educ. Member: JPA. Research and teaching psychology of language; gesture language.   M

SATO, Satoru. Akita Prefecture Central Child Welf. Cen, Nakakamenocho, Akita. b. 14 July 1929 Sendai. Bungakushi '52 Tohoku Univ, Japan. CLIN. PSYCH'T, Akita Prefecture Central Child Welf. Cen. Member: JPA, Tohoku Psych. Assn. Testing, psychotherapy, child guidance; projective techniques.   M

SATO, Prof. Tadashi. Dept. of Psych, Tokyo Univ. of Liberal Arts and Educ, Setagaya, Tokyo. b. 20 Jan 1917 Takasaki. Bungakushi '41 Tokyo Bunrika Univ, Japan. ASST. PROF, Tokyo Univ. of Liberal Arts and Educ. Member: JPA, JSAP. Educational psychology, teaching, consulting; group process, attitude measurement.   M

SATO, Prof. Tetsuo. Dept. of Educ, Nanzan Univ, Gokenya-cho, Showa-ku, Nagoya. b. 6 Apr 1920 Oita-ken. Bungakushi '42 Keio Univ, Japan. ASST. PROF. of EDUC.

PSYCH, Nanzan Univ. Member: JPA, JSAP. Testing, research, teaching; learning theory, perception.   M

SATO, Toshiaki. Lab. of Psych, Fukushima Med. Coll. Shinhama-cho, Fukushima. b. 20 Sept 1930 Sagae. Bungakushushi '55 Tohoku Univ, Japan. INSTRUCTOR, Fukushima Med. Coll; EDITOR, *Tohoku Journal of Experimental Psychology.* Member: JPA, Tohoku Psych. Assn. Teaching, research, consulting; learning theory, extinction process of conditioned response. M

SATO, Toshiro. Tohokugakuin Coll, Minami-rokkencho, Sendai. b. 28 Aug 1925 Hakodate. Bungakushi '51 Tohoku Univ, Japan. INSTR. in PSYCH, Tohokugakuin Coll. Member: JPA, Tohoku Psych. Assn. Research, teaching, consulting; thinking and learning, problem solving.   M

SATO, Tsuneo. Seiwa Univ, Kinoshita, Sendai. b. 5 Feb 1914 Miyagi Prefecture. Bungakushi '39 Tohoku Univ, Japan. INSTR. in PSYCH, Seiwa Univ. Member: JPA. Research, teaching, educational psychology; Buddhist psychology.   M

SATOW, Nozomu. 1551 Fujimidai, Meguroku Tokyo. b. 31 Oct 1919 Tokyo. Bungakushi '43 Keio Univ, Japan. CHIEF, Dept. of Classif, Tokyo Med. Reformatory, Yoyogioyama, Tokyo. Member: JPA, JSAP. Testing and classification, consulting, research; projective techniques, achievement tests, attitude measurement.   M

SAWA, Prof. Hidehisa. Dept. of Educ, Nagasaki Univ, Ohashi, Nagasaki. b. 26 Mar 1904 Hofu. Bungakushi '36 Hiroshima Univ, Japan. PROF. of PSYCH, Nagasaki Univ. Member: JPA, JAEP. Teaching, research, administration; relation of intelligence and character.   M

SAWADA, Prof. Chiuji. Dept. of Educ, Kanazawa Univ, Otemachi, Kanazawa. b. 1 Jan 1908 Hokkaido Prefecture. Bungakushi '40 Tokyo Bunrika Univ, Japan. ASST. PROF. of PSYCH, Kanazawa Univ. Member: JPA, Socy. for the Study of Educ. Teaching, educational psychology, research, consulting; personality, character.   M

SAWADA, Prof. Keisuke. Dept. of Educ. Psych, Fac. of Educ, Univ. of Tokyo, Hongo, Tokyo. b. 18 Feb 1909 Kagoshima. Bungakushi '31 Univ. of Tokyo, Japan. PROFESSOR, Univ. of Tokyo; LECTURER, Hitotsubashi Univ, Nihon Univ, and Tokyo Metrop. Univ; EDITOR, *Japanese Journal of Educational Psychology, Encyclopedia of Education.* Member: JPA, JSAP, JAEP. Teaching, research, consulting; counseling and group process in teacher-student situation.   M

SAWADA, Prof. Kohei. Dept. of Educ, Kanazawa Univ, Ote-machi, Kanazawa.

b. 10 Oct 1903 Suzu-shi. Bungakushi '39 Tokyo Bunrika Univ, Japan. PROF. of PSYCH, Kanazawa Univ. Member: JPA, Japan Socy. of Ment. Hyg, Jap. Assn. of Spec. Educ. Teaching, research, consulting; physical and mental development of children, mentality of the exceptional child.   M

SAWAI, Sachiki. Tezukayama Gakuin Jr. Coll, Sumiyoshi, Osaka. b. 16 Jan 1926 Shanghai, China. Bungakushi '50 Kwansei Gakuin Univ, Japan. INSTR. in PSYCH, Tezukayama Gakuin Jr. Coll. Member: JPA, JSAP. Teaching, research, consulting; group process, conditioning.   M

SAZI, Morio. Dept of Psych, Natl. Inst. of Ment. Health, Ichikawa City, Chiba Prefecture. b. 18 Feb 1923 Yamagata. Bungakushi '48 Univ. of Tokyo, Japan. TECH. OFF, Ministry of Hlth. and Welf, Natl. Inst. of Ment. Hlth; LECTURER, Dept. of Educ, Univ. of Tokyo. Member: JPA. Consulting, personality measurement, psychotherapy, teaching; personality structure, personality change during psychotherapy, abnormal behavior in rats.   M

SEGAWA, Prof. Yoshio. Dept. of Educ, Aoyamagakuin Univ, Shibuya, Tokyo. b. 28 May 1913 Owasi. Bungakushi '37 Univ. of Tokyo, Japan. PROF. of PSYCH, Aoyamagakuin Univ. Member: JPA, JSAP. Teaching, research, professional writing; social psychology, group process.   M

SEGAWA, Prof. Yoshiro. Dept. of Psych, Iwate Univ, Ueda, Morioka. b. 20 Sept 1910 Hanamaki. Bungakushi '40 Tokyo Bunrika Univ, Japan. ASST. PROF, Iwate Univ. Member: JPA, JSAP, JAEP. Teaching educational and adolescent psychology, research, consulting; figural similarity in perception, learning theory, attitude measurement.   M

SEKI, Prof. Kanshi. Obama-machi, Nagasaki. b. 3 Dec 1890 Nagasaki. Bungakushi '14 Univ. of Tokyo, Japan. PROFESSOR, Junshin Women's Coll, Ieno-machi, Nagasaki; PROFESSOR, Tamaki Women's Coll; LECTURER, Univ. of Nagasaki. Member: Kyushu Psych. Assn. Research, teaching, professional writing; religious development of the child.   M

SEKI, Prof. Kazuo. Dept. of Psych, Kyushu Univ, Hakozaki, Fukuoka. b. 22 Mar 1906 Tokyo. Bungakushi '43 Tokyo Bunrika Univ, Japan. PROFESSOR, Kyushu Univ; EDITOR, *Education and Medicine.* Member: JPA, JAEP. Teaching, educational and developmental psychology, research; reward and punishment, inferiority feelings, psychology of music and painting.   M

SEKOGUCHI, Prof. Kazuo. Dept. of Vocat. Guid, Kyoto Univ. of Liberal Arts and Educ, Koyama-Minami Ohna Cho, Kita-

ku, Kyoto. b. 8 Apr 1909 Kyoto. Bungakushi '36 Kyoto Univ, Japan. ASST. PROF, Kyoto Univ. of Liberal Arts and Educ. Member: JPA, SCP, Kansai Psych. Assn. Research, teaching vocational guidance, testing, counseling; vocational aptitude tests, counseling.   M

SERA, Prof. Masatoshi. Dept. of Psych, Chuo Univ, Kanda, Tokyo. b. 8 Feb 1918 1918 Hiroshima. Bungakushi '42 Univ. Tokyo, Japan. ASST. PROF, Chuo Univ. Member: JPA, JSAP. Teaching, research; projective techniques.   M

SERIZAWA, Isamu. 1545 Tomioka-cho, Kanazawa, Yokohama. b. 11 Mar 1911 Yokohama. Bungakushi '35 Univ. of Tokyo, Japan. ADMINISTRATOR, Tsurumi Ward, Yokohama. Member: JPA. Consulting, personnel psychology, administration; administrative efficiency.   M

SEYA, Masatoshi. Dept. of Psych, Fac. of Letters, Univ. of Tokyo, Hongo, Tokyo. b. 26 Dec 1922 Tokyo. Bungakushi '48 Univ. of Tokyo, Japan. ASSISTANT, Univ. of Tokyo. Member: JPA. Research, teaching, applied psychology; perception. M

SHIBAHARA, Prof. Kyoji. Dept. of Psych, Mie Univ, Marunouchi Tsu, Mie. b. 5 June 1910 Hamajima. Bungakushi '46 Tokyo Bunrika Univ, Japan. ASST. PROF, Mie Univ. Member: JPA. Teaching, research, educational psychology; perception of personality.   M

SHIBAHARA, Sadao. Dept. of Liberal Arts, Tottori Univ, Tatekawa-cho, Tottori. b. 17 May 1924 Hyogo Prefecture. Bungakushi '50 Kyoto Univ, Japan. INSTRUCTOR, Tottori Univ. Member: JPA, JAEP, Kansai PSYCH. Assn. Research, teaching, testing; retroactive and proactive interference in memory, projective techniques.   M

SHIBAYAMA, Prof. Tsuyoshi. Dept. of Educ, Okayama Univ, Tsushima, Okayama. b. 1 Aug 1905 Okayama. Bungakushi '39 Tokyo Bunrika Univ, Japan. ASST. PROF. of PSYCH, Okayama Univ. Member: JPA, JAEP. Research, teaching child psychology, consulting; perception, experience and other factors in productieve thinking.M

SHIGEMATSU, Tsuyoshi. Dept. of Psych, Aichi Univ. of Liberal Arts and Educ, Okazaki, Aichi. b. 12 July 1919 Tokyo. Bungakushi '43 Univ. of Tokyo, Japan. INSTRUCTOR, Aichi Univ. of Liberal Arts and Educ. Member: JPA. Teaching developmental psychology; learning theory. M

SHIINA, Shinichi. Dept. of Indus. Relat, Jujo Paper Mfg. Co, Ltd, 4 Ginza-Higashi 3-chome, Chuo-ku, Tokyo. b. 1 Sept 1921 Singapore, Malaya. Bungakushi '46 Keio Univ, Japan. RES. CHIEF, Personnel Div, Dept. of Indus. Relat, Jujo Paper Mfg. Co, Ltd. Member: JPA, JSAP. Industrial psychology, personnel testing, job analysis, research; attitude measurement, aptitude and personality testing. M

SHIKATA, Prof. Jitsukazu. Kyoto Univ. of Liberal Arts and Educ, Kitaku, Kyoto. b. 25 May 1907 Ayabe. Bungakushi '35 Tokyo Bunrika Univ, Japan. PROF. of PSYCH, Kyoto Univ. of Liberal Arts and Educ. Member: JPA, JSAP. Teaching, research, educational psychology; learning theory applied to mathematics, logic. M

SHIKATA, Tetsutaro. 3-chome 97, Yamasaka-cho, Higashi-Sumiyoshi-ku, Osaka. b. 28 Aug 1893 Ayabe. DIRECTOR, Jr. High Sch. of Momoyama Academy, Abeno-ku, Osaka. Member: JPA. Teaching, sociology; child psychology. M

SHIMADA, Prof. Kazuo. Dept. of Psych, Seishin Univ, Miyashirocho, Shibuya-ku, Tokyo. b. 5 Mar 1923 Iwate. Bungakushi '49 Tokyo Bunrika Univ, Japan. ASST. PROF, Seishin Univ. Member: JPA, JSAP. Research, teaching, consulting; visual sensation, perception, attitude measurement. M

SHIMADA, Shigeo. Dept. of Psych, Tokyo Bunrika Univ, Otsuka, Tokyo. b. 27 Jan 1926 Utsunomiya. Bungakushi '50 Tokyo Bunrika Univ, Japan. TEACHER, Utsunomiya Girls' High Sch, Utsunomiya, Tochigi. Member: JSAP. Teaching educational psychology, guidance; abnormal personality. M

SHIMAKURA, Kenji. Dept. of Psych, Nihon Univ, Misakicho, Tokyo. b. 28 Feb 1905 Tokyo. Bungakushi '53 Nihon Univ, Japan. CHIEF, Classif. Sect, Osaka Juv. Detention and Classif. Off, Minamidori, Osaka. Member: JPA. Testing and classification of delinquents; projective techniques, social perception, attitude measurement. M

SHIMAZU, Hoshin. Kyoto Child Welf. Cen, Senbon-Higashi, Takeyamachi-Dori, Kamikyo-ku, Kyoto. b. 1 Mar 1914 Fukui. Bungakushi '40 Kyoto Univ, Japan. CHIEF, Consultation and Day Nursery Sect, Kyoto Child Welf. Cen; LECTURER, Kyoto Women's Univ. Member: JPA, Kansai Psych. Assn. Consulting, clinical practice, testing, teaching; psychiatry, social maturity. M

SHIMAZU, Prof. Kazuo. Dept. of Psych, Yokohama City Univ, Mutsuura, Kanazawa-ku, Yokohama. b. 27 Aug 1914 Ueda. Bungakushi '38 Univ. of Tokyo, Japan. PROFESSOR, Yokohama City Univ. Member: JPA. Research, teaching educational psychology; perception of depth. M

SHIMAZU, Teiichi. 110 Yayoi, Kushiro, Hokkaido, b. 22 Oct 1916 Japan. Bungakushi '41 Waseda Univ, Japan. DIRECTOR, Kushiro Juv. Classif. and Detention Cen, Kushiro, Hokkaido. Member: JPA, Kansai Psych. Assn. Testing, consulting, guidance;

projective techniques. M

SHIMIZU, Prof. Eicho. Obihiro Zootechnical Coll, Hokkaido. b. 1 Jan 1901 Asahigawa. Bungakushi '24 Univ. of Tokyo, Japan. PROF. of PSYCH, Obihiro Zootechnical Coll, Inada, Obihiro. Member: JPA. Teaching, educational psychology, research; physical and mental tempo. M

SHIMOYAMA, Prof. Tokuji. 607 Yoyogi-Hatsudai, Shibuya-ku, Tokyo. b. 5 July 1919 Tokyo. Bungakushi '24 Univ. of Tokyo, Japan; PH.D, Bonn Univ, Germany. ASST. PROF, Sophia Univ, Kioicho, Chiyoda-ku, Tokyo. Member: JPA. Teaching, research, consulting; personality, existential analysis of neurotic anxiety. M

SHINAGAWA, Prof. Fujiro. 1-8 Toyotama-kita, Nerima-ku, Tokyo. b. 15 Apr 1916 Okayama. Bungakushi '42 Tokyo Bunrika Univ, Japan. ASST. PROF. of PSYCH, Tokyo Univ. of Liberal Arts and Educ, Shimouma, Setagaya, Tokyo; PSYCH. CONSULT, Tanaka Inst. for Educ. Res; EDITOR, *Journal of Educational Psychology*. Member: JPA, JSAP. Teaching educational, clinical and child psychology, research, consulting, guidance; WISC Intelligence Test, psychotherapy, parent-child relationship. M

SHINOMIYA, Prof. Akira. Dept. of Psych, Chiba Univ, Ichiba-cho, Chiba. b. 3 1921 Chiba. Bungakushi '45 Tokyo Bunrika Univ, Japan. ASST. PROF. Chiba Univ. Member: JPA, JSAP. Applied psychology, teaching, research; social development. M

SHINOZUKA, Akira. Dept. of Stud. Welf, Chiba Univ, 824 Konakadai, Chiba. b. 22 June 1913 Tsu City. Bungakushi '48 Tokyo Bunrika Univ, Japan. STUD. COUNSELOR, Dept. of Stud. Welf, Chiba Univ. Member: JPA, JSAP. Consulting, guidance, research, teaching; conversation and emotion. M

SHIODA, Prof. Takehiko. Fac. of Liberal Arts and Educ, Gunma Univ, Seioji-machi, Maebashi, Gunma-ken. b. 6 July 1919 Karatsu City. Bungakushi '45 Waseda Univ, Japan. ASST. PROF. of PSYCH, Gunma Univ. Member: JPA. Teaching developmental and experimental psychology, research; projective techniques, study of thought processes using the Word Association Test. M

SHIOIRI, Prof. Enyu. Dept. of Neuropsychiat, Keio Univ, Shinanomachi, Shinjuku, Tokyo. b. 1 Nov 1906 Kanazawa. Igakuhakushi '49 Keio Univ, Japan. ASST. PROF. of PSYCHIAT, Keio Univ. Member: JPA, JSAP Consulting, research, teaching psychiatry and medical psychology; amnesia and pseudo-dementia in hysteria, personality tests. M

SHIOKAWA, Prof. Takewo. Dept. of Psych, Shizuoka Univ, Oiwa, Shizuoka. b. 21

Nov 1908 Fujinomiya. Bungakushi '41 Tokyo Bunrika Univ, Japan. ASST. PROF, Shizuoka Univ; PRINCIPAL, Kindergarten and Elementary Sch. of Shizuoka Univ. Member: JPA, JSAP, JAEP. Teaching educational and social psychology, research; the school class and its members, group process. M

SHIOSE, Miss Teiko. Dept. of Psych, Keio Univ, Mita, Tokyo. b. 2 Jan 1927 Tokyo. Bungakushushi '54 Keio Univ, Japan. LECTURER, Seijo Univ, Seijo, Tokyo. Member: JPA, JSAP. Research, teaching, testing; color perception. F

SHIOTA, Prof. Prof. Yoshihisa. Dept. of Educ, Nagoya Univ, Minami-Sotobori, Nagoya. b. 20 Sept 1912 Tadotsu. Bungakushi '37 Tokyo Bunrika Univ, Japan. ASST. PROF. of EDUC. PSYCH, Nagoya Univ. Member: JPA, JSAP. Research, teaching educational psychology and testing, consulting; readiness factor in learning, social factors in classroom learning, sociometry. M

SHIRAI, Prof. Tsune. Dept. of Psych, Tokyo Woman's Christian Coll, Iogi 3-chome, Suginamiku, Tokyo. b. 31 Oct 1910 Tokyo. Bungakushi '41 Tokyo Bunrika Univ, Japan; PH.D '54 Univ. of Toronto, Canada. PROF. and HEAD, Dept. of Psych, Tokyo Woman's Christian Coll. Member: JPA, ICWP. Teaching, research, administration; development of thinking, learning theory, personality theory. F

SHIRAISHI, Prof. Kazushige. Dept. of Educ, Nagoya Univ, Minamisotobori-cho, Nakaku, Nagoya. b. 19 Aug 1914 Kyoto. Rigakushi '38 Univ. of Tokyo, Japan. PROFESSOR, Nagoya Univ; LECT. in STAT, Osaka Univ. Member: JPA, JSAP. Research, teaching educational statistics, testing; achievement tests, attitude measurement, social perception. M

SHUTO, Prof. Sadami. Fac. of Liberal Arts, Oita Univ, Danoharu, Oita. b. 3 Sept 1910 Oita. Bungakushi '37 Kyushu Univ, Japan. PROF. of EDUC. PSYCH, Oita Univ. Member: Kyushu Psych. Assn, Japan Socy. of Grp. Dynam. Teaching, research, administration; group process, audio-visual method. M

SOEJIMA, Prof. Yokichiro. Dept. of Psych, Saga Univ, Akamatu machi, Saga. b. 15 Apr 1908 Saga. Bungakushi '37 Tokyo Bunrika Univ, Japan. ASST. PROF, Saga Univ. Member: JPA, JSAP. Research, teaching, testing; learning theory applied to mathematics, achievement tests. M

SOFUE, Takao. Dept. of Sociol. and Soc. Anthrop, Tokyo Metrop. Univ. Fusuma-cho, Meguro-ku, Tokyo. b. 5 Nov 1926 Tokyo. Rigakushi '49 Univ. of Tokyo, Japan. RES. FELLOW in ANTHROP, Tokyo Metrop. Univ; RES. FELLOW, Inst. of Oriental Cultures, Univ. of Tokyo; LECT. in ANTHROP, Toyo Univ. Member: JPA. Research in anthropology, teaching; cross-cultural study of personality and human relations, use of projective techniques in anthropology. M

SOMA, Motohiro. Health Superv. Sect, Jap. Natl. Railways, Marunouchi, Chiyodaku, Tokyo. b. 11 Feb 1915 Tokyo. Bungakushi '38 Univ. of Tokyo, Japan. RES. MEMBER, Hlth. Superv. Sect, Jap. Natl. Railways. Member: JPA, JSAP. Industrial psychology, testing, psychotherapy; counseling, group process, aptitude tests. M

SONOHARA, Prof. Taro. Dept. of Psych, Kyoto Univ, Yoshida, Kyoto. b. 26 Dec 1908 Kanazawa. Bungakushi '31 Kyoto Univ, Japan. PROFESSOR, Kyoto Univ; LECTURER, Ritsumeikan Univ. and Osaka Munic. Univ. Member: JPA, Kansai Psych. Assn. Teaching, research, administration; comparative and genetic study of perception and cognition. M

SOTOBAYASHI, Prof. Daisaku. City Univ. of Yokohama, 4646 Mutuura Kanazawaku, Yokohama. b. 11 Oct 1916 Fukuyama. Bungakushi '41 Univ. of Tokyo, Japan. PROF. of PSYCH, City Univ. of Yokohama. Member: JPA, JSAP. Teaching clinical and social psychology, research, professional writing; projective techniques, sociometry. M

SUEHIRO, Dr. Ken. Seishin-Igaku Inst, Moro-machi, Tokyo. b. 21 May 1917 Tokyo. Igakushi '41 Keio Univ, Japan. ASST. DIR, Seishin-Igaku Inst; ASSISTANT, Med. Dept, Keio Univ, Tokyo. Member: JPA, Jap. Assn. of Psychiat. and Neur. Research, psychiatric clinical practice; psychotherapy, testing. M

SUENAGA, Prof. Toshiro. Dept. of Psych, Coll. of Gen. Educ, Univ. of Tokyo, Komabamachi, Meguroku, Tokyo. b. 31 May 1921 Kobe. Bungakushi '43 Univ. of Tokyo, Japan. ASST. PROF, Univ. of Tokyo. Member: JPA, JSAP. Teaching, research; group process. M

SUETOSHI, Prof. Hiroshi. Aichi Univ. of Liberal Arts and Educ, Myodaigi, Okazaki. b. 2 Sept 1916 Okayama. Bungakushi '48 Tokyo Bunrika Univ, Japan. ASST. PROF, Aichi Univ. of Liberal Arts and Educ. Member: JSAP. Teaching tests and measurements in physical education, applied psychology, research; achievement tests, group process, attitude measurement. M

SUGA, Toshio. Dept. of Psych, St. Paul Univ, Ikebukuro, Tokyo. b. 22 Sept 1916 Okayama. Bungakushi '41 St. Paul Univ, Japan. CHIEF, Tottori Juv. Classif. Off, Yudokoro, Tottori. Member: JPA, JSAP. Clinical guidance, consulting, testing, teaching; personality. M

SUGAHARA, Kaoru. Recruitment Bur, Natl. Pers. Authority, 1-2 Kasumigaseki, Chiyoda-ku, Tokyo. b. 13 Apr 1914 Tokyo. Bungakushi '41 Nihon Univ, Japan. CHIEF, Exam. Res. Sect, Natl. Pers. Authority. Member: JPA, JSAP. Administration, personnel psychology, research on test construction; personnel management, selection and classification. M

SUGAZAKI, Akio. Hakodate Juvenile Classif. Off, Nakajima-chyo, Hakodate. b. 14 Jan 1930 Hakodate. CHIEF, Hakodate Juv. Classif. Off. Member: JPA. Testing, classification and clinical diagnosis of juvenile delinquents; projective techniques, Kraepelin-Uchida Test. M

SUGIHARA, Prof. Tamotsu. 1 Tsunofuri, Nara. b. 13 Nov 1917 Nara. Igakuhakushi '50 Osaka Univ, Japan. PROF. of SOC. WORK, Kanseigakuin Univ, Uegahara, Nisinomiya; LECTURER, Osaka Univ. Member: SCP. Teaching clinical psychology, mental hygiene, and psychiatry, research, consulting; projective techniques. M

SUGITA, Jiro. Takasu, Furutamachi, Hiroshima-shi. b. 15 Feb 1913 Hiroshima. Bungakushi '41 Hiroshima Univ, Japan. CHIEF, Hiroshima Child Welf. Cen, Moto-Machi, Hiroshima. Member: JPA, JAEP. Administration, guidance, testing, teaching; projective techniques. M

SUGITA, Yukata. Dept. of Spec. Educ, Tokyo Univ. of Educ, Otsuka, Bunkyo, Tokyo. b. 7 Sept 1921 Tokyo. Bungakushi '48 Univ. of Tokyo, Japan. INSTR. in PSYCH. and EDUC, Tokyo Univ. of Educ; EDITOR, *Japanese Journal of Child Psychology and Mental Hygiene.* Member: JPA, JSAP, Jap. Assn. for Spec. Educ. Research and teaching on education of mentally retarded children, testing; social maturity, learning readiness, intelligence testing. M

SUGITANI, Kiyotoki. Dept. of Liberal Arts, Yokohama Natl. Univ, Kamakura, Kanagawa. b. 29 Mar 1922 Tokyo. Bungakushi '47 Univ. of Tokyo, Japan. INSTR. in PSYCH, Yokohama Natl. Univ. Member: JPA, JSAP. Teaching child psychology and mental hygiene, research, guidance; counseling techniques, family relationships. M

SUGIYAMA, Yoshio. Dept. of Psych, Fac. of Letters, Hokkaido Univ, Hokkaido, Sapporo. b. 8 Dec 1930 Senzaki. Bungakushi '54 Hokkaido Univ, Japan. STUDENT. Member: JPA, Hokkaido Psych. Assn. Jap. Assn. of Psychiat. and Neur. Research; emotion, anxiety. M

SUMI, Kiroku. Yazaka 2626, Okayama City. b. 31 Jan 1910 Tokusima Prefecture. Bungakushi '39 Nihon Univ, Japan. SUPERINTENDANT, Child Welf. Cen. of Okayama Prefecture, Agasaki, Tamasima;

LECTURER, Okayama Univ. Member: JPA, JSAP. Administration, guidance, testing; projective techniques. M

SUMI, Prof. Kohei. Dept. of Soc. Welf, Osaka Women's Univ, Tetsukayama, Sumiyoshi-ku, Osaka. b. 21 Oct 1914 Nagoya. Bungakushi '41 Tohoku Univ, Japan. PROFESSOR, Osaka Women's Univ. Member: JPA. Research, educational psychology, teaching; child psychology, psychology of the deaf. M

SUMIO, Minoru. Dept. of Psych, Tokyo Univ. of Liberal Arts and Educ, Shimouma, Tokyo. b. 1 Nov 1922 Osaka. Bungakushi '47 Tokyo Bunrika Univ, Japan. INSTRUCTOR, Tokyo Univ. of Liberal Arts and Educ; LECTURER, Kawamura Coll. Member: JPA, JSAP. Teaching educational and child psychology, research, professional writing; projective techniques, group process. M

SUMITA, Prof. Katsumi. Kyoto Univ. of Liberal Arts and Educ, Minami-Ohnocho, Kita-Ku, Kyoto. b. 9 Apr 1906 Hyogo Prefecture. Bungakushi '32 Tohoku Univ, Japan. PROF. of PSYCH, Kyoto Univ. of Liberal Arts and Educ. Member: JPA, Kansai Psych. Assn. Consulting, teaching, research; intelligence theory and testing, personality tests, factor analysis. M

SUSUKITA, Prof. Tsukasa. Dept. of Educ. Psych, Kanazawa Univ, Ote-machi, Kanazawa. b. 6 Jan 1907 Fukushima. Bungakushi '31 Tohoku Univ, Japan. PROF. of PSYCH, Kanazawa Univ; HEADMASTER, Elementary School of Kanazawa Univ. Member: JPA, JSAP. Research, teaching educational psychology; memory, personality. M

SUTO, Yoji. Dept. of Psych, Tokyo Univ. of Educ, Otsuka-kubomachi, Bunkyoku, Tokyo. b. 25 Aug 1926 Niigata. Bungakushi '51 Tokyo Bunrika Univ, Japan. ASSISTANT, Tokyo Univ. of Educ. Member: JPA, JSAP, JAEP. Research, teaching, professional writing; sensory and spatial perception. M

SUWA, Prof. Nozomi. Dept. of Neuropsychiat, Hokkaido Univ. Sch. of Med, Kita-12, Nishi-5, Sapporo, Hokkaido. b. 20 July 1912 Tokyo. Igakuhakushi '47 Univ. of Tokyo, Japan. PROF. of PSYCHIAT, Hokkaido Univ. Sch. of Med. Member: Hokkaido Psych. Assn. Teaching and research in psychiatry and neurology, consulting; intelligence tests, projective techniques. M

SUYAMA, Prof. Kikuji. 5932 Suidocho I, Niigata. b. 15 Feb 1896 Ikeda. Bungakushi '25 Univ. of Tokyo, Japan. PROF. of PSYCH, Niigata. Univ, Nishi ohata machi, Niigata. Member: JPA, JAEP. Teaching, research, administration; attitude measurement. M

SUZUKI, Dr. Harutaro. 3-37 Yamasaka-machi, Sumiyoshi-ku, Osaka. b. 4 Apr 1875 Siga. Bungakuhakushi '50 Kyoto Univ, Japan. LECT. in EDUC. PSYCH, Tezukayama Coll, Osaka. Retired, teaching, research; mental testing. M

SUZUKI, Katsuji. Juvenile Dept, Sendai Family Court, Omachigashira, Sendai, Miyaga. b. 25 Mar 1917 Miyagi. Bunga-kushi '48 Tohoku Univ, Japan. PROBAT. OFF, Sendai Fam. Ct. Member: JPA, JSAP, Tohoku Psych. Assn. Clinical practice and guidance of juvenile delinquents, testing, administration; personality of the criminal, social casework. M

SUZUKI, Kiyoshi. Bentenmachi, Senbonde-mizu, Kamigyo, Kyoto. b. 8 May 1926 Kyoto. Bungakushi '50 Ritsumeikan Univ, Japan. CLIN. PSYCH'T, Classif. Sect, Kobe Detention and Classif. Off, Shimogiomachi, Kobe. Member: JPA. Classification of juvenile delinquents, teaching, consulting, research; psychological testing, projective techniques. M

SUZUKI, Prof. Kiyoshi. Dept. of Psych, Tokyo Univ. of Educ, Bunkyoku, Tokyo. b. 15 Oct 1906 Shizuoka. Bungakushi '36 Tokyo Bunrika Univ, Japan. PROFESSOR, Tokyo Univ. of Educ. Member: JPA, JSAP. Research, teaching, psychotherapy; ego development, personality tests, counseling. M

SUZUKI, Prof. Makoto. Dept. of Vocat. Guid, Osaka Univ. of Liberal Arts and Educ, Minami-Kawabori Tennoji, Osaka. b. 31 Oct 1901 Utsunomiya. Bungakushi '25 Kyoto Univ, Japan. PROFESSOR, Osaka Univ. of Liberal Arts and Educ. Member: JPA, JSAP. Educational and applied psychology, testing, vocational guidance; aptitude tests. M

SUZUKI, Prof. Osamu. Dept. of Psych, Tokyo Univ. of Liberal Arts and Educ, Setagayaku, Tokyo. b. 6 Feb 1912 Suka-gawa. Bungakushi '41 Tokyo Bunrika Univ, Japan. ASST. PROF, Tokyo Univ. of Liberal Arts and Educ. Member: JPA, JSAP. Teaching developmental and educational psychology; research; development of thinking in children. M

SUZUKI, Prof. Saburo. Egamuro, Kameya-ma, Mie. b. 13 Sept 1909 Tokyo. Bunga-kushi '36 Nihon Univ, Japan. ASST. PROF, Mie Univ, Marunouchi, Tsu. Member: JPA. Teaching, research, consulting; perception of movement, development of exceptional children. M

SUZUKI, Prof. Tatsuya. Psych. Lab, Kana-zawa Univ, Ohte-machi, Kanazawa. b. 18 Oct 1913 Hiroshima. Bungakushi '37 Univ. of Tokyo, Japan. ASST. PROF, Kana-zawa Univ. Member: JPA, Hokuriku Psych. Assn. Teaching, research, applied psychology; aptitude tests, industrial fatigue and eff ciency, accidents. M

SUZUKI, Yoshio. Supervisory Trng. Sect, Employment Security Bur, Ministry of Labor, Ohte-machi, Tokyo. b. 27 Apr 1919 Okayama. Bungakushi '41 Kwansei Gakuin Univ, Japan. DIRECTOR, Super-visory Trng. Sect, Employment Security Bur. Member: JPA, JSAP. Industrial consulting, research, personnel psychology; human relations in industry, training of supervisors. M

TACHIBANA, Prof. Kakusho. Dept. of Psych, Osaka Univ, Shibahara, Toyonaka, Osaka. b. 17 Feb 1900 Osaka. Bungakuha-kushi '52 Univ. of Tokyo, Japan. PRO-FESSOR, Osaka Univ. Member: JPA, JSAP, SCP, Kansai Psych. Assn. Research, teaching, editorial; psychological approach to gerontology. M

TACHIBATA, Prof. Takuo. Dept. of Psych, Fukuoka Univ. of Liberal Arts and Educ, Tagawa Br, Tagawa, Fukuoka. b. 20 Feb 1906 Hiroshima. Bungakushi '33 Hiroshima Univ, Japan. ASST. PROF, Fukuoka Univ. of Liberal Arts and Educ. Member: JPA. Teaching, research, educational psychology; mental hygiene. M

TAGAWA, Prof. Keiichi. Dept. of Psych, Hyogo Univ. of Agric, Sasayama, Hyogo. b. 23 Sept 1924 Osaka. Bungakushi '48 Kwansei Gakuin Univ, Japan. ASST. PROF, Hyogo Univ. of Agric. Member: JPA, Kwansei Psych. Assn. Research, teaching; learning theory, conditioning. M

TAGO, Akira. 2 Kamicho, Nakano-ku, Tokyo. b. 25 Feb 1923 Medan, Indonesia. Bungakushi '50 Univ. of Tokyo, Japan. ASST. in PSYCH, Tokyo Inst. of Tech, 1 Okayama, Meguro-ku, Tokyo. Member: JPA, JSAP. Research, testing, guidance; theory and mesurement of personality, family and marital problems. M

TAGUCHI, Prof. Takayuki. 34 Wateri-Yamashita, Fukushima. b. 16 Feb 1909 Tokyo. Bungakushi '31 Tokyo Bunrika Univ, Japan. PROF. of PSYCH, Fukushima Univ, Hamada-cho, Fukushima. Member: JPA, JSAP, JAEP. Research, teaching, educational psychology; guidance of learning activities. M

TAII, Dr. Shunzo. Dept. of Neuropsychiat, Kitano Hosp, Nishi Ogi Machi, Osaka. b. 22 June 1914 Himeji. Igakuhakushi '45 Kyoto Univ, Japan. ACTING CLIN. DIR, Kitano Hosp; LECT. in PSYCHIAT, Kansai Med. Coll; LECT. in MENT. HYG, Osaka Munic. Univ. Sch. of the Sci. of Living. Member: JPA, Jap. Assn. of Psychiat. and Neur. Clinical practice, teaching, research; environmental factors in psychiatry, personality development in the psycho-path. M

TAKADA, Rishin. Dept. of Psych, Fukui

Univ, Makinoshima, Fukui. b. 24 July 1915 Shikaura. Bungakushi '39 Univ. of Tokyo, Japan. INSTRUCTOR, Fukui Univ. Member: JPA, JSAP, Jap. Pedagogical Assn. Research, teaching, guidance; learning theory, conditioning.   M

TAKADA, Yoichiro. Dept. of Psych, Fac. of Letters, Hokkaido Univ, Kita 8, Nishi 5, Sapporo. b. 21 Dec 1925 Tokyo. Bungakushi '48 Univ. of Tokyo, Japan. INSTRUCTOR, Hokkaido Univ. Member: JPA, Hokkaido Psych. Assn. Teaching, research, applied psychology; theory of human behavior, group process, learning theory.   M

TAKAGI, Prof. Kanichi. Dept. of Psych, Hiroshima Univ, Higashi-Senda, Hiroshima. b. 4 May 1900 Takayama. Bungakushi '25 Univ. of Tokyo, Japan. PROF. and CHMN, Dept. of Psych, Hiroshima Univ. Member: JPA, JSAP. Research, teaching, applied psychology; visual perception.   M

TAKAGI, Prof. Masataka. Psych. Inst, Kobe Univ, Mikage-Shihan 925, Higashi-Nada-Ku, Kobe. b. 12 Mar 1913 Tokyo. Bungakushi '36 Univ. of Tokyo, Japan. ASST. PROF, Kobe Univ. Member: JPA, JSAP. Teaching social psychology, research; research on twins, heredity and environment, national character.   M

TAKAGI, Prof. Sadaji. 480 Shinden, Koganei-cho, Tokyo. b. 3 Dec 1893 Osaka. Bungakushi '18 Univ. of Tokyo, Japan. PRESIDENT and PROF. of PSYCH, Tokyo Woman's Christian Coll, Iogi, Suginami-ku, Tokyo; EDITOR, *Japanese Journal of Psychology*; ED. BD, *Journal of Social Psychology* (USA). Member: JPA, JSAP, Jap. Socy. for Animal Psych. Administration, teaching, research; visual space perception, learning theory, psychometrics.   M

TAKAHARA, Aritoshi. Yamaguchi Women's Jr. Coll, Miyano, Yamaguchi. b. 25 Jan 1919 Manchuria, China. Bungakushi '45 Univ. of Tokyo, Japan. INSTRUCTOR, Yamaguchi Women's Jr. Coll. Member: JPA. Teaching, child psychology, research, guidance; study of delinquent girls.   M

TAKAHASHI, Prof. Kazutoshi. Shokei Women's Jr. Coll, Nakajimacho, Sendai. b. 24 Mar 1919 Fukushima. Bungakushi '50 Tohoku Univ, Japan. ASST. PROF. of PSYCH, Shokei Women's Jr. Coll. Member: JPA, JSAP, Tohoku Psych. Assn. Teaching educational psychology, research, guidance; group dynamics, personality.   M

TAKAHASHI, Dr. Kiyohiko. Sakai Ment. Hosp, Sakai, Osaka. b. 18 Feb 1920 Osaka. Igakuhakushi '54 Osaka Univ, Japan. PRESIDENT, Sakai Ment. Hosp. Member: Jap. Assn. of Psychiat. and Neur. Psychotherapy, clinical analysis, research;

group Rorschach test.   M

TAKAHASHI, Masaharu. Daido-cho, 1-1, Hyogo-ku, Kobe. b. 20 Mar 1926 Osaka. Bungakushi '50 Kyoto Univ, Japan. CHIEF, Classif. Sect, Kobe Detention and Classif. Off, Shimo-gionmachi, Kobe. Member: JPA. Consulting, guidance, teaching, research; projective techniques. M

TAKAHASHI, Prof. Seiki. Dept. of Educ. Psych, Kobe Univ, Kobe. b. 12 Jan 1911 Himeji. Bungakushi '34 Univ. of Tokyo, Japan. ASST. PROF, Kobe Univ. Member: JPA, Kwansei Psych. Assn. Teaching, research, guidance; projective techniques, counseling.   M

TAKAHASHI, Shigeo. Dept. of Psych, Kagawa Univ, Saiwai-cho, Takamatsu. b. 1 Oct 1915 Kanonji. Bungakushi '44 Hiroshima Bunrika Univ, Japan. ASST. PROF, Kagawa Univ. Member: JPA, JSAP. Teaching, educational and clinical psychology; projective techniques, diagnostic study of abnormal behavior.   M

TAKAHASHI, Susumu. 1-Kiridoshi, Sakamachi, Yushima, Bunkyo-ku, Tokyo. b. 26 Jan 1928 Tokyo. ASST. in PSYCHIAT, Med. Sch, Keio Univ, 35-Shinanomachi, Shinjuku-ku, Tokyo; EDITOR, *Japanese Journal of Psychoanalysis*. Member: JPA, Japan Psychoanal. Socy, Jap. Psychiat. Assn. Psychotherapy; psychoanalysis.   M

TAKAHASHI, Tetsu. 2-chome, Tokiwadai, Itabashi Ku, Tokyo. b. 2 Nov 1907 Tokyo. Bungakushi '40 Nihon Univ, Japan. PRESIDENT, Japan Life Psych. Socy, Tokiwadai, Tokyo; EDITOR, *Seishin Report*. Member: JSAP, Japan Psychoanal. Socy. Professional writing, consulting, testing; psychology of sex, sexual neuroses, psychoanalysis.   M

TAKAHASHI, Prof. Yutaka. Dept. of Philos, Gakushuin Univ, Mejiro, Tokyo. b. 4 May 1885 Kagawaken. Bungakuhakushi '48 Tohoku Univ, Japan. PROF. and HEAD, Dept. of Philos, Gakushuin Univ; COEDITOR, *Annual of Ethics*. Member: JPA, JSAP. Teaching, research, administration; analysis of moral attitudes.   M

TAKANO, Eijiro. Gunma Child Welf. Cen, Koyanagi-cho, Maebashi, Gunma.   b. 25 Aug 1910 Shibukawa. Bungakushi '38 Tokyo Bunrika Univ, Japan. CHIEF, Gunma Child Welf. Cen. Member: JPA, JSAP. Administration, counseling, testing, psychotherapy; counseling of problem children.   M

TAKANO, Kenji. Coll. of Arts, Nara Women's Univ, Kita Uwoya Nishi Machi, Nara. b. 22 Aug 1921 Ichimiyamura. Bungakushi '47 Tokyo Bunrika Univ, Japan. INSTR. in PSYCH, Nara Women's Univ; LECTURER, Coll. of Physical Educ, Tenri Univ. Member: JPA. Teaching and re search in psychology of physical education; kinesthetic sensation, body orientation in space, motor learning, acquisition of skills.M

TAKASE, Tsuneo. Dept. of Psych, First Coll. of Arts and Sci, Tohoku Univ, Tomizawa, Sendai. b. 10 Mar 1926 Aizu-Wakamatsu. Bungakushi '50 Tohoku Univ, Japan. INSTRUCTOR, First Coll. of Arts and Sci, Tohoku Univ. Member: JPA, JSAP, Tohoku Psych. Assn. Teaching, research, editorial; social psychology, dynamics of cultural change. M

TAKATSUKI, Toichi. 421 4-chome Matsubara-cho, Setagaya-ku, Tokyo. b. 24 Feb 1919 Hanoi, French Indo-China. Bungakushi '45 Univ. of Tokyo, Japan. RES. DIR, Assn. of Pub. Opinion Sci, 676 4-chome Sendagaya, Shibuya-ku, Tokyo; LECTURER, Japan Women's Univ. Member: JPA, JSAP. Research design for public opinion studies, market research, industrial relations, teaching; opinion, attitude and motivation measurement, mass communication, group dynamics. M

TAKEDA, Prof. Masanobu. 119 Midorigaoka Ashiya-shi, Hyogo. b. 29 Jan 1913 Amagasaki. Bungakushi '38 Kwansei Gakuin Univ, Japan. ASST. PROF. of PSYCH, Osaka Furitsu Univ, Sakai, Osaka. Member: JPA, JSAP. Teaching industrial psychology and vocational guidance, research; vocational aptitude. M

TAKEDA, Prof. Toshio. 1297 Kichijoji, Tokyo. b. 24 May 1907 Tokyo. Bungakushi '30 Univ. of Tokyo, Japan. PROF. of PSYCH, Tokyo Bunka Jr. Coll, Nakano, Tokyo. Member: JPA, JSAP. Teaching child psychology, research, clinical practice; behavior problems in children. M

TAKEGAMI, Prof. Kaoru. Dept. of Educ. Psych, Aichi Univ. of Liberal arts and Educ, Taikocho, Higashiku, Nagoya. b. 13 Apr 1913 Kagawa-Ken. Bungakushi '42 Tokyo Bunrika Univ, Japan. ASST. PROF, Aichi Univ. of Liberal Arts and Educ. Member: JPA, Tokai Psych. Assn. Research, teaching educational psychology, guidance; psychology of adolescence, educational clinics. M

TAKEMASA, Prof. Taro. 221 Shimohoya, Hoyacho, Kitatamagun, Tokyo. b. 13 Jan 1887 Okayama. Bungakushi '26 Univ. of Tokyo, Japan. PROF. of PSYCH, Otsuma Women's Coll, 12 Sabancho, Tokyo. Member: JPA, Jap. Socy. for Animal Psych. Teaching educational psychology; developmental and comparative psychology, theories of development and learning. M

TAKENAKA, Haruhiko. Dept. of Psych, Hokkaido Univ, Sapporo. b. 22 Oct 1927 Tokyo. Bungakushi '53 Univ. of Tokyo. Japan. ASSISTANT, Hokkaido Univ.

Member: JPA, Jap. Socy. for Animal Psych. Research, teaching, consulting; discrimination and partial reinforcement in learning. M

TAKETANI, Dr. Masao. 3035 Makamiya, Hirakata-shi, Osaka. b. 16 Feb 1914 Osaka. Igakuhakushi '55 Osaka Univ, Japan. CHIEF PSYCHIATRIST, Ment. Hyg. Clin, Osaka Prefectural Consultation Cen. of Ment. Hlth, 38 Ikudamamae-cho, Tennoji-ku, Osaka. Member: JPA, SCP, Jap. Assn. of Psychiat. and Neur. Psychotherapy, research, clinical practice, consulting; projective techniques, group dynamics, mental health. M

TAKEUCHI, Prof. Katashi. Dept. of Educ, Shinshu Univ, Nishinagano, Nagano-shi. b. 20 Dec 1905 Fukui. Bungakushi '32 Tokyo Bunrika Univ, Japan. PROF. of EDUC. PSYCH, Shinshu Univ. Member: JPA. Teaching, research, educational psychology; personality theory. M

TAKEUCHI, Prof. Takeshi. Hanazono-cho, 53, Chiba-shi, Chiba-ken. b. 13 Feb 1915 Fukui. Bungakushi '41 Hiroshima Bunrika Univ, Japan. ASST. PROF. of PSYCH, Fac. of Educ, Univ. of Chiba, Ichiba-cho, Chiba. Member: JPA, JAEP. Teaching, research, educational psychology; psychometric study of personality. M

TAKEUCHI, Prof. Terumune. Dept. of Psych, Hirosaki Univ. Shimoshiroganecho, Hirosaki. b. 1 Mar 1923 Ibaraki. Bungakushi '50 Tohoku Univ, Japan. Ass. Prof. Hirosaki Univ, Member: JPA, Jap. Socy. for Animal Psych. Research, teaching, testing; learning theory, group process. M

TAKEYAMA, Dr. Tsunehisa. Dept. of Psychiat, Jikei-kai Med. Coll, Shiba, Minato-ku, Tokyo. b. 21 Sept 1910 Tokyo. Igakuhakushi '45 Jikei-kai Med. Coll, Japan. LECT. in PSYCHIAT, Jikei-kai Med. Coll. Member: JSAP. Teaching, psychotherapy, consulting; projective techniques, criminal psychology. M

TAKINO, Prof. Chiharu. Dept. of Psych, Nara Univ. of Liberal Arts and Educ, Noborioji, Nara. b. 30 Mar 1924 Kyoto. Bungakushi '49 Kyoto Univ, Japan. ASST. PROF, Nara Univ. of Liberal Arts and Educ. Member: JPA, Kansai Psych. Assn. Research, teaching experimental psychology, testing; figural after-effects in perception, statistical methods. M. M

TAKUMA, Taketoshi. Dept. of Psych, Gakushuin Univ, Mejiro, Tokyo. b. 30 June 1927 Chiba. Bungakushi '51 Univ. of Tokyo, Japan. INSTRUCTOR, Gakushuin Univ. Member: JPA, JAEP. Research, teaching, testing; personality development. M

TAMAI, Shusuke. Dept. of Child Ment.

Health, Inst. of Ment. Health, Konodai, Ichikawa-shi, Chiba-ken. b. 28 July 1923 Gifu. Bungakushi '48 Univ. of Tokyo, Japan. TECH. OFF, Natl. Inst. of Ment. Hlth; LECT. in EDUC. PSYCH, Sch. of Nursing, Konodai Natl. Hosp, and Tokyo Coll. for Domes. Sci. Clinical research, psychotherapy, teaching, child psychotherapy.   M

TAMAKI, Prof. Osamu. Dept. of Liberal Arts, Wakayama Univ, Masagocho, Wakayama. b. 2 Feb 1905 Wakayama. Bungakushi, Kyoto Univ, Japan. DEAN and PROF. of PSYCH, Wakayama Univ. Member: JPA. Teaching child psychology, administration, educational psychology; developmental process, social attitude, learning. M

TAMANYU, Michitsune. Juvenile Classif. Home, Urawa, Tokyo. b. 15 July 1914 Tsuchiura. Bungakushi '35 Univ. of Tokyo, Japan. SUPERINTENDENT, Urawa Juv. Classif. Home, Urawa City, Saitamaken; LECT. in CLIN. PSYCH, Aoyama Gakuin Univ, Aoyama, Tokyo. Member: JPA, JSAP, Japan Socy. of Criminol. and Crim. Law. Research, administration, consulting, clinical practice, guidance; personality study of juvenile delinquents.   M

TAMAOKA, Prof. Shinobu. Kyoritsu Women's Coll, Kanda, Toyko. b. 25 June 1909 Saseho. Bungakushi '34 Hiroshima Bunrika Univ, Japan. PROF. of PSYCH, Kyoritsu Women's Coll; LECTURER, Chuo Univ. Member: JPA, JSAP. Teaching, research, editorial; psychology of genius and feeblemindedness, musical tests.   M

TANAKA, Haruchika. Takamatsu Juvenile Classif. Home, 87 Fujitsuka-cho, Takamatsu. b. 29 Oct 1902 Hoygo-ken. Bungakushi '37 Kyoto Univ, Japan. TECH. OFF, Takamatsu Juv. Classif. Home. Member: JPA. Testing and case studies of juvenile delinquents, research, teaching; projective techniques, learning theory, psychotherapy.   M

TANAKA, Prof. Hideo. Dept. of Psych, Defense Acad, Yokosuka, Kanagawa. b. 28 Aug 1905 Tokyo. Bungakushi '33 Tohoku Univ, Japan. PROFESSOR, Defense Acad. Member: JPA. Research, consulting, teaching; group psychology, ethics and values.   M

TANAKA, Jinemon. Nishitarumicho 1445-6, Tarumiku, Kobe. b. 6 Feb 1916 Kobe. Bungakushi '39 Keio Univ, Japan. CHIEF, Pers. and Labor Sect, Kobe Kogyo Corp, Wadayama-Dori, 1-chome, Kobe. Member: JPA. Industrail and personnel psychology; perception, psychological problems and training in industry.   M

TANAKA, Prof. Kan-ichi. Dept. of Psych, Nihon Univ, Kanda, Tokyo. b. 20 Jan 1882 Okayama. Bungakuhakushi '19

Univ. of Tokyo, Japan. PROFESSOR, Nihon Univ; DIRECTOR, Tanaka Inst. for Educ. Res. Member: JPA, JSAP. Research, teaching educational and industrial psychology; intellegence tests, character tests.   M

TANAKA, Prof. Kazushiro. Dept. of Psych, Coll. of Educ, Kochi Univ, 1000 Asakura, Kochi. b. 22 Oct 1903 Wakayama. Bungakushi '35 Kyushu Univ, Japan. PROFESSOR, Kochi Univ; PRINCIPAL, Jr. High Sch. of Kochi Univ. Member: JPA. Teaching, testing, educational psychology; child psychology, tests and measurements.   M

TANAKA, Keiji. Dept. of Psych, Shizuoka Univ, Oiwa, Shizuoka. b. 22 Oct 1916 Maebashi. Bungakushi '48 Tokyo Bunrika Univ, Japan. INSTRUCTOR, Shizuoka Univ. Member: JPA, JSAP. Teaching, research, educational psychology; visual perception, language of the infant. M

TANAKA, Prof. Kumajiro. Dept. of Educ. Psych, Tokyo Univ. of Liberal Arts and Educ, Setagaya-ku, Tokyo. b. 2 Jan 1910 Niigata-k^n. Bungakushi '42 Tokyo Bunrika Univ, Japan. ASST. PROF, Tokyo Univ. of Liberal Arts and Educ. Member: JPA, JSAP. Teaching child and educational psychology, administration, research; social development, sociometric research, group process.   M

TANAKA, Prof. Kunio. Dept. of Psych, Kobe City Univ. of Foreign Studies, Nada, Kobe. b. 11 Feb 1926 Hyogo Prefecture. Bungakushi '48 Hiroshima Bunrika Univ, Japan. ASST. PROF, Kobe City Univ. of Foreign Studies; LECTURER, Kwansei Gakuin Univ. Member: JPA. Research, teaching, educational psychology; attitude measurement, factor analysis techniques.   M

TANAKA, Prof. Masaru. Dept. of Educ, Ehime Univ, Matsuyama-Shi, Ehime Prefecture. b. 10 Apr 1908 Matsuyama. Bungakushi '35 Tokyo Bunrika Univ, Japan. PROF. of PSYCH, Ehime Univ. Member: JPA. Teaching adolescent and educational psychology, research; motivation in learning, attitude measurement, projective techniques.   M

TANAKA, Prof. Seigo. Dept. of Educ, Fac. of Literature, Osaka Univ, Toyonaka, Osaka. b. 4 June 1918 Yamaguchi. Bungakushi '42 Univ. of Tokyo, Japan. ASST. PROF. of EDUC. PSYCH, Osaka Univ. Member: JPA, JAEP. Research, teaching educational psychology; intelligence, aptitude and achievement tests, theory of test construction.   M

TANAKA, Prof. Shoichi. Dept. of Psych, Aichi Univ. of Liberal Arts and Educ, Okazaki, Aichiken. b. 18 Apr 1913 Toyohashi. Bungakushi '44 Tokyo Bunrika

Univ, Japan. ASST. PROF, Aichi Univ. of Liberal Arts and Educ. Member: JSAP, Japan Socy. of Physical Educ. Teaching psychology of physical education and industrial psychology, research; cooperation in group learning.   M

TANAKA, Prof. Tarō. Dept. of Soc. Welf, Osaka Women's Coll, Tezukayama, Sumiyoshi-ku, Osaka. b. 3 Feb 1912 Shiga. Bungakushi '35 Univ. of Tokyo, Japan. PROF. of PSYCH, Osaka Women's Coll. Member: JPA. Teaching child psychology, guidance, testing; personality of problem children.   M

TANAKA, Prof. Tetsuya. Hamamatsu Br, Fac. of Educ, Shizuoka Univ, Nagori, Hamamatsu. b. 15 Apr 1922 Mie Prefecture. Bungakushi '45 Tokyo Bunrika Univ, Japan. ASST. PROF. of PSYCH, Shizuoka Univ. Member: JPA, JSAP. Teaching developmental psychology, research, testing; emotional development. M

TANAKA, Toshitaka. Dept. of Psych, Osaka Univ. of Liberal Arts and Educ, Tennoji, Osaka. b. 11 Dec 1921 Osaka. Bungakushi '49 Tokyo Bunrika Univ, Japan. INSTRUCTOR, Osaka Univ. of Liberal Arts and Educ. Member: JPA, JSAP. Research, teaching, consulting; developmental psychology, development of thinking.   M

TANAKA, Prof. Yoshihisa. Dept. of Psych, Univ. of Tokyo, Motofuji-cho, Bunkyo-ku, Tokyo. b. 27 Feb 1917 Yahata. Bungakushi '41 Univ. of Tokyo, Japan. ASST. PROF, Univ. of Tokyo. Member: JPA, Jap. Socy. for Animal Psych. Teaching, research; psychometric and psychophysical methods, comparative study of perception.   M

TANAKA, Yutaka. Natl. Rehab. Cen. for the Physically Handicapped, 1 Toyamacho, Shinjuku-ku, Tokyo. b. 20 Aug 1921 Hiroshima. Bungakushi '45 Keijo Univ, Japan. TECH. OFF, Ministry of Welf, Natl. Rehab. Cen. for the Physcially Handicapped. Member: JPA, JSAP. Guidance and counseling, testing, psychotherapy with the physically handicapped.M

TANIMOTO, Prof. Kiichi. Tokyo Univ. of Agric. and Tech, Fuchu, Tokyo. b. 18 Jan 1902 Hyogo-ken. Bungakushi '26 Univ. of Tokyo, Japan. PROF. of PSYCH, Tokyo Univ. of Agric. and Tech. Member: JPA. Teaching, research, administration; personality, aptitude tests, social attitudes.   M

TASHIRO, Prof. Tokichi. Dept. of Psych, Osaka Univ, Toyonaka, Osaka. b. 27 Jan 1914 Utsunomiya. Bungakushi '37 Univ. of Tokyo, Japan. ASST. PROF, Osaka Univ. Member: JPA, JSAP, Kwansei Psych. Assn. Teaching, industrial psychology, research; fatigue and attitude

studies in industry.   M

TATSUMI, Prof. Toshio. 2319 Kichijoji Musashinoshi, Tokyo. b. 3 Mar 1919 Tokyo. Bungakushi '46 Tokyo Bunrika Univ, Japan. ASST. PROF, Tokyo Univ. of Liberal Arts and Educ, Shimouma Setagayaku, Tokyo. Member: JPA, JSAP. Research, teaching, testing; factor analysis of personality.   M

TATSUNO, Prof. Chitoshi. Dept. of Psych, Tokyo Univ. of Educ, Bunkyoku, Tokyo. b. 31 May 1920 Naganoken. Bungakushi '36 Tokyo Bunrika Univ, Japan. ASST. PROF, Tokyo Univ. of Educ. Member: JPA, JSAP. Research, teaching; learning, proactive and retroactive inhibition. M

TAZAKI, Prof. Masashi. Juntendo Univ, Fujisaki, Narashino, Chiba-ken. b. 28 Sept 1898 Miyazaki. Bungakushi '33 Tokyo Bunrika Univ, Japan. PROF. of PSYCH, Juntendo Univ. Member: JPA, JSAP. Teaching, testing, applied psychology; vocational counseling, effective study methods, test construction.   M

TERADA, Hiroyuki. Central Child Guid. Clin. of Fukuoka Prefecture, Sunoko, Fukuoka. b. 6 June 1921 Kumamoto. Bungakushi '50 Kyushu Univ, Japan. CHIEF of DIAGNOSIS, Cen. Child Guid. Clin. of Fukuoka Prefecture. Member: JPA, JAEP. Testing, consulting, clinical practice, educational psychology; developmental psychology.   M

TERANISHI, Ryunen. Dept. of Exper. Psych, Fac. of Letters, Hokkaido Univ, Kita-8, Nishi-5, Sapporo, Hokkaido. b. 15 June 1927 Osaka. Bungakushi '50 Univ. of Tokyo, Japan. ASSISTANT, Hokkaido Univ. Member: JPA, Hokkaido Psych. Assn. Research, designing laboratory equipment, teaching; perception, accoustical communication.   M

TERAZAWA, Prof. Izuo. Dept. of Psych, Kyoritsu Women's Coll, Tokyo. b. 19 Oct 1881 Tokushima. Bungakuhakushi '50 Kyoto Univ, Japan. PROFESSOR, Kyoritsu Women's Coll. Member: JPA, JSAP. Research, teaching, educational psychology; subconsciousness.   M

TODA, Masanao. Dept. of Exper. Psych, Fac. of Letters, Hokkaido Univ, Kita-8, Nishi-5, Sapporo, Hokkaido. b. 27 Jan 1924 Ogaki. Rigakushi '46 Univ. of Tokyo, Japan. INSTRUCTOR, Hokkaido Univ. Member: JPA, Hokkaido Psych. Assn. Research, teaching experimental and social psychology, operations research; theory of decision making, information theory, group process.   M

TOGAWA, Prof. Yukio. Dept. of Psych, Waseda Univ, Totsuka, Tokyo. b. 1 Feb 1903 Tokyo. Bungakushi '29 Waseda Univ, Japan. PROFESSOR, Waseda Univ;

EDITOR, *Japanese Journal of Psychology.* Member: JPA, JSAP. Teaching, research; projective techniques. M

TOGO, Prof. Toyoharu. Dept. of Psych, Osaka Univ. of Foreign Languages, Tennaji-ku, Osaka. b. 28 Apr 1905 Tsuruga. Bungakushi '30 Kyoto Univ, Japan. PROFESSOR, Osaka Univ. of Foreign Languages. Member: JPA. Administration, teaching, educational psychology; personality, projective techniques. M

TOKIWAI, Gyoki. Isshinden Tsu, Mie Prefecture. b. 26 Nov 1905 Tsu. Bunga-kushi '30 Kyoto Univ, Japan. LORD ABBOT of SHINSHU-TAKADAHA, Senshuji, Isshinden, Tsu; PROFESSOR, Nagoya Coll. of Elec. Engr. Member: JPA, Tokai Psych. Assn. Research, teaching, testing; social psychology of religious movements. M

TOKUDA, Yasutoshi. Dept. of Psych, Fukushima Univ, Hamadacho, Fukushima. b. 2 Mar 1922 Shuri. Bungakushi '45 Tokyo Bunrika Univ, Japan. INSTRUCTOR, Fukushima Univ; LECTURER, Fukushima Sch. of Nursing. Member: JPA, JSAP. Research, teaching, consulting; learning theory. M

TOMITA, Satoru. Coll. of Genl. Educ, Tokyo Univ, Komaba, Tokyo. b. 8 Dec 1930 Hokkaido. Bungakushi '53 Univ. of Tokyo, Japan. ASST. in PSYCH, Coll. of Genl. Educ, Tokyo Univ. Member: JPA, JSAP. Student, research, counseling; sound localization in perception, interviewing techniques. M

TOMODA, Prof. Fujio. Kokugakuin Univ, Shibuya-ku, Tokyo. b. 1 Jan 1917. Bunga-kushi '41 Tokyo Bunrika Univ, Japan. ASST. PROF. of PSYCH, Kokugakuin Univ; DIRECTOR, Tokyo Couns. Cen. Member: JSAP. Research, guidance, teaching; client-centered counseling. M

TOYODA, Kunio. 2189 Shukugawara, Kawasaki-Shi, Kanagawa-Ken. b. 3 Mar 1917 Tokyo. Bungakushi '43 Hosei Univ, Japan. TEACHER, Hosei Univ. Second High Sch, Kizuki, Kawasaki. Member: JPA, JSAP. Educational psychology, testing, teaching sociology; achievement tests. M

TOYOHARA, Prof. Tsuneo. Dept. of Psych. and Educ, St. Paul Univ, Ikebukuro, Tokyo. b. 28 Sept 1909 Tokyo. Bungakushi '32 Univ. of Tokyo, Japan. CHMN. and PROF, Dept. of Psych. and Educ, St. Paul Univ; LECTURER, Chiba Univ. and Tokyo Toritsu Univ. Member: JPA, JSAP. Teaching, research, industrial psychology; industrial fatigue and accidents, aptitude tests and accidents in aeronautics. M

TSUBOTA, Masao. 1185 Zoshigaya 6-chome, Toshima-ku, Tokyo. b. 30 Jan 1917 Tokyo. INVESTIGATOR, Tokyo Family Court, Hibiya, Tokyo. Member: JPA, JSAP.

Research, psychotherapy, clinical analysis; relation between juvenile delinquents and their stepmothers. M

TSUDZUKI, Prof. Prof. Aritsune. Dept. of Educ. Psych, Nagoya Univ, Minamisoto-bori, Nakaku, Nagoya. b. 15 Dec 1914 Sendai. Bungakushi '38 Univ. of Tokyo, Japan. PROFESSOR, Nagoya Univ. Member: JPA, JAEP. Teaching, research, editorial; research methods in educational psychology. M

TSUJI, Prof. Shozo. Dept. of Psych, Tokyo Metrop. Univ, Fusuma-cho, Meguro-ku, Tokyo. b. 24 Feb 1913 Tokyo. Bungakushi '35 Univ. of Tokyo, Japan. ASST. PROF, Tokyo Metrop. Univ. Member: JPA, JSAP. Teaching social and industrial psychology, research, professional writing; human relations, interpersonal perception, socialization. M

TSUJIMURA, Taien. 11 Chuin-cho, Nara. b. 18 Jan 1919 Takamatsu. Bungakushi '41 Kyushu Univ, Japan. MANAGER, Aizen-Ryo Orphanage, Ikoma-Cho, Nara; MANAGER, Ikoma Nursery Sch, and Gokura-kuin Nursery Sch. Member: Kansai Psych. Assn. Administration, guidance, testing; group process. M

TSUJIMURA, Yasuo. Spec. Educ. Sect, Ministry of Educ, Chiyoda-ku, Tokyo. b. 10 Jan 1913 Tokyo. Bungakushi '35 Univ. of Tokyo, Japan. CHIEF, Spec. Educ. Sect, Ministry of Educ; LECTURER, Tokyo Univ. and Ochanomizu Women's Univ. Member: JPA, JSAP. Administration, educational psychology, consultung; personality of the mentally and physically handicapped child, social factors in personality formation. M

TSUJIOKA, Bien. Dept. of Psych, Kansai Univ, Suita, Osaka. b. 16 Dec 1925 Osaka. Bungakushi '50 Kyoto Univ, Japan. INSTRUCTOR, Kansai Univ. Member: JPA, SCP, Kansai Psych. Assn. Research, teaching, testing; factor analysis, statistics, personality tests. M

TSUKADA, Prof. Takeshi. Dept. of Educ. Psych, Fac. of Educ, Tohoku Univ, Katahiracho, Sendai. b. 24 Mar 1910 To-mioka. Bungakushi '33 Univ. of Tokyo, Japan. PROF. of EDUC. PSYCH, Tohoku Univ. Member: JPA, JAEP, Jap. Pedagogical Assn. Teaching, research, testing; adjustment and social values, homeostasis and ego-constancy. M

TSUKISHIMA, Kenzo. 23 Nichome, Sakae-cho, Nakano-ku, Tokyo. b. 24 Jan 1911 Naze. Bungakushi '41 Univ. of Tokyo, Japan. RES. MEMBER, Inst. for Oriental Culture, Univ. of Tokyo, 56 Otsuka-machi Bunkyo-ku, Tokyo; LECTURER, Nanzan Univ, Nagoya. Member: JPA, Jap. Socy. for Animal Psych. Research, teaching language and culture, culture and personality. M

TSUKIZOE, Masaji. Omigakuen, Ishiyama Nangocho, Otsu City. b. 28 Feb 1913 Dairen, China. Bungakushi '38 St. Paul Univ, Japan. CHIEF of LAB, Omigakuen. Member: JPA, JSAP, SCP. Consulting, teaching, research; developmental psychology of pre-school children. M

TSUKUI, Prof. Sakio. Dept. of Psych, Otaru Univ. of Commerce, Midoricho, Otaru, Hokkaido. b. 22 Dec 1918 Kawagoe. Bungakushi '42 Univ. of Tokyo, Japan. ASST. PROF. in INDUS. PSYCH, Otaru Univ. of Commerce. Member: JPA, JSAP, Jap. Educ. Socy. Teaching industrial and educational psychology, research; group process, industrial behavior. M

TSUMAKURA, Shotaro. Dept. of Psych, Nihon Univ, Chiyoda-ku, Tokyo. b. 1 Aug 1915 Tokyo. Bungakushi '44 Nihon Univ, Japan. INSTRUCTOR, Nihon Univ. Member: JPA, JSAP. Research, teaching, guidance; family problems, marriage counseling. M

TSUMORI, Prof. Makoto. Dept. of Child Study, Ochanomizu Women's Univ, 35 Otsuka-cho, Bunkyo-ku, Tokyo. b. 9 Jan 1926 Tokyo. Bungakushi '48 Univ. of Tokyo, Japan; MA '53 Univ. of Minnesota, USA. ASST. PROF, Ochanomizu Women's Univ; RES. MEMBER, Aiiku Inst. of Child Welf; EDITOR, *Education of Early Childhood*. Member: JPA, JSAP, Japan Early Childhood Assn. Research, teaching, editorial; social factors in value formation in children, child development, social development of the feebleminded. M

TSURU, Prof. Hiroshi. Dept. of Educ, Kobe Univ, Kobe. b. 10 July 1915 Tokyo. Bungakushi '41 Tokyo Bunrika Univ, Japan. ASST. PROF, Kobe Univ. Member: JPA. Teaching educational psychology, research, administration; adolescent psychology, personality of the Japanese. M

TSURUTA, Shoichi. 1114 Kamiishiwara, Kumagaya, Saitama. b. 29 July 1908 Nagano. Bungakushi '33 Univ. of Tokyo, Japan. CHIEF ENGR, Dept. of Psych, Labor Sci. Res. Off, Jap. Natl. Railways, Tabata, Kita, Tokyo; LECT. in PSYCH, St. Paul Univ. Member: JPA, JSAP, Japan Socy. of Aviat. Med. and Psych. Industrial and applied psychology, research, testing; aptitude tests for railway employees. M

TSUSHIMA, Prof. Tadashi. 71-9 Kitazonocho, Shimogamo, Sakyo-ku, Kyoto City. b. 1 Aug 1923 Kyoto. Bungakushi '49 Kyoto Univ, Japan. ASST. PROF, Kyoto State Saikyo Univ, Katsura, Ukyoku, Kyoto City; ADVISOR, Kyoto State Child Guid. Clin. Member: JPA, SCP, Kansai Psych. Assn. Teaching, research, clinical practice,

consulting; psychotherapy, projective techniques, learning theory. M

UCHIDA, Prof. Yasuhisa. Dept. of Literature and Educ, Ochanomizu Women's Univ, Otsukamachi, Bunkyo-ku, Tokyo. b. 30 Jan 1899 Maebashi. Bungakushi '25 Univ. of Tokyo, Japan. PROF. of PSYCH, Ochanomizu Women's Univ. Member: JPA, JAEP. Teaching educational guidance and psychology, administration; learning theory. M

UCHIDA, Yuzabura. 1000 Yoyogi Nishihara Sibuya-ku, Tokyo. b. 15 Dec 1894 Tokyo. Bungakushi '21 Univ. of Tokyo, Japan. PROFESSOR, Nihon Univ, 3 Simoumamachi, Setagaya-ku, Tokyo. Member: JPA, JAEP. Teaching, research on Uchida-Kraepelin Test, testing; personality. M

UCHIYAMA, Prof. Kikuo. Dept. of Psych, Gunma Univ, Seioji, Maebashi, Gunma. b. 25 June 1920 Sakai. Bungakushi '44 Tokyo Bunrika Univ, Japan. ASST. PROF, Gunma Univ; ED. COMM, *Journal of Educational Psychology*. Member: JPA, JSAP. Research, teaching clinical psychology, guidance; behavior problems, psychotherapy. M

UCHIYAMA, Michiaki. Dept. of Psych, Nagoya Univ, Minami Sotobori, Nagoya. b. 19 Oct 1924 Nagoya. Bungakushi '51 Nagoya Univ, Japan. ASSISTANT, Nagoyo Univ. Member: JPA, JSAP. Research, teaching, consulting; visual perception. M

UEDA, Prof. Toshimi. Dept. of Psych, Nara Univ. of Liberal Arts and Educ, Noborioji, Nara City. b. 25 Sept 1921 Nara-ken. Bungakushi '45 Tokyo Bunrika Univ, Japan. ASST. PROF, Dept. of Psych, and HEAD, Stud. Pers. Off, Nara Univ. of Liberal Arts and Educ. Member: JPA, Kansai Psych. Assn. Teaching, research, guidance; social and emotional development, diagnosis and treatment of maladjustment. M

UEMATSU, Prof. Tadashi. 1 3-chome, Nishiogikubo, Suginami-ku, Tokyo. b. 21 Jan 1906 Togane. Bungakushi '29 Nihon Univ, Japan; Hogakushi '35 Tokoku Univ, Japan. PROF. of CRIM. LAW, and CRIMINOL, Hitotsubashi Univ, Kunitachi, Tokyo; VIS. PROF. of CRIM. PSYCH, Nihon Univ; ED. STAFF, *Japanese Journal of Legal Medicine and Criminology*. Member: JPA, JSAP, Jap. Assn. of Criminol. Research, applied psychology, teaching; criminal behavior, judges' behavior and testimony. M

UENO, Prof. Yōzō. Dept. of Med, Nihon Univ, Itabashi, Tokyo. b. 6 Aug 1913 Tokyo. Igakuhakushi '46 Keio Univ, Japan. ASST. PROF. of PSYCHIAT, Nihon Univ. Member: JSAP, Jap. Assn. of Psychiat. and Neur. Teaching, research, consulting,

clinical practice; psychopathology. M
UMEMOTO, Prof. Takao. Lab. of Educ.
Psych, Fac. of Educ, Kyoto Univ, Yoshida-
honmachi, Sakyo-ku, Kyoto. b. 10 Oct
1921 Kyoto. Bungakushi '48 Kyoto Univ,
Japan. ASST. PROF, Kyoto Univ; LECTURER,
Heian-jogakuin Univ. Member: JPA,
Kansai Psych. Assn, Japan Educ. Socy.
Research, teaching, educational psychology
verbal learning, thinking, psychology of
music, intelligence tests. M
UMEOKA, Prof. Yoshitaka. Dept. of Exper.
Psych, Fac. of Letters, Hokkaido Univ,
Kita 8, Nishi 5, Sapporo, Hokkaido. b.
25 July 1920 Tokyo. Bungakushi '43
Univ. of Tokyo, Japan. ASST. PROF,
Hokkaido Univ. Member: JPA, Jap. Socy.
for Animal Psych, Hokkaido Psych. Assn.
Teaching experimental psychology, re-
search, administration; learning theory,
group process. M
UMEZU, Prof. Hachizo. Dept. of Psych,
Univ. of Tokyo, Motofuji-cho, Bunkyo-
ku, Tokyo. b. 5 Dec 1906 Hanamaki.
Bungakushi '31 Univ. of Tokyo, Japan.
PROFESSOR, Univ. of Tokyo; EDITOR,
Japanese Journal of Psychology. Member:
JPA. Research, teaching experimental
psychology, editorial; spatial perception,
verbal communication in the deaf-blind,
techniques in psychological research. M
URASHIMA, Jōji. Dept. of Psychiat,
Gifu Med. Univ, Tsukasamachi, Gifu. b.
13 July 1925 Hiroshima. ASSISTANT,
Gifu Med. Univ. Member: SCP. Research,
psychotherapy, teaching; neurotic person-
ality. M
URUNO, Fujio. 1425 1-chome Meguro-ku,
Tokyo. b. 27 Apr 1917 Tokyo. Bungakushi
'49 Tokyo Bunrika Univ, Japan. ASST. in
PSYCH, Tokyo Inst. of Tech, 1 Ookayama
Meguro-ku, Tokyo; LECTURER, Dept. of
Psych, International Coll. Member: JPA,
JSAP. Research, teaching, guidance; phy-
siological psychology, criminal psychology
and lie detection. M
USHIJIMA, Prof. Yoshitomo. Dept. of Educ,
Kyushu Univ, Hakozaki, Fukuoka. b.
19 Jan 1906 Nagasaki. Bungakuhakushi
'54 Nihon Univ, Japan. PROF. of PSYCH,
Kyushu Univ. Member: JPA, JSAP, Japan
Educ. Socy. Research, teaching educational
psychology, testing; child development,
family relations, mental tests. M
USUI, Prof. Kazuaki. Dept. of Psych,
Shimane Univ, Sotonakabara, Matsue.
b. 5 Sept 1909 Kochi. Bungakushi '32
Kyoto Univ, Japan. ASST. PROF, Shimane
Univ. Member: JPA, Chugoku-Shikoku
Psych. Assn. Teaching, educational psy-
chology, research; group dynamics, social
tension. M
USUI, Prof. Toshitomo. Dept. of Management

Engr, Univ. of Electro-Communications,
1-5 Shimomeguro, Meguroku, Tokyo. b.
7 July 1920 Tokyo. Bungakushi '47 Univ.
of Tokyo, Japan. ASST. PROF. of PSYCH,
Univ. of Electro-Communications. Member:
JPA, JSAP. Research, teaching, industrial
psychology; group processes in industry. M
UTSUGI, Mrs. Etsuko. Miyagi Child Guid.
Clinic, Kitahachiban-cho, Sendai. b.
13 Dec 1925 Mizusawa. Bungakushi '48
Tohoku Univ, Japan. CHIEF COUNS,
Miyagi Child Guid. Clin. Member: JPA,
JSAP, JAEP. Consulting, psychotherapy,
testing, teaching; play techniques in
psychotherapy. F
UTSUKI, Prof. Tamotsu. Dept. of Literature
and Sci, Ehime Univ, Mochida, Matsuyama.
b. 26 July 1911 Tokyo. Bungakushi '32
Univ. of Tokyo, Japan. ASST. PROF. of
PSYCH, Ehime Univ. Member: JPA.
Teaching, research. M
UTSUNOMIYA, Prof. Sentaro. 36-chome,
Kikuzonocho, Showa-ku, Nagoya. b.
30 Mar 1900 Kyoto. PROF. of PSYCH, Aichi-
gakuin Univ, Suemoridori, Nagoya.
Member: JPA, JSAP. Teaching, applied
psychology, research in industrial psychology; behavioral perception, theory construction on relationship between physiological processes in the brain and motor
responses. M
UYENO, Prof. Yoichi. Coll. of Indus. Mamage-
ment, 3 Todoroki, Setagaya, Tokyo. b.
28 Oct 1883 Tokyo. Bungakushi '08 Univ.
of Tokyo, Japan. PRESIDENT, Coll. of
Indus. Management. Member: JPA, JSAP.
Administration, teaching, management
consulting, editorial; industrial psychology. M
WADA, Prof. Yōhei. Dept. of Psych, Tokyo
Metrop. Univ, Fusumacho, Meguro-ku,
Tokyo. b. 23 Oct 1907 Yokohama. Bungakushi '32 Univ. of Tokyo, Japan. PRO-
FESSOR, Tokyo Metrop. Univ. Member:
JPA. Teaching experimental psychology,
research, professional writing; visual and
auditory perception. M
WAKI, Prof. Katsuka. Coll. of Educ, Kago-
shima Univ, Shimoishiki-cho, Kagoshima
City. b. 1 Feb 1908 Kagoshima. Bungakushi '31 Kyoto Univ, Japan. PROF.
of PSYCH, Kagoshima Univ. Member:
JPA, JAEP. Teaching educational and clini-
cal psychology, consulting, research; social
character and its social formation, ego-
involvements, personality measurement. M
WATANABE, Prof. Eiichi. Doshisha
Women's Coll. of Liberal Arts, Kyoto.
b. 29 Oct 1919 Hiroshima. Bungakushi '42
Doshisha Univ, Japan. ASST. PROF. of
PSYCH, Doshisha Women's Coll. of Liberal
Arts. Member: JPA, JSAP, JAEP. Reserach
teaching educational and child psychology,

consulting; projective techniques, attitude measurement. M

WATANABE, Prof. Hidetoshi. 181 Oka-Shinmachi, Hirakata, Osaka. b. 25 Oct 1919 Hakodate. Bungakushi '42 Tokyo Bunrika Univ, Japan. ASST. PROF. of PSYCH, Osaka Univ. of Liberal Arts and Educ, Jonancho, Ikeda. Member: JPA, JSAP, Kansai Psych. Assn. Research, teaching, educational psychology; development of perception and memory in children, psychology of learning. M

WATANABE, Prof. Kokuei. Dept. of Psych, Utsunomiya Univ, Mine-machi, Utsunomiya. b. 17 June 1899 Yamagata. Bungakushi '22 Toyo Univ, Japan. ASST. PROF, Utsunomiya Univ. Member: JPA, Tohoku Psych. Assn. Teaching, research, administration, family counseling; learning theory and animal behavior. M

WATANABE, Prof. Shigeru. Wakayama Med. Coll, Misono-cho, Wakayama. b. 8 Dec 1920 Kobe. Bungakushi '42 Kwansei Gakuin Univ, Japan. PROF. of PSYCH, Wakayama Med. Coll. Member: JPA. Teaching, research, testing; psychological and physiological effects of emotion. M

WATANABE, Sukeyuki. 5-41 Miyazonodori, Nakano-ku, Tokyo. b. 13 Aug 1914 Fujiyoshida. Bungakushi '49 Tokyo Bunrika Univ, Japan. TEACHER, Ryogoku High Sch, 1-4 Kotobashi, Sumida-ku, Tokyo. Member: JSPA. Teaching, research, counseling; psychology of youth. M

WATANABE, Tsutomu. Dept. of Educ. Psych, Oita Univ, Danohara, Oita. b. 19 Oct 1921 Fukuoka. Bungakushi '49 Kyushu Univ, Japan. INSTRUCTOR, Oita Univ. Member: JPA, Kyushu Psych, Assn, Jap. Socy. of Grp. Dynam. Testing, teaching child psychology; psychology of language, projective techniques, principles of development. M

WATANABE, Yasushi. 938 Shinohara-cho, Kohoku-ku, Yokohama. b. 19 Sept 1911 Tokyo. Bungakushi '38 Univ. of Tokyo, Japan. CHIEF DIAGNOSTICIAN, Kanagawa-ken Central Child Guid. Clin, 9-1 Takashima-dai, Kanagawa-ku, Yokohama. Member: JPA. Consulting, guidance, testing, psychotherapy; counseling maladjusted children, projective techniques, speech pathology. M

YABUKI, Prof. Shiro. 1 Hishiya-nishi Fuse, Osaka. b. 24 Oct 1913 Osaka. Bungakushi '41 Hiroshima Bunrika Univ, Japan. ASST. PROF, Osaka Univ. of Liberal Arts and Educ, Hirano Br, Hirano Nagaremachi, Higashisumiyoshi Osaka. Member: JPA. Teaching child psychology, research, guidance; personality development of children. M

YAGI, Prof. Ben. Dept. of Psych, Univ.

of Tokyo, Bunkyo-ku, Tokyo. b. 16 July 1915 Kyoto. Bungakushi '38 Univ. of Tokyo, Japan. ASST. PROF, Univ. of Tokyo. Member: JPA, Jap. Socy. for Animal Psych. Teaching, research; learning theory, motivation, and animal behavior. M

YAMADA, Hisayoshi. 26 Fuei-nishi-jutaku 186-Otoshi, Neyagawashi. b. 8 Feb 1923 Osaka. Bungakushi '48 Kyoto Univ, Japan. INSTRUCTOR, Kinki Univ, Kowakae, Fuse. Member: JPA, JSAP, JAEP. Research, teaching, educational psychology; child development. M

YAMADA, Kojun. 32 2-chome, Nakamuraku, Nagoya. b. 5 Jan 1900 Nagoya. Bungakushi '39 Hiroshima Bunrika Univ, Japan. DIRECTOR, Guid. Clin, Aichi Child Welf. Cen, Ojimachi, Nagoya. Member: JPA. Consulting, guidance, testing, teaching; aptitude tests. M

YAMADA, Naoshi. Tokyo Family Court, Kasumigaseki, Tokyo. b. 6 Sept 1927 Tokyo. Bungakushi '52 Univ. of Tokyo, Japan. ASST. INVESTIGATOR, Tokyo Fam. Ct. Member: JPA. Consulting, case work, research; personality. M

YAMAGUCHI, Kaoru. 2123 5-chome, Kamitakaido, Suginami-ku, Tokyo. b. 31 Oct 1924 Tokyo. Bungakushi '50 Univ. of Tokyo, Japan. TECH. OFF, Ministry of Educ, Kojimachi, Chiyodaku, Tokyo. Member: JPA, JAEP, Jap. Socy. for Spec. Educ. Educational psychology, consulting, guidance, research; psychology of the mentally retarded. M

YAMAGUCHI, Prof. Tatsuro. Dept. of Psych, Fukuoka Univ. of Liberal Arts and Educ, Fukuoka. b. 15 May 1897 Fukuoka. Bungakushi '29 Kyushu Univ, Japan. PROFESSOR, Fukuoka Univ. of Liberal Arts and Educ. Member: Kyushu Psych. Assn. Teaching, research, administration; perception, learning process in children. M

YAMAKAWA, Prof. Michiko. Seiwa Jr. Coll, Okadayama, Nishinomiya. b. 1 May 1905 Kumamoto. Bungakushi '50 Kwansei Gakuin Univ, Japan. PROFESSOR, Seiwa Jr. Coll. Member: JPA, JSAP, Jap. Educ. Socy. Teaching child education and psychology, consulting and counseling with Kindergarten staff, research, administration; social development of the child, problem of left-handedness, readiness in learning. F

YAMAKAWA, Prof. Noriko. Kobe Coll, Okadayama, Nishinomiya. b. 17 Aug 1910 Oita. Bungakushi '42 Hiroshima Bunrika Univ, Japan; MA '50 Univ. of Michigan, USA. PROF. of PSYCH, Kobe Coll. Member: JPA, JSAP. Teaching, research, administration; child development, sex differences in development. F

YAMAMATSU, Prof. Tadafumi. Dept. of

Child Study, Osaka City Univ, Nishinaga-hori-Minamidori, Nishiku, Osaka. b. 24 Feb 1913 Tokyo. Bungakushi '38 Kyoto Univ, Japan. ASST. PROF. of CHILD PSYCH, Osaka City Univ, LECTURER, Osaka-Shoin Women's Coll. Member: JPA, Kansai Psych. Assn. Teaching, research, consulting musical talent, development of rhythm perception. M

YAMAMOTO, Haruo. Tokyo Family Court, Hibiya, Chiyoda-ku, Tokyo. b. 15 Jan 1903 Nagasaki. Bungakushi '27 Univ. of Tokyo, Japan. HEAD and INVES. OFF, Dept. of Scientific Res, Tokyo Fam. Ct; PROFESSOR, Seikei Univ. Member: JSAP. Testing, clinical analysis, research, teaching; clinical research on delinquency and marital problems. M

YAMAMOTO, Prof. Saburo. Dept. of Psych, Fukuoka Univ. of Liberal Arts and Educ, Shiobara, Fukuoka. b. 16 Aug 1906 Yamaguchi. Bungakushi '38 Hiroshima Bunrika Univ. Japan; Igakuhakushi '55 Kyushu Univ, Japan. PROFESSOR, Fukuoka Univ. of Liberal Arts and Educ; PRINCIPAL, Shiinomigakuen (experimental school for feebleminded children). Member: JPA. Teaching educational psychology, testing, psychotherapy, consulting; clinical analysis, intelligence tests. M

YAMANE, Prof. Kaoru. 179 Street 4, Takasago-cho, Urawa. b. 14 June 1902 Shimane Ken. Bungakushi '28 Univ. of Tokyo, Japan. PROF. of PSYCH, Saitama Univ, Tokiwa, Urawa. Member: JPA, JSAP. Research, teaching educational and developmental psychology, testing; learning theory applied to sports, achievement and personality tests. M

YAMANE, Kiyomichi. 1272 Midarebashi-zaimokuza, Kamakura. b. 5 Aug 1911 Okayama. Bungakushi '35 Univ. of Tokyo, Japan. SUPERINTENDENT, Yokohama Juvenile Classif. Home, Hodogaya-ku, Yokohama; ED. COMM, *Japanese Journal of Correctional Policy*. Member: JPA, JSAP, Jap. Assn. of Correctl. Psych. Administration, guidance, consulting, research; criminal and correctional psychology, psychological case work. M

YAMASHITA, Prof. Toshio. Dept. of Pych, Tokyo Metrop. Univ, Fusuma-cho, Meguro, Tokyo. b. 4 Dec 1903 Kagoshima. Bungakushi '28 Univ. of Tokyo, Japan. PROFESSOR, Tokyo Metrop. Univ; LECT. in CHILD STUDY, Tokyo Domes. Sci. Coll. Member: JPA, JSAP. Teaching developmental psychology, research, applied psychology; child development. M

YAMAZAKI, Prof. Masashi. Dept. of Psych, Fukui Univ, Makinoshima, Fukui-shi. b. 7 Nov 1915 Fukui. Bungakushi '44 Tokyo Bunrika Univ, Japan. ASST. PROF,

Fukui Univ. Member: JPA. Teaching, research, educational psychology; psychosomatics. M

YASUDA, Prof. Haruya. Fac. of Educ, Tottori Univ, Tachikawacho, Tottori. b. 7 Apr 1907 Tottori. Bungakushi '41 Nihon Univ, Japan. ASST. PROF. of PSYCH, Tottori Univ. Member: JPA, JSAP. Teaching educational psychology, research, psychotherapy; children with special adjustment problems, play therapy. M

YASUDA, Prof. Minoru. Dept. of Educ, Shiga Univ, Zeze, Otsu. b. 8 May 1911 Kyoto. Bungakushi '38 Tokyo Bunrika Univ, Japan. ASST. PROF. of PSYCH, Shiga Univ. Member: JPA, Jap. Educ. Socy. Teaching educational psychology, research, guidance; projective techniques. M

YASUDA, Prof. Seijiro. Dept. of Psych, Nagoya City Univ, Tanabe-dori, Mizuho-ku, Nagoya. b. 3 Nov 1901 Nagoya. Bungakushi '28 Univ. of Tokyo, Japan. PROFESSOR, Nagoya City Univ; PROFESSOR, Aichigakuin Coll. Member: JPA. Teaching educational psychology, research, consulting; trait and attitude measurement, group process. M

YASUDA, Takashi. Dept. of Psych. Exam. Wakayama Central Child Guid. Clin, Mina-todori, Wakayama. b. 4 Nov 1927 Wakayama. HEAD of PSYCH. DIAGNOSIS, Wakayama Cen. Child Guid. Clin. Member: JSAP. Testing, clinical analysis, guidance, psychotherapy; projection and frustration. M

YASUI, Masaichi. Judicial Sect, Central Child Guid. Clin, Sapporo, Hokkaido. b. 18 July 1920 Hokkaido. Bungakushi '50 Hokkaido Univ; Japan. PSYCHOLOGIST, Cen. Child Guid. Clin. Member: Hokkaido Psych. Assn. Testing, clinical analysis, guidance, psychotherapy. M

YATABE, Prof. Tatsuro. Dept. of Psych, Kyoto Univ, Yoshida, Sakyoku, Kyoto. b. 24 Oct 1893 Tokyo. Bungakuhakushi '43 Kyushu Univ, Japan. CHMN. and PROF, Dept. of Psych, Kyoto Univ; EDITOR, *Japanese Journal of Psychology*; ED. BD, *Journal of Genetic Psychology* (USA). Member: JPA, Kansai Psych. Assn. Teaching, research, administration; perception, thinking, language. M

YODA, Prof. Arata. Dept. of Educ, Nagoya Univ, Minami-Sotobori-cho, Naka-ku, Nagoya. b. 30 Sept 1905 Tokyo. Bungakushi '29 Univ. of Tokyo, Japan. PROF. of EDUC. PSYCH, Nagoya Univ. Member: JPA, JSAP. Research, teaching, consulting; personality theory, parent-child relationship, adolescence. M

YOGI, Kiyoshige. Dept. of Classif, Fukuoka Shonenin, Roji, Fukuoka. b. 15 Jan 1914 Okinawa, Naha. HEAD, Dept. of Classif, Fukuoka Shonenin. Member: JPA. Testing clinical analysis, research, psychotherapy; study of care given to juvenile criminals after release. **M**

YOGO, Toshinobu. Central Child Guid. Clin, Sapporo, Hokkaido. b. 20 May 1906 Hokkaido. PSYCHOLOGIST, Cen. Child Guid. Clin. Member: Hokkaido Psych. Assn. Clinical analysis. **M**

YOKOSE, Prof. Zensho. Dept. of Psych, Nagoya Univ, Naka-ku, Nagoya, Aichi. b. 2 Jan 1913 Nagoya. Bungakuhakushi '36 Univ. of Tokyo, Japan. PROFESSOR, Nagoya Univ. Member: JPA, JSAP. Research, teaching, consulting; visual perception, frustration. **M**

YOKOTA, Shouichiro. 574 Tsuruda, Utsunomiya. b. 23 Aug 1912 Tokyo. Bungakushi '39 Waseda Univ, Japan. HEAD, Classif. Off. and Psych. Clin, Utsunomiya Diagnostic Cen, Tsuruda, Utsunomiya. Member: JPA, JSAP. Consulting, guidance, testing, clinical analysis, research; research on classification of juvenile offenders. **M**

YOKOYAMA, Prof. Matsusaburo. Dept. of Psych, Keio Univ, Mita, Tokyo. b. 9 Feb 1890 Mito. PH.D '21 Clark Univ, USA. PROFESSOR, Keio Univ; ADVISOR, Inst. for Psycho-Med. Res; EDITOR, *Japanese Journal of Psychology*; ED. BD, *Journal of General Psychology* (USA). Member: JPA, JSAP, Jap. Socy. for Animal Psych, Japan Socy. of Aviat. Med. and Psych, Psychomet. Socy. (USA). Teaching experimental psychology, research, editorial; affective processes, spatial perception, psychophysics of sensation. **M**

YOKOYAMA, Shinpei. Keio High Sch, Hiyoshi, Yokohama. b. 8 July 1906 Fukui. Bungakushi '31 Keio Univ, Japan. TEACHER, Keio High Sch. Administration, teaching, public opinion and market research; social perception, attitude measurement. **M**

YONEDA, Hiroshi. Fukuyama, Br. Sch, Hiroshima Univ, Okinogami-cho, Fukuyama. b. 20 July 1923 Hiroshima. Bungakushi '49 Hiroshima Univ, Japan. ASST. in VOCAT. GUID, Hiroshima Univ, Higashi-Senda, Hiroshima. Member: JPA. Research, teaching, educational psychology; evaluation of vocational attitudes and interests.M

YOSHIDA, Hiroshi. 34 Kakuchu-machi, Toyama City. b. 13 Nov 1919 Toyama. Bungakushi '43 Hiroshima Univ, Japan. ASST. PROF, Toyama Univ, Gofuku, Toyama INSTRUCTOR, Toyama Jr. Coll. of Nursing. Member: JPA. Teaching educational psychology, research; personality problems, treatment of maladjusted children. **M**

YOSHIDA, Masaaki. Dept. of Psych, Univ. of Tokyo, Hongo, Tokyo. b. 29 June 1928 Keijo, Korea. Bungakushi '52 Univ. of Tokyo, Japan. ASSISTANT, Univ. of

Tokyo. Member: JPA, Jap. Socy. for Animal Psych. Research, teaching; animal experiments in learning and motivation. M

YOSHIDA, Prof. Masakichi. Psych. Lab, Prefectural Univ. of Mie, Otanicho, Tsu, Mie Prefecture. b. 1 Jan 1911 Yokkaichi. Bungakushi '36 Hosei Univ, Japan. ASST. PROF, Prefectural Univ. of Mie. Member: JPA, JSAP. Research, teaching, consulting; emotional problems of children and youths. **M**

YOSHIDA, Masaru. 12 Kajiya-cho, Akashi-City, Hyogo. b. 7 June 1922 Akashi. Igakushi '45 Osaka Univ, Japan. PSYCHIAT. STAFF, Mukogawa Hosp, Nishinomiya. Member: SCP. Clinical practice, testing, student; projective techniques. **M**

YOSHIDA, Prof. Senkichi. Dept. of Educ, Niigata Univ, Asahimachi-dori 2, Niigata. b. 18 Nov 1908 Shibata. Bungakushi '39 Tokyo Bunrika Univ, Japan. ASST. PROF. of EDUC. PSYCH, Niigata Univ; LECTURER, Niigata Sch. for the Blind. Member: JPA, JSAP. Teaching, research, testing; psychology of the blind, mental testing of the blind, social maturity test, guidance of exceptional children. **M**

YOSHIDA, Teigo. Res. Inst. of Comp. Educ. and Culture, Kyushu Univ, Hakozaki, Fukuoka City. b. 26 Feb 1923 Tokyo. Bungakushi '47 Univ. of Tokyo, Japan. INSTR. in ANTHROP, Kyushu Univ. Member: JPA, Jap. Socy. of Ethnology, Amer. Anthrop. Assn. Teaching cultural anthropology, research; cultural change, value systems, culture and personality. **M**

YOSHIDA, Toshiro. Dept. of Psych, Keio Univ, Mita, Tokyo. b. 2 Dec 1926 Yokohama. Bungakushi '50 Keio Univ, Japan. ASSISTANT, Keio Univ. Member: JPA, JSAP. Research, teaching, consulting; perception, learning theory, measurement. **M**

YOSHII, Prof. Naosaburo. Second Dept. of Physiol, Osaka Univ. Med. Sch, Joancho, Kitaku, Osaka. b. 20 Feb 1911 Osaka. Igakuhakushi '39 Osaka Univ, Japan. PROF. of PHYSIOL, Osaka Univ. Med. Sch. Member: JPA, Physiol. Socy. of Japan. Research, teaching general and neurophysiology, consulting; electroencephalography and conditioned behavior. **M**

YOSHIMI, Yoshihiro. Dept. of Educ, Aoyamagakuin Univ, Shibuya, Tokyo. b. 6 June 1928 Hamamatsu. Bungakushi '51 Univ. of Tokyo, Japan. INSTR. in PSYCH, Aoyamagakuin Univ. Member: JPA, Japan Socy. for Animal Psych. Research, teaching; learning theory. **M**

YOSHIMO, Sonosuke. 1004 Ofuna, Kamakura-shi, Kanagawa-ken. b. 20 July 1893 Odawara. Bungakushi '29 Nihon Univ, Japan. Member: JPA. Teaching. **M**

YOSHIMOTO, Keiso. Dept. of Psych,

Suzugamine Women's Coll, Inokuchimura, Saikigun, Hiroshimaken. b. 22 Oct 1926 Hiroshima. Bungakushi '50 Hiroshima Univ, Japan. INSTRUCTOR, Suzugamine Women's Coll. Member: JPA. Research, teaching educational and adolescent psychology, testing; conditioning in language. M

YOSHIMURA, Mitsuo. Kyoto Prefectural Sonobe High Sch, Funai-gun, Kyoto. b. 23 Nov 1907 Kyoto. Bungakushi '37 Tokyo Bunrika Univ, Japan. PRINCIPAL, Kyoto Prefectural Sonobe High Sch. Member: JPA, Kansai Psych. Assn. Administration, teaching, consulting, guidance relation between personality and climate of country, school evaluation. M

YOSHIMURA, Shiro. Indus. Relat. Dept, Seiko-sha Plant, Hattori Watch and Clock Co, 2 4-chome, Taihei-cho, Sumida-ku, Tokyo. b. 2 Nov 1926 Tokyo. Keizaigakushi '48 Keio Univ, Japan. CHIEF of RES, Indus. Relat. Dept, Seiko-sha Plant, Hattori Watch and Clock Co. Member: JPA, JSAP. Industrial psychology, testing, administrative research in business administration; group process, morale, attitude, and opinion measurement, administrative technique. M

YOSHIMURA, Tadayuki. Bd. of Educ. of Hokkaido, Kita 3, Nishi 6, Sapporo. b. 30 Dec 1915 Kyoto. Bungakushi '43

Hiroshima Bunrika Univ, Japan. CONSULT. to TCHRS, Bd. of Educ, Hokkaido. Member: Hokkaido Psych. Assn. Teaching, administration, consulting, guidance; projective techniques. M

YOSHIO, Naosumi. Nara Juvenile Detention and Classif. Home, Hannyaji-cho 265, Nara. b. 16 June 1918 Takamatsu. Bungakushi '41 Kwansei Gakuin Univ, Japan. CHIEF, Nara Juv. Detention and Classif. Home. Member: JPA, SCP, Kansai Psych. Assn. Testing, clinical analysis, consulting, guidance, psychotherapy; projective techniques. M

YUKI, Prof. Kinichi. Psych. Inst. Fac. of Letters, Hokkaido Univ, Sapporo. b. 21 Apr 1901 Kobe. Bungakuhakushi '43 Univ. of Tokyo, Japan. PROF. of PSYCH, Hokkaido Univ; EDITOR, *Japanese Journal of Psychology*, *Psychological Research*. Member: JPA, JSAP. Teaching experimental psychology, research, administration; auditory perception. M

YUMOTO, Prof. Nobuo. Dept. of Educ. Psych, Tokyo Univ. of Liberal Arts and Educ, Koganei, Tokyo. b. 10 May 1916 Nagano Prefecture. Bungakushi '42 Tokyo Bunrika Univ, Japan. ASST. PROF, Tokyo Univ. of Liberal Arts and Educ. Member: JSAP. Teaching educational psychology, research, consulting; intelligence, psychology of science learning in children. M

JORDAN

SHAFIQ, Mohammad Nuri. Amman Teachers Coll, Amman. b. 11 June 1927 Tafila. MA '54 Teachers Coll, Columbia Univ, USA. PROF. of EDUC, Amman Teachers

Coll; EDITOR, *Risalat al Mu'llim.* Teaching, supervision, editorial, professional writing; problems of Arab adolescents. M

KOREA

CHUNG, Prof. Bom Mo. Coll. of Educ, Seoul Natl. Univ, Seoul. b. 11 Nov 1925 Seoul. MA '52 Univ. of Chicago, USA. ASST. PROF. in EDUC. and PSYCH, Coll. of Educ, Seoul Natl. Univ. Member: KPA, Korean Socy. for the Study of Educ. Research, teaching, professional writing; achievement testing, personality assessment, group dynamics. M

HAN, Prof. Joung Woo. 130 Taebong-dong, Taegu City. b. 28 Mar 1915 Kyongju. BA '48 Taegu Normal Coll, Korea. ASSOC. PROF. and DIR, Dept. of Educ. Psych, Kyong-puk Natl. Univ, San-kyok-dong, Taegu City; MEMBER, Advis. Comm. on Secondary Educ, Kyong-puk. Member: KPA. Teaching, research, educational psychology; learning theory, achievement tests, attitude measurement. M

IN-SUP, Miss Kim. 722-2 Sangwangsip-ri, Songtong-ku, Seoul. b. 27 July 1931 Wonju. BA '56 Seoul Natl. Univ, Korea. INVESTIGATOR, The American Embassy, Refugee Relief Program, Ulchiro Ipku, Seoul. Member: KPA. Student, testing children of mixed parents for adoption, research, applied psychology. F

KIM, Hak Soo. Kyongpuk Natl. Univ, Taegu. b. 5 Sept 1919 Taegu. BA '49 Kyongpuk Natl. Univ, Korea. ASST. PROF, Teacher's Coll, Kyongpuk Natl. Univ. Teaching, research, testing; learning theory, mental tests. M

KOH, Prof. Soon-Duk. Dept. of Psych, Ewha Women's Univ, Seoul. b. 25 July 1917 Ham-Ham. MA '50 Occidental Coll, USA. PROF. and CHMN, Dept. of Psych, Ewha Women's Univ; EDITOR, *Studies in*

Psychology; VIS. SCHOLAR, Harvard Univ, Harvard-Yenching Inst, Cambridge, Mass, USA. Member: KPA. Teaching, research, administration; experimental esthetics, test development. M

LEE, Prof. Chin-Sook. Dept. of Psych, Coll. of Liberals Arts and Sci, Seoul Natl. Univ, Dong-soong Dong, Seoul. b. 11 Oct 1907 Seoul. MA '33 Keijo Imperial Univ, Korea. PROF. and CHMN, Dept. of Psych, Coll. of Liberal Arts and Science, Seoul Natl. Univ. Member: KPA. Teaching, research, testing; personality, psychometric methods, social behavior. M

SUNG, Prof. Baiksun. Dept. of Psych, Korea Univ, Anam, Seoul. b. 11 Oct 1914 Sangju. Bungakushi '40 Waseda Univ, Japan. PROFESSOR, Korea Univ; LECTURER,

Ewha Women's Univ. Member: KPA, JPA, JSAP. Applied psychology, teaching, research; projective techniques, group process, attitude measurement. M

TAI RIM, Yoon. 233 Nai ja Dong, chongno Ku, Seoul. b. 6 Aug 1908 Seoul. MA '31 Seoul Univ, Korea. HEAD, Dept. of Educ. Psych, Coll. of Educ, Seoul Natl. Univ. Member: KPA. Teaching; psychoanalysis, personality. M

YIM, Prof. Suk-jay. Coll. of Educ, Seoul Natl. Univ. Seoul. b. 1 May 1903 Seoul. BA '29 Kyung Sung Univ, Seoul. HEAD, Div. of Educ, Coll. of Educ, Seoul Natl. Univ. Member: KPA, Korean Socy. for the Study of Educ. Teaching, research, professional writing, supervision; group process in education. M

LEBANON

ABI-DIWAN, Youssef. 14 Place Denfert Rochereau, Paris, Fr. b. 4 Dec 1921 Baabdat-Sefaïla, Lebanon. L.PS '54 Sorbonne, Fr. STUDENT, Sorbonne, Paris. Research, educational psychology; projective techniques, social perception, attitude measurement. M

ANTOUN, Joseph. Achrafiée, Rue Forn-el-Hayek, Beirut. b. 13 Mar 1927 Mtaïn. Diplôme, Univ. of Paris, Fr. RES. WRKR, Educ. Res. Cen, Ministry of Educ, UNESCO Palace, Beirut. Research, guidance, testing; achievement and aptitude tests. M

DEBUT, Gilbert André. Ecole Supérieure des Lettres, Rue de Damas, Beirut. b. 21 Dec 1919 Buxières, Fr. Licence ès lettres '45 Univ. of Algiers, Algeria. EDUC. COUNS. and DIRECTOR, Ecole de Jardinières d'Enfants, Mission Culturelle Française, Beirut. Teaching, research, educational psychology; learning, bilingualism, experimental education. M

FERRAND, Prof. Jean. Place de l'Etoile, Beirut. b. 9 June 1903 Toulouse, Fr. Docteur en Droit '28 Univ. of Toulouse, Fr. PROFESSOR, Ecole Supérieure des Lettres, Rue de Damas, Beirut; ADVOCATE, Court of Appeals of Beirut; HONORARY PROF, Fac. of Law. Teaching, research, educational psychology; social psychology. M

JENSEN, Dr. John Alexander. Dept. of Psych, American Univ, Beirut. b. 16 Mar 1921 Marshall, Texas, USA. PH.D '51 Vanderbilt Univ, USA. ASST. PROF. of SOC. and EXPER. PSYCH, American Univ; RES. ASSOC, Associates for Int. Res. Member: APA. Teaching, research, administration; values, roles, leadership, communications, attitudes. M

KEEHN, Dr. Jack Dennis. Psych. Dept,

American Univ, Beirut. b. 8 Feb 1925 London, Eng. PH.D '53 Univ. of London, Eng. ASST. PROF. of CLIN. PSYCH, American Univ. Member: BPA, APA. Teaching, research, administration; personality theory, projective and achievement tests. M

KHAZA'AL, Mrs. Ada. Beirut Coll. for Women, Rue Mme. Curie, Beirut. b. 12 Oct 1907 Kerbet. MA '48 Columbia Univ, USA. TEACHER, Beirut Coll. for Women. Teaching; learning theory, group process, attitude measurement. F

MELIKIAN, Levon Hagop. American Univ, Beirut. b. 17 May 1917 Jerusalem, Jordan. PH.D '55 Columbia Univ, USA. ASST. PROF. of PSYCH. and STUD. COUNS, American Univ. Member: APA. Teaching, guidance, psychotherapy; social perception, cross-cultural research, counseling. M

NAÏM, Joseph. Educ. Res. Cen, Ministry of Educ, UNESCO Palace, Beirut. b. 15 June 1930 Torza. Diplôme '54 Inst. Natl. d'Orientation Profes, Fr. RES. PSYCH'T, Educ. Res. Cen; MEMBER, Bur. Psycho-Pédagogique, Coll. des Apôtres, Jounieh. Psycho-pedagogical research, testing, guidance; statistical analysis, achievement and mental ability tests, performance. M

NAJARIAN, Prof. Dr. Miss Pergrouhi. American Univ, Beirut. b. 11 Nov 1918 Kharput, Turkey. PH.D '52 Cornell Univ, USA. ASST. PROF, American Univ. Member: APA. Teaching and research in educational psychology and child development; social perception, attitude measurement, measurement of development. F

NASSR, Dr. César-Georges. Lebanese Ministry of Educ, UNESCO Palace, Beirut. b. 26 Dec 1927 Beirut. PH.D '55 Univ. of Paris, Fr. HEAD, Educ. Res. Cen, Ministry of Educ. Administration, teaching, research; religious prejudices, adaptation and adjustment, social psychology.   M

ORME, Miss Rhoda. Beirut Coll. for Women, Beirut. b. 6 Aug 1899 Wayne, Pennsylvania, USA. ED.D '48 Columbia Univ, USA. ACADEMIC DEAN and PROF, Beirut Coll. for Women. Administration, educational and vocational counseling and guidance, teaching; mental hygiene.   F

PROTHRO, Prof. Edwin Terry. American Univ. of Beirut, Beirut. b. 11 Dec 1919 Robeline, Louisiana, USA. PH.D '42 Loui-

siana State Univ, USA. PROF. of PSYCH, American Univ. Member: APA. Research administration, teaching; cross cultural studies, cultural effects on personality, social psychology.   M

SIDAWI, Ahmad. Educ. Res. Cen, Ministry of Educ, UNESCO Palace, Beirut. b. 5 Aug 1928 Hasbaya. MA '54 Michigan State Univ, USA. RESEARCH, Ministry of Educ. Research, testing, guidance; guidance services, intelligence tests, counseling techniques.   M

LUXEMBOURG

BRAUNSHAUSEN, Prof. Dr. N. Rue des Roses 34, Luxembourg. b. 16 Oct 1874 Garnich. PROF. EMER, Univ. of Liège, Bel.

Teaching, research, administration, editorial, professional writing, retired; memory, achievement tests, social perception.   M

MALAYA

WILSON, Vayro William. Med. Dept, Palmer Rd, Singapore. b. 18 Jan 1912 Toowoomba, Austl. MA '39 Univ. of Queensland, Austl. CHIEF PSYCH'T, Med. Dept. Member: BPS. Testing, clinical analysis, applied psychology, teaching; vocational and educational guidance, projective techniques, group dynamics.   M

ZAKI BADAWI, Mohamed Aboulkheir. Univ. of Malaya, Singapore. b. 11 Aug 1922

Sharkia, Egypt. MA '49 Al Azhar Univ, Egypt. LECT. in ISLAMIC STUDIES, Univ. of Malaya; LECT. in PSYCH, Muslim Coll, Klang Selangor, Malayan Fed; VIS. BD. MEMBER, Cungie Busi Approved Sch. for Boys. Member: Malayan Psych. Socy, BPS. Teaching, research, public lectures; perception, learning, educational psychology.   M

MEXICO

BEJARLE PALACIOS, Miss Gloria María. Edgar Allan Poe 344, Colonia Polanco, Mexico, D.F. b. 26 Mar 1932 Mexico, D.F. PSYCH'T. and PSYCHOMET, Juvenile Court, Obrero Mundial 76, Mexico, D.F. Applied psychology, testing, student; projective techniques, intelligence tests, aptitude measurement.   F

BODEK, Mrs. Ruth. 2 Cerrada de Ameyalco 39-4, Mexico 12, D.F. b. 17 June 1928 Frankfurt a/M, Germany. MA '56 Natl. Univ. of Mexico. PSYCHOLOGIST, Guardería Infantil, Secretaría de Comunicaciones y Obras Públicas, Niño Perdido y Xola, Mexico, D.F. Member: SIP. Student, applied psychology, testing, guidance of problem children; mother-child relationship, culture and personality.   F

BUENTELLO Y VILLA, Dr. Edmundo. Ave. Madero 72-12, Mexico, D.F. b. 10 Dec 1908 San Luis Potosí. MD, Natl. Univ. of Mexico. ASST. CHIEF, Dept. of Social Welfare, Insurgentes Ave. 97, Mexico, D.F.; PSYCHIATRIST, priv. prac; DIRECTOR, Cholula Men's Sanitar. Member: Mexican Psych. Socy, Neuropsychiat. Assn. Psy-

chotherapy, consulting, clinical practice, guidance, teaching, treatment of adult and juvenile delinquents; social perception, group process.   M

CABILDO y ARELLANO, Dr. Héctor Miguel. Petén 466, Mexico 13, D.F. b. 8 Jan 1928 Mexico, D.F. MD '52 Natl. Univ. of Mexico. DIRECTOR, Ment. Hyg. Clin, Centro de Salud Beatrix Velasco de Alemán, Esquina Ave. Rastro y Peluqueros, Mexico, D.F.; PSYCHIATRIST, Rehabilitation Dept. Member: Mexican League of Ment. Hyg, Mexican Pub. Hlth. Socy. Research, clinical practice, teaching; group tests, questionnaire construction, mental hygiene education.   M

CÁRDENAS OJEDA, Prof. Mauro. Motolinía 8-208, Mexico, D.F. b. 7 Nov 1927 Veracruz. M.PS '48 Natl. Univ. of Mexico. DIR. of HUMAN RELAT. RES, Bank of Mexico, 5 de Mayo 2, Mexico, D.F.; PROF. of EXPER. PSYCH, Escuela Normal Superior; PRESIDENT, Inst. of Indus. Relat. Member: SIP. Applied and industrial psychology, teaching, planning and directing research; personnel administration, opinion and attitude

measurement, projective techniques. M
CIÓFALO ZÚÑIGA, Dr. Francisco. Río Hudson 20, apt. 13, Mexico 5, D.F. b. 30 June 1918 Germania, Costa Rica. M.PS '51 Natl. Univ. of Mexico. CHIEF PSYCH'T, Cinematográfica Latina, Estudios Churubusco, Calzada Talpam y Río Churubusco, Mexico, D.F. Member: SIP, Mexican Psych. Socy. Consulting, clinical practice, psychotherapy, testing; psychological theory, problems of psychotherapy, biotypology. M
DÍAZ-GUERRERO, Dr. Rogelio. Georgia 123, Mexico 18, D.F. b. 3 Aug 1918 Guadalajara. PH.D '47 State Univ. of Iowa, USA; MD '43 Natl. Univ. of Mexico. PROF. of EXPER. PSYCH, Natl. Univ. of Mexico; PSYCHIATRIST, priv. prac. Member: SIP, APA. Psychotherapy, teaching, research; experimental psychopathology, national character, psychological theory. M
DÍAZ Y DÍAZ, Dr. José F. Rébsamen 519, Colonia Narvarte, Mexico 12, D.F. b. 13 Aug 1907 Mérida. MD '35 Natl. Univ. of Mexico. PROF. of CHILD PSYCHIAT, Sch. of Psychiat, Univ. of Mexico; CHILD PSYCHIATRIST, Hospital Infantil, Calle Dr. Marquez, Mexico, D.F. Psychotherapy, consulting, clinical practice, teaching, research; psychoanalysis. M
ELIZONDO GARZA, Dr. Manuel. Ave. de la Univ. 10, Mexico 20, D.F. b. 23 May 1925 Linares. MD '52 Univ. of Nuevo Leon, Mexico. ASST. PSYCHIATRIST, Sanatorio Español, Ave. Ejercito Nacional 637, Mexico; DIR. of REHABILITATION and PSYCHIAT, Centro de Valoración de Aptitudes. Clinical practice, therapy, teaching; evaluation of aptitudes, psychotherapy. M
ESCOBAR VILLATORO, Dr. Luis Felipe. Apartado 10434, Mexico, D.F. b. 22 May 1920 Mexico, D.F. PH.D, Natl. Univ. of Mexico. PSYCHOANALYST, priv. prac, Artes 28, dpto. 6, Mexico, D.F. Member: Spanish psychoanal. Assn. Teaching, testing, clinical analysis, psychotherapy; projective techniques, therapeutic and didactic psychoanalysis. M
FALCON, Dr. Manuel. Insurgentes 774, Mexico, D.F. b. 9 Sept 1910 Mexico, D.F. MD 33 Univ. of Louvain, Belgium. DIRECTOR, Neuropsychiatric Clinic, Ixtaccihuatl 180, Villa Obregón, Mexico, D.F. Member: APA, SIP, Mexican Socy. of Neur. and Psychiat. Consulting, clinical practice, teaching; psychopathology, psychiatric therapy. M
FÉDER, Dr. Luis. Clínica Mexicana de Psicoterapia, Puebla 194, Mexico, D.F. b. 18 Apr 1921 Nieswiez, Poland. PH.D '56 Univ. of Mexico. CHIEF CLIN. PSYCH'T, Clínica Mexicana de Psicoterapia; PROF. of PROJECTIVE TECHNIQUES, Univ. Ibero-

Americana; RES. FELLOW, Natl. Univ. of Mexico. Member: SIP, Mexican Socy. of Neur. and Psychiat, Int. Group Psychother. Assn. Psychotherapy, psychodiagnostic testing, teaching, research; projective testing, individual and group psychotherapy, psychodynamic process in cross-cultural contacts. M
FORTES, Dr. Abraham. Río de la Plata 56, Dcho. 203, Mexico, D.F. b. 8 July 1914 Kupel, Ikraine. MD '42 Natl. Univ. of Mexico. NEUROPSYCHIATRIST, Inst. Mexicano del Seguro Social; ASST. PROF, Clin. of Neur. and Psychiat, Fac. of Med, Natl. Univ. of Mexico. Member: Mexican Socy. of Psychoanal, Mexican Socy. of Neur. and Psychiat. Psychotherapy, teaching; learning theory. M
FREEMAN, Dr. Albert Vincent. Investigaciones Psicológicas, A. en P., Calle de Génova 16, Mexico 6, D.F. b. 7 Oct 1914 Portland, Oregon, USA. PH.D '48 Columbia Univ, USA. TECH. DIR, Investigaciones Psicológicas, A. en P. Member: APA. Administration, planning and direction of research, clinical consultation, psychotherapy; interdisciplinary research on creativity, malnutrition, violence, application of clinical techniques to non-psychiatric problems. M
GALVIS SPINOLA, Mrs. Luz María. Ave. Chapultepec 332-22, Mexico 7, D.F. b. 20 Mar 1930 Mexico, D.F. Pasante, Fac. of Philos. and Letters, Mexico. RES. PSYCH'T, Serv. of Psychopedagogy, Ciudad Universitaria, Mexico 20, D.F. Research on educational testing, student, professional writing; statistics, theory of intelligence test construction. F
GARCÍA MILLÁN DE RIVERA, Prof. Beatriz Elsa. Ave. Coyoacán 745-18, Mexico 12, D.F. b. 7 Aug 1927 Mexico, D.F. Pasante '54 Univ. of Mexico. CRIM. PSYCH'T, Women's Prison, Kilómetro 16½ Carretera Mexico-Puebla, Mexico, D.F. Member: SIP. Applied and educational psychology, guidance, psychotherapy; social readjustment of delinquent women, psychodynamics of delinquency. F
GÓMEZ ROBLEDA PELAYO, Carlos. Banco de Comercio, Venustiano Carranza 40, piso 5, Mexico 1, D.F. b. 24 June 1923 Mexico, D.F. M.PS '53 Natl. Univ. of Mexico. HEAD, Personnel Dept, Banco de Comercio; PSYCHOTECHNICIAN, Dept. of the Navy. Industrial psychology, teaching, research, planning programs for personnel selection. M
GUEVARA-OROPESA, Dr. Manuel. Calle Queretaro 132, Mexico, D.F. b. 23 May 1899 Orizaba. Prof. '26 Natl. Univ. of Mexico. PROF. of PSYCHIAT, School of Med, Natl. Univ. of Mexico; PSYCHIATRIST,

priv. prac. Member: APA, Mexican Socy. of Neur. and Psychiat, Société Médico-Psychologique (Paris). Teaching, psychotherapy. **M**

HOFFS, Dr. Eugenia S. de. Campos Eliseos 93-2, Mexico, D.F. b. 4 Feb 1920 Vilna, Poland. PH.D '50 Natl. Univ. of Mexico. PROF. of PSYCH, Natl. Univ. of Mexico; CHIEF CLIN. PSYCH'T, Inst. of Soc. Security of Mexico, Naranjo 110, Mexico, D.F. Member: SIP, Mexican Psych. Socy. Testing, teaching, clinical practice, psychotherapy; mental testing, projective techniques, child psychotherapy, counseling. **F**

LEMBERGER, Miss Mathilde. Estrasburgo 5-C, Mexico 6, D.F. b. 27 May 1921 Amsterdam, Neth. PH.M '47 Univ. of Mexico. LECT. in INDUS. and EXPER. PSYCH, Univ. of Mexico; PSYCHOLOGIST, Dept. of Child Placement, Ministry of Pub. Assistance. Member: SIP, League for Ment. Hlth. of WFMH. Applied and industrial psychology, testing, professional writing; vocational guidance and selection tests, use of testing for diagnostic purposes, psychotherapy. **F**

LLOPIS DE PEINADO, Prof. Luz. Antonio Sola 32, Mexico, D.F. b. 14 Jan 1921 Alicante, Spain. M.PS Natl. Univ. of Mexico. PSYCHOLOGIST, Centro Materno-Infantil „Gral. Max. Avila Camacho," Calzada Maderero 240, Tacubaya, Mexico, D.F.; PSYCHOLOGIST, Natl. Inst. of Audiology, Ave. Centenario, Colonia Merced Gómez, Mexico, D.F. Member: SIP. Clinical practice, guidance, testing, psychotherapy; child psychopathology, problems of learning, emotional balance and conduct. **F**

MACÍAS AVILÉS, Prof. Raymundo. Campeche 94, Mexico 7, D.F. b. 27 Nov 1933 Mexico, D.F. Pasante '56 Natl. Univ. of Mexico. COUNSELOR, Preparatory School No. 2, Natl. Univ. of Mexico, Lic. Verdad 2, Mexico, D.F. Member: SIP. Psychotherapy, clinical practice, educational and vocational guidance, student; projective techniques. **M**

MEKLER KLACHKY, Prof. Sara. Gutenberg 231, Mexico 5, D.F. b. 11 Dec 1923 Vilno, Russia. M.PS '50 Univ. of Mexico. MUSIC THERAPIST. Member: SIP, Natl. Assn. for Music Therapy, Mexican Socy. of Musicology. Research, professional writing, student; psychology of music, music therapy. **F**

MENDIZÁBAL CALDERÓN, Dr. Joaquín. Sonora 62, Mexico, D.F. b. 20 May 1916 Mexico, D.F. MD '44 Med. Milit. Sch, Mexico. COORDINATOR, Serv. of Ment. Hyg, Secy. of Sanitation, Mexico, D.F.; CHIEF of PSYCHIAT, Outpatient Dept, Central Milit. Hosp; PHYSICIAN, Neuropsychiat. Unit, Mexican Inst. of Soc. Security; EDITOR, *Psiquis*. Member: SIP,

Mexican League of Ment. Hyg, Latin Amer. Psychiat. Assn, Mexican Socy. of Neur. and Psychiat. Consulting, clinical practice, teaching, psychotherapy. **M**

NÚÑEZ, Dr. Rafael. Dept. of Psych, Natl. Univ of Mexico, Mexico, D.F. b. 22 Feb 1924 Rivas, Nicaragua. PH.D '54 Natl. Univ. of Mexico. PROF. of CLIN. PSYCH, Inst. of Psych, Natl. Univ; ED. *Revista de Psicología*. Member: APA, Socy. of Mexican Psychologists, Columbian Fed. of Psych'ts. Teaching, psychotherapy, clinical practice; projective techniques, group process. **M**

PADRÓN PONCE, Dr. Pedro. Unión 25, dpto. 8, Colonia Escandón, Mexico 18, D.F. b. 28 June 1921 San Luis Potosí. MD, Natl. Univ. of Mexico. PSYCHOMETRICIAN, Bank of Mexico, Edificio Guardiola Despacho 202, Mexico 1, D.F.; PROF. of LEGAL MED, Natl. Univ. of Mexico. Testing, clinical practice, industrial psychology; aptitude measurement, projective techniques, socio-economic studies, forensic and child psychiatry, legal medicine. **M**

PALACIOS LÓPEZ, Dr. Agustín Tomás. Sinaloa 10, Despacho 101, Mexico, D.F. b. 26 Dec 1926 Mexico, D.F. MD '50 Escuela Superior de Medicina Rural, Mexico. PROF. of PSYCHIAT. and PSYCHOTHER Escuela Superior de Medicina Rural, Mexico, D.F. and Escuela Normal de Especialización, Parque Lira, Mexico; VISITING PSYCHIATRIST, Children's Hosp; ED. ADVIS, Neuropsychiat. Sect, *Revista Medica de la Escuela Superior de Medicina Rural*. Member: SIP, Mexican Socy. of Neur. and Psychiat, Latin Amer. Central Comm. on Child Neuropsychiat, Amer. Rehab. Assn. Psychotherapy, teaching, research. **M**

PARRES, Dr. Ramón. Víctor Hugo 76-C, Mexico 5, D.F. b. 21 May 1920 Tapachula. MD '45 Natl. Univ. of Mexico. ASSOC. CLIN. PROF. of PSYCHIAT, Med. Sch, Natl. Univ. of Mexico, Mexico 20, D.F. Member: SIP, Amer. Psychiat. Assn, Assn. for Psychoanal. Med. (New York), Mexican Socy. of Neur. and Psychiat, Int. Psychoanal. Assn. Psychotherapy, teaching, research; psychoanalytic treatment, research on social problems. **M**

PASCUAL DEL RONCAL, Prof. Dr. Federico. Ave. Emerson 242, Mexico 5, D.F. b. 13 Feb 1903 Saragosse, Spain. MD '30 Univ. of Madrid, Spain. PROF. of PSYCHOTHER, Univ. of Mexico, Ciudad Universitaria, Mexico; HEAD of MED. STAFF, Inst. Médico-Pedagógico; CONSULT. PSYCH'T, Inst. Seguín; PSYCHIATRIST, priv. prac. Member: SIP, Int. Rorschach Socy, Mexican Psych. Socy, Argentine Socy. of Psych, Mexican Psychiat. Socy. Psychotherapy, teaching, testing; projective techniques, psychology of prejudice. **M**

PEINADO-ALTABLE, Prof. José. Amado Nervo 34, dtpo. 15, Mexico 4, D.F. b. 18 Feb 1909 Valladolid, Spain. M.PS '47 Univ. of Mexico. PSYCHOLOGIST, Centro Materno-Infantil „Gral. Maximino Avila Camacho", Madereros 240, Tacubaya, Mexico, D.F; CHEIF PSYCH'T, Diagnostic Dept, Natl. Inst. of Audiology, Ave. Centenario, Colonia Merced Gómez, Mexico. Member: SIP, Latin Amer. Comm. of Child Neuropsychiat. Clinical practice, guidance, testing, psychotherapy, teaching; projective techniques, learning theory, child psychopathology, education of abnormal children. M

PICHARDO NAVA, Prof. María de la Luz. Prolongación Melchor Ocampo 142, Colonia Romero de Terreros, Coyoacán 21, Mexico, D.F. b. 16 Mar 1916 Mexico, D.F. CLIN. PSYCH'T, Clínica de Conducta, Hosp. Infantil de México, Londres y Niza, Mexico, D.F. Member: SIP. Testing, student, teaching, psychometric and projective tests and their use in clinical psychology. F

POLA TORRES, Miss Yolanda. Circular de Morelia 2, Colonia Roma, Mexico 7, D.F. b. 23 Jan 1932 Mexico, D.F. PSYCHOMETRIST, Centro Psicopedagogico de Orientación, Ave. Reforma 2300, Mexico, D.F. Member: SIP. Applied psychology, testing, student; theory and method of projective techniques, learning difficulties in problem children. F

PRADO-HUANTE, Dr. Hector. San Pedro 14, Coyoacán 21, Mexico, D.F. b. 14 Apr 1920 Mexico, D.F. MD '43 Univ. of Mexico. PSYCHIAT. CONSULT, Neuropsychiat. Clin. of Mexican Red Cross Hosp, Monterrey and Durango, Mexico, and Neuropsychiat. Clin. of Social Security, Naranjo 110, Mexico, D.F. Member: SIP, Mexican Psych. Socy, Mexican Socy. of Neur. and Psychiat. Psychotherapy, consulting, clinical practice teaching; aptitude measurement, learning theory, achievement tests, vocational adjustment and rehabilitation. M

QUIROZ CUARON, Dr. Alfonso. Edificio Guardiola, Despacho 202, Mexico, D.F. b. 9 Feb 1910 Jinénez. Doctor '39 Natl. Univ. of Mexico. HEAD, Dept. of Special Research, Bank of Mexico, 5 de Mayo 2, Mexico, D.F.; PROF. of LEGAL MED, Escuela Nacional de Medicina. Member: Mexican Psych. Socy, Int. Socy. of Criminol. Applied and personnel psychology, teaching legal medicine, biotypology and criminology, testing; use of aptitude measurement in personnel selection, psychiatric study of criminal cases, use of the lie detector. M

QUIROZ GARCÍA, Prof. Alicia. Civilización 124-2, Mexico, D.F. b. 29 July 1930 Pachuca. MA, Natl. Univ. of Mexico. MED. PSYCH'T, Clínica de Conducta del Distrito Sanitario No. 11, Benjamín Hill 14, Mexico, D.F. Member: SIP. Testing, clinical analysis, research, educational psychology; psychotherapy, industrial psychology. F

RAMIREZ, Dr. Santiago. Puebla 259-3, Mexico, D.F. b. 6 Oct 1921 Mexico, D.F. MD '45 Univ. of Mexico. PROF. TITULAR of MED. PSYCH, Fac. of Med, Ciudad Universitaria, Mexico, D.F. Member: SIP, Int. Psychoanal. Assn, Argentine Psychoanal. Assn. Psychotherapy, teaching; psychoanalytic therapy, taeching psychology to doctors and medical students. M

RAMOS PALACIOS, Dr. Mario Inst. „Molino de Bezares," Carretera. Mexico-Toluca Km. 13, No. 1319, Mexico, D.F. b. 19 Oct 1925 Comalcalco. MD '49 Natl. Univ. of Mexico. DIRECTOR, Inst. „Molino de Bezares." Member: SIP. Administration, consulting, teaching at training school for the feebleminded; learning theory, problems of memory and learning in mental defectives. M

RINCÓN DE DUEÑAS, Mrs. Cassandra. Sor Juana Inés de la Cruz 39, Mexico, D.F. b. 14 May 1922 Puebla. PSYCHOLOGIST, Dept. of Sel. and Profes. Guid, Secy. of Communications, Xola and Universidad, Colonia Narvarte, Mexico, D.F. Member: SIP, Mexican Socy. of Ment. Hyg, Socy. of Profes. Studies. Industrial personnel testing, clinical analysis, guidance; child and adult psychotherapy, projective techniques, psychoanalytic training. F

RIVERA TAPIA, Luis. Ave. Coyoacán 745-18, Mexico, D.F. b. 13 Dec 1921 Mexico, D.F. Pasante '54 Univ. of Mexico. CRIM. PSYCH'T, Women's Prison, Kilómetro 16½ Carretera Mexico-Puebla, Mexico 9, D.F. PSYCHOTHERAPIST, priv. prac. Member: SIP. Individual psychotherapy, research, guidance, student; psychodynamics of delinquency, role of education in the prevention of delinquency, professional and vocational guidance. M

ROBLES, OCHOA, Dr. Oswaldo. Violeta 29, Mexico 3, D.F. b. 8 Mar 1905 Monterrey. PH.D '36 Natl. Univ. of Mexico; Dr. Soc. Sci. '52 Univ. of Guadalajara, Mexico. PROF. of CLIN. PSYCH, Dept. of Psych, Natl. Univ. of Mexico, Ciudad Universitaria Mexico, D.F. Member: Int. Inst. of Psychosynthesis, Inst. of Psychosynthesis and Human Relations (Venezuela). Teaching, psychotherapy, consulting, clinical practice; projective techniques, dynamics of personality, personality and values, existential therapy. M

SACRISTÁN DE GARRIDO, Prof. Luisa. Calle de Niño Perdido 23-11, Mexico, D.F. b. 10 Jan 1930 Madrid, Spain. MA '56 Natl. Univ. of Mexico. PSYCHOLOGIST,

Guardería Infantil, Secretaría de Comunicaciones y Obras Públicas, Xola y Ave. Univ. Mexico, D.F. INTERNE in PSYCH, Centro Materno-Infantil "Gral. Maximino Avila Camachö, Calzada Maderero 240, Tacubaya Mexico, D.F. Member: SIP. Testing, child guidance, psychotherapy; child development and guidance. F

SÁNCHEZ, Prof. Emma. San Carlos 79 D, Colonia Campestre, Mexico 20, D.F. b. 22 Jan 1918 Mexico, D.F. Prof. '45 Univ. of Mexico. CHIEF OFFICER, Mexican League for Ment. Hlth, Villalongin 118-1, Mexico 5, D.F; EDITOR, Psiquis. Member: SIP, Mexican League for Ment. Hlth. Teaching, editorial, professional writing; popular dissemination of psychological principles for betterment of human relations and mental health. F

SCHMIDT CAMELO, Miss Emma Augusta. Misantla 44, Colonia Roma Sur. b. 2 Dec 1931 Veracrux. M.PS, Natl. Univ. of Mexico. REHAB. COUNS, Direccion General de Rehabilitacion, S.S.A., Londres, Mexico, D.F; CLIN. PSYCH'T, Clin. of Ment. Hyg, Centro de Salud Mexico-España. Member: SIP, Socy. of Profes. Studies, Mexican Assn. of Rehabilitation. Testing, guidance, treatment and rehabilitation of the handicapped; mental tests, psychotherapy, professional guidance. F

SHORE, Dr. Aaron. Anaxagoras 428, Mexico 12, D.F. b. 20 Jan 1915 New York City, USA. PH.D '54 Natl. Univ. of Mexico. PSYCHOTHERAPIST, priv. prac. Member: SIP, New York Socy. of Clin. Psych'ts. Psychotherapy, research, consulting, clinical practice; research on authoritarian personality. M

SOLIS QUIROGA, Dr. Roberto. Medellín 21, Despacho 1, Mexico 7, D.F. b. 15 Feb 1898

Mexico, D.F. MD '22 Natl. Univ. of Mexico. DIRECTOR, Inst. Médico-Pedagógico, Parque Lira 128, Tacubaya, Mexico, D.F. Member: SIP, Mexican Socy. of Neur. and Psychiat, Amer. Socy. on Mental Deficiency. Consultant in child neuropsychiatry, clinical practice and psychotherapy with mentally ill, maladjusted, and delinquent children; diagnosis of mental illness in children, childhood neuroses. M

VALDÉS, Dr. Juan Ignacio. Altamirano 6-2, Mexico 4, D.F. b. 22 Aug 1931 Ocotlán. MD '55 Natl. Univ. of Mexico. PSYCHIAT. and VOCAT. GUID. COUNSELOR, Natl. Univ. of Mexico, Justo Sierra 16, Mexico 1, D.F; CONSULTANT, priv. prac; PHYSICIAN, Secretaría del Trabajo. Member: SIP. Diagnosis, psychotherapy, guidance; attitude measurement, projective techniques, logotherapy. M

VELASCO ALZAGA, Dr. Jorge Manuel. Puebal 325, Mexico 7, D.F. b. 1 Sept 1923 Guadalajara. MD '46 Excuela Médico-Militar, Mexico. CHIEF, Mental Health Dept. Hosp. Infantil, Mexico, D.F.; PROF. of PSYCHIAT, Natl. Univ. of Mexico. Member: SIP, Mexican Socy. of Psychoanal. Assn. of Pediatric Res, Mexican Socy. of Neur. and Psychiat. Psychotherapy, teaching, research; child psychopathology, mental hygiene. M

VIQUEIRA DE PALERM, Prof. Carmen. 323 James St, Falls Church, Virginia, USA. b. 20 Aug 1923 Badajoz, Spain. M.PS '51 Natl. Univ. of Mexico. Member: Mexican Psych. Socy, Mexican League for Ment. Hlth. Research, testing, teaching; projective techniques, culture and personality, history of clinical psychology. F

MOROCCO

BOPPE, Pierre. 3 Rue d'Auvergne, Khouribga. b. 3 Sept 1929 Nancy, Fr. Diplôme, Inst. of Psych, Univ. of Paris, Fr. PSYCHOTECHNICIAN, Office Cherifien des Phosphates, Khouribga. Member: APPD. Applied psychology, research on physical type and criminology; psychomotor tests, electroencephalography, morphology and temperament, tests of behavior. M

MAZEROL, Marie-Thérèse. 4 Rue de Valence, Rabat. b. 10 Dec 1928 Clermont-Ferrand, Fr. Licence ès lettres '55 Univ. of Paris, Fr. PSYCHOLOGIST, Ministry of Pub. Instruction of Morocco, 309 Ave. Mohamed V, Rabat; PSYCH. EXPERT, Children's Court; CONSULTANT, priv. prac. Testing, clinical analysis, research, teaching;

achievement tests, projective techniques, social perception. F

MORIN, Jacques. 3 Ave. d'Auvergne, Khouribga. b. 1 Apr 1920 Lille, Fr. Diplôme '51 Inst. of Psych, Univ. of Paris, Fr. DIRECTOR, Psychotech. Lab, 150 Blvd. Ney, Casablanca. Member: AIPA, APPD. Applied psychology, testing; research; achievement tests, industrial selection applied ot Moroccan workers, factor analysis. M

PIDOUX, Dr. Charles Louis. Immeuble Miramonte, Ave. Menéndez y Pelayo, Tangiers. b. 14 June 1917 Tunis, Tunisia. MD '44 Univ. of Montpellier, Fr. PSYCHIATRIST, priv. prac; EDITOR, Revue Internationale d'Ethnopsychologie; LECT. in PSYCH, Cen. des Hautes Etudes, Admin. Musulmane et d'Outre Mer, Univ. of Paris; Inst. of Ethnology, Univ. of Paris. Member: Fr. Psychoanal. Socy, Int. Socy. of Ethnopsych. Psychotherapy, consulting, clinical practice, guidance, research, editorial; personality formation, comparative psychopathology, Melano-African processes of individual and group therapy.   M

PIROT, Henri. Psychotech. Lab, 150 Blvd. Ney, Casablanca. b. 12 Oct 1924 Le Portel, Fr. Diplôme d'état '48 Inst. Natl. d'Orientation Professionnelle, Fr.   DIRECTOR, Psychotech. Lab; TEACHER, State Sch. for Nurses and Soc. Workers. Member: APPD. Applied and industrial psychology, research, administration; professional selection and orientation, study of the Moroccan environment.   M

ROCCHI, Miss Anne. 33 Rue de Pont à Mousson, Casablanca. b. 28 Mar 1914 Cambia, Corsica. Diplôme '51 Inst. Natl. d'Orientation Professionnelle, Fr.   EDUC. GUID. COUNS, Centre d'Orientation Professionnelle, 3 Rue du Docteur Baur,

Casablanca. Member: ACOF. Consulting, guidance, testing, clinical analysis, research; projective techniques, character study.   F

SELOSSE, Jacques Paul. Route de Meknès, Sale. b. 12 Apr 1923 Lestrem, Fr. Diplôme d'études supérieures '52 Univ. of Paris, Fr.   HEAD, Bur. for Abandoned Children, Ave. des Touarga, Rabat; PSYCHOLOGIST, Courts of Morocco; CONSULTANT, priv. prac. Administration, consulting, guidance, research; projective techniques, social psychology, juvenile crime.   M

TRYSTRAM, Prof. Jean-Paul. Moroccan Inst. for Higher Studies, Rabat. b. 10 Apr 1912 Paris, Fr. Docteur ès lettres '55 Univ. of Paris, Fr. DIR. of SOCIOL. STUDIES, Inst. for Higher Studies; DIRECTOR, Inst. for Appl. Psych. and Sociol, 150 Blvd. Ney, Casablanca. Member: APSLF, APPD. Teaching, research, applied psychology; psychosociological job evaluation, test construction, statistical research.   M

NETHERLANDS

ABBAS, Drs. Jacobus Hendrik. Boulevard Evertsen 48 Vlissingen. b. 15 Aug 1924 Winschoten. Doctorandus '51 Univ. of Groningen, Neth. INDUS. PSYCH'T, Kon. Mij „De Schelde" Vlissingen. Member: NIPP. Testing, industrial psychology; intelligence tests, industrial relations.   M

ABBAS-ROELFSEMA, Dra. Nantke Gerda. Boulevard Evertsen 48 Vlissingen. b. 12 Mar 1930 Groningen. Doctoranda '53 Univ. of Groningen, Neth. CLIN. PSYCH'T, Ment. Hosp. Beileroord, Beilen. Member: NIPP. Testing, clinical analysis, consulting; projective techniques, psychopathology.   F

ACHTERBERGH, Drs. Leopold Johannes. Boslaan 57, Son (N.B.). b. 5 July 1921 Paree, Java, Indonesia. Doctorandus '50 Univ. of Nijmegen, Neth. HEAD, Psych. Dept, Van Doorne's Automobielfabrieken N.V. Geldropseweg 303, Eindhoven; TEACHER, Cath. Trng. Sch. for Soc. Work, Eindhoven. Member: NIPP, Neth. Indus. Psych. Socy, Psych. Sect. of Thijmgenootschap. Personnel psychology, testing, guidance; industrial human relations, group process, status.   M

ACHTTIENRIBBE, Dra. Hanna Margaretha. Oude Loosdrechtse Weg 94, Hilversum. b. 4 July 1913, Amsterdam. Doctoranda '54 Univ. of Amsterdam, Neth. PSYCHOLOGIST, Medisch Opvoedkundig Bur, Emmastr. 62, Hilversum. Member: NIPP. Testing, applied psychology; psychoanalysis, learning theory, remedial

teaching.   F

ALBERTS, Drs. Albert Pieter. Veenendaalkade 440, The Hague. b. May 1922 Haren. Doctorandus '49 Univ. of Groningen, Neth. INDUS. PSYCH'T, Psych. Serv. of the PTT, Zeestr. 5, The Hague. Member: NIPP. Industrial psychology, testing, personnel selection, research; susceptibility to accidents, personality structure tests.   M

ASPEREN DE BOER, Dr. S. R. van. Jan van Eyckstr. 31B, Amsterdam Z. b. 8 June 1901 Drachten. D.SC '27 Univ. of Utrecht, Neth. CHEMISTRY TCHR, Hervormd Lyceum, Amsterdam; CONSULT. PSYCH'T, priv. prac. Member: NIPP, Neth. Psych. Assn. Teaching, consulting, testing; child and adolescent psychology, intelligence tests, projective techniques.   M

ASSELBERGHS, Drs. Victor Eduard. Martinusstr. 25, Venlo. b. 30 Dec 1920 Esschen, Bel. Doctorandus '51 Univ. of Nijmegen, Neth. PSYCH. CO-WRKR, Child Guid. Clin, Medisch Opvoedkundig Bur; PSYCH. ADVIS, St. Thomas Coll, and R.C. Bur. for Marriage Couns, Venlo; TEACHER, R.C. Sch. for Soc. Work, Sittard. Member: NIPP. Applied and educational psychology, consulting, teaching; developmental psychology, marriage counseling.   M

BAARS, Drs. Andries François. Soestdijkseweg 82N, Bilthoven. b. 23 Dec 1912 Amsterdam. Doctorandus '52 Univ. of Utrecht, Neth. HEAD, Soc. Psych. Bur, K.L.M., Airport Schiphol; PSYCH. CONSULT, priv. prac. Member: NIPP, Neth. Indus.

Psych. Socy. Industrial psychology, consulting, guidance, testing; achievement tests, social perception, attitude measurement. M

BAERENDS, Prof. Dr. Gerard P. Univ. of Groningen, Rijksstraatweg 78, Haren. b. 30 Mar 1916 The Hague. Doctor '41 Univ. of Leiden, Neth. PROF. of ZOOL, Univ. of Groningen; EDITOR, *Behaviour.* Teaching, research; comparative psychology, animal behavior. M

BAKKER, Dra. J. E. M. Emmastr. 11, Alkmaar. b. 16 July 1923 Appingedam. Doctoranda '53 Univ. of Groningen, Neth. PSYCHOLOGIST, Found. for Ment. Hlth. in N. Holl., Oudegracht 182, Alkmaar. Member: NIPP. Testing, educational psychology, consulting, guidance; projective techniques, play therapy, testing for reading and writing disability. F

BARENDREGT, Dr. Johan Teunis. Joh. Verhulststraat 29b, Amsterdam. b. 16 Feb 1924 Nieuwerkerk Zld. PH.D '54 Univ. of Amsterdam, Neth. PSYCHOLOGIST, Psychosomatic Res. Grp, Wilhelmina Hosp, Amsterdam; RES. PSYCH'T, Inst. of the Neth. Psychoanal. Socy, J.W. Brouwersplein 21, Amsterdam. Member: NIPP. Research, clinical analysis; psychosomatic specificity, effectiveness of psychotherapy, validation of psychological and psychiatric reports. M

BEETS, Dr. Nicolaas. Julianalaan 9, Utrecht. b. 17 May 1915 Arnhem. PH.D '54 Univ. of Utrecht, Neth. SCI. CO-WRKR, Paedagogisch Inst, Univ. of Utrecht, Trans 14, Utrecht. Psychotherapy, consulting, testing; psychology of adolescence. . M

BEGEMANN, Dra. M. J. Dan. de Langestr. 12 hs, Amsterdam Z. b. 28 Aug 1910 Lawang, Indonesia. Doctoranda '53 Univ. of Amsterdam, Neth. CLIN. PSYCH'T, Psychiat. Clin. Hulp en Heil, Veursche Achterweg 133, Leidschendam. Member: NIPP. Testing and clinical analysis; projective techniques, learning theory, achievement tests. F

BENDERS, Drs. H. J. Akerstr. N. 13, Hoensbroek-Treebeek. b. 7 July 1915 Schinveld. Lic. '41 Univ. of Louvain, Bel. HEAD, Psych. Dept, Dutch State Mines, v. der Maessenstr, Heerlen; BD. MEMBER, Psych. Inst. Limburg; BD. MEMBER, Cath. Cen. Inst. for Vocat. Guid. Member: NIPP. Industrial psychology, testing, research; selection and personnel problems in industry, psychometric tests, projective techniques. M

BENDIEN, Drs. Johannes. Spuistr. 108, Amsterdam. b. 19 Oct 1923 Arnhem. Doctorandus '52 Univ. of Amsterdam, Neth. CLIN. PSYCH'T, Provinciaal Ziekenhuis, nabij Santpoort. Member: NIPP,

Clin. Psych. Assn. Testing, research, teaching; projective tests, extra-sensory perception, psychoanalytic theory. M

BERG, Prof. Dr. Jan Hendrik van den. Willemsplantsoen 5, Utrecht. b. 11 June 1914 Deventer. MD '46 Univ. of Utrecht, Neth. PROF. of PSYCH, Univ. of Leiden; PROF. of PASTORAL PSYCH, Univ. of Utrecht; DIRECTOR, Inst. of Conflict Psych, Rapenburg 82, Leiden. Teaching, psychotherapy, applied psychology; psychology of human conflict, human relations, psychiatry. M

BERGER, Dr. L. H. M. Bachmanstr. 43, The Hague. b. 18 Dec 1899 Venlo. Doctor '27 Univ. of Utrecht, Neth. INSPECTOR of EDUC, Ministry of Justice, The Hague. Member: NIPP, Neth. Psych. Assn. M

BERGER, Drs. Willibrordus Johannes. Abt. Ludolfweg 89, De Bilt. b. 9 Jan 1919 Utrecht. Doctorandus '54 Univ. of Nijmegen, Neth. PASTORAL PSYCH'T, Dr. H. van der Hoeven Clin, Agnietenstr. 2, Utrecht. Member: NIPP. Pastoral psychology, consulting, child guidance, testing; projective techniques, social perception, group process. M

BERNARD, Drs. Frits. Mispelstr. 3, The Hague. b. 28 Aug 1920 Rotterdam. Doctorandus '50 Univ. of Amsterdam, Neth. PSYCHOLOGIST, Defense Dept, The Hague. Member: NIPP. Applied psychology, consulting, guidance, research; intelligence testing, psychoanalysis, developmental psychology. M

BLADERGROEN, Dra. Wilhelmina Johanna. Emmalaan 6, Haren. b. 12 July 1908 Amsterdam. Dotoranda '40 Univ. of Amsterdam, Neth. LECT. in CHILD PSYCH, Univ. of Groningen; DIRECTOR, Psycho-Pedagogical Inst. Amsterdam, Van Eeghenstr. 179, Amsterdam. Member: NIPP, APSLW, ICWP. Teaching, research, testing, consulting; clinical approach to children with learning difficulties, projective tests, developmental measurement. F

BLITS, Dra. Miss Annie Johanna. Dunklerstr. 32, The Hague. b. 20 Sept 1903 Djakarta, Java, Indonesia. Candidaat '43 Rijks Univ. of Utrecht, Neth. PSYCHOTHERAPIST, priv. prac. Member: NIPP. Psychoanalysis; unconscious processes, psychology of religion, personality development. F

BLONDEN, Drs. Fr. H. P. van Goyenstraat 18, Brunssum L. b. 25 Oct 1925 Amsterdam. Doctorandus '54 Univ. of Amsterdam, Neth. INDUS. PSYCH'T, Cokesfabrieken, Staatsmijnen in Limburg, van der Maesenstr. 2, Heerlen. Member: NIPP. Personnel administration, consulting, testing; needs and attitudes, problems of family and education, philosophical background of psychology. M

BOEKE, Drs. Johan Filip. Wijnoldy Daniëlslaan 21, Santpoort. b. 25 May 1922 Schoorl. Doctorandus '54 Univ. of Amsterdam, Neth. PSYCHOLOGIST, Stichting voor Geestelijke Volksgezondheid, De Hoost, Veesen. Member: NIPP. Testing, applied psychology, educational and vocational guidance, consulting; projective techniques, child psychotherapy, psychology of music.M

BOEKE, Drs. Pieter E. Dilgtweg 30, Haren. b. 27 Nov 1920 Schoorl. Doctorandus '50 Univ. of Amsterdam, Neth. CHIEF CLIN. PSYCH'T, Psychiat. Clin, Univ. of Groningen; LECTURER, Sch. for Soc. Work, Groningen; LECT. in CLIN. PSYCH, Univ. of Groningen. Member: NIPP, Clin. Psych. Assn. Testing, clinical analysis, psychotherapy, teaching; projective techniques, abnormal psychology, psychoanalysis. M

BOLTE-CORNELISSEN, Mrs. Dra. Hendrika M. Churchillaan 109 hs, Amsterdam Z. b. 13 May 1922 Zaandam. Doctoranda '46 Univ. of Amsterdam, Neth. STAFF MEMBER, Child Guid. Clin, Prinsengracht 717, Amsterdam; PSYCHOLOGIST, priv. prac. Member: NIPP. Testing, clinical analysis, guidance, psychotherapy; diagnosis of neuroses. F

BOS, Drs. H. G. Lorentzkade 534, Haarlem. b. 12 Jan 1921 Gaasterland. Doctorandus '49 Univ. of Utrecht, Neth. SCH. PSYCH'T, Gemeentelijk Schoolpsych. Bur, Zijlstr. 70, Haarlem. Member: NIPP. Guidance, psychotherapy, testing; educational psychology, projective techniques. M

BOUMA, Dra. Helen a. Nassaukade309III, Amsterdam. b. 11 Mar 1924 Groningen. Doctoranda '50 Free Univ. of Amsterdam, Neth. SCH. PSYCH'T, Gemeente Haarlem. Member: NIPP. Testing, clinical analysis, educational psychology, guidance; remedial education, school and learning, difficulties of the neurotic child, play therapy. F

BOUMAN, Dr. M. A. Breitnerlaan 14, Utrecht. b. 29 Mar 1919 Utrecht. PH.D '49 Univ. of Utrecht, Neth. EXEC. DIR, Res. Inst. for Perception, Kampweg 3, Soesterberg. Research, administration, professional writing; psychophysiology. M

BOUT, Drs. J. Th. Weteringschans 22, Amsterdam. b. 25 Apr 1925 Amsterdam. Doctorandus '51 Univ. of Amsterdam, Neth. CONSULT. PSYCH'T, priv. prac; TCHNG. ASST, Soc. Pedagogical Inst, Univ. of Amsterdam. Member: NIPP. Applied psychology, teaching, consulting; group process, psychoanalytic techniques, group behavior. M

BREMER, Drs. B. J. G. Julianalaan 11, Utrecht. b. 8 July '24 Utrecht. Doctorandus '49 Rijks Univ. of Utrecht, Neth. CHILD PSYCH'T, Utrechtse Katholieke Stichting voor Geestelijke Volksgezondheid, Biltstr. 112, Utrecht; EDUC. COUNS, priv. prac. Member: NIPP. Consulting, guidance, testing, psychotherapy, educational psychology; projective techniques, psychopathology, learning process. M

BREMER, Drs. Joost Jan Christiaan Benedikt. Hogerbeetsstr. 1, Wassenaar. b. 13 Feb 1928 Utrecht. Doctorandus '52 Rijks Univ. of Utrecht, Neth. CLIN. PSYCH'T, St. Ursula Kliniek and St. Jacobusstichting, Eikenlaan, Wassenaar. Member: NIPP, Neth. Clin. Psych. Assn. Testing, clinical practice, psychotherapy; psychological changes caused by organic-brain damage, projective techniques, nondirective counseling. M

BREUKERS, Dr. Eugenie Maria Josephine. St. Canisiussingel 25, Nijmegen. b. 21 Mar 1913 Roermond. PH.D '41 Cath. Univ. of Nijmegen, Neth. PSYCHOLOGIST, Child. Clin, Observatiehuis Mokerheide, Mook (L). Member: NIPP, Psych. Sect. of Thijmgenootschap, Clin. Psych. Assn. Consulting, clinical practice, psychotherapy, testing; projective techniques, achievement tests, attitude measurement. F

BROEK, Dr. Pieter van den. Houtlaan 54, Leiden. b. 2 Oct 1924 Delft. MD '49 Univ. of Leiden, Neth. SCI. ASST, Rijks Univ, Psych. Inst, Binnenvestgracht 22, Leiden. Member: NIPP, Neth. Psych. Assn. Research, educational psychology, testing; projective techniques, intelligence tests, technical abilities. M

BRUGMANS, Prof. Dr. Henri Johan Frans Willem. Hondsruglaan 25, Groningen. b. 5 June 1884 Brussels, Bel. PH.D '13 Univ. of Groningen, Neth. PROF. EMER, Univ. of Groningen. Member: NIPP, Neth. Psych. Assn. Teaching, research; meaning of truth, foundations and postulates of psychology, the unconscious and subconscious, achievement tests. M

BRUIJN, Dra. Miss Wilhelmina J. de. Jan van Eyckstraat 8II, Amsterdam. b. 13 Mar 1923 Vlaardingen. Doctoranda '52 Rijks Univ. of Utrecht, Neth. PSYCHOLOGIST, Gemeentelijk Paedotherapeutisch Inst, Niasstr. 59, Amsterdam. Member: NIPP. Testing, educational psychology; graphology, projective techniques, learning theory. F

BURGH, Drs. Aart van der. Gallenkamp Pelsweg 21, Soest-Zuid. b. 5 Jan 1926 Hazerswoude. Doctorandus '52 Univ. of Amsterdam, Neth. CHIEF ASST, Psych. Traffic Lab, Stationsstr. 8, Utrecht; EDITOR, *Verbond Voor Veilig Verkeer*. Member: NIPP. Applied psychology, research, professional writing; group dynamics, driver and traffic psychology, psychosomatics. M

BUYTENDIJK, Prof. Dr. Frederik Jacobus Johannes. Psych. Lab, Wittevrouwenstr. 9,

Utrecht. b. 29 Apr 1887 Breda. MD '09 Univ. of Amsterdam, Neth. PROF. EMER. Psych. Lab, Univ. of Utrecht; PROF. of PSYCH, Univ. of Nijmegen. Member: APSLF, SFP. Teaching, research; perception, psychological sex differences, phenomenological research. M

CALON, Prof. Dr. P. J. A. Nijmeegsebaan 86, Nijmegen. b. 23 Apr 1905 Oud-Beyerland Z.H. Doctor '50 Cath. Univ. of Nijmegen, Neth. PROF. of DEVEL. PSYCH, Cath. Univ. of Nijmegen; SCI. ADVIS, Paedological Inst. St. Joseph, Hengstdal, Nijmegen. Member: NIPP. Teaching, research, consulting, educational and medical psychology; emotions and drives. -M

CASSEE, Drs. A. P. Torenlaan 38, Hilversum. b. 26 July 1924 Haarlem. Doctorandus '49 Univ. of Amsterdam, Neth. PSYCH. DIR, Dist. Het Gooi der Stichting voor Geestelijke Volksgezondheid in N.H., Emmastr. 62, Hilversum. Member: NIPP. Applied psychology, testing, psychotherapy; conflictuology, projective techniques. M

CATE, Prof. Dr. Jasper ten. Merwedeplein 15, Amsterdam. b. 1 Oct 1887 St. Petersburg, Russia. Prof, Univ. of Amsterdam, Neth. PROF. of PHYSIOL, Physiol. Lab, Univ. of Amsterdam, Rapenburgerstr. 136, Amsterdam. Member: APSLF. Teaching, research, administration; physiology of the nervous system, conditioned reflexes, comparative psychology. M

CEHA, Miss Dra. Maria M. Th. Oostersingel 118a, Groningen. b. 18 Sept 1926 Heerlen. Lic. '51 Univ. of Louvain, Bel. PSYCHOLOGIST, Psychiat. and Neur. Clin, Univ. Hosp, Oostersingel 59, Groningen. Member: NIPP, Clin. Psych. Assn. Testing, clinical analysis, consulting, research; projective techniques, achievement tests, psychotherapy. F

CHORUS, Prof. Dr. A. M. J. Rijngeesterstraatweg 11, Oegstgeest, Leiden. b. 18 Apr 1909 Munstergeleen. PH.D '40 Univ. of Nijmegen, Neth. PROF. and HEAD, Dept. of Psych, Univ. of Leiden, Rapenburg 32, Leiden. Member: NIPP. Teaching, research, consulting, guidance; psychology of youth, aptitude tests, characterology. M

COLIJN, Drs. Petrus Johannes Hendrikus. Breedelaan 10, Heiloo. b. 30 Aug 1918 The Hague. Doctorandus '52 Free Univ. of Amsterdam, Neth. DIRECTOR, Zaanse Stichting voor Bedrijfspsychologie en Personeelsbeleid, Zaanweg 46, Wormerveer. Member: NIPP. Industrial psychology, testing, teaching; leadership and group process, learning theory, attitude measurement. M

CROMBACH, Miss Dra. Johanna Hendrika Maria. Pelikaanlaan 6, Eindhoven. b.

26 Apr 1924 Arnhem. Doctoranda '54 Cath. Univ. of Nijmegen, Neth. STAFF MEMBER, Child Guid. Clin, Vestdijk 45a, Eindhoven. Member: NIPP. Guidance, educational psychology, research; projective techniques, social perception, attitude measurement. F

CRIJNS, Drs. Arthur Gerard Joannes. Schoolstr. 2, Brunssum. b. 22 Feb 1930 Brunssum. Doctorandus '55 Univ. of Nijmegen, Neth. PSYCH. RES. WRKR, Staatsmijnen in Limburg, Psych. Dienst, van der Maesenstr. 2, Heerlen. Member: NIPP. Research; projective techniques, achievement tests, group process. M

DAEL, Dr. Joannes Jacobus van. Hoofdweg 12, Amsterdam. b. 24 Sept 1900 Stamproy. Lic, Univ. of Louvain, Bel. CHIEF, Psych. Sect, Gemeentelijke Geneeskundige en Gezondheidsdienst, Nieuwe Achtergracht 100, Amsterdam. Member: NIPP. Applied, industrial and personnel psychology. M

DANIELS, Drs. Mathé. Sterreschansweg 47, Nijmegen. b. 6 Feb 1920 Nijmegen. Doctorandus '46 Univ. of Nijmegen, Neth. HEAD, Res. Dept, Joint Inst. for Appl. Psych, Berg en Dalseweg 101, Nijmegen. Member: NIPP. Research, administration, industrial psychology; training and selection of industrial supervisors, industrial counseling. M

DECHESNE, Drs. Georgus Jozephus. Reigerstr. 32, Tilburg. b. 6 Nov 1924 Franeker. Doctorandus '54 Univ. of Leiden, Neth. SCH. PSYCH'T, Schoolpsych. Dienst, Schoolstr. 25, Tilburg. Member: NIPP. Testing, research, educational psychology; school readiness, standardization of vocational guidance tests. M

DEGEN, Drs. Hendrikus Jacobus Petrus. Nassaukade 376 hs, Amsterdam W. b. 29 Feb 1924 Nijmegen. Doctorandus '54 Univ. of Nijmegen, Neth. PSYCHOLOGIST, Munic. Med. and Hlth. Serv, Amsterdam. Member: NIPP, Psych. Sect. of Thijmgenootschap. Consulting, testing, personnel psychology; projective techniques. M

DEKKER-SCHIPPER, Mrs. Dra. Helena Louise. Adrianalaan 335, Rotterdam. b. 4 Jan 1929 Zaandam. Doctoranda '54 Univ. of Amsterdam, Neth. PSYCHOLOGIST, Medisch Opvoedkundig Bur, Claes de Vrieselaan 145b, Rotterdam. Member: NIPP. Testing, educational guidance; projective techniques, psychoanalysis, psychotherapy. F

DELHEZ, Drs. François. Loonerstraat 88a, Assen. b. 5 Mar 1920 Dordrecht. Doctorandus '55 Rijks Univ. of Groningen, Neth. PROVINCIAL SCH. PSYCH'T, Sch. Med. Off. Serv. Drenthe, Zuidersingel 15, Assen. Member: NIPP. Educational and applied psychology, testing, research; remedial teaching, projective techniques, learning theory. M

DEUR, Miss Dra. Ermina. Jan van Scorelstr. 38, Utrecht. b. 19 Mar 1927 Schoonhoven. Doctoranda '53 Free Univ. Amsterdam, Neth. ASSISTANT, Psych. Verkeerslaboratorium, Stationsstr. 5, Utrecht. Member: NIPP. Applied psychology, testing; projective techniques, vocational guidance, psychology of religion, mental deficiency. F

DIX, Drs. P. G. Hyacintenlaan 1, Haarlem. b. 13 Feb 1918 Utrecht. Doctorandus '47 Univ. of Amsterdam, Neth. CHILD PSYCH'T, Gemeentelijk Pedotherapeutisch Inst, Niasstr. 59, Amsterdam O. Member: NIPP, Int. Rorschach Socy. Research, applied psychology, psychotherapy, teaching; graphology. M

DOHMEN, Drs. Nicolaas Jozef Petrus. G. K. van Hogendorpplaan 13, Hilversum. b. 3 Jan 1921 Stoutenburg. Doctorandus '51 Univ. of Amsterdam, Neth. INDUS. PSYCH'T, N. V. Philips Telecommunicatie Industrie, Jan van der Heydenstr. 41, Hilversum. Member: NIPP, Int. Rorschach Socy. Industrial psychology, testing, guidance; achievement tests, attitude measurement, industrial adaptation of rural population. M

DOOREN, Prof. Dr. Frans Joseph van Franklin Rooseveltlaan 29, Breda. b. 3 Mar 1921 Weert. Doctor '54 Cath. Univ. of Nijmegen, Neth. PROF. of PSYCH, Cath. Univ. for Econ. and Soc. Sci, Bosscheweg, Tilburg; SCI. ADVIS, Gemeenschappelijk Inst. voor Toegepaste Psych. Member: NIPP. Teaching, research, industrial psychology; psychology of the working group, adjustment of the worker to work and organization, social behavior. M

DOYER, Drs. Chr. F. W. Anna van Saksenlaan 6, Santpoort. b. 3 Apr 1913 Amsterdam. Doctorandus '49 Free Univ. of Amsterdam, Neth. BIOL. TCHR, Chr. Lyceum Marnix van Sint Aldegonde, Planetenlaan 5, Haarlem. Member: NIPP. Teaching, educational psychology, psychotherapy; guidance; intelligence measurement, projective techniques, psychoanalysis. M

DUNGEN-MOLENAAR, Mrs. Dra. van der. Henriëtta Margaretha. Slotlaan 34III, Zeist. b. 28 Mar 1929 Amsterdam. Doctoranda '53 Free Univ. of Amsterdam, Neth. PSYCHOLOGIST, Medisch Opvoedkundig Bur, Korenmarkt 69, Delft. Member: NIPP. Testing, psychotherapy; child and educational psychology. F

DUIJKER, Prof. Dr. Hubertus Carl Johannes. Joh. Verhulststr. 135, Amsterdam. b. 10 Oct 1912 Leiden. Doctor '46 Univ. of Amsterdam, Neth. PROF. of PSYCH. and DIR. of PSYCH. LAB, Univ. of Amsterdam;

DIRECTOR, Inst. for Soc. and Indus. Psych; EDITOR, *Acta Psychologica*; CO-EDITOR, *International Directory of Psychologists*; ED. BD, *Nederlands Tijdschrift voor de Psychologie*. Member: NIPP, IUSP, Neth. Psych. Assn, APSLF. Teaching, research, administration. editorial; crosscultural comparative research, social perception, psychology of language. M

DIJK, Dra. Miss Amelia Wilhelmina van. J. W. Brouwersplein 14, Amsterdam Z. b. 25 May 1907 Teteringen. Doctoranda '40 Free Univ. of Amsterdam, Neth. CHIEF ASST, Paedologisch Inst, Vossiusstr. 56, Amsterdam. Member: NIPP. Research, guidance, psychotherapy; psychology of learning, child therapy, achievement tests. F

DIJK, Drs. Engbert Wiebe. Noorder Sanatorium, Zuidlaren. b. 26 May 1926 The Hague. Doctorandus '52 Free Univ. of Amsterdam, Neth. CLIN. PSYCH'T, Psychiat. Hosp. Dennenoord, Zuidlaren. Member: NIPP, Clin. Psych. Assn. Testing, consulting, research; clinical analysis, teaching. M

DIJKHUIS, Drs. J. H. Koningslaan 16, Utrecht. b. 20 Feb 1929 Borne. Doctorandus '53 Univ. of Utrecht, Neth. HEAD ASST., Inst. for Clin. and Indus. Psych, Trans 14, Utrecht. Member: NIPP. Psychotherapy, student consulting, clinical practice. M

DIJKHUIS, Drs. J. J. Kennemerstraatweg 632, Heiloo. b. 30 Mar 1921 Odoorn. Doctorandus '47 Univ. of Utrecht, Neth. CHIEF CLIN. PSYCH'T, Willibrordusstichting Psychiat. Hosp, Heiloo; CO-EDITOR, *DUX*. Member: NIPP, APSLF, Neth. Clin. Psych. Assn. Testing, clinical analysis, consulting, editorial, research; projective techniques, psychotherapy, social perception, group process and education, information theory. M

EEGHEN, Mr. Pieter van. Amstel 97/III, Amsterdam C. b. 28 June 1911 Amsterdam. Doctorandus '49 Univ. of Amsterdam, Neth. ASSISTANT, Inst. for Soc. and Indus. Psych, Univ. of Amsterdam, Keizersgracht 611-613, Amsterdam. Member: NIPP. Teaching, testing, applied psychology; projective techniques, artistic perception, juvenile delinquency. M

EEKELEN, Drs. Willem Frederik van. Parnassusweg 26I, Amsterdam Z. b. 22 May 1923 Tiel. Doctorandus '54 Univ. of Amsterdam, Neth. HEAD of PSYCH. DEPT, Raadgevend Efficiency Bur, Ir P. H. Bosboom en F. C. Hegener, Joh. Vermeerstr. 20, Amsterdam; TEACHER, Nederlands Opleidings Inst. voor het Buitenland Nijenrode, Breukelen. Member: NIPP. Industrial psychology and testing, teaching, consulting, research; testing. M

EGTEN, Drs. Edo van. Waalstraat 2 IJmuiden. b. 30 Nov 1923 Amsterdam. Doctorandus '54 Univ. of Utrecht, Neth. PSYCHOLOGIST, Rekkense Inrichtingen, Rekken. Member: NIPP. Consulting, testing, clinical analysis, teaching; problems of the feeble-minded and dull normal, statistical analysis in clinical psychology, social maladjustment. M

ELIËNS, Drs. P. A. M. Zilvermeeuwlaan 23, Eindhoven. b. 20 Mar 1920 Arnhem. Doctorandus '48 Univ. of Nijmegen, Neth. CLIN. PSYCH'T, R.K. Binnenziekenhuis, Vestdijk, Eindhoven; DOCENT, Cath. Sch. for Soc. Work, Eindhoven. Member: NIPP. Testing, clinical analysis, consulting, teaching. M

ELLERBECK, S. J. Prof. Dr. Joh. Paul W. Canisius Coll, Stijn Buysstraat 11, Nijmegen. b. 11 Nov 1908 Groenlo. PH.D, Univ. of Nijmegen, Neth. CONSULT. PSYCH'T, priv. prac; PROF. of PASTORAL PSYCH, Canisianum, Maastricht; PROF. of RELIG. PSYCH, Berchmanianum, Nijmegen. Member: NIPP. Consulting, teaching, administration; development of religious experience and morals, community life of religious orders. M

ELSBERG-KIEWIED, Mrs. Dra. M. T. C. van. Meyenhagen 3, de Bilt. b. 27 Nov 1920 Haarlem. Doctoranda '46 Univ. of Nijmegen, Neth. PSYCHOLOGIST, Hoogveld Inst, Stikke Hezelstr. 1, Nijmegen. Member: NIPP. Research, testing, guidance; training young workers, family life, institutional children. F

ELSEN-SCHLÖSSER, Mrs. Dra. Joséphine Maria Sophia. Burg. Elsenlaan 116, Rijswijk Z.H. b. 8 Sept 1928 Kerkrade. PSYCHOLOGIST, Gemeentelijke Dienst Waldeck Pyrmontkade 3, 's Gravenhage. Member: NIPP. Testing, educational psychology, administration; intelligence measurement, projective techniques. F

ENGELBERTS, Mr. Drs. J. J. Dr. Letteplein 15, de Bilt. b. 25 May 1912 Zwolle. Doctorandus '55 Univ. of Utrecht, Neth. SCI. STAFF MEMBER, Inst. of Clin. and Indus. Psych, Trans 14, Utrecht. Member: NIPP, Clin. Psych. Assn. Testing, clinical Psych. Assn. Testing, clinical analysis, teaching, consulting; personality description, psychopathic personality, scientific value of comprehending description. M

ENGELS, Drs. Paul M. J. Abtenlaan 24, Kerkrade. b. 25 Mar 1930 Schaesberg. Doctorandus '56 Univ. of Nijmegen, Neth. SOC. PSYCH'T, Hoogveld Inst, Stikke Hezelstr. 1-3, Nijmegen. Research, applied psychology, teaching; human relations research, opinion and attitude research. M

EYNDEN-NABER, Dra. Emmanuela van den. Laplacestr. 57/II, Amsterdam. b. 25 Dec 1929 Amsterdam. Doctoranda '55 Univ. of Amsterdam, Neth. PSYCHOLOGIST, Kath. Stichting voor Geestelijke Volksgezondheid, 2e Constantijn Huygensstr. 77, zorg en Gezinswerk, Keizersgracht 19, Amsterdam; PSYCHOLOGIST, R. K. Jeugd-Amsterdam. Member: NIPP, Psych. Sect. of Thijmgenootschap. Applied and educational psychology, testing, consulting, guidance; psychodiagnostics, projective techniques, psychotherapy. F

EX, Dr. Jacques. Psych. Lab, Cath. Univ. of Nijmegen, Berg en Dalseweg 105, Nijmegen. b. 14 May 1922 Goirle. PH.D '49 Cath. Univ. of Nijmegen. SCI. CHIEF ASST, Psych. Lab, Cath. Univ. of Nijmegen. Member: NIPP, APSLF, Neth. Indus. Psych. Socy. Research, teaching, professional writing; experimental study of social interaction, perception, psychological problems of immigrants. M

FAFIÉ, Dra. Miss Christiana M. F. M. Buitenrustplein 19, Voorburg, Z.H. b. 18 Feb 1917 Rotterdam. Doctoranda '48 Univ. of Amsterdam, Neth. CHILD PSYCH'T, Haags Hervormd Weeshuis, Scheveningseweg 78, The Hague. Member: NIPP. Applied psychology, guidance, testing; projective techniques, group process, social perception. F

FOKKEMA, Dr. Sipke Dirk. Keizer Karelweg 385, Amstelveen. b. 5 Aug 1925 Utrecht. Doctor '54 Free Univ. of Amsterdam, Neth. LEADER, Psych. Res. Lab, Free Univ. of Amsterdam. Member: NIPP, Neth. Indus. Psych. Socy, Int. Rorschach Socy, Western European Assn. for Aviat. Psych. Applied psychology, research, administration; personality, aptitude tests, methodology. M

FORTMANN, Prof. Dr. H. M. M. Sterreschansweg 43, Nijmegen. b. 15 June 1912 Amersfoort. Professor '45 Univ. of Nijmegen, Neth. YOUTH COUNS, Genl. Council of Dutch Cath. Youth, Stationsplein 15 bis, Utrecht. Member: NIPP. Consulting, guidance, professional writing, teaching; psychology of adolescence. M

FOURNIER, Miss Dra. E. P. Michel Angelostr. 61, Amsterdam Z. b. 4 Apr 1924 Djakarta, Indonesia. Doctoranda '54 Univ. of Amsterdam, Neth. ASSISTANT, Psych. Lab, Univ. of Amsterdam, Keizersgracht 613, Amsterdam, C. Member: NIPP. Research, testing, educational psycho.ogy: children with learning difficulties. F

FRAIKIN, Drs. Frans J. H. Sittarderweg 79b, Heerlen. b. 30 Nov 1920 Roermond. Lic. '43 Univ. of Louvain, Bel. LEADER, Psych.

Dept, N.B. Oranje-Nassau Mijnen, Heerlen. Member: NIPP, AIPA, Neth. Indus. Psych. Socy, Psych. Sect. of Thijmgenootschap. Industrial psychology, testing, consulting, guidance; professional ability, motivation in industry, labor-turnover. M

FRANKEN, Drs. Bernard Rudolf. Julianalaan 2, Utrecht. b. 15 Sept 1927 Loosdrecht. Doctorandus '54 Univ. of Amsterdam, Neth. FELLOW, Neth. Found. for Psychotechnics, Wittevrouwenstr. 6, Utrecht; TCHR. of PSYCH, Art Academy, Utrecht. Member: NIPP. Industrial psychology, teaching, research; psychology of organization-talent, children's drawings, projective techniques for vocational guidance. M

FROHN-DE WINTER, Mrs. Dra. Marie Louise de. Prinsengracht 512, Amsterdam C. b. 9 July 1929 Amsterdam. MA '54 Univ. of Amsterdam, Neth. CLIN. PSYCH'T, Univ. Clin, Wilhelmina Ziekenhuis, Helmersstr. 2, Amsterdam; PSYCHOLOGIST, Child Guid. Clin. Member: NIPP, Psych. Sect. of Thijmgenootschap. Clinical practice, diagnostic testing; projective techniques, psycho-neurological research. F

FRIJDA, Dr. Nico Henri. Keizersgracht 466, Amsterdam. b. 1 May 1927 Amsterdam. PH.D '51 Univ. of Amsterdam, Neth. RES. ASST, Psych. Lab, Univ. of Amsterdam. Member: NIPP, APA. Research, testing; psychology of expression and social perception, group process, theory of emotion and psychodynamic process. M

GEER, Dr. Johan P. van de. Burggravenlaan 177, Leiden. b. 21 June 1926 Rotterdam. PH.D '57 Univ. of Leiden, Neth. ASSISTANT, Psych. Inst, Rijks Univ, Rapenburg 32, Leiden. Member: NIPP. Teaching, research, consulting; thought processes, social perception, theoretical psychology. M

GELDER, Dr. Leon van. Statensingel 42c, Rotterdam. b. 3 Mar 1913 Amsterdam. Doctorandus '53 Rijks Univ. of Utrecht, Neth. SCI. DIR, Educ. Cen, Herengracht 56, Amsterdam; LECT. in PSYCH. of HANDICAPPED CHILD, Nuts Acad, Rotterdam. Educational psychology, testing, teaching; evaluation of learning results, learning difficulties. M

GIESSEN, Dr. Roelof Willem van der. Gerrit van der Veenstr. 175, Amsterdam. b. 3 May 1910 Kampen. PH.D '53 Free Univ. of Amsterdam, Neth. HEAD of SEL. DEPT, Royal Neth. Navy, Induction Cen, Voorschoten. Member: NIPP. Applied and personnel psychology, testing, research; written aptitude and classification tests, validity and prediction, selection and classification. M

GOVERS, Drs. Albert Jan. Meppelweg 395, The Hague. b. 20 Apr 1922 Maastricht. Doctorandus '49 Rijks Univ. of Utrecht, Neth. CHILD PSYCH'T, Child Guid. Clin, Josef Israëlslaan, The Hague; PSYCHOTHERAPIST, Inst. for Emotionally Disturbed Children, De Lindenhof, Schiedam. Member: NIPP. Testing, psychotherapy, research; learning difficulties, sociometry. M

GOVERS-SCHUITEMA, Mrs. Dra. Marlène. Meppelweg 395, The Hague. b. 15 Aug 1924 Rotterdam. Doctoranda '51 Rijks Univ. of Groningen, Neth. CHILD PSYCH'T, Medisch Paedagogisch Bur, Jozef Israëlslaan, The Hague; TSTNG. DIAGNOSTICIAN, Observatiehuis voor Jongens, The Hague. Member: NIPP. Testing, consulting; emotional disturbances and learning difficulties in children. F

GRAAF, Drs. Albert A. de. Courbetstr. 10, Amsterdam. b. 5 Jan 1924 Groningen. Doctorandus '49 Free Univ. of Amsterdam, Neth. CHIEF PSYCH'T, Amsterdam Lab. of Psychotechnics, Verdistraat 6, Amsterdam; PROF. of VOCAT. GUID, Tech. High. Sch. Member: NIPP. Educational and applied psychology, guidance, teaching; attitude measurement, dyslexia, dyscalculia. M

GRAAF, Mr. Drs. Menno H. K. van der. Reigerlaan 2, Eindhoven. b. 31 Oct 1914 Ginneken. Doctorandus '42 Free Univ. of Amsterdam, Neth. HEAD of PSYCH. DEPT, Philips Works, Eindhoven; LECT. on HUMAN RELAT, Delft Tech. Univ. Member: NIPP. Industrial psychology, consulting; group process, counseling. M

GRAEFF-WASSINK, Mrs. Dra. Mieke. C.E.P.A.M., B.P. 2, Bikfaya (Libanon). b. 13 Nov 1926 Amsterdam. Doctoranda '53 Univ. of Amsterdam, Neth. RES. ASST, Member: NIPP. Research, student, educational psychology; social perception, transcultural education. F

GREWEL, Dr. Frits. Willemsparkweg 44, Amsterdam. b. 19 Nov 1898 Amsterdam. MD '35 Univ. of Amsterdam, Neth. HEAD, Children's and Psych. Dept, Psychiat. Clin, Univ. of Amsterdam; LECT. in CHILD PSYCHIAT, Wilhelmina Hosp; CO-EDITOR, *Mens en Maatschappij*. Member: NIPP, APSLF. Teaching, research, consulting, clinical practice; projective and expressive techniques, neuropsychological disturbances, psychology of the feeble-minded. M

GROND, Drs. Ignatius Franciscus Ant. Vondellaan 21, Geleen. b. 4 Oct 1924 Heerlen. Lic. '49 Cath. Univ. of Louvain, Bel. INDUS. PSYCH'T, Staatsmijnen in Limburg, van der Maessenstr, Heerlen. Member: NIPP. Industrial psychology, consulting;

interviewing, methodology and statistics, group process, informal channels of communication in industry.   M

GROOT, Prof. Dr. Adriaan D. de. Roemer Visscherstr. 11, Amsterdam. b. 26 Oct 1914 Santpoort. Doctor '46 Univ. of Amsterdam, Neth. PROF. of APPL. PSYCH, Univ. of Amsterdam, Psych. Lab, Keizersgracht 611, Amsterdam. Teaching, research, applied psychology.   M

HAAN, Drs. C. M. G. de. Riouwstraat 127, 's-Gravenhage.   b. 19 Dec 1925 Goes. Doctorandus '53 Univ. of Utrecht, Neth. SOC. PSYCH'T, Rijks Psychologische Dienst, Korte Beestenmarkt 4, 's Gravenhage. Member: NIPP. Applied psychology, consulting, testing; social perception, group process, individual adaptation and intrapsychic conflicts.   M

HABETS, Drs. Jan Jozef Gerard Marie. Burg. v.d. Mortelplein 46, Tilburg. b. 2 Jan 1924 Oirsbeek. Doctorandus '50 Univ. of Amsterdam, Neth.   PSYCHOLOGIST, Medisch Opvoedkundig Bur, Gasthuisstraat 35, Tilburg. Member: NIPP. Clinical analysis, testing and psychotherapy of children, applied psychology; achievement and intelligence tests, projective techniques, psychotherapy, social adaptation. M

HAENEN, Drs. Maurice Pierre Marie. Pettelaarseweg 21, 's Hertogenbosch. b. 3 June 1924 Heerlen. Doctorandus '53 Univ. of Leiden, Neth.   PSYCHOLOGIST, Medisch Opvoedkundig Bur, Luykenstr. 25, 's Hertogenbosch. Member: NIPP. Consulting, testing, guidance, psychotherapy; learning play therapy, projective techniques.   M

HAER, B. van der. Prins Hendriklaan 81, Utrecht.   b. 17 Nov 1915 The Hague. Doctorandus '53 Univ. of Utrecht, Neth. PSYCHOLOGIST, Heldring Gestichten, Zetten Member: NIPP. Consulting, vocational guidance, testing, applied psychology; mental deficiency, mental maturity of children, child therapy.   M

HART DE RUYTER, Prof. Dr. Theodoor. Rijksstraatweg 249, Haren.   b. 3 July 1907 Kediú, Indonesia. MD '33 Univ. of Amsterdam, Neth.   PROFESSOR, Child Psychiat. Clin, Univ. of Groningen, Oostersingeldwarsstr. 10, Groningen. Member: NIPP, Dutch and Int. Psychoanal. Assn, Int. Assn. of Child Psych. and Allied Professions.   Teaching, psychotherapy, clinical practice; juvenile delinquency, psychosomatics.   M

HOUT, Drs. Harry P. M. van den. Nieuwe Bosseweg 79, Tilburg.   b. 10 Nov 1925 Son. Doctorandus '56 Univ. of Nijmegen, Neth. SOC. PSYCH'T, Hoogveld Inst, Stikke Hezelstr. 1, Nijmegen. Research, applied psychology, teaching; cultural anthropology, attitude research.   M

HAVE, Prof. Dr. Tonko Tjarko ten. Herman Gorterstraat 20, Amsterdam.   b. 5 Oct 1906 Noordbroek.   Doctor '40 Univ. of Groningen, Neth.   PROFESSOR, Univ. of Amsterdam; DIRECTOR, Sociaal-Paedagogisch Inst; ED. STAFF, *Social-Paedagogische Reeks, Paedagogische Monografieën.* Member: NIPP,   Neth.   Psych.   Assn. Teaching, research, administration; personality theory, theory of values and norms, communication theory.   M

HEIJSTER, Dr. Francisca Catharina. Hollandseweg 80, Bennekom. b. 22 Nov 1909 Tiel.   Doctor '42 Univ. of Utrecht, Neth. Member: NIPP,   Neth.   Psych.   Assn. Teaching, psychotherapy, editorial; child psychology, mental health.   F

HELBING, Drs. Johan Christiaan. Einsteinstraat 10c, Amersfoort.   b. 7 Jan 1928 Assen. Doctorandus '55 Univ. of Amsterdam, Neth. PSYCHOLOGIST, Dept. of Vocat. Guid. and Indus. Psych, Stichting voor Geestelijke Volks Gezondheid, Hellestr. 8a, Amersfoort; SEL. OFF, Royal Dutch Air Force. Member: NIPP. Testing, research, consulting, industrial psychology; job analysis, test validity, social psychology.   M

HEROLD, Dr. Joseph Louis M. Psych. Inst, St. Lambertuslaan 9, Maastricht.   b. 21 May 1912 Maastricht.   Doctor '40 Univ. of Utrecht, Neth. DIRECTOR, Psych. Inst. Member: NIPP, Neth. Indus. Psych. Socy. Consulting, industrial relations, vocational guidance, psychotherapy.   M

HESKES, Drs. Hans. Sophiastraat 17, Aalst (Neth.). Psych. Dept, N.V. Philips, Eindhoven. b. 31 Aug 1926 Woerden. Doctorandus '51 Univ. of Amsterdam, Neth. INDUS. PSYCH'T, N.V. Philips. Member: NIPP.   Industrial psychology, research, consulting, testing; integration of new impressions, influences on attitudes, industrial relations.   M

HILGERS, Drs. Emile Marie. Fransestr. 1, Nijmegen.   b. 1 May 1928 Nijmegen. Doctorandus '55 Univ. of Nijmegen, Neth. PSYCHOLOGIST, Gemeenschappelijk Inst. voor Toegepaste Psych, Berg en Dalseweg 101, Nijmegen. Member: NIPP. Testing, educational and vocational guidance; achievement tests, projective techniques, learning theory, psychology of colors.   M

HILLEGE, Drs. Hendrikus W. T. Cornelis, M. J. M., Burgerlaan 11, Zeist. b. 28 Mar 1926 Dordrecht. MA '52 Univ. of Louvain, Bel. CLIN. PSYCH'T, Militair Neurose Hosp, Woudenbergsche Weg 39, Zeist. Member: NIPP, Neth. Clin. Psych. Assn. Testing, teaching, psychotherapy; projective techniques, psychoanalysis, human relations. M

HOESEL, Dr. Aloysius Franciscus Gerardus van. Velperweg 45a, Arnhem. b. 18 Sept 1920 Apeldoorn. Doctor '48 Univ. of Utrecht, Neth. HEAD of PSYCH DEPT, A.K.U., Velperweg 76, Arnhem. Member NIPP. Industrial psychology, testing; group discussion, logic and creative thinking. M

HOF, Mr. Drs. Edward A. Psych. Inst, Van Weede van Dijkveldstr. 101, 's Gravenhage. b. 21 June 1914 Rotterdam. Doctorandus '47 Free Univ. of Amsterdam, Neth. CONSULT. PSYCH'T, Psych. Inst. Member: NIPP, Neth. Indus. Psych. Socy. Industrial psychology, personnel selection. M

HOGENDOORN, Drs. Dick Marius. Joseph Haydnlaan 28, Utrecht. b. 16 Dec 1921 Rotterdam. Doctorandus '49 Univ. of Amsterdam, Neth. SECOND PSYCH'T, Nederlandsche Spoorwegen, Moreelse Park, Utrecht. Member: NIPP. Personnel psychology, testing; projective techniques, job analysis and evaluation. M

HOORENS, Drs. Victor H. W. St. Jozefslaan 85, Weert. b. 20 Dec 1924 Maastricht. Doctorandus '55 Univ. of Amsterdam, Neth. Member: NIPP. Applied psychology, testing, consulting. M

HORNSTRA, Dr. Leo. Slingerweg 9, Wassenaar. b. 2 Feb 1908 Rotterdam. PH.D '51 Free Univ. of Amsterdam, Neth. PSYCHO-THERAPIST, priv. prac, Sweelinckstr. 32, The Hague. Member: NIPP, Neth. Psychoanal. Socy. Psychotherapy, consulting, testing; psychoanalysis, projective techniques for diagnostic purposes, psychology of the fine arts. M

HORST, Drs. A. P. J. M. van den. Ohmstraat 1, Amsterdam. b. 3 Mar 1924 Teteringen. Doctorandus '54 Rijks Univ. of Groningen, Neth. PSYCHOLOGIST, Ned. Inst. v.h. Dove en s.h. Kind; PSYCHOLOGIST, Inst. St. Mary, Eindhoven. Member: NIPP. Consulting, research, testing, guidance; psychology of the deaf and hard of hearing, brain-injured children. M

HORST, Prof. Dr. Lammert van der. Apollolaan 166, Amsterdam. b. 20 Jan 1893 Sneek. Doctor '24 Univ. of Groningen, Neth. PROF. of PSYCHIAT, Munic. Univ. of Amsterdam and Free Univ. of Amsterdam; DIRECTOR, Valerius Clin; HEAD, Psychiat. and Neur. Clin, Univ. of Amsterdam; ED. BD, *Ned. Tijdschrift voor Psychologie*. Member: NIPP, Neth. Psych. Assn, Clin. Psych. Assn. Clinical practice, professional writing, teaching; clinical psychology, perception, temporal and spatial orientation. M

HOUWINK, Drs. Roelof Hubertus. Parklaan 3, Zeist. b. 23 Nov 1927 Amsterdam. Doctorandus '52 Univ. of Utrecht, Neth. HEAD of RES. SECT, Inst. of Clin. Psych, Trans 14, Utrecht. Member: NIPP. Research, teaching, testing; projective techniques, personality, research techniques and statistics. M

HUISKAMP, Jan. Oelerweg 110, Hengelo (O). b. 11 Nov 1904 Beemster. DIRECTOR, Twents Inst. for Indus. Psych, Grundellaan 18, Hengelo. Member: NIPP, Neth. Indus. Psych. Socy. Industrial psychology, testing, research, guidance. M

HUT, Dr. Lambertus Jan. Willem Arntsz Ment. Clin. 2 Agnietenstr, Utrecht. b. 28 Oct 1908 Enschede. MD '36 Univ. of Groningen, Neth. MED. SUPT, Willem Arntsz Ment. Clin; CHIEF ED, *Annual Reports of the Willem Arntsz Ment. Clin*. Member: NIPP, Neth. Assn. for Psychiat. and Neur, Amer. Grp. Psychother. Assn. Consulting, clinical practice, psychotherapy, applied psychology; topological psychology, group psychotherapy and psychodrama, sociotherapy. M

HUTTE, Prof. Dr. Hermanus Albertus. 't Vierkant, Schipborg Gem. Anlo. b. 21 Aug 1917 Heemstede. Doctor '53 Univ. of Amsterdam, Neth. PROF. and DIR, Dept. of Soc. Psych, Univ. of Groningen, Oude Boteringestr. 34, Groningen; INDUS. PSYCH'T, priv. prac. Member: NIPP, Neth. Indus. Psych. Socy. Industrial psychology, research, teaching; social perception, leadership-phenomena and training group processes. M

JANSSE DE JONGE, Dr. Adriaan L. W. Kesstr. 21, Amsterdam. b. 24 Apr 1917 Middelburg. MD, Univ. of Amsterdam, Neth. PSYCHIATRIST, Valerius Clin, Valerius Plein, Amsterdam. Member: NIPP, Neth. Psychiat. and Neur. Assn. Teaching, research; medical psychology, psychopathology. M

JANSEN, Miss Dra. Mathilda Johanna. Jan Luykenstr. 30, Amsterdam Z. b. 9 Nov 1916 Rotterdam. Doctoranda '53 Univ. of Amsterdam, Neth. PSYCHOLOGIST, Human Relat. Inst, Univ. of Amsterdam, Singel 453, Amsterdam. Member: NIPP. Research, teaching, consulting; group process, reading habits, psychology of international relations and travel. F

JANSSEN, Dr. H. J. M. N. St. Willebrordplein 4, Tilburg. b. 5 Dec 1910 Cuyk a/d Maas. Doctor '55 Cath. Univ. of Nijmegen, Neth. CLIN. PSYCH'T, Psychiat. Inst. Voorburg, Boxtelse weg 48, Vught; PSYCH. CONSULT, priv. prac. Member: NIPP, Clin. Psych. Assn. Testing, clinical analysis, research, consulting, teaching; validity and reliability of tests. M

JANSSEN, Miss Dra. Maria Cornelia. Kralingseweg 189, Rotterdam. b. 18 June 1918 Hoorn. Doctoranda '51 Univ. of Amsterdam, Neth. CLIN. PSYCH'T, Coolsingel Ziekenhuis, Broederstr. 92, Rotterdam.

Member: NIPP. Testing, consulting, teaching, research; projective techniques, children's drawings. F

JONGE, Drs. Max E. de. Parklaan 102, Katwijk aan Zee. b. 17 Oct 1918 The Hague. Doctorandus '55 Univ. of Leiden, Neth. PSYCHOLOGIST, Rijkspsychologische Dienst, Rijnsburger Weg 96, Leiden. Member: NIPP. Personnel psychology, testing, research; intelligence and personality tests, personnel selection. M

JONG-WITTEBOON, Mrs. Dra. Marianne de. Heemraadssingel 210, Rotterdam. b. 31 Jan 1901 Amsterdam. Doctoranda, Univ. of Amsterdam, Neth. PSYCHOLOGIST, Civil Hosp. Zuider Ziekenhuis, Groeneveld, Rotterdam. Member: NIPP. Testing, clinical analysis, psychotherapy, teaching, research; psychosomatics, juvenile delinquency. F

KALSBEEK, Johan Wilhelm Hendrik. Emmalaan 4, Oegstgeest. b. 5 Apr 1921 Terschelling. Lic. '55 Sorbonne, Fr. PSYCHOTECHNICIAN, Inst. of Appl. Psych. and Sociol. 150 Blvd. Ney, Casablanca, Morocco. Applied and industrial psychology, research, student; adjustment of workers in underdeveloped areas to modern industry and assembly-line tasks. M

KAM-BOUMA, Mrs. Dra. Annie Maria de. Vosmaerstr. 3, Goes. b. 2 Nov 1926 Groningen. Doctoranda '50 Free Univ. of Amsterdam, Neth. LEADER, Chr. Vocat. Bur. for Zeeland. Member: NIPP. Testing, clinical analysis, educational and industrial psychology; educational and professional choice, psychic conflicts. F

KELLERMANN, Drs. Robert Ivan. Julianalaan 2/II, Utrecht. b. 1 Jan 1929 Budapest, Hungary. Doctorandus '56 Univ. of Utrecht, Neth. PSYCHOLOGIST, Nederlandsche Stichting voor Psychotechniek, Wittevrouwenkade 6, Utrecht. Member: NIPP. Testing, applied and personnel psychology, research, vocational guidance; social and self-perception, non-projective personality testing, assessment of pilots. M

KEMA, Drs. Gerard. Mr. B. van Royenlaan 55, Groningen. b. 10 Mar 1924 Groningen. Doctorandus '54 Rijks Univ. of Groningen, Neth. Groninger Instituut voor Toegepaste Psychologie en Psychotechniek, Groningen. Member: NIPP. Educational psychology, testing, consulting, guidance; social perception, projective techniques, achievement tests. M

KEUSKAMP, Drs. Edze. Sweelinckstr. 83, The Hague. b. 5 Aug 1919 The Hague. Doctorandus '56 Rijks Univ. of Leiden, Neth. SOC. PSYCH'T, Rijkspsychologische Dienst, Korte Beestenmarkt 4, The Hague. Research, applied psychology, testing; group process, police problems. M

KLEISEN, Drs. Gerard. Sonsbeekweg 20, Arnhem. b. 19 Sept 1925 Baarn. Doctorandus '53 Uni.v of Utrecht, Neth. PSYCHOLOGIST, Med. Paed. Inst, Burg. Weertsstr 30, Arnhem; PSYCHOLOGIST, priv. prac. Member: NIPP. Testing, consulting, psychotherapy; psychopeadagogy. M

KLINKHAMER-STEKETEE, Mrs. Dra. Henriette Tony. Nieuwe Herengracht 23/I, Amsterdam. b. 18 Apr 1919 Deventer. Doctoranda '45 Univ. of Leiden, Neth. CHILD PSYCH'T, Lab. for Appl. Psych, Vossiusstr. 54, Amsterdam. Member: NIPP. Educational and applied psychology, psychotherapy, clinical analysis, testing; play therapy, projective techniques for children, directive parental consulting. F

KNOOK, Drs. Ary L. C. Torenstr. 36, The Hague. b. 30 Sept 1911 Andel. Doctorandus '48 Free Univ. of Amsterdam, Neth. CHIEF PSYCH'T. and HEAD, Div. of Vocat. Couns, Ministry of Soc. Affairs and Pub. Hlth, The Hague. Member: AIPA, AIOP. Applied and personnel psychology, testing, consulting, job classification; vocational and educational guidance, development of semi-group tests, psychology and technology of occupations. M

KOCH, Miss Dr. Louise Willemina. Witte Singel 79, Leiden. b. 10 July 1926 Buitenzorg, Indonesia. PH.D '54 Univ. of Zurich, Switz. CLIN. PSYCH'T, Psychiat. Clin, Univ. of Leiden. Testing; projective techniques, psychology of traffic and motion. F

KOENE, Gerardus Bartholomeus M. L. Guido Gezellelaan 8, Geleen. b. 15 Aug 1926 Hoensbroek. L.PS '50 Univ. of Louvain, Bel. INDUS. PSYCH'T, Staatsmijnen, Heerlen. Industrial psychology; ergonomic research, group process. M

KOOIJ, Dra. Djoeke. Bankastraat 82, The Hague. b. 22 Dec 1925 Arnhem. Doctoranda '53 Univ. of Amsterdam, Neth. SCHOOL PSYCH'T, City Hlth. Serv, Surinamestr. 25, The Hague. Member: NIPP. Testing, educational psychology, psychotherapy; psychoanalytic therapy for children, pseudo-debilitas and feeblemindedness, progressive didactics. F

KOUWER, Prof. Dr. Benjamin Jan. Univ. of Groningen, Academieplein, Groningen. b. 26 July 1921 Groningen. Doctor '49 Univ. of Utrecht, Neth. PROF. of APPL. PSYCH, Univ. of Groningen; DIRECTOR, Groningen Inst. of Appl. Psych. and Psychotechniques. Member: NIPP, Int. Assn. of Psychotechnics. Research, teaching, consulting, personality judgment theory, validation of selection techniques, philosophical foundation of psychological theory. M

KROES, Miss Dra. Jacoba Christina. Minervalaan 83/III, Amsterdam Z. b. 21 May 1911

Rotterdam. Doctoranda '50 Univ. of Utrecht, Neth. PSYCHOLOGIST, Psych. Paedagogisch Inst, Van Eeghenstr. 179, Amsterdam Z. Member: NIPP. Testing, consulting, research; learning difficulties. F

KRUIJSEN, Drs. Bernard. Tiboel Siegenbeekstr. 1, Leiden. b. 25 Sept 1916 Oploo. Lic., Univ. of Louvain, Bel. SCI. COLLABORATOR, Rijkspsychologische Dienst, Korte Beestenmarkt 4, The Hague. Member: NIPP. Social and industrial psychology, guidance; measurement of attitudes toward work and working conditions, social organization. M

KUIPER, Miss Dra. Catherine M. Nieuwe Heerengracht 97, Amsterdam. b. 20 May 1926 Alkmaar. Doctoranda '54 Univ. of Amsterdam, Neth. CHILD PSYCH'T, Child Guid. Clin, Stichting Geestelijke Volksgezondheid, Constantijn Huygensstr. 2, Amsterdam. Member: NIPP. Testing, educational and professional selection, psychotherapy; projective techniques, achievement tests, attitude measurement. F

KUNZE, Dr. Johanna Maria Louise. Pettelaarseweg 14, Den Bosch. b. 5 July 1908 Rotterdam. Doctoranda '49 Univ. of Nijmegen, Neth; LittD '46 Univ. of Amsterdam, Neth. PSYCHOLOGIST, Psychiat. Inrichting Coudewater, Rosmalen. Member: NIPP. Teaching, clinical practice.F

KUYER, Drs. H. J. M. Van Nispenstr. 1, Nijmegen. b. 31 Oct 1922 Schalkwijk, Utrecht. Doctorandus '54 Univ. of Nijmegen, Neth. PSYCHOLOGIST, Res. Dept, Joint Inst. for Appl. Psych. Stikke Hezelstr. 1, Nijmegen; VOCAT. GUID. and PERS, SELECTN, Joint Inst. for Appl. Psych, Berg en Dalseweg 101, Nijmegen. Member: NIPP. Research, industrial psychology, testing; maladjustment in industry, attitude measurement, psychology of language. M

KUYPER, Drs. Siem. Dickenslaan 31, Utrecht. b. 26 Nov 1924 Wormerveer. Doctorandus '54 Univ. of Utrecht, Neth. CLIN. PSYCH'T, Dr. H. van der Hoeven Clin, Agnietenstr. 2, Utrecht; CLIN. PSYCH'T, Acad. of Physical Trng, Amsterdam. Clinical analysis, psychotherapy, teaching; phaenomenological theory of movement, psychology of sex, adolescent psychology. M

KUYPERS, Drs. H. M. M. C. Langevelderweg 16, Noordwijkerhout. b. 8 Oct 1926 Nijmegen. Doctorandus '54 Cath. Univ. of Nijmegen, Neth. CLIN. PSYCH'T, Psychiat. Inst. St. Bavo, Langevelderweg 27, Noordwijkerhout. Member: NIPP, Clin. Psych. Assn. Consulting, clinical practice, testing; projective techniques, intelligence testing. M

LANGE, Drs. Jacobus Johannes Bonaventura

de. Izaak Evertslaan 70, Arnhem. b. 14 July 1922 Alkmaar. Doctorandus '55 Gem. Univ. of Amsterdam, Neth. FIRST ASST, Psych. Dept. A.K.U., Arnhem. Member: NIPP. Industrial psychology, testing, research; group discussion techniques, attitude measurement, psychosomatics, psychotherapy. M

LANGE, Mr. Drs. Michiel Johan de.Plaswijcklaan 31, Rotterdam. b. 3 Sept 1914 Scherpenzeel. Doctorandus '45 Univ. of Utrecht, Neth. CLIN. PSYCH'T, Psych. Lab, Ment. Hosp. Maasoord, Albrandsw. dijk 74a, Poortugaal. Member: NIPP, Neth. Rorschach Study Grp. Testing, clinical analysis, research, teaching; projective techniques, expression techniques, phenomenological psychology. M

LANGEVELD, Prof. Dr. Martinus Jan. Univ. of Utrecht. b. 30 Oct 1905 Haarlem. Doctor '34 Univ. of Amsterdam, Neth. PROF. and DIR, Inst. of Educ. Res. and Ther, Univ. of Utrecht; CO-EDITOR, Acta Psychologica, International Review of Education. Member: Neth. Psych. Assn. Research, educational psychology, teaching, genetic psychology, child guidance, projective techniques for children. M

LARSEN, Miss Dra. Paula F. C. M. Old Hickoryplein 82/B, Maastricht. b. 4 Mar 1916 Amsterdam. Lic. '49 Univ. of Louvain; Bel. TCHR. of PSYCH, Cath. Sch. Soc. Wrk, Gouverneur van Hövellstr. 2, Sittard. Member: NIPP, Psych. Sect. of Thijmgenootschap. Teaching, consulting, testing, student; projective techniques, counseling, psychological conditioning of religious life. F

LEENT, Drs. J. A. A. van. Bloklandenplein 3, The Hague. b. 24 Oct 1926 The Hague. Doctorandus '55 Univ. of Leiden, Neth. HEAD ASST, Psych. Inst, Univ. of Leiden, Rapenburg 32, Leiden. Teaching, testing, research; interaction and communication processes, social perception and prejudice, integration of sociological and psychological theory. M

LEERSCHOOL, Drs. Jan J. M. Moergestelseweg 46, Berkel-Enschot. b. 22 Sept 1920 Meerssen. Doctorandus '47 Univ. of Nijmegen, Neth. CLIN. PSYCH'T. and HEAD, Psych. Dept, St. Elisabeth Ziekenhuis, Jan v. Beverwijkstr. 2a, Tilburg. Member-NIPP, Clin. Psych. Assn, Psych. Sect. of Thijmgenootschap. Testing, consulting, psychotherapy; projective techniques, psychosomatic diseases, intra-personal conflicts. M

LENNEP, Prof. Jhr. Dr. David Jacob van. Inst. of Clin. and Indus. Psych, Trans 14, Utrecht. b. 28 Dec 1896 Flims, Switz. PH.D '48 Univ. of Utrecht, Neth. PROF. of PSYCH, Inst. of Clin. and Indus. Psych,

Univ. of Utrecht; DIRECTOR, Neth. Inst. of Indus. Psych, Utrecht; CO-EDITOR, *Tijdschrift voor de Psychologie*. Member: NIPP, APA, Neth. Indus. Psych. Socy. Research, teaching, consulting; projective tests research, traffic psychology, phenomenology, psychology of aging. M

LICHER, Drs. Henri Joseph. Koningin Emmalaan 14 Ermelo. b. 9 June 1929 Amsterdam. Doctorandus '53 Free Univ. of Amsterdam, Neth. CLIN. PSYCH'T, Valerius Clin, Valeriusplein 9, Amsterdam. Member: NIPP, Clin. Psych. Assn. Testing, teaching, clinical practice; clinical diagnostic tests, projective techniques, character and attitude analysis. M

LIENDEN, Dr. Herman Johan Hendrik van. Dolderseweg 158, Den Dolder. b. 11 Mar 1898 Rotterdam. MD '24 Univ. of Groningen, Neth. PSYCHIATRIST, Willem Arntsz Stichting, Agnietenstr. 2; PSYCH. and PSYCHIAT. ADVIS, Ct. of Justice, Rotterdam. Member: NIPP. Research, applied psychology, clinical practice, consulting; typology, social perception, criminology. M

LINSCHOTEN, Prof. Dr. Johannes. Stadhouderslaan 37, Utrecht. Psych. Lab, Wittevrouwenstr. 9, Utrecht. b. 21 Sept 1925 Utrecht. PH.D '56 Univ. of Utrecht, Neth. PROF. OF PSYCH. Psych. Lab. Rijksuniv; CONSULT. PSYCH'T, Cath. Natl. Inst. for Ment. Hlth, Wilhelminapark 26, Utrecht; ED. SECY, *Situation*. Member: NIPP, Psych. Sect. of Thijmgenootschap. Research, teaching, professional writing; theoretical foundations and methodology, visual perception, history of psychology. M

LITJENS, Drs. Gerard. Heuvel 2, Oosterhout b. 3 July 1927 Tilburg. Doctorandus '52 Univ. of Nijmegen, Neth. CHILD PSYCH'T, Medisch Opvoedkundig Bur, Sophiastr. 24, Breda. Member: NIPP. Guidance; psychology of the family. M

LOO, Dr. K. J. M. van de. St. Annastr. 163, Nijmegen. b. 4 June 1922 Dieren. Doctor '52 Univ. of Nijmegen, Neth. LECTOR of CLIN. PSYCH, Cath. Univ. of Nijmegen, Wilhelminasingel 13, Nijmegen; CLIN. PSYCH'T, St. Canisius Hosp, St. Annastr. 289, Nijmegen. Member: NIPP. Research, testing, clinical analysis, teaching; projective techniques, achievement tests, experimental research on drawing and psychosomatics. M

LOOS, Drs. Cornelis C. H. de. Maasoord Psychiat. Inst, Albrandwaardse dijk 118, Poortugaal Z-H. b. 11 June 1908 Arnhem. Doctorandus '49 Free Univ. of Amsterdam, Neth. CLIN. PASTOR, Maasoord, Psychiat. Inst; PSYCHOLOGIST, de Ganzensprong Inst, Rotterdam. Member: NIPP. Pastoral work, testing, guidance, applied psychology; projective techniques, group process, social

perception. M

LUNING PRAK, Dr. Jacob. Psych. Inst, Laan Copes van Cattenburch 8, The Hague. b. 20 Oct 1898 Ter Apel. PH.D '25 Univ. of Groningen, Neth. INDUS. PSYCH'T, Psych. Inst. Personnel selection, educational guidance, testing, research; technical and mathematical tests, learning process. M

LYSEN, Drs. Adriaan. Goeman Borgesiuslaan 12, Amstelveen. b. 1 May 1921 Breda. Candidaat '52 Univ. of Utrecht, Neth. PSYCHOLOGIST, K.L.M. Schiphol. Testing, psychotherapy, student; projective techniques, child psychology, counseling. M

LYSEN-KIST, Mrs. Dra. L. H. B., Goeman Borgesiuslaan 12, Amstelveen. b. 22 Feb 1916 The Hague. Doctoranda '55 Univ. of Amsterdam, Neth. CHILD PSYCH'T, Rachel Steyn Huis, Hoge Duin en Dalseweg, Bloemendaal; PSYCHOLOGIST, priv. prac. Member: NIPP. Testing, teaching, psychotherapy; counseling. F

MARTENS-WARTENA, Mrs. Dra. Jansje Gelske. Acacialaan 25 Rijswijk. b. 3 Feb 1928 Kattendijke. Doctoranda '53 Univ. of Amsterdam, Neth. PSYCHOLOGIST, Med. Psych. Inst, Scheveningseweg 3, The Hague. Member: NIPP. Testing, guidance, psychotherapy; projective techniques, play therapy. F

MENGES, Drs. L. J. Roodenburgerstraat 38, Leiden. b. 7 Jan 1926 Utrecht. Doctorandus '51 Free Univ. of Amsterdam, Neth. SECT. CHIEF PSYCH'T, Rijkspsychologische Dienst, Rijnsburgerweg 96, Leiden. Member: NIPP. Applied psychology, teaching, psychotherapy and clinical analysis; problems of youth, work adaptation, emigrability, religion. M

MEUSER BOURGOGNION, Miss Dra. Anneke Vismarkt 8, Utrecht. b. 13 Feb 1927 Nijmegen. Doctoranda '53 Univ. of Utrecht Neth. CLIN, PSYCH'T, Dr. H. van der Hoeven Clin, Agnietenstr. 2, Utrecht. Member: NIPP. Clinical analysis and testing, group psychotherapy, research; projective techniques, structural character change due to psychotherapy. F

MINNEMA, Drs. Jan. Christelijk Bur. voor Toegepaste Psych, H.W. Mesdagplein 12, Groningen. b. 25 Feb 1925 Rotterdam. Doctorandus '52 Free Univ. of Amsterdam, Neth. DIRECTOR, Christelijk Bur. voor Toegepaste Psych. Member: NIPP. Applied psychology, consulting, testing; achievement tests, projective techniques, group process. M

MOLENAARS, Drs. Frederik M. Th. A. Le Sage ten Broeklaan 23, Eindhoven. b. 4 Nov 1924 Breda. Doctorandus '56 Cath. Univ. of Nijmegen, Neth. STAFF TCHR, Sch. for Soc. Work, Stichting R.K. Scholen v. Maatschappelijk Werk, Le

Sage ten Broeklaan 15, Broeklaan, Eindhoven. Member: NIPP. Teaching, applied and educational psychology, testing; prejudice, social perception, attitude measurement, mental health. M

MOLL, Miss Dra. Adèle W. E. Bergweg 10, Doetinchem. b. 9 May 1902 Arnhem. Doctoranda '41 Univ. of Utrecht, Neth. EDUC. and PSYCH. COUNS, City of Doetinchem; GUID. COUNS, Arnhemse Stichting voor Psych. en Beroepskunde, Stationsplein, Arnhem. Member: NIPP, Int. Assn. of Psychotechnics. Teaching, educational and personnel psychology, consulting; educational guidance, traffic psychology. F

MONTESSORI, Drs. Mario Montesano. Prins Hendriklaan 2B, Amsterdam-Z. b. 22 Apr 1921, Barcelona, Spain. Doctorandus '49 Free Univ. of Amsterdam, Neth. PSYCHOANALYST, priv. prac; CHILD THER, Child Guid. Clin. Prinsengracht 717, Amsterdam C; CLIN. PSYCH'T, Psychoanal. Inst, J.W. Brouwersplein 21, Amsterdam Z. Member: NIPP, Neth. Psych. Assn, Clin. Psych. Assn, Neth. Psychoanal. Socy. Psychotherapy, clinical practice, teaching; psychoanalysis, projective techniques, educational psychology. M

MUIJEN, Drs. Abram Reinier Willem. P. de Hooghstr. 42/III, Amsterdam. b. 7 Sept 1921 Heemskerk. Doctorandus, Univ. of Amsterdam, Neth. PSYCH. ASST, Inst. for Soc. and Indus. Psych, Univ. of Amsterdam, Keizersgracht 611-613, Amsterdam. Member: NIPP. Applied and industrial psychology, testing, teaching; projective techniques, achievement tests, perception theory. M

MULDER, Drs. Maurits. Kanaalweg 118, Leiden. b. 29 Sept 1922 Gorinchem. Doctorandus '51 Univ. of Amsterdam, Neth. SCI. COLLABORATOR in SOC. PSYCH, Neth. Inst. of Preven. Med. Member: NIPP. Research, teaching; group dynamics, behavior theories, field study. M

MULDER, Drs. R. A. C. Postweg 37, Achterveld. b. 17 May 1915 Groningen. Doctorandus '45 Free Univ. of Amsterdam, Neth. DIRECTOR, Rudolph Stichting, Postweg, Achterveld. Member: NIPP. Educational psychology, testing; orthopedagogy, attitude measurement. M

MUNNICHS, Drs. Joep M.A. Marialaan 113, Nijmegen. b. 20 May 1927 Roermond. Doctorandus '55 Keizer Karel Univ, Neth. PSYCHOLOGIST, Joint Inst. for Appl. Psych, Berg en Dalseweg 101, Nijmegen; EDITOR, *Gawein.* Member: NIPP. Research, student, professional writing; teaching, developmental psychology, psychology of old age.M

NIEUKERKE, Drs. Karel Herman Paul. New Zealand Management Consultants, 54 Hillside Rd, Auckland SE7, N.Z. b. 14 Aug 1914 The Hague. PH.D '49 Univ. of Utrecht, Neth. MANAGING DIR, N.Z. Management Consult. Member: NIPP, BPS. Industrial psychology, teaching, research; industrial relations, projective techniques, psychology of mathematics. M

NOORDEN, Drs. Henri van. Kerkpad NW 1, Venray. b. 10 May 1920 's Hertogenbosch. Doctorandus '53 Cath. Univ. of Nijmegen, Neth. CLIN. PSYCH'T, Ment. Hosp. St. Anna, St. Annalaan 5, Venray. Member: NIPP, Clin. Psych. Assn, Psych. Sect. of Thijmgenootschap. Testing, clinical analysis, consulting, teaching; projective techniques, intelligence and attitude measurement, psychomotor functions. M

NOORDZIJ, Drs. Yacobus Christinus. Brederoodseweg 56, Santpoort. b. 8 June 1920 Rotterdam. MD '48 Univ. of Amsterdam, Neth. PSYCHIATRIST and NEUROLOGIST, Provinciaal Ziekenhuis, Santpoort; STAFF MEMBER, Psychother. Inst, Amsterdam. Clinical practice, psychotherapy, applied psychology. M

NIJHUIS-TERMOS, Mrs. Dra. Christina Wilhelmina. Mariniersweg 37D, Rotterdam. b. 13 Jan 1924 Hilversum. Doctoranda '55 Univ. of Amsterdam, Neth. PSYCHOLOGIST, Munic. Med. Hlth. Serv, Baan 170, Rotterdam. Member: NIPP. Testing, applied psychology, psychotherapy; group dynamics, psychoanalysis, projective techniques. F

OUDEMANS-VAN DELDEN Mrs. Dra. Margaretha. Laantje van Van Iperen 9, Leerdam. b. 26 Oct 1927 Enschede. Doctoranda '53 Univ. of Amsterdam, Neth. CHILD PSYCH'T, Pro Juventute, Voorstr. 106, Dordrecht. Member: NIPP. Testing, applied psychology, guidance; projective techniques, child psychotherapy. F

OUDSHOORN, Drs. Johannes C. Parkweg 312, Voorburg Z.H. b. 10 May 1918 The Hague. Doctorandus '53 Univ. of Leiden, Neth. CONSULT. PSYCH'T, priv. prac, Groothandelsgebouw B.7, Rotterdam. Member: NIPP. Industrial and personnel psychology, research, testing; personality theory, intelligence. M

OUWELEEN, Prof. Hendrik Willem. Joh. Verhulststr. 153, Amsterdam. b. 15 June 1914 Amsterdam. Doctorandus '40 Gem. Univ. of Amsterdam, Neth. HEAD PSYCH. SERV, Post Tel. and Telegraph Serv., Zeestr. 5, The Hague; PROF. in INDUS. PSYCH, Ned. Economische Hoogeschool, Rotterdam. Member: NIPP, Neth. Indus. Psych. Socy, Int. Assn. of Psychotechnics. Industrial psychology, teaching, testing; industrial tensions, relation between the psychologist and the organization specialist, personnel techniques. M

OUWELEEN-SOPPE, Mrs. Dra. Margaretha Geertrude Elisabeth. Joh. Verhulststr. 153, Amsterdam. b. 20 Mar 1910 Meppel. Doctoranda '48 Univ. of Amsterdam, Neth. PSYCHOTHERAPIST, priv. prac. Member: NIPP, Neth. Psychoanal. Socy, Int. Psychoanal. Assn. Psychoanalysis, testing, clinical analysis. F

PARREREN, Dr. Carel Frederik van. Rivierenlaan 229II, Amsterdam Z. b. 17 Jan 1920 Amsterdam. Doctor '51 Univ. of Amsterdam, Neth. SCI. ASST, Psych. Lab, Univ. of Amsterdam, Keizersgracht 611-13, Amsterdam; PSYCH. TCHR, Pedagogical Seminar, Utrecht; CO-EDITOR, *Acta Psychologica*. Member: NIPP, Neth. Psych. Assn. Teaching research, editorial; psychology of learning and thinking. M

PELT-GOOSKENS, Mrs. Dra. L. M. J. van. Walramstr. 33, Sittard. b. 25 Mar 1921 Eindhoven. Doctoranda. PSYCHOLOGIST, priv. prac. Member: NIPP. Consulting, testing, applied psychology; projective techniques. F

PENDERS, Drs. Huub. J. Fahrenheitstr. 65, Amersfoort. b. 11 Oct 1926 Voerendaal. Doctorandus '52 Rijks Univ. of Utrecht, Neth. DIR. and PSYCH'T, Roman Cath. Inst. for Ment. Hlth, Muurhuizen 217, Amersfoort. Member: NIPP. Child guidance, testing, applied psychology, psychotherapy. M

PERELAER-PARFUMEUR, Mrs. Dra. Henrietta. Geerdinksweg 122, Hengelo. b. 8 Nov 1908 Sneek. Doctoranda '53 Univ. of Amsterdam, Neth. PSYCHOLOGIST, Child Guid. Clin, Medisch Opvoedkundig Bur, Almelo en Enschede, Woltersweg 1, Hengelo STAFF MEMBER, Sch. of Soc. Work, Grundellaan 17, Hengelo. Member: NIPP. Testing, teaching, psychotherapy; social perception, projective techniques, group process. F

PERK, Drs. Albertus. Rembrandtweg 357, Amstelveen. b. 12 July 1924 Baarn. Doctorandus '55 Univ. of Amsterdam, Neth. PSYCHOLOGIST, Stichting voor Geestelijke Volksgezondheid, Oude Gracht 182, Alkmaar. Member: NIPP. Applied and educational psychology, testing; achievement tests, projective tests, projective techniques. M

PERQUIN-GERRIS, Mrs. Dra. Jeanne Marie. Schubertstraat 40, Amsterdam. b. 9 Mar 1919 'sHertogenbosch. Doctoranda '46 Univ. of Utrecht, Neth. PSYCHOLOGIST, Child Guid. Clin, 2de Constantyn Huygensstr, Amsterdam. Testing, psychotherapy, child guidance. F

PESSERS, Drs. Aug. Franc. Corn. Spoorlaan 80, Tilburg. b. 26 July 1921 Tilburg. Lic. '49 Univ. of Louvain, Bel. PSYCHOLOGIST, priv. prac. Member: NIPP. Applied psychology, testing, consulting; projective techniques, achievement tests, attitude measurement. M

PEYPE, Dr. Willem Frederik van. Van Lyndenlaan 14, Soestduinen. b. 8 Feb 1907 Den Helder. Doctor '38 Univ. of Leiden, Neth. PSYCHOLOGIST, Nederlandse Stichting voor Psychotechniek, Wittevrouwenkade 6, Utrecht. Member: NIPP. Testing, research, applied psychology. M

PLOMP, Drs. Pieter Jan. Linnaeusparkweg 57, Amsterdam. b. 29 June 1919 Brummen. Doctorandus '52 Univ. of Amsterdam, Neth. PSYCHOLOGIST, House of Detention and Prison of Haarlem, Ministry of Justice, The Hague; CONSULT. PSYCH'T, priv. prac. Member: NIPP, Clin. Psych. Assn. Testing, psychotherapy, consulting; projective techniques, attitude measurement, social perception. M

RAALTE, Drs. Carol R. van. Michel Angelostr. 52III, Amsterdam Z. b. 1 Nov 1921 The Hague. Doctorandus '51 Free Univ. of Amsterdam, Neth. INDUS. PSYCH'T, Rijks Psychologische Dienst, Rijnsburgerweg 96, Leiden. Member: NIPP, Neth. Indus. Psych. Socy. Industrial psychology testing, teaching, professional writing; group process, sexology, interviewing techniques. M

RAEVEN, Drs. Fredericus Mathieu. 56 Soerense Weg, Apeldoorn. b. 31 May 1910 Roermond. Doctorandus '46 Free Univ. Amsterdam, Neth. CLIN. PSYCH'T, St. St. Joseph Stichting, Deventerstr, Apeldoorn. Member: NIPP, Psych. Sect. of Thijmgenootschap, Clin. Psych. Assn. Testing, clinical analysis, research, consulting, educational psychology; projective techniques. M

RATINGEN, Drs. J. R. M. van. Waldeck Pyrmontkade 6, Utrecht. b. 17 Aug 1924 Susteren. Doctorandus '49 Univ. of Utrecht, Neth. CHIEF, Psych. Dept, Psychiat. Observation Clin, Ministry of Justice, Gansstr. 164, Utrecht; SR. PSYCH'T, Dr. H. van der Hoeven Clin. Member: NIPP, Psych. Sect. of Thijmgenootschap. Testing, clinical analysis, administration, psychotherapy; forensic psychology, projective techniques, criminal psychology. M

RIEM-VIS, Drs. Adriaan Pieter. Joh. Verhulststraat 151 hs, Amsterdam. b. 14 Aug 1910 The Hague. Doctorandus '49 Free Univ. of Amsterdam, Neth. SCI. COLLABORATOR, Laboratorium voor Toegepaste Psychologie, Vossiusstr. 54-55, Amsterdam. Member: NIPP. Personnel psychology, testing, consulting; achievement tests, social perception, group process. M

ROEM, Dr. Hans Andreas Cornelius. Mauvestr. 5, The Hague. b. 11 May 1918 Zalt-Bommel. PH.D '52 Free Univ. of Amsterdam, Neth. Member: NIPP, Neth. Indus. Psych. Socy, Clin. Psych. Assn. Testing, clinical analysis, applied psychology; projective techniques, phenomenological and anthropological psychology, characterology. M

RÜMKE, Prof. Dr. H. C. Mariahoek 4, Utrecht. b. 16 Jan 1893 Leiden. Prof, Univ. of Utrecht, Neth. DIRECTOR Psychiat. Clin, Nic. Beetsstr. 24, Utrecht; PROF. of PSYCHIATRY, Rijks Univ. Member: NIPP, Neth. Assn. for Psychiat. and Neur. Teaching, research, professional writing; psychiatry. M

RUTTEN, Prof. Dr. F. J. Th. Pater Brugmanstraat 1, Nijmegen. Psych. Lab, Univ. of Nijmegen, Berg en Dalseweg 105, Nijmegen. b. 15 Sept 1899 Schinnen. Doctor '30 Univ. of Utrecht, Neth. DIRECTOR, Psych. Lab, Univ. of Nijmegen. PROF. of PSYCH. Member: Roman Cath. Assn. for Ment. Hlth. NIPP. Research, teaching, industrial psychology; human relations, social perception, group process, attitude measurement. M

RUTTEN, Drs. Josephus Wilhelmus. Mariastraat 19, Maastricht. b. 25 Nov 1921 Maastricht. Doctorandus '48 Univ. of Nijmegen, Neth. CLIN. PSYCH'T, Psychiat. Inst, Abtstr. 6, Maastricht; CLIN. PSYCH'T, Town Hosp, St. Annadal, Maastricht. Member: NIPP. Applied and educational psychology, testing, clinical analysis, consulting; lateral dominance of psychomotoric. M

RUIJSCH VAN DUGTEREN, Drs. Jan Hendrik. Lyceumlaan 8, Zeist. b. 22 June 1903 Ritthem. Doctorandus '30 Rijks Univ. of Utrecht, Neth. MANAGER, Nederlands Inst. voor Personeelsleiding, Hoofdstr. 57, Driebergen. Member: NIPP, Neth. Psych. Assn, Neth. Indus. Psych. Socy. Industrial psychology, research, teaching; group process, attitude measurement, supervisory development. M

RIJK VAN OMMEREN, Mrs. Dra. Marie Jacqueline. J. W. Brouwersstr. 18, Amsterdam Z. b. 28 Jan 1916 Paramaribo, Suriname. Doctoranda '47 Univ. of Amsterdam, Neth. PSYCHOANALYST, priv. prac. Member: NIPP, Neth. Psychoanal. Socy. Psychotherapy, consulting; child guidance, projective techniques, psychoanalysis. F

SANDERS, Dr. Cornelis. Louise de Colignylaan 14, Oegstgeest. b. 5 Jan 1921 Rijswijk. Doctor '53 Rijks Univ. of Leiden, Neth. DIRECTOR, Rijks Psychologische Dienst, Rijnsburgerweg 96, Leiden. Member: NIPP. Testing, research, industrial psychology; mental tests, projective techniques. M

SCHAAP, Drs. Hendrik Bernard. Pernéstraat 46, Castricum. b. 15 Oct 1924 Groningen.

CLIN. PSYCH'T, Prov. Hosp. Duin en bosch. Member: NIPP, Clin. Psych. Assn. Testing, clinical analysis, research; clinical psychology, psychoanalysis. M

SCHOUTEN, Dr. Jan. Nassau Dillenburgstraat 18. 's Gravenhage. b. 29 Oct 1893 Capelle aan de IJssel. Doctor '35 Univ. of Utrecht, Neth. PSYCHOLOGIST, priv. prac. Member: NIPP. Applied psychology, psychotherapy; psychology of instincts, emotions and will. M

SCHRAVENDIJK-LAMBERT, Mrs. Dra. Else van. Randweg 107, Bussum. b. 1 Apr 1925 Rotterdam. Doctoranda '52 Univ. of Amsterdam, Neth. CHILD PSYCH'T, priv. prac. Member: NIPP. Applied and educational psychology, testing, consulting; backward children, achievement tests, projective techniques. F

SCHUITEMAKER, Drs. Cornelis. Nieuwstr. 5a, Eindhoven. b. 27 Feb 1924 Werwershoof. Lic. '49 Univ. of Louvain, Bel. PSYCHOLOGIST, priv. prac. Member: NIPP, Psych. Sect. of Thijmgenootschap. Educational psychology, vocational guidance, teaching, testing; educational testing, learning process, aptitude and achievement tests. M

SCHRIJER, Drs. H. J. Schuurmanstraat 39, Zwolle. b. 11 Mar 1921 Zwolle. Doctorandus '54 Univ. of Amsterdam, Neth. PSYCHOLOGIST, Child Guid. Inst, R:K. Medisch Opvoedkundig Bur, Burg. Jansenplein 8a, Hengelo; PSYCHOLOGIST, Inst. for Child. from Broken Homes. Educational psychology, diagnostic testing, psychotherapy, teaching; abnormal psychology, psychosomatics, child psychology. M

SETERS, Miss Dra. Jentine W. van. Hofbrouckerlaan 31, Oegstgeest. b. 22 June 1926 Rotterdam. Doctoranda '53 Univ. of Amsterdam, Neth. CONSULT. PSYCH'T, Study Home Bethanie, Korte Kade, Rotterdam. Member: NIPP. Testing, guidance, group and environmental therapy; projective and therapeutic techniques, philosophy and ethics of psychological practice. F

SILVA, Drs. Daniel Jo da. Raadgevend Bur, Prof. Ir. B. W. Berenschot, Room 49, Central Station Amsterdam. b. 23 Sept 1911 Amsterdam. Doctorandus '41 Univ. of Amsterdam, Neth. MANAGEMENT CONSULT, Raadgevend Bur. Prof. Ir. B. W. Berenschot; ED. BD, Baas boven Baas. Member: NIPP, Socy. of Management Consultants. Industrial psychology, research; vocational training, of operatives, job evaluation. M

SMEETS, Drs. Peter Ant. Hub. Mgr. Schrynenstr. 2, Heerlen. b. 6 July 1916 Kerkrade. Doctorandus '52 Univ. of Amsterdam, Neth. PSYCHOLOGIST, priv. prac. Member: NIPP. Educational psychology, testing,

consulting, guidance; school psychology. M
SMIT, Drs. Hein. Louis Couperusstraat 31,
Voorburg.   b. 1 Sept 1922 Semarang,
Indonesia.   Doctorandus '53 Univ. of
Leiden, Neth. HEAD of PSYCH, SECT, Bur.
of Pers. Management, Union of Neth.
Municipalities, Paleisstr. 5, The Hague.
Member: NIPP. Industrial and personnel
psychology, testing, research; group dy-
namics, Szondi test, financial rewards for
government personnel. M
SMITS, Drs. W. C. M. 25 Elzentlaan,Eind-
hoven. b. 9 Feb 1921 Nijmegen. Docto-
randus, Univ. of Nijmegen, Neth. PSY-
CHOLOGIST, Psychiat. Clin, Boekel; PSY-
CHOLOGIST, Hosp. St. Antonius, Helmond.
Member: NIPP. Clinical analysis, testing,
research, clinical practice; developmental
and abnormal psychology, color psy-
chology. M
SMULDERS, Drs. Frank J. H. Jeroen Bosch-
laan 163, Eindhoven. b. 22 Oct 1926 's
Hertogenbosch. Doctorandus '54 Rijks
Univ. of Groningen, Neth. STAFF PSYCH'T,
Child Guid. Clin, Medisch Opvoedkundig
Bur, Vestdijk 45A, Eindhoven. Member:
NIPP, Clin. Psych. Assn. Guidance, con-
sulting, teaching; philosophic aspects of
psychology, projective techniques, social
conflict. M
SNIJDERS, Prof. Dr. J. Th. de Savornin
Lohmanlaan 1, Groningen. b. 14 May 1910
Alkemade. PH.D '46 Univ. of Nijmegen,
Neth. PROF. and DIR, Psych. Inst, Univ.
of Groningen, Oude Boteringestr. 34,
Groningen; CO-EDITOR, *Acta Psychologica,
Nederlands Tijdschrift voor de Psychologie.*
Member: NIPP, APA, APSLF, AIPA, Neth.
Psych. Assn. Teaching, research; thought,
intelligence, psychology of the deaf. M
SNIJDERS-OOMEN Mrs. Dr. A. W. M.
de Savornin Lohmanlaan 1, Groningen.
b. 20 Dec 1916 Nijmegen. Doctor '43
Univ. of Nijmegen, Neth. PSYCHOLOGIST,
priv. prac; CONSULTANT, Cath. Children's
Home, Schiermonnikoog; CO-EDITOR, *Opvoeding.* Member: NIPP, APSLF, Neth.
Psych. Assn. Professional writing, educational psychology, testing, consulting;
non-verbal intelligence tests, religious
development and education, psychology
of the deaf. F
SPEK, Dr. Johannes van der. Van Alkemade-
laan 15, 's Gravenhage. b. 14 Oct 1886
Maasdam. MD, Rijks Univ. of Utrecht,
Neth. LECTOR, Neth. Econ. Coll, Rotterdam; PRIV. DOCENT, Rijks Univ. of Utrecht.
Member: NIPP, Neth. Assn. for Psychiat.
and Neur, Neth. Assn. for Psychother.
Psychotherapy, clinical practice, teaching,
applied psychology; pastoral psychology
and psychopathology. M
SPIRO, Drs. Marcel. Pastoor Bloemstr. 63,

Oss. b. 13 Sept 1924 Hilversum. Docto-
randus '54 Univ. of Amsterdam, Neth.
PSYCHOLOGIST, Soc. Dept, N.V. Konink-
lijke Zwanenberg-Organon, Gasstr. 5, Oss.
Member: NIPP. Industrial psychology,
counseling; testing; personnel management,
group process, projection. M
SPITZ, Drs. Johannes Christiaan. Psych.
Lab, Univ. of Amsterdam, Keizersgracht
611-613, Amsterdam C. b. 23 Mar 1919
Amsterdam. Doctorandus '51 Univ. of
Amsterdam, Neth. CHIEF ASST, Psych. Lab,
Univ. of Amsterdam; CHIEF ASST, Soc.
Pedagogical Inst, Univ. of Amsterdam,
Singel 451-453, Amsterdam C. Member:
NIPP. Teaching, consulting, research;
statistics, measurement theory, per-
ception. M
STAM, Drs. N. Wijttenbachstr. 41, Amster-
dam. b. 20 Oct 1923 Amsterdam. Docto-
randus '52 Univ. of Amsterdam, Neth.
PSYCHOLOGIST, Gemeentelijke Genees-
kundige en Gezondheidsdienst, Nieuwe
Achtergracht 100, Amsterdam. Member:
NIPP. Educational psychology, testing,
guidance; projective techniques, achievement and intelligence tests, group
process. M
STEFFEN, Drs. Cornelis. Bergselaan 302,
Rotterdam. b. 12 June 1924 Rotterdam.
Doctorandus '55 Univ. of Leiden, Neth.
PSYCH'T and SCI. WRKR, Rijks Psychologische Dienst, Rijnsburgerweg 96, Leiden.
Member: NIPP. Applied psychology, testing,
research; achievement tests, projective
techniques, traffic psychology, accident
proneness. M
**STEGEREN, Miss Dr. Willemina Frederika
van.** Olympiaplein 71/III, Amsterdam Z.
b. 11 Aug 1926 Almelo. PH.D '57 Free
Univ. of Amsterdam, Neth. CLIN. PSYCH'T,
Valerius Clin, Valeriusplein 9, Amsterdam;
PSYCHOLOGIST, Child Guid. Clin. Member:
NIPP, Clin. Psych. Assn. Testing, clinical
analysis, consulting, teaching; projective
techniques, group work, psychopathology.F
STOK, Drs. Th. L. de Lairessestraat 51,
Amsterdam. b. 20 Apr 1928 Amsterdam.
Doctorandus '55 Univ. of Amsterdam,
Neth. CO-WORKER, Inst. for Soc. and
Indus. Psych, Univ. of Amsterdam, Kei-
zersgracht 611–613, Amsterdam. Member:
NIPP. Educational and industrial psy-
chology, teaching, reasearch; testing,
personnel selection, social psychological
problems in industry. M
STOKVIS, Dr. Berthold. 1e Weteringplant-
soen 2, Amsterdam. b. 24 Mar 1906 Am-
sterdam. Doctor '37 Univ. of Leiden,
Neth. CHIEF, Psychosomatic Cen, Psychiat.
Clin, Univ. of Leiden; PSYCHIATRIST,
Jelgersma Clin, Oegstgeest-Leiden; DOCENT
in MED. PSYCH, Univ. of Leiden; EDITOR,

Acta Psychotherapeutica, Psychosomatica et Orthopaedagogica. Member: NIPP, Neth. Assn. for Psychother, Neth. Psychoanal. Socy, Neth. Assn. of Psychiat. and Neur. Clinical practice, teaching, research, editorial; physio-psychology, medical psychology, psychosomatics, testing. M

STOLKER, Drs. P. J. Zoeterwoudsesingel 4, Leiden. b. 21 Mar 1923 Enschede. Doctorandus '52 Univ. of Leiden, Neth. PSYCHOLOGIST, priv. prac. Member: NIPP. Applied and educational psychology, consulting, teaching; child psychology, professional attitude testing. M

STRIEN, Drs. Pieter J. van. Florakade 286, Groningen. b. 15 Oct 1928 Veere. Doctorandus '53 Univ. of Groningen, Neth. PSYCHOLOGIST, Groningen Inst. of Appl. Psych, H. W. Mesdagplein 6, Groningen; ASST. TCHR, Univ. of Groningen. Member: NIPP, Neth. Indus. Psych. Socy. Industrial psychology, personnel selection, teaching, research; personality, human relations in industry. M

THOENES, Miss Dra. Greta Marie. Laan van Leeuwensteyn 57, Voorburg. b. 17 Aug 1920 Djakarta, Indonesia. Doctoranda '49 Univ. of Utrecht, Neth. PSYCHOLOGIST, priv. prac. Member: NIPP. Testing, consulting, psychotherapy; projective techniques, achievement tests, attitude measurement. F

TIMMERS, Drs. Jan Johannes. De Kempenaerstr. 8, Delft. b. 22 Feb 1914 Rijnsburg. Doctorandus '49 Free Univ. of Amsterdam, Neth. INDUS. PSYCH'T, N.V. Ned. Kabelfabriek, Delft. Member: NIPP. Industrial psychology, testing, consulting; projective techniques, achievement tests, social perception. M

UBBINK, Dr. Gerard. v. Lawick v. Pabststr. 3, Arnhem. b. 20 Apr 1900 Doesburg. Doctorandus '46 Free Univ. of Amsterdam, Neth. PSYCHOLOGIST, Gelders Psych. Inst; ADVISER, Gelder Christelijke Stichting voor School- en Beroeps-keuze-voorlichting. Member: NIPP. Industrial psychology, vocational guidance; achievement and projective tests. M

UYTERLINDE, Drs. Bartholomeus. Corn. Krusemanstraat 66/III, Amsterdam. b. 8 Dec 1929 Rotterdam. Doctorandus '53 Free Univ. of Amsterdam, Neth. CLIN. PSYCH'T, Valerius Clin, Valeriusplein, Amsterdam. Member: NIPP. Testing, research, guidance; projective techniques, achievement tests, fingerpainting as a therapeutic technique, psychotherapy. M

VERMEER, Mrs. Dr. Edith A. A. Prins Hendriklaan 64 bis, Utrecht. b. 17 May 1908 Utrecht. Doctor '55 Univ. of Utrecht, Neth. SCI. OFF, Inst. for Educ, Univ. of Utrecht, Trans 14, Utrecht. Teaching,

consulting, guidance, psychotherapy; play therapy. F

VERSCHUREN, Drs. Wilhelmus H. Prof. van Kanstr. 27, Maastricht. b. 6 Nov 1923 Haps. Doctorandus '51 Univ. of Nijmegen, Neth. DIRECTOR, Medisch Opvoedkundig Bur, Frans v.d. Laarplein 1, Maastricht. Member: NIPP. Educational psychology, psychotherapy, testing. M

VERSTER, Drs. Justus. Grote Leliestraat 45, Groningen. b. 9 Sept 1924 Heumen. Doctorandus '52 Univ. of Groningen, Neth. HEAD ASST, Psych. Inst. Heijmans, Univ. of Groningen, Oude Boteringestr, Groningen. Student, research, teaching. M

VERSTRAELEN, Drs. Maria Adrien Michel Ghislain. Mgr. Nolensplein 10, Venray. b. 12 Sept 1923 Heel. Lic. '50 Univ. of Louvain, Belg. CLIN. PSYCH'T, Psychiatrische Inrichting, St. Servatius, Stationsweg, Venray. Member: NIPP, Clin. Psych. Assn. Clinical analysis and practice, group psychotherapy, research; projective techniques, parapsychology, attitudes, group process. M

VLES, Dr. S. J. Ave. Concordia 52/A, Rotterdam. b. 6 May 1911 Zalt-Bommel. D.SC '39 Univ. of Utrecht, Neth. SOC. PSYCH'T, Dept. of Soc. Psychiat, Munic. Hlth. Serv, Baan 170, Rotterdam. Member: NIPP, Neth. Psych. Assn, Neth. Psychoanal. Socy. Psychotherapy, consulting, applied psychology, psychoanalysis, group process, projective techniques. M

VLIEGENTHART, W. E. Oudenoord 77 bis A, Utrecht. b. 29 Dec 1904 Zaandam. Doctorandus '51 Univ. of Utrecht, Neth. SCI. ASST, Inst. of Educ, Rijks Univ. of Utrecht, Trans 14, Utrecht; PSYCH. ADVIS, Inst. for the Deaf, Rotterdam. Educational psychology, clinical practice, guidance, orthopedagogy; learning difficulties, problems of the deaf and hard of hearing, educational theory. M

VOLLEBERGH, Drs. Joseph J. A. Prof. De Langen Wendelstr. 13, Nijmegen. b. 10 Oct 1925 Venray. Doctorandus '50 Univ. of Nijmegen, Neth. DIRECTOR, Inst. for Appl. Psych, Bergendalseweg 101, Nijmegen; ASSISTANT, Univ. of Nijmegen. Member: NIPP, Psych. Sect. of Thijmgenootschap. Testing, applied psychology, consulting; attitudes and social perception, education. M

VRIES, Drs. Willem Hubert Maria de. Park Welgelegen 11, Driebergen. b. 1 Feb 1925 Cuyk. Doctorandus '54 Cath. Univ. of Nijmegen, Neth. PSYCHOLOGIST, Rijks Observatiehuis voor Meisjes, Verlengde Slotlaan 115, Zeist; PSYCHOLOGIST, Kamp Overberg, Amerongen. Member: NIPP. Testing and clinical analysis, guidance; projective techniques, group process, attitude measurement. M

VUNDERINK, Drs. J. C. v. Breestr. 16, Amsterdam. b. 31 Jan 1904 Hoogeveen. Doctorandus '48 Free Univ. of Amsterdam, Neth. CHIEF ASST, Lab. for Appl. Psych, Vossiusstr. 54, Amsterdam. Member: NIPP. Testing, educational psychology, consulting, guidance; social psychology, adjustment problems. M

VUYK, Miss Dr. Rita. Reyer Anslostr. 29, Amsterdam W. b. 22 Jan 1913 London, Eng. Doctor '45 Univ. of Amsterdam, Neth. LECTOR, Univ. of Amsterdam. Member: NIPP, ICWP. Teaching, testing, guidance; projective techniques, student problems. F

WASSER, Drs. J. M. J. M. Jan van Beverwijckstr. 9, Tilburg. b. 15 Sept 1925 Deurne. Doctorandus '52 Univ. of Nijmegen, Neth. VOCAT. COUNS. and INDUS. PSYCH'T, Gemeenschappelijk Inst. voor Toegepaste Psych, Wilhelminapark 25, Tilburg; PSYCHOLOGIST, Huize De Goede Herder, Tilburg. Member: NIPP, Neth. Indus. Psych. Socy. Industrial psychology, guidance, research. M

WEMELSFELDER-NOLST TRENITÉ, Mrs. Dra. Gerardina. Laan van Minsweerd 38, Utrecht. b. 23 June 1917 Buitenzorg, Indonesia. Member: NIPP. Industrial psychology, testing; industrial safety, prognosis of individual development. F

WETSELAAR, Drs. Anton Marius. Nieuwegracht 24 bis, Utrecht. b. 7 Feb 1909 Utrecht. Doctorandus '42 Univ. of Utrecht, Neth. PSYCHOLOGIST, Psych. Sect, Munic. Med. Serv, Nieuwe Achtergracht 100, Amsterdam; CONSULT. PSYCH'T, priv. prac. Member: NIPP. Personnel psychology, testing, consulting, guidance; projective techniques, parapsychology, analytical and educational psychology. M

WIDDERSHOVEN-PINCKAERS, Mrs. Dra. Colette, A. A. V. M. J. Burchtstr. 120, Nijmegen. b. 24 Oct 1929 Maastricht. Doctoranda '53 Cath. Univ. of Nijmegen, Neth. Member: NIPP, Clin. Psych. Assn, Psych. Sect. of Thijmgenootschap. Research, testing, student; projective techniques, achievement tests, character analysis, personality. F

WIEGERSMA, Drs. Sies. Zoeter Woudsesingel 90, Leiden. b. 29 May 1919 Zevenaar. Doctorandus '46 Univ. of Groningen, Neth. RES. WRKR, Neth. Inst. for Preven. Med, Wassenaarseweg 56, Leiden. Member: NIPP. Research in educational psychology, vocational guidance; counseling methods, vocational aptitude, test development and validation. M

WILDERVANCK DE BLÉCOURT, Drs. Jacob Harmen. Observation Home Aaborg, van Heemskerckstr. 52, Groningen. b. 7 Apr 1919 Zutphen. Doctorandus '49

Univ. of Amsterdam, Neth. DIRECTOR, Aaborg Observation Home for Delinquent Boys; TEACHER, Sch. for Soc. Wrkrs, Groningen. Member: NIPP. Administration, guidance, teaching; diagnosis and therapy of maladjusted children, orthopedagogy. M

WILLEMS, Drs. Paul John. Merellaan 7, Valkenswaard. b. 26 Dec 1924 Kerkrade. Doctorandus '52 Cath. Univ. of Nijmegen, Neth. INDUS. PSYCH'T, Philips Elec. Co, Eindhoven. Member: NIPP. Industrial psychology, research, consulting; achievement testing, psychosomatics in industry, measurement techniques. M

WILLEMS, Dr. Willem J. P. Pijnsweg 22, Heerlen. b. 20 Oct 1909 Ruremonde. Doctor '35 Univ. of Louvain, Belg. CHIEF, Pers. Sect, Staatsmijnen in Limburg, Heerlen. Member: NIPP, APSLF, Int. Assn. of Psychotechnics. Applied and industrial psychology, research, consulting. M

WINSEMIUS, Dr. Willem. Conradstr. 8, Leiden. b. 30 Jan 1917 Meppel. MD '51 Univ. of Leiden, Neth. CHIEF RES. WRKR, Neth. Inst. of Preven. Med, Wassenaarseweg 56, Leiden; HON. LECT. in APPL. PSYCH, Fac. of Med, Univ. of Leiden. Member: NIPP. Research, industrial psychology, teaching; industrial accidents, general theory and methodology, physiological psychology. M

WIT, Drs. Gerardus Antonius de. Canisiussingel 2, Nijmegen. b. 20 Jan 1917 Helmond. Doctorandus, Univ. of Nijmegen, Neth. EDUC. PSYCH'T, Wit-Gele Kruis, Gasthuisstr. 35, Tilburg. Member: NIPP. Educational and clinical psychology, guidance, research; personality tests for children, social perception, psychology of public relations. M

WIT, Drs. Jan de. Waalstraat 83/1, Amsterdam. b. 20 Apr 1928 Voorburg. Doctorandus '53 Free Univ. of Amsterdam, Neth. PSYCHOLOGIST, Found. for Ment. Hlth, Oudegracht 182, Alkmaar; LECTURER, Educ. Semin. Member: NIPP. Applied psychology, teaching, psychotherapy; educational psychology, vocational guidance. M

WOLFF, Drs. Charles J. de. Frederik Hendriklaan 66, Voorschoten. b. 22 Jan 1930 Amsterdam. Doctorandus '53 Free Univ. of Amsterdam, Neth. PERS. ADVIS, Marine Opkomst Centrum, Voorschoten. Member: NIPP, Neth. Indus. Psych. Socy. Personnel psychology, research, testing; aptitude and achievement tests, attitude measurement, statistics. M

WOUDE, Drs. Gerben van der. Breestr. 85, Leiden. b. 17 June 1926 Groningen. Doctorandus '55 Stedelijke Univ. of Amsterdam, Neth. PSYCHOLOGIST, Rijks Psych. Dienst, Rijnsburgerweg 96, Leiden. Member: NIPP. Personnel psychology, diagnostic testing, research; methodological statistical and validation problems, political psychology, aptitude and achievement tests. **M**

WIJLEN, Drs. Hendrik Andries van. Luciënsteeg 25a, Amsterdam C. b. 22 May 1915 The Hague. Doctorandus '52 Free Univ. of Amsterdam, Neth. SUPERINTENDENT, Amsterdam Munic. Orphanage, Burgerweeshuis en Inrichting voor Stadsbestedelingen; TEACHER, Fed. of Organiz. for the Care of Alcoholics. Member: NIPP. Educational psychology, guidance, teaching; projective techniques, counseling, institutional psychology. **M**

WIJNBERGEN, Dr. Jaap. Schiedamsedijk 7D, Rotterdam. b. 10 June 1922 's Gravenhage. Doctor '52 Univ. of Zurich, Switz. YOUTH PSYCH'T, Gemeentelijke Geneeskundige en Gezondheidsdienst, Baan 170, Rotterdam. Member: NIPP. Testing, guidance, applied psychology; child and youth psychology, psychoanalytic theory. **M**

WIJNGAARDEN, Prof. Dr. Hendrik R. Michel Angelostr. 35 bov, Amsterdam. b. 13 Nov 1912 Spijk. PH.D '50 Free Univ. of Amsterdam, Neth. MANAGING DIR, Lab. for Appl. Psych, Vossiusstr. 54-55, Amsterdam; PROFESSOR, Free Univ. of Amsterdam; TEACHER, Univ. of Leiden. Member: NIPP. Psychotherapy and consulting, applied psychology, testing, teaching; counseling, industrial psychology. **M**

ZEE, Drs. Johan H. van der. Wegedoornlaan 8, Eindhoven. b. 20 July 1918 Leeuwarden.

Doctorandus '49 Univ. of Nijmegen, Neth. CONSULT. PSYCH'T, priv. prac. Member: NIPP. Applied psychology, testing, consulting; group process, projective techniques, attitude measurement. **M**

ZEEUW, Drs. Joh. de. Nachtegaallaan 10, Leiden. b. 1 Sept 1921 Zutphen. Doctorandus '56 Univ. of Leiden, Neth. CONSULT. PSYCH'T, Rijks Psych. Dienst, Rijnsburgerweg 96, Leiden. Member: NIPP, Neth. Rorschach Grp. Educational and industrial psychology, child psychotherapy, research; projective techniques. **M**

ZELDENRUST, Drs. David. Mariniersweg 51E, Rotterdam. b. 27 Nov 1920 Amsterdam. Doctorandus '48 Univ. of Amsterdam. Neth. LEADER, Psych. Lab, Munic. Med. Dept, G.G. en G.D. Baan 170, Rotterdam. Member: NIPP. Applied psychology, testing, guidance; projective techniques, psychotherapy, group process. **M**

ZELDENRUST-NOORDANUS, Mrs. Dr. Mary. Mariniersweg 51E, Rotterdam. b. 8 Apr 1928 The Hague. Doctor '56 Univ of Amsterdam, Neth. PSYCHOLOGIST, priv. prac. Member: NIPP. Testing, psychotherapy, teaching; projective techniques, social psychology. **F**

ZWETSLOOT, Drs. Joannes Th. P. C. Industriesingel 29, Oss. b. 18 Oct 1925 Baarn. Doctorandus '51 Cath. Univ. of Nijmegen, Neth. PSYCHOLOGIST, Prov. Nrd. Brabantse Bond Wit-Gele Kruis, Gasthuistr. 35, Tilburg. Member: NIPP. Educational psychology, consulting, teaching; vocational guidance, learning problems and pupil's attitude toward school **M**

NETHERLANDS WEST INDIES

KENDALL, Dr. William E. P.O. Box 545, Lago Colony, Aruba. b. 6 Sept 1914 New Holland, Illinois, USA. PH.D '46 Univ. of Minnesota, USA. PERS. STUDIES COORDINATOR, Lago Oil and Transport Co, Aruba. Member: APA. Industrial relations research, administration; employee attitudes, labor-management relations, selection, training and evaluation of supervisors and managers. **M**

WOOD, James D. P. O. Box 620, Lago Colony, Aruba. b. 31 Jan 1921 Lordsburg, New Mexico, USA. PH.D '57 New York Univ, USA. PERS. PSYCH'T, Lago Oil and Transport Co, Aruba. Member: APA, IRRA. Industrial and personnel psychology, testing, research; learning theory; achievement, intelligence, and aptitude tests, selection of employees and supervisors, performance rating techniques. **M**

NEW ZEALAND

ADCOCK, Dr. Cyril John. Victoria Univ. Coll, Box 196, Wellington. b. 15 June 1904 Manchester, Eng. PH.D '47 Univ. of London, Eng. SR. LECT, Victoria Univ. Coll. Member: BPS-NZ, APA, Psychomet. Socy. (USA). Teaching, research; aptitude, interest, and temperament measurement, related factorial studies, psychological theory. **M**

ALLEN, Alexander Bertram. Dept of Educ, Psych. Serv, P.O. Box 1011, Christchurch. b. 26 Oct 1917 Christchurch. MA '48 Univ. of New Zealand. DIST. PSYCH'T, Dept. of Educ; CONSULT. PSYCH'T, Child Health Clinic, Dept. of Health, Christchurch. Member: BPS-NZ. Educational psychology, testing, consulting, guidance to schools, parents and social agencies; psychometrics, remedial education counseling. M

BALLIN, Dr. Jack. 34 Ensors Rd, Opawa, Christchurch. b. 18 May 1910 Auckland. MB, CH.B '44 Univ. of Otago, N.Z. PSYCHO-THERAPIST, priv. prac; ASSOC. PHYS, Clinic for Med. Psych, 29 Andover St, Merivale, Christchurch. Member: BPS-NZ. Analytic psychotherapy; direct reductive analysis. M

BARNEV, Dr. William David. Dept. of Educ, Auckland Univ. Coll, Princess St, Auckland. b. 15 July 1920 Timaru. PH.D '52 Univ. of London, Eng. LECTURER, Univ. of N.Z. Auckland Univ. Coll; GUID. COUNS, Guidance Clinic, Univ. of N.Z. Member: PBS-NZ. Teaching educational psychology, guidance; children's art, performance of sub-normal children, learning and teaching of reading. M

BEAGLEHOLE, Prof. Ernest. Victoria Univ, Box 196, Wellington. b. 25 Aug 1906 Wellington. LittD '40 Univ. of London, Eng. PROF. and CHMN, Dept. of Psych, Victoria Univ; EDITOR, *Victoria University College Publications in Psychology.* Member: BPS-NZ. Teaching, research, administration; projective techniques, group process, value measurement. M

BERNARDELLI, Mrs. Betty. Univ. of Otago, Dunedin. b. 7 Nov 1919 London, Eng. MA '41 Univ. of Cambridge, Eng. LECTURER, Univ. of Otago. Member: BPS-NZ. Teaching, testing, clinical analysis, research; gerontology, brain injuries, experimental psychology of skill. F

BEVAN-BROWN, Dr. Maurice. 29 Andover St, Merivale, Christchurch. b. 29 July 1886 Christchurch. MB, CH.B '21 Univ. of New Zealand; MA '12 Univ. of Cambridge, Eng. MED. DIR, Clin. of Med. Psych; DIR. of CLIN. and CLIN. PSYCHIATRIST, Timaru Hosp, Timaru. Member: BPS-NZ, N.Z. Assn. of Psychother. Teaching, psychotherapy, professional writing; mental hygiene, technique in analytic psychotherapy, trained childbirth. M

BINDON, Miss Dorothy Marjorie. Inst. for Language Disorders in Children, Sch. of Speech, Northwestern Univ, Evanston, Illinois, USA. b. 7 July 1929 Whangarei. MA '56 Univ. of New Zealand. TEACHING ASST, Sch. of Speech, Northwestern Univ. Member: BPS. Teaching, clinical consulting and research with the deaf, student; psychological problems of the deaf, psychopathology of language, personality measurement. F

BLACKWELL, Miss Margeret May. 23 Glenfell Rd, Epsom, Auckland. b. 21 May 1908 Katapoi. Cert. in Child Devel. '36 Univ. of London, Eng. PSYCHOMETRIST,

Auckland Hosp. Bd, Park Rd, Auckland. PLAYTHERAPIST, Child. Hlth. Clin, Hlth. Dept, Auckland. Member: BPS-NZ, N.Z. Assn. of Psychother. Testing, play therapy, consulting, guidance, supervising preschool play activities and occupational therapy students; attitude measurement. F

BOURNE, Dr. Harold. Dept. of Psychiat, Univ. of Otago Med. Sch, Dunedin. b. 9 Apr 1923 London, Eng. MB, BS '54 Univ. of London, Eng. LECTURER, Univ. of Otago Med. Sch. Guidance, teaching, research; psychotherapy of psychosis, protophrenia. M

BOWIE, George Henderson. Ardmore Teachers' Coll, Auckland. b. 25 Jan 1903 Cromwell. MA '29 Univ. of New Zealand. VICE-PRINCIPAL, Ardmore Teachers' Coll. Member: BPS-NZ. Administration, teaching education and child psychology; learning theory, achievement and diagnostic testing, psychology of the adolescent. M

BREW, Quentin Heath. Psych. Div, 7th Floor, Hope Gibbons Bldg, Dixon St, Wellington. b. 2 Dec 1919 Auckland. MA '51 Univ. of New Zealand. PSYCHOLOGIST, Cen. Dist, Dept. of Educ, N.Z. Govt, Wellington. Member: BPS-NZ, N.Z. Assn. of Psychother. Educational and applied psychology, consulting, guidance, administration; preventive mental hygiene and parent education, play therapy, guidance for handicapped children and their parents. M

BROWN, Dr. Laurence Binet. 31 Lawrence St, Wellington S. 1. b. 13 Aug 1927 Wellington. PH.D '54 Univ. of London, Eng. RES. PSYCH'T, N.Z. Def. Sci. Corps, Dept. of Sci. and Indus. Res, Wellington; HONORARY LECT, Victoria Univ. Coll, Wellington. Member: BPS-NZ. Research, industrial psychology, testing, teaching; assimilation of migrants, projective techniques, job satisfaction. M

BUNBY, Mrs. Phyllis Irene. 12 Marua Rd, Auckland S.E. 6. b. 9 Feb 1907 Auckland. BA '38 Auckland Univ. Coll, Auckland. COUNSELOR, Family Guid. Cen, Victoria Arcade Shortland St, Auckland. Member: BPS-NZ, N.Z. Assn. of Psychotherapists. Child guidance, interviewing parents, testing, play therapy; intelligence and achievement tests. F

CALVERT, Mrs. Barbara. 5 Signal Hill Road, Opoho, Dunedin. b. 19 Oct 1918 Waipawa. MA '44 Univ. of Otago, N.Z. Member: BPS-NZ. Retired, research; intelligence testing, statistical methods. F

CAUGHLEY, James Gilfillan. 21 Boundary Rd, Kelburn, Wellington W.1. b. 2 Jan 1905 New Zealand. MA '38 Canterbury Univ. Coll, N.Z. CHIEF PSYCH'T, Dept. of Justice, Wellington. Member: BPS-NZ.

Administration, testing, clinical analysis, psychotherapy, consulting, guidance; rehabilitation of offenders. M

CLARK, William Johnson Hamilton. Vocat. Guid. Cen, Educ. Dept, P.O. Box 1449, Auckland. b. 15 Dec 1908 Lumsden. MA '51 Univ. of New Zealand. DIST. VOCAT. GUID. OFF, Vocat. Guid. Cen. Member: BPS-NZ, Natl. Vocat. Guid. Assn. (USA). Administration, vocational guidance, testing; educational and vocational guidance of post-primary pupils. M

CLAY, Mrs. Marie M. 15 Vaughan Crescent, Murrays Bay, Auckland. b. 3 Jan 1926 Wellington. MA '49 Univ. of New Zealand. CHILD PSYCH'T, priv. prac. Member: BPS-NZ. Diagnosis and treatment of educational and emotional problems of children; adjustment problems of school children, pre-school developmental difficulties, parent counseling. F

COHEN, Harry Eyre. 287 Withells Rd, Christchurch N.W. 3. b. 10 July 1923 Sydney, Austl. MA '51 Univ. of New Zealand. PSYCHOLOGIST, Paparua Prison, Private Bag, Christchurch; EDITOR, Publications of Clinic for Medical Psychology, Christchurch. Member: BPS-NZ. Assn. of Psychotherapists. Psychotherapy, administration, counseling, prisoner classification, crimonological research; psychopathology, analytic psychotherapy, mental hygiene. M

CONGALTON, Athol Alexander. Dept. of Psych, Victoria Univ. Coll, Wellington. b. 29 Apr 1914 Palmerston North. MA '47 Victoria Univ. Coll, N.Z. LECTURER, Victoria Univ. Coll. Member: BPS-NZ. Teaching, research, administration, consulting; social stratification, community analysis. M

CONNOR, Dr. David Vincent. Univ. of Otago, Dunedin. b. 23 Aug 1918 Rockhampton Austl. PH.D '52 Univ. of London, Eng. LECT. in EDUC, Univ. of Otago. Member: BPS-NZ, APA, AERA. Teaching, guidance, testing; personality measurement, intra-individual variability, educational guidance, experimental education and research. M

COOK, Dr. Enid Florence. 58 Armagh St, Christchurch. b. 25 Jan 1900 London, Eng. MB, CH.B '22 Univ. of Liverpool, Eng. CONSULT. PSYCHIATRIST, priv. prac. Member: BPS-NZ. Clinical practice, psychotherapy; anxiety states. F

CROWTHER, Dr. Alan. Canterbury Univ. Coll, Box 1471, Christchurch C.1. b. 6 Mar 1913 Cambridge, Eng. PH.D '47 Univ. of Cambridge, Eng. LECT. in CHARGE and HEAD, Dept. of Psych, Canterbury Univ. Coll. Member: BPS-NZ. Teaching, administration, research; theory of personality,

tests and testing. M

DALE, Dr. William S. 146 Gillies Ave, Epsom, Auckland S.E. 3. b. 12 Aug 1900 Woking, Hants, Eng. PH.D '36 Yale Univ, USA. PRINCIPAL, Educ. Bd, Wellesley St, Auckland; MEMBER, Sr. Seminar in Anthrop, Auckland Univ. Coll; EDITOR, *New Zealand Psychological Bulletin.* Member: BPS-NZ. Administration, consulting, teaching, editorial; achievement tests, learning theory, personality. M

DICK, Miss Nada Margaret. 27 Thorrington Rd, Cashmere, Christchurch. b. 8 May 1930 Christchurch. BA '55 Canterbury Univ. Coll, N.Z. REMED. READING TCHR, Remedial Reading Clin, Phillipstown Sch, Canterbury Educ.Bd, Oxford Terrace, Christchurch. Member: BPS. Teaching retarded readers, research, student; methods of studying personality, learning theory, remedial reading. F

DOBSON, Dr. John Robert Earle. Ashburn Hall, Dunedin. b. 26 Jan 1920 Christchurch. DPM '50 Univ. of London, Eng. ASST. MED. SUPT, The Proprietors, Ashburn Hall; ASST. LECT. in CHILD PSYCH, Otago Univ, Dunedin. Member: RMPA, BPS-NZ, Psych. Med. Grp. of British Med. Assn, Australasian Assn. of Psychiatrists. Clinical practice, psychotherapy, teaching; clinical psychiatry. M

DONALD, Mrs. Marjorie N. 404 Wildwood, Ann Arbor, Michigan, USA. b. 6 Oct 1918 Dunedin. MA '49 Univ. of New Zealand. ASST. STUDY DIR, Survey Res. Cen, Univ. of Michigan, Ann Arbor, Michigan. Member: BPS-NZ. Student, research, teaching; social organization and cross-cultural comparison. F

ENTWISTLE, Dr. William Harry. 40 Rodrigo Rd, Kilbirnie, Wellington E.3. b. 18 Dec 1898 Auckland. PH.D '32 Univ. of London, Eng. TUTOR, Correspondence Sch, Clifton Terrace, Wellington. Member: BPS-NZ. Teaching, research, testing; aspects of mental work, fatigue. M

FERGUSON, Alan Logan. 12 Takutai St, Parnell, Auckland C. 4. b. 12 Dec 1906 Palmerston South. BA '45 Univ. of New Zealand. VOCAT. GUID. OFF, Dept. of Educ, Wellington; ASSOC. ED, *New Zealand Bulletin of Psychology.* Member: BPS-NZ. Vocational and educational guidance, testing; counseling theory, testing, adjustment to the work situation. M

FIELD, Prof. Henry Edward. Canterbury Univ. Coll, Christchurch. b. 11 July 1903 New Zealand. PH.D '33 Univ. of London, Eng. PROF. of EDUC. Canterbury Univ. Coll; CONSULTANT, Girl's Trng. Cen, Burwood, Christchurch. Member: BPS-NZ. Teaching, administration, consulting; psychology of delinquency, educational guidance. M

FITT, Prof. Arthur Benjamin. 15 Ridings Rd, Remuera, Auckland S.E. 2. b. 1 Oct 1887 Invercargill. PH.D '14 Univ. of Leipzig, Germany. PROF. EMER. and MEMBER of COUNCIL, Auckland Univ. Coll. Member: BPS-NZ. Retired, research, professional writing, library; seasonal fluctuatons in growth and function, attitude measurement, achievement tests. M

FLEISCHL, Marianus W. Druids Chambers, Wellington C. 1. b. 3 July 1905 Lwow, USSR. Certificat d'études soc. et écon. '25 Académie Int. des Hautes Etudes, USSR. HONORARY LECT, Victoria Univ. Coll, Wellington. Member: BPS-NZ. Psychotherapy, teaching. M

FORD, Clarence Thomas. Canterbury Univ. Coll, Christchurch. b. 11 Aug 1912 Christchurch. MA '50 Univ. of New Zealand. SR. LECT. in EDUC, Canterbury Univ. Coll. Member: BPS-NZ. Teaching, consulting, guidance, testing; remedial education, achievement testing, educational diagnosis. M

FREYBERG, Peter Stuart. Teachers' Coll, Princess St, Palmerston North. b. 11 July 1924 Hawera. MA '49 Univ. of New Zealand. LECT. in EDUC, Teachers' Coll. Member: BPS-NZ. Teaching, educational psychology, research; educational techniques, child guidance. M

GEDDES, Dr. William Robert. Dept. of Anthrop, Auckland Univ. Coll, Box 2553, Auckland. b. 29 Apr 1916 New Plymouth. PH.D '48 Univ. of London, Eng. SR. LECT. in SOC. ANTHROP, Auckland Univ. Coll; EDITOR, *Journal of the Polynesian Society*. Member: BPS-NZ. Teaching, research on social change; culture and personality, group process, learning theory. M

GIBBS, Dr. David Norris. 11 Dominion Park St, Raroa, Johnsonville, Wellington. b. 9 Mar 1926 Christchurch. PH.D '55 Univ. of London, Eng. RES. OFF. in PSYCH, N.Z. Def. Sci. Corps, Army Hq, Featherston St, Wellington. Member: BPS-NZ. Consulting and research, personnel psychology, testing; interviewing, aptitude tests, prediction methods. M

GORDON, Mrs. Joan Grace. Flat 3, 70 Hill St, Wellington. b. 14 Feb 1915 N.Z. BA '46 Victoria Univ. Coll, N.Z. SR. SPEECH THER, Wellington Educ. Bd. and Wellington Hosp. Bd, Wellington. Consulting and guidance in speech therapy, teaching, psychotherapy. F

GREY, Alexander. 224 St. George St, Papatoetoe, Auckland. b. 28 May 1919 Wellington. MA '48 Victoria Univ. Coll, N.Z. LECT. in CHILD DEVEL, Auckland Teacher's Coll, Epsom Ave, Auckland; DIR. of SUPER. TRNG, Auckland Nursery Play Centres. Member: BPS-NZ. Teaching, educational and applied psychology, consulting; behavioral studies to establish non-test norms for pre-school children, permissive free play programs for young children, permissive non-directive interview techniques with parents of young children. M

HAYR, Kenneth James. 151 St. Andrews Rd, Auckland S.E. 3. b. 23 Sept 1906 Auckland. BA '48 Univ. of New Zealand. INSPECTOR of SCHOOLS, Educ. Dept, Auckland. Member: BPS. Administration, teaching, research; learning theory, achievement tests, group process. M

HENDRY, James A. Psych. Serv, Dept. of Educ, Wellesley St, Auckland. b. 2 Aug 1918 Whangarei. MA '49 Auckland Univ. Coll, N.Z. PSYCHOLOGIST, Dept. of Educ. Organization of psychological services in Auckland, testing, clinical analysis; attitude measurement, achievement and diagnostic tests. M

HOLDEN, Bertrand Cecil. Clin. for Med. Psych, 29 Andover St, Christchurch. b. 28 Feb 1911 Cromwell. L.TH '38 Coll. House, N.Z. SR. PSYCHOTHERAPIST, Clin. for Med. Psych. Member: Christchurch Psych. Socy, N.Z. Ass. of Psychotherapists. Psychotherapy, guidance, teaching, administration; reductive analysis, counseling. M

HOUNSELL, John Durrant. Howick Rd, Blenheim. b. 27 Feb 1924 Blenheim. MA '55 Canterbury Univ. Coll, N.Z. PERS. OFF, Felt and Textiles of N.Z., Ltd, 201 Lamblon Quay, Wellington; TEACHER, N.Z. Primary Schools. Member: BPS-NZ. Testing, administration, teaching; personnel selection and placement, group relantionschips. M

JEFFERY, Raymond James. N.Z. Dept. of Educ, Auckland Educ. Bd, Auckland. b. 14 Mar 1922 Bristol, Eng. MA '54 Univ. of New Zealand. PSYCHOLOGIST, Psych. Serv, Educ. Dept, Wellington; LECT. in PSYCH, Auckland Univ. Coll, Auckland. Member: BPS-NZ. Testing, guidance for parents and schools, teaching; social differentiation in young children, small group studies, adolescent behavior problems. M

JENKIN, Prof. Noël Stanley. Dept. of Psych, Univ. of New Brunswick, Fredericton, New Brunswick, Can. b. 15 May 1918 Wanganui. MA '52 Univ. of New Zealand. ASST. PROF, Univ. of New Brunswick. Member: BPS-NZ, APA, Maritime Psych. Assn. Teaching, research, consulting; cognitive processes, personality theory and measurement. M

JENNINGS, John Rannard. 80 Messines Rd, Wellington W. 3. b. 5 May 1904 Thoresway,

Eng. MA '47 Univ. of Cambridge, Eng. RES. and TESTING OFF, N.Z. Dept. of Educ; LECT. in OCCUPAT. PSYCH, Victoria Univ. Coll. Member: BPS-NZ. Applied, educational psychology, research, administration; development of procedures in vocational guidance and selection. M

JOHNSTONE, Gilbert Carswell. c/o J. Muir Esq, MacKenzie Ave, Onerahi, Whangarei. b. 23 Nov 1920 Napier. MA '49 Univ. of New Zealand. LECT. in ADULT EDUC, Auckland Univ. Coll, Princes St, Auckland. Member: BPS-NZ. Teaching; projective techniques, attitude measurement. M

LAWRENCE, Dr. Philip John. Educ. Dept, Canterbury Univ. Coll, Christchurch C. 1. b. 6 Feb 1921 Christchurch. PH.D '56 Univ. of New Zealand. LECT. in EDUC, Canterbury Univ. Coll. Member: BPS-NZ. Teaching educational psychology, research; nature of intelligence, reasoning and problem solving, learning theory. M

LIVINGSTONE, Dr. David Henry North. 110 Park Terrace, Christchurch. b. 9 May 1919 Christchurch. MB, CH.B '45 Univ. of Otago, N.Z. PSYCHIATRIST, priv. prac. Member: BPS-NZ. Psychotherapy, clinical practice, research; psychotherapy, electrocerebral stimulation, early mother-child relationships. M

MacKENZIE, Donald Finlay. H. M. Prison, Auckland. b. 9 Oct 1913 Bualnaluib, Scot. MA '35 Univ. of Edinburgh, Scot. PSYCHOLOGIST, H. M. Prison. Member: BPS-NZ. Research, testing, psychotherapy, guidance; social perception, attitude measurement, prediction. M

MacKENZIE, Mrs. Judith Mary. 19 Ascot Flats, Newton Rd, Auckland. b. 28 Sept 1920 Hunterville. BA '52 Victoria Univ. Coll, N.Z. PSYCHIAT. SOC. WRKR, Auckland Mental Hosp, Great North Rd, Auckland. Member: BPS. Case work, guidance, applied psychology, psychotherapy; abnormal personality, personality testing, child welfare. F

MALCOLM, Miss Yvonne. Psych. Serv, Educ. Dept, Auckland Educ. Bd, Auckland. b. 27 July 1918 Timaru. MA '51 Univ. of New Zealand. PSYCHOLOGIST, Psych. Serv, Educ. Dept. Member: BPS-NZ. Testing, clinical analysis, consulting, guidance, applied psychology; acculturation processes, projective techniques, mental deficiency. F

MANDER, Dudley Victor. 69 Orlando St, Stratford. b. 16 May 1924 Tauranga. MA '52 Victoria Univ. Coll, N.Z. TEACHER, Stratford Tech. High Sch, Swansea Rd, Stratford. Member: BPS-NZ. Teaching; social perception, projective techniques, learning theory. M

MANNING, Arthur Edward Bruce. 90 Valley Rd, Mt. Eden, Auckland N. 2. b. 11 Jan 1900 Coromandel. MA '43 Univ. of New Zealand. PSYCHOTHERAPIST, priv. prac. Member: N.Z. Assn. of Psychotherapists. Psychoanalysis, psychotherapy, clinical analysis, educational psychology; abnormal psychology, psychosomatic medicine, schizoid personality problems. M

McCREARY, John Rushforth. Victoria Univ. Coll, Box 196, Wellington. b. 14 Jan 1920 Dunedin. MA '48 Univ. of New Zealand. LECTURER, Sch. of Soc. Sci, Victoria Univ. Coll. Member: BPS-NZ. Teaching, research, testing, counseling; attitude study, cross-cultural testing, gerontology. M

McLAUCHLAN, Capt. Alan C. L. 18 Coast Rd, Wainui-o-mata, Wellington. b. 18 Feb 1921 Greenhills. BA '47 Univ. of Otago, N.Z. SR. PERS. SEL. OFF, N.Z. Army, Featherston St, Wellington. Member BPS-NZ. Administration of personnel selection, testing; work study and selection techniques. M

McLAY, Mrs. Lorna Alice. 46 Arney Crescent, Remuera, Auckland. b. 8 Dec 1921 Temuka. BA, Dipl. Ed. '44 Univ. of New Zealand. CLIN. PSYCH'T, Educ. Dept, Wellington; PSYCHOLOGIST, priv. prac. Member: BPS-NZ. Clinical practice, diagnostic testing and therapeutic work with children, advisor to parents and teachers; projective and therapeutic techniques, intelligence and achievement testing. F

MEDLICOTT, Dr. Reginald Warren. Ashburn Hall, Dunedin. b. 10 Aug 1913 Waimate. MB, CH.B, Otago Univ, N.Z. MED. SUPT, Ashburn Hall Hosp; PSYCHIATRIST, priv. prac; LECT. in PSYCHIAT, Otago Univ. Med. Sch. Member: BPS-NZ, RMPA, Australasian Assn. of Psychiatrists. Psychotherapy, administration, teaching; psychiatric diagnosis and treatment. M

MINOGUE, Dr. W. J. D. Auckland Univ. Coll, Auckland. b. 26 Mar 1920 Auckland. PH.D '50 Ohio State Univ, USA. SR. LECT. in EDUC, Auckland Univ. Coll. Member: BPS-NZ. Teaching, research, testing; race relations, group process, mental measurement. M

MITCHELL, Prof. Frank Wyndham. Univ. of Otago, Dunedin. b. 8 Aug 1906 Adelaide, Austl. PH.D '37 Univ. of London, Eng. PROF. and HEAD, Dept. of Educ, Univ. of Otago. Member: BPS-NZ. Teaching, research, guidance; ability tests, delinquency and behavior problems. M

MONEY, Dr. John. Johns Hopkins Hosp, Baltimore 5, Maryland, USA. b. 8 July 1921 Morrinsville. PH.D '52 Harvard Univ. USA. ASST. PROF. of MED. PSYCH, Johns Hopkins Univ. Research, professional writing; relationship of endocrine and psychologic functions, psychological development in hermaphroditism, personality theory. M

MULLIGAN, David Glenn. Dept. of Psych, Victoria Univ. Coll, Wellington. b. 15 Feb 1934 Wellington. BA '54 Victoria Univ. Coll, N.Z. DEMONSTRATOR, Victoria Univ. Coll. Research, teaching, testing; use of projective tests in culture and personality studies, psychology of small groups, measurement of stress. M

NIEUKERKE, Dr. Karel Herman Paul. N.Z. Management Consultants, 54 Hillside Rd, Auckland S.E. 7. b. 14 Aug 1914 The Hague, Neth. PH.D '49 State Univ. of Utrecht, Neth. MANAGING DIR, N.Z. Management Consultants. Member: NIPP, BPS. Industrial psychology, teaching, research; industrial relations, projective techniques, psychology of mathematics. M

NIXON, Allan Johnston. 33 Maungarei Rd, Remuera, Auckland S.E. 2. b. 12 Sept 1921 Auckland. MA '48 Univ. of New Zealand. LECT. in PSYCH, Auckland Univ. Coll, Princes St, Auckland. Member: BPS. Teaching, research, administration; analysis of broken marriages in New Zealand, marital relations. M

PARKYN, George William. N.Z. Counc. for Educ. Res, 22 Brandon St, Wellington. b. 17 June 1910 Christchurch. MA '37 Univ. of Otago, N.Z. DIRECTOR, N.Z. Counc. for Educ. Res; EDITOR, Publications of N.Z. Counc. for Educ. Res. Member: BPS-NZ. Educational research, editorial, professional writing; psychology of gifted children, selection for university entrance, construction and use of standardized aptitude and attainment tests. M

PICKFORD, Mrs. Ellen Mary. 14 Bristol St, St. Albans, Christchurch. b. 2 Jan 1911 Waimate. PSYCHOTHERAPIST, Clin. of Med. Psych, 29 Andover St, Christchurch. Member: N.Z. Assn. of Psychotherapists, Christchurch Psych. Socy. Psychotherapy, clinical practice, administration, lecturing; extra-sensory perception, reductive analysis. F

PINDER, Bryan Morgan. N.Z. Dept. of Educ, Wellington. b. 18 Sept 1914 Dunedin. MA '47 Univ. of New Zealand. OFF. for SPEC. EDUC, N.Z. Dept. of Educ; EDITOR, New Zealand *Special Class Teachers' Bulletin*; ED. BD, *The Slow Learning Child*. Member: BPS-NZ. Administration of schools and services for exceptional children, educational psychology, consulting; ability and attitude measurement, learning problems of exceptional children, maladjustment. M

RHODES, Lancelot George. P.O. Box 485, Hamilton. b. 9 Nov 1919 Napier. MA '52 Univ. of New Zealand. PSYCHOLOGIST, N.Z. Educ. Dept, Govt. Buildings, Welling-

ton. Member: BPS-NZ. Selection for special educational treatment, testing, educational psychology, guidance, consulting; exceptional children, marital happiness and parent-child relationships, reading readiness. M

RITCHIE, James Ernest. Dept. of Psych, Victoria Univ. Coll, Box 196, Wellington. b. 12 Dec 1929 Wellington. MA '55 Victoria Univ. Coll, N.Z. LECTURER, Victoria Univ. Coll. Member: BPS-NZ, Polynesian Socy. Teaching experimental psychology, research in psychoethnology, testing; projective testing in psychoethnological research, personality assessment, community study, effects of technological change. M

ROBB, Dr. James Harding. 15 Connaught Terrace, Wellington S.W. 1. b. 28 Apr 1920 Gisborne. PH.D '51 Univ. of London, Eng. LECTURER, Sch. of Soc. Sci, Victoria Univ. Coll, Wellington. Member: BPS-NZ, BRF. Teaching, supervision of casework training, research, testing; marriage and family, projective techniques, race relations. M

ROGERS, Dr. Cyril Alfred. Auckland Univ. Coll, Auckland. b. 10 Aug 1923 Auckland. PH.D '52 Univ. of London, Eng. SR. LECT. in EDUC, Auckland Univ. Coll. Member: BPS-NZ. Teaching educational psychology, research, testing, administration; personality testing, measurement in education, objective tests. M

ROSS, David Hargreaves. Psych. Serv, Dept. of Educ, P.O. Box 400, Palmerston North. b. 24 Nov 1921 Wellington. MA '54 Victoria Univ. Coll, N.Z. PSYCHOLOGIST, Psych. Serv, Dept. of Educ. Member: BPS-NZ. Guidance, testing, psychotherapy, administration; learning theory, child personality development, achievement tests. M

RYAN, James Patrick. Dept. of Psych, Victoria Univ. Coll, Box 196, Wellington. b. 29 Aug 1927 Wellington. BA '54 Victoria Univ. Coll, N.Z. JR. LECT, Victoria Univ. Coll. Teaching, research, testing; psychometrics, physiological psychology, conditioned response therapy. M

SAUNDERS, Miss Marion Elizabeth. Clinic for Med. Psych, 29 Andover St, Merivale, Christchurch. b. 27 June 1891 Dounby, Orkney, Scot. Teacher's Cert. '23 Christchurch Tchrs. Trng. Coll, N.Z. PSYCHOTHERAPIST, Clin. for Med. Psych. Member: N.Z. Assn. of Psychotherapists, Christchurch Psych. Socy, N.Z. Speech Therapists Assn. Psychotherapy, clinical practice, guidance; speech therapy. F

SCOTT, Dr. Thomas Henry. Psych. Dept, Canterbury Univ. Coll, Christchurch. b. 10 Nov 1918 Featherston. PH.D '54 McGill Univ, Can. SR. LECT, Canterbury Univ. Coll. Member: BPS-NZ, CPA, APA. Teaching, supervision of student research, research, professional writing; thinking and cognitive functioning, effects of perceptual isolation on behavior, social organization of infra-human animals. M

SEDDON, Dr. Richard. Univ. of Otago, Dunedin. b. 5 Jan 1912 Dunedin. PH.D '49 Univ. of London, Eng. SR. LECT. in EDUC, Univ. of Otago. Member: BPS-NZ. Teaching, clinical practice, research; child development, educational maladjustment, factorial analysis. M

SOMERSET, Hugh Crawford Anthony. Sch. of Soc. Sci, Victoria Univ. Coll. Box 196, Wellington. b. 19 Jan 1931 Oxford. MA '54 Univ. of New Zealand. RES. ASST, Sch. of Soc. Sci, Victoria Univ. Coll. Research in constitutional psychology, projective testing, statistical analysis; projective techniques, gerontology, social surveys. M

SOMERSET, Hugh Crawford Dixon. 32 Kelborn Parade, Wellington W. 1. b. 29 Aug 1895 Christchurch. MA '32 Univ. of New Zealand. SR. LECT. in EDUC, Victoria Univ. Coll, Box 196, Wellington. Member: BPS-NZ. Teaching, research, educational and applied psychology, professional writing; social perception in adolescence, rural sociology, child growth and development. M

STROOBANT, Raymond. Victoria Univ. Coll, Box 196, Wellington. b. 2 July 1922 Wellington. MA '52 Canterbury Univ. Coll, N.Z. LECT. in EDUC, Victoria Univ. Coll; LECT. in PSYCH, Wellington Kindergarten Assn. Member: BPS-NZ, Assn. for Study of Childhood, N.Z. Speech Ther. Assn. Teaching, educational psychology, research; projective techniques, child development, speech disorders. M

TAYLOR, Antony James William. Box 8020, Dept. of Justice, Wellington. b. 14 Aug 1926 London, Eng. BA '55 Victoria Univ. Coll, N.Z. PRISON PSYCH'T, Dept. of Justice. Member: BPS-NZ. Group therapy, counseling, testing, teaching; motivation, effect of imprisonment on personality, care of discharged prisoners. M

THOMPSON, Richard Hubert Thurlow. Psych Dept, Canterbury Univ. Coll, Christchurch. b. 9 Oct 1924 London, Eng. MA '54 Univ. of New Zealand. LECTURER, Canterbury Univ. Coll. Member: BPS-NZ. Teaching, research, educational psychology; group process, attitude measurement, racial prejudice. M

USSHER, Walter Percival. 54 Evesham

Crescent, Spreydon, Christchurch. b. 20 May 1925 Christchurch. MA '55 Canterbury Univ. Coll, N.Z. PSYCHOLOGIST, Dept. of Educ, Govt. Bldgs, Wellington; CONSULT. CLIN. PSYCH'T, Child Health Clin, Dept. of Health. Member: BPS-NZ. Educational and vocational guidance, diagnostic testing, consulting; intelligence and achievement testing, statistical psychology, projective techniques. M

WAITE, Squadron Leader Ralph McFarlane. Royal N.Z. Air Force HQ, Air Dept, Wellington. b. 13 Apr 1918 Dunedin. MA '42 Univ. of New Zealand. RES. OFF, Royal N.Z. Air Force. Member: BPS-NZ. Research on personnel and training problems, testing, consulting, military psychology; learning theory, personality diagnostic testing, job analysis. M

WATSON, John E. N.Z. Council for Educ. Res, Southern Cross Bldg, 22 Brandon St, Wellington. b. 8 Apr 1924 Wellington. MA '49 Univ. of Otago, N.Z. RES. OFF, Council for Educ. Res; ED. ASST, publications of N.Z. Council for Educational Research. Member: BPS-NZ. Research, editorial, testing, consulting; educational psychology, achievement tests and attitude scales, group dynamics. M

WILLIAMS, Rev. Dr. David Owen. Trinity Methodist Theological Coll, 138 Grafton Rd, Auckland C. 3. b. 13 Jan 1908 Waimangaro. LittD '43 Univ. of New Zealand. LECT. in PASTORAL THEOLOGY, Trinity Methodist Theological Coll. Member: BPS-NZ. Teaching, psychotherapy, research; mental organization, learning theory, inter-personal relations. M

WINTERBOURN, Prof. Ralph. Auckland Univ. Coll, Auckland C. 1. b. 10 Feb 1909 Kaiapoi. PH.D '40 Univ. of London, Eng. PROF. of EDUC, Auckland Univ. Coll. Member: BPS-NZ. Teaching, administration, testing, guidance; backward children, juvenile delinquency, educational and vocational guidance. M

WRIGLEY, Prof. Charles Frederick. Dept. of Psych, Univ. of California, Berkeley 4, California, USA. b. 23 Feb 1917 Auckland. PH.D '49 Univ. of London, Eng. VIS. ASSOC. PROF, Univ. of California; CONSULT. ED, *Journal of Abnormal and Social Psychology*. Member: APA, BPS-NZ, CPA, Amer. Stat. Assn, Psychomet. Socy. Research, teaching, editorial; factor analysis, electronic computation, beliefs and attitudes. M

NIGERIA

BEIER, Horst Ulrich. University Coll,
Ibadan. b. 30 July 1922 Glowitz, Ger.
BA '48 Univ. Coll, London, Eng. LECTURER,
Univ. Coll, Ibadan; EDITOR, *ODU.*
Member: Int. Socy. of Ethnopsych.
Teaching, research, administration, edi-
torial; ethnopsychology, art therapy.   M
LAMBO, Dr. Thomas Adeoye. Aro Hosp,
Abeokuta. b. 29 Mar 1923 Abeokuta.

MD '54 Univ. of Birmingham, Eng. PHYS.
and SUPT, Ministry of Pub. Hlth, W.
Region, Ibadan; PROF. of PSYCH. and
PSYCHIAT, Univ. Coll, Ibadan. Member:
RMPA, Int. Socy. of Ethnopsych. Clinical
practice, consulting, guidance, testing,
clinical analysis, research, teaching; projective techniques, group process.   M

NORWAY

ÅS, Cand. Psychol. Arvid. Rektorhaugen 19,
Oslo U.H. b. 21 Mar 1925 Hurum. Cand.
Psychol. '48 Univ. of Oslo, Nor. LECT. and
RES. FELLOW, Univ. of Oslo, Karl Johansgt.
47, Oslo; CLIN. PSYCH'T, Oslo City Hosp.
Member: NP. Teaching, research, testing;
experimental study of psychoanalytic
theories, personality theory, projective
techniques.   M
ÅS, Cand. Psychol. Mrs. Berit Skarpaas.
Selvbyggerveien 163/I, Grefsen, Oslo.
b. 10 Apr 1928 Frederikstad. Cand. Psy-
chol. '53 Univ. of Oslo, Nor. VOCAT.
PSYCH'T, Inst. of Occupat. Psych. Akersgt
55, Oslo. Member: NP. Consulting, testing,
personnel psychology; vocational guidance,
attitude measurement, psychology of sex
differences.   F
ALFSEN, Cand. Psychol. Aslaug Irene. Dr.
Odd Solems Klinikk, Mai Lindegaards
Stiftelse, Eidene, Tjøme. b. 7 Apr 1926
Oslo. Cand. Psychol. '53 Univ. of Oslo,
Nor. PSYCHOLOGIST, Dr. Odd Solems
Klinikk. Testing, clinical practice, psycho-
therapy; play therapy.   F
AMUNDSEN, Cand. Psychol. Arvid. Fram-
nesveien 6, II, Oslo. b. 3 Feb 1929 Oslo.
Cand. Psychol. '53 Univ. of Oslo, Nor.
CONSULTANT, Inst. for Soc. Res, Arbiens-
gate 4, Oslo. Member: NP. Research,
consulting, psychometry, journalism; per-
sonality testing, attitude measurement,
causes of alcoholism.   M
ASKILDSEN, Cand. Psychol. Mrs. Margarethe.
Buskerud Folkehøyskole, Darbu. b. 4 May
1928 Oslo. Cand. Psychol. '53 Univ. of
Oslo, Nor. TEACHER, Buskerud Folkehøyskole. Educational psychology, teaching,
testing; child psychology, cultural and
ethnographical aspects of adolescent psychology.   F
AURSAND, Cand. Psychol. Inger Marie.
Hagelundvn. 5, Grorud, Oslo. b. 4 Jan
1923 Rjukan. Cand Psychol, Univ. of
Oslo, Nor. VOCAT. GUID. OFF, Arbeids-
direktoratet, Parkvn. 8, Oslo. Member:
NP. Administration, research, industrial

psychology.   F
BAADE, Cand. Psychol. Eivind. Eiksveien
58, Røa, Oslo. b. 28 Nov 1921 Oslo. Cand.
Psychol. '52 Univ. of Oslo, Nor. CON-
SULTANT, Nor. Armed Forces, Psych. Div,
Sannergt. 14, Oslo; LECTURER, Univ. of
Oslo. Member: NP. Research, psychometry,
applied psychology, teaching; personnel
selection and classification, group dy-
namics, attitude measurement.   M
**BERG KRISTOFFERSEN, Cand. Psychol.
Martin.** Bogstadvn. 53B/II, Oslo. b. 3 Oct
1917 Bø i Vesterålen. Cand. Psychol. '51
Univ. of Oslo, Nor. PERS. MGR, Norsk A/S
Philips, Kirkevn. 64, Oslo. PERS. CONSULT,
Nor. Ministry of Foreign Affairs. Member:
NP. Applied psychology, teaching; person-
nel selection and rating, attitude measure-
ment.   M
BERG-LARSEN, Cand. Psychol. Rolf. Ka-
pellveien 44, Grefsen, Oslo. b. 31 Dec 1927
Oslo. Cand. Psychol, Univ. of Oslo, Nor.
MED. STUD, PSYCHOLOGIST, Nor. Armed
Forces. Applied psychology, testing; pro-
jective techniques, social perception, psy-
chiatry, group process.   M
BEVERFELT, Cand. Psychol. Mrs. Eva.
Ullevålsvn. 85 A, Oslo. b. 6 Mar 1924 Oslo.
Cand. Psychol. '54 Univ. of Oslo, Nor.
RES. ASST, Psych. Inst, Univ. of Oslo, Karl
Johans gt. 47, Oslo. Research; testing and
observation of children.   F
BJARTMANN, Cand. Psychol. Sölve. Florö.
b. 22 Oct 1925 Florö. Cand. Psychol. Univ.
of Oslo, Nor. SEKRETAR, Nor. Armed
Forces, Psych. Div, Sannergt. 14, Oslo.
Applied psychology.   M
BJORDAL, Cand. Psychol. Erling. Industriens
Arbeidslederinstitutt, Kristian Augustsgt.
23, Oslo. b. 12 July 1922 Bjordal, Sogn.
Cand. Psychol. '50 Univ. of Oslo, Nor.
INDUS. PSYCH'T, Industriens Arbeidsleder-
inst. Member: NP. Industrial psychology,
teaching, human relations, selection of
supervisors; industrial relations, personnel
administration.   M
BLESSING, Mag. Art. Sissel. Arbeidspsykolo-

gisk Inst, Akersgt. 55, Oslo. b. 23 Aug 1903 Oslo. Mag. Art. '33 Univ. of Oslo, Nor. INDUS. PSYCH'T, Inst. of Occupat. Psych. Testing, vocational guidance, professional writing. F

BØDAL, Cand. Psychol. Kåre. Berg Arbeidsskole, Box 96 Tønsberg. b. 11 Jan 1926 Kolvereid. Cand. Psychol. '51 Univ. of Oslo, Nor. SOSIALKURATOR, Berg Arbeidsskole. Testing, applied psychology, psychotherapy for young delinquents. M

BOYSEN, Cand Psychol. Audun. Ekebergveien 186, Oslo. b. 10 May 1929 Norway. Cand. Psychol. '54 Univ. of Oslo, Nor. PERS. MGR, Aanonsen Fabrikker, Lörenveien 68, Oslo. Member: NP. Personnel management; motivation in industry, management education, personnel selection and evaluation, rating techniques. M

BRUN, Dr. Mrs. Astri. Parkveien 41b, Oslo. b. 18 Nov 1889 Oslo. Dr. phil. '37 Greifswald Univ, Ger. PSYCHOANALYST, priv. prac. Psychotherapy. F

BYE, Cand. Psychol. Knut. Syrinveien 3, Fredrikstad Ø. b. 9 June 1928 Levanger. Cand. Psychol. Univ. of Oslo, Nor. ASST. PSYCH'T, Yrkesveiledningen i Østfold, Inst. of Occupat. Psych, Fredrikstad. Member: NP. Vocational guidance, industrial consulting, research, testing; projective techniques, aptitude tests, human relations. M

CHRISTENSEN, Cand. Psychol. Berit. Jomfrúbråtveien 78, Bekkelagshøgda, Oslo. b. 20 Aug 1924 Oslo. Cand. Psychol. '50 Univ. of Oslo, Nor. CLIN PSYCH'T; THERAPIST, Nic Waals Inst, Munkedamsveien 84, Oslo. Member: NP, Nor. Assn. of Psychiat. and Clin. Child Psych. Clinical analysis, testing, psychotherapy, administration; projective techniques, individual and group psychotherapy. F

CHRISTENSEN, Cand. Psychol. Mrs. Meta. Midtåsen 59, Ljan, Oslo. b. 15 Feb 1922 Inderøy. Cand. Psychol. '49 Univ. of Oslo, Nor. TRNG. CANDIDATE in PSYCHOTHER, Dr. Nic Waal's Inst, Munkedamsveien 87, Oslo. Member: NP. Psychotherapy, clinical analysis, consulting. F

CHRISTENSEN, Cand. Psychol. Ragnar. Gaustad Ment. Hosp, Vinderen. b. 8 Sept 1922 Fana. Cand. Psychol. '48 Univ. of Oslo, Nor. CLIN. PSSCH'T, Gausted Ment. Hosp; TEACHER, Univ. of Oslo. Member: NP. Clinical analysis, testing, research, teaching; projective techniques, criminal psychology. M

CHRISTIANSEN, Cand. Psych. Bjørn. Inst. for Soc. Res, Arbiensgt. 4, Oslo. b. 6 Aug 1927 Norway. Cand. Psychol. '50 Univ. of Oslo, Nor. RES. ASSOC, Nor. Counc. for Sci. and Humanities, Lökkevn. 7, Oslo; RES. CONSULT, CLIN. PSYCH'T, Dr. Nic

Waals Inst, Munkedamsvn. 7, Oslo. Member: NP. Research, psychotherapy, applied psychology; personality theory, projective techniques. M

COUCHERON JARL, Vidken. Risbakken 24, Vinderen, Oslo. b. 6 Nov 1912 Narvik. MA '36 Columbia Univ, USA. CHIEF PSYCH'T, Nor. Armed Forces, Psych. Div, Sannergt. 14, Oslo. Member: NP. Administration, research; environmental factors in intelligence, reaction time methodology, history of differential psychology. M

DANNEVIG, Cand. Psychol. Einar Tellef. Haslekroken 7B, Oslo. b. 1 Dec 1924 Oslo. Cand. Psychol. '51 Univ. of Oslo, Nor. CLIN. PSYCH'T, priv. prac, Parkveien 41B, Oslo. Member: NP. Psychotherapy, consulting, clinical practice, testing; psychosomatic research and therapy, projective techniques, experiential psychology. M

DRIVDAL, Cand. Psychol. Nerolf Leonhard. Schweigaardsvei 11/c, Bergen. b. 26 June 1921 Klepp, Rogaland. Cand. Psychol. '50 Univ. of Oslo, Nor. INDUS. PSYCH'T, Inst. of Occupat. Psych, Nyagten 2, Bergen. Member: NP. Testing, vocational guidance. M

DYRBORG, Cand. Psychol. Odd. Lybekkv. 46/b, Oslo. b. 1 Apr 1926 Oslo. Cand. Psychol. '49 Univ. of Oslo, Nor. HUMAN RELAT. CONSULT, Nor. Productivity Inst, Schwensensg. 6, Oslo. Member: NP. Administration, industrial psychology; aptitude tests. M

EBELTOFT, Cand. Psychol. Arne. Ymers Vei 9, Lofthus, Oslo. b. 11 Nov 1926 Narvik. Cand. Psychol. '52 Uiv. of Oslo, Nor. CONSULTANT, Nor. Inst. of Tech, Akersvn. 24/c, Oslo. Industrial psychology, teaching, testing; technological training and research. M

EGELAND, Cand. Psychol. Josef. Chr. Fredriksgt. 6, Tönsberg. b. 7 Sept 1928 Kuinesdal. Cand. Psychol. '52 Univ. of Oslo, Nor. EDUC. PSYCH'T, Sch. Psych. Dept, Tönsberg. Member: NP, Nor. Assn. for Child Psychiat. and Child Psych. Testing, consulting and guidance, administration. M

ELDEGARD, Cand. Psychol. Sigurd. Bjørnebekk kursted, Ås st. b. 9 June 1918. Cand. Psychol. '52 Univ. of Oslo, Nor. SOC. WRKR, Björnebekk kursted. Member: NP. Consulting, testing, research; social rehabilitation of alcoholics, causes of alcoholism. M

ENG, Prof. Dr. Miss Helga. Bregnevn. 27, Sogn hageby, Oslo. b. 31 May 1875 Rakkestad. Dr. philos. '13 Univ. of Oslo, Nor. Member: NP. Research, retired; psychology of language, thought, emotion and drawing. F

ENGH, Cand. Psychol. Selma Margrethe. Kirkeveien 90 A, Oslo. b. 2 Jan 1921

Bergen. Cand. Psychol. Univ. of Oslo, Nor. PSYCHOLOGIST, Child Psychiat. Div. Rikshosp, Stensberggaten, Oslo. Member: NP. Testing, clinical analysis, psychotherapy, research. F

EVJEN, Cand. Psychol. Sissel. Hedemarksgt. 10 D/I, Oslo. b. 24 Sept 1930 Tromsø. Cand. Psychol. '56 Univ. of Oslo, Nor. CAND. PSYCH, Off. of Psych, Kr. Augustsgt. 21, Oslo. Member: NP. Interviewing and analysis of data for attitude research; projective techniques, personality theory, psychotherapy. F

FRØYLAND NIELSEN, Dr. phil. Ruth. Maridalsveien 144 B IV, Oslo. b. 5 Oct 1902 Eau Claire, Wisconsin, USA. PH.D Univ. of Geneva, Switz. DIR. of SPEC. EDUC, Oslo. Member: Nor Assn. of Child Psychiat. and Clin. Child Psych. Administration, educational psychology, teaching; social adaptation problems, emotional implications of bilingualism, school readiness and adjustment. F

GAUSLAA, Cand. Psychol. Jakob. Selvbyggervn. 68, Grefsen, Oslo. b. 6 Mar 1927 Solum. Cand. Psychol. '55 Univ. of Oslo, Nor. PSYCHOLOGIST, Rehab. Cen, Sinsenvegen 70, Oslo. Member: NP. Testing, applied psychology, clinical practice; projective techniques, industrial psychology, guidance. M

GERHARDT, Cand. Psychol. Rolf G. Eiksveien 60, Röa, Oslo. b. 4 Sept 1916 Sarpsborg. Cand. Psychol. '49 Univ. of Copenhagen, Den. SECT. LEADER, Nor. Armed Forces, Psych. Div, Sannergt. 14, Oslo. Administration, teaching, research; leader selection and training, perception, psychomotor functions. M

GJESSING, Mag. Art. Hans Jørgen. Off. of Educ. Guid, Hauges gt. 100, Drammen. b. 1 Apr 1920 Drammen. Mag. art. '51 Univ. of Oslo, Nor. EDUC. PSYCH'T, Off. of Educ. Guid. Member: Norsk Pedagogikklag. Research, guidance, educational psychology, testing; reading problems, achievement tests, problems of left handedness. M

GJESVIK, Cand. Psychol. Arnljot. Svoldergt. 7, Oslo. b. 19 July 1924 Oslo. Cand. Psychol. '50 Univ. of Oslo, Nor. SCI. ASST, Univ. Psychiat. Inst, Vinderen, Oslo. Member: NP. Research, testing, clinical analysis, teaching; organic brain disorders, projective techniques, psychotherapy. M

GJESVIK, Cand. Psychol. Mrs. Elisabeth K. Svoldergt. 7, Oslo. b. 5 Oct 1926 Oslo. Cand. Psychol. '50 Univ. of Oslo, Nor. CONSULTANT, priv. prac. Member: NP. Testing, consulting, guidance, research; diagnostic testing of preschool children, effect of institutional living on the development of young children. F

GLASØ, Cand. Psychol. Johannes Henrik. Hansteensgt. 5, Oslo. b. 12 Nov 1925 Tromsö. Cand. Psychol. Univ. of Oslo, Nor. PSYCHOLOGIST, Nor. Armed Forces, Psych. Div, Sannergt. 14, Oslo. Member: NP. Teaching, applied psychology, testing; clinical interviewing, projective techniques, psychosomatic medicine. M

GRAF, Odny Ingeborg. Cort Adlersgate 12, Oslo. b. 11 Aug 1918 Arendal. MA '49 State Univ. of Iowa, USA. RES. FELLOW, Nor. Res. Counc. for Sci. and the Humanities, Løkkeveien 7, Oslo. Member: NP. Research, educational psychology, testing, student; entrance examinations for teacher training colleges, achievement tests, interviewing methods, criteria analysis. F

GRAVDAHL, Cand. Psychol. Gunnar. Bregnevegen 48, Sogn hageby, Oslo. b. 17 Aug 1927 Stokke. Cand. Psychol. '54 Univ. of Oslo, Nor. RES. ASST, Nor. Inst. of Productivity, Schwensens gate 6, Oslo. Member: NP. Research, industrial psychology, testing; human relations in industry, personality diagnosis, projective techniques. M

GREBER, Cand. Psychol. Ulf. Dalenenggt. 16 b, Oslo. b. 30 Sept 1912 Oslo. Cand. Psychol. '55 Univ. of Oslo, Nor. CLIN. PSYCH'T, Ullevål Sykehus, Psychiat. Div, Kirkeveien 166, Oslo. Member: NP. Clinical analysis, testing, psychotherapy; projective techniques, psychoanalysis, psychosomatic ailments. M

GUNVALD, Mrs. Gori. Bjerketun off. skole, Sandvika, pr. Oslo. b. 26 Nov 1917 Aalborg, Den. MA '51 Univ. of Washinton, USA. CHIEF PSYCH'T, Bjerketun off. skole. Member: NP, ICWP, Nor. Assn. for Child Psychiat. and Clin. Child Psych. Testing, clinical analysis, guidance, psychotherapy; projective techniques, individual guidance of maladjusted children, group process. F

HAGA, Cand. Psychol. Einar Martin. Idrettsveien 43, Tromsø. b. 14 June 1921 Baldersheim. Cand. Psychol. '52 Univ. of Oslo, Nor. VOCAT. REHAB. OFF, Fylkesarbeidskontoret i Troms, Torget 1, Tromsø; SCH. PSYCH'T, Tromsø Elem. Sch. Vocational rehabilitation of disabled persons, consulting, testing, teaching; projective techniques, intelligence tests, social perception. M

HALLERAKER, Cand. Psychol. Sigurd. Box 2028, Oslo. b. 5 July 1928 Bremnes. Cand. Psychol. '52 Univ. of Oslo, Nor. MILIT. PSYCH'T, Nor. Armed Forces, Psych. Div, Sannergaten 14, Oslo. Member: NP. Military spsychology, testing, personnel selection and interviews; group dynamics, mental health problems, industrial relations. M

HALS, Cand. Psychol. Adolf. Gjøvikgaten

3 c/I, Oslo. b. 30 June 1916 Måløy. Cand. Psychol. '50 Univ. of Oslo, Nor. COUNSELOR, Ministry of Soc. Welf, Dir. of Pub. Hlth, Bjørnstjerne Bjørnsons Plass 1, Oslo. Member: NP, Int. Union of Sci. Psych. Teaching, professional writing, consulting; group process, attitude measurement, projective techniques, control of narcotics. M

HAMBRO, Cato. Eikstubben 9, Eiksmarka, Oslo. b. 22 Aug 1911 Oslo. Mag. art. '51 Univ. of Oslo, Nor. SECY. GENL, Nor. Natl. Assn. for Ment. Hlth, Bygdøy Alle 12, Oslo; EDITOR, *Mental Health.* Member: NP. Administration, editorial, consulting; counseling, educational and adolescent psychology. M

HANSEN, Cand. Psychol. Finn. Dronningensgate 9, Moss. b. 20 May 1918 Moss. Cand. Psychol. '54 Univ. of Oslo, Nor. CLIN. PSYCH'T, priv. prac; CLIN. PSYCH'T, Psychosomatic Div, Univ. Policlinics, Munich, Ger. Member: NP. Psychotherapy, consuling, clinical practice, testing; counseling, projective techniques, psychosomatic medicine. M

HAUGAA, Cand. Psychol. Einar. Munthesgt. 35/III, Oslo. b. 4 Mar 1926 Bygland. Cand. Psychol. '54 Univ. of Oslo, Nor. SCH. PSYCH'T, Skolepsykologisk kontor, Herslebs gate 20/B, Oslo. Member: NP. Consulting, testing, clinical practice, psychotherapy; projective techniques, guidance, teacher-pupil relations. M

HAUGEN, Cand. Psychol. Olav Arne. Lijordveien 22, Lijordet, Røa, Oslo. b. 22 Dec 1919 Hornindal. Cand. Psychol. '54 Univ. of Oslo, Nor. SECRETARY, Nor. Armed Forces, Psych. Div. Sannergt. 14, Oslo. Member: NP. Industrial psychology, testing, teaching, selection and training of military leaders; industrial management training. M

HAVELIN, Cand. Psychol. Arnold. Bentsebrugt. 11A/III, Oslo. b. 9 Nov 1928 Kirkeness. Cand. Psychol. '55 Univ. of Oslo, Nor. SECRETARY, Nor. Armed Forces, Psych. Div, Sannergt. 14, Oslo. Member: NP. Administration, testing, applied psychology; personnel evaluation in industry. M

HAVIN, Mag. Art. Henry. Løvenskioldsvei 12, Jar near Oslo. b. 8 Sept 1902 Stavanger. Mag. art. '28 Univ. of Oslo, Nor. CHIEF PSYCH'T, Inst. of Occupat. Psych, Akersgt. 55, Oslo. Member: NP, AIPA. Applied and industrial psychology, research, teaching; characterological typology and vocabulary, humanistic approach in psychology, psychological theory. M

HERNES, Miss Ragnhild. Ostadalsveien 34 A III, Röa, pr. Oslo. b. 28 Jan 1919 Frosta. MA '51 Boston Univ. USA. SCH. PSYCH'T,

Skolepsykologisk kontor, Herslebs gate 20, Oslo. Member: NP. Testing, guidance, psychotherapy, clinical analysis; projective techniques, counseling. F

HESTMANN, Cand. Psych. Mrs. Karen-Margrethe Wolff. Ludvig Musts vei 16, Trondheim. b. 19 Nov 1927 Trondheim. Cand. Psych. '55 Univ. of Oslo, Nor. Member: NP. Psychotherapy. F

HOLTER, Miss Borghild. Fredensborgveien 22, Oslo. b. 18 Mar 1927 Voss. Cand. Psychol. '53 Univ. of Oslo, Nor. PSYCH. INTERNE, Neuropsychiat. Inst, Univ. Hosp, 1313 E, Ann Arbor, Mich, USA. Member: NP. Testing, diagnosis, clinical practice, student; personality theory, psychopathology, projective techniques. F

HOLTER, Cand. Psychol. Peter Andreas. Wergelandsveien 5, Oslo. b. 18 May 1927 Oslo. Cand. Psychol. '53 Univ. of Oslo, Nor. MANAGEMENT TRNG. CONSULT, Den Polytekniske Forenings Rasjonaliseringsgruppe, Rosenkrantzgt. 7, Oslo. Member: NP. Industrial psychology, administration, teaching; industrial relations, personnel selection, group training methods. M

HOV, Dir. Bergsvein. Berg Arbeidsskole, Tønsberg. b. 28 Nov 1910 Vefsn. Cand. Psychol. '50 Univ. of Oslo, Nor. DIRECTOR, Berg Arbeidsskole, Tønsberg. Member: NP. Teaching, administration of a juvenile penal institution. M

HOVE, Cand. Psych. Cand. theol. Peter. Laksevåg/Bergen. b. 12 June 1904 Stordal. PASTOR, Parishof Laksevåg; PSYCH. TCHR, High Sch. and Student Nurses' Sch. Guidance, administration, teaching, consulting. M

HVATTUM, Mag. Art. Gunnar. Skolepsykologisk kontor, Lillehammer. b. 21 Jan 1922 Gran. Mag. art. '55 Univ. of Oslo, Nor. SCH. PSYCH'T, Skolepsykologisk kontor. Member: NP. Teaching, student, testing. M

IRGENS JENSEN, Cand. Psychol. Olav. Kastellveien 20, Nordstrand, Oslo. b. 4 Dec 1927 Oslo. Cand. Psychol. '54 Univ. of Oslo, Nor. PSYCHOLOGIST, Nor. Armed Forces, Psych. Div, Sannergt. 14, Oslo. Applied psychology, testing, student. M

IVERSEN, Cand. Psychol. MA Eva Schibbye. Ostadalsvei 34 A, Røa, Oslo. b. 7 Mar 1928 Oslo. Cand. Psychol. '51 Univ. of Oslo, Nor; MA ,Wayne Univ, Detroit, Mich, USA. CONSULTANT, Emma Hjorth's Hjem, Sandvika, Baerum. Member: NP, Nor. Child Psychiat. Socy. Testing, clinical analysis, consulting, guidance, teaching; projective techniques, intelligence testing, normal and neurotic personality, retarded and feebleminded children. F

IVERSEN, Cand. Psychol. Kjell. Ostadalsvei 34 A, Røa, Oslo. b. 10 May 1928 Bergen. Cand. Psychol. '53 Univ. of Oslo, Nor.

SECRETARY, Akers Mek. Verksted, Dokkveien 1, Oslo. MEMBER: NP. Industrial personnel psychology; interviewing, testing and attitude measurement, personnel administration. M

JACOBSEN, Cand. Psychol. Gerd. Flekkefjord b. 10 Oct 1920 Volda. Cand. Psychol. '50 Univ. of Oslo, Nor. PSYCHOTHERAPIST, James Jackson Putnam Child. Cen, Roxbury, Mass. Member: NP, Nor. Assn. for Med. Child Psych. Child psychotherapy, consulting, testing; group process, projective techniques, learning theory. F

JANGÅRD, Cand. Psychol. Rolf. Seiersbjerget 17, Bergen. b. 12 Aug 1921 Ålesund. Cand. Psychol. '48 Univ. of Oslo, Nor. SECRETARY, Norges Handelshøyskole, Bergen. Member: NP. Industrial psychology, research, teaching; motivation, group process, management. M

JOHANSSON, Cand. Psychol. Eva. Tråkka 1, Slemdal, Oslo. b. 20 Sept 1922 Stavanger. Cand. Psychol. '53 Univ. of Oslo, Nor. INTERN, Nor. Ment. Hyg. Assn, Bygdøy Allé 12, Oslo. Member: NP. Diagnostic testing, clinical analysis, parental guidance; therapeutic methods with children, adult counseling, projective techniques. F

JOHNSEN, Cand. Psychol. Hans Petter. Eiksveien 70, Røa, Oslo. b. 31 May 1925 Oslo. Cand. Psychol. '52 Univ. of Oslo, Nor. MILIT. PSYCH'T, Nor. Armed Forces, Psych. Div, Sannergaten 14, Oslo. Member: NP. Administration, industrial and military personnel psychology, testing; psychological problems in industrial personnel administration. M

JOHNSTAD, Cand. Psychol. Trygve. Box 84, Hvalstad. b. 1 Sept 1921 Haugesund. Cand. Psychol. '49 Univ. of Oslo, Nor. CONSULTANT, Natl. Tech. Inst, Akersvn. 24/c, Oslo; REHAB. COUNS, Mo i Rana Hosp; EDUC. CONSULT, Mo i Rana Primary Sch. Member: NP. Management training, testing, teaching; projective techniques, cultural and psychological determinants of ethics and social norms, industrial relations. M

JOREM, Cand. Psychol. Per. Box 1415, Oslo. b. 23 Nov 1919 Bergen. Cand. Psychol. '49 Univ. of Oslo, Nor. COMMANDER, Royal Nor. Navy, Grev Wedels pl. 6, Oslo; RES. PSYCH'T, Ministry of Commerce. Member: NP. Administration, research, testing; personality inventories, psychological screening methods for sailors, interviewing. M

JØRGENSEN, Cand. Psychol. Else. Oppsaltoppen 2, Oppsal pr. Oslo. b. 17 July 1927 Kragerø. Cand. Psychol. '55 Univ. of Oslo, Nor. PSYCHOLOGIST, Nor. Res. Counc. for Sci. and Humanities, Løkkevn. 7, Oslo. Member: NP. Consulting, group

therapy, clinical analysis, testing; psychotherapy, projective techniques. F

KILE, Cand. Psychol. Svein M. Admin. Res. Found, Seiersbjerget 17, Bergen. b. 13 Jan 1828 Volda. Cand. Psychol. '52 Univ. of Oslo, Nor. GRP. LEADER, Admin. Res. Found. Industrial psychology, teaching, research, student; human relations in industry, attitude measurement, psychotherapy. M

KILLINGMO, Cand. Psychol. Bjørn. Colletts gate 17 /II, Oslo. b. 8 Jan 1927 Oslo. Cand. Psychol. '51 Univ. of Oslo, Nor. CLIN. PSYCH'T, Univ. Psychiat. Clin. Vinderen, Oslo. Member: NP. Diagnostic testing, psychotherapy, research; projective techniques, psychoanalytic therapy. M

KLØVE, Cand. Psychol. Hallgrim. Dept. of Neur, Indiana Univ. Med. Cen, 1100 W. Michigan St, Indianapolis 7, Ind, USA. b. 22 June 1927 Moss. Cand. Psychol. '52 Univ. of Oslo, Nor. INSTR. in NEUR, Indiana Univ. Sch. of Med. Member: NP. Neuropsychological research, teaching; relationship between organic brain function and behavior, physiological psychology. M

KOHT, Jan Andrew. Ekraveien 35, Röa, Oslo. b. 18 July 1924 Narvik. Dipl. Psych. '53 Univ. of Munich, Ger. PSYCH'T. and SOSIALKURATOR, Town of Oslo, Akersgt. 55 H, Oslo. Research, psychotherapy, guidance; learning theory, social perception, group process, juvenile crime. M

KROGH, Cand. Psychol. Kjell von. Dikemark sykehus, Asker. b. 19 Nov 1927 Oslo. Cand. Psychol. '52 Univ. of Oslo, Nor. CLIN. PSYCH'T, Dikemark Ment. Hosp, Oslo Kommune, Asker; CONSULT. PSYCH'T, Mødrehygienekontoret, Storgt. 23, Oslo; PSYCH. CONSULT, Magister Carl-Martin Borgen, Dr. Dedichens priv. clin. Member: NP. Clinical analysis, group and individual psychotherapy, research; major clinical tests, group therapy with schizophrenic patients, personality and social psychology. M

KULLMANN ELSNER, Cand. Psychol. Jacob Edgar. Psychiat. Inst, Univ. of Bergen, Bergen. b. 3 Jan 1923 Bergen. Cand. Psychol. '52 Univ. of Oslo, Nor. CLIN. PSYCH'T, Neevengården Ment. Hosp; and Psychiat. Inst. Univ. of Bergen; CONSULT. PSYCH'T, West Norway Sanatorium for Nerv. Disorders; and Neur. Dept, Haukeland Genl. Hosp, Univ. Clin. Member: NP. Psychodiagnosis, clinical practice, psychotherapy, teaching, projective techniques, mental hygiene in industry, forensic psychiatry. M

KVILHAUG, Cand. Psychol. Bjarne. Box 96, Tønsberg. b. 12 Oct 1928 Tønsberg. Cand. Psychol. '54 Univ. of Oslo, Nor. SOSIAL-

KURATOR, Berg Arbeidsskole, Tønsberg·
Member: NP. Research, testing, group
psychotherapy; problem solving behavior,
psychic research, personality and aptitude
testing, group therapy with criminals. M
LANGSET, Cand. Psychol. Miss Marit. Dr.
Nic Waals Inst, Munkedamsv. 84, Oslo.
b. 13 July 1924 Øksendal. Cand. Psych.
'50 Univ. of Oslo, Nor. PSYCHOTHERAPIST,
Dr. Nic Waals Inst; CHILD PSYCH'T,
Ribshosp. Child. Clin, Oslo. Member:
NP, Nor. Child Psychiat. Assn. Psychotherapy, clinical practice, testing, research,
teaching; family relationships, projective
techniques, therapy and teacher training. F
LARSEN, Cand. Psychol. Kaj Petter. Kongensgt. 14/v, Fylkesarbeidskontoret, Oslo.
b. 3 June 1924 Rjukan. Cand. Psychol.
'53 Univ. of Oslo, Nor. VOCAT. GUID. OFF,
County Labour Off. of Akershus. Member:
NP. Industrial psychology, testing,
teaching. M
LARSSON, Cand. Psychol. Kjell. Rödbergvn.
43, Grefsen, Oslo. b. 8 July 1926 Oslo.
Cand. Psychol. '53 Univ. of Oslo, Nor.
PSYCHOLOGIST, Rehab. Cen, Sinsenvn.
70, Oslo. Member: NP. Testing, clinical
analysis, guidance; projective techniques,
group process. M
LILLEGÅRD, Cand. Psychol. Arthur. Yrkes-
veiledningen i Östfold, Arbeidspsykologisk
Inst, Fredrikstad. b. 18 Mar 1922 Bodö.
Cand. Psychol. '50 Univ. of Oslo, Nor.
DIRECTOR, Inst. of Occupat. Psych, Yrkes-
veiledningen i Östfold. Member: NP.
Vocational guidance, testing, adminis-
tration; aptitude tests, personnel manage-
ment, industrial training. M
LILLESTØLEN, Robert. Skolepsykologisk
Kontor, Sandnes. b. 6 June 1925 Arendal.
Mag. art. '56 Univ. of Oslo, Nor. SCH.
PSYCH'T, Skolepsykologisk Kontor.
Member: NP. Guidance, educational psy-
chology, teaching; internalization of norms,
psychology of religion. M
LØCHEN, Cand. Psychol. Einar. Gamle
Drammensvei 205, Sandvika i Bærum.
b. 26 Nov 1915 Trondheim. Cand. Psychol.
'52 Univ. of Oslo, Nor. PSYCH. COUNS,
Univ. Clin. of Oslo, Dept. of Neur, Riks-
hosp, Oslo; LIEUT, Nor. Army. Member:
NP. Testing, clinical analysis, teaching
mental hygiene; projective techniques,
education, counseling. M
LUND, Cond. Psychol. Bente. Tuengen
allé 9, Vinderen. b. 13 Mar 1921 Oslo.
Cand. Psychol. '53 Univ. of Oslo, Nor.
TEACHER, Studentersamfundets Fri Under-
visning, Munchs gt. 4, Oslo. Member: NP.
Teaching. F
LUNDE, Cand. Psychol. Eivind. Holteveien
42 c, Kolbotn, Oslo. b. 14 Apr 1926 Oslo.
Cand psychol, Univ. of Oslo, Nor. INDUS.

CONSULT, Industriforbundets Ration-
aliseringskontor A/s, Munkedamsveien 53
b, Oslo. Industrial and personnel psychology, testing, consulting, guidance,
professional writing. M
LUNDEN, Mrs. Turi Sverdrup. Barnevernskolen, Øvregt. 41, Bergen. b. 26 Apr 1923
Kongsberg. Mag. art. '49 Univ. of Oslo, Nor.
SCH. DIR, Barnevernskolen. Member: NP,
ICWP, Norsk Pedagozikklag.. Teaching,
training kindergarten teachers, administration, guidance; projective techniques,
intelligence testing, mental hygiene,
guidance techniques. F
LUNDGREN, Erik Adrian. Forsvarets Psy-
kologiske Avdeling, Sannergaten 14, Oslo.
b. 8 Aug 1908 Copenhagen, Den. Cand.
Psych. '47 Univ. of Copenhagen, Den.
SECY. and PSYCHOMET. ADVIS, Nor. Armed
Forces, Psych. Div. Member: NP, Psychomet. Socy. Research, test construction,
teaching, professional writing; measurement
theory, psychology and physiology of
language and handwriting, aptitude and
achievement evaluation. M
MARSTRANDER, Nils Peter. A/s Norsk Jernverk, Mo i Rana. b. 12 Oct 1923 Oslo.
Cand. Psychol. '49 Univ. of Oslo, Nor.
TRNG. MGR, A/s Norsk Jernverk. Member:
NP. Planning training programs, industrial
psychology; test construction, attitude
measurements, personnel administration. M
MELING, Cand. Psychol. Mildrid. Arbeids-
spykologisk Inst, Nygaten 2, Bergen. b.
13 June 1925 Austre Amøy, Hetland.
Cand. Psychol. Univ of Oslo, Nor. VOCAT.
COUNS, Inst. of Occupat. Psych. Member:
NP. Vocational guidance, testing, personnel
psychology. F
MOE, Cand. Psychol. Einar. Hoffsjef Lövens-
kjolds vei 49, Övre Ullern, Oslo. b. 3 May
1926 Oslo. Cand. Psychol. '54 Univ. of
Oslo, Nor. TRAINEE in CLIN. PSYCH, Dr.
Nic Waal's Inst, Munkedamsveien 84, Oslo.
Member: NP, Nor. Assn. for Psychiat. and
Clin. Child Psych. Child psychotherapy,
testing, clinical analysis, administration;
projective techniques, research on therapeutic process in the treatment of psychotic
children, etiologic factors in the development of psychoses. M
MURPHY, Mag. Art. Ingrid Cecilie. Nesodden B.B.L, Tangen II, Oksvall, Nesodden. b. 15 July 1918 Oslo. MA '46
Univ. of Oslo, Nor. RES. ASST, Nor. Res.
Counc. for Sci. and Humanities, Lökkeveien
7, Oslo. Teaching, research, guidance;
intelligence tests, children's attitudes in
institutions, school achievement and intelligence. F
MYKSVOLL, Dosent Birger. Noregs Laerar-
høgskole, Trondheim. b. 26 Nov 1912
Lindås. PH.D '51 Univ. of Maryland, USA.

DOSENT, Noregs Lærarhøgskole; EDITOR, *Norsk Pedagogisk Årbok*. Member: Norsk Pedagogikklag. Teaching, editorial, educational psychology; psychology of adolescence, personality, social psychology. M

NATVIG AAS, Cand. Psychol. Mrs. Randi. Drammensveien 527/B, Blommenholm, Bærum. b. 19 Sept 1928 Bærum. Cand. Psychol. Univ. of Oslo, Nor. Member: NP. Child psychotherapy, research; child development. F

NEVER, Mrs. Margrete Landmark. Prof. Dahls gt. 16/III, Oslo NV. b. 23 May 1917 Trondheim. Mag. art. '46 Univ. of Oslo, Nor. CHIEF PSYCH'T, Child. Clin, Rikshosp, Pilestredet, Oslo. Member: NP, Nor. Psychoanal. Assn. Clinical analysis, psychotherapy, teaching and supervision; psychoanalysis, perception and behavior in children with organic defects, parental guidance. F

NISSEN, Mag. Art. Ingjald. Cort Adelersg. 12, Oslo. b. 2 Sept 1896 Oslo. Mag. art. '25 Univ. of Oslo, Nor. NATL. RES. FELLOW, Nor. Govt. Member: NP, APA. Research, professional writing, teaching; psychology of sex, psychosociology, psychological method. M

NØDLAND, Cand. Psychol. Thoralv K. Scheie. Tangen Terasse 40, Oksval, Bunnefjorden. b. 30 Jan 1928 Stavanger. Cand. Psychol. '54 Univ. of Oslo, Nor. RES. ASST, Nor. Res. Counc. for Sci. and Humanities, Løkkeveien 7, Oslo. Membei: NP. Research, interview analysis, observational data analysis; group process in the family, personality theory, projective techniques, interviewing. M

NØRBECH, Cand. Psychol. Preben. Svane vg. 17, Abildsø, Oslo. b. 13 Aug 1924 Asker. Cand. Psychol. '53 Univ. of Oslo, Nor. SCH. PSYCH'T, Skolepsykologisk Kontor, Herslebs gt, Oslo. Member: NP, Nor. Assn. for Child Psychiat. and Clin. Child. Psych. Testing, consulting, group and individual psychotherapy; personality development, development of reasoning. M

NORDLAND, Dr. Mrs. Eva. Blommenholm, Oslo. b. 3 Jan 1921 Bærum. Dr. philos. '55 Univ. of Oslo, Nor. TCHR. in EDUC, Pedagogisk Inst, Univ. of Oslo, Eilert Sundts gate 40/III, Oslo. Member: NP, Norsk Pedagogikklag. Research, teaching, professional writing; reading interests of children, parent-child relationships, intelligence testing. F

NØRSTEBØ, Prof. Sigurd. Lade gård, Trondheim. b. 17 Jan 1905 Lesja. MA '39 Univ. of Oslo, Nor. PROF, Norges Lærerhøgskole, Trondheim; ED. STAFF, *Norwegian Journal of Education*; *Inter-Scandinavian Journal of Education*; EDITOR, *Skrifter utgjevne av Noregs Lærarhøgskole*.

Member: Royal Nor. Socy. of Sci. and Humanities, Norsk Pedagogikklag. Teaching, research, administration; attitude measurement, educational sociology.M

NYSTUEN, Cand. Psychol. Kjell. Berger Langmoen, Brumunddal. b. 10 Dec 1928 Oslo. Cand. Psychol. '54 Univ. of Oslo, Nor. PERS. CONSULT, Berger Langmoen. Member: NP. Industrial psychology, teaching, research; industrial relations, the growth of industrial society, family relations. M

ØDEGAARD, Cand. Psychol. Gudrun. Østadalsveien 34 A, Røa, Oslo. b. 28 Aug 1924 Oslo. Cand. Psychol. '51 Univ. of Oslo, Nor. CLIN. PSYCH'T, Ment. Hyg. Assn. of Oslo, Bygdøy allé 12, Oslo. Member: NP, Nor. Med. Assn. of Child Psychiat. Clinical diagnosis, child guidance, counseling, administration; projective techniques, intelligence measurement, individual psychotherapy. F

OFTEDAL, Mag. Art. Mrs. Dagny. Bangerudsvingen 14 B, Oslo. b. 10 Feb 1920 Oslo. Mag. art. '46 Univ. of Oslo, Nor. CHIEF PSYCH'T. and DIR, Skolepsykologisk Kontor, Herslebsgt. 20 B, Oslo; CONSULTANT, Ministry of Educ. Member: NP, Nor. Assn. of Child Psychiat. and Clin. Child Psych. Administration, child psychotherapy, clinical practice; projective techniques. F

OLSEN, Cand. Psychol. Alfred Morgan. Statens Ungdoms- og Idrettskontor, Kronprinsensgate 6/III, Oslo. b. 27 Mar 1924 Door County, Wisconsin, USA. Cand. Psychol. '52 Univ. of Oslo, Nor. EDUC. CONSULT, State Off. for Sport and Youth Work; LECT. in PSYCH. and EDUC, State Sch. of Physical Educ, Oslo. Member: NP. Preparing psychological textbook for physical education, teaching, research; perception, motivation and learning in physical education. M

ØRNER, Lt. Commander, Cand. Psychol. Jan August. Vargveien 21, Ulvøya Bekkelaget. b. 27 Apr 1924 Oslo. Cand. Psychol '52 Univ. of Oslo, Nor. LT. COMMANDER, Royal Nor. Navy, Hq. Trng. and Pers. Dept, Oslo. Member: NP. Applied, educational and industrial psychology, consulting. M

ØSTBY, Mag. Art. Hans Edvard. Skolepsykologisk Kontor, Rådstaplass 8, Bergen. b. 6 Sept 1919 Eidsvoll. Mag. art '52 Univ. of Oslo, Nor. SCH. PSYCH'T, Skolepsykologisk Kontor; LECTURER, Univ. of Bergen. Member: NP. Testing, educational psychology, research, teaching; attitude measurement, group process, achievement tests. M

ØSTLYNGEN, Dr. Paul Emil Schytte. Oscars gate 49, Oslo. b. 3 Nov 1915 Skien. Dr. philos. '47 Univ. of Oslo, Nor. EDUC. SUPERV, Nor. Correspondence Sch, Arbiens gate 7, Oslo; NOR. ED, *Nordisk Psykologi*; NOR. Co-Ed, *Acta Psychologica*. Member: NP. Administration, teaching, editorial; attitude measurement, research on twins, bibliographical work. M

ØSTLYNGEN, Cand. Psychol. Mrs. Lise Heber. Oscars gate 49, Oslo. b. 11 Sept 1921 Oslo. Cand. Psychol. '50 Univ. of Oslo, Nor. SUPERVISOR, Univ. Students' Nursery Sch, Drammensveien 42/b, inng. Thomlesgate, Oslo; TEACHER, Child Welf. Acad. Member: NP. Administration, teaching children and student teachers, research, guidance; projective techniques, child development and guidance. F

PAASCHE, Cand. Psychol. Thor. Skansegt. 9, Trondheim. b. 14 Mar 1926 Trondheim. Cand. Psychol. '55 Univ. of Oslo, Nor. RES. FELLOW, Nor. Res. Counc. for Sci, and Humanities, Lökkeveien 7, Oslo. Member: NP. Research in industrial psychology, testing; test construction. M

PIENE, Mag. Art. Fiffi. Skjerstadvn 2 a, Oslo Smestad. b. 23 Sept 1918 Kristiansund Mag. art. '46 Univ. of Oslo, Nor. CLIN. PSYCH'T, Dr. Nic Waals Inst, Munkedamsvn 86, Oslo. Member: NP, Nor. Psychoanal. Assn, Nor. Assn. for Clin. Psychiat and Clin. Child Psych. Psychotherapy, teaching, clinical practice; group research on predictive value of different projective techniques. F

RAAHEIM, Cand. Psychol. Kjell. Dolvikflatens brevhus, Fana. b. 8 Oct 1920 Bergen. Cand. Psychol. '55 Univ. of Oslo, Nor. Member: NP. Applied psychology, experimental industrial research, teaching; problem solving, intelligence and aptitude evaluation. M

RAKNES, Dr. Ola. Nilserudkleiva 16, Nordberg Oslo U.H. b. 17 Jan 1887 Bergen. Dr. philos. '28 Univ. of Oslo, Nor. PSYCHOTHERAPIST, priv. prac. Member: NP, Amer. Assn. for Med. Orgonomy. Psychotherapy, psychoanalytic training, consulting, professional writing; mental health, psychology of sex, psychology of religion. M

RAMM, Cand. Psychol. Eva. Tangenåsen, Oksval i Bonnefjord. b. 23 Nov 1925 Bergen. Cand. Psychol. '55 Univ. of Oslo, Nor. PSYCH. CONSULT, Pub. Sch. of Nesodden. Member: NP. Testing, lecturing; child guidance, psychosomatic medicine, projective techniques. . F

RAND, Mrs. Gunvor Marie. Johan Sverdrupsv. 40, Økern, Oslo. b. 1 Mar 1925 Porsgrunn. Mag. art. '52 Univ. of Oslo, Nor. TEACHER, Sagene Tchr. Trng. Coll, Biermanns gt. 2, Oslo. Member: NP. Teaching, testing, research; personality and intelligence tests, socialization process. F

RAND, Per Jan. Johan Sverdrupsv. 40, Økern, Oslo. b. 19 July 1924 Porsgrunn.

Mag. art. '51 Univ. of Oslo, Nor. RES. FELLOW, Nor. Res. Counc. for Sci. and Humanities, Løkkevn. 7, Oslo; TCHR. of EDUC. PSYCH, Univ. of Oslo. Member: Nor. Pedagogikklag. Research, teaching, testing; learning theory, intelligence tests, development of number concepts. M

RIBSSKOG, Dr. phil. Bernhof. Boltelökka allé 8, Oslo. b. 25 Jan 1883 Flatanger. PH.D '31 Univ. of Oslo, Nor. Member: NP. Teaching, research, administration. M

RIESE, Miss Cand. Psychol. Ellen. Klevveien 21, Bekkestua, pr. Oslo. b. 4 May 1925 Oslo. Cand. Psychol. '54 Univ. of Oslo, Nor. MILIT. PSYCH'T, Nor. Armed Forces, Psych. Div, Sannergaten 14, Oslo. Member: NP. Psychodiagnostics, research, personnel psychology; interviewing, officer and technician selection. F

RIIS, Cand. Psychol. Erik. Guvernørens vei 10, Lilleaker, Oslo. b. 23 Sept 1923 Oslo. Cand. Psychol. '49 Univ. of Oslo, Nor. HEAD AVIAT. PSYCH'T, Royal Nor. Air Force, Myntgt. 2, Oslo. Member: NP. Research, testing, pilot selection, accident prevention, teaching; validation research on aptitude tests for pilots, therapy. M

ROGSTAD, Cand. Psychol. Carl. Lilleborg Fabrikker, Sandakervn 46/b, Oslo. b. 9 May 1930 Oslo. Cand. Psychol. '54 Univ. of Oslo, Nor. SECRETARY, Advertising and Marketing Dept, Lilleborg Fabrikker, Sandakervn 54, Oslo. Market research, applied psychology, administration. M

ROKSAND, Cand. Psychol. Bjørn. Oksval i Bunnefjord. b. 19 Apr 1921 Oslo. Cand. Psych. '50 Univ. of Oslo, Nor. VOCAT. PSYCH'T, Arbeidspsykologisk Inst, Akersgt. 55, Oslo. Member: NP. Testing, guidance, applied psychology; psychology of religion, attitude measurement. M

ROMMETVEIT, Dozent Dr. Ragnar. Dept. of Psych, Univ. of Oslo, Karl Johansgt. 47, Oslo. b. 11 July 1924 Stord. PH.D '54 Univ. of Oslo, Nor. ASSOC. PROF, Univ. of Oslo. Member: NP. Teaching, research, administration; social pressure, perception, theory construction in psychology. M

RONGVED, Cand. Psychol. Magnus. Thora Stormsvei 1, Trondheim. b. 9 Dec 1922 Bergen. Cand. Psychol. '55 Univ. of Oslo, Nor. HEAD OCCUPAT. PSYCH'T, Juv. Labor Exchange Bur, Inst. of Occupat. Psych, Kongensgt. 89, Trondheim. Member: NP, AIPA. Industrial and applied psychology, testing, guidance; intelligence and projective testing, social attitudes. M

ROTEVATN, Cand. Psychol. Jarle. Uranienborgveien 11, Oslo. b. 11 Nov 1923. Volda. Cand. Psychol. 1952 Univ. of Oslo, Nor. Member: NP. Norw. State Loan Fund, student advisor, counseling. Educational and vocational guidance. Clinical practice, testing, projective techniques. M

SÆTERSDAL, Cand. Psychol. Ulle. Solåsen 22, Nesttun, Fana. b. May 1923 Oslo. Cand. Psychol. '49 Univ. of Oslo, Nor. CONSULTANT, Child. Clin, Neur. Dept, Haukeland Sykehus, Bergen; CHILD GUID. COUNS, Bergen Ment. Hyg. Assn. Member: NP, Norsk Pedagogikklag. Consulting, testing, guidance, teaching; projective techniques, intelligence testing. F

SANDVEN, Prof. Dr. Johs. Ullernkammen 5, Oslo. b. 1 Nov 1909 Fana. PH.D '46 Univ. of Oslo, Nor. PROF. of EDUC. and DIR, Inst for Educ. Res, Univ. of Oslo, EDITOR, *Forskning og Danning*; *Pedagogisk Forskning*. Member: Nor. Educ. Socy. Research, administration, teaching; developmental psychology, problems of prediction, attitude measurement. M

SAUGSTAD, Dr. Per. Psych. Inst. Univ. of Oslo, Karl Johansgate 47, Oslo. b. 24 Oct 1920 Oslo. PH.D '52 Univ. of Chicago, USA. LECT. in EXPER. PSYCH, Psych. Inst, Univ. of Oslo. Member: NP. Research, teaching, administration; learning theory, thinking, perception. M

SCHIÖLL, Stein. Sörkedalsveien 220, Röa, Oslo. b. 10 Dec 1931 Trondheim. MS '55 Kansas State Teachers Coll, USA. APPL. PSYCH'T, Arbeidspsykologisk Inst, Akersgt. 55, Oslo. Student, selection testing, vocational guidance, applied psychology; development of high school guidance and test service program, test construction. M

SCHJELDERUP, Prof. Dr. Harald Krabbe. Kilenveien 4, Lysaker. b. 21 May 1895 Dypvaag. Dr. philos. '20 Univ. of Oslo, Nor. PROF. and CHMN, Psych. Dept, Univ. of Oslo; DIRECTOR, Psych. Inst, Univ. of Oslo. Member: NP, Nor. Psychoanal. Assn. Teaching, psychotherapy, research; personality theory, psychology of neuroses. M

SCHJELDERUP-EBBE, Prof. Dr. Thorleif. Eil. Sundtsg. 11, Oslo. b. 12 Nov 1894 Oslo. Dr. phil. '21 Greifswald Univ, Ger. PROF. of SOCIOL, Univ. Nouvelle de Paris, Blvd. St. Martin 19, Paris, Fr. Research, professional writing, applied psychology; social perception, group process, attitude measurement. M

SCHJESVOLD, Cand. Psychol. Kari Marie. Dr. Nic Waals Inst, Munkedamsveien 84, Oslo. b. 1 Apr 1928 Nøtterøy. Cand. Psychol. '52 Univ. of Oslo, Nor. TRAINEE in CLIN. PSYCH, Dr. Nic Waals Inst. Member: NP. Child psychotherapy, personality observation and testing, counseling; projective techniques, psychotherapeutic techniques, problem children. F

SCHJØTH, Cand. Psychol. Mrs. Ellen Alice. Bjørnveien 26, Slemdal, Oslo. b. 9 Oct 1897 Oslo. Cand. Psychol. '54 Univ. of Oslo, Nor. Member: NP. Student, testing,

research; projective techniques, achievement tests, graphology. F

SEIDEL, Cand. Psychol. Jan. Nobelsgt. 22/AIII, Oslo. b. 22 Feb 1931 Fredrikstad. Cand. Psychol. '56 Univ. of Oslo, Nor. CLIN. CHILD PSYCH'T, Dr. Nic Waals Inst, Munkedamsveien 24, Oslo. Member: NP. Clinical practice, teaching, testing; projective techniques, group process, social development. M

SEIM, Mag. Art. Mrs. Sol. Inndalsveien 100, Bergen. b. 8 Sept 1913 Bergen. Mag. art. '41 Univ. of Oslo, Nor. CHIEF PSYCH'T, Inst. of Occupat. Psych, Nygaten 2, Bergen; LECT. in PSYCH, Univ. of Bergen. Member: NP, AIPA. Administration, consulting, research, teaching; projective technique, achievement tests, educational and vocational counseling. F

SELJESTAD, Miss Ingegerd. Skolepsykologisk Kontor, Trondheim. b. 1 Apr 1925 Sørreisa. MA '54 Univ. of Minnesota, USA. SCH. PSYCH'T, Skolepsykologisk Kontor. Member: NP, Norges Lærerlag. Teaching, testing, consulting, clinical practice, guidance. F

SIMONSEN, Cand. mag. Mrs. Hjördis. Bygdöy allé 26, Oslo. b. 3 Apr 1899 Drammen. Cand. mag. '23 Univ. of Oslo, Nor. PSYCHOANALYST, Inst. for Dybdepsykologi, Oslo. Member: NP, Nor. Psychoanal. Assn. Psychotherapy, teaching, consulting; psychoanalytic theory. F

SIMONSEN, Dr. Kathrine. Farmannsgate 12, Frederikstad. b. 28 Oct 1903 Fredrikstad. Dr. philos. '47 Univ. of Oslo, Nor. SCH. PSYCH'T, St. Croix Sch, Fredrikstad. Member: Norsk Pedagogikklag. Educational psychology, testing, guidance, research; developmental psychology, exceptional children, achievement tests, vocabulary. F

SKAARDAL, Mag. Art. Olav. Sørkedalsveien 229, Røa, pr. Oslo. b. 12 Oct 1919 Rjukan. Mag. art, Univ. of Oslo, Nor. RES. FELLOW, Univ. of Oslo. Research, teaching; occupational guidance, social psychology. M

SKARD, Mrs. Aase Gruda. Fjellvegen 2, Lysaker. b. 2 Dec 1905 Oslo. Mag. art. '31 Univ. of Oslo, Nor. ASSOC. PROF, Inst. of Psych, Univ. of Oslo, Karl Johans gt 47, Oslo; EDITOR, *Norwegian Journal of Education*. Member: NP, ICWP, Nor. Assn. for Child Psychiat. and Clin. Child Psych. Teaching, research, editorial, administration; development of normal children, social relations in a class-room, imitation and identification in pre-school children. F

SKARD, Dr. Øyvind. Skådalsveien 24, Vettakollen, Oslo. b. 6 Nov 192 Lier. Dr. philos. '51 Univ. of Oslo, Nor. INDUS. CONSULT, priv. prac. Member: NP, Nor. Ment. Hlth. Assn. Research, industrial psychology, professional writing, aptitude testing, attitude measurement, group process. M

SKJENSTAD, Cand. Psychol. Haakon. Arbeidspsykologisk Inst, Nygaten 2, Bergen. b. 15 Apr 1923 Trondheim. Cand. Psychol. '52 Univ. of Oslo, Nor. VOCAT. COUNS, Inst. of Occupat. Psych. Member: NP. Industrial psychology, teaching, vocational guidance; nonverbal intelligence tests. M

SLETTEN, Cand. Psychol. Miss Anne Marit. Vøiensvingen 19, Oslo. b. 13 May 1919 Bergen. Cand. Psychol. '56 Univ. of Oslo, Nor. EDUC. PSYCH'T, Dr. Nic Waal's Inst, Munkedamsvei 84, Oslo. Member: Nor. Assn. of Child Psychiat. and Clin. Child Psych. Teaching, consulting, testing, psychotherapy; learning problems, emotional pathology, psychotic children. F

SLETTEN, Cand. Psych. Tormod. Fjellseterveien 34 b. Trondheim. b. 6 Mar 1927 Oslo. Cand. Psychol. '55 Univ. of Oslo, Nor. SCH. PSYCH'T, Skolepsykologisk Kontor, Munkegaten 17, Trondheim; TEACHER, Trng. Coll. for Kindergarten Tchrs. Member: NP. Child guidance, consulting, teaching, research; measurement of mental ability, social perception, therapeutic procedures. M

SMEDSLUND, Dr. Jan. Inst. for Soc. Res, Arbiens gt. 4/II, Oslo. b. 1 May 1929 Oslo. PH.D '55 Univ. of Oslo, Nor. RES. ASSOC. Inst. for Soc. Res; TEACHER, Univ. of Oslo; CONSULTANT, Dr. Nic Waal's Child Guid. Clin. Research, teaching, testing, guidance; learning, motivation, social perception, depth psychotherapy. M

SØHR, Cand. Psychol. Arvid Mosgård. Gamle Drammensvei 97, Høvik. b. 28 Apr 1916 Oslo. Cand. Psychol. '55 Univ. of Oslo, Nor. PSYCHOLOGIST, Dr. Nic Waal's Inst, Oslo. Member: NP. Testing, guidance, play therapy; projective techniques. M

SOLLID, Cand. Psychol. Reidar. Box 2028, Oslo. b. 14 Dec 1926 Drangedal. Cand. Psychol. '54 Univ. of Oslo, Nor. PERS. PSYCH'T, Nor. Armed Forces, Psych. Div, Sanner gt. 14, Oslo. Testing, personnel evaluation, administration. M

SOLUM, Cand. Psychol. Eiliv. Tangen IV, Oksval, Nesodden. b. 30 Apr 1927 Sannidal. Cand. Psychol. '50 Univ. of Oslo, Nor. SCH. PSYCH'T, Skolepsykologisk Kontor, Herslebs gate 20 B, Oslo. Member: NP. Diagnostic testing, clinical practice, guidance, psychotherapy; parent-child relations, projective techniques. M

STEEN, Mrs. Inki. Sofienberggt. 61/C, Oslo. b. 23 Mar 1919 Oslo. Mag. art. '47 Univ. of Oslo, Nor. RES. ASST, Univ. of Oslo, Karl Johansgate 47, Oslo. Member: NP. Nor. Ass. of Child Psychiatr. and Clin. Child Psych.; Nor. Psychoanalytic Ass. Ad-

ministration, teaching; projective techniques psychoanalysis. F

STEINSHOLT, Mag. Art. Odd. Johan Øydegardsvei 81, Kristiansand S. b. 19 Sept 1921 Hedrum. Mag. art '53 Univ. of Oslo, Nor. SCH. PSYCH'T, Skolepsykologisk Kontor, Kristiansand S. Member: Norsk Pedagogikklag. Educational psychology; mental deficiency, children's number concepts. M

STENSENG, Cand. Psychol. Leif Torvald. Fagerborggt. 6 c/v, Oslo. b. 21 Aug 1927 Bodø. Cand. Psychol. '54 Univ. of Oslo, Nor. MILIT. PSYCH'T, Nor. Armed Forces, Psych. Div, Sannergt. 14, Oslo. Member: NP. Personnel selection, testing, research; interview methods, achievement tests. M

STOVNER, Anna Marie. Fossveien 9, Oslo. b. 3 July 1917 Enebak. Licentia practicandi '47 Univ. of Oslo, Nor. CLIN. ASST, Nic Waal's Inst, Munkedammsveien 84, Oslo. Applied and educational psychology, testing, child guidance; learning theory. F

STRAND, Cand. Psychol. Nils Hjellup. Arbeidspsykologisk Inst, Akersgt. 55, Oslo. b. 18 Nov 1926 Trondheim. Cand. Psych. '53 Univ. of Oslo, Nor. INDUS. PSYCH'T, Inst. of Occupat. Psych. Member: NP. Testing, consulting, industrial psychology; human relations in industry, vocational, personal and educational counseling, psychotherapy. M

SUNDE, Mag. Art. Mrs. Signe. Røahagan 43, Røa, Oslo. b. 10 July 1915 Halden. Mag. art. '48 Univ. of Oslo, Nor. TEACHER, Secondary Schools, Oslo. Member: Norsk Pedagogikklag. Teaching, censorship, testing; reading deficiency, construction of reading tests, child guidance in schools. F

SYVERSEN, Cand. Psychol. John Louis. Konvallveien 2, Oksval, Nesodden. b. 5 Feb 1929 Sarpsborg. Cand. Psychol. '55 Univ. of Oslo, Nor. PSYCHOLOGIST, Nor. Air Force, Psych. Div, Sannergt. 14, Oslo. Member: NP. Selection of pilots, personnel psychology, testing, research; aviation and military psychology. M

THORBJØRNSRUD, Cand. Psychol. Guttorm. Rånåsfoss. b. 14 July 1930. Cand. Psychol. '55 Univ. of Oslo, Nor. PERS. PSYCH'T, Nor. Armed Forces, Psych. Div, Sannergt. 14, Oslo. Member: NP. Personnel selection, psychotherapy, research; group dynamics, industrial psychology. M

THORSRUD, Cand. Psychol. Einar. Nor. Inst. of Tech, Trondheim. b. 30 Apr 1923 Biri. Cand. Psychol. '48 Univ. of Oslo, Nor. LECTURER, Nor. Inst. of Tech. Member: NP. Research, teaching, industrial psychology; personnel and industrial relations, organizational processes, role relationships. M

TILLER, Cand. Psychol. Per Olav. Inst. of

Soc. Res, Arbiens gt. 4, Oslo. b. 2 July 1926 Trondheim. Cand. Psychol. '51 Univ. of Oslo, Nor. RES. DIR, Inst. for Soc. Res. Member: NP. Research, testing; family structure and personality, father role, identification, ego functions. M

TJØTTA, Cand. Psychol. Asbjórg. Johan Svendsens vei 4, Stavanger. b. 12 Jan 1928 Oslo. Cand. Psychol. Univ. of Oslo, Nor. Educational psychology; group process, projective techniques, retarded children. F

TUNOLD, Cand. Psychol. Hermod. Marinekommando Østlandet, Sanitetet, Horten. b. 29 Apr 1920 Gloppen. Cand. Psychol. '55 Univ. of Oslo, Nor. MARINE PSYCH'T, E. Nor. Marine Command, Med. Div. Horten. Member: NP. Clinical practice, testing, applied and personnel psychology; neurosis, projective techniques, industrial psychology. M

URDAL, Cand. Psychol. Bjørn. Drammensveien 56/b, Oslo. b. 17 Apr 1926 Moss. Cand. Psychol. '54 Univ. of Oslo, Nor. PSYCHOLOGIST, Dr. Nic Waal's Inst, Munkedamsveien 84, Oslo. Member: NP. Testing, psychotherapy, applied psychology. M

VALSØ, Cand. Psychol. Mrs. Inger. Holtegaten 20/III, Oslo. b. 3 Spet 1909 Tromsø. Cand. Psychol. '55 Univ. of Oslo, Nor. SCH. PSYCH'T, Skolepsykologisk Kontor, Herslebs gate 20 b, Oslo. Member: NP. Testing, clinical analysis, guidance, educational psychology; projective techniques, psychological examination for patients with organic brain disease or damage, child psychology. F

VEDELER, Cand. Psychol. Gerdt Henrik. Barnevernklinikkan, Vestfold Sentral-sykehus, Tønsberg. Cand. Psychol. '51 Univ. of Oslo, Nor. CHILD PSYCH'T, Child Guid. Clin, Vestfold Cen. Hosp. Member: NP. Nor. Assn. of Child Psychiat. and Clin. Child Psych. Child psychotherapy, diagnosis, research; projective techniques, dynamic aspects of family relations. M

VEGUM, Miss Aasta. Skilepsykologisk Kontor, Stavanger. b. 26 July 1920 Larvik. Mag. art. '48 Univ. of Oslo, Nor. SCH. PSYCH'T, Pub. Sch. of Stavanger; TCHR of EDUC. PSYCH, Statens Lærerskoleklasser, Stavanger. Member: Norsk Pedagogikklag, Nor. Assn. for Child Psychiat. and Clin. Child Psych. Testing, teaching, guidance, educational psychology; parent education, retarded children, school readiness. F

VORMELAND, Mag. Art. Oddvar. Eiksveien 53, Røa, Oslo. b. Hof in Solör. Mag. art.

'51 Univ. of Oslo, Nor. EDUC. PSYCH'T, Skolepsykologisk Kontor, Herslebsgt 20 b, Oslo; TCHR. of EDUC. PSYCH, Nor. Correspondence Sch; ED. SECY, *Prismet.* Member: Norsk Pedagogikklag. Educational psychology, guidance, testing; school readiness, educational measurement. M

WAAGE, Cand. Psychol. Jan Fredrik Holmboe. Sølvsberget, Gran. b. 24 Jan 1930 Oslo. Cand. Psychol. '54 Univ. of Oslo, Nor. TEACHER, Gran Skolekontor, Gran. Member: NP. Teaching, diagnosing educational difficulties, testing, research; education of retarded children. M

WAAL, Dr. Nic Caroline. Dr. Nic Waal's Inst. of Psychother, Munkedamsvn 84, Oslo. b. 1 Jan 1905 Oslo. DIRECTOR, Dr. Nic Waal's Inst. of Psychother; MEMBER, Pub. Hlth. Serv. Comm. on Sterilization; EDITOR, *Parent's Magazine.* Member: Int. Assn. of Child Psychiat, Int. Comm. on Grp. Psychother. Training of child psychiatrists, administration, psychotherapy, research, editorial; clinical psychology, mental hygiene, child psychiatry. F

WALLE, Cand. Psychol. Arne. Inst. of Human and Indus. Relat, Nor. Sch. of Econ. and Bus. Admin, Seiersbjerget 17, Bergen. b. 7 Dec 1926 Fredrikstad. Cand. Psychol. '53 Univ. of Oslo, Nor. SCI. ASST, Inst. of Human and Indus. Relat. Member: NP. Research in industrial psychology and personnel problems, professional writing; human relations in industry, group organization, group dynamics, psychological factors in leadership. M

WALLE, Cand. Psychol. Mrs. Erna Repenning. Ulriksdal 5, Bergen. b. 7 Feb 1926 Bergen. Cand. Psychol. '53 Univ. of Oslo, Nor. OCCUPAT. PSYCH'T, Inst. of Occupat. Psych, Nygaten 2, Bergen. Vocational guidance, testing, research; counseling, attitudes, values. F

WEGGE, Cand. Psychol. Gunnar. Eiksveien 58, Røa, Oslo. b. 19 Feb 1915 Oslo. Cand. Psychol. Univ. of Oslo, Nor. PERS. COUNS, priv. prac. Member: NP. Industrial psychology, personnel testing and counseling; group process, leadership, social perception. M

WISNES, Cand. Psychol. Miss Gerd. Skarrud Behandlingshjem, Darbu. b. 9 Feb 1928 Molde. Cand. Psychol. '53 Univ. of Oslo, Nor. PSYCHOLOGIST, Skarrud Trtmt. Home. for Nerv. Child. Testing, clinical practice, guidance; projective techniques, achievement tests. F

PAKISTAN

AHMED, Prof. Mofassiluddin. Primary Trng. Coll, Mymensingh, E. Pakistan. b. 1 Feb 1909 Gulishakhali, Barisal. MA '55 Univ. of Toronto, Can. PROF. of PSYCH. and VICE PRIN, Primary Trng. Coll. Member: CPA, All-Pakistan Assn. of Appl. Psych. and Psychoanal, Indian Psychoanal. Socy. Teaching developmental psychology, administration, psychotherapy, child psychology, child guidance; mental health and hygiene, psychopathology, perception. M

AKHTAR, Ala-ud-din. Islamia Coll, Civil Lines, Lyallpur, W. Pakistan. b. 12 Nov 1921 Sargodha. MA '53 Punjab Univ, Pakistan. ASST. PROF, Islamia Coll. Teaching general psychology, research, professional writing, adult education; projective techniques, speech defects, learning. M

ALAWI, Prof. Abdul Hayy. Dept. of Educ, Univ. of Peshawar, Peshawar, W. Pakistan. b. 12 Nov 1909 Gujranwala. MA '38 Univ. of Punjab, Pakistan. PROF. of EDUC. and DEAN of the FAC, Coll. of Educ, Univ. of Peshawar. Member: BPS. Teaching, administration, research; learning theory, personality tests. M

CHAUDHRI, Saeed Ahmed. Dept. of Child Psych, Govt. Coll, Lyallpur, W. Pakistan. b. 1 July 1926 Lahore. MA '48 Punjab Univ, Pakistan. LECTURER, Govt. Coll. Member: BPS, Pakistan Psych. Socy. Teaching, child guidance, testing; projective techniques, comparative study of social differences on intelligence tests. M

CHOUDRI, Mohammad Ali. Talim-ul-Islam Coll, Rabwah, W. Pakistan. b. 11 Dec 1918 Maseetn, Ferozepore. MA '44 Punjab Univ, Pakistan. PROF. and HEAD, Dept. of Philos. and Psych, Talim-ul-Islam Coll. Teaching, psychotherapy, vocational guidance, administration; problem children, stammering and stuttering, religious experience. M

DAS, Prof. Vincent A. Psych. Dept, Murray Coll, Sialkot. b. 22 Mar 1928 Sialkot. MA '49 Univ. of Punjab, Pakistan. HEAD, Dept. of Psych, Murray Coll; DIRECTOR, Psych. Lab, Murray Coll; FULBRIGHT SCHOLAR, Univ. of Texas, Austin, Texas, USA. Teaching general and social psychology, administration; intelligence and personality tests, audio-visual aids. M

HAMID-UD-DIN, Dr. M. Govt. Coll, Lahore, W. Pakistan. b. 4 Mar 1909 Amritsar, Punjab. PH.D '52 Columbia Univ, USA. PROF. and HEAD, Dept. of Philos. and Psych, Govt. Coll. Member: APA, Amer. Stat. Assn, Natl. Educ. Res. Assn. (USA). Teaching, research, psychotherapy, ad-

ministraion; personality testing, learning theory. M

HOSSAIN, Prof. Syed Quamr uddin. Dept. of Phil. and Psych, Edward Coll, Radhanagar, Pabna, E. Pakistan. b. 1 July 1925 Ghorasal, Dacca. MA '52 Univ. of Dacca, Pakistan. SR. PROF, Edward Coll. Member: Pakistan Psych. Socy. Teaching philosophy, psychology and logic, student, professional writing; learning theory, achievement, intelligence and personality tests. M

HUSAIN, Miss Aziz Muhammad. Husain Lodge, Calcutta Rd, Lahore Cantonment, W. Pakistan. b. 5 June 1922 Ferozepur, India. MA '55 Punjab Univ, Pakistan. TCHR. and ASST. MISTRESS, Govt. Jr. Model Sch, Educ. Dept, Lahore; LECTURER, Govt. Coll, Lahore. Teaching English and Urdu, research, testing, teaching, projective techniques; social perception, group process. F

HUSAIN, Prof. Karamat. Govt. Coll, Lahore. b. 21 May 1912 Saidpur, Sialkot. MA '33 Punjab Univ, Pakistan. PROF. of PSYCH, Educ. Dept, Govt. Coll. Teaching, administration, professional writing; projective techniques, learning, attitude measurement. M

JILANI, Dr. Ghulam. 10 Fuller Rd, Ramna, Dacca, E. Pakistan. b. 15 Dec 1911 Ferozepore. PH.D '50 Univ. of London, Eng. PROF. and HEAD, Dept. of Philos. and Psych, Univ. of Dacca, Ramna, Dacca; DIRECTOR, Pakistan Inst. of Human Relations, Dacca. Member: BPS. Research, teaching,administration; attitude measurement. M

JONATHAN, Prof. G. C. Edwardes Coll, Peshawar, W. Pakistan. b. 22 Jan 1915 Ambala, India. MA '43 Punjab Univ, Pakistan. PROF. and HEAD, Dept. of Philos. and Psych, Edwardes Coll. Teaching, research, guidance; psychic research, attitude measurement. M

KHALAF-ZAI, Nizam-ud-Din Khan. Educ. Dept, Govt. Coll, Jhang, W. Pakistan. b. 19 Sept 1925 Qasoor, Lahore. MA '49 Punjab Univ, Pakistan. LECTURER, Educ. Dept, Govt. Doll. Teaching; abnormal psychology, mental disease. M

KHAN, Lt. Col. Rafi. Pakistan Pub. Serv. Comm, Ingle Rd, Karachi. b. 1 Aug 1918 Jullundur, India. MA '40 Punjab Univ. Pakistan. PSYCHOLOGIST, Pakistan Pub. Serv. Comm; PERS. ADV, Standard Vacuum oil Co; PERS. CONSULT, Govt. of Pakistan; EDITOR, *Clinical Psychology*; *Nafsiyati Jaize*. Member: Pakistan Psych. Socy. Personnel psychology, psychotherapy, research on social and mental testing;

projective techniques, Freudian psychoanalysis, intercultural relations.	M

KHAN, Shabbir D. Union Jack Club, Victoria Rd, Karachi. b. 1 Aug 1921 Jullundur, India. MA '43 Punjab Univ, Pakistan. PERS. OFF, Oman Farnsworth Wright, Qamar Hse, Bunder Rd, Karachi. Member: Pakistan Psych. Socy. Personnel selection, administration, testing; projective techniques, achievement tests, social perception.	M

KHAN, Theodore A. R. 22 Civil Lines, Sargodha, Pakistan. b. 21 July 1921 Sukkur. MA '45 Univ. of Delhi, India. SR. LECT, Gordon Coll, Rawalpindi. Teaching general psychology, administration.	M

KHURSHID, Miss Chand. Psych. Dept, Govt. Coll, Lahore. b. 15 Aug 1926 Amritsar, India. MA '50 Punjab Univ, Pakistan. LECT. in VOCAT. PSYCH, Govt. Coll. Teaching, research, child guidance; treatment of children with emotional problems, visual perception.	F

MEHKRI, Dr. Ghulam Mohiuddin. 39 Pakistan Quarters, Lawrence Rd, Karachi 3. b. 19 Oct 1908 Bangalore City, India. PH.D '47 Univ. of Bombay, India. LABOR WELF. OFF, off. of Controller, Printing and Stationery, Karachi. Personnel management, psychotherapy, teaching, professional writing; group process, learning theory, social perception.	M

MRIDHA, Sirajuddin. M. M. Coll, Jessore, E. Pakistan. b. 1 June 1933 Wail. MA '55 Univ. of Dacca, Pakistan. LECT. in PHILOS. and PSYCH, M. M. Coll; RES. ASST, Psych. Inst. of Dacca. Teaching, research, educational psychology; projective techniques, learning theory, group process.	M

RAFIG, Said Ahmad. Govt. Coll, Quetta, W. Pakistan. b. 20 Feb 1918 Meerut, India. MA '41 Muslim Univ, Aligarh, India. LECT. in PHILOS. and PSYCH, Govt. Coll. Teaching, educational psychology, research; achievement tests in education, aesthetic experience, environment and personality.	M

RAHMAN, Prof. Fazal-ur. S. M. Coll, Karachi. b. Gujrat City, Pakistan. BA '42 Univ. of Reading, Eng. HEAD, Dept. of Philos. and Psych, S. M. Coll. Teaching, administration, educational psychology.	M

RAUF, Dr. Abdur. 47 Empress Rd, Lahore. b. 10 May 1924 Amritsar, India. PH.D '55 Univ. of London, Eng. DIRECTOR, Child Guid. Clin; HEAD, Psych. Dept, Central Trng. Coll, Lahore. Member: W. Pakistan Child. Aid Socy, Natl. Counc. of Soc. Serv. (London). Administration, guidance, lecturing, research, consulting; group tests for school children, treatment and prevention of delinquency in schools.	M

SAILER, Dr. Randolph C. Ewing Hall, Nila Gumbad, Lahore. b. 24 Aug 1898 Philadelphia, Pennsylvania, USA. PH.D '31 Columbia Univ, USA. PROF. and CHMN, Dept. of Psych, Forman Christian Coll, Punjab Univ, Lahore. Member: APA, Pakistan Psych. Socy. Teaching, professional writing, psychotherapy, consulting; culture and personality, nondirective therapy, mental hygiene.	M

SAIYED, Abdul Hai. 5 Bakhshi Bazar Lane, Dacca, E. Pakistan. b. 30 Nov 1919 Khulna. MA '41 Dacca Univ, Pakistan. LECT. in CHILD PSYCH, Eden Coll, Dacca. Teaching, administration; learning theory, achievement tests, attitude measurement.	M

SIDDIQI, Dr. Mrs. Kaniz Ataullah. Govt. Coll. for Women, Murree Rd, Rawalpindi. b. 4 Aug 1920 Ludhiana, India. PH.D '50 Univ. of Chicago, USA. PRINCIPAL, Govt. Coll. for Women, Rawalpindi. Administration, teaching, educational psychology; social class influence on the development of basic concepts, human development, learning theory.	F

ZAIDI, Dr. Syed Mohammed Hafeez. Psych. Lab, Curzon Hall, Dacca Univ, Ramna, Dacca, E. Pakistan. b. 29 Dec 1926 Faizabad, India. PH.D '55 Univ. of London, Eng. LECTURER, Dacca Univ. Member: BPS, Pakistan Philos. Assn, Pakistan Assn. for Advanc. of Sci. Teaching, research, consulting; learning theory, group process, experimental psychopathology.	M

ZOBERI, Haseenuddin. 50 Irving St, Cambridge 38, Massachusetts, USA. b. 10 Jan 1924 Marehra, India. MA '47 Aligarh Univ, India. LECTURER, Dept. of Psych, Univ. of Karachi, Princess St, Karachi. Member: Pakistan Philos. Assn. Teaching, research; psychoanalysis, child training.	M

PARAGUAY

DECOUD LARROSA, Prof. Reinaldo J. Hernan Velilla y Londres, Asunción. b. 9 Jan 1911 Asunción. Licenciado '50 Univ. of Asunción, Paraguay. PROF. of PSYCH, Univ. of Asunción, Presidente Ayala 10, Asunción; PSYCHOLOGIST, Paraguayan Armed Forces. Teaching, psychotherapy, clinical practice, consulting.	M

ZUBIZARRETA PERIS, Prof. Dr. José Ramón. Iturbe 331, Asunción. b. 8 June 1917 Asunción. MD, Univ. of Asunción, Paraguay. PSYCHIATRIST, Div. of Military Health, Bosco 339, Asunción; ADJUNCT PROF. of NEUROPSYCHIAT, Fac. of Med. Sci,

Univ. of Asunción; VICE DIR, Hosp. de Alienados, Asunción. Member: Círculo Médico Paraguayo. Teaching, psycho-

therapy, clinical practice; group psychotherapy, group process, memory and learning.   M

PERU

BLUMENFELD, Prof. Dr. Walter. Domingo Elías 245, Lima. b. 12 July 1882 Neuruppin, Germany. PH.D '13 Univ. of Berlin, Germany. PROF. PRIN. TITULAR and DIR, Inst. de Psychopedagogía, Fac. of Educ, Natl. Univ. of San Marcos, Lima. Member: SIP, DGP, AIPA, Peruvian Socy. for Psychopedagogic Studies, Peruvian Psych. Socy, São Paulo Psych. Socy. Research, teaching, educational psychology; research in psychology and pedagogy, philosophy of knowledge.   M

CANO JÁUREGUI, Dr. Arnaldo. Colmena 530, Lima. b. 13 Dec 1919 Lima. MD '46 Natl. Univ. of San Marcos, Peru. PSYCHOLOGIST, Cen. of Military Instruction of Peru, Ministry of War, Lima; MED. RESID, Psychiat. Hosp; PROF. of EXPER. PSYCH, Catholic Univ. of Peru. Member: Peruvian Psychiat. Assn, Peruvian League of Ment. Hyg. Selection and classification of military personnel, psychotherapy, teaching;sociometric tests, intelligence tests, attitude measurement.   M

CHIAPPO, Dr. Leopoldo Hipólito. Madrid 132, Lima. b. 17 Dec 1924 Lima. PH.D, Natl. Univ. of San Marcos, Peru. CATEDRATICO PRINCIPAL and CLIN. PSYCH'T, Fac. of Letters and Medicine, Natl. Univ. of San Marcos, Lima. Teaching, testing, clinical analysis, research.   M

DELGADO, Prof. Honorio. Casilla 1589, Lima. b. 26 Sept 1892 Arequipa. Dr. honoris causa, Univ. of Salamanca, Spain. CHIEF of PSYCHIAT. SERV, Hospital "Víctor Larco Herrera;" PROFESSOR, Fac. of Med, Univ. of San Marcos, Lima; PSYCHIATRIST, priv. prac; EDITOR, Revista de Neuro-Psiquiatría. Member: Peruvian Psych. Socy. Psychiatry, psychotherapy, research; psychopathology and psychology of personality.   M

GUARDIA MAYORGA, Prof. Dr. César A. Almirante Guisse 924, Lima. b. 15 May 1906 Ayacucho, Peru. PH.D '34 Univ. of San Agustín, Peru. Research, teaching, professional writing; history of psychology, reflexology, theory of knowledge.   M

LUZA, Dr. Segisfredo. Ave. Prescott 337, Lima. b. 7 Nov 1928 Arequipa. MD '56 Natl. Univ. of San Marcos, Peru. PSYCH'T. and CHIEF of PSYCHIAT, Sch. of Med, Public Health Dept, Lima. Member: Peruvian Psych. Socy, Socy. of Neuro-psychiat. and Legal Med. Teaching, consulting, clinical practice, testing, research;

projective techniques, psychological diagnosis, psychotherapy.   M

QUEROL, Dr. Mariano. Casilla 2511, Lima. b. 19 Aug 1925 Lima. MD '48 Natl. Univ. of San Marcos, Peru. ASSISTANT, Dept. of Psychiat, Fac. of Med, Univ. of San Marcos, Lima; PSYCHIATRIST, priv. prac. Member: Socy. of Neuropsychiat. Consulting, clinical practice, teaching, research; achievement tests, attitude measurement, use of electroencephalography in psychology.   M

RODRÍGUEZ MONTOYA, Dr. Modesto. Residencia Magisterial "Melitón Carvajal" 307, Lima. b. 23 Jan 1919 Usquil. ED.D, Natl. Univ. of San Marcos, Peru. PROF. of EXPER. PSYCH. and LAB. TECHNIQUES, Fac. of Letters, Natl. Univ. of San Marcos, Lima; CHIEF, Natl. Psychopedagogical Inst, Ministry of Pub. Educ, Lima. Member SIP, Peruvian Socy. of Psychopedagogic Studies. Teaching, research, applied psychology; vocational guidance, aptitude measurement, psychology of learning.   M

SAL Y ROSAS, Dr. Federico. Casilla 2076, Lima. b. 18 July 1900 Huaraz. MD, Natl. Univ. of San Marcos, Peru. CHIEF PSYCHIATRIST, Women's Dept, "Víctor Larco Herrera" Psychiat. Hosp, Magdalena del Mar, Lima; PSYCHIATRIST, priv. prac. Member: Groupement Français du Rorschach, Peruvian Psychiat. Assn, Amer. Psychiat. Assn. Consulting, clinical practice, research, professional writing; projective techniques.   M

SARDÓN, Dr. Miguel A. Fac. of Educ, Pontifical Catholic Univ. of Peru, Lima. b. 9 June 1905 Puno. PH.D '44 Natl. Univ. of San Marcos, Peru. PROF. of PSYCH, Pontifical Catholic Univ; HEAD, Vocat. Guid. Dept, Natl. Psychoped. Inst, Lima. Member: Peruvian Socy. of Psychopedagogic Studies. Administration, teaching mental measurements, consulting, student guidance; psychometrics, intelligence, aptitude and achievement tests, educational statistics.   M

SEGUIN, Prof. Dr. Carlos Alberto. Huancavelica 470, Lima. b. 8 Aug. 1907 Arequipa. MD '32 Univ. of Buenos Aires, Argentina. HEAD, Dept. of Psych, Hosp. Obrero, Lima; PSYCHIATRIST, priv. prac; EDITOR, Estudios Psicosomáticos; Revista Médica del Hospital Obrero; Revista Psiquiátrica Peruana.   Psychotherapy,

teaching, research; group psychology, projective techniques. M
SOLARI-SWAYNE, Prof. Enrique. General Borgoño 449, Lima. b. 28 July 1915 Lima. ED.B '55 Natl. Univ. of San Marcos, Peru. CHIEF PSYCH'T, Ministry of Pub. Health,

Ave. Salaverry, Lima; PROFESSOR, Natl. Univ. of San Marcos, Lima. Member: Peruvian Psych. Socy. Personnel selection, guidance, teaching; diagnosis of personality, teaching of characterology and psychotechnics, psychology of art and culture. M

PHILIPPINES

LAGMAY, Dr. Alfredo V. Dept. of Psych, Univ. of the Philippines, Diliman, Quezon City. b. 14 Aug 1919 Manila. PH.D '55 Harvard Univ, USA. ASST. PROF. and HEAD, Dept. of Psych, Univ. of the Philippines; ED. BD, *Education Quarterly*, Univ. of the Philippines. Member: APA. Teaching, consulting, research, administration; behavior in terms of reinforcement theory, behavioral therapeutic techniques, culture and behavior. M

PADILLA, Dr. Sinforoso G. 943 Gonzales, Ermita, Manila. b. 18 July 1901 Solano, Nueva Vizcaya. PH.D '30 Univ. of Michigan, USA. PROFESSORIAL LECT, Extension Div, Univ. of the Philippines; Lyceum of the Philippines; Arellano Univ; and the Far Eastern Univ, Manila; PSYCHOLOGIST, U.S. Veterans Administration, Manila. Teaching, consulting, guidance, testing; intelligence, achievement and personality tests. M

POLAND

BIEGELEISEN-ZELAZOWSKI, Prof. Dr. Bronislaw. ul. Gorska 96, m. 17, Warsaw 36. b. 3 May 1881 Lwow. DIRECTOR, Bureau de l'Etude du Travail, Inst. de l'Economie et de l'Organisation de l'Industrie, Bôite postale 153, Warsaw 10. Research, applied psychology, industrial psychology, testing; statistical methods, psychology of work, vocational guidance. M
BLACHOWSKI, Prof. Dr. Stefan. Fredry 10, Poznán. b. 19 May 1889 Opawa, Czech. PH.D '13 Univ. of Göttingen, Ger. PROF. of PSYCH, Univ. of Poznán, Stalingradzka 1, Poznán; EDITOR, *Przeglad Psychologiczny*. Member: PTP, AIPA. Teaching, research, editorial; senses, memory, thinking. M
BUDKIEVICZ, Janina. Piekna 22 m 3, Warsaw. b. 18 Sept 1896 Warsaw. PH.D '32 Univ. of Warsaw, Poland. ASSOC. PROF, Univ. of Warsaw, Krakowskie Przedmiescie 26/28, Warsaw. Member: PTP. Research, teaching, administration; history of Polish psychology, abstract thought process, applied educational psychology, vocational guidance. F
CHOYNOWSKI, Dr. Mieczyslaw. Slowackiego 66, Krakow. b. 1 Nov 1909 Zulinki. PH.D '46 Univ. of Krakow, Poland. HEAD, Psych. Lab. and Trng. Cen. for Clin. Psych'ts, State Hosp. for Mentally Ill, Krakow-Kobierzyn; CONSULTANT, Psych. Lab, Railways Res. Inst. Member: PTP, APA. Writing, teaching, research; test construction and theory, attitude measurement, personality theory. M
DYBOWSKI, Prof. Dr. Mieczyslaw. Kanclerska 17, Poznan. b. 2 Feb 1885 Kamieniec-Podolski. Prof. '39 Univ. of War-

saw, Poland. RESEARCH. Member: PTP. Research; strength and education of will, psychology of genius, psychology of inspiration. M
GEBLEWICZ, Prof. Dr. Eugène. Marymoncka 34 m 29, Warsaw. b. 13 Dec 1904 Warsaw. PH.D '31 Univ. of Warsaw, Poland. DIRECTOR, Dépt. de Psychologie, Inst. de Biologie Experimentale de M. Nencki, Pasteura 3, Warsaw; CONSULTING ED, *Przeglad Psychologiczny*. Member: PTP. Research, teaching, administration; sensation and perception, reaction times, learning, objective tests of personality. M
GERSTMANN, Docent, Dr. Phil. Stanislaw. 25/18 Chopina, Lublin. b. 28 Mar 1911 Drohobycz. PH.D, Univ. of Lwów, Poland. DOCENT, M. Curie-Sklodowska Univ, pl. Litewski 5, Lublin. Member: PTP. Research, teaching, applied psychology; emotion, character and temperament, imagination. M
GIERULANKA, Dr. Miss Danuta. 99/5 Rue Dietla, Krakow. b. 4 Mar 1909 Krakow. Doctorat '47 Univ. of Krakow, Poland. ASST. PROF, Inst. Mathématique, Univ. of Krakow. Member: PTP. Teaching, research; processes of learning mathematics, thought. F
GRZEGORZEWSKA, Maria. Inst. de Pédagogie Spéciale de l'Etat, 16 Rue Spiska, Warsaw 22. b. 18 Apr 1888 Wotueza. Doctorat, France. PROFESSOR, Univ. of Warsaw; DIRECTOR, Inst. de Pédagogie Spéciale de l'Etat. Member: PTP. Research, consulting, teaching; psychopathology of the child. F
HORNOWSKI, Dr. Boleslaw. ul. Karwows-

kiego 4 m. 5, Poznan. b. 6 May 1914 Studzianka. PH.D '50 Univ. of Poznan, Poland. ASSOC. PROF, Kathedra of Psychology, Univ. im. A. Mickiewicza, ul. Fredry 10, Poznan. Member: PTP. Applied psychology, teaching, consulting; history of psychology, childhood and adolescence, personality, child and vocational guidance, delinquency, attitudes and values. M

HULEK, Dr. Aleksander. Smiata 1 m 17, Warsaw. b. 24 Mar 1916 Bedriemysl. PH.D '51 Univ. of Poznan, Poland. CHIEF, Vocat. Rehab. Sect. Ministry of Labour and Social Welfare, Gzerniakowska 231, Warsaw. Member: PTP. Administration, research, writing; job analysis, vocational rehabilitation, vocational counseling. M

KACZYNSKA-GRZYWAK, Dr. Mrs. Marie. Rue Kielecka 48 m. 9, Warsaw. b. 10 1886 Sosnowiec. PH.D '35 Univ. of Geneva, Switz. CLIN. PSYCH, Dispensaire de la Santé Psychique, Chelmska, Warsaw. Member: PTP. Consulting, testing, research; clinical test, social attitudes, children's formation of concepts. F

KLIMOWICZ, Prof. Dr. Tadeusz. Mianowskiego 5, Radość ad Warsaw. b. 21 Feb 1886 Równe/Wolhynie. PH.D '14 Krakow Univ, Poland. PROFESSOR, Univ. of Warsaw. Member: PTP. Editorial, teaching, research; intelligence measurement, psychology of psychic evolution. M

KOWALSKI, Stanislaw. Univ. of Poznan, Fredry 10, Poznan. b. 10 Aug 1904 Trzemeszno. PH.D '45 Univ. of Poznan, Poland. DOCENT, Inst. of Psych, Univ. of Poznan. Member: PTP. Teaching, educational and personnel psychology, research; learning theory, personality, juvenile delinquency. M

KREUTZ, Prof. Dr. Mieczystaw. ul. Nowowiejska 22/4, Warsaw. b. 31 Dec 1893 Lwów. Doctor '24 Univ. of Lwów, Poland. PROF. of PSYCH, Univ. of Warsaw, Krakowskii 9, rzcolm. 26, Warsaw. Member: PTP. Teaching, research; psychological methods, will and character education. M

LEWICKI, Prof. Dr. Andrzej. Sienkiewicza 30/32, Torun. b. 29 May 1910 Lwów. Docent '51 Univ. of Wroclaw, Poland. DOCENT, A. Mickiewicz Univ, Fredry 10, Poznan; CLIN. PSYCH'T, Psychiat. Clin, Torun. Member: PTP. Research, teaching, testing, clinical analysis; application of Pavlovian theory to the psychology of perception and thinking, experimental research on thinking in oligophrenic children. M

MIELCZARSKA, Docent, Dr. Wladyslawa. Kanclerska 17, Poznan. b. 25 June 1896. Docent '47 Univ. of Poznan, Poland. Member: PTP. Teaching, research, applied psychology; resistance in the child, child

genius, reminiscence. F

NIEMIEC, Mgr. Kazimierz. ul. Reya 1, bl. I, m. 14, Piastow ad Warsaw. b. 1 Mar 1906 Mielec. Mgr. phil. '35 Jana Karim, Poland. PSYCHOLOGIST, Res. Inst. of Railways, Hoza 86, Warsaw. Member: PTP. Testing, personnel psychology, research; personnel selection, work efficiency, vocational choice. M

PIETER, Prof. Dr. Józef. Damrota 4, m. 8, Katowice. b. 19 Feb 1904 Ochaby, Silesia. PH.D '49 Univ. of Lodz, Poland. RECTOR, High Sch. of Educ, Katowice; PROF. of EDUC. PSYCH, Univ. of Warsaw. ED. BD, Naukowe Towarzystwo Pedagogiczne, Krakow, Kwartalnik Psychologiczny. Member: PTP. Research, teaching, administration, educational psychology; psychology of philosophical problems of adolescence, social environmental factors and mental development in children, psychology of reading. M

RADOMSKA STRZEMECKA, Mrs. Helena. Kieleska 48 m 9, Warsaw. b. 24 Feb 1888 Ksiezomierz. Diplôme '23 Pedagog Institute, Warsaw, Poland. RETIRED. Member: PTP. Development of concepts in children and youth, children's attitudes toward war. F

REUTT, Prof. Dr. phil. Józef. Szopena 27 m. 14, Lublin. b. 26 Aug 1907 St. Petersburg, USSR. PH.D '45 Univ. of Poznan, Poland. PROF. and DIR, Chair of Psych, Catholic Univ. of Lublin, Raclawickie 14, Lublin; EDITOR, Roczniki Filozoficzne Towarzystwa Naukowego Katolickiego Uniwversytetu Lubelskiego.. Member: PTP. Teaching, research, editorial; learning theory, will, personality. M

SCHWARZ, Prof. Dr. Jan. Noakowskiege 8, Gdánsk Oliwa. b. 27 Dec. 1901 Lasin. Dr. '31 Univ. of Poznan, Poland. LECT. in PSYCH, Coll. for Tchr. Educ, ul. Krzyweustege 19, Gdánsk Oliwa. Member: PTP. Teaching; teacher individuality, psychology of thought, temperament. M

SLONIEWSKA, Mrs. Dr. Helene. Wyspianskiego 32/6, Wroclaw. b. 12 Aug 1897 Pawlosiow. PH.D, Univ. of Lwow, Poland. DOCENT, Univ. of Wroclaw; PROFESSOR, Katheder d. Psychologie, Plac Nankiera 4, Wroclaw. Member: PTP. Teaching, research, educational psychology; psychology of interests, diagnostic methods, observational methods. F

SZEWCZUK, Prof. Dr. Wlodzimierz Ludwik. 15 Grudnia St. 12/2, Krakow. b. 2 Apr 1913 Jaslo. Docent '54 Univ. of Krakow, Poland. DIRECTOR, Lab. of Exper. Psych, Univ. of Krakow; DIRECTOR, Lab. of Psych, High Sch. for Teachers, Krakow. Member: PTP. Research, teaching, industrial psychology; memory and learning, understanding and problem solving, occupational analysis. M

SZUMAN, Prof. Dr. Stefan. Manifestu Lipcowego 13, Krakow. b. 2 Jan 1889 Torun. Prof. '28 Univ. of Krakow, Poland. DIR. of PSYCH. STUDIES, Univ. of Krakow; EDUC. CONSULT, Inst. of Educ, Warsaw. Member: PTP. Research, educational psychology, teaching; the relation of thinking and speech, esthetics. M

WITWICKI, Dr. Tadeusz. ul. Belgijska 3/32, Warsaw 12. b. 13 Sept 1902 Lwów. Doctor '27 Univ. of Lwów, Poland. LIBRARIAN, Cen. Inst. for Indus. Safety (CIOP), Tamka 1, Warsaw; LECT. in EXPER. PSYCH, Academy of Catholic Theology. Member: PTP. Gathering documents for industrial psychology and safety, teaching; conceptual thinking, mental and mechanical testing, human relations. M

WOLOSZYNOWA, Dr. Lidia. 75 Koszykowa,

m. 16, Warsaw. b. 8 Feb 1911 Petersburg, USSR. PH.D '51 Univ. of Torun, Poland. ACTING PROF. of PSYCH, Univ. of Warsaw; ED. STAFF, *Szkola i Dom.* Member: PTP. Teaching, research, editorial and professional writing; psychology of the school age child, parent teacher relations, methods of teaching psychology. F

ZEBROWSKA, Prof. Dr. phil. Maria. Katedra Psycholigii Wychowawczej, Univ. of Warsaw, ul. Krakowskie Przedmiescie 26/28, Warsaw. b. 13 Dec. 1900 Kordelowka, Ukraine. PH.D '29 Univ. of Warsaw, Poland. PROF. EXTRAORDINAIRE and DIR, Chair of Pedagogical Psych, Univ. of Warsaw; ED. BD, *Przeglad Psychologiczny.* Member: PTP. Teaching, research, educational psychology; juvenile delinquency, adolescent psychology, language and thought. F

RUMANIA

BĂLĂNESCU, Prof. Ion. Rue Bibescu Vodă 19, Bucharest. b. 30 July 1922 Iassy. Lic. '46 Univ. of Bucharest, Rumania. ASST. DIR, Inst. of Psych, Acad. R.P.R, Blvd. 6 Martie 64, Bucharest; ASST. ED, *Revue de Psychologie.* Member: APSLF. Research, teaching, editorial; conscience and subconscience, psychology of art, cybernetics. M

BOTEZ, Dr. Constantin. Inst. of Psych, Academiei R.P.R., Blvd. 6 Martie 64, Bucharest. b. 10 Nov 1904 Iassy. Docteur '36 Univ. of Iassy, Rumania. RES. DIR, Inst. of Psych. Research, applied psychology, professional writing; learning theory, collective process, social perception. M

CAZACU, Mrs. Tatiana. Calea Rahovei 108, Bucharest. b. 25 Jan 1920 Bucharest. Lic. '43 Univ. of Bucharest, Rumania. CHIEF of LAB, Inst. of Psych, Acad. R.P.R. Blvd. 6 Martie 64, Bucharest. Research, professional writing; psychology of language, relation between language and thought, psychology of art. F

FISCHBEIN, Efraim. Str. Fratil Stoenescu-Cotet 1, Bucharest. b. 20 Jan 1920 Bucharest. Lic. '45 Univ. of Bucharest, Rumania. CHIEF, Educ. Psych. Lab, Inst. of Psych; ASST. LECT, Univ. Parhon, Bucharest. Research, teaching; educational psychology. M

PAVELCO, Prof. Dr. Vasile. Univ. de Iassy. b. 4 Aug 1900 Costouleni, Russia. PH.D '36 Univ. of Iassy, Rumania. PROF. and HEAD, Dept. of Psychopedagogy, Univ.

Al. I. Cuza, 11 August 23, Calea. Teaching research, educational psychology; emotion, personality, learning. M

POPESCU-NEVEANU, Prof. Paul. Matei Millo 12, Bucharest. b. 10 May 1926 Husi. Candidat ès sciences, Univ. of Leningrad, Russia. RES. DIR, Inst. of Psych, Blvd. 6 Martie 64, Bucharest. Member: APSLF. Research, teaching, educational psychology; development of thought, temperament. M

PUFAN, Constantin. Univ. C.I. Parhon, Blvd. 6 Martie 64, Bucharest. b. 1 May 1926 Brosteni-Craiova. Candidat ès sciences '54 Univ. of Leningrad, Russia. CONFERENCE DIR, Rue 13 Decembrie 5, Bucharest. Member: Psych. Assn, Univ. of Bucharest. Teaching, research, professional writing; development of thought and language in deaf-mutes. M

ROSCA, Prof. Dr. Alexandru. Univ. V. Babeş, Cogălniceanu 1, Cluj. b. 2.' Aug 1906 Calata. PH.D '30 Univ. of Cluj, Rumania. PROFESSOR, Univ. V. Babeş. Research, teaching, educational psychology; thinking, fatigue, learning and memory. M

SCHIOPU, Ursula. Pl. Stalin 3, Bucharest. b. 30 July 1918 Turda. Lic, Univ. of Bucharest, Rumania. RES. DIR, Univ. Parhon, Lab. of Psych, Blvd. 6 Mars 64, Bucharest; STUDY DIR, Inst. of Psych, Acad. R.P.R. Teaching, research; psychology of children's thought, ontogenesis of precocity, history of child psychology. F

SPAIN

ALVAREZ DE LINERA GRUND, Prof. Anthony. Mayor, 81, Madrid. b. 26 Aug 1888 Málaga. Lic. '11 Univ. of Granada, Spain. TEACHER, Inst. of Middle Tchng. of St. Isidro, Toledo St, Madrid. Member: SEP. Professional writing and reviews, teaching, research; parapsychology, attitude measurement, achievement tests. M

CRUZ HERNANDEZ, Prof. Miguel. Gran Via Esquina San Julian, s.n. piso 4º, Dra Salamanca. b. 15 Jan 1920 Malaga. PH.D '46 Univ. of Madrid, Spain. TITULARY PROF. of PHILOS, Fac. of Philos; PROF. of PSYCH, Fac. of Med, Univ. of Salamanca. Member: SEP. Teaching, research, applied and educational psychology; Gestalt psychology, group process, social perception and behavior. M

CYMBALISTYJ, Dr. Bohdan. Galileo 67, bajo izq, Madrid. b. 8 May 1919 Lvov, Ukraine. PH.D '48 Univ. of Göttingen, Ger. WRITER, Radio Nacional de España, 42, Castellana, Madrid. Member: Spanish Psychoanal. Assn. Professional writing for press and radio, psychotherapy; development of social attitudes in the child and adolescent, political and civic education. M

FOLCH-CAMARASA, Prof. Luis. c. Ausias-March, 39, Barcelona. b. 6 Feb 1913 Barcelona. Lic, Univ. of Barcelona, Spain. DIRECTOR, Inst. Torremar, 73 rue Angel Guimera, San Ginés de Vilasar. Member: Sociedad de Neuropsiquiatria Infantil. Consulting, teaching, psychotherapy; individual and group child psychotherapy, projective techniques, child development. M

GERMAIN, Prof. Dr. José. Avenida General Mola 29, Madrid. b. 18 Nov 1897 Malaga. MD '23 Univ. of Madrid, Spain. DIRECTOR, Inst. Nacional de Psicologia Aplicada y Psicotecnia, 10, Plaza de Santa Barbara, Madrid; HEAD, Dept. of Exper. Psych, Consejo Superior de Investigaciones Cientificas, Madrid; DIRECTOR, *Revista de Psicologia General y Aplicada*. Member: SEP, AIPA, IUSP. Applied psychology, editorial, teaching, research; intelligence and aptitude tests, projective techniques, learning.M

LÓPEZ-IBOR, Juan J. Olivos, 18, Madrid. b. Valencia. Prof, Univ. of Madrid, Spain. PROF. of MED. PSYCH, Univ. of Madrid; CONSULT. PSYCHIATRIST, priv. prac; EDITOR, *Actas Luso-Españolas de Neurologia y Psiquiaria*. Consulting, research, teaching; psychotherapy, dynamics of neurosis and psychosis. M

MALLART, José. Prádena del Rincón 4, Madrid. b. 10 June 1897 Espolla-Gerona. PROF. and HEAD, Dept. of Econ. and Sociol, Inst. Nacional de Psicologia Aplicada y Psicotecnia, 10 Plaza de Santa Bárbara, Madrid. Applied psychology, editorial, teaching, research; vocational guidance and research. M

MORAGAS, Prof. Jeroni de. Iradier 26, Barcelona. b. 9 July 1901 Barcelona. MD, Univ. of Barcelona, Spain. PROF. of PSYCH, Univ. of Barcelona; DIRECTOR, Instituto de Pedagógia Terapéutica. Member: SEP, Sociedad de Neuropsiquiatria Infantil. Teaching, psychotherapy, consulting; psychology of the child and adolescent. M

MUÑOZ, Prof. Dr. Jesús, S. J. Pontifical Univ, Comillas, Santander. b. 13 Feb 1908 La Coruña. PH.D '31 Fac. of Philos, Univ. of Philos, Spain. PROF. of PSYCH, Pontifical Univ; CONSULTANT, priv. prac; ED. BD, *Erasmus* (Germany). Teaching, research, professional writing; philosophical interpretation of psychological data, psychology of religion, psychotherapy and education. M

PALMÉS VILELLA, P. Fernando M., S. J. Fac. of Philos, Colegio Máximo de San Francisco de Borja, San Cugat del Valles, Barcelona. b. 11 Mar 1879 Lérida. Dr. of Philos and Theology, Colegio Maximo de San Francisco de Borja, Spain. DIR. GENL. de Balmesiana; DEAN, Fac. of Philos, Colegio Maximo de San Francisco de Borja; EDITOR, *Pensamiento*. Member: SEP. Teaching, administration, editorial; educational psychology. M

PERDIKIDI OLIVIERI, Mrs. Hélène. Gomez Ortega 32, Colonia de la Cruz del Rayo, Madrid. b. 15 June 1929 Athens, Greece. Diplome '50 Univ. of Geneva, Switz. DIRECTOR, Psychologie Clinique Infantil. Inst. Nacional de Psicologia Aplicada y Psicotecnia, 10 Plaza Santa Barbara, Madrid. Clinical analysis, child psycho therapy, applied psychology; projective techniques, achievement tests, attitude measurement. F

PERTEJO DE ALCAMÍ, Dr. Mrs. Jesusa. San Roque, 26, Silla. b. 11 June 1920 Zamora. MD, Univ. of Madrid, Spain. RES. DIR, Departamento de Psicologia, Consejo Superior de Investigaciones Cientificas, 123 Serrano, Madrid; EDITOR, *Revista de Psicologia General y Aplicada*. Member: SEP, APSLF. Research, testing, psychotherapy; projective techniques, thought processes in schizophrenia. F

PLATA, José. Avda. Reina Victoria 37, Madrid. b. 6 Apr 1904 Mengíbar. Grad. '30 Univ. of Madrid, Spain. PSYCHO-TECHNICIAN, Colegio Nacional de Ciegos,

Platerías, 3 Charmartín, Madrid; DIRECTOR, Educ. and Vocat. Guid. Serv. for the Blind, Colegio Nacional de Ciegos, Madrid. Member: SEP, Sociedad Española de Pedagogía. Teaching, applied and educational psychology, research; the use of attitude measurement, achievement tests and vocational guidance techniques with the blind. M

SECADAS, Dr. Francisco. Calle San Martín de Valdeiglesias 5, Colonia del Pilar, Madrid. b. 6 Feb 1917 Astillero. PH.D '52 Univ. of Madrid, Spain. RES. ASSOC, Consejo Superior de Investigaciones Científicas, Serrano 127, Madrid; PSYCHOTECH. CHIEF, Inst. Sindical de Formación Profesional „Virgen de la Paloma"; PROFESSOR, Sch. of Psych, Univ. of Madrid; ED. BD, *Revista de Educación*. Member: SEP, Sociedad Española de Pedagogía. Research, applied psychology, teaching, consulting; factor analysis, test construction. M

SERRATE, Dr. Agustín. Sanclemente 22, Zaragoza. b. 23 May 1911 Huesca. MD '46 Univ. of Madrid, Spain. PSYCHIATRIST and CHIEF of CLINIC, Manicomio Nacional de Ntra. Sra. Del Pilar, Zaragoza; PSYCHOLOGIST, Hosp. de Ntra. Sra. de Gracia, Zaragoza. Member: SEP. Clinical practice, testing, research; projective techniques. M

SIGUAN, Dr. Miguel. General Mola, 274, 6º, D, Madrid. b. 2 May 1918 Barcelona. PH.D '51 Univ. of Madrid, Spain. PROF. of INDUS. PSYCH, Escuela de Psicologia, Univ. of Madrid, Calle San Bernardo, Madrid; DIRECTOR, Indus. and Soc. Psych. Sect, Consejo Superior de Investigaciones Científicas. Member: SEP. Teaching, research, industrial psychology; human factors in industry, projective techniques. M

SOTO YARRITU, Prof. Federico. Manicomio de Navarra, Pamplona. b. 1 July 1906 Santander. Diplome, Casa de Salud Valdecilla, Santander, Spain. DIRECTOR, Manicomio Provincial de Navarra; PROF. of PSYCH, Sch. of Med, Estudio General de Navarra. Member: Spanish Assn. of Neuropsychiat, Int. Assn. of Catholic Therapists. Clinical practice, guidance, testing; Szondi test. M

VALLEJO-NAGERA, Antonio. Galle Alcalá Galiano 8, Madrid. b. 20 July 1888 Paredes de Nava. Prof, Univ. of Madrid, Spain. PROF. of PSYCHIAT, Univ. of Madrid; DIRECTOR, Dept. of Psychiat, Consejo Superior de Investigaciones Científicas. Member: SEP. Research, teaching, clinical practice. M

YELA, Prof. Mariano. Virgen de Nuria, 15, B. Concepción, Madrid. b. 2 Mar 1921 Madrid. PH.D '52 Univ. of Madrid, Spain. PROF. of PSYCH, Univ. of Madrid, Ciudad Universitaria, Madrid; HEAD, Psychometric Dept, Consejo Superior de Investigaciones Científicas; ASST. DIR, *Revista de Psicologia General y Aplicada*. Member: SEP, APSLF, APA. Teaching, research, editorial; factor analysis, perception, intelligence. M

ZARAGOZÁ ANTICH, Prof. José. Corona 2, Valencia. b. 2 Aug 1921 Silla. Lic. '46 Univ. of Valencia, Spain. DIRECTOR, Escuela Especial de Orientación, Salvador Giner 5, Valencia; DIRECTOR, Cen. for Educ. Stat, Iberoamerican Off. of Educ, Madrid; ASST. PROF. of EXPER. PSYCH, Univ. of Valencia. Member: SEP, AIOP, Spanish Socy. of Pedagogy. Research, editorial, testing, professional guidance; aptitude measurement, achievement tests, vocational psychology. M

SURINAM

VEGTER, Dr. Casper Johannes. P.O. Box 1016, Paramaribo. b. 13 May 1930 Groningen, Neth. Doctorat '54 Univ. of Groningen, Neth. GOVT. PSYCH'T, Personeelsraad, Heerestraat 4, Paramaribo.

Member: NIPP. Personnel psychology, administration, teaching; achievement tests, racial differences in test results, use of statistics in psychology. M

SWEDEN

ABENIUS, Miss Ingrid Haralda Margareta. Sturegatan 28/III, Stockholm O. b. 1 July 1927 Stockholm. Fil. kand. '49 Univ. of Stockholm, Swed. GRAD. STUD, Univ. of Stockholm. Member: SP. Teaching, consulting; adult education, projective techniques, group therapy. F

AGRELL, Docent Dr. Jan. Karlsrogatan 92/A, Uppsala. b. 6 Aug 1918 Lund. Fil. dr. '49 Univ. of Lund, Swed. DIRECTOR,

Inst. of Milit. Psych, Fredrikshovsgatan 6, Stockholm. Member: SP. Administration, research, military psychology; educational psychology, mental tests. M

AHLSTRÖM, Fil. lic. Karl-Georg Johan. Studentstaden 7, Uppsala. b. 21 Sept 1929 Augerum. Fil. lic, Univ. of Uppsala, Swed. ASST. PROF, Inst. of Educ, Univ. of Uppsala, Järnbrogatan 10A, Uppsala. Member: SP. Research, testing, teaching;

learning theory, social perception, psychometrics. M

ANDERSSON, Karl Hans Ola. Gullmarsvägen 29, Johanneshov. b. 8 June 1919 Luleå. Fil. mag. '44 Univ. of Lund, Swed. PSYCHOANALYST, priv. prac. Member: SP, Swed. Psychoanal. Socy. Psychotherapy, research, teaching; theory and technique of psychoanalytic therapy, history of clinical psychology, application of psychoanalysis in cultural anthropology. M

ARDELIUS, Hans E. Smedsbacksgatan 4, Stockholm Ö. b. 22 Apr 1930 Falun. Fil. kand. '54 Univ. of Stockholm, Swed. ASSISTANT, Psych. Inst. of the Swed. Armed Forces, Fredrikshovsgatan 6, Stockholm. Member: SP. Applied psychology, student, research; psychomotor tests, aviation psychology. M

BENGTSSON, Fil. kand. Lars Olof. Ängsvägen 17 A, Kristianstad. b. ʃ22 Sept 1923 Hälsingborg. Fil. kand. '55 Univ. of Lund, Swed. PSYCHOLOGIST, Child Psychiat. Dept, V. Boulevarden 11, Kristianstad. Member: SP. Clinical testing, research; problems of rigidity. M

BERGLIND, Hans Emil. Vattravägen 27, Uttran. b. 19 Aug 1930 Stockholm. Fil. kand. '53 Univ. of Stockholm, Swed. PEDAGOGICAL CONSULT, Stockholm Läns Landsting, Råsundavägen 3, Solna 1. Member: SP. Educational psychology, teaching, student; social perception, group process. M

BERGQUIST-SÖDERBLOM, Mrs. Siv. Vivstavarvsvägen 185, Enskede. b. 17 Nov 1928 Västerås. Fil. mag. '54 Univ. of Stockholm, Swed. SECONDARY SCH. TCHR, Hallstahammar Realskola. Member: SP. Teaching, educational psychology, student; psychology of language, learning theory, education. F

BERLING, Fil. lic. Ernst-Erik (Ejje). Västerängsvägen 44, Enebyberg. b. 20 Sept 1916 Ronneby. Fil. lic. Univ. of Lund, Swed. MILIT. PSYCH'T, priv. prac; SECT. ED, Svensk Uppslagsbok; SUB-ED, *Psykologisk Pedagogisk Uppslagsbok*. Member: SP. Military psychology, professional writing, teaching; aviation psychology, criminal psychology, history of education and psychology. M

BERNER ÖSTE, Fil. lic. Mia. Bolmsövägen 24, Bromma. b. 13 June 1923 Stravanger, Nor. Fil. lic, Univ. of Stockholm, Odengat. 61, Stockholm. Member: SP. Research, professional writing; methodology, industrial psychology and sociology, small group research. F

BERNES, Fil. lic. Stig. Folkskoleseminariet, Växjö. b. 20 Oct 1912 Gothenburg. Fil.

lic. '53 Univ. of Uppsala, Swed. LECT. of EDUC. and EDUC. PSYCH, Folkskoleseminariet. Member: SP. Teaching, educational psychology, research; school adjustment, attitude measurement, motivation. M

BILLING, Fil. kand. Lars Erik Simeon. Tavastgatan 45, Stockholm. b. 5 Oct 1922 Stockholm. Fil. kand. '50 Univ. of Stockholm, Swed. CHILD PSYCH'T, Child Psychiat. Clin, Karolinska Sjukhuset, Stockholm. Clinical diagnosis, psychotherapy; projective techniques, achievement tests for handicapped children. M

BJERSTEDT, Docent Åke. St. Annegatan 1, Lund. b. 10 Apr 1930 Lund. Fil. dr. '56 Univ. of Lund, Swed. DOCENT, Univ. of Lund. Member: SP. Teaching, research; group process, social perception, personality assessment. M

BJÖRKMANN, Mats. Midgårdsvägen 18, Täby. b. 20 Oct 1926 Folkärna. Fil. lic. '56 Univ. of Stockholm, Swed. ASST. TCHR, Psych. Lab, Teknologgatan 8, Stockholm Va. Research, teaching; psychophysics, learning theory, visual perception. M

BJÖRNSSON, Carl Hugo. Bokv. 3, Sollentuna 2. b. 20 Feb 1916 Gothenburg. Fil. kand. '54 Univ. of Stockholm, Swed. SECRETARY, Stockholm Folkskoledirektion, Vasagatan 22, Stockholm. Member: SP. Educational research and psychology, administration; research in teaching methods and school organization, achievement tests. M

BJÖRSJÖ, Docent Märta. Gambrinusg. 5, Stockholm K. b. 17 Oct 1908 Halland. Fil. dr. '51 Univ. of Gothenburg, Swed. SCH. PSYCH'T, Royal Bd. of Educ, Hantverkargatan 29, Stockholm 8; ASST. PROF, Univ. of Stockholm. Member: SP. Research, administration, professional writing, constulting; abilities, curriculum, school psychology. M

BOALT, Prof. Gunnar. Odengatan 61, Stockholm. b. 26 Aug 1910 Ljusterö. Fil. dr. '47 Univ. of Stockholm, Swe. DIRECTOR, Soc. Inst, Univ. of Stockholm; EDITOR, *Stockholm Studies in Sociology*. Administration, teaching, research; differential social psychology, industrial psychology, group process. M

BORG, Fil. lic. Gunnar A.V. Sollentunavägen 207, Sollentuna. b. 29 Nov 1927 Stockholm. Fil. lic. Univ. of Stockholm, Swed. TEACHER, Folkskoleseminariet, Umeå. Member: SP. Teaching, research, applied and educational psychology; visual form perception, learning theory, military psychology. M

BÖRJESON, Gull Helga Charlotta. Fredriksdalsgat. 12c, Gothenburg. b. 17 Feb 1910 Gothenburg. Fil. lic. '53 Univ. of Gothenburg, Swed. SCH. PSYCH'T. and CHIEF,

Sch. Psych. Bur, Gothenburg Bd. of Educ, Huitfeldtsplatsen 6, Gothenburg. Member: SP. Educational psychology, testing, consulting and guidance; school maturation problems, reading, writing, and speech problems. F

BOUMAN, Fil. lic. Jan C. Kratsbodavägen 53, Marie Häll-Stockholm. b. 6 May 1912 Rotterdam, Neth. Fil. lic. '53 Univ. of Stockholm, Swed. PSYCHOLOGIST, priv. prac. Member: SP. Consulting, psychotherapy, research; perception, existential therapy, phenomenology of perception. M

BRANDT, Miss Kristina. John Ericssongatan 11, 3 tr.t.h., Stockholm K. b. 13 Mar 1923 Stockholm. CHILD PSYCH'T, Rädgivningsbyrån, Torsgatan 21/XLL, Stockholm. Member: SP, Swed. Child Psych. Assn. Child psychotherapy, guidance, clinical analysis; projective techniques, structure analysis. F

BROMAN, Miss Ulla. Mälartorget 13/III, Stockholm C. b. 3 Apr 1916 Stockholm. Fil. kand. '54 Univ. of Stockholm, Swed. CHILD PSYCH'T, Kronprinsessan Lovisas Hosp. for Children, Polhemsgatan 30, Stockholm K. Member: SP. Testing, psychotherapy, clinical practice; nervous and mental diseases, projective techniques, propaganda, music therapy. F

DAHLGREN, Fil. dr. Olov Helge. Linnégatan 32, Gothenburg. b. 1 Nov 1907 Gothenburg. Fil. dr. '47 Univ. of Gothenburg, Swed. LECT. of PSYCH. and EDUC, Tchrs. Coll, Övra Husargatan 34, Gothenburg. Member: SP. Teaching, professional writing, research; intelligence testing. M

DAHLKVIST, Ragnar. Stora Mossens Backe 24, Bromma. b. 17 July 1901 Gothenburg. Fil. lic. '49 Univ. of Gothenburg, Swed. FIRST SCH. SUPT, Stockholm Folkskoledirektion, Vasagatan 22, Stockholm. Member: SP. Administration, educational psychology; arithmetic, school level transfer, teachers' marks. M

DAHLLÖF, Urban Sigurd. Lindsbergsgatan 3a, Uppsala. b. 11 Nov 1928 Gothenburg. Fil. lic. '56 Univ. of Uppsala, Swed. ASST. TCHR. of PSYCH, Univ. of Uppsala, Psych. Inst, St. Larsgatan 2, Uppsala. Member: SP. Teaching, student, research; interviewing methodology, personality assessment, group process. M

DEINES, Fil. kand. Mrs. Märta Greta. Ersmarksgatan 34, Umeå. b. 1 Jan 1928 Stensele. Fil. kand. '53 Univ. of Gothenburg, Swed. Member: SP. Advanced studies in psychology; attitude measurement in criminal psychology. F

DUNER, Anders. Brunnsgatan 7 b, Linköping. b. 10 Apr 1925 Nora stad. Fil. kand. '55 Stockholm Högskola, Swed. TEACHER, Tchrs. Trng. Coll, Folkskolese-minariet, Limköping. Member: SP. Teaching, student, research; intelligence and achievement tests, learning theory. M

DUREMAN, Fil. lic. Ingmar. Väderkvarnsgatan 40, Uppsala. b. 19 Feb 1925 Möklinta. Fil. lic. '54 Univ. of Uppsala, Swed. RES. PSYCH'T, Psychiat. Dept, Royal Academic Hosp; TEACHER, Dept. of Educ, Univ. of Uppsala. Member: SP. Research, teaching, testing; learning theory, differential psychology of perceptual processes. M

DVORETSKY, Sigurd. Basungatan 7, Järnbrott. b. 3 Feb 1926 Stockholm. Fil. kand. '50 Univ. of Lund, Swed. PSYCHOLOGIST, Child Guid. Clin, Frölundavägan 162, Gothenburg. Member: SP. Testing, guidance, research; projective techniques, achievement tests, social perception. M

EDFELDT, Fil. lic. Åke W. Dept. of Educ, Univ. of Stockholm, Observatoriegatan 8, Stockholm Va. b. 24 Feb 1926 Stockholm. Fil. lic. '55 Univ. of Stockholm, Swed. ASST. LECT, Dept. of Educ. Univ. of Stockholm. Member: SP. Teaching, research, educational psychology; psychology of reading, school readiness tests, reading readiness. M

EDGARDH, Fil. lic. H. Bertil H. Vegagatan 24, Solna. b. 7 Feb 1918 Stockholm. Fil. lic. '51 Univ. of Lund, Swed. PSYCHO-ANALYST, priv. prac. Member: Int. Psychoanal. Assn, Swed. Psychoanal. Socy. Psychotherapy, teaching; psychoanalysis, psychology of language, speech and hearing. M

EDGARDH, Fil. kand. Mrs. Gunnel Elisabeth. Vegagatan 24, Solna. b. 25 Apr 1921 Solna. Fil. kand. '48 Stockholms Högskola, Swed. PSYCHOANALYST, priv. prac. Member: Int. Psychoanal. Assn, Swed. Psychoanal. Socy. Psychotherapy, consulting, guidance; psychoanalysis, child psychology. F

EDLUND, Prof. Sven Göran. Kastanjegatan 6 A, Lund. b. 12 Jan 1909 Svartå. Fil. dr. '47 Univ. of Lund, Swed. ASST. PROF, Univ. of Lund. Member: SP. Research, teaching, administration; school readiness, vocabulary development, history of pedagogical psychology. M

EGIDIUS, Fil. lic. Henry. Måsvägen 16, Lund. b. 29 Jah 1925 Malmö. Fil. lic. Univ. of Lund, Swed. SCH. PSYCH'T, Lunds Folkskolor, Lund. Member: SP. Educational psychology, teaching, student; educational and psychological measurement psychology of the brain-injured. M

EKMAN, Prof. A. Gösta. Psych. Lab, Teknologgatan 8, Stockholm Va. b. 3 June 1920 Lund. Fil. dr. '48 Univ. of Stockholm, Swed. PROF. and HEAD, Dept. of Psych, Univ. of Stockholm. Member: SP. Research, administration, teaching; visual

perception, psychophysics. M
EKMAN, Gustaf Einar. Tullportsgatan 4 B, Härnösand. b. 15 May 1899 Stockholm. Fil. lic, Univ. of Lund, Swed. LECT. in PSYCH. and PEDAGOGY, Folkskoleseminariet, Södra Vägen, Härnösand. Member: SP. Teaching, testing, student; character and social psychology, social pedagogy. M
ERIKSSON, Docent Karl Henrik. Geijersgatan 16 B, Uppsala. b. 11 May 1919 Shangnas. Fil. dr. '57 Univ. of Uppsala, Swed. DOCTORAL FELLOW, Psych. Inst, Univ. of Uppsala, St. Larsgatan 2, Uppsala. Research, teaching, testing. M
FÄLTHEIM, Docent Åke Alver. Terrängvägen 102, Hägersten. b. 2 Apr 1910 Hörby. Fil. dr. Univ. of Uppsala, Swed. 1956. CHIEF DIR. of EDUC, Royal Bd. of Educ, Hantverkargatan 29, Stockholm; ASST. PROF. of PSYCH, Univ. of Uppsala. Administration, research, teaching; learning theory, problem solving, psychology of mathematics. M
FRANKENHAEUSER, Fil. lic. Valborg Marianne. Backvägen 10, Solna. b. 30 Sept 1925 Helsinki, Finland. Fil. lic. '54 Univ. of Stockholm, Swed. RES. PSYCH'T, Lab. of Aviat. and Naval Med, Karolinska Inst, Solnavägen 1, Stockholm. Member: SP. Research on affects of radial acceleration on mental functions, testing; perception, brain injury. F
FRIES, Dr. phil. Hillevi Alfhild Viktoria. S. Rudbecksgatan 5, Uppsala. b. 4 Jan 1916 Uppsala. Docteur ès lettres '55 Univ. of Stockholm, Swed. TEACHER, Folkskoleseminariet, Växjö. Teaching, military psychology; psychology of personality. F
FRÖBÄRJ, Fil. lic. Gösta. Hjo. b. 2 Mar 1917 Hjo. Fil. lic. '56 Univ. of Gothenburg, Swed. LECTURER, Univ. of Gothenburg, Vasagatan, Gothenburg. Member: SP, Socy. for Collaboration between Psychiat. and Psych. Research, testing, teaching; projective techniques, theoretical psychology and philosophy. M
GÄSTRIN, Docent Jan Emanuel. Äppelviksvägen 32, Bromma. b. 30 Dec 1896 Sundsvall. Docent Univ. of Uppsala, Swed. DIR. PSYCH. COURSES, Erica Found, Odengatan 9, Stockholm Ö. Member: SP, Socy. for Collaboration between Psychiat. and Psych, Swed. Psychoanal. Socy. Teaching, psychotherapy, research, learning theory, adolescent religious life, group process. M
GERZEN, Fil. kand. Mrs. Marianne Gunhild. Frodegatan 19 A, Uppsala. b. 18 Oct 1929 Gothenburg. Fil. kand. '55 Univ. of Uppsala, Swed. PSYCH. ASST, Child Psychiat. Clin, Uppsala. Member: SP. Testing, guidance, student; intelligence testing, projective techniques, child psy-

chiatric problems. F
GILLQVIST, Bertil M. Snöbollsgränd 16, Hägersten, Stockholm. b. 22 May 1918 Eskilstuna. Fil. kand. '47 Univ. of Gothenburg, Swed. INDUS. CONSULT, Sunlight AB, Friggagatan 10, Stockholm. Member: SP, Swed. Assn. for Collaboration between Psychiat. and Psych, Swed. Assn. for Ment. Hlth. Industrial psychology, consulting, testing; employment probation, projective techniques, psychosomatic diseases. M
GORDAN, Kurt. Holbergsgatan 43, Bromma. b. 17 Sept 1922 Berlin, Ger. Fil. lic. '57 Univ. of Stockholm, Swed. PSYCHOLOGIST, Child Guid. Clin, Stockholms Läns Landsting Cen. för Psykisk Barna-och Ungdomsvård, Råsundavägen 101, Solna; TEACHER, Royal Bd. of Prisons; TEACHER, Soc. Inst, Stockholm. Member: SP, Swedish Rorschach Assn, Swed. Child Psych. Assn. Testing, teaching, research; projective and other diagnostic tests, guidance and therapy of adolescents. M
GRAN, Fil. kand. John Bertil. Jönköpingsgatan 34 B, Hälsingborg. b. 7 Oct 1926 Hälsingborg. Fil. kand. '54 Univ. of Lund, Swed. SCH. PSYCH'T, Sch. Admin, S. Storgatan 22, Hälsingborg. Member: SP. Testing, research, guidance; feelings and emotions of school age children, problems of backward and deviant children. M
GRANIT, Prof. Dagnar Arthur. Med. Nobel Inst, Neurophysiol. Dept, Stockholm 60. b. 30 Oct 1900 Helsinki, Finland. MD '27 Univ. of Helsinki, Finland. PROF. and DIR, Neurophysiol. Dept, Med. Nobel Inst; PROF. in NEUROPHYSIOL, Royal Caroline Inst, Stockholm 60. Research; sensory mechanisms. M
GUETTLER, Klas M. Bråvallavägen 12, Djursholm. b. 18 Apr 1920 Stockholm. Fil. lic. '52 Univ. of Stockholm, Swed. LECT. and PSYCHOTHER, Erica Found, Odengatan 9, Stockholm. Member: SP, Swed. Psychoanal. Socy. Psychotherapy, teaching; psychoanalysis, developmental psychology, social psychology. M
GUSTAVSSON, Fil. lic. Bengt P. G. Friherregatan 8, Stockholm-Vällingby. b. 7 Sept 1923 Ålem. Fil. lic, Univ. of Stockholm, Swed. RES. ASST, Counc. of Pers. Admin, Linnegatan 18, Stockholm Oe. Member: SP. Research, industrial psychology, teaching; aptitude and achievement tests, attitude measurement, learning theory. M
HAAGE, Fil. dr. Helge. Snäckparken 11, Bromma. b. 15 Oct 1890 Söderala. Fil. dr. '28 Univ. of Uppsala, Swed. SUPERINTENDENT, Elem. and Secondary Schools, Swed. Bd. of Educ, Hantverkargat. 29, Stockholm. Administration, research; reading and writing problems. M

364

SWEDEN

HAAK, Dr. Nils. Backskåran 10, Bromma, Stockholm. b. 18 May 1906 Gothenburg. MD '38 Univ. of Stockholm, Swed. PSYCHO-ANALYST, Stockholms Stads Mentalvårdsbyrå, Stockholm; TRNG. ANALYST and LECT, Swed. Psychoanal. Socy. Member: Int. Psychoanal. Assn, Swed. Psychoanal. Socy. psychotherapy, clinical practice, teaching; psychoanalytic techniques. M

HALLGREN, Fil. lic. Siver S. E. Karlstad. b. 27 July 1911 Esphult. Fil. lic. '39 Univ. of Lund, Swed. LEKTOR, Folkskoleseminariet, Karlstad. Member: SP. Teaching; teacher selection, intellectually subnormal children. M

HÄLLJE, Fil. dr. Börje. Råsundavägen 64, Solna. b. 11 July 1913 Malmö. Fil. dr. '53 Univ. of Stockholm, Swed. RES. DIR. and SCH. PRIN, Åtvidabergsinst, Kungsträdgårdsgatan 20, Stockholm. Member: SP. Research, educational psychology, administration; learning theory, achievement tests, theological psychology. M

HANSSEN, Prof. Sten Olof Börje. Vinterled, Laeggesta. b. 11 Aug 1917 Stockholm. Fil. dr. '52 Univ. of Stockholm, Swed. ASST. PROF. of SOCIOL, Univ. of Stockholm, Drottninggatan 116, Stockholm Va. Member: Deutsche Gesellschaft für Soziologie. Research, teaching, professional writing; borderline research between social psychology, social anthropology and social history, family relations, general methodology. M

HÄRNQVIST, Docent Kjell. Arvid Mörnes väg 1, Bromma. b. 22 Mar 1921 Kvämum. Fil. dr. '56 Univ. of Stockholm, Swed. DOCENT in PSYCH, Univ. of Stockholm, Teknologgatan 8, Stockholm, Va. Member: SP. Research, teaching, administration; mental testing, attitude measurement, experimental design. M

HECTOR, Fil. kand. Karl-Göran. Odensg. 18/III, Uppsala. b. 29 Aug 1928 Kristinehamm. Fil. kand, Univ. of Uppsala, Swed. AMANUENSIS, Psych. Inst, Univ. of Uppsala, St. Larsgatan 2, Uppsala. Member: SP. Teaching, student; differential psychology, motor tests. M

HEDBERG, Magnus. Smedsbacksgatan 7/v, Stockholm Ö. b. 11 Aug 1923 Stockholm. Fil. kand. '55 Univ. of Stockholm, Swed. RES. ASST, Counc. of Pers. Admin, Linnegatan 18, Stockholm. Member: SP. Research, applied psychology, consulting; group process, organizational theory. M

HENRICSON, Sven-Eric. Banérgatan 79/III, Stockholm Ö. b. 15 Jan 1920 Sweden. Fil. lic. '53 Univ. of Stockholm, Swed. SCH. PSYCH'T, Royal Bd. of Educ, Hantverkargatan 29, Stockholm, Member: SP. Applied educational psychology and research, administration; test construction,

attitude and interest measurement. M

HENRYSSON, Fil. dr. Sten. Björngårdsgatan 13, Stockholm. b. 13 June 1921 Linköping. Fil. dr. '57 Univ. of Uppsala, Swed. ASSOC. PROF. 'of EDUC. MSMT, Tchrs. Coll, Fredhäll, Stockholm; LECT. in PSYCH. STAT, Univ. of Stockholm; EDITOR, Meddelanden Fran Sveriges Psykologförbund. Member: SP. Research, teaching, professional writing; test construction, factor analysis, scale construction, research design. M

HESSELMAN, Miss Stina. Danderydsgatan 16, Stockholm Ö. b. 25 May 1910 Stockholm. Diploma '33 Sch. of Soc. Work, Stockholm, Swed. CHILD. THER. Ericastiftelsen, Odengatan 9, Stockholm Ö. Member: SP. Psychotherapy; child and adolescent psychoanalysis, play therapy. F

HIMMELSTRAND, Fil. kand. Mrs. Karin. Källplan 4 D/III, Uppsala. b. 18 Jan 1928 Sundsvall. Fil. kand. '49 Univ. of Uppsala, Swed. ASST. CLIN. PSYCH'T, Psychiat. Clin, Academic Hosp, Uppsala. Member: SP. Testing, Research, student; child psychology, mental and behavioral disorders, social psychology of child rearing. F

HIMMELSTRAND, Fil. lic. Ulf. Kallplan 4 D/III, Uppsala. b. 26 Aug 1924 Tirupatur, India. Fil. lic. '55 Univ. of Uppsala, Swed. ASST. PROF, Sociol. Dept, Univ. of Uppsala, Villavägen 1, Uppsala. Member: SP. Teaching, research, administration; psychology of language, social psychology and sociology of communication, political and consumer behavior. M

HJORTH, Miss Ann Mari Sofia. Styrmansgatan 21, Stockholm. b. 6 Apr 1931 Stockholm. Fil. kand. '54 Univ. of Stockholm, Swed. AMANUENS, Inst. of Appl. Psych, Univ. of Stockholm, Norrtullsgatan 2, Stockholm. Member: SP. Testing, guidance, applied psychology, research; ability tests, performance and personality tests, developmental psychology, perception, group relations. F

HOLMKVIST, Olov. Hällbyg 34A, Uppsala. b. 25 Feb 1931 Ludvika. Fil. kand. '55 Univ. of Uppsala, Swed. GRAD. STUD, Psych. Inst, St. Larsg. 2, Uppsala. Member: SP. Research, testing. M

HUSÉN, Prof. Torsten. Jungfrugatan 37/III, Stockholm Ö. b. 1 Mar 1916 Lund. Fil. dr. Univ. of Lund, Swed. PROF. of EDUC. and HEAD, Inst. of Educ. Res, Tchrs. Coll, Univ. of Stockholm; EDITOR, Research Bulletin, Inst. of Educ. Member: SP, AIPA. Research, teaching, educational psychology differential psychology, social psychology related to school problems, adolescent psychology. M

IRGENS, Hans Rutger. Birkagatan 51 a, Gothenburg Ö. b. 7 Oct 1926 Vienna, Austria. Fil. lic. '57 Univ. of Gothenburg,

Swed. Member: SP. Student, research, consulting, teaching; rigidity, film appreciation, propaganda, social perception, attitude measurement. M

ISRAEL, Docent Joachim. Vasaloppsvägen 94, Hägerston. b. 9 June 1920 Karlsruhe, Ger. Fil. dr. '56 Univ. of Stockholm, Swed. DOCENT of SOCIOL, Univ. of Stockholm, Dept. of Sociol, Norrtullsgatan 3, Stockholm; RES. ASSOC, Inst. of Soc. Res, Oslo. Member: SP. Research, editorial, teaching; group relations, industrial psychology, personality theory. M

IVERUS, Dr. Ivar. Stureparken 1, Stockholm. b. 2 Sept 1913 Helsinki, Finland. PH.D '50 Univ. of Zurich, Switz. CONSULT. PSYCH'T, priv. prac. Member: SP. Consulting, clinical practice, psychotherapy. M

JANSSON, Elsa. Västerled 24, Bromma. b. 15 Jan 1903 Uddevalla. Fil. kand, Univ. of Stockholm, Swed. CHILD PSYCH'T, Cen. for Psyckisk Barna-och Ungdomsvård, Torsgatan 21, Stockholm. Member: SP, Swed. Rorschach Assn. Testing, teaching, research; projective techniques. F

JARNE, Ragnar. Karmstolsvägen 7, Enskede. b. 5 July 1925 Stockholm. Fil. kand. '52 Univ. of Stockholm, Swed. RECORDING CLERK, Bd. of Educ, Vasagatan 22, Stockholm. Member: SP. Administration, student, applied psychology; psychophysics, learning theory, testing, educational psychology. M

JERKEDAL, Sven Åke. Tuve Skola, Gothenburg H. b. 29 Dec 1925 Kungälv. Fil. kand. '55 Univ. of Gothenburg, Swed. TEACHER, Tuve Skola. Member: SP. Research, teaching, editorial; prediction of teaching efficiency, improvement of teaching methods, children's drawings. M

JERKEDAL, Mrs. Kerstin. Tuve Skola, Gothenburg H. b. 3 Oct 1929 Sollefteå. Fil. kand. '52 Univ. of Uppsala, Swed. PSYCH. ASST, Gothenburg Sjukhusdirektion, Polhemsplatsen 5, Gothenburg. Member: SP. Clinical testing and diagonosis, consulting, child guidance, student; projective and intelligence testing, vocational guidance. F

JOHANNESSON, Docent Ingvar. Rörläggarvägen 43, Bromma. b. 26 Oct 1912 Lund. Fil. dr. '54 Univ. of Lund, Swed. LECTURER, Tchrs. Coll, Rålambsvägen 24, Stockholm. Member: SP. Educational psychology, research, teaching; social psychology of education, group dynamics in school classes, group work. M

JOHANSON, Miss Elvy. Norrtullsgatan 15, Stockholm. b. 21 Feb 1923 Sundsvall. Fil. kand. '51 Univ. of Stockholm, Swed. ASSISTANT, Inst. of Appl. Psych, Univ. of Stockholm. Member: SP. Testing, guidance; intelligence tests, performance tests, projective techniques. F

JONSSON, Carl-Otto. Kirunagatan 44, Vällingby. b. 5 Jan 1925 Sundsvall. Fil. lic. '47 Univ. of Uppsala, Swed. CLIN. PSYCH'T, Beckomberga Sjukhus, Bromma 4. Member: SP. Research, testing, teaching; validation of questionnaire and interview techniques, tests of intellectual deterioration, clinical psychology. M

KÄLLÉN, Fil. dr. Elov. Dr. Heymans gata 1, Gothenburg C. b. 18 Sept 1908 Degerfors. Fil. dr. '49 Univ. of Gothenburg, Swed. LECTOR of PSYCH, Tchrs. Coll, Guldhedsgatan 6, Gothenburg. Member: SP. Teaching, educational psychology, research; attention tests. M

KATZ, Dr. phil. Mrs. Rosa. Östermalmsgatan 97, Stockholm. b. 9 Apr 1885 Odessa, USSR. PH.D '14 Univ. of Göttingen, Ger. Member: SP, BPS, DGP. Research, testing, professional writing; child psychology. F

KEBBON, Lars Olof. Gropgränd 2A, Uppsala. b. 10 Apr 1929 Köping. Fil. kand. '53 Univ. of Uppsala, Swed. MILIT. PSYCH'T, Inst. of Milit. Psych, Fredrikshovsgatan, Stockholm. Member: SP. Student, testing, research; motivation, personality diagnosis. M

KJÄLLQUIST, Fil. kand. Hans. Bantorget 8, Lund. b. 16 May 1924 Karlskrona. Fil. kand. '50 Univ. of Lund, Swed. PSYCHOLOGIST, Child Psychiat. Clin, Univ. of Lund; PSYCHOLOGIST, Borstal Roztuna; ASST. TCHR, Pedagogic Inst, Univ. of Lund. Member: SP. Research, consulting, psychotherapy, teaching; emotional disturbances, cognitive functions, clinical diagnostic methods, etiology of neuroses. M

KLINGBERG, Fil. lic. Göte K. W. Stiernhööksvägen 1 D, Falun. b. 31 July 1918 Lovisa, Finland. Fil. lic. '45 Univ. of Lund, Swed. LECTURER, Folkskoleseminariet, Falun. Member: SP. Teaching, research, educational psychology; child psychology, elementary school testing. M

KRAGH, Fil. dr. Ulf Wilhelm Osvald. Inst. of Milit. Psych, Fredrikshovsgatan 6, Stockholm. b. 25 Feb 1920 Lund. Fil. dr. '56 Univ. of Lund, Swed. MILIT. PSYCH'T, Inst. of Milit. Psych. Member: SP. Research, testing, psychotherapy; clinical psychology, perception and personality, genetic theory, projective techniques. M

KRISTENSSON, Mrs. Inga Lisa. Kaggeledsgatan 34, Gothenburg. b. 1 July 1913 Tvååker. Fil. kand. '56 Univ. of Gothenburg, Swed. TCHR. in PRIMARY SCH, Lunden Sch, Kärralundsgatan, Gothenburg. Member: SP. Teaching, student, testing; learning theory, achievement tests, social perception. F

KÜNNAPAS, Fil. lic. Teodor Michael. Holmögaddsvägen 15, Johanneshow, Stockholm. b. 29 Apr 1902 Estonia. Fil. lic. '48

Univ. of Stockholm, Swed. ASST. TCHR, Psych. Lab, Teknologgatan 8, Stockholm Va. Member: SP. Teaching, research, administration; visual perception, learning and thinking, educational psychology. M

LAMBERGER, Miss Barbro Karin Linnea. Kronprinsessan Lovisas Barnsjukhus, Polhemsgatan 30, Stockholm K. b. Karlstad. Fil. kand. '49 Univ. of Uppsala, Swed. CHILD PSYCH'T, Kronprinsessan Lovisas Barnsjukhus. Member: SP, Swed. Child Psych. Assn. Child psychotherapy, testing; projective techniques. F

LANDIN, Lars Johan. Midsommarvägen 10, Hägersten. b. 22 Apr 1918 Gothenburg. Fil. lic. '52 Univ. of Gothenburg, Swed. HEADMASTER, Stockholms Folkskoledirektion, Vasagatan 22, Stockholm. Member: SP. Administration, teaching, educational psychology; education of exceptional children, remedial teaching. M

LEIJONHIELM, Fil. lic. Christer August. Trollesundsvägen 89, Bandhagen. b. 26 May 1924 Karlskrona. Fil. lic. '55 Stockholms Högskola, Swed. LEADER of EDUC. ACTIV, Armed Forces, Stockholm 90; ASST. TCHR. in EDUC. PSYCH, Stockholms Högskola. Member: SP. Administration, teaching, educational psychology; attitude formation, social and cultural values.M

LENNERLÖF, Lennart N.O. Frigångagatan 2 B, Gothenburg C. b. 25 Feb 1927 Lidköping. Fil. kand, Univ. of Gothenburg, Swed. Member: SP. Student, research, educational psychology; differential psychology, aptitude tests, adaptive processes. M

LILJEDAHL, Fil. lic. Nils-Axel. Reveljgatan 4, Gothenburg V. b. 23 July 1910 Gothenburg. Fil. lic. '47 Univ. of Gothenburg, Swed. MANAGING DIR, Karlstad Transport, Östra Torgatan 14, Karlstad; LECTURER, Tech. Univ. of Gothenburg. Member: SP. Industrial psychology, administration, teaching; industrial relations. M

LINDBERG, Prof. Bengt J. Psychiat. Univ. Clin, Sahlgren Hosp, Gothenburg. b. 28 Mar 1904 Gävle. MD '38 Univ. of Lund, Swed. PROF. and CLIN. DIR, Univ. of Gothenburg. Member: SP. Teaching, psychotherapy, research; personality attitudes and deviations, mental disturbances, psychopathology. M

LINDBLAD, Fil. lic. Gunnar. Doktor Liborius gata 40, Gothenburg C. b. 24 May 1904 Gothenburg. Fil. lic. '50 Univ. of Gothenburg, Swed. CITY SECY. of CULTURE and EDUC, City of Gothenburg, Stadshuset, Gothenburg. Member: SP. Administration, teaching, educational psychology; psychology of volition, child psychology, elementary education. M

LINDHE, Fil. lic. Olof. Folkhögskolan, S.

Sunderbyn. b. 10 Oct 1908 Hjortsberga. Fil. lic. '43 Univ. of Lund, Swed. SR. MASTER of PSYCH, Folkskoleseminariet, Luleå. Member: SP. Teaching, psychotherapy, research; learning theory, attitude measurement, medical psychology. M

LINDSTRÖM, Nils G. Skiljemyntsgatan 3, Gothenburg. b. 7 May 1923 Orsa. Fil. kand. '51 Univ. of Gothenburg, Swed. ASST. to HEADMASTER, Stretered, Sch. for Retarded Children, Kållered. Member: SP. Administration, intelligence testing, educational psychology; child psychology, social perception in mentally retarded children. M

LJUNG, Bengt-Olov. Ormängsgatan 53D/II, Stockholm-Vällingby. b. 24 Mar 1927 Stockholm. Fil. kand. '55 Univ. of Stockholm, Swed. RES. ASST, Tchrs. Coll, Rålambsvägen 24, Stockholm 34. Member: SP. Educational and psychological research, administration, teaching; psychometric problems, achievement tests, educational programs. M

LÖFVING, Miss Barbro Margareta. Van Dürens väg 6a, Lund. b. 27 Jan 1923, Stockholm. Fil. lic. '56 Univ. of Lund, Swed. LECT. in CLIN. PSYCH, Psychiat. Clin, Univ. of Lund. Member: SP, BPS. Clinical analysis, research, teaching; memory in senile patients, tests of brain injury and deterioration. F

LUNDGREN, Miss Marianne. Marmorgatan 11/13, Stockholm Sö. b. 30 July 1924 Ås. Fil. kand. '51 Univ. of Stockholm, Swed. CLIN. PSYCH'T, Södersjukhuset, Stockholm. Member: SP, Swed. Rorschach Assn. Testing, clinical practice, research; projective techniques, testing dementia, personality changes and improvements in psychotherapy. F

MACHL, Mrs. Margareta. Haga Parkgata 3D, Västerås. b. 19 Nov 1924 Västerås. Fil. kand. '46 Univ. of Uppsala, Swed. PSYCHOLOGIST, A.S.E.A., Västerås. Member: SP. Applied and educational psychology, statistical research, student; achievement tests, vocational guidance, school counseling. F

MAGNE, Docent Olof E. F. Prytzgatan 5, Gothenburg S. b. 18 May 1918 Visby. Fil. dr. '52 Univ. of Gothenburg, Swed. ASST. PROF, Dept. of Psych, Univ. of Gothenburg. Member: SP. Teaching, research, educational psychology; learning theory, teaching of arithmetic, special education. M

MAGNUSSON, David N. Plogvägen 7, Solna. b. 5 Sept 1925 Nässjö. Fil. kand, Univ. of Stockholm, Swed. RES. ASST, Psych. Inst, Univ. of Stockholm, Teknologgatan 8, Stockholm. Member: SP. Teaching, applied psychology, research; learning theory, group process, projective techniques. M

MALMQUIST, Fil. lic. Eve. Skräddaregatan 1, Linköping. b. 15 Nov 1915 Malmö. Fil. lic. Univ. of Lund, Swed. LEKTOR, Folkskoleseminariet, Linnégatan 11, Linköping; EDITOR, *Yggdiasik.* Member: SP. Teaching, research, administration, educational psychology; elementary school textbooks, intelligence and reading test construction. M

MÅNSSON, Miss Inga-Britt. Fruängsgatan 13 n.b., Stockholm. b. 18 Apr 1920 Lund. Fil. kand. '44 Univ. of Lund, Swed. PSYCHOLOGIST, Stockholm Stads Psykiska Barna-och Ungdomsvård. Member: SP, Swed. Rorschach Assn, Swedish Child Psych. Assn. Testing, adolescent psychotherapy; projective techniques, group process. F

MARKE, Sven. Inst. of Sociol, Univ. of Lund, Magle St, Kyrkogata 12 b, Lund. b. 15 Dec 1928 Ängelholm. Fil. lic. '54 Univ. of Lund, Swed. RES. ASST, Inst. of Sociol. Member: SP. Research, industrial psychology; attitude measurement, industrial sociology, parent-child relations. M

MOLANDER, Lars A. H. Sandhamnsgatan 13/v, Stockholm Ö. b. 29 May 1927 Stockholm. CONSULT. PSYCH'T, Karolinska Sjukhuset, Stockholm 60. Member: SP. Testing, research, consulting; memory, brain damage. M

NAESLUND, Fil. dr. Jon S. Holbergsgatan 129, Bromma. b. 3 Sept 1917 Oudmundrå. Fil. dr. '56 Univ. of Stockholm, Swed. LECTURER, Tchrs. Coll, Stockholm. Member: SP. Teaching, research, educational psychology; teacher training, methods of teaching reading, learning theory. M

NILSEN, Pastor Finar Anker. Overaas, Danskavagen 20, Gothenburg S. b. 8 July 1904 Porsgrunn, Nor. PH.D '52 Northwestern Univ, USA. PROFESSOR, Union Scandinavian Sch. of Theology. Member: NP. Teaching; personality, psychology of religion, counseling. M

NORELL, Mrs. Margit Sonja Annie. Karlbergsvägen 86 a, Stockholm Va. b. 23 Dec 1914 Uppsala. Fil. kand. '39 Univ. of Lund, Swed. PSYCHOANALYST, priv. prac. Member: Swed. Psychoanal. Socy. Psychoanalysis, psychotherapy. F

NORLIN, Sven. Åkersberga. b. 8 Dec 1919 Södertälje. Fil. kand. '54 Univ. of Stockholm, Swed. SCH. PSYCH'T, Åkersberga Central Sch. Member: SP. Teaching, guidance, testing; personality studies. M

NORLING, Mrs. Barbro Märta. Götgatan 20A, Uppsala. b. 25 Aug 1929 Karlstad. Fil. kand. '56 Univ. of Uppsala, Swed. Student, guidance, educational psychology; university student problems, psychometric methods. F

NORLING, Herman Ingemar. Götgatan 20 A, Uppsala. b. 7 Aug 1926 Lesjöfors. Fil. kand. '53 Univ. of Uppsala, Swed. FIRST ASST, Inst. for Psych, Univ. of Uppsala; INDUS. CONSULT, priv. prac. Member: SP. Research, teaching, industrial psychology, testing; psychometric methods, test construction, training problems. M

NYCANDER, Fil. kand. Berndt Gösta. Viggbyholmsvägen 56A, Viggbyholm. b. 26 Aug 1929 Uppsala. Fil. kand. '54 Univ. of Stockholm, Swed. TEACHER, Viggbyholmskolan. Teaching, psychotherapy, student; psychoanalysis. M

NYMAN-HELLBOM, Mrs. Birgit. Essingeringen 9, Stockholm K. b. 1 July 1923 Hälsingborg. Fil. kand. '54 Univ. of Lund, Swed. Member: SP. Student, applied psychology, testing. F

ÖGREN, Fil. dr. Gustaf. Cirkelvägen 22, Enskede 6. b. 8 May 1911 Falköping. Fil. dr. '53 Univ. of Gothenburg, Swed. REKTOR and HEAD, Sch. Broadcasting, Swed. Broadcasting Corp, Kungsgatan 8, Stockholm; ASST. LECT. in EDUC. PSYCH, Univ. of Stockholm. Member: SP. Teaching, planning and production of school broadcasts, research; foreign language teaching methods, comparative education, achievement tests. M

ORCHIDÉEN, Fil. kand. Gerd Gunborg. Box 108, Skara. b. 27 Aug 1930 Lidköping. Fil. kand. '51 Univ. of Gothenburg, Swed. Member: SP. Student; psychotherapy. F

ÖRNER, Fil. lic. Miss Bibi. Klippgatan 14, Uppg. 5, Stockholm S. b. 4 May 1927 Oslo, Nor. Fil. lic. Stockholms Högskola, Swed. Member: SP. Student, research, testing; research on separated twins. F

PALMÉR, Rikard Elving. Tiundagatan 53, Uppsala. b. 7 Feb 1922 Åseda. Fil. lic. '55 Univ. of Uppsala, Swed. CONSULTANT, Kungl. Skolöverstyrelsen, Hantverkargatan 29, Stockholm. Member: SP. Industrial psychology, administration, consulting; social perception, vocational development and guidance, suggestion and suggestibility. M

PETRÉN, Lektor K. J. Erik G. Majorsgatan 24 G, Gävle. b. 22 Oct 1919 Uppsala. Licence ès lettres '47 Univ. of Lund, Swed. LEKTOR, Folkskoleseminariet, Gävle; PSYCH. TCHR, Nrsng. Sch. Gävle. Member: SP. Teaching; personality traits, selection of teachers. M

PRIEN, Fil. lic. Lars. Blåsutvägen 47/II, Enskede. b. 22 July 1924 Stockholm. Fil. lic. '56 Univ. of Stockholm, Swed. CONSULT. INDUS. PSYCH'T, Sandvikens Järnverk Sandviken. Member: SP. Personnel psychology, testing, industrial sociology; leadership, psychological testing, motivations of workers. M

RAMFALK, Fil. lic. Carl Wilhelm. Sjösavägen 3, Stockholm-Bandhagen. b. 12 June 1915 Halmstad. Fil. lic. '52 Univ. of Lund, Swed. RES. WRKR, Swed. Counc. for Pers. Admin, Södra Blasieholmshamnen 4A, Stockholm; PSYCH. TCHR, Stockholm Sch. of Soc. Work and Pub. Admin. Member: SP, Int. Psychoanal. Assn. Research, psychotherapy, teaching; personality theory and measurement. M

ROSÉN, Mrs. Anne-Sofie. Långseleringen 57, Stockholm-Vällingby. b. 7 May 1927 Stockholm. Fil. kand. '54 Univ. of Stockholm, Swed. CLIN. PSYCH'T, Beckomberga Sjukhus, Bromma. Member: SP. Research, clinical testing, student. F

ROSENBERG, Fil. lic. Dr. E. Günther K. A. Kungsholmsborg 10/I, Stockholm. b. 21 May 1914 Lübeck, Ger. Fil. lic, Univ. of Stockholm, Swed. ADJUNKT, Sodra Flicklaeov, Stockholm. Member: SP. Teaching, research, testing; psychology of thinking, projective techniques, psychoanalysis. M

RUBENOWITZ, Civilingenjör Sigvard. Lövmånadsg. 3, Gothenburg N. b. 1 Oct 1925 Lund. Diploma '54 Univ. of London, Eng. INDUS. CONSULT, Svenska Arbetsgivare föreningens, Personaladministrativa Råd, Blasieholmen, Stockholm; LECTURER, Gothenburg Univ. of Bus. Admin; EDITOR, *Applied Psychology.* Member: SP, BPS. Industrial psychology, research, testing; merit rating, personnel selection. M

SÄLDE, Dr. med. Docent Henry. Psych. Clin, Akademiska Sjukhuset, Luthagsesplanaden 8B, Uppsala. b. 9 Apr 1916 Skara. MD '52 Univ. of Uppsala, Swed. DOCENT and CLIN. PSYCHIATRIST, Psych. Clin, Akademiska Sjukhuset. Member: SP, Swed. Psychiat. Assn. Clinical practice, psychotherapy, research, testing, teaching; psychometric and experimental procedures in clinical diagnosis. M

SANDELS, Fil. dr. Stina Claesdotter. Smedsbacksgatan 5, Stockholm. b. 4 Jan 1908 Mariestad. Fil. dr. '56 Univ. of Gothenburg, Swed. INSPECTOR, Preschool Trng. Coll, Kungl. Socialstyrelsen, Birger Jarls torg 2, Stockholm. Member: SP. Teaching, research, administration; genetic psychology, preschool psychology, intelligence and development tests. F

SANDSTRÖM, Docent Carl Ivar G. Artillerigatan 46/IV, Stockholm Ö. b. 14 Aug 1914 Södertälje. Fil. dr. '51 Univ. of Stockholm, Swed. DOCENT, Univ. of Uppsala; SWED. ED, *Nordisk Psykologi, Acta Psychologica.* Member: SP. Teaching, research, editorial; space perception, perceptive sex differences. M

SCHALLING, Fil. lic. Daisy S. M. Konvaljstigen 2, Solna, Stockholm. b. 10 Sept 1923 Stockholm. Fil. lic. '54 Univ. of Stockholm,

Swed. CLIN. PSYCH'T, Forensic Psychiat. Clin, Långholmen, Stockholm; HEAD CLIN. PSYCH'T, State Rehab. Clin, Karolinska Vägen, Stockholm 60; PSYCH. ASST, Prof. Gösta Rylander. Member: SP. Clinical testing, research, teaching; brain injury and language disabilities, brain injury and perception, psychological methods in psychosurgery. F

SEIFERT, Dipl. Psych. Theodor Johannes. Ringvägen 64, Saltsjöbaden. b. 9 July 1931 Zwickau, Ger. Dipl. Psych, Free Univ. of Berlin, Ger. INDUS. PSYCH'T, Inst. för Tillämpad Psykologi, Ängsvägen 7, Nacka. Industrial psychology, teaching, testing, graphology; expressive movements and handwriting, measurement of leadership and industrial attitudes, group relations in industrial and religious fields. M

SEITZ, Mrs. Gudrun Hedvig. Östermalmsgatan 93, Stockholm. b. 22 Feb 1912 Friel. Dipl. '38 Univ. of London, Eng. PLAY THERAPIST, Erica Found, Odengatan 9, Stockholm Ö. Member: SP, Swed. Child Psych. Assn. Testing, consulting, psychotherapy, research; play therapy, psychodrama. F

SIEGVALD, Prof. Dr. Herman. Univ. of Lund, Psych. Dept, Lundagård, Lund. b. 13 Feb 1894 Beddinge. Fil. dr. '44 Univ. of Lund, Swed. PROF. and HEAD, Dept. of Psych, Inst. of Psych. and Educ. Member: SP. Teaching, research, administration; differential psychology, intelligence testing, learning theory. M

SJÖSTRAND, Prof. Wilhelm. Karlsrog. 88A, Uppsala. b. 19 Aug 1909 Barnarp. Fil. dr. '41 Univ. of Uppsala, Swed. PROFESSOR, Inst. of Educ, Univ. of Uppsala. Member: SP. Teaching, research, administration, professional writing, psychology of learning, testing, history of education. M

SJÖVALL, Fil. lic. Björn Yngve Yson. Eriksviks gård, Saltsjö-Boo. b. 16 Feb 1916 Kristianstad. Fil. lic. '48 Univ. of Stockholm, Swed. HEAD PSYCH'T, NKI Sch, St-Eriksgatan 33, Stockholm; TEACHER, Swedish Naval Coll. Member: SP. Applied psychology, psychotherapy, consulting; personal adjustment. M

SMITH, Docent Gudmund John Wilhelm. Univ. of Lund, Lund. b. 29 Jan 1920 Lund. Fil. dr. Univ. of Lund, Swed. DOCENT, Univ. of Lund; EDITOR, *Stuida Psychologica et Paedagogica.* Member: SP, APA. Teaching, research, applied psychology; twin psychology, perceptual processes, attitude measurement. M

STEVENS, Fil. lic. Stig R. Lagman Eskils väg, Lerum. b. 8 Mar 1929 Port Arthur, Texas, USA. Fil. lic. '53 Univ. of Gothenburg, Swed. CONSULTANT, priv. prac. Member: SP. Industrial psychology, re-

search, teaching; personnel selection, industrial fatigue, group process. M
STOKSTAD, Cand. Psych. Johannes Bergh. Barnbyn, Skå. b. 23 Jan 1927 Trondheim, Nor. Cand. Psych. '53 Univ. of Oslo, Nor. PSYCHOLOGIST, Barnbyn. Member: NP. Group and individual psychotherapy, guidance, clinical analysis; group processes among criminal youngsters, maladjusted children. M
STUKAT, Fil. lic. Karl-Gustaf. Ungmåstargatan 8, Gothenburg. b. 1922 Gothenburg. PSYCHOLOGIST, Pedagogiska Inst, Vasa Parken, Gothenburg. Member: SP. Research, teaching, educational psychology; suggestibility, social perception. M
SVENSSON, Nils-Eric. Sjösavägen 69, Bandhagen. b. 7 Nov 1923 Tännäs. Fil, kand. '54 Univ. of Stockholm, Swed. RES. ASST, Tchrs. Coll, Rålambsvägen 24, Stockholm. Member: SP. Research, administration, teaching; achievement tests; attitude measurement, psychometric problems. M
SZÉKELY, Dr. Lajos. Setterwallsväg 19, Nacka. b. 20 Oct 1904 Budapest, Hungary. PH.D '30 Pázmány Péter Univ, Hungary. PSYCHOANALYST, priv. prac; LECTURER, Soc. Inst, Odengatan 61, Stockholm. Member: SP, APA, Swed. Psychoanal. Socy, Amer. Sociol. Socy. Psychotherapy, teaching, research, consulting; instinct theory, affects, thinking, medical and child psychology. M
TEGEN, Prof. Einar. Norrskogsvägen 3, Stockholm K. b. 4 June 1884 Gryta, Uppsala. Fil. dr. '18 Univ. of Uppsala, Swed. PROF. EMER. of PRACTICAL PHILOS, Univ. of Stockholm. Research; field theory and group process, problem of authority in history of cultures. M
TÖRNBLOM, Miss Rose Ingrid Birgitta. Frejgatan 48, I Stockholm va. b. 13 Oct 1920 Jönköping. Fil. kand. '48 Univ. of Stockholm, Swed. GRAD. STUD, Univ. of Stockholm. Member: SP. Psychotherapy, teaching; counseling, projective techniques, psychoanalysis. F
TRANKELL, Prof. Arne. Aspen. b. 28 Mar 1919 Stockholm. Fil. dr. '51 Univ. of Gothenburg, Swed. ASST. PROF, Univ. of Gothenburg; CONSULT. PSYCH'T, Scandinavian Airlines System. Member: SP, Amer. Socy. of Human Genetics, European Assn. for Aviat. Psych. Industrial psychology, research, teaching; aviation psychology, population and statistical genetics, psychology of lefthandedness. M
ULIN, Fil. dr. Carin. Östermalmsgatan 68, Stockholm Ö. b. 28 Sept 1886 Stockholm. Fil. dr. '50 Univ. of Gothenburg, Swed. PRINCIPAL, Södra KFUK:S Pedagogiska Inst, Folkungagatan 122, Stockholm Sö.

Member: World Organiza. for Preschool Educ. Research, teaching, testing; psychology of the preschool child, growth problem in children. F
ULMER-THIEME, Marion. Norra Esplanaden 13, Tierp. b. 29 Oct 1925 Hamburg, Ger. Dipl. Psych. '51 Univ. of Hamburg, Ger. PSYCHOLOGIST, priv. prac. Member: SP, BDP. Consulting, testing, psychotherapy; projective techniques, psychological stages of child development. F
VIDLUND, Lars Erik. Katrinelundsvägen 20, Västerås. b. 27 Nov 1931 Västerås. ASST. to PERS. MGR, ASEA, Västerås. Personnel work, student, research; group process, attitude measurement, achievement tests. M
WÄCHTER, Fil. lic. Walter Michael. Värmdövägen 53/I, Klinten, Stockholm. b. 26 May 1913 Hamburg, Ger. Fil. lic, Univ. of Stockholm, Swed. MILIT. PSYCH'T, Inst. of Milit. Psych, Fredrikshovsgatan 6, Stockholm Ö; CONSULTANT, Stockholm Högskolas Psykotekniska Inst. Member: SP, Swed. Rorschach Assn. Applied psychology, administration, consulting, teaching; achievement tests, projective techniques, attitude measurement, military psychology. M
WALLNER, Teut. Skutuddsvägen 5, Saltsjöbaden. b. 14 July 1923 Berlin, Ger. Dipl. Psych. '53 Free Univ. of Berlin, Ger. INDUS. PSYCH'T, Inst. för Tillämpad Psych, Lärkvägen 22, Saltsjöbaden. Teaching, testing, research; test development, handwriting characteristics, personnel evaluation and selection. M
WÄRNERYD, Dr. Karl-Erik. Agnes Lagerstedts Gata 16, Hägersten. b. 20 Dec 1927 Edsvära. PH.D '55 Univ. of Chicago, USA. RES. ASSOC, Stockholm Sch. of Econ, Sveavägen 65, Stockholm. Member: SP. Research, applied psychology, teaching; psychometrics, attitude measurement, learning theory. M
WERDELIN, Fil. lic. Carl Ingvar Kristian. Brommogatan 21, Hälsingborg. b. 1 Dec 1924 Värö. Fil. lic. '55 Univ. of Lund, Swed. ASST. PROF, Univ. of Lund. Member: SP. Research, teaching, student; factor analysis, problem solving, learning theory, intelligence testing. M
WESTERLUND, Prof. Gunnar. Sch. of Econ, Univ. of Stockholm, Sveavägen 65, Stockholm Va. b. 21 June 1911 Stockholm. Fil. dr. '52 Univ. of Stockholm, Swed. PROF. of SOC. PSYCH, Sch. of Econ, Univ. of Stockholm; DIRECTOR, Inst. of Business Res, Univ. of Stockholm; EDITOR, Publications of the Inst. of Bus. Res. Member: SP, AIPA, Amer. Sociol. Socy. Applied psychology, research, administration; field studies of work group and foreman, leadership and productivity. M

WESTMARK, Mrs. Inger Margareta. Smedsbacksg. 20, Stockholm. b. 18 Aug 1916 Gothenburg. Fil. kand. '40 Univ. of Stockholm, Swed. STUDENT, Univ. of Stockholm. Member: SP. Research in juvenile delinquency, child and adolescent psychotherapy, guidance.   F
WIKBERG, Anders Emil. Sturegatan 26, Uppsala. b. 9 Dec 1911 Arvidsjaur. Fil. lic. '54 Univ. of Uppsala, Swed. INSPECTOR of ELEM. SCHOOLS, Govt. of Sweden. Member: SP. Teaching, research, administration; visual perception, visual transposition, depth perception.   M
WINGBORG, Olof August Bruno. Västerled 23, Bromma. b. 6 Sept 1928 Stockholm.

Fil. mag. '54 Univ. of Stockholm, Swed. PSYCH. ASST, Kungl. Medicinalstyrelsen, Stockholm 3. Member: SP. Testing; achievement and intelligence tests.   M
WIRDENIUS, Fil. lic. Hans. O. Björnbo 42, Lidingö 1. b. 9 Dec 1919 Stockholm. Fil. lic. '51 Univ. of Stockholm, Swed. DEPT. HEAD, Swedish Employers' Assn. Member: SP. Research, testing, industrial psychology; personnel selection, leadership in industry, human relations training.   M
ZACKRISSON, Fil. kand. Per-Gunnar. Skårsgatan 38, Gothenburg. b. 15 Mar 1929 Gothenburg. Fil. kand, Univ. of Gothenburg, Swed. Member: SP. Student, educational psychology, research.   M

SWITZERLAND

ABRAHAM, Dr. phil. Mrs. Elisabeth. Freiestr. 155, Zurich 7/32. b. 3 July 1915 Zurich. PH.D, Univ. of Bern, Switz. PSYCHOANAL. COUNS, priv. prac. Member: SSP, Swiss Psychoanal. Assn. Psychotherapy, clinical analysis.   F
ACHTNICH, Dr. Martin. Rehweg 13, Winterthur. b. 20 May 1918 Winterthur. Dr. '46 Univ. of Zurich, Switz. VOCAT. GUID. OFF, Vocat. Guid. Cen. for Boys, Rathausdurchgang, Winterthur. Member: SSP, AIOP. Consulting, clinical analysis, applied psychology; vocational guidance for mentally and physically maladapted youth.   M
ACKERMANN, Dr. phil. Albert. C. F. Meyerstr, Kilchberg/Zch. b. 2 Sept 1897 Wolfwyl. PH.D '25 Univ. of Jena, Ger. INDUS. CONSULT, priv. prac. Member: SSP, Swiss Graphology Socy. Industrial psychology, consulting, psychotherapy; automation, human relations, personnel training.   M
AEBLI, Prof. Dr. Hans. Psych. Inst, Univ. of Saarland, Saarbrücken 15, Saar. b. 6 Aug 1923 Zurich, Switz. PH.D '51 Univ. of Geneva, Switz. VIS. PROF. and ACTING DIR, Psych. Inst, Univ. of Saarland. Member: SSP, APSLF. Teaching, research, administration; learning theory, child psychology, education.   M
AEBLY, Mrs. Marie. Bionstr. 11, Zurich 6. b. Apr 1888 Reutlingen, Ger. PSYCH. CONSULT, priv. prac. Member: Gesellschaft für Angewandte Psych. Consulting; graphology, applied psychology.   F
AFFOLTER, Miss Félicie. 17 d Varnbüelstr, St. Gallen. b. 22 Feb 1926 St. Gallen. L.PS '54 Univ. of Geneva, Switz. TEACHER, Sch. for Deaf-Mutes, St. Gallen. Member: SSP. Teaching, research; psychology of language, achievement tests, cognitive and affective development.   F
ANDINA, Dr. Rinaldo. Freiestr. 155, Zurich 32. b. 1 Aug 1925 Zurich. PH.D '50 Univ.

of Zurich, Switz. PSYCH. CONSULT, priv. prac. Member: Schweiz. Berufsverband für Angewandte Psych, Swiss Psychoanal. Socy. Consulting, testing, teaching, applied psychology; social psychology, vocational guidance.   M
ANDINA-HEIM, Mrs. Margarete. Freiestr. 155, Zurich 32. b. 30 Oct 1927 Stuttgart, Ger. Diploma, Inst. for Appl. Psych, Zurich, Switz. PSYCHOTHERAPIST, priv. prac. Member: Swiss Psychoanal. Socy. Psychotherapy, testing and clinical analysis; psychoanalysis.   F
BASH, Dr. Kenower Weimar. Kantonale Heil- und Pflegeanstalt, Wil, St. Gallen. b. 21 Aug 1913 New Glasgow, NS, Can. MD '49 Univ. of Zurich, Switz. CHIEF PHYS, Kantonale Heil- und Pflegeanstalt, Wil; EDITOR, Rorschachiana; ED. BD, Schweizerische Zeitschrift für Psychology. Member: SSP. Swiss Socy. for Appl. Psych. Psychiatric practice, psychotherapy, research; general psychopathology, Rorschach.   M
BAUER, Dr. Ernst. Mariabergstr. 20, Rorschach SG. b. 1 Nov 1915 St. Gallen. PH.D '49 Univ. of Zurich, Switz. SCH. PSYCH'T, Schulpsychologische Dienst des Kantons St. Gallen, Oberer Graben 39, St. Gallen; LECTURER, Sch. for Kindergarten Tchrs. Member: SSP. Guidance, testing; speech development, school readiness, development of expression through drawing.   M
BAUMGARTEN-TRAMER, Prof. Dr. phil. Franziska. Thunstr. 35, Bern. PH.D, Univ. of Zurich, Switz. DIRECTOR, Cen. for Labor and Vocat. Psych; EDITOR, International Journal of Professional Ethics. Member: AIPA. Professional writing, research, applied psychology, testing; social perception, group process, attitude measurement, vocational tests, tests of moral attitudes.   F

BENO, Dr. Norbert. Maison de Santé de Malévoz, Monthey. b. 14 Apr 1899 Adrianople, Turkey. MD '46 Univ. of Lausanne, Switz. ASST. DR. in PSYCHIAT, Maison de Santé de Malévoz. Member: SSP, Int. Psychoanal. Socy. Psychotherapy, clinical practice, teaching; psychoanalysis, child psychiatry. M

BERNA, Jacques. Sophienstr. 16, Zurich 32. b. 25 Mar 1911 Zurich. PSYCHOANALYST, priv. prac. Member: SSP, Swiss Psychoanal. Socy. Child psychotherapy, teaching, professional writing; psychoanalysis. M

BERTRAND, Miss Marie-Louise. Rue du Midi, Monthey, Valais. b. 15 Oct 1919 Saxon. Diplôme, Inst. of Educ. Sci, Geneva, Switz. ASST. PSYCH'T, Serv. Médico-Pédagogique Valaisan, Monthey, Valais. Member: SSP. Psychotherapy, testing, applied and educational psychology; child analysis, psychology of delinquency. F

BÉVAND, Richard Gilbert. Cours de Rive 6, Geneva. b. 30 Nov 1921 Geneva. Licence, Univ. of Geneva, Switz. PSYCHOTHERAPIST, priv. prac. Member: SSP, Swiss Socy. for Appl. Psych. Psychotherapy, applied psychology; waking dreams. M

BIÄSCH, Prof. Dr. Hans. Spiegelhofstr. 62, Zurich 7/32. b. 4 Oct 1901 Davos. Dr. sci. nat. '27 Fed. Inst. of Tech, Switz. PROF. of APPL. PSYCH, Fed. Inst. of Tech, Zurich; DIRECTOR, Inst. for Appl. Psych, Merkurstr. 20, Zurich. Member: SSP, DGP. Teaching, applied psychology, administration, research; projective techniques, group process, social perception, achievement tests. M

BINSWANGER, Dr. med. Kurt. Moussonstr. 15, Zurich 7/44. b. 15 Mar 1887 Basel. MD '13 Univ. of Basel, Switz. PSYCHIATRIST, C.G. Jung Inst, Gemeindestr. 27, Zurich. Member: SSP, Swiss Socy. for Appl. Psych. Psychotherapy, consulting, clinical practice, teaching; analytical psychology. M

BLARER, Dr. phil. Arno von. Freiestr. 72, Zurich 7/32. b. 23 Mar 1922 Fribourg. PH.D '50 Univ. of Zurich, Switz. PSYCHO-ANALYST, priv. prac. Member: SSP. Psychotherapy, clinical analysis, applied psychology; psychodynamics, social psychological process, psychodiagnostics. M

BLICKENSTORFER, Privat dozent Dr. med. Edwin. Universitätsstr. 86, Zurich 6. b. 5 Aug 1919 Zurich. Privatdozent '52 Univ. of Zurich, Switz. PSYCHOTHERAPIST, priv. prac; EDITOR, *Psychoanalytische Kasuistik*. Member: Swiss Psychoanal. Socy. Psychotherapy, consulting, research; psychosomatic medicine, psychoanalysis. M

BOLLAG, Dr. Elisabeth. Goldauerstr. 15, Zurich 6. b. 26 Feb 1906 Liestal. PH.D '48 Univ. of Zurich, Switz. PSYCHOLOGIST, priv. prac. Member: SSP. Psychotherapy,

consulting, teaching lip reading; projective techniques, analysis, child play therapy. F

BOLLER-SCHWING, Gertrud. Rämistr. 60, Zurich 1. b. 22 June 1905 Zurich. PSYCHO-ANALYST, priv. prac. Member: SSP, Int. Psychoanal. Socy. Psychotherapy, consulting, teaching; psychotherapy of schizophrenia. F

BOSS, Jean-Paul. 197 Rue Numa Droz, La-Chaux-de-Fonds. b. 7 June 1923 Neuchâtel. Dipl. Math. '47 E.P.F., Zurich, Switz. ASSISTANT, Inst. of Psych, Univ. of Neuchâtel. Research, applied psychology, teaching; mathematical statistics, aptitude tests. M

BOSS, Prof. Dr. med. Médard. Theaterstr. 12, Zurich 1. b. St. Gall. Prof. '52 Univ. of Zurich, Switz. HEAD, Dept. for Psychoanal. Trng; Psychiat. Clin, Univ. of Zurich, Lenggstr. 31, Zurich. Member: SSP, Swiss Psychoanal. Socy. Teaching, research, psychotherapy; existential analysis, psychotherapeutic techniques. M

BOSSARD, Dr. phil. Robert. Ruetistr. 21, Zollikon, Zurich. b. 1 Dec. 1920 Wattwil SG. PH.D '45 Univ. of Zurich, Switz. CHIEF, Psych. Serv, Swiss Air Lines, Zurich. Member: SSP. Applied and personnel psychology, research, teaching; development and application of aviation tests, characterology, genetic psychology, physiological psychology. M

BOVEN, Prof. William. Ave. de la Gare 2, Lausanne. b. 26 June 1887 Lausanne. MD, Univ. of Lausanne, Switz. RECTOR, Univ. of Lausanne. Member: SSP. Teaching, psychotherapy, clinical practice; neuropsychopathology, characterology. M

BOVET, Dr. Pierre. Grandchamp Areuse/ Neuchâtel. b. 5 June 1878 Grandchamp Boudry. Docteur ès lettres '02 Univ. of Geneva, Switz. RETIRED. M

BRAENDLI, Dr. Alfred. Bedastr. 12, St. Gallen-O. b. 9 Sept 1920 Davos/GR. PH.D '51 Univ. of Zurich, Switz. PSYCHOLOGIST, priv. prac. Member: SSP. Testing, consulting. M

BRÄNDLI-BARTH, Mrs. Eleonore. Marbachweg 1, Thalwil, Zurich. b. 4 Oct 1905 Munich, Ger. Dipl. Psych. '54 Inst. of Appl. Psych, Zurich, Switz. PSYCH. CONSULT, priv. prac. Testing, consulting, guidance, research; personality, projective tests, dreams. F

BRINKMANN, Prof. Dr. Donald. Dunanstr. 2, Zurich 44. b. 9 Feb 1909 Zurich. Prof. Dr, Univ. of Zurich, Switz. PROFESSOR, Univ. of Zurich. Teaching, research, educational and industrial psychology, consulting; industrial management and training, psychology of films, mass phenomena and behavior. M

BRUN, Rudolf. Zurichbergstr. 88, Zurich 7.

b. 15 Mar 1885 Zurich. MD Univ. of Zurich, Switz. NEUROLOGIST and PSYCHOANALYST, priv. prac. Member: Swiss Psychoanal. Socy, Swiss Psychiat. Socy. Research, psychotherapy, consulting, clinical practice; Freudian psychoanalysis, neurobiology. M

CHAPUIS, Dr. Frédy. Chemin de Fantaisie 1, Pully. b. 2 Feb 1913 Neuchâtel. Docteur ès sciences '49 Univ. of Neuchâtel, Switz. PERS. CHIEF, Société des Produits Nestlé, Quai Perdonnet, Vevey. Member: SSP, AIPA. Industrial personnel, testing-research; achievement tests, projective techniques. M

CHRISTOFFEL, Dr. Hans. Albanvorstadt 21, Basel. b. 27 July 1888 Aarau. MD, Univ. of Basel, Switz. PSYCHIATRIST, priv. prac. Member: SSP, Swiss Psychoanal. Socy. Research, psychotherapy, clinical practice; psychopathology and psychosomatics, history of psychiatry, comparative psychology. M

DEBRUNNER, Dr. Hugo. Stäfa-Zurich. b. 17 May 1896 Zurich. PH.D '26 Univ. of Bern, Switz. Member: Swiss Socy. for Appl. Psych. Psychotherapy, applied psychology, testing, comparative research on hand structures of men and apes, psychology of expression, depth psychology. M

DESCOMBES, Gaston. La Jaluse 13, Le Locle. b. 14 Oct 1917 La Chaux-de-Fonds. PSYCH. ANALYST, priv. prac. Psychotherapy, educational and applied psychology. M

DUBOSSON, Jacques-Maurice Henri. Micheli du Crest 11b, Geneva. b. 26 Feb 1916 Lausanne. Licence '50 Univ. of Lausanne, Switz. CHARGÉ de COURS, Inst. of Educ. Sci, 53 Rue des Paguis-Rue de Neuchâtel 47, Geneva. Member: SSP, APSLF. Teaching, research, testing; educational guidance, intellectual and emotional re-education. M

DUPONT, Jean-Blaise. Ave. Bel-Air 27, La Tour-de-Peilz/Vaud. b. 21 Sept 1926 Bex. L.PS '48 Univ. of Paris, Fr. PSYCHOLOGIST, Nestlé S.A. Vevey; TCHR. in CHILD PSYCH, Ecole Normale Cantonale, Neuchâtel. Member: SSP, AIPA, APSLF. Educational and industrial psychology, teaching, guidance; personnel selection, test evaluation. M

DUPRAZ, Prof. Dr. Laure. 190 Rue Préfecture, Fribourg. b. 16 June 1896 Geneva. PH.D '32 Univ. of Fribourg, Switz. PROF. of EDUC, Fac. of Letters, Univ. of Fribourg; EDITOR, Inst. de *Pédagogie, Orthopédagogie et Psych. Appliquée.* Member: SSP. Teaching, research, editorial; educational psychology. F

EGGMANN, Dr. phil. Otto. Langnau i.E. Bern. b. 5 Aug 1913 Biel/Bern. PH.D, Univ. of Bern, Switz. DIRECTOR, Gotthelfschule, Luisenstr. 5, Bern. Member: SSP, Schweiz. Gesellschaft für Parapsych.

Teaching, educational psychology, guidance testing; depth psychology, child psychology, parapsychology, graphology. M

ELLENBERGER, Dr. Henri Frédéric. Menninger Found, Topeka, Kansas, USA. b. 6 Nov 1905 Rhodesia, S. Africa. MD '34 Univ. of Paris, Fr. STAFF PSYCHIATRIST, Menninger Foundation. Member: SSP. Research, dynamic psychotherapy, teaching, testing; phenomenology of inspiration, creativity in normal and abnormal conditions, projective tests. M

FANKHAUSER, Dr. Gottfried. Bernastr. 68, Bern. b. 17 Jan 1908 Bern. PH.D '43 Univ. of Bern, Switz. TEACHER, Lehrerinnenseminar Bern, Waisenhausplatz 29, Bern. Member: SSP. Teaching, research, testing; developmental psychology, structural psychology. M

FAVRE, Dr. André. 84 Blvd. des Tranchées, Geneva. b. 7 Mar 1906 St. Imier. MD '30 Univ. of Lausanne, Switz. PSYCHIATRIST, priv. prac. Member: SSP, Swiss Psychiat. Socy. Psychotherapy. M

FIERZ, Dr. med. Henrich Karl. Sanatorium Bellevue, Hauptstr. 14, Kreuzlingen, Thurgau. b. 20 June 1912 Basel. MD '41 Univ. of Zurich, Switz. DEPT. HEAD, Sanatorium Bellevue. Member: SSP, Swiss Socy. for Med. Psychother, Swiss Socy. for Appl. Psych. Psychotherapy, clinical practice, professional writing; psychology of transference. M

FISCHER, Hardi. 8 Contrat Social, Geneva. b. 5 Aug 1922 Zurich. Docteur ès sciences '56 Univ. of Geneva, Switz. SCH. PSYCH'T, Secondary Schools of Geneva. Member: SSP, APSLF. Educational psychology, research, teaching; factor analysis, statistical methods. M

FISCHER, Dr. phil. Max. Heliosstr. 6, Zurich 7/32. b. 23 July 1907 Zurich. PH.D '34 Univ. of Zurich, Switz. PSYCHOTHERAPIST, priv. prac. Member: SSP. Psychotherapy, applied psychology, consulting; psychopathology of sexuality, marriage, psychosomatics. M

FRANK, Dr. Sigwart. Bergstr. 3, Zurich 44. b. 11 May 1896 Münsterlingen. MD '25 Univ. of Zurich, Switz. PSYCHOTHERAPIST, priv. prac. Member: Swiss Psychother. Socy, Swiss Psychiat. Socy. Psychotherapy. M

FREY-ROHN, Dr. Mrs. Lilian. Gladbachstr. 103, Zurich 7. b. 24 Oct 1901 Cologne, Ger. PH.D '33 Univ. of Zurich, Switz. ANAL. PSYCH'T, Inst. C. G. Jung, Gemeindestr. 28, Zurich. Member: SSP, Swiss Socy. for Appl. Psych. Analytical psychology, guidance, teaching, clinical analysis; psychoanalysis. F

FRIEDEMANN, Dr. med. A. Fischerweg 6, Biel. b. 26 May 1902 Saicourt J. B.

MD '26 Univ. of Freiburg, Ger. DIRECTOR, Inst. of Ment. Hyg, Rue Centrale 49, Biel; EDITOR, *Schweiz. Zeitschrift für Psychologie und ihre Anwendungen.* Member: SSP, DGP, Int. Rorschach Socy. Research, clinical analysis, psychotherapy; psychopathology, projective techniques, vocational guidance. M

FRIEDRICH, Dipl. Psych. Miss Dorothee. Brennofenstr. 5, Roggwil, Bern. b. 29 Mar 1923 Hannover, Ger. Dipl. Psych. '50 Univ. of Göttingen, Ger. INDUS. PSYCH'T, Textilfirma Gugelmann und Cie. AG, Langenthal. Member: Schweiz. Berufsverband für Angewandte Psych. Industrial psychology, guidance, personnel work. F

GALLUSSER, Miss Ursula Maria. Dept. of Educ, UNESCO, 19 Ave. Kléber, Paris 16, Fr. b. 29 Mar 1922 Geneva. Licence '51 Univ. of Geneva, Switz. ASSOC. OFF. in charge of EDUC. and CHILD. DEVEL, Dept. of Educ, UNESCO; PSYCH. ADVISOR, Int. Nursery School, Paris, Fr. Member: SSP. Administration, editorial, professional writing; child development, learning theory, projective techniques. F

GIROD, Prof. Dr. Roger. Univ. of Geneva. b. 24 Mar 1921 Geneva. PH.D '52 Univ. of Geneva, Switz. PROF. of SOCIOL, Univ. of Geneva; DIRECTOR, Sociol. Res. Cen. of Geneva. Member: SSP, APSLF, Swiss Sociol. Socy. Research, teaching; social stratification in attitudes and ideology, interaction between social structure, economic condition, and behavior. M

GOUMAZ, Gaston. Ave. du Mont d'Or 13, Lausanne. b. 27 June 1931 Moudon. L.PS '54 Univ. of Geneva, Switz. PSYCHOTECHNICIAN, Off. for Profes. Integration, Ave. du Mont d'Or 13, Lausanne. Member: SSP, APSLF. Testing, guidance, research; professional rehabilitation of physically handicapped workers, job evaluation, habit formation, religious psychology. M

GRABER, Dr. Gustav Hans. Humboldtstr. 49, Bern. b. 17 May 1893 Bern. PH.D '24 Univ. of Bern, Switz. PSYCHOTHERAPIST, priv. prac. Member: SSP, Swiss Socy. for Appl. Psych, Swiss Psychoanal. Socy. Psychotherapy, applied psychology, professional writing; depth psychology. M

GRESSOT, Dr. Michel. Chemin Thury 3 bis, Geneva. b. 27 Nov 1918 Porrentruy. MD '46 Univ. of Lausanne, Switz. PSYCHOANALYST, priv. prac. Member: SSP, APSLF, Int. Psychoanal. Assn. Psychotherapy, teaching, professional writing; ethnopsychology, psychology of art, psychoanalysis. M

HÄBERLI, Dr. Hans. Kantonale Erziehungs Anstalt, Aarburg. b. 17 Aug 1924 Olten. PH.D '54 Univ. of Zurich, Switz. ASSISTANT, Kantonale Erziehungs Anstalt. Education-

al psychology, guidance, administration; adolescent psychology, characterology, family sociology. M

HÄBERLIN, Dr. phil. Miss Annemarie. Gutenbergstr. 43, Bern. b. 21 Nov 1917 Bern. PH.D '52 Univ. of Bern, Switz. CHILD GUID. COUNS, Erziehungsberatung, Städtischen Schularztamtes, Hirschgraben 11, Bern; CONSULT. PSYCH'T, Observation Cen, Bern. Member: SSP. Consulting, psychotherapy; applied and educational psychology, child guidance; psychosomatics. F

HAEBERLIN, Prof. Dr. phil. Paul. Gotthardstr. 10, Basel. b. 17 Feb 1878 Kesswil. PH.D '03 Univ. of Basel, Switz. Retired; anthropology, educational psychology. M

HAESLER, Dr. Walter Th. Sonnenberg, Lenzburg AG. b. 25 Dec 1926 Baden. Dr. ès lettres '55 Univ. of Neuchâtel, Switz. PSYCHOLOGIST, Lenzburg Penitentiary. Member: SSP, Swiss Socy. for Appl. Psych. Applied and educational psychology, clinical practice, research; problem children, psychology of prison life, cultural relations. M

HALTER, Dr. Camilla. Inst. for Indus. Psych, Universitätsstr. 69, Zurich. b. 16 May 1913 Rorschach, St. Gallen. PH.D '39 Univ. of Zurich, Switz. DIRECTOR, Inst. for Indus. Psych. Member: SSP. Industrial psychology, testing, teaching; psychology of work, aptitude tests. F

HAUSER, Irene. Eichenstr. 44, Basel. b. 2 July 1922 Hottingen, Ger. PSYCHOTHERAPIST, Familienfürsorge, Augustinergasse 1a, Basel. Member: SSP. Psychotherapy, educational psychology, testing, teaching; achievement and character tests. F

HEDIGER, Prof. Dr. Heini P. Ackermannstr. 14, Zurich. b. 30 Nov 1908 Basel. PH.D '32 Univ. of Basel, Switz. ZOO DIRECTOR, Zoo and Univ, Zurich; EDITOR, *Behaviour.* Member: SSP. Animal psychology, teaching, research; effects of captivity, domestication and training of animals. M

HEGG, Dr. phil. Hans. Junkerngasse 37, Bern. b. 30 May 1893 Bern. PH.D '19 Univ. of Bern, Switz. HEAD, Erziehungsberatung, Schularztamt, Hirschgraben 11, Bern. Member: SSP. Consulting, testing, educational psychology, teaching; intelligence tests, projective techniques. M

HEYMANN, Dr. Karl. Davidsbodenstr. 27, Basel. b. 1 Mar 1901 Mainz, Ger. PH.D '33 Univ. of Marburg/L, Ger. DIRECTOR, Free Sch. for Maladjusted Children. Member: SSP. Educational psychology, teaching, professional writing; guidance; problem children, psychology of art, social psychology. M

HUBER, Hans T. Marktgasse 9, Bern. b. 22 Dec 1919 Bern. PUBLISHER, Verlag

Hans Huber. Member: SSP, Rorschach Socy. Publishing, editorial, professional writing; projective techniques, learning theory, medical psychology.   M

HULL, Dr. James. Zwinggartenweg 21, Dubendorf. b. 1 Nov 1912 Sheffield, Eng. PH.D '54 Univ. of Zurich, Switz. PSYCHO-ANALYST, priv. prac. Beethovenstr. 1, Zurich. DIRECTOR, Inst. of English Studies, Zurich. Member: SSP. Psychotherapy, teaching, clinical practice; psychoanalysis, schizophrenia, metaphysical and religious implications of depth psychology.   M

INHELDER, Prof. Dr. Miss Bärbel. Inst. of Educ. Sci, Univ. of Geneva, Palais Wilson, Geneva. b. 15 Apr 1913 St. Gallen. PH.D '43 Univ. of Geneva, Switz. PROF. of CHILD PSYCH, Univ. of Geneva. Member: SSP, APSLF. Teaching, research, professional writing; genetic psychology, cognition, social psychology.   F

JACCARD, Prof. Dr. Pierre A. 31 Ave. de Chailly, Lausanne. b. 14 Sept 1901 Morges. Doctuer ès lettres '32 Univ. of Lausanne, Switz. PROF. of PSYCH. and SOCIOL. and PRESIDENT, Grad. Sch. of Soc. and Polit. Sci, Univ. of Lausanne. Member: SSP, APSLF. Teaching, research, administration; psychology of religion, general and social psychology.   M

JACOBI, Dr. phil. Jolande. Zeltweg 66, Zurich.   b. 1890 Budapest, Hungary. PH.D '38 Univ. of Vienna, Austria. LECT. and PSYCHOTHERAPIST, C. G. Jung Inst, Gemeinde Str. 27, Zurich. Member: SSP, Swiss Socy. for Appl. Psych. Teaching, research, psychotherapy, professional writing; clinical psychology, symbolism. F

JEANNET, Maurice. Office Romand IPH, Ave. Mont d'Or 11, Lausanne. b. 23 Apr 1930 Sonvilier. L.PS '54 Univ. of Geneva, Switz. PSYCHOLOGIST, Office Romand IPH. Member: APSLF. Consulting, clinical practice, guidance, testing, research; vocational adaptation, psychology of primitives, fatigue.   M

JUD, Rév. Abbé Dr. Gallus J. A. Caviano s/ Ranzo, Ticino. b. 8 Nov 1900 St. Gallen. Dr. phil. I '35 Univ. of Fribourg, Switz. PSYCHOLOGIST, priv. prac. Member: SSP, Swiss Socy. for Appl. Psych. Consulting, guidance, applied psychology, research; pastoral psychology.   M

JUNG, Prof. Dr. med. et jur. Carl Gustav. Seestr. 228, Küsnacht-Zurich. b. 26 July 1875 Kesswil, Thurgau. Research; psychology of the unconscious.   M

JUSTITZ, Dr. Alfred. Schifflände. 3, Basel. b. 21 Dec 1904 Zurich. EDUC. and PERS. PSYCH'T, priv. prac. Member: SSP, AIPA. Applied and educational psychology, research; projective techniques.   M

KAMM, Dr. Peter. Rombach AG. b. 26 July

1907 Glarus. Doktordiplom '37 Univ. of Basel, Switz. TEACHER, Aarg. Lehrerinnen-seminar und Aarg. Tochterschule, Aarau; EDITOR, *Philosophie.* Member: SSP, Swiss Philos. Socy. Teaching, educational psychology, research; child psychology.   M

KATZENSTEIN-SUTRO, Dr. med. Erich. Stadthausquai 5, Zurich. b. 25 Apr 1893 Hannover, Ger. MD, Univ. of Bern, Switz. NEUROLOGIST, priv. prac. Member: Swiss Socy. for Appl. Psych, Swiss Neur. Socy. Psychotherapy, clinical analysis, research; projective techniques, learning theory, social perception.   M

KELLER, Prof. Dr. phil. Wilhelm. Langensteinenstr. 32, Zurich 57. b. 19 Oct 1909 Toffen, Bern. PH.D '35 Univ. of Bern, Switz. PROFESSOR, Univ. of Zurich. Member: SSP. Teaching, research; anthropology, psychological theory, psychology of will.   M

KELLER-BUSSMANN, Dr. phil. Esther. Langensteinenstr. 32, Zurich 57. b. 17 Apr 1912 Zurich. PH.D '44 Univ. of Geneva, Switz. PSYCHOTHERAPIST, priv. prac. Member: SSP. Psychotherapy, consulting, testing; psychoanalysis.   F

KIELHOLZ, Dr. med. Arthur. Rohrerstr. 28, Aarau. b. 26 Sept 1879 Travers, Neuenburg. Dr. med. '32 Univ. of Zurich, Switz. PSYCHOTHERAPIST, priv. prac. Member: SSP, Swiss Psychoanal. Socy. Retired, psychotherapy, professional writing; psychoanalysis.   M

KILCHHERR, Rector Wilhelm. Eglisesstr. 16, Basel. b. 11 Dec 1896 Frenkendorf. Volksschullehrer '18 Lehrerseminar, Basel, Switz. INSPECTOR and DIR, Knaben Primar und Sekundarschule, Münsterplatz 17, Basel 1; LECT. in PEDAGOGY, Kantonales Lehrerseminar, Schlüsselberg 17, Basel 2. Member: SSP. Teaching, guidance; educational psychology, group process, depth psychology.   M

KLAGES, Dr. Ludwig. Postfach, Kilchberg, Zurich. b. 10 Dec 1872 Hannover, Ger. Retired, psychology of expression, graphology, characterology.   M

KOCH, Charles. Inst. of Appl. Psych, Sempacherstr. 18, Lucerne. b. 14 Sept 1906 Aarau. PSYCHOLOGIST, Inst. of Appl. Psych. Member: SSP, Swiss Socy. for Appl. Psych. Applied and industrial psychology; professional guidance, graphology, projective techniques.   M

KÖCKEL, Dr. Elsa. Neptunstr. 29, Zurich 7/32. b. 12 Apr 1903 Frick. MD '30 Univ. of Zurich, Switz. PSYCHOANALYST, priv. prac. Member: swiss Socy. for Appl. Psych, Swiss Psychoanal. Socy. Psychotherapy, teaching; psychology of Freud and Jung.   F

KRAMER, Mrs. Josefine. Erziehungsbera-

tung, Gurzelngasse 14, Solothurn. b.
24 Dec 1906 Tettnand, Ger. Diplôme '38
Univ. of Fribourg, Switz. INSTRUCTOR,
Inst. of Pedagogy, Univ. of Fribourg;
EDUC. GUID. COUNS, Erziehungsberatung.
Member: SSP. Consulting, guidance,
teaching, testing; testing methods, speech
defects.   F
KREBS, Henri. Psychiat. Univ. Clin.
Burghölzli, Zurich 32. b. 11 July 1926
St. Imier. Dipl. Med. '52 Univ. of Zurich,
Switz. RESIDENT, Psychiat. Univ. Clin.
Burghölzli. Clinical practice, testing,
group psychotherapy; projective and a-
chievement tests.   M
KUNZ, Prof. Dr. Hans. Grenzacherweg 97,
Riehen bei Basel. b. 24 May 1904 Brittnau.
Prof. '51 Univ. of Basel, Switz. DOZENT,
Univ. of Basel, Petersplatz, Basel; EDITOR,
Studia Philosophica. Member: SSP. Re-
search, editorial, teaching; theoretical
psychology, phenomenology, philosophical
anthropology.   M
LARGUIER DES BANCELS, Prof. Dr. Jean.
Les Bergières, Chemin du Gray 26, Lausanne. b. 3 Apr 1876 Lausanne. Docteur ès
sciences '02 Univ. of Paris, Fr. RETIRED. M
LAUTENBACH, Dr. Kurt. Arbeitspsych.
Inst, Universitätsstr. 69, Zurich 6/33.
b. 11 Jan 1906 Basel. Dr. iur. '30 Univ.
of Basel, Switz. PSYCHOLOGIST, Arbeitspsych. Inst. Applied and industrial psychology, testing, consulting; psychological
leadership in labor unions.   M
LEBER, Dr. Willi. Solothurnstr. 56, Biel.
b. 29 June 1924 Maulburg/Baden. PH.D
'51 Univ. of Freiburg, Ger. ASSISTANT,
Inst. for Appl. Psych, Seilerstr. 22, Bern.
Applied psychology, testing, consulting;
psychological diagnosis, industrial psychology, vocational counseling.   M
LEUZINGER-SCHULER, Mrs. Amélie.
Schlossberstr. 26, Zollikon/Zurich. b. 9 Jan
1891 Glaris. Diplôme, Inst. J. J. Rousseau,
Switz. ASST. in CHILD PSYCH, Schweiz
Anstalt für Epileptische, Südstr. 120,
Zurich. Member: SSP. Clinical testing,
research, psychotherapy; projective tech-
niques, children's drawings.   F
LEVI, Dr. Rolf James. 2 Quai Philippe Godet,
Neuchâtel. b. 21 May 1918 Berlin, Ger. MD
'41 Univ. of Zurich, Switz. PSYCHIATRIST,
Hlth. Serv. of Neuchâtel; priv. prac.
Psychotherapy, clinical practice, research,
administration; child psychiatry, psycho-
somatic medicine.   M
LIENGME, Dr. André F. M. Clinique La
Rochelle, Vaumarcus, Neuchâtel. b.
28 Mar 1895 Mandlakazi, Mozambique.
MD '21 Univ. of Geneva, Switz. MED. DIR,
Clinique La Rochelle. Member: SSP.
Group psychotherapy, clinical practice,
research; psychosomatic medicine, carbon

dioxide therapy.   M
LINCKE, Dr. Harold. Neumarkt 6, Zurich 1.
b. 26 Mar 1917 Zurich. Dr. phil. II '45
Univ. of Zurich, Switz. Member: Swiss
Psychoanal. Socy. Psychotherapy, pro-
fessional writing, research; anger and
agression.   M
LOOSLI-USTERI, Marguerite. 6 Chemin de
la Tour de Champel, Geneva. b. 11 Dec
1893 Zurich. PH.D '43 Univ. of Geneva,
Switz. LECTURER, Inst. for Educ. Sci,
Univ. of Geneva, 52 Rue des Pâquis,
Geneva. Member: SSP, Int. Rorschach
Socy. Teaching, testing, psychotherapy;
child and adolescent psychology, projective
techniques.   F
MAEDER, Dr. Alphonse. Toblerstr. 60,
Zurich 7. b. 11 Sept 1882 la Chaux-de-
Fonds. MD '11 Univ. of Zurich, Switz.
PSYCHIATRIST, priv. prac. Member: SSP,
Swiss Psychiat. Socy. Psychotherapy,
professional writing.   M
MANDEL, Rodolphe. 47 Rue des Alpes,
Biel/Bienne. b. 18 Oct 1927 Freiburg,
Ger. ASSISTANT, Inst. for Ment. Hyg,
49 Rue Centrale, Bienne. Testing, student;
projective techniques, social perception. M
MASTROPAOLO, Dr. Giovanni. Inst. de
Pédagogie Appliquée, Chalet Anglais,
Champery, Valais. b. 1 Oct 1916 Foggia,
Italy. Docteur, Univ. of Rome, Italy.
FAM. CONSULT, Inst. of Appl. Pedagogy;
DIRECTOR, Inst. of Psychopedagogy;
EDITOR, Hermes. Consulting, psycho-
therapy; projective techniques, group
process, attitude measurement.   M
MEILI, Prof. Dr. phil. Richard. Jungfraustr.
21, Gümligen. b. 28 Feb 1900 Schaffhouse.
PH.D '25 Univ. of Berlin, Ger. PROF. of
PSYCH, Univ. of Bern, Falkenplatz 16,
Bern; EDITOR, Schweizerische Zeitschrift für
Psychologie. Member: SSP, APSLF, AIPA.
Teaching, research, editorial; factor ana-
lysis, mental tests, genetic psychology. M
MEILI-DWORETZKI, Dr. Gertrud. Jung-
fraustr. 21, Gümligen, Bern. b. 3 Dec
1912 Danzig. PH.D '39 Univ. of Geneva,
Switz. Member: SSP. Research, consulting,
psychotherapy; genetic psychology, Rorschach, perception.   F
MENG, Prof. Dr. med. Heinrich. Lerchenstr.
92, Basel. b. 9 July 1887 Hohnhurst.
PROFESSOR, Univ. of Basel. Member:
Swiss Psychoanal. Socy. Teaching, research, psychotherapy; medical psychology,
psychoanalysis.   M
MERIAN, Dr. phil. Doris. Witikonerstr. 221,
Zurich 7/53. b. 24 Feb 1931 Basel. PH.D
'56 Univ. of Zurich, Switz. Testing, clinical
analysis, child psychotherapy, educational
psychology; projective techniques.   F
MONARD, Hélène. Ave. L. Robert 77, La
Chaux de Fonds. b. 11 May 1907 Les

Ponts de Martel. PSYCHOANALYST, priv. prac. Member: SSP, Swiss Psychoanal. Socy. Psychotherapy, consulting; achievement tests, social perception, attitude measurement. F

MONTALTA, Prof. Dr. Eduard. Guggiweg 20, Zug. b. 8 May 1907 Grisons, Zizers. PH.D '29 Univ. of Louvain, Bel. PROFESSOR, Univ. of Fribourg; EDITOR, Inst. for Remedial Educ, Lucerne; CO-DIRECTOR, Inst. for Educ, Remedial Educ. and Appl. Psych, Univ. of Fribourg, 8 Rue St. Michel, Fribourg. Member: SSP. Teaching, research, professional writing; human development, psychological diagnosis, educational counseling, school psychology. M

MOOR, Prof. Dr. phil. Paul. Bodmerweg 12, Meilen, Zurich. b. 27 July 1899 Basel. Prof, Univ. of Zurich, Switz. HEAD, Heilpädagogisches Seminar, Kantonsschulstr. 1, Zurich. Member: SSP. Educational psychology, testing; psychology of remedial education, psychodiagnostics. M

MORGENTHALER, Dr. med. Fritz. Utoquai 41, Zurich. b. 19 July 1919 Bern. MD '45 Univ. of Zurich, Switz. PSYCHOANALYST and NEUROLOGIST, priv. prac. Member: Swiss Psychoanal. Socy. Psychotherapy, clinical practice, consulting, research; character analysis, psychosomatic medecine. M

MORGENTHALER, Dr. med. Walter. Gurtenweg 52, Muri-Bern. b. 15 Apr 1882 Ursenbach, Bern. Privat Dozent '17 Univ. of Bern, Switz. PSYCHOTHERAPIST, priv. prac. Member: SSP. Psychotherapy, consulting.M

MOSER, Dr. phil. Ulrich Freiestr. 17, Zurich 32. b. 21 Sept 1925 Winterthur. Dr. phil. I '52 Univ. of Zurich, Switz. PSYCHO-ANALYST, priv. prac. Member: SSP. Psychotherapy, testing, clinical analysis; psychoanalysis, psychology of work, psychodiagnostics. M

MÜLLER, Prof. Philippe-Henri. Ruelle Dupeyrou 2, Neuchâtel. b. 29 Dec 1916 Neuchâtel. Dr. ès lettres '46 Univ. of Neuchâtel, Switz. PROF. of PSYCH, Univ. of Neuchâtel, BOOK REVIEW ED, *Revue Suisse de Psychologie.* Member: SSP, APSLF, Socy. for Res. in Child Devel. Teaching, research, editorial; genetic psychology, projective techniques, attitude measurement. factor analysis. M

MÜNGER, Dr. phil. Werner. Biglen bei Bern. b. 9 Mar 1901 Bern. PH.D '39 Univ. of Bern, Switz. HEAD, Secondary Sch, Biglen. Member: SSP. Teaching, educational psychology and guidance; developmental psychology. M

NAEGELI-OSJORD, Hans Emil Richard. Fraumünsterstr. 8, Zurich 1. MD '38 Univ. of Zurich, Switz. PSYCHOTHER. and PHYS, priv. prac. Member: SSP, Swiss Psychiat.

Socy. Psychotherapy; dream analysis, relaxation and suggestion therapy, parapsychology. M

OSSENDORF, Dr. Karel. Psychiat. Clin, Univ. of Basel, 1 Petersgraben, Basel. b. 30 Oct 1917 Strakonice, Czech. PH.D '48 Univ. of Basel, Switz. PSYCHOLOGIST, Psychiat. Clin. Member: SSP. Testing, consulting, guidance, psychotherapy, research; projective tests, psychoanalysis. M

PARIN, Dr. med. Paul. Utoquai 41, Zurich. b. 20 Sept 1916 Linescio. MD '43 Univ. of Zurich, Switz. PSYCHOANALYST and NEUROLOGIST, priv. prac. Member: SWISS Psychoanal. Socy. Psychotherapy, clinical practice, consulting, research; psychosomatic medicine, character analysis. M

PERRET, Miss Sylvie Hélène. Rue des Jardinets 27, La Chaux-de-Fonds. b. 7 Dec 1905 Corcelles. Diplôme '46 Seminary for Remedial Educ, Zurich, Switz. PSYCHOLOGIST, Serv. Médicopédogogique Neuchâtelois, 1 Ave. du Coll, Le Locle, Neuchâtel. Member: APPD, Swiss Psychoanal. Socy. Assn. for Child Psychother. Psychotherapy, guidance, testing, clinical analysis; projective techniques, achievement tests. F

PETER, Karl Georg. Winterhalde 1, Binningen /Bl. b. 10 Apr 1931 Basel. Cand. phil, Univ. of Basel, Switz. STUD. VOLUNTEER, Univ. Psychiat. Poliklinik, Petersgraben 1, Basel. Student, clinical analysis, applied psychology; psychoanalysis, social perception, group process. M

PFISTER-AMMENDE, Dr. med. Maria. Burglistr. 29, Zurich. b. 11 June 1910 Bamberg. MD '38 Univ. of Zurich, Switz. MED. OFF, World Hlth. Organiza, Ment. Hlth. Sect, Palais des Nations, Geneva; EDITOR, *Mental Health.* Member: Swiss Psychiat. Socy, Int. Psychoanal. Socy. Psychotherapy, psychology of refugees; mental health. F

PIAGET, Prof. Dr. Jean, See page 471.

PLATTNER, Dr. Gabriel. Inst. of Appl. Psych, Greifengasse 1, Basel. b. 30 June 1922 Untervaz. PH.D '48 Univ. of Zurich, Switz. HEAD, Inst. of Appl. Psych. Member: SSP. Applied and industrial psychology, testing; graphology, selection and training of executives, professional guidance. M

PORTMAN, Prof. Dr. Adolf. Zoological Inst, Univ. of Basel, Rheinsprung 9, Basel. b. 27 May 1897 Basel. PH.D '20 Univ. of Basel, Switz. PROF. and DIR, Zool. Inst. Member: SSP. Teaching, research, administration; evolution, nervous functions, behavior of higher organisms, biometrics. M

PROBST, Prof. Dr. Ernst. Peter Ochsstr. 43, Basel. b. 10 Feb 1894 Bern. PH.D '22 Univ. of Bern, Switz. SCH. PSYCH'T, Serv. Médico-pédagogique, Münsterplatz, Basel; PROF. of APPL. PSYCH, Univ. of Basel;

EDITOR, *Psychologische Praxis.* Membe : SSP. Consulting, educational guidance, teaching, research; achievement and projective tests. M

PULVER, Johannes. 34 Muristalden, Bern. b. 21 Feb 1913 Paris, Fr. Diploma '41 Univ. of Zurich, Switz. GRAPHOLOGIST, priv. prac. Member: SSP, Assn. Suisse pour l'Orientation Profes. Applied psychology, teaching; graphology. M

RAGETH, Prof. Georges. Ecole de Commerce, Sierre, Valais. b. 3 July 1890 Domat, Grisons. Licence, Gregorian Univ, Italy. PROF. and DIR, Ecole de Commerce, Collège St. Maurice. Member: SSP. Teaching; education. M

RAMBERT, Miss Madeleine L. 9 Chemin de Mornet, Lausanne. b. 26 Oct 1900 Brassus. Diplôme, Inst. for Educ. Sci, Switz. PSYCHOANALYST, Medico-Educ. Serv, 4 Caroline, Lausanne. Member: SSP, Swiss Psychoanal. Socy. Psychoanalysis, clinical training, teaching; projective techniques. F

RAMSEYER, Frank. 18 Ave. Eug. Rambert, Lausanne. b. 1 Mar 1914 Versoix, Geneva. L.PS '48 Univ. of Geneva, Switz. PROF. of PSYCH, Ecoles Normales et Gymnase de Jeunes Filles, Lausanne. Member: SSP. Teaching, research, consulting; psychology of juvenile delinquents, psychoanalysis, guidance of secondary students. M

REY, Prof. André. 2 Place du Bourg de Four, Geneva. b. 10 Nov 1906 Lausanne. PH.D '35 Univ. of Geneva, Switz. PROF. of APPL. PSYCH, Inst. of Sci. of Educ, Univ. of Geneva; ASSOC. PROF. and LAB. CHIEF, Cantonal Hosp, Geneva. Member: SFP, APSLF, AIPA. Teaching, research, clinical analysis; neurological and psychopathological testing, motor, perceptive and memory processes. M

REYMOND-RIVIER, Mrs. Berthe. 54 Grand, 'Rue, Morges. b. 21 July 1926 Lausanne. L.PS '52 Univ. of Geneva, Switz. Member: SSP, APSLF. Research, testing; child psychology, Rorschach, social psychology. F

RIBEAUD, Jeanne. 11 Rue de la Serre, Neuchâtel. b. 25 June 1906 Porrentruy. ASSISTANT, Medico-Educ. Serv, Neuchâtel. Member: SSP. Child psychotherapy, consulting, research, testing; psychoanalysis. F

RICHARD, Dr. Gustave. Crêt-Taconnet 40, Neuchâtel. b. 19 Oct 1886 Neuchâtel. MD '15 Univ. of Bern, Switz. PSYCHOANALYST, priv. prac. Member: SSP, Swiss Psychoanal. Socy. Psychotherapy, consulting, teaching; psychoanalytic research. M

ROCHEDIEU, Prof. Edmond Robert. 7 Rue de Beaumont, Geneva. b. 20 July 1895 Brussels, Bel. PH.D '38 Univ. of Geneva, Switz. PROF. of RELIGIOUS PSYCH, Fac. of Theology, Univ. of Geneva, Rue Candolle, Geneva. Member: Swiss Socy. for Appl. Psych. Teaching, psychotherapy, research; religious psychology, characterology. M

RUEFENACHT, Dr. Mrs. Irene. Villa Aton, 11 Chemin de la Paix, Corseaux, Vevey. b. 1893 Bonfol, Bern. MD '18 Univ. of Geneva, Switz. PSYCHOTHER. and PSYCHIATRIST, priv. prac. Member: SSP. Psychotherapy, consulting. F

RUMLEY, Miss Simone. Rue du Locle 10, La Chaux-de-Fonds. b. 8 Jan 1911 Tavannes. Diplôme '54 Univ. of Geneva, Switz. ASSISTANT, Medico-Educ. Serv, Neuchâtel, La Chaux-de-Fonds. Member: Assn. of Psychoanal. Psych'ts. Testing, psychotherapy; achievement and intelligence tests, projective techniques. F

RUST, Dr. med. Franz. Pelikanstr. 19, Zurich. b. 19 May 1902 Walchwil. MD '42 Univ. of Basel, Switz. PHYSICIAN, priv. prac. Member: SSP. Medical practice, applied psychology, psychotherapy; psychosomatic medicine. M

RUTSCHMANN, Dr. J. 6 Chemin du Port Noir, Geneva. b. 4 Jan 1925 Uster. Dr. ès sciences '56 Univ. of Geneva, Switz. RES. ASSOC, Cen. Int. d'Epistémologie Génétique, Univ. of Geneva, 52 rue des Pàquis, Geneva. Member: SSP, APSLF. Research, physiological psychology, teaching; perceptual processes, psycho-physiology of vision, genetic psychology. M

SANTSCHI, Pierre. 19 Route des Cerisiers, Corseaux-Vevey. b. 13 Mar 1914 Vevey. Licence, Univ. of Lausanne, Switz. DIRECTOR, Inst. of Appl. Psych, 9 Rue Centrale, Lausanne. Applied and industrial psychology, administration, teaching; industrial management and organization, personnel selection. M

SARASIN, Dr. med. Philipp. 65 Cartenstr, Basel. b. 22 May 1888 Basel. MD '15 Univ. of Basel, Switz. PSYCHOTHERAPIST, priv. prac. Member: SSP. Psychotherapy, consulting, testing; Freudian psychoanalysis. M

SCHAER, Hans. Brunnadernstr. 36, Bern. b. 7 June 1910 Gerlafingen. Dr. Theol, Univ. of Bern, Switz. PASTOR, Reformed Church of Bern; PROF. of RELIGIOUS PSYCH, Univ. of Bern; PROFESSOR, Jung Inst, Zurich. Member: SSP, Société de la Psych. Appl. Teaching, pastor; psychology of religion, psychotherapy. M

SCHAER, Dr. K. F. Schertlingasse 6, Basel. b. 12 Sept 1895 Alt St. Johann. PH.D '21 Univ. of Bern, Switz. DIRECTOR, Res. Inst. for Grp. Typology; EDITOR, *Psychologische Rundschau; Schriften-Reihe der Psychologischen Rundschau.* Member: SSP, Berufsverband Schweiz. Gesellschaft für Praktische Psych. Research, applied and industrial psychology, clinical analysis;

blood group and character, typology, vocational choice. M

SCHLUMPF, Dr. Albert J. Zürcherstr. 102, Rapperswil, St. G. b. 5 Apr 1906 Zofingen. PH.D '34 Univ. of Zurich, Switz. RES. WRKR, Inst. for Indus. Psych. Member: SSP. Applied and industrial psychology, psychotherapy, professional writing; chromatics, graphology, professional counseling. M

SCHMID, Dr. Harald. Place de la gare 5, Bienne. b. 17 Mar 1901 Aarberg. MD '26 Univ. of Bern, Switz. CONSULT. PSYCHIATRIST and NEUROLOGIST, District Hosp, Bienne. Member: SSP, Swiss Psychiat. Socy, Schweiz. Ärztegesellschaft für Psychother. Psychotherapy, consulting, testing. M

SCHMIDT, Mrs. Trudy. Strassburgerallee 5, Basel. b. 10 Jan 1918 Basel. BOOK REVIEWER, Basler Nachrichten, Dufourstr. 40, Basel. Member: SSP. Book reviews, radio lectures, publications; psychoanalysis, educational and developmental psychology, psychodiagnosis. F

SCHMUTZ, Friedrich. Privatschulinstitut Forchwies, Forch/Zurich. b. 21 Nov 1909 Basel. DIRECTOR, Privatschulinst. Forchwies, Forch, Zurich. Educational and child psychology; remedial education, guidance. M

SCHNEEBERGER, Dr. Fritz. Im Ganzenbühl 13, Winterthur 5. b. 7 Oct 1919 Ochlenberg, Bern. Dr. phil. I '45 Univ. of Zurich, Switz. DOZENT, Heilpädagogisches Seminar, Kantonsschulstr. 1, Zurich; DIRECTOR, Sch. Psych. Serv, Zurich. Member: SSP. Teaching, educational psychology, testing, guidance; remedial education, psychology of human development, sociology of the family. M

SCHNEIDER, Prof. Dr. phil. Ernst. Rennweg 79, Basel. b. 17 Oct 1878 Langenbruck, Basel. PH.D '04 Univ. of Bern, Switz. Member: SSP, Schweiz. Gesellschaft für Psychoanal. Clinical analysis, research; psychology of human development, psychopathology, projective tests. M

SCHNYDER VON WARTENSEE, Dr. Robert J. Inst. De Psychologie Appliquée, Rue Centrale 9, Lausanne. b. 30 Mar 1917 Fribourg. Dr. '45 Univ. of Bern, Switz. INDUS. CONSULT, priv. prac. Member: SSP, Fondation Suisse de Psych. Appl, Schweiz. Berufsverband für Angewandte Psych. Industrial; human relations, organization, development of groups. M

SCHWARZMANN, Dr. Julia. Rigistr. 56, Zurich 6. b. 10 Sept 1914 Bern. PH.D '47 Univ. of Zurich, Switz. PSYCHOTHERAPIST, priv. prac. Member: Assn. Suisse de Psychoanal. Psychotherapy, teaching, professional writing; psychoanalysis. F

SECRETAN, Miss Henriette. 21 Av. du Tribunal Fédéral, Lausanne. b. 23 Aug 1892 Lausanne. Diplôme '10 Gymnase of Lausanne, Switz. PSYCHOTECHNICIAN, Inst. for Appl. Psych, 9 Rue Centrale, Lausanne. Member: SSP, Assn. Suisse de Psych. Appl. Testing, applied psychology, consulting and guidance, professional selection; projective techniques, learning theory, aptitude tests. F

SPITZ, Dr. phil. Charlotte. Hofstr. 53, Zurich 7/32. b. 7 June 1894 Berlin, Ger. PH.D '35 Univ. of Leipzig, Ger. PSYCH. CONSULT, priv. prac; LECTURER, Inst. for Appl. Psych. Merkurstr. 20, Zurich; EDITOR, *Azondi Bulletin*. Member: SSP, Schweiz. Gesellschaft für Praktische Psych. Consulting, teaching, testing; graphology, projective techniques, psychology of women, social relations. F

SPRENG, Dr. Hans. Inst. for Appl. Psych, Seilerstr. 22, Bern. b. 8 Apr 1895 Bern. Prof. '34 Univ. of Neuchâtel, Switz. DIRECTOR, Inst. for Appl. Psych. Member: SSP. Applied psychology, testing; professional selection and guidance, selection and training of executives. M

STEINER, Dr. Wilfrid. Steinerstr. 45, Bern. b. 29 Dec 1909 Rorschach. MD '39 Univ. of Bern, Switz. SPEC. for INTERNAL MED, priv. prac. Member: SSP. Psychotherapy; psychoanalysis, psychosomatic medicine. M

STERN, Prof. Dr. med, Dr. phil. Erich. Grenzsteig 3, Kilchberg/Zurich. b. 30 Oct 1889 Berlin, Ger. Prof. '24 Univ. of Giessen, Ger. EDITOR, *Handbuch der Klinischen Psychologie*. Member: Groupement français de neuro-psychopathologie infantile Retired, research, editorial, psychotherapy; projective tests, child psychology and psychopathology, social psychology, clinical psychology. M

STETTLER-V. ALBERTINI, Mrs. Barbara. Dorfstr. 57, Gümligen, Bern. b. 5 Aug 1920 Bern. Licence '50 Univ. of Geneva, Switz. Member: SSP. Research, applied psychology, testing, perceptual development, achievement tests, school problems. F

STORCH, Priv. Doz. Dr. Alfred. Niesenmatte 9, Münsingen. b. 4 Apr 1888 Hamburg, Ger. Priv. Doz. '50 Univ. of Bern, Switz. PSYCHOTHERAPIST, Kant. Heilanstalt Münsingen. Member: SSP, Schweizer. Psychoanal. Gesellschaft. Psychotherapy, research, teaching; depth psychology. M

SUTER, Prof. Dr. Jules. Guggerstr. 2, Zollikon, ZH. b. 9 June 1882 Biel, BE. a.o. Prof. '41 Univ. of Zurich, Switz. Member: Schweizer. Berufsverband für Angewandte Psych, Schweizer. Stiftung für Angewandte Psych. Applied and industrial psychology, professional writing, editorial. M

SUTERMEISTER, Dr. med. Hans Martin. Hiltystr. 26, Bern. b. 29 Sept 1907 Rued, Aargovie. MD '39 Univ. of Bern, Switz. LECTURER, Univ. of Bern; PHYSICIAN, priv. prac. Member: SSP. Teaching, research, psychotherapy, clinical practice; psychosomatics, physiological psychology, history of medicine. M

SZONDI, Dr. med. Leopold. Dunantstr. 3, Zurich 7/44. b. 11 Mar 1893 Nyitra, Ungarn. MD, Univ. of Budapest, Hungary. PSYCHOTHERAPIST, priv. prac; EDITOR, *Tiefenpsychologie; die Ueberbrückung der Tiefenpsychologie und der Genetik*. Member: SSP, Schweiz. Gesellschaft für Psychoanal. Research, psychotherapy, editorial; depth psychology, projective techniques. M

TAPONIER, Miss Suzanne. 9 rue Dassier, Geneva. b. 7 July 1930 St-Julien, Fr. L.PS '54 Univ. of Geneva, Switz. ASSISTANT, Inst. for Educ. Sci, rue des Pâquis, Geneva 14. Member: SSP, APSLF. Research; genetic psychology, development of thought. F

TAUBER, Ignaz Camillo. Salstr. 37, Winterthur. b. 28 Dec 1907 Alexandria, Egypt. MD '35 Univ. of Zurich, Switz. PHYSICIAN, priv. prac. Member: SSP. Psychotherapy, consulting; psychosomatic medicine, psychology of C. G. Jung, religion of ancient Egypt. M

TONNAC DE VILLENEUVE, Miss Lucile de. 7 Rue des Alpes, Geneva. b. 21 Mar 1927 Geneva. Licence '51 Univ. of Geneva, Switz. PSYCHOTHERAPIST, Psycho-educ. Cen, 11 Rue de Chantepoulet, Geneva. Member: SSP, Société Suisse des Psychologues, Psychoanalystes d'enfants. Child psychotherapy, consulting, testing. F

UNGRICHT, Dr. Jean. Lindenstr. 32, Zurich 8. b. 28 July 1915 Zurich. PH.D '46 Univ. of Zurich, Switz. CHIEF, Academic Vocat. Guid. Off, Kantonales Jugendamt, Kaspar-Eschernhaus, Zurich; PSYCHOLOGIST, Swissair, Zurich; LECTURER, Inst. for Appl. Psych, Zurich. Member: SSP, Schweiz. Verband für Berufsberatung und Lehrlingsfürsorge, Assn. Int. d'Orientation Profes. Applied, testing, consulting; theory and techniques of vocational guidance, selection of air personnel. M

VALKO-ELFER, Dr. Charlotte. Aarburg, Aargau. b. 1 Jan 1897 Budapest, Hungary. MD, Univ. of Vienna, Austria. PSYCHOTHERAPIST, priv. prac. Member: SSP. Psychotherapy. F

VINH-BANG, Dr. 5 Rue Sismondi, Geneva. b. 15 Nov 1922, Huê, Viêt-Nam. Doctorate '55 Univ. of Geneva, Switz. RES. ASST, Inst. of Educ. Sci, Palais Wilson, rue des Paquis, Geneva. Member: SSP, APSLF. Research, applied and educational psychology; perceptual illusions, developmental psychology. M

VOLUTER DE LORIOL, Mrs. Renée Elisabeth. 196 route de Florissant, Geneva. b. 12 Sept 1898 Newcastle-on-Tyne, Eng. MD '37 Univ. of Strasbourg, Fr. PSYCHOANALYST, priv. prac. Member: SSP. Psychotherapy, consulting, guidance; psychoanalysis. F

VON SURY, Dr. Kurt. Hackbergstr. 89, Riehen. b. 20 Nov 1882 Basel. MD '07 Univ. of Basel, Switz. PSYCHOTHERAPIST. Psychotherapy, consulting, guidance, professional writing. M

WALDER, Dr. phil. Peter. Englischviertelstr. 33, Zurich 32/7. b. 20 Sept 1919 Neuhausen, Rheinfall. PH.D '50 Univ. of Zurich, Switz. Psychotherapy, consulting, research; analytical psychology of C. G. Jung. M

WALTER, Dr. Emil. Rigistr. 2, Zurich 6/33. b. 13 Dec 1892 Winterthur. PH.D '49 Univ. of Zurich, Switz. HEAD TCHR, Pewerbeschule, Ausstellungsstr, Zurich; DOZENT, Univ. of Zurich; Handelshochschule, St. Gallen; Eidg. Tech. Hochschule, Zurich; EDITOR, *Internationale Bibliothek für Psychologie und Sociologie*. Member: SSP, Schweiz. Psychoanal. Gesellschaft. Teaching, editorial; depth psychology, social psychology. M

WALTHER, Prof. Dr. Léon. 60 Quai Gustave-Ador, Geneva. b. 28 Mar 1889 Pétrograd, USSR. PH.D '26 Univ. of Geneva, Switz. PROF. of APPL. PSYCH, Univ. of Fribourg; INDUS. PSYCH'T, priv. prac; PRIVAT DOCENT, Univ. of Geneva. Member: AIPA. Teaching, industrial psychology, research, testing; psychology of work, professional guidance. M

WELTE, Mrs. Sonja. Rigiplatz 1, Zurich. b. 20 Sept 1912 Basel. Diplôme '51 Univ. of Zurich, Switz. CHILD PSYCH'T, priv. prac. Testing, consulting, applied psychology, child psychotherapy; graphology, projective tests. F

WETTSTEIN, Pitt. J. Mutschellenstr. 118, Zurich 38. b. 2 Sept 1929 Zurich. Diploma '55 Inst. of Appl. Psych, Zurich, Switz. PSYCHOLOGIST, priv. prac. Applied and educational psychology, testing, professional writing; psychotherapy. M

WIDMER, Dr. Konrad. Scheidwegstr. 20, St. Gallen. b. 17 Dec 1919 St. Gallen. PH.D '52 Univ. of Zurich, Switz. TEACHER, Schulverwaltung, St. Gallen; PSYCHOLOGIST, Kinderheim Riedernholz, St. Gallen. Member: SSP. Teaching, educational psychology, guidance; psychosomatics, play therapy. M

WINTER, Dr. Harold. Frohburgstr. 50, Zurich. b. 22 May 1910 Richterswil, Zurich. PSYCHOANALYST, priv. prac. Member: Schweiz. Gesellschaft für Psychoanal. Psychotherapy, teaching; ego

function in neurosis, psychosis and health. M
ZANGER, Gina. Bergstr. 25, Zurich. b. 19
Oct 1911 Zurich. Diplôme '36 Univ. of
Geneva, Switz. SCHULPTOR. Member: SSP.
Clinical analysis. F
ZULLIGER, Dr. phil. Hans. Ittigen, Bern.
b. 21 Feb 1893 Mett-Biel, Bern. PH.D '53
Univ. of Bern, Switz. Member: SSP, Société
Swisse de Psychoanal. Child psycho-
analysis, teaching; projective techniques. M
ZÜRCHER, Dr. Werner. Klaraweg 12, Bern.
b. 1 Feb 1909 Christiansborg, Gold Coast.
PH.D '39 Univ. of Bern, Switz. TEACHER,
Primarschule Kirchenfeld, Aegertenstr,
Bern. Member: SSP. Teaching, educational

psychology; psychology of the school child,
achievement tests, childrens' drawing. M
ZÜST, Dr. phil. Ruth. Kirchgasse 33, Zurich.
b. 18 Dec 1917 Hauptwil, Thg. PH.D '47
Univ. of Zurich, Switz. ASSISTANT, Med.
and Psych. Couns, Dept. of Sch, Werd-
mühlestr, Zurich. Member: SSP. Testing,
consulting, research, teaching; test analysis, projective techniques. F
ZWINGMANN, Charles A. A. 44 Rue de
l'Athenée, Geneva. b. 10 June 1920 Munich,
Ger. MA '51 Stanford Univ, USA. GRAD.
STUD, Stanford Univ, California, USA.
Member: SSP. Research, student; counseling
and guidance, semantics. M

SYRIA

AKIL, Prof. Fakher. Fac. of Educ. Syrian
Univ, Damascus. b. 17 Feb 1919 Aleppo.
PH.D '48 Univ. of London, Eng. PROF. of
EDUC. PSYCH, Fac. of Educ, Syrian Univ.
Member: BPS. Teaching, research, edu-
cational psychology; learning theory, atti-
tude measurement, social perception. M
JAMAL, Muhammad Salih. 27/3 Jaber Ben
Hayan St, Bagdad Sta, Aleppo. b. 1 May
1921 Antioch. MA '51 American Univ,
Beirut, Lebanon. CHAIRMAN, Dept. of
Psych. and Educ, Teacher Training Coll,
Aleppo. Member: APA. Teaching, pro-
fessional writing; learning theory, attitude
measurement, group process. M
MARZIA, Dr. Kouatly. Ata el-Ayoubi 58,
Apt. 8, Abu-Rumanek, Damascus. b. 19
May 1919 Damascus. ED.D '51 New York
Univ, USA. TEACHER, Teacher Trng. Sch.
for Girls; SUPERVISOR, Beit el Anadel,
Damascus. Teaching. F
MILLER, Dean George. Aleppo Coll, P. O.

Box 287, Aleppo. b.29 July 1922 Oklaho-
ma City, Okla, USA. ED.M '51 Harvard
Univ, USA. ACADEMIC DEAN, Aleppo Coll.
Member: APA. Administration, research,
teaching; achievement and aptitude
testing, attitude and value formation, cross
cultural research. M
SALIBA, Prof. Djémil. Blvd. de Bagdad,
Damascus. b. 7 Feb 1902 Damascus.
Doctorat ès lettres, Sorbonne, Fr. DEAN,
Fac. of Pedagogy, Syrian Univ, Damascus;
PROF. of PHILOS, Syrian Univ; ED. in CHIEF,
Revue Pédagogique. Member: Socy. of
Comp. Psych. (Egypt). Teaching, re-
search, administration; memory, dreams,
symbolism in language, perception. M
TAJU, Abdullah. 10 Farabi St, Aleppo. b.
19 Mar 1922 Aleppo. MA '51 American
Univ. Lebanon. TEACHER, Govt. Secondary
Sch. and Tchr. Trng. Coll, Aleppo.
Teaching, educational psychology; learning
theory. M

THAILAND

AYER, Dr. Frederic L. Dept. of Educ, Fac. of
Arts and Educ, Chulalongkorn Univ,
Bangkok. b. 24 Mar 1919 Akron, Ohio,
USA. PH.D '52 Columbia Univ, USA. LECT.
in EDUC. and ENGLISH, Chulalongkorn
Univ; CONSULT. in PSYCHOMET, Educ. and
Psych. Res. Inst. Member: Natl. Educ.
res. Assn, (USA), Soc. Sci. Assn. (Thailand).
Research, teaching, test construction and
standardization; educational tests, cross
cultural attitude tests, cross cultural edu-
cational psychology. M
RATANAKORN, Dr. Prasop. Dhonburi
Govt. Ment. Hosp, Bangkok. b. 25 Apr
1919 Yala. M.SC. Med '55 Univ. of Pennsyl-
vania, USA. SR. PSYCHIATRIST, Govt.Ment.
Hosp, Dept. of Med. Serv, Ministry of
Hlth, Bangkok; PSYCHIATRIST, priv. prac;

EDITOR, *Medical Journal* of Dept. of Med.
Serv; *Medical Topics.* Member: WFMH.
Amer. Psychiat. Assn, Thailand Psychiat,
Assn, Amer. Assn. for Ment. Defic. Teaching,
editorial, clinical practice, consulting,
administration; cultural aspects of mental
illness, mental health problems. M
STEPAN, Dr. Margarete. World Hlth. Or-
ganiza, Ministry of Pub. Hlth, Devesh
Palace, Bangkok. b. 2 July 1923 Vienna,
Austria. PH.D '49 Univ. of Vienna, Austria.
W.H.O. CONSULT for MENT. HLTH, W.H.O.
Palais des Nations, Geneva, Switz.
Member: BOP, Int. Psychoanal. Socy.
Consulting, child guidance, research,
teaching clinical psychology; cross cultural
studies, mental health research and
planning, psychotherapy. F

XOOMSAI, Dr. Tooi. 4 Soi Sainambhung, Bangkapi, Bangkok. b. 28 Aug 1909 Bangkok. PH.D, Univ. of Michigan, USA. STAT. EXPERT, Cen. Stat. Off. of Thailand, Thailand Natl. Econ. Counc, Krung Kasem Rd,Bangkok; PSYCH.TCHR, Chulalongkorn Univ; PSYCH. TCHR, Buddhist Univ. Teaching, research; psychological measurement by statistical methods. **M**

TUNISIA

ABDENNEBI, Azouz. Centre d'Orientation et Documentation Scolaires et Professionnelles (BUS), 6 Rue de la Loire, Tunis. b. 21 Nov 1909 Zaghouan. Diplôme d'état, Paris, Fr. DIRECTOR, BUS. Administration, consulting, guidance, testing; achievement tests, projective techniques. **M**

FONTAINE, Claude. Ministry for Soc. Affairs, Rue Kléber, Tunis. b. 8 Oct 1928 Paris, Fr. Docteur ès lettres, Univ. of Toulouse, Fr. DIRECTOR, Centre de Sélection Psychotechnique, Ministry for Soc. Affairs.

Member: APPD. Applied psychology, testing, administration; psychophysiology, social and ethnological psychology. **M**

NIZARD, Miss Huguette. 8 Rue Beuté, Tunis. b. 12 Dec 1927 Tunis. L.PS '49 Univ. of Paris, Fr. PSYCHOLOGIST, Laboratoire de Psycho-Biologie de l'Enfant, 97 Rue Courbet, Tunis. Member: APPD, SNPPD, Fr. Rorschach Socy. Testing, clinical analysis, consulting, guidance, applied psychology; projective techniques, achievement tests, social psychology. **F**

TURKEY

ANASTASIADIS, Dr. Yani. Mis Sokak 24, Beyoglu, Istanbul. b. Oct 1919 Istanbul. PH.D '54 Univ. of Istanbul, Turkey. PSYCH. LAB. DIR, Fac. of Med. Psychiat. Clin, Univ. of Istanbul. Member: Turkish Psych. Socy, Turkish Socy. of Neuropsychiat, Int. Socy. of Ment. Hyg. Testing, clinical analysis, psychotherapy, research, teaching; projective techniques, achievement tests, applied psychology. **M**

ARI, Oğuz Necip. Iktisat Fakültesi, Beyazit, Istanbul. b. 9 Dec 1927 Istanbul. MA '55 Univ. of Calif. Los Angeles. USA. ASST. in SOCIOL, Univ. of Istanbul, Iktisat Fakültesi. Member: Psi Chi. Student, research, teaching; group process, attitude measurement, social perception. **M**

ARKUN (neé Tanç), Dr. Mrs. Nezahat. Bostan Sokak 53, Moda, Kadiköy, Istanbul. b. 18 Feb 1917 Istanbul. Docteur ès lettres '48 Univ. of Istanbul, Turkey. ASST. PROF, Dept. of Psych, Fac. of Letters, Univ. of Istanbul, Beyazit, Istanbul. Member: Turkish Psych, Socy. Teaching, research; personality, attitude measurement. **F**

AVIDOR-KEMALOF, Mrs. Sara. Kurtulus Cad. 222/7, Istanbul. b. 28 Nov 1924 Istanbul. Licence '49 Univ. of Istanbul, Turkey. STUDENT, Univ. of Istanbul. Member: Turkish Psych. Socy. Student, research, testing; emotions, memory, projective techniques. **F**

BIRAND-DIYARBAKIRLI, Dr. Mrs. Beğlân. Riza Pasa Sokak 2, Moda, Kadiköy, Istanbul. b. 1 Mar 1927 Istanbul. PH.D '54 Univ. of Istanbul, Turkey. INSTRUCTOR, Dept. of Psych, Fac. of Letters, Univ. of Istanbul. Member: Turkish Psych. Socy. Teaching,

research, administration, translations; esthetic evaluations, visual perception, social perception. **F**

DALAT, Dr. Ziya. Psikoloji Öğretmeni, Gazi Eğitim Enstitüsü, Ankara. b. June 1901 Iskilip. PH.D '38 Univ. of Halle-Wittenberg, Ger. TCHR. of PSYCH, Gazi Inst. of Educ. Teaching, research, educational psychology; failure in examinations **M**

ENÇ, Mitoit. Sok. 14, Bahcelievler 27, Ankara. b. 24 Dec 1909 Gaziantep. MA '39 Columbia Univ, USA. TEACHER, Gazi Egitim Enstitüsü, Ankara; HEAD, Sch. for the Blind, Gazi; ED. COMM, Professional Pubs, Ministry of Educ. Member: WFMH, Turkish Psych. Socy. Teaching, editorial, administration; learning, special education. **M**

EVRIM, Dr. Mrs. Selmin. Fac. of Letters, Univ. of Istanbul, Vezneciler, Istanbul. b. Istanbul. MA, Amer. Coll. of Philos. and Psych, Turkey. ASST. in GENL. PSYCH, Univ. of Istanbul. Member: Turkish Psych. Socy, Turkish Sociol. Socy. Teaching, research, consulting and clinical work; projective techniques, delinquency, personality. **F**

GÜRSEL, Prof. Fikri. Tasarruf Evleri, Akar Apt. 6/5, Bahçelievler, Ankara. b. 21 Dec 1900 Yanya, Greece. Diploma '28 Univ. of Istanbul, Turkey. PROF. of PSYCH. and HEAD, Lab. of Appl. Psych, Tech. Tchr. Trng. Coll. for Men, Ankara. Member: AIPA. Teaching, testing; educational and applied psychology. **M**

KESKINER, Dr. med. Ali. Küçüklanga Cad 10, Aksaray, Istanbul. b. 10 Mar 1929

Kirsehir. Diploma '55 Univ. of Istanbul, Turkey. ASSISTANT, Chair of Exper. Psych, Istanbul Univ, Edebiyat Fakültesi, Beyazit, Istanbul; PHYSICIAN, priv. prac. Member: WFMH, Turkish Psych. Socy. Student, research, teaching; visual perception. M

MILES, Prof. Walter Richard. Fac. of Letters, Istanbul Univ, Istanbul. b. 29 Mar 1885 Silverleaf, North Dakota, USA. PH.D '13 Univ. of Iowa, USA. PROF. of EXPER. PSYCH, Istanbul Univ, Beyazit, Istanbul. Member: APA, Natl. Acad. of Sci. (USA), Turkish Psych. Socy, American Physiol. Socy, Socy. of Exper. Psych. Teaching, research, professional writing; visual, olfactory and spatial perception. M

ONCÜL, Remzi. Özdemir Caddesi Buğday Sk. 6, Kavaklidere, Ankara. b. 6 Nov 1909 Kirklareli. MA '48 Columbia Univ, USA. MEMBER: Nat. Bd. of Educ, Ministry of Educ, Bakanliklar Yenişehir, Ankara. Educational psychology, consulting, testing, teaching, achievement tests, guidance, counseling, test construction. M

ÖZBAYDAR, Sabri Saim. Sultantepe, Kuyulu Sokak 24, Üsküdar, Istanbul. b. 8 May 1925 Istanbul. ASST. in EXPER. PSYCH, Edebiyat Fakültesi, Univ. of Istanbul. Research, student; learning theory, criminal psychology. M

ÖZDIL, Dr. Ilhan. Beşeuler Durak, Mentesoğlu Apt. 7, Bahcelieuler, Ankara. b. 1921 Oenizli. PH.D '54 Ohio State Univ, USA. ADVISOR, Genl. Off. of Tech. and Vocat. Educ, Atuhurk Blvd, Ankara; TEACHER, Tech. Tchr. Trng. Coll. for Men. Administration, teaching, professional writing; mass communications, learning theory, group process. M

ROGERS, Prof. Spaulding. Ankara Univ, Dil ve Tarih-Coğrafya Fakültesi, Ankara. b. 20 Aug 1912 Au Sable Forks, New York, USA. PH.D '41 Columbia Univ, USA. PROFESSOR, Chair of Psych. and Educ, Univ. of Ankara. Member: APA. Teaching, research, consulting; psychophysics, intercultural psychology, family relations, child rearing practices. M

SELÇIKOGLU, Prof. Hasan Şükrü. Psych. Inst. of Gazi Terbiye, Ankara. b. Apr 1916 Silifke. RES. WRKR, Psych. Serv, Gazi Terbiye, Ankara. Member: Turkish

Psych. Socy. Teaching, testing, psychotherapy, research, consulting, guidance; projective techniques, psychoanalysis. M

SIYAVUŞGIL, Prof. Sabri Esat. Edabiyal Fakültesi, Beyazid, Istanbul. b. 9 Apr 1907 Istanbul. Licence ès lettres '32 Univ. of Lyon, Fr. PROFESSOR, Edebiyat Facütesi. Member: AIPA. Teaching, research, testing; psychology of personality. M

TANER, Prof. Ali Haydar. Koca Ragip Caddesi 4, Aksaray, Istanbul. b. 15 Oct 1883 Kazanlik, Bulgaria. Diplôme '10 Univ. of Jena, Ger. PRESIDENT, Société de Pédagogie, P. O. Box 1068, Istanbul. Retired; learning theory, testing. M

TURHAN, Prof. Dr. Mümtaz. Univ. of Istanbul, Edebiyst Fakültesi, Beyazid, Istanbul. b. 29 Oct 1908 Erzurum. Dr. phil. nat. '35 Univ. of Frankfurt/M, Ger. PROF. of EXPER. PSYCH. and HEAD, Dept. of Psych, Univ. of Istanbul; LECTURER, Natl. Milit. Acad; CO-EDITOR, *Istanbul Studies in Psychology*. Member: Turkish Psych. Socy, Hellenic Psych. Assn. Teaching, administration, research; cultural changes, facial expressions, social perception, learning. M

UĞUREL-ŞEMIN, Asst. Prof. Dr. Mrs. Refia. Bozkir Sokak 5, Selâmiçeşme, Istanbul. b. 18 May 1909 Istanbul. PH.D '36 Univ. of Geneva, Switz. ASST. PROF, Fac. of Letters, Inst. of Pedagogy, Univ. of Istanbul, Beyazit, Istanbul. Member: Turkish Psych. Socy. Teaching, research, educational psychology; child behavior and development, intelligence tests, comparative psychology. F

YÖRÜKÂN, Dr. Turhan. Dept. of Sociol, Fac. of Letters, Univ. of Istanbul, Beyazid, Istanbul. b. 29 Jan 1927 Istanbul. PH.D '54 Univ. of Ankara, Turkey. ASSISTANT, Dept. of Sociol, Univ. of Istanbul. Teaching, and research in social psychology, testing; culture and personality, learning theory, projective techniques, personality tests. M

ZORLU, Resdan. Cağaloğlu, Zorlu Apt. 21/4, Istanbul. b. 14 Aug 1922 Istanbul. MA '44 Univ. of Istanbul, Turkey. SECRETARY, Turkish Tech. Info. Cen, Istanbul Tech. Univ, Taksim, Istanbul. Member: Turkish Psych. Socy. Teaching, applied psycholo gy, testing; psychological laboratory work, attitude measurement, hypnotherapy. M

UGANDA

McADAM, Mrs. Hrothgarde. Makerere Coll, Kampala. b. 12 Apr 1917 Kandy, Ceylon. MA '38 Univ. of Cambridge, Eng. LECTURER Fac. of Educ, Makerere Coll. Member:

BPS. Teaching, educational psychology, testing; African child development, race relations, selection techniques, personnel work. F

UNION OF SOUTH AFRICA

AITKEN, Miss Elizabeth Dorothy. Sch. Clin, Herbert St, Bellville, Cape Province. b. 19 Nov 1910 Durban. MA '37 Univ. of Oxford, Eng. HEAD of SCH. CLIN, Psych. Services, Cape Educ. Dept, P. O. Box 13, Cape Town. Member: SAPA. Psychotherapy, guidance, testing; psychotherapy with school children, remedial teaching, achievement tests. F

ALBINO, Ronald Charles. Howard Coll, Univ. of Natal, Natal. b. 31 Jan 1916 England. MA '49 Univ. of South Africa. SR. LECT, Univ. of Natal. Member: SAPA. Teaching, research, administration, testing; child play, stimulation studies of mesocortical systems in intact, free-ranging animals, perception of the self. M

ARBOUS, Adrian Garth. African Explosives and Chemical Industries, Ltd, 40 Fox St, Johannesburg. b. 12 July 1915 Durban. MA '40 Univ. of Natal, S. Africa. ADMIN. PERS. ASST, African Explosives and Chemical Industries. Member: SAPA, S. Africa Stat. Assn. Industrial psychology, administration, professional writing; personnel management, aptitude testing, attitude surveys, job appraisal and evaluation, personnel assessment. M

ASKEW, Clifford Creswell. 406 Alliance Hse, 48 St. George's St, Cape Town. b. 30 May 1912 Cape Town. MA '34 Univ. of Cape Town, S. Africa. OCCUPAT. PSYCH'T, priv. prac; LECT. in INDUS. PSYCH, Univ. of Cape Town. Member: SAPA. Applied psychology, vocational guidance, aptitude testing; counseling. M

BARNARD, Willem Hendrik. P. O. Box 17, Kuilsrivier, Cape Province. b. 15 Nov 1915 Ventersburg. MA '38 Univ. of Stellenbosch, S. Africa. PRINCIPAL, Jan Kriel Sch. for Epileptics. Member: SAPA. Administration, educational psychology, teaching, psychotherapy problems of epileptics, teaching methods, personality analysis, diagnostic procedures, projective techniques, electroencephalography. M

BARNETT, Eric Oliver. P. O. Box 22, Durban, Natal. b. 13 Feb 1929 Johannesburg. MA '57 Univ. of Natal, S. Africa. RES. STUD. and LECT, Univ. of Natal, King George V Ave, Durban. Member: SAPA. Research, teaching, student; social perception, ethnic prejudice, stereotyping, personality theory. M

BARSDORF, Miss Harriet. 43 Albert St, Rosettenville, Johannesburg. b. 30 Sept 1933 Johannesburg. BA '54 Univ. of South Africa. RES. ASST, Natl. Inst. for Pers. Res, Box 10319, Johannesburg. Member: SAPA. Testing, research, administration; aptitude and achievement tests, personality measurement. F

BAUMAN, Mrs. Sheila. 32 Murry St, Waverley, Johannesburg. b. 19 May 1927 Butterworth, C.P. MA '54 Univ. of Witwatersrand, S. Africa. LECT. in LOGOPEDICS, Univ. of Witwatersrand; ASST. DIR, Speech, Voice and Hearing Clin, Univ. of Witwatersrand, Milner Park, Johannesburg. Member: SAPA, Int. Assn. for Logopedics and Phoniatrics, Amer. Speech and Hearing Assn. Teaching, administration, guidance, psychotherapy; typical and atypical learning and perception in brain-injured adults and children, psychology of the handicapped, group therapy. F

BEEZHOLD, Frederik Willem. Natl. Inst. for Pers. Res, P. O. Box 10319, Johannesburg. b. 1 July 1924 Hilversum, Neth. MA '53 Univ. of Pretoria, S. Africa. RES. OFF, Natl. Inst. for Pers. Res. Member: SAPA. Industrial psychology, research, administration; human relations, psychometrics, operational research. M

BEEZHOLD, Mrs. Margaret Anstis. c/o Natl. Inst. for Pers. Res, P. O. Box 10319, Johannesburg. b. 25 Oct 1925 Bulawayo. BA '49 Univ. of South Africa. VOCAT. PSYCH. CONSULT, priv. prac. Member: SAPA. Consulting, personnel psychology, testing. F

BEHR, Dr. Abraham Leslie. Coll. of Educ, P. O. Box 1013, Johannesburg. b. 19 Oct 1911 Johannesburg. ED.D '52 Potchefstroom Univ. for Christian Higher Educ, S. Africa. SR. LECT, Coll. of Educ, Hoofd St, Braamfontein, Johannesburg; TEST PSYCH'T, Hearing and Speech Clin, Univ. of Witwatersrand, Johannesburg; ED. in CHIEF, *Paideia, Journal of Educational Opinion, Research and Methodology*. Member: SAPA. Teaching, research, testing, editorial; educational psychology, diagnostic and achievement tests, sensory training apparatus. M

BERESFORD, Harold Beaumont. Univ. of Natal, Durban, Natal. b. 29 July 1914 Huddersfield, Eng. MA '42 Univ. of Cambridge, Eng. SR. LECT. in EDUC, Univ. of Natal. Member: BPS. Teaching, research, administration; learning theory, statistical techniques, psychology of teaching. M

BESTER, Jacobus Roelof. Porter Reformatory, Retreat, Cape Town. b. 10 Aug 1926 Luckhoff, Orange Free State. MA '47 Univ. of Stellenbosch, S. Africa. PSYCH. TCHR, Dept. of Educ, Arts and Sci, Vanderstel Bldg, Pretoria. Member: SAPA. Consulting, clinical practice, guidance, psychotherapy, testing, teaching; projective techniques, clinical interviewing and diagnosis, psychomatic medicine, hypnosis.   M

BEYERS, Dr. Maria. 2 Soete Inval, Victoria St, Stellenbosch. b. 20 Jan 1912 Paarl. ED.D '54 Univ. of Stellenbosch, S. Africa. ASSOC. PROF, Dept. of Methods, Fac. of Educ, Univ. of Stellenbosch. Member: SAPA. Teaching, research, educational psychology, testing; learning theory, achievement tests, play therapy.   F

BIESHEUVEL, Dr. Simon. P. O. Box 10319, Johannesburg. b. 3 Apr 1908 Rotterdam, Neth. PH.D '33 Univ. of Edinburgh, Scot. DIRECTOR, Natl. Inst. for . Pers. Res, Empire Rd. Ext, Johannesburg; ED. in CHIEF, *Journal of the National Institute for Personnel Research*; ED. BD, *South African Journal of Social Research*. Member: SAPA, AIPA, Ergonomics Res. Socy. Administration, research, industrial psychology; aptitude testing, study of abilities of African peoples, nature of temperament. M

BILJON, Dr. Izak Johannes van. Dept. of Psych, Univ. of Stellenbosch, Stellenbosch. b. 30 Nov 1924 Cala. PH.D '53 Univ. of Stellenbosch, S. Africa. SR. LECT. in PSYCH, Univ. of Stellenbosch. Member: SAPA. Teaching, clinical analysis, research; teaching methods, psychological and speech therapy, blindness, emotional tensions.   M

BINGLE, Prof. Dr. Hendrik Johannes Jacob. Potchefstroom Univ. for Christian Higher Educ, Potchefstroom. b. 15 Aug 1910 Colesberg. PH.D '40 Univ. of South Africa. PROF. and DEAN, Faculty of Educ, Potchefstroom Univ; EDITOR, School Books for Religious Education. Teaching, research, administration; adolescent religious interests.   M

BLAKE, Mrs. Yvonne. Doornkop, P. O. Medig, E. Transvaal. b. 19 Apr 1926 Potchefstroom. BA '49 Univ. of Witwatersrand, S. Africa. STUDENT, Univ. of Witwatersrand, Milner Park, Johannesburg. Research; child development, psychotherapy, educational psychology.   F

BLIGNAULT, Prof. Dr. Hendrik. 4 Innes Ave, Bloemfontein. b. 22 May 1898 Calitzdorp. ED.D '37 Univ. of Stellenbosch, S. Africa. PROF. and DEAN, Fac. of Educ, Univ. of Orange Free State; ED. COMM, *Teacher's Journal*. Member: SAPA. Teaching, research, guidance; research on gifted children.   M

BOER, Frederick Leonard. Durban Roodepoort Deep Mining Co, P. O. Roodiep Myn, via Roodepoort, Transvaal. b. 16 Jan 1904 Cape Town. OCCUPAT. PSYCH'T. and SUPT, Native Aptitude Tstng. Cen, Durban Roodepoot Deep Gold Mining Co. Member: SAPA. Testing, personnel work, vocational guidance; group aptitude and personality testing.   M

BOTHA, Rev. David Petrus. The Parsonage, Mortimer Rd, Wynberg, Cape Province. b. 23 Feb 1925 Wellington. BA '48 Univ. of South Africa. MINISTER, Wynberg Dutch Reformed Mission Church, Aliwal St, Wynberg. Member: SAPA. Preaching, teaching, school management, research, social therapy; group process, attitude measurement, leadership, juvenile delinquency.   M

BRADLEY, Daniel James. Natl. Inst. for Pers. Res, P. O. Box 10319, Johannesburg. b. 4 Mar 1925 Pretoria. B.SC '52 Univ. of Witwatersrand, S. Africa. APPL. PSYCH'T, Natl. Inst. for Pers. Res. Member: SAPA, BPA. Research, applied psychology, testing; temperament assessment, factor analysis, ergonomics.   M

BRENNER, Dr. May Woolf. Natl. Inst. for Pers. Res, P. O. Box 10319, Johannesburg. b. 6 May 1921 Johannesburg. PH.D '53 Univ. of London, Eng. SR. BURSAR, S. African Counc. for Sci. and Indus. Res, Natl. Inst. for Pers. Res. Member: SAPA. Research; relationship between modes of perception and temperament.   F

CLOETE, Christofer de Mede. J. W. Luchoff Indus. Sch, Heideberg, Transvaal. b. 30 Dec 1931 Pretoria. MA '56 Univ. of Pretoria, S. Africa. TEACHER, Dept. of Educ, Arts and Sci, Vanderstel Bldg, Pretoria. Teaching, research, administration; personality analysis, projective techniques, psychotherapy.   M

COETZEE, Prof. Dr. Johannes Christiaan. Potchefstroom Univ. for Christian Higher Educ, Potchefstroom. b. 8 Mar 1893 Venterstad, Cape Province. PH.D '25 Univ. of South Africa. PRESIDENT, Potchefstroom Univ; EDITOR, *Onderwysblad Transvaal, Veteraan Potchefstroom*. Teaching, research, administration; the unconscious, learning, testing.   M

COWLEY, John Jefferies. Counc. for Sci. and Indus. Res, P. O. Box 395, Pretoria. b. 22 Apr 1925 Johannesburg. M.SC '49 Univ. of Natal, S. Africa. RES. OFF, Natl. Inst. for Pers. Res, Pretoria. Member: S. African Assn. for the Advancement of Sci. Research, administration; social perception, psychoanalytic theory, neurophysiology. M

DANZIGER, Dr. Kurt. Dept. of Psych, Univ. of Natal, King George V. Ave, Durban. b. 3 June 1926 Breslau, Ger. PH.D '51 Univ. of Oxford, Eng. LECT. in PSYCH, Univ. of Natal. Member: SAPA. Teaching, research; conceptual development, personality and ideology, animal motivation.   M

DU TOIT, Dr. Elizabeth Catharina Maria. Allan Memor. Inst. of Psychiat, 1025 Pine Ave W, Montreal 2, Que, Can. b. 2 Jan 1925 Zastron, O.F.S. PH.D '54 Univ. of

Pretoria, S. Africa. CLIN. PSYCH'T, Allan Memor. Inst. of Psychiat. Member: SAPA. Clinical analysis, consulting, research; projective techniques, research on psychodynamics of change, art exploration. F

DU TOIT, Dr. J. M. Dept. of Psych, Univ. of Stellenbosch, Stellenbosch. b. 23 Feb 1912 Barrydale. PH.D '52 Univ. of Cape Town, S. Africa. SR. LECT, Univ. of Stellenbosch; CONSULT. PSYCH'T, priv. prac. Member: SAPA. Research, teaching, consulting, guidance; psychophysiological measures, intelligence tests, statistical techniques. M

ERASMUS, Christoffel Petrus Johannes. Univ. of the Orange Free State, Bloemfontein. b. 3 June 1929 Enkeldoorn, Rhodesia. MA '52 Univ. of the Orange Free State, S. Africa. LECT. in PSYCH, Univ. of the Orange Free State. Teaching, educational and industrial psychology, guidance; aptitude, personality and interest tests. M

GAVRON, Dr. Sylvia Cecile. Three Oaks, Riverside Rd, Newlands, Cape Province. b. 14 Dec 1910 Oklahama, USA. Dr. of Pub. Hlth. '37 Univ. of London, Eng. MED. OFF. and PSYCH. CONSULT, Child Guid. Clin, Dept. of Psych, Univ. of Cape Town; PSYCH. MED. CONSULT, priv. prac. Member: SAPA. Consulting, testing, clinical analysis, guidance; psychosomatic ailments of children, behavior problems, temperament and physical characterstics. F

GEERE, Carl Frederik Christoffel. 318 Zoutpansberg Rd, Rietondale, Pretoria, Transvaal. b. 9 Jan 1918 Frankfort. MA '50 Potchefstroom Univ. for Christian Higher Educ, S. Africa. TEACHER, Dept. of Native Affairs, Genl. Pretorious Bldg, Paul Kruger St, Pretoria. Member: SAPA. Teaching, educational psychology, library work; projective techniques, social perception, attitude measurement. M

GLASS, Mrs. Yette. Natl. Inst. for Pers. Res, P. O. Box 10319, Johannesburg. b. 6 May 1920 Johannesburg. BA '42 Univ. of Witwatersrand, S. Africa. RES. OFF, Natl.. Inst. of Pers. Res. Member: SAPA. Research, administration, personnel psychology; developmental tests, group process, projective tests. F

GOUWS, David Johannes. 224 Christoffel St, Pretoria. b. 25 June 1926 Pretoria. M.SC '53 Potchefstroom Univ. for Christian Higher Educ, S. Africa. SR. LECT. in PSYCH, Univ. of Pretoria. Member: SAPA, Ment. Hlth. Socy. Teaching, research; dynamics, psychotherapy, statistical methods. M

GROBBELAAR, Joshua Johannes. School of Industries, Queenstown. b. 18 Jan 1924 Heidelberg, Transvaal. B.SC '46 Potchefstroom Univ. for Christian Higher Educ,

S. Africa. VICE PRIN. and HEAD, Psych. Div, School of Industries. Member: SAPA. Applied psychology, testing, guidance, psychotherapy; remedial education, juvenile delinquency, group therapy. M

GROENEWALD, Dr. Alfred Johannes. P. O. Box 432, Pretoria. b. 13 Jan 1907 George. ED.D '46 Univ. of Pretoria, S. Africa. HEAD, Educ. Bur, Transvaal Educ. Dept, Central St, Pretoria; EDITOR, Educational Bulletin. Member: SAPA. Guidance, testing, research; achievement tests, vocational guidance, projective tests. M

GROENEWALD, Barend Hermanus. P. O. Box 89, Lynnwood, Pretoria. b. 22 July 1927 Delareyville. MA '56 Univ. of Pretoria, S. Africa. PROFES. OFF, Natl. Bur. of Educ. and Soc. Res, Dept. of Educ, Arts and Sci, 534 Van der Stel Bldg, Pretorius St, Pretoria. Research, testing, applied psychology; test construction and validation, vocational guidance. M

GROVER, Dr. Vera Maud. Dept. of Psych, Univ. of Cape Town, Rondebosch, Cape Town. b. 12 Aug 1905 Kent, Eng. PH.D '47 Univ. of Cape Town, S. Africa. SR. LECT. in PSYCH, Univ. of Cape Town. Member: SAPA. Teaching, clinical practice, research; achievement tests, child psychotherapy, remidial reading. F

HALL, Henry Hudson. Natal. Educ. Dept, P. O. Box 902, Durban. b. 10 Oct 1921 Caledon. BA '47 Rhodes Univ, S. Africa. ASST. EDUC. PSYCH'T, Natal Educ. Dept; VICE PRESIDENT, Occupat. Cen. for Ineducable Child. Member: SAPA, BPS, WFMH. Educational psychology, testing, guidance; intelligence and attainment testing, remedial reading. M

HALL, Prof. Kenneth Ronald. Dept. of Psych, Univ. of Cape Town, Rondebosch, Cape Town. b. 21 July 1917 Beschill, Eng. PH.D '49 Univ. of Oxford, Eng. HEAD, Dept. of Psych, Univ. of Cape Town. Member: BPS, APA, Exper. Psych. Grp. (Eng.) Teaching, administration, research; experimental study of abnormal behavior, concept formation and deterioration, physiological psychology. M

HATTINGH, Prof. Dr. Jacobus Marais. Potchefstroom Univ. for Christian Higher Educ, Potchefstroom. b. 13 Mar 1907 Cradock. PH. D '46 Univ. of South Africa. PROF. of PSYCH, Potchefstroom Univ. Member: SAPA, BPS. Teaching, administration, research; perception, illusion and apparent movement, child guidance clinics. M

HAWKINS, Frederick. 10 Wimbledon Place, Durban North. b. 4 May 1918 Burgersdorp. BA '53 Univ. of Natal, S. Africa. TEACHER and VOCAT. GUID. OFF, Natal Educ. Dept, Loop St, Pietermaritzburg. Member:

SAPA. Teaching, consulting, guidance, applied and educational psychology; intelligence and aptitude tests, interest measurement and vocational guidance. M

HUDSON, Dr. William. Natl. Inst. for Pers. Res, P. O. Box 10319, Johannesburg. b. 23 Apr 1914 Montrose, Scot. PH.D '54 Univ. of Witwatersrand, S. Africa. PRIN. RES. OFF, Natl. Inst. for Pers. Res; ED. BD, *Journal of the National Institute for Personnel Research.* Member: SAPA. Research, industrial psychology, administration; industrial race relations, occupatoinal classification of African industrial personnel. M

HUNTER, Peter. 18 Chamberlain Rd, Pietermaritzburg. b. 24 Dec 1928 Pietermaritzburg. ED.M '54 Univ. of Natal, S. Africa. LECT. in PSYCH. and EDUC, Natal Trng. Coll, Longmarket St, Pietermaritzburg. Member: SAPA. Teaching, research, educational psychology; learning theory, educational backwardness, teacher education. M

HURST, Dr. Lewis Alfred. Sterkfontein Hosp, P. O. Box 323, Krugersdorp, Transvaal. b. 5 Apr 1911 Pretoria. PH.D '50 Univ. of Cape Town, S. Africa. PHYS. and SUPT, Sterkfontein Hosp; SR. LECT. in PSYCHIAT, Univ. of Witwatersrand, Johannesburg; ED. BD, *The South African Practitioner.* Member: SAPA, Med. Assn. of S. Africa. Administration, teaching, research; physiological psychology, electroencephalography, factor analysis and typology, projective techniques. M

JACOBS, Dr. Gidean François. 9A Sturdee Ave, Rosebank, Johannesburg. b. 21 Jan 1922 Faurfsmith. PH.D '53 Univ. of Pretoria, S. Africa. PERS. ADV, Anglo American Corp, Main St. Johannesburg; RES. OFF, Natl. Inst. for Pers. Res. Member: SAPA. Industrial psychology, testing, administration; psychometric procedures, occupational maladjustment, psychological statistics. M

KALDENBERG, Jan. Constantia Reformatory, P. O. Retreat, Cape Town. b. 23 June 1907 Herwynen, Neth. MA '52 Univ. of Cape Town, S. Africa. VICE PRIN, Constantia Reformatory, Dept. of Educ, Arts and Sci, Vanderstel Bldg, Pretoria. Member: SAPA. Administration, educational psychology, guidance; behavior theory and formation of habits, case histories, diagnostic tests and remedial teaching. M

KATZ, (née Rosen) Mrs. Esther Jill. 228 Johann St, Arcadia, Pretoria. b. 20 June 1927 Johannesburg. MA '53 Univ. of Witwatersrand, S. Africa. Member: SAPA. Research, testing, professional writing; aptitude and interest tests, psychometrics. F

KLUYTS, Gert. Reinier Johannes. 30 Laan

293, Villieria, Pretoria, Transvaal. b. 1 Dec 1908 Krugersdorp. BA '43 Univ. of South Africa. VICE PRIN, Villieria Sch, Transvaal Educ. Dept, P. O. Box 432, Pretoria. Member: SAPA. Teaching, administration, educational psychology, testing; achievement and intelligence tests. M

KGORTS, Pieter Jacobus. Natl. Bur. of Educ. and Soc. Res, Pretorius St, Pretoria. b. 5 Feb 1909 Laingsburg. MA '31 Univ. of Stellenbosch, S. Africa. ASST. DIR, Natl. Bur. of Educ. and Soc. Res. Member: SAPA. Research, administration, educational psychology; achievement tests, social perception, group process, attitude measurement. M

KOTZEE, Andries Lodewikus. 56 Fourteenth St, Menlo Pk, Pretoria. b. 26 Mar 1919 Potchefstroom, Transvaal. M.SC '53 Potchefstroom Univ. for Christian Higher Educ, S. Africa. RES. OFF, Transvaal Educ. Bur, Central St, Pretoria; ED. ASST, *Bulletin*, Transvaal Educ. Bur. Member: SAPA, S. African Assn. for the Advanc. of Sci. Research, editorial, professional writing; psychometrics, projective techniques, learning theory. M

KRIEL, Dr. Ryno Gerhard. W.G.A., P. O. Box 765, Port Elizabeth. b. 28 May 1925 Port Elizabeth. PH.D '55 Univ. of Stellenbosch, S. Africa. TEACHER, Transvaal Educ. Dept, P. O. Box 432, Pretoria. Member: SAPA. Teaching, educational psychology, testing; interest and aptitude measurement, achievement tests, projective techniques. M

KRUGER, Cornelius Francois. P. O. Box 54, Spring, Transvaal. b. 4 Jan 1930 De Aar, MA '51 Univ. of Stellenbosch, S. Africa. PERS. PSYCH'T, Anglo-American Corp. of S. Africa, Ltd, 44 Main St, Johannesburg. Member: SAPA. Testing, industrial psychology, research; group behavior and leadership, motivation, morale, attitude and adjustment problems. M

KRUGER, Mrs. Muriel Sophia. 28 O'Reilly Rd, Berea, Johannesburg. b. 19 Dec 1895 Toronto, Can. BA '15 Univ. of South Africa. PSYCHOANALYST, priv. prac. Member: SAPA. Psychotherapy, consulting, clinical practice, Freudian psychoanalysis, race prejudice. F

KRUGER, Thomas Marx Dreyer. 86 Sophiastr, Roseville, Pretoria. b. 17 Apr 1924 Queenstown. MA '53 Univ. of Pretoria, S. Africa. PROFES. OFF. for VOCAT. GUID, Dept. of Labor, Schoemanstr, Pretoria; LECTURER, Univ. of South Africa; LECTURER Adult Educ. Sect, Dept. of Educ, Arts and Sci; ED. STAFF, *My Career.* Member: SAPA. Guidance, testing, administration, applied and industrial psychology; projective techniques, interviewing and testing, personnel selection. M

LA GRANGE, Prof. Dr. Adriaan J. Dept. of Educ. Psych, Univ. of Stellenbosch, Stellenbosch. b. 29 July 1900 Middelburg. PH.D '30 Univ. of Stellenbosch, S. Africa. PROF. and HEAD, Dept. of Educ. Psych, Univ. of Stellenbosch. Member: SAPA, APA, S. African Assn. for the Advanc. of Sci. Teaching, educational psychology, psychotherapy; projective techniques, learning theory, child psychology, play therapy, counseling and guidance. M

LAKE, John Ross. Natl. Inst. for Pers. Res, P. O. Box 445, Springs, Transvaal. b. 18 June 1931 Durban. BA '56 Univ. of Witwatersrand, S. Africa. RES. ASST, Natl. Inst. for Pers. Res, S. African Counc. for Sci. and Indus. Res, Empire Road Ext, Johannesburg. Member: SAPA. Industrial psychology, research, testing; tests of physical endurance and fatigue, perception of primitive peoples, attitudes of non-Europeans toward industry. M

LANGENHOVEN, Hendrik Petrus. P. O. Box 7, Hercules, Pretoria. b. 13 Nov 1921 Mossel Bay. MA '45 Univ. of Stellenbosch, S. Africa. PRIN. PROFES. OFF, Natl. Bur. of Educ. and Soc. Res, Dept. of Educ, Arts and Sci, Pretoria. Member: SAPA. Research, applied and educational psychology, testing; test construction and validation, environment and test scores. M

LAZARUS, Arnold Allan. 8 North Ave, Riviera, Johannesburg. b. 27 Jan 1932 Johannesburg. BA '56 Univ. of Witwatersrand, S. Africa. PSYCHOLOGIST, Ment. Hlth. Socy. of the Witwatersrand, 421 Empire Bldg, Kruis St, Johannesburg; RES. WRKR, Tara Hosp. Member: SAPA, Ment. Hlth. Socy. Testing, clinical analysis, research, psychotherapy; etiology of psychoneuroses, behavior theory, personality. M

LEJEUNE, Dr. Yvonne. 134 Frances St, Bellevue, Johannesburg. b. 7 July 1917 Johannesburg. PH.D '53 Univ. of Witwatersrand, S. Africa. PSYCHOLOGIST, Johannesburg Child Guid. Clin, Salstaff Bldgs, Smit St; LECT. in CHILD and CLIN. PSYCH, Witwatersrand. Member: SAPA. Psychotherapy, testing, teaching; projective tests for children, group psychotherapy with children and adults. F

LIDDICOAT, Miss Renée. P.O. Box 10319, Johannesburg. b. 25 May 1912 Johannesburg. BA '49 Univ. of Witwatersrand, S. Africa. ASST. RES. OFF, Natl. Inst. for Pers. Res, Empire Rd. Ext, Milner Park, Johannesburg. Research, testing, administration; achievement tests, intelligence, personality and temperament. F

MacCRONE, Prof. Ian Douglas. Univ. of Witwatersrand, Milner Park, Johannesburg. b. 7 May 1898 Wellington, Cape Province. PH.D '36 Univ. of Witwatersrand, S. Africa. PROF. and HEAD, Dept. of Psych, Univ. of Witwatersrand; CHAIRMAN, Johannesburg Child Guid. Clin. Member: SAPA. Teaching, research, administration; attitude measurement, personality structure, and prejudice, group ideology and ethnocentrism. M

MALHERBE, Dr. Ernst Gideon. Campbell House, 267 King George V Ave, Durban. b. 8 Nov 1895 Luckhoff, Orange Free State. PH.D '24 Columbia Univ, Teachers Coll, USA. PRIN. and VICE-CHANCELLOR, Univ. of Natal; EDITOR, *Educational Adaptations in a Changing Society*; EDITOR, Research Series, S. African Counc. for Educ. and Soc. Res. Member: SAPA. Administration, research, teaching, educational psychology; achievement tests, aptitude measurement, student selection. M

MANN, John William. 4 Fifth Ave, Walmer, Port Elizabeth. b. 25 Sept 1928 Umtata. MA '51 Univ. of South Africa. ADVANCED SR. SCHOLAR, Inst. for Soc. Res, Univ. of Natal, King George V Ave, Durban. Member: SAPA. Research, testing; race relations, attitude measurement, vocational guidance. M

MANN, Miss Sybil. 23 Norfolk Rd, Durban. b. 7 May 1928 S. Africa. MA '49 Univ. of Natal, S. Africa. CHILD PSYCHOTHERAPIST, Meyrick Bennett Children's Cen, 191 Chelmsford Rd, Durban. Member: SAPA. Psychotherapy, testing, clinical analysis, research; family relationships, projective techniques, child development. F

MEIRING, Prof. Dr. Jacobus Gerhard. P. O. Box 13, Cape Town. b. 24 Oct 1898 Johannesburg. PH.D '24 Leipzig Univ, Ger. SUPT. GENL. of EDUC, Cape Province of S. Africa, Union Govt, Cape Town. Teaching, administration; learning theory, achievement tests, personality traits, child development. M

NECKER, Jan George Hendrik de. Genl. Hendrik Schoeman Sch, P. O. Hartebeespoort, Pretoria. b. 15 Nov 1931 Albertinia. BA '52 Univ. of Stellenbosch, S. Africa. TEACHER, Transvaal Educ. Dept, P. O. Box 432, Pretoria. Teaching, research, testing, administration; educational psychology. M

NEL, Prof. Dr. Barend Frederik. Univ. of Pretoria. b. 16 Dec 1905 Kokstad. PH.D. '46 Potchefstroom Univ. for Christian Higher Educ, S. Africa. PROF. of EDUC. PSYCH. and DEAN, Faculty of Educ; DIRECTOR, Child Guid. Clin, Univ. of Pretoria. Member: SAPA. Teaching, guidance, educational psychology; psychology of brain-injured children, behavior problems,

projective techniques.   M
O'CALLAGHAN, Mrs. Joan. 19 Barry Rd, Pietermaritzburg. b. 12 May 1911 London, Eng. BA '56 Univ. of Natal, S. Africa. PSYCHOTHERAPIST, priv. prac. Member: SAPA, S. African Psychoanal. Assn, Assn. of Occupat. Therapists (Eng). Psychotherapy, consulting, clinical practice, research; the therapeutic value of occupation in psychosis, Jungian psychology and-therapeutic methods.   F

OSMOND, William Martin Graham. P. O. Box 20, Bergvlei Dist, Johannesburg. b. 14 July 1915 Paarl. BA '56 Univ. of South Africa. SUPERINTENDENT, Northlea Retreat for Alcoholics, Rand Aid Assn, 42 Annet Rd, Cottesloe, Johannesburg; PSYCHOMETRIST, Rand Ther. Cen. Administration, guidance, student; projective techniques, group therapy.   M

POVALL, Miss Margery. Natl. Inst. for Pers. Res, P. O. Box 10319, Johannesburg. b. 5 Nov 1934 Johannesburg. BA '54 Univ. of Witwatersrand, S. Africa. RES. ASST, Natl. Inst. for Pers. Res. Research; personality and temperament, perception as related to personality.   F

PROKSCH, Dr. Francis Bruwer. 802 Colonial Mutual Bldg, West St, Durban, Natal. b. 12 Aug 1904 Kranskop, Natal. MB, B.CH '30 Univ. of Glasgow, Scot. PSYCHOSOMATIC PHYSICIAN, priv. prac. Member: S. African Psychoanal. Assn. Clinical practice, psychotherapy, professional writing; depth psychotherapy.   M

RACHMAN, Stanley. Psych. Dept, Univ. of Witwatersrand, Johannesburg. b. 19 Jan 1934 Johannesburg. BA '54 Univ. of Witwatersrand, S. Africa. GRAD. ASST, Univ. of Witwatersrand. Member: SAPA, S. African Stat. Assn. Teaching, research, psychotherapy; behaviorist therapy, selective perception, electrodermal activity.M

RAKOFF-KATZ, Mrs. Lorna. Psych. Dept, Univ. of Cape Town, Rondebosch, Cape Town. b. 19 Mar 1933 Cape Town. BA '52 Univ. of Cape Town, S. Africa. JR. LECT, Univ. of Cape Town. Member: SAPA. Teaching, testing, psychotherapy, child guidance, research, student; concept formation in young adults, learning theory, perception.   F

REICHLIN, Dr. Mrs. Bex. Charlest, Riverside Rd, Newlands, Cape Town. b. 3 Aug 1917 Mariampol, Lithuania. PH.D '51 Univ. of Cape Town, S. Africa. HONORARY PSYCH'T, Jewish Sheltered Empl. Counc, Security Bldg, Exchange Pl, Cape Town; LECTURER, Hebrew Tchrs. Semin; PSYCHOTHERAPIST, priv. prac. Member: SAPA. Psychotherapy, consulting, clinical practice, guidance, teaching; social perception, attitude measurement, learning theory.   F

REUNING, Dr. Helmut. 49 Fourth Ave, Parktown N, Johannesburg. b. 18 May 1914 Swakopmund. Dr. rer. nat. '51 Univ. of Frankfurt/M, Ger. RES. OFF, Natl. Inst. for Pers. Res, Empire Rd, Ext, Johannesburg; CO-ED, *Journal of the National Institute for Personnel Research*; EDITOR, *Proceedings of the South African Psychological Association*. Member: SAPA. Research, professional writing, editorial; personality and temperament trait measurement, mental energy, temperament and cognitive abilities.   M

ROBBERTSE, Dr. Paul Magiel. P. O. Box 1177, Pretoria. b. 20 June 1912 Rustenburg. ED.D '53 Pretoria Univ, S. Africa. INSPECTOR of EDUC, Dept. of Educ, Arts and Sci, Van der Stel Bldg, Pretorius St, Pretoria. Member: SAPA. Testing, psychotherapy, guidance; projective techniques, achievement tests.   M

ROBERTS, Alfred Oscar Hoexter. 97 Doreen St, Colbyn, Pretoria. b. 5 Sept 1917 Pretoria. B.SC. '44 Univ. of Natal, S. Africa. RES. OFF, Psychometric Dept, Natl. Inst. for Pers. Res, P. O. Box 395, Pretoria. Member: SAPA. Psychometric techniques, research, applied psychology; interest and attitude measurement, measurement methods.   M

ROOS, Johan George. 6 Deveron Pl, 472 Reitz St, Pretoria. b. 18 Nov 1928 Kroonstad. MA '55 Univ. of Pretoria, S. Africa. INDUS. PSYCH'T, Dept. of Labour, Compensation House, Schoemann St, Pretoria; LECT. in PSYCH, Univ. of S. Africa. Member: SAPA. Industrial psychology, research, consulting, vocational guidance, testing; projective techniques, situational tests, study of drives in relation to occupational adjustment and choice.   M

ROUX, Prof. Andréas Stephanus. P. O. Box 392, Pretoria. b. 1 Feb 1915 Winburg. PH.D '54 Univ. of Pretoria, S. Africa. PROF. of PSYCH, Univ. of S. Africa, 263 Skinner St, Pretoria. Member: SAPA. Teaching, research, administration; alcoholism, parapsychology, projective techniques.   M

SCHACH, Dr. Florette. 4 Wale St, Cape Town. b. 26 Mar 1917 Cape Town. PH.D '47 Univ. of Cape Town, S. Africa. CHILD PSYCH'T, priv. prac. Member: SAPA. Research, testing, consulting, clinical analysis, guidance; projective techniques, group therapy, educational achievement of superior children.   F

SCHEPERS, Johannes Magdalenus. Natl. Inst. for Pers. Res, P. O. Box 395, Pretoria. b. 2 Feb 1930 Marquard. MA '57 Univ. of Orange Free State, S. Africa. RES. ASST, Natl. Inst. for Pers. Res, De Quar Rd, Pretoria. Member: SAPA. Research, applied and industrial psychology, clinical analysis; aptitude tests, temperament assessment. M

SCHLEBUSCH, Miss Anita. 2368 Park St, Haffield, Pretoria. b. 31 July 1929 Kroonstad. MA '54 Univ. of Pretoria, S. Africa. STUDENT, Univ. of Minnesota, USA. Member: SAPA. Teaching, guidance; student counseling, projective techniques. F

SCHLEBUSCH, Prof. Dr. Barend Johannes. Dept. of Psych, Univ. of Pretoria, Pretoria. b. 5 Apr 1919 Dewetsdorp. PH.D '46 Univ. of Stellenbosch, S. Africa. HEAD, Dept. of Psych, Univ. of Pretoria. Member: SAPA. Teaching, research, psychotherapy; projective techniques, abnormal psychology, personality. M

SCHNIDT, Dr. Wilfred Heinrich Otto. Dept. of Educ. Psych, Univ. of Natal, P. O. Box 375, Pietermaritzburg. b. 21 Apr 1913 Stanger. PH.D '37 Univ. of Leipzig, Ger. SR. LECT. and HEAD, Dept. of Educ. Psych, Univ. of Natal. Member: SAPA, APA. Teaching, research, remedial education; educational backwardness, personality theory, psychology of reading. M

SCHOEMAN, Andries Johannes Lategan. J. W. Luckhoff Indus. Sch, Heidelberg, Transvaal. b. 7 Oct 1924 Frankfort. MA '53 Univ. of South Africa. TEACHER, Dept. of Educ, Arts and Sci, Vanderstel Bldg, Pretorius St, Pretoria. Member: SAPA. Applied psychology, research, testing; aptitude testing, alcoholism, institutionalized subnormal boys. M

SCHÖNFELDT, Johann Heinrich Christiaan. Porter Reformatory, P. O. Retreat, Cape Town. b. 13 Mar 1912 Orange Free State. MA Potchefstroom Univ. for Christian Higher Educ, S. Africa. VICE PRIN. and PSYCH'T, Porter Reformatory. Member: SAPA. Administration, testing, psychotherapy; values, psychodiagnosis, projective techniques. M

SCOGINGS, Timothy Peter Ralph. 163 Loop St, Pietermaritzburg, Natal. b. 30 Mar 1926 Bulawayd, S. Rhodesia. MA '50 Univ. of Natal, S. Africa. TEACHER, Natal Educ. Dept. Member: SAPA. Teaching, educational psychology, testing; techniques of remedial teaching, scholastic attainment and diagnostic tests, clinical approach to educational and emotional maladjustment. M

SEYMOUR, Dr. Alfred Harmston. P. O. Box 1639, Johannesburg. b. 17 Dec 1904 Newark, Eng. PH.D '35 Univ. of London, Eng. CHAIRMAN, Harold Whitehead and Partners Ltd, 701/3 ABC Chambers Simmonds St, Johannesburg. Member: BPS. Administration, industrial psychology, research; placement and training of executives and supervisors. M

SHERWOOD, Edward Torrance. Inst. of Soc. and Econ. Res, Rhodes Univ, Grahamstown, C. P. b. 10 Sept 1914 Winnipeg, Can. BA '36 Queen's Univ, Can. EXEC. SECY. and SR. RES. FELLOW, Inst. of Soc. and Econ. Res. Member: SAPA, Amer. Anthrop. Assn, Socy. for Appl. Anthrop. Research, administration, applied psychology; personality and culture, projective techniques, motivation. M

SHERWOOD, Mrs. Rae. 9 Harrismith St, Grahamstown. b. 10 Aug 1918 Johannesburg. MA '48 Univ. of Chicago, USA. SR. RES. OFF, Natl. Inst. for Pers. Res, Counc. for Sci. and Indus. Res, Empire Rd, Johannesburg. Research, applied psychology, professional writing. F

SHOUL, Mrs. Shirley Muriel. Natl. Inst. for Pers. Res, P. O. Box 10319, Johannesburg. b. 26 Aug 1934 Johannesburg. BA '56 Univ. of Witwatersrand, S. Africa. RES. ASST, Natl. Inst. for Pers. Res. Member: SAPA. Research, student; temperament assessment and measurement. F

SKAWRAN, Prof. Dr. Paul Robert. 303 Rupertstr, Pretoria. b. 12 Jan 1900 Bottmersdorf, Ger. PH.D '26 Univ. of Bonn, Ger. CHIEF VOCAT. OFF, African Railways, Harbours, and Airways. Member: SAPA, AIPA, DGP. Personnel psychology, testing, professional writing; psychology of the pilot, developing the personality, psychotherapy. M

SMUTS, Dr. Adriaan J. 2 Tugela Rd, Emmarentia, Johannesburg. b. 22 July 1907 Stellenbosch. PH.D '38 Columbia Univ, USA. VOCAT. and EDUC. ADVIS, Transvaal Educ. Dept, P. O. Box 432, Pretoria. Member: SAPA. Consulting, clinical and educational psychology, testing, vocational guidance, professional writing. M

SNELL, Mrs. Doreen Mary. 61 Rose St, Florida, Transvaal. b. 16 Aug 1915 Johannesburg. MA '53 Univ. of Witwatersrand, S. Africa. CHILD PSYCH'T, priv. prac; CLIN. PSYCH'T, Johannesburg Child Guid. Clin; LECTURER, Pre-School Tchr. Trng. Cen, Johannesburg. Member: SAPA. Consulting, guidance, psychotherapy, teaching. F

SONNEKUS, Marthinus Christoffel Hendrikus. Dept. of Educ. Psych, Fac. of Educ, Univ. of Pretoria, Pretoria. b. 31 Oct 1925 Standerton. ED.M '53 Univ. of Pretoria, S. Africa. LECTURER, Pretoria Univ. Educational psychology, testing, research; achievement tests, statistical methods and testing techniques, vocational and child guidance. M

STARFIELD, Mrs. Anita. 21The Braids Rd, Emmarentia Ext, Johannesburg. b. 17 Aug 1925 Cape Town. MA '45 Univ. of Cape Town, S. Africa. LECT. in PSYCH, Univ. of Witwatersrand, Johannesburg.

Member: SAPA. Teaching, research; attitude measurement, personality theory, parent-child relationship. F

STEENKAMP, Dr. Daniel Jacobus. Constantia Reformatory, P. O. Retreat, Cape Town. b. 17 Aug 1907 Griguatown. ED.D '54 Potchefstroom, Univ. of Christian Higher Educ, S. Africa. PRINCIPAL, Dept. of Union Educ, Arts and Sci, Pretorius St, Pretoria; MARRIAGE GUID. COUNC, priv. prac. Member: SAPA. Administration, psychotherapy, consulting; case history, adaptation and temperament tests, projective techniques, diagnosing and treatment. M

STEENKAMP, Willem Lucas. P. O. Box 20, Bergvlei, Johannesburg. b. 29 Mar 1930 Cape Town. Mag. art. '54 Univ. of Stellenbosch, S. Africa. ASST. SUPT, Northlea Wedge Farm and Cottesloe Retreat, Rand Aid Assn, 42 Annett Rd, Cottesloe, Johannesburg. Member: SAPA. Testing, research, psychotherapy, administration; social adaptations, personality inventories, intelligence testing. M

STEUART, Guy W. Dept. of Soc, Preven. and Family Med, Univ. of Natal Med. Sch, Durban, Natal. b. 14 Aug 1918 Durban. MA '50 Univ. of South Africa. ORGANIZER of HLTH. EDUC, Inst. of Fam. and Commun. Hlth, P. O. Merebank; SR. LECT. in HLTH. EDUC, Univ. of Natal Med. Sch. Member: SAPA. Administration, educational psychology, research; social psychological implications for community health education. M

SUGARMAN, Miss Lola Patricia. P. O. Box 10319, Johannesburg. b. 12 Apr 1931 Pretoria. BA '50 Univ. of Witwatersrand, S. Africa. RES. ASST, Natl. Inst. for Pers. Res, Empire Rd, Johannesburg. Member: SAPA, BPS. Research, psychophysiological testing, applied psychology, electroencephalography; objective personality measurement. F

SUTTON, Richard Vincent. 79 Altham Rd, Robertsham, Johannesburg. b. 11 Apr 1921 Krugersdorp. BA '41 Univ. of Witwatersrand, S. Africa. ASST. tot the DIR, Natl. Inst. for Pers. Res, S. African Counc. for Sci. and Indus. Res, Visagie St, Pretoria; EDIT. COMM, *Journal of the National Institute for Personnel Research.* Member: SAPA. Administraion, editorial, personnel work; research institute administration. M

SWARTZ, Prof. John Francis Alexander. 14 Soeteweide St, Stellenbosch. b. 4 Sept 1914 Graaff Reinet. PH.D '53 Univ. of Stellenbosch, S. Africa. PROF. and HEAD, Dept. of Method, Fac. of Educ, Univ. of Stellenbosch. Member: SAPA. Teaching, educational guidance, research; methods of study, measurement of interest, a-chievement tests. M

SWIEGERS, Dr. Daniel Jacobus. Dept. of Psych, Univ. of Pretoria, Pretoria. b. 14 Jan 1944 Louisvale, C.P. PH.D '56 Univ. of Pretoria, S. Africa. SR. LECT, Univ. of Pretoria; CONSULT. PSYCH'T, Ment. Hyg. Socy. Member: SAPA. Teaching, industrial psychology, research; projective techniques, measurement of job proficiency, human factors in industrial problems, criminal reform. M

VAN AARDE, Josef Albert. Elizabeth Conradie Sch, P. O. Diskobolos, Kimberley. b. 17 June 1928 Malmesbury. MA '51 Univ. of Stellenbosch, S. Africa. TEACHER, Elizabeth Conradie Sch. Member: SAPA. Testing, psychotherapy, teaching; intelligence tests, psychotherapy with children, psychology of the handicapped. M

VAN ANTWERP, Dr. Cornelius Marthinus. Dept. of Educ, Arts and Sci, Pretoria. b. 23 Oct 1912 Uetenhage. PH.D '38 Univ. of Cape Town, S. Africa. INSPECTOR of SCHOOLS, Dept. of Educ, Arts and Sci. Member: SAPA. Educational administration; problems of the psychology of the physically handicapped, special education. M

VAN DEN BERG, Coert Grobbelaar. P. O. Box 395, Pietermaritzburg, Natal. b. 30 May 1906 Aberdeen. ED.M '38 Univ. of South Africa. VOCAT. PSYCH'T, Natal Educ. Dept. Member: SAPA. Consulting, guidance, administration, testing; intelligence, aptitudes, interests. M

VAN DER MERWE, Prof. Abraham Beatrix. Dept. of Psych, Univ. of Stellenbosch, Stellenbosch. b. 23 Dec 1914 Philippolis. PH.D '48 Univ. of Stellenbosch, S. Africa. HEAD, Dept. of Psych, Univ. of Stellenbosch. Member: SAPA. Teaching, consulting, psychotherapy; personality measurement, temperamental stability. M

VAN DER MERWE, Dr. Johan D. G. S. African Natl. Counc. for Marriage Guid. and Family Life, Welfare House, 168 Fox St, Johannesburg. b. 15 Aug 1926 Griguatown. PH.D '50 Univ. of Stellenbosch, S. Africa. NATL. SECY. and DIR, S. African Natl. Counc. for Marriage Guid. and Fam. Life. Member: SAPA. Administration, consulting, training and supervision of counselors, psychotherapy; marriage and pastoral counseling, clinical psychometrics, personality theory. M

VAN JAARSVELD, Adriaan Albertus. High Sch. of Industries, George. b. 4 Mar 1926 Dordrecht. Mag. art. '51 Potchefstroom Univ. for Christian Higher Educ, S. Africa. PSYCHOLOGIST, Dept. of Educ, Arts and Sci, Private Bag 122, Pretoria. Member: SAPA. Educational psychology, diagnosis and psychotherapy, consulting; projective techniques, achievement tests. M

VAN KERKEN, Erris Edmond. Dept. of Educ, P. O. Box 521, Bloemfontein. b. 25 Nov 1902 Bloemfontein. MA '28 Univ. of Orange Free State, S. Africa. ADJUNCT DIR. of EDUC, Orange Free State Provincial Admin, President Brand St, Bloemfontein. Member: SAPA. Administration, research; projective techniques, achievement and educational tests. M

VAN LENNEP, Mrs. Dr. Wilhelmina Roberta. 4 Bellevue Terr, Kenilworth, Cape Town. b. 3 Jan 1921 Roermond, Neth. MA '53 Leiden's Acad, Neth. CONSULT. PSYCH'T, priv. prac. Member: SAPA. Testing, consulting; projective techniques, graphology, psychosomatics, child psychotherapy. F

VAN NIEKERK, Dr. Dorothea. 706 Koch Mansions, 7 Pietersen St, Hillbrow, Johannesburg. b. 12 May 1918 Ermelo, Transvaal. PH.D '55 Univ. of Pretoria, S. Africa. CLIN. PSYCH'T, Johannesburg Trng. and Trtmt. Cen. for Cerebral Palsied Children, Rannoch Rd, Forest Town, Johannesburg. Member: SAPA. Educational psychology, testing, psychotherapy; play therapy, psychotherapy with parents, educational problems of the cerebral palsied. F

VAN ZYL, Miss Alma Elsie. Dept. of Psych, Univ. of Witwatersrand, Johannesburg. b. 11 Feb 1928 Bloemfontein. MA '51 Univ. of Cape Town, S. Africa. LECTURER, Univ. of Witwatersrand. Member: SAPA, S. African Stat. Assn. Teaching, testing, research; learning theory, perception, psychometry and psychodiagnostics, statistics, physiology. F

VENTER, Miss A. J. E. Natl. Inst. for Pers. Res, P. O. Box 10319, Johannesburg. b. 30 Aug 1930 Pretoria. MA '56 Univ. of Pretoria, S. Africa. RES. ASST, Natl. Inst. for Pers. Res; VOCAT. GUID. OFF, Dept. of Labour. Member: SAPA. Testing, research, industrial group relations; attitude measurement, ability and achievement tests, projective techniques. F

VERWEY, Frederik Anton. Natl. Inst. for Pers. Res, P. O. Box 10319, Johannesburg. b. 29 May 1916 Schweizer-Reineke, Transvaal. BA '43 Univ. of South Africa. SR. RES. OFF. and HEAD, Group Relat. Sect, Natl. Inst. for Pers. Res. Member: SAPA. Research, industrial psychology; attitude measurement, morale surveys, personality theory and measurement, application of mathematics to problems of measurement. M

VILLIERS, Miss Carolina de. Natl. Bur. of Educ. and Soc. Res, Dept. of Educ, Arts and Sci, Pretoria. b. 21 June 1928 Adelaide. BA '49 Univ. of Stellenbosch, S. Africa. ASST. VOCAT. OFF, Natl. Bur. of Educ. and Soc. Res. Research; educational and in-telligence tests. F

VISSER, Willem Johannes Conradie. Sch. Clin, c/o Sch. Bd, Port Elizabeth. b. 16 Jan 1920 Heidelberg. ED.M '50 Univ. of Orange Free State, S. Africa. INSPECTOR, Spec. Classes and Sch. Guid, Cape Educ. Dept, P. O. Box 13, Cape Town. Member: SAPA, S. African Ment. Hlth. Socy. Testing, educational psychology, school guidance, psychotherapy; non-directive therapy and psychoanalysis, special education, juvenile delinquency. M

VLOK, Adrian. Natl. Bur. of Educ. and Soc. Res, Dept. of Educ, Arts, and Sci, Pretoria. b. 26 Apr 1933 Marquard. MA '55 Univ. of Pretoria, S. Africa. ASST. PROFES. OFF, Natl. Bur. of Educ. and Soc. Res. Research, applied psychology, testing; vocational guidance, aptitude testing, projective techniques. M

VORSTER, David Johannes Mentz. P.O. Box 1, Daggafontein, Springs, Transvaal. b. 10 Jan 1917 Steynsburg. MA, Univ. of Pretoria, S. Africa. PERS. OFF, Daggafontein Gold Mines Ltd. Member: SAPA. Industrial personnel work, guidance, testing; aptitude and achievement tests, interview techniques, leadership studies. M

WARFFEMIUS, Cornelius Adrianus Leonardus. Psych. Dept, Univ. of Witwatersrand, Milner Park, Johannesburg. b. 20 Oct 1921 Amsterdam, Neth. BA '52 Univ. of Witwatersrand, S. Africa. LECTURER, Univ. of Witwatersrand; HONORARY ED, *South African Journal of Science*. Member: SAPA, S. African Assn. for the Advanc. of Sci. Teaching, research, psychotherapy; learning theory, rehabilitation of alcoholics. M

WILD, Prof. Ernest Hamilton. Rhodes Univ, Grahamstown. b. 14 Sept 1900 East London. PH.D '26 Univ. of London, Eng. PROF. and HEAD, Dept. of Psych, Rhodes Univ; PRO-VICE CHANCELLOR and VICE-PRIN, Rhodes Univ. Member: SAPA, BPS. Teaching, administration, guidance; testing. M

WOLPE, Dr. Joseph. 318 Pan Africa House, Troye St, Johannesburg. b. 30 Apr 1915 Johannesburg. MD '48 Univ. of Witwatersrand, S. Africa. PSYCHOTHERAPIST, priv. prac; LECTURER, Dept. of Psychiat, Univ. of Witwatersrand. Member: SAPA. Psychotherapy, research, teaching; learning theory, mechanisms of neurosis production. M

WOODROW, Miss Alice Patricia. b. 7 Oct 1930 Cape Town. M.SC '54 Univ. of London, Eng. RES. ASST, Natl. Inst. for Pers. Res, De Quar Rd, Pretoria; ED. COMM, *Journal of the National Institute for Personnel Research*. Research, testing, industrial psychology; aptitude tests, pupil pilot research, personnel selection. F

WOOLFSON, Julius Omri. 29 Junction Rd, Bramley, Johannesburg. b. 23 Mar 1928 Rustenburg. MA '56 Univ. of Pretoria, S. Africa. DIRECTOR, Career Advice Bur, 16 and 17 Pasteur Chambers, 191 Jeppe St; INDUS. CONSULT. PSYCH'T, priv. prac. Member: SAPA. Consulting, vocational guidance, industrial psychology, testing; projective techniques, achievement tests, personnel selection and placement. M

WOOLLEY, David Howell. P. O. Northrand, Transvaal. b. 31 Mar 1929 Cape Town. M.SC '52 Univ. of Natal, S. Africa. EDUC.

OFF, and CHIEF SUPT, Pers. Dept, African Explosives and Chemical Industries, Ltd, P. O. Northrand. Industrial psychology, administration, teaching. M

YSSEL, Gert Johannes. Hotel Frozèno, Jacob Marè St, Pretoria. b. 2 Feb 1930 Vryburg. BA '53 Univ. of South Africa. RES. ASST, Natl. Inst. for Pers. Res, Dequar Rd, Pretoria. Member: SAPA. Research, industrial psychology, testing; aptitude tests, industrial relations, atiitude measurement. M

UNION OF SOVIET SOCIALIST REPUBLICS

ABDULLAEV, Cand. Educ. Sci. Adil K. ul. Vodopianova 22, kv. 2, Baku. b. 10 Feb 1913 Kazakhski r-n, selo 2-e Shikhly, Azerbajan. C.ESC '53 Psych. Inst, Acad. of Educ. Sci, USSR. LECTURER, Chair of Educ. and Psych, Azerbajan Tchr. Trng. Inst. after Lenin, ul. Shaumiana 39, Baku. Teaching, research; sport psychology. M

ABRAMIAN, Cand. Educ. Sci, Mrs. Elda. Prospekt Lenina 59, kv. 26, Erevan. b. 1928. C.ESC '56 Moscow Tchr. Trng. Inst. after Potemkin, USSR. SR. TCHR, Erevan Univ. Research on methods of teaching foreign languages in Armenian schools; teaching foreign languages. F

ADAMASHVILI, Cand. Educ. Sci, Lecturer, Mrs. Nina. ul. Tsilkanskaia 2-a, Tbilisi. b. 7 Sept 1913. C.ESC '46 Tbilisi Univ, USSR. LECTURER, Chair of Psych, Tbilisi Univ, Universtetskaia 1, Tbilisi. Teaching, researrch, student; child psychology. F

AKHOBADZE, Mrs. Roza I. ul. Plekhanova 117, Tbilisi. b. 16 Apr 1923 Tbilisi. ACTING SR. SCI. WKRK, OMD Inst, ul. Lenina 38, Tbilisi. Research, teaching. F

ALEKSEEVA, Cand. Educ. Sci, Mrs. Nina A. ul. Kovalikhinskaia 82, kv. 1, Gorky 24. b. 9 Mar 1925 Arzamas. C.ESC '54 Psych. Inst, Acad. of Educ. Sci. USSR. SR. TCHR, Chair of Psych, Gorky Tchr. Trng. Inst. after Gorky, ul. Ulianova 1, Gorky. Teaching, educational psychology, research; psychology of teaching foreign languages, learning rate. F

ALKHIMOV, Cand. Educ. Sci. Dmitri D. ul. Internatsionalnaia 1, kv. 23, Smolensk. b. 16 Nov 1903 Kharkov. C.ESC '47 Moscow Tchr. Trng. Inst. after Lenin, USSR. LECTURER, Chair of Educ. and Psych, Tchr. Trng. Inst, ul. Przhevalskogo 8, Smolensk. Teaching, research, professional writing; comprehension in learning. M

ANANIEV, Dr. Educ, Prof. Boris G. ul. Dibunovskaia 31, kv. 7, Novaia Derevnia, Leningrad. b. 14 Aug 1907 Vladikavkaz. ED.D, Leningrad Univ, USSR. DIRECTOR,

Inst. of Educ, Acad. of Educ. Sci, nab. Kutuzova 8, Leningrad; PROFESSOR, Chair of Psych, Leningrad Univ. Member: USSR Socy. of Psych'ts, AE. SC Presidium. Administration, student, research, teaching; theory of senses, perception, educational process. M

ANKUDINOVA, Mrs. Nina A. Oktiabrskaia 44, vtoroi etazh, Omsk. b. Dec 1916. SR. TCHR, Omsk Tchr. Trng. Inst, Internatsionalnaia 2, Omsk. Teaching; education. F

ARIAMOV, Dr. Educ., Prof. Ivan A. ul. Kazakova 18, kv. 81, Moscow B-66. b. 5 Feb 1884. ED.D '48 Moscow Univ, USSR. HEAD, Chair of Psych, Moscow Reg. Tchr. Trng. Inst. Teaching, research; child psychology. M

ARISKINA, Cand. Educ. Sci, Mrs. Kira A. Inst. of Psych, ul. Radishcheva 33, Kursk. b. 17 July 1924. C.ESC '53 Inst. of Psych, Kursk, USSR. TEACHER, Inst. of Psych, Teaching, research. F

ARKHANGELSKY, Cand. Educ. Sci. Sergei. Kolpachny per. 6, kv. 43, Moscow Centre. b. 1 July 1896 Riazan. C.ESC '48 Moscow Univ, USSR. SR. SCI. WKRK, Psych. Inst, Acad. of Educ. Sci, Mokhovaia 9, Moscow. Research, applied and educational psychology, editorial; habits of movement, psychology of the planning process. M

ARTEMOV, Dr. Educ, Prof. Vladimir A. B. Savvinski per. 13, kv. 12, Moscow G-117. b. 23 Apr 1897 Belebei. ED.D, Moscow, USSR. HEAD, Chair of Psych, Lab. of Exper. Phonetics and Psych. of Speech, First Moscow Tchr. Trng. Inst. of Foreign Languages, ul. Metrostroevskaia 38, Moscow. Research, editorial, teaching; psychology of speech and teaching foreign languages, experimental phonetics. M

ASATIANI, Cand. Educ. Sci, Mrs. Liubov M. Elektricheski per. 4, Tbilisi. b. 30 Sept 1898 Moscow. C.ESC '49 Moscow Univ, USSR. HEAD, Lab. of Pathopsych, Inst. of Psychiat, Tbilisi. Research, testing, clinical analysis, consulting; mental disease and

the pathology of thinking.　F
ASHMUTAIT, Cand. Educ. Sci, Mrs. Maria P.
ul. Bronitskaia 2, kv. 44, Leningrad.　b.
1904. c.esc '37 Tchr. Trng. Inst. after
Gertsen, Leningrad, ussr.　sr. sci. wrkr,
Inst. of Educ, Acad. of Educ. Sci, Nabe-
rezhnaia Kutuzova 8, Leningrad. Member:
Psych. Sect. of Leningrad Sci. Club. Re-
search, professional writing, educational
psychology, teaching; psychology of labor,
thought process in pupils.　F
AVALISHVILI, Cand. Educ. Sci. Akaki M.
ul. Sheroziia 5, Tbilisi.　b. 15 Apr 1906
Ordzhonikidzevski r-n, selo Kitskhi,
Georgia.　c.esc '44 Tbilisi Univ. after
Stalin, ussr. head, Chair of Educ. and
Psych, Telavski Tchr. Trng. Inst, ul.
Irakliia 2, Telavi. Teaching, research, administration; psychology of speech and
education.　M
AVRAMENKO, Cand. Educ. Sci. Alexei M.
Geroiev Revoliutsii 4- a/10, korpus 3, Kiev.
b. 23 Feb 1923. c.esc '54 Kiev Univ, ussr.
sr. sci. wrkr, Psych. Inst, ul. Lenina 10,
Kiev. Member: The Psych. Socy. Research,
professional writing; nature of psychical
activities, will, psychology of creative
work.　M
BADUDIN, Cand. Educ. Sci. Valeri T. Pedinstitut, katedra pedagogiki i psikhologii,
Kostroma.　b. 3 Nov 1923. c.esc '54
Moscow Tchr. Trng. Inst. after Potemkin.
sr. tchr, Kostroma Tchr. Trng. Inst. after
Nekrasov. Teaching, research; perception
and comprehension; age differences.　M
BAEV, Cand. Educ. Sci. Boris F. ul. Leonto-
vicha 5, kv. 21, Kiev.　b. 14 Aug 1923.
c.esc '56 Kiev. Univ, ussr. sr. sci. wrkr,
Psych. Inst, ul. Lenina 10, Kiev. Member:
The Psych. Socy. Research, professional
writing; language and thinking, individual
differences.　M
BAINDURASHVILI, Cand. Educ. Sci. Akaki.
Sovetskaia 143-a, Tbilisi.　b. 10 Feb 1924.
c.esc '55 Tbilisi Univ. after Stalin, ussr.
jr. sci. wrkr, Psych. Inst, Georgian Acad.
of Sci, ul. Dzhavakhishvili 1, Tbilisi.
Research; psychology of thinking.　M
BEIN, Dr. Biol, Mrs. Esfir S. Bersenevskaia
nab. 16, kv. 3, Moscow 72.　b. 23 Jan 1907.
Dr. of Biol. '30 Moscow Univ, ussr. sr.
sci. wrkr, Neurology Inst, Acad. of Med.
Sci, Shchipok 6/8, Moscow. Member:
Moscow Socy. of Neuropathologists and
Psychiatrists. Diagnostic testing and
clinical analysis of nervous diseases, research, clinical practice; speech defects,
perception.　F
BEKBASOV, Cand. Educ. Sci. Algazy. ul.
Uchitelskaia 61, Nukus, Kara-Kalpakskaia
assr.　b. 13 Feb 1923. c.esc '56 Psych.
Inst, Acad. of Educ. Sci, Nukus, ussr.
sr. tchr, Chair of Educ. and Psych,

Kara-Kalpakian Tchr. Trng. Inst, Nukus.
Teaching, research, educational psychology;
experimental work in education.　M
BELIAEV, Cand. Educ. Sci. Boris V. Petro-
verigski per. 6/8, kv. 180, Moscow Centre.
b. 3 Aug 1900 g. Kromy, Orlovskoi obl.
c.esc, Moscow Univ, ussr. lecturer,
Chair of Psych, First Moscow State Tchr.
Trng. Inst. of Foreign Languages, Metro-
stroievskaia 38, Moscow. Teaching, research, educational psychology; psychology
of thinking, psychology of teaching foreign
languages.　M
**BELIAEVA-EKZEMPLIARSKAIA, Cand.
Educ. Sci, Mrs. Sophia.** ul. Spartaka 49,
kv. 24, Cheliabinsk.　b. 12 May 1895.
c.esc '45, ussr. lecturer, Chair of Educ.
and Psych, Cheliabinsk Tchr. Trng. Inst;
lecturer, All-Union Socy. of Propagating
Polit. and Sci. Knowledge. Teaching,
research, educational psychology; emotions,
aesthetic perception.　F
BERKOVICH, Cand. Educ. Sci, Lect, Emil L.
Fabrichny per. 17, kv. 1, Chkalov.　b.
24 Feb 1897.　c.esc '40, Moscow, ussr.
lecturer, Chkalov Tchr. Trng. Inst,
Chkalov. Teaching, research; philosophical
foundations of psychology, history of
psychology.　M
**BEZHIASHVILI, Cand. Educ. Sci, Lect.
Vladimir D.** ul. Pasanaurskaia 17, Tbilisi.
b. 2 July 1908 Signakshki r-n, selo Anaga,
Georgia. c.esc '46 Tbilisi Univ. after Stalin,
ussr. sr. sci. wrkr, Inst. of Educ, ul.
Dzhavakhishvili 1, Tbilisi. Research in
educational psychology, teaching; analysis
of student's character and work process. M
BEZRUKOVA, Mrs. Evgeniia Z. ul. Malyshe-
va 154-21, Vtuzgorodok, Sverdlovsk.　b. 15
Mar 1922. assistant, Tchr. Trng. Inst,
Sverdlosvk. Teaching, research, education-
al psychology; study of thinking.　F
**BIKCHENTAI, Cand. Educ. Sci, Lect. Nasyb-
Iroglo A.** ul. Mendeleeva 8, Stalinabad.
b. 1 Oct 1898 Ulianovskaia obl, der.
Isantimur.　c.esc, Moscow Univ, ussr.
teacher, Stalinabad Tchr. Trng. Inst,
ul. Lenina, Stalinabad; consultant, Tchr.
Trng. Inst. for Women. Teaching, research,
educational psychology, consulting.　M
**BLAGONADEZHINA, Cand. Educ. Sci, Mrs.
Larisa V.** B. Kaluzhskaia 2-a, kv. 9,
Moscow V-49.　b. 1895 Pavlograd, Dnie-
propetrovskaia obl. c.esc ussr. sr. sci.
wrkr, Lab. of Educ. Psych, Psych. Inst,
Acad. of Educ. Sci, Mokhovaia 9, Moscow.
Research, professional writing, teaching;
personality, esthetic development.　F
BOCHORISHVILI, Dr. Educ, Prof. Angiia T.
ul. Lisi 2, kv. 19, Tbilisi.　b. 6 Dec 1902.
ed.d '46 Tbilisi Univ. after Stalin, ussr.
chairman, Soc. Sci. Sect, Georgian Acad.
of Sci, ul. Dzerzhinskogo 8, Tbilisi; head,

Chair of Educ. and Psych, Tchr. Trng. Inst. Member: Georgian Acad. of Med. Sci. Research, administration, teaching; logic. M

BOCHORISHVILI, Gela A. ul. Lisi 2, kv. 19, Tbilisi. b. 26 May 1929 Kutaisi, Georgia. SR. TCHR, Kutaisi Tchr. Trng. Inst, ul. Kirova 55, Kutaisi. Research, teaching; philosophical problems of psychology, history of French psychology. M

BODALIOV, Cand. Educ. Sci. Alexei A. ul. Polozova 14, kv. 5, Leningrad P-136. b. 13 Oct 1923 g. Sarapul, Udmurtskaia. c.ESC '54 Leningrad Univ, USSR. ASSISTANT, Chair of Psych, Leningrad Univ, Universitetskaia nab. 7/9, Leningrad. Educational psychology, research, teaching; abilities, character. M

BOGOIAVLENSKY, Cand. Educ. Sci, Lect. Dmitri N. Sivtsev Vrazhek 38, kv. 1, Moscow 2. b. 6 July 1898 Riazanskaia obl, der. Loshaki. c.ESC '43 Tchr. Trng. Inst. after Lenin, Moscow, USSR. HEAD, Lab. of Educ. Psych, Psych. Inst, Acad. of Educ. Sci, Mokhovaia 9, Moscow. Educational psychology, directing research, consulting, student; psychology of learning grammar and spelling. M

BOGUSH, Cand. Med. Sci, Lect. Nikita R. ul. Vorovskogo 15, kv. 9, Kiev. b. 10 June 1900 Vinnitskaia obl. c.ESC '45, MD '26 Kiev Inst. of Med, USSR. LECTURER, Chair of Psych, Kiev Inst. of Physical Trng, ul. Fizkultury 1, Kiev. Teaching, research, psychotherapy; psychology of movements, perception. M

BOIADZHIAN-KHACHIKIAN, Cand. Educ. Sci, Mrs. Margo Kh. ul. Kommunistov 38, kv. 5, g. Fergana. b. 8 Nov 1918 Kars, Turkey. c.ESC '52 Leningrad Univ, USSR. SR. TCHR, Tchr. Trng. Inst, ul. Stalina 17, Fergana. Teaching, research; problems of scientific thinking. F

BORISOVA, Cand. Educ. Sci, Mrs. Mira N. Mokhovaia 9, korp. V, kv. 57, Moscow K-9. b. 28 June 1925 g. Mogiliov. c.ESC '51 Psych. Inst. Acad. of Educ. Sci, Moscow, USSR. JR. SCI. WRKR, Psych. Inst, Acad. of Educ. Sci, Mokhovaia 9, Moscow. Research; individual differences. F

BORKOVA, Cand. Educ. Sci, Mrs. Taisiia N. Zatsepa 2, kv. 118, Moscow. b. 14 Aug 1920. c.ESC '52, USSR. JR. SCI. WRKR, Psych. Inst, Acad. of Educ. Sci, Mokhovaia 9, Moscow. Research, educational psychology, professional writing. F

BOSKIS, Dr. Educ, Prof. Mrs. Rakhil M. Pervaia Miusskaia 20, kv. 2, Moscow. b. 29 Mar 1902. ED.D '53 Psych. Inst, Acad. of Educ. Sci, USSR. HEAD, Sect. for Educ. of Deaf Children, Defectology Inst, Acad. of Educ. Sci, ul. Pogodinskaia 8, Moscow.

Research, administration, teaching, consulting, clinical practice. F

BOTIAKOVA, Cand. Educ. Sci, Mrs. Lidia V. Tokmakov per. 3, kv. 5, Moscow B-66. b. 5 Dec. 1924. c.ESC '55 Moscow Reg. Tchr. Trng. Inst, USSR. SR. TCHR, Stalingrad Tchr. Trng. Inst, ul. Akademicheskaia 2, Stalingrad. Teaching, research; psychology of thinking. F

BOZHOVICH, Cand. Educ. Sci, Lect, Mrs. Lidia I. il. Preobrazhenskaia 5/7, kiv. 189, Moscow. b. 1908 Kursk. c.ESC, Moscow, USSR. HEAD, Educ. Lab, Psych. Inst, Acad. of Educ. Sci, Mokhovaia 9, Moscow. Research, educational / psychology, teaching; personality. F

BUBNOVA, Cand. Educ. Sci, Mrs. Vera K. Lialin per. 26, kv. 26, Moscow B-64. b. 24 Nov 1894 Moscow. c.ESC '47 Psych. Inst, Acad. of Educ. Sci, Moscow, USSR. SR. SCI. WRKR, Lab of Educ. Psych, Psych. Inst., Acad. of Educ. Sci, Mokhovaia 9, Moscow. Research, testing, clinical analysis, editing psychology textbook; pathopsychology. F

BYZOV, Cand. Educ. Sci, Lect. Stepan A. ul. Riazhskaia 50, Riazan. b. 30 Nov 1896 Gatchina. c.ESC '46 Psych. Inst, Acad. of Educ. Sci, Moscow, USSR. LECTURER, Chair of Psych, Tchr. Trng. Inst, ul. Svobody, Riazan. Teaching, research, educational psychology; interests, guidance thinking. M

BZHALAVA, Dr. Med, Prof. Iosif. tupik Dzhavakhishvili 9, Tbilisi. b. 1904. MD '46 Tbilisi Univ, USSR. HEAD, Pathopsych. Sect, Psych. Inst. after Uznadze, ul. Dzhavakhishvili 1, Tbilisi. Research, psychotherapy, consulting, clinical practice; psychiatry. M

CHAMATA, Cand. Educ. Sci, Lect. Pavel R. ul. Saksaganskogo 34, kv. 4, Kiev. b. 16 July 1898 Kanevski r-n, s. Babichi, Kievskaia obl. c.ESC, USSR. ASST. DIR, Inst. of Psych, ul. Lenina 10, Kiev. Member: UKSSR Psych. Socy, USSR Psych. Socy. Research, administration, teaching; editing. M

CHEBYSHEVA, Cand. Educ. Sci, Mrs. Varvara V. ul. Novo-Peschanaia 24, kv. 32, Moscow. b. 17 Dec 1903. c.ESC '30 Moscow Univ, USSR. SR. SCI. WRKR, Psych. Inst, Acad. of Educ. Sci, Mokhovaia 9, Moscow. Research. F

CHERNIKOVA, Cand. Educ. Sci, Mrs. Nina A. 2-oi Neopalimovsky per. 3, kv. 3, Moscow G-117. b. 19 Apr 1899 Moscow. c.ESC '47 Psych. Inst, Acad. of Educ. Sci, Moscow, USSR. SR. SCI. WRKR, Psych. Inst, Acad. of Educ. Sci, Mokhovaia 9, Moscow. Experimental research; psychology of speech development, psychology of children's literary work. F

CHERNIKOVA, Cand. Biol. Sci, Mrs. Olga A. 2-d Neopalimovski per. 3, kv. 1, Moscow

117. b. 5 Sept 1903. c.BCS '35 Moscow, USSR. LECTURER, Chair of Psych, Inst. of Physical Trng, ul. Kazakova 18, Moscow. Teaching, research; will, emotions, personality development and sports. F

CHERNOKOZOV, Ivan I. Kotsiubinskogo 88, kv. 18, Vinnitza. b. 27 Jan 1920. TCHR. of PSYCH, Tchr. Trng. Inst, Vinnitsa. Teaching, research. M

CHERNOV, Anatoli P. Semashko 19-a, kv. 1, g. Gorki. b. 25 Jan 1922 Gorki. SR. TCHR, Chair of Educ.,Gorki Univ. after Lobachevski, g. Gorki. Teaching, research; psychology of thinking, tide of intellectual activities. M

CHISTOV, Mikhail A. Lesnaia 22-a, Chita 10. b. 27 Dec 1912. SR. TCHR, Chair of Educ, Chita Tchr. Trng. Inst, Chkalova 140, Chita. Teaching, research, professional writing; origin and development of psychical processes. M

CHKHARTISHVILI, Cand. Educ. Sci. Shalva N. Uritskogo 52, Kutaisi, Georgia. b. 1910. c.ESC '41 Tbilisi Univ, USSR. ASST. DIR, Kutaisi Tchr. Trng. Inst, ul. Kirova, Kutaisi. Administration, research, teaching; psychology of will. M

CHRELASHVILI, Cand. Educ. Sci, Mrs. Natela V. ul. Kamo 32, kv. 21, Tbilisi. b. 1 Dec 1918, Tbilisi. c.ESC Psych. Inst, USSR. SR. SCI. WRKR, Inst. of Psych. after Uznadze, Dzhavakhishvili 1, Tbilisi. Research; illusionary concepts of animals, speech and thinking of children. F

CHUCHMARIOV, Dr. Biol, Prof. Zakhari I. 1 Astradamski proezd 4, kv. 3, Moscow A-8. b. 4 Sept 1888 Voroshilovgrad. Dr. of Biol. '39 Moscow, USSR. PROF. of PSYCH, Moscow Reg. Tchr. Trng. Inst, ul. Radio 10, Moscow. Member: Moscow Psych. Socy. Research, teaching, educational psychology; development of thinking and emotions, fatigue. M

CHUDINOVA, Cand. Educ. Sci, Mrs. Maria A. Oktiabrskaia 15, kv. 22, Yakutsk. b. Mar 1908. c.ESC Ministry of Higher Educ, USSR. HEAD, Chair of Psych, Yakutsk Univ, ul. Yaroslavskogo, Yakutsk. Teaching, student, administration. F

CHUKHIN, Cand. Educ. Sci, Lect. Alexander I. ul. Maiakovskogo 11, kv. 1, Simferopol. b. 10 Oct 1896 Mosalsk. c.ESC '49 Tchr. Trng. Inst, Moscow, USSR. LECTURER, Chair of Educ, Krimea Tchr. Trng. Inst, ul. Lenina 11, Simferopol. Teaching, research, educational psychology. M

DADABAEVA, Mrs. Paiza. ul. Kirova 61, Frunze. b. 25 Dec 1930 Oshskaia obl, Dzhapalakski s/s, s. Uchar. Teacher, Moscow Tchr. Trng. Inst. after Lenin, USSR. JR. SCI. WRKR, Inst. of Educ, Frunze. Research. F

DARBINIAN, Cand. Educ. Sci, Mrs. Vera. ul.

Bagramiana 50-a, kv, 9, Erevan. b. 10 Apr 1911. c.ESC '49 Psych. Inst, Georgian Acad. of Sci. USSR. PSYCH. TCHR, Armenian Tchr. Trng. Inst, ul. Moskovskaia 5, Erevan. Teaching, research; imagination. F

DAVYDOVA, Cand. Educ. Sci, Mrs. Anna N. ul. Zhukovskaia 28, kv. 3, Leningrad D-14. b. 2 Mar 1903. c.ESC '40 Tchr. Trng. Inst. after Gertsen, USSR. LECTURER, 2-d Leningrad Tchr. Trng. Inst. of Foreign Languages, pr. Stachek 30, Leningrad. Research, teaching; child psychology, psychology of sensation. F

DMITRIEV, Cand. Educ. Sci, Lect. Grigori P. ul. Novaia 6, kv. 5, Barnaul. b. 17 Nov 1900. c.ESC '47 Inst. of Educ, Acad. of Educ. Sci, Moscow, USSR. SR. TCHR, Chair of Educ. and PSYCH, Barnaul Tchr. Trng. Inst, im. Krupskoi 124, Barnaul. Teaching, educational psychology; leadership among children, abilities, study of difficult children. M

DOBRYNIN, Dr. Educ, Prof. Nikolai F. B. Yakimanka 22, kv. 47, Moscow V-180. b. 18 May 1890 Bobruisk. ED.D.'38 Moscow, USSR. PROF. and HEAD of PSYCH, Moscow City Tchr. Trng. Inst, ul. Krasnoprudnaia, Davydov per. 4, Moscow. Teaching, research; psychology of attention. M

DRAGUNOVA, Cand. Educ. Sci, Mrs. Tatiana V. ul. 2 Borodinskaia, 10/12, kv. 19, Moscow. b. 12 July 1923 Moscow. c.ESC '51 Psych. Inst, Acad. of Educ. Sci, Moscow. USSR. SR. SCI. WRKR, Lab. of Pre-School Age Children's Educ, Psych. Inst, Acad. of Educ. Sci, Mokhovaia 9, Moscow. Research, educational psychology; age psychology. F

DRAPKINA, Cand. Educ. Sci, Mrs. Sarra E. p/101 Kirovski pr. 20/10, kv. 15, Leningrad. b. 15 Jan 1905. c.ESC '31 Tchr. Trng. Inst. after Gertsen, Leningrad, USSR. SR. SCI. WRKR, Psych. Sect, Inst. of Educ, Acad. of Educ. Sci, Naberezhnaia Kutuzova 8 Leningrad. Research, educational psychology, consulting; history of psycholog auditory and spatial perception, think and teaching. F

DUBOVIS, Cand. Educ. Sci, Lect, Mrs. De ra M. ul. Artema 9/11, kv. 7, Kharkov. 27 Mar 1910. c.ESC '44 Psych. Inst, Ac of Educ. Sci, USSR. LECTURER, Chair of duc. and Psych, Kharkov Univ, Univeitets- kaia 16, Kharkov. Teaching, r earch; thinking. F

DULNEV, Cand. Educ. Sci. Grigori N Pogo- dinskaia 8, kv. 14, Moscow G-117 b. Jan 1909. c.ESC ,USSR. HEAD, Sect. fc Study of Mentally Retarded Children, Jefect- Inst, Acad. of Educ. Sci, Pogdinskaia 8, Moscow. Directing research, educational psychology; psychology of teaching. M

DZHAVADOGLY, Cand. Educ. Sci. Megerramov **Mamedali.** 6 Kommunisticheski per. 8, kv. 31, Baku. b. 12 Dec 1909. C.ESC '49 Azerbaijan State Univ. after Kirov, USSR. LECTURER, Chair of Logic and Psych, Azerbaijan State Univ. Teaching, research, editorial. M

EGOROV, Dr. Prof. Tikhon G. 5 Verkhne-Mikhailovskii proezd 28, kv. 63, Moscow. b. 29 June 1891. Doctor '22 Smolensk Univ, USSR. Retired, educational psychology, professional writing, research. M

ELIAVA, Cand. Educ. Sci, Mrs. Nina. ul. Moskovskaia 13, Tbilisi. b. 9 Aug 1902. C.ESC '46 Psych. Inst, Georgian Acad. of Sci, USSR. SR. SCI. WRKR, Psych. Inst. after Uznadze, ul. Dzhavakhishvili 1, Tbilisi. Research; psychology of perception and thinking. F

ELINETSKI, Cand. Educ. Sci. Evgeni F. ul. K. Marxa 10-a, Khmelnitskaia obl, Kamenets-Podolski. b. 13 Apr 1907 Cherkasski r-n, selo Cherniavka, Kievskaia obl. C.ESC '53, USSR. SR. TCHR, Tchr. Trng. Inst, Kamenets-Podolski. Research; memory. M

ELKONIN, Cand. Educ. Sci. Daniil B. Psych. Inst, Mokhovaia 9, Moscow. b. 2 Feb 1904. C.ESC '41 Ministry of Higher Educ, USSR. SR. SCI. WRKR, Psych. Inst, Acad. of Educ. Sci. Research, teaching; child psychology. M

ENDOVITSKAIA, Cand. Educ. Sci, Mrs. Tatiana V. Psych. Inst, Mokhovaia 9, Moscow. b. 16 Dec 1905 Vorontsovo-Aleksandrovsk. C.ESC '47 Psych. Inst, Acad. of Educ. Sci, USSR. SR. SCI. WRKR, Psych. Lab. for Pre-School Children, Psych. Inst, Acad. of Educ. Sci. Research; development of perception and feelings in children. F

ENIKEEV, Cand. Educ. Sci. Khasan. ul. Aksakova 87, kv. 1, Ufa. b. 9 June 1905 Ufa. C.ESC '42 Molotov Tchr. Trng. Inst, Ufa, USSR. LECTURER, Bashkir Tchr. Trng. Inst, Ufa. Teaching, research; psychology of teaching. M

ERAPONOVA, Cand. Educ. Sci, Mrs. Emilia ul. Novo- Basmannaia 4/6, kv. 260, Moscow. b. 6 Oct 1926. C.ESC '53 Psych. Inst, Acad. of Educ. Sci, USSR. JR. SCI. WKR, Psych. Inst, Acad. of Educ. Sci, Mokhovaia 9, Moscow. Research; memory, perception. M

FEOFANOV, Dr. Educ, Prof. Mikhail P. B. Vlasievski per. 7/24, kv. 7, Moscow G-2. b. 30 Oct 1882. ED.D '21 Gorky Univ, USSR. MEMB, Sci. Council, and Defectology and Natl. Sch. Insts. of Acad. of Educ. Sci. Retired, research, educational psychology; children writing, emotions, senses. M

FILATOV, Dr. Phil, Prof. Vasili S. ul. Chaikovskogo 1-a, kv. 7, Yaroslavl, b. 24 Aug 1900. PH.L'53 Yaroslavl. USSR. DIRECTOR, Yaroslav Tchr. Trng. Inst. after Ushinsky,

ul. Respoblikanskaia 108, Yaroslavl. Teaching, research, administration; psychology of character. M

FRADKINA, Cand. Sci, Mrs. Frida. Mozhaiskaya 39, kv. 6, Leningrad F-147. b. 19 Aug 1909 Leningrad. C.SC '49 Psych. Inst, Acad. of Educ. Sci, Moscow, USSR. LECTURER, Chair of Psych, Leningrad State Tchr. Trng. Inst, Malaya Posadskaya 26, Leningrad. Teaching, research; psychology of play, speech development in children. F

FRENKEL, Cand. Educ. Sci. Isai A. ul. Radishcheva 56, kv. 18, Kursk. b. Zhitomirskoi obl., m. Volodarsk. C.ESC, Leningrad Tchr. Trng. Inst. after Gertsen, USSR. LECTURER, Kursk State Tchr. Trng. Inst. Teaching, research, educational psychology; history of Russian psychology in mid-nineteenth century, research methods. M

GADZHIEV, Cand. Educ. Sci. Surkhai. ul. Gogolia 3, kv. 36, Baku. b. 1904. C.ESC '51, USSR. HEAD, Chair of Psych, Foreign Languages Inst, Sameda Vurguna 24, Baku. Teaching, research on relationship of speech and action; change of psychical processes as a result of brain injuries. M

GAGAEVA, Cand. Biol. Sci, Lect. Mrs. Galina M. Arbat 35, kv. 52, Moscow G-2. b. Sept 1899. C.BSC '45, USSR. LECTURER, Central Inst. of Physical Culture, ul. Kazakova 18, Moscow. Teaching, research; sport psychology. F

GAIVAROVSKY, Prof. Alexandr A. Krasnoarmeiskaia 41, kv. 2, Kuibyshev. b. 16 Oct 1899. PROFESSOR, Chair of Psych, Kuibyshev Tchr. Trng. Inst, M. Gorkogo 65/67, Kuibyshev. Research, teaching; perception. M

GALKINA, Cand. Educ. Sci, Mrs. Olga I. Nevski pr. 184, kv. 17, Leningrad S-167. b. 9 Mar 1905 Kazan. C.ESC '43 Leningrad, USSR. SR. SCI. WRKR, Educ. Psych. Sect, Inst. of Educ, Acad. of Educ. Sci, Kutuzova 8, Leningrad. Member: Psych. Sect. of Leningrad Sci. Club. Research, educational psychology, professional writing; mental development. F

GALPERIN, Cand. Med. Sci, Lect. Piotr Y. Borovskoie shosse 1, kv. 251, Moscow V-261. b. 2 Nov 1902. C.MSC '38, USSR. LECTURER, Chair of Psych, Fac. of Philos, Moscow Univ, Mokhovaia 11, Moscow. Teaching, research; thinking process. M

GARBACHAUSKENE, Mrs. Maria I. ul. Dzhiaugsmo 14, Pavilnius, Vilnius. b. 30 May 1927. Grad. '50 Vilnius Tchr. Trng. Inst, USSR. SR. TCHR, Vilnius Tchr. Trng. Inst, ul. Gorkogo 83, Vilnius. Teaching, research, administration; development of thinking habits in the process of teaching. F

GARSIASHVILI, Mrs. Leila A. Pedinstitut, ul. Stalina 21, Sukhumi. b. 1923 Tbilisi.

SR. TCHR, Chair of Educ. and Psych, Sukhumi Tchr. Trng. Inst. after Gorky. Teaching, research, educational and psychological consulting. F

GELLERSTEIN, Dr. Biol, Prof. Solomon G. Pervy Obydensky per. 12, kv. 1, Moscow G-34. b. 2 Nov 1896 Dnepropetrovsk. Dr. of Biol, Moscow, USSR. Retired, professional writing; perception of time, training methods. M

GEODAKIAN, Cand. Educ. Sci. Irina M. ul. Chaikovskogo 14, kv. 33, Erevan. b. 10 Dec 1924 g. Stepanavan. C.ESC '55 Psych. Inst, Georgian Acad. of Sci, USSR. SR. TCHR, Russian Tchr. Trng. Inst, ul. Amiriana 28, Erevan. Teaching, research, professional writing; psychology of learning a language. F

GERD, Mrs. Maria A. ul. Durova 4, kv. 1, Moscow I-90. b. 1924. Diploma '49 Moscow Univ, USSR. SCI. DIRECTOR, Durov's Corner. Research, administration, editorial; zoo-psychology, taming and training animals. F

GODYNA, Cand. Educ. Sci. Mitrofan. ul. Institutskaia 28, kv. 3, Lvov. b. 17 June 1892 selo Alekseevka, Poltavskaia obl. C.ESC '31, Kharkov, USSR. LECTURER, Chair of Educ. and Psych, Univ, ul. Universitetskaia, g. Lvov. Teaching, educational psychology, research; history of psychology in Ukraine. M

GOLDBERG, Cand. Educ. Sci, Mrs. Avgusta M. ul. Malo-Vasilkovskaia 33, kv. 28, Kiev. b. 12 Apr 1913 Kiev. C.ESC '45 Kiev Univ, USSR. HEAD, Sect. of Special Psych, Ukrainian Psych. Inst, ul. Lenina 10, Kiev. Member: USSR Socy. of Psych'ts. Research, educational and applied psychology; thinking and speech. F

GOLNEVA, Mrs. Valentina A. Kooperativnaia 8, kv. 10, Cheboksary. b. 22 May 1925. Grad. Tchr. Trng. Inst, Saratov, USSR. SR. TCHR, Chuvashian Tchr. Trng. Inst, ul. K. Marxa, Cheboksary. Member: Socy. of Propagating Polit. and Sci. Knowledge. Teaching, educational psychology. F

GONOBOLIN, Cand. Educ. Sci. Fiodor N. Peschanaia 40/1, kv. 296, Moscow D-80. b. 4 June 1901 Novgorod. C.ESC '49 Psych. Inst, Acad. of Educ. Sci, Moscow, USSR. SR. SCI. WRKR, Psych. Inst, Acad. of Educ. Sci, Mokhovaia 9, Moscow. Research, teaching, professional writing; memory and learning, abilities. M

GORBACH, Cand. Educ. Sci, Mrs. Maria S. Voroshilova 32, Cherkassy obl. b. 28 July 1921. C.ESC '53 Kiev State Univ, USSR. LECTURER, Chair of Educ, Cherkassy Tchr. Trng. Inst, ul. Karla Marxa 24, Cherkassy. Teaching, research, educational psychology. F

GORDON, Cand. Educ. Sci, Lect, Mrs. Elena. 22 ul. Barachnaia 10, kv. 164, Kharkov. b. 3 Sept 1903 Yaroslavl. C.ESC '49 Psych. Inst, Acad. of Educ. Sci, Moscow, USSR. LECTURER, Kharkov Tchr. Trng. Inst, ul. Artema 29, Kharkov. Teaching, research; perception and memory. F

GORFUNKEL, Cand. Educ. Sci. Pavel. ul. Trud. 60, kv. 8, Ishevsk, Udmurtskaia. b. 27 Oct 1923 Leningrad. C.ESC '53 Psych. Inst, Acad. of Educ. Sci, Moscow, USSR. DEAN, Fac. of Phys. Trng. and Sports, Udmurt Tchr. Trng. Inst, Krasnogeroiski 69, Izhevsk, Udmurt. Teaching, research, administration, vocational and educational guidance; psychology of teaching, personality and motivation. M

GOZOVA, Cand. Educ. Sci, Mrs. Alexandra P. Trekhprudny per. 11/13, kv. 168, Moscow. b. 18 Aug 1923 Zhitomirskaia obl, g. Luginy. C.ESC '52 Tchr. Trng. Inst, Moscow, USSR. JR. SCI. WRKR, Defectology Inst, Acad. of Educ. Sci, Pogodinskaia 8, Moscow. Research, applied psychology, teaching; memory, perception, teaching methods. F

GRIGOLAVA, Cand. Educ. Sci. Vladimir V. ul. Melikishvili 6, kv. 6, Tbilisi. b. 22 Dec 1920 Kutaisi. C.ESC '56, USSR. JR. SCI. WRKR, Inst. of Psych, after Uznadze, Dzhavakhishvili 1, Tbilisi. Research, educational psychology; contrast illusion and the problem of fixed concepts. M

GUCHAS, Lect. Alfonsas. ul. Pervazhos 4-1, Vilnius. b. 4 Dec 1907 volost Salochai, der. Vidugiriai. Diploma '37 Univ. after Vituat the Great, Kaunas, Lithua. HEAD, Chair of Educ. and Psych, Vilnius Univ, ul. Stuokos-Guceviciaus 5, Vilnius. Teaching, research, administration; perception, thinking, psychology of art. M

GUREVICH, Prof. Lazar I. prospekt Pravdy 7, kv. 55, Kharkov. b. 18 Aug 1894 mestechko Koman, byv. Kovenskoi gubernii. Professor '36 Kharkov Univ, USSR. HEAD, Chair of Educ. and Psych, Kharkov Univ, Universitetskaia 23, Kharkov; DIRECTOR, Central Science Library. Teaching, research; psychical peculiarities and personality. M

GURIANOV, Cand. Educ. Sci. Evgeni V. 7 Rostovski per. 10, kv. 6, Moscow G-117. b. 18 Feb 1889 selo Pomary, Mariiskaia USSR. C.ESC '38 Moscow Tchr. Trng. Inst. after Lenin, USSR. HEAD, Lab. of Labor Psych, Inst, Acad. of Educ. Sci, Mokhovaia 9, Moscow. Research, applied psychology, professional writing; psychology of training. M

GURIANOVA, Mrs. Evdokiia Y. Kommunisticheskaia 78-a, kv. 1, Joshkar-Ola. b. 26 Aug 1926. SR. TCHR, Chair of Educ, Marpedinstitut, Mariiski Tchr. Trng. Inst, Joshkar-Ola. Teaching, research, professional writing; thinking, temperament, family education. F

IAROSHCHUK, Cand. Educ. Sci, Lect, Mrs. Valentina. ul. Ostrovidova 75, kv. 10, Odessa. b. 27 July 1911. c.esc '51 Psych. Inst, Acad. of Educ. Sci, Moscow, ussr. lecturer, Chair of Psych, Odessa Tchr. Trng. Inst. for Foreign Languages, ul. Pastera 42, Odessa. Teaching, research; psychology of school teaching, habits and interests. F

IBRAGIMBEKOV, Cand. Med. Sci, Lect. Fuad. Kubinskaia 33, Baku 2. b. 16 Dec 1901. cm.sc '46 Baku, ussr; c.esc '38 Ministry of Educ, Azerbaijan, ussr. lect. in psych, Azerbaijanian Tchr. Trng. Inst. after M. F. Akhundova, Plukhina 205, Baku. Teaching, research, consulting, psychiatric practice; psychology of teaching a second language. M

IBRAGIMOVA, Cand. Educ. Sci, Mrs. Railia N. ul. K. Marxa 44, kv. 22, Kazan. b. 22 Dec 1912. c.esc '53, ussr. lecturer, Chair of Educ. and Psych, Kazan Tchr. Trng. Inst, ul. Levo-Bulochnaia 44, Kazan. Teaching, research, editorial; projective techniques. F

ILTSINA, Cand. Educ. Sci, Mrs. Tamara K. per. Krylova 5, kv. 20, Leningrad 11. b. 8 Sept 1902. c.esc '51 Leningrad, ussr. acting lect, Leningrad Univ, Universitetskaia nab. 7/9, Leningrad. Teaching, research. F

ILYINA, Cand. Educ. Sci, Mrs. Valentina I. Mozhaiskoe shosse, 55/57, kv. 39, Moskovskaia obl, Kuntsevo. b. 29 Jan 1920 Kazan. c.esc '50 Moscow Tchr. Trng. Inst. after Lenin, ussr. lecturer, Chair of Psych, Moscow Tchr. Trng. Inst. of Foreign Languages, ul. Metrostroevskaia 38, Moscov. Teaching, research, editorial; psychology of mind and speech. F

ISTOMINA, Cand. Educ. Sci, Mrs. Zinaida M. Nizhniaia Pervomaiskaia 54, kv. 5, Moscow E-203. b. 17 June 1917 Arkhangelsk. c.esc '47, ussr. sr. sci. wrkr, Lab. of Educ. Psych. and Speech, Psych. Inst, Acad. of Educ. Sci, Mokhovaia 9, Moscow. Teaching, research, applied and educational psychology, professional writing. F

IVANOV, Cand. Educ. Sci. Georgi P. Pedinstitut, ul. Lenina 78, Blagoveshchensk. b. 8 May 1896. c.esc '40 Moscow Tchr. Trng. Inst. after Libknecht, ussr. lecturer, Tchr. Trng. Inst. Teaching, research. M

IVANOV, Cand. Educ. Sci. Vladimir G. ul. Tavricheskaia 7, kv. 16, Leningrad S-15. b. 23 Mar 1922 Saratov. c.esc Leningrad Univ. after Zhdanov, ussr. assistant, Chair of Educ, Leningrad Univ, Leningrad. Teaching, research, educational psychology; interests of an individual . M

IVANOVA, Cand. Educ. Sci, Lect, Mrs. Veronika S. ul. Dolgireva 60, kv. 15, Omsk. b. 6 May 1924 Kokchetav, Kazakh. c.esc '51 Leningrad Tchr. Trng. Inst. after Gertsen, ussr. lecturer, Chair of Educ, Omsk Tchr. Trng. Inst, Internatsionalnaia 2, Omsk. Teaching, research, educational psychology; thinking, abilities. F

IVASHCHENKO, Cand. Educ. Sci, Lect. Fyodor I. n/k ul. Dzerzhinskogo 120, kv. 1, Stavropol. b. 20 Feb 1920 khutor Filevo-Sorochin, Solotonishsky District, Poltava Region. Grad. '42 Tchr. Trng. Inst, Nalchik ussr. acting head, Chair of Educ. and Psych, Stavropol State Tchr. Trng. Inst. of Foreign Languages, ul. Kagonovicha 20, Stavropol. Teaching, research; study of speech and conditioned reflexes. M

KADIROV, Aladdin A. ul. Trudovaia 9, Kirovabad, Azerbajan. b. 1929 Akstafinski raion, Azerbajan. sr. tchr, Tchr. Trng. Inst. after Zardabi, ploshchad Kirova 53, Kirovabad. Teaching, research; memory, thinking. M

KADOCHKIN, Cand. Educ. Sci. Lev N. ul. Iubileinaia 60, kv. 4, Kuibyshev. b. 1 Feb 1921. c.esc '54 Psych. Inst, Acad. of Educ. Sci, Moscow, ussr. asst. dir, Kuibyshev Tchr. Trng. Inst, Kuibyshev. Teaching, administration; methods of determining personality, habit formation. M

KALMYKOVA, Cand. Educ. Sci, Mrs. Zinaida I. N. Peschanaia, kor. 86, kv. 32, Moscow D-252. b. 1914 Rostov-na-Donu. c.esc '49 Psych. Inst, Acad. of Educ. Sci, ussr. sr. sci. wrkr, Psych. Inst, Acad. of Educ. Sci, Mokhovaia 9, Moscow. Research, applied psychology; psychology of learning. F

KAPLAN, Cand. Educ. Sci, Mrs. Lidia I. Maiakovskogo 40, kv. 43, Magnitogorsk. b. 8 July 1924. c.esc '53 Psych. Inst, Acad. of Educ. Sci, Moscow, ussr. tchr. of psych, Magnitogorsk Tchr. Trng. Inst, Pr. Pushkina 21, Magnitogorsk. Teaching, research, educational psychology. F

KAPLANOVA, Cand. Educ. Sci, Mrs. Sophia G. ul. Kachalova 14, kv. 8, Moscow G-69. b. 17 July 1924 Moscow. c.esc '50 Psych. Inst, Acad. of Educ. Sci, Moscow, ussr. jr. sci. wrkr, Inst. of Theory and History of the Arts, ussr Acad. of Arts, ul. Kropotkina 21, Moscow. Research; psychology of art. F

KARANDEEVA, Mrs. Olga S. Chernyshevsky per. 1, kv. 1, Moscow A-55. b. 24 Mar 1908. jr. sci. wrkr, Psych. Inst, Acad. of Educ. Sci, Mokhovaia 9, Moscow. Research, educational psychology, professional writing. F

KARPENKO, Cand. Educ. Sci, Lect. Nikolai M. pl. Sverdlova 9, kv. 19, g. Shuia, Ivanovskaia obl. b. 1 May 1907. c.esc Leningrad, ussr. director, Shuia Tchr. Trng. Inst, Ivanovskaia obl. Member: Leningrad Psych. Socy. Teaching, research, administration; perception, imagination, memory. M

KARPOV, Cand. Educ. Sci. Ivan V. ul. Piatnitskaia 12, kv. 14, Moscow V-35. b. 1 May 1890 der. Zevnevo, Moskovskoi g. C.ESC '38, USSR. HEAD, Foreign Languages Sect, Teaching Methods Inst, Acad. of Educ. Sci, Lobkovski per. 5/16, Moscow. Research on methods of teaching foreign languages, administration, professional writing; development of mind and language, psychology of teaching. M

KARPOVA, Cand. Educ. Sci, Mrs. Sophia N. Solianka 8, kv. 18, Moscow. b. 4 Nov 1920 g. Korotoiak, Voronezhskaia obl. C.ESC '54 Moscow Univ. USSR. TEACHER, Chair of Psych, Moscow Univ, Mokhovaia 11, Moscow. Teaching, research, applied and educational psychology; development of thinking in children. F

KECHKHUASHVILI, Cand. Educ. Sci. Georgi. ul. Perovskoi 19, kv. 10, Tbilisi. b. 24 June 1920. C.ESC '51 Tbilisi Inst. of Psych. after Uznadze, USSR. ASSISTANT, Chair of Psych, Tbilisi Univ, Universitetskaia 1, Tbilisi. Teaching, research, student; psychology of music and personality. M

KEZHERADZE, Cand. Educ. Sci, Mrs. Elena. ul. Engelsa 54, Tbilisi. b. 16 Jan 1911. C.ESC '50 Inst. of Psych. after Uznadze, USSR. SR. SCI. WRKR, Psych. Inst. after Uznadze, Dzhavakhishvili 1, Tbilisi. Research; attention in the pre-school age child. F

KHACHAPURIDZE, Cand. Educ. Sci, Lect. Barnab. ul. Kazbekskaia 41, Tbilisi. b. 11 Nov 1905. C.ESC '38 Tbilisi State Univ. after Stalin, USSR. LECTURER, Chair of Psych, Tbilisi Univ, Universitetskaia 1, Tbilisi. Teaching, research on pre-school education, educational psychology; psychology of concept formation. M

KHARSHILADZE, Cand. Educ, Sci. Joseph. ul. Engelsa 54, Tbilisi. b. 3 Mar 1906. C.ESC '50 USSR Inst. of Educ, USSR. LECTURER, Gori Tchr. Trng. Inst. after Baratashvili, ul. Chavchavadze 56, Gori. Teaching, research. M

KHODZHAVA, Dr. Educ, Prof. Zosim. ul. Merkviladze 4-v, Tbilisi. b. 2 Jan 1904 Kutaisi. ED.D '51 Psych. Inst. after Uznadze, Tbilisi, USSR. HEAD, Sect. of Genl. Psych, Psych. Inst. after Uznadze, ul. Dzhavakhishvili 1, Tbilisi. Research, teaching, editorial; psychology of needs, psychology of teaching. M

KHOMENKO, Cand. Educ. Sci, Lect, Mrs. Kseniia. pl. Rudneva 32, kv. 27, Kharkov. b. 12 July 1905. C.ESC '39 Moscow Univ, Kharkov, USSR. LECTURER, Chair of Educ. and Psych, Kharkov Tchr. Trng. Inst. Teaching, research; perception and thinking. F

KHOPRENINOVA, Cand. Educ. Sci, Lect, Mrs. Nina G. ul. Pushkina 18, Chkalov. b. Mar 1925. C.ESC '53 Psych. Inst, Acad. of Educ. Sci, Moscow, USSR. LECTURER, Chair of Educ. and Psych, Chkalov Tchr. Trng. Inst, ul. Sovietskaia 19, Chkalov. Teaching, research; psychology of the blind. F

KHRAMOVSKIKH, Mrs. Agniia P. 1 proezd Shaumiana 4, Samarkand. b. 1890. SR. TCHR, Uzbek St. Univ, bulvar im. Gorkogo, Samarkand. Teaching, research; methods of determining personality. F

KHUNDADZE, Cand. Educ. Sci, Mrs. Fatma. ul. Chonkadze 5, Tbilisi. b. 17 Jan 1895 Kutaisi. C.ESC '50 Psych. Inst. after Uznadze, Tbilisi; PH.D '25 Munich Univ, Ger. SR. SCI. WRKR, Psych. Inst. after Uznadze, ul. Dzhavakhishvili 1, Tbilisi. Research, educational psychology, teaching; child psychology, genetic psychology, psychology of teaching. F

KINTSURASHVILI, Cand. Educ. Sci. Apolon. ul. Barnova 46, Tbilisi. b. 24 Apr 1907. C.ESC '54 Inst. of Psych. after Uznadze, USSR. SR. SCI. WRKR, Inst. of Psych. after Uznadze, ul. Dzhavakhishvili 1, Tbilisi. Research; general psychology, concept formation and imagination. M

KIREENKO, Cand. Educ. Sci, Lect. Vasili. ul. Sovetskaia 1, kv. 35, Stavropol Kavkazski. b. 9 May 1910. C.ESC '46, USSR. HEAD, Chair of Educ. and Psych, Stavropol Tchr. Trng. Inst. of Foreign Languages. Teaching, research; psychology of abilities. M

KISLIUK, Cand. Educ. Sci, Mrs. Galina A. ul. Gorkogo 6, kv. 250, Moscow. b. 4 Dec 1926 Moscow. C.ESC '54 Psych. Inst, Acad. of Educ. Sci, USSR. JR. SCI. WRKR, Inst. of Theory and History of Educ, Acad. of Educ. Sci, Lobkovski per 5/16, Moscow. Research, professional writing, educational psychology; thinking. F

KITAEV, Cand. Educ. Sci. Nikolai N. Dokuchaev per. 17, kv. 1, Moscow I-53. b. 26 Dec 1892 Bolkhov. C.ESC '54 Psych. Inst, Acad. of Educ. Sci. Moscow. USSR. SR. SCI. WRKR, Teaching Methods Inst, Acad. of Educ. Sci, Lobkovsky per. 5/16, Moscow. Teaching, research, professional writing; language and thinking. M

KLYCHNIKOVA, Cand. Educ. Sci, Lect, Mrs. Zinaida I. ul. Surikova 3, kv. 1, Moscow D-80. b. 10 Oct 1920 Moscow. C.ESC '49 Moscow Tchr. Trng. Inst. after Lenin, Moscow, USSR. LECTURER, Chair of Psych, First Moscow Tchr. Trng. Inst. for Foreign Languages, Metrostroevskaia 38, Moscow. Teaching, research, professional writing; linguistic psychology. F

KOCHKINA, Cand. Educ. Sci, Lect, Mrs. Alexandra F. ul. 17 Sentiabria 23, kv. 7,

Lutsk. b. 22 Apr 1914 selo Tiugash, Molotovskaia obl. c.esc '50 Psych. Inst, Acad. of Educ. Sci, Moscow, ussr. LECTURER, Chair of Educ. and Psych, Lutsk Tchr. Trng, Inst. after L. Ukrainka, Lutsk. Teaching, educational psychology, research; character and temperament. F

KOMISSARCHIK, Cand. Educ. Sci, Mrs. Keilia A. ul. Pervomaiskaia 9, kv. 19, Gomel. b. 1904. c.esc '55 Moscow Inst. of Psych, Moscow, ussr. SR. TCHR, Tchr. Trng. Inst, ul. Kirova 167, Gomel. Teaching, research; memory. F

KOMM, Cand. Educ. Sci, Mrs. Anna. 1 Akademichesky proezd 19, kv. 11, Moscow V-134. b. 22 Sept 1904. c.esc '40 Leningrad State Tchr. Trng. Inst. after Gertsen, ussr. LECTURER, Chair of Psych, Moscow Univ, Mokhovaia 11, Moscow. Teaching, research; memory, thinking, intellect. F

KORM, Cand. Educ. Sci, Mrs. Tatiana A. ul. Kirova 5, pos. Novo-Khovrino, Moskovskaia obl. b. 16 Dec 1910 g. Chaplygin. c.esc '42 Moscow Tchr. Trng. Inst. after Potemkin, ussr. LECTURER, Chair of Psych, Moscow Tchr. Trng. Inst. after Potemkin, Davydovski per. 4, Moscow. Teaching, research; memory, psychology of teaching. F

KORNILOV, Dr. Educ, Prof. Konstantin N. ul. Vereshchagina 16, kv. 1, Moscow D-80. b. 9 Mar 1879 Tiumen. ED.D, Moscow, ussr. PROFESSOR, Chair of Educ. and Psych, Moscow Tchr. Trng. Inst, M. Pirogovskaia 1, Moscow. Member: Psych. Socy. of the AESC. Teaching, research, educational psychology; personality theory. M

KOSMA, Cand. Educ. Sci, Lect, Mrs. Tatiana V. ul. Voroshilova 36, kv. 7, Kiev. b. 30 Nov 1905 Berdiansk. c.esc '47 Kiev Univ, ussr. LECTURER, Chair of Psych, Kiev Univ, Kiev. Teaching, research; development of thought. F

KOSSOV, Cand. Educ. Sci. Boris B. per. Obukha 3, kv. 59, Moscow B-120. b. 25 June 1929 g. Molotov. c.esc '55 Psych. Inst, Acad. of Educ. Sci, Moscow, ussr. JR. SCI. WRKR, Psych. Inst, Acad. of Educ. Sci, Mokhovaia 9, Moscow. Research, professional writing, applied psychology; human types of higher nervous activity, perception, psychic activity and signal systems. M

KOSTIUK, Cand. Educ. Sci, Prof. Grigori S. ul. Saksaganskogo 34, Kiev. b. 23 Nov 1899 s. Mogilno, Odesskaia obl. c.esc '29 Kiev, ussr. DIRECTOR, Inst. of Psych, Kiev, ul. Lenina 10; TCHR. of PSYCH, Kiev Tchr. Trng. Inst; ED. BD, Voprosy Psikhologi. Member: Psych. Socy. of the AESC. Research, teaching, administration; thinking, evolution and education. M

KOSTOMAROVA, Cand. Sci, Mrs. Nadezhda M. Arbat 9, kv. 3, Moscow G-19. b. 19 Mar 1895. c.sc '37 Moscow, ussr. SR. SCI. WRKR, Psych. Inst, Acad. of Educ. Sci, Mokhovaia 9, Moscow. Research, consulting, testing, clinical analysis; experimental psychology, thinking. F

KOTLIAROV, Vladimir. Tchr. Trng. Inst, Novosvetlovskaia 2, Voroshilovgrad. b. 28 July 1903, Nezhin. SR. TCHR, Tchr. Trng. Inst. Teaching, educational psychology; psychological analysis of lessons, sport psychology. M

KOTLIAROVA, Cand. Educ. Sci, Mrs. Liudmila I. ul. Krymskaia 7, kv. 4, Lvov. b. Dec 1905. c.esc '49 Psych. Inst, Acad. of Educ. Sci, ussr. LECTURER, Tchr. Trng. Inst, ul. Zelionaia 8-10, Lvov. Teaching, research; perception. F

KOVALIOV, Dr. Educ, Prof. Alexander G. Kuznetsovskaia 18, kv. 83, Leningrad. b. 6 June 1913 g. Novosil, Orlovskaia obl. ED.D '54 Moscow Psych. Inst, ussr. PROFESSOR, Chair of Psych, Leningrad Univ, Universitetskaia nab. 7, Leningrad. Teaching, research, administration; temperament, character, will, emotions. M

KOZLOV, Cand. Sci, Lect. Semyon F. Tikhvinskii per. 11, kv. 42, Moscow A-55. b. 5 June 1897. c.sc '45 Moscow State Tchr. Trng. Inst. after Lenin, ussr. LECTURER, Chair of Psych, Moscow State Tchr. Trng. Inst. after Lenin, ussr. govskaia 1, Moscow; ED. BD, Doshkolnoie Vospitanie. Teaching, research, editorial. M

KRASILSHCHIKOVA, Cand. Educ. Sci, Lect, Mrs. Dobrusia I. ul. Varfolomeeva 193/51, kv. 303, Rostov-na-Donu. b. 28 Sept 1906 Vitebskaia obl. c.esc '40 Rostov-na-Donu Tchr. Trng. Inst, ussr. LECTURER, Chair of Educ. and Psych, Rostov-na-Donu Tchr. Trng. Inst, ul. Engelsa 37, Rostov-na-Donu. Teaching, research; memory. F

KREVNEVICH, Cand. Educ. Sci, Mrs. Valentina V. ul. Chaplygina 15, kv. 170, Moscow. b. 14 Jan 1924. c.esc '53, Moscow, ussr. ASSISTANT, Chair of Psych, Moscow Tchr. Trng. Inst, M. Pirogovskaia 1, Moscow. Teaching, research, educational psychology; choice of profession, psychology of labor. F

KRUGLIAK, Cand. Educ. Sci. Mordukh. Kommunalnaia 2, Nezhin, Chernigov Region. b. 11 Sept 1898. c.esc '48 Kiev Univ, ussr; Lect. '51 Ministry of Higher Educ, ussr. LECTURER, Chair of Educ, Nezhin Tchr. Trng. Inst. after N.V. Gogol; HEAD of EDUC. SECT, Town Socy. for Popularizing Polit. and Cultural knowledge. Teaching, research; psychological problems of teaching, formation of ideas and images. M

KRUTETSKI, Cand. Educ. Sci. Vadim A. ul.

Studencheskaia 22, kv. 1, Moscow G-151. b. 17 Dec 1917 Moscow. c.esc '50 Psych. Inst, Moscow, ussr. sr. sci. wrkr, Psych. Inst, Acad. of Educ. Sci, Mokhovaia 9, Moscow. Research, teaching; character, abilities, education of personality. M

KRYLOV, Cand. Educ. Sci, Lect. Alexei N. ul. Minina 40, kv. 6, g. Gorki. b. 10 Oct 1900 s. Teplovo, Arzamasskaia obl. c.esc '50 Leningrad Inst. of Educ, ussr. lecturer, Chair of Psych, Tchr. Trng. Inst, ul. Ulianova 1, g. Gorki. Teaching, research, editorial; psychology of pupils' work. M

KRYLOV, Cand. Educ. Sci. Nikolai I. 4 Lugovoi per 5, kv. 1, Moscow G-59. b. 9 Nov 1921. c.esc '51, ussr. jr. sci. wrkr, Psych. Inst, Acad. of Educ. Sci, Mokhovaia 9, Moscow. Research, educational psychology; methods of studying students' personality. M

KULIKOV, Cand. Educ. Sci. Vladimir. N ul. Molotova 65, Ivanovo. b. 25 Sept 1922. c.esc '52 Psych. Inst, Acad. of Educ. Sci, Moscow, ussr. lecturer, Chair of Educ. and Psych, Ivanovo Tchr. Trng. Inst, ul. Ermaka 37, Ivanovo. Teaching, research, educational psychology; psychophysical problems, comprehension and attention processes. M

KURTENKOVA, Cand. Educ. Sci, Mrs. Valentina. ul. Karla Marxa 36, Arzamas-Oblastnoi. b. 7 Nov 1926 Tutaevski r-n, selo Terekhovo, Yaroslavskaia obl. c.esc '54 Moscow Tchr. Trng. Inst. after Lenin, ussr. sr. tchr, Tchr. Trng. Inst, Arzamas-Oblastnoi. Teaching, research; methods of investigating personality. F

KUSTKOV, Cand. Educ. Sci. Sergei I. ul. Grazhdanskaia 52, kv. 17, Saransk, Mordovian ssr. b. 10 July 1892. c.esc '49 ussr. lecturer, Chair of Educ. and Psych, Mordavian Tchr. Trng. Inst. Teaching. M

KUVSHINOV, Cand. Educ. Sci. Nikolai I. pr. Frunze 63, kv. 1, Tomsk. b. 25 July 1923 Muromtsevski r-n, d. Plotbishche, Omskaia obl. c.esc '54 Psych. Inst, Acad. of Educ. Sci, Moscow, ussr. sr. tchr, Chair of Educ, Tchr. Trng. Inst, Kievskaia 60, Tomsk. Teaching, research; psychology of labor and vocational training. M

LADYGINA-KOTS, Dr. Biol, Mrs. Nadezhda N. Darwin Museum, M. Pirogovskaia 1, Moscow G-21. b. 6 May 1889 Penza. Dr. of Biol. '49 Moscow, ussr. sr. sci. wrkr, Psych. Sect, Inst. of Philos, ussr Acad. of Sci, Volkhonka 14, Moscow. Research, editorial, teaching; psychology of animals. F

LARIN, Cand. Educ. Sci. Andrei P. ul. Sibirtseva 22, kv. 1, Velikie Luki. b. 8 Nov 1905. c.esc '54, ussr. acting lect, Veli-

kolukski Tchr. Trng. Inst, ul. Timiriazeva 1, Velikie Luki. Teaching, research, professional writing; problems of character. M

LEBEDINSKY, Dr. Educ, Prof. Mark S. Bolshoi Afanasievsky per 41, kv. 2, Arbat, Moscow. b. 28 Jan 1894. ed.d '39 Moscow, ussr. head, Lab. of Clin. Psych, Psychother. and Pathol, Inst. of Psychiat, ussr Min. of Hlth, Zagorodnoie Shosse 2, Moscow. Research, clinical analysis, psychotherapy; movement, thinking, perception.M

LEITES, Cand. Educ. Sci. Natan S. ul. Razina 24, kv. 20, Moscow. b. 26 June 1918 Dnepropetrovsk. c.esc '48 Psych. Inst, Acad. of Educ. Sci, Moscow, ussr. sr. sci. wrkr, Psych. Inst, Acad. of Educ. Sci, Mokhovaia 9, Moscow. Research; individual differences. M

LEONTIEV, Dr. Educ, Prof. Alexey N. ul. Novopeschanaia 24, kv. 17, Moscow D-252. b. 5 Feb 1903 Moscow. ed.d '24 Moscow Univ, ussr. head, Chair of Psych, Moscow Univ, Mokhovaia 11, Moscow. Member: aesc Presidium. Research, teaching, administration; psychology of conscience, theory of psychical development, psychology of teaching. M

LEVITOV, Dr. Educ, Prof. Nikolai D. Pochtovy iashchik 371, Moscow K 9. b. 17 Apr 1890 Riazanskaia gubernia, g. Ranenburg. ed.d, Relig. Acad, Petrograd. professor, Chair of Psych, Moscow St. Tchr. Trng. Inst. after Lenin. Research, teaching, educational psychology; psychology of character, child psychology. M

LEZHNEV, Cand. Educ. Sci, Lect. Vladimir T. ul. Pushkina 1, kv. 4, Stavropol Kraevoi. b. 1908 Baku. c.esc '37 Moscow Tchr. Trng. Inst. after Lenin, Moscow, ussr. lecturer, Chair of Educ. and Psych, Stavropol Tchr. Trng. Inst. Teaching, research, professional writing; general psychology, thinking. M

LISINA, Cand. Educ. Sci, Mrs. Maia I. Begovaia 1-2, korp. 10, kv. 8, Moscow D-284. b. 20 Apr 1919 Kharkov. c.esc '56 Psych. Inst, Acad. of Educ. Sci, Moscow, ussr. jr. sci wrkr, Psych. Inst, Acad. of Educ. Sci, Mokhovaia 9, Moscow. Research, educational psychology, professional writing; vocational training, free movements, habits. F

LIUBLINSKAIA, Cand. Educ. Sci, Mrs. Anna A. ul. Sablinskaia 13/15, kv. 28, Leningrad 3. b. 18 June 1903 Grodno. c.esc '46 Tchr. Trng. Inst. after Gertsen, Leningrad, ussr. lecturer, Chair of Psych, Leningrad Tchr. Trng. Inst. after Gertsen. Teaching, research, editing; child psychology, development of mind and speech. F

LOMOV, Cand. Educ. Sci. Boris F. ul. Serpukhovskaia 30, kv. 13, Leningrad. b. 28 Jan 1927 Gorky. c.esc '56 Leningrad

Inst. of Educ, nab. Kutuzova 8, Leningrad. Research, educational psychology; technological aptitudes.   M

LUBOVSKY, Cand. Educ. Sci. Vladimir I. ul. Kolkhoznaia 33, pos. Kraskovo, Ukhtomsky r-n, Moskovskaia obl. b. 15 Dec 1923 Vitebsk, Byelorussian SSR. C.ESC '56 Moscow Univ, USSR. JR. SCI. WRKR, Res. Inst. of Defectology, Acad. of Educ. Sci, ul. Pogodinskaia 8, Moscow. Research, testing, clinical analysis, teaching; physiology of higher nervous system, auditory perception.   M

LURIA, Dr. Med, Dr. Phil, Prof. Alexander Romanowich. 13 Frunse, Moscow. b. 16 July 1902 Kazan. MD '37 Moscow Med. Inst, USSR. PROFESSOR, Psych. Dept, Moscow Univ, DEPT. HEAD, Defectology Inst, Acad. of Pedagogical Sci, Pogodinskaia 8, Moscow. Member: USSR Psych. Assn, Assn. of Neurologists and Psychiatrists. Research, teaching, editorial; speech psychology, problems of localization of functions, physiology and pathology of higher nervous system.   M

MAKAROV, Cand. Educ. Sci. Ivan O. ul. Sadovo-Sukharevskaia 6/37, kv. 3, Moscow. b. 9 Oct 1891. C.ESC '38 Moscow Tchr. Trng. Inst, USSR. Retired.   M

MAKHLAKH, Cand. Educ. Sci, Mrs. Elena S. ul. Chernyshevskogo 19, kv. 7, Moscow. b. 25 Dec 1928 Moscow. C.ESC '56 . JR. SCI. WRKR, Educ. Lab, Psych. Inst, Acad. of Educ. Sci, Mokhovaia 9, Moscow. Research, teaching; personality formation.   F

MAKLIAK, Nikolai M. ul. Sadovaia 69, Zaporozhie. b. 18 Oct 1921, Lebedinski r-n, s. Bishkin, Sumskaia obl. TEACHER, Tchr. Trng. Inst, Zaporozhie. Teaching psychology and logics, research; psychology of teaching arithmetic, thinking and speech.   M

MAKOVELSKY, Dr. Phil, Prof. Alexander. ul. leit. Shmidta 8, kv. 76, Baku. b. 22 July 1884 Grodno. HEAD, Chair of Logics and Psych, Azerbaijan Univ. after Kirov, Kommunisticheskaia 6, Baku. Teaching, research; history of psychology.   M

MALKOV, Nikolai E. ul. Borisoglebskaia 17, kv. 18, Kiev. b. 29 Nov 1918. SR. SCI. WRKR, Psych. Inst, ul. Lenina 10, Kiev. Member: The Psych. Socy. Research; temperament.   M

MALTSEVA, Cand. Educ. Sci, Mrs. Klavdiia P. Inst. of Psych, Mokhovaia 9, Moscow K-9. b. 1910. C.ESC '48 Psych. Inst, Moscow, USSR. SR. SCI. WRKR, Psych. Inst, Acad. of Educ. Sci. Research, professional writing; memory development. F

MANUILENKO, Cand. Educ, Sci, Mrs. Zinaida V. ul. Chaikovskogo 10/14, kv. k, Moscow. b. 1906. C.ESC '49 Moscow, USSR. TEACHER, Moscow Correspondence Tchr. Trng. Inst.

Member: USSR Socy. of Psych'ts. Teaching, research, editorial; study and teaching of pre-school children.   F

MASLENNIKOV, Cand. Educ. Sci. Mikhail. ul. Lenina 86, kv. 22, Voronezh. b. 19 Nov 1899. LECTURER, Chair of Educ. and Psych, Voronezh St. Tchr. Trng. Inst, Voronezh. Teaching, research, professional writing.   M

MATIUKHINA, Cand. Educ. Sci, Mrs. Margarita V. Sovnarkomskaia 89, Stalingrad. b. 3 Apr 1928 Stalingrad. C.ESC '54 Psych. Inst, Acad. of Educ. Sci, Moscow, USSR. SR. TCHR, Stalingrad Tchr. Trng. Inst. after Serafimovich. Teaching, research; development of work habits.   F

MATIUSHINA, Cand. Educ. Sci, Mrs. Nataliia M. ul. Kuibysheva 10, Tambov. b. 6 Dec 1920 der. Darovoie, Moskovskaia obl. C.ESC '47 Moscow Tchr. Trng. Inst. after Lenin, Tambov. LECTURER, Chair of Psych, Tambov Tchr. Trng. Inst. Teaching, research; personality.   F

MATLIN, Cand. Educ. Sci. Efim. 1 Dovatora 26/9, blok 3, kv. 21, Vitebsk. b. 4 July 1905. C.ESC '45 Moscow Tchr. Trng. Inst. after Lenin, Vitebsk. HEAD, Chair of Psych. and Educ, Vitebsk Tchr. Trng. Inst, ul. Pushkina 3, Vitebsk. Teaching, research; memory, personality.   M

MCHEDLISHVILI, Georgi. ul. Varaziskhevi 7, Tbilisi. b. 10 Jan 1925. JR. SCI. WRKR, Psych. Inst. after Uznadze, ul. Dzhavakhishvili 1, Tbilisi. Research; concept formation.   M

MDIVANI, Cand. Educ. Sci, Mrs. Ketevan. ul. Kipiani 13, Tbilisi. b. 8 Oct 1902, Kutaisi. C.ESC '46 Inst. of Psych, GSSR Acad. of Sci, Moscow. SR. SCI. WRKR, Psych. Inst. after Uznadze, ul. Dzhavakhishvili 1, Tbilisi. Research, professsional writing; space perception, thought processes in schizophrenia.   F

MEDELIAN, Cand. Educ. Sci. Grigori A. ul, Stalina 294, g. Osh, Kirgiziia. b. 19 Jan 1905 selo Vossiiatskoie, Nikolaevskaia obl. C.ESC '54 Moscow, USSR. HEAD, Chair of Educ. and Psych, Tchr. Trng. Inst, ul. Raboche-Dekhkanskaia 340, g. Osh, Kirgizskaia. Teaching, research, administration; psychology of thought.   M

MEIKSHAN, Cand. Educ. Sci. Isidor A. ul. Shkolnaia 11, kv. 3, Riga. b. 19 Nov 1900. C.ESC '49 Moscow Reg. Tchr. Trng. Inst, Riga, USSR. SR. SCI. WRKR, Inst. of Schools of the Min. of Educ. of Latvian SSR, ul. Valniu 2, Riga. Teaching, educational psychology, professional writing; thinking as a form of reflecting reality.   M

MEKHTIZADE, Cand. Educ. Sci. Zakhariia M. ul. Sovietskaia 21, Baku. b. 23 Mar 1913 Dzhebrailski r-n, selo Dashkesan, Azerbajan. C.ESC '53 Psych. Inst, Acad.

of Educ. Sci, Moscow, USSR. HEAD, Sect. of Educ. and Psych, Azerbajan Inst. of Educ, Kommunisticheskaia 11/13, Baku. Research, administration, professional writing; memory, thinking. M

MELLER, Cand. Educ. Sci, Mrs. Evgeniia N. Sredni Tishinski per. 4, kv. 3, Moscow D-56. b. 27 Dec 1902, Moscow. c.ESC '26 Psych. Inst, Acad. of Educ. Sci, Moscow. SR. SCI. WRKR, Psych. Inst, Acad. of Educ. Sci, Mokhovaia 9, Moscow. Research, professional writing; educational psychology. F

MENCHINSKAIA, Dr. Educ, Prof, Mrs. Natalia A. Novo-Peschanaia, korp. 86, kv, 40, Moscow. b. 15 Jan 1905 Yalta. ASST. DIR, Psych. Inst, Acad. of Educ. Sci. Mokhovaia 9, Moscow. Research, administration; psychology of teaching. F

MESHCHERIAKOV, Cand. Educ. Sci, A-lexander I. ul. Studencheskaia 32, kv. 175, Moscow G-165. b. 16 Dec 1923 Skopinskogo r-na, Riasanskoi oblasti, d. Chumenki. c.ESC '53 Psych. Inst, Acad. of Educ. Sci, USSR. SR. SCI. WRKR, Defectology Inst, Acad. of Educ. Sci, ul. Pogodinskaia 8, Moscow. Research, educational psychology; free behavior and its physiological mechanism. M

MIASISHCHEV, Dr. Med, Prof. Vladimir. Bolshoi Prosp, 98, kv, 20, Pet. Stor, Leningrad. b. 11 July 1893 Fridrikhshtadt, Latvia. MD '46 USSR. HEAD, Chair of Psych, Leningrad Univ, Universitetskair nab, 9, Vas. Ostrov, Leningrad. Research, consulting, clinical practice, teaching; personality and character. M

MIKULINSKAIA, Cand. Educ. Sci, Mrs. Maria Y. ul. Griboedova 27, kv. 3, Batumi. b. 26 Apr 1924 Kharkov. c.ESC '51 Psych. Inst, Acad. of Educ. Sci, USSR. SR. TCHR, Batumi Tchr. Trng. Inst. after Shota Rustaveli, Batumi. Teaching, research; temperament, attention, educational psychology. F

MILERIAN, Cand. Educ. Sci. Evgeni A. Brest-Litovskoe shosse 14, kv. 7, Kiev-62. b. 19 Apr 1913. c.ESC '54, USSR. HEAD, Sect. of Labor Psych. and Polytechnical Educ, Inst. of Psych, Lenina 10, Kiev. Teaching, research, educational psychology. M

MIRONENKO, Cand. Educ. Sci. Vladimir V. ul. Zhukovskogo 26, kv. 9, Krymskaia obl, Simferopol, UKSSR. b. 22 Dec 1918. c.ESC '54 Psych. Inst, Acad. of Educ. Sci, Moscow, USSR. DEAN, Physical Trng. Fac, Crimean Tchr. Trng. Inst. after M. V. Frunze, ul, Lenina 13, Simferopol; TEACHER, Tchr. Trng. Inst. after Lenin, Simferopol. Teaching, research, administration; sports psychology, character, abilities. M

MISTIUK, Cand. Educ. Sci, Lect, Mrs. Valeriia V. ul. Saksagonskogo 110, kv. 17, Kiev.

b. 21 Nov 1907 Nikolaev. c.ESC '47 Middle-Asian St. Univ, USSR. SR. SCI WRKR, Sect of Labor Psych, Kiev Inst. of Psych, Lenina 10, Kiev. Teaching, research, educational psychology. F

MKRTYCH, Cand. Educ. Sci. Mazmanian A. ul. Koskovskaia 31, kv. 21, Erevan, Armenian SSR. b. 22 Feb 1910. c.ESC '30, USSR. HEAD, Chair of Psych, Erevan Tchr. Trng. Inst, ul. Moskovskaia 5, Erevan. Member: Socy. of Psychotechnicians and Appl. Psych'ts, Socy of Psychiatrists and Neuropathologists. Teaching, research, professional writing. M

MOROZOVA, Cand. Educ. Sci, Mrs. Natalia G. Leningradskoie shosse 62, kv. 98, Moscow. b. 28 Aug 1906 Kharkov. c.ESC '44 Psych. Inst, Acad. of Educ. Sci, USSR. ASST. DIR, Defectology Inst, Acad. of Educ. Sci, Pogodinskaia 8, Moscow. Member: Socy of Psych'ts, Psychiatrists and Neuropathologists. Research, teaching, professional writing; speech and hearing psychopathology of children, psychology of pre-school child. F

MOSKALENKO, Cand. Educ. Sci. Konstantin A. ul. Grizodubovoi 8, kv. 1, Lipetsk obl. b. 3 June 1917. c.ESC '55 Psych. Inst, Acad. of Educ. Sci, Moscow, USSR. HEAD, Chair of Educ. and Psych, Lipetsk Tchr. Trng. Inst, Klubnaia pl. 1, Lipetsk 7. Teaching, research, educational psychology; teaching methods. M

MOTSAK, Anatoli M. Tchr. Trng. Inst. of Foreign Languages, ul. Krasnoarmeiskaia 73, Kiev. b. 16 July 1916, Poltavskaia obl, selo Glshkovo. Grad, Kiev Univ, USSR. SR. TCHR, Kiev St. Tchr. Trng. Inst. of Foreign Languages. Member: Ukranian Socy. of Propagating Polit. and Sci. Knowledge. Teaching, research, educational psychology; personality, history of psychology. M

MURZAKOVA, Cand. Educ. Sci, Lect, Mrs. Zoia N. ul. Sovetskaia 61, g. Birsk. b. 12 Feb 1905. c.ESC '53, USSR. TCHR. and HEAD, Chair of Educ. and Psych, Birsk Tchr. Trng. Inst, ul. Stalina 61, Birsk. Member: All-Union Socy. of Propagating Sci. and Polit. Knowledge. Teaching, research, administration; individual differences. F

MUSTAFAEVA, Cand. Educ. Sci, Mrs. Makhtaban. ul. Chkalova 15, Baku. b. b. 28 Apr 1905. c.ESC '49 Azerbaijanian Tchr. Trng. Inst. after Lenin, USSR. LECTURER, Chair of Educ. and Psych, Azerbaijanian Tchr. Trng. Inst. after Lenin, ul. Shaumiana 39, Baku. Member: Sect. of Educ, Socy. of Propagating Polit. and Sci. Knowledge. Teaching, research, professional writing; studying the language of pre-school children. F

MYSHKO, Cand. Educ. Sci. Matvei Y. ul.

Krasnaia 16, kv. 11, Minsk. b. 22 Nov 1895. c.esc. '46 Moscow Univ, USSR. HEAD, Chair of Psych, Tchr. Trng. Inst, Sovietskaia 18, Minsk. Teaching, research, editorial; methods of investigating personality, character. M

NADIRASHVILI, Cand. Educ. Sci. Shota. Teletski per. 2, Tbilisi. b. 1926. c.esc '55 Tbilisi Univ. after Stalin, USSR. JR. SCI. WRKR, Inst. of Psych. after Uznadze, ul. Dzhavakhishvili 1, Tbilisi. Research; thinking and speech, perception, concept formation. M

NAMITOKOV, Cand. Educ. Sci. Jusuf K. ul. Zhukovskogo 14, Maikop. b. 25 Oct 1904. c.esc '51 Odessa St. Univ, USSR. HEAD, Chair of Educ. and Psych, Adygei St. Tchr. Trng. Inst, Maikop. Teaching, research, professional writing; psychological foundations of teaching methods. M

NATADZE, Dr. Educ, Prof. Revaz. ul. Kuchishvili 20, Tbilisi. b. 11 Nov 1903. ED.D '39 Tbilisi Univ, USSR. HEAD, Chair of Psych, Tbilisi Univ, Universitetskaia 1, Tbilisi; HEAD, Sect. of Genetic Psych, Psych. Inst. after Uznadze. Member: Georgian Acad. of Sci. Research, teaching, student; psychology of thinking, genetic psychology, perception. M

NAZAROVA, Cand. Educ. Sci, Mrs. Lidia K. Piatnitski per. 8, kv. 7, Moscow ZH-127. b. 20 Mar 1919 Moscow. c.esc '50 Psych. Inst, Acad. of Educ. Sci, USSR. SR. SCI. WRKR, Methods of Tchng. Inst, Acad. of Educ. Sci, Lobkovski per, 5/16, Moscow. Teaching, educational psychology, consulting; individual differences of pupils in learning orthography. F

NAZIMOV, Igor N. ul. Lenina 10, Kiev. b. 14 June 1928. SR. SCI. WRKR, Sect. of Labor Psych, Inst. of Psych. Member: The Psych. Socy. Research, educational psychology; abilities, interests. M

NEELOVA, Mrs. Antonia. ul. Chapaeva 25, kor. 1, kv. 47, Ordzhonikidze, N. Osetia. b. 17 Jan 1926. ASSISTANT, Chair of Psych, N. Osetian Tchr. Trng. Inst, ul. Markusa 24, Ordzhonikidze. Research, professional writing, teaching, consultations; investigation of pupils' attention. F

NEKRASOVA, Cand. Educ. Sci, Mrs. Kseniia A. ul. Kovalikhinskaia 4, kv. 2, Gorky. b. 5 Jan 1907. c.esc '49 Moscow Tchr. Trng. Inst. after Lenin, Moscow, USSR. LECTURER, Chair of Psych, Gorky Tchr. Trng. Inst. after Gorky, pl. Minina, Gorky. Teaching, research; psychology of pre-school childhood; psychology of thinking. F

NEVEROVICH, Cand. Educ. Sci, Mrs. Yadviga Z. Psych. Inst, Mokhovaia 9, Moscow. b. 19 Mar 1913. c.esc '41 ,USSR. SR. SCI. WRKR, Psych. Inst, Acad. of Educ. Sci. Research; formation of habits; development

of attitudes toward work. F

NEVSKI, Cand. Educ. Sci. Alexander M. ul. Kirova 25-v, Alma-Ata. b. 9 Feb 1925 Uninski r-n, s. Verkhesunie, Viatskaia guberniia. c.esc '54, USSR. SR. TCHR, Chair of Psych, Alma-Ata Tchr. Trng. Inst. after Abai, ul. Sovietskaia 28, Alma-Ata. Member: Kazakh Psych. Socy. Teaching, research, educational psychology; psychological problems of teaching history. M

NIKIFOROVA, Cand. Educ. Sci, Mrs. Olga I. ul. Gorkogo 16/2, kv. 24, Moscow. b. 24 July 1903 Irkutsk. c.esc '38, USSR. LECTURER, Chair of Psych, Moscow Univ, Mokhovaia 9, Moscow. Student, research, teaching; perception, psychology of creative work and imagination. F

NIKOLENKO, Cand. Educ. Sci. Dmitri F. ul. Tarasovskaia 19, kv. 5, Kiev. b. 26 Oct 1899. c.esc. HEAD, Chair of Psych, Kiev Tchr. Trng. Inst. after Gorky, Boulevar Shevchenko 22-24, Kiev. Teaching, research, educational psychology; post-graduate advisor. M

NORAKIDZE, Dr. Educ, Prof. Vladimir. ul. Rodena 5, Tbilisi. b. 12 Apr 1905 Zugdidi, Georgia. ED.D '51 Psych. Inst, GSSR Acad. of Sci, USSR. PROFESSOR, Psych. Inst, GSSR Acad. of Sci, Dzhavakhishvili 1, Tbilisi. Research, teaching, consulting; methods of determining personality. M

NOVOMEISKI, Cand. Educ. Sci. Abram S. ul. Spichechnikov 19, kv. 17, Sverdlovsk. b. 26 July 1919. c.esc '50 Psych. Inst, Acad. of Educ. Sci, USSR. SR. TCHR, Chair of Psych, Sverdlovsk Tchr. Trng. Inst, ul. K. Libknekhta 9, Sverlovsk. Research, teaching, educational psychology; memory and imagination. M

NUDELMAN, Cand. Educ. Sci, Lect. Mikhail M. 3 Rostovski per 1, kv. 5, Moscow. b. 26 Mar 1909 Odesskaia obl. c.esc '42 Psych. Inst, USSR. LECTURER, Chair of Educ. and Psych, Kolomenski Tchr. Trng. Inst, g. Kolomna, Moskovskaia obl. Teaching, research, student; memory. M

ONISHCHENKO, Cand. Educ. Sci. Ivan M. ul. Saksaganskogo 88, kv. 2, Kiev. b. 23 Aug 1922. c.esc '54, USSR. LECTURER, Chair of Psych, Kiev Inst. of Physical Culture. Teaching, research; psychology of education in sport. M

ORLOVA, Cand. Educ. Sci, Mrs. Anna M. ul. Novo-Peschanaia 24, kv. 37, Moscow D-252. b. 15 Feb 1892 s. Agrafenina Pustyn Ranenburgskogo r-na, Riazanskaia obl. c.esc '51 Psych Inst, USSR. SR. SCI. WRKR, Psych. Inst, Acad. of Educ. Sci, Mokhovaia 9, Moscow. Research; problems of mastering knowledge. F

OSHANIN, Dr. Phil. Cand. Educ. Sci, Prof. Dmitri A. Yaroslavskoe Shosse 26, kv. 254, Moscow I-164. b. 13 Feb 1907 Vologda

PH.D '38 Paris Univ, France. SR. SCI. WRKR, Lab. of Labor Psych, Psych. Inst, Acad. of Educ. Sci, Mokhovaia 9, Moscow. Research, educational psychology; child psychology, labor psychology; sport psychology. M

OVSEPIAN, Cand. Educ. Sci. Gaiane. ul. Nalbandiana 96, Erevan. b. 1906. C.ESC '54 Tchr. Trng. Inst. after Gertsen, Moscow, USSR. LECTURER, Chair of Psych, Tchr. Trng. Inst. after Kh. Abovian, ul. Moskovskaia 5, Erevan. Teaching, research; problems of will, methods of training pupils' will. M

PALEI, Iosif M. Kirova 65, kv. 62, Molotov. b. 13 Apr 1926 g. Rechitsa. SR. TCHR, Tchr. Trng. Inst, ul. K. Marxa 24, Molotov. Teaching, research; temperament and will. M

PARAMONOVA, Cand. Educ. Sci, Mrs. Nina P. ul. Dobrovolcheskaia 36, kv. 3, Moscow ZH-33. b. 10 Jan 1927. C.ESC '54 Moscow Univ, Moscow, USSR. JR. SCI. WRKR, Defectology Inst, Acad. of Educ. Sci, Pogodinskaia 8, Moscow. Research, consulting, clinical practice, professional writing; physiological mechanisms of free movement. F

PELEKH, Cand. Educ. Sci. Piotr M. Lvovskaia 14, Kiev-Sviatushino. b. 18 Mar 1887. C.ESC '49, USSR. SR. SCI. WRKR, Psych. Inst, ul. Lenina 10, Kiev. Research; history of psychology. M

PENSKAIA, Cand. Educ. Sci, Mrs. Antonina V. Kirova 65, kv. 62, Molotov. b. 21 Jan 1927 Leninski r-n, selo Solodovka, Stalingradskaia obl. C.ESC '53 Leningrad Univ, USSR. TEACHER, Univ. Molotov. Teaching, research; child psychology, methods of teaching psychology. F

PEROV, Cand. Educ. Sci. Anatoli K. ul. Lenina 97, kv. 13, Sverdlovsk, Oblastnoi. b. 21 Oct 1908. C.ESC '46 Psych. Inst, Acad. of Educ. Sci, Moscow, USSR. LECTURER, Chair of Psych, Tchr. Trng. Inst, Sverdlovsk, obl. Teaching, research, editorial; character formation, needs and their role in the life of man. M

PETERBURGSKAIA, Cand. Educ. Sci, Mrs. Maria S. ul. Molodogvardeiskaia 52, kv. 3, Kuibyshev, Oblastnoi. b. 29 Mar 1902. C.ESC '54 Psych. Inst, Acad. of Educ. Sci, USSR. SR. TCHR, Chair of Psych, Kuibyshev Tchr. Trng. Inst, ul. Gorkogo 65/67, Kuibyshev. Teaching, research; psychology of teaching. F

PETROV, Cand. Educ. Sci, Lect. Yakov I. Sovetskaia 2, kv. 6, Brianskaia obl, Novozybkov. b. 27 Nov 1918 g. Atbasar, Akmolinskaia obl. C.ESC '49 Tchr. Trng. Inst, USSR. LECTURER, Chair of Educ. and Psych, Novozybkov Tchr. Trng. Inst, Leninskaia 11, Novozybkov. Member:

USSR Socy. of Psych'ts. Teaching, research, applied psychology. M

PETROVA, Cand. Educ. Sci, Mrs. Vera G. ul. Venetsianova 3, kv. 1, pos. Sokol, Moscow D-80. b. 8 Dec 1921. C.ESC '51, Acad. of Educ. Sci, USSR. JR. SCI. WRKR, Defectology Inst, Acad. of Educ. Sci, Pogodinskaia 8, Moscow. Research; memory, perception, psychology of speech. F

PIETUKHOVA, Cand. Educ. Sci, Mrs. Tamara V. ul. Gogolia 6, kv. 11, Stavropolski krai, Piatigorsk. b. 1 Feb 1925 Cheliabinks. C.ESC '52 Psych. Inst, Acad. of Educ. Sci, Moscow, USSR. SR. TCHR, Chair of Educ. and Psych. Tchr. Trng. Inst, pr. Kirova 70, Piatigorsk. Teaching, research, professional writing; attention, psychology of personality. F

PINSKY, Cand. Educ. Sci. Boris I. ul. Kaliaevskaia 5, kv. 48, Moscow K-6. b. 6 Sept 1909. C.ESC '45 Acad. of Educ. Sci, USSR. SR. SCI. WRKR, Defectology Inst, Acad. of Educ. Sci, Pogodinskaia 8, Moscow. Research, educational psychology, professional writing; psychology of activities of mentally retarded children, psychology of estimation. M

PISKUNOVA, Mrs. Maria K. ul. Krasnykh Partizan 3, kv. 13, Stalinabad. b. 23 Feb 1922. TEACHER, Stalinabad Tchr. Trng. Inst, ul. Lenina 139, Stalinabad. Teaching, research, educational psychology; sport psychology. F

PLATONOV, Dr. Med, Prof. Konstantin K. ul. Gorkogo 22, kv.o,g Moscow K-1. b. 7 June 1906 Kharkov. MD '54, USSR. CHIEF, Psych. Sect, Exper. Inst. of Aviat. Med, Moscow; TEACHER, Philos. Fac, Moscow Univ, Moscow. Research, teaching, student; labor psychology, abilities, habits, e-motions. M

PODBEREZIN, Cand. Educ. Sci, Lect. Ibragim M. ul. Vatutina 46, Ordzhonikidze, Severo-Osetinskaia. b. 15 July 1910. C.ESC '48 Moscow Tchr. Trng. Inst. after Lenin, USSR. HEAD, Chair of Psych, Tchr. Trng. Inst. Teaching, research, educational psychology; moral evolution of personality. M

PONOMARIOV, Yakov A. ul. Chaikovskogo 13, kv. 34, Moscow G-242. b. 25 Dec 1920 g. Vichuag, Ivanovskaia obl. Diploma '51 Moscow Univ, USSR. LECTURER. Research, teaching, professional writing; theoretical problems of psychiatry, thinking. M

POTANINA, Cand. Educ. Sci, Mrs. Gali L. Proletarskaia pl. 21-a, kom. 13, Ulianovsk. b. 9 Apr 1908. C.ESC '55 Moscow Reg. Tchr. Trng. Inst, USSR. SR. TCHR, Ulianov Tchr. Trng. Inst, ul. Ulianova 2, Ulianovsk. Member: All-Union Socy of Propagating Polit. and Sci. Knowledge. Teaching; attention, history of Russian psychology

at end of nineteenth century.   F
PRANGISHVILI, Cand. Educ. Sci. Alexander.
ul. Dzhavakhishvili 7, Tbilisi. b. 13 Jan
1909, Georgia. c.esc '41, ussr. director,
Psych. Inst, gssr Acad. of Sci, ul. Dzhavakhishvili 1, Tbilisi.   Research, editorial,
teaching; memory, thinking, history of
psychology.   M
PRIIMAK, Mrs. Maria A. ul. Pervogo Maia
11, kv. 6, Lvov. b. 23 Apr 1922 Boguslavski
r-n, s. Sinitsa, Kievskaia. postgraduate,
Chair of Educ. and Psych, Lvov St. Tchr.
Trng. Inst. Teaching, research; attention. F
PROKOLIENKO, Cand. Educ. Sci, Mrs.
Liudmila N. ul. Suvorova 5, kv. 19, Kiev.
b. 29 Sept 1927 Mirgorodslki raion, s.
Dubrovka, Poltavskaia obl.   c.esc '56
Kiev Tchr. Trng. Inst, ussr. sr. sci. wrkr,
Psych. Inst, ul. Lenina 10, Kiev. Member:
The Psych. Socy. Research, professional
writing; evolution of children's thinking,
development and defects of children's
speech.   F
PROSETSKI, Cand. Educ. Sci. Pavel A. ul.
Lenina 86, kv. 28, Voronezh. b. 26 Jan
1913. c.esc '49 Moscow Tchr. Trng. Inst.
after Lenin, Moscow, ussr.   lecturer,
Tchr. Trng. Inst. in Voronezh. Teaching,
research, editorial; psychology of children's
group, psychology of teachers.   M
PROSETSKI, Cand. Educ. Sci, Lect. Vladimir
A. ul. Sverdlova 1, kv. 1, Lipetskaia obl,
G. Elets. b. 27 Feb 1921. c.esc '50 Moscow
Tchr. Trng. Inst after Lenin, ussr. head,
Chair of Educ. and Psych, Tchr. Trng.
Inst, ul. Lenina 83, gor. Elets. Teaching,
research, educational psychology; psy-
chology of imitation, personality.   M
PUNI, Dr. Educ, Prof. Avksenti Ts. Karpovki
19, kv. 66, Naberezhnaia r, Leningrad P-22.
ed.d '56, ussr. head, Chair of Psych,
Lesgaft Inst. of Physical Trng, ul. Deka-
bristov 25, Leningrad. Member: Psych.
Sect, Leningrad Sci. Club after Gorky.
Teaching, research, consulting; sport psy-
chology.   M
RAEVSKI, Prof. Alexander N. ul. Lenine 82,
kv. 9, Kiev. b. 22 Aug 1891. head, Chair
of Psych, Kiev Univ. after Shevchenko,
ul. Vladimirskaia 58, Kiev.   Member:
Ukranian Sect, Psych. Socy. Research,
teaching, student; personality theory.   M
RAGINSKAIA, Cand. Educ. Sci, Mrs. Ida A.
Kirovski proezd 2, kv. 9, Moscow D-78.
b. 15 Nov 1907 Baku.   c.esc '45 Tchr.
Trng. Inst. in Moscow, ussr. lecturer,
Chair of Psych, Moscow Tchr. Trng. Inst.
after Lenin, M. Pirogovskaia 1, Moscow.
Teaching, research.   F
RAMISHVILI, Cand. Educ. Sci, Mrs. Da-
pedzhan.   ul. Iak, Nikoladze 4, Tbilisi.
b. 1906. c.esc '41 Tbilisi Univ. after Stalin,
ussr. sr. sci. wrkr, Psych. Inst. after

Uznadze, ul. Dzhavakhishvili 1, Tbilisi.
Research; psychology of speech, psychology
of esthetic perception, imagination.   F
RAMUL, Prof. Dr. Konstantin. Vilde t. 3-1,
Tartu, Estonia. b. 30 May 1879 Kures-
saare. ph.d '39 Univ. of Tartu, ussr.
prof. of psych, Univ. of Tartu. Teaching,
research, professional writing; history of
psychology, laboratory methods and apparatus, teaching psychology.   M
RASTORGUEVA, Mrs. Nina A. ul. Oktiabrs-
kaia 28, Iakutsk Gos. Universitet, Yakutsk.
b. 21 Nov 1929 Yakutsk. sr. tchr, Chair
of Psych, Yakutsk Univ. Teaching, edu-
cational psychology; logic.   F
RAVICH-SHCHERBO, Cand. Educ. Sci, Mrs.
Inna V. b. Kaluzhskaia 37, kv. 87, Moscow
B-17. b. 21 Apr. 1927. c.esc '54 Moscow
Univ, ussr. jr. sci. wrkr, Psych. Inst,
Acad. of Educ. Sci, Mokhovaia 9, Moscow.
Research; individual differences.   F
REBIZOV, Cand. Educ. Sci. Dmitri G. Tchr.
Trng. Inst, ul. Svobody 46, Riazan. b. 6
Nov. 1903. c.esc '56 Moscow Tchr. Inst.
after Lenin, ussr. sr. tchr, Chair of
Psych, Riazansky St. Tchr. Trng. Inst.
Teaching, education psychology; psycholo-
gy of memory.   M
REPINA, Cand. Educ. Sci, Mrs. Tatiania A.
Psych. Inst, korpus V, Mokhovaia 9,
Moscow. b. 23 Mar 1923. c.esc '55 . jr.
sci. wrkr, Lab. of Pre-School Child,
Psych. Inst, Acad. of Educ. Sci. Research;
evolution of children's imagination, per-
ception.   F
RESHETOVA, Cand. Educ. Sci, Mrs. Zoia A.
Borovskoie shosse 1, kv. 489, Moscow V-261.
b. 15 Dec 1918 Baloshovski r-n, M. Ser-
geevka, Saratovskaia obl.   c.esc '54
Moscow Univ, ussr. assistant,Chair of
Psych, Moscow Univ, Mokhovaia 11, Moscow. Teaching, research; labor psychology,
abilities.   F
ROGINSKI, Dr. Educ, Prof. Girsha Z. Podolskaia 34, kv. 9-a, Leningrad. b. 28 Dec
1903. ed.d '46 ussr. professor, Tchr.
Trng. Inst. after Gertsen, Moika 48, Leningrad Socy. of Psych'ts. Teaching, research;
experimental studies of anthropoids and
pre-school children, evolution of brains
and psychical phenomena.   M
ROZANOVA, Cand. Educ. Sci, Mrs. Tatiana
V. ul. Chaikovskogo 13, kv. 34, Moscow
G-242. b. 20 Oct 1928 Moscow. c.esc '55
Moscow Univ, ussr. sr. sci. wrkr, Defectology Inst, Acad. of Educ. Sci, Pogodinskaia 8, Moscow. Research, editorial,
educational psychology; memory, thinking,
perception.   F
ROZENGART-PUPKO, Cand. Educ. Sci,
Mrs. Gita. ul. Taganskaia 6-B, kv. 9, Mos-
cow 4. b. 31 Dec 1894. c.esc '44 Moscow
Univ, ussr; c.nsc Liège Univ, Belgium;

c.JSC Warsaw Univ. RETIRED. Research; genetic psychology, childhood speech and psychical development. M

ROZHDESTVENSKAIA, Cand. Educ. Sci, Mrs. Valentina I. B. Yakimanka 27, kv. 30, Moscow. b. 19 Dec 1921 g. Belev. c.ESC Psych. Inst, Acad. of Educ. Sci, USSR. SR. SCI.WRKR, Psych. Inst, Acad. of Educ. Sci, Mokhovaia 9, Moscow. Research; individual differences. M

RUBINSTEIN, Dr. Educ, Prof. Sergei L. B. Kaluzhskaia 13, kv. 122, Moscow. b. 19 June 1889 Odessa. ED.D '37, USSR. HEAD, Psych. Sect, Philos. Inst, Acad. of Sci; PROFESSOR, Philos. Fac, Moscow Univ. Member: A.SC, AESC. Teaching, research, editorial; theoretical problems of general psychology, history of psychology, psychology of thinking and speech. M

RUBTSOVA, Cand. Educ. Sci, Mrs. Tamara V. Franka 5, kv. 15, Kiev. b. 22 July 1907. c.ESC '48 Kiev Tchr. Trng. Inst, USSR. SR. SCI. WRKR, Psych. Inst, Lenina 10, Kiev. Member: The Psych. Socy. Research, educational psychology, professional writing; readers' interests. F

RUDCHENKO, Cand. Educ. Sci. Ivan. ul. Nagornaia 32-a, Vinnitsa. b. 5 Oct 1898. c.ESC '56 Kiev Tchr. Trng. Inst, USSR. SR. TCHR, Tchr. Trng. Inst, ul. Kraznoznamionnaia 56, Vinnitsa. Teaching, research, educational psychology; children's thinking, professional habits. M

RUDIK, Cand. Educ. Sci, Prof. Piotr A. Savelievsky per. 10, kv. 9, Moscow G-34. b. 13 July 1893 Piatigorsk. c.ESC '31, USSR. HEAD, Chair of Psych, St. Cen. Inst. of Physical Culture, ul. Kazakova 18, Moscow. Member: AESC. Research, teaching, editorial; psychology of sports. M

RUMIANTSEVA, Mrs. Liubov I. ul. Vasilievskaia 6, kv. 9, Moscow. b. 4 Sept 1900 Moscow. JR. SCI. WRKR, Lab. of Psych. of Tchg, Psych. Inst, Acad. of Educ. Sci, Mokhovaia 9, Moscow. Research, educational psychology, professional writing; linguistics. F

RUZSKAIA, Cand. Educ. Sci, Mrs. Antonina G. ul. Tatishcheva 3, kv. 8, Moscow V-162. b. 26 Nov. 1925. c.ESC '54 Psych. Inst, Acad. of Educ. Sci, Moscow. USSR. JR. SCI. WRKR, Lab. of Perception, Psych. Inst, Acad. of Educ. Sci, Mokhovaia 9, Moscow. Research. F

RYBAKOVA, Cand. Educ. Sci, Mrs. Liubov. ul. Krestianskaia 3-a, kv. 1, Vologda. b. 20 May 1926 Vologodskaia obl. c.ESC '52 Psych. Inst, Moscow, USSR. SR. TCHR, Chair of Educ, Tchr. Trng. Inst, ul. Maiakovskogo 6, Vologda. Teaching, research. F

RYBNIKOV, Dr. Educ, Prof. Nikolai A. 1 Meshchenskaia 14, kv. 11, Moscow 10. b. 29 Oct 1880. ED.D '43, USSR. PROFESSOR, Inst. of Psych, Mokhovaia 9, Moscow. Member: AESC, All-Union Socy of Propagating Polit. and Sci. Knowledge. Research, educational psychology, professional writing; history of psychology, memory, child's speech. M

SABUROVA, Cand. Educ. Sci, Mrs. Galina G. Likhachevskoie shosse 11/5, kv. 15, Moscow A-183. b. 8 July 1924 Yaroslavl. c.ESC '52 Psych. Inst, Acad. of Educ. Sci, USSR. JR. SCI. WRKR, Psych. Inst, Acad. of Educ. Sci, Mokhovaia 9, Moscow. Research, educational psychology; learning foreign languages. F

SAKVARELIDZE, Cand. Educ. Sci, Mrs. Marine. ul. Bakradze 18, Tbilisi. b. 1926. c.ESC '54 Psych. Inst. after Uznadze, USSR. SR. SCI. WRKR, Psych. Inst. after Uznadze, ul. Dzhavakhishvili 1, Tbilisi. Research, clinical analysis. M

SAMARIN, Cand. Educ. Sci. Iuri A. ul. Vosstaniia 12, kv. 3, Leningrad D-14. b. 11 Dec 1901 Leningrad. c.ESC '41 Tchr. Trng. Inst. after Gertsen, USSR. HEAD, Sect. of Educ. Psych, Inst. of Educ, Acad. of Educ. Sci, nab. Kutuzova 8, Leningrad. Member: Psych. Sect, Leningrad Sci. Club, Sect. of Educ, All-Union Socy. of Propagating Polit. and Sci. Knowledge. Research, teaching, administration; mental activities, abilities, psychology of personality. M

SAMBROS, Cand. Educ. Sci, Georgi F. ul. Moskovskaia 11, Sverdlovskaia obl, Kamyshlov. b. 7 Apr 1894. c.ESC '55 Psych. Inst, Acad. of Educ. Sci, USSR. RETIRED. Research, educational psychology; personality development. M

SAMOKHVALOVA, Cand. Educ. Sci, Mrs. Vera I. ul. Novo-Slobodskaia 3, kv. 11, Moscow A-55. b. 22 May 1925 Sobinski r-n. Vladimirskaia obl. c.ESC '53 Psych. Inst, Acad. of Educ. Sci, USSR. JR. SCI. WRKR, Lab. of Educ, Psych. Inst, Acad. of Educ. Sci, Mokhovaia 9, Moscow. Teaching, research, educational psychology; problem of personality and its formation. F

SAMUILENKOV, Cand. Educ. Sci, Lect. Dmitri F. ul. Internatsionalnaia 1, kv. 1, Smolensk. b. 21 Oct 1895. c.ESC '35, USSR. LECTURER, Chair of Psych. and Educ, Smolensk Tchr. Trng. Inst. after K. Marx. Member: All-Union Socy. of Propagating Polit. and Sci. Knowledge. Teaching, research, educational psychology; child psychology, psychology of professions. M

SAPOZHNIKOVA, Cand. Educ. Sci, Mrs. Elka S. ul. Rognedinskaia 4, kv. 3-a, Kiev. b. 18 Apr 1924. c.ESC '55 Kiev Univ, USSR. SR. SCI. WRKR, Psych. Inst, ul. Lenina 10, Kiev. Member: The Psych. Socy. Research, educational psychology, professional writing; child development. F

SAZONTIEV, Cand. Educ. Sci. Boris. prospekt K. Marxa 24, kv. 77, Petrozavodsk. b. 23 June 1923 Gorky. c.esc '54 Psych. Inst, Acad. of Educ. Sci, Moscow, ussr. sr. tchr, Chair of Educ. and Psych, Petrozavodsk Tchr. Trng. Inst, prospekt Lenina 79, Petrozavodsk. Teaching, research, professional writing; art and literary abilities, word perception.   M
SELITSKAIA, Cand. Educ. Sci, Mrs. Elena K. ul. Marxa-Engelsa 19, kv. 4, Moscow G-19. b. 15 May 1923. c.esc '53 Moscow St. Tchr. Trng. Inst. after Potemkin, ussr. sr. tchr, Chair of Psych, First Moscow St. Tchr. Trng. Inst. of Foreign Languages, Metrostroevskaia 38, Moscow G-34. Teaching, research; psychology of speech. F
SELIVANOV, Dr. phil, Prof. Vladimir. ul. Riazhskaia 25, kv. 3, Riazan. b. 8 July 1906. ph.d '53 Philos. Inst, Acad. of Sci, Moscow, ussr. head, Chair of Psych, Riazan St. Tchr. Trng. Inst, ul. Svobody 46, Riazan. Member: All-Union Socy. of Propagating Polit. and Sci. Knowledge. Teaching, research, educational psychology; will, character, personality.   M
SEMERNITSKAIA, Cand. Educ. Sci, Mrs. Frida M. Krasnoarmeiskaia 14-v, Alushta, Crimea. b. 1 Aug 1905 Leningrad. c.esc '45 Psych. Inst, Acad. of Educ. Sci, Moscow, ussr. Teaching, research; rhythm. F
SERDIUK, Cand. Educ. Sci, Mrs. Augustina K ul. 17 Sentiabria 23-a, kv. 12, Lutsk. b. 2 Apr 1924 g. Kriukov. c.esc '53 Kiev Univ, ussr. lecturer, Chair of Educ. and Psych, Lutsk Tchr. Trng. Inst. after L. Ukrainka, Lutsk. Teaching, research, educational psychology; personality formation.   F
SERGEEVICHEV, Cand. Educ. Sci. Vasili N. ul. Lenina 4, kv. 2, g. Ivanovo. b. 11 Jan 1911. c.esc '51 Psych. Inst, Acad. of Educ. Sci, ussr. lecturer, Chair of Educ. and Psych, Ivanovo Tchr. Trng. Inst, ul. Ermaka 37, Ivanovo. Teaching, research, educational psychology; imagination.   M
SERGIEVSKI, Dr. Med, Prof. Mikhail V. ul. Leningradskaia 72, kv. 36, Kuibyshev. b. 27 Oct 1898 selo Zharenki, Mordovia. md '35, Kazan, ussr. head, Chair of Normal Physiology, Kuibyshev Inst. of Med, Artsibushevskaia 161, Kuibyshev. Member: Academy of Medical Science, Kuibyshev Sec, Physiological Socy. Research, teaching, consulting; physiology of higher nervous activities.   M
SHCHEPOTIEV, Cand. Educ. Sci. Fiodor A. ul. Pervomaiskaia 41, kv. 3, Pskov. b. 21 Feb 1917. c.esc '49 Tchr. Trng. Inst, ussr. sr. tchr, Pskov Tchr. Trng. Inst, Sovetskaia 21, Pskov. Teaching, research, educational psychology; concept formation.   M

SHEVARIOV, Cand. Educ. Sci, Prof. Piotr A. Chistyie Prudy 12, korp 2, kv. 86, Moscow. b. 12 July 1892 Riazan. c.esc '35, ussr. head, Lab. of Perception and Memory, Psych. Inst, Acad. of Educ. Sci, Mokhovaia 9, Moscow. Member: The Psych. Socy. Research; perception.   M
SHEVTSOVA, Cand. Educ. Sci, Mrs. Liudmila P. ul. Kotsiubinskogo 7, kv. 6, Chernovtsy. b. 18 Nov 1928 Zaporozhie. c.esc '54 Kiev Univ, ussr. sr. tchr. in psych, Chernovtsy Univ, ul. Universitetskaia 28, Chernovtsy. Teaching, research; education of pre-school children in family.   F
SHIF, Cand. Educ. Sci, Mrs. Zhozefina I. ul. Chaikovskogo 1/2, kv. 17, Moscow 99. b. 8 Jan 1904. c.esc '35, ussr. head, Lab. of Psych. of Mentally Retarded Children, Defectology Inst, Acad. of Educ. Sci, Pogodinskaia 8, Moscow. Research, professional writing, teaching; development of thinking and speech of normal and abnormal children.   F
SHIRBAEV, Cand. Educ. Sci, Lect. Muradbek. Uzbek St. Univ. after A. Navoi, Samarkand b. 15 July 1905. c.esc '52 Ministry of Higher Educ, ussr. lecturer, Chair of Educ. and Psych, Univ. after A. Navoi, bulvar m. Gorkogo, Samarkand. Teaching. M
SHNIRMAN, Cand. Educ. Sci, Lect. Alexander. ul. Pisareva 18, kv. 17, Leningrad F-121. b. 7 Mar 1899 Leningrad. c.esc '47 Leningrad Tchr. Trng. Inst. after Gertsen, ussr. lecturer, Chair of Psych, Leningrad Tchr. Trng. Inst, M. Posadskaia 26, Leningrad. Member: Psych. Sect, Leningrad Sci. Club. Teaching, research, editorial; personality and group, methods of investigating personality, habits.   M
SHUBERT, Cand. Educ. Sci, Mrs. Anna M. Zemledelcheski per 12, kv. 11, Moscow G-117. b. 21 Dec 1881. ph.d '09 Zurich, Switzerland, c.esc '46, ussr. Member: Sci. Council, Central Inst. of Trial Psychiat. after Prof. Serbski, Kropothinski per 23, Moscow. Consulting, research; cognition. F
SHVARTS, Cand. Educ. Sci, Mrs. Liubov. Arbat 35, kv. 78, Moscow. b. 25 Dec. 1904. c.esc '41 Psych. Inst, Acad. of Educ. Sci, ussr. sr. sci. wrkr, Psych. Inst, Acad. of Educ. Sci, Mokhovaia 9, Moscow. Research, professional writing; feelings, types of higher nervous systems.   F
SIMONOV, Boris I. ul. Pervomaiskaia 41, kv. 3, Pskov. b. 23 Oct 1917, g. Taldom, Moskovskaia gub. sr. tchr, Pskov Tchr. Trng. Inst, Sovetskaia 21, Pskov. Teaching, research, educational psychology; memory and its mechanism.   M
SINITSA, Cand. Educ. Sci. Ivan E. ul. Turgeneva 25, kv. 2, Kiev. b. 6 Aug 1910. c.esc '55 Kiev Tchr. Trng. Inst, ussr. head, Sect. of Educ. Psych, Psych. Inst,

DIRECTOR, Ust-Kamenogorsk Tchr. Trng. ul. Lenina 10, Kiev. Member: The Psych. Socy. Research, educational psychology, professional writing; thinking and speech. M
SKRIPCHENKO, Cand. Educ. Sci. Alexander V. ul. Lenina 66, kv. 29, Kiev. b. 26 Dec 1921. C.ESC '56 Kiev Univ. USSR. SR. SCI. WRKR, Psych. Inst, ul. Lenina 10, Kiev. Member: The Psych. Socy. Research, professional writing; perception and thinking.M
SLAVINA, Cand. Sci, Mrs. Liia S. 1 Meshchanskaia 43, kv. 29, Moscow I-110. b. 14 Jan 1906 Gomel. c.sc '30, 2-d Moscow St. Univ, USSR. SR. SCI. WRKR, Psych. Lab. of Educ, Psych. Inst, Acad. of Educ. Sci, Mokhovaia 9, Moscow. Research, educational psychology, professional writing; personality development. F
SMIRNOV, Dr. Educ, Prof. Anatoly A. Inst. of Psych, Mokhovaia 9, Moscow. b. 5 Nov 1894 Moscow. ED.D '51, USSR. DIRECTOR, Psych. Inst, Acad. of Educ. Sci. Member: AESC. Presidium, USSR Socy of Psych'ts. EDITOR, Voprosy Psikhologii. Administration, research, editorial; directing research, child psychology, memory. M
SMIRNOVA, Cand. Educ. Sci, Mrs. Tatiana S. Tverskoi bulvar 20, kv. 33, Moscow. b. 20 Jan 1903. C.ESC '49 Psych. Inst, Acad. of Educ. Sci, USSR. LECTURER, Moscow St. Tchr. Trng. Inst. after Potemkin, Davydovski per. 4, Moscow. Teaching, research; intellectual maturation of pupils. F
SOBIEVA, Cand. Educ. Sci, Mrs. Galina. ul. Lenina 28, gor Ordzhonikidze. b. 10 Sept 1901. C.ESC '53 Psych. Inst, Acad. of Educ. Sci, USSR. LECTURER, Chair of Psych, N. Osetian Tchr. Trng. Inst. after Khetagurov. Teaching, research, educational psychology; methods of personality investigation. F
SOKOLOV, Cand. Educ. Sci. Alexander N. Psych. Inst, Mokhovaia 9, Moscow. b. 10 Oct 1911, Riazanskaia obl. C.ESC '38 Psych. Inst, USSR. SR. SCI. WRKR, Psych. Inst, Acad. of Educ. Sci. Research; psychology of thinking and speech. M
SOLOVIOV, Cand. Educ. Sci. Ivan M. Pietrovski bulvar 8, kv. 3, Moscow 1-51. b. 2 June 1902 Penza. C.ESC, USSR. HEAD. Lab. of Studying Deaf and Dumb Children's Psych, Defectology Inst, Acad. of Educ. Sci, ul. Pogodinskaia 8, Moscow. Research, administration, editorial; teaching and memory, perception. M
SOROKUN, Cand. Educ. Sci. Prokopi A. M. Posadskaia 17, kv. 5, Leningrad P-46. b. 1921. C.ESC '54 Leningrad Univ, Leningrad, USSR. SR. TCHR, Leningrad Tchr. Trng. Inst, M. Posadskaia 26, Leningrad. Teaching, research; spatial perception in school children. M
STARZHEVSKI, Georgi L. ul. Marxa 88,

kv. 4, Krasnoiarsk. b. 3 Nov 1901. SR. TCHR, Krasnoiarsk Tchr. Trng. Inst. Teaching, research. M
STRAKHOV, Dr. Educ, Prof. Ivan V. ul. Gorkogo 6, kv. 3, Saratov. b. 1905. ED.D '42 ,USSR. HEAD, Chair of Psych, Tchr. Trng. Inst, ul. Michurina 14, Saratov. Research, teaching, educational psychology; character development. M
STYCHINSKI, Prof. Iosif. ul. Shevchenko 60, Alma-Ata. b. 2 Jan 1896 Saratov. HEAD, Chair of Psych, Tchr. Trng. Inst. in Alma-Ata, Sovetskaia 28, Alma-Ata. Member: Socy. of Neuropathologists and Psycht's. Teaching, research, educational psychology; methods of study of personality; thinking and speech. M
SUVOROVA, Cand. Educ. Sci, Mrs. Valentina V. Borovskoe shosse 1, kv. 189, Moscow V-261. b. 1 Feb 1926 g. Pavlov, Gorkovskoi obl. C.ESC '53, USSR. JR. SCI. WRKR, Lab. of Labor Psych, Psych. Inst, Acad. of Educ. Sci, Mokhovaia 9, Moscow. Research, educational psychology, professional writing; psychological aspects of work on high speed processes. F
SVERLOV, Dr. Educ. Vladimir S. ul. prof. Popova 41, kv. 59, Leningrad 137. b. 30 Mar 1898 Irkutsk. ED.D '56 Psych. Inst, Acad. of Educ. Sci, USSR. SR. SCI. WRKR, Labor for Invalids Inst, ul. Smolnogo 4, Leningrad 124. Member: All-Russian Socy. of the Blind, Leningrad Sci. Club. Research, consulting, teaching; imagination and perception of the blind, determination of personality. M
SYRKINA-FRIDMAN, Cand. Educ. Sci, Mrs. Vera Kh. Morskoi prospekt 33, kv. 10, Leningrad P-47. b. 2 Mar 1900 Leningrad. C.ESC '41 Tchr. Trng. Inst. after Gertsen, Leningrad, USSR. RETIRED. Professional writing; development of abilities and character, perception of art works. F
TABIDZE, Cand. Educ. Sci. Otar I. ul. Mardzhanishvili 26-a, Tbilisi. b. 30 Mar 1925 S. Ivandidi, Tsulukidzevski r-n, Georgian SSR. C.ESC '56, USSR. ACADEMICIAN SECY, Psych. Inst. im Uznadze, ul. Dzhavakhishvili 1, Tbilisi. Research, administration; psychological methods, psychology of thinking, habit. M
TALYZINA, Cand. Educ. Sci, Mrs. Nina F. Barovskoe shosse 1, kv. 591, Moscow V-261. b. 28 Dec 1923 Yaroslav obl. C.ESC '50 Psych. Inst, Acad. of Educ. Sci. SR. TCHR, Fac. of Philos, Moscow Univ, Mokhovaia 11, Moscow; HEAD, Parents' Univ. Teaching, research, administration; problems of teaching, thinking. F
TEMIRBEKOV, Cand. Educ. Sci. Abdulla. ul. Gogolia 2, kv. 12, Ust-Kamenogorsk, Kazakh SSR. b. 28 Nov 1904. C.ESC '55 Alma Ata Tchr. Trng. Inst. after Abai.

Inst, Stroiploshchadka, Ust-Kamenogorsk. Administration, teaching, research; psychology of teaching, relationship between morale and personality. M

TEPLOV, Dr. Educ, Honorary Sci. Prof. Boris M. 2 ul. Peschanaia 8, kv. 9, Moscow D-252. b. 20 Oct 1896 Tula. ED.D '41 Leningrad Tchr. Trng. Inst. after Gertsen. HEAD, Psych. Lab. of Indiv. Differences, Psych. Inst, Acad. of Educ. Sci, Mokhovaia 9, Moscow. Member: AESC, APSLF, USSR Socy. of Psych'ts. Research, professional writing; individual differences, senses, psychology of music. M

TEREKHOVA, Cand. Educ. Sci., Mrs. Taisiia P. ul. Kuibysheva 10, kv. 17, Tambov. b. 28 May 1918 Tabovskaia obl, d. Nizovaia. C.ESC '56 Moscow Inst. of Psych. PSYCH. TCHR, Tambov Tchr. Trng. Inst. Teaching, research; personality. F

TIAKHTY, Cand. Educ. Sci. Boris A. ul. Lenina 79, kv. 1, Petrozavodsk, Karelo SSR. b. 6 Aug 1906. C.ESC '56 Gertsen Inst. USSR. SR. TCHR. of PSYCH, Karolo Tchr. Trng. Inst; ED. COMM, Kiria, Leningrad. Teaching, applied and educational psychology; psychology of thinking, comprehension. M

TIKH, Dr. Biol, Prof, Mrs. Nina A. Podolskaia 34, kv. 9a, Leningrad. b. 13 Apr 1905 Saratov. Dr. of Biol. '50 Pavlov Inst, Acad. of Sci, Leningrad, USSR. PROF. of PSYCH, Higher Sch. of T. U. Movement, ul. Krasnaia 22, Leningrad. Member: Leningrad Psych. Socy. Teaching, experimental and theoretical research; origin of language and thinking. F

TKACHEVA, Cand. Educ. Sci, Mrs. Galina A. ul. Ofitserskaia 1, kv. 9, Kaliningrad obl. b. 1 Apr 1912. C.ESC '51 Moscow Tchr. Trng. Inst. after Lenin. HEAD, Chair of Educ. and Psych, Tchr. Trng. Inst, ul. Chernyshevskogo 56, Kaliningrad obl. Teaching, research, administration; educational psychology. F

TOKMAKOV, Cand. Educ. Sci, Lazar. Kotoroslnaia nab. 46 B, kv. 53, Yaroslavl. b. 1895. C.ESC '30. LECTURER, Yaroslavl. Tchr. Trng. Inst. after Ushinski, ul. Respublikanskaia 8, Yaroslavl. Teaching, research. M

TOMILOVA, Cand. Educ. Sci, Mrs. Maria A. ul. Sofii Kovalevskoi 18/10, kv. 1, Yaroslavl b. 1897. C.ESC '42 Molotov Tchr. Trng. Inst, USSR. RETIRED. Consulting; development of speech with deaf and dumb. F

TOSHMATOV, Asabidin. ul. Ozodi 8, kv. 20, Leninabad. b. 25 Aug 1927. SR. TCHR, Leninabad Tchr. Trng. Inst. after Kirov, ul. Ordszhonikidze 158, Leninabad. Teaching; methods of defining personality. M

TSVETKOV, Cand. Educ. Sci. Ivan M. ul. Deputatskaia 2, kv. 12, Yaroslavl. b. 17

Aug 1899l C.ESC '43 Moscow Univ. USSR. LECTURER, Tchr. Trng. Inst, ul. Respublikanskaia 108, Yaroslavl. Teaching, research, editorial; development of student's personality during the process of teaching.M

TURPANOV, Cand. Educ. Sci. Afanasi. ul. Oktiabrskaia 33, Yakutsk. b. 28 Dec 1920 Sredne-Kolymsk, Yakutskaia SSR. C.ESC '53 Moscow State Tchr. Trng. Inst. after Lenin, USSR. LECTURER, Chair of Psych, State Univ, Yakutsk. Teaching, educational psychology, research, public lecturing; psychology of teaching, imagination, interests. M

TUTUNDZHIAN, Cand. Educ. Sci. Ovsep M. prospekt Stalina 48, kv. 19, Erevan, Armenian SSR. b. 10 Aug 1918 Alexandria, Egypt. C.ESC '56 Moscow Regional Tchr. Trng. Inst, Erevan, USSR. SR. SCI. WRKR, Inst. of Schools, ul. Pushkina 38, Erevan. Research, teaching, educational psychology; personality measurement. M

VADACHKORIIA, Cand. Educ. Sci. Prokofi K. ul. Kazbekskaia 25, Tbilisi. b. 10 Oct 1904. C.ESC '36 Tbilisi Univ, USSR. LECTURER, Chair of Educ. and Psych, Staliniri Tchr. Trng. Inst, ul. Molotova 8, Staliniri. Teaching, research, professional writing; abilities, thinking. M

VASILEISKI, Prof. Serafim M. ul. Gruzinskaia 29, kv. 48, Gorky. b. 1 Mar 1888. Grade, St. Petersburg Univ. HEAD, Chair of Psych, Gorky Tchr. Trng. Inst, ul. Ulianova 1, Gorky. Teaching, research, educational psychology; psychology of creative work, invention. M

VEKKER, Cand. Educ. Sci, Lect. Lev M. Vituato 20-a, kv. 8, Vilnius. b. 4 Oct 1918 Odessa. C.ESC '47, USSR. HEAD, Chair of Psych, Tchr. Trng. Inst, ul. Gorkogo 83, Vilnius. Teaching, research, administration; senses and perception. M

VELIKORODNOVA, Cand. Educ. Sci, Mrs. Anastasiia I. Leningrad State Tchr. Trng. Inst, Leningrad 46. b. June 1922. C.ESC '53 Leningrad Univ, USSR. SR. TCHR, Leningrad State Tchr. Trng. Inst. Teaching, research, educational psychology. F

VISHNEPOLSKAIA, Cand. Educ. Sci, Mrs. Anna. ul. Kolarova, dom prepodavat, kv. 1, Komsomolsk-na-Amure. b. 14 May 1903 Kiev. C.ESC '55 Psych. Inst, Acad. of Educ. Sci, USSR. HEAD, Chair of Educ. and Psych, Tchr. Trng. Inst, ul. Pionierskaia, Komsomolsk-na-Amure. Teaching, research, administration; psychology of learning orthography. F

VITSINSKI, Cand. Educ. Sci, Lect. Alexander V. ul. Stankevicha 9, kv. 26, Moscow K-9. b. 19 Oct 1904 Sevastopol. C.ESC. LECTURER, Chair of Piano, Moscow Conservatory after Chaikovsky, ul. Gertsena 13, Moscow. Teaching, research; psychology

of music. M
VLASOVA, Cand. Educ. Sci, Mrs. Maia M.
Mokhovaia 9, Moscow. b. 23 Dec 1923
Moscow. c.esc '52 Moscow, ussr. jr. sci.
wrkr, Psych. Inst, Acad. of Educ. Sci,
Mokhovaia 9, Moscow. Research; higher
human neurodynamics. F
**VNOROVSKAIA, Cand. Educ. Sci, Lect, Mrs.
Kleopatra M.** ul. Shchorsa 50, Kishinev,
Moldavian ssr. b. 1 Nov 1911. c.esc,
Moscow Inst. of Psych. ussr. head, Chair
of Educ. and Psych, Kishinev State Tchr.
Trng. Inst. after I. Kriange: ed. bd.
Gosizdat. Teaching, research, educational
psychology; vocational preparation in
school. F
VOLF, Dr. Educ, Prof. Merlin. ul. gazety
Pravda 14, kv. 6, Molotov. b. 22 Jan 1898
Mogiliov. ed.d '50 Leningrad, ussr. pro-
fessor, Chair of Educ, Molotov Tchr. Trng.
Inst, ul. K. Marxa, Molotov. Teaching,
research, consulting; personality. M
VOLKOV, Dr. Educ. Nikolai N. 5 Monetchi-
kovski per. 5, kv. 1, Moscow ZH-54. b.
24 Aug 1897 Moscow. ed.d '51 Psych.
Inst, Acad. of Educ. Sci, Moscow, ussr.
sr. sci. wrkr, ussr Acad. of Arts, ul.
Kropotkina 21, Moscow. Research on art
theory, mathematical logic; psychology of
optical perception, psychology of art. M
**VOVCHIK-BLAKITNA, Cand. Educ. Sci, Mrs.
Maia V.** ul. Rozy Liuksemburg 7/9, kv. 19,
Kiev. b. 14 July 1923. c.esc '55 Kiev
Univ, ussr. sr. sci. wrkr, Psych. Inst,
ul. Lenina 10, Kiev. Member: The Psych.
Socy. Research, professional writing;
images and emotions of children. F
YAKOBSON, Cand. Educ. Sci. Pavel V.
Kooperativnaia 3, kv. 28/32, Moscow G-48.
b. 1 Jan 1902. c.esc '35, ussr. sr. sci.
wrkr, Psych. Inst, Acad. of Educ. Sci,
Mokhovaia 9, Moscow. Research, applied
and educational psychology, teaching;
psychology of work, psychology of
sentiments. M
YAKOVLEV, Cand. Educ. Sci. Vladimir A.
Oktiabrskaia 6, kv. 17, Tambov. b. 28
June 1904 Kokchetav. c.esc '34 Moscow
Tchr. Trng. Inst. after Lenin, ussr. asst.
dir, Voronezh Tchr. Trng. Inst. Administration, research, teaching; personality. M
**YAKOVLEVA, Cand. Med. Sci, Mrs. Ekaterina
K.** 9 Sovetskaia 39, kv. 41, Leningrad 144.
b. 21 Sept 1894 Leningrad. c.msc '41, ussr.
section head, Psychoneur. Inst. after
Bekhterev, ul. im. Bekhtereva 3, Nevskaia
zastava, Leningrad. Member: Leningrad
Socy. of Psychiatrists and Neuropatholo-
gists. Psychotherapy, research, consulting,
clinical practice, administration; personality and neuroses. F
YAKOVLICHEVA, Cand. Sci, Mrs. Anna F.
Dovostrebovania, Pcohtamt, Rostov-na-

Donu. b. 12 July 1922. c.sc '54. ussr.
tchr. of child psych, Tchr. Trng. Inst,
ul. Engelsa 37, Rostov-na-Donu. Teaching,
educational psychology, research; development of thinking in pre-school child. F
**YANKELEVICH, Cand. Educ. Sci, Lect.
Samuil.** ul. Mozhaiskogo 8, kv. 17, Ulianovsk. b. May 1902 gor. Buinaksk, Dagest.
c.esc '49, ussr. lecturer, Chair of Educ.
and Psych, Ulianovsk Tchr. Trng. Inst.
Teaching, research, educational psychology;
personality, psychology of creative work,
watchfulness. M
YARMOLENKO, Dr. Educ, Mrs. Avgusta V.
Bolshoi Prospekt 74, kv. 14, Leningrad
P-136. b. 27 Sept 1900 Leningrad. ed.d '55
Leningrad Univ, ussr. lecturer, Chair
of Psych, Fac. of Philosphy, Leningrad
State Univ. after A. A. Zhdanov, V. O.
Univers. nba. 7/9, Leningrad. Member:
Psych. Sect. of Leningrad Sci. Club. Re-
search, teaching, editorial; psychology
of speech and thinking, pathopsychology. F
YAROSHEVSKI, Cand. Educ. Sci. Mikhail G.
ul. K. Marxa 2, Kuliab, Tadjik ssr. b. 22
Aug 1916 Kherson. c.esc '45 Psych. Inst,
Acad. of Educ. Sci, ussr. asst. dir. and
head, Chair of Educ. and Psych, Kuliab
State Tchr. Trng. Inst. Teaching, research, administration; history of psy-
chology in nineteenth century, psychology
of speech and the mind. M
ZACHEPITSKI, Rafail A. 7 Sovetskaia 40,
kv. 4, Leningrad S-144. b. 1900. Leningrad
Inst. of Med, ussr. sci. wrkr, Psychoneur. Inst. after Bekhterev, ul. Kazachia 3,
Leningrad S-19. Member: Leningrad Socy.
of Psychiatrists and Neuropathologists.
Psychotherapy, research, consulting, clinical practice; personality and the development of neuroses. M
ZAKHAROV, Cand. Educ. Sci. Alexander N.
Simonovski val 9, kv. 2, Moscow. b. 1924.
c.esc '50 Psych. Inst, Acad. of Educ. Sci,
ussr. jr. sci. wrkr, Psych. Inst, Acad.
of Educ. Sci, Mokhovia 9, Moscow. Research; psychology of thinking. M
**ZAKUEV-ZAKUZADE, Dr. Phil, Prof.
Akhmed K.** ul. Miasnikova 9, kv. 104,
Baku 5. b. 1888 sel. Kumukh, Dagestan
assr. ph.d '49 Baku, ussr. professor,
Chair of Psych, Azerbaijan Tchr. Trng. Inst.
after Lenin, ul. Shaumiana 39, Baku.
Teaching, research; children's memory. M
ZALTSMAN, Cand. Educ. Sci, Mrs. Bella N.
ul. Irininskaia 3b, kv. 9, Kiev. b. 24 Feb
1908 Chernigov. c.esc '50, ussr. sr. tchr,
Chair of Psych, Kiev Tchr. Trng. Inst.
after Gorky. Teaching, research, profession-
al writing; methods of teaching psychology,
memory, imagination. F
ZANKOV, Dr. Educ, Prof. Leonid V. Tverskoi-
Yamskoi per. 10, kv. 10, Moscow D-47.

b. 23 Apr 1901 Warsaw, Poland. ED.D '46. HEAD, Lab. of Exper. Didactics, Inst. of Theory of History of Educ, Acad. of Educ. Sci, Lobkovski per. 5/16, Moscow. Member: Psych. Socy. of the AESC. Research, educational psychology, professional writing; memory and teaching, perception and speech, mental retardation. M

ZAPOROZHETS, Cand. Educ. Sci, Lect. Alexander V. Psych. Inst, Mokhovaia, 9 Moscow. b. 30 Aug 1905 Kiev. C.ESC '46, USSR. HEAD, Lab. of Pre-School Children's Psych, Psych. Inst, Acad. of Educ. Sci; LECTURER, Moscow Univ. Research, teaching; evolution of children's thinking, free movements. M

ZARKUA, Cand. Educ. Sci. Mikhail B. ul. Revoliutsii 1905, 6, Kutaisi, Georgian SSR. b. 5 Sept 1906. C.ESC '52 Psych. Inst. after Uznadze. USSR. LECTURER, Chair of Educ. and Psych, Kutaisi Tchr. Trng. Inst. Research, teaching, educational psychology; psychology of creative work. M

ZARUDNAIA, Cand. Educ. Sci, Mrs. Anna A. Pervomaiskaia 30, kv. 36, Mogiliov, BSSR. b. 10 July 1909 Yarslavskaia obl, Rostovski r-n, selo Dioboly. C.ESC '40, USSR. ASST. DIR, Mogiliov Tchr. Trng. Inst. Administration, teaching, research; teaching and the mental development of children. F

ZEMTSOVA, Cand. Biol. Sci, Mrs. Maria I. 9 Ulitsa Oktiabrskogo Polia 8, kv. 17, Moscow. b. 8 Aug 1903. C.BSC '30, USSR. HEAD, Sect. of the Blind, Defectology Inst, Acad. of Educ. Sci, Pogodinskaia 8, Moscow. Teaching, applied and educational psychology, professional writing; psychology of blindness. F

ZHAVORONKO, Cand. Educ. Sci, Mrs. A-lexandra I. ul. Engelsa 7/10, kv. 8, Kiev. b. 10 Mar 1913. C.ESC '53 Kiev Univ, USSR. SR. SCI. WRKR, Psych. Inst, ul. Lenina 10, Kiev. Member: The Psych. Socy. Research, educational psychology, professional writing. F

ZHEKULIN, Cand. Educ. Sci, Lect. Sergei. ul. Sovetskaia 86, kv. 34, Kalinin. b. 11 May 1895 Krivoi Rog. C.ESC '38 Moscow Tchr. Trng. Inst, USSR. ASST. DIR, Kalinin Tchr. Trng. Inst. Teaching, research, administration; psychology of teaching, thinking, emotions. M

ZHINKIN, Cand. Educ. Sci. Nikolai I. Briusovsky per. 2/14, kv. 90, Moscow K-9. b. 14 July 1893 Vladimir. C.ESC '47 Psych. Inst, Acad. of Educ. Sci, USSR. SR. SCI. WRKR, Psych. Inst, Acad. of Educ. Sci, Mokhovaia 9, Moscow; TEACHER, Moscow

Tchr. Trng. Inst. Research, teaching; psychology of speech. M

ZHITNIKOVA, Mrs. Larisa M. ul. Strushnia 17, Mogiliov, BSSR. b. 10 Sept 1926. B.SC '50 USSR. TEACHER, Chair of Educ. and Psych, Mogilev State Tchr. Trng. Inst. Member: All-Union Socy. of Propagating Polit. and Cultural Knowledge. Teaching, research, student. F

ZHUIKOV, Cand. Educ. Sci. Sergei F. ul. Novo-Peschanaia 24, kv. 43, Moscow 252. b. 3 Oct 1911 Udmurtskaia ASSR, Vovopsky r-n, d. Zhuikovo. C.ESC '48 Psych. Inst, Moscow, USSR. SR. SCI. WRKR, Psych. Inst, Mokhovaia 9, Moscow. Research, educational psychology; psychology of learning grammar and spelling. M

ZHURAVLEVA, Cand. Educ. Sci, Lect, Mrs. Raisa Y. ul. Mashkova 17, kv. 19, Moscow. b. 8 Aug 1911 Moscow. C.ESC '48, USSR. LECTURER, Chair of Psych, State Central Inst. of Physical Trng. after Stalin, ul. Kazakova 18, Moscow. Teaching, research; memory and teaching; psychology of sports. F

ZINCHENKO, Cand. Educ. Sci, Lect. Piotr I. ul. Barachnaia 16, kv. 60, Kharkov. b. 29 June 1903. C.ESC '36 Kharkov, USSR. LECTURER, Chair of Educ. and Psych, Kharkov Tchr. Trng. Inst. of Foreign Languages after Krupskaia, prospect Stalina 18, Kharkov. Teaching, research; memory. M

ZIUBIN, Cand. Educ. Sci. Leonid M. ul. Telezhnaia 3, kv. 11, Leningrad 24. b. 17 Jan 1925 Belgorod. C.ESC '56 Leningrad Univ, USSR. JR. SCI. WRKR, Leningrad Inst. of Educ, Acad. of Educ. Sci, nab. Kutuzova 8, Leningrad; LECTURER, All-Union Socy. of Propagating Polit. and Cultural Knowledge. Research, educational psychology, consulting; mental activity of children. M

ZVEREVA, Cand. Educ. Sci, Mrs. Maria V. ul. 4 Meshchanskaia 6, kv. 16, Moscow 1-90. b. 7 Dec 1921 Moskovskaia obl. C.ESC '48, USSR. SR. SCI. WRKR, Lab. of Exper. Didactics, Inst. of Theory and History of Educ, Acad. of Educ. Sci, Lobkovski per 5/16, Moscow. Research; perception in mentally retarded children. F

ZYKOVA, Cand. Educ. Sci, Mrs. Vera I. Petrovsko-Razumovskaia alleia 26, kv. 96, Moscow A-83. b. 7 Aug 1908 Arkhangelskaia obl. C.ESC '39 Tchr. Trng. Inst, USSR. SR. SCI. WRKR, Psych. Inst, Acad. of Educ. Sci, Mokhovaia 9, Moscow. Research, educational psychology; psychology of teaching. F

UNITED KINGDOM

ABENHEIMER, Dr. Karl Marcus. 46 Belmont St, Glasgow W. 2, Scot. b. 2 Nov 1898 Mannheim, Ger. Dr. '21 Univ. of Heidelberg, Ger. PSYCHOTHERAPIST, priv. prac. Member: BPS. Psychotherapy, consulting, guidance, clinical practice; psychoanalysis and analytical psychology. M

ABI RAFI, Dr. Amin y. St. Andrew's Hosp, Thorpe, Norwich, Eng. b. 20 June 1920 Aley, Lebanon. PH.D '53 Univ. of London, Eng. CLIN. PYSCH'T, St. Andrew's Hosp. Member: BPS. Testing, consulting, clinical practice, guidance, psychotherapy; intellectual deterioration, perceptual disturbances, projective techniques. M

ABRAMS, Mrs. Anita Rosalie. 2 Parklake Ave, Salford 7, Lancaster, Eng. b. 22 Dec 1928 Salford, Eng. BA '50 Univ. of Cambridge, Eng. Member: BPS, No. Grp. of Guid. Clinics. Testing, consulting, applied psychology; projective, attainment and intelligence testing. F

ACE, Philip William. Child Guid. Clin, Catherine St. Plymouth, Eng. b. 28 Sept 1909 Swansea, Wales. BA '45 Univ. of London, Eng. EDUC. PSYCH'T, Educ. Authority, Conbourg St, Plymouth. Member: BPS. Educational psychology, testing, teaching, clinical analysis, child guidance. M

ADAMS, Richard Henry. Tunground, Kingswood Schools, Kennard Rd, Bristol, Eng. b. 31 July 1914 London, Eng. MA '40 Univ. of London, Eng. PRINCIPAL, Kingswood Trng. and Classif. Schools. Member: BPS. Administration, educational psychology, guidance; juvenile delinquency. M

ADLER, Dr. Gerhard. 29 Welbeck St, London W. 1, Eng. b. 14 Apr 1904 Berlin, Ger. Dr. phil. '27 Univ. of Freiburg, Ger. PSYCHOTHERAPIST, priv, prac; TRNG. ANALYST, Socy. of Analytical Psych; ED. BD, *Journal of Analytical Psychology*; *Psyche*. Member: BPS, Socy. of Anal. Psych. Psychotherapy, administration, professional writing, teaching, editorial. M

ALCOCK, Miss Augusta Theodora. Tavistock Inst. of Human Relat, 2 Beaumont St, London W. 1; Eng. b. 20 Sept 1888 Berkhamsted, Eng. SR. RORSCHACH TUTOR, Tavistock Inst. of Human Relat. Member: BPS, BRF, SPT, Assn. of Child. Psychotherapists. Teaching, child psychotherapy, research, testing; asthma in childhood, teachers' attitudes, projective techniques. F

ALEXANDER, Miss Helen Campbell. Riverdale, 4 Mure Pl, Newmilns, Ayrshire, Scot. b. 18 Dec 1915 Kilmarnock, Scot. ED.B '46 Univ. of Glasgow, Scot. ASST. PSYCH'T, Educ. Comm, Ayrshire County Counc,

County Bldg, Ayr, Scot. Member: BPS. Guidance, educational psychology, testing, remedial treatment. F

ALEXANDER, Dr. William Picken. Assn. of Educ. Committees for Eng. and Wales, 10 Queen Anne St, London W. 1, Eng. b. 12 Dec 1905 Paisley, Scot. PH.D '34 Univ. of Glasgow, Scot. SECRETARY, Assn. of Educ. Committees for Eng. and Wales. Member: BPS. Educational administration; nature of ability. M

ALLAN, Miss Barbara Napier. 2 Melville Rd, Dalkeith, Midlothian, Scot. b. 3 Jan 1915 Dalkeith, Scot. ED.B '50 Univ. of Edinburgh, Scot. EDUC. PSYCH'T, Educ. Comm, E. Lothian County Counc, County Bldg, Haddington, E. Lothian. Scot. Member: BPS. Guidance, testing, educational psychology, consulting. F

ALLAN, Mrs. Joan Reed. 45 Sussex Sq, Brighton, Sussex, Eng. b. 8 Aug 1923 London, Eng. BA '50 Univ. of London, Eng. Member: BPS, BRF. Testing, applied psychology, guidance; projective techniques, intelligence testing; child development. F

ALLISON, Rev. Lewis Henry. 17 Roker Park Rd, Sunderland, Durham, Eng. b. 9 June 1900 London, Eng. MA '37 Univ. of Reading, Eng. SUPERINTENDENT, Sunderland N. Methodist Circuit, Dock St, Sunderland. Member: BPS. Minister, clinical practice, teaching; personality tests, spiritual healing. M

AMBROSE, John Anthony. Tavistock Clin, Tavistock Inst. of Human Relat, 2 Beaumont St, London W. 1, Eng. b. 15 Nov 1925 Ilkley, UK. BA '53 Balliol Coll, Univ. of Oxford, Eng. RES. PSYCH'T, Child Devel. Res. Unit, Tavistock Inst. of Human Relat. Member: BPS. Research, psychotherapy, student; psychoanalysis, human relations. M

ANDERSON, Miss Jemima Ann. 13 Henderson Park, Windygates, Fife, Scot. b. 27 Oct 1924 Windygates, Scot. ED.B '51 Univ. of St. Andrews, Scot. EDUC. PSYCH'T, Child Guid. Clin, 1 Swan Rd, Kirkcaldy, Fife, Scot. Member: BPS. Testing, educational guidance, remedial teaching, treatment of behavior problems. F

ANDERSON, Walter. 77 Russell St, Wishaw, Lanarkshire, Scot. b. 4 Dec 1913 Scot. ED.B '48 Univ. of Glasgow, Scot. H. M. INSPECTOR of SCHOOLS, Scottish Educ. Dept, St. Andrew's House, Edinburgh, Scot. Member: BPS. Inspection of special schools; mental testing of handicapped children. M

ANDREWS, Miss Pamela Monica Joan. 21 Bromeswell Rd, Ipswich, Suffolk, Eng.

b. 28 Aug 1919 Slough, Eng. MA '52 Univ. of London, Eng. EDUC. PSYCH'T, E. Suffolk Educ. Comm, E. Suffolk County Counc, Rope Walk, Ipswich, Suffolk. Member: BPS. Educational guidance, testing, teaching, backwardness in the basic skills, student placement, maladjusted school children. F

ANDRY, Dr. Robert George. 30 Brondesbury Park, London N.W. 6, Eng. b. 15 Oct 1923. PH.D '55 Univ. of London, Eng. SR. CLIN. PSYCH'T, St. Thomas' Hosp. London S.W. Eng; LECTURER, Univ. of London; SR. RES. OFF, L.S.E. Univ. of London. Member: BPS. Clinical practice, consulting, teaching; psychology and crime, psychosis, group behavior, measurement of attitudes, criminology. M

ANNETT, John. Inst. of Exper. Psych, 34 Banbury Rd, Oxford, Eng. b. 11 July 1930 Gillingham, Eng. BA '53 Univ. of Oxford, Eng. RES. WRKR, Univ. of Oxford, Univ. Chest, Broad St, Oxford. Member: BPS. Research, industrial psychology, teaching; learning theory, motor skills, industrial training, training of mental defectives. M

ANNETT, Mrs. Marian Elsie. 26 Potland Rd, Oxford, Eng. b. 28 June 1931 Whitwell, Eng. BA '52 Univ. of London, Eng. CLIN. PSYCH'T, Warneford Hosp, Oxford. Member: BPS. Diagnostic testing, research, teaching; concept formation, development of children's thinking, impairment in mental illness. F

ANSTEY, Dr. Edgar. 27 Cumberland Dr, Esher, Surrey, Eng. b. 1917 Bombay, India. PH.D '49 Univ. of London, Eng. CIVIL SERVANT, PRIN, Home Off, Whitehall, London S.W. 1, Eng. Member: BPS. Administration, professional writing, teaching; selection tests, interviewing, staff training. M

ANTHONY, Mrs. Helen Sylvia. 25 Northway, London N.W. 11, Eng. b. 15 Feb 1898 Howick, Natal. S. Africa. MA '39 Univ. of London, Eng. PRIN. PSYCH'T, Sci. 4, Air Ministry, Turnstile House, High Holborn, W.C. 1, London, Eng. Member: BPS, AIPA. Applied psychology, personnel selection, research; social development of children, psychomotor tests of personality, sociological implications of achievement test differences. F

ARGYLE, Michael. Inst. of Exper. Psych, Univ. of Oxford, 34 Banbury Rd, Oxford, Eng. b. 11 Aug 1925 UK. MA '50 Univ. of Cambridge, Eng. LECT. in SOC. PSYCH, Univ. of Oxford. Member: BPS. Teaching, research, professional writing; small social groups, industrial productivity, social theory. M

AUSTIN, Mrs. Frances May. 26 Harborne

Rd, Edgbaston, Birmingham 15, Eng. b. 19 July 1893 Belfast, N. Ire. M.SC '23 Univ. of Birmingham, Eng. Member: BPS. Retired; Thought processes, fear, learning theory. F

BACKUS, Dr. Percy Lavern. 92 Harley St, London W. 1, Eng. b. 26 Oct 1892 Welland, Can. MD. CM, McGill Univ. Can. CONSULT. PSYCHIATRIST, St. Mary's Hosp, London W. 2. Member: BPS, RMPS, Br. Med. Assn, Royal Socy. of Med. Consulting, psychotherapy, teaching. M

BAKER, Horace Charles. 61 Hallam Crange Rd, Sheffield 10, Eng. b. 10 Feb 1928 Stockton on Tees, Eng. MA '56 Univ. of Liverpool, Eng. SR. SCI. OFF, Br. Iron and Steel Res. Assn, Hoyle St, Sheffield; HONORARY TUTOR in INDUS. PSYCH, Univ. of Sheffield. Member: BPS. Research, industrial psychology, teaching; accidents, social thinking, experimental design, human relations in industry. M

BALBERNIE, Richard. 26 Kirk Close, Oxford Eng. b. 20 June 1923 Croydan, Eng. MA '47 Univ. of Cambridge, Eng. RES. WRKR, Noel Buxton Trust, London, Eng. Member: BPS, Int. Educ. Assn. Research, applied and educational psychology, teaching; creative children's community for deprived and disturbed adolescents, comparative studies of liberal and rigid communities. M

BALINT, Dr. Michael. 7 Park Sq. W, London N.W. 1, Eng. b. 12 Mar 1896 Budapest, Hungary. MD '20 Univ. of Budapest, Hungary. CONSULT. PSYCHIATRIST, Tavistock Clin, 2 Beaumont St, London W. 1. Member: BPS, Br. Psychoanal. Socy. Psychotherapy, consulting, research, teaching; psychoanalysis. M

BANISTER, Dr. Harry. Alfordesweye, Grantchester, Cambridge, Eng. b. 12 Apr 1882 St. Annes on Sea, Eng. PH.D '25 Univ. of Cambridge, Eng. Member: BPS. Retired; psychotherapy, child guidance, professional writing; hearing, vision. M

BANNON, William J. 47 Sandhurst Ave, Birmingham 34, Eng. b. 23 May 1905 Glasgow, Scot. ED.B '48 Univ. of Glasgow, Scot. SR. EDUC. PSYCH'T, Birmingham Educ. Comm, Margaret St, Birmingham 3; LECT. in CHILD PSYCH, Hlth. Visitors Course, Univ. of Birmingham. Member: BPS. Educational psychology, administration, clinical practice, testing; preventive measures in mental health, intelligence and achievement tests. M

BARBOUR, Dr. Robert Freeland. Hill House, Iron Acton, Bristol, Eng. b. 27 Mar 1904 Colinton, Midlothian. MB, CH.B '29 Univ. of Edinburgh, Scot. CONSULT. PSYCHIATRIST, Bristol Tchng. Hosp. Grp, Univ. of Bristol, Queens Rd, Bristol; DIRECTOR, Child Guid. Clin; PSYCHIAT. SPEC, Ministry of Natl. Ins; PSYCHIAT.

SPEC, Civil Serv. Member: BPS, RMPA. Clinical practice, psychotherapy, teaching; child guidance, teaching normal psychology to medically oriented groups. M

BARBU, Dr. Zevedei. 12 Univ. Gardens, Glasgow W.2, Scot. b. 28 Jan 1914 Sibiu, Rumania. PH.D '54 Univ. of Glasgow, Scot. LECT. in PSYCH, Univ. of Glasgow. Member: BPS, Br. Sociol. Assn. Teaching, research, professional writing; political psychology, social perception, psychotherapy. M

BARCLAY, Miss Catherine Weir. 5 Balfleurs St, Milngavie, Glasgow, Scot. b. 30 Oct; 1906 Milngavie, Scot. ED.B '45 Univ. of Glasgow, Scot. SR. ASST. PSYCH'T, County Counc. of the County of Lanark, 191 Ingram St, Glasgow. Member: BPS. Educational psychology, psychotherapy, testing, child guidance, administration. F

BARKER, Mrs. Matilda Mary Helena. 6 Horn Beams, Welwyn Garden City, Herts, Eng. b. 17 May 1925 Kirkcaldy, Scot. ED.B '54 Univ. of Edinburgh, Scot. EDUC. PSYCH'T, Herts County Child Guid. Serv, Hill End, St. Albans, Herts. Member: BPS. Testing, clinical practice, teaching; educational research and methods. F

BARTLETT, Prof. Sir Frederic Charles. 161 Huntingdon Rd, Cambridge, Eng. b. 20 Oct 1886 Stow-on-the-Wold, Eng. MA '17 Univ. of Cambridge, Eng. MEMBER: Appl. Psych. Res. Unit, Med. Res. Counc, 15 Chaucer Rd, Cambridge, Eng. Member: SFP, Amer. Philos. Socy, Swed. Psych. Socy, Spanish Psych. Socy. Retired, research, applied psychology, consulting; remembering and thinking. M

BARTLETT, Robert John. 41 Warrington Rd, Harrow, Middlesex, Eng. b. 2 Apr 1897 Sudbury, Middlesex, Eng. M.SC '21 Univ. of London, Eng. Member: BPS, Royal Inst. of Philos, Assn. for the Study of Animal Behavior. Retired; teaching, research. M

BARTOSHUK, Dr. Alexander Karl. Burden Neur. Inst, Bristol, Eng. b. 8 Jan 1928 Montreal, Can. PH.D '54 McGill Univ, Can. EXPER. PSYCH'T, Burden Neur. Inst. Member: CPA, APA. Research; physiological measures of motivation and emotion during learning and performance of motor tasks. M

BATHURST, Dr. Georgina Campbell. 9 Wildwood Grove, Hampstead, London N.W. 3, Eng. b. 20 June 1891 Belfast, N. Ire. PH.D '40 Univ. of London, Eng. PSYCHOLOGIST, Warlingham Park Hosp, Warlingham, Surrey Eng. Member: BPS. Testing, clinical analysis, applied psychology, vocational guidance, remedial teaching. F

BEECH, Harold Reginald. 4 Bramcote Ct, Bramcote Ave, Mitcham, Surrey, Eng. b. 9 Oct 1925 Doncaster, Eng. BA '52

Univ. of Durham, Eng. RES. ASST, Inst. of Psychiat, Denmark Hill, London S.W. 5, Eng. Member: BPS. Clinical research, applied psychology; individual and group differences in perception. M

BEEDELL, Christopher John. 3 Windsor Terr, Bristol 8, Eng. b. 14 Dec 1924 Highbridge, Eng. B.SC '47 Univ. Coll, London, Eng. RES. FELLOW, Inst. of Educ, Univ. of Bristol. Member: BPS. Research, teaching, psychotherapy, clinical analysis; social control in small groups, assessment of auditory disorders. M

BELSON, William Albert. 41 York Mansions, Prince of Wales Dr, London, S.W. 11, Eng. b. 10 Mar 1921 Brisbane, Austl. BA '49 Univ. of Sydney, Austl. SR. RES. PSYCH'T, Br. Broadcasting Corp, Portland Pl, London. Member: BPS. Research, applied psychology, survey administration; attitude assessment, communication research, prediction techniques, test construction. M

BENE, Dr. Eva Mary. 143 Harley St, London W. 1, Eng. b. 4 Oct 1912 Budapest, Hungary. PH.D '54 Univ. of London, Eng. RES. ASST, Inst. of Psychiat, London Univ, Maudsley Hosp, Denmark Hill, London S.E. 5. Member: BPS. Research, development of new diagnostic techniques; projective techniques, emotional attitudes. F

BERLYNE, Dr. Daniel Ellis. Cen. for Advanc. Study in the Behavioural Sciences, Stanford California, USA. b. 25 Apr 1924 Salford, Eng. PH.D '53 Yale Univ. USA. LECT. in PSYCH, Univ. of Aberdeen, Scot. Member: BPS, Exper. Psych. Grp. Teaching, research, psychotherapy; behavior theory, symbolic processes, motivation. M

BERNSTEIN, Mrs. Marian. 11 Park Mansions, S. Lambeth Rd, London S.W. 8, Eng. b. 30 Sept 1931 Manchester, Eng. BA '52 Univ. of Manchester, Eng. PSYCHOTHER. TRAINEE, Tavistock Inst. of Human Relat, 2 Beaumont St, London W. 1. Member: BPS. Child Psychotherapy, testing, clinical analysis, research; psychoanalytic theory and practice, semantics. F

BEVANS, Herbert Gordon. Flat 3, Willerby Hall, Willerby, Nr. Hull, York, Eng. b. 27 Jan 1920 London, Eng. B.SC '49 Univ. of London, Eng. VOCAT. OFF, Indus. Rehab. b. 27 Jan 1920 London, Eng. B.SC '49 Univ. Unit, Ministry of Labour and Natl. Serv, Chamberlain Rd, Hull. Member: BPS. Applied and industrial psychology, testing, student; errors of judgment in cognitive problem solving, psycho-motor tests, vocational guidance of the handicapped. M

BIRCH, Lewis Bernard. 272 Abbeydale Rd. S, Totley Rise, Sheffield, Eng. b. 24 Feb 1913 Burton on Trent, Eng. MA '51 Univ. of Birmingham, Eng. DEPUTY DIR. and

LECT. in EDUC. PSYCH, Inst. of Educ, Univ. of Sheffield, Western Bank, Sheffield; ASST. ED, *British Journal of Educational Psychology*. Member: BPS. Teaching, research, testing, administration, editorial; educability of handicapped pupils, physical disabilities and intelligence, effect of birth injuries upon future development.   M

BIRKETT, Nichol Thomson.   Child Guid. Cen, Corner House, 2 Atholl St, Perth, Scot. b. 8 Oct 1920 Macduff, Scot. ED.B '50 Univ. of Aberdeen, Scot. EDUC. PSYCH'T, Educ. Comm, Perth and Kinrose Joint County Counc, County Off, York Pl, Perth. Member: BPS. Educational psychology, parental guidance, testing, child therapy.   M

BLACK, Miss Elizabeth Marguerite.   75 Prince of Wales Mansions, London S.W. 11, Eng. b. 17 Jan 1914 London, Eng. MA '51 Univ. of London, Eng. EDUC. PSYCH'T, Middlesex Educ. Comm, 10 Great George St, London E.C. 1. Member: BPS. Educational psychology, testing, clinical analysis.   F

BLAIN, Dr. Isabel Janet.   33 Frognal, Hampstead, London N.W. 3, Eng. b. 29 Mar 1912 Turriff, Scot. PH.D '38 Bryn Mawr Coll, USA. SCI. STAFF, Natl. Inst. of Indus. Psych, 14 Welbeck St, London W. 1. Member: BPS. Industrial psychology, research; training industrial workers, methodology of industrial investigation.   F

BLOCK, Lionel Victor.   Hollymoor Hosp, Birmingham 31, Eng. b. 16 Aug 1910 London, Eng. BA '45 Univ. of Reading, Eng. SR. CLIN. PSYCH'T, Hollymoor and Rubery Hill Hosps, No. 6 Grp, Northfield, Birmingham. Member: BPS, APA, Assn. of Profes. Psychother. Clinical testing, psychotherapy, research; behavior as a function of physiology and biochemistry, drug therapy, learning theory, projective techniques.   M

BLUNDEN, Dr. Ruth.   7, North Ct, Gt. Peter St, London S.W. 1, Eng. b. 30 Mar 1904 Stuttgard, Ger. PH.D '27 Univ. of Giessen, Ger. CLIN. PSYCH'T, St. Francis Hosp, Haywards Heath, Sussex, Eng. Member: BPS. Testing, and clinical analysis, applied psychology; learning theory, theory of diagnostic tests.   F

BLYTHEN, Miss Kathleen.   Educ. Dept, Somerset County Counc, Trull Rd, Taunton Somerset, Eng. b. 5 Jan 1909 Hayes, Middx, Eng. BA '37 King's Coll, London, Eng. EDUC. PSYCH'T, Somerset County Counc. Educational psychology, clinical child guidance, administration.   F

BOREHAM, John Lionel.   17 Arterberry Rd, London S.W. 20, Eng. b. 10 Jan 1924 UK. BA '48 Univ. of London, Eng. SR. CLIN. PSYCH'T, Tavistock Clin, 2 Beaumont St,

London W. 1. Member: BPS, BRF. Clinical diagnosis, teaching, psychotherapy, research; projective techniques, marital tensions, effects of psychotherapy.   M

BOSTON, Mrs. Christine Mary.   5 Kingsbridge Rd, London W. 10, Eng. b. 27 May 1923 London, Eng. BA '44 Univ. of London, Eng. Member: BPS, Assn. of Child Psychotherapists. Child psychotherapy; child development.   F

BOWLBY, Dr. Edward John Mostyn.   Tavistock Clin, 2 Beaumont St, London W. 1, Eng. b. 26 Feb 1907 London, Eng. MA '32 Univ. of Cambridge, Eng. DEPUTY DIR, Tavistock Clin; DIRECTOR, Dept. for Child. and Parents, and Child Devel. Res. Unit, Tavistock Clin. Member: BPS, RMPA, Royal Med. Socy, Amer. Psychiat. Assn, Br. Psychoanal. Socy, Assn. of Psychiat. Soc. Wrkrs, Assn. of Child Psychotherapists. Clinical practice, psychotherapy, administration, teaching, research; social responses in infants and young children, early social experience and personality development. M

BOWLEY, Dr. Agatha Hilliam.   39 Temple Fortune Hill, London N.W. 11, Eng. b. 3 Oct 1909 Reading, Eng. BA '30 Univ. of London, Eng. EDUC. PSYCH'T, Queen Elizabeth Hosp, Haikey Rd, London E. 2; EDUC. PSYCH'T, R.N.I.B. 224 Gr. Portland St, London W. 1; EDUC. PSYCH'T, Cheyne Spastic Cen, 61 Cheyne Walk, London S.W. 3; LECTURER, Natl. Child. Home; LECTURER, Banstead Hosp. Member: BPS, Natl. Assn. for Ment. Hlth. Clinical analysis, educational guidance, teaching, research; blind, spastic and maladjusted pre-school children, problems of assessment and adjustment, parental attitudes.   F

BOWYER, Miss Laura Ruth.   Dept. of Psych, Univ. of Bristol, 27 Belgrave Rd, Bristol, Eng. b. 4 Dec 1907 Brechin, Scot. ED.B '45 Univ. of Glasgow, Scot. LECTURER, Univ. of Bristol. Member: BPS, Amer. Socy. for Res. in Child Devel. Teaching, student counseling, clinical analysis, psychotherapy, research; projective techniques, perception, personality theory, social psychology.   F

BRADDOCK, Albert Parcy.   126 Selly Park Rd, Birmingham 29, Eng. b. 10 Feb 1877 Hove, Sussex, Eng. MA '17 King's Coll, London, Eng. Member: BPS. Retired; advertising.   M

BRADFORD, Edouard Jules Gaston.   7 Taptonville Rd, Sheffield 10, Eng. b. 4 Feb 1888 London, Eng. M.SC '19 Univ. of London, Eng. SR. PSYCH'T, Management Comm, Sheffield Hosps, No. 1 and No. 2, Sheffield Regional Hosp. Bd, Middlewood Hosp, Middlewood, Sheffield 6. Member: BPS. Testing, consulting, teaching; test construction, educational guidance, clini-

cal diagnosis. M
BRADLEY, Noel Clifton. 1194 Crafmont
Ave, Berkeley 8, California, USA. b. 2 Dec
1916 Christchurch, N.Z. PH.D '52 Univ. of
London, Eng. PSYCHOANALYST, priv. prac.
Member: BPS, Br. Psychoanal. Socy, Inst.
for Study and Trtmt. of Delinquency.
Psychotherapy, research; psychoanalysis. M
BRADSHAW, Miss Joyce Buckley. 26 Mossley
Rd, Crasscroft near Oldham, Lancaster,
Eng. b. 22 Feb 1921 Oldham, Eng. B.SC
'48 Univ. of Manchester, Eng. EDUC.
PSYCH'T, Local Educ. Authority, Chapel
St, Salford 3, Eng. Member: BPS, Natl.
Assn. for Ment. Hlth. Clinical testing
and analysis, administration, teaching
student nurses; educationally subnormal
children. F
BRENGELMANN, Dr. Johannes Clemens.
Inst. of Psychiat. Maudsley Hosp. Den-
mark Hill, London S.E. 5, Eng. b. 15 Feb
1920 Essen/Oldenburg, Ger. MD '45 Univ.
of Göttingen, Ger. RES. ASST, Inst. of
Psychiat. Member: BPS, APA, DGP, BDP.
Research, professional writing, teaching;
expressive movement, learning and perception in abnormal personality. M
BRIERLEY, Harry. 30 Moor Hey Rd, Mag-
hull near Liverpool, Eng. b. 2 Feb 1927
Clitheroe, Eng. BA '51 Univ. of Cambridge,
Eng. PSYCHOLOGIST, Her Majesty's Prison,
Hornby Rd, Liverpool 9. Member: BPS.
Clinical testing, applied psychology,
guidance; achievement testing of mental
defectives, attitude measurement of crimi-
nals, training and treatment of specific
criminal groups. M
BRIERLEY, Dr. Marjorie Flowers. Rowling
End, Newlands, Keswick, Cumberland, Eng
b. 24 Mar 1893 London, Eng. B.SC '20
Univ. of London, Eng. HONORARY ASST.
ED, *International Journal of Psycho-
Analysis.* Member: BPS, Br. Psychoanal.
Socy. Retired, editorial, professional
writing; theory of psychoanalysis, feminine
psychology. F
BRIERS, John Michael. Kingswood Trng.
Sch, Kennard Rd, Kingswood, Nr. Bristol,
Eng. b. 30 May 1922 Geraldton, Austl.
BA '48 Univ. of Western Australia. RESID.
CLIN. PSYCH'T, Kingswood Trng. Sch.
Member: BPS-A. Clinical practice and
guidance, individual and group psycho-
therapy, testing, clinical analysis; juvenile
delinquency, projective techniques, group
process. M
BROADBENT, Donald Eric. Med. Res. Counc,
Appl. Psych. Unit, 15 Chaucer Rd, Cam-
bridge, Eng. b. 6 May 1926 Birmingham,
Eng. MA '51 Univ. of Cambridge, Eng.
PSYCHOLOGIST, Sci. Staff, Med. Res.
Counc, Appl. Psych. Unit. Member: BPS,
Exper. Psych. Grp, Ergonomics Res. Socy.

Research on acoustic problems, professional
writing, applied psychology; prolonged
work, attention, learning theory. M
BROADHURST, Dr. Anne. 6 Hampstead
Grove, London N.W. 3, Eng. b. 14 Feb
1930 Belfast, N. Ire. PH.D '56 Univ. of
London, Eng. SR. CLIN. PSYCH'T, Springfield
Hosp, Beechcroft Rd, London S.W. 17.
Member: BPS. Psychiatric research, clinical
testing, consulting; learning theory and
objective psychotherapy, remedial teaching
market research techniques. F
BROADHURST, Dr. Peter Lovell. Animal
Psych. Lab, Inst. of Psychiat, Bethlem
Royal Hosp, Beckenham, Kent, Eng. b.
2 Feb 1924 Teddington, Eng. PH.D '56
Univ. of London, Eng. RES. PSYCH'T,
Univ. of London, Inst, of Psychiat,
Maudsley Hosp, Denmark Hill, London
S.E. 5, Eng. Member: BPS, APA, Socy. for
the Study of Animal Behavior, Socy. for
Exper. Biology. Research, professional
writing, administration; abnormal animal
behavior, psychogenetics, behavioral effects
of drugs. M
BROLLY, Maxwell Hall. Westminster
House, 7 Millbank, London S.W. 1, Eng.
b. 10 Jan 1914 Wednesbury, Eng. ED.B
'48 Univ. of Glasgow, Scot. PSYCHOLOGIST,
Pers. Dept, British-American Tobacco Co.
Ltd. Member: BPS. Industrial psychology,
research, teaching; personnel selection. M
BROMLEY, Dennis Basil. Dept. of Psych,
Univ. of Liverpool, 7 Abercromby Sq,
Liverpool 7, Eng. b. 18 Apr 1924 Stoke-
on-Trent ,Eng. BA '50 Univ. of Manchester,
Eng. LECTURER, Univ. of Liverpool.
Member: BPS. Research, teaching, adminis-
tration; gerontology, cognition, social
interaction. M
BROWN, Miss Janet Robertson. 59 Titwood
Rd, Glasgow S. 1, Scot. b. 12 Oct 1914
Glasgow, Scot. ED.B '46 Univ. of Glasgow,
Scot. ASST. EDUC. PSYCH'T, Glasgow Corp.
Educ. Authority, 129 Bath St, Glasgow C. 2.
Member: BPS. Child guidance, testing
psychotherapy, lecturing; left-handedness,
intelligence and attainment tests, pro -
jective techniques. F
BROWN, Dr. John. Dept. of Psych, Birk-
beck Coll, Univ. of London, London
W.C. 1, Eng. b. 2 Aug 1925 London, Eng.
PH.D '55 Univ. of Cambridge, Eng.
LECTURER, Birkbeck Coll. Member: BPS.
Teaching, research, administration; memo-
ry, perception, experimental design. M
BRUCE, David James. Dept. of Psych, Univ.
of Reading, London Rd, Reading, Berks,
Eng. b. 7 Nov 1928 Rickmansworth, Eng.
BA '52 Univ. of Reading, Eng. LECTURER,
Univ. of Reading. Member: BPS. Teaching,
research; speech perception, recall of visual
and verbal material, organization of sym-

bolic material, visual aids in teaching. M
BUCHANAN, Miss Margaret Pettigrew. 101
Whitehall Pl, Aberdeen, Scot. b. 5 June
1907 Glasgow, Scot. ED.B Univ. of Glasgow
Scot. PRIN. PSYCH'T, Aberdeen Child Guid.
Cen, Corp. of Aberdeen Educ. Comm, 66
Carden Pl, Aberdeen. Member: BPS.
Clinical diagnosis and treatment, applied
and educational psychology, teaching;
child psychology, family relationships,
maladjusted children. F
BUCHER, Miss Sheila. 48 Champion Hill,
London S.E. 5, Eng. b. 2 Oct 1926 Geneva,
Switz. MA '53 Univ. of London, Eng.
EDUC. PSYCH'T, E. Ham County Borough
Counc, The Town Hall, London E. 6.
Member: BPS. Educational guidance and
treatment, testing; projective techniques,
child psychology, learning theory, edu-
cational problems. F
BUCK, Leslie John. 32 Eashing Point,
London S.W. 15, Eng. b. 12 Oct 1929
London, Eng. B.SC '52 Univ. of London,
Eng. MEMBER of SCI. STAFF, Indus. Psych.
Res. Grp, Med. Res. Counc, 38 Old Queen
St, London S.W. 1. Member: BPS. In-
dustrial psychology, research; group
process, motivation, attitude measure-
ment, human behavior in industry. M
BURKE, Mrs. Joyce Mary Gibson. 468
Footscray Rd, Eltham, London S.E. 9,
Eng. b. 27 Oct 1928 Hillegersberg-Rotter-
dam, Neth. BA '50 Univ. of London, Eng.
EDUC. PSYCH'T, Kent Educ. Comm, Cray-
ford Child Guid. Clin, Woodside Rd,
Barnehurst, Kent, Eng. Member: BPS.
Testing, guidance, educational psychology;
projective techniques, group process, case-
work with psychoanalytic orientation. F
BURNS, Charles. 29 Frederick Rd, Bir-
mingham 15, Eng. b. 20 Dec 1894 Chile.
SR. PSYCHIATRIST, Reg. Hosp. Bd, 10
Augustus Rd, Birmingham 15; PSYCHIA-
TRIST, Pediatric Unit, Dudley Rd. Hosp;
LECT. in CHILD GUID, Med. Sch, Queen
Elizabeth Hosp. Member: BPS. Psycho-
therapy, child guidance, consulting; malad-
justed children. M
CABOT, Dr. P. Sidney de Q. P.S. Cabot and
Co, 37-41 Bedford Row, London W.C. 1,
Eng. b. 18 July 1900 New Zealand. PH.D
'36 Harvard Univ, USA. DIRECTOR, P. S.
Cabot and Co; ED. BD, *Child Development
Abstracts.* Member: BPS, APA. Manage-
ment consulting, industrial psychology,
administration; human relations and
communication in industry, group behavior,
clinical assessment of executives. M
CALVERT, Miss Rhoda Margaret. 4 Latta St,
Dumbarton, Scot. b. 4 May 1921 Aberdeen,
Scot. ED.B '44 Univ. of Aberdeen, Scot.
PRIN. EDUC. PSYCH'T, Educ. Comm,
County Counc. of Dunbarton, 18 Park

Circus, Glasgow C. 3, Scot. Member: BPS.
Educational psychology, testing, child
guidance; intelligence and attainment tests,
remedial education. F
CAMERON, John Alexander. Fassiefern,
Conon Bridge, Ross Shire, Scot. b. 12
Mar 1914 Inverness, Scot. ED.B '51 Univ.
of Glasgow, Scot. EDUC. PSYCH'T, Ross
and Cromarty Educ. Comm, Educ. Off,
High St, Dingwall, Ross Shire. Member:
BPS. Applied and educational psychology,
administration, guidance; intelligence and
attainment testing, learning theory, re-
medial teaching techniques, speech thera-
py. M
CAMERON, Miss Mary Young. Wauchope
Cottage, Langholm, Dumfriesshire, Scot.
b. 19 June 1907 Glasgow, Scot. ED.B '47
Univ. of Glasgow, Scot. EDUC. PSYCH'T,
Carlisle Corp, 2 George St, Carlisle, Eng.
Member: BPS. Child and parent guidance,
testing, educational psychology, treatment
of emotionally disturbed children. F
CAMPBELL, Dugal. 45A Brockley View,
London S.E. 23, Eng. b. 12 Jan 1929
London, Eng. BA '52 Univ. of Oxford,
Eng. RES. ASST, Inst. of Psychiat, Den-
mark Hill, London S.E. 5. Member: BPS.
Research student; learning theory, slow-
ness of psychological functions in psychia-
tric patients. M
CAMPBELL, Dr. Isabelle Erskine. 2 Enner-
dale Rd, Reading, Berks, Eng. b. 7 June
1894 Penicuik, Midlothian, Scot. PH.D
'43 Univ. of Reading, Eng. LECT. in EDUC,
Univ. of Reading, London Rd, Reading.
Member: BPS. Teaching, research, edu-
cational psychology, testing; learning
theory, achievement and intelligence tests,
attitude measurement. F
CARR, Albert. 3 Chapel Lane, Standlake,
Witney, Oxon, Eng. b. 6 Sept 1920
Liverpool, Eng. B.Litt '49 Merton Coll,
Oxford, Eng. EDUC. THERAPIST, Mulberry
Bush Sch. Ltd, Standlake. Member: BPS.
Educational psychology, research, teaching
emotionally disturbed children; social
perception, group process, projective tech-
niques. M
CARR, Mrs. Janet Gould. 18 Park Ave,
Woodford Green, Essex, Eng. b. 31 Mar
1927 Peking, China. BA '48 Univ. of
Reading, Eng. Member: BPS. F
CARRIGAN, Miss Mary Drummond. Dundee
Corp, Child Guid. Cen, 8A Nelson St,
Dundee, Scot. b. 3 Aug 1918 Glasgow,
Scot. ED.B '41 Univ. of Glasgow, Scot.
SR. ASST. EDUC. PSYCH'T, Dugdee Corp,
Child. Guid. Cen. Member: BPS. Guidance,
testing, teaching. F
CASSIE, Alexander. 88 Broom Rd, Tedding-
ton, Middlesex, Eng. b. 22 Dec 1916
Queenstown, S. Africa. MA '38 Univ. of

Aberdeen, Scot. PRIN. PSYCH'T. and DEPUTY HEAD, Psych. Br, Air Ministry, Sci. 4, Turnstile House, High Holborn, London W.C. 1, Eng. Member: BPS. Testing, military personnel selection, research, administration; training and assessment. M

CAST, Miss Beatrice Maud Dale. 8 Cavendish Rd, Clapham Common, London S.W. 12, Eng. b. 24 Sept 1905 London, Eng. MA '39 Univ. Coll, London, Eng. ASST. MISTRESS, Owen's Sch, The Brewers' Co. Ltd, Owen St, London. Member: BPS. Teaching, research, educational psychology; selection procedures. F

CASTLE, Dr. Peter Francis Charles. 4 Chemin des Bougeries, Conches, Geneva, Switz. b. 12 Jan 1922 London, Eng. PH.D '52 Univ. of London, Eng. MEMBER of DIV, Int. Labour Off, Rue de Lausanne, Geneva, Switz. Member: BPS. Personnel administration, applied and industrial psychology; social psychology. M

CATLIN, Mrs. Kathleen Mary. Fair View, Campsell, Doncaster, Eng. b. 3 June 1909 London, Eng. BA '33 Univ. of London, Eng. H.M. INSPECTOR, Ministry of Educ, Curzon St, London W. 1, Eng. Member: BPS. Inspector of educational institutions. F

CAWS, Dr. Allan George. 48 Links Rd, W. Wickham, Kent, Eng. b. 28 June 1903 Portsmouth, Eng. PH.D '33 Univ. of London, Eng. DEPUTY HEAD, Pub. Hlth. Dept, Battersea Polytechnic, London S.W. 11, Eng. Member: BPS. Teaching, administration, applied psychology, professional writing; learning theory, perception, social relationships in hospital situations, child study. M

CHAMBERS, Eric Gordon. Psych. Lab, Cambridge, Eng. b. 28 June 1900 Stoke-on-Trent, Eng. MA '25 Univ. of Cambridge, Eng. RES. STAFF, Appl. Psych. Unit, Med. Res. Counc, 38 Old Queen St, London S.W. 1, Eng; ASST. DIR. of RES. in INDUS. PSYCH, Univ. of Cambridge; LECT. in PSYCH. and STAT, Univ. of Cambridge. Member: BPS, Royal Stat. Socy. Research, statistical consultant, industrial psychology, teaching; accident proneness, personnel selection. M

CHAZAN, Maurice. 35B Croxteth Rd, Liverpool 8, Eng. b. 20 Nov 1922 Cardiff, Wales. MA '51 Univ. of Birmingham, Eng. EDUC. PSYCH'T. and LECT. in CHILD PSYCH, Child Guid. Cen, Liverpool Educ. Comm, Liverpool. Member: BPS. Testing, guidance, remedial teaching, administration; intelligence and achievement tests, projective techniques, social development of children, group play therapy. M

CHEN, Miss Anita King-Fun. Remed.

Educ. Cen, Univ. of Birmingham, Selly Wick Rd, Birmingham 29, Eng. b. 7 Aug 1930 Hong Kong. BA '51 Lake Forest Coll, USA. RES. STUD, Univ. of Birmingham. Child guidance, research, applied psychology; projective techniques, play therapy. F

CHESTERS, Miss Gwendolen Ella. 86 Ladbroke Rd, Holland Park, London W. 11 Eng. b. 28 Mar 1905 Blackburn, UK. BA '28 Univ. Coll, Nottingham, Eng. INSPECTOR, Children's Dept, Home Off, Horseferry House, London S.W. 1. Member: BPS, Assn. of Child Psychotherapists. Applied psychology, personnel guidance; child psychotherapy, group process, child development. F

CHILD, Hubert A. T. 3 N. Hill, London N. 6, Eng. b. 18 Dec 1904 Harrow, Eng. BA, Univ. of Cambridge, Eng. SR. EDUC. PSYCH'T, London County Counc, County Hall, London S.E. 1. Member: BPS. Educational psychology, testing, guidance, administration; group process, achievement tests, social development, cultural influences. M

CLARIDGE, Dr. Gordon Sidney. Hambledon, 69 Princes Ave, Walsall, Staffs, Eng. b. 23 Jan 1932 Walsall, Eng. PH.D '56 Inst. of Psychiat, London, Eng. CLIN. PSYCH'T, Leavesden Hosp, Abbots Langley, Watford, Herts, Eng. Member: BPS. Clinical testing, research, psychotherapy; learning theory, rehabilitation of mental defectives, motivation, personality. M

CLARK, David Findlay. Glenesk, 77 Greengate Lane, Birstall near Leicester, Eng. b. Aberdeen, Scot. MA '51 Univ. of Aberdeen, Scot. VOCAT. OFF, Indus. Rehab. Unit, Ministry of Labour and Natl. Serv, Humberstone Lane, Leicester. Member: BPS. Testing, rehabilitation and guidance of the handicapped; personality measurement, group structure and therapy, work attitudes. M

CLARK, Mrs. Hilda Mary. 40 St. Margaret's Rd, London, S. E. 4, Eng. b. 23 Jan 1905 Stoke-on-Trent, Eng. MA '55 King's Coll, London, Eng. TUTOR, Inst. of Educ, Univ. of Reading, Eng. Teaching, research, guidance. F

CLARK, Robert Peter. 38 Whitehall Terr, Aberdeen, Scot. b. 9 Mar 1910 Leven, Scot. ED.B '46 Univ. of Edinburgh, Scot. PRIN. LECT. in EDUC. SCI, Trng. Coll, St. Andrew St, Aberdeen. Member: BPS. Teacher training, educational consulting and psychology; learning theory, mental testing. M

CLARKE, Dr. Alan Douglas Benson. 22 Dalmeny Rd, Carshalton, Surrey, Eng. b. 21 Mar 1922 Carshalton, Eng. PH.D '50 Univ. of London, Eng. SR. CLIN. PSYCH'T, The Manor Hosp, Epsom, Surrey; TUTOR in

PSYCH, Univ. of London. Member: BPS. Applied psychology, research, teaching objective personality tests, factors influencing intellectual growth, learning, rehabilitation of the mentally deficient. M

CLARKE, Dr. Ann Margaret. 22 Dalmeny Rd, Carshalton, Surrey, Eng. b. 3 Nov 1928 Madras, India. PH.D '50 Univ. of London, Eng. CLIN. PSYCH'T, The Manor Hosp, Epsom, Surrey. Member: BPS. Applied psychology, clinical assessment, research, teaching; perceptual measurement of temperament, factors influencing intellectual growth, education of the subnormal. F

CLARKE, Miss Lilian Margaret. 22 Minto St, Edinburgh, Scot. b. 24 Sept 1924 Irvinestown, N. Ire. ED.B '51 Queen's Univ. of Belfast, N. Ire. ASST. EDUC. PSYCH'T, Child Guid. Clin, 7 Merchiston Park, Edinburgh. Member: BPS. Educational psychology, testing, guidance. F

CLAY, Miss Hilary Mary. 32 Newton Rd, Cambridge, Eng. b. 27 Nov 1920 New York City, USA. MA '54 Univ. of Cambridge, Eng. RES. WRKR, Nuffield Unit for Res. into Problems of Ageing, Psych. Lab, Univ. of Cambridge, Cambridge, Eng. Member: BPS, Ergonomics Res. Socy. Research; thinking in relation to age changes, industrial survey of skilled craftsmen. F

CLAYTON, Miss Eileen. 31A Post St, Godmanchester, Hunts, Eng. b. 18 Feb 1926 Darlington, Eng. BA '50 Univ. of Durham, Eng. EDUC. PSYCH'T, Local Educ. Authority, Market Sq, Hunts. Member: BPS. Educational psychology, testing, guidance. F

CLEUGH, Dr. Mary Frances. 36 St. Margaret's Rd, London S.E. 4, Eng. b. 22 June 1913 Whittington, Salop, Eng. PH.D '36 Univ. of London, Eng. SR. LECT, Inst. of Educ, Univ. of London, Malet St, London W.C. 1. Member: BPS. Teacher training, administration, research; education of subnormal children. F

CLYDE, Mrs. Janet Watt McKinnon. 38 Elmlands Grove, Stockton Lane, York, Eng. b. 12 July 1904 Dundee, Scot. MA '26 Univ. of St. Andrews, Scot. SR. PSYCH'T, Rowntree and Co, Ltd, The Coca Works, York. Member: BPS, Natl. Assn. of Ment. Hlth. Personnel psychology, research, guidance; placement of operatives, training methods, factors influencing production. F

COATS, Stephen Hartley. 50 Coolhurst Rd, London N. 8, Eng. b. 5 June 1918 Nelson, Eng. MA '43 Univ. of Cambridge, Eng. SR. CLIN. PSYCH'T, Middlesex Hosp, Mortimer St, London W. 1. Member: BPS, BRF, Assn. of Child Psychotherapists. Clinical analysis and practice, psychotherapy, teaching; psychoanalysis, Ror-

schach techniques, intelligence, testing. M

COCKETT, Dr. Reginald. 23 Netheravon Rd, Chiswick, London W. 4, Eng. b. 13 Nov 1915 London, Eng. PH.D '50 Univ. of London, Eng. PRIN. PSYCH'T, H. M. Prison Comm, N. M. Borstal Reception Cen, Latchmere House, Ham Common near Richmond, Surrey, Eng. Member: BPS. Clinical analysis and testing, administration: learning problems, penal and criminal psychology, psychopathology, training and therapy. M

COHEN, Prof. John. Dept. of Psych, Univ. of Manchester, Manchester 13, Eng. b. 20 Jan 1911 Tredegar, Eng. PH.D '40 Univ. of London, Eng. PROFESSOR, Univ. of Manchester. Member: BPS. Research, teaching, administration, broadcasting; thought processes, developmental psychology, group behavior. M

COLLINS, Joseph Edward. Piran Round, Playing Pl, Truro, Cornwall, Eng. b. 22 Oct 1916 Foster, Austl. PH.D '46 Univ. of Birmingham, Eng. EDUC. PSYCH'T, Cornwall County Counc, County Hall, Truro. Member: BPS, BRF. Educational psychology, child guidance; learning theory, educational retardation, projective techniques. M

COLLINS, Dr. Mary. Psych. Dept, Univ. of Edinburgh, S. Bridge, Edinburgh, Scot. b. Edinburgh, Scot. PH.D '23 Univ. of Edinburgh. Reader in Psych, Univ. of Edinburgh. Member: BPS, ICWP. Teaching, research, clinical testing, professional writing; color blindness, child psychology. F

COLLMANN, Dr. Robin Dickinson. 10 Glenlock Ct, Glenlock Rd, London N.W. 3, Eng. b. 6 Jan 1896 Melbourne, Austl. PH.D '31 Columbia Univ, USA. RES. PSYCH'T, Royal Eastern Counties Hosp, Colchester, Essex, Eng; MEMBER, Psychiat. Res. Comm, Essex, Eng, BPS. Research; mental deficiency. M

COLOQUHOUN, William Peter. Br. Med. Res. Counc, Appl. Psych. Res. Unit, 15 Chaucer Rd, Cambridge, Eng. b. 18 Aug 1928 Weymouth, Eng. MA '52 Univ. of Edinburgh, Scot. PSYCHOLOGIST, Sci. Staff, Br. Med. Res. Counc, Appl. Psych. Res. Unit. Member: BPS. Research, applied psychology, student; skilled performance, human engineering, effects of drugs. M

CONRAD, Dr. R. Appl. Psych. Res. Unit, 15 Chaucer Rd, Cambridge, Eng. b. 6 July 1916 London, Eng. PH.D '53 Univ. of Cambridge, Eng. RES. WRKR, Med. Res. Counc, 38a Old Queen St, London S.W. 1, Eng. Member: BPS, Ergonomics Res. Socy. Research, applied psychology, consulting; Visual perception, pacing and timing in sensory motor skills. M

COSTELLO, Charles Gerard. Dept. of Psych,

St. George's Hosp, Morpeth, Northumber-
land, Eng. b. 24 Sept 1929 Manchester,
Eng. BA '52 Univ. of Manchester, Eng.
SR. PSYCH'T, St. George's Hosp. Member:
BPS. Clinical analysis, research, adminis-
tration; visual imagery, projective tech-
niques, deterioration tests. M
COVENTRY, Miss Isabel Anderson. 16 Over-
toun Dr, Rutherglen, Glasgow, Scot. b. 22
Jan 1906 Glasgow, Scot. ED.B '52 Univ. of
Glasgow, Scot. ASST. PSYCH'T, Child Guid.
Serv, Educ. Comm. of Lanarkshire, 7
Clydesdale St, Hamilton, Lanarkshire,
Scot. Member: BPS. Child guidance,
educational and psychological testing, ad-
ministration; intelligence and achievement
tests. F
COVERDALE, Ralph. 44 Lonsdale Rd,
Oxford, Eng. b. 13 Oct 1918 Ingatestone,
Essex, Eng. B.Litt '49 Univ. of Oxford,
Eng. EXEC. DEVEL. OFF, Steel Co. of Wales
Ltd, Abbey Works, Port Talbot, Gla-
morgan, Wales. Member: BPS, Br. Oper-
ational Res. Socy. Personnel psychology,
research, testing; group dynamics, in-
dustrial morale, consumer research, pro-
jective and standardized testing. M
COWAN, Miss Margaret McQueen. 16 Elie St,
Glasgow W. 1, Scot. b. 23 Mar 1906 Glas-
gow, Scot. ED.B '45 Univ. of Glasgow,
Scot. TEACHER, Glasgow Corp, 129 Bath
St, Glasgow C. 2. Member: BPS. Teaching.F
COWE, Miss Marjory M. Moray House Trng.
Coll, Holyrood Rd, Edinburgh 8, Scot. b.
23 Feb 1913 Edinburgh, Scot. ED.B '48
Univ. of Edinburgh, Scot. LECT. in PSYCH,
Moray House Trng. Coll. Member: BPS.
Teacher training, educational psychology,
testing; child guidance, handicapped
children. F
COWIE, Dr. Flora Margaret Valda. 1 The
Knapp, Earley, Reading, Berks, Eng. b.
1 Feb 1913 Richmond, Surrey, Eng. PH.D
'40 Univ. of London, Eng. Member: BPS.
Retired; subjective judgement of theo-
logical properties of matter. F
COX, Dr. John William. Wentsland House,
Pontypool, Mon, S. Wales. b. 17 Jan 1893
London, Eng. D.SC '28 Univ. of London,
Eng. COUNTY EDUC. PSYCH'T, Monmouth-
shire, S. Wales. Member: BPS. Educational
psychology, testing, guidance; factor ana-
lysis, mechanical aptitude and manual skill,
psychotherapy. M
CRANE, Dr. Sybil Mary. Riverscourt, Park
Ave, Worcester, Eng. b. 27 Apr 1913
Shrewsbury, Eng. PH.D '50 Univ. of
London, Eng. PSYCHOLOGIST, Powick
Hosp, Worcester, Member: BPS. Testing,
consulting, guidance; esthetics, Rorschach,
intelligence and personality tests. F
CRAWFORD, Dr. Agnes. Dept. of Psych,
Univ. of Liverpool, 7 Abercromby Sq,

Liverpool 7, Eng. b. 7 Nov 1909 Lugar,
Scot. PH.D '50 Univ. of London, Eng.
LECTURER, Univ. of Liverpool. Member:
BPS. Teaching, research; backwardness in
reading, color blindness; learning theory. F
CRAWFORD, Dr. Alan. Road Res. Lab,
Hamondsworth, Middlesex, Eng. b. 11
May 1928 Darlington, Eng. PH.D '55 Univ.
of Edinburgh, Scot. SR. SCI. OFF, Road
Res. Lab, Dept. of Sci. and Indus. Res,
Lower Regent St, London W. 1, Eng.
Member: Ergonomics Res. Socy. Research
on human factors in highway transpor-
tation, industrial psychology; communi-
cation theory, learning theory and per-
ceptual set, electroencephalography. M
CROCKET, Dr. Richard Wilfred. Ingrebourne
Cen. for Psych. Med, St. George's Hosp,
Hornchurch, Essex, Eng. b. 9 Feb 1914
Kilmacolm, Scot. HEAD. Ingrebourne Cen.
for Psych. Med; CONSULT. in PSYCH. MED,
Oldchruch Hosp, Romford; CONSULT. in
PSYCH. MED, St. George's Hosp; PSYCHIA-
TRIST, London County Counc. Member:
BPS, RMPA. Consulting, clinical practice,
psychotherapy; psychosomatic medicine,
social psychiatry. M
CULLEN, Dr. John Henry. Psych. Lab, Univ.
of Cambridge, Downing Place, Cambridge,
Eng. b. 19 July 1929 Dublin, Eire. MB,
B.CH '52 Univ. Coll, Dublin, Eire. RES. ASST.
in PSYCHIAT, Med. Res. Counc, Univ. of
Cambridge; HONORARY CLIN. ASST, Adden-
brookes and Fulbourn Hosps, Cambridge.
Member: BPS. Research, guidance, con-
sulting, psychotherapy; disorders of per-
ception, psychosomatic diseases. M
CUMMINGS, Dr. Jean Dorothea. 31 Private
Rd, Sherwood, Notts, Eng. b. 29 Jan 1912
Darlington, Eng. PH.D '38 Univ. of London,
Eng. EDUC. PSYCH'T, Nottinghamshire
Child Guid. Clin, 3 Fletcher Gate, Nottingham. Member: BPS. Guidance, testing,
teaching; projective techniques, preventive
work in diagnosis of backwardness. F
CUNNINGHAM, Morris Anskar. 25 Leonard
Ave, Sherwood, Notts, Eng. b. 11 Mar
1916 Cambridge, Eng. MA '48 Univ. of
London, Eng. EDUC. PSYCH'T, Nottinghamshire County Counc, County Hall,
Nottingham. Member: BPS. Guidance,
testing, remedial teaching, educational
psychology; intelligence and achievement
tests, juvenile delinquency, maladjusted
children. M
CURR, William. Educ. Dept, Univ. of Birmingham, Birmingham 3, Eng. b. 28 Jan
1914 Paisley, Scot. ED.B '39 Univ. of
Glasgow, Scot. LECTURER, Univ. of Birmingham. Member: BPS. Teaching, administration, research; mental measurement, learning processes in mathematics,
remedial education of retarded children. M

CURRIE, Mrs. Jeanne Margaret. 20 Douglas St, Hamilton. Lanarkshire, Scot. b. 3 Mar 1926 London, Eng. B.SC '52 Univ. of London, Eng. ASST. PSYCH'T, Renfrewshire Educ. Authority, 16 Glasgow Rd, Paisley, Scot. Member: BPS. Educational psychology, testing, teaching, child guidance.   F

DAINOW, Morley. 3 Russell Sq. Mansions, 122 Southampton Row, London W.C. 1, Eng. b. 1 Apr 1886 London, Eng. B.SC '09 King's Coll, London, Eng. PSYCHOLOGIST, priv. prac. Member: BPS. Research, vocational guidance, consulting, professional writing; personality, psychology and politics.   M

DALE, Reginald Rowland. Univ. Coll. of Swansea, Wales. b. 1 Apr 1907 Widnes, Eng. ED.M '36 Univ. of Leeds, Eng. LECT. in EDUC, Univ. Coll. of Swansea. Member: BPS. Research, teaching, professional writing; co-education, selection of university students and teachers, psychology of music.   M

DANIELS, John Clifford. Inst. of Educ, Adams Hill, Derby Rd, Nottingham, Eng. b. 29 Nov 1915 Audley, Eng. ED.M '48 Univ. of Durham, Eng. TUTOR in charge of RES. and PSYCH. TESTS, Inst. of Educ, Univ. of Nottingham. Member: BPS. Teaching, research, professional writing; methods of teaching reading and numbers, learning theory, educational selection and guidance.   M

DANIELS, Miss Peggy Elizabeth. Dovedale, Bowling Green Rd, Stourbridge, Worcester, Eng. b. 4 Nov 1929 W. Bromsich, Staffs, Eng. BA '52 Bedford Coll, London, Eng. Member: BPS. Clinical cognitive and objective tests.   F

DARROCH, Dr. Jane. 9 Falcon Gardens, Edinburgh 10, Scot. b. 18 Apr 1907 Scot. PH.D '36 Univ. of Edinburgh, Scot. EDUC. PSYCH'T, CHILD PSYCHOTHER, Davidson Clin, 58 Dalkeith Rd, Edinburgh; EDITOR, *Davidson Clinic Bulletin.* Member: BPS. Play therapy, remedial teaching, research, testing; mental defectives with emotional problems, child psychology.   F

DAVIDSON, Miss May Alison. 7B Bradmore Rd, Oxford, Eng. b. 14 Nov 1914 Bulawayo, Rhodesia, S. Africa. M.SC '35 Univ. of Cape Town, S. Africa. CONSULT. CLIN. PSYCH'T, Wameford Park Hosp. Management Comm, Wameford Park Hosps, Headington, Oxford; LECTURER, Univ. of Oxford. Member: BPS. Testing, research, clinical practice, administration; learning theory, projective techniques, achievement tests.   F

DAVIES-EYSENCK, Mrs. Margaret Malcolm. 15 Alleyn Park, Dulwich, London. S.E. 21, Eng. b. 22 Nov 1909 Winnipeg, Can. MA '38 Univ. of London, Eng. LECT. in PSYCH, W.

End Hosp. Speech Ther. Trng. Sch, 26 Holland Park, London W. 11; CLIN. PSYCH'T, W. End Hosp; CLIN. PSYCH'T, Moor House Sch. for Speech Defectives. Member: BPS. Teaching, testing, educational psychology; language development, intellectual deterioration in old age.   F

DAVIS, Dr. Derek Russell. Med. Sch, Tennis Ct. Rd, Cambridge, Eng. b. 20 Apr 1914 London, MD '46 Univ. of Cambridge, Eng. READER in CLIN. PSYCH, Univ. of Cambridge, CONSULT. PSYCHIATRIST, United Cambridge Hosps; EDITOR, *Quarterly Journal of Experimental Psychology.* Member: BPS, Exper. Psych. Group. Research, teaching, psychotherapy; disorders of mental development in childhood, disorders of perception and recall in adult patients.   M

DAY, Michael. 8 Bargrove Ave, Boxmoor, Herts, Eng. b. 23 Mar 1928 Ilfracombe, UK. B.SC '52 Univ. of London, Eng. ASST. TRNG. OFF, Br. Petroleum Co. Ltd, Finsbury Circus, London E.C. 2, Eng. Member: BPS. Personnel psychology, administration, testing; personnel training and selection. M

DEARNALEY, Edmund John. Dept. of Psych, Univ. of Manchester, Manchester 13, Eng. b. 30 Apr 1933 Manchester, Eng. B.SC '54 Univ. of Manchester, Eng. RES. ASST, Univ. of Manchester. Member: BPS. Research, student, teaching; subjective probabilities, risk taking behavior, creative thinking.   M

DE BERKER, Paul Udo. 411 Upper Richmond Rd, Putney S.W. 15, Eng. b. 8 Sept 1919 London, Eng. B.Litt '51 Univ. of Oxford, Eng. SR. PSYCH'T, H. M. Prison Comm, Horseferry House, Dean Ryle St, London S.W. 1, Eng; PSYCH. COUNS, priv. prac. Member: BPS, Assn. of Profes. Psychotherapists. Testing, group psychotherapy, guidance, professional writing; counseling, delinquency.   M

DE MONCHAUX, Miss Cecily. 32 Fitzroy Sq, London W. 1, Eng. b. 13 June 1922 Sydney, Austl. PH.D '51 Univ. of London, Eng. LECT. in PSYCH, Univ. Coll, Gower St, London W.C. 1; PSYCHOANALYST, priv. prac; RES. WRKR. and LECT, Hampstead Child Ther. Clin; EDITOR, *Bulletin of British Psychological Society*; *Psychology Series,* Hutchinson's Univ. Library; ED. BD, *Psycho-analysis and Social Sciences.* Member: BPS, ICWP, Br. Psychoanal. Socy. Teaching, psychotherapy, research; psychoanalysis, psychology of small groups. F

DEMPSIE, Miss Jeanie. 24 Agnew Ave, Coatbridge, Lanarkshire, Scot. b. 5 May 1917 Coatbridge, Scot. ED.B '50 Univ. of Glasgow, Scot. ASST. PSYCH'T, Educ. Dept, Corp. of Glasgow, 129 Bath St, Glasgow, Scot. Member: BPS. Clinical practice,

testing, educational psychology. F
DENTON, Dr. Eva Rose. Bronte Hall, Avery Hill Training Coll, Bexley Rd, Eltham, London S.E. 9, Eng. b. 21 Dec 1902 Warlingham, Surrey, Eng. PH.D '49 Univ. of London, Eng. SR. LECT. in EDUC, Avery Hill Trng. Coll. Member: BPS. Lecturing, supervision of student teachers; fluctuation in mental work, intelligence testing. F
DESAI, Dr. Maheshchandra Maneklal. 16 Meadow Rd, Sutton, Surrey, Eng. b. 21 Sept 1903 Baroda, India. PH.D '37 Univ. of London, Eng. CONSULT. CLIN. PSYCH'T and HEAD, Psych. Dept, Belmont Hosp, Brighton Rd, Sutton. Member: BPS. Testing, clinical practice, administration, research; projective techniques, rehabilitation of psychiatric cases. M
DICKS, Dr. Henry Victor. Tavistock Clin, 2 Beaumont St, London W. 1, Eng. b. 27 Apr 1900 Parnu, Estonia. MD '30 Univ. of Cambridge, Eng. CONSULT. PSYCHIATRIST, Tavistock Clin; LECT. and MED. ADVIS, N.A.M.H., Eng; PSYCHOLOGIST, priv. prac; ED. BD, *Human Relations*. Member: BPS, RMPA. Psychotherapy, clinical practice, teaching, research; psychopathology, marital breakdown and its socio-psychological etiology, national character. M
DIXON, Dr. Norman Frank. Dept. of Psych, Univ. Coll, Gower St, London W.C. 1, Eng. b. 19 May 1922 Cheam, Eng. PH.D '56 Univ. of Reading, Eng. ASST. LECT, Univ. Coll. Member: BPS. Research, teaching, administration; cybernetics, psychoanalysis. M
DODWELL, Peter C. Birkbeck Coll, Univ. of London, Malet St, London W.C. 1, Eng. b. 13 Mar 1930 Ootacamund, India. BA '53 Univ. of Oxford, Eng. ASST. LECT. in PSYCH, Birkbeck Coll. Member: BPS. Teaching, research, professional writing; perception, thinking, child psychology. M
DOW, Miss Elizabeth Faulds. 1 Marchmont Terr, Glasgow W. 2, Scot. b. 20 Sept 1905 Glasgow, Scot. ED.B '50 Univ. of Glasgow, Scot. EDUC. PSYCH'T, Dunbartonshire Educ. Comm, 18 Park Circus, Glasgow C. 3. Educational psychology, testing, child guidance; intelligence and achievement testing. F
DRASPA, Dr. Leon Julian. Deva Hosp, Liverpool Rd, Chester, Eng. b. 14 June 1911 Warsaw, Poland. PH.D '55 Univ. of Edinburgh, Scot. CLIN. PSYCH'T, Deva Hosp. Member: BPS. Clinical analysis, and practice, psychotherapy, guidance; learning and personality theory, psychosomatic disorders, personality assessment. M
DREVER, Prof. James. 2 Dick Pl, Edinburgh, Scot. b. 29 Jan 1910 Edinburgh, Scot. MA '32 Univ. of Edinburgh, Scot. PROF.

of PSYCH, Univ. of Edinburgh, S. Bridge, Edinburgh; EDITOR, *British Journal of Psychology*. Member: BPS. Teaching, administration, research; theoretical experiments of early learning. M
DREW, Prof. George Charles. Dept. of Psych, Univ. of Bristol, 27 Belgrave Rd, Bristol 8, Eng. b. 10 Dec 1911 Bristol, Eng. MA '47 Univ. of Bristol, Eng. PROF. and HEAD, Dept. of Psych, Univ. of Bristol; ED. BD, *British Journal of Psychology, Quarterly Journal of Experimental Psychology*. Member: BPS, APA, Exper. Psych. Grp, Socy. for the Study of Animal Behavior. Teaching, research, administration; learning theory, skills, effects of drugs. M
DUNCAN, David Conochie. 65 Briar Crescent, Northolt, Middlesex, Eng. b. 26 Apr 1926 Blairgowrie, Scot. MA '50 Univ. of St. Andrews, Scot. INDUS. INVES, Natl. Inst. of Indus. Psych, 14 Welbeck St, London W. 1. Member: BPS. Industrial psychology, research, teaching; recruitment, selection and training in industry, measurement of industrial absence, accidents and labor loss rates, psychology and economics. M
DUNSDON, Dr. Marjorie Isabel. Burden Ment. Res. Dept, Stoke Park Hosp, Stoke Lane, Stapleton, Birstol, Eng. b. 1 Dec 1906 London, Eng. PH.D '52 Univ. of London, Eng. CHIEF PSYCH'T, Burden Ment. Res. Dept. Member: BPS. Research, consulting, clinical analysis; mental and physical handicaps, large sample survey work, delinquency. F
DURANT, Dr. Henry William. Social Surveys, Ltd. 59 Brook St, London W. 1, Eng. b. 23 Oct 1902 London, Eng. PH.D '39 Univ. of London, Eng. DIRECTOR, Gallup Poll of Great Britain, Soc. Surveys Ltd. Member: BPS. Research, public opinion measurement, applied psychology; attitude measurement, scaling, motivation, forecasting behavior. M
DURNING Miss Margaret Gray. 18 Newton St, Glasgow C.2, Scot. b. 17 Dec 1908 Glasgow, Scot. ED.B '48 Univ. of Glasgow, Scot. EDUC. PSYCH'T, Educ. Dept, Corp. of Glasgow, 129 Bath St, Glasgow. Teaching, psychotherapy, guidance. F
DURWARD, Miss Marjorie. Natl. Hosp. for Nerv. Diseases, Maida Vale, London W. 9, Eng. b. 18 May 1918 Christchurch, N.Z. MA '44 Victoria Univ. Coll, N.Z. SR. PSYCH'T Natl. Hosps. for Nerv. Diseases, ASSISTANT, Dept. of Psych, Univ. Coll, London, Eng. Member: BPS. Clinical analysis, research, teaching; organic brain damage, localization of brain function, remedial reading. F
DYCE-SHARP, Miss Katharine May. Waternish House, Isle of Skye, Scot. b. 12 Mar

1923 London, Eng. B.SC '48 Univ. of London, Eng. LECTURER, Loughborough Coll. of Tech, Loughborough, Leicester, Eng. Member: BPS, Ergonomic Res. Socy. Industrial psychology, teaching, professional writing; selection work, market research, personnel and management relations in industry. F

DYMOND, Miss F. Louise. 50 Palace Mansions, Earsby St, London W. 14, Eng. b. 12 June 1911 Bideford, Eng. BA '34 Univ. of Bristol, Eng. PSYCHOLOGIST, London County Counc, Brixton Child Guid. Unit, Brixton, London S.W. 2. Member: BPS. Child psychotherapy, testing, guidance. F

EAGLESIM, Miss Martha Thomsom. 6 Baronscourt Dr, Paisley, Scot. b. 16 Jan 1922 Paisley, Scot. ED.B '47 Univ. of Glasgow, Scot. ASST. EDUC. PSYCH'T, Educ. Dept, Corp. of Glasgow, 129 Bath St, Glasgow, Scot. Member: BPS. Child psychotherapy, guidance, testing; maladjusted children, projective techniques, diagnostic tests. F

EATTELL, Miss Eleanor Amy. Cen. Hosp, Warwick, Eng. b. 26 July 1902 Malmesbury, Eng. M.SC '46 Birkbeck Coll, London, Eng. SR. CLIN. PSYCH'T, Cen. Hosp. Member: BPS. Testing, psychotherapy, administration, teaching; diagnostic and therapeutic work. F

EDDISON, Dr. Herbert Wilfred. 76 Shipton Rd, York, Eng. b. 5 Apr 1893 Leeds, Eng. DPM '23 Univ. of Cambridge, Eng. PSYCHIATRIST, Clifton Hosp, York; PSYCHIATRIST, Leeds Reg. Hosp. Bd, Park Parade, Harrogate, Eng; PSYCHIATRIST, Scarborough Child. Guid. Clin. and Scarborough Hosp. Member: BPS. Guidance, clinical practice, psychotherapy, testing. M

EDE, Derek Arthur. First Admiralty Interview Bd, c/o HMS Sultan, Gosport, Hants, Eng. b. 21 Nov 1922 Hayle, Cornwall, Eng. MA '53 Univ. of Cambridge, Eng. SR. PSYCH'T, S. P. Dept, Queen Anne's Mansions, St. James Park, London S.W. 1, Eng. Member: BPS. Personnel psychology, testing; group selection, mental testing, personnel selection. M

EDWARDS, Reginald. 182 Carter Knowle Rd, Sheffield 7, Eng. b. 25 Feb 1913 Oldham, Eng. ED.M '50 Univ. of Manchester, Eng. LECT. in EDUC. PSYCH, Univ. of Sheffield. Member: BPS. Teaching, research, educational psychology; learning theory, test construction. M

ELLINGHAM, Mrs. Eily Gwendolyn. White Corner, Meerut Rd, Brockenhurst, Hants, Eng. b. 26 Dec 1905 London, Eng. Dipl. Psych. '43 Univ. of London, Eng. LAY THERAPIST, Child Guid. Clin, Southampton Sch. Hlth. Serv. and Local Educ. Authority, Civic Cen, Southampton, Eng.

Member: BPS. Play therapy, testing, educational psychology. F

ELLIOTT, Edward. Greenwood, Mogador Rd, Lower Kingswood, Surrey, Eng. b. 19 Oct 1920 London, Eng. B.SC '48 Univ. of London, Eng. SR. PSYCH'T, Dept. of Sr. Psych'ts, Admiralty, Whitehall, London, Eng. Member: BPS. Research, applied psychology; psychoacoustics, vigilance problems, psychological statistics. M

ELLIOTT, Mrs. Elsie Souter. 127 Hermitage Lane, Aylesford, Maidstone, Kent, Eng. b. 29 Apr 1922 Elgin, Scot. MA '42 Univ. of Aberdeen, Scot. Member: BPS. Retired, projective techniques, tests of conceptual thinking, tests of mental deterioration and impairment. F

EMERSON, Anthony Roy. Dept. of Soc. Sci, Univ. of Nottingham, Univ. Park, Notts, Eng. b. 9 Dec 1925 London, Eng. BA '52 Univ. of Nottingham, Eng. LECT. in SOC. SCI, Univ. of Nottingham. Member: BPS. Research, teaching, applied psychology; research methods in social psychology. attitude measurement, sociometry, social class, gerontology. M

ERNEST, Mrs. Elna. 13-15 Frognal, London N.W. 3, Eng. b. 18 Apr 1920 Gothenburg, Swed. BA '43 Cornell Univ, USA. SR. CLIN. PSYCH'T, Westminster Hosp, St. John's Gardens, London S.W. 1. Member: BPS. Testing, clinical practice, psychotherapy; personality tests, therapeutic techniques, remedial teaching. F

EVANS, Dr. Ellis George Shacklock. 24 Luccombe Rd, Upper Shirley, Southampton, Eng. b. 27 Nov 1918 Gisborne, N.Z. PH.D '51 Univ. of Birmingham, Eng. LEDT. in EDUC. PSYCH, Univ. of Southampton, Univ. Rd, Southampton. Member: BPS. Educational psychology, lecturing, research; psychology of cognition, formation of concepts. M

EVANS, Dr. Kathleen Marianne. 33 Axminister Rd, Roath, Cardiff, Wales. b. 25 Feb 1911 Pembrey, UK. PH.D '52 Univ. of London, Eng. LECT. in EDUC. PSYCH. and RES. WRKR, Univ. Coll. of S. Wales and Monmouthshire, Cathays Park, Cardiff. Member: BPS. Teaching, research, professional writing; attitude and interst measurement, teaching ability. F

EYSENCK, Prof. Hans Jurgen. Inst. of Psychiat, Maudsley Hosp, Denmark Hill, London S.E. 5, Eng. b. 4 Mar 1916 Berlin, Ger. PH.D '40 Univ. of London, Eng. PROF. of PSYCH, Inst. of Psychiat, Maudsley Hosp; PSYCHOLOGIST, Maudsley and Bethlem Royal Hosps. Member: BPS, APA. Research, teaching, administration; personality, learning theory, psychometrics. M

EYSENCK, Dr. Sybill Bianca Giuletta. 10 Dorchester Dr, Herne Hill, London S.E. 24,

Eng. b. 16 Mar 1927 Vienna, Austria. PH.D '55 Inst. of Psychiat, London, Eng. RES. WRKR, Inst. of Psychiat, Maudsley Hosp, Denmark Hill, London S.E. 5, Eng. Member: BPS. Research, testing; personality, psychometrics, abnormal psychology. F

FAIRBAIRN, Dr. William Ronald Dodds. Grosvenor Crescent, Edinburgh 12, Scot. b. 11 Aug 1889 Edinburgh, Scot. MD '29 Univ. of Edinburgh, Scot. Member: BPS, RMPA, Br. Psychoanal. Socy. Psychotherapy; psychoanalytical theory, psychology of art. M

FALK, Dr. Gertrud Edith. 47 Pembroke Pl, Chelmsford, Essex, Eng. b. 6 Aug 1911 Vienna, Austria. PH.D '35 Univ. of Vienna, Austria. EDUC. PSYCH'T, Mid-Essex Child Guid. Clin, Essex Educ. Comm, 146 Broomfield Rd, Chelmsford. Member: BPS. Testing, administration, remedial teaching, guidance; Rorschach testing, reading, difficulties, problems of adolescence. F

FARMER, Eric. Chantry Cottage, W. Row, Bury St. Edmunds, Eng. b. 7 Oct 1888 Northampton, Eng. MA, Univ. of Cambridge, Eng. Member: BPS. Retired; industrial psychology. M

FARNWORTH, Miss Mary. BM/LSW.FR., London W.C. 1, Eng. b. 28 Aug 1911 Leek, Staffs, Eng. B.SC '47 Univ. of London, Eng. LECT. in MENT. HLTH, St. Charles's Hosp, London. Member: BPS. Research, teaching; vocational psychology, recruitment of nurses. F

FERGUSON, Henry Hall. Dept. of Psych, St. Salvator's Coll, Univ. of St. Andrews, Scot. b. 18 Oct 1906 Comrie, Scot. MA '29 Univ. of St. Andrews, Scot. HEAD, Dept. of Psych, Univ. of St. Andrews. Member: BPS, APA. Teaching, administration, research; incentives, intelligence tests, skill. M

FIELD, Mrs. Elinor M. 67 Harley St, London W. 1, Eng. b. 23 Dec 1926 London, Eng. MA '48 Univ. of Edinburgh, Scot. CLIN. PSYCH'T, Warneford Hosp, Oxford, Eng. Member: BPS. Testing, clinical analysis, research, teaching; effects of neurosurgical operations, organic and psychogenic factors in speech defects. F

FIELD, Jack. 13a Dacres Rd, London S.E. 23, Eng. b. 29 Apr 1929 Vienna, Austria. MA '54 Univ. of Glasgow, Scot. RES. ASST, Dept. of Psych, Inst. of Psychiat, Denmark Hill, London. Member: BPS. Research, testing, student; geriatics, visual perception, motor skills. M

FISH, John Reginald. 3 Towncroft Ave, Middleton near Manchester, Eng. b. 27 Sept 1922 Chelmsford, Eng. B.SC '49 Univ. Coll, London, Eng. SR. PSYCH'T, Child Psychiat. Cen, Booth Hall Hosp, Charlestown Rd, Manchester 9. Member: BPS.

Testing, child guidance, research; educational guidance, cognitive and projective techniques. M

FISK, Edward. Burnside ,Kippen, Stirlingshire, Scot. b. 5 Dec 1925 London, Eng. ED.B '51 Univ. of Glasgow, Scot. EDUC. PSYCH'T, Child Guid. Clin, Educ. Authority, Viewforth, Stirling, Scot. Member: BPS. Educational psychology, child guidance, teaching; development of preschool children, reading attitudes. , M

FITCH, John Horace. 72 St. Alban's Rd, Westbury Park, Bristol 6, Eng. b. 21 Aug 1924 London, Eng. BA. '50 Univ. of Reading, Eng. SR. PSYCH'T, Prison Comm, Horseferry House, Dean Ryle St, Westminster, London, Eng. Member: BPS. Testing, clinical practice, guidance, research; cognitive testing, projective techniques, psychotherapy. M

FITZPATRICK, Miss Florence Kathleen. 211 Connaught Rd, Brookwood, Surrey, Eng. b. 14 Aug 1901 Stratford-on-Avon, Eng. BA '50 Univ. of London, Eng. SR. CLIN. PSYCH'T, Botleys Park Hosp, Chertsey, Surrey, Eng. Member: BPS. Clinical analysis, testing, vocational guidance, professional writing; mental deficiency, learning theory. F

FLEMING, Dr. Charlotte Mary. 7 Granard Ave, Putney, London S.W. 15, Eng. b. 17 May 1894 Middlesbrough, Eng. PH.D '30 Univ. of Glasgow, Scot. READER in EDUC, Univ. of London, Malet St, London W.C. 1; CHIEF EXAM, Lancashire County Counc, Worcesterchire and Kesteven County Couns; CONSULTANT, Local Educ. Authorities and Univ. of London, Birmingham and Hull. Member: BPA, APA. Teaching, professional writing, consulting, research; child and adolescent development, group process in education, achievement tests. F

FLEMING, Miss Elizabeth. 7 Baronald Dr, Glasgow W. 2, Scot. b. 1 Aug 1908 Glasgow, Scot. ED.B '51 Univ. of Glasgow, Scot. EDUC. PSYCH'T, Educ. Dept, Glasgow Corp, Glasgow. Member: BPS. Psychotherapy, child guidance, testing. F

FLOOK, Alfred John Melsom. 20 Melbourne Pl, St. Andrews, Fife, Scot. b. 29 Sept 1918 Bristol, Eng. BA '48 Univ. of London, Eng. LECT. in PSYCH, Univ. of St. Andrews. Member: BPS. Teaching, research, administration; group dynamics, psychology of humor, family problems. M

FONTAINE, Bernard Leon Stark. 20 Brunswick, Gons, Kensinton, London W. 8, Eng. b. 27 June 1914 London, Eng. M.SC '41 Univ. of London, Eng. MANAGEMENT CONSULT, Urwick Orr and Partners Lts, Park Lane, London. Member: BPS. Administration, industrial and personnel psychology; consulting, executive development, training methods. M

FORDHAM, Dr. Michael Scott Montagne. 1 St Katherine's Precinct, Regent's Park, London N.W. 1, Eng. b. 4 Aug 1905 London, Eng. MD '47 Univ. of Cambridge, Eng. DIRECTOR, C. G. Jung Clin, Socy. of Anal. Psych, 25 Park Crescent, London W. 1; ASST. DIR, Child Guid. Clin, St. Marylebone Hosp; EDITOR, *Journal of Analytical Psychology.* Member: BPS, RMPA, Socy. of Anal. Psych. Clinical practice, editorial, teaching; analytical. psychology. M

FORRES GRUENBAUM, Dr. phil. Hildegard. 41 Woodhall Rd, Penn, Wolverhampton, Eng. b. 4 Dec 1888 Wraczlaw, Poland. PH.D '18 Univ. of Jena, Ger. Member: BPS. Retired, lecturing, guidance, psychotherapy; social psychology, psychology and religion. F

FORREST, Dr. Derek William. Dept. of Psych, Bedford Coll, Univ. of London, Regent's Park, London N.W. 1, Eng. b. 15 Feb 1926 Liverpool, Eng. PH.D '56 Univ. of London, Eng. LECTURER, Bedford Coll. Member: BPS, Ergonomics Res. Socy. Research, teaching, professional writing; muscular tension, perceptual defence, human memory and learning. M

FOSS, Brian Malzard. Birkbeck Coll, Malet St, London W.C. 1, Eng. b. 25 Oct 1921 Eng. MA '45 Univ. of Cambridge, Eng. LECT. in PSYCH, Birkbeck Coll; EXPER. PSYCH'T, Market Res. Organiza. Member: BPS, Assn. for the Study of Animal Behavior, Exper. Psych. Group. Teaching, research, administration; cognition, physiological psychology. M

FOSTER, Patrick Michael. 24 The Park Ealing, London W. 5, Eng. b. 4 June 1921 Hastings, Eng. ED.B '51 Queens Univ. of Belfast, N. Ire. LECTURER, Acton Tech. Coll, High St, Acton, London W. 3. Member: BPS. Consulting, student guidance teaching, industrial psychology; group process and industrial change, operator training. M

FOULDS, Dr. Graham Alexander. Rosebank, Vicarage Hill, S. Benfleet, Essex, Eng. b. 1 June 1914 Liverpool, Eng. PH.D '53 Univ. of London, Eng. DIRECTOR, Psych. Dept, Runwell Hosp, Wickford, Essex, Eng; ADVIS. BD, *International Journal of Social Psychiatry.* Member: BPS. Research, clinical testing; projective techniques, visuo-motor techniques, cognitive abilities. M

FOXLEV, Benjamin Worthington. 34 Baring Rd, Bournemouth, Eng. b. 6 Oct 1917 Handsworth, Eng. B.SC '49 Univ. of London, Eng. EDUC. PSYCH'T, County Borough of Bournemouth; EDITOR,

Abstracts and Information. Member: BPS. Psychotherapy, testing, editorial, teaching; physiological psychology, community psychological services. M

FRANGLEN, Mrs. Sheila. 41 Primrose Gardens, London N.W. 3, Eng. b. 12 Aug 1921 London, Eng. B.SC '49 Univ. of London, Eng. SR. CLIN. PSYCH'T, St. Marley Bone Hosp. for Psychiat. and Child Guid, Cosway St, London; SR. CLIN. PSYCH'T, W. End Hosp. of Neur. and Neurosurgery; EDITOR, *Rorschach Newsletter.* Member: BPS. Clinical testing and analysis, consulting, teaching; projective techniques, assessment of organic intellectual and personality deterioration. F

FRANKS, Dr. Cyril Maurice. Inst. of Psychiat, Maudsley Hosp, Denmark Hill, London S.E. 5, Eng. b. 26 July 1923 Neath, Wales. PH.D '54 Univ. of London, Eng. RES. PSYCH'T, Inst. of Psychiat, Univ. of London; CLIN. and EDUC. PSYCH'T, The Church of Eng. Cnildren's Socy; LECT. in SOC. PSYCH, Univ. of London. Member: BPS. Personality and market research, testing, teaching; conditioning, personality questionnaires, delinquency. M

FRASER, Dr. Elizabeth D. 2 Clark's Lane, Old Aberdeen, Scot. b. 13 Nov 1920 Inverness, Scot. PH.D '55 Univ. of Aberdeen, Scot. LECT. in PSYCH, Univ. of Aberdeen, High St, Old Aberdeen. Member: BPS. Teaching, research, student research supervision; personality factors in perception, effects of environment on intelligence and achievement, model psychosis produced by drugs. F

FRASER, John Munro. Orchard House, Whitehouse, Common Rd, Sutton, Coldfield, Warwick, Eng. b. 24 Nov 1907 Kilmarnock, Scot. MA '34 Univ. of Glasgow, Scot. SR. LECT. in HUMAN RELAT, Coll. of Tech, Gosta Green, Birmingham, Eng. Member: BPS. Teaching, industrial psychology; group dynamics, attitude research. M

FREEMAN, Miss Josephine Murielle. Ingrams Copse, Farnham Common, Bucks, Eng. b. 19 June 1914 Corby, Eng. BA '52 Univ. of London, Eng. EDUC. PSYCH'T, Slough Dist. Child Guid. Clin, Buckinghamshire Educ. Comm, County Off, Aylesbury, Bucks, Eng. Member: BPS. Testing, educational psychology, remedial teaching; guidance; projective techniques, learning theory, achievement tests. F

FREYMAN, Richard. 26 Oakdale Close, Downend, Bristol, Eng. b. 10 June 1912 Leipzig, Ger. BA '45 Univ. of London, Eng. EDUC. PSYCH'T, Child Guid. Clin, Gloucestershire Educ. Comm, Morley Rd, Staple Hill, Bristol. Member: BPS. Educational psychology, testing, remedial teaching, psychotherapy; developmental aspects of education and learning. M

FRIEDMANN, Susanna. 166 Wymering Mansions, London W. 9, Eng. b. 1 Apr 1924 Berlin, Ger. PH.D '52 Univ. of London, Eng. EDUC. PSYCH'T, City of Oxford Educ. Comm, George St, Oxford, Eng. Member: BPS. Diagnostic testing, educational psychology, child guidance, teaching; influence of emotional factors on learning. F

FRISBY, Dr. Clifford Brook. 4A Keats Grove, London N.W. 3, Eng. b. 21 July 1902 London, Eng. PH.D '47 Univ. of London, Eng. DIRECTOR, Natl. Inst. of Indus. Psych, 14 Welbeck St, London. Member: BPS, AIPA. Administration, research, applied and industrial psychology; sources of satisfaction and attitudes in working life, work organization, methods and equipment. M

FROST, Mrs. Sybil Margaret. 29 Rudall Crescent, London N.W. 3, Eng. b. 28 Aug 1910 London, Eng. MA '40 Univ. of Cambridge, Eng. RES. ASST, Political and Econ. Planning (P.E.P.), 16 Queen Anne's Gate, London. Interviewing and survey research. F

FUCHS, Dr. Leo Gerog. Philips Croydon Works Ltd, Commerce Way, Purley Way, Croydon, Surrey, Eng. b. 20 Oct 1900 Iglau, Czech. MA '49 Univ. of London, Eng. TRNG. OFF, Philips Croydon Works Ltd; CONSULTANT, Express Diary. Member: BPS. Applied psychology, teaching, research; perception, psychophysical training methods, rehabilitation of the disabled. M

FURNEAUX, Walter Desmond Charles. Nuffield Res. Unit, Inst. of Psychiat, Maudsley Hosp, Denmark Hill, London S.E. 5, Eng. b. 10 June 1919 London, Eng. B.SC '49 Univ. of London, Eng. PSYCH'T. and HEAD, Nuffield Res. Unit, Inst. of Psychiat. Member: BPS, American Socy. for Clin. and Exper. Hypnosis. Research, applied psychology, teaching; cognitive testing, selection of univeristiy students, hypnosis, suggestibility, psychical research. M

GARDEN, Miss Ruth J. M. Child Guid. Clin, 9 Newbould Lane, Sheffield 10, Eng. b. 27 June Aberdeen, Scot. ED.B '49 Univ. of Aberdeen, Scot. EDUC. PSYCH'T, Child Guid. Cen. Member: BPS. Applied and educational psychology, testing, psychotherapy. F

GARDNER, Miss Dorothy Ellen Marion. Lindfield, Shalford Rd, Guildford, Surrey, Eng. b. 27 July 1900 Secunderabad, India. MA '40 Univ. of Leeds, Eng. HEAD, Dept. of Child Devel, Inst. of Educ. Univ. of London, Malet St, London W.C. 1, Eng; UNIV. READER, Univ. of London. Member: BPS, Socy. for Res. in Child Devel. (USA). Teaching, research, administration; a-

chievement tests, attitude measurement, longitudinal child study. F

GARDNER, Dr. Godfrey James. Inst. of Exper. Psych, Univ. of Oxford, 34 Branbury Rd, Oxford, Eng. b. 13 Feb 1913 Croydon, Eng. PH.D '56 Univ. Coll, London, Eng. RES. OFF, Inst. of Exper. Psych, Univ. of Oxford; LECTURER, Univ. of Maryland Overseas Program. Member: BPS. Research, teaching, administration; human relations in industry, group dynamics, leadership. M

GARDNER, Leslie. 4 Camp View, Wimbledon Common, London S.W. 19, Eng. b. 25 Dec 1925 London, Eng. B.SC '50 Univ. of London, Eng. PSYCHOLOGIST, Dept. of Psych. Med, Hosp. for Sick Children, Great Ormond St, London W.C. 1. Member: BPS. Testing, clinical analysis, guidance, educational psychology; learning theory, play interviewing, intelligence testing of young children, handicapped children. M

GARSIDE, Roger Forbes. 61 Holly Ave, Newcastle-upon-Tyne 2, Eng. b. 13 Sept 1917 Liverpool, Eng. B.SC '38 Univ. of London, Eng. LECT. in APPL. PSYCH, Dept. of Psych. Med, King's Coll, Newcastle-upon-Tyne. Member: BPS. Testing, consulting, research, teaching; intelligence and achievement test, projective techniques. M

GARVIE, Elizabeth Dorothy Findlay. Aldavock, 2 Prospect Ave, Cambuslang, Glasgow, Scot. b. 12 Apr 1909 Fordoun, Scot. ED.B '36 Univ. of Edinburgh, Scot. ASST. PSYCH'T, Lanarkshire Educ. Comm, 191 Ingram St, Glasgow. Member: BPS. Applied and educational psychology, testing, child guidance. F

GASCOYNE, Miss Sylvia Barbara. 75 Prince of Wales Mansions, Prince of Wales Dr, London S.W. 11, Eng. b. 11 Dec. 1919 Worcester, Eng. BA '52 Birkbeck Coll, London, Eng. EDUC. PSYCH'T, Ilford Child Guid. Clin, Loxford Hall, Loxford Lane, Ilford, Eng. Member: BPS. Educational psychology, testing, teaching; intelligence and achievement tests. F

GASKILL, Peter. Royal Cross Schs. for the Deaf, Preston, Lancs, Eng. b. 17 Oct 1914 Doncaster, Eng. ED.M '52 Univ. of Manchester, Eng. HEADMASTER and SUPT, Royal Cross Schs. for the Deaf; LECTURER, Deaf Children's Socy. Member: BPS. Administration, research, teaching; intelligence and achievement tests, projective techniques. M

GATELY, Dr. Grace Mary. 1 Saxon Way, Southgate, London N. 14, Eng. b. 24 May 1907 Salford, Eng. PH.D '54 Univ. of London, Eng. EDUC. PSYCH'T, Middlesex C. C. Educ. Comm, 10 Great George St, Westminster S.W. 1, Eng. Educational psychology and guidance, testing, administration, treatment of retarded and maladjusted children.   F

GAUL, Miss Mary. Educ. Dept, County Hall, Chichester, W. Sussex, Eng. b. 23 Feb 1922 Mount Abu, India. MA '54 Univ. Coll, London, Eng. SR. EDUC. PSYCH'T, W. Sussex Educ. Comm, Chichester. Member: BPS. Educational and clinical psychology, guidance, psychotherapy, administration; maladjusted children, education of mentally handicapped children, mental health education of parents.   F

GERHARD, Derek James Jeremy. The Flat, Peppard   Rectory,   Henley-on-Thames, Oxon, Eng. b. 16 Dec 1927 London, Eng. MA '53 Univ. of Cambridge, Eng. SR. PSYCH'T, Air Ministry, Sci. Advis. Dept, Whitehall Gardens, London, Eng. Member: BPS.   Applied psychology, research, administration.   M

GIBBS, John Morel. Sea Roads, Cliff Parade, Penarth, Wales. b. 17 Aug 1912 Penarth, Wales. MA '40 Univ. of London, Eng. LECT. in SOC. PSYCH, Univ. Coll, Cathays Park, Cardiff, Wales; PSYCH. CONSULT, S. Wales Marriage Guid. Counc; SUPERVISOR, Approved School, Inst. for Juv. Offenders. Member: BPS. Teaching, consulting, educational and applied psychology; group process, group therapy, counseling, family relations.   M

GIBBS, Miss Norah Louise. 37 Montagu Sq, London W. 1, Eng. b. 21 July 1902 London, Eng. MA '37 Univ. of London, Eng. PSYCH. CONSULT, Child Guid. Trng. Cen, 6 Osuaburgh St, London W. 1; PSYCHOLOGIST, Cerebral Palsy Unit, Hosp. for Sick Children, Great Ormond St, London. Member: BPS. Testing, consulting, research, teaching; comparative development of normal and physically handicapped children, psychological and psychiatric implications of neurological abnormalities, non-visual projective techniques.   F

GILL, Miss Ruth. 19 Grange Rd, Sutton, Surrey, Eng. b. 6 Dec 1927 Swansea, Wales. B.SC '48 Univ. Coll, London, Eng. EDUC. PSYCH'T, Child Guid. Clin, Surrey County   Counc,   Kingston-on-Thames, Surrey. Member: BPS. Educational psychology, remedial teaching, testing; correlation of intelligence and school attainment, school attendance related to emotional disturbances, problems of first school experience.   F

GILLESPIE, Dr. William Hewitt. 73 Carlton Hill, London N.W. 8, Eng. b. 6 Aug 1905 Pei-Tai-Ho, China. MD '34 Univ. of Edinburgh, Scot. CONSULT. PHYS, Maudsley Hosp, Denmark Hill, London S.E. 5; CONSULT. PSYCHIATRIST and PSYCHOANAL, priv. prac. Member: BPS, RMPA, Br.

Psychoanal. Socy.   Psychoanalysis, child psychiatry, clinical teaching; sexual perversions.   M

GLADSTON, Dr. Elaine Rosslyn. 48 Porchester Terr, London W. 2, Eng. b. 11 June 1925 London, Eng. PH.D '55 Birkbeck Coll, London, Eng. CLIN. STUD, Maudsley Hosp, Denmark Hill, London. Member: BPS, BRF. Testing, student, clinical and educational   psychology,   professional writing; projective techniques, personality theory, culture and personality.   F

GLEAVES, Dr. Edward. 12 St. John St, Manchester 3, Eng. b. 4 Apr 1892 Bolton, Lancaster, Eng. M.SC, Victoria Coll, Manchester, Eng. CONSULT. PSYCHIATRIST, priv. prac. Member: BPS. Psychotherapy, consulting.   M

GLOVER, Dr. Edward. 18 Wimpole St, London W. 1, Eng. b. 13 Jan 1888 Lesmahagow, Scot. MD '15 Univ. of Glasgow, Scot.   CHAIRMAN, Sci. Comm, Inst. for Study   and   Trtmt. of Delinquency, 8 Bourdon St, London W. 1; CO-ED, British Journal of Delinquency. Member: BPS, Swiss Psychoanal. Socy, Amer. Psychoanal. Socy.   Consulting, psychotherapy, professional writing, editorial; psychoanalysis.   M

GLOVER, George Kendal. 26 Morningside Dr, E. Didsbury, Manchester 20, Eng. b. 20 Oct 1918 Leyland, Eng. ED.M '54 Univ. of Manchester, Eng. TEACHER, Lancashire Educ. Comm, Worsley Haysbrook Sch, Worsley, Lancaster, Eng. Member: BPS. Teaching, research, student; motor ability, test construction, retarded children.   M

GOLDMAN-EISLER, Dr. Frieda. Dept. of Phonetics, Univ. Coll, Gower St, London W.C. 1, Eng. b. 9 June 1915 Tarnow, Poland. PH.D '37 Univ. of Vienna, Austria. HONORARY RES. ASSOC, Med. Res. Counc, Old Queen St, London S.W. 1. Member: BPS.   Research, teaching; psychology of speech and language, measurement of expressive behavior, experimental research with psychoanalytical concepts.   F

GOMULICKI, Dr. Bronislaw Rudolf. 1 Nevern Rd, Earls Ct, London S.W. 5, Eng. b. 14 Dec 1913 Zberów, Poland. PH.D '52 Univ. of Oxford, Eng. Member: BPS.   Research, professional writing, design of research equipment; memory, theory, visual perception.   M

GOOD, Dr. Rankine. Ashgrove, Hartwood, Shotts, Lanarkshire, Scot. b. 13 Mar 1912 Hamilton, Scot. MD '42 Univ. of Glasgow, Scot.   CONSULT. PSYCHIATRIST and DEPUTY SUPT, Scottish Western Reg. Hosp. Bd, Hartwood Ment. Hosp, 64 W. Regent St, Glasgow, Scot. Member: BPS. Psychotherapy, clinical practice, administration, research; psychopathological research.   M

GOODALL, Dr. George William. The Glen, Ramelton, Donegal, Eire. b. 12 Aug 1879 Leeds, Eng. PH.D '38 Univ. of London, Eng. Member: BPS. Retired, communication, occupation, temperament. M

GORDON, Dr. Rosemary. 111 Gloucester Pl, London W. 1, Eng. b. 16 Apr 1923 Wiesbaden, Ger. PH.D '52 Univ. of London, Eng. SR. CLIN. PSYCH'T, Napsbury Hosp. near St. Albans, Herts, Eng. Member: BPS. Clinical analysis, teaching, research, psychotherapy; relationship of social attitudes and personality, projective techniques, marketing and advertising. F

GORODKIN, Miss Anita Sylvia. 6 Queen's Dr, Prestwich, Lancs, Eng. b. 13 Apr 1930 Buenos Aires, Argentina. BA '52 Univ. of Manchester, Eng. CLIN. PSYCH'T, Ingrebourne Cen, St. George's Hosp, Suttons Lane, Essex. Eng. Member: BPS. Clinical evaluation, guidance, psychotherapy; projective techniques, attitudes and values in personality, language and feeling. F

GOULD, Mrs. Elisabeth McCaw. 1 Bassett Crescent W, Southampton, Hants, Eng. b. 26 Oct 1928 Edinburgh, Scot. M.Litt '54 Girton Coll, Cambridge, Eng. Member: BPS. Vocational and educational guidance, testing, selection for university education, experimental esthetics. F

GRAHAM, Douglas. Dept. of Psych, Kepier Terr, Gilesgate, Durham, Eng. b. 13 Jan 1920 Glasgow, Scot. ED.B '48 Univ. of Glasgow, Scot. LECTURER, Durham Colleges, 38 N. Bailey, Durham; ASST. ED, *Durham Research Review*; ED. BD, *British Journal of General Psychology.* Member: BPS. Teaching, research, administration; perception, educational testing, social theory. M

GRAHAM WHITE, John. Dept. of Studies in Psych. Med. Univ. of Liverpool, 77 Bedford St. S, Liverpool 7, Eng. b. 12 Oct 1913 Birkenhead, Chester, Eng. ED.M '42 Harvard Univ, USA. LECT. in CLIN. PSYCH, Dept. of Studies in Psych. Med, Univ. of Liverpool. Member: BPS, APA. Teaching, research, clinical duties; teaching psychology to psychiatrists, prediction of social adjustment in mentally defective delinquents. M

GRANGER, Dr. George William. 15 Torrington Ct, Westwood Hill, London S.E. 26, Eng. b. 4 July 1922 Kingslynn, Eng. PH.D '51 Univ. Coll, London, Eng. LECT. in PSYCH, Univ. of London Inst. of Psychiat, Maudsley Hosp, Denmark Hill, London S.E. 5. Member: BPS. Research, teaching; visual perception, experimental visual esthetics, visual disfunction in psychiatric disorders. M

GREEN, John Lawrance. South Side, The Mount, Shrewsbury, Eng. b. 30 Oct 1908 London, Eng. BA '34 Univ. of London, Eng. SR. EDUC. PSYCH'T, Shropshire County Counc, County Bldgs, Shrewsbury. Child guidance, testing, applied and educational psychology, adult education. M

GREEN, Dr. Robert. 15 Clifton Gardens, London NW 11. b. 27 Feb 1927 London. PH.D '56 Univ. of London, Eng. LECTURER, Univ. Coll, Gower St, London WC 1. Member: BPS. Teaching, research, advertising consulting, professional writing; attention and memory, learning theory, interviewer selection and training. M

GREGORY, Richard Langton. Psych. Lab, Univ. of Cambridge, Downing Pl, Cambridge, Eng. b. 24 July 1923 London, Eng. MA '53 Univ. of Cambridge, Eng. DEMONSTRATOR in EXPER. PSYCH, Univ. of Cambridge; INDUS. CONSULT, priv. prac. Member: Exper. Psych. Group. Designing optical and recording instruments, research, teaching, consulting; perception, probability and induction in learning, applied psychological problems. M

GRENSTED, Prof. Laurence William. 9 Shepherds Way, Cirencester, Glos, Eng. b. 6 Dec 1884 Liverpool, Eng. DD '31 Univ. of Oxford, Eng. Member: BPS. Retired, counseling; psychological theory, psychology of religion. M

GRIEW, Stephen. Dept. of Psych, Univ. of Bristol, 27 Belgrave Rd, Bristol 8, Eng. b. 13 Sept 1928 London, Eng. B.SC '49 Univ. of London, Eng. RES. ASST, Univ. of Bristol. Member: BPS, Ergonomics Res. Socy. Research, teaching, industrial psychology; gerontology, experimental psychology, perception, equipment design. M

GRIMWOOD, Dr. Frank Southgate. Gateways, Headington Hill, Oxford, Eng. b. 14 July 1904 London, Eng. PH.D '56 McQueen's Coll, Oxon, Eng. RES. STUD, Univ. of Oxford. Member: BPS. Research, teaching, group psychotherapy; Christian doctrine. M

GRYGIER, Mrs. Patricia Ann. 3 Spring House, Spring St, Ewell, Surrey, Eng. b. 12 Dec 1922 Simla, India. BA '49 Univ. Coll, London, Eng. CLIN. PSYCH'T, Horton Hosp, Epsom, Surrey. Member: BPS. Clinical testing, research, teaching; projective techniques, personality testing. F

GRYGIER, Dr. Tadeusz. Banstead Hosp, Sutton, Surrey, Eng. b. 10 Feb 1915 Warsaw, Poland. PH. D '50 Univ. of London, Eng. SR. PSYCH'T. and HEAD, Dept. of Clin. Psych. and Res, Banstead Hosp; ABSTRACT ED, *British Journal of Delinquency.* Member: BPS. Research, clinical diagnosis, psychotherapy, administration; projective techniques, experimental validation of dynamic personality theories. M

GULLIFORD, Ronald. 68 Howard Rd, Kings Heath, Birmingham 14, Eng. b. 8 Dec 1920 Manchester, Eng. BA '44 Univ. of London, Eng. TUTOR, Educ. Dept, Univ. of Birmingham, Edmund St, Birmingham 3. Member: BPS. Teaching, educational psychology, research; mental assessment of retarded and defective children.   M

GUNTRIP, Dr. Henry James Samuel. 20 Montagu Dr, Oakwood, Leeds 8, York, Eng. b. 29 May 1901 London, Eng. PH.D '53 Univ. of London, Eng. PSYCHOTHERAPIST and LECT, Univ. of Leeds, Dept. of Psychiat, Blundell St, Leeds. Member: BPS. Psychotherapy, professional writing, teaching; object relations theory applied to psychoanalytic therapy, history of psychoanalytic theory.   M

GÜNZBURG, Dr. Herbert Charles. 49 Prospect Rd, Moseley, Birmingham 13, Eng. b. 17 Aug 1914 Wr. Neustadt, Austria. PH.D '48 Univ. of Vienna, Austria. SR. PSYCH'T, Monyhull Hall Hosp, Kings Heath, Birmingham 14; ED. BD. Journal of Midland Mental Deficiency Society. Member BPS, Amer. Assn. on Ment. Defic. Clinical analysis, psychotherapy, professional writing, research; projective techniques, psychotherapy with mental defectives, educational problems of the adult mental defective.   M

GURNEY, Miss Margaret Elizabeth. Alder Hey Hosp, Liverpool 12, Eng. b. 1 Nov 1901 Eastbonrue, Eng. Dipl. Psych. '37 Univ. of London, Eng. CHILD PSYCHOTHERAPIST, Alder Hey Hosp. Member: BPS, Assn. of Child Psychotherapists. Psychotherapy; psychosomatic disorders. F

HALDANE, Ian Rodger. Sythwood, Old Woking Rd, Pyrford, Surrey, Eng. b. 31 July 1922 Edinburgh, Scot. MA '49 Univ. of St. Andrews, Scot. SR. PSYCH'T, Army Operational Res. Grp, War. Dept, AORG Broadoaks, Parvis Rd, W. Byfleet, Surrey. Member: BPS. Research, applied psychology, testing; training methods, intelligence test construction, attitude and opinion surveys.   M

HALL, Miss Valentine Norah. The College, Ripon, York, Eng. b. 14 Feb 1904 Ashley, Chester, Eng. MA '32 Univ. of London, Eng. PRINCIPAL, Ripon Trng. Coll. for Tchrs. Member: BPS. Administration, teaching, research.   F

HALSTEAD, Dr. Herbert. 113 Manor Lane, Birmingham 32, Eng. b. 14 Mar 1904 Bradford, York, Eng. PH.D '56 Univ. of Birmingham, Eng. SR. CLIN. PSYCH'T, All Saints' Hosp, Lodge Rd, Birmingham. Member: BPS. Clinical analysis, applied psychology, research; epilepsy in children, memory function, aptitude tests.   M

HAMER, Mrs. Grace Mary. Rydal Mount, 91 Brockwell Lane, Chesterfield, Derby, Eng. b. 19 Feb 1904 Tibshelf, Eng. MA '26 Univ. of Sheffield, Eng. SR. EDUC. PSYCH'T, Chesterfield Borough Educ. Comm. Town Hall, Chesterfield. Member: BPS. Testing, psychotherapy, remedial teaching; learning, secondary school selection, projective techniques.   F

HAMILTON, James Alexander. 10 Sherwood Ave, Uddingston, Glasgow, Scot. b. 11 Jan 1921 Glasgow, Scot. ED.B '50 Univ. of Glasgow, Scot. EDUC. PSYCH'T, Lanarkshire Educ. Comm, Lanarkshire House, 191 Ingram St, Glasgow. Member: BPS. Educational psychology, testing, guidance, administration; intelligence testing, nonlearning in above average children, problem children.   M

HAMILTON, John More. Mkt. Res. Dept, Thomas Hedley and Co. Ltd. Gosforth, Newcastle upon Tyne, Eng. b. 6 May 1927 Bellshill, Scot. MA '50 Univ. of Glasgow, Scot. PSYCH'T. and PLNG. SUPERV, Thomas Hedley and Co. Ltd. Member: BPS. Industrial psychology, motivation research, administration; manual skill training, attitude measurement, aptitude tests.   M

HAMILTON, Dr. Vernon. 31 Glasslyn Rd, London N. 8, Eng. b. 15 Apr 1922 Hamburg. Ger. PH.D '56 Univ. of London, Eng. CLIN, PSYCH'T, Banstead Hosp, Sutton, Surrey, Eng; LECT. in PSYCH, Univ. of London. Member: BPS. Clinical analysis, teaching, research; perception, objective measurement of clinical symptoms, experimental tests of psychoanalytical theories. M

HAMMOND, Miss Dorothy. 19 The Promenade, Peacehaven, Sussex, Eng. b. 10 Jan 1907 London, Eng. B.SC '32 Univ. of London, Eng. EDUC. PSYCH'T, Brighton Local Educ. Authority, 62 Grand Parade, Brighton Eng. Member: BPS. Clinical practice, guidance, testing, teaching; maladjusted children, ability assessment, selection for special education.   F

HANSEL, Charles Edward Mark. Dept. of Psych, Univ. of Manchester, Oxford Rd, Manchester, Eng. b. 12 Oct 1917 Bedford, Eng. MA '53 Univ. of Cambridge, Eng. LECTURER, Univ. of Manchester. Member: BPS. Research, teaching; perception, learning, subjective probability.   M

HARBORTH, Augustus William Martin. County Off, Sleaford, Lincolnshire, Eng. b. 9 Dec 1911 Edinburgh, Scot. ED.B '51 Univ. of Edinburgh, Scot. EDUC. PSYCH'T, Kesteven County Counc, Eastgate, Sleaford. Member: BPS. Testing, educational psychology, remedial teaching; child guidance. M

HARDCASTLE, Mrs. Evelyn Mary Katherine. 32 Hadlam Rd, Bishops Stortford, Herts, Eng. b. 30 May 1909 Birkenhead, Eng. Diplôme '30 Inst. J. J. Rousseau, Switz.

PSYCHOLOGIST, Divisional Educ. Off, Springfield Dukes, Springfield Green, Chelsmford, Essex, Eng. Member: BPS. Research, teaching, guidance, consulting; psychological factors influencing breast feeding. F

HARDING, Prof. Denys Clement Wyatt. Bedford Coll, Univ. of London, Regent's Park, London N.W. 1, Eng. b. 13 July 1906 Lowestoft, Eng. BA '28 Univ. of Cambridge, Eng. PROF. of PSYCH, Bedford Coll. Member: BPS. Teaching, research, administration. M

HARNETT, Miss Sylvia C. Sotwell Hse, New Wallingford, Berks, Eng. b. 5 Aug 1897 Wolverton, Bucks, Eng. Dipl. Psych. '39 Univ. Coll, London, Eng. PSYCHO-THERAPIST, Middlesex Hosp, London; City of Oxford Child Guid. Clin; Oxfordshire County Counc. Child Guid. Clin; SR. CLIN. PSYCH'T, Chailey Heritage Sch. and Hosp. Member: BPS, Assn. of Child Psychotherapists. Psychotherapy, testing, clinical analysis. F

HARPER, Dr. Raymond Sydney. Trentvale, Holland Rd, Hove 2, Sussex, Eng. b. 1881, Brighton, Eng. M.R.C.S, L.R.C.P. '06 Coll. of Surgeons, Eng. PHYSICIAN, priv. prac. Member: BPS, RMPA. Consulting, general clinical practice; psychotherapy. M

HARPER, Dr. Roland. Dept. of Psych, Univ. of Leeds, Leeds 2, Eng. b. 23 Mar 1916 Uttoxeter, Eng. PH.D '49 Univ. of Reading, Eng. LECT. in INDUS. PSYCH, Univ. of Leeds. Member: BPS, AIPA, Exper. Psych. Grp, Ergonomics Res. Socy. Teaching, industrial psychology, research; psychophysics, psychology of human senses, social and technological change. M

HARRIS, Miss Lilian Edith. 3 Southbourne Close, Pinner, Middlesex, Eng. b. 22 July 1914 Willesden, Eng. B.SC '50 Univ. of London, Eng. SR. PSYCH'T, Ockendon Grp. Hosp. Management Comm, Leytonstone Hse, High Rd, Leytonstone E. 11, Eng. Member: BPS, Natl. Assn. for Ment. Hlth. Intelligence and personality assessment of mentally defective patients, consulting, research, student; social perception, group therapy. F

HARRIS, Trevor. 98 Fairfax Bd, Teddington, Middlesex, Eng. b. 19 May 1913 Mountain Ash, Wales. B.SC '49 Univ. of London, Eng. EDUC. PSYCH'T, Middlesex County Counc, 10 Great George St, London, S.W. 1, Eng. Member: BPS. Educational psychology, child guidance, teaching, administration; achievement tests, learning theory, causes of academic failure. M

HARRISON, Arthur Lewis. 4 Derwen Rd, Cyncoed, Cardiff, Wales. b. 22 Feb 1917 St. Helens, Eng. B.SC '39 Univ. of Manchester, Eng. SR. LECT, Cardiff Coll. of Tech. and Commerce, Cathays Park, Cardiff; LECT. in INDUS. PSYCH, Univ. of Wales, Cardiff. Member: BPS. Teaching management studies, industrial psychology, consulting; administration; industrial selection techniques, work rating, measurement of merit, job evaluation. M

HARRISON, Dr. Kenneth. 7 Ormiston Dr, Knock, Belfast, N. Ire. b. 27 Jan 1906 Wrexham, Wales. PH.D '35 Trinity Coll, Dublin, Eire. SR. EDUC. PSYCH'T, Belfast Educ. Authority, Acad. St, Belfast. Member: BPS. Educational psychology, testing, administration; projective techniques, educational and industrial selection, juvenile delinquency. M

HARRISON, Prof. Michael. 65 Langdon St, Cambridge, Massachusetts, USA. b. 2 Feb 1915 London, Eng. Dipl. Psych. '46 Univ. of London, Eng. ASSOC. PROF. of PSYCH, Boston Univ, 700 Commonwealth Ave, Boston 15, Massachusetts, USA. Member: BPS, APA, Socy. for Study of Animal Behavior. Research, teaching, administration; relation between structure and function of nervous system and behavior. M

HASSAN, Miss Janet Wilson McFarlane. Royal Hosp. for Sick Children, Dept. of Child Psychiat, 70 Univ. Ave, Glasgow W. 2, Scot. b. 20 Jan 1915 Glasgow, Scot. ED.B '49 Univ. of Glasgow, Scot. CHILD THER, Royal Hosp. for Sick Children. Member: BPS. Analytic psychotherapy, consulting, testing, guidance. F

HAWARD, Dr. Lionel Richard Charles. Dept. of Psych. Med, Winterton Hosp, Sedgefield, Durham, Eng. b. 4 Nov 1920 London, Eng. PH.D, Rijksuniv. of Leiden, Neth. SR. CLIN. PSYCH'T, Winterton Hosp; PSYCHOLOGIST, priv. prac. Member: BPS. Administration, research, teaching, professional writing; psychophysiological measurement, brain pathology and its psychological concomitants, projective techniques. M

HAWKEY, Miss Lawry. Milsey Bank, Holly Park, Crouch Hill, London, N.4, Eng. b. 27 Dec 1912 Retford, Eng. B.SC '36 Univ. of London, Eng. PSYCHOTHERAPIST, Child Guid. Unit, Woodberry Down Health Cen, London County Counc, County Hall, London. Member: BPS, Assn. of Child Psychotherapists. Child psychotherapy; analytical psychology, educational guidance. F

HEARD, Arthur Oswald. 46 Springfield Rd, Etwall near Derby, Eng. b. 11 Aug 1907 Moscow, Russia. MA '47 Univ. of Glasgow, Scot. CLIN. PSYCH'T, The Pastures Hosp, Mickleover near Derby. Member: BPS. Consulting, psychotherapy, teaching, clinical testing, projective techniques, socialization and rehabilitation of

patients.   M
HEARNSHAW, Prof. Leslie Spencer. Dept.
of Psych, Univ. of Liverpool, 7 Abercromby
Sq, Liverpool, Eng. b. 9 Dec 1907 South-
ampton, Eng. BA '30 Univ. of Oxford,
Eng. PROFESSOR, Univ. of Liverpool.
Member: BPS, AIPA. Teaching psychology,
research, industrial psychology; psychology
of thinking, history of British psychology,
occupational aspects of ageing.   M
HEBRON, Dr. Miriam Ethel. The Rectory,
Cottingham, E. York, Eng. b. 14 Oct 1904
Grays, Essex, Eng. PH.D '51 Univ. of
London, Eng. LECT. in EDUC, Univ. of Hull,
York, Eng. Member: BPS.   Research,
teaching, statistics; diagnostic uses of
intelligence, arithmetic and reading tests,
psychological theory and school organi-
sation, curricular problems.   F
HEDGES, Mrs. Pamela Edith. 12 Tarlington
Rd, Coventry, Warwick, Eng. b. 5 Mar
1920 Coventry, Eng. B.SC '47 Univ. of
London, Eng. EDUC. PSYCH'T, Coventry
Educ. Authority, Counc. Off, Earl St,
Coventry. Member: BPS. Child and edu-
cational guidance, testing; projective tech-
niques, achievement tests, child de-
velopment.   F
HEIM, Dr. Alice Winifred.   Psych. Lab,
Cambridge, Eng. b. 19 Apr 1913 London,
Eng. PH.D '39 Univ. of Cambridge, Eng.
PSYCHOLOGIST, Sci. Staff, Med. Res.
Counc, 38 Old Queen St, London S.W. 1,
Eng. Member: BPS, Exper. Psych. Grp.
Research, teaching, mental testing; thought
processes and craft formation.   F
HEMMING, Clifford James. 31 Broom Water,
Teddington, Middlesex, Eng. b. 9 Sept
1909 Stalybridge, Chester, Eng. BA '49
Univ. of London, Eng. RESEARCHER,
Birkbeck Coll, Malet St, London; CON-
SULTANT, Longmans Green and The Hulton
Press. Member: BPS. Research, professional
writing, industrial psychology; social ad-
justment, group process, adolescent psy-
chology, genesis of individual value
systems.   M
HERD, Miss Jessie Whyte. 26 Dinmont Rd,
Glasgow S. 1, Scot. b. 30 Oct 1906 Glasgow,
Scot. ED.B '46 Univ. of Glasgow, Scot.
SR. ASST. PSYCH'T, Educ. Off, Corp. of
Glasgow, 129 Bath St, Glasgow C. 2.
Member: BPS. Clinical practice, adminis-
tration, child guidance.   F
HERON, Dr. Alastair. 7 Abercromby Square,
Liverpool 7, Eng. b. 10 Oct 1915 Edin-
burgh, Scot. PH.D '51 Univ. of London,
Eng. DEPUTY DIR, Med. Res. Counc, Grp.
for Res. on Occupat. Aspects of Ageing;
HONORARY LECT. in PSYCH, Univ. of Liver-
pool. Member: BPS, APA, CPA. Research,
administration, teaching; adult develop-
ment and ageing, evaluation and measure-

ment, individual differences.   M
HERZBERG, Miss Irene.   60 Arden Rd,
London N. 3, Eng. b. 9 Sept 1918 Berlin,
Ger. BA '52 Univ. of London, Eng. EDUC.
PSYCH'T, Devon County Counc, St. David's
Hill, Ivybank, Exeter, S. Devon, Eng.
Member: BPS, Natl. Assn. for Ment. Hlth.
Child guidance, testing, psychotherapy;
projective techniques, attitude measure-
ment, group process.   F
HETHERINGTON, Dr. Ralph Railton. Crich-
ton Royal, Dumfries, Scot. b. 10 Sept 1917
Dumfermline, Scot. PH.D '54 Univ. of
London, Eng. SR. CLIN. PSYCH'T, Crichton
Royal. Member: BPS. Diagnostic testing,
psychotherapy, research, teaching; pro-
jective techniques, group psychology,
thought and memory disorders.   M
HICK, Dr. William Edmund. 66 Bishop's
Rd, Trumpington, Cambridge, Eng. b. 1
Aug 1912 Tynemouth, Eng. MD '49 Univ. of
Durham, Eng. READER in EXPER. PSYCH,
Univ. of Cambridge; CHAIRMAN, Manual
Control Sub-Comm, Ministry of Supply;
PSYCHOLOGIST, Appl. Psych. Res. Unit,
Med. Res. Counc, 15 Chaucer Rd, Cam-
bridge. Member: BPS, Exper. Psych. Grp.
Research, teaching, psychotherapy; motor
skill, manual control of machinery, cyber-
netics, human engineering.   M
HIGHAM, Thomas Martin. Selectn. and Trng.
Dept, Rowntree and Co. Ltd, The Cocoa
Works, York, Eng. b. 2 Dec 1921 Oxford,
Eng. B.Litt '50 Univ. of Oxford, Eng.
CHIEF INDUS. PSYCH'T, Rowntree and Co.
Ltd. Member: BPS. Personnel psychology,
administration, writing, teaching; industrial
training and selection, communication
theory and practice, rumor and remember-
ing.   M
HILL, John Campbell.   280 Kew Rd, Kew
Gardens, Surrey, Eng. b. 25 Apr 1888
Glasgow, Scot. M.SC '22 Kings Coll,
Durham, Eng. Member: BPS.   Retired
inspector of schools, psychotherapy,
teaching; application of Freudian psy-
chology to education.   M
HILLMAN, Horatio Henry. 16 Windsor Terr,
Jesmond, Newcastle on Tyne, Eng. b. 18
Dec. 1916 Portsmouth, Eng. M.SC '56 Univ.
of Durham, Eng. ADMIN. OFF, Spec. Schs.
and Handicapped Pupils Dept, Durham
County Counc. Educ. Dept, Shire Hall,
Durham, Eng. Member: BPS, BRF. Ad-
ministration, educational psychology, re-
search; handicapped children, reading in-
struction and method.   M
HIMMELWEIT, Dr. Hilde. London Sch. of
Econ, Univ. of London, Houghton St,
London W.C. 2, Eng. b. 20 Feb 1918 Berlin,
Ger. PH.D Univ. of London, Eng. READER
in SOC. PSYCH. and HEAD, Psych. Dept,
London Sch. of Econ; SR. CLIN. PSYCH'T,

Kings Coll. Hosp. Member: BPS. Teaching, research, testing, administration; personality, communication research, social class differences in attitudes and values.   F

HINCHCLIFFE, Dr. Ronald. 86 Gloucester Terr, London W. 2, Eng. b. 20 Feb 1926 Bolton, Eng. MD '55 Univ. of Manchester, Eng. RES. WRKR, Sci. Staff, Med. Res. Counc, 38 Old Queen St, London S.W. 1. Research in hearing and deafness, clinical otolaryngology, otology; psycho-acoustics.   M

HINDLEY, Dr. Colin Boothman. Child Study Cen, Inst. of Educ. and Child Hlth, Univ. of London, 41 Brunswick Sq, London W.C. 1, Eng. b. 4 July 1923 Bolton, Eng. MB, B.CH '46 Univ. of Manchester, Eng. RES. PSYCH'T, Child Study Cen; PSYCH. ADVIS, Int. Child. Cen, Paris. Member: BPS. Longitudinal research on child development, administation, testing; parental methods and attitudes, infant feeding.   M

HITCHFIELD, Miss Elizabeth Mary. 16 Highwood Crescent, Harraby, Carlisle. b. 2 Oct 1924 Newcastle-on-Tyne, Eng. BA '49 Univ. of London, Eng. EDUC. PSYCH'T, Bedfordshire County Counc, Shire Hall, Beds, Eng. Member: BPS. Educational psychology, testing, psychotherapy.   F

HODGKINS, Rev. William. 17 Park Crescent, Westcliff-on-Sea, Essex, Eng. b. 22 Sept 1903 Bolsover, Derby, Eng. MA '38 Univ. of Manchester, Eng. MINISTER, Cliff Town Congregational Church, Nelson St, Southend-on-Sea; TCHR. of PSYCH, Adult Educ. Sect, Munic. Coll, Southend-on-Sea, Essex. Member: BPS. Minister of religion, consulting, teaching; aphasia, re-education and social rehabilitation of alcoholics, juvenile delinquents, social significance of the church.   M

HOLDEN, Mrs. Una Philomena. 236 Newton Rd, Winwick, Warrington, Lancs, Eng. b. 20 Nov 1930 Waterloo, Liverpool, Eng. BA '51 Univ. of Manchester, Eng. CLIN. PSYCH'T, Winwick Ment. Hosp. Member: BPS. Clinical diagnosis, research; organic damage, experimental method applied to individual cases, cognition.   F

HOLDING, Dennis H. Dept. of Indus. Hlth, Med. Sch, King's Coll, Univ. of Durham, Newcastle-on-Tyne, Eng. b. 6 Dec 1925 London, Eng. MA '52 Univ. of Edinburgh, Scot. RES. PSYCH'T, Dept. of Indus. Hlth. Member: BPS. Research, experimental and applied psychology; human engineering, learning theory, perception.   M

HOLMAN, Leonard Joseph. 69 Woodlands Ave, W. Byfleet, Weybridge, Surrey, Eng. b. 14 Apr 1901 London, Eng. B.SC '33 Univ. Coll, London, Eng. PRIN. PSYCH'T, Army Operational Res. Grp, Parvis Rd, W.

Byfleet, Weybridge. Member: BPS. Military operational research, personnel psychology; selection testing, training, management and morale.   M

HOOD, Henry Blair. Messrs. Allan-Lowson and Hood, S.S.C., 118 Hanover St, Edinburgh, Scot. b. 19 Oct 1912 Edinburgh, Scot. MA '40 Univ. of Edinburgh, Scot. EDUC. PSYCH'T, Chumberland Educ. Comm, 5 Portland Sq, Carlisle. Member: BPS. Educational psychology, testing, research, teaching; achievement tests, learning, theories of Piaget.   M

HOOPER, Miss Patricia Mary Florendiyne. 5 Alwyne Place, Canonbury, London N. 1, Eng. b. 23 Sept 1924 Sherburn-in-Elmet, Eng. BA '45 Univ. of London, Eng. PSYCHOLOGIST, H. M. Prison, Holloway, Parkhurst R, London N. 7. Member: BPS. BRF. Testing, applied psychology, research, teaching; personality, projective techniques, therapy, institutions as treatment groups. F

HOPE, Thomas. Park View, Beechgrove, Moffat. Dumfries shire, Scot. b. 12 June 1890 Edinburgh, Scot. ED.B '21 Univ. of Edinburgh, Scot. RETIRED. Member: BPS.   M

HOPKINS, John. 7 Alwyne Villas, Islington, London N. 1, Eng. b. 21 Jan 1924 Paris, France. PH.D '56 Univ. of London, Eng. RES. PSYCH'T, Univ. Coll, London, Gower St, London W.C. 1. Member: BPS. Research, testing, educational psychology; projective techniques, experimental psychopathology, mental defects.   M

HORNE, Miss Edna. 32/A Burgate, Canterbury, Kent, Eng. b. 5 June 1906 Swinton, Manchester, Eng. Dipl. Psych. '47 Univ. of London, Eng. LECT. in EDUC. and PSYCH, Whitelands Trng. Coll, Putney, London S.W. 15, Eng. Member: BPS. Teaching, testing, research; remedial work with children.   F

HOTOPF, William Hugh Norman. London Sch. of Econ, Houghton St, Aldwych, London W.C. 2, Eng. b. 18 June 1914 London, Eng. MA '46 Univ. of Cambridge, Eng. LECT. in PSYCH, London Sch. of Econ. Member: BPS, Exper. Psych. Grp. Teaching, research; language, vocational guidance.   M

HOWARD, Ian Porteous. Dept. of Psych, Univ. of Durham, 7 Kepier Terr, Gilesgate, Durham City, Eng. b. 20 July 1927 Rochdale, Eng. B.SC '52 Univ. of Manchester, Eng. LECTURER, Univ. of Durham. Member: BPS. Teaching, research; physiological psychology, perception.   M

HOWE, Eric Draham. 14/C Upper Wimpole St, London W. 1, Eng. b. 3 Feb 1897 London, Eng. MB, BS '27 Univ. of London, Eng. Member: BPS. Research, professional writing, psychotherapy, consulting; psycho-dynamism. M

HOWIE, Miss Margaret Muir. Educ. Off, Stewartry of Kirkcudbright, Educ. Comm, Castle Douglas, Kirkcudbrightshire, Scot. b. 27 Apr 1910 Glasgow, Scot. ED.B '49 Univ. of Glasgow, Scot. EDUC. PSYCH'T, Stewartry of Kirkcudbright. Member: BPS. Educational psychology, testing, child guidance; projective techniques, intelligence testing, treatment of maladjusted children. F

HOY, Richard Malcolm. Dept. of Clin. Psych, Bellsdyke Ment. Hosp, Larbert, Stirlingshire, Scot. b. 18 Aug 1930 Altringham, Eng. BA '53 Univ. of Cambridge, Eng. SR. CLIN. PSYCH'T, Bellsdyke Ment. Hosp. Member: BPS. Clinical analysis, research, teaching; diagnostic testing, social psychology of the mental hospital. M

HOYLE (née McFarlane), Mrs. Alice Muriel. 63 South Drive, Chorltonville, Manchester 21, Eng. b. 4 Mar 1920 Glasgow, Scot. ED.B '45 Univ. of Glasgow, Scot. ANAL. PSYCH'T, priv. prac. Member: BPS. Psychotherapy, consulting, testing; Jungian psychology, attitude measurement, intelligence and achievement testing. F

HUGHES, Mrs. Doreen Mary. Lynwood, Station Rd, Otley, York, Eng. b. 18 Mar 1924 Preston, Eng. BA '47 Univ. of London, Eng. PSYCH'T-IN-CHARGE, Leeds Educ. Authority Child Guid. Clin, 3 Hyde Terr, Leeds 2, York, Eng. Member: BPS. Consulting, child guidance, administration, testing; learning theory, reading skills, selection for secondary education, personality assessment. F

HUMPHREY, Prof. George. Inst. of Exper. Psych, 34 Banbury Rd, Oxford, Eng. b. 17 July 1889 Bourton-under-Blean. PH.D, Harvard Univ, USA. PROF. and DIR, Inst. of Exper. Psych. Teaching, research, administration; nature of learning, thinking. M

HUMPHREY, Michael Edward. Fair Mile Hosp, Wallingford, Berks, Eng. b. 6 May 1926 London, Eng. B.SC, Univ. of Oxford, Eng. SR. CLIN. PSYCH'T, Reading Area Dept. of Psychiat, Fair Mile Hosp. Member: BPS. Clinical analysis, consulting, research; handedness, learning and problem solving, abilities of sub-normal children. M

HUMPHREY, Peter Barnard. A.O.R.G., Broadoaks, Parvis Rd, W. Byfleet, Surrey, Eng. b. 12 May 1920 Slough, Bucks, Eng. BA '51 Univ. of Cambridge, Eng. SR. PSYCH'T, A.O.R.G. Member: BPS, Ergonomics Res. Socy. Operational research, industrial psychology, testing, clinical analysis; achievement tests, human engineering, learning theory. M

HUNTER, Dr. Ian Melville Logan. Psych. Dept, Old Coll, Univ. of Edinburgh, Edin-

burgh. Scot. b. 14 Oct 1927 Largs, Scot. PH.D '53 Univ. of Oxford, Eng. LECTURER, Univ. of Edinburgh; ASST. ED, *British Journal of Psychology*. Member: BPS, Exper. Psych. Grp. Teaching, research, editorial; perceiving, learning, thinking. M

HUTTON, Geoffrey John. 157 Whitehorse Rd, W. Croydon, Surrey, Eng. b. 2 May 1928 Croydon, Eng. B.SC '51 Univ. Coll, London, Eng. PSYCHOLOGIST, Tavistock Inst. of Human Relat, 2 Beaumont St, London W. 1, Eng. Member: BPS. Industrial consulting, research, personnel selection; human relations, group behavior, role, personality. M

IKIN, Miss Alice Graham. Shangri La, Eskdale Green, Holmrook, Cumberland, Eng. b. 12 Feb 1895 Stanhope, Durham, Eng. MA, Univ. of Cambridge, Eng; M.SC, Univ. of Manchester, Eng. Member: BPS. Retired, professional writing; psychology of religion, depth psychotherapy and religious healing. F

INGHAM, Dr. John Gordon. Neuropsychiat. Res. Cen, Whitechurch Hosp, Cardiff, Glamorgan, Wales. b. 22 Aug 1923 St. Annes-on-Sea, Eng. PH.D '48 Univ. of London, Eng. PSYCHOLOGIST, Neuropsychiat. Res. Cen. Member: BPS. Research, professional writing, teaching; perception, suggestion, neurosis. M

INGLIS, James. 18 Honor Oak Rd, Forest Hill, London S.E. 23, Eng. b. 12 Aug 1927 Edinburgh, Scot. MA '52 Univ. of Edinburgh, Scot. LECT. in PSYCH, Inst. of Psychiat, Maudsley Hosp, Denmark Hill, London S.E. 5. Member: BPS. Teaching abnormal psychology, research, testing; learning theory, psychology of ageing, motivation. M

INGRAM, Mrs. Mary Margaret. Medicine Hat, 20 Redfern Close, Cambridge, Eng. b. 9 July 1924 Wembley, Eng. BA '45 Univ. of London, Eng. Member: BPS. Child guidance, projective techniques. F

INMAN, William Samuel. 22 Clarendon Rd, Southsea, Portsmouth, Hants, Eng. b. 14 Mar 1876 Sheffield, Eng. MB 1900 Univ. of Sheffield, Eng. OPHTHALMIC SURGEON, Portsmouth and S. Hants Eye and Ear Hosp, Grove Rd. N, Southsea, Portsmouth. Member: BPS, Br. Psychoanal. Socy. Psychotherapy, research, consulting, clinical practice; psychosomatic medicine in eye diseases. M

IRVINE, Dr. Douglas. Trollseter, Burnhams Rd, Little Bookham, Leatherhead, Surrey, Eng. b. 8 Sept 1920 Ootacamund, India. PH.D '55 Univ. of London, Eng. SR. PSYCH'T Army Operational Res. Grp, Broadoaks, Parvis Rd, W. Byfleet, Surrey. Member: BPS. Research, military and social psychology, testing; attitude measurement and social processes, training, psycho-acoustics, fatigue. M

ISAACS, Dr. Evelyn Mary. 30 Primrose Hill Rd, London, Eng. b. 31 Dec 1892 Walton-on-Thames, Eng. PH.D '29 Univ. of London, Eng. HONORARY DIR, Natl. Froebel Found, 2 Manchester Sq, London W. 1; EDITOR, *National Froebel Foundation Bulletin.* Member: BPS. Administration, editorial, teaching; educational psychology, inheritance of intelligence, vocational guidance. F

JACKSON, Clifford Vivian. Jewell House Cottage, Marden, Tonbridge, Kent, Eng. b. 30 Oct 1924 London, Eng. B.SC '52 Univ. of Oxford, Eng. MANAGEMENT CONSULT, 29 Hartford St, London W. 1, Eng. Member: Br. Operational Res. Socy, Ergonomics Res. Socy. Consulting; neurological psychology, human engineering, personnel selection. M

JACKSON, Dr. Mrs. Lydia. 370 Russell Ct, Woburn Pl, London W.C. 1, Eng. b. 6 Oct 1899 Moghilev, Russia. PH.D '49 Univ. of Oxford, Eng. CHILD PSYCHOTHERAPIST, London County Counc. Child Guid. Unit, 25 Straford Rd, London W. 8. Member: BPS, ICWP, ASSN. of Child Psychotherapists. Psychotherapy, professional writing, research; play therapy, projective test construction. F

JAHODA, Dr. Gustav. Dept. of Psych, Univ. of Glasgow, Glasgow W. 2, Scot. b. 11 Oct 1920 Vienna, Austria. PH.D '52 Univ. of London, Eng. SR. LECT, Univ. of Glasgow. Member: BPS. Teaching and research in social psychology; culture contacts, race attitudes, social class. M

JAMES, Cyril Benjamin Edmund. Carmarthenshire County Counc, County Hall, Carmerthen, S. Wales. b. 24 June 1915 Llanelly, UK. ED.B '47 Univ. of Edinburgh, Scot. PSYCHOLOGIST, Carmarthenshire County Counc; CONSULTANT, Pembrokeshire County Counc. Member: BPS. Psychotherapy, guidance, administration, educational psychology and testing; learning theory, achievement tests, effects of bilingualism on mental development. M

JAMES, Harold Ernest Oswald. Inst. of Educ, Univ. of London, Malet St, London W.C. 1, Eng. b. 1 Oct 1896 W. Houghton, Eng. M.SC '24 Univ. of Manchester, Eng. READER in PSYCH, Univ. of London. Member: BPS. Teaching, research, professional writing; group process, social attitudes, learning. M

JAMES, Miss Valerie Mary Wallwyn. Flat 4, 80 N. Walls, Winchester, Hants, Eng. b. 25 Sept 1924 Gillingham, Kent, Eng. MA '52 Univ. of St. Andrews, Scot. ASST. EDUC. PSYCH'T, Hampshire County Counc, The Castle, Winchester, Eng. Member:

BPS. Educational psychology and guidance, testing, play therapy, remedial teaching, school advising. F

JARVIE, Dr. Hugh Forrest. Dept. of Studies in Psych. Med, Univ. of Liverpool, 77 Bedford St. S, Liverpool 7, Eng. b. 21 Apr 1918 Coatbridge, Scot. MD '54 Univ. of Glasgow, Scot. SR. LECT. in PSYCH. MED, Univ. of Liverpool; CONSULT. PSYCHIATRIST, Liverpool Royal Infirmary; CONSULT. PSYCHIATRIST, Liverpool Psychiat. Clin. Member: BPS, RMPA. Teaching, research, clinical practice, consulting; clinical research in psychological medicine, relations of cerebral functions to behavior and intelligence. M

JEFFRIES, Cyril Robert. Inglenook, 103 Greenstead Rd, Colchester, Essex, Eng. b. 26 Feb 1893 Colchester, Eng. Cert. in Appl. Psych. '39 Univ. of London, Eng. Member: BPS. Editorial, applied psychology, professional writing. M

JENKIN, Dr. Annie Mabel. St. Katherine's Coll, White Hart Lane, Tottenham, London N. 17, Eng. b. 18 Dec 1897 Devonport, Eng. PH.D '33 Univ. of London, Eng. SR. LECT. in EDUC, St. Katharine's Coll. Member: BPS. Teaching, testing; imagery and learning. F

JESSOP, Prof. Thomas Edmund. 73 Park Ave, Hull, Eng. b. 10 Sept 1896 Huddersfield, Eng. B.Litt '24 Univ. of Oxford, Eng. PROF. of PHILOS, Univ. of Hull. Member: BPS. Teaching. M

JOHN, Miss Enid Margaret. Child Guid. Clin, Birmingham Educ. Comm, 280 Birchfield Rd, Perry Barr, Birmingham 20, Eng. b. 16 Sept 1915 Stockton-on-Tees, Eng. M.SC '42 Univ. Coll, London, Eng. EDUC. PSYCH'T, Birmingham Educ. Comm. Member: BPS. Psychotherapy, intelligence testing, educational guidance, administration; projective techniques, child psychology. F

JOHNSON, Miss Erica Muriel Christine. 13 Trebovir Rd, London S.W. 5, Eng. b. 20 May 1919 Essex, Eng. BA '41 Univ. Coll, London, Eng. EDUC. PSYCH'T, London County Counc, Waterloo, London S.E. 1. Testing, remedial teaching, psychotherapy, liaison work with schools. F

JOHNSTON, Miss Janey Alison Donald. 39 Donmouth Crescent, Bridge of Don, Aberdeen, Scot. b. 17 Apr 1927 Peterhead, Scot. ED.B '51 Univ. of Aberdeen, Scot. ASST. CLIN. PSYCH'T, Aberdeen Educ. Comm. Child Guid. Clin, 66 Carden Pl, Aberdeen. Member: BPS. Child psychotherapy and guidance, clinical psychology; projective tests, anthropology. F

JONES, Mrs. Alice Marie. 49 Kelston Rd, Whitchurch, Cardiff, Wales. b. 16 Apr 1906 Pueblo, Colorado, USA. ED.B '37

Univ. of Colorado, USA. SR. PSYCH'T, Child Guid. Clin, Whitchurch Hosp, Whitchurch, Cardiff, Wales; EDUC. PSYCH'T, Med. Advis. Panel, Craig-y-Park Spastic Sch. Member: BPS. Testing, educational psychology, research, child guidance; projective techniques, child development, psychotherapy. F

JONES, Dr. Ernest. The Plat, Elsted, Midhurst, Sussex, Eng. b. 1 Jan 1897 Llwchwr, Wales. MD '04 Univ. of London, Eng. EDITOR, International Psychoanalytical Library. Member: BPS, RMPA, Int. Psychoanal. Assn, Amer. Psychoanal. Assn, Br. Psychoanal. Socy, Amer. Psychiat. Assn. Research, professional writing, clinical practice, consulting; psychoanalysis. M

JONES, H. Gwynne. 103 Turney Rd, Dulwich, London S.E. 21, Eng. b. 1 Aug 1918 Llanelly, Wales. B.SC '51 Univ. of London, Eng. LECT. in PSYCH, Univ. of London, Inst. of Psychiat, Maudsley Hosp, Denmark Hill, London S.E. 5. Member: BPS. Teaching, clinical practice, research; experimental methods in clinical investigation and treatment, learning theory, diagnostic testing. M

JONES, Dr. Howard. 21 Palmerston Blvd, Leicester, Eng. b. 23 Nov 1918 W. Bromwich, Eng. PH.D '53 Univ. of London, Eng. LECT. in SOC. STUDIES, Univ. Coll. of Leicester. Member: BPS, Br. Sociol. Assn. Teaching, research, professional writing; group process, criminology, psychoanalysis, juvenile delinquency. M

JONES, Dr. Llewelyn Wynn. Collinwood, Tree Lane, Iffley, Oxon. b. 23 Apr 1897 Pwllheli, Wales. D.SC '39 Univ. of Wales. Member: BPS, Int. Union of Sci. Psych. Professional writing, research; absolute color threshold, group process. M

JONES, Mrs. Margaret Eleanor. Bathafarn Hall, Ruthin, Denbighshire, Eng. b. 1 June 1920 London, Eng. BA '42 Univ. Coll, London, Eng. Member: BPS. Educational psychology, clinical practice, child guidance. F

JONES, Thomas. 9 Church Close, Croesyceiliog, Cwmbran, Mon, Eng. b. 28 Sept 1918 Crickhowell, Wales. MA '51 Univ. of Birmingham, Eng. EDUC. PSYCH'T, Educ. Comm, Civic Cen, Newport, Mon. Member: BPS. Testing, educational psychology, child guidance; performance tests, remedial techniques, psychotherapy. M

JOYCE, Miss Mary Patricia. 6 Buile Hill Ave, Little Hulton, Walkden, Lancaster, Eng. b. 29 Mar 1928 Blackpool, Lancaster, Eng. B.SC '53 Univ. of London, Eng. EDUC. PSYCH'T, Bolton, Lancaster Local Educ. Authority; SR. CLIN. PSYCH'T, Bolton and Dist. Hosp. Management Comm, Bolton Genl. Hosp, Bolton, Lancaster, Eng.

Member: BPS. Educational psychology, testing, clinical diagnosis, guidance. F

JOYNSON, Robert Billington. Dept. of Psych, Univ. of Nottingham, Nottingham, Eng. b. 5 Sept 1922 Norwich, Eng. B.Litt '49 Univ. of Oxford, Eng. LECTURER, Univ. of Nottingham. Member: BPS. Teaching, research; constancy studies. M

JUDE, Sister. Notre Dame Child Guid. Clin, 20 Athole Gardens, Glasgow W. 2, Scot. b. 1 Feb 1912 Glasgow, Scot. ED.B '44 Univ. of Glasgow, Scot. DIRECTOR, Notre Dame Child Guid. Clin. Member: BPS, Natl. Assn. for Ment. Hlth. Consulting, administration, testing, guidance; projective techniques, achievement tests. F

KALDEGG, Dr. Ann. 14B Landdowne Rd, Wimbledon, London S.W. 20, Eng. b. 19 May 1899 Vienna, Austria. PH.D '53 Univ. of London, Eng. SR. CLIN. PSYCH'T, Dept. of Psych. Med. Guy's Hosp, London S.E. 1; SR. CLIN. PSYCH'T, Cane Hill Hosp, Coulsdon Surrey, Eng. Member: BPS, BRF. Clinical analysis, guidance, research; projective techniques, psychosomatic disorders, comparative studies of national attitudes and characteristics. F

KANTER, Victor Ben. Flat D, 15 Frognal, London N.W. 3, Eng. b. 20 Feb 1918 Johannesburg, S. Africa. MA '43 Univ. of Oxford, Eng. CLIN. PSYCH'T, Br. Hosp. for Functional Nerv. Disorders, Camden Rd, London; STUDENT, Inst. of Psychoanal. Member: BPS, BRF. Clinical testing, psychotherapy, vocational guidance; psychoanalysis, projective techniques, psychosomatic medicine, dyspepsia and duodenal ulcer. M

KAY, Dr. Brian Ross. Dept. of Psych, Univ. of New Hampshire, Durham, NewHampshire, USA. b. 8 May 1922 Gisborne, N.Z. PH.D '52 Univ. of London, Eng. ASST. PROF, Univ. of New Hampshire. Member: BPS. Teaching, research, consulting; communications, stress, self concept. M

KAY, Dr. Julius. 38 Moore Rd, Mapperley, Notts, Eng. b. 16 Apr 1902 Warsaw, Poland. PH.D '33 Univ. of Warsaw, Poland. SR. CLIN. PSYCH'T, No. 3 Hosp. Management Comm, Nottingham Area, Porchester Rd, Notts. Member: BPS. Testing, clinical practice, psychotherapy, lecturing; psychometric measurements, projective techniques. M

KELLY, Joseph. Brown Hall, Mid-Lodge, Glencaple Rd, Dumfries, Scot. b. 9 May 1911 Glasgow, Scot. ED.B '48 Univ. of Glasgow, Scot. SR. CLIN. PSYCH'T, Crichton Royal Inst, Dumfries. Member: BPS. Consultant to school for maladjusted children, psychotherapy, clinical testing, research; projective techniques, play therapy. M

KENDALL, Dr. David Carr. Flat 9, 65 Warwick Rd, Earl Court, London S.W. 5, Eng. b. 9 Sept 1925 London, Eng. PH.D '53 Univ. of Manchester, Eng. RES. WRKR, Carnegie United Kingdom Trust, Comely Park House, Dumfermline, Scot. Member: BPS. Consulting, clinical testing, research on handicapped children; child development, audiology. M

KENNA, John Corbett. Univ. of Manchester, Dept. of Psychiat, Manchester Royal Infirmary, Oxford Rd, Manchester 13, Lancaster, Eng. b. 28 July 1913 Moss Vale, Austl. MA '50 Univ. of California, USA. LECT. in CLIN. PSYCH, Univ. of Manchester; PSYCHOLOGIST, Advis. Comm, Manchester Marriage Guid. Counc. Member: BPS, BRF. Clinical psychology, research, guidance, teaching; personality theory and measurement, psychopathology of memory, history of British psychology. M

KENNEDY, Prof. Dr. Alexander. 2 George Sq, Edinburgh, Scot. b. 16 Jan 1909 London, Eng. MD '34 Univ. of London, Eng. PROF. of PSYCH. MED. and DEPT. HEAD, Univ. of Edinburgh, Old College, Edinburgh; NEUROPSYCHIATRIST, priv. prac; ED. BD, *Scottish Medical Journal*. Member: BPS, RMPA. Teaching, research, administration, clinical practice, professional writing; diagnostic psychiatry, electroencephalography, delinquency, industrial applied psychology. M

KERR, Dr. Madeline. Ty Draw, Efenechtyd near Ruthin, N. Wales. b. 6 July 1907 Altrincham, Eng. PH.D '38 Univ. of London, Eng. SR. LECT. in SOC. SCI, Univ. of Liverpool, 19 Abercromby Sq, Liverpool, Eng. Member: BPS, BRF. Teaching, research, testing; culture analysis and conflict, culture and personality, projective techniques. F

KIDD, Miss Jane S. H. Norwich Educ. Comm. Off, City Hall, Norwich, Norfolk, Eng. b. 15 July 1925 Dundee, Scot. ED.B '50 Univ. of St. Andrews, Scot. EDUC. PSYCH'T, Norwich Educ. Comm. Member: BPS. Testing, educational psychology, administration. F

KING, Cyril. Pennyfold Steep, Petersfield, Hants, Eng. b. 10 Aug 1896 London, Eng. MA '29 King's Coll, Cambridge, Eng. SR. MASTER, Bedales Sch, Petersfield. Member: BPS. Teaching, testing, guidance, educational selection; intelligence and personality tests. M

KINGERLEE, Miss Patricia Eileen. Frilford Heath nr. Abingdon, Berks, Eng. b. 1 June 1929 Oxford, Eng. B.SC '51 Univ. of Manchester, Eng. PSYCHOLOGIST, Ingrebourne Cen, St. George's Hosp, Horn Church, Essex, Eng. Member: BPS. Clinical analysis, consulting; diagnostic testing, projective techniques. F

KITCHENER, Philip. 42 Crompton Ave, Glasgow S 4, Scot. b. 28 June 1913 Glasgow Scot. ED.B '50 Univ. of Glasgow, Scot. EDUC. PSYCH'T, Glasgow, Corp Educ. Dept, 129 Bath St, Glasgow. Member: BPS. Educational psychology, psychotherapy, consulting; young criminals, maladjusted children, projective techniques, testing. M

KNIGHT, David Arthur. Menston Hosp, Leeds, Eng. b. 12 Mar 1921 Grimsby, Eng. MA '46 Univ. of Cambridge, Eng. SR. CLIN. PSYCH'T, Menston Hosp; CLIN. PSYCH'T, Stanley Royd Hosp, Wakefield; CLIN. PSYCH'T, Bootham Hosp, York. Member: BPS. Clinical analysis and practice, consulting, administration; brain damage, projective techniques, learning theory. M

KRAEMER, Dr. Wilhelm Guenther Paul. Davidson Clin, 58 Dalkeith Rd, Edinburgh, Scot. b. 22 Mar 1911 Essen, Ger. MD '37 Sienna Univ. Italy. MED. DIR, Davidson Clin. Member: BPS, RMPA. Psychotherapy, consulting, marriage guidance, administration; individual and group analysis. M

KRAS, Mrs. Sara. Marlborough Day Hosp, 38 Marlborough Pl, London NW 3, Eng. b. 1 Jan 1901 Hungary. BA '48 Birkbeck Coll, London, Eng. SR. CLIN. PSYCH'T, Cen. Middlesex Hosp. Bd, Acton, London. Member: BPS. Clinical assessment, psychotherapy, professional writing; didactic groups, prevention of mental illness. F

KRAUSS, Dr. Stephen. Fair Mile Hosp, Wallingford, Berks, Eng. b. 22 June 1902 Budapest, Hungary. MD '34 Univ. of Basel, Switz. SR. PSYCHIATRIST, Oxford Reg. Hosp. Bd, Fair Mile Hosp. Member: BPS, RMPA. Clinical practice, research, testing, clinical analysis; personality development after brain lesions, experimental psychopathology, color vision and flicker response. M

KRIKLER, Mrs. Berenice. Psych. Dept, Inst. of Psychiat, Denmark Hill, London SE 5, Eng. b. 21 Apr 1930 Johannesburg, S. Africa. BA '51 Univ. of Witwatersrand, S. Africa. ASST. LECT, Inst. of Psychiat. Member: BPS. Teaching, testing, clinical research; therapeutic techniques derived from learning theory, remedial teaching. F

KRONHEIMER, Mrs. Else Fanny. 26 St. Margarets Rd, Oxford, Eng. b. 3 June 1898 Frankfurt, Ger. B.SC '42 Univ. of Oxford, Eng. PSYCHOTHERAPIST and GRAPHOLOGIST, priv. prac, 95 Regency House, London NW 3, Eng. Member: BPS. Psychotherapy, research, applied psychology; schizophrenia, personality theory, graphology. F

LANER, Dr. Stephen. BISRA, OR Dept. 11 Park Lane, London W. 1, Eng. b. 11 May 1920. PH.D '56 Univ. of Reading, Eng.

SR. SCI. OFF, BIRSA. Member: BPS. Research, industrial psychology, lecturing; perception, skill acquisition, group process, industrial accidents.   M

LANGAN, Dr. Winifred. The Outspan, Park Gates Dr, Cheadle Hulme, Chester, Eng. b. 5 Feb 1909 London, Eng. PH. D '49 Univ. of Reading, Eng. LECT. in CHILD PSYCH, Univ. of Manchester, Oxford Rd, Manchester 13; PSYCHOLOGIST, priv. prac. Member: BPS. Teaching, consulting, educational psychology, research; educational problems, remedial reading, development of handicapped children.   F

LANGDON, Dr. James Norman. Albrighton Hall, Broad Oak, Shrewsbury, Eng. b. 27 Mar 1902 Aldershot, Eng. PH.D '33 Univ. of London, Eng. PRIN. and SECY, Royal Normal Coll. for the Blind, Broad Oak, Shrewsbury. Member: BPS. Administration, teaching, research; problems of blindness, achievement tests, learning theory.   M

LATIF, Dr. Israil. 126 Streatfield Rd, Kenton, Harrow, Middlesex, Eng. b. 13 Nov 1891 Zaffarioal, India. PH.D '33 Princeton Univ, USA. PSYCHOANALYST, priv. prac. Member: BPS, Br. Psychoanal. Socy. Consulting, psychotherapy, professional writing; psychopathology, personality tests, linguistic development of the child.   M

LAWLOR, Miss Monica Mary. Bedford Coll, Univ. of London, Regents Park, London NW 1, Eng. b. 2 May 1926 London, Eng. BA '48 Univ. of London, Eng. LECT. in PSYCH, Bedford Coll. Member: BPS. Teaching, research; social behavior of animals, experimental aesthetics, child development.   F

LAYARD, Dr. John. 1 Northmoor Rd, Oxford, Eng. b. 28 Nov 1891 London, Eng. D.SC '44 Univ. of Oxford, Eng. ANAL. PSYCH'T, Socy. of Anal. Psych, 25 Park Crescent, London, Eng; ASST. ED, Journal of Analytical Psychology. Member: BPS, Socy. of Anal. Psych. Psychotherapy, editorial, professional writing, research; depth psychology, psychosomatics, homosexuality.   M

LEE, Dr. Sidney Gillmore McKenzie. Dept. of Psych, Bedford Coll, Univ. of London, Regents Park, London, Eng. b. 26 Dec 1920 Durban, S. Africa. PH.D '55 Univ. of London, Eng. ASST. LECT, Bedford Coll. Member: BPS. Teaching, research, professional writing; group processes in psychopathology, culture and personality, projective techniques.   M

LEE, Dr. Terance Richard. Dept. of Psych, Univ. of St. Andrews, St. Andrews, Fife, Scot. b. 30 Nov 1924 London, Eng. PH.D '53 Univ. of Cambridge, Eng. LECTURER, Univ. of St. Andrews. Member: BPS.

Teaching, research, applied and educational psychology; attitude measurement, urban and rural social psychology, personnel selection.   M

LEONARD, Dr. John Alfred. 24 St. Andrews Rd, Cambridge, Eng. b. 27 Oct 1922 Frankfurt/M, Ger. PH.D '52 Univ. of Cambridge, Eng. SCI. RES. WRKR, Med. Res. Counc. Appl. Psych. Res. Unit, 15 Chaucer Rd, Cambridge. Member: BPS, Exper. Psych. Grp. Research, professional writing; acquisition and transmission of information, reaction times, transfer of training, discrimination of visual figures.   M

LEWIS, Prof. Aubrey Julian. Inst. of Psychiat, Maudsley Hosp, Univ. of London, Denmark Hill, London SE5, Eng. b. 8 Nov 1900 Adelaide, S. Austl. MD '31 Adelaide Univ, Austl. PROFESSOR, Inst. of Psychiat; CO-EDITOR, Maudsley Monograph Series. Member: BPS, RMPA. Research, teaching, consulting; social and occupational psychiatry, behavior of chronic psychotic patients.   M

LEWIS, David Howell. Flat 4, Court Rd, Bridgend, Glamorgan, Wales. b. 10 Feb 1923 Carmarthen, Wales. B.SC '50 Univ. of Manchester, Eng. SR. CLIN. PSYCH'T, Morgannwg Hosp. Grp, Bridgend. Member: BPS. Testing, clinical analysis, applied psychology, child guidance; testing, projective techniques, psychometric diagnostic assessment of intracranial pathology, psychotherapy.   M

LEWIS, Mrs. Eve. Child Guid. Cen, Exeter Educ. Comm, St. David's Hill, Exeter, Devon, Eng. b. 28 July 1894 Cotherstone, Eng. MA '28 Univ. of Birmingham, Eng. EDUC. PSYCH'T, Exeter Educ. Comm. Member: BPS. Research, testing, psychotherapy, learning theory, effects of emotional disturbance on learning, problems of partially sighted.   F

LIEBMANN, Dr. Susanne. Pewsey Hosp, Pewsey, Wilts, Eng. b. 29 Feb 1897 Berlin, Ger. PH.D '27 Univ. of Berlin, Ger. CLIN. PSYCH'T, Pewsey Hosp. Member: ICWP. Psychotherapy, testing.   F

LIGGETT, John. 220 Jesmond Dene Rd, Newcastle on Tyne, Eng. b. 18 June 1923 Manchester, Eng. B.SC '51 Univ. of London, Eng. LECT. in APPL. PSYCH, Dept. of Psych. Med. King's Coll, Univ. of Durham, Newcastle, Eng; CONSULT. PSYCH'T, St. Nicholas Hosp. Mgmt. Comm, Northumberland, Eng. Member: BPS. Research, teaching, testing; object relationships, social perception, phenomenology.   M

LIGHTFOOT, Dr. William. 5 The Crescent, Beckenham, Kent, Eng. b. 22 Oct 1912 Stockton-on-Tees, Eng. PH.D '50 Univ. of London, Eng. SR. LECT. in EDUC, St. Mary's Coll, Inst. of Educ, Twickenham,

Middlesex, Eng. Member: BPS. Teaching, testing, research; learning theories. M

LINKLATER, John Roy. 9 Drumsheugh Gardens, Edinburgh 3, Scot. b. 6 Jan 1917 Orkney, Scot. ED.B '40 Univ. of Aberdeen, Scot. ASST, DIR. of EDUC, Midlothian County Counc, George IV Bridge, Edinburgh 1. Member: BPS. Administration, educational psychology, consulting; achievement tests, personality, teaching. M

LIVINGSTON, Miss Amelia Annie. Mayfield, Dunlop, Aryshire, Scot. b. 9 Aug 1920 Dunlop, Scot. ED.B '45 Univ. of Glasgow, Scot. EDUC. PSYCH'T, Kilmarnock Child Guid. Clin, Ayrshire County Counc, Educ. Dept, County Bldgs, Ayrshire. Member: BPS. Guidance, testing, teaching; projective techniques, learning theory. F

LLOYD, Arthur Wynne. Shenley Hosp, Shenley near St. Albans, Herts, Eng. b. 23 Apr 1926 Holyhead, Wales. BA '52 Univ. of Bristol, Eng. CLIN. PSYCH'T, Shenley Hosp. Member: BPS. Testing, clinical analysis, consulting, research; personality assessment. M

LOCK, Harold Frank. 33 Chester Rd, Northwood, Middlesex, Eng. b. 20 Sept 1905 Cheltenham, Eng. B.SC '27 Univ. of Bristol, Eng. PERS. ADVIS, The Rank Organiza, 11 Belgrave Rd, London SW 1, Eng. Member: BPS. Personnel psychology, administration, consulting; personnel selection, testing, group observation techniques. M

LOMAX-SIMPSON, Dr. Josephine Mary. c/o The Midland Bank, 25 Wigmore St, London W1, Eng. b. 3 Nov 1925 London, Eng. MB, CH.B '48 Univ. of Aberdeen, Scot. PSYCHOTHERAPIST, S. London Hosp. for Women, Clapham, London; PSYCHIATRIST, London County Counc. Member: BPS. Psychotherapy, consulting, student, teaching; clinical psychiatry. F

LOVE, Peter Carvell. 46 Greystock Ave, Fulwood, Preston, Lancaster, Eng. b. 30 Jan 1925 Portsmouth, Eng. ED.B '53 Univ. of St. Andrews, Scot. EDUC. PSYCH'T, Lancashire County Counc, E. Cliff County Off, Preston. Member: BPS. Testing, educational guidance, teaching; child development, mental health in infancy, testing of handicapped children. M

LOVELESS, Norman Ernest. Lindisfrane, Northumberland Rd, Ryton, Durham, Eng. b. 9 Oct 1921 London, Eng. MA '51 Univ. of Edinburgh, Scot. LECT. in PSYCH, Nuffield Dept. of Indus. Hlth, King's Coll, Univ. of Durham, Newcastle-upon-Tyne, Eng. Member: BPS, Assn. for Study of Animal Beh, Ergonomics Res. Socy. Research for Royal Air Force, teaching, educational psychology; human engineering, psychophysics, learning theory. M

LOVELL, Dr. Kenneth. 10 Sudbury Ct. Dr, Harrow, Middlesex, Eng. b. 14 Oct 1915 Exeter, Eng. PH.D '54 Univ. of London, Eng. LECT. in EDUC. PSYCH, Borough Rd. Coll, Univ. of London, Inst. of Educ, Borough Rd. Isleworth, Middlesex. Member: BPS. Teaching, educational psychology, testing; mental testing, personality assessment, learning theory. M

LOWE, Dr. Marianne. 13 Montenotte Rd, London N 8, Eng. b. 15 Mar 1913 Prague, Czech. PH.D '45 Univ. Coll, London, Eng. RETIRED. Member: BPS. Psychology of early childhood. F

LOWENFELD, Dr. Margaret. 6 Pembridge Villas, London W 11, Eng. b. 4 Feb 1890 London, Eng. M.R.C.S, L.R.C.P. '18 Eng. CHIEF. PHY. and DIR. of TRNG, Inst. of Child Psych; PSYCHIAT. and PSYCHOTHER, Exper. Sch, Hengrove Sch, St. Leonards, Herts, Eng. Member: BSP, ICWP, Assn. of Child Psychother. Child psychotherapy, teaching, research, professional writing; psychosomatics, projective techniques. F

LOWY, Dr. Samuel. 23 W. 73rd St, New York 23, N.Y. USA. b. 12 Dec. 1900 Levôca, Czech. MD '26 Univ. of Prague, Czech. TUTOR in NEUROPHYSIOLOGY, N.P.A.P., W. 72 St, New York 23, N.Y, USA. Member: BPS, Assn. for Advanc. of Psychother. Psychotherapy, consulting, teaching; psychosomatics, dream problems, modified analytical therapies. M

LUBBOCK, Ronald William Hendry. 7 Madison Gardens, Bromley, Kent, Eng. b. 27 July 1927 London, Eng. B.SC '51 Univ. of London, Eng. TECH. STAFF OFF, Sperry Gyroscope Co. Ltd, Great West Rd, Brentford, Middlesex, Eng. Member: BPS. Administration, personnel selection, testing; training in technical and human relations skills. M

LUMSDEN, James. Ministry of Educ, Curzon St, London W1, Eng. b. 3 Oct 1904 Dundee, Scot. ED.B '28 Univ. of Edinburgh, Scot. H. M. INSPECTOR of SCH, Ministry of Educ. Member: BPS. Administration, educational psychology, consulting; child guidance, mental retardation, sense deprivation. M

LUSH, Dr. Dora. 4 Harman Dr, London NW 2, Eng. b. 22 May 1929 Brussels, Belg. PH.D '53 Univ. of London, Eng. STUDENT, Tavistock Clin, 2 Beaumont St, London W1. Member: BPS. Student, research; child analytical psychotherapy, psychological aspects of feminism. F

MACCALMAN, Prof. Douglas Robert. Ridgefield, N. Hill Rd, Leeds 6, Eng. b. 4 Dec 1903 Dunoon, Scot. MD '33 Univ. of Glasgow, Scot. PROF. of PSYCHIAT, Univ. of Leeds; CONSULT. PSYCHIAT, St. James Hosp, Leeds. Member: RMPA, BPS. Teaching pharmacalogical research, psychotherapy; projective techniques, mental health. M

MACDONALD, Allan. 17 Broomhall Rd, Edinburgh 12, Scot. b. 11 Mar 1916 Bellshill, Scot. ED.B '53 Aberdeen Univ, Scot. SR. ASST. PSYCH'T, Child Guid. Serv, Edinburgh Educ. Comm, St. Giles Street, Edinburgh. Member: BPS. Educational psychology, testing, child guidance; projective techniques with children, achievement tests, remedial education. M

MACDONALD, Dr. Allan. Newlands, York Rd, Haxby, York, Eng. b. 6 Sept 1912 Edinburgh, Scot. PH.D '39 Univ. of Edinburgh, Scot. PERS. MGR, Rowntree and Co. Ltd, Haxby Rd, York. Member: BPS. Administration, personnel psychology, testing; vocational guidance, selection and training. M

MACDONALD, John Edwin. Graylingwell Hosp, Chichester, Sussex, Eng. b. 31 Oct 1924 Inverness, Scot. MA '51 Univ. of Edinburgh, Scot. SR. PSYCH'T, Graylingwell and Summersdale Hosp. Member: BPS. Testing, clinical analysis, research, teaching; hypnosis, psychomotor reactions. M

MACDONALD, Ronald Annandale. 23A Aberdare Gardens, London NW 6, Eng. b. 23 May 1899 Beattock, Scot. MB, CH.B '24 Univ. of Edinburgh, Scot. PSYCHOANALYST, priv. prac. Member: BPS, Br. Psychoanal. Socy. Psychotherapy, consulting; psychoanalysis. M

MACE, Prof. Cecil Alec. Birkbeck Coll, Univ. of London, Malet St, London WC 1, Eng. b. 22 July 1894 Norwich, Eng. D.Litt '37 Univ. of London, Eng. PROF. of PSYCH, Birkbeck Coll; EDITOR, *Methuens Manuals of Psychology*; *Penguin Psychological Series*. Teaching, administration, research, editorial; philosophical psychology, theories and experimental studies of motivation. M

MACFARLANE, Miss Jean Crystal. 30 Dellside, Harefield, Middlesex, Eng. b. 12 Nov 1913 Pinner, Eng. MA '50 Inst. of Educ, London, Eng. EDUC. PSYCH'T, Middlesex County Counc, 10 Great George St, London, Eng. Member: BPS. Testing, psychotherapy, consulting, administration; vocational guidance, remedial teaching, psychotherapeutic techniques. F

MACKWORTH, Dr. Norman Humphrey. Med. Res. Counc, Appl. Psych. Res. Unit, 15 Chaucer Rd, Cambridge, Eng. b. 2 Dec 1917 Bareilly, India. PH.D '47 Univ. of Cambridge, Eng. DIRECTOR, Appl. Psych. Res. Unit, Med. Res. Counc, 38 Old Queen St, London SW 1, Eng. Member: BPS, Exper. Psych. Grp. Administration, research, applied psychology; measurement of human performance under stress. M

MACLAY, Dr. The Honorable Walter Symington. Ministry of Hlth, Savile Row, London

W 1, Eng. b. 29 Oct 1901 Glasgow, Scot. FRCP '55 Univ. of London, Eng. MED. SR. COMMR, Bd. of Control, H. M. Queen of England. Member: BPS, Amer. Psychiat. Assn. Administration, consulting. M

MACLEAN, Dr. Isabella Clark. Broomlee Clin, 1 Swan Rd, Kirkcaldy, Fife, Scot. b. 5 Apr 1915 Edinburgh, Scot. PH.D '53 Univ. of Edinburgh, Scot. PRIN. PSYCH'T, Fife Educ. Comm. Wemyssfield, Kirkcaldy. Member: BPS, ICWP, Assn. of Ment. Hlth. Administration, testing, child guidance, remedial teaching, psychotherapy; projective techniques, learning theory, diagnostic techniques with retarded children, visual perception. F

MACPHERSON, Euan Lachlan Robert. Royal Edinburgh Hosp. for Ment. and Nerv. Disorders, 40 Colinton Rd, Edinburgh, Scot. b. 17 May 1926 Edmonton, Can. MA '50 Univ. of Edinburgh, Scot. SR. CLIN. PSYCH'T, Bd. of Management for Royal Edinburgh Hosp. Member: BPS. Clinical practice and analysis, research; projective techniques, physiological psychology, delinquency. M

MADDOX, Dr. Harry. 19 Leasowes Rd, Birmingham 14, Eng. b. 28 June 1918 Hereford, Eng. PH.D '56 Univ. of London, Eng. LECT. in EDUC. PSYCH, Univ. of Birmingham, Edmund St, Birmingham 3. Member: BPS. Teaching, educational psychology, research; social class, mental tests, electron equipment. M

MAHER, Dr. Brendan Arnold. Dept. of Psych, Northwestern Univ, Evanston, Ill, USA. b. 31 Oct 1924 Widnes, Eng. PH.D '45 Ohio State Univ, USA. ASST. PROF. of PSYCH, Northwestern Univ. Member: BPS, APA. Teaching, clinical research, guidance; personality theory, physiological psychology, projective techniques. M

MAHONEY, Francis Gerard. 50 Woodside Rd, Huncoat, Accrington, Lancaster, Eng. b. 25 Mar 1911 Carlisle, Eng. BA '52 Univ. of London, Eng. EDUC. PSYCH'T, Educ. Comm, Elizabeth St, Burnley, Eng. Member: BPS. Testing, applied and educational psychology, administration; intelligence testing, attitude measurement, child development. M

MAIN, Mrs. Elizabeth Watson. 23 Bentinck St, Glasgow C 3, Scot. b. 9 June 1904 Glasgow, Scot. ED.B '49 Univ. of Glasgow, Scot. ASST. EDUC. PSYCH'T, Dunbarton County Counc, Educ. Comm, 18 Park Circus, Glasgow C 3, Scot. Member: BPS. Educational psychology, testing, child guidance; projective techniques, learning theory, achievement tests. F

MAINWARING, Dr. James. Belvedere House, Braddons Hill Rd. W, Torovay, Devon, Eng. b. 21 Aug 1892 Kidsgrove, Staffs,

Eng. D.Litt '40 Univ. of Birmingham, Eng.
RETIRED, Member: BPS. Professional
writing; musicology, learning theory, aes-
thetics. M
MALIPHANT, Rodney. 38 Lower Kings
Ave, Exeter, Devon, Eng. b. 19 Apr 1925
Bristol, Eng. BA '53 Univ. of London, Eng.
EDUC. PSYCH'T, Devon County Educ.
Comm, Topsham Rd, Exeter. Member:
BPS. Educational and applied psychology,
clinical analysis, child guidance; emotional
factors in learning, remedial techniques,
projective techniques. M
MANNHEIM, Dr. Max Josef. 96 Greencroft
Gardens, London NW 6, Eng. b. 10 Apr
1898 Cologne, Ger. MD '22 Univ. of Cologne,
Ger. CONSULT. PSYCHIAT, North-West
Hosp. Bd, 11A Portland Pl, London W 1.
Member: BPS, BRF. Consulting, clinical
practice, psychotherapy, child guidance;
projective techniques, graphology. M
MARCUS, Bernard. 138 Balne Lane, Wake-
field, York, Eng. b. 28 Mar 1922 London,
Eng. BA '51 Univ. of London, Eng. SR.
PSYCH'T, H. M. Wakefield Prison, H. M.
Prison Comm, Horseferry House, Dean
Ryle St, London SW 1, Eng. Member:
BPS. Testing, personnel selection, research,
group therapy; criminology. M
MARKHAM, Miss Margaret Irene. 43 The
Moors, Kidlington, Oxford, Eng. b. 30
Mar 1905 Aughton, Eng. BA '39 Univ. of
London, Eng. EDUC. PSYCH'T, Oxfordshire
Educ. Comm, New Rd, Oxford. Member:
BPS. Educational psychology, testing,
child guidance. F
MARRIOTT, Reginald. 90 Bedford Ave,
Barnet, Herts, Eng. b. 3 July 1897 York,
Eng. M.SC '46 Univ. of Manchester, Eng.
ASST. DIR, Indus. Psych. Res. Grp, Med.
Res. Counc, 38 Old Queen St, London SW 1,
Eng. Member: BPS. Research, adminis-
tration, professional writing; incentives in
industry, workers' attitudes, interviewing
methods. M
MARSHAK, Dr. Mildred D. 17 Yaw Tree
Ct, Bridge Lane, London BW 11, Eng.
b. 9 Dec 1923 Chicago, USA. PH.D '56 Univ.
of London, Eng. LECTURER, Univ. Coll.
London, Gower St, London; PSYCHO-
THERAPIST and CONSULT. PSYCH'T, Queen
Elizabeth Hosp. for Sick Children, Hackney
Rd, London. Member: BPS. Teaching,
educational psychology, research, testing,
group psychotherapy; delinquency, learning
process in child development. F
MARSHALL, Miss Annie Margaret. 7 Orleans
Rd, London N 19, Eng. b. 27 Jan 1911
Hull, York, Eng. BA '41 Univ. Coll,
London, Eng. EDUC. PSYCH'T, Essex
County Counc, County Off, Chelmsford,
Essex, Eng. Member: BPS. Testing,
educational guidance, teaching; remedial

reading, intelligence tests. F
MARSZALEK, Kazimierz Stanislaw. St.
Luke's Hosp. Middlesbrough, York, Eng.
b. 5 Nov 1912 Radziszów, Poland. CLIN.
PSYCH'T, St. Luke's Hosp. Member: BPS.
Testing, clinical analysis; projective tech-
niques. M
MARTIN, Dr. Alec Owen. 4 Redberry Grove,
London SE 26, Eng. b. 5 Nov 1922
Thaxted, Essex, Eng. PH.D '55 Univ. of
London, Eng. TRNG. OFF. and SR. INSTR,
Genl. Post Off. HQ, St. Martins-le-Grand,
London EC 1. Member: BPS. Adminis-
tration, teaching, research, industrial;
learning theory, manual skill training,
incentive. M
MARTIN, Dr. Frederick Morris. Usher Inst,
Warrender Park Rd, Edinburgh 9, Scot.
b. 2 Oct 1923 London, Eng. PH.D '52 Univ.
of London, Eng. LECTURER, Dept. of Pub.
Hlth. and Soc. Med, Univ. of Edinburgh,
Old College, S. Bridge, Edinburgh 8.
Member: BPS. Research, teaching; social
stratification, psychological and social
medicine, social psychiatry. M
MARTIN, Dr. Irene Doris. 4 Redberry Grove,
Sydenham SE 26, Eng. b. 10 Mar 1926
Ilford, Eng. PH.D '55 Inst. of Psychiat,
London, Eng. RES. ASST, Inst. of Psychiat,
Denmark Hill, London SE 5, Eng. Member:
BPS. Psychophysiological, research, testing;
theories of emotion. F
MARTIN, Miss Margaret. 11 Berridale Ave,
Cathcart, Glasgow, Scot. b. 17 Sept 1903
Glasgow, Scot. B.SC '25 Univ. of Glasgow,
Scot. LECTURER, Jordanhill Trng. Coll,
Southbrae Dr, Glasgow. Member: BPS.
Educational psychology, research, testing;
ability and attainment tests, learning
theory, handicapped children. F
MATHIE, Miss Georgina Paterson. 24 Dal-
morglen Park, Stirling, Scot. b. 12 Jan 1905
Glasgow, Scot. ED.B '56 Univ. of Glasgow,
Scot. PRIN. EDUC. PSYCH'T, Stirlingshire
County Counc, Viewforth, Stirling. Clinical
practice, child guidance, testing, adminis-
tration; achievement tests, projective
techniques, psychotherapy. F
MATHIESON, Miss Constance Mina. Little
Plumstead Hosp, nr. Norwich, Norfolk,
Eng. b. 7 Oct 1927 Aberdeen, Scot. ED.B
'49 Univ. of Aberdeen, Scot. SR. CLIN.
PSYCH'T, Little Plumstead Hosp. Member:
BPS, APA. Testing, research, teaching;
intelligence and achievement tests, pro-
jective techniques, elementary motor and
social development. F
MAULE, Dr. Henry Gordon. 3 Brockham
Warren, Boxhill Rd, Tadworth, Surrey,
Eng. b. 20 Mar 1911 London, Eng. PH.D
'49 Univ. of London, Eng. SR. LECT. in
OCCUPAT. PSYCH, London Sch. of Hyg.
and Tropical Med, Keppel St, London WC

1, Eng. Member: BPS. Teaching, research, administration; industrial psychology, management training and selection, vocational selection, adapting work to worker.   M

MAXWELL, Albert E. 64 Herne Hill, London S.E. 24, Eng. b. 7 July 1916 Eire. ED.B '51 Univ. of Edinburgh, Scot. LECT. in PSYCH. STAT, Inst. of Psychiat, Denmark Hill, London S.E. 5. Member: BPS. Teaching, research, professional writing; statistical design of experiments, factor analysis, learning theory.   M

McALLISTER, Dr. Anne Hutcheson. 31 Rowallan Gardens, Glasgow W 1, Scot. b. 29 Nov 1892 Biggar, Scot. D.SC '37 Univ. of Glasgow, Scot. PRIN. LECT, Jordanhill Coll, 96 Southbrae Dr, Glasgow W 3. Member: BPS. Teacher training, lecturing, mental testing, administration; learning theory, achievement tests, therapy with handicapped children.   F

McALLISTER, Miss Brigid. 61 Airlie St, Glasgow W 2, Scot. b. 7 Aug 1910 Glasgow, Scot. ED.B '50 Univ. of Glasgow, Scot. EDUC. PSYCH'T, Glasgow Educ. Comm, 129 Bath St, Glasgow. Member: BPS. Testing, child guidance, psychotherapy; learning theory, achievement tests, projective techniques.   F

McARTHUR, Mrs. Millicent Mary Magdalene. 12 Mount Ararat Rd, Richmond, Surrey, Eng. b. 6 Mar 1914 Aberdeen, Scot. BA '38 Univ. of Cambridge, Eng. PRIN. PSYCH'T, Civil Serv. Selectn. Bd, 9-10 Savile Row, London W 1, Eng. Member: BPA. Personnel selection, administration, research; group selection procedures, test construction.   F

McCLELLAND, Mrs. Marilyn Alice. Dept. of Psych, Runwell Hosp, nr. Wickford, Essex, Eng. b. 30 Jan 1931 London. MA '54 Univ. of Western Ontario, Can. STAFF PSYCH, Ont. Hosp, St. Thomas, Ont, Can. Testing, research, psychotherapy; projective techniques, personality testing research,.   F

McCLELLAND, William John. Dept. of Psych, Ont. Hosp, St. Thomas, Ont. b. 26 May 1931 Toronto. MA '55 Univ. of Toronto Can. PSYCHOLOGIST, Ont. Hosp. Member: CPA, APA, Ont. Psych. Assn. Testing, therapy, research, clinical practice; longitudinal studies of psychotics, projective techniques, Lowenfeld mosaic, comparative psychology, early experience in sub-human species.   M

McCLELLAND, William Wither. Fra-Mor, Castlelaw Rd, Colinton, Edinburgh 13, Scot. b. 10 June 1889 Newton-Stewart, Scot. ED.B '18 Univ. of Edinburgh. Scot. EXEC. OFF, Natl. Comm. for the Trng. of Tchrs, 140 Princes St, Edinburgh, Scot. Member: BPS. Administration of Scottish

teacher training system; selection for secondary education, statistical methods in educational and psychological research.   M

McCLEMENTS, Miss Catherine Verrier. Cordova, Castle Douglas Rd, Dumfries, Scot. b. 24 June 1904 Johnstone, Renfrewshire, Scot. ED.B 'Univ. of Glasgow, Scot. PRIN. EDUC. PSYCH'T, Educ. Comm, County Bldgs, Dumfries. Member: BPS. Child guidance, administration, testing; speech therapy, educational psychology.   F

McFARLANE, Miss Margaret Mary. Breen Banks, Painswick, Gloucestershire, Eng. b. 16 June 1886 London, Eng. PH.D '24 Bedford Coll, London, Eng. RETIRED. Member: BPS. Research; development of mental tests of practical ability.   F

McGHIE, Andrew. 12 Clydeford Dr, Tollcross, Glasgow, Scot. b. 4 Feb 1926 Glasgow Scot. MA '51 Univ. of Glasgow, Scot. SR. CLIN. PSYCH'T, Glasgow Royal Ment. Hosp, Great Western Rd, Glasgow. Member: BPS. Testing, clinical research, teaching, group psychotherapy; group process, psychotic process, personality theory and assessment.   N

McGLASHAN, Dr. Alan Fleming. 21 Wimpole St, London W 1, Eng. b. 20 Oct 1898 Nottingham, Eng. MA '21 Univ. of Cambridge, Eng. CONSULT. PSYCHOTHERAPIST, St. Marylebone Hosp, 48 Cosway St, London NW 1. Psychotherapy, consulting, professional writing.   M

McINTOSH, Dr. Douglas Moul. 39 Balwearie Rd, Kirkcaldy, Fife, Scot. b. 27 Sept 1909 Dundee, Scot. PH.D, Univ. of St. Andrews, Scot. DIR. of EDUC, Fife County Counc, Wemyssfield, Kirkcaldy. Member: BPS. Administration, research, editorial; prognostic value of tests, statistical techniques, mental and scholastic surveys.   M

McKELLAR, Dr. Thomas Peter Huntly. Psych. Lab, Univ. of Sheffield, Eng. b. 24 May 1921 Dunedin, NZ. PH.D '49 Univ. of London, Eng. LECT. in CHARGE, Univ. of Sheffield, Western Bank, Sheffield. Member: BPS, CPA. Teaching, research, administration; psychological theory, psychopathology, introspection.   M

McKENZIE, Roderick M. 29 Buccleuch Pl, Edinburgh 8, Scot. b. 9 Jan 1922 Nagpur, India. MA '49 Univ. of Edinburgh, Scot. LECT. in SOC. and OCCUPAT. PSYCH, Univ. of Edinburgh. Member: BPS. Research, teaching, testing; occupational and organizational satisfactions, relations of psychology with sociology and anthropology, vocational guidance.   M

McKINNON, Donald. 44 Brora St, Riddrie, Glasgow, Scot. b. 16 Aug 1915 Glasgow, Scot. ED.B '39 Univ. of Glasgow, Scot. EDUC. PSYCH'T, Renfrewshire Educ. Comm, 16 Glasgow Rd, Paisley, Scot. Member:

BPS. Testing, child guidance, psychotherapy; learning theory, achievement tests. M

McKNIGHT, Robert Kennedy. 3 Deeside Gardens, Aberdeen, Scot. b. 1 Oct 1922 Dalbeattie, Scot. ED.B '50 Univ. of Glasgow, Scot. PSYCHOLOGIST, Child Guid. Cen, Aberdeen Educ. Authority, Garden Pl, Aberdeen. Member: BPS. Psychotherapy, guidance, testing; nonanalytical child psychotherapy, projective techniques, achievement tests. M

McLAREN, Dr. Violet Mitchell. Minniebank, 14 Braeside Ave, Rutherglen, Lanarkshire, Scot. b. 24 May 1899 Kirkevdbright, Scot. PH.D '50 Univ. of Glasgow, Scot. PRIN. EDUC. PSYCH'T, County of Renfrew Educ. Comm, 16 Glasgow Rd, Paisley, Scot. Member: BPS, ICWP. Clinical and educational psychology, testing, teaching, research; intelligence and achievement tests, learning theory, retardation in normally intelligent pupils. F

McLEISH, John. 8 Hazelhurst Rd, Bradford 9, Eng. b. 21 May 1917 Glasgow, Scot. ED.B '47 Univ. of Glasgow, Scot. LECTURER, Univ. of Leeds, Univ. Rd, Leeds 2, Eng; EDITOR, *Quarterly Bulletin of Soviet Psychology.* Member: BPS, Assn. for Study of Animal Beh. Research, teaching, professional writing, translating and editing; cognitive tests, Soviet psychological theory, adult learning. M

McLEOD, John. 51 Higher Rd, Hunts Cross, Liverpool, Eng. b. 26 Feb 1925 Blackburn, Eng. ED.B '50 Univ. of St. Andrews, Scot. EDUC. PSYCH'T, Wallasey Local Educ. Authority, Town Hall Annex, Brighton St, Wallasey, Chester, Eng. Member: BPS. Consulting, educational psychology, teaching, administration; achievement and ability testing, test standardization, secondary school selection. M

McMAHON, Denis. 31 Bucclench Pl, Edinburgh, Scot. b. 7 Nov 1908 Harthpore, Durham, Eng. MA '33 Univ. of Durham, Eng. SR. LECT. and DIR, Appl. Psych. Unit, Univ. of Edinburgh; PSYCHOLOGIST, Child Guid. Clin. Member: BPS. Educational and vocational guidance, teaching, consulting; interviewing, cognitive testing, assessment procedures. M

McNALLY, Joseph. 49 Bamford Rd, Didsbury, Manchester 20, Eng. b. 4 July 1914 Glasgow, Scot. ED.B '49 Univ. of Glasgow, Scot. SR. PSYCH'T, and CHIEF, Child Guid. Serv, Manchester Educ. Authority, Deansgate, Manchester; PSYCHOLOGIST, Salford Royal Hosp. Member: BPS. Consulting, educational psychology, testing, administration; projective techniques, achievement and diagnostic tests, remedial education. M

McRAE, Hugh. 32 Belvidere Crescent,

Aberdeen, Scot. b. 16 Dec 1902 Glasgow, Scot. ED.B Univ. of Glascow, Scot. EDUC. PSYCH'T, Town Counc. of Aberdeen, Castle St, Aberdeen. Member: BPS. Testing, psychotherapy, administration, lecturing; emotional maladjustment in children, dream interpretation, group testing. M

MELROSE, Herbert Rex. Educ. Dept, County Hall, Trowbridge, Wiltshire, Eng. b. 2 Apr 1912 Exeter, Eng. BA '33 Univ. of Oxford, Eng. CONSULT. PSYCH'T, Wiltshire County Counc, Trowbridge. Member: BPS, Natl. Assn. for Ment. Hlth. Child guidance, educational counseling, research; intelligence and personality assessment, teacher guidance, juvenile delinquency. M

MENZIES, Miss Isabel Edgar Punton. 24 B Eton Ave, London NW 3, Eng. b. 12 Sept 1917 Dysart, Scot. MA '39 Univ. of St. Andrews, Scot. PSYCHOANALYST, priv. prac; SR. STAFF MEMBER, Tavistock Inst. of Human Rel, London. Member: BPS, Br. Psychoanal. Socy. Psychotherapy, industrial psychology, research; interdisciplinary research and consultancy, application of psychoanalytic findings to industrial problems. F

MERCER, Dr. Edith Olive. Hillside, Deepdene Dr, Dorking, Surrey, Eng. b. 28 June 1905 Ilford, UK. PH.D '35 Univ. of London, Eng. PRINCIPAL, Colonial Off, Churchhouse, Great Smith St, London SW 1, Eng. Member: BPS. Retired; personnel selection, vocational guidance, interviewing, aptitude testing, projective methods. F

MESSER, William James. Cheshire County Trng. Coll, Alsager, Near Stoke-on-Trent, Staffs, Eng. b. 26 Mar 1898 Reading, Eng. M.SC '26 Univ. of London, Eng. DEPUTY PRIN, Cheshire County Trng. Coll. Member: BPS. Teaching, educational psychology, consulting; manual dexterities. M

METCALFE, Mrs. Maryse. 87 Linden Gardens London W. 2, Eng. b. 2 Oct 1920 Alexandria, Egypt. Diplôme '47 Inst. Rousseau, Geneva, Switz. RES. ASST, Maudsley and Bethlem Royal Hosps, Denmark Hill, London S.E. 5, Eng. Member: BPS. Research; emotional reactions in schizophrenic or psychosomatic patients. F

MEYER, Victor. 48 Westbere Rd, London N.W. 2, Eng. b. 1 Sept 1920 Piotrkowtryb, Poland. BA '51 Univ. of Manchester, Eng. RES. ASST, Guy's-Maudsley Neurosurgical Unit, Inst. of Psychiat, De Grespiginy Rd, Denmark Hill, London S.E. 5. Member: BPS. Research, testing, clinical analysis; theory of brain function, learning theory, achievement tests, research on cognitive changes following brain surgery. M

MICHAELS, Mrs. Barbara. 36 Haven Green, Ealing, London W 5, Eng. b. 21 Dec 1917

444 UNITED KINGDOM

London, Eng. BA '47 Univ. of London, Eng. Member: BPS. F
MIDGLEY, Mrs. Jane Dewhurst. 19 Fford Euryn, Mochdre, Colwyn Bay, N. Wales. b. 27 May 1924 Stockton on Tees, Eng. M.SC '51 Univ. of Manchester, Eng. TUTOR in PSYCH, Colwyn Bay Workers' Educ. Assn, 33 College Rd, Bangor, N. Wales. Member: BPS. Temporarily retired, teaching; psychology of deafness, audiometry, tests of hearing in young children. F
MILBANKE, Miss Ethel Margaret. 20 Thornhill Terr, Sunderland, Eng. b. 29 Feb 1920 Newcastle, Eng. MA '52 Univ. of Cambridge, Eng. EDUC. PSYCH'T, N. Riding Child Guid. Serv, Yorkshire County Counc, County Hall, Northallerton, Eng. Member: BPS. Clinical analysis, child guidance, administration; educational counseling. F
MILES, Thomas Richard. Univ. Coll. of N. Wales, Bangor, Wales. b. 11 Mar 1923 Sheffield, Eng. MA '49 Univ. of Oxford, Eng. LECT. in PSYCH, Univ. Coll. of N. Wales; PSYCHOLOGIST, Bangor Child Guid. Clin. Member: BPS. Teaching, research, testing, professional writing; philosophy and psychology. M
MILLER, Dr. Emanuel. 77 Harley House, Regents Park, London W 7, Eng. b. 1893 London, Eng. MA '23 St. Johns Coll, Cambridge, Eng. PHY. and DIR, St. Georges Hosp, Hyde Park, London; JOINT ED, *British Journal of Delinquency*. Member: BPS, RMPA. Clinical practice, teaching, research, editorial; child psychiatry, juvenile delinquency, psychopathology, neuro-psychological relationships, learning theory. M
MILLS, Dr. Leslie Fife. 36 Langholm Crescent, Darlington, Durham, Eng. b. 19 Aug 1911 Tynemouth, Eng. PH.D '52 Univ. of Durham, Eng. EDUC. PSYCH'T, Child Guid. Clin, County Borough of Darlington Educ. Authority, Educ. Off, Darlington. Member: BPS. Testing, child guidance, psychotherapy; intelligence testing, teaching of reading. M
MILNER, Mrs. Marion. 12 Provost Rd, London N.W. 3, Eng. b. 1 Feb 1900 London Eng. B.SC '23 Univ. of London, Eng. PSYCHOANALYST, priv. prac. Member: BPS, Br. Psychoanal. Socy. Consulting, research, training analysis, the development of the capacity for creating symbols in the child, artist, neurotic and psychotic. F
MITCHELL, Alexander. 6 Hillcrest Ave, Temple Fortune, London NW 11, Eng. b. 11 Sept 1911 New Cumnock, Scot. MA '33 Univ. of Glasgow, Scot. MANAGER, Res. and Info. Div, Lintas Ltd, Hesketh House, Portman Sq, London W 1. Member: BPS. Personnel psychology, advertising,

research, administration; attitude measurement, qualitative aspects of consumer behavior, learning theory applied to propaganda. M
MITCHELL, Miss Elizabeth Horner Bell. 93 Carthmore Rd, Paisley, Scot. b. 23 Feb 1922 Belfast, N. Ire. ED.B '47 Univ. of Glasgow, Scot. ASST. PSYCH'T, Child Guid. Serv, Corp. of Glasgow, Educ. Dept, 129 Bath St, Glasgow C 2, Scot. Member: BPS. Guidance, testing, teaching; projective techniques, attitude measurement, learning theory. F
MITCHELL, Geoffrey Duncan. Univ. of Exeter, Eng. b. 5 June 1921 Lancaster, Eng. B.SC '49 Univ. of London, Eng. LECT. in CHARGE, Sub-Dept. of Sociol, Univ. of Exeter. Member: BPS. Teaching, administration, research; social perception, group dynamics, attitude measurement. M
MITTLER, Peter. Warneford Hosp, Oxford, Eng. b. 2 Apr 1930 Vienna, Austria. BA '53 Univ. of Cambridge, Eng. CLIN. PSYCH'T, Warneford and Park Hosp, Management Comm, Oxford; LECT. in PSYCH, Workers Educ. Assn. Member: BPS. Diagnostic mental testing, research, teaching; intelligence testing, projective techniques, vocational guidance, rehabilitation of psychiatric patients. M
MOORE, Terence Willoughby. 43 Rosebery Rd, London N 10, Eng. b. 22 Nov 1915 Kansas City, Mo, USA. BA '41 Univ. of London, Eng. RES. PSYCH'T, Child Study Cen, Univ. of London, Inst. of Educ, Malet St, London WC 1; TESTING, Hosp. for Sick Child, Great Ormond St, London WC 1. Member: BPS. Research, testing, teaching; child development, family relationships, projective techniques. M
MOORE, William Edmund. Nantesholme, Newsham Lane, Woodplumpton, Preston, Lancaster, Eng. b. 18 June 1915 Lancaster, Eng. B.SC '37 Univ. of Manchester, Eng. SR. EDUC. PSYCH'T, Preston Educ. Authority, Preston Corp, Munic. Bldg, Preston. Member: BPS. Educational and child guidance, testing. M
MORGAN, Albert Henry. 2 Lansdowne Rd, Chingford, London E 4, Eng. b. 17 Dec 1914 Newcastle-on-Lyme, Eng. MA '51 Univ. of London, Eng. EDUC. PSYCH'T, Middlesex County Counc, Great George St, Westminster, London. Member: BPS. Educational psychology, testing, administration; learning theory, achievement tests, remedial education. M
MORGAN, Dr. Griffith Arthur Vincent. 45 Lawson Rd, Colwyn Bay, Denbighshire, S. Wales. b. 9 Aug 1925 Cllybebyll, Pontardawe, Wales. PH.D '53 Univ. of London, Eng. SR. PSYCH'T, N. Wales Child Guid. Clin, Denbigh Ment. Hosp.

Management Comm, Cardiff, S. Wales. Member: BPS. Clinical analysis, educational psychology, child psychotherapy, administration; psychology of special abilities, achievement tests, handicapped children. M

MORREY, Miss Dora. Selber, Heald Rd, Bowdon, Chester, Eng. b. 31 July 1903 Manchester, Eng. B.SC '25 Univ. of Manchester, Eng. EDUC. PSYCH'T, St. Helens Educ. Comm, Lancaster, Eng; ADVIS. OFF, Lancaster Educ. Authority. Member: BPS. Clinical testing, educational guidance, · administration; intelligence testing, causes and treatment of backwardness, child guidance. F

MORRIS, Prof. Benjamin Stephen. Univ. of Bristol, Inst. of Educ, Lyndale House, 19 Berkeley Sq, Bristol 8, Eng. b. 25 May 1910 Sherborne, Dorset, Eng. ED.B '37 Univ. of Glasgow, Scot. PROF. of EDUC. and DIR, Inst. of Educ, Univ. of Bristol. Member: BPS, Assn. for Wrkrs. with Maladjusted Child. Administration, teaching, educational research; relationship of psychoanalytic and anthropological knowledge to educational research. M

MORRIS, Dr. John Frederick. Dept. of Psych, Univ. of Manchester, Eng. b. 16 Aug 1923 London, Eng. PH.D '55 Univ. of London, Eng. LECT. in SOC. PSYCH, Univ. of Manchester. Member: BPS. Research, teaching, occupational psychology; adult education, moral judgment in adolescence, role theory in occupational psychology. M

MORRIS, John Gamble. 73 Douglas Park Crescent, Bearsden, Dumbartonshire, Scot. b. 28 Oct 1921 Glasgow, Scot. ED.B '49 Univ. of Glasgow, Scot. LECT. in PSYCH, Jordanhill Trng. Cen, 76 Southbrae Dr, Glasgow, Scot. Member: BPS. Teaching, educational psychological research; learning theory, intelligence tests. M

MORRISON, Robert Lang. 32 Hertford Ave, Esheen, London SW 14, Eng. b. 27 Nov 1916 Paisley, Scot. ED.B '46 Univ. of Glasgow, Scot. PRIN. PSYCH'T, H. M. Prison Wormwood Scrubs, H. M. Prison Comm, Horseferry House, Dean Ryle St. Westminster, London SW 1. Member: BPS, BRF. Guidance, applied psychology; group psychotherapy, interdisciplinary approach to crime and delinquency, group processes. M

MORTON-WILLIAMS, Miss Roma. 12A Parliament Hill Mansions, Lissenden Gardens, London NW 5, Eng. b. 26 Jan 1924 Carnarvonshire, UK. B.SC '45 Univ. of London, Eng. PSYCHOLOGIST, Civil Serv. Comm, 9-10 Savile Row, London W. Member: BPS. Personnel selection, research, teaching; intelligence and achievement tests, merit rating techniques, test construction, industrial training methods. F

MOWBRAY, Robert Murdoch. Dept. of Psych. Med, Southern Genl. Hosp, Govan Rd, Glasgow SW 1, Scot. b. 7 Aug 1924 Ayr, Scot. MA '50 Univ. of Glasgow, Scot. SR. CLIN. PSYCH'T, Southern Genl. Hosp; LECT. in CLIN. PSYCH, Univ. of Glasgow, Scot. Member: BPS. Teaching, clinical practice, research; psychophysiology, psychiatric treatment, psychotherapeutic relationships. M

MUNDY, Mrs. Lydia. Amersham Corner, Beaconsfield, Bucks, Eng. b. 12 June 1912 Vienna, Austria. M.SC '55 Univ. of London, Eng. SR. CLIN. PSYCH'T, Fountain Grp. Hosp. Management Comm, Tooting Grove, London SW 17, Eng. Member: BPS, ICWP, Assn. of Child Psychotherapists. Clinical analysis, psychotherapy, research, teaching; social perception, development of subnormal and handicapped children. F

MURRAY, Hugh. 144 Motspur Park, New Malden, Surrey, Eng. b. 27 June 1919 W. Hartlepool, Eng. M.SC '49 Univ. of Sheffield Eng. PSYCHOLOGIST, Tavistock Inst. of Human Relat, 2 Beaumont St, London W 1, Eng. Member: BPS. Industrial psychology, research, consulting, testing; social perception, group process, attitude measurement. M

MURRAY, K. A. G. Civil Serv. Comm, Burlington Gardens, London W 1, Eng. b. 17 June 1916 Aberdeen, Scot. ED.B '49 Univ. of Aberdeen, Scot. PRIN. PSYCH'T, Civil Serv. Comm. Member: BPS. Personnel selection, testing, administration; test construction. M

NATHAN, Mrs. Esther. 67 Harley St, London W 1, Eng. b. 16 Aug 1894 Dolginovo, Lithuania. Dipl. Psych. '36 Univ. of London, Eng. EDUC. PSYCH'T, West Ham Child Guid. Clin, Borough of West Ham, Credon Rd, E 13. Member: BPS. Testing, guidance, educational psychology; remedial teaching methods, backward and handicapped children, assessment of young infants. F

NELL, Mrs. Mildred Joy. 18 Catherine Rd, Surbiton, Surrey, Eng. b. 19 May 1922 Johannesburg, S. Africa. MA '46 Natal Univ. Coll, S. Africa. SR. PSYCH'T, Army Operational Res. Grp, Parvis Rd, W. Byfleet, Surrey. Member: BPS, S. Africa Psych. Assn. Research, professional writing, student; military aptitude tests, attitude measurement, span of control. F

NELSON, Dr. Elizabeth Hawkins. 32 Pembridge Gardens, London W 2, Eng. b. 27 Jan 1931 Rockville Cen, New York, USA. PH.D '53 Univ. of London, Eng. MKT. RES. MGR, Lambe and Robinson Ltd, 169 Regent St, London W 1. Member: BPS. Market research, survey administration, industrial psychology; attitude and opinion measure-

ment, projective techniques, group be-
havior. F
NEVILL, Miss E. Mildred. Moorlands,
Croydon Rd, Reigate, Surrey, Eng. b. 20
Aug 1889 London, Eng. Dipl. Psych.
'28 Univ. of London, Eng. PSYCHOLOGIST,
priv. prac. Member: BPS. Testing, re-
medial teaching, lecturing; measurement
of intelligence, special abilities and edu-
cational attainment. F
NEWHAM, Victor Francis William. 5
Douglas Rd, Hollywood, nr. Birmingham,
Eng. b. 29 June 1925 London, Eng.
BA '52 Univ. of Nottingham, Eng. EDUC.
PSYCH'T, St. Francis Residential Spec.
Sch, City of Birmingham Educ. Authority,
Kings Heath, Birmingham. Member: BPS.
Educational psychology, clinical analysis,
psychotherapy; therapeutic and counseling
techniques, social training, education of
subnormal children. M
NEWSON, Laurence John. Psych. Dept,
Univ. of Nottingham, Nottingham, Eng.
b. 10 Dec 1925 London, Eng. B.SC '51
Univ. Coll, London, Eng. LECTURER, Univ.
of Nottingham. Member: BPS. Teaching,
research, testing; child development, per-
ception, experimental design. M
NISBET, Dr. John Donald. Dept. of Educ.
Univ. of Aberdeen, Old Aberdeen, Scot.
b. 17 Oct 1922 Dunfermline, Scot. PH.D '52
Univ. of Aberdeen, Scot. LECT. in EDUC,
Univ. of Aberdeen. Member: BPS.
Teaching, research, administration; in-
telligence testing, secondary school se-
lection, differential fertility. M
NISBET, Prof. Stanley Donald. 6 Victoria
Park Corner, Glasgow W 4, Scot. b. 26
July 1912 Isafjordur, Iceland. ED.B '40
Univ. of Edinburgh, Scot. PROF. of EDUC,
Univ. of Glasgow. Member: BPS. Teaching,
administration, educational research; psy-
chometrics, educational guidance and
selection, child development. M
NORTON, Dr. Walter Anthony. 27 Ella Rd,
London N. 8, Eng. b. 13 Feb 1923 Liver-
pool, Eng. PH.D '53 Univ. of London, Eng.
SR. PSYCH'T, H.M. Prison Brixton, Jebb
Ave, London S.W. 2. Member: BPS. Testing,
applied psychology, guidance; achievement
tests, diagnostic testing, criminology. M
OAKELY, Charles Allen. 64 Kelvingrove St,
Glasgow C3, Scot. b. 30 Sept 1900 Portsmouth, Eng. ED.B '29 Univ. of Glasgow,
Scot. LECT. in INDUS. PSYCH, Univ. of
Glasgow; MANAGEMENT CONSULT, priv.
prac. Member: BPS. Consulting, teaching,
industrial psychology; testing, accident
prevention, movement study. M
OATES, Dr. David William Rowland. Aely-
bryn. 13, Dewsland Park Rd, Newport,
Mon. b. 19 Apr 1883 Maesteg, Wales.
D.SC '30 Univ. of Wales. RETIRED. EDUC.

ADVIS, Wolsey Hall, Oxford, Eng; AREA
CHMN. of APPEALS, Ministry of Pensions
and Natl. Assistance. Member: BPS.
Professional writing; educational psycholo-
gy, temperament. M
O'CONNOR, Dr. Neil. Soc. Psychiat. Res.
Unit, Inst. of Psychiat, Maudsley Hosp,
London S.E. 5, Eng. b. 23 Mar 1917
Geralton, Australia. PH.D '53 Univ. of
London, Eng. RES. PSYCH'T, Inst. of
Psychiat. Member: BPS. Research,
teaching, consulting; learning and moti-
vation in mental defectives and chronic
psychotics. M
O'CONNOR, Dr. William Albert. Ashwood
House, Kingswinford, Staffs, Eng. b. 9
Feb 1897 London, Eng. DPM '38 Univ. of
London, Eng. MED. SUPT, Ashwood House.
Member: BPS. Analytical psychotherapy,
administration, professional writing; hyp-
nosis, depth psychology. M
OLDHAM, Dr. Hilda. 16 St. James' Sq,
Bath, Eng. b. 8 Apr 1881 Newcastle-
under-Lyme, Eng. PH.D '36 Univ. of
Reading, Eng. RETIRED. Member: BPS.
Research, professional writing, retired;
achievement tests, psychology of children's
drawings. F
OLIVER, Prof. Richard Alexander Cavaye.
7 Spring Gardens, Manchester 20, Eng.
b. 9 Jan 1904 Lockerbie, Scot. PH.D '33
Univ. of Edinburgh, Scot. PROF. and DIR,
Univ. of Manchester; ED. BD, *British
Journal of Educational Psychology.* Member
BPS. Administration, teaching, research;
attitude measurement, achievement tests. M
OPPENHEIM, Dr. Abraham Naftali. 91 S.
Side, London SW 4, Eng. b. 25 Nov 1924
Haifa, Palestine. PH.D '56 Univ. of London,
Eng. LECT. in SOC. PSYCH, London Sch.
of Econ. and Polit. Sci, Houghton St,
London WC 2. Member: BPS. Research,
teaching, administration; effects of mass
media, parental attitudes and behavior,
social learning and class. M
OPPENHEIMER, Mrs. Dorothy. 9 Ashbourne
Ave, London NW 11, Eng. b. 27 May 1911
London, Eng. BA '32 Univ. of London,
Eng. SR. PSYCH'T, Portman Clin, Pad-
dington Grp. Hosp. Management Comm,
8 Bourdon St, Davies St, London W 1;
EDUC. PSYCH'T, Hertford Child Guid.
Serv. Member: BPS, Assn. of Child Psychother. Group child psychotherapy, testing,
consulting; emotional factors in intellectual
retardation. F
ORME, John Edward. Crichton Royal, Dum-
fries, Scot. b. 7 July 1927 Margate, Eng.
BA '51 Univ. of Manchester, Eng. SR. CLIN.
PSYCH'T, Crichton Royal. Member: BPA.
Clinical analysis, research, psychotherapy;
personality theory and assessment, normal
and abnormal ageing, personality and

EEG. M
OUSELEY, Maurice Henry. 33 Purley Bury Close, Purley, Surrey, Eng. b. 19 Mar 1906 Burton Bradstock nr. Bridport, Eng. MA '48 Univ. of London, Eng. LECT. in EDUC, Battersea Polytechnic, Battersea Park Rd, London SW 11, Eng. Member: BPS. Teaching, research, educational psychology; learning theory, group process, attitude measurement. M

PAJACZKOWSKA DYDYNSKA, Mrs. Dorothea Mary. 24 Torphin Rd, Colinton, Edinburgh, Scot. b. 9 Sept 1905 Rivington, Lancaster, Eng. BA '27 Univ. of London, SR. ASST. PSYCH'T, Edinburgh Corp. Educ. Dept, St. Giles St, Edinburgh. Member: BPS. Testing, consulting, educational psychology; speech. F

PARNABY, Miss Mary Cragg. Churchwood, Beckett Park, Leeds 6, York, Eng. b. 8 Mar 1910 Edinburgh, Scot. ED.B '35 Univ. of Edinburgh, Scot. VICE PRIN, City of Leeds Trng. Coll, Beckett Park, Leeds 6. Member: BPS. Administration, teaching; learning theory, mental testing, social perception. F

PARRY, Dr. John Butler. 3 Wychcombe Studios, England's Lane, London NW 3, Eng. b. 30 Dec 1905 London, Eng. PH.D '40 Univ. of London, Eng. ASST. SCI. PERS. ADVIS, Air Ministry, 94/99 High Holborn, London WC 1. Member: BPS. Direction of psychological program, research; personnel selection, training methods, aesthetics and criticism. M

PATERSON, Dr. Arthur Spencer. 2 Devonshire Pl, London W 1, Eng. b. 22 Feb 1900 Aberdeen, Scot. MD '34 Univ. of Edinburgh, London, Eng. CHIEF PHY. and LECT, London Hosp, London W 6. Member: BPS, RMPA. Research, teaching, consulting; psychological state before and after electrocerebral treatment, psychosexual development. M

PAYNE, Dr. Robert Walter. 24 High View Close, Upper Norwood, London SE 19, Eng. b. 5 Nov 1925 Calgary, Can. PH.D '54 Univ. of London, Eng. LECTURER, Inst. of Psychiat, Univ. of London, Maudsley Hosp, Denmark Hill, London SE 5. Member: BPS. Teaching, clinical practice and research; thought disorder in psychotics, psychometrics, methodology in clinical psychology. M

PEAR, Prof. Tom Hatherley. Shirkoak House, Woodchurch, Ashford, Kent, Eng. b. 22 Mar 1886 Walpole, Norfolk, Eng. B.SC, Univ. of London, Eng. EMER. PROF., Univ. of Manchester, Eng. Member: BPS. Teaching, research, retired; psychological problems of peace and war, personality, appearance and speech, English social differences. M

PEARSON, Frederick James. 20 Piercing

Hill, Theydon Bois, Epping, Essex, Eng. b. 11 Oct 1893 London, Eng. M.SC '49 Univ. of London, Eng. HEADMASTER, L.C.C. Acland Sch, Fortess Rd, London NW 5, Eng. Member: BPS. Teaching, administration. M

PEEL, Prof. Edwin Arthur. Educ. Dept, Univ. of Birmingham, Edmund St, Birmingham 3, Eng. b. 11 Mar 1911 Liverpool, Eng. PROF. and HEAD, Educ. and Res. Depts, Univ. of Birmingham; ED. BD, British Journal of Statistical Psychology; British Journal of Educational Psychology; EDITOR, Educational Review. Member: BPS. Research, teaching, editorial; psychometric methods, learning theory, teacher training. M

PENTON, Dr. James Christopher. 4 Heath Rd, Weybridge, Surrey, Eng. b. 11 Jan 1910 London, Eng. BM, B.CH '35 Univ. of Oxford, Eng. SUPERINTENDENT, Psych. Br, Army Operational Res. Grp, Broadoaks, Parvis Rd, W. Byfleet, Surrey. Member: BPS, RMPA. Administration, research, teaching; selection techniques, morale, training methods. M

PERCIVAL, Raymond. The Cottage, The Royal Philanthropic Socy's. Sch, Redhill, Surrey, Eng. b. 27 Mar 1922 Warrington, Eng. BA '53 Univ. of Nottingham, Eng. DEPUTY PRIN. and EDUC. PSYCH'T, The Royal Philantropic Socy's. Sch. Member: BPS. Assessment and placement of juvenile delinquents, testing, administration. M

PHILLIPS, Charles Joseph. 246 Bristol Rd, Edgbaston, Birmingham 5, Eng. b. 19 Sept 1914 London, Eng. BA '52 Birkbeck Coll, London, Eng. LECT. in EDUC, Univ. of Birmingham Edmund St, Birmingham 3; EDUC. PSYCH'T, Remedial Educ. Cen, Univ. of Birmingham, Selly Wick House, Birmingham 29. Member: BPS. Teaching, testing, educational psychology; intelligence and attainment tests, intellectual, social and emotional development in children, learning theory. M

PHILLIPS, Miss Margaret. Home Farm House, Bledington, Oxford, Eng. b. 13 Dec 1891 Nottingham, Eng. MA '18 Univ. of Birmingham, Eng. EXTERNAL EXAM, Insts. of Educ, Bristol, Birmingham, Exeter, Decester and Nottingham. Member: BPS. Teaching, research, educational psychology; sentiment development, group psychology, teacher training. F

PHILLIPSON, Herbert. Tavistock Clin, 2 Beaumont St, London W 1, Eng. b. 16 Mar 1911 Barnsley, Eng. MA '53 Birkbeck Coll, London, Eng. SR. CLIN. PSYCH'T, Tavistock Clin. Member: BPS, BRF. Psychodiagnostic testing, teaching, research; marital case work, vocational guidance, projective techniques, group psycho-

therapy.   M
PHILP, Rev. Dr. Howard Littleton. Yetminster Vicarage, Sherborne, Dorset, Eng. b. 11 June 1902 Cornwall, Eng. PH.D, Kings Coll, London, Eng. VICAR, Yetminster with Ryme Intrinseca. Member: BPS. Teaching, professional writing, administration, clergyman; social psychology.   M
PICKARD, Miss Phyllis Marguerite. 72 Howards Lane, London SW 15, Eng. b. 7 May 1904 London, Eng. MA '52 Univ. Coll, London, Eng. SR. EDUC. LECT, Middlesex County Counc, Great George St, London SW 1, Eng. Member: BPS. Lecturing, guidance, educational psychology, professional writing; intelligence and scholastic tests, psychoanalytical approach to play, teacher training techniques.   F
PICKETT, Kenneth. 50 Redbridge Lane W, Wamstead, London E 11, Eng. b. 29 May 1912 Rhomdoa, Wales. b. 29 May Oxford, Eng. EDUC. PSYCH'T, Essex Educ. Comm, County Hall, Chelmsford, Essex, Eng. Member: BPS. Educational psychology, clinical analysis, psychotherapy; psychometric techniques, educational guidance.   M
PICKFORD, Prof. Ralph William. Psych. Dept, Univ. of Glasgow, Univ. Ave, Glasgow W 2, Scot. b. 11 Feb 1903 Bournemouth, Eng. D.Litt '47 Univ of Glasgow, Scot. PROF. of PSYCH, Univ. of Glasgow. Member: BPS, Assn. of Child Psychother. Teaching, administration, research, psychotherapy; color vision and color blindness, analytic psychotherapy and personality, psychology of art.   M
PICKLES, Dennis Greenwood. 62 Common Rd, Staincliffe, Batley, W. Riding, York, Eng. b. 21 Dec 1925 Rochdale, Eng. MA '52 Univ. of Cambridge, Eng. CLIN. PSYCH'T, W. Riding County Pub. Hlth. Dept, Wood St, Wakefield, W. Riding. LECT. and EXAM. in PSYCH, Natl. Assn. for Ment. Hlth. Member: BPS. Child guidance, diagnostic testing, teaching; occupational potentialities of the mentally deficient, psychological and sensory deprivation, projective techniques.   M
PIDGEON, Douglas Alfred. 79 Wimpole St, London W 1, Eng. b. 6 Aug 1919 London, Eng. B.SC '49 Univ. of London, Eng. SR. RES. OFF, Natl. Found. for Educ. Res. in Eng. and Wales, 79 Wimpole St, London. Member: BSP. Educational research, administration; national surveys of attainment, ability and attainment test construction.   M
PILKINGTON, Geoffrey Walter. Psych. Lab. Univ. of Sheffield, Sheffield 10, York, Eng. b. 16 July 1928 Preston, Eng. BA '54 Univ. of London, Eng. ASST. LECT,

Univ. of Sheffield. Member: BPS. Teaching, research, administration; methodology, history of psychology, learning theory.   M
PLASTOW, Miss Dorothy Anne. 2 Oaklawn, Arthur Rd, Wimbledon SW 19. b. 8 May 1902 London, Eng. B.SC '37 Univ. of London, Eng. ASST. OFF, Spec. Serv, London County Council, County Hall, London SE 1, Eng. Administration; education of handicapped children.   F
PLAUT, Dr. Alfred B. J. 10 Devonshire Pl, London W 1, Eng. b. 8 Feb 1913 Dusseldorf, Ger. MB, B.CH '37 Univ. of Witwatersrand, S. Africa. CHIEF MED. OFF, Child Guid. Clin, Middlesex Hosp, London W 1, Eng. Member: BPS, RMPA, Socy. of Anal. Psych. Psychotherapy, clinical practice, teaching; child psychology, analytical psychology.   M
PLOWMAN, David Eric Garth. Univ. Coll, Singleton Park, Swansea, Glam, Wales. b. 16 Mar 1929 Southend-on-Sea, Eng. MA '52 Univ. of California, USA. LECT. in SOC. PSYCH, Univ. Coll. of Swansea. Member: BPS. Teaching, research; psychology of politics, social status, group process.   M
POLLOCK, Alexander Brian. 2 Keats Grove, London NW 3, Eng. b. 16 June 1926 Glasgow, Scot. MA '49 Univ. of Glasgow, Scot. PSYCHOLOGIST, Tavistock Inst. of Human Relat, 2 Beaumont St, London W. 1, Eng. Member: BPS. Industrial psychology and personnel, research, testing; socio-technical interaction in working groups, projective techniques, selection and training.   M
POPPER, Dr. Erwin. 21 Wimpole St, London W 1, Eng. b. 20 Dec 1890 Prague, Czech. MD '15 Univ. of Prague, Czech. CONSULT. PSYCHIATRIST, Tavistock Clin, London; CONSULT. PSYCHOTHER, London Hosp; PSYCHOTHERAPIST, priv. prac. Member: BPS, RMPA, Br. Med. Assn. Psychotherapy, consulting, clinical practice; group psychology, sexual disorders, problems of individual psychology, psychology of humor.   M
POPPER, Mrs. Yana. Tavistock Clin, 2 Beaumont St, London W 1, Eng. b. 24 Apr 1898 Prague, Czech. PH. D '22 Univ. of Prague, Czech. SR. CLIN. PSYCH'T, Tavistock Clin. Member: BPS, BRF, Assn. of Child Psychother. Teaching, clinical analysis, research, child psychotherapy; psychology of cognition, projective techniques, psychoanalysis.   F
PORTEOUS, William Scobie. Rountree and Co. Ltd, The Cocoa Works, York, Eng. b. 3 Oct 1913 Bo'ness, Scot. ED.B '37 Univ. of Edinburgh, Scot. ADV. MGR, Rountree and Co. Member: BPS. Administration, industrial psychology;

psychology in advertising and market research. **M**

PORTWOOD, Peter Francis. 433 Redmires Rd, Sheffield 10, Eng. b. 31 Jan 1928 London, Eng. EDUC. PSYCH'T, Sheffield Child Guid. Cen, City of Sheffield Educ. Comm, Town Hall, Sheffield 1. Member: BPS. Guidance, clinical analysis, lecturing, research; intelligence and achievement tests, constancy of IQ of sub normal children. **M**

POULTON, Miss Irene Alice. 45 Kavanaghs Rd, Brentwood, Essex, Eng. b. 3 Sept 1918 Shenfield, Eng. BA '50 Univ. of London, Eng. EDUC. PSYCH'T, Essex County Counc, Duke St, Chelmsford, Eng. Member: BPS. Educational psychology, testing, guidance; learning theory, projective techniques, achievement tests. **F**

PRESTON, Mrs. Phyllis. 131 Carshalton Park Rd, Carshalton, Surrey, Eng. b. 19 Dec 1922 Cairo, Egypt. MA '46 Univ. Coll, London, Eng. EDUC. PSYCH'T, Kent. County Counc, County Hall, Springfield, Maidstone, Kent, Eng. Member: BPS. Psychotherapy, clinical testing, remedial teaching, educational psychology; projective techniques with children, differential diagnostic tests for early psychoses, play therapy. **F**

PRICE, Emrys James John. 27 Lawrence Gardens, Mill Hill, London NW 7, Eng. b. 30 May 1914 Swansea, Wales. B.SC '39 Univ. of Oxford, Eng. CLIN. PSYCH'T, Friern Hosp. Management Comm, New Southgate, London N 11. Member: BPS. Clinical analysis, teaching, research; learning theory, intellectual deterioration.M

PRINGLE, Dr. Mia Lilly Kellmer. 38 Spring Rd, Edgbaston, Birmingham 15, Eng. b. 20 June 1920 Vienna, Austria. PH.D '50 Univ. of London, Eng. LECT. in EDUC, DEPUTY HEAD, Remed. Educ. Cen, Univ. of Birmingham, Selly Wick Rd, Selly Oak, Birmingham 29; GOVERNOR, Condover Hall Sch. for Blind Child; Mulberry Bush Sch. for the Maladjusted. Member: BPS, ICWP. Teaching, clinical practice, research; child development, educational retardation, remedial work, social maturity and growth. **F**

PROCTER, Miss Margaret. 36 Belmont Rise, Cream, Sutton, Surrey, Eng. b. 18 May 1914 London, Eng. EDUC. PSYCH'T, London County Counc, Westminster Bridge RD, London SE 1, Eng. Member: BPS. Administration, educational psychology, clinical analysis; maladjusted and backward children, remedial teaching techniques. **F**

PROVINS, Kenneth A. 43 Beech Crescent, Kidlington, Oxford, Eng. b. 8 July 1923 London, Eng. BA '49 Univ. of Oxford, Eng. MEMBER of SCI. STAFF, M.R.C. Unit for Res.

on Climate and Working Efficiency, Dept. of Human Anat, Univ. Museum, Oxford. Member: BPS, Ergonomics Res. Socy Research, applied psychology; motor skills, kinesthetic sensibility, laterality. **M**

PUGH, Derek. Soc. Sci. Res. Cen, Univ. of Edinburgh, Edinburgh 8, Scot. b. 31 Aug 1930 London, Eng. MA '53 Univ. of Edinburgh, Scot. RES. ASST, Soc. Sci. Res. Cen. Member: BPS, BRF. Research, industrial psychology; industrial organization, attitude and personality measurement, scientific method. **M**

PUTZEL, Miss Johanna Renate. Child Guid. Clin, 3 Hyde Terr, Leeds 2, York, Eng. b. 26 Feb 1923 Karlsruhe, Ger. MA '42 Univ. of Capetown, S. Africa. EDUC. PSYCH'T, Child Guid. Clin. Member: BPS. Educational psychology, guidance, diagnostic testing; child therapy, projective techniques. **F**

RAINE, Dr. Stanley Greenaway. 56 Wincanton Rd, Southfield, London SW 18, Eng. b. 16 Sept 1898 London, Eng. PH.D '35 Univ. of London, Eng. HEADMASTER, London County Counc, London; LECT. in PSYCH, and EXPER. PSYCH, Dept. of Extra Mural Studies, Univ. of London. Member BPS. Teaching, administration, educational psychology, character, intelligence. **M**

RAMSAY, Squadron Off. Marjorie. Flat 3, 140 A Camden High St, London NW 1, Eng. b. 21 Jan 1907 Plymouth, Eng. MA '39 Univ. of London, Eng. SQUADRON OFF, Womens Royal Air Force, Air Ministry, London. Member: BPS. Testing, research, teaching; aptitude testing, interviewing. **F**

RAMSAY, Stanley George. 128 North St, St. Andrews, Scot. b. 17 Oct 1923 Edinburgh, Scot. B.SC '51 Univ. of Edinburgh, Scot. LECT. in PSYCH, Univ. of St. Andrews. Member: BPS. Teaching, research, administration; mental testing, vocational selection and guidance, methodology. **M**

RAPHAEL, Mrs. Winifred. 28 Clareville Grove, London SW 7, Eng. b. 21 Nov 1898 London, Eng. B.SC '20 Univ. of London, Eng. ASST. DIR, Natl. Inst. of Indus. Psych, 14 Welbeck St, London W 1; LECTURER, London Sch. of Econ. and Polit. Sci; LECTURER, Royal Coll. of Nrsng. Member: BPS, AIPA. Applied and industrial psychology, research, teaching; personnel selection and training, morale, attitude surveys. **F**

RAVEN, John Carlyle. 20 Castle St, Dumfries, Scot. b. 28 June 1902. M.SC '36 Univ. of London, Eng. DIR. of PSYCH. RES, Crichton Royal. Member: BPS, Br. Socy. for Psych. Res. Research, administration, teaching; determination of normal mental development, assessment of abnormal mental

conditions.   M
RAYNER, Dr. Eric Hurbert. Cassel Hosp,
Ham Common, Richmond, Surrey, Eng.
b. 1 Aug 1926 Harrow, Eng. PH.D '56
Univ. of London, Eng. CLIN. PSYCH'T,
Cassel Hosp. Member: BPS. Clinical ana-
lysis, research; projective techniques,
psychoanalytic theory, problem solving
and thought process.   M
REED, Graham Frederick. 28 Victoria Ave,
Hull, York, Eng. b. 13 Mar 1923 Coventry,
Eng. MA '50 Univ. of Cambridge, Eng.
EDUC. PSYCH'T, Kingston-upon-Hull Educ.
Comm, Guildhall, Hull. Member: BPS,
Royal Stat. Socy. Educational psychology,
testing, psychotherapy, remedial teaching;
auditory weakness, projective techniques.M
REEVE, Major Ernest Gavin. 14 Dingwall
Ave, Croyden, Surrey, Eng. b. 17 June
1908 Croydon, Eng. M.SC '48 Univ. Coll,
London, Eng. CONSULT. in APPL. STAT,
priv. prac. Member: BPS. Applied sta-
tistics; validation.   M
REEVES, Dr. Joan Wynn. Bedford Coll,
Regents Park, London NW 1, Eng. b. 26
Apr 1910 Enfield, Eng. PH.D '34 Univ. of
London, Eng. LECT. in PSYCH, Bedford
Coll; SUB EDITOR, *British Journal of
Psychology*; ASST. ED, *Occupational Psy-
chology*. Member: BPS. Teaching, research,
professional writing; personnel selection,
aesthetics in relation to personality study,
history of psychology.   F
REID, Miss Lorna Ward. Woodlands, Old
Kilpatrick, Glasgow, Scot. b. 18 Jan 1918
Clyde Bank, Scot. ED.B '49 Univ. of
Glasgow, Scot. EDUC. PSYCH'T, Dunbarton
County Counc, 18 Park Circus, Glasgow C3.
Member: BPS. Educational psychology,
testing, child guidance; learning theory,
intelligence, achievement and attainment
tests.   F
REID, Robert Leslie. Dept. of Psych, Univ.
of Aberdeen, Scot. b. 19 Mar 1924 Pol-
mont, Scot. MA '49 Univ. of Edinburgh,
Scot. LECTURER in PSYCH, Univ. of Aberdeen. Member: BPS. Teaching, research,
administration; learning theory, perception, comparative psychology.   M
REID, Robert Scott. 107 Malvern Rd, St.
John's, Worcester, Worcs, Eng. b. 3 Mar
1914 Aberdeen, Scot. ED.B '47 Univ. of
Glasgow, Scot. EDUC. PSYCH'T, Worcester-
shire County Counc. Educ. Comm, Castle
St, Worcester. Member: BPS. Educational
psychology, testing, guidance; achievement
and intelligence tests, projective techniques.   M
REINER, Dr. Joanna Elizabeth. 37 Carpenter
Rd, Edgbaston, Birmingham 15, Eng.
b. 16 Apr 1906 Lemberg, Austria. PH.D '30
Univ. of Vienna, Austria. EDUC. PSYCH'T,
City of Birmingham Child Guid. Clin,

George Rd, Birmingham. Member: BPS.
Testing, psychotherapy, educational
guidance; personality, projective tech-
niques, mental deficiency, play therapy. F
RESIDE, Miss Sheena Main Mackay. 10
Woodburn Terr, Edinburgh, Scot. b.
4 June 1917 Edinburgh, Scot. ED.B '46
Univ. of Edinburgh, Scot. EDUC. PSYCH'T,
Stewarting of Kirkcudbright Educ. Comm,
Castle Douglas, Scot. Member: BPS.
Clinical analysis, psychotherapy, teaching.F
REYNELL, Miss Joan Katharine. 30 Spring-
field Rd, London NW 8, Eng. b. 6 Nov
1918 Newton Abbot, Eng. B.SC '54 Univ.
of London, Eng. ASST. EDUC. PSYCH'T,
W. Sussex County Counc, Sussex, Eng.
Member: BPS. Educational psychology. F
RICHARDSON, Dr. Alan. Bedford Coll,
Univ. of London, Regent's Park, London
NW 1, Eng. b. 4 Dec 1923 Letchworth,
Herts, Eng. PH.D '56 Univ. of London, Eng.
ASST. LECT. in PSYCH, Bedford Coll; LECT.
in PSYCH, St. Bartholomew's Hosp,
London EC 1. Member: BPS. Teaching,
research, professional writing; attitude
change in assimilation of immigrants,
personality, perceptual processes.   M
RICHARDSON (née Bichan), Mrs. Helen Jane.
Croham Hurst, 5 Greenway, Appleton near
Warrington, Lancaster, Eng. b. 15 July
1918 Orkney, Scot. ED.B '54 Univ. of
Edinburgh, Scot. EDUC. PSYCH'T, Shaw
Classifying Approved Sch, Appleton near
Warrington. Member: BPS. Testing and
clinical analysis; projective techniques,
personality and intelligence testing, atti-
tude measurement with delinquent ado-
lescents.   F
RICHARDSON, Dr. Mrs. Sylvia Camroux.
Thornlea, New North Rd, Exeter, Eng.
b. 18 Mar 1912 London, Eng. PH.D '56
Univ. of London, Eng. LECT. in PSYCH,
The Univ, Exeter; CHIEF EXAM, Plymouth
Educ. Comm. Member: BPS. Teaching,
educational and industrial psychology;
educational and occupational selection,
aesthetics.   F
RITCHIE, Miss Mary Elizabeth. 36 Duchy
Ave, Fulwood, Preston, Lancaster, Eng.
b. 27 Feb 1928 Ipswich, Eng. B.SC '54
Univ. of London, Eng. ASST. EDUC.
PSYCH'T, Preston Educ. Comm, Munic.
Bldgs, Preston. Member: BPS. Educational
psychology, testing, guidance; intelligence
testing, backward children, play therapy. F
RIVETT, Mrs. Catherine Mary. 28 Oakland
Ave, Salford 6, Lancaster, Eng. b. 10 May
1904 London, Eng. MA '47 Univ. of Man-
chester, Eng. EDUC. PSYCH'T, County
Borough of Warrington, Educ. Authority,
Warrington, Sankey St, Warrington, Eng;
LECTURER, Univ. of Manchester, Eng;
LECTURER, Manchester Reg. Hosps. Bd,

Manchester. Member: BPS. Testing, educational psychology, teaching, psychotherapy; child development, intelligence and achievement tests, projective techniques, social adjustment. F

ROBERTS, Mrs. Muriel. 7 Charlotte St, W 1. b. 27 Sept 1924 London, Eng. B.SC '51 Univ. of London, Eng. EDUC. PSYCH'T, Reigate Child Guid. Clin, Surrey County Counc, County Hall, Kingston-upon-Thames, Surrey, Eng. Member: BPS. Educational psychology, testing; backwardness, remedial teaching. F

ROBERTSON, Dr. James Patrick Shinnie. 21 Searchwood Rd, Warlingham, Surrey, Eng. b. 31 Oct 1912 Olds, Calgary, Can. PH.D '50 Unv. of London, Eng. SR. CLIN. PSYCH'T. and HEAD, Psych. Dept, Netherne Hosp, Coulsdon, Surrey. Member: BPS. Research, teaching, testing; perception, language and thinking, objective tests in neuropsychiatric research. M

ROBERTSON, John David Cochrane. c/o Official Secy, Australia House, Strand, London W.C. 2, Eng. b. 27 Dec 1916 Melbourne, Australia. MA '53 Univ. of London, Eng. RES. OFF, Natl. Found. for Educ. Res. in Eng. and Wales, 79 Wimpole St, London W. 1. Member: BPS. Research, testing, educational psychology; learning theory, projective techniques, achievement tests. M

ROBERTSON, William. 29 Mountfields Rd, Taunton, Somerset, Eng. b. 23 June 1914 Glasgow, Scot. ED.B '38 Univ. of Glasgow, Scot. SR. EDUC. PSYCH'T, Somerset County Counc, County Educ. Off, Trull Rd, Taunton, Eng. Member: BPS. Educational psychology, testing, administration, research; achievement tests, projective techniques, attitude measurement. M

RODGER, Alec. Birkbeck Coll, Univ. of London, Malet St, London W.C. 1, Eng. b. 22 Nov 1907 Scotland. MA '32 Univ. of Cambridge, Eng. READER in PSYCH, Birkbeck Coll; CONSULT. PSYCH'T, Ministry of Labour and Ministry of Supply; EDITOR, *Occupational Psychology.* Member: BPS, Br. Sociol. Socy. Teaching, research, industrial psychology; vocational guidance, personnel selection, job analysis. M

RODGER, Prof. Thomas Ferguson. 25 Campbell Dr, Bearsden, nr. Glasgow, Scot. b. 4 Nov 1907 Glasgow, Scot. MB, CH.B '29 Univ. of Glasgow, Scot. PROF. of PSYCH. MED, Univ. of Glasgow, Glasgow; ED. BD, *British Journal of Medical Psychology and Human Relations.* Member: BPS, RMPA, Amer. Psychiat. Assn, Br. Med. Assn. Teaching, administration, group psychotherapy; clinical and social psychiatry. M

ROONEY, Sister Mary. Notre Dame Trng.

Coll, 74 Victoria Crescent Rd, Glasgow W 2, Scot. b. 14 June 1904 Kilmarnock, Scot. ED.B '35 Univ. of Glasgow, Scot. PRINCIPAL, Notre Dame Trng. Coll. Member: BPS. Administration, teaching, counseling; child guidance, intelligence testing, projective techniques. F

RORKE, Miss Kate. Bridge House, Aylesford, Maidstone, Kent, Eng. b. 13 Jan 1907 Kingston-on-Thames, Eng. BA '46 Univ. of London, Eng. EDUC. PSYCH'T, Kent Educ. Comm, Springfield, Maidstone. Member: BPS. Educational psychology, testing, remedial teaching; learning theory, achievement tests, emotional factors in learning. F

ROSENBLUTH, Miss Dina. 25/C Cannon Pl, London NW 3, Eng. b. 9 May 1919 Berlin, Ger. BA '40 Univ. Coll, London, Eng. SR. CLIN. PSYCH'T, Tavistock Clin, 2 Beaumont St, London W 1. Member: BPS, Assn. of Child Psychother. Child psychotherapy. F

ROSS, Miss Elizabeth L. S. 45 Forrester Rd, Corstorphine, Edinburgh 12, Scot. b. 1887 Edinburgh, Scot. MA '09 Univ. of Edinburgh, Scot. RETIRED. Member: BPS. Handicapped and maladjusted children. F

ROYSE, Arthur Bates. 36 Highfield, Sutton, Hull, York, Eng. b. 4 June 1918 Bolton, Eng. M.SC '50 Univ. of Manchester, Eng. LECT. in PSYCH, The Univ, Hull; CLIN. PSYCH'T, De La Role Hosp, Willerby, E. York, Eng. Member: BPS. Teaching, research, clinical analysis; objective personality tests, psychological scaling techniques, measurement of judgement. M

RUSHTON, Cyril Stephenson. Child Guid. Clin, Brunswick House, Buckland Hill, Maidstone, Kent. Eng. b. 29 Jan 1922 Bolton, Eng. BA '55 Univ. of London, Eng. EDUC. PSYCH'T, Kent Educ. Comm, Springfield, Maidstone. Member: BPS. Diagnostic testing, remedial teaching; educational psychology, consulting; intelligence testing, personality assessment, adolescent delinquents. M

RUSSELL, Prof. Roger Wolcott. Dept. of Psych, Univ. Coll, London, Gower St, London WC 1, Eng. b. 30 Aug 1914 Worcester, Mass, USA. D.SC '54 Univ. of London, Eng. PROF. and HEAD, Dept. of Psych, Univ. Coll, London; EDITOR, *The American Psychologist*; EXEC. SEC, APA. Member: BPS, APA, Exper. Psych. Grp. Research, administration, teaching; experimental psychopathology, effects of biochemical lesions on behavior, effects of environment on performance. M

SAMPSON, Miss Olive Christian. 13 Trueway Rd, Leicester, Eng. b. 3 Jan 1905 Durhan, Eng. ED.B '32 Univ. of Edinburgh, Scot. SR. EDUC. PSYCH'T. and HEAD,

Leicester Sch. Psych. Serv, Leicester Educ. Comm, Newarke St, Leicester. Member: BPS. Testing, clinical analysis, administration, teaching; speech development, reading problems, intelligence testing. F

SANDLER, Dr. Joseph John. 96 Portland Pl, London W. 1. Eng. b. 10 Jan 1927 Cape Town, S. Africa. PH.D '50 Inst. of Psychiat, Univ. of London, Eng. SR. PSYCH'T, Tavistock Clin, 2 Beaumont St, London W. 1; PSYCHOANALYST, priv. prac; EDITOR, *British Journal of Medical Psychology.* Member: BPS, Br. Psychoanal. Socy, Socy. for Res. in Psychosomatic Med. Psychoanalysis, research, editorial; psychosomatic medicine, application of experimental and statistical methods to psychoanalytic theory. M

SANDON, Frank. 142 Rotton Park Rd, Edgbaston, Birmingham 16, Eng. b. 3 June 1890 London, Eng. MA '20 Univ. of Cambridge, Eng. CHIEF EXAMINER, Somerset Educ. Comm, Somerset, Eng; LECT. in STAT, Birmingham Coll. of Comm. Member: BPS, Eugenics Socy. Retired, educational psychology, testing; selection techniques for secondary education, methods of teaching mathematics. M

SANTS, Hector John. Lilac Cottage, Lickey Sq, Rednal, near Birmingham, Eng. b. 26 May 1923 Bath. Eng. MA '53 Univ. of Oxford, Eng. EDUC. PSYCH'T, Birmingham Educ. Comm, Counc. House, Margaret St, Birmingham. Member: BPS. Psychotherapy, administration, testing, child guidance; intelligence and personality testing, child psychotherapy. M

SARGENT, Dr. William Ewart. 51 Ash Grove, Leeds 6, York, Eng. b. 17 June 1898 Maesteg, Wales. PH.D '42 Univ. of Edinburgh, Scot. MINISTER, Trinity Congregational Church, Woodhouse Lane, Leeds 2; CHAIRMAN, Leeds Hostel for Girls. Member: BPS, Leeds Psychiat. Assn. Psychotherapy, professional writing, pastoral work. M

SAUNDERS, Robert Valentine. 14 Coombe Bridge Ave, Bristol 9, Eng. b. 14 Feb 1913 Ipswich, Eng. ED.B '47 Univ. of Edinburgh, Scot. SR. EDUC. PSYCH'T, Bristol Educ. Comm, Coll. Green, Bristol. Member: BPS. Educational psychology, testing; teaching; assessment of handicapped children, selection for secondary education, learning theory. M

SCHAFFER, Heinz Rudolph. 1 Belmont Crescent, Glasgow W. 2 Scot. b. 21 July 1926 Berlin, Germany. BA '50 Univ. of London, Eng. SR. CLIN. PSYCH'T. Royal Hosp. for Sick Children, Glasgow; EXTRA-MURAL LECT. in CHILD PSYCH, Univ. of Glasgow. Member: BPS. Research, testing, clinical analysis, teaching; developmental

functions in infancy, brain injuries, psychosomatics. M

SCHONFIELD, Ahron Eliezer David. 8 Canterbury Close, Cambridge, Eng. b. 31 Aug 1920 Baden, Austria. MA '51 Univ. of Cambridge, Eng. SR. CLIN. PSYCH'T, Child Psychiat. Clin, Chesterton Hall, Chesterton Rd, Cambridge. Member: BPS. Applied psychology, diagnostic testing, clinical analysis, research; development of individual differences, memory in children, reading and arithmetical difficulties. M

SCHOTTLANDER, Mrs. Adel. 19 Fitzjohn's Ave, Hampstead, London N.W. 3, Eng. b. 24 Mar 1920 Berlin, Ger. BA '43 Univ. of London, Eng. LECT. in PSYCH, Guildlok Sch. of Music and Drama, John Carpenter St, London. Member: BPS. Psychotherapy, child guidance, testing, clinical analysis, teaching; play therapy, projective techniques, psychology and the arts. F

SCOBBIE, Lawrence. Shenley Hosp, Shenley, near St. Albans, Herts, Eng. b. 20 Sept 1914 Edinburgh, Scot. ED.B '44 Univ. of Edinburgh, Scot. SR. PSYCH'T, Shenley Hosp. Member: BPS, BRF. Testing, applied psychology, consulting, psychodiagnosis; projective techniques, cognitive testing, analytical psychology. M

SCOTT, Miss Diana Vandeleur. Highcroft, Spratton, Northants, Eng. b. 12 Apr 1919 London, Eng. MA '51 Univ. Coll, London, Eng. EDUC. PSYCH'T, The Educ. Comm, The County and County Borough of Northampton, Eng. Member: BPS. Educational psychology, testing, child guidance; education of handicapped and retarded children, the maladjusted child. F

SCOTT, Dr. Eileen Mcinroy. 3 Great Stuart St, Edinburg 3, Scot. b. 7 Jan 1921 Dundee, Scot. PH.D '54 Univ. of Edinburgh, Scot. Member: BPS, Br. Sociol Assn. Retired; attitude measurement, intelligence and personality testing, social perception. F

SCOTT, Miss Margaret Campbell. Craigrothie, 223 Nithsdale Rd, Glasgow S. 1, Scot. b. 1 May 1905 St. Andrews, Scot. ED.B '41 Univ. of Glasgow, Scot. SR. LECT. in EDUC, The Glamargan Trng. Coll, Barry, Wales. Member: BPS. Teaching, educational psychology, teacher training. F

SCOTT BLAIR, Mrs. Margaret Florence. Applecroft, Shinfield, Reading, Eng. b. 10 Mar 1903 Norwood, Dickoya, Ceylon. MA ,Univ. of Oxford, Eng. PSYCHOLOGIST, Berks Child Guid. Clin, 27 Kidmore Rd, Caversham, Reading. Testing, guidance, applied and educational psychology. F

SECRETAN, Peter Norman Max. 8 Cambridge Rd, Wimbledon S.W. 20, Eng. b. 21 Oct 1913 Freudenstadt, Württemberg, Germany. MA '39 Emmanuel Coll, Eng. EDUC. PSYCH'T, Middlesex County Counc,

Staines Clin, Gresham Rd, Staines, Middlesex, Eng; PSYCHOLOGIST, St. Michael's Coll, Tenbury, Eng. Member: BPS, Natl. Assn. for Mentally Handicapped Children. Educational psychology, testing, psychotherapy; psychology of authoritarian structures, psychological tensions in the family and in teacher-pupil relationships, intellectual inhibitions in average and gifted pupils. M

SELWOOD, Dr. Ernest Henry. 3 Folly Lane, Caddington, Luton, Beds, Eng. b. 1876 Bristol, Eng. PH.D, Univ. of London, Eng. Member: BPS. Research, teaching, retired.M

SEMEONOFF, Dr. Boris. 4 Morningside Park, Edinburgh 10, Scot. b. 20 Mar 1910 Leningrad, Russia. PH.D '36 Univ. of Edinburgh, Scot. SR. LECT, Univ. of Edinburgh, S. Bridge, Edinburgh. Member: BPS, Exper. Psych. Grp. Teaching, research, testing; projective techniques, statistical methods, personnel selection. M

SERGEAN, Robert. 17 Gordon Sq, London W.C. 1, Eng. b. 3 Apr 1919 Wolstanton, Staffs, Eng. MA '52 Univ. of Edinburgh, Scot. RES. WRKR, Indus. Psych. Res. Grp, Med. Res. Counc, 38 Old Queen St, London S.W. 1; HONORARY RES. ASST, Dept. of Psych, Univ. Coll, London. Member: BPS, Br. Sociol. Assn. Research; communication. M

SHACKEL, Brian. The Frith, Brockenhurst Rd, Ascot, Berks, Eng. b. 9 Jan 1927 Kidbrooke, Eng. MA '51 Univ. of Cambridge, Eng. RES. PSYCH'T, E.M.I. Electronics Ltd, Victoria Rd, Feltham, Middlesex, Eng. Member: BPS, Ergonomics Res. Socy. Research, student, industrial psychology; electro-oculography, sensory-motor skills, human engineering. M

SHAPIRO, Dr. Monte Bernard. 8 Stanley Rd, Orpington, Kent, Eng. b. 31 May 1912 Germiston, South Africa. PH.D '56 Inst. of Psychiat, London, Eng. SR. LECT, Inst. of Psychiat, Maudsley Hosp, Denmark Hill, London S.E. 5, Eng. Member: BPS. Administration, teaching, research, clinical practice, professional writing; psychology of design reproduction by drawing, speed of psychological functions, experimental method in clinical psychology. M

SHAW, Miss Agnes MacGregor. 12 Terregles Ave, Glasgow S. 1, Scot. b. 20 Mar 1904 Scot. ED.B '44 Univ. of Glasgow, Scot. DEPUTE CLIN. PSYCH'T, Educ. Authority, 129 Bath St, Glasgow; LECT. in INDIV. PSYCH, Sch. of Soc. Study and Trng, Univ. of Glasgow. Member: BPS. Administration, educational psychology, guidance; child guidance. F

SHAW, Miss Anne Gillespie. The Anne Shaw Organization Ltd, Beech House, Heald Green, Cheadle, Chester, Eng. b. 28 May 1904 Uddingston, Scot. MA '27 Univ. of Edinburgh, Scot. MANAGING DIR, The Anne Shaw Organiza. Ltd. member: BPS. Industrial consulting, administration; motion study, personnel management. F

SHEPPARD, Dr. David. 15 Westlands Ave, Redding, Berks, Eng. b. 31 Oct 1925 Camberlay, Surrey, Eng. PH.D '54 Univ. of Reading, Eng. HEAD of PSYCH. SECT, Natl. Inst. for Res. in Dairying, Slimfield, Berks. Member: BPS. Research, industrial psychology; psychophysics,attitude studies, educational problems. M

SHIELDS, Dr. Robert Wylie. 56 Alleyn Rd, London S.E. 21, Eng. b. 31 May 1919 Worthing, Eng. PH.D '50 Univ. of London, Eng. PSYCHOTHERAPIST, London County Counc, London S.E. 1, Eng. Member: BPS, Assn. of Child Psychother, Assn. of Profes. Psychother. Psychotherapy, professional writing, clinical practice. M

SHIMMIN, Miss Sylvia Bambury Nixon. Indus. Psych. Res. Grp, Univ. Coll, 17 Gordon Sq, London W.C. 1, Eng. b. 26 Feb 1925 Guiseley, Eng. B.SC '46 Univ. of London, Eng. SCI. RES. WRKR, Med. Res. Counc, 38 Old Queen St, London S.W. 1; EXT. LECT, Univ. of London. Member: BPS. Research, teaching, applied and industrial psychology; motivation and incentives in industry, social perception, small group research. F

SHOOTER, Mrs. Antonia M. N. 1 Redgrave Rd, Putney S.W. 15, Eng. b. 20 Mar 1927 Cambridge, Eng. MA '51 Univ. of Cambridge, Eng. TRAINEE CLIN. PSYCH'T, Tavistock Clin, 2 Beaumont St, London W. 1, Eng. Member: BPS. Testing and clinical analysis; diagnostic clinical testing, family casework, social psychology. F

SHORT, Philip Lionel. Cummunic. Res. Unit, Lintas Ltd, Hesketh House, Portman Sq, London W. 1, Eng. b. 1 May 1923 Bath, Eng. MA '53 Univ. of Oxford, Eng. COMMUNIC. RES. OFF, Lintas Ltd. Member: BPS. Advertising research, applied psychology, administration; psychophysiological studies, test techniques in advertising and propaganda, projective techniques. M

SHOUKSMITH, George Albert. Appl. Psych. Unit, Univ. of Edinburgh, 39 George Sq, Edinburgh 8, Scot. b. 2 Nov 1931 York, Eng. MA '54 Univ. of Edinburgh Scot. UNIV. TCHR, Univ. of Edinburgh; PSYCH. ADVIS. to PERS. SECT, Br. European Airways. Member: BPS. Applied psychology, research, teaching; group dynamics, personnel selection, scientific methodology applied to behavioral sciences, management training. M

SIDDALL, Gerald James. 7 Chiltern Close, Cove, Farnborough, Hants, Eng. b. 8 Aug

1926 Manchester, Eng. MA '55 Univ. of Cambridge, Eng. PSYCHOLOGIST, Ministry of Supply, Royal Aircraft Establishment, Farnborough. Member: BPS, Ergonomics Res. Socy. Industrial psychology, research, administration; vigilance and perceptual problems, human engineering of equipement, industrial skills. M

SILVER, Miss Alice Mary. St. James Hosp, Portsmouth, Eng. b. 20 Aug 1904 Cravesand, Eng. MA '44 Univ. of London, Eng. SR. CLIN. PSYCH'T, St. James Hosp. Member BPS. Testing, psychotherapy, consulting; projective techniques. F

SIMM, Trevor. 80 Heath Rd, Widnes, Lancaster, Eng. b. 26 Dec 1923 Widnes, Eng. B.SC '50 Univ. of Manchester, Eng. EDUC. PSYCH'T, Lancaster County Council, Sch. Hlth. Serv. East Cliff County Off, Preston, Eng. Member: BPS. Remedial education, testing, clinical analysis, psychotherapy; intelligence and achievement tests, mentally handicapped children, delinquency. M

SIMMINS, Miss Constance Amy. 15 Mountfield Gardens, Tunbridge Wells, Kent, Eng. b. 28 June 1886 S. Norwood, Surrey, Eng. MA '11 Univ. of Cambridge, Eng. Member: BPS, Natl. Assn. for Ment. Hlth. Retired, teaching, testing, research; intelligence tests, intelligence of abnormal adults. F

SINGLETON, William Thomas. 36 Buckfast Sq, Corby, Northampton, Eng. b. 3 Mar 1924 Haslingden, Eng. MA '50 Univ. of Cambridge, Eng. HEAD of ERGONOMICS, Br. Boot, Shoe and Allied Trades Res. Assn, Rockingham, Rd, Kettering, Northampton. Member: BPS, APA, Ergonomics Res. Socy. Industrial psychology, administration, research; design of machinery on human engineering principles, factory organization and work flow, industrial skills. M

SKEMP, Richard Rowland. Dept. of Psych, The Univ, Manchester 13, Eng. b. 10 Mar 1919 Bristol, Eng. MA '55 Univ. of Oxford, Eng. ASST. LECT, Univ. of Manchester. Member: BPS. Research, teaching, professional writing; learning theory, educational psychology. M

SLUCKIN, Dr. Wladyslaw. Dept. of Psych, Univ. of Durham, Kepier Tce, Gilesgate, Durham, Eng. b. 20 Mar 1919 Warsaw, Poland. PH.D '55 Univ. of London, Eng. LECTURER, Univ. of Durham. Member: BPS. Teaching, research, professional writing; statistics, occupational psychology, cybernetics. M

SLUPINSKI, Leon. Prudhoe and Monkton Hosp, Prudhoe on Tyne, Northumberland, Eng. b. 7 Dec 1914 Warsaw, Poland. MA '53 Univ. of Cambridge, Eng. CLIN. PSYCH'T, Prudhoe and Monkton Hosp. Member: BPS. Clinical analysis, research, psycho-

therapy; skilled performance, experimental study of movement, education of mental defectives. M

SMITH, Bernard Babington. 34 Banbury Rd, Oxford, Eng. b. 26 Oct 1905 London, Eng. MA '31 Univ. of Cambridge, Eng. SR. LECT. in EXPER. PSYCH, Oxford Univ, Eng. Teaching, research, applied psychology; experimental psychology. M

SMITH, Miss Christina Anne. 18 Woodmill Terr, Dunfermline, Fife, Scot. b. 23 Apr 1920 Dunfermline, Scot. ED.B '43 Univ. of Edinburgh, Scot. ASST. EDUC. PSYCH'T, Fife County Counc. Educ. Comm, Wemyssfield, Kirkcaldy, Scot. Member: BPS. Clinical testing and analysis, consulting, educational psychology. F

SMITH, Miss Edith Mary. 9 Beech Ave, Buckhurst Hill, Essex, Eng. b. 31 Mar 1907 Wolverhampton, Eng. MA '46 Univ. of Birmingham, Eng. EDUC. PSYCH'T, Educ. Comm, Walthamstow, Essex, Eng. Member: BPS. Educational psychology, testing, child guidance; learning theory, remedial education. F

SMITH, Prof. Frederick Viggers. Dept. of Psych, Univ. of Durham, 7 Kepier Terr, Gilesgate, Durham, Eng. b. 24 Jan 1912 Newcastle, Australia. PH.D Univ. of London, Eng. PROFESSOR, Univ. of Durham; EDITOR, *The Durham Research Review*. Member: BPS. Teaching, administration, research; systems of psychology, perception, clinical psychology. M

SMITH, James Gauld. 71 Morton Lane, Beverley, E. Yorkshire, Eng. b. 14 Nov 1920 Uphall, Scot. ED.B '49 Univ. of Aberdeen, Scot. EDUC. PSYCH'T, E. Riding of Yorkshire Educ. Comm, County Hall, Beverley; EDUC. CONSULT, priv. prac; CLIN. PSYCH'T, Broadgate Ment. Hosp, Beverley; LECTURER, Coll. of Handicraft, Hull Coll. of Commerce, Beverley Tech. Inst. Member: BPS. Educational psychology, guidance, testing; industrial selection and training, family and group structure, learning theory and methods. M

SMITH, Dr. James W. D. 94 Southbrae Dr, Glasgow W. 3, Scot. b. 2 Mar 1899 Glasgow, Scot. ED.B '27 Univ. of Glasgow, Scot. PRIN. LECT. in RELIG. EDUC, Natl. Comm. for the Trng. of Tchrs, Jordonhill Trng. Cen, Glasgow W. 3. Member: BPS. Teaching psychology and religion in personal development. M

SMITH, John Angus. Jordanhill Trng. Cen, Glasgow W. 3, Scot. b. 28 June 1911 Inverness, Scot. B.ED '44 Univ. of Edinburgh, Scot. DEPUTY DIR. of STUDIES, Jordanhill Trng. Cen. Member: BPS. Administration, teaching, educational psychology; teacher training, attitudes to teaching, psychology of handicapped

children. M
SMITH, Margaret Metcalfe. Inst. of Educ, The Univ, Leeds 2, Eng. MA '43 Univ. of Leeds, Eng. LECT. in PRIMARY EDUC, Univ. of Leeds. Teaching; development and education of young children. F
SMITH, Dr. Mrs. Mary Hannah Gibson. 21 Woodlands Park Rd, King's Norton, Birmingham, Eng. b. 5 Aug 1875 Bishop Auckland, Durham, Eng. PH.D '09 Univ. of Jena, Germany. Retired. F
SMITH, Miss May. 37 Abbey Gardens, London N.W. 8, Eng. b. 29 Aug 1879 Manchester, Eng. D.SC '30 Univ. of London, Eng. Member: BPS. Retired. F
SMITH, Thomas. 47 St. Vincent Crescent, Glasgow C. 3, Scot. b. 14 June 1905 Crocketford, Scot. ED.B '43 Univ. of Glasgow, Scot. PRIN. PSYCH'T, Lanarkshire Child Guid. Serv, County Counc. of Lanark, Lanarkshire House, Glasgow C. 1. Member: BPS. Administration, guidance, consulting, testing. M
SNEATH, Frank Archer. Wayside, Thurlby, Bourne, Lincoln, Eng. b. 27 Jan 1927 Thurlby, Eng. Diploma '51 Univ. of London, Eng. SR. VOCAT. OFF, Ministry of Labour and Natl. Serv, Ebury Bridge Rd, London S.W. 1. Member: BPS. Guidance, industrial rehabilitation, testing; vocational counseling, aptitude testing, group dynamics. M
SPENCER, Dr. Seymour Jamie Gerald. 1 The Drive, Gosforth, Newcastle upon Tyne 3, Eng. b. 4 May 1920 London, Eng. D.PM '51 Univ. of London, Eng; MD, B.CH, Univ. of Oxford, Eng. FIRST ASST, Dept. of Psych. Med, King's Coll, Univ. of Durham, Queen Victoria Rd, Newcastle upon Tyne 1. Member- BPS, RMPA, Royal Socy. of Med. Clinical practice, psychotherapy, teaching, research; relationship between physique and psychological illness, psychological illness among undergraduates. M
SPRENT, Richard Anthony. Blenheim Cottage, Bears Hill, Oxford, Eng. b. 25 May 1919 London, Eng. MA '41 Univ. of Oxford, Eng. SR. TUTOR and LECT, Dept. of Educ, Oxford Univ, 15 Norham Gardens, Oxford. Member: BPS. Teaching, research; child development, educational psychology. M
SPROTT, Prof. Walter John Herbert. 116 Portland Rd, Nottingham, Eng. b. 19 Apr 1897 Crowborough, Sussex, Eng. MA '22 Univ. of Cambridge, Eng. PROF. of PHILOS, Univ. of Nottingham. Member: BPS. Teaching, professional writing, administration; group process. M
STANDEN, John Lucas. 33 Arundel Gardens, London W.1, Eng. b. 11 Oct 1923 London, Eng. BA '47 Univ. Coll, London, Eng. CLIN. PSYCH'T, St. Bernard's Hosp, Ux-

bridge Rd, Southall, Middlesex, Eng. Member: BPS. Testing, student, vocational guidance, consulting; objective testing, projective techniques, methodology. M
STAR, Dr. Leonard Paul. Copplestone, Crediton, Devon. Eng. b. 5 Nov 1914 Bristol, Eng. PH.D '42 Trinity Coll, Eire. SR. COUNTY EDUC. PSYCH'T. Devon County Counc, 45 St. David's Hill, Exeter, Devon. Member: BPS. Educational psychology, consulting, teaching; educational and clinical psychology. M
STAUNTON, Gerard Joseph. Saxondale Hosp, Radcliffe on Trent, Nottingham, Eng. b. 23 June 1925 Galway, Eire. BA '48 Univ. of London, Eng. SR. CLIN. PSYCH'T, Nottingham No. 4 Hosp. Management Comm, Saxondale Hosp. Member: BPS, BRF. Testing, consulting, research; projective techniques, diagnostic assessment, personality development. M
STEINBERG, Dr. Hannah. Pharmacology Dept, Univ. Coll, Gower St, London W.C. 1, Eng. b. 16 Mar 1924 Vienna, Austria. PH.D '53 Univ. of London, Eng. LECTURER, Univ. Coll, London; EDITOR, *Bulletin* of the British Psychological Society. Member: BPS. Research, teaching, editorial; psychological effect of drugs, learning, measurement of emotions. F
STEPHEN, Miss Jean Elspeth Murray. Westminster Bank, Oxford St. Br, 67 New Oxford St, London W.C. 1, Eng. b. 21 Aug 1911 Dundee, Scot. MA '33 St. Andrews Univ, Scot. SR. CLIN. PSYCH'T, Chailey Heritage Craft Sch. and Hosp, Chailey, Sussex, Eng. Member: BPS. Consulting, research, testing; psychological effect of cerebral palsy. F
STEPHENSON, Arthur. 43 Charleville Mansions, London W. 14, Eng. b. 12 Dec 1889 Low Fell, Durham, Eng. B.SC '21 Univ. of London, Eng. Member: BPS. Retired, industrial psychology, research; application of learning theory to industrial training, visual perception, industrial accidents. M
STEVENS, Mrs. Jean Fulbrook. 32 Grasmere Gardens, Ilford, Essex, Eng. b. 18 Oct 1923 Dunedin, New Zealand. MA '49 Otago Univ, New Zealand. PSYCH'T. in CHARGE, E. Ham Child Guid. Cen, Shrewsbury Rd. Sch, London E. 7, Eng. Member: BPS. Testing, psychotherapy, educational psychology; child guidance. F
STEVENSON, Miss Margaret Scott. 290 Fir Tree Rd, Epsom Downs, Surrey, Eng. b. 22 July 1920 Wimbledon, Eng. M.SC '44 Univ. of London, Eng. SR. PSYCH'T, H. M. Civil Serv. Comm, 6 Burlington Gardens, London W. 1, Eng. Member: BPS. Applied and personnel psychology, research; intelligence and achievement tests, person-

nel selection. F
STEWART, Alan Harrison. 220 Station Rd, Beeston, Notts, Eng. b. 14 July 1904 Newcastle on Tyne, Eng. BA '29 Univ. of London, Eng. LECT. in EDUC, Univ. of Nottingham, Eng. Member: BPS. Teaching, applied and educational psychology, testing; intelligence and attainment tests, psychology of groups, psychology of language. M
STEWART, David John. Med. Res. Counc, Grp. for Res. on Occupat. Aspects of Ageing, Univ. Dept. of Psych, 7 Abercromby Sq, Liverpool 7, Eng. b. 27 June 1930 Croydon, Eng. BA '54 Univ. of Bristol, Eng. MEMBER of SCI. STAFF, Med. Res. Counc. Member: BPS. Research, applied and industrial psychology, teaching; general control theory in psychology, psychological changes with age. M
STEWART, Miss Magdalene M. 14 Circus Dr, Glasgow E. 1, Scot. b. 19 Apr 1909 Glasgow, Scot. ED.B '46 Univ. of Glasgow, Scot. PSYCHOLOGIST, Child Guid. Clin, Corp. of Glasgow, 194 Renfrew St, Glasgow C. 3. Member: BPS. Guidance, testing, research. F
STEWART, Miss Nancy Pearl. 17 Crediton Hill, London N.W. 6, Eng. b. 15 July 1919 Perth, Austl. BA '40 Univ. of Western Australia. CHILD PSYCHOTHER, County Counc. of Middlesex and County Borough of E. Ham, Eng. Member: BPS, Assn. of Child Psychother. Psychotherapy with disturbed children, consulting, guidance, student; psychoanalystic techniques in child psychotherapy, projective techniques, mental testing. F
STIRLING, Isobel Millicent. 94 Morningside Dr, Edinburgh, Scot. b. 25 Apr 1900 Poona, India. MA, Oxon, Eng. Member: BPS. Psychotherapy, professional writing, testing. F
STOCKBRIDGE, Hugh Charles Walter. Clothing and Stores Exper. Establishment, c/o R.A.E, S. Farnborough, Hants, Eng. b. 27 Apr 1925 Cambridge, Eng. MA '55 Univ. of Reading, Eng. SR. PSYCH'T, Clothing and Stores Exper. Establishment, Ministry of Supply. Member: BPS, Ergonomics Res. Socy. Research, industrial psychology, administration; human engineering, controls and displays, questionnaires. M
STONEMAN, Miss Audrey Marion. 6 Constable House, Chalk Farm, London N.W. 3, Eng. b. 4 Nov 1919 Teddington, Eng. BA '47 Univ. of London, Eng. EDUC. PSYCH'T, Woking Child Guid. Clin, Surrey County Counc, 28 Claremont Ave, Woking, Surrey, Eng; EDUC. PSYCH'T, Psychiat. Outpatient Dept, Bromley Dist. Hosp, Bromley, Kent, Eng. Member: BPS. Testing, educational psychology, psychotherapy, remedial

teaching. F
STOTT, Dr. Denis Herbert. 13 Maurice Rd, Bristol 6, Eng. b. 31 Dec 1909 London, Eng. PH.D '50 Univ. of London, Eng. RES. FELLOW, Inst. of Educ. Univ. of Bristol, 19 Berkeley Sq, Bristol 8, Eng. Member: BPS. Research, professional writing, testing; scolastic backwardness, social adjustment of children, delinquency. M
STOTT, Miss Mary Boole. 40 Priory Gardens, Highgate, London N. 6, Eng. b. 11 Sept 1893 Liverpool, Eng. BA '16 Univ. of London, Eng. SR. VOCAT. ADVIS, Natl. Inst. of Indus. Psych, 14 Welbeck St, London W. 1, Eng. Member: BPS, Assn. of Psychiat. Soc. Wrkers. Vocational guidance. F
STRAKER, Dermot. 35 Caldy Rd, W. Kirby, Wirral, Chester, Eng. b. 2 June 1912 London, Eng. MA '49 Univ. of Cambridge, Eng. LECT. in PSYCH, Univ. of Liverpool, Brownlow Hill, Liverpool, Eng. Member: BPS. Teaching, research, administration; vocational guidance, personnel selection, industrial training. M
STRAUSS, Dr. Eric Benjamin. 45 Wimpole St, London W. 1, Eng. b. 18 Feb 1894 London, Eng. MD '30 Univ. of Oxford, Eng. PHYSICIAN and LECT. in PSYCH. MED, St. Bartholomew's Hosps, London; PHYSICIAN for PSYCH. MED, The N. Middlesex Hosp. and St. Andrew's Hosp, Dollis Hill. Member: BPS, RMPA, Royal Socy. of Med. Teaching, clinical practice, administration; psychological medicine. M
STRAUSS, Frederick Henry. 11 Dunraven St, London W. 1, Eng. b. 13 Apr 1902 Berlin, Germany. BA '48 Univ. of London, Eng. SR. CLIN. PSYCH'T, Belmont Hosp, Brighton Rd, Sutton, Surrey, Eng. Member: BPS. Testing, clinical analysis, psychotherapy, research; projective techniques, group process, analytical psychology. M
STUART, Miss Mary. 49 The Fairway, Blaby, Leicester, Eng. b. 8 June 1913 Wolverhampton, Eng. ED.M '44 Univ. of Manchester, Eng. CHILDREN'S OFFICER, Leicester City Counc, Town Hall, Leicester. Member: BPS. Educational psychology, administration, teaching; social and emotional development of children, learning theory. F
STURROCK, George Wright. Woodmuir Terr, Newport on Tay, Fife, Scot. b. 18 May 1907 Kirriemuir, Scot. ED.B '36 Univ. of Edinburgh, Scot. PRIN. EDUC. PSYCH'T, Educ. Comm. of City of Dundee, 14 City Sq, Dundee, Scot. Member: BPS. Educational psychology, testing, administration; intelligence and achievement testing, child guidance. M
SUMMERFIELD, Arthur. 4 Leaside Ave,

London N. 10, Eng. b. 31 Mar 1923 Wilmslow, Eng. B.SC '49 Univ. of London, Eng. LECT. in PSYCH, Univ. coll, Gower St, London W.C. 1. Member: BPS, Exper. Psych. Grp. Teaching, research; statistical methods, experimental psychology of perception and learning. M

SUTHERLAND, Dr. John. 8 Glenisla Gardens, Edinburgh 9, Scot. b. 14 June 1910 Edinburgh, Scot. PH.D '49 Univ. of Edinburgh, Scot. LECT. in EDUC. and PSYCH, Moray House Trng. Coll, Holyrood Rd, Edinburgh. Member: BPS. Teaching, research, educational psychology, testing; learning theory, achievement tests, factor analysis.M

SUTHERLAND, Dr. Margaret Brownlie. Dept. of Educ, Queen's Univ, Belfast, N. Ire. b. 19 May 1920 Glasgow, Scot. PH.D '55 Queen's Univ, N. Ire. LECTURER, Queen's Univ. Member: BPS. Teaching, research, professional writing; imagination, attitude measurement, aptitude testing. F

SWAINSON, Dr. Mary. Inst. of Educ, 328 London Rd, Leicester, Eng. b. 23 Mar 1908 Weston super Mare, Eng. PH.D '49 Univ. of Oxford, Eng. PSYCHOLOGIST, Psych. Advisory Serv, Inst. of Educ; LECT. in EDUC. PSYCH, Dept. of Educ, Univ. Coll. of Leicester. Member: BPS, Natl. Assn. for Ment. Hlth, Assn. of Profes. Psychother. Guidance, psychotherapy, teaching; student problems, application of depth psychology to education, psychology and religion. F

SYMONS, Norman Jelinger. 25 Honor Oak Rd, Forest Hill, London S.E. 23, Eng. b. 12 Aug 1889 Southport, Lancastar, Eng. MA '15 Pembroke Coll, Oxford, Eng. Member: BPS. Retired. M

SZAFRAN, Dr. Jacek. Univ. of Exeter, Exeter, Eng. b. 25 Oct 1920 Warsaw, Poland. PH.D '53 Univ. of Cambridge, Eng. LECT. in PSYCH, Univ. of Exeter. Member: BPS, Exper. Psych. Grp, Ergonomics Res. Socy. Teaching, administration, research; psychological and physiological aspects of development and ageing, perceptual learning, psychopathology. M

TAJFEL, Henri. Univ. of Oxford, Delegacy for Soc. Trng, Barnett House, Wellington Sq, Oxford, Eng. b. 22 June 1919 Wloclawek, Poland. MA '56 Univ. of Oxford, Eng. TUTOR in PSYCH, Univ. of Oxford. Member: BPS, Assn. for the Study of Animal Behaviour. Teaching, research, administration; social perception, motivation and learning, perception, group tensions. M

TANNER, Miss Margaret Florence. 51 Calton Ave, Dulwich, London S.E. 21, Eng. b. 11 Nov 1925 London, Eng. B.SC '52 Birkbeck Coll, London, Eng. EDUC. PSYCH'T, Middlesex County Counc, 10 Great George St, London. Member: BPS. Educational psychology, testing, child

guidance; child development, school adjustment, educational retardation. F

TAYLOR, Herbert John Fenton. 7 Plough Lane, Harefield, Middlesex, Eng. b. 8 Mar 1923 Bedford, Eng. MA '50 Univ. of Cambridge, Eng. EDUC. PSYCH'T, Child Guid. Cen, Lannock Rd, Hayes, Middlesex. Member: BPS. Educational psychology, guidance, teaching, administration. M

TAYLOR, Roy Shrewsbury. 12 Arterberry Rd, Wimbledon S.W. 20, Eng. b. 28 Feb 1925 Wallington, Surrey, Eng. MA '54 Univ. of Cambridge, Eng. SR. PSYCH'T, Wandsworth Prison, Prison Comm, Horseferry House, Dean Ryle St, Westminster S.W. 1, Eng. Member: BPS. Testing, interviewing, applied psychology, administration; projective techniques, delinquent behavior. M

TENEN, Dr. Cora. 135 Grosvenor Rd, Epsom Downs, Surrey, Eng. b. 31 Oct 1902 Manchester, Eng. PH.D '48 Univ. of Manchester, Eng. SR. LECT, London County Counc, Furzedown Coll, Welham Rd, London S.W. 17, Eng. Member: BPS. Teaching, research; psychology of adolescence, industrial psychology. F

THOM, Miss Mary. 38 Edgemont St, Glasgow S. 1, Scot. b. 21 Dec 1918 Glasgow, Scot. ED.B '46 Univ. of Glasgow, Scot. ASST. PSYCH'T, The Glasgow Corp. Educ. Dept, 129 Bath St, Glasgow. Child guidance, psychotherapy, testing, educational psychology. F

THOMASSON, Frank Hope. 79 Sandford Rd, Moseley, Birmingham 13, Eng. b. 4 July 1923 Manchester, Eng. BA '51 Univ. of Cambridge, Eng. TRAINING OFF, Albright and Wilson Ltd, Trinity St, Oldbury, Birmingham. Member: BPS. Industrial and personnel psychology, administration, testing. M

THOMPSON, Miss Margaret Irene. 9 Harlescott Crescent, Shrewsbury, Eng. b. 22 Oct 1926 near Goole, York, Eng. BA '47 Univ. of Birmingham, Eng. EDUC. PSYCH'T, Salop County Counc, Educ. Comm. Member: BPS. Testing, educational psychology, guidance. F

THOMPSON, Miss Veronica Joan. Child Guid. Clin, Belgrave Hosp. for Children, 1 Clapham Rd, London S.W. 9, Eng. b. 13 Nov 1930 Daunhauser, Natal. MA '54 Univ. of Natal, S. Africa. SR. PSYCH'T, King's Coll. Hosp, Denmark Hill, London S.E. 5. Member: BPS. Psychotherapy, testing; play therapy. F

THOMPSON, Walter Gerald. Child Guid. Cen, Shapethorpe Hall, Hall Rd, Wakefield, York, Eng. b. 23 Aug 1919 Hamburg, Germany. MA '55 Univ. of London, Eng. EDUC. PSYCH'T, Educ. Comm, 27 King St, Wakefield. Member: BPS. Educational psychology, testing, child guidance; intelligence and attainment testing, personality assessment, vocational guidance.　M

THOMSON, Miss Edith Isobel Miller. 145 Dalkeith Rd, Edinburgh, Scot. b. 3 July 1894 S. Ronaldshay, Orkney, Scot. ED.B '19 Univ. of Edinburgh, Scot. LECT. in EDUC, Moray House Trng. Coll, Holyrood Rd, Edinburgh. Member: BPS. Teaching, testing, consulting; intelligence and achievement tests.　F

THOMSON, Robert Alexander. The School House, Three Mile Lane, New Costessey, Norwich, Eng. b. 29 July 1925 Edinburgh, Scot. ED.B '50 Univ. of Edinburgh, Scot, EDUC. PSYCH'T, Child Guid. Serv, Norfolk Educ. Comm, Norfolk County Counc, Stracey Rd, Norwich. Member: BPS. Educational psychology, guidance, testing; intelligence and achievement testing, projective techniques, play therapy, educational techniques for the physically handicapped.　M

THORLEY, Stanley. 2 Mansfield Mews, Harley St, London W. 1, Eng. b. 7 Apr 1925 Warrington, Eng. MA '54 Univ. of Michigan, USA. SOC. PSYCH'T, Natl. Inst. of Indus. Psych, 14 Welbeck St, London W. 1. Member: BPS. Industrial psychology, research, teaching; group processes, attributes of power, attitude measurement.　M

THORPE, Dr. James Geoffrey. 59 Monks Orchard Rd, Beckenham, Kent, Eng. b. 18 Mar 1924 Huddersfield, Eng. PH.D '53 Univ. of London, Eng. SR. PSYCH'T, Banstead Hosp, Sutton, Surrey, Eng. Member: BPS. Research, clinical analysis and testing, professional writing; diagnostic testing, achievement tests, personality theory.　M

THORNTON, Dr. Mrs. Peggie K. Upcott House, Bishops Hull, Taunton, Somerset, Eng. b. 16 Aug 1909 London, Eng. PH.D '56 Univ. of Reading, Eng. PERS. OFF, Simon-Carves Ltd, Cheadle Heath, Chester, Eng. Member: BPS. Research in industrial psychology, testing; inter-cultural comparisons in visual perception, learning theory, achievement tests and projective techniques.　F

THOULESS, Dr. Robert Henry. 2 Leys Rd, Cambridge, Eng. b. 15 July 1894 Norwich, Eng. SC.D '54 Univ. of Cambridge, Eng. READER in EDUC. PSYCH, Univ. of Cambridge; EDITOR, *Psychological Monographs*. Member: BPS, Socy. for Psychical Res. Teaching, editorial, research; perception, parapsychology, religion.　M

THYNE, James Morrison. 2 Lochend Crescent, Bearsden, Dunbartonshire, Scot. b. 8 Oct 1914 Glasgow, Scot. ED.B '39 Univ. of Glasgow, Scot. PRIN. LECT. in PSYCH, Jordanhill Trng. Coll, Southbrae Dr, Glasgow, Scot. Member: BPS. Teaching,

administration, research; application of learning theory to education, psychological theory.　M

TINBERGEN, Prof. Nikolaas. Department of Zool. University Museum, Oxford, Eng. b. 15 Apr 1907 The Hague, Neth. PH.D '32 Leiden Univ, Neth. LECTURER, Dept. of Zool, Univ. of Oxford, Eng; CO-EDITOR, *Behaviour, British Journal of Animal Behaviour*. Member: Assn. for the Study of Animal Behavior. Teaching, research, editorial; perception prior to conditioning, multiple motivation, social behavior.　M

TIZARD, Dr. Jack. Maudsley Hosp, Denmark Hill, London S.E. 5, Eng. b. 25 Feb 1919 New Zealand. PH.D '51 Univ. of London, Eng. SCI. STAFF, Soc. Psychiat. Res. Unit, Med. Res. Counc, Maudsley Hosp; HONORARY LECT, Inst. of Psychiat. Member: BPS. Research; mental deficiency, schizophrenia.　M

TODD, Geoffrey Burkett. Kingswood Classifying Sch, Kingswood, Bristol, Eng. b. 16 Oct 1922 London, Eng. BA '50 Univ. of Cambridge, Eng. EDUC. PSYCH'T, Kingswood Classifying Sch. Member: BPS. Educational psychology, testing, guidance; projective techniques, interview techniques, dynamics of family relationship, personality assessment.　M

TONG, John Edward. Psych. Dept, Rampton Hosp, Retford, Notts, Eng. b. 12 Dec 1921 Wolverhampton, Eng. BA '52 Univ. of Bristol, Eng. SR. PSYCH'T, Rampton Hosp. Member: BPS. Clinical analysis and testing, research, administration; application of physiological psychology, learning theory and projective techniques to the adult criminal.　M

TOZER, Arthur Humphrey Denny. Univ. of Liverpool, Liverpool 3, Eng. b. 16 Aug 1908 Gillingham, Eng. MA '34 Univ. of Cambridge, Eng. LECT. in EDUC, Univ. of Liverpool. Member: BPS. Teaching, research, educational psychology; psychological tests, learning theory, educational selection and guidance.　M

TRAILL, Miss Phyllis Maud. Inst. of Child Psych, 6 Pembridge Villas, London W. 11, Eng. b. 14 Oct 1907 Cullercoats, Eng. MA '32 Univ. of Cambridge, Eng. CHILD PSYCHOTHER, Inst. of Child Psychother. Member: BPS, Assn. of Child Psychother. Child psychotherapy, teaching, research; diagnostic and therapeutic techniques.　F

TRASLER, Dr. Gordon Blair. 2 White Shute Lane, St. Cross, Winchester, Hants, Eng. b. 7 Mar 1929 Bournemouth, Eng. PH.D ''55 Univ. of London, Eng. PSYCHOLOGIST, H. M. Prison, Romsey Rd, Winchester. Member: BPS, Natl. Assn. for Ment. Hlth. Clinical testing, research, professional writing; criminal behavior, effects of

maternal depriviation, projective techniques. M
TRIST, Eric Lansdown. Tavistock Inst. of Human Relations, 2 Beaumont St, London W. 1, Eng. b. 11 Sept 1909 Dover, Eng. MA '35 Univ. of Cambridge, Eng. DEPUTY CHMN, Tavistock Inst. of Human Relat; BR. ED. COMM, *Human Relations*; CONSULT. ED, *Psychological Review*. Member: BRF, Exper. Psych. Group. Applied psychology, research, administration; group process, social organization, projective techniques, social applications of psychoanalysis, management selection and training. M
TYERMAN, Dr. Maurice Joseph. 10 Heneagg Rd, Grimsby, Eng. b. 24 May 1922 Middlesbrough, Eng. PH.D '55 Univ. of London, Eng. CLIN. and EDUC. PSYCH'T, Grimsby Educ. Comm, Eleanor St, Grimsby; LECTURER, Dept. of Adult Educ, Univ. of Hull. Member: BPS. Child guidance, applied and educational psychology, administration; irregular school attendance, delinquency, attainment and intelligence tests. M
UNDERWOOD, Mrs. Vera. Brentwood, Melton Rd, Sprotborough near Doncaster, York, Eng. b. 30 July 1910 Ipswich, Eng. BA '32 Univ. of Reading, Eng. EDUC. PSYCH'T, Doncaster Educ. Comm, Whitaker St, Doncaster; LECTURER, Workers' Educ. Assn. Member: BPS. Educational psychology, guidance, administration; use of achievement tests for secondary school selection. F
UNGERSON, Bernard. 65 Ralph Ct, Queensway, London W. 2, Eng. b. 1 May 1912 London, Eng. B.SC '34 Univ. of London, Eng. DIRECTOR, The Anne Shaw Organiza, Beech House, Heald Green, Cheadle, Chester, Eng. Member: BPS. Industrial consulting, administration, teaching; motion study, personnel selection, human relations in industry. M
URQUHART, Miss Helen. Rosslea, 6 Luss Rd, Alexandria, Dumbartonshire, Scot. b. 20 Oct 1904 Coatbridge, Scot. ED.B '50 Univ. of Glasgow, Scot. ASST. EDUC. PSYCH'T, Child Guid. Serv. Glasgow Corp. Educ. Dept, 129 Bath St, Glasgow, Scot. Member: BPS. Child guidance, psychotherapy, testing, teaching. F
VALENTINE, Prof. Emer. Charles Wilfred. The White House, Wythall, near Birmingham, Eng. b. 16 Aug 1879 Runcorn, Eng. PH.D '13 Univ. of St. Andrews, Scot. PROF. EMER. of EDUC, Univ. of Birmingham. Member: BPS, Société Française d'Esthétique. Professional writing, teaching, consulting; child psychology, educational psychology, tests. M
VALENTINE, Hugh Brian. 13 Meadowlands Ave, Barrow in Furness, Lancaster, Eng.

b. 27 Mar 1921 Birmingham, Eng. MA '55 Univ. of Birmingham, Eng. EDUC. PSYCH'T, Barrow in Furness Educ. Comm, Town Hall, Barrow in Furness. Member: BPS. Educational psychology, testing, guidance; remedial education, intelligence and attainment testing. M
VANCE, Right Rev. Monsignor John Gabriel. Crawley St. Mary, Crawley Downs, Sussex, Eng. b. 12 Nov 1885 London, Eng. PH.D '12 Univ. of Louvain, Belgium. CATH. PRELATE. Member: BPS. Consulting, educational psychology, administration; retired; psychological theory and cognitive and volitional processes. M
VENABLES, Dr. Peter Henry. 62 Whyteleafe Rd, Caterham, Surrey, Eng. b. 3 Apr 1923 Ilfracombe, Eng. PH.D '53 Univ. of London, Eng. SCI. STAFF, Med. Res. Counc. 38 Old Queen St, London S.W. 1, Eng. Member: BPS. Research, professional writing, applied psychology; learning theory, abnormal psychology, human engineering. M
VENESS, Miss Winifred Thelma. Birkbeck Coll, Malet St, London W.C. 1, Eng. b. 28 Apr 1919 London, Eng. BA '45 Univ. of London, Eng. LECT. in PSYCH, Birkbeck Coll. Member: BPS. Research, teaching; motivation, joint consultation, national character. F
VERNON, Dr. Magdalen Dorothea. The Univ, Reading, Berks, Eng. b. 25 June 1901 Oxford, Eng. D.SC '53 Univ. of Cambridge, Eng. READER in PSYCH, Univ. of Reading. Member: BPS, Exper. Psych. Grp. Research, teaching, applied psychology; visual perception, reading. F
VERNON, Prof. Philip Ewart. 30 Sherrardspark Rd, Welwyn Garden City, Herts, Eng. b. 6 June 1905 Oxford, Eng. D.SC '52 Univ. of London, Eng. PROF. of EDUC. PSYCH, Inst. of Educ. Univ. of London, Malet St, London W.C. 1, Eng; EDITOR, *British Journal of Educational Psychology.* Member: BPS, APA. Teaching, research, editorial; mental and personality testing, music. M
VICKERS, W. 10 Caledon Rd, Parkstone, Dorset, Eng. b. 25 Jan 1890 Bolton, Eng. ED.M '16 Univ. of Manchester, Eng. INTERVIEWER, Dorset Educ. Comm, Dorset, Eng. Member: BPS. Retired, testing; student selection for schools, mental testing. M
WALKER, Dr. David Arnold. 63 William St, Kirkcaldy, Scot. b. 9 May 1905 Newcastle on Tyne, Eng. PH.D '37 Univ. of Edinburgh, Scot. DEPUTY DIR. of EDUC, Fife County Counc, Wemyssfield, Kirkcaldy. Member: BPS. Administration, research, educational psychology; mental test construction, selection techniques for secondary education. M

WALKER, Dr. Norman Thomson. Dept. of Educ, Univ. of Aberdeen, Broad St, Aberdeen, Scot. b. 11 Mar 1895 Alexandria, Dunbartonshire, Scot. PH.D '29 Univ. of Glasgow, Scot. READER, and HEAD, Dept. of Educ, Univ. of Aberdeen; ED. BD, *British Journal of Educational Studies.* Member: BPS. Scot. Counc. for Res. in Educ. Teaching, administration, research, editorial and professional writing; achievement tests, mental measurement, child guidance. M

WALL, Dr. William Douglas. Natl. Found. for Educ. Res. in Eng. and Wales, 79 Wimpole St, London W. 1, Eng. b. 22 Aug 1913 Wallington, Surrey, Eng. PH.D '48 Univ. of Birmingham, Eng. DIRECTOR, Natl. Found. for Educ. Res. Member: BPS. Administration of research in educational psychology, professional writing; learning theory, achievement tests, group processes. M

WALLERSTEIN, Dr. Harvey. London House, Guilford St, London W.C. 1, Eng. b. 16 Sept 1928 Montreal, Canada. PH.D '53 McGill Univ, Canada. SR. RES. FELLOW, Post off. Engr. Dept, Res. Station, Dollis Hill, London N.W. 2, Eng. Member: BPS. Research, industrial psychology. M

WALLIS, Donald. 54 Outwood Lane, Chipstead, Surrey, Eng. b. 24 July 1923 London, Eng. B.SC '50 Univ. of London, Eng. SR. PSYCH'T, Admiralty, Queen Anne's Mansions, London S.W. 1, Eng; LECT. in INDUS. PSYCH, City of London Coll, Eng. Member: BPS, Ergonomics Res. Socy. Personnel and industrial psychology, research, administration; human engineering, perceptive-motor skills, synthetic training methods. M

WALTON, Donald. 23 Windle Grove, Windle, St. Helens, Lancaster, Eng. b. 22 Aug 1926 St. Helens, Eng. BA '51 Univ. of Liverpool, Eng. SR. CLIN. PSYCH'T, Rainhill Hosp. and Winwick Hosp, Rainhill Hosp. Management Comm, Rainhill, near Liverpool, Eng. Member: BPS. Clinical practice, consulting, research, teaching; perception and relation to psychological diagnosis, cognitive tests, diagnosis of brain damage by psychological tests. M

WALTON, Robert Denison. Tasman, Castle Douglas Rd, Dumfries, Scot. b. 16 July 1909 Glasgow, Scot. ED.B '35 Univ .of Glasgow, Scot. SCHOOLMASTER, Dumfries Acad, Dumfries, Scot. Member: BPS. Teaching, administration, educational psychology; achievement tests in mathematics, learning theory, oscillation as a mental factor. M

WARBURTON, Dr. Francis William. Waldon, Richmond Rd. Bowdon, Chester, Eng. b. 9 July 1909 London, Eng. PH.D '45 Univ. of London, Eng. LECT. in EDUC.

PSYCH, The Univ. Manchester, Eng. Member: BPS. Research, teaching, professional writing; educational selection, factor analysis, theory of measurement, learning theory. M

WARD, Douglas Frank. 14 St. Helena Rd, Colchester, Essex, Eng. b. 28 Nov 1913 London, Eng. M.SC '39 Univ. of London, Eng. EDUC. PSYCH'T, N.E. Essex Child Guid. Clin, Winsleys House, High St, Colchester, Essex, Eng. Member: BPS. Educational psychology, testing, guidance; achievement tests, projective techniques. M

WASON, Peter Cathcart. Flat 7, 12 Morden Rd, Blackheath, London S.E. 3, Eng. b. 22 Apr 1924 Bath, Eng. PH.D '57 Univ. of London, Eng. INVESTIGATOR, Med. Res. Counc, Indus. Psych. Res. Grp, 17 Gordon Sq, London W.C. 1, Eng; HONORARY RES. ASST, Psych. Dept, Univ. Coll, London, Eng. Member: BPS. Research, industrial psychology, teaching; thinking, psycholinguistics, administrative skills. M

WATSON, Dr. Ralph Harry Johnston. 2 Galesway, Woodford Bridge, Essex, Eng. b. 27 Oct 1920 London, Eng. PH.D '54 Univ. of London, Eng. SR. RES. PSYCH'T, Med. Res. Counc, 38 Old Queen St, London S.W. 1, Eng. Member: BPS. Research, teaching, administration; brain chemistry and behavior, behavior measures of toxicity. M

WATSON, Thomas Edward. Smuggler's Pightle, The Meadow, Chislehurst, Kent, Eng. b. 25 May 1926 Wallsend-on-Tyne, Eng. MA '51 Univ. of Edinburgh, Scot. SUPERVISOR, Job Eval. Sect, Ford Motor Co. Ltd, Dagenham, Essex, Eng. Member: BPS. Applied and industrial psychology, research, administration; job evaluation, personnel selection, management development. M

WEBSTER , Miss Janet Speed. c/o Miss M. Clarke, The Cabin, Lympstone, nr. Exmouth, Devon, Eng. b. 20 Nov 1926 Glenduckie, Fife, Scot. ED.B '50 Univ. of St. Andrews, Scot. EDUC. PSYCH'TDevon, County Counc, Larkbearl, Topsham Rd, Exeter, Devon. Member: BPS. Educational psychology, testing, clinical practice and guidance. F

WELFORD, Alan Traviss. Psych. Lab, Downing St, Cambridge, Eng. b. 27 Jan 1914 London, Eng. MA '39 Univ. of Cambridge, Eng. LECT. in EXPER. PSYCH, Univ. of Cambridge; HON. DIR, Nuffield Unit for Res. into Problems of Ageing; EDITOR, Publications of Ergonomics Res. Socy; ED. COMM, *Perception and Motor Skills.* Member: APA, Exper. Psych. Grp, Ergonomics Res. Socy. Research, teaching, administration; human skilled performance, changes of human performance with age, psychology of religion. M

WESTBY, George. Dept. of Psych, Univ. of Hull, Eng. b. 30 Mar 1909 Presten, UK. MA '31 Univ. of Oxford, Eng. HEAD, Dept. of Psych, Univ. of Hull. Member: BPS, AIPA. Teaching, applied psychology, research; intelligence and personality assessment, psychotherapy of exceptional children. M

WHELLER, Emer. Prof. Dame Olive Annie. Woodlands, 65 Bettws-y-coed Rd, Cardiff, Wales. b. 4 May 1886 Brecon, Wales. D.SC '15 Univ. of London, Eng. EMER. PROF. of EDUC, Univ. of Wales. Member: BPS. Retired, professional writing. F

WHILDE, Noel Elvidge. 5 Taptonville Rd, Sheffield 10, Eng. b. 11 Dec 1905 Alfreton, Derby, Eng. M.SC '54 Univ. of Nottingham, Eng. EDUC. PSYCH'T. and HEAD, Sheffield Child Guid. Cen, Sheffield Educ. Comm, Leopold St, Sheffield. Member: BPS. Psychotherapy, administration, educational psychology, professional writing; symbolism in psychotherapy. M

WHILES, Dr. William Herbert. Woodsmoke, Sandford, Wareham, Dorset, Eng. b. 6 Sept 1908 Newark, Eng. MRCS, LRCP, Kings Coll, London, Eng. CONSULT. CHILD. PSYCHIATRIST, Bournemouth and Dorset Child Guid. Serv, S.W. Metrop. R.H.B, Portland Pl, London, Eng; CONSULTANT, priv. prac; LECTURER, Univ. of London. Member: BPS, RMPA. Clinical child guidance, psychotherapy, teaching. M

WHINNOM, Mrs. Marie. 3A Holmesdale Close, S. Norwood, London SE 25, Eng. b. 3 June 1918 Plymouth, Eng. B.SC '44 Univ. of London, Eng. RETIRED; ASSOC. ED, *International Journal of Social Psychology*. Member: BPS. Psychometrics, play therapy, group dynamics. F

WHITE, Miss Eunice A. Child Guid. Clin, 33 St. Luke's Rd, Cheltenham, Glos, Eng. b. 23 Nov 1927 Fairlie, Scot. EDUC. PSYCH'T,Child Guid. Clin, Gloucestershire Educ. Authority, Shire Hall, Gloucester, Eng. Member: BPS. Educational psychology; child guidance. F

WHITE, Dr. Harold Dinely Jennings. BM/HDJW, London WC 1, Eng. b. 7 Sept 1894 London, Eng. PH.D '26 Univ. of London, Eng. Member: BPS. Professional writing, psychotherapy, consulting; child psychology, ethics and religion, aesthetics. M

WILKINSON, Norman William. 79 Green Ridge, Withdean, Brighton 5, Sussex, Eng. b. 4 Dec 1925 London, Eng. ED.B '52 Univ. of Edinburgh, Scot. EDUC. PSYCH'T, E. Sussex County Counc, Pub. Hlth. Dept, County Hall, Lewes, Sussex. Member: BPS. Child guidance, educational psychology, testing; projective techniques, personality dynamics, perceptual tech-

niques, scholastic retardation. M

WILLIAMS, Mrs. Celia Heather. Warley Hosp, Brentwood, Essex, Eng. b. Vermilion, Can. BA '50 Univ. of London, Eng. CLIN. PSYCH'T, Warley Ment. Hosp. Member: BPS, BRF. Clinical testing; projective techniques. F

WILLIAMS, David Charles Steyning. Fuller's Earth Lodge, Woburn, Bletchley, Bucks, Eng. b. 31 May 1923 Epsom, Eng. MA '50 Univ. of Cambridge, Eng. LECT. in MANAGEMENT STUDIES, Coll. of Tech, Oxford, Eng. Member: BPS. Teaching, industrial psychology, research; industrial personnel. M

WILLIAMS, Ioan Samuel. 184 Limpsfield Rd, Warlingham, Surrey, Eng. b. 30 Oct 1911 Narayanganj, India. B.SC '50 Univ. Coll, London, Eng. VOCAT. OFF, Ministry of Labour and Natl. Serv, Stafford Rd, Wadden, Surrey. Member: BPS. Guidance, testing, applied and industrial psychology; rehabilitation and vocational guidance of disabled adults. M

WILLIAMS. Dr. James Godfrey Lee. Woodman's Cottage, Sydenham Rd, London SE 26, Eng. b. 28 Nov 1920 Batley, York, Eng. PH.D '56 Univ. of London, Eng. RES. under GRANT, NUFFIELD FOUND, Sherrington Sch. of Physiol, St. Thomas's Hosp, London SE 1. Member: BPS, APA, Assn. for the Study of Animal Behavior. Research, teaching, professional writing; physiological psychology, experimental neurosis, learning theory. M

WILLIAMS, Mrs. Janette Roxburgh. 356 Jersey Rd, Isleworth, Middlesex, Eng. b. 18 July 1907 Glasgow, Scot. ED.B '38 Univ. of Glasgow, Scot. GRAD. STUD, Inst. of Psychiat, Maudsley Hosp, Denmark Hill, London, Eng. Member: BPS. Teaching, educational psychology, student, psychotherapy. F

WILLIAMS, Mrs. Jessie Melville. Griffins, Abinger Hammer, nr. Dorking, Surrey, Eng. b. Pudsey, Eng. MA '45 Univ. Coll, London, Eng. SR. CLIN. PSYCH'T, Guy's Hosp, St. Thomas St, London SE 1, Eng; PSYCHOLOGIST, Surrey County Counc. Reception Cen. Member: BPS, BRF, APA, Amer. Socy. for Projective Techniques. Testing, clinical practice, research; projective techniques, personality, development and learning capacity in brain damaged and emotionally deprived children. F

WILLIAMS, John Arthur Charles. 85 Elwill Way, Beckenham, Kent, Eng. b. 2 Dec 1915 Portsmouth, Eng. M.SC '55 Univ. of London, Eng. HEAD of ENGR. TRNG, Indus. Relat. Dept, Natl. Coal Bd, Grosvenor Pl, London SW 1, Eng. Member: BPS, Ergonomics Res. Socy. Administration, industrial psychology, professional writing; operator training and selection, ergonomics, control design, work study.   M

WILLIAMS, Dr. Moyra. Stones Farm, Standlake, Oxon, Eng. b. 5 Dec 1917 London, Eng. PH.D '54 Oxford, Eng. PSYCHOLOGIST, Nuffield Ment. Hlth. Res. Team, Cowley Rd. Hosp, Oxford, Eng. Member: BPS. Research, clinical analysis; organic basis of mental functions.   F

WILLS, Miss Annie Rankin. Netherby, Greenhill Crescent, Elderslie, Renfrewshire, Scot. b. 22 May 1911 Paisley, Scot. ED.B '37 Univ. of Glasgow, Scot. SR. ASST. EDUC. PSYCH'T, Dunbartonshire Educ. Comm, 18 Park Circus, Glasgow C 3, Scot. Member: BPS. Mental testing, educational psychology, child guidance; learning theory, a-chievement tests, education of backward children.   F

WILSON, Dr. Alexander Thomson Macbeth. 2 Beaumont St, London W 1, Eng. b. 15 Nov 1905. MD '40 Univ. of Glasgow, Scot. CHAIRMAN, Management Comm, Tavistock Inst. of Human Relat; ED. COMM, *Human Relations.* Member: BPS. Applied research, administration, teaching; methodology of field research, interplay of role and personality in small groups, psycho-analytic concepts in social psychology.   M

WILSON, Dr. Mary Dixon. 23 E. Churchfield Rd, London W 3, Eng. b. 17 Sept 1909 Whitehaven, Eng. PH.D '52 Univ. of London, Eng. EDUC. PSYCH'T, Middlesex L.E.A. Great George St, London. Testing, child guidance, educational psychology. F

WILSON, Dr. Norman A. B. 12 Bray Rd, Cobham, Surrey, Eng. b. 5 Dec 1908 Edinburgh, Scot. PH.D '35 Univ. of St. Andrews, Scot. SR. PSYCH'T, The Admiralty, Whitehall, London SW 1, Eng. Member: BPS, Ergonomics Res. Socy. Adminis-tration, personnel psychology; testing; attitude surveys, training research, human engineering.   M

WINCH, Miss Margaret Florence. 5 Croham Park Ave, S. Croydon, Surrey, Eng. b. 27 Aug 1919 London, Eng. BA '46 Univ. of London, Eng. EDUC. PSYCH'T, London County Counc, Woodberry Down Child Guid. Clin, Green Lanes, London N 6, Eng. Member: BPS, BRF, Natl. Assn. for Ment. Hlth. Guidance, educational psychology, testing; projective techniques, achievement tests, learning theory.   F

WING, Dr. Herbert. City of Sheffield Trng. Coll, Sheffield 10, Eng. b. 25 Aug 1904 London, Eng. PH.D '41 Univ. Coll, London, Eng. PRINCIPAL, City of Sheffield Trng. Coll. Member: BPS. Administration, edu-cational psychology, testing; measurement of musical aptitude.   M

WINNICOTT, Dr. Donald Woods. 87 Chester Sq, London SW 1, Eng. b. 4 July 1896 Plymouth, Eng. MA, Univ. of Cambridge, Eng. PHYSICIAN, Paddington Green Children's Hosp, St. Mary's Hosp. Grp, London W 2; PHYSICIAN, Inst. of Psycho-anal, London. Member: BPS, RMPA, Br. Psychoanal. Socy. Psychotherapy, clinical practice, teaching; psychoanalysis, pedia-trics, child development.   M

WISEMAN, Dr. Stephen. 382 Slade Lane, Manchester 19, Eng. b. 1 Sept 1907 Durham, Eng. PH.D '52 Univ. of Man-chester, Eng. DIRECTOR, Sch. of Educ, Univ. of Manchester. Member: BPS. Ad-ministration, research, teaching; edu-cational measurement and selection, a-chievement and intelligence testing.   M

WOLFF, Bear Berthold. 311 W. 95th St, New York 25, New York, USA. b. 9 Apr 1926 Berlin, Ger. Dipl. Psych. '52 Univ. of London, Eng. STAFF CLIN. PSYCH'T, Neurological Inst, Columbia Presbyterian Med. Cen, Fort Washinton Ave. and W. 168 th St, New York 32, New York, USA. Member: BPS. Testing, clinical practice, research; hypothetico-deductive method in clinical diagnosis, objective behavior tests, group therapy.   M

WOLFF, Dr. Charlotte. 69 Harcourt Terr, London SW 10, Eng. b. 30 Sept 1897 Poland. MD, Univ. of Berlin, Ger. PSYCHO-THERAPIST, priv. prac. Member: BPS. Psychotherapy, research; diagnosis from hand traits, expressive movements.   F

WOOD, Miss Dorothy Kathleen. 5 The Walk, Merthyr Tydfil, Glamorganshire, Wales. b. 24 Apr 1924 Halifax, Eng. BA '45 Univ. of Reading, Eng. EDUC. PSYCH'T, Merthyr Tydfil Educ. Comm, Educ. Dept, Pontmor-lais, Merthyr Tydfil. Member: BPS. Applied and educational psychology, guidance, administration; intelligence testing, remedial reading, secondary school selection.   F

WOODWARD, Dr. Winifred Mary. 62 A Belsize Park Gardens, London NW 3, Eng. b. 25 July 1921 Stamford, Eng. PH.D '56 Univ. of London, Eng. CLIN. PSYCH'T, Fountain Hosp, Tooting Grove, London SW 17. Member: BPS. Testing, research, applied and educational psychology; parent-child relations, delinquency, child develop-ment, mental deficiency.   F

WORSLEY, James Laurence. Psych. Dept, Park Prewett Hosp, Basingstoke, Hants, Eng. b. 17 Oct 1925 Delph, Eng. SR, PSYCH'T, Park Prewett Hosp. Member: BPS. Clinical analysis, research, guidance; intellectual abilites and deterioratiion, personality, treatment in schizophrenia. M

WORTHINGTON, Dennis Bernard. 14 Parrs Wood Ave, Didsbury, Manchester 20, Eng. b. 22 Jan 1927 Manchester, Eng.

MA '54 Univ. of Liverpool, Eng. PSYCHOLO-
GIST, Pub. Hlth. Dept, Town Hall, Oldham,
Eng. Member: BPS. Testing, applied psy-
chology, guidance, lecturing; projective
techniques, intelligence and achievement
tests, training of mental defectives. M
WOTHERSPOON, Miss Jean Russell. 2
Crown Mansions, N. Gardner St, Glasgow
W 1, Scot. b. 14 May 1907 W. Calder, Scot.
ED.B '46 Univ. of Glasgow, Scot. SR. ASST.
PSYCH'T, Child Guid. Serv, Corp. of Glasgow,
Educ. Dept, Glasgow; LECT. in EDUC.
THEORY and PRAC, Stud. Hlth. Visitors,
Univ. of Glasgow. Member: BPS. Teaching,
psychotherapy, testing. F
WRENN, Mrs. Margaret Helen. Flat 2, 47
Netherhall Gardens, London NW 3, Eng.
b. 5 May 1918 Glasgow, Scot. MA '44 Univ.
of Glasgow, Scot. SR. PSYCH'T, Cassel
Hosp, Ham Common, Richmond, Surrey,
Eng. Member: BPS. Clinical testing,
teaching, administration; projective tech-
niques, experimental studies of thinking and
concept function, attitude measurement. F
WRIGHT, Dr. George Gibson Neil. Southfield,
Dunbar, E. Lothian, Scot. b. 31 Aug 1890
Haddington, Scot. D.Litt '33 Univ. of
Edinburgh, Scot. RETIRED. Member: BPS.
Teaching, research, child guidance; psy-
chology and pedagogy of handwriting,
psychological structure of small groups. M
WRIGHT, Hubert. 44 Fairway, Leigh-on-Sea,
Essex, Eng. b. 25 Apr 1915 Bath, Eng.
B.SC '38 Univ. of London, Eng. EDUC.
PSYCH'T, Southend Educ. Comm, Warrior
Sq, Southend-on-Sea, Eng; LECT. in SOC.
and EDUC. PSYCH, Univ. of London, Eng.
Member: BPS. Guidance, testing, education-
al psychology; learning theory, theory of
human abilities, remedial education. M
WRIGLEY, Dr. Jack. 31 Dunlambert Dr,
Belfast, N. Ire. b. 8 Mar 1923 Oldham,
Eng. PH.D '56 Queen's Univ. of Belfast,
N. Ire. LECT. in EDUC, Queen's Univ,
Belfast. Member: BPS. Teaching, re-
search; psychometrics, achievement tests,
factor analysis. M
WYLIE, Miss Margaret Fyfe. Child Guid.
Clin, Nelson Terr, Stockton-on-Tees,
Eng. b. 17 July 1901 Johnstone, Ren-
frewshire, Scot. ED.B '50 Univ. of Glasgow,
Scot. EDUC. PSYCH'T, Comm. for Educ,
Dorecot St, Stockton-on-Tees, Durham,
Scot. Member: BPS. Teaching, testing,
guidance; educational psychology, in-
telligence tests, projective techniques. F
XAVIER, Sister Margaret. Notre Dame R.C.
Trng. Coll, Dowanhill, Glasgow W 2, Scot.
b. 18 Sept 1906 St. Helens, Lancaster, Eng.
PRIN. LECT. of EDUC. SCI, Natl. Comm. for
Trng. of Tchrs, Princes St, Edinburgh, Scot.
Member: BPS. Teaching, testing; a-
chievement and intelligence testing, play

therapy. F
YATES, Alfred. 79 Wimpole St, London W 1,
Eng. b. 17 Nov 1917 Farnworth, Eng.
ED.B '50 Queens Univ. of Belfast, N. Ire.
SR. RES. OFF, Natl. Found. for Educ. Res.
in Eng. and Wales; EDITOR, Bulletin of
National Foundation for Educational Re-
search in England and Wales. Member: BPS.
Research, administration, editorial; child
development, ability and achievement
tests, group process. M
YATES, Dr. Aubrey James. Dept. of Psych,
Inst. of Psychiat, Maudsley Hosp, Den-
mark Hill, London SE 5, Eng. b. 16 Dec
1925 Liverpool, Eng. PH.D '55 Univ. of
London, Eng. LECTURER, Inst. of Psychiat.
Member: BPS. Teaching, research, clinical
analysis; psychomotor function, learning
theory, brain damage. M
YEAXLEE, Basil Alfred. 42 Chalfont Rd,
Oxford, Eng. b. 2 Dec 1883 Southampton,
Eng. PH.D '25 Univ. of London, Eng.
RETIRED; EDITOR, Religion in Education.
Member: BPS. Research, editorial, psycho-
therapy; psychology of religion, educational
psychology. M
YEO, Miss Mary Elizabeth. 27 Goldhurst
Terr, London NW 6, Eng. b. 24 June 1914
London, Eng. Diploma '47 Univ. of
Oxford, Eng. PSYCHOLOGIST, Devon
County Med. Dept, Devon County Counc,
Ivy Bank, St. Davids, Exeter, Eng.
Member: BPS. Psychotherapy, clinical
practice and guidance, testing; physically
handicapped children, residential tech-
niques of treatment. F
YOUNG, Anthony John. Dept. of Psychiat,
27 Blundell St, Leeds 2, Eng. b. 8 Aug
1915 Edinburgh, Scot. ED.B '47 Univ. of
Edinburgh, Scot. SR. PSYCH'T, LECT. in
CLIN. PSYCH, Univ. of Leeds. Member:
BPS. Testing, teaching, psychotherapy;
intelligence testing, diagnostic clinical
testing, projective techniques. M
YOUNG, Miss Margaret. 15 Hillside Rd,
Dundee, Scot. b. 14 Sept 1896 Edinburgh,
Scot. MA '19 Univ. of Edinburgh, Scot.
LECTURER, Dundee Trng. Coll. for Tchrs,
Natl. Comm. for Trng. Tchrs, 140 Prince
St, Edinburgh; ASSISTANT, Dept. of Educ.
Univ. of St. Andrews, Scot. Member: BPS.
Teaching, educational psychology, re-
search; educational guidance. F
ZANGWILL, Prof. Oliver Louis. Psych. Lab,
Downing St, Cambridge, Eng. b. 29 Oct
1913 E. Preston, Eng. MA '39 Univ. of
Cambridge, Eng. PROF. of EXPER. PSYCH,
Univ. of Cambridge; VIS. PSYCH'T, Natl.
Hosp. for Nerv. Diseases, Queen Sq,
London, Eng; ADVIS. ED. BD, Brain;
Quarterly Journal of Experimental Psych;
Journal of Neurology, Neurosurgery and
Psychiatry. Member: BPS, Exper. Psych.

Grp. Teaching, research, administration, clinical analysis; analysis of brain damage in human neurological cases, general experimental psychology. M
ZAUSMER, Dr. David Moses. 9 Oldstead Rd, Bromley, Kent, Eng. b. 28 Dec 1921 London, Eng. DPM '51 Inst. of Psychiat,

London, Eng. MED. DIR, Crayford Child Guid. Clin, Woodside Rd, Barnehurst, Kent. Member: BPS, RMPA. Clinical practice, psychotherapy, research; tics and motor disorders in childhood, electrophysiology, projective techniques. M

URUGUAY

BARANGER, Prof. Madeleine. Asociación Psicoanálitica del Uruguay, Luis de la Torre 919, Montevideo. b. 23 Jan 1920 Aubin, France. Lic. '42 Univ. of Toulouse, France. PSYCHOANAL. and TRNG. DIR, Asociación Psicoanálitica del Uruguay. Member: Argentine Psychoanal. Assn, Uruguayan Psychoanal. Assn, Argentine Assn. of Group Psychother. Psychotherapy, teaching, research; didactic psychoanalysis, group dynamics, psychoanalysis of children, problems of insight. F
BARANGER, Prof. Willy. Asociación Psicoanálitica del Uruguay, Luis de la Torre 919, Montevideo. b. 13 Aug 1922 Bône, Algeria. Agrégation '45 Univ. of Paris, France. PSYCHOANALYST, Asociación Psicoanálitica del Uruguay; ED. COMM, *Revista Uruguaya de Psicoanalisis*. Member Argentine Psychoanal. Assn, Uruguyan Psychoanal. Assn. Psychotherapy, teaching, research; theoretical problems of psychic structure, analysis of ideologies, character. M
CAPITÓN, Dr. Peter de. Br. España 2573 bis, apt. 19, Montevideo. b. 1 Feb 1905 Novocerkassk, Ukraine. PH.D '30 State Univ. of Bulgaria. ASST. MGR, Dept. of Pub. Relat, State Airlines (P.L.U.N.A.), Colonia 1021, Montevideo. Teaching, research, administration; parapsychology. M
CARBONELL DE GROMPONE, Mrs. María Angélica. Obligado 1384, Montevideo. b. 3 Sept 1907 Montevideo. DIRECTOR, Psychopedagogic Lab. "Sabastián Morey Otero," Calle Ciudadela 1393, Montevideo; PROF. of CHILD and EDUC. PSYCH, Inst. de Profesores de Enseñanza Secundaria; EDITOR, *Archivos del Laboratorio de Psicopedagogía Sebastián Morey Otero*. Member: Psych. Socy. of Uruguay. Testing, conculting, teaching; projective techniques, psychology of child development. F
CARRASCO, Prof. Juan Carlos. Millán 2480, Montevideo. b. 26 May 1923 Montevideo. Prof, Fac. of Med, Univ. of Montevideo, Uruguay. PSYCH. TCHR, Fac. of Med, Hosp. de Clinicas, piso 13, Montevideo; PSYCHOLOGIST, Psychiat. Clin, Fac. of Med; PSYCHOLOGIST, Consejo del Niño. Member: Psych. Socy. of Urugay. Testing, clinical analysis, teaching, research; projective

techniques, psychopathology and personality, readjustment of the injured. M
CARVE, Sister María del Divino Corazón. Establecimiento Correccional para Mujeres, Cabildo 1998, Montevideo. b. 11 June 1908 Montevideo. Dr. en Psych. '55 Fac. Libre de Psicología de Montevideo, Uruguay. DIRECTOR, Psychotech. Lab, Establecimiento Correccional para Mujeres. Applied psychology, testing, clinical analysis, psychotherapy; psychological tests, projective techniques. F
DOMÍNGUEZ FERNÁNDEZ, Prof. Miss María Esther. Emilio Raña 2966, Montevideo. b. 26 Dec 1911 Montevideo. Psychologist '47 Fac. Libre de Psicología de Montevideo, Uruguay. PSYCH. TECH, Clínica Psicotécnica, 18 de Julio 1507, Montevideo; DIRECTOR, Facultad Libre de Psicología de Montevideo. Member: IUSP. Guidance, clinical analysis, teaching, psychotherapy; functional interpretation of tests, child psychology, projective techniques. F
FAÍLDE NOGUÉS, Prof. Enrique. Reconquista 473, Montevideo. b. 1 July 1896 Sarandí del Yi. Psychologist '53 Fac. Libre de Psicología de Montevideo, Uruguay. CHIEF, Psychotech. Lab, Inst. of Criminol, Penal Institutes, Ellauri 306, Montevideo. Member: Latin Amer. Coordinating Comm. on Psych, Psych. Socy. of Uruguay. Consulting, guidance, testing, teaching educational psychology and psychotechnics; projective techniques, achievement tests, attitude measurement. M
FERNÁNDEZ, Dr. Célica Perdomo de. 21 de Setiembre 3043, Montevideo. b. 18 Mar 1916 Canelones. MD '44 Univ. of Montevideo, Uruguay. CHIEF PHYSICIAN, Dispensario Central Antituberculoso, Durazno 1242, Montevideo. Clinical practice, psychotherapy, administration; social readjustment, vocational guidance, projective techniques. F
HERNÁNDEZ PENELA, Miss Carmen. Canelones 1012, apt. 1, Montevideo. b. 16 Oct 1928 Montevideo. '55 Univ. of Birmingham, Eng. TCHR. of REMEDIAL EDUC, Natl. Counc. of Primary Educ, Soriano 1658, Montevideo; PSYCHOLOGIST, Consejo del Niño, 25 de Mayo 520, Montevideo, Member: Assn. for Psychopedagogic

Studies. Remedial teaching, education of mental defectives, testing, clinical psychology; behavior problems of children, juvenile delinquency, projective techniques.   F
LORENZO, María Eloisa García de. Buschental 3347, Montevideo. b. 8 July 1923 Montevideo. MA '47 Univ. of Michigan, USA. PRINCIPAL, Escuela de Recuperación Psíquica, 19 de Abril 1130, Montevideo; PROF. of EDUC. PSYCH, Teacher's College. Member: APA, Psych. Socy. of Uruguay. Teaching, guidance and training of personnel, educational research, testing; achievement tests, learning theory, group process.   F
LOUZÁN, Prof. Magda. Brito del Pino 1423, Montevideo. b. Montevideo. Catedrática, Inst. Normal de Montevideo, Uruguay. PROF. of CHILD PSYCH, Inst. Normales, Cuarein 1381, Montevideo; PROF. of ADOLESCENT PSYCH, Inst. de Profesores "Artigas," Sarandí 420, Montevideo; DIRECTOR, "Jean Piaget" Clinic, Duvinioso Terra 1657, Montevideo. Teaching child psychology and testing methods, research; intelligence and achievement tests, psychology of adolescence.   F
MOLNOS, Dr. Angela. Inst. de Profesores, Calle Sarandí 420 Montevideo. b. 2 July 1923 Budapest, Hungary. PH.D '47 Univ. of Genoa, Italy. LECT. in GENL. PSYCH,

Inst. de Profesores. Teaching, research, student; general psychology, characterology.   F
NIETO GROVE, Miss Marta. Cololó 2865, Montevideo. b. 19 Nov 1922 Montevideo. BA '40 Univ. of Montevideo, Uruguay. PSYCHOTECHNICIAN, Clinica Médico-Psicologica, Hospital "Pedro Visca," Gonzalo Ramirez 1926, Montevideo. Member: APA. Consulting, clinical practice, testing, teaching.   F
PASEYRO, Prof. Marina. Francisco Muñoz 3223, apt. 2, Montevideo. b. 11 Oct 1911 Rivera. Maestra Normalista '31 Inst. Normales, Uruguay. PRIMARY SCH. TEACHER, Escuela de Segundo Grado No. 77, Ave. San Martin 2211, Montevideo. Teaching, educational psychology, testing; achievement tests, projective techniques, social readjustment.   F
PEREIRA ANAVITARTE, Prof. Juan. San José 825, apt. 11, Montevideo. b. 17 Apr 1927 Montevideo. Bachelor, Univ. of Montevideo, Uruguay. PSYCHOANALYST, Maciel Hospital, Montevideo; PROF. of PSYCH, Inst. Normal, Montevideo; ED. COMM, Revista Uruguaya de Psicoanálisis. Member: AIPA, Uruguayan Psychoanal. Assn, São Paulo Psych. Socy. Research, psychotherapy, testing, clinical analysis, teaching; group psychotherapy, psychology of the unconscious.   M

VENEZUELA

ATENCIO R., Prof. Luis Alberto. Escuela Normal Rural Interamericana (ENRI), Rubio, Táchira. b. 10 Apr 1926 Maracaibo. Lic. '52 Univ. of Chile. PROF. of PSYCH. and HEAD, Dept. of Psychopedagogy, ENRI. Member: Chilean Assn. of Psych'ts. Teaching, educational psychology, testing; projective techniques, social perception. M
BERBIN, Miss Lesbia Josefina. Ave. América, Quinta "Por Fin", Los Rosales, Caracas. b. 16 June 1930 La Asunción. MA '55 Univ. of Michigan, USA. CHIEF PSYCH'T, Children's Clinic of Ment. Hyg, Venezuelan League of Ment. Hyg, Ave. Los Jabillos 20, La Florida Caracas. Clinical analysis, child psychotherapy, guidance; standardization of tests for Venezuela, projective techniques, group process.   F
BOULGER, John R. Apartado 246, Caracas. b. 21 June 1919 St. Paul, Minnesota, USA. PH.D '52 Univ. of Minnesota, USA. TRNG. ADMIN, Socony Mobil Oil of Venezuela, Salas a Caja de Agua, Caracas; CONSULTANT, Venezuelan Inst. of Neur. and Cerebral Res. Member: APA, IRRA, SIP, Natl. Vocat. Guid. Assn. Administration and evaluation of training programs, industrial psychology,

testing; personnel research, employee morale and attitude surveys, psychological tests and measurements.   M
BRACHFELD, Prof. Dr. Francis Oliver. Inst. of Psychosynthesis and Human Relations, Apartado 2192, Caracas. b. 18 Feb 1908 Budapest, Hungary. PH.D '30 Univ. of Budapest, Hungary. DIRECTOR, Inst. of Psychosynthesis and Human Relat; EDITOR in CHIEF, Universitas Emeritensis; ED. BD, Psyché, Acta Psychotherapeutica, Psychosomatica and Orthopaedagogica. Member: SIP, Int. Assn. for Indiv. Psych, Inst. de Sociologie Economique et de Psychologie des Peuples (Le Havre). Professional writing, research, teaching; measurement of international attitudes, social tensions, Latin American character, Adlerian psychology.   M
COOK, Dr. David W. Creole Petroleum Corp, Apartado 889, Caracas. b. 11 Oct 1904 Yarmouth, Nova Scotia, Canada. PH.D '35 New York Univ, USA. CHIEF, Indus. Psych. Sect, Creole Petroleum Corp. Member: APA. Administration, research, industrial psychology; aptitude and achievement tests, rating techniques.   M

DEMBO, Mrs. Miriam. Ave. Bucare, Qta. „Ida," La Florida, Caracas. b. 19 May 1927 Bendzin, Poland. BA '49 Bard College, USA. ASST. INDUS. PSYCH'T, Socony Mobil de Venezuela, Salas a Caja de Agua 69, Caracas. Member: Venezuelan Psych. Assn. Applied psychology, administering and analyzing tests, research; aptitude tests, attitude measurement, child psychology, vocational guidance.   F

GIMÉNEZ PÉREZ, Tulio. Sur 21, No. 9, Los Caobos, Caracas. b. 15 Dec 1928 Quíbor. Psychologist '54 Univ. of Chile. PSYCHOLOGIST, Physical Med. and Rehabilitation Center, Venezuelan Inst. of Social Security, Edif. Sur, Centro Bolivar, Off. 410, Caracas. Member: Chilian Assn. of Psych'ts. Guidance, clinical analysis, psychotherapy; attitude measurement, achievement tests, projective techniques, human relations and personnel evaluation.   M

KARLOWSKI, Dr. T. C. Creole Petroleum Corp, Apartado 889, Caracas. b. 16 Jan 1917 Sylvan Grove, Kansas, USA. PH.D '48 Ohio State Univ, USA. SUPERVISOR, Personnel Dept, Creole Petroleum Corp. Membei: APA. Applied psychology, personnel research, administration; industrial testing, attitude measurement.   M

LÁREZ, Prof. Belarmino A. Apartado 6074, Caracas. b. 23 Feb 1922 La Asunción. Bachellor '50 Liceo "Juan Vicente Gonzáles", Venezuela. PRINCIPAL, Inst. of Psych. and Psychotechnics, Fac. of Humanities, Univ. Central, Caracas; PRINCIPAL, Interamer.

Educ. Inst. Teaching, research, student; projective techniques, attitude measurement, achievement tests.   M

MORETTI GARANTÓN, Dr. Juan Baustista. Creole Petroleum Corp, Apartado 889, Caracas. b. 23 June 1922 Caicara de Maturín. MS '49 Purdue Univ, USA. PLACEMENT SUPERV, Dept. of Indus. Relat, Creole Petroleum Corp; PROF. of PSYCH, Sch. of Sociol, Fac. of Econ, Central Univ. of Venezuela. Member: APA, Socy. for Appl. Anthrop. (USA). Industrial, educational, and applied psychology, personnel selection; social psychological approach to education and industry.   M

OLMO, B., Francisco del. Creole Petroleum Corp, Apartado 889, Caracas. b. 13 Mar 1907 Barcelona, Spain. Lic. en Droit '33 Univ. of Zaragoza, Spain. ASST. SUPERV, Indus. Psych. Sect, Creole Petroleum Corp. Member: APA, AIPA, Psychometric Socy. Personnel selection and guidance, research in industrial psychology, test development; aptitude and intelligence tests, psychometry.   M

TROMPIZ, Prof. Gabriel. Apartado Este 4319, Caracas. b. 7 Mar 1907, Coro. MD; Prof. of Internal Med, Central Univ. of Venezuela. PROFESSOR, Fac. of Med, Central Univ. of Venezuela, Los Caobos, Ave. Valparaiso "Los Gabrieles," Caracas; PHYSICIAN, Inst. of Internal Med, Caracas; ED. DIR, Revista de la Facultad de Medicina. Member: SIP. Teaching, psychotherapy, clinical analysis; study of neurosis, psychosomatic medicine.   M

YUGOSLAVIA

AGAPOFF, Prof. Maxime. Baba Višnjina 17/III, Belgrade IV. b. 3 Feb 1890 Moscow, USSR. Diplôme '14 Univ. of Moscow, USSR. LECT. in RUSSIAN LANGUAGE, Fac. of Natural Sci. and Math, Belgrade; PSYCHOLOGIST, priv. prac. Member: YPA. Teaching, testing, educational psychology; development of mental functions, characterology, psychometrics.   M

AHTIK, Vitomir. Livarska 6, Ljubljana. b. 5 May 1926 Celje. Dipl. Psych. '54 Univ. of Ljubljana, Yugo. RES. ASST, Zavod za proučevanje organizacije dela in varnosti pri delu L.R.S, Parmova 33/2, Ljubljana. Member: YPA. Applied and industrial psychology, testing, research; aptitude testing, factor analysis, vacational guidance, interviewing.   M

AHTIK-KNEZ, Mrs. Desanka. Livarska 6, Ljubljana. b. 5 Mar 1927 Ljubljana. Dipl. Psych. '54 Univ. of Ljubljana, Yugo. PSYCHOLOGIST, Zavod za proučevanje organizacije dela L.R.S. Parmova 33/2,

Ljubljana. Member: YPA. Industrial psychology, testing, consulting; advertising, infant behavior.   F

ARNAUTOVIĆ, Prof. Štefanija. Krajiška 13/I, Zagreb, N.R. Hrvatska. b. 1 Aug 1904 Donji Miholjac, N.R. Hrvatska. Diplôme '48 Univ. of Zagreb, Yugo. PROFESSOR, Viša Pedagogška Škola, Savska Cesta 77/III Zagreb. Teaching; mentally deficient children, education of deaf-mutes.   F

BAJIĆ, Prof. Dr. Baja. Dr. Kestera 17, Belgrade. b. 24 Dec 1896 Zagreb. Docteur ès lettres '28 Sorbonne, Fr. PROFESSOR, Fac. of Philos, Studentski Trg. 1, Belgrade. Member: YPA. Teaching, student, professional writing; methodology, perception, imagination.   M

BERGER, Josip I. Kosmajska 19, Belgrade. b. 15 June 1929 Novi Sad. Diplôme, Univ. of Belgrade, Yugo. CLIN. PSYCH'T, Neuropsychiat. Clin. of Med. Fac, Univ. of Belgrade. Member: YPA. Testing, clinical analysis, research, consulting; projective

techniques, intelligence tests, pathology of behavior. M
BERTONCELJ, Ivan. Zupančičeva 2, Ljubljana. b. 7 Apr 1914 Ljubljana. Diplôme '52 Univ. of Ljubljana, Yugo. HEAD, Psych. Dept, Zavod za proučevanje organizacije dela in varnosti pri delu LRS, Parmova 33/2, Ljubljana. Member: YPA. Teaching, administration, industrial psychology; training of industrial supervisors, industrial schools, human relations. M
BREGANT, Leopold. Črevljarska ulica 1, Ljubljana. b. 6 Nov 1926 Maribor. MA '54 Univ. of Ljubljana, Yugo. CLIN. PSYCH'T, Psychiat. Hosp, Polje, Ljubljana. Member: YPA. Consulting, testing, clinical analysis, psychotherapy; counseling, projective techniques, criminal psychology. M
BUJAS, Prof. Ramiro. Psych. Inst, Marulićev trg 19, Zagreb. b. 23 Aug 1879 Budva. PH.D '06 Univ. of Graz, Austria. EMER. PROF, Psych. Inst, Univ. of Zagreb; DIR. of PUBLICATION, Acta Instituti psychologici Universitatis zagrebiensis; COOPERATING ED, The Psychological Register. Member: YPA, SFP. Research, editorial, lecturing; contrast phenomena, attention, suggestion theory, sensory perception, concomitant phenomena. M
CAR-GAVRILOVIĆ, Mrs. Ivana. Ribnjak 20 c, Zagreb. b. 23 May 1914 Jastrebarsko. Diplôme, Univ. of Zagreb, Yugo. EDUC. PSYCH'T, 14th Lycee Experimentale,Dobojska b.b, Zagreb. Member: YPA. Educational psychology, consulting, guidance, teaching; achievement tests, educational guidance, problems of grading students. F
CUCULOVIĆ, Mrs. Katarina. Njegoševa 63, Belgrade. b. 22 Feb 1920 Štip. Diplôme '47 Univ. of Belgrade, Yugo. PSYCHOLOGIST, Vocat. Guid. Cen, Zmaja od Noćaja 12, Belgrade. Member: YPA. Personnel psychology, testing, consulting, vocational guidance; attitude measurement, achievement tests, social perception. F
DJORDJEVIĆ, Mrs. Bosiljka. Stanoja Glavaša 34, Belgrade. b. 11 Jan 1922 Banja Luka. Diplôme '49 Univ. of Belgrade, Yugo. SCHOOL PSYCH'T, Dept. of Natl. Educ. for Belgrade, Sremska 6, Belgrade. Member: YPA. Educational psychology, testing, educational inspection of schools; social perception, achievement tests, attitude measurement. F
DJORDJEVIĆ, Ducan. Prizrenska 15/I, Belgrade. b. 27 Feb 1928 Belgrade. Dipl. Psych. '53 Univ. of Belgrade, Yugo. PSYCHOLOGIST, Vasa Stajic, Home for Juv. Delinquents, Tvornička 1, Zemun. Member: YPA. Applied and educational psychology, teaching, research, social work; psychology of delinquents, psychotherapy, clinical psychology. M

DOBRINAC-SUSMEL, Jelka. 3 Ljubljanska, Zagreb. b. 1 Aug 1914 Rijeka. Diplôme '45 Univ. of Zagreb, Yugo. TEACHER, Commercial Sch, 77 Savska, Zagreb. Member: YPA. Teaching English; intelligence. F
GODLER, Mrs. Ljubica. Prilaz JNA 25, Zagreb. b. 16 Apr 1897 Tovarnik. Diplôme '36 Univ. of Zagreb, Yugo. Research, educational psychology, professional writing, retired; child development, study of children's toys. F
GOJKOVIĆ, Prof. Nadežda. ul. Narodnih heroja 5/II, Novi Sad. b. 3 Sept 1925 Paraćin. Diplôme '51 Univ. of Belgrade, Yugo. CLIN. PSYCH'T, Med. and Pedagogical Inst, Poštanska 3, Novi Sad. Member: YPA. Administration, applied psychology, testing; learning, achievement tests, social perception. M
HUDINA-POTUŠEK, Prof. Ela. Medvešćak 13, Zagreb. b. 12 Jan 1924 Sarajevo. Diplôme '50 Univ. of Zagreb, Yugo. CHILD PSYCH'T, Savjetovalište za majku i dijete Dom Narodnog Zdravlja Trešnjevka, Nehajska 15, Zagreb. Member: YPA. Testing, guidance, applied and educational psychology; achievement tests. F
IVANČEVIĆ, Milivoj. Sime Šolaje 41, Belgrade. b. 6 Oct 1910 Stara Pazova. Diplôme '36 Univ. of Belgrade, Yugo. PSYCHOLOGIST, Vocat. Guid. Cen, Zmaja od Noćaja 12, Belgrade. Member: YPA. Personnel psychology, testing, consulting, vocational guidance; attitude measurement, achievement tests, social perception. F
JEVTIĆ, Prof. Dr. med. Dušan. Kursulina 2, Belgrade. b. 18 Sept 1899 Belgrade. Dr. med. habil; Diplôme '28 Univ. of Belgrade, Yugo. PROFESSOR, Juristische Fakultät, Pravni fakultet, Bulevar Revolucije br. 67, Belgrade. Member: YPA, Socy. of Criminology, Paris. Teaching, professional writing; criminal psychology, criminal psychopathology. M
JOVANOVIĆ, Prof. Svetislav. Med. and Pedagogical Inst, Poštanska 3, Novi Sad. b. 6 June 1930 Svetozarevo. Diplôme, Univ. of Belgrade, Yugo. PSYCHOLOGIST, Med. and Pedagogical Inst. Member: YPA. Testing; achievement tests. M
JOVIČIĆ, Miloc. Hadži-Ruvimova 7, Belgrade. b. 19 Aug 1914 Bošnjane. Diplôme '39 Univ. of Belgrade, Yugo. RES. ASSOC. DIR, Inst. for Educ. Res. of Peoples' Republic of Serbia, Knez Mihailova 35/IV, Belgrade. Member: YPA, Yugo. Assn. for Profes. Orientation. Administration, research, teaching; children's thinking, achievement tests. M
JURAS, Prof. Zvonko. Kozarska Poljana Br. 1. stan 21, Zagreb. b. 12 Aug 1924 Čakovec. Diplôme '52 Univ. of Zagreb, Yugo.

PSYCH'T. for the DEAF, Zavod za Odgoj Gluhonijeme Djece, Ilica 83, Zagreb. Member: YPA. Applied and educational psychology, testing, consulting, parental guidance; intelligence testing and auditory training, audiometric testing. M

KAJFEŠ, Prof. Jelena. Cvjetno Naselje 6, Zagreb III. b. 17 Sept 1907 Zagreb. Diplôme '30 Univ. of Zagreb, Yugo. DIRECTOR, Vocat. Guid. Cen, Socijalističke Revolucije 15/III, Zagreb. Member: YPA. Applied psychology, testing, vocational guidance; attitude measurement, a-chievement tests, educational guidance. F

KANONI, Prof. Dr. Janez John. Studenec 23, Ljubljana-Polje. b. 24 Feb 1904 Vordern-berg-Leoben, Austria. MD '29 Univ. of Zagreb, Yugo. DIRECTOR, Psychiat. Clin, Med. Fac, Univ. of Ljubljana. Member: YPA. Teaching, research, administration, psychotherapy; criminology, psychopa-thology, forensic psychiatry. M

KOGEJ, Pavle. Dolnji Logatec, Slovenia. b. 10 Sept 1927 Mokronog. Dipl. Psych. '55 Univ. of Ljubljana, Yugo. VOCAT. COUNS, Vocat. Guid. Serv, OLO Nova Gorica, Nova Gorica. Member: YPA. Testing, personnel psychology, guidance; test construction, industrial supervision, job analysis, sexology. M

KOLBIČ-BAHOVEC, Prof. Dr. Mrs. Ana. Metelkova 3, Ljubljana. b. 16 May 1910 Ljubljana. PH.D '44 Univ. of Graz, Austria. Member: YPA. Child psychology, research, testing; psychology of art, child's creative art, personality. F

KOPAJTIĆ, Mrs. Neda. Gjorgjićeva 11/II, Zagreb. b. 7 Dec 1926 Zagreb. BA '49 Univ. of Zagreb, Yugo. PSYCHOLOGIST, Savjetovalište za odgoj djece i omladine, Kukuljevićeva 19, Zagreb. Member: YPA. Applied psychology, testing, clinical ana-lysis, guidance; causes, diagnosis and guidance of mental deficient persons. F

KOPAJTIĆ, Nikola Josip. Gjorgjićeva 11/II, Zagreb. b. 28 Sept 1926 Krasica. BA '50 Univ. of Zagreb, Yugo. VOCAT. COUNS, Vocat. Guid. Cen, Ulica Socijalističke Revolucije 15, Zagreb. Member: YPA. Research, applied psychology, guidance; aptitude test construction and use, tests and measurements in physical education. M

KOVAČEVIĆ, Prof. Vojislav. Antunovac 7, Zagreb. b. 18 Jan 1924 Stari Grad. Prof. '49 Univ. of Zagreb, Yugo. PSYCHOLOGIST, Reception Cen. for Juv. Delinquents, Prilar J.N.A. 9, Zagreb. Member: YPA. Testing, guidance, applied psychology; juvenile delinquency, achievement tests, projective techniques. M

KRAMAR, Miss Meta. Pražakova 11, Ljublja-na. b. 13 June 1931 Ljubljana. ASSISTANT, Sch. for Soc. Work, Župančičeva 6,

Ljubljana. Student, teaching, counseling; human relations, diagnostics, interviewing. F

KRKOVIĆ, Andjelko. Psych. Inst, Univ. of Zagreb, Marulićev Trg 19, Zagreb. b. 21 Nov 1931 Osijek. Diplôme '55 Univ. of Zagreb, Yugo. ASST. in PSYCH, Psych. Inst, Univ. of Zagreb. Member: YPA. Research, teaching, applied psychology; sensory mechanisms, fatigue, electro-dermal reaction. M

KUČERA, Dr. phil. Elsa. Mallinova 27, Zagreb. b. 22 Oct 1883 Vinkovci. PH.D '09 Univ. of Zurich, Switz. LIBRARIAN, Retired. Member: YPA, DGP. Research, editorial; psychology of emotion and will. F

LAZIĆ, Mrs. Branka. Psych. Inst, Marulićev trg 19, Zagreb. b. 4 Aug 1908 Otočac. BA '31 Univ. of Zagreb, Yugo. LECTURER, Psych. Inst, Univ. of Zagreb. Member: YPA. Teaching, research, student; socio-metric techniques. F

LESJAK, Vladimir. Šenoina 3, Zagreb. b. 11 May 1914 Zagreb. Diplôme '41 Univ. of Zagreb, Yugo. PSYCHODIAGNOSTICIAN, Vocat. Guid. Cen, Ul. Socijal Revolucije 15, Zagreb. Member: YPA. Psychodiagnosis, guidance, professional writing; attention research, psychodiagnostic methods applied to psychomotor activity and thinking. M

MIJUĆA, Prof. Nebojša. 80/II. Palmotićeva. b. 3 Mar 1915 Vršac-Dupljaja. Diplôme, Univ. of Zagreb, Yugo. CLIN. PSYCH'T, Hosp. for Ment. and Nerv. Pathology, Zagreb-Vrapče. Member: YPA. Testing, psycho-diagnostics, clinical analysis, con-sulting, teaching; emotions, projective techniques, sexual psychopathology. M

MIKAČIĆ-BUSIJA, Zlata. Heinzelova 11, Zagreb. b. 7 Mar 1911 Ivanec, Hrvatska. Diplôme '35 Univ. of Zagreb, Yugo. Retired. F

MILA, Mrs. Ilic. Svetozara Markovica 60, Belgrade. b. 25 Feb 1928 Bajina Basta. Diplôme '53 Univ. of Belgrade, Yugo. CHILD PSYCH'T, Child Guid. Clin, Prole-terskih brigada 57, Belgrade. Member: YPA, Serbian Ment. Hyg. Socys. Testing, educational psychology, psychotherapy, guidance; play therapy, group process, achievement tests. F

MILETIĆ, Miss Ljubica. Obilićev Venac 13/IV, Belgrade. b. 16 May 1927 Čačak. Diplôme '54 Univ. of Zagreb, Yugo. PSYCHOLOGIST, Vasa Stajić, Home for Juv. Delinquents, Tvornička, 1, Zemun. Member: YPA. Applied and educational psychology, guidance, testing, research; vocational guidance of juvenile delinquents, attitude measurement, causes of delin-quency. F

MITROVIĆ, Mrs. Melita. Tkalčićeva 44, Zagreb. b. 19 July 1921 Zagreb. Diplôme '49 Univ. of Zagreb, Yugo. PHONETIST,

Orl Clinic, Šalata, Zagreb. Member: YPA. Psychotherapy, testing, guidance, speech therapy; projective techniques, child psychotherapy, testing. F

MOLL, Josip. Miramarska 26, Zagreb. b. 20 Mar 1927 Zagreb. BA '53 Univ. of Zagreb, Yugo. PSYCHOLOGIST, Savjetovalište zaodgoj djecei omladine, Kukvljeviceva 19, Zagreb. Member: YPA. Diagnostic testing of mental deficiency and deafness, applied psychology, guidance; achievement tests, interest measurement, emotional expression. M

MUHEK, Prof. Šimunec Jelena. Trg Maršala Tita 9, Zagreb. b. 21 Nov 1915 Marija Bistrica. Diplôme '46 Univ. of Zagreb, Yugo. CLIN. PSYCH'T, Hosp. Dr. M. Stojanovic, Neuropsychiat. Dept, Vinogradska 29, Zagreb. Member: YPA. Testing, teaching; achievement tests, attitude measurement, projective techniques. M

NEUMAN, Zdravko. Lončarska 10, Ljubljana. b. 6 Sept 1924 Jesenice. Dipl. Psych. '52 Univ. of Ljubljana, Yugo. VOCAT. GUID. COUNS, Zavod za Proučevanje organizacije dela in varnosti pri delu L.R.S., Parmova 33/2, Ljubljana. Member: YPA. Testing, consulting, guidance, personnel psychology; aptitude tests, statistics, interviewing. M

NOVOSEL, Mrs. Maria. Vlaska 75/8, Zagreb. b. 6 July 1928 Zagreb. Diploma '52 Univ. of Zagreb, Yugo. ASST. INDUS. PSYCH'T, Central Inst. for Hyg, Mirogojska Cesta 4, Zagreb. Member: YPA. Industrial psychology, research, testing; group process, accident proneness, human relations in industry. F

OSTOIĆ, Mrs. Neda. Jurjevska 63a, Zagreb. b. 7 Aug 1930 Zagreb. Diploma '55 Univ. of Zagreb, Yugo. HEAD, Programme Off, Radio Zagreb, Jurisiceva 4, Zagreb. Member: YPA. Audience research and program analysis, applied psychology, testing; attitude measurement, social perception and group process, clinical analysis. F

PEČJAK, Vid. Staničeva 37, Ljubljana. b. 7 Jan 1929 Ljubljana. Diplôme '56 Univ. of Ljubljana, Yugo. PSYCHOLOGIST, Prehodni mladinski dom, Kodeljevo, Ljubljana. Member: YPA. Testing, child guidance, applied psychology; personality measurement, case study, projective techniques, mental hygiene. M

PETROVIĆ, Miss Milica. Kosovska 11, Belgrade. b. 15 Jan 1920 Arilje. Diplôme '51 Univ. of Belgrade, Yugo. CLIN. PSYCH'T, Univ. Neuropsychiat. Clin, Pasterova 14, Belgrade. Member: YPA, Assn. for Ment. Hyg, Yugo. Med. Assn. Testing, clinical analysis, consulting, research; achievement tests, projective techniques, delinquency and neuroses. F

PETROVITCH, Vladimir. Gospodar Jovanova 6, Belgrade. b. 17 June 1919 Belgrade. Diplôme '53 Univ. of Belgrade, Yugo. CHILD PSYCH'T, Child Guid. Clin, Proleterskih brigada 57, Belgrade. Member: YPA. Serbian Socy. for Ment. Hyg. Testing, educational psychology, psychotherapy, guidance; group process, achievement tests, projective techniques. M

PETZ, Dr. Boris. Mose Pijade 158, Zagreb, Yugoslavia. b. 26 Nov 1919 Bjelovar, Yugo. PH.D '45 Yugo. PSYCHOLOGIST Inst. for Med. Res, Mose Pijade 158, Zagreb. Member: AIPA. Teaching, applied, research, accidents and absences in industry measurement of fatigue; human relations. M

POPOVIĆ, Prof. Dr. Slobodan. Vele Nigrinove 11, Belgrade. b. 12 Jan 1896 Kruševac. PH.D '33 Univ. of Belgrade, Yugo. PROF. of EDUC, Fac. of Philos, Univ. of Belgrade, Studentski trg, Belgrade. Member: YPA. Teaching, research, educational psychology; introspection, adolescent psychology, psychology of literary creativeness. M

RAKIĆ, Prof. Branko. Skerlićeva 24, Belgrade. b. 22 April 1912 Sarajevo. CONSULT. PSYCH'T, Inst. for Health Educ, Skerlićeva 24, Belgrade. Member: YPA. Applied psychology, research, teaching; group process, attitude measurement, projective techniques. M

ROT, Nikola. Kralja Milutina 23, Belgrade. b. 10 June 1910 Osijek. Diplôme, Univ. of Zagreb, Yugo. INSTR. in PSYCH, Psych. Inst, Fac. of Letters, Knez Mihajlova 40, Belgrade. Member: YPA. Teaching, research; social perception, attitude measurement, psychology of thought. M

ROTER, Mihajlo. Palmoticeva 24/III, Belgrade. b. 29 Jan 1919 Dubrovnik. Diplôme '51 Univ. of Belgrade, Yugo. ASST. LECT, Fac. of Philos, Stud. trg I, Belgrade; LECTURER, State Inst. of Physical Culture, Belgrade. Member: YPA. Teaching, applied psychology, professional writing; motivation, frustration and conflict, sexual behavior. M

ŠEBEK, Dipl. Psych. Levin. Vrtača 10, Ljubljana. b. 12 June 1922 Maribor. Dipl. Psych. '54 Univ. of Ljubljana, Yugo. ASSISTANT, Univ. Psych. Inst, Parmova 33, Ljubljana. Member: YPA. Student, teaching, research, psychodiagnostics; social perception, aptitude testing, group process. M

SMILJANIĆ-ČOLENOVIĆ, Vera. Kralja Milutina 7, Belgrade. b. 25 Feb 1923 Čibutkovica. BA '50 Univ. of Belgrade, Yugo. ASST. and CONDUCTOR of PRACTICUM, Inst. of Psych, Fac. of Philos, Knez Mihajlova 40/II, Belgrade. Member: YPA. Teaching, research; sociometry, projective techniques, measurement of individual

differences. F
SMOLIĆ-KRKOVIĆ, Dr. Nada. Psych. Inst, Marulićev Trg 19, Zagreb. b. 17 June 1923 Vinkovci. PH.D '53 Univ. of Zagreb, Yugo. PSYCH. ASST, Psych. Inst, Univ. of Zagreb. Member: YPA. Research, teaching, applied psychology; sensory mechanisms, interest measurement, methods of learning. F
SOROKIN, Boris. Grahorova ul. 16/II, Zagreb. b. 25 July 1927 Zagreb. Dipl. Psych. '55 Univ. of Zagreb, Yugo. Member: YPA. Psychodiagnostic methods, statistical and factorial analysis of tests, personnel selection, psychological development. M
STEVANOVIĆ, Prof. Dr. P. Borislav. Kneza Miloša 6, Belgrade. b. 12 Feb 1891 Aleksinac. PH.D '26 London Univ, Eng; Diplôme '19 Univ. of Belgrade, Yugo. PROF. and HEAD, Psych. Dept. and Inst. of Psych, Fac. of Philos, Univ. of Belgrade, Knez Mihaila 40, Belgrade. Member: YPA, AIPA. Teaching, research, administration, professional writing; learning and thinking, mental testing, influence of socio-cultural change on mentality. M
SUPEK, Dr. Rudi. Psych. Inst, Fac. of Letters, Marulicev trg 19, Zagreb. b. 8 Apr 1913 Zagreb. Agrégé, Univ. of Zagreb, Yugo. PROF. AGRÉGÉ and DOCENT, Psych. Inst, Univ. of Zagreb; PSYCH. TCHR, Académie des arts dramatiques, Zagreb. Member: YPA. Teaching, research, testing; attitude measurement, imagination, psychology of cultural values and aesthetics. M
TERSTENJAK, Prof. Dr. Anton. Resljeva 7, Ljubljana. b. 8 Jan 1906 Radgona. PH.D '29 Univ. of Innsbruck, Austria. PROFESSOR, Fac. of Theology, Poljanska 4, Ljubljana. Member: AIPA. Research, teaching, applied psychology; visual and time perception, feelings and emotions, human relations. M
TOLIČIĆ, Dipl. Psych. Ivan. Psych. Inst, Parmova 33, Ljubljana. b. 17 Dec 1922 Starše. Dipl. Psych. '52 Univ. of Ljubljana, Yugo. ASSISTANT, Psych. Inst, Univ. of Ljubljana. Member: YPA. Teaching, research, educational psychology; achievement tests, child play and development. M
TOMEKOVIĆ, Tomislav Antuna. Sekspirova 31, Belgrade. b. 8 Dec 1909 Špišić-Bukovica

Dist. Virovitica. MA '34 Univ. of Edinburgh, Scot. SECONDARY SCH. TCHR, X Beogradska Gimnazije, Belgrade. Member: YPA. Teaching, educational and industrial psychology; relation between intelligence and school success, workers' attitude towards technical change. M
VIDAČEK, Mrs. Branka. Trg Žrtava fašizma 15, Zagreb. b. 25 Nov 1928 Križevci. BA, Univ. of Zagreb, Yugo. PSYCHOLOGIST, Savjetovalište za odgoj djece i omladine, Kukuljevićeva 19, Zagreb. Member: YPA. Testing, clinical analysis, applied and educational psychology, guidance; diagnosis and causes of mental deficiency, juvenile delinquency. F
VUČIĆ, Miss Lidija. Lepenička, 2, Voždovac, Belgrade. b. 14 Jan 1932 Belgrade. Dipl. Psych. '55 Univ. of Belgrade, Yugo. ASST. in APPL. PSYCH, Psych. Inst, Fac. of Philos, Univ. of Belgrade, Knez Mihajlova 40/II, Belgrade. Member: YPA. Applied and educational psychology, teaching, testing; mental tests, individual adjustment, children and films. F
VUČIĆ, Dr. Mrs. Marija. Lepenička 2, Voždovac, Belgrade. b. 25 Dec 1891 Zagreb. Dr. '24 Univ. of Zagreb, Yugo. DIR. and PSYCH'T, Psych. and Educ. Guid. Clin, Jove Ilića 150, Voždovac, Belgrade. Member: YPA. Retired, consulting, editorial; family influences on child evolution, influence of emotions on pregnancy, interpersonal relations, psychosomatics. F
VUKANOVIĆ, Prof. Radmila. Vojvode Babunskof 7 paviljon 6, Belgrade. b. 23 Mar 1930 Odžaci. Diplôme '54 Univ. of Belgrade, Yugo. PSYCHOLOGIST, Psych. and Educ. Guid. Clin, Jove Ilića 150, Belgrade. Member: YPA. Applied and educational psychology, testing, clinical analysis; achievement tests, social perception. F
ZAJEC, Mrs. Marija. Riharjeva 8, Ljubljana. b. 14 July 1914 Zagorje ob Savi. Dipl. Psych. '54 Univ. of Ljubljana, Yugo. VOCAT. GUID. COUNS, Zavod za Proučevanje Orfanizacije dela in varnosti pri delu LRS, Parmova 33/2, Ljubljana. Member: YPA. Guidance. testing, personnel psychology; interviewing, aptitude and developmental testing. F

ADDENDA

COSTA RICA

ADIS-CASTRO, Dr. Gonzalo. Departamento de Bienestar y Orientacion, Univ. of Costa Rica, San José. b. 28 Dec 1927 Guatemala. PH.D '57 Univ. of Calif, USA. CHIEF COUNSEL. SERV, Univ. of Costa Rica, CHIEF CLIN. PSYCHOL. Neuro-Psychiatric Hospital, San José. Clinical practice, research, psychotherapy; test construction, learning theory, psychotherapy.   M

HUNGARY

TOTH, Dr. Bela. Verpeleti-ut 4-6, Budapest 11, Hungary. b. 16 Oct 1913 Hungary. PH.D '39 Univ. of Szeged, Hungary. PROF., Teachers' Coll, Kiss Janos altb. u. 40, Budapest; CONSULT. MEMBER, Inst. Child Psych, MTA Gyermeklelektani Intezete, Rippl Ronai utca 26, Budapest. Teaching, research, writing; child psychology, speech analysis, pedagogics.   M

INDIA

SHAH, Dr. Madhuri R. Ed. Dept. Mun. Corp,, Cruikshank Road, Bombay. b. 13 Dec 1919 Bombay.   PH.D '54 London, UK. DIR, Psych. Res. Inst, RES. OFFICER, Bombay Mun. Corp, Cruikshank Road, Bombay 1. Research, educational, testing; adolescent vocational counseling, intelligence and achievement testing.   F

ITALY

FERRACUTI, Dr. Franco. Via Ugo Balzani 57, Rome, b. 1 Apr 1927 Italy. MD '51, Univ. of Rome. ASSIST, Inst. of Psych, Univ. of Rome, Citta Universitaria, Rome. Member: It. Psych. Assoc, IAPA, APA. Research, teaching, clinical practice; fosensic psychology, criminology, market research.   M
FERRARI DI VALBONA, Carlo Alberto. Viale Bruno Buozzi 102, Rome. b. 6 Jan 1920, It. Libera Docenza '29 Univ. of Rome, It. MEMB. of the BOARD, Cartiere del Maglio e di Brodano, Bologna, Mediano,

Trieste. Member: It. Psych. Assoc., AIP. DIR. Rivista di Psicologia. Manpower engineer, editor, applied; learning theory, social perception, habits.   M

SPAIN

PINILLOS, Prof. Dr. Jose Luis. Alonso Cano 52, Madrid. b. 11 Apr 1919. PH.D '49 Univ. of Madrid, Spain. LECT. School of Psych, Univ. of Madrid. Member: SEP, BPS. Teaching, research, applied; personality, attitudes, learning.   M

SWITZERLAND

PIAGET, Jean. Institut des Sciences de l'Education de l'Université de Genève, Palais Wilson, Genève. Switz. b. 8 Aug., 1896, Neuchâtel, Switz. Docteur ès Sciences 1918. Dr. h.c. Univ. Harvard (U.S.A.). Sorbonne (France), Chicago (USA), Prof. h.c. Univ. Rio de Janeiro. PROFESSOR Univ. of Genève (Switz.) and Sorbonne (Paris). DIRECTOR Psych. sect. Institut des Sciences de l'Education and of the Psych. Lab., Univ. of Genève; Centre Intern. d'Epistémologie; Bureau Intern. d'Education. ED Archives de Psychologie. Member: IUSP, APSLF, SSP. Research, teaching; developmental psychology, epistemonology, logic; development of cognitive functions (perception, intelligence, logic.)   M

THAILAND

BOESCH, Prof. Dr. Ernest E. International Institute for Child Study, Chulalongkorn University, Bangkok. b. 26 Dec 1916 Switz. PH.D '46 Univ. of Geneva, Switz. DIR. International Institute for Child Study, Chulalongkorn, Univ, Bangkok. PROF. DIR, Department of Psychology, University of Saarbruecken, Germ. Member: SSP, DGP, Swiss Psychoanal. Assn. Research, teaching, clinical practice; cross-cultural research in child psychology, developmental psychology.   M

INDEX OF COUNTRIES
AND OF ABBREVIATIONS USED IN
THE INDEX OF NAMES

INDEX OF NAMES

Rabitz, J.	Ger. 204	Rasmussen, I.	Den. 114
Rachman, S.	S.Afr. 388	Rasmussen, K. J.	Den. 114
Rad, P. M.	Iran 248	Rasmussen, L.	Den. 114
Radaelli, A. L. de	Arg. 7	Rasmussen, O. W. H.	Den. 114
Radbruch, M. L.	Ger. 204	Rastorgueva, N. A.	USSR 406
Radcliffe, J. A.	Austl. 23	Ratanakorn, P.	Thail. 380
Radecka, H.	Arg. 7	Rath, R.	India 243
Radespiel, H. M.	Ger. 204	Ratingen, J. R. M. van	Neth. 330
Radford, W. C.	Austl. 23	Rauch, B.	Ger. 204
Radomska Strzemecka, H.	Pol. 357	Rauf, A.	Pak. 354
Raether-Goetze, L. M.	Ger. 204	Rauhala, L. M.	Fin. 123
Raeven, F. M.	Neth. 330	Rausch, E.	Ger. 204
Raevski, A. N.	USSR 406	Rausch de Traubenberg, N.	Fr. 153
Rafig, S. A.	Pak. 354	Ravagnan, L. M.	Arg. 7
Rageh, A. E.	Eg. 119	Ravaschino de Vázquez, O. T.	Arg. 7
Rageth, G.	Switz. 377	Raven, J. C.	U.K. 449
Raginskaia, I. A.	USSR 406	Ravich-Shcherbo, S. V.	USSR 406
Raguneau E.	Fr. 153	Ravnmark, A. N.	Den. 114
Rahier, A. M.	Belg. 42	Rawat, K. S.	India 243
Rahman, F.-u.	Pak. 354	Ray-Chowdhury, K.	India 243
Rahmel, R.	Ger. 204	Rayner, E. H.	U.K. 450
Rahn, G.	Ger. 204	Read, L. M.	Can. 84
Raine, S. G.	U.K. 449	Read, W. H.	Can. 84
Rainho, O.	Braz. 52	Rebizov, D. G.	USSR 406
Rainio, K.	Fin. 123	Reche-Ackermann, H.	Ger. 204
Raivio, Y. A.	Fin. 123	Record, M. A.	Can. 84
Rajan, K. V.	India 242	Reed, G. F.	U.K. 450
Raja, P. T.	India 242	Reese, I.	Ger. 205
Rakić, B.	Yug. 469	Reeve, E. G.	U.K. 450
Raknes, O.	Nor. 349	Reeves, J. W.	U.K. 450
Rakoff-Katz, L.	S.Afr. 388	Rehm, R.	Ger. 205
Ramanujachari, R.	India 242	Reich, E.	Austria 34
Rambert, M. L.	Switz. 377	Reich, E. L.	Austria 34
Ramfalk, C. W.	Swed. 368	Reichardt, K. W.	Ger. 205
Ramirez, S.	Mex. 315	Reichlin B.	S.Afr. 388
Ramishvili, D.	USSR 406	Reid, L. W.	U.K. 450
Ramm, E.	Nor. 349	Reid, R. L.	U.K. 450
Ramos Palacios, M.	Mex. 315	Reid, R. S.	U.K. 450
Ramsay, M.	U.K. 449	Reineke, H. H. F.	Ger. 205
Ramsay, S. G.	U.K. 449	Reiner, J. E.	U.K. 450
Ramseyer, F.	Switz. 377	Reinert, G. R. M.	Ger. 205
Ramul, K.	USSR 406	Reinhard, W.	Ger. 205
Ramzia, E. G.	Eg. 119	Reitberger, G.	Ger. 205
Rand, G. M.	Nor. 349	Remplein, H.	Ger. 205
Rand, P. J.	Nor. 349	Rémy, M.	Fr. 153
Rands, S.	Can. 84	Renaud, M. M. C.	Fr. 153
Rangachar, C.	India 242	Renaud, P. A.	Can. 84
Ranke, O. F.	Ger. 204	Rendo, R.	Arg. 7
Rankin, W. B.	Can. 84	Rennes, P.	Fr. 153
Rao, D. G.	India 243	Renthe-Fink, L. von	Ger. 205
Rao, K. U.	India 243	Renwick, I. D.	Austl. 23
Rao, L. N.	India 243	Repina, T. A.	USSR 406
Rao, M. N.	India 243	Repp, G.	Austria 34
Rao, N. C. S. N.	India 243	Rérat, G.	Fr. 153
Rao, S. K. R.	India 243	Resag, K.	Ger. 205
Raphael, W.	U.K. 449	Reside, S. M. M.	U.K. 450
Rasch, W. D.	Ger. 204	Reshetova, Z. A.	USSR 406
Rascovsky, A.	Arg. 7	Resta, G.	It. 256
Rassmann, W.	Ger. 204	Retz, K.	Ger. 205
Rasmussen, E. T.	Den. 114	Reuchlin, M.	Fr. 153
Rasmussen, H. C.	Den. 114	Reuning, H.	S.Afr. 388
Rasmussen, H.	Den. 114	Reutt, J.	Pol. 357
Rasmussen, H.	Den. 114	Revers, W. J.	Ger. 205

Wills, A. R.	U.K. 462
Wilson, A. T. M.	U.K. 462
Wilson, F. S.	Can. 92
Wilson, J.	Can. 92
Wilson, M. D.	U.K. 462
Wilson, N. A. B.	U.K. 462
Wilson, V. W.	Malaya 312
Wiltrup, J.	Den. 117
Winch, M. F.	U.K. 462
Windey, R. A. G.	Belg. 43
Wing, H.	U.K. 462
Wingborg, O. A. B.	Swed. 370
Winkelmann, G.	Ger. 223
Winkelmann, R.	Ger. 223
Winkler, W.	Ger. 223
Winnefeld, F.	Ger. 223
Winnicott, D. W.	U.K. 462
Winsemius, W.	Neth. 334
Winter, H.	Switz. 379
Winter, I.	Ger. 223
Winter, K. B.	Austl. 29
Winterbourn, R.	N.Z. 341
Wirdenius, H. O.	Swed. 370
Wiseman, S.	U.K. 462
Wisler, J. E.	Fr. 158
Wisner, A.	Fr. 158
Wisnes, G.	Nor. 352
Wit, G. A. de	Neth. 334
Wit, J. de	Neth. 334
Witte, W.	Ger. 223
Wittig, H.	Ger. 223
Wittkower, E. D.	Can. 92
Wittlich, B.	Ger. 223
Witvrouw, M.	Belg. 44
Witwicky, T.	Pol. 358
Wobeser-Warnstedt, M. G. von	Ger. 223
Wogatzki, R.	Ger. 223
Wohlfahrt, E.	Ger. 224
Woldrich, C.	Ger. 224
Wolf, H. E.	Ger. 224
Wolf-Doettinchem, H. O. R.	Ger. 224
Wolfe, S. W.	Can. 92
Wolff, B. B.	U.K. 462
Wolff, C.	U.K. 462
Wolff, C. J. de	Neth. 334
Wolff, W.	Ger. 224
Wolfrum, E.	Ger. 224
Wölker, H.	Ger. 224
Woloszynowa, L.	Pol. 358
Wolpe, J.	S.Afr. 391
Wong Hop-Do	Chin.M. 98
Woo Chiang-Lin	Chin.M. 99
Wood, D. K.	U.K. 462
Wood, J. D.	Neth. W.I. 335
Wood, W.	Austl. 29
Woodhouse, H. M.	Austl. 29
Woodrow, A. P.	S.Afr. 391
Woodward, W. M.	U.K. 462
Woolfson, J. O.	S.Afr. 392
Woolley, D. H.	S.Afr. 392
Worsley, J. L.	U.K. 462
Worthington, D. B.	U.K. 462
Worthington, R. N.	Austl. 29
Wotherspoon, J. R.	U.K. 463
Woude, G. van der	Neth. 334
Wrenn, M. H.	U.K. 463
Wright, B. R.	Hongkong 228
Wright, G. G. N.	U.K. 463
Wright, H.	U.K. 463
Wright, H. W.	Can. 92
Wright, J. M. von	Fin. 125
Wright, M. J.	Can. 92
Wright, M. W.	Can. 92
Wrigley, C. F.	N.Z. 341
Wrigley, J.	U.K. 463
Wu Hwei-ling	Chin.M. 99
Wu Tzi-chiang,	Chin.M. 99
Wübbe, C.	Ger. 224
Wunsch, W.	Austria 37
Wurmbach, E.	Ger. 224
Wyatt, W.	Austl. 29
Wyeth, E. R. H.	Austl. 29
Wijlen, H. A. van	Neth. 335
Wylie, M. F.	U.K. 463
Wijnbergen, J.	Neth. 335
Wijngaarden, H. R.	Neth. 335
Xavier, M.	U.K. 463
Xoomsai, T.	Thail. 381
Xydias, N.	Fr. 158
Yabuki, S.	Jap. 307
Yagi, B.	Jap. 307
Yahn, M.	Braz. 54
Yakobson, P. V.	USSR 411
Yakovlev, V. A.	USSR 411
Yakovleva, E. K.	USSR 411
Yakovlicheva, A. F.	USSR 411
Yamada, H.	Jap. 307
Yamada, K.	Jap. 307
Yamada, N.	Jap. 307
Yamaguchi, K.	Jap. 307
Yamaguchi, T.	Jap. 307
Yamakawa, M.	Jap. 307
Yamakawa, N.	Jap. 307
Yamamatsu, T.	Jap. 307
Yamamoto, H.	Jap. 308
Yamamoto, S.	Jap. 308
Yamane, K.	Jap. 308
Yamane, K.	Jap. 308
Yamashita, T.	Jap. 308
Yamazaki, M.	Jap. 308
Yankelevich, S.	USSR 411
Yarmolenko, A. V.	USSR 411
Yaroshevski, M. G.	USSR 411
Yasuda, H.	Jap. 308
Yasuda, M.	Jap. 308
Yasuda, S.	Jap. 308
Yasuda, T.	Jap. 308
Yasui, M.	Jap. 308
Yatabe, T.	Jap. 308
Yates, A.	U.K. 463
Yates, A. J.	U.K. 463
Yeats, L. C.	Can. 92
Yeaxlee, B. A.	U.K. 463
Yeh Ling,	Chin.M. 99